ENCYCLOPEDIA OF CONTEMPORARY CHINESE CULTURE

'Made in China' has become a tag familiar to all Westerners, but China's shift to a market economy in the early 1980s released not only the industrial but also the vast creative energies of China's citizens to produce a cultural renaissance unique in the contemporary world. In the last quarter-century, communist ideology has been in rapid retreat and the cultural resources of China's pre-socialist past have been rediscovered and combined with current influences from home and abroad to construct competing responses to China's ever-changing present.

The *Encyclopedia of Contemporary Chinese Culture* is the first reference book to digest this vast cultural output and make it accessible to the English-speaking world. The *Encyclopedia* contains nearly 1,200 entries written by an international team of specialists to enable readers to explore a range of diverse and fascinating cultural subjects from prisons to rock groups, underground Christian churches to TV talk shows and radio hotlines. Experimental artists with names such as 'Big-Tailed Elephant' and 'The Pond Society' nestle between the covers alongside entries on lotteries, gay cinema, political jokes, sex shops, theme parks, 'New Author-itarians' and 'little emperors'. These, as well as more traditional subjects and biographical entries, are indexed under the following eighteen categories for easy thematic reference:

- architecture and space
- education
- ethnicity and ethnic identity
- fashion and design
- film
- food and drink

- health
- language
- literature
- media
- music
- performing arts

- political culture
- religion
- society
- sports and recreation
- visual arts
- women and gender

While the focus of the *Encyclopedia of Contemporary Chinese Culture* is on mainland China since 1980, the *Encyclopedia* also includes longer, specially commissioned entries on various aspects of contemporary culture in Hong Kong and Taiwan. Most entries include full and up-to-date references for further reading, making the *Encyclopedia* an indispensable reference tool for all teachers and students of contemporary Chinese culture. It is also likely to be warmly embraced as an invaluable source of cultural context by tourists, journalists, business people and others who visit China.

Edward L. Davis is Associate Professor of History at the University of Hawai'i, USA.

ENCYCLOPEDIA OF CONTEMPORARY CHINESE CULTURE

Edited by Edward L. Davis

Routledge
Taylor & Francis Group

LONDON AND NEW YORK

First published 2005 by Routledge
First published in paperback 2009 by Routledge
2 Park Square, Milton Park, Abingdon, Oxon, OX14 4RN

Simultaneously published in the USA and Canada
by Routledge
270 Madison Avenue, New York, NY 10016, USA

Routledge is an imprint of the Taylor & Francis Group, an informa business

© 2005, 2009 Routledge

Typeset in Baskerville and Optima by Newgen Imaging Systems (P) Ltd, India

Printed and bound in Great Britain by TJ International Ltd,
Padstow, Cornwall

British Library Cataloguing in Publication Data
A catalogue record for this book is available from the British Library

Library of Congress Cataloging in Publication Data
Encyclopedia of contemporary Chinese culture / edited by Edward L. Davis.
p. cm.
Includes index.
1. China-Civilization-1976-2002-Encyclopedias.
2. China-Civilization-2002-Encyclopedias. I. Davis, Edward L. (Edward Lawrence), 1954-
DS779.23.E53 2009
951.0603-dc22
2008021956

ISBN10: 0–415–24129–4 (hbk)
ISBN10: 0–415–77716–X (pbk)
ISBN10: 0–203–64506–5 (ebk)
ISBN13: 978–0–415–24129–8 (hbk)
ISBN13: 978–0–415–77716–2 (pbk)
ISBN13: 978–0–203–64506–2 (ebk)

Contents

Editorial team

General editor

Edward L. Davis
University of Hawai'i

Contributors

Daniel B. Abramson
University of Washington

Fiorella Allio
Université de Provence, Marseilles

Alain Arrault
École Française d'Extrême-Orient, Beijing

Ying Bao
University of California, Los Angeles

Nimrod Baranovitch
Hebrew University of Jerusalem

A. W. Barber
University of Calgary

Maria Barbieri
University of Hong Kong

Geremie R. Barmé
Australian National University

Daniel Bays
Calvin College

Robert Bernell
Publisher, Timezone 8, Beijing

Michael Berry
University of California, Santa Barbara

Brigitte Berthier-Baptandier
Centre National de la Recherche Scientifique, Paris

Sébastien Billioud
University of Paris 7

Susan D. Blum
University of Notre Dame

Mathieu Borysevicz
The Church of Unintentional Wisdom (Brooklyn, N.Y.) and mabz productions

Yomi Braester
University of Washington

Susan Brownell
University of Missouri–St Louis

Cai Shuqin
Bowdoin College

Chang Hui-mei
University of Hawai'i

Emily Chao
Pitzer College

Isabelle Charleux
Centre National de la Recherche Scientifique, Paris

Adam Yuet Chau
Skidmore College

Timothy Cheek
University of British Columbia

Chen Jianhua
Hong Kong University of Science and Technology

Lily Chen
University of Sheffield

Nancy N. Chen
University of South Carolina

Tina Mai Chen
University of Manitoba

Chen Xiaomei
Ohio State University

Matthew Chew
Princeton University

Chou Yuting
independent scholar, Madeira (Portugal)

Matthew Clark
beijingband.com

Paul Clark
University of Auckland

Donald Clarke
University of Washington

Philip Clart
University of Missouri-Columbia

Jeffrey W. Cody
Chinese University of Hong Kong

Claude Comtois
University of Montreal

Claire Conceison
University of Michigan

Ralph Covell
Denver Seminary

Remy Cristini
Sinological Institute, Leiden

Cui Shuqin
Bowdoin College, Southern Methodist University

Annie Curien
Centre National de la Recherche Scientifique, Paris

Francesca Dal Lago
McGill University

Sarah Dauncey
Sheffield University

Ursula Dauth
Queensland Theatre Company, Australia

Gloria Davies
Monash University

Edward L. Davis
University of Hawai'i

Jeroen de Kloet
University of Amsterdam

Kenneth Dean
McGill University

Frank Dikötter
School of African and Oriental Studies, University of London

Stephanie Hemelryk Donald
University of Technology, Sydney

Du Wenwei
Vassar College

Du Yaxiong
Hangzhou Normal University

Thomas DuBois
National University of Singapore

Isabelle Duchesne
New York University

Mercedes M. Dujunco
New York University

Bettina S. Entell
Director/Producer,
Mediamondo Productions

Megan Evans
University of Hawai'i

Frederik Fällman
Stockholm University

C. Cindy Fan
University of California, Los Angeles

Fan Pen Chen
University at Albany,
State University of New York

Judith Farquhar
University of North Carolina

Mary Farquhar
Griffith University

James Farrer
Sophia University

Megan M. Ferry
Union College

Peter M. Foggin
University of Montreal

Fu Hongchu
Smith College

Gao Minglu
University at Buffalo,
State University of New York

Ge Congmin
University of Leeds

Vincent Goossaert
Centre National de la Recherche Scientifique,
Paris

Edward Gunn
Cornell University

Nancy Guy
University of California,
San Diego

John Christopher Hamm
University of Washington

Han Kuo-Huang
Northern Illinois University

Han Xiaorong
Butler University

He Donghui
University of British Columbia

Ho Puay-peng
Chinese University of Hong Kong

Lisa M. Hoffman
University of Washington

David Holm
University of Melbourne

Hu Mingrong
Chongqing Technology and Business University

Hu Ying
University of California, Irvine

Huang Yibing
Connecticut College

William Jankowiak
University of Nevada, Las Vegas

Maria Jaschok
University of Oxford

Lionel M. Jensen
University of Notre Dame

Jia Wenshan
State University of New York at New Paltz

Alice Ming Wai Jim
Vancouver International Centre for
Contemporary Asian Art

Jin Ping
State University of New York, New Paltz

Perry Johansson
Columbia University

Andrew F. Jones
University of California, Berkeley

Ellen R. Judd
University of Manitoba

Eric I. Karchmer
University of North Carolina

Paul R. Katz
Academia Sinica

Ke Ping
Nanjing University

Michael Keane
Queensland University of Technology

Scott Kennedy
University of Indiana

Kim Kwang-ok
Seoul National University

Jason Kindopp
George Washington University

Andrew Kipnis
Australian National University

Carla Kirkwood
Southwestern College

Deirdre Sabina Knight
Smith College

Martina Köppel-Yang
Independent art historian

Kuo Wen-hua
Massachusetts Institute of Technology

Lars Laamann
School of Oriental and African Studies,
University of London

John Lagerwey
École Pratique des Hautes-Études

Stefan Landsberger
University of Leiden

Kevin Latham
School of African and Oriental Studies,
University of London

Beatrice Leanza
CAAW (China Art Archives and Warehouse),
Contemporary and Experimental Art Centre,
Beijing

Joanna C. Lee
University of Hong Kong

Lily Xiao Hong Lee
University of Sydney

Leung Laifong
University of Alberta

Steven W. Lewis
Rice University

Li, Dian
University of Arizona

Li Jiwen
Central Academy of Drama, Beijing

Li Ruru
University of Leeds

Li Xianting
independent scholar and curator, Beijing

Li Zhang
Northern Illinois University

Lin Wei-yü
University of Hawai'i

Birgit Linder
Peking University

Alan P. L. Liu
University of California, Santa Barbara

Liu Chang
University of Mary Washington

Gordon Liu
University of North Carolina

Liu Meng
Chair, Department of Social Work
Women's College, Beijing

Rosa Lombardi
Università degli Studi Roma Tre

Kam Louie
University of Queensland

Eriberto P. Lozada, Jr
Butler University

Lu Hongwei
University of Oregon

Colin Mackerras
Griffith University

Meg Maggio
Director, CourtYard Gallery

Paul Manfredi
Pacific Lutheran University

Meng Qing
Université de Montréal

Miao Pu
University of Hawai'i

Ming Fengying
California Institute of Technology

Kalpana Misra
University of Tulsa

Barbara Mittler
University of Heidelberg

Thomas Moran
Middlebury College

Christina Neder
Ruhr Universität Bochum

Cynthia Y. Ning
University of Hawai'i

Lucie Olivová
Palacky University

David A. Palmer
École Française d'Extrême-Orient, Hong Kong

Clifton W. Pannell
University of Georgia

Simon Patton
University of Queensland

Veronica Pearson
University of Hong Kong

Peng Hsiao-yen
Academia Sinica

Morgan Perkins
State University of New York, Potsdam

Michael R. Phillips
Director, National Centre for Suicide Research
and Prevention, Huilongguan Hospital, Beijing

Cesare Polenghi
University of Hawai'i

Judy Polumbaum
University of Iowa

Pitman Potter
University of British Columbia

William Powell
University of California, Santa Barbara

Qian Zhijian
Institute of Fine Arts,
New York University

Qiu Peipei
Vassar College

Dennis Rea
musician, composer

Ren Hai
Bowling Green State University

Bérénice Reynaud
School of Film/Video, CalArts

Claire Roberts
Senior curator, Asian Decorative Arts and Design,
Powerhourse Museum, Sydney

Carlos Rojas
Columbia University

Sang Tze-lan
University of Oregon

Louisa Schein
Rutgers, State University of New Jersey

Jonathan Schwartz
State University of New York at New Paltz

Simon Shen
University of Oxford

Michael Shoenhals
Lunds University

Shui Jingjun
Chinese Academy of Social Sciences,
Henan Branch

Cathy Silber
Williams University

Jerome Silbergeld
University of Washington

Richard VanNess Simmons
Rutgers, State University of New Jersey

Richard J. Smith
Rice University

Richard B. Stamps
Oakland University

Andreas Steen
University of Berlin

Daniel B. Stevenson
University of Kansas

Jonathan P. J. Stock
University of Sheffield

Marina Svensson
Lunds University

Michael Szonyi
University of Toronto

Tan Hwee-san
School of Oriental and African Studies,
University of London

Tang Di
Writer and curator, Beijing

Tao Hongyin
University of California, Los Angeles

Alan R. Thrasher
University of British Columbia

Martine Torfs
independent scholar and translator,
contemporary Chinese literature

Marion Torrance
Medical Director, Plateau Perspectives

L. L. Tsai
Harvard University

Sue-Han Ueng
National Taipei University

Jonathan Unger
Australian National University

Robin Visser
Valparaiso University

Natascha Vittinghoff
University of Frankfurt

Alan L. M. Wachman
Tufts University

Margaret Baptist Wan
University of Notre Dame

Michael Weidong Wan
University of Notre Dame

Wang Chang
University of Illinois

Wang Jing
Massachusetts Institute of Technology

Wang Qi
University of California, Los Angeles

Wang Xiaolu
Sichuan University

Wang Xiaoming

Wang Yiman
Duke University

Eduardo Welsh
independent scholar, Madeira (Portugal)

Timothy Weston
University of Colorado

Elizabeth Wichmann-Walczak
University of Hawai'i

Sabine Wilms
University of Arizona

James Dale Wilson
Columbia University

Cynthia P. Wong
Columbia University

Linda Wong
City University of Hong Kong

Helen Xiaoyan Wu
University of Toronto

Xu Xiaoqun
Francis Marion University

Yang Guobin
University of Hawai'i

Yang Lan
University of Leeds

Mayfair Mei-hui Yang
University of California, Santa Barbara

Nora Yeh
American Folklife Center, Library of Congress

Yip Ka-che
University of Maryland

Yu Shiao-ling
Oregon State University

Yuan Haiwang
West Kentucky University

Yue Gang
University of North Carolina

Rik Zak
Alberta College of Art and Design

Paola Zamperini
Amherst College, University of California,
Berkeley

Everett Zhang
University of California, Berkeley

Zhang Yulong
Ohio State University

Zhao Dingxin
University of Chicago

Thomas Zimmer
Chinese German College,
Tongji University, Shanghai

Preface

When asked by Routledge to contribute to its series of reference books with an *Encyclopedia of Contemporary Chinese Culture*, two issues surfaced immediately and have remained in play even as the project has been completed – what should be meant by 'contemporary' and what should be meant by 'Chinese'. The first was the easier to deal with and to justify. In contrast to other encyclopedias in the series, some which reach back to WWII and others which even encompass most of the last century, the end of the Cultural Revolution and death of Mao in 1976 set in motion a series of events and socio-political transformations of such startling contrast to China's socialist past that the late 1970s became the natural *terminus a quo* for a definition of the contemporary. The Chinese themselves refer to the period since 1979 as the 'New Period' or 'New Era', though technically these terms denote only the first decade, and many have suggested that we adopt 'post-Tiananmen' for the years since 4 June 1989. Readers will find that the contributors to this volume also employ several synonyms for the entire period: the 'post-Mao', 'post-Cultural Revolution' or, simply, 'reform' period. The *Encyclopedia*, therefore, covers the years from 1979 to the present and takes the first date seriously – any important writer, for example, whose work was produced largely in the 1970s or before, is excluded. The second issue – how to take the word 'Chinese' – was the more intractable problem, and even I am willing to admit that my decision to limit this encyclopedia to cultural developments in the People's Republic is open to rebuttal, not least because it has been impossible to live up to. A strong argument has been made over the last decade for the existence of a 'Greater China', a 'Cultural China', a 'China' that includes not only the political entities of Hong Kong, Taiwan and Singapore in addition to the PRC, but the Chinese 'diasporic' communities in Europe, North America, Southeast Asia and Australia as well, 50 million strong. The analysis of this 'Cultural China' largely falls under the purview of the now robust and exciting academic discipline known as Cultural Studies. Yet the 'discursive space' constructed by the notion of a 'Cultural China' presents a difficult conundrum for the encyclopedist. On the one hand, 'Cultural China' is not 'Chinese Culture' and the limited subject matter and urban secular bias of the former cannot serve as a guide for what should be included under the latter. On the other hand, a single-volume encyclopedia cannot possibly do justice to the cultures of the transnational space designated by 'Cultural China' and to try to do so would only reduce the content of such an encyclopedia to an argument for such a space – a worthy enterprise, to be sure, but one more efficiently made in a different format. Nonetheless, the intricate contestations over cultural identity that characterize 'Cultural China' are very much part of the contemporary scene on the mainland, especially since the mid 1990s, and cannot be ignored. The *Encyclopedia*, therefore, makes a serious nod in this direction in the content of many of the entries, in the choice of recommended readings, in the inclusion of long entries on aspects of the culture of Taiwan, Hong Kong and Singapore and of shorter ones on cultural producers who spent their formative period on the mainland, but now live in the diaspora. In this encyclopedia, a single, authorial (editorial) voice has been avoided. Writers were encouraged, beyond a statement of the 'facts', to analyze, to make judgments, and even to editorialize in the restricted space available to them. The reader will therefore find a range of points of view expressed – from cultural boosterism to weary scepticism to moral indignation. The anthropologist Liu Xin has recently argued for the development of a sense of the 'now' in the PRC and my editorial policy has been to capture this sense of the today-ness of the contemporary. This, of course, increases the risk of missing some of the trees in the forest, if not the forest itself, but this risk is otherwise unavoidable, and as the passing of time highlights the inadequacies of this volume as a secondary source, it might augment its value as a primary one. Still, slots that were supposed to be filled, but for one reason or another were not, weigh heavily on the mind of the editor pressed by publication deadlines. There are no entries for the Hui and Kazak nationalities, Islam among minorities, Reportage literature (*Baogao wenxue*) or calligraphy, among other, less obvious lacunae.

Those who have contributed to this volume are many, but I must first thank my colleague at the University of Hawai'i, Mingbao Yue, who was first solicited by Routledge to edit the *Encyclopedia* and was kind enough to include me as co-editor. Mingbao wrote the initial proposal, contacted many of the consultants, and made a significant contribution to the first version of the entry list. Unfortunately, she needed to withdraw from the project just as it was getting underway, but it is important to note that without her there would have been no *Encyclopedia*. All the consultants provided enthusiastic support, but I must single out Yue Daiyun, who shared the first draft of the entry list with her colleague at Peking University, Dai Jinhua, and together they provided a long list of suggestions that were eventually incorporated. As the list evolved, the intervention of Bérénice Reynaud, Alan Thrasher, Elizabeth Wichmann-Walczak and Paola Zamperini was decisive, perfecting the lists of film, traditional music, performing arts and fashion entries, respectively. All four were extremely generous with their time, secured many superb writers for the volume, and, indeed, wrote many entries

themselves. Isabelle Duchesne, Nancy Guy, Joanna Lee and Jonathan Stock all saved me from some bad choices, Kirk Denton provided technical help, and the peripatetic Geremie Barmé responded to all my queries in between lectures and movie premieres and provided some of the most provocative entries in the volume (this is a good place to thank Reaktion Books for allowing me to include an adaptation of Barmé's essay in Peter Wollen and Joe Kerr (eds), *Autopia: Cars and Culture* (London: Reaktion, 2003) and the editors of the *IIAS Newsletter* 27 (March 2002) for allowing me reprint Sang Tze-lan's 'Restless Longing: Homoerotic Fiction in China'). My 'handler' at Routledge, Dominic Shryane, was a constant source of encouragement and accepted my pleas for more time with equanimity and understanding. Elizabeth Jones provided sure and efficient copy-editing. The Chun Fong and Grace Ning Fund of the Center for Chinese Studies at the University of Hawai'i twice provided generous support for research assistants, and I would like to thank Meilan Frame and Meishi Huang for their editorial assistance at the beginning and end of this project, respectively. Indeed, Meilan's enthusiasm for Beijing was infectious and proved a great source of inspiration as I pondered what to include in this volume. When the last entries were submitted and I began to edit the manuscript in the summer of 2003, Ashley Maynard, Kevin Groark and friends at Café Lom Lek in San Cristóbal de Las Casas, Chiapas, provided the ideal environment (Bush es terrorista! Vivan los Simpson!).

Last, but by no means least, I must thank the inimitable Francesca Dal Lago, who mercifully agreed to make sense of the contemporary art scene for me, and, after re-fashioning the list of entries, brought together an international group of critics, curators and historians to write them. All this was accomplished at great cost to her own personal projects, and not only I but the field are in her debt. Below, I have asked Francesca to provide an additional preface, in which she explains her choices.

Of course, most of the choices were ultimately my own and I take responsibility for all of them. Readers are encouraged to email their criticisms and suggestions (including omissions and errors) to me at edavis@hawaii.edu in the event of a second edition. I dedicate my portion of this project to the other members of the now extinct Con Brio Trio – Niels Herold (violin) and Chris Haight (piano) – and to our manager, Bojidar Yanev, who has made a career of supporting failing structures.

Ned Davis

Honolulu, February 2004

The Visual Art entries

When Ned Davis asked me to compile the Visual Art entries for the *Encyclopedia of Contemporary Chinese Culture*, my first reaction was to decline: listing and categorizing a phenomenon that is still very much in the making appeared to me as a pointless task and a project inevitably associated with canon formation. I did not wish to be held responsible for what could only be a very partial selection. And yet here I am now, after nearly two years, explaining the rationale that has guided me in the accomplishment of this project. While the most relevant methodological and historical problems have been pointed out by Ned in his Preface and more could be said to provide a theoretical justification for the work, I must confess that my acceptance of the project was in large part inspired by those same motives that will be likely considered to be its main flaw. To wit, it was my personal investment in the material discussed by these entries that convinced me to accept Ned's proposal: relaying 'subjective' information on the Chinese art world during the last twenty years was, more than just 'historically useful', a profoundly personal feat. I was intrigued by the vaguely disruptive idea of infusing a supposedly 'scientific' work with the kind of subjective involvement that derives from the experience gathered in nine years of residence in China and nearly two decades of intimate familiarity with most of the people and issues presented in these entries – a familiarity that has still not liberated me from the perspective of, in the words of art historian Wu Hong, 'observers who look from the outside in'.

Aware of the possible usefulness of such an outlook, I first began by heatedly discussing Ned's original list of names and trends with Qian Zhijian, a fellow graduate student at the Institute of Fine Arts and former editor of the magazine *Meishu*. We decided that we would include only those individuals or groups of individuals who had been actively producing 'new' forms of art and had been influential in the artistic output of mainland China during the last twenty years. Important historical figures, while still very influential in the dynamics of contemporary Chinese art, were thus not considered, while individual artists were chosen for the larger and continuous influence they have exerted during the contemporary period and for their critically accepted status in the art-historical narrative of the post-Mao period.

The most exciting part of the project has been my interaction with the contributors. Had it not been for the professionalism of this group, and for Ned's Zen patience in moving deadlines forward, the meticulous task of editing the entries and compiling the bibliographic references might have prevailed over my original commitment. It is therefore mainly to thank these individuals for their enthusiasm and support that I am writing today. For her availability at the very early stages of the project I would like to thank Alice Jim – formerly of Montreal, now of Vancouver – who set the scholarly and critical tone for the entries. I would also like to express my gratitude to: Mathieu Borysevicz in New York, whose work as a photographer and with photographers in Beijing for a period of five years made him the favourite 'reporter' of this new and exciting genre; Tang Di, a close friend, half-sister, and cultural officer in Beijing, who dutifully checked most of her information and comments with the artists and critics about whom she wrote; Eduardo Welsh, in Madeira (Portugal), a pioneering scholar and the first ever to have received a PhD in contemporary Chinese art (from the School of African and Oriental Studies), who took painstaking care in compiling most of the 1980s entries; and Yuting Chou, who contributed on Fang Lijun, the subject of her Master's thesis from the University of Leiden. My attempt at providing some 'first-hand authenticity' comes through the contributions of two of the protagonists of the events discussed in the visual arts entries – Gao Minglu and Li Xianting. Both deserve an entry under their own name and both wrote for this volume on phenomena and movements that they were instrumental in launching and/or defining. Gao Minglu, now at SUNY Buffalo, wrote on the 1989 Avant-Garde Exhibition in Beijing, for which he was main curator, and on the 1985 [Art] Movement, of which he was one of the main engines. Li Xianting in Beijing contributed on the two currents that he named and presented to the world, 'Political Pop' and 'Cynical Realism', as well as on the first avant-garde movement of the post-Mao period, the Stars, that he bravely introduced to the general public in the pages of *Meishu*, the most authoritative art periodical in China. Robert Bernell, a Texan in Beijing who has connected China's experimental art scene to the world through his invaluable website (Chinese-art.com) contributed entries on some of the most important contemporary critics; Martina Köppel-Yang wrote on Paris-based artists and critics whom she has known and worked with for years; Lucie Olivová of Charles University in Prague offered her help with some of the *Zhongguohua* entries, a subject on which she organized an exhibition and wrote a catalogue in 2001; Morgan Perkins, an anthropologist of art in upstate New York, wrote on artistic institutions, art academies and displaying practices – the topic of his PhD dissertation from Oxford; Meg Maggio, director of the Courtyard Gallery in Beijing, offered her expertise on auction houses and the art market; and finally, Beatrice Leanza of the Chinese Art Archives and Warehouse in Beijing enthusiastically responded to my last-minute panic by contributing many entries that had not yet been completed and by checking relevant data in the first-class archives of her institution and often directly with the artists. In brief, the same principle of personal connection that led me to accept this task also guided me in the selection of this dedicated group of people, whose shared asset is their deep involvement in the subjects that they were asked to write about.

Last but not least, I would like to remember three protagonists who are directly or indirectly quoted in the entries and who would have certainly contributed to them had they lived. Critic and art historian Alice Yang, curator and critic Hans van Dijk and artist Chen Zhen all died before they could complete the major tasks they had set for themselves. It is to their memory and to the great contributions that they made to this very young field that I wish to dedicate my efforts and, if I may presume, the efforts of all the people that have helped me with this project.

Francesca Dal Lago
Montréal, March 2004

Classified entry list

Architecture and space

ancestral halls/lineage temples
architectural criticism and theory
architectural journals
architectural styles
bridges
Buddhist monasteries (Chinese)
Buddhist monasteries (Tibetan)
Children's Palace
cities
cultural landscapes
cultural zones (urban)
Daoist monasteries/abbeys
department stores
development zones (urban)
domestic space
environment, perceptions of
foreign enclaves (urban)
geography of disease
geography of health care
highways
historical and cultural cities
home refurbishing
hospitals
hotels
housing
hukou
Islamic mosques
migration and settlement patterns
monuments and public sculpture
museums
parks and squares
prisons
public libraries
residential districts (urban)
restoration districts (urban)

retail and business districts (urban)
ring roads
shopping malls
skyscrapers
streets
theme parks
Tiananmen Square
tombs and cremation
towns and townships
train stations
urban planning/renewal
villages
World Heritage sites
Yuanming Yuan

Education

bilingual education
bulletin board systems
Central Academy of Fine Arts
Central Radio and Television University
Central University for Nationalities
China People's University
Chinese Academy of Sciences
Chinese Academy of Social Sciences
Cultural Revolution (education)
elite schools
examinations for self-paced higher education
foreign students
higher education through self-paced study
HSK
Islamic schools
literacy (and illiteracy)
Lu Xun Literary Institute
memorization
Ministry of Education
Nanjing University

Food and drink

Health

acupuncture and moxibustion
aphrodisiacs
barefoot doctors
birth control and contraception
culture-bound syndromes
disabilities
geography of disease
geography of health care
herbal medicine
HIV/AIDS and STIs
massage
medical doctors
medical insurance
mental health
pharmacies
physical fitness and sports clubs
public health care
Qigong (history)
Qigong (masters)
reproductive health
Western-style Chinese medicine
Yan Xin

Language

baihua/Guoyu
Chinese as a foreign language
curses and maledicta
dialects
dictionaries
foreign language acquisition and teaching
Indo-European language speakers
Institute of Linguistics
neologisms
political slogans
simplified characters
Sino-Tibetan language speakers
State Working Commission on Language
terms of address
translation industry
Tungusic language speakers
Turkic language speakers
urban slang
writing reform movements
writing systems
Xinhua zidian,
    Xinhua cidian

Literature

Ah Cheng
Alai
Aniwar, Mamat
avant-garde/experimental literature
Bai Hua
Bai Xianyong
Beauties' Literature
Bei Dao
Bo Yang
Butterfly literature
Can Xue
Chen Pingyuan
Chen Ran
Chi Zijian
children's literature
Dai Houying
detective fiction
Duoduo
ethnic minority literary collections
Fang Fang
Feng Jicai
Foreign Languages Press
Gao Xingjian
Ge Fei
Gu Cheng
Guo Lusheng
Haizi
Han Shaogong
He Dun
He Jingzhi
Hong Ying
Huang Chunming
Huang Xiang
Ji Xianlin
Jia Pingwa
Jiang He
Jin Yong
journalistic literature
Ke Yunlu
Kong Jiesheng
Leung Ping-kwan
Li Jie
Li Qingxi
Li Rui
Li Yongping
Lin Bai
literary awards

Media

Performing arts

Political culture

Religion

Society

Sports and recreation

Women and gender

A Jia

b. 1907, Jiangsu; d. 1994

Theatre director

A Jia was a brilliant director, playwright and theatre theorist who devoted his impressive fifty-year career to the study and practice of **Xiqu** (sung-drama/opera). He made the first major systematic study of Xiqu's aesthetic principles, and is perhaps most famous for his work as director and head writer of *Red Lantern* (*Hongdengji*), the first of the model revolutionary modern plays (*yangbanxi*) of the **Cultural Revolution**.

A Jia studied poetry and calligraphy in his youth. Before joining Mao in Yan'an in 1938, he spent time as a teacher, reporter, labourer and even briefly as a monk. He also participated in many amateur Xiqu performances. At Yan'an he entered the Yan'an Academy of Arts and Literature and joined the Communist Party in 1941, serving as director and later vice president of the Yan'an Pingju (also known as **Jingju**, 'Peking Opera') Research Academy, which was established in 1942. Involved in hundreds of productions, he became one of the area's most renowned Xiqu performers, wrote and directed many new plays, and adapted traditional plays to conform with his Communist ideals. After 1949 he studied at the Central Academy of Drama (Zhongyang xiju xueyuan) which broadened his understanding of major schools or styles of Xiqu performance as well as Western theories of performance. These ideas he incorporated into a prolific body of theoretical writing.

A Jia held numerous leading positions in the arts, including Director of the People's Government Research Institute to Reform Xiqu (Zhongyang renmin zhengfu wenhuabu xiqu gaijinju yishuchu yanjiushi zhuren) and Head Director of the China Jingju Company (Zhongguo jingju yuanzong daoyan). He is known for his deep practical and theoretical understanding of traditional Xiqu and for being one of the most successful innovators of the genre as he discovered ways to portray modern life on the Xiqu stage.

Further reading

A, Jia (1999). 'Truth in Life and Truth in Art'. In F. Fei (ed.), *Chinese Theories of Theater and Performance from Confucius to the Present*. Ann Arbor: University of Michigan Press, 146–53.

Liu, Y. (1988). Trans. D. Hu *et al*. 'Ah Jia's Theory of Xiqu Performance'. *Asian Theatre Journal* 5.2: 111–31.

MEGAN EVANS AND ELIZABETH
WICHMANN-WALCZAK

academic e-journals

The late 1990s saw the rapid growth of electronic Chinese-language journals that published articles on a diverse range of issues in the social sciences and humanities. *China News Digest* (*Huaxia wenzhai*) was one of the earliest (US-based) Chinese e-journals to feature several scholarly essays among those on popular topics that it normally carried. Since

2000, PRC-based academic e-journals have become highly significant in the Chinese intellectual world. In that year alone, websites like *Century China (Shiji Zhongguo)*, *The Realm of Ideas (Sixiang de jingjie)*, *Cultural China (Wenhua Zhongguo)* and *Critical Inquiry (Sixiang pinglun)* provided an increasingly global Chinese-language readership with unprecedentedly up-to-the-minute information and commentary on topics of both scholarly and public interest.

Unlike academic e-journals in the English language which largely adhere to the format of their print versions, Chinese-language e-journals, like the influential *Century China*, feature both academic articles and informal 'discussions' on topical issues and current affairs. These 'discussions' may include one-sentence opinions, pithy commentaries or lengthy excurses by both known and pseudonymous authors. The immediacy of cyber-publication and its relative freedom from official censorship, coupled with the willingness of most Chinese e-journal editorial boards to accommodate different views and to accept pseudonymous submissions, have led many Chinese intellectuals to celebrate the dawning of a virtual public sphere in the Chinese-speaking world. Critics of the vitriolic exchanges that have appeared in these e-journals, such as the controversy surrounding the 'Cheung Kong – *Reading* Awards'(Changjiang *Dushu* jiang) in 2000, fear that the relative ease of cyber-publication may also undermine intellectual responsibility and academic professionalism.

GLORIA DAVIES

Academy of Chinese Culture

(Zhongguo wenhua shuyuan)

The Academy of Chinese Culture is an independent entity founded in 1984 by a group of scholars from **Peking University** (Beijing daxue) including Zhang Dainian, Tang Yijie, **Ji Xianlin** and Wang Shouchang, among others. It was also supported by prominent intellectual figures such as Feng Youlan and Liang Shuming.

The purpose of the Academy is the promotion, beyond the academic world, of the study of Chinese traditional culture, the understanding of

its historical specificity, and the fostering of cultural dialogue with the outside world. Activities of the academy include publications, organization of symposia, and teaching programmes. For two years, between 1986 and 1988, more than 12,000 people from extremely different backgrounds (engineers, doctors, military personnel, students) enrolled in its courses, some of which were broadcast nationwide.

The Academy's activities had a strong impact on the intellectual debates of the second half of the 1980s. As it encouraged the rehabilitation of traditional culture, the Academy was subject to fierce criticism and accusations of conservatism from intellectual circles that considered tradition to be an obstacle to modernization. Nonetheless, several scholars linked to the Academy published articles requesting the liberalization of the political system beyond the economic sphere and also participated in the student movement of 1989. This in turn generated strong criticism from the regime. From 1989 to 1991 the Academy almost ceased its activities as the authorization to operate was not renewed. It was reactivated afterwards, yet has since concentrated on academic research.

See also: Research Institute for National Studies

SÉBASTIEN BILLIOUD

acting (drama schools and training)

There are two routes to train for acting in the PRC: through professional and state-run schools or informally. According to official figures, there were 210 educational institutions for the performing arts in 1989, with 19,674 employees; by 1999 the number had risen slightly to 238, with 20,432 employees. Among these, most either include acting and performance skills in their purview or are specifically dedicated to them. In 1999, there were also nearly 300,000 mass art centres, cultural centres and cultural stations, which among other functions ran classes in acting and other performance skills like storytelling.

There are three main criteria for accepting students into full-time drama schools. These are voice, physical features and artistic ability. Potential students must also take an examination before auditioning. Competition is extremely keen, and acceptance rates usually well below 10 per cent. In special cases, including exceptional ability or coming from an acting family, students may enter acting school as young as five years old, but the great majority must graduate from primary school before applying. Acting schools run courses on culture and general knowledge, as well as performance skills. This is to avoid illiteracy in the acting profession, which was once universal.

In classes or schools for traditional forms of drama, boys outnumber girls, reflecting the male dominance of the casts. However, this is not the case in the more modern theatre styles. Teaching techniques are traditional for the classical forms of drama. For modern theatre, they were strongly influenced by Russian methods, but have accepted techniques from other Western countries. Until the 1980s, acting schools were fully funded by the state. Although the state still gives substantial subsidies and schools offer scholarships, fees became more or less universal during the 1990s. These are quite large, especially since students live on the spot.

COLIN MACKERRAS

acupuncture and moxibustion

Acupuncture and moxibustion constitute one of the most distinctive branches of Chinese medicine. Acupuncture refers to the therapeutic manipulation of needles at specific sites on the body, and moxibustion to the therapeutic warming or cauterizing of these sites with slow-burning moxa leaves. They are commonly used together in clinical practice, although acupuncture is the predominant technique. Acupuncture and moxibustion have a history of 2,500 years of practice in China and continue to be vibrant, evolving medical practices today.

Acupuncture and moxibustion practice first emerged during the late Warring States and early Han dynasty eras (c. 475 BC to AD 24). The oldest extant medical text in China, the *Yellow Emperor's Inner Canon* (*Huangdi neijing*), a collection of some of the most important medical writings of this period, devotes considerable space to expounding the basic principles of acupuncture and moxibustion. The innovations of subsequent generations of scholars have relied heavily on the theoretical foundations laid down in this classic. In contemporary practice, acupuncture doctors must master the basic theory of Chinese medicine (see **herbal medicine**), with a particular emphasis on meridian theory, acupoint location, and needle and moxa manipulation techniques. Meridian theory describes the pathways and relationships that link specific organs, tissues and regions of the body. It constitutes the essential diagnostic and therapeutic guide for acupuncture practice. Most acupoints, the sites of therapeutic application, lie along meridian pathways. Therefore skilful needle or moxa manipulation not only produces local physiological responses, but also operates through the meridian pathways to effect changes in distant corporeal sites.

Chinese Communist Party (CCP) health care policies have deeply influenced the contemporary practice of Chinese medicine. Reversing Republican era policies, the CCP incorporated Chinese medicine into the state health care system, creating medical schools, **hospitals**, research institutes, academic journals and administrative bodies specifically for Chinese medicine. Today acupuncture doctors can be found working both in Chinese medicine hospitals (in acupuncture and moxibustion departments) and in general hospitals (in Chinese medicine departments).

One of the greatest challenges confronting Chinese medicine practitioners today is the global hegemony of biomedicine. Health policy-makers and Chinese medicine institutions have responded to this challenge by encouraging integration of the two practices, in spite of the vast epistemological differences that separate them. Chinese medicine schools provide basic training in biomedicine, in addition to standard Chinese medicine curriculum. Many acupuncturists reinterpret their knowledge of meridian theory and modify their acupoint selection according to knowledge of the nervous, circulatory and lymphatic systems. In addition to traditional adjunct therapies, such as cupping and scraping, acupuncturists also employ new modern forms of acupuncture that are based in part on biomedicine, such as ear acupuncture and head acupuncture. Electromagnetic energy sources – electrical current, magnetic fields, infrared light, lasers, etc. – are widely incorporated in clinical practice. But the growing authority of the biomedicine continues to encroach on Chinese medicine. In spite of their traditionally wide range of use, acupuncture and moxibustion are increasingly reserved for a narrow range of chronic illnesses that don't respond well to biomedical interventions.

ERIC I. KARCHMER

Administrative Litigation Law

Law in China has traditionally been viewed as a tool for carrying out the will of the rulers, not as a vehicle for the exercise of citizen control over them, and this view remained dominant in the first three decades of the People's Republic. Rules about the functioning of government were a method of top-down control designed to ensure that officials carried out their assigned tasks. Citizens with complaints about an official's behaviour could only make complaints to that official's superiors through an informal 'letters and visits' system, and had no legal right to relief.

During the first decade of the post-Mao reform era, however, the idea grew that bottom-up supervision also had a role to play, and that citizens aggrieved by bureaucratic arbitrariness and lawlessness ought to have a law-based avenue of relief. A number of laws and regulations passed in the 1980s made specific provision for the appeal to the courts of various decisions by government bodies. Finally, 1989 saw the passage of the Administrative Litigation Law (ALL), which provides that administrative decisions may be appealed to courts except where the law specifically states otherwise. While the ALL permits challenges to the application of specific rules and regulations, it does not in general allow challenges to the propriety or lawfulness of the rules themselves.

While complainants prevail at least in part in over 40 per cent of cases, the overall impact of the ALL on official behaviour is difficult to measure. On the one hand, the number of administrative litigation cases brought to courts has risen steadily from 13,000 in 1990 to 86,000 in 2000. On the other hand, these numbers are still quite small relative both to overall court caseloads and to the number of challengeable administrative acts.

Further reading

Peerenboom, R. (2002). *China's Long March Toward Rule of Law*. Cambridge: Cambridge University Press.

DONALD CLARKE

adoption

A traditional form of adoption in China is called *lisi*, literally 'establishing an heir', which usually involves the naming of a child, most likely a boy, as the descendant of couples who do not have biological children or sons of their own. This practice may or may not be legally binding, and as its main purpose is to continue the family's name it is rendered by the PRC as 'feudalistic'. By contrast, the PRC has established an Adoption Law that clearly states that the main purpose of adoption is to enrich the development of the child. The Law restricts adoption to children under fourteen who are: (1) orphans; (2) abandoned children whose birth parents are not found; or (3) children of birth parents who for hardship reasons are unable to raise them. Though abandonment of children is illegal in China, it is believed to be a major source of children in orphanages, also known as 'social welfare institutes'. It is widely known that the **one-child policy** has accelerated the abandonment of girl babies. Indeed, the children in orphanages are predominantly girls.

Official statistics report a total of about 900 orphanages in China caring for approximately 200,000 children. The Adoption Law applies similarly to domestic and international adoptive parents – they must be at least 30 years of age, must not have major illnesses, and must have a demonstrated capacity to raise a child. Single persons, but not homosexuals, are also eligible to be adoptive parents. As of 2000, there were roughly 14,000 domestic adoptions in China. It appears that among Chinese a negative connotation continues to be associated with adoption, which in part explains the relatively low number of domestic adoptions. Chinese adoptive parents also tend to hide the adoption from the child, using strategies such as moving to new communities where neighbours are not aware of the family's history.

By contrast, the international adoption of Chinese children is the focus of some of the most colourful and widely read stories about China since the early 1990s. In 2000, approximately 10,000 Chinese children were adopted by families from other countries. US families adopted a mere twenty-nine Chinese children in 1990 but by the late 1990s were adopting approximately 5,000 per year, 95 per cent of them girls. Since 1995, China has been ranked first or second (to Russia) as the largest source of adopted children in the USA. Canada and England are among the other prominent countries adopting Chinese children. Many Western adoptive parents see international adoption as an opportunity to further expand the family, and in China's case also as a response to the heavily criticized one-child policy and allegations of girl infanticide. The China Centre of Adoption Affairs in Beijing centralizes all international adoptions of Chinese children. Only a small number of orphanages are included in the international adoption system and their revenues are abundantly augmented by the 'donations', usually a predetermined sum, by adoptive parents. Children in other orphanages, such as those in remote locations, are much less likely to be adopted internationally.

Further reading

Families with Children from China website: http://www. fwcc.org

Johnson, Kay Ann (2003). *Wanting a Daughter, Needing a Son: Abandonment, Adoption, and Orphanage Care in China*. St Paul, MN: Yeong & Yeong.

C. CINDY FAN

adultery

Rejecting the polygamous sexual double standard of pre-socialist China, the Maoist state sought to prohibit adultery by both sexes. An adulterer might be forced to make a public self-criticism, or be demoted or even dismissed from a work unit. More rarely adulterers were imprisoned for hooliganism or rape. With the 'opening and reform' in the early 1980s some voices in the Chinese media began to argue for more tolerance, especially in cases in which the marriage was effectively dead. By the 1990s adultery had come to be seen as a national social problem contributing to rapidly rising divorce rates. According to sociologist Xu Anqi, more than 40 per cent of divorced couples in Shanghai cited adultery by one or both of the partners as a direct cause of their divorce. Chinese surveyed in the 1990s overwhelmingly disapproved of extramarital sex. However, in various sample surveys, between 10 and 30 per cent of Chinese married men and women said they had engaged in sex outside marriage. Moreover, in some areas of social life extramarital relations were tolerated or even condoned. A flood of novels, films and television serials treated 'extramarital love' with considerable sympathy and moral ambiguity. Popular commercial dance halls allowed both married men and women a convenient place to begin affairs. Business entertainment often featured hostesses who were available for further sexual services. A revision of the Marriage Law passed in 2001 (see **Marriage Law of the PRC (1 January 1981) and revisions (2001)**) explicitly prohibited cohabitation with a third person, attempting to rein in the practice of rich men keeping mistresses as secondary wives (**bao ernai**).

Further reading

Farrer, James (2002). *Opening Up: Youth Sex Culture and Market Reform in Shanghai*. Chicago: University of Chicago Press.

Zha, Bo and Geng, Wenxiu (1992). 'Sexuality in Urban China'. *The Australian Journal of Chinese Affairs* 28: 1–20.

JAMES FARRER

advertising

Advertising in the broadest sense of making goods publicly known developed as early as commodity exchange took shape in human society. In China, as elsewhere, the earliest medium of advertising was oral and even musical. *The Book of Odes* recorded an entry in the 'Hymns to Zhou' which tells anecdotes of street pedlars playing bamboo flutes to sell candies. Other variations of musical ads such as tinkers' clappers, waste-collectors' bells and the copper gongs of travelling sundriesmen are still heard all over China. Human voice is another commercial medium that hardly went out of date. Those growing up in 1950s and 1960s Taiwan will recall the melodious voice of soft bean curd vendors resonating through the night and at dawn. And today, tourists strolling down the bustling Snack Street at Wangfujing in downtown Beijing are still earnestly saluted by young shop clerks hawking their culinary specialties.

When the market developed further, the written word overtook the oral medium as a means of publicity. Signboards inscribed in calligraphy went up as another popular form of advertising that has persisted since the Song Dynasty (960–1279) and still exists today. Two of the historic store tablets in Beijing today, 'Tongren tang' for Chinese medicine and 'Quanjude' for **Beijing Roast Duck**, first greeted the consumer public during the Qing dynasty (1644–1911). Numerous rhymed couplet commercials mounted on scrolls and hung up at taverns enjoyed their own heyday during the same period. However, the first Chinese commercial in the genuine modern sense, complete with copywriting and a logo, is said to be a print ad made by a needle shop of the Liu family in Jinan during the Northern Song dynasty (960–1127). The ad extolled the fine quality of the Liu needles and used the visual of a white rabbit holding a medicine pounder as its store insignia.

Modern advertising in China came into being after the Opium War (1840). It departed from the random endeavours of individual advertisers to evolve into an organized guild commanding a vast network of commercial information and persuasion depending upon modern mass media such as radio and the paper. Modern print ads in China first appeared in foreign-owned papers *Shanghai xinbao*

(*Shanghai New Post*, c. 1861) and *Shen bao* (1872). But in the early twentieth century, the Chinese masses had limited access to radio and print media. Therefore, foreign advertisers resorted to a different medium, one most familiar to the common folk. These were Chinese New Year Poster (*nianhua*) ads, which remain popular today. They cover a wide range of subjects – scenic spots, portraits, historical figures, Confucian legends of filial piety, religious rituals, and still lifes of flowers, fish and animals. In most instances, these early modern poster ads bore little relationship to the product being sold, which occupied an obscure corner of the canvas. A notable example was an ad portraying a traditionally dressed young woman breast-feeding her mother-in-law, while the product advertised was a flashlight. Commodities featured frequently in those *nianhua* ads were cigarettes, of both foreign and domestic brands.

Print ads also appeared in pop magazines and journals during the May Fourth period (1917–21). Notable examples include *Dongfang Magazine* and *Good Companion* (*Liangyou*). Even Communist publications (e.g. Li Dazhao and Chen Duxiu's *Weekly Review* (1918) and Mao Zedong's *Xiang River Review* (1919)) courted advertisers and used ads as instruments of a political ideology promoting Chinese goods, progressive journals and anti-imperialism. In the commercial hub of Shanghai, a booming industry of advertising design and *nianhua* art rose to meet the demands of commercial clients. Most famous among those designer artists were Zhang Guangyu, Liang Dingming and Zheng Mantuo. But the **Cultural Revolution** (1966–76) brought an abrupt end to commercial advertising. A small handful of advertising agencies that flourished in Shanghai and other cities in the 1930s were also nipped in the bud. It was not until the early 1980s that the agency would re-emerge as a dominant player of commercial communications.

The first TV commercial of post-Mao China – for a domestic tonic wine – was aired by Shanghai Television Station in January 1979. Later that year, the municipal government of Beijing moved the Democracy Wall at Xidan to Yuetan Park and turned the original site into an advertising wall. Outdoor billboards began to mushroom. Shanghai, Guangzhou and Beijing soon became the three pillars of advertising. The Association of Chinese

Advertising (Zhongguangxie) was founded in 1983, mediating between agencies and the official regulator of the sector – the State Administration of Industry and Commerce. The Advertising Law came into effect in 1995. Regulation was focused on deceitful advertisements. Comparative advertising is banned. So are tobacco ads. But, with the exception of medicine, the law is not considered cumbersome for most product categories. More important were rules governing the entry of transnational agencies in the mid 1980s, whose presence – 328 companies at the end of 2000 – has had a beneficial impact on local talent training. Increasingly, however, as local agencies became more seasoned practitioners, a discursive contestation between local and transnational practice developed. The year 2001 marked the height of the controversy over the American model of the 4A (Association of Accredited Advertising Agency) and the publication of other critical literature challenging Western marketing concepts. But the industry's craving for foreign models and methodologies has also given birth to several trade magazines that are instrumental to the shaping of the guild consciousness of Chinese ad men and women – *Chinese Advertising* (1981), *International Advertising* (1985) and *Modern Advertising* (1994). By early 2000, China had more than 64,800 advertising units with a total billing expected to rise up to US$11 billion. The top five categories of highest advertising business volume are household appliances, food and beverages, medicines, cosmetics and real estate.

Media in post-Mao China have also grown in parallel. Besides tier 1 cities, radio coverage is relatively low. Online advertising is still young. Television is the most popular medium for advertisers. In Guangzhou and Shenzhen, however, the newspaper has upstaged TV as the most advantageous medium of advertising. The national TV audience amounts to 1 billion, with an average viewing time for adults stretched to 175 minutes daily. The 2001 state policy of consolidating cable and terrestrial network will shrink China's astounding number of 3,280 TV stations into a more controllable pool. This decree, however, has weakened significantly the bargaining power of ad agencies to negotiate with provincial media vendors. In China, where media are

state owned, changing media policies impacts advertising in a way unprecedented in world advertising history.

Post-socialist media policy is a double-edged sword. In fact, a decisive momentum that helped jump-start the advertising industry also came from a historic policy change. In 1993, Beijing gave freer rein to news media to run their operations as businesses rather than public institutional units. With decreasing state subsidies, the media had to court advertisers for new sources of revenue. **CCTV (Chinese Central Television)**, for instance, held public auctions between 1994 and 2000 to crown an annual 'champion bidder' who paid world record-breaking prices for prime-time spots. The most publicized scandal was the bid made by Qinchi Liquor Distillery in 1996 – 320 million RMB (approximately $40 million) for a five-second spot. For more than a decade, the agency–media relationship was tilted in the latter's favour. Toward the end of the 1990s, however, proliferating media outlets turned the media market from a seller's to a buyer's market. The old scenario of 'weak agency, strong media' is now in flux. Since early 2001, the media landscape has been framed in new terms of competition. It was CCTV and its emerging rival – a united front of elite provincial stations – who were busy vying for clients who now enjoy the luxury of making media choices strategically. The old relationship between media and agency was further adjusted because of the rise of powerful media-buying networks in the mid 1990s. Primarily subsidiaries belonging to joint-venture agencies (e.g. Ogilvy, J. P. Thompson, Saatchi and Saatchi, and Grey, etc.), these networks have the advantage of buying advertising spots in bulk, thus offsetting to a certain degree the weak negotiating power of transnational agencies in their dealings with traditionally **Guanxi**-based Chinese media. MindShare, Zenith Media and Mediacom are a few examples. They gain an edge over local media brokers because they provide media planning strategies based on quantitative media research and analysis. Increasingly, clients are keen on understanding brand relationships and the media consumption patterns of consumer segments through those research tools.

The media, of course, were not the lone determining factor for the swift development of post-Mao advertising. Another momentum came from the industrial/commercial sector. In the late 1980s, Apollo (Taiyang shen), a health-drink company in Guangdong, imported a new management system, CIS (Corporate Identity System), from Japan. Its investment on the sub-system VI (visual identity) brought about a huge success. The company logo was turned into a household image overnight. Corporate China has been fascinated with the cash value of the VI ever since. Commercial logos abound in all mediums. Together with the notion of brand names, they fed the imagination of the commercial sector for a 'corporate culture' (qiye wenhua) that is rooted in the concept of 'culture as capital'.

Increasingly, Chinese advertisers were coached to comprehend the links between branding and a corporate culture that sells. To better serve and communicate the brand value, transnational agencies in China have been busy making a transition from ad agencies into communications companies since the mid 1990s. The 360-degree brand stewardship of Ogilvy is a notable example. The integration of various disciplines within an agency – account service, planning, creative, accounting, public relations and direct/interactive marketing – is now the going model for full-service agencies of the future. Although local clients are slow to buy the trend, China's entry into the World Trade Organization (2002) will move advertising in the direction of brand-building rather than simple ad production.

See also: Party advertising and self-promotion

Further reading

Wang, Jing (2001). 'Introduction'. In idem (ed.), Chinese Popular Culture and the State. Special issue of positions: east asia cultures critique 9.1.

—— (2001). 'Culture as Leisure, Culture as Capital'. positions: east asia cultures critique 9.1: 69–104.

Yu, Hong and Zhengqiang, Deng (2000). Zhongguo dangdai guanggaoshi [The History of Contemporary Chinese Advertising]. Changsha: Hunan kexue jishu chubanshe.

Zhao, Shen (2001). Zhongguo jindai guanggao wenhua [The Culture of Modern Chinese Advertising]. Changchun: Jilin kexue jishu chubanshe.

WANG JING

Ah Cheng

(né Zhong Acheng)

b. 1949, Beijing

Writer

During the **Cultural Revolution**, Ah Cheng spent some time in Inner Mongolia before going to the Xishuangbanna region of Yunnan in the tropical southwest. He returned to Beijing in 1979. In 1984 he wrote 'The King of Chess' (Qiwang), an award-winning short story that earned him universal acclaim. In the following year, he wrote two more 'King' stories as well as a series of sketches entitled Romances of the Landscape (Biandi fengliu) which describe the scenery and customs of border areas far from 'civilization'. In 1986, Ah Cheng emigrated to the USA, where he continued to write, though never attracting the attention that the 'King' stories received.

The most striking feature of both the 'King' stories and his 'landscape romances' is Ah Cheng's use of language and narrative, which borrow heavily from traditional storytelling techniques. Closely related is the skilful introduction of ideas drawn from Confucianism and Daoism, philosophies that had been attacked vehemently in the previous three decades. His descriptions of life in the countryside are also remarkable, avoiding both the self-pity of **Scar literature** and the idealized images of orthodox and pastoral writers. Because of his debt to traditional Chinese culture, Ah Cheng is usually included among the **Root-seeking school** of writers (xungenpai). However, in the 'King' stories, he avoids their excessive emphasis on violence and brutality.

Further reading

Ah, Cheng (1990). Three Kings. Three Stories from Today's China. Trans. Bonnie McDougall. London: Collins Harvill.

Ah, Cheng (1992). 'The First Half of My Life: A Boy from the City Struggling for Survival in Far-Away Yunnan'. Trans. Linette Lee. In Helmut Martin (ed.), *Modern Chinese Writers: Self-portrayals*. Armonk, NY: M. E. Sharpe, 107–17.

KAM LOUIE

Ai Jing

b. 1969, Shenyang, Dongbei

Pop singer, actress

Ai Jing was one of the first in a series of music stars packaged by the Chinese recording industry. Ai Jing's musical style is influenced by her parents who were able to play many kinds of traditional instruments, especially her mother who was also an actress of Peking opera. After receiving music training in Shenyang Special School of Art, she entered the Shenyang Performance Troupe in 1985 and became a contracted singer for the Oriental Performance Troupe (Dongfang gewutuan) in 1987.

Since 1992, Ai Jing (www.aijing.com) has recorded more than seven albums, including *My 1997* (*Wo de 1997*, 1992), *Once Upon a Time in Yanfen Street* (*Yanfenjie de gushi*, 1995) and *Made in China* (1998). In addition, Ai Jing has also acted in films such as *Five Girls and a Rope* (Yeh Hung-Wei, dir., 1991), **Beijing Bastards** (Zhang Yuan, dir., 1993) and *From the Queen to the Chief Executive* (Herman Yao Lai-to, dir., 2000).

Her songs exude the light-heartedness of an ordinary girl. Her tunes are plain, a little understated, with a touch of humour on political issues. Her simple autobiographical rhetoric is very popular with Chinese audiences. The famous song 'My 1997' was issued four times between 1992 and 1997, both in China and in Hong Kong and Japan. It tells the story of a young mainland-born woman who anxiously waits for the return of Hong Kong to China in 1997 so that she can visit her boyfriend in Hong Kong.

Further reading

Baranovitch, Nimrod (2003). *China's New Voices: Popular Music, Ethnicity, Gender, and Politics*. Berkeley: University of California Press, 161–73.

REN HAI

Ai Weiwei

b. 1957, Beijing

Exhibition organizer, artist

Not long after his graduation from the **Beijing Film Academy**, in 1981 Ai Weiwei moved to New York City where he lived until 1993. Through exposure to art museums and contemporary exhibition practices in New York, he formed the idea of establishing his own art gallery and art magazine in Beijing. He then became the publisher and chief editor of *Heipi shu* (Black-cover Book, 1994), *Baipi shu* (White-cover Book, 1995) and *Huipi shu* (Grey-cover Book, 1997), a series of privately published journals focusing on emerging installation and performance artists, who would not get a chance otherwise to be exposed in the Chinese media. The three 'books' included translations of modernist and contemporary art documents. Since the late 1990s, Ai has been one of the directors of China Art Archives and Warehouse, a contemporary art exhibition space in Beijing (see **van Dijk, Hans**). In 2000, he co-organized with **Feng Boyi** the exhibition *Bu hezuo fangshi* (Uncooperative Method) for which the English translation of 'Fuck Off' was used. With about fifty artists, including Ai Weiwei himself, the show tried to expose current trends of contemporary art in China of the 1990s, from performance to installation, from painting to video and photography.

As an artist, Ai Weiwei's work is often related to his antique collecting. The major theme in many of his works deals with issues of authenticity, displacement of meaning of reproduction of a traditional object in a changed form of existence. This is the case of his porcelain- and furniture-related works such as *Blue and White after Kangxi, Qianlong and Yongzhen* (1997) which are replicas of the finest crafts in China's porcelain tradition, as well as the

Table series (1996) where traditional furniture styles and shapes are subverted and reassembled. Ai Weiwei has exhibited extensively worldwide featuring in shows such as 'The Star: Ten Years' (Hanart Gallery, Hong Kong, 1989), 'Configura 2-Dialog der Kultur' (Germany, 1995), the 48th Biennale of Venice (Italy, 1999) and 'New Zone – Chinese Art' at the Zecheta National Gallery of Art (Warsaw, 2003).

Further reading

Chang, Tsong-zung *et al.* (1989). *The Stars: Ten Years*. Hong Kong: Hanart 2 Gallery.

De Matté, Monica (1999). 'Ai Weiwei'. In *La Biennale di Venezia, 48a Esposizione d'Arte, d'Apertutto, Aperto Over All*. Marsilio: La Biennale di Venezia, 122–23.

Hua, Yianxue *et al.* (eds), (2000). *Fuck Off* (exhibition catalogue). N.p.

Merewether, Charles (ed.) (2003). *Ai Weiwei, Works: Beijing 1993–2003*. Beijing: Timezone 8.

Pachnicke, Peter and Mensch, Bernhard (2002). *CHINA Tradition und Moderne*. Oberhausen: Ludwig Galerie-Schloss Oberhausen.

Zeng, Xiaojun, Ai, Weiwei and Xu, Bing (1994). *The Red Flag – the Black Cover Book*, 43–51.

QIAN ZHIJIAN

works have been translated into several foreign languages. The 2002 publication of the English translation of his novel was a landmark event for Tibetan writers in the PRC.

Alai's writings are set mostly in his homeland, the Tibetan region of Kham, historically beyond the rule of Lhasa. They exhibit a deep love of the land and its independent folk spirit combined with soul-searching reflections on the environmental degradation, social decay and cultural displacement in modern times. *Red Poppies* describes the turbulence and collapse of a traditional chiefdom prior to 1949. It is narrated by an idiot, born to a Tibetan father and a Han Chinese mother, and highlights the hybrid culture of the border region. Epical in historical scope yet poetic in prose, this novel of 'idiocy' evokes a similar experience to reading Faulkner or Marquez.

See also: Tibetans, culture of; Ma Yuan

Further reading

Alai (2003). *Red Poppies: A Novel of Tibet*. Trans. Howard Goldblatt and Sylvia Li-chun Li. Boston: Mariner Books.

YUE GANG

Alai

b. 1959, Maerkang, Sichuan

Writer

Alai is a Tibetan writer publishing in Chinese. He was born into a peasant family and taught both primary and middle school after graduating from college in 1980. He began to publish in 1982 and became a professional writer in 1984. He later moved to Chengdu and has since worked as an editor for a science fiction magazine. His first collection of short stories was published in 1989, and his first volume of poetry in 1990. *Red Poppies* (*Chen'ai luoding*), his first novel, appeared in 1998 and won the Mao Dun prize (see **literary awards**). He has also published volumes of essays and interviews and produced television scripts. His

All-China Women's Federation

Established in March 1949 as the All-China Democratic Women's Federation, it was renamed Women's Federation of the People's Republic of China in 1957. The current name was first used in 1978. All-China Women's Federation is a non-governmental organization (under CCP leadership) of women from all walks of life and ethnic backgrounds. Its mission is to strive for women's equal opportunities and to encourage them to participate in the nation's economic and social development. It also teaches women to become self-respectful, self-confident, self-reliant and self-aspiring. It engages them in the process of decision-making in national affairs. It also works to strengthen the unity of Chinese women from all circles and ethnic groups, from various regions and foreign soils for the purpose of China's reunification and world peace.

The highest decision-making body of the federation is the National Women's Congress, with branches at all levels throughout China, governed with the principle of democratic centralism: Women's Committees in governmental departments and non-profit organizations, and Trade Union Women Workers' Councils in factories and mines. Branches in cities usually take the city's name, such as Beijing Women's Federation and Shanghai Women's Federation. On the one hand, branches report to the national federation, fulfilling its mission; on the other, they initiate activities and events befitting their local circumstances. Beijing Women's Federation, for example, has organized 'Women Establishing Themselves', reading parties and training classes for unemployed women. Projects on research into women's issues by the Shanghai branch are marked with that city's characteristics.

Further reading

Hsiung, Ping-chun, Jaschok, Maria and Milwertz, Cecilia (eds) (2002). *Chinese Women Organizing*. Oxford: Berg.

Judd, Ellen (2002). *The Chinese Women's Movement between State and Market*. Stanford: Stanford University Press.

HU MINGRONG

An Hong

b. 1963, Beijing

Photographer

An Hong studied graphic design at the Central Academy of Arts and Design in Beijing, graduating in 1985. From 1985 to 1994 his modern, highly stylized calligraphy and ink paintings caught the attention of both national and international audiences. From 1992 to 1994 he went to the Lahti Academy of Design in Finland to lecture on Chinese calligraphy, and travelled around Europe.

An Hong's most indelible mark on the Chinese art scene is to be found in his Buddha performance pieces and photographs, also known as *JG2* or *Jingang*, a reference to a class of indestructible divine warriors who protect the Buddha and his doctrine. In these works, An Hong cloaks his own gold-painted body in an elaborate costume of his own design and construction and takes on the persona of a modern-day living Buddha, often appearing in sexually provocative poses. The series is formed from an eclectic mix of Buddhism, Chinese opera, popular culture and kitsch iconography. An Hong's 'living Buddha' provides cures for modern-day ailments such as stress, AIDS or a lack of love. Messages of this nature are incorporated into his performances or photographic images through actual propaganda signs and absurd humour. During performances he often gives massage therapy or distributes concoctions of Coca-Cola and Chinese medicine to audience volunteers.

An Hong has performed his living Buddha in 'Fortune Cookies' at the Institute of Contemporary Art, London, and exhibited his photographs in the 1999 Biennale de Lyon (France) and in 'Portraits, Figures, Couples and Groups from the Mcaf Foundation' (BizArt, Shanghai, 2000). He teaches Graphic Design at the Beijing Arts and Design Academy.

Further reading

Schmid, Andreas (1997). *Zeitgenössische Fotokunst aus der Volksrepublic China*. Heidelberg: Edition Braus, 32–7.

Spada, Clayton (1999). *Hsin: A Visible Spirit – Contemporary Photography from the People's Republic of China* (exhibition catalogue). Cypress, CA: Cypress College.

MATHIEU BORYSEVICZ

ancestral halls/lineage temples

Ancestral halls are often the largest and most elaborate buildings in a Chinese village. With the initiation of economic liberalization in the early 1980s, ancestral halls began reclaiming their pre-revolutionary significance as community centres, ritual sites and focal points of lineage authority.

Although most ancestral halls were either destroyed or secularized to function as village schools or granaries during the land reform of the 1950s and the **Cultural Revolution** of the 1960s, norms and networks of lineage unity have remained resilient. In most reconstruction projects the majority of households make voluntary donations. The rebuilding of community ancestral halls is especially prevalent in southeastern China, where lineage organizations were historically more developed and where more communities enjoy donations from relations overseas.

The revival of lineage activities and ancestral halls has occurred despite the opposition of local officials in some areas and with their implicit or active support and participation in others. In the more liberalized areas, the committees formed to oversee ancestral hall reconstruction projects often evolve into permanent lineage councils that organize religious, social and philanthropic activities, though none preside over collective land as in the past. The local governments in these areas reason that such non-official (**minjian** (popular space)) social institutions help finance public services such as road building and village education as well as promote social stability by keeping the behaviour of its members within prescribed bounds. In other areas, lineages may promote norms of unity through organized activities and rituals but lack a formal association.

Lineage halls serve as sites for collective rituals and festivals in which people make obeisance to their ancestors with offerings of food and other material items. **Weddings**, betrothals, **funerals**, lineage feasts and meetings of lineage elders may also take place at lineage halls, which are now also used as polling booths for village elections (see **democracy and elections**) and recreational centres for children and the elderly.

Lineage halls vary immensely in their level of grandeur, necessarily depending on the wealth and ritual needs of lineage members. But they all have certain elements in common, such as furniture and ritual objects and their placement. Smaller halls consist of a main room flanked by two smaller rooms. Larger lineage halls are recessed more deeply behind one or more rectangular courtyards that may also be lined with side halls. Inside the lineage hall, altars take the form of either a shelf accessible by a short ladder or a high narrow table placed against the back wall and facing the entryway. Ancestral tablets embodying the ancestral spirits are organized by seniority, and ritual items such as incense censers, divination blocks, statues and souvenirs from visits to related-lineage halls typically clutter one or more square tables placed in front of the altar and various rectangular tables to the sides. Brightly painted lineage halls may have ornate carvings, paintings and hangings which adorn the pillars and walls. As community centres, contemporary lineage halls may also display group photographs of lineage members at festivals or on sightseeing trips, awards and banners won by village sports teams or performance groups, and government plaques bestowed on the village for model behaviour.

See also: Ghost Festival; Qingming Festival; villages; weddings (rural)

Further reading

Faure, David (1986). *The Structure of Chinese Rural Society*. Hong Kong: Oxford University Press.

Knapp, Ronald G. (1989). *Chinese Vernacular Architecture: House Form and Culture*. Honolulu: University of Hawai'i Press.

—— (1999). *China's Living Houses: Folk Beliefs, Symbols, and Household Ornamentation*. Honolulu: University of Hawai'i Press.

Tsai, Lily (2002). 'Cadres, Temple and Lineage Organizations, and Governance in Rural China'. *The China Journal* 48: 1–33.

L. L. TSAI

animation

(donghuapian)

The Shanghai Animation Studio (Shanghai meishu dianying) is probably the best-known animation studio in China. Founded in the northeast in 1947, the studio was renamed and moved to Shanghai in 1950. It has excelled in both puppet animation (*mu'ou pian*) and drawn animation, with a particular expertise in adapting popular visual styles (paper cuts, soft ink-wash brush painting, New Year style wood-cuts or *nianhua* and so on) for animated film. The soft ink-wash style (*shuimo donghua*) is exemplified in *Little Tadpoles Look for Mummy* (*Xiao kedou zhao mama*, 1960/1). This story of little creatures unable to recognize their mother (a frog, of course!) is an entirely familiar narrative to children the world over, and marks a moment of classic storytelling in the Chinese animation tradition.

Puppet animation was famously exploited by the *Little Wooden Head* or *Little Ding Dong* series (*Xiao Ling Dang*, Beijing Film Studio, 1964). This film, directed by Xie Tian, the revered actor and director of 'small children's films', takes two children into the streets of Beijing for an adventure with a living boy-puppet. They end up in the **Children's Palace** (*Shaoniangong*) in the centre of the city, before finally going home. The significance of the film may lie in its portrait of a safe, publicly oriented and child-friendly city, bringing together the romance of the puppet character with the naïveté of childhood.

Recently, animation has undergone a crisis in the face of imports from Disney and Japan (including the Pokémon phenomenon), the pressure of more sophisticated audiences, and the need to digitize production. The crisis has led the **State Administration for Radio, Film and Television**, beginning in 2000, to reserve a ten-minute time-slot on televisions across China for domestic animation. The huge cost of this requirement has encouraged co-productions with foreign content providers, but also some excellent work, including an all-new *Journey to the West* (*Xiyouji*, 2000), and an increasingly strong profile for animation-based storytelling on television and in film. *The Lotus Lantern* (*Bao lian deng*, 1999), a feature-length animation and recent hit, marked a watershed in the commercial expression of this national art. It continues the narrative of child heroism explored earlier in such films as *Nezha Calms the Sea* (Wang Shuchen, Shanghai, 1979) and *Hailibu* (Huang Wei, Shanghai, 1985), but there is also a distinct sense of Disneyfication. Some of the characters display an anachronistic, self-deprecating irony, which smacks of the Eddie Murphy funny-guy gags in *Mulan* and *Shrek*. At one point a Qin tomb soldier falls back into place in Xi'an and – almost – raises an eyebrow at his own bad luck. Furthermore, the depiction of 'indigeneity' and

'primitivism' has become sleek and somewhat removed from the more clearly naïve romanticism of earlier films. The heroine strongly resembles the faux innocence of Disney's Pocahontas.

Further reading

Donald, Stephanie (2000). *Public Secrets, Public Spaces: Cinema and Civility in China*. Lanham, MD: Rowman and Littlefield.

—— (2001). 'History, Entertainment, Education and *Jiaoyu*: A Western Australian Perspective on Australian Children's Media, and Some Chinese Alternatives'. *International Journal of Cultural Studies* 4.3: 279–99.

Gao, Fang (1999–2000). 'Minzu fengge de tansuo – zhongguo donghua dianying' [The Pursuit of a National Style in Chinese Animation Film]. In Gao Fang, 'Xuni de shijie: donghua dianying lilun tansuo' [A Fictitious World: Looking for Theory in Animation] (unpubl. ms).

Internal documents (2000). *Handbook of Directors (1900–1999)*, Shanghai Animation Studio.

—— (nd, 2000–1?). *Handbook of Films*. Shanghai Animation Studio.

Lent, John (2000). 'Animation in Asia: Appropriation, Reinterpretation, and Adoption or Adaption'. *Screening the Past* 11. Online journal, available at http://www.screen@latrobe.edu.au

Lent, John and Xu, Ying (2001). 'Animation in China Yesterday and Today – The Pioneers Speak Out'. *Asian Cinema* 12.2 (Fall/Winter): 34–49.

Xu, Ying (2000). 'Animation Film Production in Beijing'. *Asian Cinema* 11.2 (Fall/Winter): 60–6.

STEPHANIE HEMELRYK DONALD

Aniwar, Mamat

b. 1962, Kashgar

Painter

Mamat Aniwar is an independent Uighur painter living in Beijing, best known for his large and mainly abstract oil paintings that incorporate motifs of Uighur culture (see **Uighurs (Weiwu'er), culture of**). He has also painted a large number of paintings with ink and watercolour on Korean paper and worked with more figurative and universal motifs related mainly to sexuality and life, such as sperms, sex organs and female bodies. Aniwar is hailed as one of China's most innovative and bold artists and his work has been presented in numerous exhibitions in China and abroad. Since the late 1990s, he has been affiliated with the famous Courtyard Gallery in Beijing (see **art galleries (private, commercial)**).

After a short period of study in 1980 at the Tianjin Institute of Art and Design, he worked between 1981 and 1984 as a carpet designer in the Xinjiang Woven Carpet Design Centre. Between 1985 and 1987 he studied oil painting at the **Central University for Nationalities** in Beijing, and he is currently teaching at the School of Arts and Design in the capital. Aniwar's oil paintings combine modern Western techniques and styles with patterns, forms, colours and textures that draw upon traditional Central Asian and Islamic architecture, carpets and textiles. Another source of inspiration evident in his work is the landscape, fauna, and flora of the deserts of Xinjiang. In this unique combination Aniwar offers an important alternative to the dominant visual representation of Uighur culture in China, which either sticks to the revolutionary socialist realist style, or tends to paint it with orientalistic, exotic colours.

NIMROD BARANOVITCH

aphrodisiacs

The reform era in China has been marked by a growing interest in aphrodisiacs, which has often been misunderstood by foreign observers in terms of a purely instrumentalist notion of sexual stimulation. 'Adult health shops', selling birth control supplies, sexual aids and a variety of sexual stimulants, are now common in urban areas. Restaurants, featuring deer antler wine, animal male genitalia or other dishes to stimulate (usually male) sexual desire are not hard to find. And a new discipline of Chinese medicine, *Nanke* or Men's Medicine, that explicitly treats male sexual disorders, was officially established in the 1980s. Although there is a decidedly male bias to the

current interest in sexual stimulants, it is also important to recognize its deep historical links with Chinese conceptions of health. The ancient practitioners of China's bedchamber arts (*fangzhongshu*) were as much interested in prolonging life as they were in exploring sexual pleasures. Ancient predecessors of today's Chinese medicine *Nanke* doctors treated sexual disorders by redressing imbalances in the body and not by directly stimulating sexual desire. Pfizer's revolutionary new drug, Viagra, has yet to shake this more holistic understanding of sexual function. Chinese medicine *Nanke* doctors have incorporated Viagra into their regimen of male impotency treatments. But many impotency patients see it as merely temporary relief and believe that Chinese herbal remedies still offer the best hope for achieving a permanent solution to their debilitating condition.

Further reading

Farquhar, Judith (2002). *Appetites: Food and Sex in Post-Socialist China*. Durham and London: Duke University Press.

ERIC I. KARCHMER

arbitration law

Arbitration of disputes has emerged as a workable alternative to reliance on the judicial system. Arbitration of disputes involving Chinese domestic enterprises is handled by various administrative departments with jurisdiction over the subject matter: for example, labour disputes are handled by the local Labour Administration, while contract disputes are under the authority of the State Administration for Industry and Commerce. Under both the revised Economic Contract Law (1993) and the Unified Contract Law (1999), significant encouragement was given to arbitration of contract disputes. Chinese courts have actively engaged in arbitration as a more flexible alternative to the litigation process requirements of the Civil Procedure Law. Maritime disputes are subject to the China Maritime Arbitration Commission. Under the Arbitration Law of the PRC (1995), arbitration of domestic commercial disputes has devolved from administrative agencies such as the State Administration for Industry and Commerce (SAIC) to local chambers of commerce and other quasi-civil organizations.

Arbitration and conciliation between Chinese and foreign parties in economic and trade matters were traditionally under the exclusive jurisdiction of the China International Economic and Trade Arbitration Commission (CIETAC) under the China Council for the Promotion of International Trade (CCPIT) in Beijing and its sub-councils in Shanghai and Shenzhen. The CIETAC Arbitration Rules have been amended several times over the past few years, to accommodate the concerns of foreign parties and to accord with the requirements of the PRC Arbitration Law (1995). Unlike the situation at the People's Courts, CIETAC permits foreign lawyers to represent their clients directly in arbitration proceedings. Pursuant to the Arbitration Law, local arbitration committees linked with local people's governments are authorized to handle foreign-related disputes. While this has the potential to expand and diversify the venues available for foreign dispute settlement, concerns have been raised about the effectiveness and impartiality of the new provincial arbitration bodies.

CIETAC practices reflect the internationaliza-tion of China's official legal culture. By virtue of its hearing process in which foreign lawyers can par-ticipate and at which foreign and international law can be pleaded as governing law, and through the inclusion of foreign specialists on its panel of arbi-trators, CIETAC is constantly exposed to interna-tional norms. Moreover CIETAC's audience includes foreign firms, which have the opportunity to select or reject CIETAC as an arbitration venue. These factors exercise a powerful influence, drawing CIETAC increasingly into the ambit of interna-tional norms. CIETAC arbitration decisions reflect an increased willingness to follow international legal norms in other cases where specific provisions of Chinese law are either unavailable or unclear. CIETAC's rules for arbitrators proscribe *ex parte* contact and other improprieties. CIETAC arbitral awards are subject to enforcement internationally pursuant to the New York Convention on the Recognition and Enforcement of Foreign Arbitral Awards, to which China acceded effective 1987. Also influential has been the 'Understanding on Rules and Procedures Governing the Settlement of Disputes' appended to the Marrakech Agreement establishing the World Trade Organization. While practice in each of these areas remains inconsistent, the pattern is one of steady internationalization, mediated by norms of local legal culture.

PITMAN POTTER

architectural criticism and theory

Forced to dance to the government's tune during the Mao era, architectural writing since the 1979 reform has gained freedom but is also dominated by Western concepts. Pre-reform China shunned modern Western theory in its struggle against the capitalist world. The Soviet doctrine of 'national form with socialist content' was borrowed in the 1950s and embraced by most leading Chinese architects, due to their nationalist feeling and beaux-arts education in the 1920s USA. Liang Sicheng of **Qinghua University** even proposed a theory of using traditional forms as vocabularies in any architectural composition. The doctrine, too expensive to implement, was replaced in 1959 by an architecturally meaningless principle which stated that buildings should be 'functional, eco-nomic and aesthetic when conditions permit'. A few lone Modernist voices did exist in this period, such as Feng Jizhong at Tongji University in Shanghai. Trained in the Bauhaus system, Feng discussed the four basic space types and their functional implications in *An Outline of Spatial Principles* (*Kongjian yuanli shuyao*, 1964). This period also saw the completion of several excellent surveys of historical buildings and gardens under the direction of Liu Dunzhen. After 1979, the state no longer tightly controlled architectural discussions. However, architects generally lost interest in theory in an increasingly market-oriented China after the 1990s. Development since the reform can be outlined in four aspects.

First, Western architectural theory is being trans-lated and published in **architectural journals** and books at an unprecedented pace. Chinese scholars, some of whom have been educated in the West since 1978 (e.g. Wang Tan, Xue Qiuli and Shen Kening), have also produced competent analyses of new developments in Western architectural thought. Such were the most popular reading among architecture students until the market replaced theory as the guiding light in the 1990s.

Second, numerous research monographs on traditional architecture have emerged. They provide systematic analysis, fresh perspectives and methods, and substantial new data, especially the work of Chen Congzhou, Guo Husheng and several younger historians. Many of these projects study vernacular architecture, scenic area planning and village forms, topics previously ignored by the academy.

Third, in the search for a direction for today's Chinese architecture, the debate between traditional and modern styles again dominated the scene until the mid 1990s, at which time the consensus shifted towards the latter. Using methods borrowed from the West, Xu Ping and Miao Pu examined the deep structure of traditional architecture rather than its superficial styles. There are also writings attempting to construct frameworks for general theories of architecture and for new fields of research. Many of these efforts could be improved by introducing more original concepts, rigorous methods and updated data. Surprisingly, few works have been done in quantitative research on basic functional and technological issues, much needed in a developing country.

And finally, in a culture which values personal connections and sees academic criticism as a form of disrespect, architectural criticism is largely eulogistic. Nevertheless, a few critics, such as Zeng Zhaofen and Chen Zhihua, have broken the taboo. Their sharp diagnostics, especially Chen's *Notes at the North Window* (*Beichuang zaji*), attack both the revivalist and market-oriented design approaches and call for a return to the true Modernist tradition.

MIAO PU

architectural journals

Three periodicals published in Beijing form the core of Chinese architectural journals. Sponsored by the Architectural Society of China and the state, *Architectural Journal* (*Jianzhu xuebao*) is the only one established before the Reform and available in libraries all over the world. The *Journal* provides the only comprehensive coverage of all major Chinese architectural projects. It publishes designs as well as theory and governmental policy studies.

The 1979 Reform ushered in a proliferation of architectural journals. The most important newcomer is *Architect* (*Jianzhushi*), issued as a book series. Focusing on architectural criticism and theory, it single-handedly introduced major Western theoretical works to Chinese architects and provides the only venue for Chinese scholars to publish substantial research papers. It also pioneered the promotion of experimental designs by young Chinese architects.

Since the 1990s, Chinese architects have increasingly relied on fashionable Western architectural examples to produce quick schemes in a booming economy. This explains why *World Architecture* (*Shijie jianzhu*), established in 1979 and specializing in architectural designs outside of China, has become the most widely read publication, even surpassing *Architectural Journal*. There are several national journals published in other major cities. Often subsidized by large local design firms, their formats look better but their editorial policies tend to be swayed by the sponsors and by the popular interest. These journals frequently devote equal if not more space to the foreign architectural scene than to the domestic one. Articles are usually shorter and centre around images.

MIAO PU

architectural styles

The majority of buildings erected in China between 1949 and 1979 appeared as simple boxes: not, however, in a conscious pursuit of Modernism, but as the result of a poor economy. As for the small number of public buildings intended as architecture (e.g. the 'Ten Grand Projects' in Beijing during the 1950s), Soviet classicism and Chinese classical revivalism were the official styles, reflecting both government control and the taste of leading architects. The only exception was Guangzhou's 'New Architecture' in the 1960s and 1970s which combined Modernist form with traditional Chinese garden space. Since the 1979

Reform, material prosperity and more artistic freedom have produced a freewheeling variety of styles which can be described according to the following three characteristics.

First, 'imitation', a trait inherited from the pre-Reform era, remains the chief design approach. In many designs viewers can easily identify the original building from which they were copied. Even avant-garde designers cannot do away with replicating Western avant-garde. The favoured models used to be Chinese classical and vernacular architecture, causing many high-rise buildings to wear the hats of traditional roofs. But with an increasingly modernized and younger China, other forms like Western classicism, Modernism, and high-tech styles have entered the mainstream since the mid 1990s.

Second, architectural design tends to focus on the visual image of a building. This is because the available construction budget, material, technology and many other factors often do not match those of the model that is being imitated. To quickly satisfy the demands of clients, architects produce eye-catching facades with abundant add-ons which often bear little relationship to internal functions, spatial layouts or actual systems of construction, such as a brick-bearing wall dressed in glass curtains.

Third, contemporary Chinese architecture emphasizes instant sensations. Popular design treatments include monumental compositions with grand scales, or dynamic curvilinear forms with exotic ornaments and bright colours. In some cases, entire buildings are made into giant symbols to resemble a boat or ancient bronzeware.

These three characteristics can be attributed to the unique contemporary Chinese culture. Due to the cultural destruction between 1949 and 1979, the majority of the public are poorly educated. Today's China also displays uncertainty and cynicism in its cultural and political beliefs, and in the absence of coherent ideals, the society is absorbed in immediate material wealth and political power at both the personal and the national level. What patrons demand most are not artworks exploring lasting cultural values but billboards to generate a quick commercial or political sale. Such goals can be achieved most effectively by using well-established skin-deep but eye-catching forms.

The current state of architectural affairs also has to do with the lack of a Modernist tradition.

Architectural education (such as at **Qinghua University**) is dominated by a system established by architects who were trained in the beaux-arts tradition in the United States during the 1920s. When China opened its doors after 1979, postmodern architecture was at its peak in the West. Both events reinforced the Chinese habit of revering established things and seeing architecture as decoration.

Further reading

Gandelsonas, Mario (2002). *Shanghai Reflections: Architecture, Urbanism, and the Search for an Alternative Modernity*. Princeton: Princeton Architectural Press.

Liu, Ermin and Yi, Feng (eds) (1997). *Chinese Architecture since 1980*, 3 vols. Beijing: Encyclopedia of China Publishing House. [Covers the work of both young and established Chinese architects and that of foreign firms; in Chinese and English.]

Miao, Pu (1995). 'In the Absence of Authenticity: An Interpretation of Contemporary Chinese Architecture'. *Nordic Journal of Architectural Research* 3: 7–24.

Rowe, Peter G. and Seng, Kuan (2002). *Architectural Encounters with Essence and Form in Modern China*. Cambridge, MA: MIT Press.

MIAO PU

art academies

Art academies have played a fundamental role in the development of contemporary Chinese art, and to this day the majority of contemporary artists are a product of the academic system of art education. In the early twentieth century, the education reformer Cai Yuanpei promoted the establishment of art academies and the importance of 'aesthetic education' (*meigan jiaoyu*). During the first half of the century the artists Lin Fengmian and Xu Beihong, who had both studied in Europe, were particularly influential in establishing the art education system on European models, and sought a synthesis of Western and traditional Chinese styles. At the first and second National Congress of

Literature and Art Workers in 1949 and 1953 respectively, educational goals for the academies were readjusted in accordance with Mao Zedong's 1942 *Yan'an Talks* focusing on the production of art as a political tool. Under the supervision of printmaker and educator Jiang Feng the academy system was transformed to conform more closely to Soviet educational models. To this day, late nineteenth-century European and Soviet models continue to inform most art education at the university level.

Most academies were closed or had a restricted curriculum during the **Cultural Revolution** while students and teachers were sent down to the countryside to 'learn from the masses'. When most academies re-opened, by 1979, several thousand applicants competed for admission, contributing greatly to the level and range of work produced during the 1980s (see **85 New Wave [Art] Movement**; **art exhibitions (experimental, 1980s)**). The academies offered otherwise restricted information on foreign art through visits from foreign teachers, artists and students as well as publications and travel. Artistic expressive freedom decreased significantly in the academies in the years following 1989 but became more tolerant later in the 1990s as the boundary between official and unofficial art became less distinct.

While the range of departments in the academies varies, they normally include departments of *Zhongguohua* (Chinese traditional painting), oil painting, printmaking and sculpture. Some academies also include art history, photography, media art, environmental art, crafts or design, folk art and ceramics as well as music and drama. Many cities also have painting academies (*huayuan*) and painting research academies (*yanjiuyuan*) that employ artists and art researchers but do not teach students. All academies function as a work unit (*danwei*) and are integrated into the political structure (the Central Academy of Art in Beijing being under the direct supervision of the Ministry of Culture). Academic administration is often responsible for setting restrictions on artistic production and exhibitions. While academies continue to concentrate on training artists in officially accepted art forms, there have been significant levels of privatization in both institutional and personal activities. Many provinces and cities

have art education institutions on a range of levels. The following list includes some of the most influential academies:

(1) The Central Academy of Fine Arts (Zhongyang meishu xueyuan) was founded in 1918 as the Beijing National School of Fine Arts and acquired its current name in 1950 under the directorship of Xu Beihong. Former students include **Fang Lijun**, **Feng Mengbo**, **Liu Wei**, **Liu Xiaodong**, **Lu Shenzhong**, **Xu Bing**, **Yu Hong**, **Zhao Bandi**, **Zeng Hao** and **Chen Ping**.

(2) The China Academy of Art (Zhongguo meishu xueyuan) was established as the West Lake National Art Academy in 1928 by Lin Fengmian and acquired its present name in 1994. Since the founding of the PRC it has been called the Hangzhou National Art College (1928–50), East China College of Central Academy of Fine Arts (1950–6), Hangzhou Academy of Fine Arts (1956–8) and Zhejiang Academy of Fine Arts (1958–93). Former students include **Chen Haiyan**, Chen Xiangxun, Chen Yanyin, **Geng Jianyi**, **Gu Wenda**, **Huang Yongping**, Liu Dahong, Ni Haifeng, **Shi Hui**, **Song Yonghong**, **Qiu Zhijie**, **Wang Guangyi**, **Wang Jinsong**, Wu Shanzhuan, **Wu Meichun**, **Zhang Peili**, Wang Qiang and **Zhang Huan**.

(3) The Academy of Arts and Design, **Qinghua University** (Qinghua daxue meishu xueyuan) was established in 1956 by Pang Xunqin and was named the Chinese Central Academy of Arts and Crafts until 1999. Former students include **Yu Youhan** and **Zhang Hongtu**.

(4) Sichuan Academy of Fine Arts (Sichuan meishu xueyuan) was established in 1953 as the Southwest College of Fine Arts and was given its present name in 1959. Former students include Guo Wei, Shen Xiaotong, Wang Chuan, Xin Haizhou, Ye Yongqing and **Zhang Xiaogang**.

(5) Lu Xun Academy of Fine Arts (Lu Xun meishu xueyuan) in Shenyang was founded as the Northeast Lu Xun Art College in 1953 and was given its present name in 1958. Former students include Ren Jian and Shu Qun.

(6) The Nanjing Art Institute (Nanjing yishu xueyuan) was founded in 1958 and was given its present name in 1959. Former students include **Li Xiaoshan**, **Ding Fang**, Liu Ming and Ren Rong.

(7) Guangzhou Academy of Fine Arts (Guangzhou meishu xueyuan) was established in 1953 as the South Central China Fine Arts College and was given its present name in 1959. Former students include Chen Shaoxiong, Fang Tu and Lin Weimin.

(8) Hubei Institute of Fine Arts (Hubei meishu xueyuan) was initially founded as the Wuchang Fine Arts School in 1920. Former names include Wuchang Fine Arts College, Wuchang Private Fine Arts College, Art Department of the Hubei Education Institute, and the Department of Drawing and Cartography of the Central China Normal College. Former students include **Ma Liuming**, Shang Yang and **Zeng Fangzhi**.

(9) Xi'an Academy of Fine Arts (Xi'an meishu xueyuan) was first established in 1948 as the Northwest People's School of Arts. Former names include the Art College of Northwest Military and Political University and the Northwest Art Institute.

Further reading

Andrews, Julia (1994). *Painters and Politics in the People's Republic of China*. Berkeley: University of California Press.

Pang, Gongkai and Xu, Jiamu (eds) (1998). *Shiji zhuanxin* [The Flames of Art: The 70th Anniversary of the Founding of China Academy of Art]. Hangzhou: Zhongguo meishu xueyuan chubanshe.

Song, Zhongyuan (1988). *Yishu yaolan* [The Cradle of the Arts]. Hangzhou: Zhejiang meishu xueyuan chubanshe.

Sullivan, Michael (1996). *Art and Artists of Twentieth-Century China*. Berkeley: University of California Press, 42–51.

Zheng, Shengtian (1991). 'The Avant-Garde Movement in Chinese Art Academies'. In Richard E. Strassberg (ed.), *'I Don't Want to Play Cards with Cezanne' and Other Works: Selections from the Chinese 'New Wave' and 'Avant-Garde' Art of the Eighties*. Pasadena: Pacific Asia Museum, 19–22.

—— (1994). 'Modern Chinese Art and the Zhejiang Academy in Hangzhou'. In Jochen Noth (ed.), *China Avant-Garde: Counter-currents in Art and Culture*. Hong Kong/New York: Oxford University Press, 51–4.

Zhonghua renmin gongheguo wenhuabu jiaoyu keji si (ed.) (1991). *Zhongguo gaodeng yishu yuanxiao jianshi ji* [A Collection of the Concise Histories of the Chinese Art Academies]. Hangzhou: Zhejiang meishu chubanshe.

MORGAN PERKINS

art exhibitions (experimental, 1980s)

The 1980s saw a surge in exhibitions showing innovative experimental art which fell outside the accepted political and ideological conventions. This art drew on an ongoing link with a pre-1949 modernism that had subsequently been discouraged and often violently suppressed in the three decades after 1949. A wave of modernist-inspired experimentation began to re-emerge after the downfall of the Gang of Four in 1976 by means of the underground exhibitions of the Anonymous Painting Society (Wuming huahui) and other groups, the quasi-official exhibitions of the 'Beijing Spring' in 1979, and the **Stars**' open demands for alternative exhibition space later that year. The growth of self-initiated art groups and the liberalization of cultural institutions led to a new spate of exhibitions which fell outside the system of state-initiated shows and explored new and often sensitive styles and subject matters.

Thematically, experimental-art exhibitions began by tackling forbidden areas: abstraction, self-expression and early modernist styles such as Impressionism, Cubism and Fauvism. Once stylistic diversity was available, artists turned to explore their social contexts in a variety of new ways. The Advancing Young Artists Exhibition (Qianjinzhong de zhongghuo qingnian meizhan, May 1985) was remarkable for the range of its novel approaches, of which the painting *In the New Era, Revelation of Adam and Eve* by Meng Luding and Zhang Qun represented a striking example. In October of 1985, the Jiangsu Youth Art Week (Jiangsu qingnian yishuzhou) exhibition drew together over three hundred works by more than a hundred artists. Statistically, the number of modern art exhibitions rose from a constant of under fifteen per year prior to 1985, to around 110 in 1986, largely due to the activity of youth groups. This nationwide phenomenon became known as the **85 New Wave [Art] Movement**.

Two broad approaches defined the art of this period. One tendency was to adopt largely expressive styles and an intense, intuitive or romantic attitude to life, often expressed in relation to nature and non-Han cultures. This was typical of the **Southwest Art Research Group** (Xinan yishu yanjiu qunti) and in particular the vibrant works of Mao Xuhui, **Zhang Xiaogang**, Ye Yongqing and Zhou Chunya. The other tendency was a more conceptual and perhaps cynical approach that emphasized 'rationality' and employed crisp, almost sterile modernist styles of painting, such as those of the 1985 New Space Exhibition (1985 nian xinkongjian zhanlan) and of the **Northern Art Group** (Beifang yishu qunti). Both currents were disposed to avoid or subvert the narrative, illustrative and didactic conventions of Socialist art, and required a greater level of personal interpretation. At times, when works were considered too controversial yet not altogether unacceptable, exhibitions were closed partially or completely to the general public and reserved for select audiences only.

The format of exhibitions during this period was also marked by the advent of performance art. The Southern Artists Salon First Experimental Art Exhibition (Nanfang yishujia shalong diyihui shiyanzhan, September, 1986) in Guangzhou combined paintings, music and performance to create a new all-encompassing artistic experience. Body-bondage, body-painting and performances became popular as a way to experience and convey an altered state of existence. They allowed for greater spontaneity and interaction with the audience, while simultaneously circumventing the restrictions regulating public art exhibitions. Events like the Concept 21 (Guannian 21) action art at Beijing University in December 1986 had the effect of 'breaking the ice'. The artists participating in this 'happening' collaborated in 1988 with the director Wen Pulin on an experimental, multi-media documentary, *The Great Earthquake (Da dizhen)*.

Further reading

Li, Xianting (1993). 'Major Trends in the Development of Contemporary Chinese Art'. In Valerie C. Doran (ed.), *China's New Art, Post-1989, with a Retrospective from 1979 to 1989*. Hong Kong: Hanart T Z Gallery, x–xxii.

Lü, Peng and Yi, Dan (1992). *Zhongguo xiandai yishushi 1979–1989* [A History of China Modern Art]. Changsha: Hunan meishu chubanshe.

van Dijk, Hans (1991/1992). 'Painting in China after the Cultural Revolution: Style Developments and Theoretical Debates'. *China Information* 6.3 (Winter): 25–43 and 7.4 (Spring): 1–18.

EDUARDO WELSH

art exhibitions (experimental, 1990s)

The decade of the 1990s witnessed major socio-economical transformations as a consequence of Deng Xiaoping's reforms, pushing the growth of metropolitan centres and bringing in flocks of rural migrants. If the 1989 show **China Avant-Garde** was a landmark of the new tide of the 1980s, it also framed the context for new experiments that would increasingly convey social and cultural critiques. The urban mobility typical of the period after 1989 also affected artistic circles, which had begun to move and cluster in major urban centres such as Shanghai, Hangzhou, Guangzhou and especially Beijing, where since the very beginning of the 1990s residential communities of artists were established. These included the **Yuanming Yuan** – the Garden of Perfect Brightness – village (on the outskirts of the Beijing near the ruins of the Old Summer Palace, active since 1991) and **Dongcun** [East Village], active between 1992 and 1994.

Departing from the stylistic diversity of the 1980s and nurtured through collective experiences emerging on a local basis, artistic experimentation shifted to individualization, the development of personal artistic languages and the voicing of autonomous ideas. Performance and installation art became more popular, in part as a response to the growing exposure to the international art scene and as a form of direct confrontation with Western art practices. In the first half of the decade, shows were often held in private spaces and studios (so-called Apartment Art/*Gongyu yishu*) or inside foreign embassies. The receptiveness to Chinese art from abroad was also attested by a growing number of exhibitions featuring Chinese art: the first Chinese participation at the Venice Biennale (1993), the show 'China Avant-Garde' at the Haus der Kulturen der Welt in Berlin (1993) and the 22nd Sao Paolo Biennale (1994). Yet exhibitions and public performances within China were still suffering under the restricted atmosphere that followed Tiananmen, which forced the cancellation and/or early termination of many exhibitions by the authorities and even led to the detention of performance artist **Ma Liuming** and the dispersion of the East Village group in 1994. At the same time, globalization and its psychological impact linked to the expanding and pervasive consumerism within China itself were questioned, along with the annihilation of the individual and the loss of ideals, all of which helps explain the emergence of **Cynical Realism** (*Popi, Wanshi xianshi*) and **Gaudy Art** (*Yansu yishu*) as signs of the ennui typical of the early 1990s.

The second half of the 1990s witnessed a deepening interest in the use of new media and paths of expression, culminating in the artistic outburst known as **Sensationalism. Shock Art** in 1999. Video and conceptual photography also began to be pursued by artists like Hong Lei, **Zhuang Hui**, Zhu Jia, and **Big-Tailed Elephant**, among others. In 1995 the Gallery of the National Academy of Fine Arts in Hangzhou hosted 'Image and Phenomena', the first show dedicated to video art; curated by **Wu Meichun**, it was accompanied by a series of lectures and conferences on the topic of art and mass culture in the information age.

With the beginning of the second half of the decade, attempts were also made to establish a national market system for contemporary art supported by the growth of a critical and academic corpus. Curators started to work with semi-official museums and institutions and formed a new generation of entrepreneurs providing financial assistance for artistic events. Such attempts began with the 1st Guangzhou Biennale in 1992 and were later revived in the Guangzhou Art Fair (1994), the 1st Shanghai Biennale (1996), the 1st Academic Exhibition of Chinese Contemporary Art in Beijing (1996), and 'A Chinese Dream' (1997), the first auction (see **auctions (art and antiquities)**) held in Beijing for contemporary Chinese art. In fact, artists in the 1990s began to take control of their own work as professionals, outside of the art academies and institutional frameworks. On the one hand, many artists were forced to give up their jobs by their affiliated institutions because of unorthodox approaches or irregular schedules and lifestyles; on the other hand, the artists themselves became more aware of the economic potential of their work and how to realize this potential on their own, especially in view of the increasing number of foreign curators and collectors attracted by China's artistic development.

Further reading

Dreissen, Chris and van Mierlo, Heidi (1997). *Another Long March – Chinese Conceptual and Installation Art in the Nineties* (exhibition catalogue). Breda: Fundament Foundation.

Gao, Minglu (1996). 'From the Local Context to the International Context: An Essay on the Critique of Art and Culture'. In *The First Academic Exhibition of Contemporary Chinese Art: 1996–97*. Hong Kong: Hong Kong Arts Centre, 23–9.

—— (1998). 'Toward a Transnational Modernity: An Overview of "Inside Out: New Chinese Art"'. In Gao Minglu, *Inside Out: New Chinese Art* (exhibition catalogue). Berkeley: University of California Press, 28–33.

Lü, Peng (2000). *Zhongguo dangdai yishushi 1990–1999/90s Art China*. Hunan: Hunan Meishu Chubanshe (Hunan Fine Arts Ed.).

Sang, Ye (1997). 'Fringe-Dwellers: Down and Out in the Yuan Ming Yuan Artists' Village'. Trans. Geremie R. Barmé. *ART AsiaPacific* 15 (June).

Wu, Hung (2000). *Cancelled: Exhibiting Experimental Art in China*, Chicago: The Smart Museum of Art.

Wu, Hung, Wang, Huangsheng and Feng, Boyi (eds) (2002). *The 1st Guangzhou Triennal-Reinterpretation: A Decade of Chinese Experimental Art*. Guangdong: Guangdong Museum of Art.

BEATRICE LEANZA

art galleries (private, commercial)

Up until the mid 1990s, there were very few private or commercial contemporary art galleries in China, with the majority of buyers being expatriates from the diplomatic and journalistic communities, as well as patrons from Hong Kong and Taiwan. Since then, with the increase of interest and market value, there has been an explosion of new galleries for contemporary art opening up in most major Chinese cities, including Beijing and Shanghai, as well as in Chengdu, Kunming and Guangzhou. In Beijing, the first privately owned contemporary art gallery was the Red Gate Gallery at the Dongbianmen Watchtower, founded by Australian Brian Wallace in 1991. On its tenth anniversary, Red Gate expanded its role within the local art community by hosting foreign artists in China through its affiliation with the Beijing Art Academy and its recently established artist-in-residence programme. Located in a traditional 150-year old courtyard house across the moat from the East Gate of the Forbidden City, the CourtYard Gallery was established in 1996 by Handel Lee, a Chinese-American lawyer, and is currently directed by Meg Maggio. In 1999, **Hans van Dijk** joined with collector Frank Uytterhaegen and artist **Ai Weiwei** to found China Art Archives and Warehouse, focusing mainly on installation and media art. In Shanghai, the first private gallery devoted entirely to Chinese avant-garde art was ShangART, established in 1995 by Swiss gallerist Lorenz Helbling. Since then many other galleries have opened, including: BizArt founded in 1998 by Huang Yuanqing, Davide Quadrio and Katelijn Verstraete, the first art centre in Shanghai specializing in media art; and Eastlink Gallery founded by Li Liang in 1999. Many of these galleries show a broad range of contemporary Chinese art and have been instrumental in providing more public exposure to local Chinese and international audiences. In the late 1990s, however, alternative, non-profit (or even semi-commercial) spaces have emerged as experimental grounds in between galleries and art museums, heightening the competition for cutting-edge contents. Another recent phenomenon likely to impact the local art market in the near future has been the establishment of branch galleries with main operations based outside mainland China, such as the Schoeni Art Gallery of Hong Kong in Beijing, the Soka (Beijing) Art Centre of Taiwan, the Beijing Tokyo Art Projects owned by the Tokyo Art Gallery (see **798**), and Shanghai Contemporary, Albrecht, Ochs and Wei, a collaboration between gallerists from Frankfurt, Berlin and Shanghai. These new overseas galleries are soon likely to profit from the foreseeable relaxation of customs restrictions and scrutiny by the **Ministry of Culture** on the sale of foreign artworks into China.

Further reading

BizArt: www.biz-art.com
China Art Archives and Warehouse: www.archivesandwarehouse.com
CourtYard Gallery: www.courtyard-gallery.com
Red Gate Gallery: www.redgategallery.com
ShangART: www.shangart.com
Shanghai Contemporary, Albrecht, Ochs and Wei: www.shanghai-contemporary.com Soka (Beijing) Art Centre of Taiwan: www.soka-art.com.tw

ALICE MING WAI JIM WITH MEG MAGGIO

auctions (art and antiquities)

Auctions, no longer rejected as capitalist, were reintroduced in China in the early 1990s. In May 1991, China's National Cultural Conference decided that auction markets of artworks might be established in China in an effort to curb illicit trade and regularize the market, and the first auction of artworks took place in Xi'an on 8 September 1992.

The establishment of fine art and antiquities auction companies in major Chinese cities followed shortly thereafter. In Beijing, China Guardian Auctions Co., Ltd., the first state-level professional auction company in China, obtained approval to operate in 1993, and since then has held spring and autumn auctions that reportedly sold more than 10,000 pieces of antiques and jewellery, with total earnings of about 700 million yuan (US$84.34 million) by the year 2000. Guardian's president is Ms Wang Yannan, daughter of former Chinese leader Zhao Ziyang.

Today, the four major auction companies in Beijing are China Guardian, Sungari, Huachen and Hanhai. Hanhai, established shortly after Guardian, is closely linked to the Beijing Municipal Cultural Relics Bureau, and initially obtained most of its items from PRC state-run antiquities stores. Rongbaozhai, one of Beijing's most famous Chinese traditional painting restorers, collectors and mounters, also runs a Beijing-based fine arts auction company.

In Shanghai, Duo Yun Xuan Art Auctioneers, founded in 1992, remains the most well known, and belongs to the 100-year-old Duo Yun Xuan Company located on Nanjing Dong Lu, which also runs a traditional Chinese art gallery and a store for art supplies. In Duo Yun Xuan's first years of auctioneering, most of the items on the block came from their own in-house collection, and generated intense local interest. Three of the more active Shanghai auction companies are Guotai Art Auction, Shanghai International Commodity Auction and Shanghai New Century Auction, all of which have been operating since the early to mid 1990s. Auction companies have also been established in many of China's major cities. Items typically on auction include Chinese ancient and modern paintings and calligraphy, porcelain items, ancient furniture, Chinese oil paintings and sculpture, rare books, folk art, jewellery, stamps and coins. Since the late 1990s, auctions have also regularly included works of contemporary art, often contributing to the rapid increase in the market value of such productions.

Further reading

Dewar, Susan (1994). 'Report from Beijing', *Orientations* 25: 49.

Zhou, Lin (1998). *Chinalaw Web – Art Law in China*, available at http://www.qis.net/chinalaw/prcartlaw.htm (last modified 25 June 1998).

Auction house websites

Duo Yun Xuan Art Auction: www.duoyunxuan-sh.com

Guardian: www.guardianauctions.com; on-line auctions portal: www.guaweb.com

Shanghai International Commodity Auction Co., Ltd: www.alltobid.com

Shanghai New Century Auction Co., Ltd: http://mind.sq.sh.cn/xsjpm.htm

MEG MAGGIO

autonomous regions, prefectures, counties and banners

These are the three main levels of autonomous administrative areas for the PRC's minority nationalities. There are five autonomous regions (*zizhiqu*), which are equivalent in level to provinces. They are the Inner Mongolian Autonomous Region (set up 1 May 1947), Xinjiang Uygur Autonomous Region (1 October 1955), Guangxi Zhuang Autonomous Region (15 May 1958), Ningxia Hui Autonomous Region (25 October 1958) and Tibet Autonomous Region (9 September 1965). In 2001, the number of autonomous prefectures (*zizhizhou*) was thirty, while autonomous counties (*zizhixian*; termed 'banners' for Mongolians) numbered 119.

The principle behind these areas is autonomy for minorities living in concentrated communities. China describes itself as a multinational unitary state. However, there are also 'preferential policies' (*youhui zhengce*) for the minorities in education (see **bilingual education**, **family planning**). In May 1984, the PRC adopted its Law on Regional National Autonomy, amended on 28 February 2001, spelling out precisely what autonomy means. For instance, it specifies that the government head of an autonomous area must belong to the minority exercising autonomy there, and requires privileges for the minorities in training administrative personnel. It also gives autonomous rights in the framing of the budget and in the management of culture, education and health delivery.

There are, however, great limitations on autonomy, which makes no pretence to resemble independence, the Law itself (Article 5 of the 2001 version) demanding that the organs of self-government of autonomous areas 'must uphold the unity of the country'. Two examples suffice to illustrate the limitations. First, although an autonomous area's government head must belong to the minority exercising autonomy, there is no such rule for the CCP secretary, and the CCP actually holds far more power than the government. Second, there is a national curriculum in China, with which no autonomous education system may conflict. Many ethnic groups have adopted a curriculum covering their own culture, but it is *in addition* to the national curriculum, not instead of it. These and other restrictions have led some scholars to consider this system of autonomy a sham. Yet over the years it has proved generally beneficial to the minorities. It has contributed to improving their administrative and professional skills and given them some say in their economy. It has helped raise the ethnic consciousness of most of the minorities, despite generally helping integrate them with the Chinese economy and state.

See also: one-child policy; state policies on minority cultures

Further reading

Gladney, Dru (1991). *Muslim Chinese: Ethnic Nationalism in the People's Republic*. Cambridge, MA, and London: Council on East Asian Studies, Harvard University Press.

Kaup, K. P. (2000). *Creating the Zhuang: Ethnic Politics in China*. Boulder: Lynne Rienner [covers the most populous of the minorities, but includes a great deal of material on policy and autonomy issues].

Mackerras, Colin (1994). *China's Minorities: Integration and Modernization in the Twentieth Century*. Hong Kong: Oxford University Press.

COLIN MACKERRAS

avant-garde/experimental literature

(xianfeng wenxue/shiyan wenxue)

The first examples of avant-garde literature appeared towards the middle of the 1980s in Shanghai magazines [*Harvest (Shouhuo)* and *Shanghai Literature (Shanghai wenxue)*] with the works of authors such as **Ma Yuan**, **Can Xue** and **Mo Yan**. However, this tendency spread between 1987 and 1988 and established its reputation thanks to the publications of works by writers such as **Su Tong**, **Ge Fei**, **Yu Hua**, Hong Feng and **Sun Ganlu** who were born during the 1960s and with whom experimentation took on more definite connotations and major visibility, thanks also to the increased attention of the media. However, the emergence of the trend of avant-garde literature dates back to the thematic exploration and stylistic experimentation launched by the younger generation of so-called **Misty poetry** (*menglong shi*) (**Bei Dao**, Mang Ke) at the end of the 1970s.

The new narrative was initially defined by the Chinese critics as 'new-trend literature' (*Xinchao xiaoshuo*). Some years later, when formal experimentation intensified and took on a more extreme and provoking stance, it was called 'avant-garde literature' (*xianfeng wenxue*) or 'experimental literature' (*shiyan wenxue*).

Various factors contributed to the emergence of this new narrative: on the one hand the changing social climate, resulting from the politics of overture and reform starting at the beginning of the 1980s that permitted the spread, throughout China, of modern Western theories of philosophy and aesthetics (psychoanalysis, structuralism, formalism, existentialism) and, above all European, American and Latin American literary works. On the other hand, the beginning of a cultural renewal process started a few years before with previously mentioned Misty poetry, with the **Root-seeking school** (*Xungen pai*) (**Han Shaogong**, **Ah Cheng**) and, then with the 'modernist narrative' group (**Xu Xing**, **Liu Suola**, **Wang Shuo**).

The spirit of the avant-garde group expresses itself in strong experimental tension, in the search for stylistic forms and methods that release new expressive possibilities into the language, in the fragmentation and diversification of the positions and voices as a reaction to the unitary and disciplined vision of literature that had dominated the cultural scene in the preceding forty years under the so-called Socialist Realism. It is this diversification of style and expression that the young authors appear to be anxious to tackle, the element that will give vital birth to and feed all the literature of the period between 1985 and 1989. The reflection on, and experimentation with language respond to a dual requirement: the demand to overcome the schematic and standardized language used in political communication, made up of slogans and formulas, that in itself had, for decades, informed and saturated every aspect of daily life; and the renewed interest in the Chinese language and its expressive and suggestive possibilities. The creation of stories that develop on parallel planes through leaps in time and space (Mo Yan), of stories lacking a plot, a beginning or an end, where the narration appears fragmented, bordering between reality and imagination (Ma Yuan), the vision of mirages and enchanted worlds (Sun Ganlu) and of labyrinths of memories (Ge Fei, Bei Cun) have the challenging task of presenting works that escape traditional decoding methods, inducing the reader to think, not merely to accept the text passively but to investigate and discover alternative perspectives and the numerous possibilities of interpretation.

Unlike the preceding root-searching generation still solidly anchored to positive ideals, to a literature steeped in history and the vision of literary work as commitment, the avant-gardists refuse ideals and values they perceive as anachronistic and artificial. They refuse above all to play the role of social or political guides, a burden that writers have always taken on. Therefore in the avant-garde literature the great social themes disappear, attention shifts towards the discovery of individual experience and the emotional world, ignored for so long. This tendency will be developed to the extreme in the literature written in the 1990s. If history appears in the works of authors such as Mo Yan, Su Tong and Yu Hua, it takes on a subversive significance, suggesting a radical change in perspective, showing the desire to deconstruct the official history and offer new interpretation of the events, as they were experienced by the common people. In the avant-garde narrative works lacking a central core or intent appeared, where the representation and psychology of the characters are fragmented and deepened, thus overcoming the naïve Manichean vision in which the positive hero is to be emulated and 'villains' to be condemned. Often the characters and the plot no longer take on a central position in the story, but recede to the background, giving space to the story make-up, whereby its form and narrative style become the true basis and expressive values of the work.

Further reading

Huot, Marie Claire (2000). 'Literary Experiments: Six Files'. In Marie Claire Huot, *China's New Cultural Scene: A Handbook of Changes*. Durham, NC: Duke University Press, 7–48.

Jones, Andrew F. (2003). 'Avant-Garde Fiction in China'. In Joshua Mostow (ed.) and Kirk A. Denton (China section, ed.), *Columbia Companion to Modern East Asian Literatures*. New York: Columbia University Press, 554–60.

Lu, Tonglin (1995). *Misogyny, Cultural Nihilism, and Oppositional Politics: Contemporary Chinese Experimental Fiction*. Stanford: Stanford University Press.

Wang, Jing (ed.) (1998). *China's Avant-Garde Fiction*. Durham, NC: Duke University Press.

Yang, Xiaobin (2002). *The Chinese Postmodern: Trauma and Irony in Chinese Avant-Garde Fiction*. Ann Arbor: University of Michigan Press.

Zhang, Xudong (1997). *Chinese Modernism in the Era of Reforms: Culture Fever, Avant-Garde Fiction, and the New Chinese Cinema*. Durham, NC: Duke University Press.

Zhao, Yiheng (1992). 'The Rise of Metafiction in China'. *Bulletin of African and Oriental Studies* 55.1.

ROSA LOMBARDI

avant-garde/experimental theatre

(xianfeng xiju/shiyan xiju)

With regard to **Huaju** (spoken drama), the concepts *xianfeng xiju* and *shiyan xiju* are generally interchangeable, because experimental theatre works are often regarded as avant-garde theatre works. However, only experimental theatre has been given a conceptual definition and recognized as an actual theatre movement by Huaju scholars. This movement arose in the early 1980s and since the mid 1980s has been considered by many to be a mainstream theatrical genre.

Some proto-experimental theatre plays were created in the late 1970s and the very early 1980s. For example, *A Warm Current Outside the House* (*Wuwai you reliu*) by Ma Zhongjun and Jia Hongyuan, staged in Shanghai in 1980, was innovative in its use of dream scenes and stream of consciousness technique. In 1982, **Gao Xingjian**'s *Alarm Signal* (*Juedui xinghao*), directed by **Lin Zhaohua**, was able to completely break from the old-style realism in Huaju. This play was staged in a rehearsal room of the **Beijing People's Art Theatre** (Beijing renmin yishu juyuan), with the audience seated on three sides of the stage and without any realistic scenery. Furthermore, it broke the fourth wall by having actors converse with the audience during the performance. *Alarm Signal* is regarded as the first influential and mature experimental theatre production, as well as the beginning of the experimental theatre movement.

The most important traits of experimental theatre are: (1) breaking with the dramatic forms of realism and the fourth wall, in order to depart from traditional realistic Huaju; (2) a tendency towards theatricalism in production, generating theatrical effects and emphasizing artistic techniques so as to urge the audience to see plays as artistic works rather than as real life; and (3) suppositionality, the tendency to avoid duplicating real life on stage, and to rely instead on the actor's ability to present that which is less concrete visually but more real in feeling, such as an old and feeble heart or an abstract river. Following these traits, experimental theatre directors usually adopt methods such as *wuchangci* (without act or scene breaks) structure, a bare stage, a non-proscenium stage, the use of a narrator, and the pursuit of communication between the actor and the audience.

Famous experimental theatre plays include: **Bus Stop** (*Chezhan*, 1981), by Gao Xinjian; *Old B Hanging on the Wall* (*Gua zai qiangshang de Lao B*, 1984) by Sun Huizhu; **WM (W[o]m[en])** by Wang Peigong and Wang Gui; **Uncle Doggie's Nirvana** (*Gou'er ye niepan*, 1986) by Jin Yun; *Jesus, Confucius, and John Lennon* (*Yesu, Kongzi, Yuehan Lannong*, 1987) by **Sha Yexin**; *Thinking of Worldly Pleasures* (*Sifan*, 1992) by **Meng Jinghui**; and *File Zero* (*Ling dang'an*, 1994) by **Yu Jian**. Important experimental theatre directors include Xu Xiaozhong, Lin Zhaohua, Meng Jinghui, Wang Xiaoying and **Mou Sen**.

See also: Hu Xuehua; Tian Qinxin; Western theatre

Further reading

Meng, J. (1999). *Xianfeng xiju dang'an* [Avant-Garde Theatre Files]. Beijing: Zuojia chubanshe.

Wang, X. (2000). *Zhongguo dangdai huaju yishu yanbianshi* [Evolution of Contemporary Huaju Art]. Hangzhou: Zhejiang daxue chubanshe.

Zhao, Y. (1999). *Jianli yizhong xiandai chanju: Gao Xingjian yu Zhongguo shiyan xiju* [Establishing a Type of Modern Dhyana Play – Gao Xingjian and Experimental Chinese Theatre]. Taipei: Erya.

LIN WEI-YÜ AND
ELIZABETH WICHMANN-WALCZAK

B

Bai, culture of

Bai is the name of a Yunnan ethnic minority, with a population of nearly 1.6 million, according to the 1990 census. The Bai are focused on the Dali Bai Autonomous Prefecture (capital, Dali City) in central-western Yunnan. Set up in 1956, the prefecture had a population of about 3.3 million in 1999, of whom about half belonged to a minority, the Bai being far the most numerous. There are small Bai populations elsewhere, notably in other parts of Yunnan, Guizhou and Hunan.

The Bai spoken language belongs to the Yi branch of the Tibeto-Burman family, but most Bai nowadays also speak Chinese. The Bai people are mainly agricultural, though urbanization has accelerated in the period of reform. Their main staple crops are rice and wheat. Their houses are two-storeyed, with the family living on top and livestock below. The style is characteristic, with mud bricks, graceful eaves and tiled roofs.

The main Bai religion is worship of local tutelary spirits. These include national heroes and ancestors, and natural phenomena like fish, conches, the sun and moon, rivers and mountains. Buddhism and Daoism have also penetrated Bai society. The **Cultural Revolution** saw widespread destruction of religious buildings, but many temples and other religious structures have been restored or built in the period of reform. Although socialism has produced a significant effect on Bai society, traditional religious thinking remains strong, especially in the country-side. Some people still associate sickness with offence to tutelary spirits, and, along with modern personnel, religious specialists can function as doctors. The most important Bai festival is the Third Month Fair, focused at the foot of a mountain near Dali City. Linked with the religious **Guanyin** Festival, the traditional ceremonies are still alive. Nowadays, the festival is most important for markets, performances, competitions and games.

The most famous remaining art objects among the Bai, and possibly created by them, are three pagodas outside the town of Dali, the largest of them being 60 metres high and over 1,000 years old. They are similar in style to the Great Gander Pagoda in Xi'an, built about the same time. These three pagodas are certainly Dali Prefecture's main tourist attraction, and in 1998 contributed to bringing the number of foreign and domestic tourists to the prefecture past the three million mark for the first time.

There is also a tradition of Bai literature using Chinese characters. The Bai are among the minority nationalities with their own style of drama. In the period of reform, there have been attempts to 'nationalize' it by adapting it to traditional Bai stories, dances and song styles. Even when the CCP took control in 1949, the Bai were among the most acculturated with the Han of China's minorities. Although the system of autonomy has allowed the growth of a distinct Bai identity, the process of acculturation has gathered momentum, despite the persistence of indigenous cultural characteristics.

Further reading

Mackerras, C. (1988). 'Aspects of Bai Culture: Change and Continuity in a Yunnan Nationality'. *Modern China* 14.1: 51–84.

Wu, David H. Y. (1990). 'Chinese Minority Policy and the Meaning of Minority Culture: The Example of the Bai in Yunnan, China'. *Human Organization* 49.1 (March): 1–13.

COLIN MACKERRAS

Bai Fengxi

b. 1934, Wen'an, Hebei

Theatre actress, playwright

Bai Fengxi became an actress in the China Youth Art Theatre in 1954 and played more than forty dramatic characters, such as the title heroines in *Liu Hulai* (1951) and *Prince Wencheng* (*Wencheng gongzhu*, 1960). She began writing plays after 1976 and became the first woman playwright in the PRC who focused on the experiences and uncertain roles of women in real life. *The Women Trilogy* depicts the concerns of intellectual women in the transition from the Maoist (1949–76) to post-Maoist (1976–present) eras. The first play, *First Bathed in Moonlight* (*Mingyue chu zhao ren*, 1981), represents a microcosm of PRC women, relating the lives of three generations of mothers and daughters who struggle between their official roles as liberated women and their private search for love, happiness and freedom. It portrays Fang Ruoming, a Party official in charge of women's affairs, whose efforts to help rural women with arranged marriages coincides with her endeavour to understand her own daughters' fight against social prejudice and traditional values. Bai's second play, *An Old Friend Comes on a Stormy Night* (*Fengyu guren lai*, 1983), probes more deeply into women's protest against a sexist society. Xia Zhixian finds success in her career as a gynaecologist at the expense of her family life. She lives alone, having divorced her husband, who proved unable to support her total devotion to a career. As the play unfolds, her daughter faces a similar dilemma: when she is ranked first in a graduate school entrance examination to study abroad, her mother-in-law urges her to give up her plans, since a family with a PhD husband seems to be more acceptable than a family with a PhD wife. After much torment, Xia encourages her daughter to pursue her journey abroad, saying, 'A woman is not a moon. She does not need to depend on someone else's light to glow'.

This line was frequently repeated in the effort to raise public consciousness of women's issues. Her third play, *Where is Longing in Autumn?* (*Buzhi qiusi zai shui jia*, 1986), staged a group of courageous women whose unconventional decisions shocked their audiences. The mother, Su Zhongyuan, was puzzled by the choices of her children: her elder daughter left her husband solely to take better care of herself; her second daughter remained a spinster to avoid a loveless marriage; and her son opted for a business career instead of taking college entrance examinations and was engaged to a fashion model. The play ends with no closure and no resolution of a mother's anguish. The seemingly irreconcilable conflicts between mother and children suggest the moral tribulations of a society in flux, caught between a problematic tradition and the uncertainties of Westernization and commercialization.

Further reading

Bai, Fengxi (1991). *The Women Trilogy*. Trans. Guan Yuehua. Beijing: Chinese Literature Press.
—— (1994). 'Friend on a Rainy Day'. Trans. Diana B. Kingsbury. In Diana B. Kingsbury (ed.), *I Wish I Were a Wolf: The New Voice in Chinese Women's Literature*. Beijing: New World Press, 64–122.
Chen, Xiaomei (1997). 'A Stage of Their Own: The Problematics of Women's Theatre in Post-Mao China'. *Journal of Asian Studies* 56.1: 3–25.

CHEN XIAOMEI

Bai Hua

(né Chen Youhua)

b. 1930, Xinyang, Henan

Writer, poet, playright

Labelled a 'rightist' during the Anti-Rightist Campaign in 1957, Bai Hua was silenced for twenty-two years. His work combines poetic sensitivity and a preoccupation with socio-political criticism. The misfortune of intellectuals, the condemnation of bureaucratic corruption and dogmatism and the call for individual freedom are among his key themes.

His best-known film script, *Bitter Love* (*Kulian*, 1979) was made into a film entitled *The Sun and the*

People (*Taiyang yü ren*, 1980), but was denounced nationwide in 1981, making him the first Chinese writer to be singled out for criticism after Mao's death. *Unrequited Love* portrays the misfortune of a patriotic painter who returned to China from the United States with his family after the CCP's victory, only to be persecuted and die in misery. His 1980 novella *The Mothers* (*Mama a, mama*) is among the early works critical of the CCP's alienation from the people. His symbolic novella *Death of a Fisherman* (*Yige yübashi zhi si*) of 1982 portrays the psychological struggle between a cormorant and its master, the stubborn and domineering fisherman. His long novel *The Remote Country of Women* (*Yuanfang you ge nu'er guo*, 1988) contrasts the hypocrisy of Han culture under Mao with the carefree spirit of the Moso minority, which practises matriarchy. In the 1990s, he continued to show his social concern through fiction eliminate in the novel *River of No Return* (*Liushui wu guicheng*, 1995), which depicts moral degradation.

Further reading

Bai, Hua (1992). 'China's Contemporary Literature: Reaching Out to the World and to the Future'. Trans. Howard Goldblatt. In Helmut Martin (ed.), *Modern Chinese Writers: Self-Portrayals*. Armonk, NY: M. E. Sharpe, 42–52.

—— (1994). *The Remote Country of Women*. Trans. Wu Qingyun and Thomas O. Beebee. Honolulu: University of Hawai'i Press.

Spence, Jonathan. 'Film and Politics: Bai Hua's *Bitter Love*'. In Jonathan Spence, *Chinese Roundabout: Essays in History and Culture*. New York: Norton, 277–92.

LEUNG LAIFONG

Bai Xianyong

(Pai Hsien-yung)

b. 1937, Guilin, Guangxi

Writer, professor

Widely regarded as 'arguably the most accomplished contemporary writer of fiction in China' and 'a master of portraiture', Bai Xianyong's

fiction has been appreciated by readers throughout the Chinese-speaking world. Some of his stories have been made into films and plays.

The son of Bai Chongxi, a general of the Nationalist Government, Bai moved to Taiwan with his family in 1952. With classmates from the National Taiwan University, he founded the magazine *Modern Literature* (*Xiandai wenxue*) in 1961 which played an important role in introducing Western writers and literary trends to Taiwan. Upon graduation, he went to study at the University of Iowa where he obtained an MFA and taught Chinese language and literature on the Santa Barbara campus of the University of California until his retirement in 1998.

The uncertainties of life and history are prominent in his fiction. Past glory and present decline are sensitively embodied in many memorable characters who escaped to Taiwan after the Communist takeover in 1949, as exemplified in the fourteen short stories collected in *Wandering in the Garden, Waking from a Dream: Tales of Taibei Characters* (*Taibei ren*, 1971). Old KMT generals, poor professors, unhappy widows and faded prostitutes are delineated with keen pathos, occasional humour and highly allusive language. Bai's novel *Crystal Boys* (*Niezi*, 1983) is the first modern Chinese fiction to focus on homosexuality (see **homosexuality and tongzhi culture**).

Further reading

Bai, Xianyong (1990). *Crystal Boys*. San Francisco: Gay Sunshine Press.

—— (1999). *Taipei People* (bilingual edition). Trans. Bai Xianyong and Patia Yasin. Hong Kong: The Chinese University Press.

LEUNG LAIFONG

baihua/Guoyu

(semi-colloquial language)

The philosopher Hu Shi employed the term *baihua* in public exchanges with Qian Xuantong in 1917 during the movement to adopt a vernacular writing style for educated discourse. Hu stated that the '*bai*' (white) signified writing that is vernacular, clear, and clean (unadorned, aphelia). Hu's promotion of *baihua* style included local dialects, such as the Shanghai dialect represented in the novel *Flowers of Shanghai* (*Hai shang hua liezhuan*, 1897). However, he conceded that since the Song dynasty, Mandarin (*guanhua*) had been used in most vernacular texts and constituted the only practical replacement for the classical literary styles used in educated discourse.

In 1928, following the consolidation of a central government by the Nationalist Party, Mandarin was standardized by linguists for education and adopted as the 'National Language', or *Guoyu*. This language also came to dominate the media. However, as a spoken language Mandarin was divided among several distinct geographical groupings, and the standardized form that spread through education and the media was a language spoken by few without the benefit of education. As inherited from classic novels it contained a great deal of classical language, which newspapers continued to use. Moreover, as a vehicle for modernizing China, it was saturated with imported loan words and phrases, many from English by way of Japanese, that were, at the outset, the written style of a small educated elite. Hence, the distance between *baihua* as a Mandarin national language and the many local languages spoken by most Chinese made it a semi-colloquial language. Although there were proposals for writers to adopt a 'language of the masses' to overcome the linguistic barriers, *Guoyu* was widely adopted and preserved as the 'common language' (*putonghua*) by the Communist Party after the founding of the People's Republic in 1949. *Guoyu* or *putonghua* has remained the style or language of cultural production orally and in print.

EDWARD GUNN

ballroom dancing

In Mandarin Chinese, ballroom dancing is called 'social dance' (*jiaoyiwu/hejiaowu*) or 'international dance' (*guoji biaozhunwu/guojiwu*), and it has been associated with Western cosmopolitanism since its introduction into China, particularly Shanghai, in the early part of the last century. It was largely

forbidden during the **Cultural Revolution**, but after the era of reform began, it was among the recreational dance forms that replaced the mass calisthenics of the Maoist era as daily exercise. Commercial ballrooms were first allowed in Beijing in May 1987, although they appeared in other cities a few years earlier. In Beijing by the mid 1990s, several hundred dancers, the majority of them middle-aged or elderly retirees, convened from dawn until about 8.00 a.m. in the large parking lot across from the Capitol Gymnasium, and smaller groups occupied parks and grassy islands around the city.

In the college dances of the mid to late 1980s, students typically danced with same-sex partners. Starting in the mid 1990s, in classes at colleges and universities, males danced with females, with the goal of teaching students how to interact with the opposite sex in a 'civilized' manner, and of preparing them for the newly emerging job market by developing their social poise and their cosmopolitan refinement. By the new millennium, ballroom dancing had become a fixture of social life in the dance halls of the multi-functional recreational clubs, where state officials and private entrepreneurs formed and cemented their social networks.

See also: leisure culture

SUSAN BROWNELL

Bangzi

(Clapper opera)

regional Xiqu (sung-drama/opera) genre

Bangzi is a major style of opera prominent in northern, western and central China in several dozen regional genres. Originally designating a pair of woodblock percussion instruments marking the main beat, the term defines by metonymy genres based on a modular system of arias known as *bangziqiang* or 'melodies for Bangzi'. The arias are composed in modes both melodic and rhythmic. Melodies are essentially heptatonic with lyrics structured in parallel distichs of seven or ten characters that often start on the second part of the main beat. Arias also incorporate extra ornamented and melismatic phrases like the *shisan hai*, a series of thirteen vocables which highlight singing skills in Hebei bangzi. Bangzi music consists also of traditional 'labelled melodies' (*qupai*) and folk melodies, along with instrumental interludes and percussion patterns. Bangzi operas share the two-string fiddle (*banhu*) as the lead melodic instrument and large portions of repertory.

The characteristically high-pitched, loud and animated 'sound' of Bangzi music conjures up its folk roots and the harsh open spaces of its northwestern origins. Interpretation also thrives in tragic and highly emotional scenes. Individual dialects, particular artistic idiosyncrasies and repertoire provide for the diversity of genres. *Qinqiang* from Shaanxi provides an outstanding example of the versatile rhythmic forms and colours that can be found in Bangzi modes, with its 'happy sound' (*huanyin*) and 'sad sound' (*kuyin*). Bangzi's modular system of arias brought a major artistic innovation to Chinese opera, since its musical/poetic units could easily be rearranged from one play to the next, allowing for more flexibility than the music of earlier opera genres.

The accessibility, local flavour and emotional impact of Bangzi facilitated its broad expansion. Its earliest forms, Qinqiang and Puzhou bangzi, were born three and half centuries ago around the Shaanxi and Shanxi areas. Through exposure to other cultures during their progression, they absorbed local dialects, artistic features and new plays, thereby creating new genres. The Qing dynasty (1644–1911) marks the years of prosperity for Bangzi, during which it penetrated to Sichuan, Henan, Shandong, Hubei, Anhui, Zhejiang, and even further south, to form separate genres or influence other operas. By the late eighteenth century, the style reached Beijing, Tianjin and the surrounding Hebei province. Supported by rich merchants and bankers from Shaanxi and Shanxi and appreciated by the lower classes, including peasants, what would later become Hebei bangzi took root successfully in the area.

Bangzi's traditional repertory, adapted from historical novels, folk stories or oral literature, exceeds several thousand plays. Qinqiang's 'Yisu she', a progressive theatrical institution created by intellectuals in Xi'an 'to make changes in customs and traditions', as its name indicates, has spearheaded the renewal of Bangzi repertoire since 1912. Their 1977 creation of *The Xi'an Incident* (*Xian shibian*), depicting the 1936 kidnapping of Chang Kai-Shek on a visit to Xi'an by mutinous troops in order to force him to form a united front with the Communists against Japan, illustrates how new productions can use a significant moment in China's recent history to serve a didactic purpose. The standard repertoire has undergone successive revisions in the 1930s, 1950s or 1980s, and plays inspired by classic drama in which the heroine achieves retribution, such as *The Injustice to Dou E* (*Dou E yuan*) and *Qin Xianglian*, have remained popular. Contemporary adaptations of world classics like Shakespeare or Greek tragedies have toured abroad; Hebei bangzi's *Medea* has been performed in Athens and at La Scala in Milan in the 1990s.

The future prospects of genres like Hebei bangzi is hard to predict. Despite the recent national and international acclaim of actresses like Pei Yanling (b. 1947), known as the demon-queller Zhong Kui on stage and screen, and the effort to adapt the singing so that male parts can join female roles in duets, dwindling resources have led many actors to turn at least partially to other professions. Hebei bangzi's audiences have shrunk, and its most loyal base is now to be found in the countryside. Qinqiang has fared rather well throughout the twentieth century, as has Yuju opera from Henan, thanks to its accessible language and melodies.

See also: Xiqu musical structure

ISABELLE DUCHESNE

bao ernai

[Cant. *bau yi lai*] ('keeping a second wife')

Monogamy has been the sole legal form of **marriage** in China since 1950 and in Hong Kong (HK) since 1971. Monogamy has been widely accepted by women as they believe it to be to their advantage. However, men have been considerably more reluctant to change the habits and prerogatives of thousands of years and rich men in HK routinely keep and exchange mistresses. Ordinary men have more usually been constrained by the lack of financial resources to keep to the bonds of matrimony.

However, since the relocation of HK's manufacturing base to Guangdong province managers, technicians, supervisors and truck drivers from HK have been using the opportunity to establish *yi lai* relationships. Young female migrant workers from rural Guangdong and neighbouring provinces are preferred workers in the factories because they are cheap, malleable and easy to train, creating a gender imbalance. Men from HK, while not highly desirable in HK, acquire greater exchange value in Guangdong because their salaries look larger and they can offer lifestyle and financial benefits otherwise unavailable to the young women who are consequently willing to enter into liaisons even without marriage. The phrase *yi lai* has entered HK slang to describe an easy-pull opening on a can of herbal drink.

The publicity in HK given to *yi lai* relationships has created a great sense of unease among wives whose husbands work in China. In 1998, a woman killed her two sons and then herself when she discovered her husband had a mistress in China. An HK legislator suggested making adultery a criminal offence, and the Guangdong Women's Federation lobbied vigorously and successfully to have the definition of bigamy expanded to cover *yi lai* liaisons.

The phenomenon is also prevalent on the mainland, though the phrase, 'keeping a second wife' (*bao ernai*) can also refer to the less stable practice of booking or keeping a mistress, in which case it is also sometimes associated with the phrase 'Miss Three Accompanies' (*Sanpeinü*), which refers to escorts. In either case, the keeping of mistresses, concubines or second and even third wives (*bao sannai*) is common, and the high-ranking officials who were prosecuted for **corruption** – Chen Xitong, Wang Baosen, Hu Changqing or Cheng Kejie – all had at least one.

Further reading

De Mente, B. L. (1996). *NTC's Dictionary of China's Cultural Code Words*. Lincolnwood: National Textbook Company.

Lang, Graeme and Smart, Josephine (2002). 'Migration and the "Second Wife" in South China: Toward Cross-Border Polygyny'. *International Migration Review* 36 (Summer): 546–69.

VERONICA PEARSON

barefoot doctors

In 1958, during the Great Leap Forward, health care was organized in health stations at the commune level, which employed peasants to work as part-time doctors. In 1965 Chairman Mao was concerned that the large peasant population had no access to medical services. Urban doctors were sent out to rural areas, where many trained paramedics. These 'barefoot doctors' were given a three-month training and a comprehensive manual was developed for their use. They worked part-time in agriculture (hence their name) and part-time in health care, receiving payment similar to other peasants. It was the village collective which ran and financed clinics and paid doctors' salaries. Consistent with the basic guidelines of the First National Congress, the emphasis was on preventative medicine and the integration of traditional and Western medicine. The services included health education, immunizations, communicable disease reporting and basic medical care. The almost universal access to health with its emphasis on prevention (with the improvement of social conditions and stability after decades of war) contributed to vast reductions in mortality and morbidity.

In the 1980s the financing of, along with the popular and political support for, the cooperative medical system diminished. Although the basic tenets of health care policy were retained, after 1978, the economic reforms affected the financing and running of the health services. An examination was established for all barefoot doctors and all those who passed became 'township doctors' who could charge for services. Some moved to more lucrative jobs, some moved into other areas of health care and others who failed examinations returned to agriculture.

It is very difficult to generalize for the whole of China as to what became of the 1.8 million barefoot doctors, but the system as it was no longer exists. The health bureau is responsible for provision of health care services at all levels and patients pay for their medication and hospital care. Immunizations and preventative health are organized by the Centres for Epidemic and TB Control. Private clinics and medicine shops also provide much of the health care. With the loss of the barefoot doctor, achieving universal accessibility to health care continues to present a major challenge.

Further reading

Zhu, Naisu *et al.* (1989). 'Factors Associated with the Decline of the Cooperative Medical System and Barefoot Doctors in China'. *Bulletin of the World Health Organisation* 67.4: 431–41.

Shi, Leiyu (1993). 'Health Care in China: a Rural–Urban Comparison after the Socio-economic Reforms'. *Bulletin of the World Health Organisation* 71.6: 723–36.

MARION TORRANCE

basketball

The Young Men's Christian Association introduced basketball to China in the mid 1890s. More than a century later, Chinese hoops player Yao Ming became a cross-cultural celebrity when a US professional team chose him as the number one pick in the National Basketball Association's 2002 draft. Yao was not the first Chinese to play pro basketball in the US – two men and one woman preceded him – but perhaps more than any other single event, his arrival illuminates China's growing importance in the global sports marketplace.

Although basketball has been an important component of Chinese sports throughout its modern history, played in Republican and Communist eras alike, only recently has the game truly gained the status of a national sport. Its potential as a route to international recognition now overshadows that of table tennis, while its popularity as both participant and spectator sport certainly rivals that of soccer.

In political terms, basketball already is a vehicle for Chinese regional assertion through the Asian Games, with men's and women's teams regularly winning regional championships over the past two decades. In economic terms, basketball is seen as an emerging profit centre for both Chinese and multinational capital. The NBA already has a large fan base among young Chinese consumers, while China's professional men's league, launched in 1995, has attracted commercial sponsorship from a range of domestic and foreign companies. With foreign-born players increasingly important on NBA teams, and China recognized as a logical source of talent, the Chinese pro league is acquiring additional practical and symbolic significance as a training ground for world-calibre players.

Further reading

Polumbaum, Judy (2002). 'From Evangelism to Entertainment: The YMCA, the NBA, and the Evolution of Chinese Basketball'. *Modern Chinese Literature and Culture* 14.1 (Spring): 178–230.

JUDY POLUMBAUM

bayinhui

Traditional music ensemble

Bayinhui (eight-tone associations) is a term used in many parts of China to refer to a variety of ensemble types, most of which serve ritual and ceremonial functions. Eight-tone associations may comprise combinations of wind and string instruments, as is the case in northern Shanxi, or mixed groupings of wind, string and percussion instruments, as is the case in much of Guangdong. In some rural regions of China *bayinhui* are formed by groups of villagers for self-cultivation and entertainment. Across wide areas of China, **weddings**, **funerals** and other events have been traditionally marked by *bayinhui* performances.

The repertoire of *bayinhui* is frequently related to that of regional opera, reflective of a widespread interpenetration of opera and ritual in China. In rural parts of the Pearl River Delta near Guangzhou there is a long history of unstaged Cantonese operas being performed by eight-tone associations, particularly in conjunction with ritual events.

Usually opera repertoire, when used, is adapted to particular ritual contexts.

The significance of *bayin* performance must also be understood in terms of sponsorship. In regions of the Pearl River Delta funeral custom dictates that *bayin* ensembles, known in the region as *bayinban* (eight-sound bands), be hired by familial and social sectors as tributes to the deceased. In Taishan, just west of Guangzhou, there are instances of multiple ensembles being hired for a single funeral.

Further reading

Jones, Stephen (1995). *Folk Music of China: Living Instrumental Traditions*. Oxford: Clarendon.

JAMES DALE WILSON

Beauties' Literature

(Meinü wenxue)

Beauties' Literature refers to a 1990s literary genre of a group of women writers who were born in the 1970s. They are, or write about, pretty women. Representative of these writers are Mianmian (or Mian Mian, b. 1970), a high school dropout; Zhou Wenhui (a.k.a. Wei Hui), a graduate of Fudan University and a dance-party queen of Shanghai; and finally Beijing's Jiu Dan. Some of their work has been so controversial that it has been banned in China, but pirated copies are commonly available. Most of their work has actually been published in China, and some of it has been translated into English, French and other languages. The bans have been justified by the antinomian subject matter: a base lust for drugs, unmarried young women having sex with Chinese and foreign men, both married and unmarried, prostitution, suicide, and so forth. *LaLaLa*, a collection of short stories, and *Candy*, a novel, are Mian Mian's semi-autobiographies. Her other works include *Every Good Kid Deserves Candy* and *Acid Lover*. In addition to her semi-autobiographical *Shanghai Baby*, Wei Hui's books include *A Virgin in the Water* and *As Crazy as Wei Hui*. Both writers, though jealous of each other, see their own work as alternative love stories

and are in fact proud of being China's first banned drug-and-pornography novelists. Jiu Dan's novel *Crows* (*Wuya*) describes the prostitution of female students from China in Singapore, and *A Woman's Bed* (*Nüren chuang*, 2002), her latest novel, was a big hit. In response to her critics, Jiu Dan has described the work of such well-established female writers as Bing Xin, **Chen Ran** and **Wang Anyi** as only 'so-so'. Serious writers and even most readers do not take Beauties' Literature seriously, but turn to it out of curiosity and amusement. Nonetheless, some severely criticize these self-proclaimed pretty and artistic writers, calling their work 'sub-literature', 'prostitutes' literature' or 'privacy literature', while others take their work to be a form of **avant-garde/experimental literature**.

See also: bestsellers; sexuality and behaviour; web literature

Further reading

Lyne, Sandra (2002). 'Consuming Madame Chrysanthème: Loti's "dolls" to *Shanghai Baby*'. *Intersections: Gender, History and Culture in the Asian Context* 8 (October). Online journal, available at http://www.sshe.murdoch.edu.au/intersections/default/htm

Mian, Mian (2003). *Candy: A Novel*. Trans. Andrea Lingenfelter. Back Bay Books.

Shi, Anbin (2003). 'Body Writing and Corporeal Feminism: Reconstructing Gender Identity in Contemporary China'. In Anbin Shi, *A Comparative Approach to Redefining Chineseness in the Era of Globalization*. Lewiston: Mellen Press, 129–206.

Wei, Hui (2001). *Shanghai Baby*. Trans. Bruce Humes. New York: Simon and Schuster.

HELEN XIAOYAN WU

beauty contests

In the early 1980s the 'pursuit of beauty' was part of a backlash against the repressive Maoist state. Banned by the state since 1949, beauty contests were quickly co-opted to stimulate the growth of consumer culture.

Beijing Television Studio attempted to hold the first post-Liberation beauty contest in June 1988. Although it included a talent contest and questions about knowledge and morals, it was cancelled due to official pressure. The first post-Liberation beauty contest was held in Guangzhou in 1988 and subsequent years; not until 1991 were contests held in Tianjin, Shanghai and elsewhere. In Beijing in 1991, the first Chinese Supermodel Contest selected a representative to the Elite Model Look world contest, one of the most important international modelling competitions. The state approved it due to the promotion of high fashion in order to stimulate the textile and garment industries (see **cashmere industry**; **silk industry**). This opened the door for beauty contests, and in 1992 they burst onto the scene nationwide; by one estimate, over seventy contests sponsored by over fifty newspapers and nearly one hundred television stations were held in that year. China achieved its first top finish in a major international contest with a third place in the 2002 Miss Universe contest.

Further reading

Lan, C. (2000). *Zhongguo mote qishilu* [The Story of Chinese Models]. Shanghai: Shanghai renmin chubanshe.

Wang, S. (1993). *Zhongguo xuanmei dachao jiemi* [Revealing the Secrets of the High Tide of Beauty Contests in China]. Beijing: Shijieyu chubanshe.

SUSAN BROWNELL

beauty magazines

When 'femininity', 'fashion' and 'beauty' reappeared in the public discourse of the early reform era, there existed no media devoted to subjects like these. However, the magazines run by the **All-China Women's Federation** were already producing occasional pieces on how to dress and behave like a 'real woman' in the 1980s. The paper of those magazines was of low quality, greyish and with hand-drawn black-and-white illustrations. In the 1990s the authorities cut magazine subsidies. More ads appeared, and the editors focused on the readers' wants. Magazines such as *Women's Friend* (*Nüyou*), run by the Shaanxi Provincial Women's Federation, devoted larger sections to beauty and fashion and increased the sections with colour to glossy paper.

With the aim of developing the textile industry, magazines like *Fashion* (*Shizhuang*), published by the branch organization China Silk Import and Export General Corporation and *Modern Dress* (*Xiandai fuzhuang*) appeared in the early 1980s. These magazines could not compete in popularity with the more expensive, international, glossy magazines that arrived in the 1990s. The French multinational fashion magazine *Elle* was the first, published as a joint venture with Shanghai Translation Publishing House. *Elle* has three Chinese language editions. The PRC *Elle* is also called *The Garden of World Fashion* (*Shijie shizhuang zhi yuan*) and it fills the magazine mainly with fashion features from Western editions. *Cosmopolitan* has also entered the Chinese market, teaming up with the Chinese *Shishang*, a lifestyle and fashion magazine with a distinct East Asian flavour.

Further reading

Andrews, Julia and Shen, Kuiyi (2002) 'The New Chinese Woman and Lifestyle Magazines in the Late 1990s'. In Perry Link, Richard Madsen and Paul Pickowicz (eds), *Popular China: Unofficial Culture in a Globalizing Society*. Lanham, MD: Rowman and Littlefield, 137–62.

Evans, Harriet (2000). 'Marketing Femininity: Images of the Modern Chinese Woman'. In Timothy Weston and Lionel Jensen (eds), *China Beyond the Headlines*. Lanham, MD: Rowman and Littlefield, 217–44.

Johansson, Perry (1998). 'White Skin, Large Breasts: Chinese Beauty Product Advertising as Cultural Discourse'. *China Information* 12.2/3 (Autumn/Winter): 59–84.

—— (2001). 'Selling the New Chinese Woman: Consumer Culture and the Chinese Politics of Beauty'. In Shoma Munshi (ed.), *Modern Asian Woman: Global Media Local Meaning*. Richmond: Curzon.

PERRY JOHANSSON

Bei Dao

b. 1949, Beijing

Poet

Several times nominated for the Nobel Prize for literature, Bei Dao is best known as a founder of **Misty poetry** (*Menglong shi*) and co-founder of the dissident literary magazine *Today* (*Jintian*) which appeared during the brief Beijing Spring in late 1978 and early 1979, and was suppressed after the collapse of the movement, but resumed in Europe in 1990 when Bei Dao was in exile.

Bei Dao began writing poetry when he was a sent-down youth in Baiyangding, Hebei, during the **Cultural Revolution**. As underground literature, his poems were circulated among friends in the countryside. Drastically different from the high-flown propagandistic language of the state discourse, his poems with their original images, structure, and syntax express a powerfully individual voice of bitterness, despair and defiance. Regarded as incomprehensible, his poems (along with those of his fellow poets) were condemned in the 1980s by orthodox critics, but were highly praised by the liberal critics Xie Mian, Sun Shaozhen and Xu Jingya. Bei Dao's only novella to date is *Waves* (*Bodong*, 1974), which deals with the despair of sent-down youth (see **xiafang, xiaxiang**) and is regarded as a forerunner of post-Mao modernistic fiction.

Bei Dao was active in promoting democracy and human rights. He was in Berlin when the 4 June Massacre occurred. Since then, he has been in exile in several European countries and is currently teaching at the University of California at Davis. His poetry has been translated into many languages.

See also: Tianya

Further reading

Bei, Dao (1985). *Waves: Stories*. Ed. Bonnie McDougall and Susette Ternent Cooke. Hong Kong: Chinese University Press.

—— (1990). *The August Sleepwalkers*. Trans. Bonnie McDougall. New York: New Directions.

Pan, Yuan and Jie, Pan (1985). 'The Non-Official Magazine *Today* and the Younger Generation's Ideals for a New Literature'. In J. Kinkley (ed.), *After Mao: Chinese Literature and Society*, 1978–1981. Cambridge: Harvard University Press, 193–219.

LEUNG LAIFONG

Beijing Bastards

[Beijing zazhong, 1993]

Film

Beijing Bastards was the second feature film by independent director **Zhang Yuan**. Censored in China and first shown at the Locarno Film Festival and the Singapore Film Festival, it gave 'underground film' its name in Chinese cinema. Based on a loose script, the film is deeply honest in dealing with a group of young aspiring artists in the Beijing semi-underground of the 1990s. A painter, a writer, a bar owner and a musician – the latter played by the famous rock-star **Cui Jian** – deal with issues of relationships, pregnancy, abortion, money problems and future worries. Without a finished script and featuring Zhang Yuan's friends as actors, it is a highly improvised film, much as the lives portrayed in it are. Nevertheless, the drifting and sense of loss of this subculture youth is not presented as a dead end. Ultimately, the characters come to the painful but life-changing realization that they only care about themselves.

Released in 1993, it has established director Zhang Yuan as a leading member of the **Sixth Generation** of independent filmmakers in the 1990s. His exploration of aspects of contemporary city life in China made him the main representative of urban realism. The dark energy of frustration and alienation in *Beijing Bastards*, the semi-documentary style, the handheld camera and the gloomy lighting initiated the departure from the largely epic and allegorical visions of the **Fifth Generation** directors before him.

Further reading

Jaivin, Linda. (1995). 'Beijing Bastards – the New Revolution'. *Chime* 8 (Spring): 99–103.

Kuoshu, Harry (1999). 'Beijing Bastards, the Sixth Generation Directors, and "Generation-X" in China'. *Asian Cinema* 10.2 (Spring/Summer): 18–28.

BIRGIT LINDER

Beijing Children's Film Studio

(Zhongguo ertong zhipianchang)

The Beijing Children's Film Studio was the brain-child of Yu Lan (b. 1921), a famous film actress of the 1950s and 1960s. Her acting pedigree includes *Lin Family Shop* (*Lin jia puzi*,1959), *Revolutionary Family* (*Geming jia*) and *Living in the Flames of War* (*Liehuo zhong yongsheng*, 1965). Her experience in the **Cultural Revolution** was not happy and, tellingly, this extraordinarily beautiful and talented person made just one more film, in 1974. The Film Studio, which Yu Lan founded on Children's Day, 1 June 1981, was, unsurprisingly, a work of passionate commitment and professional investment. She has stated that it was founded to transmit moral stability in a time of great change, and many of the films made in the late 1980s and 1990s dealt with divorce, melded families and the pressures of being a single child in the first generation of the **one-child policy** era. One of the best in this genre was the study of a child who cares for his emotionally distraught mother (*Don't Cry Mummy*/*Bie ku mama*, 1990). The film demonstrated a nuanced understanding of a child protagonist in an adult world, and skilfully employed camera angles and locations to create a child's perspective on the dark, wet world of marital breakdown in Beijing. Other films revived the theme of schoolchildren and teacher loyalty (*Four Schoolmates*/*Sige xiaohuoban*, 1982) or focused on minority themes (*Red Elephant*/*Hongxiang*, 1982). *Red Elephant* is a typical film about minorities insofar as it weaves together a romantic, dare we say infantilized, portrait of a minority people with a quasi-mythical animal (a similar format is found in animation of the same period – see, for example, *Hailibu*, 1985). The studio also brought in female directors as diverse in scope as **Peng Xiaolian** and

Guang Chunlan. The former is one of the few female names that emerged out of the **Fifth Generation (film directors)**, while the latter made her name as a minority director with a keen interest in children's drama. The Studio has been under-funded for most of its existence and is currently trying to make alliances with external production houses in an attempt to widen its creative scope and its appeal to the new televisually sophisticated audience. This initiative produced *Crazy Rabbit*, the story of a real and breathing computer virus shaped like a rabbit. Other part live-action, part computer-animation films are being planned.

Further reading

Chinese Teenage Research Institution (2000). 'Julang de chongji: meijie yü dangdai shaonian ertong' [Contemporary Media and Children]. In *Xin faxian: dangdai Zhongguo shaonian ertong baogao* [New Discoveries: Reports of Contemporary Chinese Children]. Zhongguo shaonian ertong chubanshe.

Donald, Stephanie (2002). 'Crazy Rabbits! Children's Media Culture and Socialization'. In Stephanie Donald, Michael Keane and Yin Hong (eds), *Media in China: Consumption, Content and Change*, London: Routledge Curzon, 128–38.

STEPHANIE HEMELRYK DONALD

Beijing Film Academy

(Beijing dianying xueyuan)

The Beijing Film Academy (BFA: http://www.bfa.edu.cn/) was founded in 1950 and has since become China's premier institution for film studies. An outgrowth of the film department of the Central Cultural Ministry Graduate School of Acting and Arts, it attained its final name as Beijing Film Academy in 1956. After a forced hiatus during the **Cultural Revolution**, the academy was completely re-established in 1977.

In 1979, the Youth Film Studio was established, which enabled the academy to produce its own films. It is one of the cinema studios officially approved by the Chinese government and a foundation for the production activities of students and teachers. It is also where films are dubbed and television programmes produced. In 1995, noted director **Jia Zhangke** established the well-received Youth Experimental Film Group there.

According to the most recent data, BFA consists of seven departments, two institutes, four centres and a separate College of Photography. These offer degrees in twelve disciplines: cinematography, production, directing, advertising, dramaturgy, performance studies, recording art, TV broadcasting and advertising, TV and film production design and management, animation, film theory, and screenwriting and editing.

As the only institute of higher learning for film studies in China, BFA has brought forth a large contingent of famous directors, actors, and film technicians, and it is the alma mater of most of the filmmakers known as the **Fifth Generation** and **Sixth Generation** directors, most notable among them **Zhang Yimou**, **Chen Kaige**, **Zhang Yuan**, **Ning Ying** and Jia Zhangke.

See also: Xi'an Film Studio

BIRGIT LINDER

Beijing People's Art Theatre

(Beijng renmin yishu juyuan)

Beijing People's Art Theatre (BPAT) was established in 1952, shortly after the founding of the People's Republic. From the very beginning, both the Chinese government and BPAT's prominent founders, including the playwright Cao Yu and the director **Jiao Juyin**, wanted to make it the flagship of Chinese drama companies on a par with the Moscow Art Theatre.

The development of BPAT over the past fifty years may be divided into three periods. The first period (1952–9) marked the formation and maturation of this theatre's unique style of performance. Under the guidance of its director Jiao Juyin, BPAT developed a system of performance that combined Western realism with China's own theatrical tradition and produced a number of plays that employed the methods of the Stanislavsky system and the techniques of Chinese opera.

During these eight years, BPAT mounted seventy productions, including such modern classics as Cao Yu's *Thunderstorm* (*Leiyu*), *Sunrise* (*Richu*) and *Peking Man* (*Beijing ren*), and Lao She's *Teahouse* (*Chaguan*).

During the second period (1960–76), BPAT's output declined in the quantity and quality, as art became a victim of political campaigns. The impact of the **Cultural Revolution** was devastating. From 1967 to 1972 not a single play was performed. Lao She committed suicide; Jiao Juyin died from persecution and cancer.

The third period (1977 and currently) brought revival and new developments to Beijing People's Art Theatre. *Teahouse* was restaged in 1979 with its original cast and toured Europe the following year. Several new 'Beijing flavour' plays in the style of Lao She's masterpiece were also performed. More important was the emergence in the 1980s of an **avant-garde/experimental theatre** that challenged the dominance of socialist realism and the Stanislavsky system. Collaboration between playwright **Gao Xingjian** and director **Lin Zhaohua** in the production of Gao's plays *Alarm Signal* (*Juedui xinhao*, 1982) and **Bus Stop** (*Chezhan*, 1983) led BPAT in a new direction – its tradition of realism infused with theatre of the absurd and Berthold Brecht's epic theatre. The government's 'open door' policy also enabled BPAT to stage a large number of Western plays (see **Western theatre**), providing Chinese dramatists with models and inspiration. The Western influence manifested itself in the adaptation of foreign plays as a method of dramatic creation. Many of the young director Meng Jinghui's works produced in the 1990s belonged to this category.

During the fifty years of its existence, Beijing People's Art Theatre has fulfilled the vision of its founders in becoming the leading company of spoken drama in China. Several factors account for its pre-eminence. First, it has developed its own theory and system of performance. Second, it has trained a group of top actors. Third, it has produced a body of works that exemplify its style and spirit. Last but not least, BPAT has continued to grow, absorbing new theories and techniques in the creation of a new Chinese theatre that is both modern and rooted in the Chinese tradition.

YU SHIAO-LING

Beijing Roast Duck

Only Bianyifang and Quanjude in Beijing, along with their branch restaurants, make the authentic Beijing Roast Duck. The restaurants represent two distinct duck-roasting cuisines. Bianyifang, founded in 1855, roasts its ducks by the radiant heat from the oven walls heated with sorghum stalks. Ducks thus roasted are crisp and golden brown. Quanjude, which opened nine years later but became more famous, cooks its ducks by hanging them over a flame fed with wood from date, peach or pear trees. When roasted, the duck looks brilliantly dark red, its skin crisp and meat tender. The duck skin and meat are sliced off the duck before served in a pancake with green onions and beanpaste.

The earliest roasting duck in China was recorded in the thirteenth century and later became the Ming dynasty's royal delicacy. As the Yongle emperor relocated Ming's capital from Nanjing to Beijing in 1419, the dainty came along with him. The opening of Bianyifang and Quanjude restaurants made Beijing Roast Duck available to the public.

To guarantee the quality of their ducks, the restaurants used designated sources of force-feed ducks as their supply. Raised with an ancient method, a new breed of Beijing force-feed ducks came into existence known for its white feather, plump body and tender meat. Today, the stock has already become extinct and 90 per cent of the duck supply for the Beijing Roast Duck is from the British Cherry Valley stock, the offspring of a hybrid of Beijing ducks with foreign breeds.

YUAN HAIWANG

Beijing yinyue

(Capital/Beijing music)

Regional traditional music genre

Beijing music is Buddhist instrumental music played by a wind and percussion band (see **drumming and blowing**). Its repertoire includes over one hundred labelled melodies (*qupai*), which musicians arrange into suites of ten or more tunes. The musical instruments used are two cylindrical reed-pipes (*guanzi*), double

mouth-organs (*sheng*), two bamboo flutes (**dizi**), two frames of gongs (*yunluo*), and percussion, including cymbals, drums and a small gong, called *dangzi*. This genre, which originated in the Beijing area, is historically related to the palace ceremonial music and Buddhist music used by the imperial family. In the twentieth century it was played not only by Buddhist monks in the temples of Beijing, but also by many local musicians within the rural triangular area whose points are Beijing, Tianjin and Baoding. As a ceremonial music, it is played mainly for **funerals** and various other ceremonies, such as praying for rain and driving ghosts and spirits out from villages. Pieces in the repertoire can be played independently, but they are usually grouped into suites having four parts. Since music accompanies a ceremony, the suites must necessarily fit the length of the ritual steps, resulting in pieces of variable length. All pieces of Beijing music are essentially pentatonic; there is no contrast from phrase to phrase or from one section to another. Ensemble 'harmony' is emphasized over individual achievement.

Further reading

Jones, Stephen and Xue, Yibing (1991). 'The Music Associations of Hebei Province, China'. *Ethnomusicology* 35.1: 1–29.

Yang, Yinliu (1981). *Zhongguo gudai yinyue shigao* [Draft History of Ancient Chinese Music]. 2 vols. Beijing: Renmin yinyue chubanshe.

—— (1996). 'The Capital Music of the Zhinhua Temple'. *Sonus* 17.1: 20–6.

Yuan, Jingfang (1999). *Yuezhongxue* [A Study of Instrumental Music Genres]. Beijing: Huayue chubanshe.

DU YAXIONG

Beijingers in New York

[Beijingren zai Niuyue, 1993]

Television serial

Beijingers in New York was the most controversial television drama serial (*dianshi lianxuju*) produced in China during the 1990s. The serial, adapted from

Cao Guilin's novel, delivered a range of propositions to Chinese viewers, not only about the West, but about the changing nature of Chinese society. It was the first Chinese television serial to receive a government bank loan, the first production filmed outside China, and the first Chinese television drama touching on cross-cultural sexual relationships. *Beijingers* provided the first television role for celebrated actor **Jiang Wen** who portrayed Wang Qiming, a casualty of Western 'spiritual pollution'. Soon after arriving in New York Wang's wife leaves him for the American boss of a garment sweatshop. Humiliated, he plots revenge in business, in the process engaging in immoral activities: he takes a de-facto lover, uses alcohol to excess, procures a prostitute, gambles, and engages in stock market speculation. Portrayed as an anti-hero, Wang Qiming is generally remembered as an entrepreneur prepared to take a risk, albeit with financial help from A Chun, a Taiwanese businesswoman who becomes his de-facto lover. The portrayal of Western decadence titillated, while the obsession with materialism reflected China's changing society. Notable performances included Wang Ji as A Chun, Yan Xiaopin as Wang's wife Guo Yan, and Robert Daly as David McCarthy, the scheming sweatshop boss. The series was co-produced by **CCTV (Chinese Central Television)**'s China Television Drama Production Centre and the Beijing Television Arts Centre. The directors were Zheng Xiaolong and **Feng Xiaogang**.

Further reading

Huot, Claire (2000). *China's New Cultural Scene: A Handbook of Changes*. Durham: Duke University Press, 60–4.

Keane, Michael and Tao, Dongfeng (1999). 'Conversations with Feng Xiaogang, Director of the TV Series "Beijingers on New York"'. *positions: east asia cultures critique* 7.1: 193–200.

Liu, Lydia (1999). 'Beijing Soujourners in New York: Postsocialism and the Question of Ideology in Global Media Culture'. *positions: east asia cultures critique* 7.3: 763–97.

MICHAEL KEANE

bestsellers

The bestseller (*changxiao shu*) is a relatively new phenomenon in contemporary Chinese society. Although there had been titles with high print runs before the reform period started in 1978, commercial money-spinners were rather frowned upon in the socialist book sector. In fact, the term 'bestseller' was not included in Chinese dictionaries at the end of the 1980s. The transformation of the book and publishing sector, which led to an economically liberalized, pluralistic book market, also produced bestsellers and 'bestseller bulletins' (*paihangbang*) in the early 1990s. Since then, lists of top sellers from the state-owned Xinhua book stores in different regions have been announced regularly in well-known journals such as *China Book Review* (*Zhongguo tushu pinglun*) and sporadically in the country biggest **newspapers, People's Daily** (*Renmin ribao*) and *Enlightenment Daily* (**Guangming ribao**). The allegedly first national bestseller bulletin was published in 1995. Moreover, the bestsellers of private bookstores and kiosks have also been determined by the *Beijing Youth Daily* (*Beijing qingnian ribao*).

The changes in Chinese book publishing and marketing have had an impact on the nature of best and long sellers. While texts by and about important personalities from CCP history and Marxism–Leninism (Mao Zedong, Deng Xiaoping, etc.) as well as reference books, had high print runs and allegedly high sales figures in the Xinhua bookstores even until the 1990s, the transformation of the book sector established new trends. Since the beginning of the reform era, fictional bestsellers no longer mirrored socialist realism, but centred on a critical treatment of society (e.g. **Mo Yan, Su Xiaokang, Wang Meng**). After several political campaigns during the 1980s and particularly since the suppression of the 1989 mass protest movement, Chinese fictional bestsellers have reflected the growing *ennui* in Chinese society which expressed the disillusioned urban lifestyle of an estranged, depoliticized and consumption-addicted young generation. Writers like **Wang Shuo** and **Jia Pingwa** in the early 1990s and young, self-willed women like Mian Mian and Wei Hui at the end of the 1990s (see **Beauties' Literature**) became bestselling authors. Entertainment fiction, such as the popular love stories by the Taiwanese female writers San Mao and **Qiong Yao**, has been attracting a large readership since the 1980s. The Chinese bestseller has been promoted by increasingly wide reception in all media sectors (radio, film, television and Internet) and strongly influenced by international trends. Since the beginning of the reform era, Western literature of the eighteenth and nineteenth centuries, modern Western authors like Kafka and Sartre, and also popular titles like *Gone with the Wind*, *Titanic* and *Harry Potter* headed the bestseller lists. Besides, at least the unofficial bestseller lists have been dominated by the genre of **martial arts fiction**. This genre, which is closely linked to Chinese history and tradition, is a reminiscence of China's cultural heyday. Its clear normative frame provides orientation and meaning – rather like the great traditional novels *Dream of the Red Chamber* (*Honglou meng*), *Water Margin* (*Shuihui zhuan*) and so forth, which have remained long sellers in various adapted versions (comics) on the book market.

The ambivalence between national and Western (post)modern trends is also reflected in the non-fictional sector. Bill Gates' *The Road Ahead* and **Zhongguo keyi shuo bu** (*China Can Say No*) – a chauvinistic pamphlet against the international superiority of the US and for strengthening China's own national power – were front-runners in the 1990s. Computer handbooks, English textbooks and biographies of famous (and successful) personalities but also self-help books based on Chinese traditional philosophy were also among the top sellers. During the 1980s, by contrast, Western philosophers and sociologists like Max Weber, Kant, Nietzsche had dominated the book market with print runs of hundred of thousands of copies. We might conclude that, at the turn of the century, the Chinese bestseller bulletins are headed by either entertainment and success-promising consumer 'products' or books that propagate China's national greatness and traditional values.

See also: book publishing; consumerism; morality; nationalism; Olympics; socio-political values; xiahai

Further reading

Link, Perry (2000). *The Uses of Literature*. Princeton: Princeton University Press.
Neder, Christina (1999). *Lesen in der VR China*. Hamburg: Institut für Asienkunde.

CHRISTINA NEDER

Beyond

Rock group

In both journalistic and academic discourse, Hong Kong and (to a lesser extent) Taiwan are considered commercial places where only pop music prospers. In contrast to Beijing, the perceived cultural centre of 'Greater China', the commercial spirit of both places allows little or no room for the 'alternative' sound of rock music. The example of the Hong Kong rock band Beyond upsets such spatial division of musical genres. Formed in 1983, Beyond quickly became a main thrust of the 'band movement' of Hong Kong during the late 1980s, together with **Tat Ming Pair**, Taichi and Raidas. As a rock band considered to be 'underground', even after signing with a major label, Beyond embodies a rebellious, angry and youthful spirit typical of the 1960s flower-power idealism of, for example, Bob Dylan.

Beyond was formed around lead vocalist Wong Ka-Kui (b. 1962). His sudden death during a performance in Japan in 1993 shocked audiences and became metaphoric for the death of the spirited 'band movement' and a young daring generation. The three remaining band members remained active, and were subsequently contracted by the Taiwanese label Rock Records. According to a 1997 survey, Beyond was the most popular rock band among Beijing youth. Nonetheless, having used up all their artistic resources, and increasingly dissatisfied with their record company, Beyond released their last album *Goodtime* in 1999 and the members went solo. It is of interest to note the almost contemporary emergence of a new band, Lazy Muthafucka. The rebellious idealism of Beyond was replaced by a more aggressive, streetwise hip-hop sound that would certainly be awarded a parental warning in the US.

JEROEN DE KLOET

Big-Tailed Elephant

Artist group

The Big-Tailed Elephant was formed by a quartet of artists in 1990: Xu Tan (b. 1957, Wuhan, Hubei), Chen Shaoxiong (b. 1962, Shantou, Guangdong), Lin Yilin (b. 1964, Guangzhou) and Liang Juhui (b. 1957, Guangzhou). Later, the group was joined on occasion by Zheng Guogu and Wang Huimin. Keeping their distance from the more conceptual and socio-political art of northern China (i.e. Beijing), these artists asserted the value of the individual artistic body as an autonomous being with a more sense-oriented approach to life. Despite the absence of a specific unifying artistic agenda, they were all reacting to the high-speed transformations that had characterized the regions surrounding the Pearl River Delta since Deng Xiaoping's creation of Special Economic Zones, in which a growing commercial environment was saturating cities with consumerism, and ephemeral desires were redefining the relationship between humans and their environment.

Working in video and photography (Chen Shaoxiong), installation (Lin Yilin, Liang Juhui) and interactive projects (Xu Tan), the group uses ready-made objects found in the new, highly mediated, postmodern urban reality – industrial rejects, construction materials, TV screen-sets, neon lights, scaffoldings, and so forth. Annual joint exhibitions were held in 1991 (Guangzhou Workers Palace), 1992 (Guangdong Broadcast/Television University), 1993 (Red Ants Bar, Guangzhou) and 1996 (basement of Zhongguang Building, Guangzhou). The group participated in the 1st China Art EXPO in Guangzhou (1994) with an extra-mural show entitled *No Room*, an installation realized for the Hanmo Centre (Beijing) in a run-down villa. In 1998 the group received international recognition with the 'Grosz Schwanze Elefant' show held at the Kunsthalle Bern in Germany. In 2003 they were part of the section 'Z.O.U. – Zone Of Urgency' curated by Hou Hanru at the 50th Venice Biennale.

Further reading

(1998). *Grosz Schwanze Elefant* [Big-Tailed Elephant](exhibition catalogue). Kunsthalle Bern.

Hou, Hanru (1996). 'Beyond the Cynical: China Avant-Garde in the 1990's'. *ART AsiaPacific* 3.1: 42–51.

Lü, Peng (2000). *Zhongguo Dangdai Yishushi 1990–1999* [History of Contemporary Art in China, 1990–1999]. Hunan: Hunan Fine Art Publ. House, 283.

Napack, Jonathan (2000). 'Yang Yong and the Four Elephants – The Emerging Avant-Garde of China's Pearl River Delta is Raising Eyebrows with Multimedia Journeys Through an Urban Underworld of Sex, Drugs, and Rock 'n' Roll'. *ARTnews* 128 (March).

BEATRICE LEANZA

bilingual education

Bilingual education (*shuangyu jiaoyu*) is an official policy adopted by the Chinese government in areas inhabited by minority groups. It aims at promoting the use of the languages both of the minority groups and of the **Han** Chinese among the minority people. In 1951, the government decided that for those groups that had well-developed writing systems, including the Mongols, Koreans, Uighurs, Kazaks and Tibetans, the native language should be used as the media of instruction in elementary and secondary schools. For those groups that had their own languages but not writing systems, the government would help them create their own writing systems. At the same time, they may choose to use Han Chinese as the media of instruction in schools. All minority groups may choose to offer Chinese classes in their schools. Based on this policy, fourteen writing systems were created for twelve minority groups in the 1950s.

The development of bilingual education entered a new stage in the 1980s when the policy was written into law. Accordingly, all students should learn standard Chinese; schools and classes that mainly enrol minority students should use the language both of the minority and of the Han Chinese as media of instruction; if the minority group does not have a writing system, Han Chinese should be used as the media of instruction, and the language of the minority group can be used as a supplementary media of instruction.

Based on the new laws, governments in the minority areas began to promote bilingual education. The Tibetan Autonomous Region, for example, has adopted the policy of using the Tibetan language as the main medium of instruction in the lower grades, while using both Tibetan and Chinese in the upper grades. The aim is for the students to master both Tibetan and Chinese when they graduate from high school. Similar policies have been adopted in other minority areas.

See also: Koreans, culture of; Mongols, culture of; Tibetans, culture of; Uighurs (Weiwu'er), culture of

Further reading

Postiliglioni, Gerard (ed.) (1998). *China's National Minority Education: Culturecide, State, Schooling and Development*. Levittown: Garland.

HAN XIAORONG

birth control and contraception

Birth control, or 'birth planning' (*jihuashengyu*), is one of the more controversial issues in contemporary China, entangling state policy and cultural mobilization. From the establishment of the PRC, a large-population policy was favoured by the CCP leader Mao Zedong; birth control was thus unnecessary. Although this idea was challenged by some intellectuals in the late 1950s, including the economist Ma Yingchu, their arrests turned birth control into a taboo subject for almost a decade. Thus, in contrast to other Asian countries that paid serious attention and took action towards their over-populations, PRC, then about 900 million people in population, hesitated to deal with its overgrowth until the removal of its iron curtain. Population studies resumed secretly, and presentations to the UN were made in 1973 and 1974. Birth control was now incorporated into China's economic programme, and a policy of 'marrying late, waiting longer between births, and having fewer children' (*wan xi shao*) was adopted.

However, this suggestion soon became a compulsive **one-child policy** (*yitaihua jence*) that has been in practice since 1979. This state policy, which asks couples to have at most only one child, became notorious in the UN's international population conference in 1984 where reports of the inhumane murders of unwanted children and abortions were released and were followed by harsh criticisms. The birth rate declined as expected, from 2.23 per cent in 1981 to 1.71 per cent in 1994. Although the PRC later loosened its regulations so that under certain situations (e.g. the first child is handicapped) a couple may have a second, the United Nations Fund for Population Activities (UNFPA), the big supporter for China's birth control, held back its aid until 1993 under some religious, cultural and political controversies in the name of women's human rights. The other related issue is a Malthusian debate on the balance between population growth and economic development. While hosting about 22 per cent of the world's population, China only has 7 per cent of the world's farms to support them. Whether it can survive this burden until its population reaches the peak of 1.6 billion, as claimed, in the 2030s, will be a question for demographers and policy researchers.

As state policy and a token to connecting with the world, from the beginning China's birth control was never claimed to be purely for women's health. However, it should be noted that China is a large country comprised of various racial and religious populations, rendering policy making on a national level painful for the government. Second, population distribution and economic development are severely unequal in China. The attitude towards birth control thus differs in accordance with each couple's socio-economic status and education. While well-educated people in major cities have voluntarily restricted their births, in rural areas very few are aware of the need. Third, emphasis on the 'quality' of the family appeared in the official policy after 1995: the *sanjiehe* ('three combinations': birth control combines with the state's economic development, the family's economic sufficiency and cultural happiness) and *sanweiju* ('three focuses' of population control: public education, contraception and routine work). Although achievements are made in selected villages, researchers are not optimistic, as with the breakdown of farming structures an increased number of *heihu* (people without proper registration) were found in big cities.

After imposing birth control on its people for over twenty years, China finally enacted the Law for Population and Birth Control in the fall of 2002. Yet whether birth control can be a tool for improving not only China's economy but also the quality of life for its citizens will remain a tough task in the coming decades.

Further reading

Peng, Peiyun (ed.) (1997). *Zhongguo juhua shengyu chuangshu* [A Sourcebook on Birth Control in China]. Beijing: Zhongguo renkou chubanshe. [There are also almanacs published by the Institute of Population Studies, Chinese Academy of Social Science, available since 1985, providing up-to-date data and information on this topic.]

KUO WEN-HUA

Blacklist Studio

(Heimingdan gongzuo shi)

Pop musicians

Formed in the wake of the Nationalist Party's (KMT) 1987 lifting of martial law, Blacklist Studio played a seminal role in the popularization and politicization of popular song sung in Taiwanese dialect. Their 1989 album *Songs of Madness* (*Zhuakuang ge*) remains a landmark in the history of popular music in Taiwan, and a crucial sonic document of the upsurge in nativist consciousness and democratic activism which characterized the period. Fronted by the now prominent Taiwanese singer and composer Chen Ming-chang (b. 1956), who had made a name for himself by tirelessly promoting Taiwanese folksong on the campus circuit as well as writing an award-winning soundtrack for new wave filmmaker **Hou Hsiao-hsien**'s *Dust in the Wind* (*Lianlian fengchen*, 1986), the band was composed of a group of self-described 'musical dissidents', including vocalist Wang Ming-hui and lyricist Chen Ming-yu.

Rebelling against forty years of Mandarin hegemony in Taiwanese popular musical production, and at the same time distancing themselves from the undeniably strong influence of Japanese enka on local Taiwanese folksong, Blacklist Studio fused native folk idioms and instruments (including elements of Hakka and aboriginal (*yuanzhumin*) Taiwanese music) with rock and roll and synthesizer-driven new wave to create a new sound. Straying from what had been seen as the 'vulgar' preoccupation of previous Taiwanese-language popular song with the lives and loves of the working class and the underworld, Blacklist Studio's lyrically sophisticated songs such as 'Imperial Taipei' (*Taipei diguo*) and 'Democracy Bumpkin' (*Minzhu acao*) provided epic and politically pointed testimony to the tribulations of modern Taiwanese history, confronting issues as diverse as Japanese and US colonialism, KMT repression and the decidedly mixed blessings of the island's breakneck economic development, all through a defiantly local lens. Although their follow-up album, *Cradle Songs* (*Yaolan qu*, 1996), was a commercial and critical failure, Blacklist is widely recognized for having paved the way not only for a new generation of alternative Taiwanese folk and rock musicians, but also for the entrance of Taiwanese language into the mainstream as exemplified by the runaway success of the aboriginal pop chanteuse Ah-Mei in the late 1990s.

See also: music in Taiwan

ANDREW F. JONES

Bo Yang

(né Guo, Yidong)

b. 1920, Kaifeng, Henan

Writer, cultural critic

Bo Yang is known in Taiwan as a poet, novelist, essayist and historian. After graduation from Northeast University, he became the proprietor of the *Youth Daily* (*Qingnian ribao*) and an instructor. In 1949 he went to Taiwan as an instructor. In 1966 he became the director of the Pingyuan Publishing House and edited the cartoon page of *China Daily* (*Zhonghua ribao*). He was jailed for ten years in Taiwan for translating into Chinese a Popeye cartoon that the authorities found offensive. After his release in 1977, he began delivering speeches on the 'Ugly Chinaman' phenomenon, which is the subject of his popular book *The Ugly Chinaman* (*Choulou de zhongguoren*). In it he asks why it is so hard to be a Chinese. He believes that every country has been through bad times and has its own history of humiliations. China's bad times, however, seem to have lasted longer than most other countries'. Bo Yang believes that when the face-saving Chinese start calling their compatriots 'Ugly Chinaman' in public, this will mark the birth of a new era and Chinese will be able to free themselves from their own ugliness. This book has become popular on the mainland, too. Most of his writings are satirical and reveal the dark side of society.

Further reading

Bo, Yang (1992). 'The Chinese Cursed'. In Geremie Barmé (ed.), *New Ghosts, Old Dreams: Chinese Rebel Voices*. New York: Times Books, 210–15.

—— (1992). *The Ugly Chinaman and the Crisis of Chinese Culture*. Trans. Don J. Cohn and Jing Qing. North Sydney: Allen and Unwin.

WANG XIAOLU

book publishing

After the founding of the PRC in 1949, the book-publishing (*chuban*) sector was economically and institutionally re-organized within the framework of a planned economy and a socialist public administration. The state's monopoly and the task of the publishing sector to serve as a propaganda medium for CCP authority were ensured by means of a new institutional structure. From the late 1950s through the early 1980s, only state-owned central and regional publishing houses were permitted. These comprised the general People's Publishing Houses (*Renmin chubanshe*) and a handful of specialist publishers. The state-owned Xinhua Bookstore (*Xinhua shudian*) became sole distributor and guaranteed the control of books both in terms of content and quantity. These measures reduced the number of publishing houses from 356 private firms in 1949 to 87 state-owned firms in 1965.

However, the economic reforms introduced in the early 1980s have stimulated the transformation from a monopolistic to a competitive book market.

Through the reforms of the early 1980s the publishing houses regained decision-making authority over their publishing programme and number of titles and printed copies. Tax reforms gradually brought autonomy in the area of management and with it the responsibility for profit and loss. Further regulations allowed the founding of new publishing houses and strengthened the position of regional publishers. By the late 1980s the publishers had complete autonomy with respect to management, publishing programme, production and distribution, as well as the opportunity to hold shares based on a kind of lease system (*chengbao*). Although their legal status as state-owned enterprises remained unchanged, the acceptance of 'cooperative' (*hezuo chuban*) and 'self-funded publishing' (*zifei chuban*) projects by associations, but not by private individuals, brought structural diversification and prosperous commercialized publishing programmes and also paved the way for semi-legal and illegal publishing projects. Not only did the number of publishing houses increase from 75 in 1976 to 553 in 1995, but the number of published titles also soared from around 15,000 in 1978 to 140,000 at the turn of the century. China is now the world's largest book producer. Book prices have increased by 600 per cent since the early 1980s after the lifting of price controls in 1992, the virtual elimination of subsidies, and the enactment of a copyright law in 1999 (*zhuzuo quan*, see **intellectual property**).

In the book-trade sector (*faxing*) the changes have been even more profound. The reform of the Xinhua Bookstore (the first channel – *diyi qudao*) and the gradual development of a collective and private distribution channel (the second channel – *di'er qudao*) had already been decided by the CCP government in the early 1980s. By the end of the 1980s the decentralization of the Xinhua Bookstore, the introduction of the *chengbao* system in state-owned bookstores, the establishment of wholesale centres (*pifa zhongxin*) in the cities, and the acceptance of cooperatives between publishers and bookstores, of collective and private bookstores and of book kiosks, made for a pluralistic, sales-oriented book market in China. While the Xinhua

Bookstore held a monopoly on book distribution until the 1970s, it has since lost 20 per cent of book sales to the 'second channel'– even according official statistics. Unofficial statistics put the figure much higher. The Xinhua Bookstore has reacted by improving customer service and management, as well as by setting up big modern book malls in main cities.

The book-publishing sector faces more far-reaching changes following China's entry to the World Trade Organization (WTO) in December 2001. While foreign book companies were previously barred from doing business in China except in the framework of cooperation projects with indigenous partners, they are now admitted, albeit to a controlled degree. Some prestigious publishing houses and book traders have merged in an effort to counter foreign competition.

See also: bestsellers; shuhao; state control of media; State Press and Publication Administration (State Copyright Bureau)

Further reading

Baensch, Robert E. (2003). *The Publishing Industry in China.* New Brunswick: Transaction Publishers.

Feldman, Gayle (1986). 'The Organization of Publishing in China'. *China Quarterly* 102: 519–29.

Lynch, Daniel (1999). *After the Propaganda State.* Stanford: Stanford University Press.

Neder, Christina (1999). *Lesen in der VR China* [Reading in the People's Republic of China]. Hamburg: Institut für Asienkunde.

Nielsen, Inge (2000). 'Modern Chinese Literature Sells Out'. *Tamkang Review* 30.3 (Spring): 89–110.

CHRISTINA NEDER

bosom friends

When it comes to personal relationships, the Chinese never lack for terminology. *Tongchuang* refers to friends made at school; *wangnianjiao*, to friends of different generations; and *monizhijiao*, to bosom friends, or literally 'friends of no betrayal'. The best-known example is the three legendary warriors Liu Bei, Guan Yu and Zhang Fei, who vowed to die for each other, although from different families. Such friendship still exists, although rapid economic and social changes are gradually eroding its original innocence.

Traditionally, *monizhijiao* referred to friends of the same sex. With a more open society, even China's official media has become tolerant of the debate on whether different sexes can have bosom friends. The consensus sees a difference between *hongyanzhiji* and **xiaomi**, the former being a close female friend void of sexual contact outside a man's marital relationship. A convenient example is found in a female friend of Bora Milutinovic, former coach of China's soccer team. Apparently feeling uncomfortable using the term for the friendship between the two greatest contemporary Chinese man and woman of letters, Ba Jin and Bing Xin, people would rather call it *monizhijiao*.

Lanyanzhiji (a male bosom friend) emerged corresponding to *hongyanzhiji*. Some independent white-collar women argue that if men can have *hongyanzhiji*, they see no reason why they cannot have men as their *lanyanzhiji* so that they can enjoy a *qingshanzhijiao* (friendship with someone in a suit). However, as some ask in a world of patriarchy, how many men would be cool enough to be a *lanyanzhiji*?

YUAN HAIWANG

Bouyei (Buyi), culture of

The Buyi or Bouyei (in their own language) have a population of nearly 3 million. They live mainly in two Bouyei-Miao autonomous prefectures in Guizhou province: Qiannan and Qianxinan, where several famous sightseeing spots are situated: the awe-inspiring Huangguoshu Waterfall, Asia's largest; the Huaxi Scenic Resort; and the labyrinthine limestone cave called Longgong (Dragon Palace). The region has become an important hydro-electric development zone planned by the central government. Some Bouyei people are scattered over Yunnan, Sichuan and Guangxi. The Bouyei language had no script until the Roman alphabet was introduced in the 1950s. The Bouyei live in houses on stilts or stone houses by the river or on mountain slopes. They are farmers, but are also migrant workers during the off-season. The Bouyei hand-woven and batik are well known, one of the best-selling handicrafts in the region. Typical costumes are blue and black and they wear turbans with a blue and white chequered pattern. The Bouyei 'ground drama' is similar to the mask play in which performers use masks carved of poplar-wood and they perform on the ground. The *suona*, a Han instrument, is also popular among the Bouyei, and produces the main music in the band playing in simple but energetic rhythms. The Bouyei traditional religion is a mixture of animism and Daoism. They participate in the Han festivals but also have their own, such as the Ox King's Day to honour oxen for their hard work in the past year, and song festivals which are gatherings for socializing and romantic purposes.

HELEN XIAOYAN WU

bridges

China has a long history of building bridges. The country is famous for its expertise in stone arch construction. Significant breakthroughs in technological processes have permitted China to leap into the world's advanced ranks in bridge-building capacity under varied geological conditions. Bridges of various types have been built to stride across the country's main rivers. The Wuhan Bridge, completed in 1957, was the first major highway–railway bridge with a main structure consisting of continuous steel trusses. The first pre-stressed concrete rigid-frame bridge dates back to 1964 when the Yanhe River Bridge in Jiangsu province opened to traffic. The Yunyang Bridge in Sichuan province, completed in 1975, is the earliest cable-stayed bridge in China. Suspension bridges and pre-stressed concrete arch bridges have been built in remote mountainous areas and over the deep valleys of Yunnan, Guizhou and Sichuan provinces. By 2000, China had 240,630 highway bridges totalling 8,655,112 metres in length. Crossing river junctions have improved traffic networks between cities along the Yangzi and the Yellow Rivers. Bridges have been instrumental in facilitating the construction of dam power plants,

the development of farm production, and the exploitation of mineral resources. Bridges have also created a favourable environment for the development of the tourist industry. In the 1990s China built a record number of city river bridges, two-deck rail and highway bridges, interchanges, fly-overs and overpasses. The grade-separation bridges in cities with different transport capacities are transforming China's urban landscape.

CLAUDE COMTOIS

Buddhism in Inner Mongolia

Since 1978, as a minority, the Inner Mongols have enjoyed a more favourable religious policy than the **Han** (see **state policies on minority cultures**). In the 1980s, the state financed the first large restoration of Buddhist temples to promote tourism and conceal the destruction of Mongolian culture. But in the 1990s, fearing Tibetan Buddhism's potential as an expression of nationalism, it limited authorizations for re-opening monasteries, and promoted non-Buddhist 'ethnic markers', such as the symbol of Gengis Khan. The current Buddhist revival is threatened by the generation gap within the clergy, the superficial training of young monks, the 'mummification' of the monasteries, and the impoverishment of rural Mongols.

Buddhism is tolerated within the restricted framework of an 'orthodoxy' defined by the state, and controlled by local branches of the 'patriotic' Buddhist association. There are more than 5,000 registered monks (1984 census), 3,854 of whom are old monks who took their vows again, but often live at home. Since 1987, 120 young monks have been educated in the official Buddhist school (located near Hohhot), which organizes a three-year training including lectures on socialism, basic Buddhism and management. Many more novices receive a minimum education from old monks, or are ordained outside Inner Mongolia, in the monasteries of Wutaishan, Beijing and in Kumbum (Qinghai). However, Mongol monks cannot go to the Buddhist Institute of Lhasa, which delivers the highest academic degree (*geshe*). A quota of monks is fixed per monastery. In theory one has to be eighteen years old to enter the monkhood, but there is a tolerance for younger novices (twelve to thirteen years old). In the poorest areas, their status is enviable: in 1999, novices received a government pay of 300 yuan per month, and ordained monks received 900 yuan per month.

The institution of reincarnated monks is disappearing. About fifty 'patriotic' reincarnations played an important role in the modern revival, but when they die, the state does not 'authorize their rebirth', except for a few who are trained in Beijing's Yellow Temple. The most important religious personality of Inner Mongolia is the Eleventh *Siregetü qutu-tu*, the head of the Buddhist association of Hohhot. The recent reincarnation abroad of the Sixth *lCang-skya qutu-tu*, recognized by the Dalai Lama, does not pose a serious problem to the Chinese state because of the past unpopularity of this figure in Inner Mongolia.

During the 1980s, monks and worshippers took private initiatives, organized fundraising and worked together to re-open or rebuild monasteries. More than a hundred monasteries, plus unofficial ones, are active (with generally fewer than ten monks, and a maximum of forty): there are, on average, two monasteries per banner, compared with twenty per banner in the nineteenth century. The official monasteries, even when reconstructed above ruins, are protected as 'cultural heritage' (*wenwu*) and sometimes turned into museums with an entrance fee. In the few tourist areas (Hohhot, Wudang zhao, Xilinhot), monks seem to be part of the ethnic folklore on display in mummified monasteries. The new urban Mongol identity, facing sinicization, does not seem to include Buddhism any more.

By contrast with institutional Buddhism, manifestations of a popular Buddhism which survived underground in the countryside are difficult to measure but seem more genuine. The Mongols used to gather during festivals in rural temples and regularly perform Buddhist and non-Buddhist practices (prostration, circumambulation, donations, pilgrimage to Wutaishan, *ovoo* worship). In the domestic sphere, Buddhist icons and photographs of the Panchen Lama are seen on family altars. The clergy remains exclusively male, but some older women take vows and shave their heads, though they continue to live in their family. Han devotees also participate in festivals, because they have very few temples of their own.

See also: autonomous regions, prefectures, counties and banners; Buddhist monasteries (Tibetan); ethnicity, concepts of; Mongols, culture of

Further reading

Hurelbaatar, A. (1996). 'Grass-Roots Buddhist Practices in Inner Mongolia'. MPhil thesis, Department of Social Anthropology, University of Cambridge.

Mackerras, Colin (1994). 'Religion, Politics and the Economy in Inner Mongolia and Ningxia'. In H. Kaplan and Donald W. Whisenhunt (eds), *Opuscula Altaica: Essays Presented in Honour of Henry Schwarz*. Bellingham: Centre for East Asian Studies, Western Washington University.

Sneath, David (2000). *Changing Inner Mongolia. Pastoral Mongolian Society and the Chinese State*. Oxford: Oxford University Press.

ISABELLE CHARLEUX

Buddhist calendar

The Buddhist calendar was established in classical times and set to the traditional Chinese lunar calendar. The Buddhist calendar is used throughout the Chinese Buddhist cultural sphere as well as in other countries like Japan. Events noted on the Buddhist calendar can be divided into two major groups: shared and exclusive holidays.

The shared holidays begin with the **New Year Festival** held in the first month on the first day (1/1) of the Chinese lunar calendar (see **calendars and almanacs**). This is celebrated by Buddhists as the Bodhisattva Maitreya's birthday. This is followed by the Dipamkara Buddha's birthday on the sixth day (1/6), Yama's on 1/8, and Indra's on 1/9, which is the last day of the Chinese New Year. However, the **Lantern Festival** on 1/15 is also widely celebrated at Buddhist temples.

Shakyamuni's Great Renunciation is celebrated on 2/8, while 2/15 is considered his day of extinction/nirvana and is also considered the birthday of the Chinese deity Guan Di. The Bodhisattva Avalokiteshvara's birthday is on 2/19 (see **Guanyin**), the Bodhisattva Samantabhadra's birthday on 2/21, and the Bodhisattva Chundi's birthday on 3/16. The next holiday is on 4/4, which is the Bodhisattva Manjusri's birthday. This is followed by Shakyamuni Buddha's birthday on 4/8, Bodhisattva Bhaisajaraja's birthday on 4/28, and Bodhisattva Sangharama's birthday on 5/13.

The Bodhisattva Weito's birthday is on 6/3, the Dragon King's day on 6/13, the Bodhisattva Avalokiteshvara's realization day on 6/19, and the Bodhisattva Mahasthamaprapta's birthday on 7/13. These are all single-day events. The celebration of Ullambana takes place on 7/15, but is usually accompanied by many activities for a couple of weeks in and around this date (see **Gongde**). On 7/24 the founder of the Madhyamaka school Nagarjuna's birthday is celebrated. On 7/30 the Bodhisattva Ksitigarbha-raja's birthday is celebrated.

The remote Buddha Dipamkara's birthday is held on 8/22. On 9/19 the Bodhisattva Avalokiteshvara's ordination is celebrated. On 9/30 is the Medicine Buddha Bhaisajaguru's birthday. The tenth month has no holiday and 11/17 is considered Buddha Amita's birthday. The last month of the year has two celebrations: on 12/8 is the day of Buddha Shakyamuni's 'awakening', and 12/29 is the Bodhisattva Avatamsaka's birthday. This concludes the shared holidays.

However, there are also exclusive holidays for the Patriarch Huineng's ordination on 1/15, Bodhidharma's birthday on 10/8, and the Patriarch Pu'an's birthday on 7/21. These are all important to the Chan tradition. The Tiantai master Zhiyi's anniversary is held on 11/4, while the death of the Pure Land Master Huiyuan is remembered on 8/6. Days are also set aside for the founders of temples, monasteries, schools and sects, and there are other holidays exclusive to specific lineages that are of concern primarily to monks and nuns.

For personal cultivation, either the 1st, 8th, 14th, 15th, 18th, 23rd, 24th and the last three days of each month, or, alternatively, the 8th, 14th, 15th, 23rd and the last three days of each month are considered days of abstinence. Furthermore, 1/8, 2/7, 2/9, 2/19, 3/3, 3/6, 3/13, 4/22, 5/3, 5/17, 6/16, 6/18, 6/19, 6/23, 7/13, 8/16, 9/19, 9/23, 10/2, 11/19, 11/24 and 12/25 are considered special abstinence days in honour of the Bodhisattva Avalokiteshvara.

A. W. BARBER

Buddhist monasteries (Chinese)

The last quarter of the twentieth century saw both increases in Buddhist monastic construction and changes in construction materials when compared to earlier periods. The adaptive nature of Buddhism architecture is demonstrated in the modern Asian setting as well as in the diaspora. The last quarter of the twentieth century well demonstrates progressive and conservative aspects within Chinese Buddhist architecture.

The pleasing style of Chinese monasteries during the Tang–Song dynasties that have become familiar through classical paintings, preserved structures in China (e.g. Fogong Si) and representations of these period pieces located in Japan, were gradually replaced by architectural innovations during the Ming and thereafter. The early classic period monasteries were constructed out of natural materials like stone, wattle-and-daub and wood. Joinery was employed in a timbered frame construction. Heavy tiled roofs with large overhangs were standard. Although brick was available it was seldom employed and stone structures were also known. The complex layout was divided on a north–south axis incorporating **fengshui** ideas, and included an enclosing roofed high wall. An example of pre-Chan layout can be found in Chengdu's Wenshu Si. An example of a modern Tang Style complex is seen in the Chilin Si in Hong Kong.

In the late classic period, both building materials and style changed. The Ming dynasty saw increasing use of brick and mortar in many architectural projects. This began a slow process of replacing the timbered-framed construction in the monastic complexes. This slow replacement process was far from complete as ample evidence of timbered-framed complexes still existed in the early part of the twentieth century. These changes indicate the adaptive and progressive nature of Buddhist architecture.

Brick construction brought about stylistic changes. The elaborate wood roof bracketing and supports were no longer needed as outer brick walls allowed load bearing, and metal bracing and nails were employed. Although the new materials would allow the creation of very different structures in terms of style, wood construction features were imitated instead. Plaster was employed in imitation of the daub surfaces. These aspects demonstrate the conservative nature. One of the best examples of brick monastic complexes is the famed White Horse Monastery (Baima Si) located in Luoyang.

There was significant destruction of Buddhist sites during World War II, the establishing of the PRC and the **Culture Revolution**. However, in the last few years of the 1970s, changed government policies and the return of seized sites allowed a modern period of rebuilding. Various branches of the government even helped finance rebuilding. Buddhist architecture has changed significantly, beginning at this time, but there have only been radical departures from set standards in special situations.

Most modern monastery reconstruction in China employs bricks and mortar with the Chan ground plan. Local geographic conditions and settings may act as mitigating factors. Many of the reconstructed buildings are exact duplications of the structures that existed before the mid-century destruction. Some documented early twentieth-century timber-framed constructions have been replaced by brick construction. In construction techniques, materials and style, these complexes employ the patterns developed in the Ming dynasty. However, steel-reinforced concrete is the material of choice in the construction of foundations.

Some innovation has been brought about because of general technical improvements in China's construction industries. Almost all buildings have made adjustments to allow for electricity and lighting. All complexes now have running water and many have installed modern toilets. Kitchen complexes generally employ gas stoves instead of wood or coal burners. However, these technical innovations have not altered the stylistic considerations in most cases.

Real adaptability and innovation have taken place in the larger cities and in the diaspora. With the increasing urbanization in Taipei, Hong Kong, Singapore, etc., and land at a premium, building traditional monasteries within the city became cost-prohibitive. In such locales it is common to find a large monastery consisting of several floors preferably at the top of an otherwise unremarkable multi-storied building housing secular facilities. Typically, a very large room will act as the main shrine hall with side rooms being dedicated to various Bodhisattvas, the Founder's Hall, etc., incorporating many of the traditional features. Perhaps another floor will contain the Meditation Hall and even housing for the monks or nuns.

Architectural style and materials are the same as for modern high-rises in these countries and have to comply with building codes. These complexes can display interior traditional stylistic features or features appealing to contemporary aesthetic values – for example, using etched glass as partitioning walls or decorative lighting to create intended atmospheres.

As Chinese Buddhism became a world phenomenon, architecture reflected the diverse settings. Many Chinese Buddhist monasteries in North America are older pre-existing structures that now function as monasteries. Sometimes a larger house or an industrial structure was converted. An example of the later is the Huayen Si, located in Calgary, which was a camping supply outlet. Often older churches are converted to serve Buddhist purposes. An example of this is the Berkeley Buddhist Monastery in Berkeley, which was a Nazarene church.

An excellent example of both the progressive and the conservative aspects in Buddhist architecture can be found in Shilai Si, located in the Los Angeles area. The construction technique and materials are thoroughly modern. The complex is steel framed, employing reinforced concrete, etc., with a state-of-the-art cooling system and many energy-saving features. However, from the outside it appears as a very traditional Chinese monastery. The intricate roof bracketing and painted ceiling panels were reproduced in fibreglass sheets that were installed as decorative features applied to the underlying surface. What appears as marble work in fact is only a marble facade, and the exterior is wire-mesh-reinforced stucco. Although these same architectural features can be found in many other monasteries in and out of Asia, because of the demanding building codes in the Los Angles area the sophistication is higher at Shilai Si than at most locales.

Further reading

Birnbaum, Raoul (2003). 'Buddhist China at the Century's Turn'. In Daniel Overmyer (ed.),

Religion in China Today. Cambridge: Cambridge University Press, 122–44.

Prip-Moller, J. (1982). *Chinese Buddhist Monasteries*. Hong Kong: Hong Kong University Press.

A. W. BARBER

Buddhist monasteries (Tibetan)

The last quarter of the twentieth century has witnessed considerable expansion in architectural changes and adaptations of Tibetan monastic architecture in China. Whereas architectural adaptability was never an important factor in early periods, in the present it has become of key significance.

Traditionally, Tibetan monastic buildings are constructed of mortar and stone or sometimes sun-dried bricks, and if possible a plaster is applied. Tall buildings have walls with a narrowing upward slope. Protruding and sloping door and window jambs are also used. The combined effect makes buildings appear taller than they really are. The stone walls are load-bearing and large wooden beams support a wattle and plaster floor. Large expanses between walls have pillars with stone footings to support beams. Often the first floor does not have windows, and staircases are external to the building. Most buildings are whitewashed with the jambs in burgundy, although other colour combinations are commonly found. Most of the buildings have flat roofs. However, when possible, the shrine and other buildings will have a Chinese-style roof made of metal. These could be multi-layered and decorated. Many of these traditional-style buildings can be found in the Chinese provinces near Tibet. An excellent example is Maigui Monastery in Hongyuan county, Sichuan.

In addition, stupas are constructed. These too are traditionally made of stone or sun-dried brick with an outer plaster. The Tibetans prefer a style that has a square base with a series of steps sloping towards the top. Below the midpoint, a cylindrical structure sloping out towards a flat top is located. Above this is the stylized umbrella in a pyramid shape topped with a crescent moon and flame symbol. The location of the stupa within the complex seems to follow no set pattern. In general, stupas containing the remains of esteemed lamas are placed on an elevated spot. An excellent example is the great stupa at Mt Wutai.

The layout of monastic complexes follows the Indian pattern, although Chinese influences are noted. The shrine is in the centre, with the monks' cells and other functional buildings on both sides and the whole forming an enclosure with a gated entrance. Walls were used as in-fills between buildings and surrounding them. Because, of the organic growth in these complexes the pattern becomes broken. An example of this would be Changqing Chunke e Monastery in Litang county, Sichuan. In the later quarter of the twentieth century this pattern was still followed when possible. In these Chinese areas, the largest changes have been the increased use of oven-baked bricks and accommodating electricity, plumbing and air-conditioning.

The adoptive nature in Tibetan Buddhist architecture is well demonstrated at the famous Guanhai Si at Wutai Mountain. This is a completely Chinese-looking temple in architectural form, yet the inside is very Tibetan, with a large Yamantaka (a wrathful bodhisattva). Another example from Wutai Mountain is Pusa Dian, one of the main pilgrimage sites, a Gelugpa temple on the inside but very Chinese in outer architectural style.

Combinations of Chinese and Tibetan styles can also be found, as in Mt Wutai's Guanyin Dong. The lower section of the temple, which straddles the mountainside, is completely Chinese in style. However, as one climbs the thousands of stairs, Tibetan architectural elements are clearly noted.

Further reading

Denwood, Philip (1972). 'The Tibetan Temple – Art in its Architectural Setting'. In W. Watson (ed.), *Mahayanist Art after AD 900*. London: University of London.

A. W. BARBER

Buddhist music

Since the period of the Northern and Southern dynasties (420–589), Chinese Buddhist music has developed different regional emphases. In the north, a rich legacy of instrumental music exists at many temples or temple complexes, while in large monasteries of learning in the south, vocal liturgical music predominates.

The mainstream of northern Buddhist music is 'mouth-organ and reed pipe' music (*shengguan*). The ensemble consists of the double-reed pipe (*guanzi*), mouth-organ (*sheng*), transverse flute (*di*), framed pitched gongs (*yunluo*) and ritual percussion instruments, including the drum (*gu*), bronze bowl (*qing*), wooden fish (*muyu*), cymbals (*hazi*), hand-held gong (*dangzi*) and hand-held stick bowl (*yinqing*). Instrumental music pervades temples in the northern provinces of Hebei, Henan and Shanxi, and the northeastern provinces of Shandong and Liaoning (see **bayinhui**, **Shandong guchui**, **Shanxi badatao**).

Beijing is an important centre for this tradition (see **Beijing yinyue**). The discovery by Chinese musicologists such as Yang Yinliu in the mid 1950s of the 'Capital music' (*jingyinyue*) of Zhihuasi temple brought Buddhist instrumental music to the fore. Musical notations found in Zhihuasi date back to 1694, and its *gongche* notation system predates the standard *gongche* used today. Capital Music is further exalted by its use of the seventeen-reed mouth-organ (*sheng*) and the small nine-hole reed pipe (*guanzi*), rather than the fourteen-reed *sheng* and eight-hole *guanzi* more common today; both, however, can be traced back to the Song dynasty (960–1279). The instrumental tradition of Zhihuasi, with its refined and elegant style, has since become the representative of Capital Music. However, *shengguan* music has also been found in temples on Wutaishan in Shanxi and in the Beiwanshousi temple in Shenyang. Since the **Cultural Revolution** hiatus, renewed research has found *shengguan* music in other temples in Beijing such as the Jiuding niangniangmiao; similar traditions also survive in temples in Tianjin, Shandong, on Qianshan in Liaoning province, and at the Daxiangguosi temple in Henan.

During imperial times, 'art monks' (*yiseng*) were the main practitioners of instrumental music. They belonged to the category of monks who perform rituals for the dead in return for fees. Major political upheavals at the turn of the twentieth century, culminating in the Cultural Revolution, have greatly affected Buddhism. Monastic modernization, which eschewed instrumental music performance because of its link with rituals for the dead, along with a decrease in the number of *yiseng*, led to the decline of *shengguan* music in temples. Since the 1980s, scholars have sought out *yiseng* monks who had returned to laity; Buddhist ensembles comprising elderly monks were formed, and the young were recruited from villages to learn the tradition from this older generation. Conservatoire-trained musicians now promote this music in commercial recordings (e.g. *Qianshan Foyue*,1990). Despite these efforts, instrumental music within the Buddhist tradition today is weaker than before. However, the strong influence of Buddhist instrumental music on folk music means that shadows of the former tradition can be found in the latter. For example, the 'Eight Great Suites' (*Badatao*) folk music of Shanxi (see **Shanxi badatao**) is closely related to the instrumental ritual music of Wutaishan.

Apart from the more exalted Capital Music, a more robust style of Buddhist *shengguan* music known as 'rustic music' (*qieyinyue*) also exists in the north. In this, the large eight-hole reed pipe is used, and the music shows a stronger folk influence. In Capital Music, instrumentation consists of pairs of the four main melodic instruments (*sheng*, *guan*, *di* and *yunluo*), but the 'rustic style' may add other instruments. This style of *shengguan* ritual music is best preserved among folk musicians and by 'music associations' (*yinyuehui*), which serve in life-cycle rituals in northern villages. **Daoist music** throughout northern China is also closely related to Buddhist and folk *shengguan* music. In the east-central Zhejiang and Jiangsu provinces and in the southeastern provinces of Fujian and Guangdong, instrumental music is rarely found in large monasteries; smaller temples, however, may use instruments to accompany liturgical singing or to perform para-liturgical music in **Gongde** or other rituals for the dead.

Monastic liturgical singing is known as *fanbei*, which may be loosely translated as 'Indian singing'. The term is used exclusively to refer to melodious metrical pieces, while the chanting of sutras and other texts was once known as 'undulated reading' (*zhuandu*), but is now simply called 'recitation' (*niansong*). According to Buddhist historical sources, the first composer of *fanbei* in China was Cao Zhi, the son of Cao Cao, the ruler of the Wei Kingdom

(221–65 CE). Scholars have found that from the third to the fifth centuries, Indo-Central Asian monks and laymen were disseminating *fanbei*. From the fifth century onward, Buddhist music gradually underwent syncretic fusion, assimilating court and folk music as it evolved. Vocal liturgy became an essential component of the daily and calendrical rituals in monasteries.

Zhejiang and Jiangsu provinces have historically been the epicentres of monastic Buddhism. Several large monasteries such as Tianningsi, Tiantongsi and Longchangsi in the Baohuashan mountains were, and still are, major ordination centres and institutions of monastic training. The *fanbei* of these monasteries came to be acknowledged as the quintessence of vocal liturgical music. By the end of the nineteenth century, monasteries and temples all over China had adopted the *fanbei* repertory of this region in their 'morning and evening lessons' (*zhaomu kesong*). This national repertory is also widely disseminated among Chinese Mahayana temples overseas. The vocal style of Tianningsi is considered by Buddhist clerics and scholars to be the representative of monastic *fanbei*.

Fanbei comprises 'praises' (*zan*) and 'gathas' or 'verses' (*ji*) and is accompanied only by ritual percussion. The melodies of *zan* praises, in particular, are melismatic, with long cadences, and sung to a slow tempo strictly regulated by the percussion. *Ji* verses have shorter melodies and a smaller melodic and textual repertory than *zan*. In theory, *fanbei* singing is in unison, but as a result of oral–aural transmission, some degree of heterophonic variation may be heard in performance practice.

Today, in monasteries in the south, including Gushan Yongquansi in Fuzhou, Guanghuasi in Putian, Kaiyuansi in Quanzhou, Nanputuosi in Xiamen, Nanshansi in Zhangzhou and monasteries in Guangzhou and Chaozhou, the unified national *fanbei* repertory is more expedient than ever because monks-in-residence often come from different parts of China. Traditionally local or regional repertories of *zan* and *ji* have existed. These are often used in rituals for the dead. These may come in the form of different melodies sharing the same texts as the national repertory, or different corpora of texts and melodies typical to a region (see Yuan 1997). A repertory which developed in the Fuzhou area is widely diffused in the Minnan area, Taiwan,

Singapore, Malaysia, the Philippines and may even be found among Chinese Buddhist communities in parts of North America.

See also: Shifan (Shifan gu, Shifan luogu)

Further reading

Beijing lianhua foyuetuan (1990). *Qianshan foyue* (cassette). Taipei: Music in China Publishing.

Hu, Yao (1992). *Fojiao yü yinyue yishu*. Tianjin: Tianjin renmin chubanshe.

Jones, Stephen (1998). *Folk Music of China: Living Instrumental Traditions*, 2nd edn with CD. Oxford: Oxford University Press.

Ling, Qizhen (1957). 'Shenyang diqu fanyue de chutan'. *Minzu yinyue lunwenji* 3. Beijing: Beijing yinyue chubanshe, 69–74.

Tian, Qing (1999/2000). 'The Sinicization of Buddhist Music'. Translated by Tan Hwee-San. *Chime* 14/15: 8–30.

Ya, Xin *et al.* (1955). *Siyuan yinyue*. Chengdu: Zhongguo Yinyuejia Xiehui Chengdu Fenhui.

Yuan, Jingfang (1997). *Zhongguo fojiaojing yinyue yanjiu*. Taipei: Ciji wenhua chubanshe.

TAN HWEE-SAN

bulletin board systems

Bulletin board systems (BBSs) are one of the network services provided on the Internet. They are asynchronous online discussion forums classified by topics. Internet users in China may access at least five types of BBSs. The first type is affiliated with official media agencies. The best known of this type is the 'Strengthening the Nation Forum' (*Qiangguo luntan*) affiliated with the online edition of **People's Daily**. The second type comes as part of the services offered by commercial portal sites. For example, *sina.com*, *netease.com* and *sohu.com* all run BBS forums. The third type is run by individuals on free web space. Some BBSs in this category attract many visitors; most have a small circle of users. Fourth, users in China may access some BBS forums on overseas computer servers. Finally, the fifth type of BBSs is run by professional and educational institutions. The most popular among these are the numerous university-run BBSs.

China's first university BBS was set up in 1995 at **Qinghua University**. Others quickly followed at **Peking University**, Xi'an Jiaotong University and so forth. By November 2000, the top-ranking portal site, sohu.com, had listed seventy university-based BBSs. In almost all cases, one bulletin board system supports many different forums. For example, as of 8 December 2000, **Peking University** had 149 forums in its BBS (http://bbs.pku.edu.cn/) and Xi'an Jiaotong University (http://bbs.xjtu.edu.cn/cgi-bin/bbsall) had 129 forums. The total number of university-based BBS forums can easily be estimated in the thousands.

BBSs became popular among Chinese university students because they provide several useful functions. People may use the BBS to follow current affairs, seek and share information, discuss academic questions, socialize and make friends, and even lodge complaints. At times, the postings may engage social problems, touch on politically sensitive issues, or directly criticize the government. In several documented cases, online bulletin boards have been used for popular protest.

There is an elaborate set of rules and regulations concerning Internet uses and services in China, which apply to the university BBSs directly or indirectly. One regulation promulgated in November 2000 explicitly targets the use of BBSs. It stipulates, for example, that all BBS users are responsible for the information they release, that users cannot release information deemed harmful to national interests, and that bulletin board services should follow a licensing procedure. A complete list of Internet regulations in China is available at the official website of the China Internet Network Information Centre, http://www.cnnic.net.cn. Despite these regulations, the actual management of BBSs varies a great deal in terms of control and censorship.

Further reading

Hartford, Kathleen (2000). 'Cyberspace with Chinese Characteristics'. *Current History* (September): 255–62.

Harwit, Eric and Clark, Duncan (2001). 'Shaping the Internet in China: Evolution of Political Control over Network Infrastructure and Content'. *Asian Survey* 41.3: 377–408.

Yang, Guobin (2003). 'The Impact of the Internet on Civil Society in China: A Preliminary Assessment'. *Journal of Contemporary China* 12.36. Available at http://www.tandf.co.uk/journals/Leaflets/CJCC.PDF

YANG GUOBIN

Bus Stop

[*Chezhan*, 1981]

Spoken drama (Huaju)

Bus Stop is the first play of the Chinese writer and Nobel laureate **Gao Xingjian**. Written in 1981, the play was considered unacceptable by the **Beijing People's Art Theatre** due to its non-realistic tendencies, and shelved for two years. In July 1983, Gao Xingjian and **Lin Zhaohua**, Deputy Director of the People's Art Theatre, after a successful run of Gao's second play *Absolute Signal* (*Juedui xinhao*), worked to mount a production of *Bus Stop*. As a prelude to the performance, Lu Xun's short text *The Passerby* was performed. Staged in the Loft Space at the People's Art Theatre, *Bus Stop* had a brief run of thirteen performances. The government, under the banner of the 'Anti-Spiritual Pollution' campaign, ordered the production closed and heavily criticized the text for deviating from the government-sanctioned cultural model of 'socialist realism'.

The play was viewed as politically ambiguous with no clear heroes, no affirmation of political policy and a questionable symbolic representation of the socialist system.

Bus Stop tells the story of eight characters, each archetypes representing different elements of Chinese society: Old Man, Mother, Young Woman, Carpenter, Manager Ma, Man Wearing Glasses, Brash Young Man and Silent Man. Each character has hopes for the future, which can only be realized by moving forward into the city. However, their means of transport, a public bus, repeatedly passes by without stopping.

One character, the Silent Man, finally decides to stop waiting and walks into town. The other seven characters remain at the bus stop, passing the time by complaining about the ills of society and their own lack of accomplishment. Failing to take initiative, they wait in line for ten years. At the end of the play the characters resolve their individual differences and, following in the footsteps of the Silent Man, walk together into the city.

Gao's introductory note to the text indicates that the plot must be driven by musical rhythms. He indicates that this influence in his work is derived from the traditional Chinese opera, which utilizes strong rhythmic patterns to move a plot forward. This technique was a total rejection of the most common form of spoken drama (**Huaju**) practised in China in 1981, which, influenced by the work of Henrik Ibsen, dictated that the external action be more or less static and that characters perceive everything through internal crisis. In Gao's text we see exactly the opposite: a character is moved forward primarily by external elements.

Gao encourages the actors to play the characters as abstractions of real life – 'to be alike in spirit', not realistic in detail. Gao once again makes reference to traditional Chinese opera, where characterization, while based upon the reality of life, does not recreate that reality on stage but instead elevates it to a higher plane through exaggeration. Critics often compare the play to Beckett's *Waiting for Godot* and identify it as the first play in China to incorporate techniques from the Theatre of the Absurd. However, seeing *Bus Stop* as merely a Chinese *Waiting for Godot* limits a Western audience's ability to understand the dynamic synthesis of Western and Chinese theatrical traditions present in the play and perpetuates the practice of defining non-Western artistic work through a strictly Western 'lens'.

Bus Stop has been staged in Yugoslavia, Hong Kong, Austria, Romania, Sweden and the United States. The first English-language production was performed in 1986 at the Workshop Theatre at the University of Leeds and was translated and directed by Carla Kirkwood.

Further reading

Gao, Xingjian (1996). 'The Bus Stop'. In Yu Shiao-ling (ed.), *Chinese Drama after the Cultural Revolution, 1979–1989*. Lewiston: Edwin Mellen Press, 233–90.

—— (1998). Trans. Kimberley Besio. 'Bus Stop: A Lyrical Comedy on Life in One Act'. In Yan Haiping (ed.), *Theater and Society: An Anthology of Contemporary Chinese Drama*. Armonk, NY: M. E. Sharpe, 3–59.

CARLA KIRKWOOD

Butterfly literature

(Yuanyang hudiepai)

Literary revival

In the 1980s and 1990s, along with a nostalgic ethos for the flowering urban life and culture in the Republican era (1912–49), numerous reprints of that era's 'Mandarin Duck and Butterfly fiction' (*Yuanyang hudiepai xiaoshuo*) appeared. Among the multi-volume collections of Butterfly literature, the most impressive were those edited by literary historians Fan Boqun, Wei Shaochang, Yuan Jin and Yu Runqi. While commercially catering to general readers, these collections served scholarly use, as the selected texts were noted for their original sources.

Rooted in the sentimental romance of early twentieth century, Butterfly fiction developed in later decades into diverse genres such as social fiction, science fiction, detective story and knight-errant fiction; it was popular in Chinese urban centres as it primarily entertained city-dwellers in their needs of diversion or pleasure. After 1949 Butterfly literature was condemned by literary historians as feudalistic, decadent and poisonous, and disappeared. So its revival suggests nothing less than an ironic turn after its repression and neglect for half a century.

The appearance of innumerable reprinted works and academic re-evaluations seems more than a literary phenomenon; it signifies a revival of popular print culture, reading pleasure and generic pluralism, a nostalgia for the bygone splendour of urban life and freedom from Communist ideology. Commercially, the label appeals to the reader not only with its images of 'small cute animals' as a kind of soft literature embedded in metropolitan nostalgia; implied is also a political message: Butterfly literature is a victim of May Fourth literature or the Chinese revolution.

Further reading

Chow, Rey (1986/87). 'Rereading Mandarin Ducks and Butterflies: A Response to the "Postmodern' Condition"'. *Cultural Critique* 5 (Winter): 69–95.

Fan, Boqun (ed.) (1991). *Yuanyang hudie – 'Libailiu' pai zuopinxuan* [Mandarin Ducks and Butterflies – Selected Works of the 'Saturday' School]. Beijing: Renmin wenxue.

—— (1993). *Yuanyang hudie pai yanqing xiaoshuo jicui* [A Collection of Love Stories of the Mandarin Duck and Butterfly School]. 3 vols. Beijing: Zhongyang minzu xueyuan.

Wei, Shaochang (ed.) (1982). *Yuanyang hudiepai yanjiu ziliao* [Research Materials for Mandarin Duck and Butterfly School]. 2 vols. Shanghai: Wenyi chubanshe.

CHEN JIANHUA

C

cable television

Since the early 1990s, when cable television networks were first introduced to China, they have become one of the principle modes of television reception in China's major cities. The significance of cable television is enhanced by the fact that direct-to-home **satellite television** is banned, and all legal reception of satellite channels is through local cable television relays. However, cable television also has a key role to play in the development of broadband services in China.

Cable networks generally supply between twenty and forty channels to subscribers in large cities, including relays of local and national terrestrial channels as well as provincial satellite offerings. The first networks were launched in Guangzhou, Shanghai and Beijing in 1992. By 1996 there were already some 1,300 cable television networks nationwide.

Key to the development of China's cable television networks is their emergence from the city, town or county level under the direct control of local offices of the **State Administration for Radio Film and Television** (SARFT). Cable television networks have often proven to be lucrative sources of revenue for these local television administrators whether through subscriptions, which are modest, or through advertising.

In the early 2000s, SARFT has been keen to unify and centralize the country's cable television networks, in order to wrest control over content and revenues away from the local level in preparation for the provision of broadband, Internet and multimedia services. It also hopes to strengthen its hand in relation to its rival, the **Ministry of Information Industry**, which controls telecom operations in the country and currently dominates the small but developing broadband market. However, SARFT faces significant challenges in the task of network unification due to the enormous cost involved both in laying the necessary infrastructure and buying out local operators. The project also faces resistance from vested local interests.

KEVIN LATHAM

Cai Guoqiang

b. 1957, Quanzhou, Fujian

Installation artist

Trained as a theatrical set designer, Cai Guoqiang graduated in 1985 from the Department of Stage Design at the Shanghai Drama Institute. In late 1986, he moved to Japan where he began to attract public attention as the Chinese 'gunpowder artist', making abstract paintings by leaving traces of gunpowder on paper and canvas. In the first half of the 1990s, Cai had frequent solo shows in Japan and overseas at important venues, such as the Osaka Contemporary Art Centre (1990) and the Museum of Modern Art in Oxford (1993). In 1995, Cai moved with his family to New York City to participate in the International Studio Programme at P.S.1, the Institute for Contemporary Art. Gaining increasing international success, Cai's solo shows were organized at major institutions such as the

Queens Museum of Art, New York (1997), the Taiwan Museum of Art (1998), the Kunsthalle, Vienna (1999), and the Fondation Cartier pour l'Art Contemporain, Paris (2000). In 1999 he won the International Prize at the Venice Biennale with his work *Venice Rent-Collection Courtyard*, a literal remake of the most famous sculptural model canonized during the **Cultural Revolution**.

Using iconic Chinese references–fireworks, paper lanterns, medicinal herbs, **Taihu rocks**, junks terracotta warriors and traditional proverbs – in theatrical installations, Cai reinterprets rather than explores ancient Chinese concepts and cultural values, questioning their contemporary impact. His internationally acclaimed work has sometimes been criticized as catering to a Western taste for the exotic. For his part, he wilfully exacerbates obvious marks of national identity to demystify the necessity of cultural belonging imposed on non-Western artists in the international sphere.

Further reading

Cai, Guo-Qiang (1994). 'On Thought and Action'. In *The Potential of Asian Thought: Contemporary Art Symposium, 1994*. Tokyo: Japan Foundation ASEAN Culture Centre.

Chang, Tsong-zung (1998). 'Beyond the Middle Kingdom: An Insider's View'. In Gao Minglu (ed.), *Inside Out: New Chinese Art* (exhibition catalogue). Berkeley: University of California Press, 67–75.

Dal Lago, Francesca (2000). 'Chinese Art at the Venice Biennale: The Virtual Reality of Chinese Contemporary Art'. In John Clark (ed.), *Chinese Art at the End of the Millennium*. Hong Kong: New Media, 158–66.

Fei, Dawei and Ujica, Andrei (2000). *Cai Guo-Qiang. Fondation Cartier pour l'art contemporain*. London: Thames and Hudson.

Friis-Hansen, Dana Octavio Zaya and Serizawa, Takashi (2002). *Cai Guo-Qiang*. New York: Phaidon Press.

Hou, Hanru (1994). 'Entropy; Chinese Artists, Western Art Institutions: A New Internationalism'. In Jean Fisher (ed.), *Global Visions: Towards a New Internationalism in the Visual Arts*. London: Kala Press, 79–88.

Hou, Hanru and Gao, Minglu (1998). 'Strategies of Survival in the Third Space: A Conversation on the Situation of Overseas Chinese Artists in the 1990s'. In Gao Minglu (ed.), *Inside Out: New Chinese Art*. Berkeley: University of California Press, 183–9.

Musée d'Art Contemporain de Lyon (2002). *Cai Guo-Qiang: Une Histoire arbitraire*. Milan: 5 Continents Editions.

Venice Biennale (1997). Available at http://www.labiennale.it/visual_ar...vii/mostre_en/Guo_Qiang/caiguo.htm

QIAN ZHIJIAN

Cai Jin

b. 1965, Anhui

Oil painter

Cai Jin graduated from the Art Department of Anhui Normal University (1986) and, from a specialization course in the Oil Painting Department of the **Central Academy of Fine Arts** in Beijing (1991). She was then hired as a professor in the Education Department of the Tianjin Art Academy, a position she still holds, after having spent several years in New York City.

Since the early 1990s, Cai Jin has been obsessively painting a single theme, entitled *(Beauty) Banana Series (Meirenjiao)*. She traces her inspiration to the dried and contorted shapes of banana leaves, common to her native southern Anhui, which sag and curl around the trunks during winter. The supposedly vegetal matter referred to in the title is processed into a flesh-like substance, rotten and yet vital, which is then painted on soft surfaces such as mattresses, shoes, bicycle seats and cushions, suggesting the image of a wound that cannot heal. Alternatively, her disturbing compositions also suggest an experience of descending into the deep realms of the soul, offering graphic descriptions of unsuspected inner turbulence.

Cai Jin has often associated her work with painstaking and obsessive practices, similar to traditional feminine chores such as sewing or knitting, where the creative process, not the final product, is the goal. She has taken part in numerous exhibitions in China and overseas, including 'Century-Woman' in Beijing (Spring, 1998) and 'Die Hälfte des Himmels' [Half of the Sky] at the Frauenmusuem in Bonn, Germany (1998). She lives in Beijing and New York.

Further reading

Dal Lago, Francesca (1999). 'Embroidering with Paint'. In *Off the Canvas* (exhibition catalogue). Beijing: The Courtyard Gallery. [Reprinted in Wu Hong (ed.) (2001). *Chinese Art at the Crossroads: Between Past and Future.* Hong Kong: New Art Media.]

Wu, Hung (1999). 'Rotten Red'. In *idem, Transience: Chinese Experimental Art at the End of the 20th Century.* Chicago: University of Chicago/David and Alfred Smart Museum, 83–7.

FRANCESCA DAL LAGO

calendars and almanacs

The Chinese lunar-solar calendar (*liri* or *lishu, nongli* or *huangli*) is one of the few calendars in the world with a history dating back more than 2,000 years. It was first inscribed on bamboo slips and wooden strips in the third century AD, and from the fifth century onwards it was written on paper. During the ninth and tenth centuries, it acquired the form and content that we know today, as perfectly illustrated by the calendars found among documents at Dunhuang.

However, this continuity is not without variations or modifications. Two radical changes took place, one at the founding of the Republic in 1912 and the other after the establishment of the People's Republic of China in 1949. The Republican government officially adopted the Western calendar, with its system of weeks, running parallel to the traditional Chinese calendar. Mao Zedong's government, with its policy of eradicating all forms of 'superstitions', removed the almanac aspect of the calendar, i.e. the day-by-day indication of auspicious or inauspicious activities.

This aim of placing the calendar on a 'scientific' basis did not go unchallenged. The producer of a 1953 calendar, published with the permission of the local authorities in Hunan, pleading that the calendars contained many popular traditions, mostly retained for daily activities, those elements concerned with agricultural work. The calendar is peppered with political slogans: 'Let us eagerly apply ourselves to production, increasing our strength for the struggle against the Americans and for supporting the Koreans' (during the Korean War); 'Let us plant more valuable crops like cotton, hemp tea . . .' or 'Let us increase production and economize in order to reinforce the defence of our country' (to prove the revolutionary spirit of the author).

With the economic liberalization of the 1980s, traditional calendars and modernized calendars began to appear simultaneously. In 2002, two types of daily almanacs are now available in Beijing bookshops, both using the Western calendar as a base, but indicating the concordance with the Chinese calendar and its twenty-four solar periods (*ershisi jieqi*). The traditional type of daily almanac, imported from Taiwan or Hong Kong, following a long line of traditional almanacs, indicates auspicious days for various activities (marriage, building, travel, business transactions, social events), auspicious and inauspicious times of day (*jishi*), and the location of auspicious spirits (*jishen*), and so forth. The modern calendar, printed in Hubei province, is more 'politically correct'. Although it retains a few traditional festivals (e.g. Chinese **New Year Festival**, **Lantern Festival**, **Dragon-Boat Festival**, **Mid-Autumn Festival**), it also takes care to include Western holidays (e.g. Christmas, New Year's Day, Valentine's Day), national holidays (e.g. Youth Day on 4 May; Founding of the People's Liberation Army on 1 August; Teachers' Day on 10 September; National Holiday on 1 October), and international days (e.g. Workers' Day on 1 May; Children's Day on 1 June). The picture would not be complete without a mention of the wholesale introduction of 'memorial days' (*nianri*), recalling both the most important events of the People's Republic (the demonstrations on 11 October 1911; the foundation of the CCP on 1 July 1921; the victory over the Japanese on 3 September 1945) and famous Communist personalities (birth and death days of Marx, Lenin, Sun Yatsen, Lu Xun, Stalin, Liu Shaoqi, Zhu De, Zhou Enlai and Mao

Zedong). This new calendar is also embellished with recipes and advice on diet, hygiene and fashion.

See also: Buddhist calendar; divination and fortune-telling; holidays (Western)

Further reading

Morgan, Carole (1980). *Le Tableau du boeuf du Printemps. Etude d'une page de l'almanach chinois.* Paris: Collège de France, Institut des Hautes Études Chinoises.

Smith, Richard J. (1992). *Chinese Almanacs.* Hong Kong: Oxford University Press.

ALAIN ARRAULT

Campaign against Bourgeois Liberalization

(Fandui zichangjie ziyouhua, 1987)

Ideological movement

The Campaign against Bourgeois Liberalization was a movement to oppose tendencies related to Western freedoms and in defence of the CCP's rule. Authorities believed that 'bourgeois liberalization' stood in opposition to the 'four cardinal principles' enunciated by Deng Xiaoping (1904–97) on 30 March 1979, the main one of which was to uphold the leadership of the CCP. In September 1986, a CCP Plenum defined 'bourgeois liberalization' as 'negating the socialist system in favour of capitalism'.

In November, student demonstrations for greater freedoms began in Anhui, where the noted academic Fang Lizhi had called for democracy, and spread to Shanghai and Beijing. These were suppressed by the CCP authorities as a threat to their rule. Early in January 1987, China's main newspaper, **People's Daily**, printed several articles opposing 'bourgeois liberalization' and defending the 'four cardinal principles'. It also attacked the idea of 'complete Westernization', a typical product of 'bourgeois liberalization',

arguing that this meant abandoning socialism in favour of capitalism.

Deng Xiaoping held CCP General Secretary Hu Yaobang (1917–89) chiefly responsible for the student demonstrations, accusing him of espousing 'bourgeois liberalization'. On 16 January 1987, Hu resigned, after having made a self-criticism of his mistakes. His fall made him a hero to liberal causes thereafter. At about the same time, several prominent intellectuals, journalists and writers, including Fang Lizhi, were expelled from the CCP for their 'bourgeois liberalization'. Though quite short, the campaign affected China's later history. Hu Yaobang's death in mid-April 1989 was the spark that set off the fire of new student demonstrations, which culminated in their violent suppression early in June.

COLIN MACKERRAS

Can Xue

(née Deng Xiaohua)

b. 1953, Changsha, Hunan

Writer

Can Xue is one of the first avant-garde writers to have emerged in the 1980s, and is the only female author attributed to this group. She began writing in 1981 and is best known for her two novellas, *Old Floating Cloud (Canglao di fuyun)* and *Yellow Mud Street (Huangni jie)*, as well as many short stories. Her writing emphasizes the hallucinations of largely female protagonists who have turned the violence of a socially ordered world into mental and fictitious images. Her work constructs and deconstructs language, evoking a surreal and strangely disordered world that has no grounding in real-life experience or history. Her characters thus speak in abstract dialogue, provide nonsensical or irrelevant answers, and ultimately fail to communicate. Her work has been compared to that of Franz Kafka because many of her protagonists suffer from paranoia. She has written commentaries on the work of Franz Kafka and Jorge Luis Borges. She is also an outspoken critic of the male-dominated literary world that has narrowly defined what the literary content of a woman's text can be. Can Xue is an honorary member of the International Writing Programme at the University of Iowa.

See also: avant-garde/experimental literature

Further reading

Can, Xue (1989). *Dialogues in Paradise*. Trans. R. Janssen and J. Zhang. Evanston: Northwestern University Press.

—— (1991). *Old Floating Cloud: Two Novellas*. Trans. R. Janssen and J. Zhang. Evanston: Northwestern University Press.

—— (1997). *The Embroidered Shoes*. Trans. R. Janssen and J. Zhang. New York: Henry Holt.

—— (1998). 'Hut on a Mountain'. Trans. J. Zhang and R. Janssen. In Wang Jing (ed.), *China's Avant-Garde Fiction*. Durham: Duke University Press.

Lu, Tonglin (1993). 'Can Xue: What is So Paranoid in Her Writing?' In *idem*, *Gender and Sexuality in Twentieth Century Chinese Literature and Society*. Albany: SUNY Press.

Posborg, Susanne (1993). 'Can Xue: Tracing Madness'. In Wendy Larson and Anne Wedell-Wedellsborg (eds), *Inside Out: Modernism and Postmodernism in Chinese Literary Culture*. Aarhus, Denmark: Aarhus University Press.

Solomon, Jon (1988). 'Taking Tiger Mountain: Can Xue's Resistance and Cultural Critique'. *Modern Chinese Literature* 4: 235–62.

Wedell-Wedellsborg, Anne (1994). 'Ambiguous Subjectivity: Reading Can Xue'. *Modern Chinese Literature* 8: 7–20.

MEGAN M. FERRY

Cankao xiaoxi (Reference News) and neibu [internal] publications

Reference News is a national daily newspaper published by the **Xinhua News Agency**. It contains translations of news articles and commentaries from foreign news agencies and newspapers. The original intention of this publication was to provide foreign news to a select political elite.

The first editions appeared under different titles in Ruijin (Jiangxi) in 1931 and were renamed *Reference News* (*Cankao xiaoxi*) in 1942. Production and distribution were guided by various Party directives (1957, 1958, 1971 and 1985). Although it began as an 'internally distributed' publication (*neibu faxing*), since 1985 its distribution has been widened under the rubric 'restricted to inland distribution' (*xian guonei faxing*) and it can be subscribed to and purchased in bookshops.

Neibu materials are marked with a stamp and contain the word *neibu* or phrases such as 'reference for leading cadres' (*gong lingdao ganbu cankao*). Such classifications imply restriction to an authorized readership in order to prevent uncontrolled dissemination of information and public discussion. *Neibu* materials contain discussions of major domestic policy and social issues. As they are subjected to a simplified censorship procedure, they allow for the speedy circulation of new information. Many foreign books translated into Chinese are *neibu*. The full scope of internal materials touches upon a broad range of areas like technology, history, politics, culture and sciences, as is revealed by the *National Bibliography of Internally Distributed Works 1949–1986*, a *neibu* publication itself.

Further reading

Li, Paoguang and Zhao, Huachun (eds) (1988). *Quanguo neibu faxing tushu zongmu 1949–1986*. Beijing: Zhonghua shuju.

NATASCHA VITTINGHOFF

Cantonese music

(Guangdong yinyue)

The term 'Cantonese music' (*Guangdong yinyue*) refers to the instrumental version of a genre called *xiaoqu* or 'short songs', which began in the Pearl River Delta as instrumental interludes during performances of Cantonese opera (see **Yueju (Guangdong, Guanxi opera)**) and narrative singing (**quyi**), and gradually merged with music from other regions in the early twentieth century.

Cantonese music is usually performed by small **Silk and Bamboo** (*sizhu*) ensembles of string and wind instruments, dominated by the Cantonese two-stringed fiddle (*yuehu* or *gaohu*). The music is fluid, natural and lively, often with flowery ornamentation and a wide ambitus or register between notes. The repertory, consisting of some five hundred tunes, keeps being enriched by musicians and composers who arrange existing tunes or compose new pieces.

Most notable is Cantonese music's facility of adaptation to modern urban life. In its heyday in the 1920s and 1930s, it prospered in Hong Kong and in treaty ports such as Canton, Shanghai and Tianjin, and also among overseas Chinese communities, where it is still played today. Played as incidental music for operas or silent movies, or as music in dance halls, it has had broad commercial success, relayed by modern media and transmitted by amateurs practising in specialized societies. Cantonese music's ability to assimilate Western and jazz instruments (including the saxophone and jazz rhythm section) and popular tunes, and to experiment, explains its continuing popularity. While some pieces composed in the 1930s and 1940s have been criticized by the current regime for their decadence, Cantonese music is largely supported by the authorities. Its orchestration has become a model for professional folk music in contemporary China.

ISABELLE DUCHESNE

Cao Cao and Yang Xiu

[Cao Cao yü Yang Xiu, 1988]

Xiqu (sung-drama/opera)

This 'newly written historical play' (*xinbian lishiju*) may be the most celebrated **Jingju** (Peking opera) created since the **Cultural Revolution**. Written by Chen Yaxian, it was revised and mounted in 1988 at the Shanghai Jingju Company (Shanghai jingjuyuan) by a team of artists led by director **Ma Ke** and the painted-face actor **Shang Changrong**. It entered the permanent repertory of the company and has been further revised several times, most extensively in 1995.

This play was created specifically for urban intellectual audiences, who fill theatres whenever and wherever it is performed. Both politically and philosophically daring, it is based on incidents in the historical novel *The Romance of the Three Kingdoms* (*Sanguozhi tongsu yanyi*). It concerns the relationship between the emperor Cao Cao and his brilliant minister Yang Xiu which, in the play, clearly parallels that of Mao Zedong and Peng Dehuai on the eve of the Cultural Revolution, as well as that of Deng Xiaoping and Zhao Ziyang just prior to 4 June 1989. The play concludes with a genuine and very moving heart-to-heart talk between Cao and Yang just before Cao has Yang beheaded.

The production is staged with strikingly imagistic scenery and original, historically based costumes. Its music incorporates contemporary material from outside the Jingju form and innovative instrumentation into eloquently applied Jingju traditions. *Cao Cao and Yang Xiu* won most major national awards given between 1988 and 1996, including the grand prize at the 1995 National Festival of Jingju Art, constituting official recognition as the finest Jingju created since the Cultural Revolution.

See also: Xiqu; Xiqu musical structure

ELIZABETH WICHMANN-WALCZAK

cars and taxis

Despite the newfound prominence of the private sedan in post-socialist China, the history of the motorized vehicle in China has been one marked by scorn, rejection and opprobrium. If the slick, latest-model cars of the 1990s and the new millennium are a mobile advertisement for the branding of international capital, throughout Chinese modern history the car has equally been a moving target for popular discontent, protest and defacement.

Although the Empress Dowager Cixi was offered and rejected the use of a German Benz to motor out to her beloved Summer Palace, early suspicions of the motor vehicle were far from being restricted to issues of courtly protocol. In June 1907, when the first Beijing–Paris car marathon was held, the Chinese press speculated that what lay behind such a seemingly innocuous sporting event was a Western plot to survey the geography of inland China so as both to gauge popular sentiment and to facilitate the imperial powers building communications and trade routes into the nation's heartland.

Such suspicions and concerns (many of which were well founded) continued throughout the century. The sense of aggrieved nationalism that flourished at the time of the economic opening-up of the 1980s (and that fed into the incipient patriotism of the 1990s and beyond) found particular expression in the highly popular tele-documentary **River Elegy**, made in 1988. One of the authors of that programme, Su Xiaokang, later a prominent dissident-in-exile, gave voice to the widespread disquiet in the following way:

> Over the past century we have continually been losers. First we lost to England, then to the eight powers during the Boxer Rebellion, then to the Japanese. Having finally got rid of the Japanese, New China enjoyed a short period of pride and achievement. Who was to guess that when we woke up from the thirty-odd years of internal turmoil we had created, we found ourselves in the company of nations like Tanzania and Zambia. Even South Korea and Singapore were ahead of us. And as for the Japanese, they were the ones laughing now that they were back with their Toshibas, Hitachis, Toyotas, Crowns, Yamahas and Cassios.

This sense of frustration, reflecting as it did a consumerist imperative that was both fuelled and enraged by the lure of foreign goods, had only a few years earlier sparked an outbreak of violence aimed against the motor vehicle. On 19 May 1985, a soccer riot broke out in Beijing after the local team was trounced by visitors from Hong Kong. Gangs of angry young men roamed the streets outside the stadium after the game, detaining every passing taxi to shout and jeer at the drivers. One particularly vociferous rioter screamed: 'Fuck it, while I spend my hard-earned money to go to some lousy game, these guys are sitting in their cars pulling in a coupla hundred bucks a night. Get the bastards!' The mob soon set to spitting on windows, kicking doors and beating bonnets.

Foreign journalists who observed the mayhem drew parallels between the brutish anti-foreignism and the Boxer rebels of 1900 whose xenophobia led to the occupation of Beijing by the colonial powers. But Liu Xinwu, a novelist who wrote a 'reportage' account of the 1985 riot, 'Zooming In on May 19', remarked that the Boxers had sworn an oath starting with the words 'Heavenly spirits, earthly wraiths/We beg all masters to answer our call', and ending with a plea for the spirits of traditional China 'to lead 100,000 heavenly troops' to support their anti-foreign cause. The rioters of 1985, however, were far from being such a fanatical group of protesters. 'If there were to have been a chant', Liu observed, 'it would probably go like this':

> Heavenly spirits, earthly wraiths
> We all want to have a good time,
> Let's evoke Xi Xiulan, Zhang Mingmin,
> Wang Mingquan, Xu Xiaoming;
> Let's watch [the TV series] *Huo Yuanjia*
> and *Love Ties Together the Rivers and Mountains*
> We want jeans,
> We want discos and Washi Cosmetics,
> We want Sharp, Toshiba and Hitachi electrical appliances,
> We want Suzuki, Yamaha, plus Seiko and Citizen.

They are the most ardent consumers of popular Hong Kong culture and Japanese products. The real reason they targeted foreigners and Hong Kong people during the incident was that they dislike the way these people enjoy special privileges in Beijing and flaunt their superiority. What the mob was expressing was a long-repressed resentment and jealousy. The rioters eventually managed to overturn a vehicle or two and numerous arrests and police action finally quelled the disturbance.

It was little surprise that taxis attracted such ire, for they provided the first privileged private space in reformist China, for both drivers and passengers alike. Long before the self-driving car owner appeared in the 1990s, taxi drivers were a class apart: they were mobile, free from the fetters of their original work units, and their wages were based on kilometres travelled, rather than according to the old rigid socialist pay scale.

Initially, taxi drivers were recruited from among former government chauffeurs or lorry drivers, but as the urban economic reforms took hold during the 1980s, many men and women quit their state jobs to drive taxis, attracted by the promise of better pay and relative freedom. Soon the taxi driver, a kind of entrepreneur with state backing, became one of the most liminal figures in the urban landscape. Not only did they transport more traditional fares around the city, they also ferried prostitutes (members of another newly visible class of entrepreneur) from hotel to hotel, and provided the covert environment for illicit contacts of all descriptions.

Taxi drivers also constituted one of the most garrulous and outspoken groups in the society: they could declaim on issues of the moment with little thought of being caught out or penalized as they coursed their way around the city streets, spreading gossip and generating innuendo as they went. For foreign journalists working in the restrictive media environment of Deng Xiaoping's China, the taxi driver was a boon companion, and he or she provided many of the *vox populi* quotes that peppered international news reports issuing from Beijing.

The interior of those early taxis was particular. Prior to the advent of car-washing stations in the early 1990s (including 'digital and computerized' car cleaning), a feather-duster for the daily removal of urban grime was a feature of the rear window of virtually every taxi (now they are generally relegated to the rear boot), and the drivers would don grubby white gloves to carry out the operation. Day-Glo-coloured and sickly-sweet air-freshener would feature on the front dash, and a large jar (*cha gangzi* – usually an old Nescafé instant-coffee jar) of thickly-brewed Chinese tea would ride shotgun near the handbrake by the driver. The passenger windows were often cloaked with green or brown gauze shades, the back seat covered in tan cloth with fussy antimacassars, and woven mat seat coverings were (and still are) often features on the seats – the taxi a miniaturized version of the official audience hall or meeting room, always open for a session the minute a new fare gets in. These appointments presaged the busy interiors of the future: deodorizers, tinted windows, rear-view mirror adornments, frilly tissue boxes and head-wagging dogs.

Since 1989, however, the taxi has also been dragooned into more direct service for the state. Starting with the preparations for the 1991 Asian Games in Beijing, taxi drivers have regularly been used as hospitality representatives and propagandists for official campaigns aimed at international visitors and foreign residents. For years, taxi companies have been required to festoon their vehicles with public service announcements (or, to use the language of the past, 'propaganda slogans'). In the more quotidian realm, the taxi has also given birth its own particular vocabulary. The Cantonese sinicization of the word 'taxi', *diksee*, has been in common use in the former colony of Hong Kong for many decades. When the cultural influence of south China began to expand northward in the 1980s, the standard Chinese pronunciation of the term, *dishi*, as opposed to the official term for taxi, *chuzuche* (vehicle available for rent), became fashionable. In Beijing slang, an argot renowned for abbreviations and humorous word play, this was simply reduced to *di*. Thus, 'to hail a taxi' or 'take a cab' became *dadi* (travel by taxi). Soon *di* was being used to describe a range of locomotive possibilities unrelated to its Hong Kong Cantonese origins: *tui'rdi* (leg taxi) meant to walk; *rendi* (human taxi) was a new word for pedicab. *Juedi* (crippled taxi) indicated a motorized wheelchair; while *miandi* or 'bread taxi' indicated a mini-bus taxi (the shape of the vehicle being likened to a loaf of bread or *mianbao*). *Qiongdi* (pauper's taxi) was another name for Xiali-make vehicles, the cheapest taxi in Beijing from the late 1990s; and, last but not least, there is the *boyindi* (Boeing taxi) for 'plane'

From 1991 until the mid 1990s, a new taxi and car craze hit China when laminated portraits of Mao Zedong started appearing hanging in the windscreens or set up on the dashboards of vehicles throughout the country. The fad reportedly originated in Guangdong province after a person or people miraculously avoided injury in a traffic accident because, it was said, their vehicle had been protected by a portrait of Mao placed on the dash. Like the door gods and lucky talismans that were traditionally used to adorn the home to ward off malign influences, the Mao portrait was suddenly recognized as a way to ensure safety and good fortune in the fast-paced urban environment of highway and car.

The laminated Mao mobiles were simply called *guawu* (hangings). During the height of the fad, they were sold all over the country and by a range of outlets: from street-side stalls and temple stores to the Mao Mausoleum in the heart of **Tiananmen Square** itself. In design they varied widely. The more austere simply featured a picture of Mao, the most popular representations being of 'the young Mao': that is, the retouched picture of Mao in a Red Army uniform taken by Edgar Snow in the 1930s, or the official portrait of the aged Mao, although Mao in a PLA uniform dating from the early Cultural Revolution was also common. More elaborate hangings had the Mao picture framed in mock-Chinese temples, or with gold ingots hanging from the picture, with more traditional benedictions, like 'May the winds fill your sails' (*yifan fengshun*) or 'May you make a fortune' (*gongxi facai*) on the reverse side (see **Neo-Maoism and Mao Fever**).

But luck can also be a matter of numbers. Although cars might not legitimately require the ministrations of **fengshui** specialists (geomancers), the wrong number plate (with too many 4s – *si*, a homophone for 'death', for instance) can be challenging. That is why plates with the digit 8 (*fa* or *fat* in Cantonese, 'prosper/thrive') sell for such a premium at auctions, not only in the Chinese cultural world but internationally as well. In 2002, there was an abortive attempt to market personalized number plates, but rakish drivers wanted plates reading 'IAM:007' or 'TMD' (Theatre Missile Defence) and the plan was shelved.

The melding of hoary traditions, old socialist icons and new commercial practices became possible in just this environment of economic boom and retro fashion. By employing the tropes of nostalgia typified by the 1990s Mao cult or the numerological fixation on number plates, state enterprises increasingly attempted to cast themselves as the representatives both of national and of consumer interests. An egregious example of this style of agitprop appeared in early 1997 when the Number One Automobile Plant (suitably renamed 'The Number One Automobile Production Consortium of China') in Changchun, Jilin province, now a joint venture invested with a new lease on life, initiated a national competition for an advertising slogan to launch the remodelled Maoist-era

limousine, the Red Flag, re-branded as the 'Audi-Chrysler-Red Flag'. The advertisement took up nearly half a page in the weekend edition of *Beijing Youth News* in early 1997:

All Chinese celebrated the birth of the original 'Red Flag' limousine. All Chinese have been proud of the brilliant glories of the 'Red Flag'. Today, we are appealing to every Chinese to take up their pens and celebrate the great leap of a new generation of 'Red Flag' cars.

In 1958, designers at the Number One Plant combined their extraordinary talents to create the first generation of Chinese luxury limousine, the 'Red Flag'. They wrote the first page in the history of China's automotive industry.

As the paramount make of Chinese vehicle, the 'Red Flag' is not merely a legend in motoring history. She crystallizes the ceaseless faith, the tireless struggles, and the fiery emotion of the whole country over a period of dozens of years and a number of generations. She symbolizes the eternal glories of the wisdom and the spirit of the Chinese nation.

The 'Red Flag' is a National Car of the latest international standard.

We are determined to create a new slogan for the 'Red Flag' that will resonate everywhere. We want to raise high the bright red banner of Chinese-manufactured cars, the banner of our national industry. We need a slogan from every warm-blooded Chinese. If you want to make your contribution to the resurgence of the national automotive industry then pick up your pen and participate in our advertising slogan campaign!!

The retooling of the lumbering limos of high socialism was not restricted to the Red Flag. In 2001, General Motors in Shanghai was producing a Buick GLX, for, as the journalist Lynne O'Donnell remarked, 'the cadre who knows what he wants in luxury road travel'. The sedan was designed for specific Chinese road and bureaucratic conditions to be, as O'Donnell wrote, a:

'rear-passenger oriented' luxury vehicle that was targeted at chauffeur-driven officials and executives. The leg room for the back seat was extended, a head-rest was added, pockets were put on the back of the front seats and the panel between the two front seats had controls for the air conditioning and heating as well as the radio, and a fancy ashtray was thrown in for good measure.

In keeping with adjustment to China's cadre-culture, Volkswagen went to work on the Audi A6 (like the Red Flag, also manufactured in Changchun) and added nine centimetres of legroom for the lounging comfort of the back-seat passengers.

> We bleed and sweat, earning millions for the factory.
> They go buy a tortoiseshell [sedan], and sit like tortoises [bastards] inside.
> No matter how small the village, the head gets a Bluebird;
> Regardless of their rank, they all take to Audis.
> Even when the business is broke, the bosses flaunt their Hondas;
> The workers might get zilch, but they still buy Santanas.
> (late 1990s **shunkouliu** (rhyming doggerel) on official **corruption**)

In the mid 1990s there were 30 million car licence holders in China; by mid 2001 that number had more than doubled and was approaching 75 million. With over 60 million motor vehicles on the country's roads, and with an increase of some 18 per cent annually, there was speculation that by the end of the first decade of the new century one in three urban families would be motorized. Not surprisingly, driving schools are a growth industry, and they attract customers of all ages with such advertising hooks such as 'I might not have a car yet, but I do have a licence' and 'Wanquan Driving School will set you on the road to the future'. Even the precipitous increase in road fatalities has done little to detract from the car boom. There were some 94,000 deaths in 2000, nearly a 10 per cent increase over 1999. If nothing else, this was a boon for car security and safety specialists, and airbags and seatbelts are only some of the new features in cars that are more often than not becalmed in the traffic snarls that choke the country's urban roads. On-board domestic luxuries – TVs, digital links, elaborate sound systems, DVD players, game

platforms, and the like – are also not the stuff of some future utopia, but something just around the next bend.

Finally, the vast boulevards envisaged as futuristic highways for socialist modernity since the avowal of socialism in all but name have been filling up with the joint-venture vehicles of international capitalism. In Canton and Shanghai the narrow streets and old suburbs have been giving way to a new urban architecture of the flyover, the bypass and the tunnel, in which there is sparse room for the bikes that were once a trademark of mainland Chinese life – although attempts to outlaw bicycles in some Chinese cities in favour of motorized traffic have generally failed. And everywhere there are traffic jams and road rage.

If nothing else, this has all been a boost for radio programmes targeted at frustrated motorists who can ring up talk-back shows on their mobiles and participate in the imagined community of migratory white-collar workers.

See also: bridges; highways; ring roads; streets; transportation patterns (urban)

GEREMIE R. BARMÉ

cashmere industry

Thanks largely to the grasslands that cover much of Inner Mongolia and the vast western hinterland of Gansu, Ningxia and Xinjiang, China is the world's largest producer of cashmere, the fine wool produced by goats and specifically associated with one breed native to the Himalayas. In China cashmere is sometimes dubbed 'soft gold'. Many goat breeders made their fortunes in the 1990s, when the country's cashmere industry mushroomed to meet world demand. More than 2,000 cashmere factories had sprouted across China. At its highest point in 2000, one kilo of cashmere sold for 530 yuan (US$63.85).

Since the late 1990s, however, cashmere prices have fallen dramatically because of unfair competition, a lack of co-ordination, and poor management. And raw cashmere now garners less than 100 yuan (US$12.04) per kilo. To make matters worse, environmentalists in China complained that allowing goats to graze wild was having a disastrous ecological impact on the grasslands, leaving them barren. From the point of view of the Chinese government, however, the cashmere industry employs too many workers to let the industry go under or shrink dramatically. The St Edenweiss Cashmere Fashion Trading Co. Ltd, for example, one of the most profitable companies in the Chinese industry, employs a staff of nearly 10,000 in various branches across the nation. Each year it sells 1.2 million pieces of cashmere to native and foreign consumers, and in Beijing alone it clears 10 million yuan (US$1.2 million) per year in profits. In recent years, therefore, the government has taken steps to solve the dilemma and has instituted a new policy that encourages herdsmen to raise their goats in folds and fences, rather than allowing them to roam free. This may offer a compromise between saving nature and satisfying the demand for cashmere, which remains one of the most favoured textiles of Western designers like Laura Biagiotti and Giorgio Armani.

See also: clothing industry; fashion designers; fur fashion; silk industry

PAOLA ZAMPERINI

Catholic villages

While rural Catholicism has provided a source of continuity for the Chinese Catholic Church through difficult times of persecution, it has also been a source of change: villagers have adapted many Catholic practices to better fit Chinese culture. While many key Catholic institutions (hospitals, universities, publishing houses) have been located in the cities, especially prior to 1949, rural Catholic strongholds have provided the clergy (priests and sisters) and the most active parishioners for the Chinese Church. There are Catholic villages scattered throughout the Chinese countryside; in many cases all the villagers are nominally Catholic, but in others Catholics make up only part of a village population (perhaps a lineage in a multi-lineage village, or lineage segment in a uni-lineage village). Catholic missionary strategies were especially well suited for the rural setting because of their emphasis on family, as opposed to individual, conversion (the latter being the historical strategy of Protestant missionaries). Many Catholic villages were actually established by missionaries, who bought land for their converts; these Catholic villages are unusual in the countryside because they may contain twenty or thirty different surname groups (as opposed to the more typical village, which consists of only one or two lineages). In the countryside, family ties and ritual events maintain village solidarity and provide for wider social networks, and Catholicism has adapted to meet these social needs. For example, while non-Catholic villagers use calendrical rituals such as the **Qingming Festival** (communal celebration of the ancestors) and the Chinese **New Year Festival** (*chunjie*) to bring scattered family members together, Catholic villages use All Soul's Day and Christmas for similar gatherings. Rural Catholic practices have also found a way to incorporate the ancestors, through Masses for the Deceased and Catholic funerary ritual, while the church provides a focal meeting place for Catholic villagers in lieu of an ancestral hall (see **ancestral halls/lineage temples**).

See also: Catholicism; Document 19 (1982)

Further reading

Lozada, Eriberto P (2001). *God Aboveground: Catholic Church, Postsocialist State, and Transnational Processes in a Chinese Village*. Stanford: Stanford University Press.

Madsen, Richard (1998). *China's Catholics: Tragedy and Hope in an Emerging Civil Society*. Berkeley: University of California Press.

Tang, Edmond and Wiest, Jean-Paul (eds) (1993). *The Catholic Church in Modern China: Perspectives*. Maryknoll: Orbis Books.

ERIBERTO P. LOZADA JR

Catholicism

Throughout its turbulent history, the Catholic Church in China has survived many movements of persecution because of the persistent faith of rural Catholic communities. In good times, the

Chinese Catholic Church flourishes politically and intellectually in the cities; but in bad times, which have been frequent since the Franciscans first arrived during the Yuan dynasty (1279–1321 CE), the Catholic Church has maintained a presence in China through its rural strongholds. The earliest evidence of Roman Catholicism in China (not including the Nestorian Christians) is John of Montecorvino's mission during the Yuan dynasty (1279–1321) and the creation of the Archdiocese of Beijing in 1307. By the Ming dynasty (1368–1644), the Jesuits and other missionary organizations arrived in China, establishing a Catholic presence that has continued up to the present.

Unlike other Catholic mission groups such as the Franciscans or Dominicans, the Jesuits sought to spread Catholicism through the Chinese political and intellectual elites, a strategy initiated in China by Matteo Ricci (1552–1610). The Jesuits grounded themselves in the Confucian classics, used Confucian-style philosophical debates to present Christianity, and introduced Western science and technology to win the support of the Chinese literati; for example, Jesuits Adam Schall (1591–1666) and Ferdinand Verbiest (1623–88) wrote definitive treatises on gunnery and designed cannons for both the Ming and Qing (1644–1911) imperial courts. An important legacy of Ricci was his translation of the word 'God' as 'Master of Heaven' (*tianzhu*) in an attempt to distinguish the Catholic notion of God from other Chinese concepts. Catholics still use the term today, and Catholicism is called 'the teachings of the Master of Heaven' (*Tianzhu jiao*) as distinct from Protestant Christianity, which is known as 'the teachings of Jesus' (*Jidu jiao*). The Jesuits also tried to reconcile Catholic doctrine with Confucianism by accommodating Chinese funerary and Confucian rituals as civil rituals. However, the Vatican rejected this mission strategy in the 'Rites Controversy', which resulted in the Kangxi emperor's proscription of foreign missionary activity and the worldwide disbanding of the Jesuit order in 1773.

A resurgence of Catholic missionary activity in China accompanied the concessions granted to Western imperialist powers through the unequal treaties of the Opium War (1839–42). With the strong support of the French government, Catholic missionaries expanded their activities throughout China. Because of extraterritoriality for Catholic missionaries and Western imperialist expansion in China, Catholic missionaries (and through missionary patronage, their converts) had strong political influence in both city and countryside. In south China, many Han Chinese who had converted to Catholicism after emigrating to various parts of southeast Asia returned to their villages and invited Catholic mission orders to send missionaries and support (financial and political) to the Chinese countryside. In north China, these Catholic communities became targets for rebels during the Boxer Rebellion (1899–1900). With the fall of the Qing dynasty and the establishment of the Republic of China (1911–45, in the mainland), the Catholic Church in China continued to expand and achieved strong linkages to the ruling Nationalist Party (Guomindang) through the continued support of foreign missionaries (backed by foreign states) and the Church's institutional expansion (schools, universities and hospitals) in Chinese society.

Because of the dominance of foreign missionaries in the Chinese Catholic Church when the People's Republic of China was established, the Church was targeted by the Chinese Communist Party (CCP) first for co-optation through a United Front, and then later for nationalization due to the worldwide Catholic Church's anti-Communist stance. In 1957, the CCP established the Chinese Catholic Patriotic Association as the official institution of the Chinese Catholic Church, forcing many Catholic communities who retained allegiance to the Vatican to go underground. With the 'reform and opening' (*gaige kaifang*) of Deng Xiaoping starting in 1979, CCP restrictions over religion were loosened, and in 1982 through a directive called Document 19, a new religious policy promoting state tolerance for officially recognized religions (including Catholicism) allowed for the resurgence of the Chinese Catholic Church. In 1992, the Chinese Catholic Bishops' Conference was established as the highest Catholic organization in China (superseding the Patriotic Association), thus aligning the structure of the Chinese Catholic Church to the structure of the worldwide Catholic Church. In 2002, some underground churches have resurfaced, and others continue to remain underground because of historical infighting, while the worldwide Catholic Church fosters its relationships with the above-ground Church. One of the main obstacles to full reconciliation of the Chinese Catholic Church with the Vatican is the lack of normalized relations between the Vatican and the PRC; in 2002, the Vatican still had diplomatic relations with the Republic of China on Taiwan. Although it is impossible to get precise numbers of Catholics, in 2002 there were probably around 10 million Chinese Catholics (the CCP claims there are 4 million Chinese Catholics, while the Vatican says 12 million). Catholicism continues to grow in an increasingly open and globalized China.

See also: Catholic villages; house churches; Document 19 (1982)

Further reading

Lozada, Eriberto P. (2001). *God Aboveground: Catholic Church, Postsocialist State, and Transnational Processes in a Chinese Village*. Stanford: Stanford University Press.

Madsen, Richard (1998). *China's Catholics: Tragedy and Hope in an Emerging Civil Society*. Berkeley: University of California Press.

—— (2003). 'Catholic Revival during the Reform Era'. In Daniel Overmyer (ed.), *Religion in China Today*. Cambridge: Cambridge University Press, 162–83.

Tang, Edmond and Wiest, Jean-Paul (eds) (1993). *The Catholic Church in Modern China: Perspectives*. Maryknoll: Orbis Books.

ERIBERTO P. LOZADA JR

CCTV (Chinese Central Television)

Chinese television is defined by the organization CCTV or Chinese Central Television. The national sector was split into a four-level system in 1982/3 – national, provincial, prefectural city and county – all under the aegis of the newly instituted Ministry for Broadcasting and Television (now subsumed into SARFT – **State Administration for Radio, Film and Television**). Although each level enjoys varying degrees of local programming content, each is linked to the CCTV network, and is obliged to screen CCTV news at least once a day.

The Chinese television industry began on 1 May 1958. Beijing TV, which would later became CCTV, was the first to broadcast, followed in the same year by Shanghai TV and Harbin TV. Beijing TV became a discrete entity in 1960 and was the leader in a rapid expansion of television access across China. Unsurprisingly perhaps, there was a significant hiccough in the late 1960s, when the chaos of the **Cultural Revolution** curtailed creative foreign imports. Nevertheless, Beijing TV began to broadcast in colour in the early 1970s, and its programming had become available in twenty-five provinces by the death of Mao in 1976. The station changed its name to CCTV in 1978, and an alternative municipal station (the current BTV) was set up to take over local-interest broadcasting for Beijing. The broadcaster is distinguished not only by its privileged access to public funding and screening quotas, but also by its breakdown of content by channel: for example, Channel 1 is the main news channel, Channel 5 carries sport and special events, Channel 4 is partly current affairs and partly English language summaries (now superseded by Channel 9). Channel 6 is a movie channel, and indicates the lasting but irritable relationship between the film and television arms of SARFT. Although SARFT is a single organization, it is bifurcated according to medium, and it is rumoured to be much easier to get content approvals for television than for film, so many talented filmmakers are moving to work in television.

Channel 9 (Zhongguo zhongying dianshetai) is the newest addition to the CCTV stable. It is an English-language channel and is devoted to highlighting international issues and the 'basic policies and principles of the Chinese Government'. Its dictum is to provide a 'reliable and authoritative source of information about China for a worldwide English-speaking audience'. The channel is therefore both fascinating and in need of decoding. It is explicitly designed to give the diplomatic, tourist and business communities information about China that is accurate in the neatest sense of the term. It is likely that the fiercest debates behind the scenes will be whether to employ media graduates with English or American accents and presentational style.

CCTV is a publicly funded service but it does carry advertising and it is also working to make links with foreign content providers, the idea being to exchange access to the Chinese market for Chinese programming in the American and European markets. This is where CCTV 9 would be most useful, but also where it needs to be reinvented if it wants to make an impact on foreign audiences.

See also: television programmes

Further reading

Keane, Michael. 'Send in the Clones: Television Formats and Content Creation in the People's Republic of China'. In Donald, Keane and Yin Hong (eds), *Media in China: Consumption, Content and Crisis*. London: RoutledgeCurzon, 80–90.

Yin, Hong (2002). 'Meaning, Production, Consumption: The History and Reality of Television Drama in China'. In Donald, Keane and Yin Hong (eds), *Media in China: Consumption, Content and Crisis*. London: RoutledgeCurzon, 28–39.

Yu, Hang and Green, Anthony (2000). 'From Mao to the Millennium: 40 Years of Television in China'. In David French and Michael Richards (eds), *Television in Contemporary Asia*. New Delhi: Sage.

STEPHANIE HEMELRYK DONALD

cellular phones

The cellular phone (*yidong dianhua*, or *shouji* as it is known colloquially) has become both a compulsory fashion accessory and an alternative to fixed-line telephony in China. *Shouji* were initially made popular by businessmen from Hong Kong and Taiwan during the mid 1980s. They soon became known as *dageda*, although this term is now rarely used. *Shouji* usage is most prominent among men between the ages of thirty-one and forty. However, market analysts predict that falling prices of wireless technology enabled by Wireless Application Protocol (WAP), together with localized content provided by Chinese Internet Content Providers (ICPs), will make the technology more appealing to the female and youth markets, replicating consumer patterns elsewhere in Asia. The WAP *shouji* is expected to outpace the sales of PCs in China.

A more ubiquitous but rapidly diminishing personal communications device is the *bibiji*, also known as *chuanhuji*, or *CALL-ji*. A 2000 survey of residents in twenty-two cities found that 42.7 per cent of families owned a cell phone while 60.4 per cent used pagers. According to the **Ministry of Information Industry** (MII), the number of *shouji* users in China had reached 139.9 million by November 2001. The cellular phone industry is regulated by the MII, which in 1999 subdivided the basic telecom service industry into four state-owned companies: China Telecom, China Mobile, China Satellite and China Unicom. Of these China Mobile and China Unicom are the main operators, and Kejian, Bird and Hai'er rank as the bestselling domestically made appliances.

MICHAEL KEANE

Central Academy of Fine Arts

(Zhongyang meishu xueyuan)

The Central Academy of Fine Arts (CAFA) is the only fine art institution of higher education directly subordinate to the **Ministry of Education**. It was founded in April 1950 on the basis of the Beiping National Art School dating back to 1918 and of the Department of Fine Arts of North China University, whose predecessor was the 'Lu Yi' Fine Art Department established in Yan'an in 1938. CAFA's first president was the famous Chinese painter and fine art educator, Xu Beihong.

CAFA has four undergraduate programmes in painting, sculpture, art and design, and art studies; two master's programmes in art studies and the art of design; and one doctoral programme in art studies. The programmes are offered in seven departments: Chinese Painting, Western Painting, Engraving, Mural Painting, Sculpture, Design, and Art History. In addition, CAFA also has a 101 Plastic Arts Seminar and an Adult Education Unit. There are over 1,000 undergraduate and graduate students, including over one hundred visiting students from a few dozen countries and regions.

The Library of CAFA is the largest of its kind in China, holding almost 300,000 albums of paintings and books on various subjects. Its art gallery has collected a vast array of rare artwork and hosts annual exhibitions of works created by the faculty and students. CAFA pays great attention to international exchanges, exhibitions and forums for artists at home and abroad. CAFA publishes two journals: *Art Studies* and *World Art*.

See also: art academies

HU MINGRONG

Central Propaganda Department

Created in May 1924, the Central Propaganda Department is one of only two Party organizations from the earliest years of the CCP to have survived into the twenty-first century, the other being the Central Organization Department. It peaked in power and importance at the start of the **Cultural Revolution**. With the beginning of the reform era in 1979, it entered a period of slow and steady decline as the core of the correct ideology, which it was meant to propagate, became increasingly hollow.

In the 1980s, the department launched a succession of largely ineffective propaganda campaigns to neutralize the impact of heretic ideology and 'spiritual pollution'. In the 1990s, its futile attempts to promote the sanctity of the 'eternal truths of Marxism–Leninism' have lost out to an explosive growth of **consumerism** as a competing discourse that is easily winning the hearts and minds of increasing numbers of PRC citizens. Today, as the CCP attempts to redefine its relationship to the revolutionary praxis of the past, the Central Propaganda Department is regarded by more and more Party members as an archaic institution ill-suited to the needs of a political force operating in a world of open borders, the increasingly free

flow of information, and sophisticated techniques of mass persuasion that make George Orwell's *1984* look like the picture of an age of innocence by comparison (see **Party advertising and self-promotion**).

See also: Campaign against Bourgeois Liberalization; cultural purges; socialist spiritual civilization

Further reading

Schoenhals, M. (ed.) (1992). Selections from 'Propaganda Trends', Organ of the CCP Central Propaganda Department. Published as *Chinese Law and Government* 24.4. Armonk: M. E. Sharpe.

MICHAEL SCHOENHALS

Central Radio and Television University

(Zhongyang guangbo dianshi daxue)

China's radio and television university system encompasses the Central Radio and Television University (CRTVU), local remote education institutions, and centres that manage their routine operations. This system adopts a mechanism of integrating centralized planning with management of specific operations by local governments. Its mission is to complement regular undergraduate education and to provide training to people who seek continuing education and life-long learning and who need to improve their on-the-job skills. Open to anyone who applies, radio and TV education is a combination of self-paced study and teaching by correspondence and/or face-to-face. Courses and syllabi are nationally standardized and school largely opens and closes at the same pace. Enrolment is decided by nationally standardized entrance examinations. A million students are graduated each year in accordance with the central government's regulations related to exams for those who seek higher education through self-paced studies to get associate or undergraduate degrees (see **examinations for self-paced higher education**).

China is one of the pioneers in remote education, its first correspondence university established in July 1958 in Tianjin. The momentum was cut short by the **Cultural Revolution**. On 6 February 1978, the Central Radio and Television University was opened. On 10 October 1986, the China Education TV channel started to offer CRTVU courses via satellite. In August 1995, the State Education Commission issued its guidelines on 'How to Implement China's Outline for Educational Reform and Development in RTVUs', thus turning over a new leaf for China's open school system, now enhanced by the Internet technology.

HU MINGRONG

Central University for Nationalities

(Zhongyang minzu daxue)

Central University for Nationalities (CUN), renamed on 30 November 1993, was established as the Central College for Nationalities (Zhongyang minzu xueyuan) on 2 May 1950 in Beijing. Characterized by programmes that focus on China's minority nationalities, CUN is a comprehensive university emphasizing the humanities and social sciences. Other subjects include engineering, education, medicine, finance, management and fine arts. CUN is recognized as the nation's best among comparable institutions, offering more programmes and graduating the best students

CUN has ten colleges with twenty-nine departments providing forty-one undergraduate, twenty-four master's and nine doctoral programmes. There are also three post-doctoral centres. Of the 6,000 full-time students, over 350 are pursuing graduate degrees. With 85 per cent of the students from minority nationality backgrounds, CUN is the only campus in China embracing all fifty-six nationalities recognized by the government. Many of the 1,454 faculty and staff are well versed in their languages, histories and cultures. The university has graduated over 60,000 students. Many have become leading members of their communities.

CUN attaches great importance to research, having established forty-two research centres and institutes studying Anthropology, Economy of Minority Nationalities, and Diversity and Foreign Language Teaching. Research on ethnicity, language, religion, history and the fine arts of minority nationalities remains at the forefront of such research in China.

CUN's library holds 110,000 books in over twenty languages, including Mandarin, Mongolian, Tibetan, Kazak and Korean. CUN's Ethnic Museum houses 20,000 items. CUN has exchange programmes with over fifty universities throughout the world and enrols over 550 foreign students annually.

See also: autonomous regions, prefectures, counties and banners; ethnic groups, history of

HU MINGRONG

Chan, Jackie

(né Chen Gangsheng; a.k.a. Cheng Long)

b. 7 April 1954, Hong Kong

Film actor, director, screenwriter, producer, stunt coordinator, pop singer

Jackie Chan appeared in his first motion picture in 1962 at the age of seven, while still a student at Hong Kong's China Drama Academy. There he practised Peking-opera *jing* (warrior) roles (see **Xiqu role types**) and **martial arts** alongside classmates Sammo Hung and Yuen Biao. Through 1977, he appeared in several films as one of the actors groomed to replace the late Bruce Lee (Li Xiaolong, 1940–73), to whom Chan has been contrasted ever since his breakthrough successes of 1978 through 1983. These included *Snake in the Eagle's Shadow* (*Shexing diaoshou*), *Drunken Master* (*Zuiquan*) and *Project A* (*A jihua*). Jackie Chan's *kungfu* comedies of the 1980s and early 1990s feature inventive action choreography, showcase the star's acrobatic skill and physical daring (not least in outtakes), and establish Chan's screen persona as the indefatigable, likeable underdog. Bruce Lee was threatening and sexy; Jackie Chan is neither.

Chan's films, including his police dramas and globe-trekking adventures, are entertaining, well-crafted, formulaic and solidly middle-class in taste and values. Chan was a pan-Asian film star by the release of *Young Master* (*Shidi chuma*) in 1980, but did not succeed in North America until *Rumble in the Bronx* (1996) and *Rush Hour* (1998). Jackie Chan typifies transnational Chinese cinema in an era of globalization in that his Hollywood triumph required the sacrifice of some of what marked his early films as culturally and aesthetically unique to Hong Kong.

Further reading

Cheung, Mabel (dir.) (2003). *Traces of the Dragon* [documentary on the life and family of Jackie Chan].

THOMAS MORAN

Chan, Peter

(né Chan Ho-sun; Chen Kexin)

b. 1962, Hong Kong

Film director/producer

The author of sophisticated comedies of manners, Chan is one of the most eloquent voices in Hong Kong cinema in the 1990s and 2000s. His characters, often floating between several cultures, struggle to decipher the mysteries of their own hearts as well as the enigmas of modernity.

Born in a displaced family of Thai Chinese intellectuals (his father is the filmmaker Chan Tung-man), Chan grew up both in Hong Kong and Bangkok, and later studied in the USA. Back in Hong Kong, he worked as an assistant director for Golden Harvest, then co-founded the United Filmmakers Organization (UFO), an independent production company for which he directed highly successful comedies: *Alan and Eric: Between Hello and Goodbye* (*Shuangcheng gushi*, 1991), *He's a Woman, She's a Man* (*Jinzhe yuye*, 1994) and others. *Comrades: Almost a Love Story* (*Tian Mimi*, 1996), a bittersweet comedy of love lost and regained in a post-colonial, pan-Chinese context, won many awards.

In 1999, Chan directed *Love Letters*, shot in New England for Dreamworks, and then started commuting between the US and Asia. In 2000, he co-founded Applause Pictures, a pan-Asian production company based in Hong Kong designed to foster emerging talent in East Asia. Having produced a series of internationally well-received films by directors from Hong Kong, China, Thailand, Korea, Singapore and Japan, Chan directed *Coming Home* (*Huijia*) for the omnibus horror film *Three* (*Sangeng*, 2002) which is considered by critics as the most successful of the three episodes.

BÉRÉNICE REYNAUD

Chan Fruit

(né Chan Goh/Chen Guo)

b. 1959, Guangzhou

Film director

Chan directed his first film, *Finale in Blood* (*Danao guangchang long*) in 1991, but it was only with *Made in Hong Kong* (*Xianggang zhizao*, 1997), one of the first independent features produced in the territory, that he developed his idiosyncratic style: a form of neo-realism involving the frequent use of non-professional actors and a mixture of popular street culture, lively vulgarity and nostalgia for a vanished world.

Chan was ten years old when his family emigrated from Guangzhou, and his characters are often torn between the multiple strands of their Chinese identity. *Made in Hong Kong* shows confused, semi-delinquent youths in working-class dwellings once built for immigrants. *The Longest Summer* (*Qunian yanhua tebie duo*, 1998) is an expressionist reconstitution of the darker social effects of the 1997 handover. In *Little Cheung* (*Xilu Xiang*, 2000), *Durian, Durian* (*Liulian Piao Piao*, 2000) and *Hollywood, Hong Kong* (*Xianggang you ge Helihuo*, 2001), Chan follows the plight, wanderings and erratic destinies of immigrants from Shenzhen or northern China and their interaction with Hong Kong natives – focusing on the resilience of mainland prostitutes, who work till exhaustion in the red districts of Kowloon only to lead a completely different existence later. Finally, *Public Toilet* (*Renmin gongce*, 2002) is an ambitious, baroque, pan-Asian fresco in which the different characters – in China, Hong Kong, Korea, India and New York – are linked by various narratives having to do with the strange poetry of public toilets and the ecological effects on the planet of human waste.

Further reading

Huber, Christopher (2003). 'Curious about Crap: Fruit Chan's *Public Toilet*'. *Senses of Cinema* 24 (Jan./Feb.). Available at http://www.sensesofcinema.com

BÉRÉNICE REYNAUD

Chang, Sylvia

(née Zhang Aijia/Cheung Ngai-kar)

b. 1953, Chiayi, Taiwan

Actress, producer, director, screenwriter

A well-known star and multi-talented filmmaker, Chang has worked in Taiwan, Hong Kong and, briefly, in the United States (for television) and England (Mike Newell's *Soursweet*, 1988). In Taiwan, Chang was a teenage TV actress, won two Golden Horse awards (1976 and 1981) and contributed to the genesis of the New Cinema by producing the TV series *Eleven Women* (*Shi yige nüren*, 1981), which triggered Edward **Yang**'s directing career. She also starred in Yang's first feature, *That Day on the Beach* (*Haitan de yitian*, 1993), as well as in several major films, including Ang **Lee**'s US co-production *Eat Drink Man Woman* (*Yin shi nan nü*, 1994).

In Hong Kong she was cast in action comedies, especially the popular series *Aces Go Places* (*Zuijia paidang*, 1982, 1983, 1984, 1986). She produced and starred in Ann **Hui**'s first feature, *The Secret* (*Feng Jie*, 1979), and worked with Li Hanxiang, King Hu/Hu Jinquan, **Tsui Hark**, Johnny To Kei-fung, Clifton Ko Chi-sum, Mabel Cheung Yuen-ting, Stanley **Kwan**, Lawrence Ah Mon/ Lau Kwok-cheong, and so forth. In 1981, she started writing screenplays and directing films

focusing on female protagonists. She appears in some of her films – *Passion* (*Zui Hai*, 1986), *Tempting Heart* (*Xin Dong*, 1999) – while gracefully yielding centre-stage in others – *Mary from Beijing* (*Mengxing shifen*, 1992), *Siao Yu* (*XiaoNü Xiao Yu*, 1994), *Nobody Wants to Go Home* (*Jintian bu huijia*, 1996), *Princess D* (*Xiang Fei*, 2002).

See also: cinema in Taiwan

BÉRÉNICE REYNAUD

Chang Tsong-zung

b. 1951, Hong Kong

Independent curator, art critic, gallery director

Chang Tsong-zung opened the Hanart T Z Gallery in Hong Kong in 1993 and Hanart (Taipei) Gallery in Taiwan in 1988, the latter having changed its operations in 2001, becoming a curatorial and consultancy service. Over the past twenty years, Hanart has represented a large number of contemporary Chinese artists, including Ju Ming from Taiwan, Luis Chan from Hong Kong, and, from mainland China, the **85 New Wave [Art] Movement** artist Wu Shanzhuan and 'China's New Art Post-89' artists such as **Fang Lijun**, Zhang Xiaogang and **Qiu Zhijie**.

Chang has also played a major role in curating and promoting contemporary Chinese art since the 1980s. In this capacity he first began to organize exhibitions of Hong Kong and Taiwan art, expanding by the late 1980s to include art from mainland China. In early 1989, Chang organized 'The Stars: 10 Years' on the tenth anniversary of the first unofficial art exhibition held in China after the **Cultural Revolution**. In 1993 with **Li Xianting**, he co-curated and organized the seminal exhibition 'China's New Art, Post-1989' in Hong Kong, one of the first large shows of experimental art. In 1994 and 1996, he curated the Special Chinese Exhibitions for the 22nd and 23rd São Paulo Bienniels in Brazil, and, in 1995 he selected the Chinese artists for the Venice Biennale centenary exhibition. In 1996, with Graeme Murray he curated 'Reckoning with the Past: Contemporary Chinese Painting' (Fruitmarket

Gallery, Edinburgh, Scotland), the first exhibition to present to an overseas audience artists from China, Hong Kong and Taiwan. Other major exhibitions include: 'Faces and Bodies of the Middle Kingdom' (Galerie Rudolfinum, Prague, 1997); 'Power of the Word' (Taiwan Art Museum and various US venues, 1999); 'Polypolis: Art from Asian Pacific Megacities' (Kunsthaus, Hamburg, 2001) and 'Magic at Street Level' (Hong Kong–China Exhibition, 49th Venice Biennale, 2001); and, with Jean-Marc Decrop, 'Paris–Pekin' (Espace Cardin, Paris, 2002), the largest exhibition to date of Chinese art in Europe. An advocate of the presentation of artistic movements rather than just individual artists, Chang has also written numerous articles and catalogue essays, including 'Into the Nineties' (*China's New Art*, 1993), 'The Other Face' (*Identity and Alterity*, 1995) and 'A New Era for Chinese Art' (*Made by Chinese*, 2001).

ALICE MING WAI JIM

Chaozhou-Hakka sixian

regional traditional music genre

Chaozhou-Hakka sixian refers to a genre of music common to both the Chaozhou and Hakka Chinese subcultures inhabiting the contiguous areas centred respectively in the cities of Shantou and Dabu in eastern Guangdong province. It is typically performed in an intimate indoor setting on an ensemble comprised largely of untempered plucked and bowed string instruments – hence the term *sixian* (silk strings) – as opposed to the balanced combination of wind and string instruments collectively known as **Silk and Bamboo** (*sizhu*). Occasionally, three small percussion instruments and a vertical bamboo notched flute are added.

The genre is likewise defined by a small core repertoire of pieces based on ancient melodies (e.g. *Zhaojun yuan*) as well as shorter stock tunes (e.g. *Liuqingniang*) also known in other parts of China. However, a complex system of modes, certain melodic and rhythmic motifs and techniques of ornamentation, and the manner and the extent to which the melodies are subjected to different types of variation in performance distinguish Chaozhou-Hakka sixian from other regional string ensemble music styles.

Since 1980, with the reopening of music clubs and other traditional presocialist sites for this music, Chaozhou-Hakka sixian has been flourishing again. In some counties of eastern Guangdong, there are a dozen or more clubs devoted to this music within a ten-mile radius. Playing a key role in its revitalization are Chaozhou and Hakka Chinese overseas whom the government is wooing with tax incentives as well as ethnic and nostalgic appeals to invest in the mainland. Higher levels of income and the increasingly open sociopolitical atmosphere today are undoubtedly contributing factors.

See also: string ensemble

Further reading

Dujunco, Mercedes M. (1994). *Tugging at the Native's Heartstrings: Nostalgia and the Post-Mao 'Revival' of the Xian Shi Yue String Ensemble Music of Chaozhou, South China*. Ann Arbor: UMI.

MERCEDES M. DUJUNCO

Cheang Shu-lea

b. 1954, Tainan, Taiwan

Film and video-filmmaker, multi-media and net installation artist

From community-based video to 'art porn' film to high-tech digital installations, Cheang Shu-lea's brilliant international career defies easy characterization, crossing the boundaries of genre, traditional authorship, aesthetic medium, national and sexual identity. After studying at NYU (1977–9), Cheang became involved with Paper Tiger TV (1980–90) and Deep Dish TV (1990–4), two alternative media public access organizations in downtown Manhattan. Her trip to Beijing in June 1989 inspired two critical deconstructions of the media representation of the event in the US, Taiwan and the PRC: *Making News/Making History* (installation, 1989) and *How Was History*

Wounded (*Lishi ruhe chengwei shangkou*, video, 1990). She produced the series *Will Be Televised* (1990), in collaboration with artists in five Asian countries, including Hong Kong (the performance art group **Zuni Icosahedron**), Taiwan (the agit-prop organization Green Team) and the PRC (a selection from the banned television series **River Elegy**/*Heshang*, 1988). In the early 1990s, she presented ground-breaking multi-media installations: *Colour Schemes* (Whitney Museum, 1990), an ironical commentary on US multiculturalism, and *Those Fluttering Objects of Desire* (Whitney Biennale, 1993), a collaboration with twenty-five women artists on sex, pornography and interracial desire.

Her first feature, *Fresh Kill* (1994), was a witty, transgressive variation on ethnicity, sexuality, ecology and urban political resistance. Then Cheang opted to become a 'digital drifter', creating web-based interactive installations throughout the world: *Bowling Alley* (Minneapolis, 1995), *Elephant Cage Butterfly Locker* (Tokyo, 1996), *Brandon* (Guggenheim Museum, New York, 1998–9), *Carry On* (Hanover, 2000), *Baby Play* (Tokyo, 2001), *GARLIC = RICH AIR* (New York, 2002), *Burn* (2003, Liverpool). In Japan, she directed *I.K.U.* (2000), a science-fiction digital porn feature – polysexual, queer-inspired, and visually stunning.

See also: New Documentary Movement; gay cinema and video

Further reading

Marchetti, Gina. (2001). 'Cinema Frames, Videoscapes, and Cyberspace: Exploring Shu Lea Cheang's *Fresh Kill*'. *positions: east asia cultures critique* 9.2: 401–22.

Tomes, K. S. (1996). 'Shu Lea Cheang: Hi-Tech Aborigine'. *Wide Angle* 18.1.

BÉRÉNICE REYNAUD

chefs

In the early 1960s, China began to grant titles to chefs based on testing and evaluation. In 1963, over a hundred chefs obtained such 'special-class' certificates. Another 800 achieved this status in 1982 and thousands more in the 1990s. On 6 March 2001, the government issued a set of 'Standards for Chinese Professionals and Skilled Workers.' According to the document, chefs are classified as Master of Chinese Cuisine, Master of Western Cuisine, Master of Chinese Bakery, Master of Western Bakery, and Restaurant Servers. Each of these five titles is further divided into three levels: junior, intermediate and senior, and each level requires a year of formal training and a year of learning on the job. The training integrates traditional apprenticeship with a modern education offered by a dozen national training centres in major cities (e.g. Wuhan, Chongqing and Xi'an) and in numerous local culinary schools and college programmes throughout the country. Heilongjiang College of Business, for example, graduated China's first Masters of Culinary Art.

Since 1983, half a dozen national cooking contests have been organized to enhance culinary skill and encourage innovation. In half a century, Chinese chefs have created over ten thousand recipes. They have participated and excelled in a number of international culinary Olympics. The job of chef has become a respectable and lucrative profession. Several thousands have been entered in the *Who's Who of Famous Chefs* (*Mingchu dadian*). Lack of training in nutrition, however, is still a weakness of Chinese culinary education, which nonetheless produces chefs of superb skill.

YUAN HAIWANG

Chen, Joan

(née Chen Chong)

b. 1961, Shanghai

Actress, film director

In her debut, *Youth* (*Qingchun*, 1977), Chen Chong plays Yamei, a teenager who overcomes difficulty to become a Party member. Director **Xie Jin** picked Chen because of her expressive eyes (Yamei is mute). As the eponymous heroine of *Little Flower* (*Xiaohua*, 1979), Chen charmed fans and won China's best actress award. She moved to the US in 1981. She played May-May in *Tai-Pan* (1986), Empress Wan Jung (Wanrong) in *The Last Emperor*

(1987), and femme fatale Josie Packard in *Twin Peaks* (1990). As an Asian, Chen has had limited opportunity in Hollywood (she plays an Eskimo in a Stephen Segal film), but she has succeeded (she has directed Richard Gere).

Chen's looks and distinctive pose – head titled, eyes dreamy, full lips smiling faintly – have made her popular. In early films, Chen is demure; in later work, she is alluring; but whether as the wholesome Zhao Xiaohua in *Little Flower* or the adulterous Wang Jiaorui in *Red Rose, White Rose* (*Hongmeigui baimeigui*, 1994), Chen accepts the audience's gaze. Chen's intriguing, opaque screen persona is typified by her character in *Temptation of a Monk* (*Youseng*, 1993), a sweet, flirtatious princess whose alter-ego is a seductress–assassin.

Chen won Taiwan's Golden Horse for her first film as director, *The Sent-Down Girl* (*Tianyu* or *Xiu Xiu*, 1998), about a girl sent to Tibet during the **Cultural Revolution**. The refracted outline of Chen's career emerges in her direction of sixteen-year-old Lu Lu, who as Xiu Xiu goes from chaste naïveté to resigned promiscuity with jarring rapidity and explicitness. Xiu Xiu's misfortune is to become a sexual object, but the film uses sex to sell us her story.

THOMAS MORAN

Chen Danqing

b. 1953, Shanghai

Oil painter

Chen's naturalist paintings of Tibetans broke the conventions of socialist realism. Troubled by his family's political persecution during the **Cultural Revolution** and denied entry to art school, Chen tried his luck in Tibet, where his future wife, the painter Huang Suning, had been posted. There, he collaborated with Nawang Choedrak to paint *The Workers Weep though the Harvest is Good, 1976/9/9* (*Leishui saman fengshoutian*, 1976), showing Tibetans mourning the death of Mao Zedong. A masterpiece of Soviet-style socialist realism, all details and colours are worked out to convey a particular message. In 1978, after his family's political rehabilitation, Chen was admitted as

a research student to the **Central Academy of Fine Arts**, graduating in 1982. His *Tibetan Series* (*Xizang zuhua*, 1980), was to have a tremendous influence on the emerging **Native Soil Painting**. These works dropped the monumental size of his earlier social-realist painting in favour of the intimate style and scale of the nineteenth-century French naturalist school. They portrayed the Tibetans in a dignified, forthright way, avoiding the patronizing depictions of propaganda images. *Pilgrimage* (*Chaosheng*) depicts Tibetans at prayer. His *Khampa Men* (*Khampa Hanzi*) show none of the usual indications of the benefits of socialism; they seem totally untouched and indifferent to it. Chen left for the United States in 1982 where he continued painting grand, transcultural themes in a realistic style. He now teaches at **Qinghua University** Art College, Chen Danqing studio.

See also: art academies

Further reading

Abbas, Ackbar (1995). *Chen Danqing: Painting after Tiananmen* (exhibition catalogue). Hong Kong: University of Hong Kong.

Galikowski, Maria (1998). *Art and Politics in China, 1949–1984*. Hong Kong: Chinese University Press, 193–207.

Lü, Peng and Yi, Dan (1992). *Zhongguo xiandai yishushi* [A History of China Modern Art]. Changsha: Hunan meishu chubanshe, 51–7.

EDUARDO WELSH

Chen Haiyan

b. 1955, Fushun, Liaoning

Printmaker

Chen Haiyan is a female printmaker best known for her dream series of wood-block prints begun as a private art project in the early to mid 1980s. She is professor of printmaking at the China Academy of Art (Zhongguo meishu xueyuan; see **art academies**).

Chen Haiyan entered the Zhejiang Academy of Art (now China Academy of Art) in 1980. She studied printmaking and specialized in etching, which she continues to practise. After graduation in 1984 she was retained as a teacher. Chen Haiyan was one of the earliest contemporary Chinese artists to pursue an interest in dreams and the unconscious mind. Since 1980 she has kept a diary of dreams. Her first dream works were small, boldly carved wood blocks incorporating image and text that used the traditional 'penetrating ink' (*touyin*) method of printing. Whilst Chen Haiyan's dream works are stylistically unique they resonate in an interesting, questioning manner with China's long tradition of wood-block printing, which includes Buddhist sutras, book illustration, New Year prints and twentieth-century revolutionary prints. She also acknowledges the inspiration of German expressionist art, Western philosophy and Chinese mystical and philosophical traditions. Since 1999 Chen Haiyan has also experimented with brush and ink painting and large five-ply sheets, which she has carved and painted with her dream narratives. Chen Haiyan's works have been collected by Chinese and international art museums and galleries. She continues to be one of China's most inspiring artists.

CLAIRE ROBERTS

Chen Kaige

b. 1956, Beijing

Film director

One of China's internationally best-known film directors, Chen Kaige was the son of a prominent director (Chen Huaikai) and scriptwriter (Liu Yanchi). Well-educated into his teenage years, Chen's work was deeply influenced by his experiences while sent down to the countryside in Yunnan province during the **Cultural Revolution**. Subsequently, Chen entered the **Beijing Film Academy** and graduated in 1982 with first class honours to emerge since the early 1960s, the so-called Fifth Generation (see **Fifth Generation (film directors)**).

In his first independent directing role, for **Yellow Earth** (1984), Chen and cinematographer **Zhang Yimou** electrified the Asian film world with their subtle artistry and daring political stance. Replacing the melodrama of PRC film style with slow-paced intellectual contemplation, *Yellow Earth* describes a historical stalemate between People's Liberation Army rhetoric and the intransigence of a traditional-minded peasantry. After appearing in the 1985 Hong Kong Film Festival, *Yellow Earth* sold a million tickets in six days and heralded the arrival of a new era in PRC filmmaking.

Chen's next films, *The Big Parade* (1985) and *King of the Children* (1987), fared poorly with the public despite their formal beauty and intellectual gravity, and his career foundered. Not until 1993, with the lavishly produced *Farewell My Concubine*, did Chen revise his style to meet popular demand and revive his fortunes. *Farewell* shared the Palm d'Or at Cannes and won an Academy Award nomination for best foreign film. Following a pair of actors from childhood to death, through Nationalist Chinese, Japanese and Communist eras of control, the film pitted art against the harshness of twentieth-century politics. None of Chen's subsequent films, including *Temptress Moon* (1995) and *The Emperor and the Assassin* (1999), have rivalled his earlier achievements.

Further reading

Braester, Yomi (2003). 'Farewell My Concubine: National Myth and City Memories'. In Chris Berry (ed.), *Chinese Films in Focus: 25 New Takes*. London: BFI, 89–96.

Chow, Rey (1993). 'Male Narcissism and National Culture: Subjectivity in Chen Kaige's *King of Children*'. In Ellen Widmer and David Der-Wei Wang (eds), *From May Fourth to June Fourth: Fiction and Film in Twentieth Century China*. Cambridge: Harvard University Press, 327–59.

—— (2000). 'The Seduction of Homecoming: Place, Authenticity, and Chen Kaige's *Temptress Moon*'. In Yeh Wen-hsin (ed.), *Cross Cultural Readings of Chineseness: Narratives, Images, and Interpretations of the 1990s*. Berkeley: Centre for Chinese Studies, 8–26.

Xu, Ben (1997). '*Farewell My Concubine* and Its Nativist Critics'. *Quarterly Review of Film and Television* 16.2: 155–70.

JEROME SILBERGELD

Chen Ping

b. 1960, Beijing

Traditional Chinese painter

Trained privately in traditional Chinese painting, calligraphy and seal carving from his youngest years, Chen Ping received from the start the education of a classic literatus. In 1984 he graduated from the Traditional Chinese Painting Department of the **Central Academy of Fine Arts** in Beijing, with a specialization in landscape painting. In 1987 he was hired as staff of the same department, where in 1989 he began teaching in the newly founded Calligraphy Research Workshop. A leading representative of the **New Literati Painting**, Chen Ping is unanimously considered one of the most talented and promising artists to have emerged in the field of traditional Chinese painting during the post-Mao period. His works are close to old literati practice and yet endowed with a distinctive modern look. Chen spends long periods of time engaged in the orthodox practice of 'learning from nature', yet it is the modern countryside that he observes. In his compositions, specific if studiously naïve references to modernization – buses, cars and bicycles – appear without ostentation. Chen Ping's most impressive technique – the depiction of clouds and the treatment of dark monochrome ink – is extremely new in its prominent three-dimensional effects reminiscent of Western modernism, while hinting at a similar technique found in the work of the seventeenth-century Chinese painter Gong Xian (1618–89) in which the layering of black-and-white surfaces provides a sculptural texture to volatile elements such as clouds, fog and foliage. Since 1989, Chen Ping has regularly participated in New Literati Painting exhibitions of which the largest was held in Beijing in 1997. He has also widely exhibited in Taiwan, Japan and Singapore.

Further reading

Andrews, Julia and Shen, Kuiyi (1998). 'Chinese Painting in the Post-Mao Era'. In *idem* (eds), *A Century in Crisis. Modernity and Tradition in the art of Twentieth-Century China*. New York: Guggenheim Museum, 278–89.

Dal Lago, Francesca (1998). ' "New Literati Painting", China Art Gallery, Beijing' (exhibition review). *ART AsiaPacific* 19 (July): 32–4.

Dal Lago, Francesca and Trombetta Panigadi, Laura (1991). 'Il volto nuovo di una pittura antica' [The New Face of an Ancient Tradition – on the New Literati Painting]. *ARTE* 224 (December).

Tang, Shikang (ed.) (1992). *Chen Ping*. Hong Kong: DaYe Publishing House.

FRANCESCA DAL LAGO

Chen Pingyuan

b. 1954, Chaozhou, Guangdong

Literary theorist

Chen Pingyuan is a literary scholar and **Peking University** professor whose innovative work on twentieth-century Chinese literature greatly influenced the field of Chinese studies and humanities research. Chen Pingyuan has contributed to Chinese scholarship in two important ways. Beginning with his PhD thesis in 1987, his meticulous and in-depth research methods have become a model to students and scholars alike. His wide-ranging research is entirely based on original material, which he references in a clear and detailed manner and encompasses the history of Chinese fiction and prose, theories of narrative, Ming and Qing prose, genre theory, literature and learning, popular fiction and **martial arts fiction**.

Second, Chen is known for his groundbreaking re-evaluation of the history of modern Chinese literature. He was the first literary scholar to introduce a division of modern Chinese literature based on influences other than political ones. Instead, he proved the importance of traditional Chinese elements as well as Western literature and modernity in the development of modern Chinese literature. Also of importance is his new history of the May Fourth movement. As a study of the relationship between image and text, it includes hitherto unknown and unconventional materials such as newspaper clippings and photographs and offers a novel approach to this important period in modern Chinese history. Chen's scholarship is also marked by a dynamic exchange with experts from Europe, the USA and Japan, which has further established his reputation as a leading scholar in the field.

See also: Liu Dong; National Studies; Research Institute for National Studies

Further reading

Chen, Ping-yuan (1999). 'Literature High and Low: Popular Fiction in Twentieth-Century China'. In Michel Hockx (ed.), *The Literary Field of Twentieth-Century China*. Richmond: Curzon, 113–34.
—— (2003). 'Scholarship, Ideas, Politics'. In Wang Chaohua (ed.), *One China, Many Paths*. London: Verso, 108–27.

BIRGIT LINDER

Chen Qigang

b. 1951, Shanghai

Composer

Chen Qigang, a composer of the Chinese 'New Wave' (see **Third Generation (composers)**), now lives and works in Paris. He graduated from the affiliate middle school of the Central Conservatory of Music in 1973 as a clarinet student. In 1978, he enrolled in the first composition class at the reopening of the Central Conservatory in the post-Cultural Revolution era, along with fellow students **Tan Dun**, **Qu Xiaosong**, **Chen Yi** and **Zhou Long** (see **music conservatories**).

In 1984, Chen Qigang received a grant from the French government to study in Paris, where Olivier Messiaen accepted him as his last and only student. At the Paris Conservatory, Chen's teachers included Ivo Malec, Claude Ballif and Betsy Jolas. Apart from orchestral and chamber works, Chen also experimented with electronic music, working at IRCAM and in 1993 producing *Dream of a Recluse* (*Rêve d'un solitaire*) for instrumentalists

and electronics. In 2001, he composed the ballet music for *Raise the Red Lantern*, a collaboration with film director **Zhang Yimou**, based loosely on the novella by **Su Tong** that first inspired Zhang to make the feature film. Chen's music mixes East and West effectively, with sensitive instrumental timbres reminiscent of French impressionists. However, he is definitely a representative of the Chinese 'New Wave'. His musical language incorporates a transnational range, from traditional **Jingju** (Peking opera) to pointillistic avant-garde idioms, including works that refer specifically to Chinese culture, such as *Wu Xing* (*Les 5 elements*).

JOANNA C. LEE

Chen Ran

b. 1962, Beijing

Writer

A writer of psychological novels, Chen Ran is known as the only Chinese woman writer who identifies herself as a feminist. Chen started to publish in 1985 and toured England, Australia and Germany before she returned and settled down in Beijing as a freelance writer. As one of the few writers of **avant-garde/experimental literature** in China, she presents herself as writing from the margin even after she became a member of the Chinese Writers' Association in 1990. Since the publication of her short story 'The Disease of the Century' (*Shiji bing*, 1986), Chen has held critics' attention because of her modernist exploration of female subjectivity as well as her inventive style and perspective.

Chen diverges from the literary mainstream in that she tries to go beyond a social and historical interest in women's experiences to write from an essential female subjectivity. Informed by dreams and fantasies, her analysis often focuses on the female body or domestic space. At the same time, Chen's writing features a highly personal and sensual use of language: the abstract is described using words of sensual and sexual texture while multiple descriptions of physical reality offset the workings of the narrator's psyche. This defiance of plot-oriented narration highlights Chen's painstaking efforts to escape the accepted norms of literacy. Her amoral and apolitical approach to literature and her refusal to accommodate the public's reading habits contribute to her singularity in contrast to other forms of woman-authored literature, which were increasingly submerged within 'middle brow' literature in the 1990s.

See also: Lin Bai; lesbianism in literature

Further reading

Chen, Ran (1995). 'Sunshine between the Lips'. Trans. Shelley Wing Chan. In Howard Goldblatt (ed.), *Chairman Mao Would Not Be Amused: Fiction from Today's China*. New York: Grove Press, 112–29.
—— (2001). 'Breaking Open'. Trans. Paola Zamperini. In Patricia Sieber (ed.), *Red Is Not the Only Color: Contemporary Chinese Fiction on Love and Sex between Women, Collected Stories*. Lanham, MD: Rowman and Littlefield, 49–72.
Huot, Claire (2000). 'Literary Experiments: Six Files'. In *idem, China's New Cultural Scene: A Handbook of Changes*. Durham: Duke University Press, 7–48.
Larson, Wendy (1997). 'Women and the Discourse of Desire in Postrevolutionary China: The Awkward Postmodernism of Chen Ran'. *Boundary 2* 24.3: 201–23.
Visser, Robin (2002). 'Privacy and its Ill Effects in Post-Mao Urban Fiction'. In Bonnie S. McDougall and Anders Hansson (eds), *Chinese Concepts of Privacy*. Leiden: Brill, 171–94.

HE DONGHUI

Chen Rong

b. 6 January 1929, Harbin, Heilongjiang

Theatre director

Chen Rong, one of China's foremost female directors, escaped to Beijing from Japanese-controlled Harbin at the age of twelve. At sixteen she joined the People's Liberation Army and was assigned to a performing arts troupe during the Chinese Civil War (1945–9). The troupe performed classical Chinese Operas for audiences composed of workers, peasants and soldiers. In 1950 she studied acting at the newly established Central Drama Academy, in Beijing.

After graduation she worked at the Chinese Traditional Opera Institute in Beijing, collaborating with famous Chinese Opera actor, Mei Lanfang. In 1954 she was accepted as a student at the National Dramatic Arts Academy in Moscow and five years later graduated with a degree in stage direction. She joined the China Children's Art Theatre in 1960 where she became well known for her direction of the Chinese play *Flower Malan*. In 1962 she was assigned to the China Youth Art Theatre in Beijing and in 1988 became the Artistic Director of the company. Her productions of Bertholt Brecht's plays *Galileo, The Caucasian Chalk Circle* and *The Three Penny Opera* have had a major impact on contemporary Chinese theatre. These productions reflect Chen Rong's unique style of infusing modern **Huaju** (spoken drama) with classical Chinese Opera techniques. Her work has been presented in Hong Kong, Taiwan and Japan. In 1991, Chen Rong resigned her position as Artistic Director to become a national political consultant for the government. She currently lives in Beijing and continues to direct plays for the China Youth Art Theatre.

See also: Western theatre

CARLA KIRKWOOD

Chen Yi

b. 1953, Guangzhou

Composer

In 1977, Chen Yi was admitted to the Central Conservatory of Music, studying composition with Wu Zuqiang. In 1980 she became one of a handful of students selected from Beijing and Shanghai to study at the British composer Alexander Goehr's composition workshop in Beijing, which had a lasting impact on her music. In 1986 she became the first woman ever in China to receive a master's degree in composition, and went to the

United States to study at Columbia University with Chou Wen-chung and Mario Davidovsky, receiving her doctorate in 1993. From 1993 to 1996, Chen served as Composer-in-Residence for the Women's Philharmonic, the vocal ensemble Chanticleer, and the Aptos Creative Arts Centre. She was on the composition faculty of Peabody Conservatory, Johns Hopkins University in Baltimore, from 1996 to 1998 before she became the Cravens/Millsap/Missouri Distinguished Professor at the Conservatory of the University of Missouri–Kansas City in 1998.

Chen is recognized as one of the leading composers in the United States. Her composition is a profound integration of Chinese and Western music. Although her music always unmistakably reveals her joyful and energetic personality, it is also subtle and exquisitely eloquent. Chen is the recipient of the Charles Ives Living Award, a large grant paid over three years (2001 to 2004) from the American Academy of Arts and Letters. She has received numerous grants and commissions from prestigious organizations and major orchestras, and her music has been recorded on major labels.

JIN PING

Chen Yifei

b. 1946, Zhenhai, Zhejiang

Artist

The artist Chen Yifei has evolved from a painter into a genuine cultural entrepreneur. Chen graduated from the Shanghai Painting Academy in 1965. In the years following, he specialized in Socialist Realist oil painting. Many of the paintings he produced in the 1970s initially met with official criticism, but as an indication of their later acceptance have been included in various national collections. Chen studied at Hunter College (New York) in 1981, and held a number of one-man exhibitions in the USA in the 1980s where his works fetched high prices.

Although still painting, Chen has become active in other cultural sectors through his Yifei Group. His motion picture, *Evening Liaison*, was screened at the Cannes Film Festival (1995), where it received special recognition. In 1999, Chen launched

a clothing brand named Leyefe (or Layefe), which evolved into a trendy fashion store with more than 162 branches nationwide. A year later, he set up home furnishing outlets in Shanghai and Beijing (see **clothing industry**). He acted as manager for several successful Chinese fashion models and was the modelling coach for Zhuo Ling, Miss China 2002 (see **fashion shows and modelling**).

Chen was the brain behind, and one of the financial backers of, China's thickest fashion magazine, *Vision Magazine*, which was sponsored by *China Youth Magazine* under the Central Committee of the Communist Youth League. The first issue of the monthly, weighing two kilograms and numbering more than 400 pages, carried articles on art, fashion, cosmetics and technology. It was published in December 2001 (see **beauty magazines**).

STEFAN LANDSBERGER

Chen Zhen

b. 1955, Shanghai; d. 2000, Paris

Installation artist

Throughout his artistic career Chen Zhen was concerned with what he called 'rongchao jingyan' or 'transexperience'. This not only describes his personal experience as a Chinese artist living in France since 1986 and working internationally, but also alludes to his concept of art and method of creation. Situated in between East and West, he employed materials, signs and concepts original to the Chinese tradition – including the most recent revolutionary tradition – and to contemporary Western culture. The interplay of material and conceptual juxtapositions in his mixed media installations aims at releasing a dynamic balance, to which he referred as 'synergy'. He therefore sought to explore the correlation between technology and nature, community and individual, the body and the self, or again the material and the spiritual, aiming to propose a cure to the basic problems of mankind. One of his most compelling works, *Fifty Strokes to Each* (*Juechang*, 1998), a set of large drums made from beds and chairs resembling a traditional Chinese musical instrument, invites the audience to perform, taking place in a kind of homeopathic ritual. His late works, such as *Zen Garden* (2000) – an ensemble of five translucent inner organs, arranged in the model of a Zen garden – or *Inner Body Landscape* (2000), use the human body as metaphor. Chen's work has been exhibited at venues around the world, including exhibitions such as the First Shanghai Biennial (1996), the Second Johannesburg Bienniale (1997), the 48th Venice Bienniale (1999) and finally 'A Tribute' at the P.S.1 Contemporary Art Center in New York (2003).

Further reading

(1998) *Chen Zhen*. Montreal: Centre International d'Art Contemporain.

(2000). *Chen Zhen – In Praise of Black Magic.* GAM Galleria Civica d'Art Moderna e Contemporanea, Turin.

De Matté, Monica (1999). 'Chen Zhen'. In *d'Apertutto- Aperto Over All* (exhibition catalogue). Venezia: Edizioni La Biennale di Venezia, Marsilio, 98–9.

Uslip, Jeffrey and Zur, Rachel (eds) (2003). *Chen Zhen: A Tribute.* New York: P.S.1 Contemporary Art Center.

Yang, Alice (1998). 'Chen Zhen'. In *idem, Why Asia?* New York: New York University Press, 57–9.

MARTINA KÖPPEL-YANG

Cheng Conglin

b. 1954, Wan county, Sichuan

Oil painter

Cheng Conglin specializes in contemporary history painting. He entered the Sichuan Academy of Art in 1978 where he soon emerged as an important interpreter of emerging social change. His *1968 X month X day* (*1968 nian X yue X ri xue*, 1979) captured the absurdity of the struggle between Red Guard factions by renegotiating the conventions of the 'three prominences' (*san tuchu*): the defeated faction are given centre-stage, while the apprehension and mixed emotions of the surrounding figurants undermines the heroism of the central drama. The fanaticism of the **Cultural Revolution** is thus contained by the humanism of the observers.

The huge painting, *Summer Evening 1978 – Beside Me I Felt the Yearning of a Nation* (*1978 nian xiaye – shenpang wo gandao minzu zai kewang*, 177 cm x 415 cm, 1980), refers to the resumption of enrolment of university students by examination after the Cultural Revolution (see **Cultural Revolution (education)** and **laosanjie**). The hesitation, hopes and excitement of a generation are caught through the portrayal of hundreds of figures in different attitudes. Its composition was controversial at the time for lacking a central focus.

Cheng Conglin graduated in 1982, taught at the Sichuan Academy and continued his studies at the Central Academy. In 1984 he applied his mass portrait technique to a grim series of historical paintings about exploitation entitled *1844 China Coast Port* (*1844-nian Zhongguo yanhai kou'an*). These, however, lacked the immediacy of his earlier works. His later subject matter, though also quite sombre in tone, dealt with tranquil scenes of countryside life and life among the ethnic minorities.

See also: Scar art

Further reading

Galikowski, Maria (1998). *Art and Politics in China, 1949–1984.* Hong Kong: Chinese University Press, 193–207.

Lü, Peng and Yi, Dan (1992). *Zhongguo xiandai yishushi* [A History of Modern Art in China]. Changsha: Hunan meishu chubanshe, 34–41.

EDUARDO WELSH

Cheng Jihua

b. 1921, Hubei

Film historian, critic

Cheng Jihua is best known for his monumental book *The History of the Development of Chinese Cinema* (1963). In two volumes and over a thousand pages, Cheng provides the most comprehensive work to trace the evolution of film production and perception in China from 1896 to 1949. The extensive filmography (over 2000), for instance, stretches from the first production in 1905 to 1949 and offers detailed information on production studio and cast. Composed chronologically, the book begins with the origin and development of Chinese cinema (1896–1931), focuses on Communist leadership over the film cultural movement (1931–7), and ends with an introduction to the progressive people's cinema (1937–49).

Cheng had to write his *History* from the standpoint of Marxism, Leninism and Mao's thought – criteria considered promising in socialist China yet problematic today. As a result, film history is made subordinate to China's revolutionary history, national salvation and class struggle. Understandably, there was no alternative way to write at a time when art and literature had to serve political interests and follow the dictates of socialist discourse. Despite its appropriate political stance, however, the book failed to secure final official publication. After a trial printing of a small quantity of its first version, the project received the 'death penalty' because of the **Cultural Revolution**. Its second edition did not reach readers until 1981.

Cheng also served as chief editor for different film journals and held a professorship at the **Beijing Film Academy**. In 1983, the University of California at Los Angeles invited Cheng Jihua and his colleague Chen Mei to teach Chinese cinema. Their visit led to an academic exchange programme that enabled a number of American film scholars to go to China to offer a series of lectures on film theory to Chinese audiences.

See also: film criticism; Li Shaobai

Further reading

Cheng, Jihua (1963). *Zhongguo dianying fazhan shi* [History of the Development of Chinese Cinema], 2 vols. Beijing: Zhongguo dianying.

Hu, Ke (1998). 'Contemporary Film Theory in China'. Trans. Ted Wang, Chris Berry and Chen Mei. *Screening the Past* 3. Available at http://screeningthepast.media

Semsel, George (1999). 'Cheng Jihua and Li Shaobai, Pioneers in Chinese Film Studies: Interview II'. *Asian Cinema* 10.2 (Spring/Summer): 90–5.

Shen, Vivian (1999). 'Cheng Jihua, Pioneer in Chinese Film Studies: Interview I'. *Asian Cinema* 10.2 (Spring/Summer): 87–90.

CUI SHUQIN

Cheung, Leslie

(né Cheung Kwok Wing; Zhong Guorong)

b. 12 September 1956, Hong Kong; d. 2003

Pop singer/film actor

Leslie Cheung has enjoyed more than two decades of popularity as a singer-actor with audiences in and outside Hong Kong. Unlike his rival Alan **Tam**, with his ever-increasing commercial tone, Leslie Cheung was a pop idol who transformed himself into an artistic icon. After graduating from Leeds University, Cheung returned to Hong Kong, his place of birth, and emerged as the first runner-up at the Second Asian Song Contest. Despite joining the local television channel Rediffusion as early as 1976, Leslie was practically unknown until his first solo album *The Wind Blows On* (1981, released in 1983), catapulted him into an enduring career as one of Hong Kong's most popular singers. He was recognized as a top star after the overwhelming success of his single 'Monica' in 1984, and soon became Alan Tam's only competitor. His 1989 farewell concert resulted in an even more prolific comeback.

As an amphibious figure, he was also actively involved in film acting. From 1978, when he debuted in *Erotic Dreams of the Red Chamber* (*Honglou chun shang chun*), he acted in some sixty films. He worked with such directors as: John **Woo** in *A Better Tomorrow* (*Yingxiong bense*); Stanley **Kwan** in *Yanzhi ko* (*Rouge*); **Tsui Hark** (Xu Ke) in *A Chinese Ghost Story* (*Qiannu youhun*); **Wong Kar-wai** in *Days of Being Wild* (*A Fei zhengzhuan*, for which Cheung won 'best actor' from the Hong Kong Film

Academy in 1990) and *Happy Together* (*Chunguang zhaxie*); **Chen Kaige** in *Bawang bieji* (*Farewell My Concubine*, which made Cheung's international reputation after the movie won the Palme d'Or at Cannes in 1993); and Ronny Yu in *The Bride with White Hair* (*Baifa monü zhuan*) and *Phantom Lover* (*Yeban gesheng*). Taking advantage of his musical talent, he composed and sang the theme songs of some of these films. His directorial debut came in 2000 with *From Ashes to Ashes* (*Yanfei yanmie*). His recent films were *Sword Master* (*San shaoye de jian*) and *The Unicorn Hunt*. Other than films, he also acted in sixteen TV mini-series and three music dramas. Cheung's film roles established his public image as a sentimental romantic lover, which simultaneously contradicts and complements his feminized singing persona. Leslie eventually returned to the music world in the mid 1990s, but with his open acknowledgement of being a bisexual, his singing style – like that of *Red* (*Hong*, 1996) – turned to unconventionality, too. Yet despite moving into his forties, none of Leslie's transformations to the artistic lobby distanced him from his massive worldwide fans, who were shocked by his suicide in 2003.

See also: pop music in Hong Kong

Further reading

www.lesliecheung.com

WANG YIMAN AND SIMON SHEN

Cheung, Maggie

(née Zhang Manyu)

b. 20 September 1964, Hong Kong

Actress

Born in Hong Kong, emigrating to England with her family at eight, returning to Hong Kong and emerging as the runner-up in the 1983 Miss Hong Kong Contest, Maggie Cheung moved on to a career in the movie and TV industry. Her superb performance of a variety of characters, both

historical and fictional, in some seventy films since 1984 enables her to become the most awarded Hong Kong actress.

Starting as a 'flower vase' (*huaping*) actress, she gradually matured and began to play more sophisticated characters. Her first collaboration with Stanley **Kwan** in *Full Moon in New York* (*Renzai niuyue*, 1989) won her the Best Actress Award at the Golden Horse competition in Taiwan. Their second collaboration in *Centre Stage* (*Ruan Lingyu*, 1991), a filmic reconstruction of the life and films of the 1930s Shanghai tragic star Ruan Lingyu, won her a 1992 HK Film Award as Best Actress, an award at the 1992 Chicago International Film Festival, and a Silver Bear award at the 1992 Berlin Film Festival. Another film that has garnered multiple awards is *Comrades, Almost a Love Story* (*Tian mimi*, 1996), which deals with diasporic Chinese people. Her most recent internationally recognized film is *In the Mood for Love* (*Huayang nianhua*), directed by **Wong Kar-wai**.

Unlike Hong Kong actors such as Jackie **Chan** and **Chow Yun-fat** who underwent a clear transition from the Hong Kong to the Hollywood stage, Cheung has demonstrated a deeper range of international experience, collaborating with French director Olivier Assayas in *Irma Vep* (1996) and with Wayne Wang in *Chinese Box* (with **Gong Li**, 1997). Cheung has also continued her earlier career as model, walking the runway for Hermès during Paris Fashion Week, March 1998.

WANG YIMAN

Chi Zijian

b. 1964, Mohe, Heilongjiang

Writer

Chi Zijian began her literary career in 1983 when she was a junior at college. From the beginning, critics noted her extraordinary narrative power which renders otherwise ordinary things interesting. Whether set in the historical past or in contemporary time, her stories always give a vivid sense of place, portraying the far north with its extreme climate and its crowd of finely drawn people. More than lending her stories local colour, heavy snow, dense fog and white night, typical phenomena of the far north, often give her narrative a touch of the magical.

Some of Chi Zijian's stories are set earlier in the twentieth century. Peopled by folk dancers, bandits and those who love them, these stories are suffused with a legendary glow. 'Folk Dance' (*Yangge*) tells the story of a hugely popular dancer through the eyes of a young girl, who herself grows up to be a strong-minded woman in the course of the story. Chi Zijian's contemporary fiction is noted for its psychological incisiveness. 'Comet' (*Huixing*) tells the story of a cosmopolitan young woman travelling back to her native village in the north to watch Haley's Comet. En route, she gathers up a motley crowd of other stargazers, each with quirky life of his or her own. Chi's fiction has been translated into English, French and Japanese. Representative of her work are the novels *Under the Tree* (*Shuxia*) and *Morning Bells Ringing at Dusk* (*Chenzhong xiangche huanghun*), and the novellas *Fairytales from a Village of the North Pole* (*Beijicun tonghua*) and *Marching Toward the White Night* (*Xiangzhe baiye liuxing*).

Further reading

Chi, Zijian (1998). 'Silver Plates'. *Chinese Literature* (Winter).

HU YING

Chiao, Peggy

(neé Chiao Hsiung-ping)

b. 1953, Taipei, Taiwan

Film critic, historian, educator, producer

A tireless advocate of 'new cinemas' in Taiwan, Hong Kong and mainland China, Peggy Chiao first reached prominence in international circles for her critical work on ground-breaking Taiwanese directors such as **Hou Hsiao-hsien**, before turning to film production. Chiao studied film and television at UT Austin (1977–81), then at UCLA (1983–5). A film critic for some of the major Taiwanese newspapers – *United Daily News* (*Lien Ho Pao*), *China Times* (*Chung Kuo Shi Pao*), *China Times Express* (*Chung Shi Wan Pao*) – she has also been teaching at the Taipei National University of Arts since 1985. She wrote a number of books, including: *New Taiwan Cinema* (*Xin Taiwan dianying*, 1987) *Hong Kong New Wave* (*Xianggang dianying xinchao*, 1987) and *Aspects of New Asian Films* (*Xin Yachu dianying mianmian guanguan*, 1991).

In 1990, she established the *China Times Express* Awards for young cinema, then founded the Taiwan Film Centre in 1994, to help develop an international network for local filmmakers, and, in 1997, opened Arc Light, a production company with pan-Chinese ambitions. Among the films thus produced are: in Hong Kong, the series *A Personal Memoir from Hong Kong* (1997), Ann **Hui**'s *Qu Ri Ku Duo* and Stanley **Kwan**'s *Nian Ni Hao Xi*; in Taiwan, **Ts'ai Ming-liang**'s *The Hole* (*Dong*, 1998), Lin Chen-sheng's *Betelnut Beauty* (*Ai Ni Ai Wo*, 2001) and Yee Chih-Yen's *Blue Gate Crossing* (*Lanse damen*, 2002); and in China, Wang Xiaoshuai's *Beijing Bicycle* (*Shiqisui de danche*, 2001).

See also: cinema in Taiwan

Further reading

Chiao, Hsiung-Ping (1991). 'The Distinct Taiwanese and Hong Kong Cinemas'. In Chris Berry (ed.), *Perspectives on Chinese Cinema*. London: BFI, 141–54.

—— (1993). 'Reel Contacts Across the Taiwan Straits: A History of Separation and Reunion.' In K. Eder and D. Rossell (eds), *New Chinese Cinema*. London: National Film Theatre, 48–57.

—— (2001). 'Academic Roundtable with Peggy Chiao: Contemporary Chinese Cinema in China, Taiwan, and Hong Kong: A Collective Force in the Global Market'. Baker Institute, Rice University: Transnational China Project (online). Available at http://www.rice.edu/tnchina/index.html

BÉRÉNICE REYNAUD

children's feature film

Children's feature film in China is distinguished by the seriousness with which pressing, political and social issues are addressed, and by the dedication of key film-workers to the survival and expansion of this sector of the industry. It can be divided in six periods for convenience. Roughly these are: the 'waifs' of the 1920s; the 'seventeen years' 1949–1966, when film explored the meaning of new China; the empty years of the **Cultural Revolution** – when the only movie made in the genre was *Shining Red Star* (*Shanshan hongxin*); the new spring 1976–8, when older artists returned to the industry; and the 1979 apogee of post-Cultural Revolution creativity led by **Xie Jin** and Wang Junzheng (*The Cradle*, *A Yaolan* and *Miaomiao*), and the founding of the Children's Film Studio in 1981.

Film for children is classically traced back to Cai Chusheng's *Lost Lambs* (*Mitu de gaoyang*, 1935). This is a wrenching tale of urban poverty, and deals with the strength of children and their continual betrayal by adults. It is hardly a 'children's film' in the light entertainment genre in that it deals directly with suffering. Arguably, however, it is that quality which lends it the high status that it enjoys in film history (an argument supported by key children's film scholar Li Suyuan and tying in with a recent re-evaluation of the importance of silent film to the Chinese tradition). The next milestone is the film version of *Sanmao's Travels* (*Sanmao liulangji*, dir. Zhao Ming, 1949). Based on a newspaper cartoon strip, this film also deals with corruption and child poverty in Shanghai, but with a much more humorous touch. Sanmao (Three Hairs), an urchin with three hairs on his head and a bulbous nose, is not far off from a puppet animation, and bridges the styles of storytelling later developed in animation and latterly in children's television. Lesser versions of the Sanmao stories were made on film and for television, but the verve of the original has not been surpassed. In the post Liberation period, children's feature films were also 'family films', with an emphasis on children as rural heroes (*Good Children*/*Hao haizi*, 1959; *Red Children*/*Hong haizi*, 1958) and occasionally heroines (*Liu Hulan*, 1950), children as (somewhat psychopathic) young soldiers, and children as Party messengers (*Chicken Feather Letter*/*Jimaoxin*, 1954; *Little Soldier*

Zhang Ga/*Xiaobing Zhang Ga*, 1963). Films also tackled the political education of young people in the school system, making links between soldierly duty and the responsibility of young pioneers to live and study within the moral remit of the young People's Republic. A typical story might bring together a soldier and young school students to provide mutual inspiration one for the other (*Flowers of the Motherland*/*Zuguo de hua'rduo*, 1955). More recently the school system has been implicitly criticized. *Childhood in Ruijin* (*Tongnian zai Ruijin*, 1989) tells of a group of children whose hopes of a full education are systematically crushed by the requirements of work at home, rising costs and rural poverty. Although it was set as a period piece, Chinese educational commentators and film workers recognized that the film was dealing with current issues. In this way children's feature films continue to be indicative of the political world. There is a strong drive towards entertainment media for children, but the relationship between national concerns and the child audience is still apparent in texts of the late twentieth century.

See also: Peng Xiaolian

Further reading

Donald. S. H. (2002). 'Children's Day: The Fashionable Performance of Modern Citizenship in China'. In Wendy Parkins (ed.): *Fashioning the Body Politic*. Oxford: Berg, 205–16.

Farquhar, Mary (1999). *Children's Literature in China*. Armonk, NY: M. E. Sharpe.

Xiao, Yu (2002). 'Hai ertong bu ertong le?' [To be a child, or not?]. *Sanlian shenghuo zhoukan* 6–7.

Zheng, Zhenqin (1999). 'Buduan chengzhang de xinshiqi ertong dianying chuangzuo' [The Growth of Contemporary Children's Film]. *Dangdai dianying* 5.

STEPHANIE HEMELRYK DONALD

children's literature

Children's literature is called 'literature for children and adolescents' (*shaonian ertong wenxue*). Another term, which encompasses a wider range of genres, is 'literature and art for children and adolescents' (*shaonian ertong wenyi*), but this was more commonly used in the mainland in the Maoist period. Officially, children's literature encompasses prose, fiction, film, plays, poems and picture books and animation for the young.

Children's literature is an industry. It caters to children between three and fifteen years, that is from kindergarten to lower middle school. It has a vast audience, an established range of genres from songs to science fiction, and a complex infrastructure in all Chinese-speaking countries. The industry includes writers, publishing houses, distribution networks, television, libraries and prizes. Rhetorically at least, the primary function of this industry is educational, but modern mass media is reshaping children's literature around commercial entertainment and consumer choice. The commercial aspect of children's literature is a new feature of the contemporary field in the People's Republic of China but a continuing feature in the children's literature of Taiwan, Hong Kong and Singapore.

Contemporary children's literature is made up of three strands: a living Confucian tradition, a modern canon that is institutionalized in the education system, and new works, forms and formats.

Confucian children's literature is almost a thousand years old, beginning with one of the world's great children's books: *The Three Character Classic* (*Sanzijing*, AD 1242). Together with *The One Hundred Family Names* (*Baijiaxing*), *The Thousand Character Classic* (*Qianziwen*) and *The Three Hundred Thousand* (*Sanbaiqian*) were the foundation of the Confucian education system. Traditionally, children also read from China's rich popular literature. Such works, often abridged and rewritten, remain a part of children's literature, especially in Taiwan and other Chinese-speaking countries that emphasize Confucian values.

There is also a modern canon that varies across the Chinese-speaking world. Chinese reformers created a vernacular children's literature on Western models in the May Fourth period. Much of this work was banned in the People's Republic of China during the Cultural Revolution. After 1979, the history of children's literature was reassessed and a canon of major works established as part of the PRC's contemporary

children's literature, including its revolutionary heritage. Work by such luminaries as Ye Shengtao (fairytales), Bing Xin (prose) and Wan Laiming (animations such as *Monkey Creates Havoc in Heaven* (*Sun Wukong danao tiangong*) are recognized as classics of children's literature today.

Finally, there is new work. Some involves the return or revitalization of established genres, such as science fiction on the mainland in the post-Mao period. Some is in new formats, such as television and the Internet, and part of a transnational children's literature across Chinese-speaking regions. Finally, some work is in translation making Chinese children's literature part of a global field. Chinese children watch Disney cartoons and, in the new millennium, they demand more of J. K. Rowling's *Harry Potter* series in translation, surpassing sales of other Western translations of children's literature. With China's accession to the World Trade Organization, more global fare will become part of the contemporary scene.

See also: animation; children's feature film; serial picture books

Further reading

Farquhar, Mary Ann (1999). *Children's Literature in China*. New York: M. E. Sharpe.

MARY FARQUHAR

Children's Palace

(Shaoniangong)

Also called the Youth Palace (Qingshaoniangong) in some places, the Children's Palace is an after-school educational institution implemented by the PRC government to enhance moral education and extracurricular activities for primary and secondary school students. A non-profit organization, the operation of the Children's Palace is under the supervision of the local Communist Youth League committee or, in some cases, under the Bureau of Education. The Children's Palace was first established in the capital city and a few big cities in the mid 1950s, when most of the elementary schools had to divide the students into morning and afternoon classes to meet the rapid increase in enrolments. The Children's Palace played an instrumental role in providing the students with educational activities during the long out-of-school hours. In the 1960s, many provincial capitals established the Children's Palace, but its operation was virtually stopped during the **Cultural Revolution**. The Children's Palace flourished again in the 1980s after the fall of the Gang of Four. By the end of the 1990s, it was found in most major cities of the PRC, and some cities had more than one in different districts.

The Children's Palace offers a rich array of enrichment programmes, such as science, music, performing and visual arts, creative writing, computer technology and sports. It also provides special training programmes for the talented. Many young talents trained there later became the nation's leading artists, athletes and specialists in different fields. The Children's Palace also takes the role of coordinating convocations and contests among the schools in the area.

QIU PEIPEI

children's television

Children's television should properly be the fastest growing sector of the television market in China. There are over 350 million people under the age of sixteen in China today, many of whom have access to a television. Children's broadcasting is reportedly a key issue for **CCTV (Chinese Central Television)**, which needs to woo and retain an audience as the macro-competition steps up from regional conglomerates – in particular Shanghai Oriental Pearl and Star (Phoenix). However, whilst there are timeslots and quotas (two to eight hours per day plus ten minutes of 'new' domestic animation) in operation for kids' shows, CCTV 7 broadcasts dedicated children's programming on the same channel as military extravaganzas and sport. This miscellany develops a confused sense of targeted programming, and certainly does not speak to middle school aspirations, nor to the possibilities of using children's

TV in imaginative forays into rural issues, urban education stresses and exciting dramas. Rather, there is an assortment of game shows, short documentaries, storytelling features and cartoons, which serve a junior school very adequately, but which leave the middle school years without much to go on. Recent research describes the channel as 'a Pure Land full of knowledge, wisdom, lofty character, and sentiments'. It does not explain, however, where the over-tens will go to continue their spiritual education once they tire of *Big Pinwheel* (a magazine format rather like *Saturday Disney*). In this, Chinese children's TV is similar to other TV regimes the world over. There are real difficulties facing Chinese broadcasters, however. Children's programming is expensive, especially as the standard of (a) animated content and (b) interactive content relies on strong recent experience in the relative creative fields and also a dynamic response to American and Japanese products that are susceptible to localization and are highly popular with young audiences. Shanghai and Jiangsu TV have taken the lead here with co-productions, but CCTV also has created transborder shows (again for younger viewers) such as the Australian/Chinese co-production *Magic Mountain*. Meanwhile, advertising is not highly regulated so there can supposedly be any number of ads inserted into children's programmes to make them more profitable (CCTV carries ads despite being the main public broadcaster and free-to-air service in China). In practice, though, and probably because of the emphasis on younger children, there is little will to sponsor or buy space in these slots. On the positive side, children's TV does produce success stories. There are well-known presenters who now work to promote films for children through their popularity; there are also merchandizing ventures capitalizing on TV shows, and therefore deepening the local industry (*Blue Cat/Lanmao* and *Journey to the West/Xiyouji* are examples from 2000–2). These consumerist ventures complement the more worthy impulses of the medium and reach out to the urban child elites (but not to the poorer rural children, for whom merchandizing is not an option). Children's TV in China is at a point of transition. It needs to take on the interactive, high production values that are informing shows worldwide, but avoid the junk food broadcasting that comes along as quota fodder in many media systems.

Further reading

Research Team of the Centre for Documentation and Information (CASS) (2000). 'An Assessment of Children's TV Programmes in the People's Republic of China'. In A. Goonasekera, C. Z. Huang, L. Eashwer, B. Guntarto, S. Bairaj-Ambigapathy, J. Dhungana, A. Lin, A. Chung and V. T. M. Hanh (eds), *Growing up with TV: Asian Children's Experience*. AMIC: Singapore, 12–47.

Huang, Yufu, Liu, Ni and Shi, Ying (2001). 'Portrayal of Children in the News: A Case Study of China'. In A. Goonasekera (ed.), *Children in the News: Reporting of Children's Issues in Television and the Press in Asia*. AMIC: Singapore.

STEPHANIE HEMELRYK DONALD

China Art Gallery

(Zhongguo meishuguan)

The China Art Gallery was founded in 1959. The architectural design incorporates both traditional and modern elements. It functions at state level as the primary official exhibition space for modern art and it is the one of the largest art galleries in China with fourteen exhibition halls covering a surface of 6,000 square metres. Exhibitions and publications of Chinese art sponsored by the China Art Gallery concentrate on modern and contemporary works in a wide range of styles. Over a hundred exhibitions of foreign modern art have been organized, while exhibitions based on works from the Gallery's own collection are frequently shown abroad, one of the most notable being the Guggenheim show, 'A Century in Crisis' (1998).

During its early years the focus was primarily on revolutionary art and positive expressions of nationalism continue to dominate its exhibitions.

The number of exhibitions displaying both traditional and modern styles of Chinese art as well as work by foreign artists has increased steadily since the 1980s. Despite the official nature of the gallery – which remains the site of display of the final, prize-winning selection of the national exhibitions – many works have been shown there that have stretched the range of official acceptability. While in 1979 for the first avant-garde art exhibition organized by the **Stars** (*Xingxing huapai*) the artists hung their works on the railings outside the gallery in protest at their exclusion from official exhibition spaces, in 1980 they were allowed to show inside the gallery for their second show. The landmark event breaking for the first and last time the gallery's limits of acceptability came with the **China Avant-Garde** exhibition of 1989. The 7th National Art Exhibition that followed the same year marked a radical return to conservatism that has been slow to change. With the radical reduction in government funding for the arts in the late 1990s, moreover, the gallery has been run along commercial lines, hosting for the most part paid exhibitions of often questionable artistic quality.

Further reading

Wu, Hung (2000). *Exhibiting Experimental Art in China*. Chicago: The Smart Museum of Art, 26–9.

MORGAN PERKINS

China Avant-Garde

Art exhibition

The 'China Avant-Garde Exhibition' took place in the **China Art Gallery** in Beijing on 5–19 February 1989, two months before the beginning of the Tiananmen Square Student Democratic Movement, and four months before the governmental shut-down of the movement on 4 June 1989.

The first call for organizing a nationwide avant-garde exhibition was initiated by **Gao Minglu** in the conference entitled 'Zhuhai '85 New Wave Large-Scale Slides Exhibition' (Zhuhai bawu meishu sichao daxing huandengzhan) curated by Gao Minglu, 15–19 August 1986. Representatives from avant-garde groups and critics from all over China attended the event. The exhibition was originally scheduled to take place in the National Agricultural Museum in Beijing in July 1987. Three months before the opening, the officials from the Chinese Art Association ordered the exhibition's organizer Gao Minglu to cease preparatory work because of the political **Campaign against Bourgeois Liberalization**. The result was the abortion of the exhibition, although most of the preparatory work had already been completed.

When the political situation eased in the early 1988, Gao Minglu started again to organize the exhibition and many artists and critics joined him. The organizational committee was founded in Beijing on 8 October 1988. Gao Minglu was elected as the head, or the chief curator of the committee. The committee consisted of fourteen members among active scholars and critics, including **Gan Yang**, Zhang Yaojun, **Liu Dong**, Liu Xiaochun, Zhang Zuying, **Li Xianting**, Tang Qingnian, Yang Lihua, Zhouyan, Fan Dian, Wang Mingxian, Kong Changan and **Fei Dawei**.

Though there were in total six open-minded official units willing to sponsor the exhibition, they mostly offered the formal support without which the National Art Gallery would not allow the exhibition to be held in the gallery. All the funds for the exhibition were raised by the organizer and the artists themselves.

The exhibition opened in the National Art Gallery in Beijing on 5 February 1989, on the eve of Chinese New Year. The works in the exhibition were distributed over six galleries that occupied three floors, and included 297 pieces in the various media of painting, sculpture, photography, video and installations. All the classic Chinese avant-garde artworks of the 1980s, such as **Xu Bing**'s *The Book from the Sky*, **Wang Guangyi**'s *Mao Zedong No. 1*, **Huang Yongping**'s *History of Chinese Painting* and *Concise History of Western Painting in Washing Machine for Two Minutes*, were displayed in the exhibition.

Three hours after the opening, the exhibition was shut down due to several provocative performance works, particularly the two gun-shots performance by **Xiao Lu** and Tang Song at their installation work *Dialogue*. After the reopening of the show in three days, the exhibition was forced to close again because of an anonymous letter threatening to place three bombs in the China Art Gallery unless the exhibition was shut down. As a result, the China Art Gallery punished the Organizational Committee with a fine of 2,000 yuan. Some conservative critics criticized the exhibition as 'bourgeois liberalism'. Particularly after the 4 June Tiananmen Square Event, a few critics even named the exhibition a 'small Tiananmen Square'.

Further reading

(1988) 'Zhongguo xiandai yishuzhan chouzhan tonggao, diyihao' [Announcement of the organization of 'China Avant-Garde)'] *Zhongguo meishubao* 44 (31 October), 1.

Gao, Minglu (1999). 'Fengkuang de yijiubajiu – zhongguo xiandai yishuzhan shimo' [1989 – A Crazy Year: A Description of the Beginning and End of the 'China Avant-Garde' Exhibition] *Qingxiang* [Tendency] 12: 43–76.

Lü, Peng and Yi, Dan (1992). *Zhongguo xiandai yishushi* [A History of Modern Art in China]. Changsha: Hunan meishu chubanshe, 325–53.

Tyson, Ann Scott (1989). 'Avant-Garde Bursts onto Chinese Art Scene – Action Art Symbolizes Artist Determination to Brashly Take Advantage of Eased State Censorship'. *The Christian Science Monitor* (7 February), 6.

Wu, Hung (2000). *Exhibiting Experimental Art in China*. Chicago: David and Alfred Smart Museum of Art/University of Chicago, 11–23.

Zhou, Yan (1989). 'Zhongguo xiandai yishuzhan de dansheng' [The Birth of the 'China

Avant-Garde' Exhibition]. *Beijing qingnianbao* (10 February).

GAO MINGLU

China Christian Council

(Zhongguo jidujiao xiehui)

The China Christian Council (CCC) is the officially authorized representative organization for China's Protestant population. Established in 1980, the CCC was designed to work alongside the **Three-Self Patriotic Movement (TSPM)**, purportedly to tend to the Church's internal and ecclesiastical affairs as opposed to the TSPM's explicitly political function of serving as a 'bridge' between the CCP and China's Protestants. Headquartered in Shanghai, the CCC maintains a nationwide representative system, but its national agenda is set by a small group of elites who comprise its Executive Committee and Standing Committee. The Executive Committee is made up of the CCC's President, eight Vice-Presidents and a General Secretary, who also preside over the forty-two-member Standing Committee. Its top leaders have all been active in the TSPM since the early 1950s, most notably former CCP Presidents **Ding Guangxun** (currently Honorary President) and Han Wenzao (currently Director of the CCC Advisory Committee), and the current President Cao Shengjie. The committees oversee a hierarchically ordered organizational structure that extends to the district/municipal level. At lower levels, the CCC and the TSPM share the same officials, and the two organizations are commonly identified together as the 'two committees' (*lianghui*).

Together with the TSPM, the CCC supervises the country's eighteen Protestant theological schools and its 12,000 registered churches, and manages several printing presses, which print Bibles, hymnals and other Christian literature and publish the journal **Tianfeng** [Heavenly Wind]. In 1996, the joint CCC/TSPM Standing Committee issued a 'Church Order', which aimed at establishing organizational, doctrinal and ritual boundaries for China's entire Protestant population. The China Christian Council is a member church of the World Council of Churches.

Further reading

(n.d.) *About the China Christian Council*. Available at http://www.amityfoundation.org/ANS/AboutCCC.htm

(28 December 1996) 'Zhongguo jidujiao jiaohui guizhang' (Church Order for Chinese Protestant Christian Churches) *Tianfeng* 2 (1997). Reprinted in *Chinese Law and Government* 33: 6 (2000): 43–51.

JASON KINDOPP

China dolls

One fascinating way in which transnational images of both Chinese and Western fashion trends and bodily dictates circulate is through toys, and specifically dolls. As Inderpal Grewal has shown, the links of the doll-market to the fashion industry and modelling world are complex and problematic. Doll-designers market their products in response to both global and local trends, and in turn the response of consumers of this commodity, from little girls to their parents, is informed by and informs global trends and bodily and clothes fashion.

The first doll-icon to 'go Chinese' could not be anyone but Barbie, from Mattel Inc. Barbie is the reigning global and transnational queen of dolls. Barbie dolls and accessories take in about $1.5 billion a year worldwide and account for about 30 per cent of Mattel's sales. It was in 1981 that Mattel issued the Oriental (Hong Kong) Barbie with the 'the new oriental head mould' and a Cheongsam dress. In 1993 Mattel released Chinese Barbie in a two-piece cherry-blossom dress with long black hair. In 1998 Fantasy Goddess of Asia Barbie, holding a fan, made her debut, along with an 1998 exclusive Barbie called Golden Qi-Pao Barbie, designed to commemorate the first anniversary of the British hand-over of Hong Kong to the Chinese. A Qing dynasty princess and a doll in 'China chic' **Shanghai Tang**-style clothing are planned, but apart from the costumes and dark hair, the dolls are meant to look like the original Barbie.

The Chineseness of the transnational Barbie is only skin- and clothes-deep. In this sense, at least at a first glance, Barbie's global 'queendom' is being challenged by Yue-Sai Wa Wa, the doll-child of Yue-Sai Kan. Recently voted in a national poll in China as one of the most influential women in the last twenty years, Emmy-award winner Yue-Sai Kan is the founder of Yue-Sai Kan Cosmetics, China's leading cosmetics company, as well as the bestselling author of, among other works, *Etiquette for the Modern Chinese*. Yue-Sai Kan launched the Yue-Sai Wa Wa doll line in order to 'serve as a role model for girls everywhere and help merge Eastern and Western cultures'. Yue-Sai is the name of the character, from the doll's creator, and *wa wa* is a way to say 'doll' in Chinese. In the intention of her designer, this doll 'is an Asian role model designed with shiny black hair, almond-shaped eyes, and porcelain skin tone'. She is also 'an Asian-American girl, who studies hard in school, respects her parents, and is kind and generous to her friends, and was designed to enrich the lives of children around the world'. Each doll is packaged with a sophisticated wardrobe, designed to reflect both Eastern and Western fashion. So Yue-Sai Wa Wa can also be the 'Panda Protector', who comes with a backpack full of polar-tech gear and her own panda bear to tend to, or the fashionable Shanghai girl, dressed up in 'silken Kung-fu pink pyjamas'. Though she says that she created the doll in response to the fact that there were no 'Chinese dolls', only blue-eyed blondes, Kan also admitted that she learned from Barbie that the doll itself had to be curvaceous. Kan said that she needed to create an exaggerated body for Yue-Sai Wa Wa, with Barbie-like long legs and expansive breasts, in order for the clothes to fit well. 'Short legs and a small chest just didn't work,' Kan said. In the end, even Yue-Sai Wa Wa has to bow to the standards of fashion and bodily beauty set by Barbie and the Western capitalist market.

Further reading

Grewal, Inderpal (1999). 'Travelling Barbie. Indian Transnationality and New Consumer Subjects'. *positions, east asia cultures critique* 7.3 (Winter).
www.yuesaiwawa.com

PAOLA ZAMPERINI

China Dream

[Zhongguo meng, 1987]

Spoken drama (Huaju)

Penned in both English and Chinese by playwright couple Sun Huizhu (William Sun) and Fei Chunfang (Faye Fei) and performed in separate productions in Shanghai and New York, *China Dream* (*Zhongguo meng*) was a ground-breaking production when it premiered in Shanghai in 1987. The Chinese production ran through 1989 and toured Beijing and other Chinese cities, as well as Singapore. The American version of the play was staged at the Henry Street Theatre in 1987. The play was also translated and produced in Tokyo. Its main contribution is its attempt, both in the playwrights' vision and the approach of the three directors in Shanghai (**Huang Zuolin**, **Hu Xuehua**, Chen Tijiang), to realize Huang Zuolin's theatrical theory of *xieyi* on stage. Its staging calls for a bare set and performance elements borrowed from Chinese **Xiqu** (sung-drama/opera). The play is intercultural in both form and content, influenced by experiences and aesthetics encountered by its authors when they moved to the USA in 1984 and 1985. The story (told through eight temporally alinear 'episodes' that occur in various locations) centres on Mingming, a Chinese actress who opens a restaurant in the USA, and her American boyfriend John Hodges, a lawyer with a PhD in Chinese philosophy. The actor who plays John also plays several other male roles, including another American suitor, Mingming's grandfather and her lost love back in China.

Further reading

Conceison, Claire (1999). 'Between Orient and Occident: The Intercultural Spoken Other in *China Dream*'. *Theatre InSight* 1: 14–26.
Entell, Bettina (1994). '*China Dream*: A Chinese Spoken Drama'. *Asian Theatre Journal* 2: 242–59.
Sun, Huizhu (1999). 'Aesthetics of Stanislavsky, Brecht, and Mei Lanfang'. In Faye Chunfang Fei (ed./trans.), *Chinese Theories of Theater and Performance from Confucius to the Present*. Ann Arbor: University of Michigan Press, 170–8.

CLAIRE CONCEISON

China Federation of Literary and Arts Circles

(Zhongguo wenxue yishujie lianhehui)

Founded in 1949, the China Federation of Literary and Art Circles (CFLAC; Zhongguo wenlian, for short; www.cflac.org.cn) is a national network with forty-nine regional branches (e.g. Shanghai Federation of Literary and Arts Circles; Shanghai wenlian, for short) and more than two million registered members. The CFLAC is composed of twelve member associations in literature, film, drama, fine arts, music, folk-art forms (including **quyi**), dance, photography, calligraphy, folk art and literature (*minjian wenyi*), acrobatics and TV art (see **Xiqu on television**). Among these associations, the Chinese Writers' Association (CWA), which also has thirty-nine local associations, is the largest group. Collaboration enables the CFLAC to conduct many large-scale activities, including national conferences and forums, art exhibitions and international exchanges. Though characterized as a non-governmental organization or 'people's group' (*renmin tuanti*), its major associations, like the CWA, are government organizations. In fact, the CFLAC is treated as a government organization under the direct supervision of the CCP. The CFLAC runs over forty literary and arts publications (see **literary periodicals**), including newspapers, and also owns businesses such as the CFLAC Press (*Zhongguo wenlian chubanshe*), multi-media presses, travel agencies and hostels. These businesses generate revenue in addition to the state allocation and membership dues.

HELEN XIAOYAN WU

China National Symphony Orchestra

(Zhongguo guojia jiaoxiang yuetuan)

The China National Symphony Orchestra's predecessor, the Central Philharmonic Orchestra (Zhongyang jiaoxiang yuetuan), played a major role in the cultural life of post-1949 China until the 1980s, when other Beijing and regional orchestras rivalled its pre-eminence. The Central Philharmonic Society of China was founded in 1956 in Beijing, when the Orchestra and the chorus were to serve the role of national and international cultural ambassadors. New Chinese orchestral works were specifically written for and by members of the Central Philharmonic Orchestra to incorporate Chinese elements into a Western idiom. Such works have remained popular among Chinese audiences, and have been recorded extensively. For example, the symphonic poem *Lady Martial* (*Mu Guiying*, 1959) was written by four musicians of the Central Philharmonic Orchestra, proclaimed as the first symphonic composition derived from tunes from Beijing opera and incorporating Chinese instruments. Similarly, during the Cultural Revolution, the *Yellow River Piano Concerto* was composed by committee.

Renamed and restructured as the China National Symphony Orchestra in 2000, the Orchestra continues its tradition in national and international performing and recording. Between 2000 and 2002, a succession of internationally established Chinese conductors, including Chen Zuohuang and Tang Muhai, have served as its music director. The Orchestra has also hired professional musicians from abroad to strengthen certain instrumental sections. Apart from its regular orchestral season, the China National Symphony Orchestra has specialized in recording orchestral soundtracks for many of China's 'Fifth Generation' filmmakers, among them **Chen Kaige** (see **Fifth Generation (film directors)**). The composer **Zhao Jiping** also has a long-standing working relationship with the Orchestra.

JOANNA C. LEE

China People's University

(Zhongguo renmin daxue)

Among China's top-notch universities, the People's University is known for its close affiliation with the Communist Party and government. The name of the university well indicates this political connection. The university traces its origins to the Shanbei College founded in Yan'an in 1937 and some other revolutionary universities and colleges created by the Chinese Communist Party in northern China before 1949. The school was officially founded in the western suburbs of Beijing in 1950, and it is said to be the first formal university created by the newly proclaimed People's Republic. Two senior Communist revolutionaries, Cheng Fangwu and Wu Yuzhang, served as its first and second presidents, respectively. In the 1950s, the university led the nation in importing curriculum from the Soviet Union. Its graduates have been favoured by the Party and government, and many of them have become high- and middle-ranking Party or government officials.

The curriculum of the university, which emphasizes the social sciences, humanities and political education, reflects its special relationship with the Party. The university is well known for its programmes in the history of the Chinese Communist Party, Marxist philosophy and theory, history of the Qing dynasty, and so forth. In 1977, the then paramount Party leader Deng Xiaoping reiterated the mission of the university as training specialists in finance and economic management, and Marxist theory. Since then, the university has developed its strength in economics and management, legal studies and other areas. The university does not offer programmes in the natural sciences, which helps keep its size relatively small.

HAN XIAORONG

China Philharmonic Orchestra

(Zhongguo aiyue yuetuan)

A national 120-member full-time professional orchestra established in May 2000, the China Philharmonic Orchestra was founded on the basis of the former China Broadcasting Symphony Orchestra. Yu Long, a native of China trained in Germany, is the China Philharmonic Orchestra's founding artistic director and has been principal conductor since its inception.

Modelled after major international orchestras, the China Philharmonic Orchestra has a forward-thinking philosophy in repertoire and programming, both in its annual season and as

orchestra-in-residence at the annual Beijing Music Festival. At the 2001 Festival, the China Philharmonic performed the world premiere of Philip Glass's *Cello Concerto* as well as the Chinese premiere of **Tan Dun**'s *Crouching Tiger Concerto*. The China Philharmonic Orchestra also has extended new commissions to such figures as Krzysztof Penderecki (who also serves as the Orchestra's principal guest conductor). In the Beijing Music Festival 2002, the China Philharmonic performed a complete new music programme by **Chen Qigang**, part of its ongoing commitment to Chinese **New Music**.

The Orchestra's annual season includes works from the Western orchestral canon (e.g. Beethoven, Berlioz, Brahms, Mahler), Chinese symphonic favourites (works from the 1930s on) and New Music. It has toured extensively nationally and internationally since its founding, having visited Taiwan in September 2001 and Puerto Rico's Casals Festival in June 2002. In 2001 and 2002, the Orchestra released two CDs for Deutsche Grammophone. While the first is devoted to German repertoire (Wagner's Overture to *Tannhäuser* and Brahms's *Piano Quartet in G minor* as orchestrated by Arnold Schoenberg), the second featured Chinese orchestral favourites.

JOANNA C. LEE

China's New Art, Post-89 (Hong Kong, 1993) and China Avant-Garde (Berlin, 1993)

Art exhibitions

'China's New Art, Post-1989', curated by **Chang Tsong-zung** and **Li Xianting** and co-presented by the Hong Kong Arts Centre, the Hong Kong City Hall and the Hong Kong Arts Festival Society in February 1993, was the first major survey exhibition of Chinese avant-garde art to take place outside of mainland China. It was originally conceived four years earlier when Chang met Li at the Beijing **China Avant-Garde** exhibition, but historical circumstances postponed its opening to 1993. Organized by Hanart T Z

Gallery, the exhibition sought to sum up the cultural sensibilities emblematic of the avant-garde in the 1990s, contrasting the more exhilarating but less focused explorations of the 1980s with works done in the intervening years between 1989 and 1991 in the post-Tiananmen era. Underscoring the current of malaise, disillusionment and cynicism that had followed the New Wave movement of the mid 1980s, it emphasized art as a force that developed creative responses to sociocultural situations.

The exhibition adopted Li's original terms **Political Pop** (*zhengzhi popu*) and **Cynical Realism** (*Popi*) and introduced four other categorical distinctions – 'Wounded Romantic Spirit' (**Ding Fang**, Xia Xiaowan, Zhang Xiaogang); 'Emotional Bondage' (**Zhang Peili**, **Cai Jin**); 'Endgame Art' (**Gu Wenda**, **Xu Bing**); and 'New Abstract Art' (Shang Yang, Wang Chuan, Liu Ming, **Ding Yi**) – that were principally proposed by Chang and finalized in curatorial discussions. It featured fifty-one artists and some 200 works including paintings, mixed media installations and sculptures, with examples of Political Pop and Cynical Realism dominating and attracting instant attention abroad.

This highly successful exhibition subsequently travelled for five years, first in a reduced form and with a new title, 'Mao Goes Pop', to the Museum of Contemporary Art, Sydney, Australia, and the Melbourne Arts Festival. From 1994 to 1997, with the original title restored, a reduced exhibition travelled to the Vancouver Art Gallery, Canada, and five venues in the USA, organized by the American Federation of Art in New York.

'China Avant-Garde', a similar retrospective exhibition organized by **Hans van Djik**, Jochen Noth and Andreas Schmid for the Haus der Kulturen der Welt in Berlin (January 1993), brought the existence of Chinese avant-garde art to the attention of European audiences. Consisting of cinema, music, theatre, poetry and visual arts (sixteen avant-garde artists were featured), this exhibition attempted to relate Chinese experimental art since the late 1970s to other avant-garde movements in contemporary Chinese culture. It subsequently toured Rotterdam and Odense, and was reshaped to focus more on installation art for the Museum of Modern Art in Oxford.

Both 'China's New Art, Post-1989' and 'China Avant-Garde' were pivotal in creating public awareness of Chinese experimental art and helped its post-1989 revival. They also created immediate discourses exposing the prevalent tendency of Western institutions to stress the dissident aspect of such art. The circulation of substantial, multi-authored catalogues further enhanced the reach and reading of both these exhibitions.

See also: art exhibitions (experimental, 1980s)

Further reading

Doran, Valerie, C. (ed.) (1993). *China's New Art, Post-1989, with a Retrospective from 1979 to 1989*. (exhibition catalogue). Hong Kong: Hanart T Z Gallery. (Reprinted in 2001 by Asia Art Archive, Hong Kong).

Noth, Jochen, Pöhlmann, Wolfger and Reschke, Kai (eds) (1994). *China Avant-Garde: Counter-Currents in Art and Culture*. (exhibition catalogue). Berlin and Hong Kong: Haus der Kulturen der Welt and Oxford University Press.

ALICE MING WAI JIM

Chinese Academy of Sciences

(Zhongguo kexueyuan)

The Chinese Academy of Sciences (CAS), China's supreme institution of science and technology, grew out of the former Central Academy and Beiping Academy in November 1949. CAS has over 650 academicians at home and abroad. The General Congress of Academicians serves as its top decision-making body, with the Presidium of the Academic Divisions as its standing agent, and the CAS President as its executive chair. The Academic Divisions – Mathematics and Physics, Chemistry, Biology, Earth Science, and Technological Sciences – were formed on 1 June 1955, and function as the leading academic bodies. In 1984, the State Council made them the nation's highest advisory bodies for science and technology.

In 1987, CAS initiated the concept of 'One Academy, Two Operational Mechanisms', namely organizing the main forces to serve national economic and social development, while retaining crack teams for basic research and high-tech innovation. One hundred and seventeen laboratories have been created. Their numerous achievements include a heavy ion accelerator, a 2.16m optical telescope, and the discovery of fauna that is 580 million years old. CAS also collaborates with fifteen provinces and cities on economic and technology development projects and has exchange and cooperative programmes with over sixty countries and regions in the world.

Since 1978, CAS has established graduate schools, with 431 master's degree and 276 doctoral degree programmes, graduating about 12,000 students each year. CAS publishes over a thousand books and 290 periodicals annually, in addition to several hundred electronic publications. Of the more than 2,000 faculty members (most affiliated with the University of Sciences and Technology of China), 250 occupy leading roles in international organizations. CAS has also invited over 140 foreign experts as visiting professors.

HU MINGRONG

Chinese Academy of Social Sciences

(Zhongguo shehui kexueyuan)

The Chinese Academy of Social Sciences (CASS) was founded in 1977 in Beijing and grew out of the Department of Philosophy and Social Sciences of the **Chinese Academy of Sciences** (Zhongguo kexueyuan zhexue shehui kexue xuebu). CASS is the nation's highest academic research organization in the social sciences and humanities, and is administered and sponsored by the government. From 1977 to 2002, CASS expanded from the fourteen research institutes within the former Department of Philosophy and Social Sciences to thirty-one institutes and more than fifty research centres. As of May 2001, there were 3,767 staff members, of whom 2,975 were professional researchers. CASS's library, or the Centre for Documentation and Information, has China's largest collection in the humanities and social sciences, consisting of some 5,500,000 volumes, including a considerable number of rare books. The collection increases by over 100,000 volumes each year. CASS established a Graduate School in 1978, which offers doctoral and master's degrees in the humanities and social sciences. Directly affiliated with CASS are three publishing agencies: China Social Science Publishing House, Editorial Office of Social Sciences in China, and the Social Sciences Documentation Publishing House.

CASS plays an instrumental role in the theoretical, and many of its research results are taken into consideration in the formation of government policy. It carries out research projects sponsored by the National Social Sciences Fund and actively conducts research projects assigned by the Central Committee of the CCP and by government departments.

QIU PEIPEI

chinese-art.com

The site at http://www.chinese-art.com (officially titled *Chinese Type Contemporary Art Magazine*) is a non-profit bimonthly online magazine initiated and managed by Robert Bernell (Luobote Bonaou), an American resident in Beijing. Launched in December 1997, this web portal is subdivided into traditional and contemporary Chinese art and designed to provide collectors, historians, curators, dealers and critics outside of China with English documentation on some of the art making history in China. The site includes a free monthly e-bulletin with over 4,000 subscribers worldwide. Each issue has commissioned a guest editor, among them such notable curators, art historians and art critics as Wu Hung, Hou Hanru, Francesca Dal Lago and Wu Meichun. In the last five years, the in-depth and highly professional information provided over the Internet by chinese-art.com, with 150 essays, reviews and articles and over 10,000 images related to contemporary Chinese art, has fuelled the growing international interest in the field. Published by New Art Media Limited (founded by Bernell), chinese-art.com is supported by galleries in New York, Paris, London, Hong Kong, Beijing and Shanghai. In 2000, New Art Media Limited began to publish print compilations of articles, essays and other text materials from the website from 1998 to 1999 (John Clark (ed.), *Chinese Art at the End of the Millennium*) and 2000 (Wu Hong (ed.), *Chinese Art at the Crossroads*).

In 2002, Bernell started Time Zone 8 Limited, a physical book publishing company and a monthly e-newsletter, *What's On*, with a focus on contemporary art, design, photography, architecture and urban culture in Asia. Maintaining an arm's length approach, Bernell continues to research, compile, commission and translate materials related to contemporary Chinese art for chinese-art.com and various book publications.

ALICE MING WAI JIM

Chinese as a foreign language

The term *Duiwai Hanyü jiaoxue* (*Huayüwen jiaoxue* in Taiwan) may be translated as 'teaching Chinese to foreigners' or 'teaching Chinese as a foreign language' (TCFL). The field has developed rapidly since reform and China's opening to the outside world. Beijing Language University (Beijing yüyan daxue, or Beiyü for short; formerly known as Beijing Language and Culture University from 1996 to 2002 and Beijing Language Institute from 1964 to 1996) leads the country in teaching Chinese to **foreign students**, in training teachers in TCFL, and in promoting the **HSK** (Chinese Proficiency Test) designed for foreigners. Almost all major universities across the country have a department or a college for TCFL but those who hold a teaching certificate in TCFL or a degree from the BLU have an edge in employment. The Mandarin Centre at the Taiwan Normal University also runs MA programmes in TCFL. The International Association for Chinese Language Teaching (Shijie Hanyü jiaoxue xuehui) in Beijing and the World Chinese Language Society (Shijie Huayüwen jiaoyu xuehui) in Taipei are the professional organizations in the field, each holding an international conference every three years. The highest state organization governing the teaching of Chinese to foreigners on the mainland is the

National Office for Chinese as a Foreign Language or NOCFL (Guojia duiwai Hanyü jiaoxue lingdao xiaozu bangongshi; Guojia Hanban or simply Hanban for short; see www.hanban.edu.cn). It is composed of eleven departments and commissions under the State Council, including the **State Working Commission on Language** (Guojia Yüwei), the PRC's language legislator.

HELEN XIAOYAN WU

Chow, Stephen

(né Chow Sing Chi/Zhou Xingchi)

b. 22 June 1962, Hong Kong

Film actor, scriptwriter, director, producer

Often compared to Jim Carrey, the Hong Kong born, Shanghai native Stephen Chow embodies *wulitou* (*mo lei tau* in Cantonese, meaning 'nonsensical humour') acting, infused with Bruce Lee spirit. His 2001 comeback comedy *Kung-fu Soccer*, a.k.a. *Shaolin Soccer* (*Shaolin zuqiu*), shot on the mainland, which Chow wrote, directed and acted (with **Zhao Wei**), surpassed all box-office hits (grossing HK$67.26 million) in Hong Kong. Cashing in on the film's popularity, Chow, along with the film's other actors, did a special celebrity edition of *Who Wants to be a Millionaire?* as a philanthropic fund-raising project. The film's copyright was bought by Miramax and was scheduled for release in the USA in 2003.

Chow attended TVB's acting school in Hong Kong, and entered showbiz by hosting the children's show with Tony Leung. He won the 1988 Best Supporting Actor Golden Horse Award (*Jinma jiang*) for his performance in *Final Justice* (*Pili xianfeng*). He played his first leading role in the 1990 box-office hit *All for the Winner* (*Du Xia 2*), which parodies **Chow Yun-fat**'s 1989 *God of Gamblers* (*Dushen*) and introduced *wu li tou* acting to Hong Kong audiences. During the 1990s his popularity increased, with no fewer than forty-four films which he acted in and occasionally wrote and directed. The best-known of these are: *Justice, My Foot* (*Shen si guan*), which won him the Best Actor Award at the 1992 Pacific Film Festival; *From Beijing with Love* (*Guochan linglingqi*, 1994), a parody of James Bond movies; and *Gorgeous* (*Boli zun*, 1999), a Jackie **Chan** movie in which Chow made a guest appearance.

Further reading

http://www.chowsingchi.sphosting.com/chow-facts.html [a profile of the life and career of Stephen Chow]

WANG YIMAN

Chow Yun-fat

(Jau Yun Faat; Zhou Runfa)

b. 1955, Lamma Island, Hong Kong

Film actor

Along with Jackie **Chan**, Chow Yun-fat is the most popular actor in Hong Kong. And like Chan, Chow has 'crossed over' to the West, especially in Ang **Lee**'s pan-Chinese/US **martial arts** co-production, *Crouching Tiger, Hidden Dragon* (*Wohu canglong*, 2000). A versatile, charismatic performer, Chow has worked in a variety of genres – television, comedies, romances – before reaching international fame as an action hero.

At sixteen, Chow enrolled in the TVB actors training programme. From 1976 to 1985, he appeared in twenty TV series, the most popular being *The Bund* (*Shanghai tang/Sheung Hoi Tan*, 1980). In the 1980s, he worked with important film *auteurs*, such as Stanley **Kwan**, Tony Au Ting-ping and Ann **Hui**, who skilfully exploited both his romanticism and physicality in *The Story of Woo Viet* (*Hu Yue de gushi*, 1981) and *Love in a Fallen City* (*Qingcheng zhi lian*, 1984). The turning point of his career came through his work with John **Woo**: *A Better Tomorrow* (*Yingxiong bense*) Part I (1986) and II (1987), *The Killer* (*Diexue shuangxiong*, 1989), *Once a Thief* (*Zhongheng sihai*, 1990) and *Hard-Boiled* (*Lashou shentan*, 1992).

Though he continued to make romantic comedies, such as Mabel Cheung's *An Autumn's Tale* (*Qiutang de tonghua*, 1987), in the second stage of his career he was mostly cast in action films by the likes of Ringo Lam Leng-tung (the *City on Fire/ Longhu fengyun* series, 1987), Wong Jing (the *God of*

Gamblers/Dushen series, 1989, 1994) and Wai Ka-fai (*Peace Hotel/Heping fandian*, 1995). In the USA, Chow worked with directors Antoine Fuqua, James Foley, Andy Tennant and Paul Hunter in the film *Bulletproof Monk* (2003), which was produced by John Woo.

BÉRÉNICE REYNAUD

Christianity (Protestantism)

Protestant Christianity is the fastest-growing religion in China. In 1949, the number of Protestant Christians was only around 700,000; but by 2000 the official estimate had reached approximately 15 million. Reliable unofficial sources claim at least double this figure, and there are probably many more.

After 1949, missions were forbidden in the PRC, and Premier Zhou Enlai met with Christian leaders in the spring of 1950 to discuss the future of Christianity in China. The meetings resulted in what came to be known as the 'Christian Manifesto' (*Sanzi gexin xuanyan*), which is counted as the starting point for the **Three-Self Patriotic Movement (TSPM)**.

In 1958, all denominations were abolished after a decision of the TSPM National Committee. The TSPM also led criticism and denunciation campaigns against **house churches** and other non-TSPM groups and leaders during the 1950s and 1960s. This led to severe conflicts and mistrust between Christians of different groups. The government and the CCP also imposed restrictions on what could be preached and who could be accepted as a pastor or evangelist. Already in the early 1960s, many churches were forcibly closed and used for other purposes, but during the **Cultural Revolution** religion in general was prohibited. Many Christians were persecuted. All churches were closed or taken over by the authorities, and the TSPM was disbanded. Christians could at best meet in small groups. The churches were again allowed to open in the late 1970s. In October 1980 the third National Christian Conference was held in Nanjing and bishop **Ding Guangxun** was elected both the chairman of the TSPM and president of the newly established

China Christian Council (CCC). The CCC was formed to be a more church-like counterpart to the TSPM and to deal with theological matters and questions more directly related to church life.

Both house churches and the TSPM have experienced a strong revival during the 1980s and 1990s, and the growth in the number of Christians has been enormous. The majority of Protestants in the PRC live in the countryside and have a low level of education. They often have an evangelical and biblical faith in contrast to leading persons in the TSPM and the CCC who frequently represent a more liberal theology. In the countryside, faith healing is an important factor in the quick growth (see **faith healing (Christian)**). Relations between the TSPM, the CCC and the house churches have improved on local levels but mistrust still exists on the national level.

One problem for all Christians in China is the lack of educated pastors and evangelists to take care of all new believers, leading to a rise of pseudo-Christian sects. Theological education thus became the focus of attention in the 1990s, and the house churches also set up training centres around the country. In 2000 there were eighteen official Protestant theological seminaries in the PRC, of which five were regional and one, **Jinling Union Theological Seminary** in Nanjing, was national.

The period after 1980 can be divided in three stages for the Church in China. First, the period of formation with building and re-opening of churches; second, training of pastors and evangelists, which is still going on. The third stage is that of raising the level of theological education where the goal is a contextualized Chinese theology.

See also: house churches

Further reading

Bays, Daniel (2003). 'Chinese Protestant Christianity Today'. In Daniel Overmyer (ed.), *Religion in China Today*. Cambridge: Cambridge University Press, 182–98.

Chan, Kim-kwong and Hunter, Alan (1993). *Protestantism in Contemporary China*. Cambridge: Cambridge University Press.

Kupfer, Kristin (2002/2003). 'Christlich inspirierte, spirituell-religiöse Gruppierungen in der VR China seit 1979, 1–4'. *China heute* 21.4–5: 119–127; 21.6: 169–75; 22.1–2: 27–32; 22.3: 81–3.

Malek, R. (ed.) (1996). *Fallbeispiel' China: ökumenische Beiträge zu Religion, Theologie, und Kirche im chinesischen Kontext*. Sankt Augustin: China-Zentrum.

FREDERIK FÄLLMAN

Christianity among national minorities

In general, all minority nationalities in northern China are Muslims, with the exception of the Mongols, who adhere to Lamaism, a form of Buddhism. Even though minority nationalities committed to Islam or Buddhism have traditionally been resistant to the Christian faith, efforts going back eight hundred years have been made to evangelize them.

Roman Catholic missionaries sought to penetrate Tibet in the Yuan dynasty (1276–1368), but more successful efforts were made during the latter years of the Ming dynasty (1368–1644). From that time until the present, Catholic missionaries have tried to evangelize Tibet, whether from India, from the northwest corner of Yunnan or from western Sichuan. Protestant evangelization in Tibet began much later, in the nineteenth century, and has not been as successful as that of the Catholics. Some Protestant Tibetan Christians may be found in the scattered **house churches** in Tibet and Qinghai and in far western Yunnan. Even in these areas, however, they often worship together with Chinese Christians. Nestorian Christianity came to China and Mongolia in the late Tang dynasty (618–906), but its early influence was largely among the Han Chinese. Following its demise in the tenth century, many of its followers were dispersed to the north among Turkic-Mongolian groups in Mongolia. As a result, Christian communities developed among the Kerait, Naiman and possibly Uighur peoples. As far as we know, however, no present Christian communities exist among these minority nationalities today. However, in the People's Republic of Mongolia, no longer a part of China, Christian churches have sprung up in a climate of religious freedom. Over the last two or three hundred years, Catholics have also evangelized among China's minorities who are followers of folk religion. In general, however, Roman Catholic authors, apart from what they say about Tibet and Mongolia, do not highlight Catholic work among minorities. They treat such groups as citizens of China and as being on the same level as the **Han** Chinese.

One of the earliest Protestant efforts among traditional folk religionists was the Dutch evangelistic attempts among several minorities of Taiwan early in the seventeenth century. And in the late nineteenth century, workers from several Protestant mission agencies began to work among minority nationalities in southwest China. The results have been far greater among the resistant groups adhering to such major religions as Islam and Buddhism. Among the eleven original inhabitant nationalities in Taiwan, the proportion of the Christian population, both Protestant and Catholic, is about 75 per cent. The Korean nationality in China, living largely in the Yanbian Korean autonomous prefecture in Jilin province, are known for the vigour of their Protestant faith. Miao churches – largely among the Flowery Miao and the Great Flowery Miao – have grown equally well. At present, there is an estimated number of 3,000 in Guizhou province and possibly as many as 50,000 in Wuding and Luquan counties in Yunnan province. Local government officials in the Nujiang Lisu autonomous prefecture in Yunnan claim that one half of the total Lisu population of 500,000 is Christian and that it would be accurate to call them a 'Christian people'.

Today, several other minority nationalities (Zhuang, Tujia, Yao, Bouyei, Jing, Yi, Vai, Lahu, Va, Hani and Jingpo) have Christian populations numbering at least 10,000. In most instances their churches are well established and their members continue to evangelize among their own peoples. Other minority nationalities (Dai, Manchu, Dong, Li, Mulao, Nu, Zan, Drung, and Maonan) have Christian communities numbering fewer than a thousand adherents and with no strong, vibrant churches. Some nationality groups, even those following folk religion, have proved to be very resistant. For example, the Black Yi of Yunnan

have several thousand believers, while their cousins among the Shengzha independent Yi in Sichuan are only now beginning to respond to the gospel.

As has been the case with Han Chinese churches, many of the minority nationality churches, whether small or large and whether associated with the government-registered **China Christian Council** or the more covert autonomous churches, have faced varying degrees of government interference and pressure. They are no longer dependent on the presence of outsiders, although workers associated with Christian and philanthropic organizations are helping in education, medicine, compassionate service and translation of the Bible.

Why has there been such a positive response to the Christian faith among so many of the minority nationalities of Taiwan, Yunnan, Guizhou, Guangxi and Sichuan? The very nature of their own religions has been important – traditionally not as resistant worldwide as the more classical religions with holy books, a priesthood and a unifying social structure. With most groups there has been a charismatic proclaimer of the message – whether local or an outsider – who has identified with the people, helped to meet their needs and, in some instances, defended them against all types of oppression. Anthropologists and sociologists talk about the ways in which the coming of a new religion is able to 'revitalize' a society that has been destabilized by some external challenge, as has been the case with many southwest Chinese minorities. This leads to developing a new corporate identity centred in the Christian faith. This enables the minority nationality – usually a subordinate group in a dominant society – to assert itself in establishing the new identity. Those proclaiming the new faith have usually latched on to indigenous concepts, such as a millennial hope for the coming of a future king among the Miao. There has always been a better response when the message has been contextualized in such a way. It becomes their message, and, subsequently, their church.

How will these minority nationality churches face future challenges? At least three dangers confront them. Will the churches have sufficient numbers of trained pastors to lead them in the development of their faith in a changing China? Will the Chinese government try to assimilate the minority peoples or continue to help them to use their own cultures and languages? How will churches and individual Christians deal with the pressures of modernization, even in isolated mountain communities? As compared with several decades ago when these peoples were largely rural and feudal in social life, many of the younger generation are well educated, technologically literate and working as dentists, doctors, lawyers and educators. Some have forsaken their language and culture and entered fully into Han society. Will they be able to maintain their Christian commitment and help their less fortunate co-villagers enter with them into the modern world? Or will there be many residual rural enclaves who continue to live in the past?

Further reading

Covell, Ralph (1995). *The Liberating Gospel in China: The Christian Faith Among China's Minority Peoples*. Grand Rapids, MI: Baker.

—— (1998). *Pentecost of the Hills in Taiwan: The Christian Faith Among the Original Inhabitants*. Pasadena, CA: Hope.

Harrell, Steven (ed.) (2001). *Ways of Being Ethnic in Southwest China*. Seattle: University of Washington Press.

Hattaway, Paul (2000). *Operation China: Introducing All the Peoples of China*. London: Piquant.

RALPH COVELL

Chuanju

(Sichuan opera)

Regional Xiqu (sung-drama/opera) genre

Sichuan opera, or Chuanju, is the form of traditional Chinese sung-drama found in the southwestern province of Sichuan as well as in some regions of the neighbouring provinces of Yunnan and Guizhou. One of the most famous and favoured traditional theatre forms in China, Sichuan opera is a fusion of five different musical systems, with four of these systems introduced from other regions (see **Xiqu musical structure**).

Gaoqiang, a variant of the music of the *yiyang*-style of Jiangxi, was brought to Sichuan in the seventeenth century. Its significant characteristics are the use of the *bangqiang*, or 'helping chorus', and the dominance of percussion instruments. In contemporary performance, *gaoqiang* is the most dominant and most frequently performed musical style. A second musical system belonging to the 'Clapper opera' was also introduced to Sichuan in the seventeenth century. Originating in Shaanxi, it has developed into the Sichuanese version known as *tanxi* or 'plays for stringed instruments'. The third musical system introduced to Sichuan is the *huqinqiang*, a variant of the *pihuang* musical system from the operas of Hunan and Hubei provinces. Its name derives from the *huqin*, a two-stringed spiked fiddle, and indicates that the orchestra is dominated by string instruments. The last system brought to Sichuan is that of the **Kunqu** opera of Jiangsu province, a refined drama form popular with the elite. It was introduced to Chengdu, Sichuan, in 1663, when a visiting Kunqu troupe performed in one of the major guildhouses. The *dengxi* (lantern theatre) is the fifth and only musical form native to Sichuan. It is a small-scale folk opera, which developed from shamanic rituals for exorcizing evil spirits and beseeching the gods for good harvests. The melodies of *dengxi* are derived from the folksongs of Sichuan and neighbouring regions.

The integration of these five styles did not occur until the beginning of the twentieth century, when the famous Sanqing Company began to reform and enhance the performance styles and musical systems. Though an 'integrated' opera can include elements from as many as three of the above five musical systems, one system always remains dominant, and the repertoire is categorized according to the style dominant in each play.

In performance, stagecraft and repertoire Sichuan opera is in general similar to other regional opera styles, including **Jingju** (Peking opera). However, Sichuan opera is famous for its unique stunts, such as sword-swallowing, fire-breathing, juggling with burning candles, and the sudden appearance of a third eye on an actor's forehead. The latter is a breathtaking skill in which the actor kicks up his foot for a split second, attaching a fake third eye to his forehead. But the most closely guarded secret, and certainly the local style's signature spectacle, is a special effect known as 'face-changing' (*bianlian*), whereby painted full-face silk masks are changed up to fourteen times in magically quick succession.

The foundation of the People's Republic of China in 1949 ushered in a new era for the art of Sichuan opera, interrupted only by the ten years of the **Cultural Revolution** (1966–76), during which all performances of traditional Sichuan opera were forbidden. It was one of the first regional styles to be revived after the fall of the 'Gang of Four' in 1976 and began to flourish again quickly. However, the Cultural Revolution and the rapid modernization process after 1978 have taken a heavy toll on traditional theatre. Alarmingly decreasing audience numbers and the dwindling popularity of traditional theatre with younger audiences made Sichuan the first province to implement strategies to rejuvenate its local opera style. In 1982 the provincial government launched a reform movement under the slogan 'rejuvenating Sichuan opera' (*zhenxing chuanju*). The main objectives have focused on 'saving' (*qiangjiu*), 'inheriting' (*jicheng*), 'reforming' (*gaige*) and 'developing' (*fazhan*) the art form.

See also: Xiqu

Further reading

Dauth, Ursula (1997). 'Strategies of Reform in Sichuan Opera since 1982: Confronting the Challenge of Rejuvenating a Regional Opera'. PhD diss., Griffith University.

Hu, Du, Liu, Xingming and Fu, Ze (1987). *Chuanju cidian* [Dictionary of Sichuan Opera]. Beijing: Zhongguo xiju chubanshe.

Kalvodová, Dana (1972). 'Theatre in Szechwan'. *Interscena* 1–II: 42–64; 2–II: 32–55; 3–II: 31–59; 4–II: 43–59.

URSULA DAUTH

Chuanju troupes

Until the twentieth century, opera troupes in Sichuan specialized in only one or, at most, two of the five different musical systems and performance

styles that would come to define the modern genre. But in 1912, the founding of the Sanqing Company in Chengdu integrated these five systems in order to achieve a standardized performance art. This art is now known as **Chuanju** or Sichuan opera. After Liberation, both amateur and state-run troupes flourished, performing traditional and contemporary plays. But the prosperity of Sichuan opera suffered a severe setback with the beginning of the **Cultural Revolution** in 1966. By 1971, nearly all professional and amateur troupes had been disbanded.

The sudden revival of traditional opera after the fall of the 'Gang of Four' resulted in the re-establishment of 130 professional Sichuan opera troupes with about 17,000 theatre workers. The reform of the economic and political systems in December 1978 also sparked a rethinking of the structure of the performing arts troupes. This included abandoning the **iron rice bowl**, such that theatre workers would no longer be kept on and paid without actively contributing to the troupe. Moreover, with less state funding, opera troupes were now expected to expand or contract in response to market demand. A ranking system for artists and opera troupes was introduced during the early 1980s to regulate their status and state subsidies. The highest-ranking troupes, such as the Sichuan Province Sichuan Opera Company, came to be administered by the Provincial Cultural Department. Troupes on a city, municipal or autonomous-prefectural level were ranked second and administered by the Cultural Bureaux. Troupes at the county level, the lowest rank, were administered by the county Cultural Offices. Since 1982 all troupes have recruited their actors from the provincial professional opera school in Chengdu or its deputized institutions in the regions.

The number of active professional troupes has dramatically decreased since the early 1990s, as many troupes have been disbanded due to financial difficulties and an increasing lack of public interest and support. Already by 1982, the number of troupes had shrunk to 119, and by 1992 only eighty-six remained. The number of active Sichuan opera troupes in 1997 was estimated to be between forty and fifty, with the majority of these troupes state-run. The estimated number of active troupes in 2000 was about twenty. The number of Sichuan opera workers decreased from 10,900 in 1982 to only 2,000 in 2000, with 1,500 older than forty-five. With the decrease in the number of troupes, and thus in the employment opportunities for artists, the annual enrolment of opera students has also decreased dramatically.

An interesting example of how troupes have responded to the changing social and economic environment is provided by the Third Chengdu City Sichuan Opera Troupe, one of the most acclaimed Sichuan opera troupes. The troupe ceased regular performances in 1997 due to lack of audiences and the destruction of its home, the Jinjiang Theatre, the oldest and most famous theatre in Chengdu. Since then, the troupe has successfully toured overseas, introducing the art of Sichuan opera, as part of China's cultural heritage, to foreign audiences and returning to profitability at the same time. Nowadays many cities and towns in Sichuan have modern entertainment centres but in most cases these are not played by opera troupes. The Jinjiang Theatre, as the 'cradle' of Sichuan opera, has been rebuilt recently: a positive sign for the continuation of the opera's long tradition. There are also a small number of semi-professional or amateur groups performing in public parks, **teahouses** and even at official functions or family celebrations, still performing almost every day. The environment for Sichuan opera is now governed less by state cultural policies and more by social and economic forces. Theatre workers today must deal with their art as a 'cultural commodity'.

See also: Chuanju

Further reading

Dauth, Ursula (1997). 'Strategies of Reform in Sichuan Opera since 1982: Confronting the Challenge of Rejuvenating a Regional Opera'. PhD diss., Griffith University.

Mackerras, Colin (1990). *Chinese Drama. A Historical Survey.* Beijing: New World Press.

URSULA DAUTH

cinema in Taiwan

As Taiwan was occupied by Japan from 1895 to 1945, its national cinema only started after the liberation of the island. First, it was used as a propaganda tool by the ruling party, the Kuomintang, who gradually eradicated the production of Taiwanese-language films. In the 1970s, the industry, producing mostly 'escapist' films, was in crisis. The 'New Taiwan Cinema' (*Taiwan xindianying*) revitalized it in the early 1980s, and directors such as **Hou Hsiao-hsien** and Edward **Yang** won fame in international film festivals. However, the small size of the local market, increased competition from Hong Kong and Hollywood, and the Asian economic crisis have created difficult conditions for Taiwanese filmmakers. While the most famous survive, some have gone into exile or stopped production. Nonetheless, a younger generation is emerging, exploring new media and new formats.

When the Japanese withdrew in 1945, they left Taiwan in a profound political, social and cultural crisis. Kuomintang supporters were arriving *en masse*; the tension between 'Mainlanders' and 'Native Taiwanese' climaxed in the 28 February 1947 incident, and a Martial Law was enacted. In 1949, the Kuomintang arrived with a million and a half refugees, declared Taipei to be the 'provisional capital' of China, and imposed the use of Mandarin.

The Taipei Cinemathèque (founded in 1976) estimates that between the late 1940s and the early 1970s, about 1,000–1,500 Taiwanese-language films were produced. Representing less than one-fifth of the national production, these films nevertheless dominated the market between 1955 and 1958. Directors like Ho Gi Ming and the Japanese-educated Lin Pao Chiao, or the independent Big Mountain Studio (Husang) played an important role, but this grass-root industry, being denied government subsidies, was long considered artistically 'inferior' and is barely mentioned in official histories. By the late 1970s it had yielded to Mandarin-speaking cinema.

The government set production structures, such as the Kuomintang-owned CMPC (Central Motion Picture Company/Zhongyang Dianying Qiye Gufen Youxian Gongsi), the country's biggest studio. The first films thus produced were propaganda pieces. In 1955, substantial tax advantages and subsidies were granted to Hong Kong filmmakers who directed a Cantonese *and* a Mandarin version of their films – thus intertwining the two national cinemas. In 1962, the Golden Horse Award was instituted on an annual basis for the best Hong Kong and Taiwan movies. Films from the PRC remained banned until the mid 1990s.

In the early 1960s, two major Hong Kong filmmakers (both born in pre-1949 China), Li Han Hsiang (Li Hanxiang) and King Hu (Hu Jinquan), settled in Taiwan. Li opened his own studio, the Grand Motion Picture Company (Guolian), where he directed the costly two-part historical epic, *The Beauty of Beauties* (*Xi Shi*, 1965), and the more intimate *The Winter* (*Dong Nuan*, 1967), now considered a forerunner of the 'New Cinema'. Hired by the Union Film Company (Lianbang), King Hu (with his martial arts director, Han Yingyie) trained young actors, including Hsu Feng, the future star of some of his films and the future producer of **Chen Kaige**'s *Farewell My Concubine* (*Bawang bieji*, 1993). He directed two **martial arts** masterpieces, *Dragon Inn* (*Longmen kezhan*, 1967) and *A Touch of Zen* (*Xianü*, 1970). In 1970, Lee and Hu returned to Hong Kong. Back in Taiwan in 1979, Hu made *The Juvenizer* (*Zhongshen Dashi*, 1981), his only comedy, produced by Sylvia **Chang**, and *All the King's Men* (*Tianxia Diyi*, 1982), before leaving for the USA.

His Taiwanese-born colleague, Lee Hsing (Li Xing), first directed Taiwanese-language films in the 1950s, before switching to Mandarin with *Life in a Small Alley* (*Jietou xiangwei*, 1963). Then, embracing the KMT's slogan of 'healthy realism' (*jiankang xieshi zhuyi*), he made optimistic movies narrating the daily life struggles of plain people striving for happiness, such as *Beautiful Ducklings* (*Yangya renjia*, 1964). He also directed adaptations of romances by the popular female novelist Chiung Yao, like *The Silent Wife* (*Yaqi*, 1965). His career continued till the mid 1990s and includes forty-nine feature films, including *Execution in Autumn* (*Qiujue*, 1972) and *Good Morning, Taipei* (*Zao'an Taibei*, 1979), scripted by Hou Hsiao-hsien and shot by Chen Kun-hou. Among Lee's contemporaries, Pai Ching-jui (one of the first Taiwanese directors

to have studied abroad) directed adaptations of **Qiong Yao**'s novels, such as *Lonely Seventeen* (*Jimo de shiqi sui*, 1967), while Sung Tsun-shou (Song Cunshou) was dealing with controversial psychological subjects, including a teacher–student love affair in *Outside the Window* (*Chuanwai*, 1973, starring Brigitte **Lin**).

In the 1970s, Taiwanese film production (including subsidized Hong Kong films) reached 300 movies a year – the third place after Japan and India – but 42 per cent were mediocre kung fu films. It was a period of social and political crisis. The 'Taiwan economic miracle' had caused a major rural exodus, industrial pollution, pockets of poverty and delinquency. In 1971, Taiwan was expelled from the United Nations. In 1975 Chiang Kai-shek died. In 1979, the USA severed diplomatic ties with Taiwan, triggering a long period of diplomatic isolation (until the 1996 first democratic elections and the threat of Chinese missiles over the Taiwan straits).

In the early 1980s, a literary movement, Nativist Literature (*Xiangtu wenxue*), was striving to depict Taiwanese reality as distinct from the history of the mainland; returning to local dialects (Hakka, Minnanhua) and using colourful profanities and slang, it sought to depict the plight of 'little people' victimized, displaced or reduced to petty crimes by industrialization. Meanwhile, as cinema was disconnected from Taiwanese reality and losing audiences, the CMPC sought to revitalize the industry and hired two young writers influenced by the *Xiangtu Wenxue*, Wu Nien-jen (see **Wu Nien-chen**) and Hsiao Yeh (Xiao Ye). In 1982, they produced *In Our Times* (*Guangyin de gushi*), a film in four episodes, one directed by Edward Yang and another by Chang Yi. Wu and Hsiao's next project, *Sandwich-Man* (*Ezri de da wan'ou*, 1983) is considered the birth of the New Taiwan Cinema; its three episodes are adapted from stories by the most famous *Xiangtu wenxue* writers, **Huang Chunming**; its three directors are Hou Hsiaohsien, Wan Jen and Tseng Chuang-hsiang (Zeng Zhuangxiang). Still in 1983, the CMPC produced Chen Kun-hou's *Growing Up* (*Xiao Bi de gushi*), written by Hou Hsiao-hsien and the young female novelist Chu Tien-wen, as well as Edward Yang's first feature, *That Day on the Beach* (*Haitan de yi tian*), starring Sylvia Chang and written by

Wu Nien-jen, that explores the contradictions of Taiwanese modernity – also a theme of Yang's next films, *Taipei Story* (*Qingmei zhuma*, 1985, starring Hou Hsiao-hsien) and *The Terrorizer* (*Kongbu fenzi*, 1986). Meanwhile, Hou started a long-lasting screenwriting collaboration with Wu Nien-jen and Chu Tien-wen to delve into Taiwan's recent popular memories, with *The Boys from Fengkuei* (*Fenggui lai de ren*, 1983), *A Summer at Grandpa's* (*Dongdong de jiaqi*, 1984), *A Time to Live, a Time to Die* (*Tongnian wangshi*, 1985) and *Dust in the Wind* (*Lianlian fengchen*, 1987).

The 'New Cinema' continued throughout the 1980s, with a series of modern melodramas that explored the female condition, the plight of delinquent youths or the changing status of the Taiwanese family: Wan Jen's *Ah Fei* (*Youma caizi*, 1984, written by Hou Hsiao-hsien), *Super Citizen* (*Chaoji shimin*, 1985) and *The Farewell Coast* (*Xibie de hai an*, 1987); Chang Yi's *Jade Love* (*Yuqing sao*, 1984), *Kuei-Mei, a Woman* (*Wo zheyang guole yisheng*, 1985) and *This Love of Mine* (*Wo de ai*, 1988); Chen Kun-hou's *The Matrimony* (*Jiehun*, 1985) and *Osmanthus Alley* (*Guihua xiang*, 1987, written by Wu Nien-jen); or Tseng Chuang-hsiang's *The Woman of Wrath* (*Sha fu*, 1984) – also written by Wu Nien-jen, who authored a great number of screenplays at the time, including Li You-ning's *Lao Mo's Second Spring* (*Lao Mo de di erge chuntian*, 1984), about the marriage of a displaced war veteran to a young aboriginal woman.

By the end of the decade, the honeymoon between the CMPC and the New Cinema was over, and alternative solutions had to be found, from local independent companies to foreign financing. In 1987, the forty-year-old Martial Law was lifted, allowing filmmakers to delve into some taboo aspects of Taiwanese history – the Japanese occupation, the taking over by the Kuomintang, the 'White Terror' of the early 1950s, or the difficult modernization of the country in the 1960s. In this vein, Hou Hsiao-hsien directed his *Taiwan Trilogy: A City of Sadness* (*Beiqing chengshi*, 1989), *Puppetmaster* (*Ximeng Chensheng*, 1993) and *Good Men, Good Women* (*Haonan, haonü*, 1995). Edward Yang made a similarly ambitious work, *A Brighter Summer Day* (*Giuling jie shaonian sha ren shijian*, 1991); and Wan Jen directed *Super Citizen Ko* (*Chaoji da guomin*, 1995).

Another filmmaker to benefit from the lifting of the Martial Law was Wang Tun, who had started to make movies in 1981; in 1983, he adapted a Huang Chun-ming story, *Flower in the Rainy Night* (*Kanhai de rizi*, 1983). His first explorations of Taiwanese history, *Strawman* (*Daocao ren*, 1987) and *Banana Paradise* (*Xiangjiao tiantang*, 1989), were written by Wang Shaudi (Wang Xiaodi), a director herself. The third part of Wang Tung's trilogy, *Hill of No Return* (*Wuyan de shanqiu*, 1992), was the last screenplay written by Wu Nien-jen before he turned to directing, inspired by his own past – *A Borrowed Life* (*Duo-Sang*, 1993) – or by recent history – *Buddha Bless America* (*Tai Ping, Tian Guo*, 1996). Wang Tung kept following his historical inspiration with *Red Persimmon* (*Hong Shih Zi*, 1996).

Not always successful at the box-office, the New Cinema had nevertheless profoundly renewed the industry, put Taiwan on the international cultural map, fostered formal experiments (such as the use of long takes, real locations, available lighting and non-professional actors) and opened the path to a plurality of cinematic voices. The former critic Chen Kuo-fu made his first feature, *Junior High School Girl*, in 1988. Ed Yang's collaborator/producer Yu Weiyen directed *Gang of Three Forever* (*Tongdang wansui*, 1989) and *Moonlight Boy* (*Yueguang shaonian*, 1993), while Hsu Hsiao-ming (Xu Xiaoming), a former assistant of Hou Hsiao-hsien, became a director with *Dust of Angels* (*Shaonian ye, an la!*, 1992) and *Heartbreak Island* (*Qunian dongtian*, 1995). The theatre and television director Stan Lai (**Lai Shengchuan**) made *Peach Blossom Land* (*An lian taohuayuan*, 1992) and *Red Lotus Society* (*Fei Xia A-Da*, 1994). The baker-turned-comic-actor Lin Cheng-sheng turned to filmmaking with a series of ground-breaking films such as *A Drifting Life* (*Chuen hua mon lu*, 1995) or *Betelnut Beauty* (*Ai Ni Ai Wo*, 2001). Wang Shau-di opened a television production studio where she trained a bevy of young filmmakers, including Tsai Ming-liang and Chen Yu-Hsun (Chen Yuxun). Then she turned to directing features with *Accidental Legend* (*Fei Tian*, 1996), *Yours and Mine* (*Wo de Shenjinbing*, 1997) and the animated film *Grandma and Her Ghosts* (*Mo-Fo A-Ma*, 1998).

As Taiwanese society evolved, filmmakers started to deal more with the ever-changing modernized urban space. Edward Yang directed two urban comedies, *A Confucian Confusion* (*Duli Shidai*, 1994), *Mahjong* (*Maijiang*, 1996) and the splendid *A One and a Two* (*Yi Yi*, 2000, staring Wu Nien-jen), which explores the existential and emotional unease of the modern Taiwanese man. Hou Hsiao-hsien's gangster anti-heroes still roam the countryside in *Goodbye, South, Goodbye* (*Zaijian, nanguo, zaijian*, 1996), and the claustrophobic abstract *Flowers of Shanghai* (*Hai shang hua*, 1998) is a *kammerspiel* in costume – but with *Millennium Mambo* (*Qianxi Manbo*, 2001), Hou signed his first great contemporary urban drama, embracing the point of view of female subjectivity, as in his earlier *Daughter of the Nile* (*Niluohe nüer*, 1987), or the modern-time sequences of *Good Men, Good Women*.

Paradoxically, the most inspired descriptions of contemporary Taipei come from Malaysian-born **Ts'ai Ming-liang**. In *Rebels of the Neon God* (*Qing shaonian nezha*, 1992) and *Vive l'Amour* (*Aiqin wansui*, 1994) he acutely depicts the (often sexual) confusion of lost young marginalized urbanites. *The River* (*He liu*, 1996) locates the origin of the malaise in the nuclear urban family. Both *The Hole* (*Dong*, 1998) and *What Time Is It Here?* (*Ni Neibian Jidian*, 2001) open new vistas – one by combining science fiction and musical, the other by taking the wanderings of one of the protagonists to France, as well as beyond death itself.

One of the most interesting directors of the 1990s is Chang Tso-chi (Zhang Zuoji), who turns his camera towards disenfranchised strata of the population – young delinquents, petty gangsters, hard-working yet impoverished families. His films – *Ah Chung* (*Zhong Zai*, 1996), *Darkness and Light* (*Heian zhi guang*, 1999) or *The Best of Times* (*Meili Shiguang*, 2002) – combine a warm, realistic approach with unexpected oneirism. Other directors worth mentioning are Ho Ping (*18/Shibu*, 1993; *The Rule of the Game/Wa Dong Ren*, 2002), Chen Yu-Hsun (*Tropical Fish* (*Redai yu*, 1995); *Love Go-Go/Aiqing laile*, 1998) and Chen Yiwen (*Jam/Guojiang*, 1998; *The Cabbie/Yun Zhuanshou de Lian*, 2000).

Like Edward Yang, Wan Jen or Tseng Chuang-hsiang, a number of people active in the film industry studied or lived in the USA. This is particularly true for women – such as the powerful critic Peggy **Chiao**; Wang Shau-di; the feminist director Huang Yu-chang (*The Peony Birds/Mu dan niao*, 1990); or the independent filmmaker Chen Jo-Fei. Another influential woman is the star Sylvia Chang, who, though living mostly in Hong Kong, has produced and directed a number of features in her native Taiwan. Two significant directors did not return home after studying in the USA. In 1991 Ang **Lee** struck an ongoing collaboration with New York independent producer James Schamus, and directed films in the USA and Europe, while making *Eat Drink Man Woman* (*Yinshi nannü*, 1994) in Taiwan and *Crouching Tiger, Hidden Dragon* (*Wo Hu Zang Long*, 2000) in China. More hybrid and experimental, the multi-media artist **Cheang Shu-lea** has worked in the USA, Europe and Japan.

There is a lively queer scene in Taiwan, and the first gay Taiwanese movie was Yu Kanping's *The Outcasts* (*Niezi*, 1986), an adaptation of Pai Hsien-Yung's (**Bai Xianyong**) novel *Crystal Boys*. It is, however, telling that, with the exception of Lin Cheng-sheng's *Murmur of Youth* (*Meili za changge*, 1997), most films involving gay/lesbian themes or issues are directed either by foreign-born filmmakers – Tsai Ming-liang's *Vive l'Amour* and *The River* – or people who have spent time abroad: Huang Yu-chang's *Twin Bracelets* (*Shuangzhuo*, 1990); Ang Lee's *The Wedding Banquet* (*Xiyan*, 1992); Yin Chi's *Fleeing by Night* (*Ye ben*, 2000 – co-directed with former CMPC director Hsu Li-Kong); Yee Chih Yen (Yi Zhiyan)'s *Blue Gate Crossing* (*Lanse damen*, 2002); Sylvia Chang's *Tempting Heart* (*Xin Dong*, 1999) – not to mention the sexually transgressive films and videos directed abroad by Cheang Shu-lea. The development of an independent scene also fostered the emergence of original gay work, such as Chen Jo-Fei's *Where Is My Love* (*Qiangpo puguang*, 1995) and *The Accidental Journey* (*Hai jiao tianya*, 2000); or *The Love of Three Oranges* (*Sanju zhilian*, 1999) by the poet/screenwriter/stage director Hung Hung (Yan Hongya, a former collaborator of Edward Yang).

The first independent Taiwanese movie was *Man from Island West* (*Xibu laide ren*, 1990), followed by *Bodo* (*Baodao dameng*, 1993), in which the director, Huang Mingchuan (who had spent ten years in the US), coins an experimental language to express the Taiwanese imaginary. In 2000, a young woman, Singing Chen (Chen Xinyi) directed *Bundled* (*Wo Jiao A-Ming-la*), a non-conventional narrative about the plight of the homeless, and in 2001, Hsiao Ya-Chuan, a former Hou Hsiao-hsien assistant, gathered much attention for his daring, witty *Mirror Image* (*Ming Dai Zhui Zhu*).

At the beginning of the twenty-first century, the Taiwanese film industry is ailing. Major production companies such as the CMPC or ERA International (which had produced *A City of Sadness* and **Zhang Yimou**'s *Raise the Red Lantern/Da hongdenglong gaogao gua*, 1991) have reconverted to television. Even the most famous directors find it difficult to raise money and become dependent on international financing and distribution. Yet the younger generations are organizing parallel circuits of exhibition/distribution, and find solutions for independent, low-budget, alternative financing.

See also: Wang Tong

Further reading

Chen, R.-R. S. (1998). 'Taiwan Cinema'. In Zhang Yingjin and Xiao Zhiwei (eds), *Encyclopedia of Chinese Film*. London: Routledge.

Chiao, P.-H. P. (1987). *Xin Taiwan dianying* [New Taiwan Cinema]. Taipei: Shibao chuban gongsi.

Reynaud, B. (1999). *Nouvelles Chines, nouveaux cinémas*. Paris: Cahiers du cinéma.

BÉRÉNICE REYNAUD

cities

There are approximately 700 urban areas that are classified as cities (*shi*) in China (668 in 1997), including the four municipally organized areas that report directly to the central government (Beijing, Shanghai, Tianjin and Chongqing). These four metropolitan regions (all of which include in their territory counties and smaller cities or towns) form the summit of an urban hierarchy, followed by approximately ten other cities with a population of over 2 million, twenty-three with a population between 1 and 2 million, forty-four with populations between 500,000 and 1 million, 159 with a population between 200,000 and 500,000, popularly referred to as 'middle-sized cities'; and

finally, 393 cities with populations of less than 200,000. There is also a very large number of smaller towns (*zhen*) of sub-regional or local importance (see **towns and townships**). Cities and towns combined make up a population that is well over 500 million. However, these kinds of numbers can be misleading since *within* the areas of many municipalities one often finds a number of satellite towns and rural counties, and invariably a significant proportion of the labour force that is made up of agricultural workers. Chongqing in Sichuan province is an extreme example of this reality: the municipality of the same name has an area of 82,400 sq km (almost the size of an eastern province – for example, this is about 80 per cent of the area of Jiangsu province) and has a total population of over 30 million, whereas the hilly city of Chongqing itself, spread over the promontory formed by the confluence of the Jialing and the Yangzi rivers, has a population of the order of 5 million. The rest of Chongqing's population is spread out among smaller cities, towns and agricultural areas falling within the boundaries of this immense municipality. Approximately 40 to 50 per cent of the population of the municipalities of Beijing and Shanghai also live outside the main built-up city areas. This trend can also be seen frequently in large and middle-sized cities. Wenzhou municipality, for example, in southern Zhejiang province, has a population of well over 6 million, while the actual city of the same name on the Ou River has a population of only around 600,000. Nevertheless, it is hard to define the geographical limits of most cities because of a historically recent trend – the spread of urbanization from cities into rural areas to form a new type of urban-rural landscape in the highly urbanized areas of China as elsewhere in Asia. The term used for this phenomenon is *desakota*, taken from the Malay-Indonesian words for village and city (McGee 1991).

Compared to other developing countries, urbanization has been relatively slow in China, and up until the 1990s reasonably controlled by making it officially very difficult to move from the countryside and towns into the city (see **hukou**; **migration and settlement patterns**). Another characteristic that is not, however, unique to China is that certain regions show much greater urban growth than others. One of these, for example, is the southern part of Jiangsu province called Sunan. In general, such urbanizing regions owe their great economic and demographic growth to the proliferation of rural township and village enterprises – once again resulting in the mixed *desakota* type of rural-urban landscape.

Further reading

Davis, S. D. (2000). *The Consumer Revolution in China.* Berkeley: University of California Press.

Davis, S. D., Kraus, R., Naughton, B. and Perry, E. J. (1995). *Urban Spaces in Contemporary China: The Potential for Autonomy and Community in Post-Mao China.* Cambridge: Cambridge University Press.

Hu, Zhouliang and Foggin, Peter (1995). 'Chinese Cities after Reform and Opening to the Outside World'. *China City Planning Review* 11: 12–24.

McGee, T. G. (1991). 'The Emergence of *Desakota* Regions in Asia: Expanding a Hypothesis'. In Norton Ginsburg, Bruce Koppel and T. G. McGee (eds), *The Extended Metropolis: Settlement Transition in Asia.* Honolulu: University of Hawai'i Press.

Solinger, Dorothy, J. (1999). *Contesting Citizenship in Urban China: Peasant Migrants, the State, and the Logic of the Market.* Berkeley: University of California Press.

Tang, Wenfang and Parish, William (2000). *Chinese Urban Life Under Reform: The Changing Social Contract.* New York: Cambridge University Press.

Yeung, Yue-Man (ed.) (2000). *Urban Development in Asia.* Hong Kong: Chinese University of Hong Kong.

PETER M. FOGGIN

classics publishing houses

With a long and well-documented history, China takes classics publishing seriously. Apart from dedicated classics publishing houses, other presses such as the Commercial Press in Hong Kong also devote much of their efforts to classics publication. Major players like Zhonghua Book Company established in 1912 and Shanghai Classics

Publishing House started in 1956 have been very active in classics publication.

China's opening to the outside world with its massive economic reform programme resulted in a surge of interest in re-evaluating Chinese ancient heritage. Classics publishing houses mushroomed: Beijing Classics Publishing House and Zhong Zhou Ancient Books in 1979, and Tianjin Ancient Books and Mao Wen Ancient Books in 1983. Focusing on local chronicles, regionally collected classics and various reference books on ancient Chinese literature and history, they also publish learning aids related to their published classics. They also take on classics-publishing projects assigned by the central government. Take Zhonghua Book Company, for example. Since its relocation to Beijing in 1954, it has processed, compiled and published over 2,000 kinds of Chinese classics covering the areas of literature, history and philosophy. They include *Taiping yujian* [Lessons for Emperors in Times of Peace], *Yongle dadian* [Yongle Canon] and *Siku quanshu zongmu* [Accumulative Index to the Complete Library in Four Branches of Literature]. The Commercial Press, on the other hand, specializes in publishing rare books of classics. In 1980, the Chinese Traditional Medicine Classics Publishing House was established, specializing in the publication of classics on Chinese traditional medicine.

HU MINGRONG

clothing industry

Since 1994, China has been the world's largest manufacturer and exporter of textiles and clothing. In 2000, China's trade volume of textiles and clothing accounted for almost 15 per cent of the world total. This is a figure that is expected to get even larger over coming years as export quotas will have gradually been lifted by 2005 in accordance with WTO protocols. Statistics show that China's textile and garment industries exported US$52.1 billion worth of products in 2000. Over the past twenty years, garment production in China has increased nearly fifteen-fold, with an annual growth rate of 14.4 per cent. Currently, 45,000 garment businesses in China produce more than 310 articles of clothing per second and make profits of US$60,000 per minute.

The state still runs most clothing companies. However, in the past two decades, there has been a steady increase in the number of joint-venture companies, as well as in the number of Chinese designers venturing in clothing manufacture and entrepreneurs who have hired local designers to develop clothing lines that they sell to local stores. The government has also played a fundamental role in the development of the fashion industry. The China Garment Association and China Garment Designers' Association organize events such as Fashion Week that attract designers and buyers from both China and abroad. Such events have become media magnets: the annual designer awards night is now featured on prime-time television. Several years ago, only a few dozen journalists turned up at the press centre for China Fashion Week. Last season, the number topped 500.

Foreign investors are multiplying rapidly. High-end Italian designers are prominent in their enthusiasm for the Chinese market. Moschino recently created Moschino Far East, a joint venture with Bluebell, its local partner. Their goal is to increase their business in East Asia by 25 per cent within four years. Moschino already has fifteen retail centres in Japan, Korea, Hong Kong, Taiwan, Singapore, Thailand and China. Recently they opened two big stores in Shanghai and in Beijing. Italy is also the main importer of shoes into China.

The international clothing industry stands out for its constant global search for the cheapest, most compliant labour force. The apparel industry is now organized into buyer-driven commodity chains. Corporations such as Nike, Reebok, Liz Claiborne and The Gap design and market but do not manufacture the products they sell. Thus, they rely on an intricate network of contractors that perform almost all their specialized tasks. Contractors around the globe with low profit margins engage in fierce competition for contracts with such retailers that tend to prefer to contract in countries, such as China, where independent labour organizing is suppressed by the state.

Millions of rural Chinese women and children are recruited to toil in the nation's factories making products for Western consumers. Both government officials and foreign factory owners routinely ignore China's wage, hour, health and safety laws. Employees work twelve-hour days, sometimes seven days a week, and pay can be as low as 12 cents an hour, with wages sometimes withheld for months. The workers are forced to do overtime, adding up to eighty-four-hour work-weeks, sometimes without the legally required overtime premium. There is complete secrecy about how their wages and deductions are calculated. No benefits, even legally required ones, are granted to the workers, who are housed in cramped quarters, ten to twelve people to a room, under twenty-four-hour surveillance of guards. Corporal punishment is common: in the worst factories, workers endure beatings, insults, arbitrary fines for breaking rules, body searches, restricted use of the bathroom and few or no holidays. They are exposed to dangerous chemicals and hazardous working conditions.

See also: cashmere industry; fashion designers; fur fashion; silk industry

Further reading

http://english.peopledaily.com.cn/200203/30/ eng20020330_93092.shtml
http://www.cctv.com/lm/933/13/72205.html
http://www.fashion.org.cn/
http://www.phm.gov.au/hsc/evrev/
http://www.sh.com/custom/cgea.htm
www.cleanclothes.org
www.nlcnet.org
www.sweatshopwatch.org
Chen, Tina Mai, and Zamperini, Paola (eds) (2003). *Fabrications*. Special issue of *positions: east asia cultures critique* 11.2 (Fall).
Roberts, C. (1997). *Evolution and Revolution: Chinese Dress 1700s–1900s*. Sydney: Powerhouse Museum.
Steele, Valerie and Major, J. S. (1999) *China Chic: East Meets West*. London: Yale University Press.

PAOLA ZAMPERINI

Cobra

(Yanjingshe)

Rock band

Founded in the spring of 1989 by four women musicians in Beijing, Cobra began as a cover band playing English-language pop/rock songs and popularized versions of Chinese folksongs. Their debut appearance at the 'Concert of Modern Music' in Beijing (1990) launched their career – this landmark event was the first large-scale unveiling of local rock to the Chinese public. After the band's initial success, the members began writing their own material. Cobra released their first original, 'My Own Paradise', on a compilation called *Rocking Beijing* in 1992. After replacing one member and adding a new instrumentalist, Cobra's membership has remained unchanged since 1992, allowing for a musical camaraderie that has led, over time, to the band's eclectic 'The Cure-meets-Nirvana' sound.

Cobra's unique status as China's only all-female rock band from 1989 to 1999 brought the members much attention, especially from the news media and Westerners, who tended to see Cobra as a progressive force for Chinese feminism. The women's private and public lives have been profiled in a number of press articles and documentaries, including *1966: My Time in the Red Guards* by **Wu Wenguang** and *Rockin' the Great Wall* by Victor Huey.

Cobra released two self-produced albums: *Hypocrisy* (1994, re-released as *Cobra* in mainland China, 1996) and *Cobra II* (2000). After twelve years of struggling in a fledgling rock scene with few economic rewards, and fewer opportunities for artistic recognition, the group finally disbanded in late 2000, shortly after the release of their second and final album. The members of the group are: Wang Xiaofang (drums/vocals, songwriter), Xiao Nan (guitar/vocals/songwriter), Yu Jin (keyboard/manager), Lin Xue (saxophone, 1992–9), Yang Ying (bass, 1989–92) and Suo Yi (bass, 1992–2000).

See also: New Documentary Movement; rock music, rock bands

Further reading

http://www.niubi.com/cobra/

CYNTHIA P. WONG

Confucian ritual music

The Confucian ritual maintained in Taiwan is one of the few surviving symbols of traditional Chinese government and ideology. The accompanying music, however, with its ponderously slow melodies, openly ideological texts and ancient ritual instruments, has the most minimal entertainment value in today's world and is not well known outside a small circle of government functionaries and traditionally educated literati.

Confucius (551–479 BC) is remembered and worshipped for his high educational and philosophical ideals. While performances in his honour are mentioned in texts dating from the Han dynasty (206 BC–AD 220), it was not until about the thirteenth century that Confucianism became firmly established as official state ideology. Subsequently, Confucian shrines were located in every district of the empire, and rituals were scheduled during the spring and autumn of each year. With the fall of the imperial system in 1911, the ritual and its music slowly disappeared on the Chinese mainland. Many shrines were destroyed before and during the **Cultural Revolution** (1966–76), but there has been some resumption of ritual activity at the shrine in Qufu (the birthplace of Confucius) and elsewhere, though a large part of this activity has been oriented towards the entertainment of tourists. In Taiwan, the ritual has been maintained, though with early twentieth-century war-time interruptions and later revisions. Known in Taiwan as the 'Confucian sacrificial ceremony' (*jikong dianli*), it is held only once a year on 28 September, which is named 'Teacher's Day' in honour of the legacy of Confucianism and its educational ideals.

In Taiwan there are several active shrines, the largest being the Taipei Kongmiao. The Taipei shrine is a cluster of buildings and courtyards enclosed by a wall. Attached to the front of the main temple is a broad platform on which the very large sets of bells and stone chimes are positioned.

Extending out from this platform is a performance terrace on which ceremonial dancers and other musicians perform. The Taipei ritual begins at dawn. Consecration officers, dignitaries, musicians and dancers march into position in the central courtyard and onto the raised performance terrace. They are accompanied by drum rolls sounded on the *jingu* (large barrel drum) and strokes on the very large *yongzhong* (bell). Following the offering of sacrificial animals, the ceremony continues with a performance of the first of six hymns, 'Welcoming the Spirit' (*yingshen*), in which the 'spirit' of Confucius is invited to descend into the shrine for recognition. As with all hymns, the ancient text promotes Confucian ideology, notably virtuous behaviour, welfare for the country and performance of the proper rituals.

Each hymn is organized in eight phrases, four words per phrase, each held four beats. It is introduced by three-stroke consecutive patterns on the *paiban* (wooden clapper), *zhu* (resonant wooden box) and *taogu* (small pole-mounted drum), and a single stroke on the *bozhong* (medium bell). The hymn is sung by a chorus of (usually) six male voices in unison, accompanied heterophonically by an ensemble consisting of wind instruments, zithers and struck idiophones. The wind instruments are traditionally of six types: *xun* (globular flute of clay), *chi* (transverse flute), **dizi** (transverse flute with membrane), *xiao* (vertical notched flute), *paixiao* (panpipes) and *sheng* (mouth-organ) – normally with several or more performers on each part. The zithers employed are of two types: the **qin** (seven-string bridgeless zither) and the *se* (twenty-five-string bridged zither), the popular **zheng** zither not traditionally employed in ritual music. Bells and stone chimes punctuate the melody at fixed time intervals, the *bianzhong* (frame of clapperless bells) alternating with the *bianqing* (frame of resonant stones).

Particularly characteristic of the Taipei ritual is the employment of percussion interludes between phrases, patterns of alternating strokes between *jiangu* and *yinggu* (large barrel drums mounted on poles), together with strokes on the *teqing* (single stone chime) and *bozhong* (medium bell). The end of the hymn is signalled by three strokes on the back of an instrument called *yu*, a wooden idiophone in the shape of a crouching tiger. The symbolic implications of this act are powerful, for the tiger was traditionally the most feared of all animals in China. Stroking its back is believed to represent the subjugation of the beast and conquering of evil.

See also: Confucius (recent interpretations); New Confucianism

Further reading

Kishibe, Shigeo (1980). 'China: II. Court Traditions'. *The New Grove Dictionary of Music and Musicians*, 6th edn, vol. 4. London: Macmillan: 250–3.

Lam, Joseph (1998). *State Sacrifices and Music in Ming China: Orthodoxy, Creativity, and Expressiveness*. Albany: State University of New York.

Moule, G. E. (1901). 'Notes on the Ting-Chi, or Half Yearly Sacrifice to Confucius'. *Journal of the Royal Asiatic Society, North China Branch* 33: 120–56.

Thrasher, Alan (2000). *Chinese Musical Instruments*. Hong Kong: Oxford University Press.

ALAN R. THRASHER

Confucius (recent interpretations)

From 1949 to 1978, the new regime explicitly sought to replace traditional culture with a Communist one. As the most influential philosopher in pre-Communist China whose teachings represented the core of Chinese tradition, Confucius suffered a steady decline in stature. In the 1950s and early 1960s, attempts were made by neo-Confucians such as Feng Youlan to 'inherit' elements of his philosophy that were compatible with socialism. By the Cultural Revolution period, however, Confucius was denounced as an arch villain and paramount reactionary. When the Cultural Revolution ended, attempts were made to reinterpret both the man and his teachings as progressive and useful.

In post-1949 China, education was the one area where many intellectuals felt Confucius could still provide a model. This became patent as soon as the Cultural Revolution ended. As early as 1980,

Confucian moral education was proposed as a means of filling the 'moral vacuum' left by the political chaos of the previous decade. Thus, Confucius was held up as a man upon whom young people could model themselves. By highlighting the perception that the moral and educational situation had reached a crisis point, Confucius was hailed as a sagely thinker and scholars and intellectuals were seen as indispensable elements of the social fabric.

The reinstatement of Confucius as the paragon of teachers was no surprise. This was done many times before. However, in the 1980s and 1990s a totally new interpretation of Confucius' role in the modern world emerged. Given the fact that for centuries Confucius had been associated with the scholar class and seen to be hostile to commerce and monetary concerns, it seems inconceivable that he could be portrayed as a business guru. Yet this is precisely what happened. The new interpretations were partly initiated by 'contemporary New Confucians' (*dangdai xinrujia*), scholars such as Tang Junyi and Tu Wei-ming, who lived outside mainland China. They attempted to modernize and internationalize Confucianism by linking Confucian education with the economic prosperity in East Asia.

The economic growth of the Asia-Pacific region throughout most of the 1980s and 1990s generated increasing interest in the search for 'Asian values', of which Confucianism was an integral feature. Scholars and intellectuals who for many years had called for the 'inheritance' of Confucian philosophy were understandably very quick to cash in on the economic boom in East Asia. In the PRC, a similar shift in emphasis took place. In quick succession, a series of articles appeared showing how Confucianism had been essential for modernization in industrial countries in East Asia such as Japan and Korea. Throughout the 1980s and 1990s, there was a concerted effort to show that Confucius' ideas were beneficial to economic growth. Using the generally accepted view that the central core of Confucius' teaching is *ren*, and that *ren* meant the discovery of humanity in human relationships, scholars tried to show that this emphasis on the centrality of man was the essential element that had been missing in modern management. Thus, it was argued, in a developing socialist market economy, Confucian ethics should be used to combat the corrupting influence of the lust for money. By such means, the traditional antipathy between Confucianism and capitalism was dissolved, and Confucius was said to have been a management and entrepreneurial guru, whose words set the benchmark for good business practice. This new assessment of Confucius continued to gain popularity in the beginning of the twenty-first century.

See also: New Confucianism; political culture in Singapore; socialist spiritual civilization

KAM LOUIE

Conjugation

[Dongci bianwei, 2001]

Film

In her masterfully directed first feature film, Emily Tang (Tang Xiaobai), one of the few female directors of the **Sixth Generation**, draws a subtle yet harrowing picture of the despair that struck her generation after Tiananmen Square.

In the cold winter of 1989, Guo Song and Xiao Qing, a young couple who have met while demonstrating on the Square, sneak into empty buses to make love at night. Later, they move in together (illegally, for they're not married) in a hovel they try to turn into a shelter against the outside world. Guo Song, a recent graduate, has been assigned a factory job. Xiao Qing, a student, moonlights in a 'new-style' cappuccino bar. When Guo Song gets drunk with his buddies, they talk about one of them, nicknamed 'Foot Finger', still 'missing', and they read aloud the poems he left behind – letters addressed to an imaginary 'sister':

> Sister, sister! I am cold and lonely
> Shrouded in darkness.

Conjugation's elliptic structure is made of seemingly disconnected vignettes: the pathetic dance celebrating the upcoming Asian Olympic games that Guo Song and his co-workers are forced to perform; Xiao Qing's joyless encounter with a businessman who takes her to a hotel; or Guo Song's blank stare when the man drops her at their door. Keeping all violence off-screen, Tang focuses on small gestures, mundane situations, the fragile pursuit of personal happiness and the unbearable silence of repression, sometimes broken by a glimpse of hope.

BÉRÉNICE REYNAUD

consumerism

Consumerism, both as the mass consumption of commercial goods and as an ideology of the Chinese economy, has significantly shaped the lives of the ordinary Chinese since the end of the 1970s. Since the end of the 1970s, 'mass consumption' (*dazhong xiaofei*), a characteristic of consumption, came to refer to the rapid spread of durable goods such as refrigerators, televisions and washing machines into every household within a few years. If one family purchased an item, all families in the neighbourhood followed suit. Also, mass consumption was manifest at the ideological level. Because the individual was not allowed to own productive materials under the system of planned distribution, ownership of consumer goods became the major form of personal wealth. Hence, in the mid 1980s when reform began in the cities, 'make money, spend hard' (*nengzheng huihua*) became a fashionable new lifestyle widely reported in the media.

As incomes rise and new products enter the market, Chinese households steadily redefine which household purchases are considered 'major items' (*dajian*). During the 1970s, bicycles, sewing machines and watches were considered substantial household purchases. In the 1980s, colour televisions, refrigerators and washing machines were the new status objects. In the 1990s, stereo sets, air conditioners, microwaves and personal computers became the new indicators. Housing and home improvement are currently a major area of consumption. All-in-one housing units – self-contained apartments with their own entrance, private bath and kitchen – have become the norm in new buildings and the standard in most renovations.

The development of consumption has also been shaped by the significant increase of leisure time. Before the 1980s, there was hardly differentiation between 'work time' (*gongzuo shijian*) and 'rest time' (*xiuxi shijian*), between 'individual activities' (*geren huodong*) and 'collective activities' (*jiti huodong*), and between 'material pleasure/entertainment' (*wuzhi xiangshou/yule*) and 'spiritual pleasure/entertainment' (*jingshen xiangshou/ yule*). By the 1990s, the boundaries between 'work for wages' (*gongzuo*) and 'leisure' (*xiuxian*) had been clearly marked. Moreover, leisure time has been increased significantly since 1994 when the Chinese government reduced weekly work hours from forty-eight to forty. Since 1999, the national holidays, including Chinese **New Year Festival**, May Day and National Day (1 October), have been significantly expanded so that Chinese have more time to consume and travel. May Day celebration, for example, has been extended from a one-day to a seven-day holiday. The total number of holidays in a year has currently reached to 114 days.

The Chinese government has also encouraged the development of the 'rights of the consumers' (*xiaofeizhe*). The first consumer rights organization began in Xingle county, Hebei province in 1983. The Chinese Association of Consumers was established in Beijing in 1984, and 15 March has been recognized as International Consumer's Day since 1985. An Act for Protecting the Rights of Consumers (*Xiaofeizhe quanyi baohufa*) was passed in 1993. There are now over 20,000 consumer rights organizations across the nation.

See also: department stores; advertising; shopping malls

Further reading

Dai, Jinhua (1996). 'Redemption and Consumption: Depicting Culture in the 1990s'. *positions: east asia cultures critique* 4.1 (Spring): 127–43.

Davis, Deborah (ed.) (2000). *The Consumer Revolution in Urban China*. Berkeley, CA: University of California Press.

Hooper, Beverly (2001). 'Consumer Voices: Asserting Rights in Post-Mao China'. *China Information* 14.2: 92–128.

Schein, Louisa (2001). 'Chinese Consumerism and the Politics of Envy: Cargo in the 1990s?' In Zhang Xudong (ed.), *Whither China? Intellectual Politics in Contemporary China*. Durham: Duke University Press, 285–314.

Zhao, Bin and Murdock, Graham (1996). 'Young Pioneers: Children and the Making of Chinese Consumerism'. *Cultural Studies* 10.2: 201–17.

REN HAI

corruption

Post-Mao China is an era of corruption as well as reform. Corruption has accelerated partly because the changes in the economy have provided officials with a much greater incentive and opportunity to embezzle funds or accept bribes. Taking advantage of the 'double price track policy' (*jiage shuanggui zhi*) in the 1980s, official-profiteers obtained raw materials for production and scarce goods at the government-fixed prices and sold them at much higher prices in the market. During the Tiananmen movement in 1989, student demonstrators indignantly shouted, 'Down with official profiteering!' but since then corruption has only worsened.

Chen Xitong (b. 1930), Politburo member and Beijing's Party Secretary, was sentenced to sixteen years of imprisonment in 1998 for depriving the city's coffers of an equivalent of over US$2 billion. His fall was presaged by the suicide of Wang Baosen (1935–95), the vice-mayor of Beijing, during his investigation for corruption. The two cases suggested that the entire Beijing municipal leadership had grown fat on ill-gotten money and bribes. Hu Changqing (1948–2000), Vice-Governor of Jiangxi, was executed on 8 March 2000 for taking 5.44 million yuan ($657,200) in bribes and possessing 1.61 million yuan ($195,000) worth of property whose origin he could not explain. Cheng Kejie, Vice-Chairman of the National People's Congress and Governor of Guangxi, was executed on 14 September 2000 for taking bribes of an equivalent of $5 million. He is the most senior person ever executed in the history of the PRC. All of them, by the way, had a mistress or mistresses.

The sentences signal a determination to eradicate official corruption, but the motives seem rooted more in politics than in the rule of law (*fazhi*). To complement China's traditional 'rule by **morality**' (*dezhi*), which Jiang Zemin still emphasizes, some localities are even setting regulations that hold officials responsible, along with the perpetrators, for failing to prevent corruption-related crimes. When we look at the corruption cases exposed in China's media, from the top leaders mentioned above to the case of Lai Changxing, who went from rags to riches by bribing numerous high-ranking officials for **Guanxi** and smuggling and then fled to Canada, which of these cases is not committed by officials themselves or not official-related? A growing number of corrupt officials have found safe haven in Western countries with their astonishing hauls. China's leaders realize the dangers of corruption, openly and repeatedly acknowledging that it is a life-and-death matter. Ironically, some officials even embezzled Party membership fees and the funds for study material related to the propagation of Jiang Zemin's ideology of the **Sange daibiao** (Three Represents). These cases, most of which are understandably not publicized, are considered 'alternative corruption' (*lingyilei tanwu*), according to an article in **Xinmin Evening News** (16 December 2001). The authorities face a stark dilemma, neatly summed up in a snippet of doggerel verse (**shunkouliu**): 'If you control corruption, you'll destroy the Party/If you don't control corruption, you'll destroy the State (*Fan fubai wangdang/bu fan fubai wangguo*)'.

Further reading

Kwong, Julia (1997). *The Political Economy of Corruption in China*. Armonk, NY, and London: M. E. Sharpe.

Lü, Xiaobo (2000). *Cadres and Corruption: The Organizational Involution of the Chinese Communist Party*. Stanford: Stanford University Press: 154–227.

HELEN XIAOYAN WU

cosmetic surgery

In 1943, during the Anti-Japanese War, a medical school student was sent to the University of Pennsylvania to study plastic and reconstructive surgery so that he could bring back advanced treatments for wounded soldiers. His name was

Song Ruyao, and he became the founder of plastic surgery in China and its offshoot, cosmetic surgery.

Only a few cosmetic surgery operations were performed before Liberation. It was denounced during the **Cultural Revolution** for its 'bourgeois' attention to form over function. When the 'pursuit of beauty' became acceptable in the 1980s, cosmetic surgery grew rapidly in popularity, reflecting changing beauty ideals. Due to a long-standing ideal of smooth white skin, techniques for whitening skin and removing moles and freckles were by far the most popular. Perhaps reflecting the influence of Western ideals, next popular was the 'double eyelid' operation to add a crease above the eye opening, which was considered naturally characteristic of European eyes as well as of a minority of Chinese eyes. This was followed by nose implants to increase the height of the nose bridge. Breast augmentation was not nearly as popular as in the USA, and the average size of the implants was smaller; but it became more popular over time, perhaps due to the influence of Hollywood ideals.

Further reading

Song, R. (1987). 'Woguo zhengxing waike fazhande lishi huigu' [A Look Back at the History of the Development of Our Nation's Plastic Surgery]. *Zhonghua zhengxing shaoshang waike zazhi* [Chinese Journal of Plastic and Burn Surgery] 3.4 (December).

SUSAN BROWNELL

crazes

China's 1978 reform opened the door of a formerly repressive and isolated society. The ensuing loosening of state control and influx of new information induced waves of crazes in urban areas, especially in the 1980s. The crazes can be categorized into three types: socioeconomic crazes, high culture crazes and popular culture crazes. Socioeconomic crazes were a result of people's reactions to the sudden emergence of new economic and political freedoms after the reform. Both the high culture craze and the popular culture craze resulted from a sudden influx of new information from the West and

a rediscovery of China's past. High culture crazes can be further divided into three subtypes: Western culture crazes, (Chinese) culture criticism crazes and traditional Chinese culture crazes. The first two subtypes are two sides of the same coin. While the culture criticism crazes saw Chinese culture as a major hurdle to modernization, the Western culture crazes looked to the West for solutions.

The frequent crazes have created great uncertainties for urban life. Culture crazes introduced new values and ways of life incompatible with the prevailing orthodoxy, while socioeconomic crazes often turned past winners into losers. Thus, although crazes came into being under the impetus for change, they also brought great pain to both those inside and those outside of them. Crazes have been a vital part in China's sociopolitical life since the reform. For example, the 1989 pro-democracy movement was induced in part by the culture crazes of the mid 1980s, and Li Hongzhi's **Falun gong** was a product of the Qigong craze (a traditional Chinese culture craze; see **Qigong (history)**). While the 1989 Movement is arguably one of the largest rebellions in Chinese history, Falun gong is currently a big headache for the Chinese regime.

Major social fevers in urban China during the 1980s

1   Socio-economic fevers

    (a)   Study fever and diploma fever: arose because early reform policies emphasized the role of intellectuals in economic reform and greatly elevated the political status of intellectuals.

    (b)   Political career fever (*Congzheng re*): arose due to massive recruitment of state cadres among university graduates during the early 1980s, and diminished as state offices became saturated by the mid 1980s.

    (c)   Business fever: arose with the opportunities created by the market-oriented reform, and peaked in 1988, when some intellectuals and students, many in a protesting mood, got involved in commercial ventures.

    (d)   Going abroad fever: students and some young urban workers tried any means to work abroad in order to have a better life and career and to escape from Chinese realities. Peaked in the late 1980s when the opportunities to go abroad increased and the reform was in crisis.

(e) Special Economic Zones (SEZs) fever: massive numbers of people flooded the SEZs looking for better opportunities. The most infamous such fever was in Hainan in the late 1980s, when hundreds of thousands moved to this newly founded island province and SEZ.

2   High culture fevers

(a) Sartre, Nietszche and Freud fevers: a series of social fevers found Chinese intellectuals and students searching for meaning in the wake of the decline of Marxism.

(b) Religion fever: in cities, mainly the fever for Christianity. People looked for alternative faiths after Marxism, although many followed just out of pro-Western curiosity.

(c) Culture fever: culture criticism started in the mid 1980s and peaked in 1988 with the TV series *Heshang* (**River Elegy**) and the earth citizenship discussion. The central idea was that Chinese culture should be held responsible for the failed development and tragedies of Mao's era.

(d) Searching-for-roots fever (*Xungen re*); roots-searching literature (see **Scar literature**; **Scar art**), **New Confucianism**, **Yijing** and Qigong fevers: most of these fevers were apolitical. They marked the revival of Chinese culture after the death of Mao and were led by intellectuals absorbed by features of traditional Chinese culture.

3   Popular culture fevers

(a) The Hong Kong/Taiwan pop song fever: during the early 1980s, Hong Kong and Taiwan songs flooded the mainland. The state initially tried to resist but eventually acquiesced (see **Kong-Tai style**).

(b) Jeans fever, brand-name dress fever, make-up fever: Western and Hong Kong–style dress and ideas of beauty dominated Chinese cities and coastal areas during and after these and other similar fevers.

(c) Western food and holiday fevers: eating Western food and celebrating Western holidays such as Christmas became very popular from the mid 1980s, especially among students (see **fast food (Western); holidays (Western)**).

(d) Pop and movie star fever: Since the late 1980s, fans of movie stars and pop singers have acted more and more like their Western counterparts.

(e) **Mahjong** fever: **mahjong** fever represented the revival of many traditional recreational activites, rituals and superstitions.

(Adapted from Zhao Dingxin 2001: 44–5)

Further reading

Wang, Jing (1996). *High Culture Fever*. Berkeley: University of California Press.

Zhao, Dingxin (2001). *The Power of Tiananmen: State–Society Relations and the 1989 Beijing Student Movement*. Chicago: University of Chicago Press, ch. 2.

ZHAO DINGXIN

Criminal Procedure Law (and revisions)

For the first three decades of its existence, the People's Republic of China had neither a general Criminal Law nor a general Criminal Procedure Law. Crimes and their punishments were defined, if at all, in a variety of documents ranging from individual legislative acts to Communist Party documents. Procedure was seen as distinctly secondary, and indeed as not the kind of matter about which rules were necessary or desirable.

The post-Mao leadership, however, saw a need for a firmer legal foundation for China's criminal law regime, and quite quickly (in 1979) promulgated both a Criminal Law and a Criminal Procedure Law (CPL). The 1979 CPL was substantially revised in 1996 in order to bring its provisions in line both with the vast changes in

Chinese society that had taken place since the original law was promulgated and with demands for greater rationalization. On the whole, the revised CPL is more hospitable to defendants' rights. It allows earlier access to **lawyers**, and makes court proceedings somewhat more transparent than before. It does not, however, allow the defence the right either to obtain witnesses under the same conditions as the prosecution or to examine all witnesses against him or her. Whatever its provisions, the CPL plays only a limited role in governing state-initiated punitive procedures, as it governs only proceedings under the Criminal Law. It is of no effect, for example, in proceedings under which sentences of up to fifteen days of 'administrative detention' or up to four years of 'rehabilitation through labour' can be imposed.

Further reading

Hecht, J. (1996). *Opening to Reform? An Analysis of China's Revised Criminal Procedure Law*. New York: Lawyers Committee for Human Rights.

DONALD CLARKE

Cui Jian

b. 2 August 1961, Beijing

Rock singer

Cui Jian was born into an ethnically Korean musician's family. He started learning the trumpet at age fourteen and worked with the Beijing Philharmonic Orchestra from 1981 to 1987. In late 1984, he recorded his first album, *Return of the Prodigal Son* (*Langzi gui*). Cui did not contribute the lyrics, and the music followed the mainstream of popular light music. In 1986, his song '**I Have Nothing**' ('*Yiwu suoyou*') became an instant hit. The following year he began working with ADO, a young Beijing band, with which he released the PRC's first rock album, *Rock 'n' Roll on the New Long March* (*Xin changzhang lushang de yaogun*, 1988). Despite the absence of any media coverage, difficulties in organizing concerts and censorship problems, the album sold nationwide and his lyrics

very much gave voice to the sentiments of many young Chinese during that period in the PRC's history.

Cui is the first rock musician who has given concerts outside the PRC (Seoul 1988; London, Paris 1989, etc.) and, since 1993, has also been engaged in a number of film projects: **Beijing Bastards** (*Beijing zazong*) was jointly produced with film director **Zhang Yuan**. In 2000 he composed the music for **Jiang Wen**'s movie, *Devils at the Doorstep* (*Guizi laile*), and acted in Yu Zhong's *My Brothers and Sisters* (*Wo de xiongdi jiemei*). In December, the Netherlands honoured him with the Prince Claus Award for outstanding contributions to culture and society. The experimental dance musical *Show Me Your Colours* (*Gei wo yidian yanse*), a collaboration with the Hong Kong Modern Dance Company, had its premiere in February 2001.

While he emphasizes individualism and self-reflection, the music shifted from rock towards rhythm-oriented digital avant-rock, still bearing significant Chinese elements. Although his later albums could not compete with the success of 1988, Cui continues to be critical of society, recognized both abroad and in the PRC, where he played twenty-eight shows in 2001.

See also: rock music, rock bands

Further reading

Baranovitch, Nimrod (2003). *China's New Voices: Popular Music, Ethnicity, Gender, and Politics*. Berkeley: University of California Press.

Chong, Woei Lien (1991). 'Young China's Voice of the 1980s: Rock Star Cui Jian'. *China Information* 6.1 (Summer): 55–74.

Cui, Jian and Zhou, Guoping (2001). *Ziyou fengge* [Free Style]. Guangxi shifan daxue chubanshe.

Jones, Andrew (1992). *Like a Knife. Ideology and Genre in Contemporary Chinese Popular Music*. Ithaca: Cornell University.

Steen, Andreas (1996). *Der Lang Marsch des Rock 'n' Roll. Pop- und Rockmusik in der Volksrepublik China*. Hamburg: Lit-Verlag.

www.cuijian.com

ANDREAS STEEN

Cui Zhiyuan

b. 1963, Beijing

Political economist, intellectual

A political economist trained at the University of Chicago and based overseas, Cui is among the most influential expatriate scholars in China. Although his work is constituted in the mode of Western social sciences, his views are read and debated in Chinese intellectual circles. Of particular impact upon recent Chinese thought is his thesis on 'institutional innovation and the second intellectual liberation' which marked the arrival of the **New Left**. The first intellectual liberation led to the post-Mao economic reforms. Its basic assumptions about central planning versus the free market, Cui argues, have evolved into a new dogmatism that involves the wholesale repudiation of socialism in favour of absolute capitalism. This dogmatism was most forcefully pursued in Eastern Europe and the former USSR with catastrophic consequences, and China was dangerously moving in this direction. Given these circumstances, Cui's intervention has been timely.

Cui sets out to demystify the free market by highlighting recent legal and political changes in the United States that have strengthened the state regulation of corporations and the protection of stakeholders and community interests, thus undermining the very sources of the free-market fantasy. He further connects American innovations in workplace democracy and economic justice to his constructive revaluation of some Maoist experiments and to the success stories of collective rural and township enterprises in China. Cui's intervention is dialectical, simultaneously uncovering egalitarian elements in the unlikely system of American capitalism and unpacking a similarly monolithic image of Chinese socialism in order to transcend reductive dichotomies and establish a new-leftist politics.

YUE GANG

cultural Christians

The phenomenon of cultural Christians (*wenhua jidutu*) developed in the PRC in the 1980s. The term is often used in a wider context to describe the increasing number of researchers in the PRC doing varied studies about Christianity. They can be roughly divided into three groups: first, intellectuals researching Christianity in various ways without having a faith; second, intellectuals professing Christian faith but not associating with any church; and third, intellectuals who are active, baptized members in a congregation. A majority of the first group may not even consider themselves cultural Christians. The second group can be considered the core of cultural Christians, while the third group is quite marginal.

One of the most prominent cultural Christians is Liu Xiaofeng (b. 1956, Chongqing), theologian and philosopher. Other well-known names are He Guanghu and Zhang Zhiyang. Liu wrote several books in the 1980s and the 1990s that attracted much attention in academic and church circles in the PRC, Hong Kong and Taiwan as well as abroad. Liu's and others' theological and ethical reflections for a change in modern Chinese society have been seen by some other Chinese intellectuals as attempts to 'save China'. Liu and others deny this but personal and national salvation is undoubtedly an important part of all aspects of the cultural Christian phenomenon.

Cultural Christians are few in number and have not developed any network or particular form of worship but are influential through their academic positions and publications. They have a decisive role to play in contemporary Chinese society and specifically for Christian development in China.

Further reading

Zhuo, X. (2001). 'Discussion on "Cultural Christians" in China'. In S. Uhalley and X. Wu (eds), *China and Christianity: Burdened Past, Hopeful Future*. Armonk, NY: M. E. Sharpe.

FREDERIK FÄLLMAN

cultural discussion

(wenhua taolun)

Intellectual debate

'Cultural discussion' refers to the major academic debate during the **culture fever** of the 1980s.

The debate was stimulated by the ongoing economic reforms. Frustrated by various problems encountered in the reform, intellectuals were eager to find the roots of and solutions to these problems. Culture was believed a crucial factor in social and economic transition. What role Chinese traditional culture was playing in the reform and modernization thus became the dominant issue in the discussion. Two opposing views emerged. One believed that China's traditional culture, more specifically its core, Confucianism, could become a very positive spiritual resource for China's modernization. The other condemned Confucianism and Chinese traditional culture as incompatible with modern society and therefore to be got rid of, and argued that modern culture originated in the West should be introduced to transform Chinese society and mindset. To a large extent these two opinions echoed those debated in the New Culture movement seventy years before; however, unlike the earlier situation, the opinion favouring Chinese traditional culture seemed to win a more sympathetic hearing and attract more attention. Overseas Chinese scholars have played a significant role in this cultural discussion. Chinese-American scholar Tu Wei-ming, for example, lectured in Beijing and Shanghai several times in the mid 1980s, arguing that Confucianism had played a very positive role in the modernization of East and Southeast Asia, and it could play a similar role in China's modernization. His arguments greatly stimulated the discussion and convinced people to pay more attention to the positive elements in China's tradition. This discussion continued to attract scholarly attention until the end of the decade, and it has greatly deepened and widened people's understanding of tradition and modernization.

Further reading

Wang, Jing (1996). 'High Culture Fever: The Cultural Discussion in the Mid-1980s and the Politics of Methodologies'. In *idem*, *High Culture Fever: Politics, Aesthetics, and Ideology in Deng's China*. Berkeley: University of California Press, 37–117.

LIU CHANG

cultural landscapes

Over thirty years ago one of the twentieth century's greatest human geographers wrote:

> The Chinese earth is pervasively humanized through long occupation ... Even in the rugged parts of China, in areas that look like untouched wildernesses, subtle evidences of human presence occur ... Landscapes depicted by Chinese artists ... owe their expressive grammar at least in part to the special character of the Chinese environment.
>
> (Tuan 1970: 1)

In human geography, cultural landscapes are seen both as the material expression of culture and as 'texts' that inform us regarding cultural values, meanings and characteristics. In one sense they form the link between the natural environment and human experience.

For example, the soft, yellow earth of the *loess* plateau (*huangtu gaoyuan*) in the dry north is the backdrop to a contemporary cultural landscape that has been in the making for more than thirty centuries. This is the region that is often referred to as the cradle of Chinese civilization. Although the city walls are gone (with a few exceptions such as Pingyao in Shanxi province; see Knapp 1992), various models of cave-like, underground dwellings are still actively built and used in large areas. Estimates vary greatly, but a reasonably conservative one places the number at some 30 million people in the provinces of Shanxi, Henan, Shaanxi and Gansu who live in underground homes that are either dug down from the surface, carved into soft *loess* cliff-faces or are combinations of above-ground and *loess*-covered dwellings. In spite of certain drawbacks, there are considerable advantages to this traditional type of dwelling: they are cool in the summer, warm in the winter, and relatively inexpensive to build.

Although cityscapes in China tend to be rather similar to each other, two-thirds of the people still live in rural areas where there are indeed a variety of cultural landscapes. In central and south China there are some village types that are frequently found, depending on the basic physical features of the landscape mixed with local history and tradition. A common one is the village built around a man-made pond that serves practical (e.g. fish farming, water supply), aesthetic and/or religious (see **fengshui**) needs. Then there is the village that is typical of the 'water country' found in Jiangsu province, northern Zhejiang province, and the municipality of Shanghai. Here, dwellings are strung along the ubiquitous canals so that villages take on a linear (as opposed to compact) form. These villages tend to be smaller than those on the Northern Plain (the lower reaches of the Yellow River), where settlements are compact and many times as large. One of the more unifying features of the rural landscape is that of burial grounds. Even though officially discouraged, rural China places a high premium on a suitable burial place for the departed: most often, where possible, on a hill not far outside of the village or town (see **tombs and cremation**). Finally, there is a kind of village landscape found in low mountainous areas in the centre, south and southwest of China where there always seems to be a multi-purpose central 'square' (for drying, threshing, winnowing and other agricultural or social activities), as often as not one or several drum towers (see **Dong, culture of**) and often traditional waterwheels or other water-lifting devices to take maximum advantage of the river along which so many villages are built (see **Miao, culture of**).

Further reading

Tuan, Yi-fu (1970). *China*. London: Longman.

Knapp, Ronald, G. (1992). *Chinese Landscapes: The Village as Place*. Honolulu: University of Hawai'i Press.

—— (2000). *China's Walled Cities*. Oxford: Oxford University Press.

PETER M. FOGGIN

cultural purges

A purge often takes place as part of a 'rectification' (*zhengdun*), a means for the Party mechanism to right itself by wronging its members or individuals outside its ranks. In the past, cultural purges were often a weathervane for larger political ructions. The denunciation of a film or play in the press could be the prelude to a larger political campaign (the press attacks on Sun Yu's 1951 film *A Life of Wu Xun*, for example, accompanied the elimination of bourgeois ideology and its supposed champions in the educational realm). Anti-Party messages were often detected in the most obscure works, and often the most asinine reasons were given for denunciations and bans; but the effects on individuals and the culture as a whole could prove devastating.

As the sanctions against writers and artists who had erred became more cosmetic, and the effects of cultural purges less long-lived following the 1970s, canny creators began to exploit the potential of being attacked in the Party. By the late 1980s, an official ban in the mainland could lead to lucrative sales in Hong Kong, Taiwan and further afield. By the 1990s, rock artists, painters and some writers and filmmakers positively thrived on official opprobrium. Meanwhile, within the Party's culture attacking negative social and cultural trends could still bolster bureaucratic careers and be used as an excuse to pad the budgets of propaganda organizations. The Party-state mechanisms for launching cultural purges or denunciation campaigns (from the late 1990s these were often patriotic education campaigns) were not dismantled, and they could function with impressive gusto when the need arose.

Following 4 June 1989, a series of cultural purges aimed at the supposed intellectual and culture progenitors of the political turmoil were launched. The writers who had worked on **River Elegy**, the astrophysicist Fang Lizhi, the journalists Liu Binyan, Wang Ruowang and **Dai Qing**, and the literary critic **Liu Xiaobo**, among others (a list originally compiled by the rogue conservative writer **He Xin**), were vilified in the mass media, and edited collections of their poisonous writings were produced to illustrate the official attacks. These crude, Maoist-style media criticisms did more to extol rather than extirpate the heinous influence of these individuals. Eventually, younger, more media-savvy apparatchiks would eschew such methods; instead, they dressed up positive Party messages in the language of commercial advertising and the hard sell.

The purge, either individual or collective, can still be initiated by the remarks of a political leader, the tenor of a Party meeting, or as the result of some external stimulus (international notoriety, factional jealousy, as part a diversionary tactic used by politicians, or out of sheer bureaucratic bloody-mindedness). While many cultural figures can make a comeback from a cultural putsch, or may re-launch flagging careers as a result of one, those purged for political reasons, in particular for political or religious dissent, more often than not languish in exile or suffer interment for many years.

GEREMIE R. BARMÉ

Cultural Revolution

With little agreement on when it began (1964, late 1965 or mid 1966), how long it lasted (three years, 1966–9, or a decade, 1966–76), what it was about (culture, revolution, power struggles, or simply Mao Zedong's monomania), or what it achieved (that it was a true Marxist–Leninist revolution, the prelude to the extraordinary post 1978 reform era, or just a historical vacuum), and a general official ban on in-depth research or analysis of the period, the Cultural Revolution remains one of the most ill-understood and controversial periods in modern Chinese history.

After the socialist transformation of China in the mid 1950s, Mao Zedong and his key supporters were mindful of the fragile nature of the revolution that they had initiated. Utopian agricultural policies and inefficient industrialization directed by political fiat rather than determined by socio-economic realities, coupled with an anti-market ethos that resisted the development of a consumer economy threatened the stability and viability of the People's Republic. Mao believed that ideological rectitude and revolutionary thinking would in the long run bolster the socialist state. Following the Great Leap Forward period of the late 1950s, when 'instant Communism' was attempted with disastrous results and an enormous loss of life, efforts to ameliorate those extreme policies led to a mild shift towards a mixed economy in the early 1960s. A concomitant social and cultural relaxation engendered a relative flourishing of the arts, but alerted Mao, who had been

sidelined politically because of his earlier baleful Communist adventurism, to the dangers of corrupting thoughts, cultural works and the insufficiently political educational system. Through directives, comments and the support of army leaders like Lin Biao, as well as his own wife Jiang Qing, Mao began to make a series of oblique interventions in national politics. He now proposed a cultural revolution (in the spheres of education, the media, the legal system and within state power itself) that would reinforce and safeguard the economic and political revolution that had taken place. The immediate evidence of these efforts was a series of new theatrical works, what was hailed in the media as 'modern Beijing revolutionary opera' among others, that would see traditional themes and heroes swept aside by worker, peasant and soldier protagonists.

The widespread sense of internal paranoia and embattlement was dramatically exacerbated as a result of the economic and ideological rupture with the Soviet Union (now declared to be a 'revisionist' socialist state) in the early 1960s, and the continued hostilities with the Nationalist government on Taiwan. The Nationalists were supported by a bellicose USA, a country that was regarded as being an imperialist aggressor in Korea, Japan, Taiwan, Vietnam, a nation that had engineered a veritable 'arc of aggression' against socialist China.

Mao and his colleagues encouraged a belief that apart from the external economic and military threats to the regime, there was a more long-term and insidious threat lurking within China itself. That was that culture itself (the legal system, the media, the arts and education) was subject to erroneous political thinking authored by many leaders and public figures. These figures, it was felt, were actively insinuating bourgeois and feudal (that is, traditional) ideas and values among the populace, in particular the young. It was believed that these corrupting ideas could well prepare the way, either intentionally or unintentionally, for a counter-revolution that would see the re-privatization of agricultural land, industry and business, the creation of an educational and cultural meritocracy that privileged entrenched traditional elites, and a political reversal that would undermine the rights of the proletariat and peasantry, and that would witness a quasi-capitalist and feudal regime rule in the name of the Communist Party itself.

The rise of the Red Guards from May 1966 (the movement was founded by a small group of students at the ruins of the Jesuit-designed rococo palaces in the old imperial garden palace of the **Yuanming Yuan** to the north-west of Beijing) marked both a spontaneous student response to broader political tensions and an elite contestation over the future of the nation and revolution itself. Mao Zedong and the Party's open support for these rebels in July–August 1966 led to a mass uprising of young, and not-so-young, people against the Party nomenklatura. The result over the following months was the collapse of Party and government rule.

The original rebels, having played a role in inciting nationwide rebellion by travelling the country in mock-imitations of the Red Army's Long March, and through overt and often violent attacks on all aspects of the 'old society', were in turn condemned. Contending groups vied for the mantle of true revolutionary and all swore to the death to defend Chairman Mao's revolutionary line. The contestation led to clashes and in some cases open warfare fuelled by an environment of virtual anarchy. The old power structures had been toppled, and new groupings sanctioned by Mao and his cohort grabbed power. Eventually the restive young population of the cities with no jobs or educational opportunities was dispatched to the countryside to learn about revolution through manual labour. For many this internal exile only ended in the mid to late 1970s. State cadres and intellectuals of all kinds were also rusticated as part of a policy to transform the bourgeois thinking of urban elites. Radical agricultural, industrial and cultural policies formulated in the past were now implemented with results that are generally regarded as calamitous. In the arts, model works inspired by the Beijing opera reform of the 1950s and early 1960s held sway. While the 'Beijing model theatrical works' attempted a striking amalgam of Chinese and Western culture that involved highly talented writers (like the noted novelist **Wang Zengqi**) and performers, the paucity of cultural variety and inventiveness, not to mention the stigma of their champion, Madam Mao, Jiang Qing, led to a wholesale rejection of these experiments.

Meanwhile, power struggles in Beijing and cities throughout China saw the fall of entrenched leaders and their bureaucratic supporters, all now condemned as followers of the now-defunct state president Liu Shaoqi, 'China's Khrushchev'. Revolutionary committees comprising rebels, reliable cadres and military personnel were formed to rule in their place, but they proved to be no less bureaucratic than their predecessors. An extravagant Mao cult had been promoted making it sacrilegious (and punishable) to question his omniscience and the universal wisdom of Mao Thought. With the demise of Mao's one-time staunch military supporter, Lin Biao, in 1971, supposedly following a failed assassination attempt, the extravagances of the Mao cult were curtailed, and the chairman initiated a return to regularized government by recalling Deng Xiaoping, Liu Shaoqi's close bureaucratic comrade-in-arms, to work with the premier Zhou Enlai, one of the only older Party leaders to have survived the maelstrom of the preceding years.

Infighting continued, however, with radical Maoist leaders (later dubbed 'the Gang of Four') constantly attempting to undermine both Zhou and Deng who were cautiously introducing policies aimed at reinvigorating education, the sciences, culture and the economy. Following Zhou's death in early 1976, Deng Xiaoping was purged once more. Yet another campaign in what was still being called the Cultural Revolution in the state media was unfolding when Mao Zedong himself died in September 1976. Shortly thereafter, his most radical followers were toppled from power and over the following years the policies and practices of the Cultural Revolution era, officially called a 'ten-year blank', were negated and Mao's role in the period was formally criticized in a Party decision passed in 1981. Although there are no officially published figures, it is generally recognized that during that decade millions of people's lives were disrupted, countless people were tortured or killed, and incalculable damaged was inflicted on the material legacy of Chinese civilization.

The Cultural Revolution and Mao's role in it inspired many imitators and much theoretical discussion internationally. Mao himself foresaw a time following his death when his radical attempt to maintain revolutionary momentum in a one-party socialist state would be negated, but he predicted that its value would one day be realized.

The Cultural Revolution was also a critical event in the shaping of contemporary China. The attitudes and alliances, the culture and the politics of that period led directly to the economic reforms launched by Deng Xiaoping and his supporters over twenty years ago, reforms which have changed the face and fate of the People's Republic. The cadres currently in positions of leadership in China – those running China's leading companies and much of its government, as well as those shaping its popular culture, its art and its intellectual life – came of age in the Cultural Revolution.

Since the mid 1980s, Cultural Revolution retro-chic has played a role in the contemporary arts (fashion, music, film and art); it has also led to a flourishing of 'victim literature' with only the occasional confession of heinous deeds perpetrated in the name of revolution. From the early 1990s a number of Sinophone writers and academics on both sides of the Pacific have reaffirmed the value of the period and searched in it for answers for China's post-socialist dilemmas. While neo-liberal reformist thinkers argue that the follies of the Cultural Revolution era laid the way for the economic reforms of the past decades and China's integration in the global capitalist system, a long-term benefit for China, for new left-wing commentators and neo-Marxists, all of Mao's fears about the fate of the revolution and the need for the kind of bottom-up purge of the system that he encouraged in the 1960s were justified. For them, China is indeed in the grip of a reactionary monopoly – Party bourgeois counter-revolution that has enmeshed the nation with the global economy and the US-led 'new world order'.

The Communist Party's 1981 evaluation of the Cultural Revolution (and the events that led to it) was seen as the final official verdict on the period, speaking as it did of an era of waste, 'extreme leftism' and futile infighting. When in 1989 rebellious students took to the streets of China's capital once more protesting against the power-holders, for many Party leaders it signalled a dangerous return to the iconoclasm of the past when a wave of destruction had unseated Party-state rulers and pulverized their emblems of power. This time they

did not hesitate to use maximum force to terminate a rebellion that they argued would have brought down the People's Republic itself.

GEREMIE R. BARMÉ

Cultural Revolution (education)

Schooling in China during the period 1968–76 underwent radical changes, to an extent rarely witnessed elsewhere in modern times.

In the 1960s, China's school structure had largely resembled the educational structures of other late-developing countries. Entrance examinations helped determine which of the students were able to enter each higher level of education; the competition among secondary school students was tight; and many secondary schools, especially in the cities, competed to attain a high university entrance rate.

In the aftermath of the 1966–8 Cultural Revolution turmoil, the education line favoured by Mao Zedong destroyed this earlier school structure. A principal motive was to provide better opportunities to young people from proletarian families. Since the children of the pre-revolution intellectuals and merchants were among the academically best-equipped students, the examination system had favoured them. Thus all entrance examinations and all other tests that sorted and stratified students were to be abolished. Schooling was restructured so as to level out the gaps between students from different backgrounds, and school lessons were made considerably easier.

An effort was also made to universalize education in the countryside. Villages that did not contain primary schools were pushed to establish one, largely using their own funds, while prosperous villages that already contained primary schools were encouraged to expand village schooling up through the seventh grade. The content of rural schooling no longer was influenced by efforts to send a fortunate minority of the students onward to higher education. Instead, the children were supposed to be educated solely for lives within the villages, and rural textbooks were revamped in line with this. The quality of teaching by the untrained teachers often was poor, but the rate of literacy rose noticeably.

In the major cities during the 1970s, an education was supplied to all young people through senior high school. Financially this was made possible by shortening the school curriculum from twelve years to nine or ten. Then, so as to sever entirely the links between classroom achievements and subsequent employment, all of the young graduates were assigned directly to jobs, with no account taken of their academic records when devising these job postings. A substantial proportion were allocated to work as ordinary peasants in the countryside, as China's cities were producing more school graduates than there were urban job openings. The choice of which young people could subsequently go on to a tertiary education was left to the places of work, purportedly on the basis of a young worker's or young peasant's on-the-job performance.

Though this new scheme was intended to improve the chances of working-class young people, it had a deleterious effect on a great many students' classroom behaviour, regardless of class background. According to urban schoolteachers of that era, between 1968 and Mao's death in 1976 most of their students stopped paying attention in class, and discipline in the schools became a problem. The teenagers reportedly felt it was 'useless to study' because success or failure at their schoolwork would have no bearing on their futures.

Among other things, many of them reportedly felt that a higher education was all but closed off to them. In the absence of entrance examinations or other regularized means for selecting new university students from workplaces, officials had begun pulling strings to secure a university seat for their own children. A substantial percentage of the young people who had been assigned to the countryside and who subsequently got admitted to university came from the families of urban officials, and many of the peasant entrants were closely related to commune or village officials.

Most of the new university students were ill-prepared for tertiary studies, as they had graduated from Cultural Revolution-era schools after only seven to nine years of simplified classes. Mathematics professors often needed to teach simple arithmetic to first-year students who could not add fractions. The university curriculum was also made shorter. Medical training, which had formerly been a six-year course, was reduced to three years by teaching mostly about symptoms and prescriptions, and only for the less exotic ailments. The curricula of many other specialties were reduced to three to three and a half years, and 30 per cent of this scheduled schoolwork was supposed to be devoted to labour and political study.

After Mao's death in 1976, the new leadership moved quickly to overturn almost all of the innovations in education. The competitive school ladder was reintroduced, with entrance examinations for senior high school as well as university. The new structure stresses academic 'talent' even more than the pre-Cultural Revolution system had.

When university entrance examinations were reintroduced in 1977–8, the former secondary students of pre-Cultural Revolution times were allowed to sit them. Unlike the students of the 1970s, this older generation had received a rigorous academic education, and they did disproportionately well in the exams. They were very heavily represented in the universities' intakes – especially the children of the pre-revolution intellectuals. Chinese education had come full circle.

Further reading

Pepper, Suzanne (1996). *Radicalism and Education Reform in 20th-century China*. Cambridge: Cambridge University Press: chapters 15 and 16.
Unger, Jonathan (1982). *Education Under Mao: Class and Competition in Canton Schools, 1960–1980*. New York: Columbia University Press. chapters 7–10.

JONATHAN UNGER

cultural zones (urban)

Since the early 1980s several Chinese urban administrators have designated certain streets or neighbourhoods where it has been determined that culture (*wenhua*, variously defined) is a significant element characterizing the identity (*gexing*) of that area. One important example was Liulichang in

Beijing, where the traditional identity of that street and its environs was linked to bookselling, inkstones, brushes and other paraphernalia associated with calligraphy and ink painting. Municipal authorities sanctioned both the rehabilitation and the restoration of the shops along Liulichang so that both foreign tourists and domestic patrons would revitalize the area.

In the past twenty years similar kinds of cultural zones have become fashionable throughout many Chinese cities where, because of either deliberate government intervention, private entrepreneurship or both, selected spaces associated with heritage and history have become fashionable places associated with commodities and commerce. In some cases these zones have unclear boundaries, such as the Beijing's Qianmen neighbourhood south of Tiananmen Square where, although traditional handicrafts, kitchen goods and foodstuffs are still sold from famous stores, there are no rigidly enforced guidelines associated with architectural rehabilitation. In other cases, such as Nanjing's Fuzimiao neighbourhood, the design strategies are more standardized (in this case, historicist) and the spatial boundaries more clearly defined. In other cases, as in the Barkor area of Lhasa, the spectrum constituting what is 'culture' is wide and diffuse (i.e. Han as well as Tibetan).

Further reading

Wu, Liangyong (1999). *Rehabilitating the Old City of Beijing: A Project in the Ju'er Hutong Neighbourhood.* Vancouver: University of British Columbia Press.

JEFFREY W. CODY

culture-bound syndromes

Culture-bound syndromes refer to the recurrent patterns of illness experiences only found in the Chinese societies. Some of the symptoms of a culture-bound syndrome may resemble symptoms of mental disorders found throughout the world, but there is seldom a one-to-one equivalence of any culture-bound syndrome with any mental disorder defined by DSM-IV published by the American Psychiatric Association. The most acknowledged culture-bound syndromes in China include four illnesses: (1) Koro (*Suoyang*, 'shrinking of yang'), referring to an episode of sudden and intense anxiety that the penis (or, in females, the vulva and nipples) will recede into the body and possibly cause death. Koro is increasingly rare, but occurred as an epidemic in Hainan in the mid 1980s. (2) Qigong psychotic reaction (*Zouhuo rumo*, 'go wild as though possessed'), referring to delusional reactions due to misguided practices or overpractice of Qigong. (3) *Shenjing shuairuo* (debilitation of nerves, or neurasthenia), referring to a condition characterized by physical and mental fatigue, dizziness, headaches, other pains, concentration difficulties, sleep disturbance and memory loss. Partially due to the trend in the West, *shenjing shuairuo* has been gradually replaced by other categories such as depression. (4) *Shenkui* (depletion of renal yang), referring to a condition marked by anxiety with accompanying somatic complaints attributed to excessive semen loss. Some culture-bound syndromes were documented in ancient literature of Chinese medicine (e.g. *suoyang*); others resulted from the mixing and transforming of both Chinese and foreign categories (e.g. *shenjing shuairuo*) in modern times.

See also: geography of disease

Further reading

Chen, N. (2003). *Breathing Spaces.* New York: Columbia University Press.

Kleinman, A. (1999). 'The Moral Economy of Depression and Neurasthenia in China'. *Culture, Medicine and Psychiatry* 23: 389–92.

Lee, S. (1999). 'Diagnosis Postponed: Shenjing-shuairuo and the Transformation of Psychiatry in Post-Mao China'. *Culture, Medicine and Psychiatry* 23: 349–80.

Wang, Q. (1997). *Wang Qi nankexue.* Zhengzhou: Henan kexuejishu chubanshe.

EVERETT ZHANG

culture fever

(wenhua re)

The term refers to the intellectual and cultural movement in the 1980s. This movement aroused great interest and enthusiasm among intellectuals on various cultural issues. It also reached a larger audience beyond academic institutes and college campuses, and had very wide repercussions in society. It is therefore called a fever over culture. Basically an urban phenomenon, the so-called fever emerged around 1984 when economic reforms in urban China entered a critical moment. The situation was deemed necessary for new thinking to break the spell of ossified official ideology and also for structural measures to further and deepen the reform. Intellectuals, especially young ones, were very eager to make a breakthrough in theoretical thinking, to influence public opinion and social mentality, and to help move the reform forward. Cultural issues occupied intellectual debates because intellectuals generally agreed that problems encountered in the reform were deep-rooted in China's cultural tradition. The discussion on Chinese culture and its role in modernization dominated intellectual debate from 1984 and ended in 1989 due to the sudden change of political climate. During this period, quite a few research institutes and societies for cultural studies were established, most of them semi-official or unofficial, many conferences for **cultural discussion** were convened, and numerous scholarly works on cultural issues were published. The movement secured some official support and sponsorship, but it was nevertheless the first independent intellectual movement since 1949. It introduced and encouraged new ideas and theories, opened people's minds, promoted freedom in thinking and research, fostered an independent spirit among intellectuals, and also furthered liberalization in academic and cultural life.

See also: Li Zehou; Liu Zaifu

LIU CHANG

curses and maledicta

The Chinese word for 'curses' is *majie*, meaning literally 'curses in the street'. In early rural China a woman would even broadcast her curses on the roof of her house. Curses like this aimed at vilifying the victim by character-assassination. The extension of 'street' could be any public space or situation. Bullies used the streets to vent their diatribes, which could be very vulgar with extensive references to the human genitalia. Other means of humiliation were to banish the victim to 'hell' or reduce him to the abuser's 'posterity'. Cause of this type of curses could be alleged hurt feelings or simply pure suspicions. They usually lacked a specific target. Therefore, 'referring to A while attacking B' was the normal tactic. Sometimes accusations were point blank. The abuser could run out of steam if the victim remained calm. A rebuttal, however, could trigger a verbal confrontation, which would lead to a tribal war if family members and relatives were involved.

As society progresses, *majie* in its real sense has become a thing of the past, no longer acceptable to an increasingly educated public. Maledicta as mannerism still exist: the worst equivalent to the f-words in English, the milder comparable to the moderated sh-word, such as *daomei*, which connotes bad luck.

Curses are dialectical. An alleged bad person is called *suizai* in Canton, but *biesan* in Shanghai, and *gui erzi* in Sichuan. Some curses are gender-sensitive: only a woman would call someone harassing her *chouliumang*, meaning 'a foul rascal'.

YUAN HAIWANG

Cynical Realism

(Popi)

Art movement

Popi is a colloquial expression whose original meaning is close to 'bored', 'senseless', 'rogue', 'small ruffian'. The term also bears the reference to 'dissipated', 'cynical', 'indifferent to everything' and 'jaded'. I first used it as an art critical term in 1990 in my article 'Apathetic Feelings in

Contemporary Chinese Art Trends: An Analysis of the Cynical Realist Current' to define a widespread attitude prevalent in Chinese society after the Tiananmen events of 1989 and the resulting artistic current. The works in this style often display fortuitous fragments of daily experience using a *popi* attitude to describe the bored feelings of their characters. The term has also been translated as 'hippy spirit', which nonetheless contrasts with the anti-idealistic trend expressed by *popi*: the *popi* is grey in his or her approach to life, in a way that recalls the attitude of traditional scholar-gentry frustrated in their official careers.

The main exponents of this trend were artists who were born in the 1960s and who in the 1980s were still largely studying in the **art academies**. With little idealism left to hold on, they gave up all sense of mission typical of the previous **85 New Wave [Art] Movement** generation, espousing a view of contemporary society marked by a sense of malaise. The work normally displays a high level of realist technique mastered during the artists' training at art academies, in particular the **Central Academy of Fine Arts**, and seemingly rejecting the modernist experimentations typical of the artists belonging to the generation who were the protagonists of the 85 [Art] Movement. One of the most representative works of this current is **Fang Lijun**'s portrait of a 'Bold Rogue'. Other artists include **Liu Wei**, **Song Yonghong**, **Wang Jingsong**, **Liu Xiaodong** and **Yu Hong**.

Further reading

Dal Lago, Francesca (1993). 'Il realismo critico della giovane arte cinese' [The Critical Realism of Young Chinese Art]. In *Punti Cardinali dell'Arte, Catalogo della XLV Esposizione Internazionale d'Arte Venezia*: Edizioni La Biennale di Venezia, 538.

Li, Xianting (1992). 'Apathetic Feelings in Contemporary Chinese Art Trends: An Analysis of the Cynical Realist Current', *Ershiyi shiji* [originally published in *Yishu chaoliu* in 1990].

—— (1993). 'Major Trends in the Development of Contemporary Chinese Art'. In Valerie C. Doran (ed.), *China's New Art, Post-1989* (exhibition catalogue), Hong Kong: Hanart Gallery, x–xxii.

LI XIANTING (TRANS. FRANCESCA DAL LAGO)

D

Dai Houying

b. 1938; d. 1996, Nanzhao, Anhui

Writer

Much criticized for her novels defending humanist values, Dai Houying was among the first to portray the traumatic legacy of the Anti-Rightist Campaign and the **Cultural Revolution**. Dai earned a degree in Chinese and worked as a literary critic in Shanghai until her persecution as a rightist in 1969. From 1979 until her murder in 1996, Dai taught literature at Fudan and Shanghai Universities.

Dai began writing fiction in 1978 with her trilogy on the fate of intellectuals, *Death of a Poet* (*Shiren zhi si*), *Stones on the Wall* (*Ren a'ren*), and *Footsteps in the Void* (*Kongzhong de zuyin*). Her momentous novel, *Stones on the Wall* (1980), inspired intense controversy for its advocacy of a **Marxist Humanism** and was banned between 1983 and 1986. Told through ten points of view, direct dialogue and some stream-of-consciousness narration, the novel takes place after the fall of the 'Gang of Four' but invokes dreams, regrets and extended flashbacks to confront the deep scars left by repressive political movements and their consequences for interpersonal relations. The novel confronts harsh cynicism and opportunism but also insists on the possibility for forgiveness, integrity and stalwart idealism. These values also inform Dai's many novellas, short stories and essays. Especially perceptive is her novella *Soft is the Chain* (*Suolian, shi rouruande*, 1982) about a peasant woman's bewilderment as the changing norms of her children's generation repay with an empty honour her sacrifices to rules against remarriage that she had accepted as immutable.

Further reading

Dai, Houying (1985). *Stones of the Wall.* Trans. Frances Wood. London: Michael Joseph.
—— (1992). 'On Behalf of Humanism: The Confession of a Former Leftist'. Trans. Frances LaFleur. In Helmut Martin (ed.), *Modern Chinese Writers: Self-Portrayals.* Armonk, NY: M. E. Sharpe, 27–33.
Pruyn, Carolyn S. (1988). *Humanism in Modern Chinese Literature: The Case of Dai Houying.* Bochum: Studienverlag Brockmeyer.

DEIRDRE SABINA KNIGHT

Dai Jinhua

b. 1959, Beijing

Film and culture critic

Dai Jinhua is a leading Marxist feminist scholar of Chinese literature, film and popular culture. She graduated from **Peking University** in 1982 and has since taught at the **Beijing Film Academy** and Peking University. Dai Jinhua's research and writing is informed by various Western theories of literature and culture. During the 1980s, while teaching at the Beijing Film Academy, she was the first to study Western literary theory, structuralism and feminism in particular, and apply them to her analysis of Chinese cinema. This made her a pioneer in both feminist and film studies. In addition to setting up the first countrywide major in film theory in 1986, she was also instrumental in the establishment of various research institutes for popular and comparative culture.

Prompted by the widespread social and cultural changes during the 1990s, Dai increasingly focused her research on issues of popular culture. Her representative writings address such topics as cultural research and criticism, **feminism**, urban culture, modernity, Orientalism, popular and independent film, the role of television and **advertising**, the representation of the Chinese Diaspora, and cultural implications of **consumerism**, capitalism and globalization. Her innovative experiments with different critical approaches and the feminist perspective with which she re-examined dominant theories of literature, film and popular culture, introduced a new way of critical analysis far beyond her field in China. The development of her own dynamic cultural critique also addressed a growing audience in Taiwan, Hong Kong and the West.

See also: film criticism

Further reading

Dai, Jinhua (1995). 'Invisible Women: Contemporary Chinese Cinema and Women's Film'. *positions: east asia cultures critique* 3.1 (Winter): 255–80.

—— (1996). 'Redemption and Consumption: Depicting Culture in the 1990s'. *positions: east asia cultures critique* 4. 1 (Spring): 127–43.

—— (1999). 'Invisible Writing: The Politics of Chinese Mass Culture in the 1990s'. *Modern Chinese Literature and Culture* 11.1 (Spring): 31–60.

Wang, J. and Barlow, T. (eds) (2001). *Cinema and Desire: Feminist Marxism and Cultural Politics in the Work of Dai Jinhua*. Verso Press. [Reviewed by Gina Marchetti (2003). 'Chinese Feminist Film Criticism'. *Jump Cut: A Review of Contemporary Media* 46 (Summer).]

BIRGIT LINDER

Dai Qing

(neé Fu Xiaoping)

b. 1942

Journalist, culture critic, writer

The daughter of an underground Party worker and an engineer, Dai Qing was raised for the most part in the family of Ye Jianying, one of the founders of the PLA and one of the ten great marshals of the People's Republic. After schooling in Beijing and training in missile technology at Harbin, she became a technician working for the Public Security Bureau and subsequently, for a short time, an undercover cadre in the Chinese Writers' Association working for the security organs. Her post-Cultural Revolution career in writing and journalism was inspired by the works of Liu Binyan and the US oral historian Studs Terkel, and she eventually found employment with the leading newspaper **Guangming ribao**.

During the 1980s, as literary innovation changed the face of Chinese letters – and the old censorship system gave way to a more complex and nuanced *ad hoc* regime of commercial publishing – she became a leading practitioner of 'historical investigative journalism'. In a number of popular studies of intellectual and cultural figures (the neo-Confucian Liang Shuming, the writer Wang Shiwei and the journalist Chu Anping), Dai Qing challenged Party rulings and offered her own running commentary on contemporary Chinese politics and society. Some of these writings, which are masterful prose pieces, were the first to excite discussion among the intelligentsia about the revival of the long-ignored liberal democratic tradition in Chinese politics.

An irascibly independent figure, Dai was a unique journalistic voice in the second half of the 1980s. She was a key activist crucially in the founding of China's first environmental lobby group in 1988 and went on to become a vocal opponent of the Three Gorges Dam project. Jailed in 1989 following 4 June on nebulous charges related to inciting the protesters, she was released the following year and immediately published an account of her imprisonment in Hong Kong. Banned for the most part from publication in

China, she continued to act as an independent critique of the authorities. Her freedom to write and travel overseas following her 1990 release have occasioned many comments among the dissident community about her supposed continued affiliation with the security apparat.

Further reading

Barmé, Geremie R. (ed.) (1992). *New Ghosts, Old Dreams: Chinese Rebel Voices*. New York: Times Books. ['From Lin Zexu to Chiang Ching-kuo', 'The Case of Chu Anping' and 'A Sexy Lady' (with Luo Ke).]

Dai, Qing (1984). 'Anticipation'. Trans. Billy Bikales. In Perry Link (ed.) *Roses and Thorns: The Second Blooming of the Hundred Flowers in Chinese Fiction*. Berkeley: University of California Press, 146–67.

—— (1985). 'No!'. Trans. Dale R. Johnson. In Michael S. Duke (ed.), *Contemporary Chinese Literature: An Anthology of Post-Mao Fiction and Poetry*. Armonk, NY: M. E. Sharpe, 109–14.

—— (1992). 'My Imprisonment: An Excerpt'. Trans. Geremie Barmé. *Index on Censorship* 8: 20–7.

—— (1995). 'How I Experienced the Cultural Revolution'. In Feminist Press (ed.), *China for Women: Travel and Culture*. New York : Feminist Press, 79–85.

—— (comp.) (1998). *The River Dragon Has Come! The Three Gorges Dam and the Fate of China's Yangtze River and Its People*. Trans. Yi Ming. Ed. John G. Thibodeau and Philip B. William. Armonk, NY: M. E. Sharpe.

GEREMIE R. BARMÉ

dakou culture

By the end of the twentieth century a new generation emerged in urban China, named after the cut CDs, dumped from the West to be used as surplus plastic, available at illegal markets in Chinese cities. The cut at the margin of these *dakou* CDs, as they are called in Chinese, brings this young generation to the centre of a global music culture. *Dakou* stands for far more than just an illegal CD, it stands for a lifestyle very much *en vogue*

among China's urban youth. *Dakou* is not just a metaphor for the ambiguity of the globalization of popular music, the CDs also cut open a new era for what is coined in Beijing as the New Sound Movement (see **New Sound Movement, Modern Sky Records**).

When China moved on from the 1980s towards the 1990s, the idea of being *liumang* (a hooligan) was celebrated in the work of **Wang Shuo**. At the start of the new century the term has lost its aura. The *dakou* label is unsuitable for such 'oldies' as **Cui Jian** and Wang Shuo, as it refers to the generation born during or after the **Cultural Revolution**. What is strikingly different between the *liumang* and the *dakou* generation is not only the direct reference to music, but also – and especially – the inclusion of the illegal West in a 'Chinese' concept. The *dakou* culture challenges established binaries such as local/global, as the CD is both specifically Western and specifically Chinese. To be *dakou* is to be both global (the music) and local (the cut). The cut deforms the circle; something is missing, yet as a listener one gets more, because through this CD Chinese youth enter a domain of illegality.

JEROEN DE KLOET

dance (ethnic)

Dance is essential to the cultures of all China's ethnic groups and most important among the performing arts forms of most of the minorities. Ethnic minorities with distinguished dance traditions include the Tai, Koreans, Miao, Mongols, Tibetans and Uighurs (see **Tai, culture of**; **Koreans, culture of**; **Miao, culture of**; **Mongols, culture of**; **Tibetans, culture of**; **Uighurs (Weiwu'er), culture of**).

Dance plays a vital social role in such matters as courtship, celebration and national festivals. In China, the Cultural Revolution tried to suppress cultural traditions, but the period of reform has seen large-scale revival. Although modernization has again exercised a deleterious effect on dance traditions, researchers have commented on their tenacity among some minorities, especially in Xinjiang and Tibet. It is quite likely that traditional dance forms play a role in intensifying ethnic identities.

Among the Uighurs collective song and dance gatherings are termed *mexrep*. The largest in scale take place at festival time, but smaller occur at weddings. They continue to exist in contemporary society. Reed-pipe dances are still frequent among the Miao and many other ethnic minorities of Guizhou, Yunnan, Guangxi and western Hunan. These feature a young man playing the reed-pipe to a young woman, dancing as he does so, the music providing the rhythm. The integration of dance and instrumental playing is common among not only the Miao but the Koreans and other minorities. Still today, Miao villages have special public spaces for courtship reed-pipe dance gatherings.

In contemporary China, authorities have set up professional troupes to perform ethnic dances, training young dancers. Revived in the early 1980s, these troupes have declined since the 1990s, but remain popular among tourists.

COLIN MACKERRAS

dance troupes

Dance troupes in China consist of three kinds of groups: ballets concentrating on an artistic form which originated in the West; companies, such as the Oriental Song and Dance Company (Dongfang gewu tuan), focusing on both Chinese and foreign folk arts of song and dance; and a great number of troupes popular in China, featuring the performances of dance in modern and traditional style. With many nationalities and minorities living in different places in China, troupes of dance that embody diverse Chinese national flavours have been established as professional artistic organizations at the levels of the country, province, district, city as to county.

China Central Ballet and Shanghai Ballet are well known not only in China but also in the world. China Central Ballet, the ballet at Chinese national level, was established in 1959. The eminent ballet dancer Dai Ailian made a considerable contribution to its organization. The Ballet cherishes the tradition of classical ballets, of which the performances of

famous Russian works such as *Swan Lake* and *Giselle* have laid a solid foundation for its development. The renowned programmes of the troupe also include George Balanchine's *Serenade*, Kenneth MacMillan's *Concerto* as well as *Don Quixote, Romeo and Juliet* and *The Last Four Songs*. On the other hand, the artists of the Ballet care about depicting Chinese people's life with this Western artistic form. Their creations, such as *The Red Detachment of Women, The New-Year Sacrifice* and *Lin Daiyu* based on modern and classical Chinese stories, have been in the repertoire of the Ballet. Shanghai Ballet was named in 1979, achieving instant fame with the performance of *The White Haired Girl*. In addition to classical ballets, the troupe also created the ballets *Thunderstorm*, based on Cao Yu's play, and *Regret for the Past*, originally a Lu Xun story. The ballet dancers Wang Qifeng, Yang Xinhua, Tang Min and Zhang Weiqiang have won awards in international ballet competitions.

In terms of performing Chinese national dances, the China National Song and Dance Ensemble, the Chinese Opera and Dance Theatre, and the China Central Song and Dance Troupe of Minorities are influential. The Out of China Central Song and Dance Company was set up in China in 1952, and won first awards for *Locus Dance, Peacock Dance* and so on in international dance competitions. The dance group of the China National Song and Dance Ensemble is famous for performing Chinese national and folk dances. Established in the 1950s, the Chinese Opera and Dance Theatre has had a good reputation in its programmes of dance drama on a big scale, such as *Princess Wencheng* and *Dreams of Red Mansions*. Inheriting and developing the tradition of the colourful art of song and dance of minorities, the China Central Song and Dance Troupe of Minorities has performed a great number of dances with various artistic styles and has fostered more than 400 professional performers from different minorities for other troupes. Local troupes of provinces and autonomous regions – Xinjiang, Xizang, Inner Mongolia, Guangxi, Ningxia, Yunnan and so on – provide song and dance programmes with the particular national flavour of the minorities of Uygur, Zang, Meng, Zhuang, Hui, Bai, and so forth.

See also: Wuju

GE CONGMIN

Daoism (Daojiao), recent history of

Daoism is among five religions, including Buddhism, Islam, Catholicism and Protestantism, recognized by the PRC (what might be called 'Chinese religion' is condemned as 'superstition'). And like the other four recognized religions, Daoist activities must be organized by a National Association. The various Daoist associations created during the Republican period were disbanded at the creation of the PRC, although one continued on Taiwan. A new Daoist Association was created in Beijing in 1957, ceased all activities in 1966, and was reactivated in 1980. The Association is headquartered in Beijing's White Cloud Abbey (Baiyunguan), a monastery of the Quanzhen order (see **Daoism (Quanzhen order)**). Most of the Association's dignitaries are Quanzhen Daoists, but it also includes Zhengyi clerics and laymen (see **Daoism (Zhengyi tradition)**). The Association runs a periodical, *Chinese Daoism* (*Zhongguo daojiao*, from 1987), and since 1982 has managed a school at the White Cloud Abbey that enrols novices for a two-year apprenticeship. Branches of the Association are being created in provinces and districts in ever greater numbers.

The relationship of the Association with the renewal of Daoist practice is ambiguous. On the one hand, the Association applies the official policy whereby the religion is a distinct sphere of activity within society: clerics should live in monasteries, supported by the income derived from entrance fees, cultural activities, rituals, shops and handicrafts, along with stipends official clerics receive from the state. The government does not approve of the traditional place of Daoism within society, i.e. a class of priests serving temple communities and families, paid for by performing **Jiao** ('offering') rituals in popular community temples, and **funerals**. The Association has to support the official policy whereby certain rituals performed within the monastery are permitted, while 'superstitious activities', such as practising **divination and fortune-telling** or burning paper money, are forbidden. Policies on certain sensitive questions such as the practice of death rituals at the deceased's home vary according to texts and to local implementation.

On the other hand, the Association provides status and protection to its members and plays a positive role in allowing old Daoists to resurface and practise anew. It is only through the Association, moreover, that Daoists may regain control of their former temples and monasteries. The Daoist Association, like its Buddhist counterpart, has been in competition to regain control of temples that were managed before 1949 by clerics and then appropriated by the various Heritage Bureaux (Wenwuju) or other government outfits afterwards. During the 1980s, it has managed to recover most of the large Quanzhen monasteries, but so far very few temples, which have often been turned over to **museums** or to other tourism outfits.

The renewal of Daoist practice during the 1980s and 1990s has been strong but unequal. It is largely hampered by the absence of an institutional basis for Chinese religion, i.e. the temples and their lay cult communities which were the major venue for the grand Jiao ('offering') rituals. In some parts of the country (notably in the southern coastal provinces), temples are tolerated, and **temple fairs** and **pilgrimage**s are organized once again. Elsewhere, especially in many (but not all) districts of the Yellow River basin, almost no temple is active, and few if any **Daoist priests** (*Daoshi*) can be found. As a result, this field has been taken over by **sectarian religion**s and Qigong (see **Qigong (masters)**).

The Association and the institutional development of Daoism are of course affected by the **religious policies of the state**. During the last twenty years, the trend has been towards more tolerance, but the evolution is far from steady. Periodically, the room for manoeuvre by Daoists is reduced by a general anti-religious backlash, such as the **Falun gong** affair. One of the main assets of the Daoist Association is its strong links to Daoist milieux in Taiwan and Hong Kong; formal ties with Daoist organizations in the West also exist, but are not significant. The prestige of the White Cloud Abbey and of its court music and liturgy have caused the Daoists there to be invited regularly to perform in Taiwan and Hong Kong. Money for the restoration of monasteries and the organization of rituals flows in the reverse direction. Although the solicitation of subscriptions is not permitted, the Daoist Association also raises considerable finance through festivals: it has the resources to restore and run many more monasteries and temples than is allowed.

Unofficial, grassroots Daoism is tentatively supported by the official, monastic structure, which in turn receives some legitimization from scholarly circles, Chinese as well as foreign. Daoist studies is growing very fast in China. After 1980, it began modestly at the **Chinese Academy of Social Sciences**, and then developed in the institutes or departments of religious studies at several universities (notably **Peking University** and Sichuan University) and in various provincial academies of social sciences. Major dictionaries and encyclopedias of Daoism were edited in the mid 1990s, and quite a lot of material published (especially rare editions or manuscripts of spiritual and liturgical practice). Daoist clerics themselves still play only a minor part in Daoist studies, although some eminent clerics have played a crucial role in the contemporary transmission and diffusion of the Daoist spiritual tradition, notably inner alchemy (*neidan*), which is only recently being recognized as one of the jewels of the Chinese intellectual heritage. Daoists and scholars of Daoism want to distinguish Daoism from sectarian groups (a vital necessity), and from 'superstition' – the intellectuals of the Qing and Republican periods mostly identified Daoism with 'superstition', hence the particularly harsh treatment Daoism received from the state over the last century. Daoists are presently working at defining a place for Daoism in China's future, but to do so they focus almost exclusively on its speculative, intellectual aspects. More generally, Daoism has caught the attention of many Chinese intellectuals in their nationalist quest for a superior **socialist spiritual civilization**. However, these non-specialists tend to focus on their modern interpretation of texts such as the *Book of the Way and Its Power* (*Daodejing*). The real role and ritual practice of Daoism in Chinese society before 1949 is not a question that elicits much interest beyond a few specialists. The fateful notion that 'philosophical Daoism' (*daojia*) is different from 'religious Daoism' (*daojiao*) still prevents many intellectuals from reappraising Daoism seriously.

Further reading

Ding, H. (2000). 'The Study of Daoism in China Today'. In Livia Kohn (ed.), *Handbook of Daoism*. Leiden: Brill, 765–91.

Lagerwey, John (1997). 'A propos de la situation actuelle des pratiques religieuses traditionnelles en Chine'. In C. Clémentin-Ojha (ed.), *Renouveau religieux en Asie*. Paris: EFEO, 3–16.

Lai, Chi-Tim (2003). 'Daoism in China Today, 1980–2002'. In Daniel Overmyer (ed.), *Religion in China Today*. Cambridge: Cambridge University Press, 107–21.

Li, Y. (1993/2000). *Dangdai daojiao*. Beijing: Dongfang chubanshe.

VINCENT GOOSSAERT

Daoism (Quanzhen order)

Quanzhen was created during the late twelfth century and ever since has constituted one of the two orders of the Daoist clergy, the second one being the Zhengyi tradition (see **Daoism (Zhengyi tradition)**). Quanzhen clerics are celibate and they are ordained collectively during ceremonies that bear some resemblance to Buddhist ordinations. They are trained in large ecumenical monasteries (about twenty-five of which were active in the early twentieth century) and frequently travel around the country visiting different masters and sacred sites. They belong to a number of lineages (mere spiritual families, not 'sects'), the most prestigious and common of which is Longmen. The Quanzhen order is strong in northern China, and in a few other parts of the country, notably Jiangsu and Zhejiang, and the Guangzhou area. In Taiwan, there are lay Quanzhen adepts, but no Quanzhen clerics. Being a well-organized order, and not only a class of priests serving the local religion like the Zhengyi tradition, the Quanzhen has often been favoured by political authority, which it is still the case today. Nuns are less numerous than monks, but their place is more important than in Zhengyi Daoism. Monks and nuns often live in the same monasteries, and nuns practise a specific tradition of 'female alchemy'.

Before 1949, there existed over 20,000 Quanzhen clerics, with perhaps one quarter of them female. The number in 2000 was probably in the range of 5,000–10,000. Novices are accepted with the approval of parents and local officials at the age of eighteen. Traditionally, novices joined earlier, in their early teens. Most of the former large monasteries are now active again under the supervision of the Daoist Association. However, the largest part of the Quanzhen clergy used to be in the service of local temple lay communities, a situation not permitted by the current regime. The monasteries have also changed their organization and regimen in accordance with the government's instructions. They formerly relied on landed endowments and were closed to visitors except on festival days. Now, however, they must sustain themselves, and the monks are busy catering to visitors, making handicrafts, running shops and the like. Quanzhen clerics are assigned to a monastery, but may travel quite easily.

The institutional foundation of the Quanzhen order is the ordination. Quanzhen ordinations had to wait longer than their Buddhist counterparts to be authorized anew: the first ordination since the 1930s occurred in 1989 at the White Cloud Monastery (Baiyunguan) in Beijing (seventy-five ordinees), and a second one was organized in 1995 in Sichuan (546 ordinees). In addition to liturgical practice and music, and the individual and collective discipline taught in monasteries, especially during ordinations, novices also try to learn the immortality techniques (or inner alchemy, *neidan*) that have contributed to Quanzhen's reputation as a summit of Chinese spirituality. In this realm, the transmission has always been extra-institutional, between one master and one disciple. Novices find it difficult to find masters both accomplished enough and willing to transmit their art; the older generation, ordained in the 1930s, has not seen disciples for a very long time and sometimes doubts the sincerity and resolve of the new generation. On the other hand, the popularity of traditional spiritual techniques, fanned by the Qigong (see **Qigong (masters)**) craze, has encouraged Quanzhen vocations far beyond the traditional recruits though healing of sick children and within Daoist families.

VINCENT GOOSSAERT

Daoism (Zhengyi tradition)

Zhengyi is a very loosely organized Daoist lineage that combines an ancient and very sophisticated liturgy, named *Qingwei Lingbao*, and the nominal authority of the Zhang Heavenly Master (*Zhang tianshi*), who held court on Mount Longhu in Jiangxi until the 1930s. Both the liturgy and the Heavenly Master institution can be traced back to the second century and both took their modern form during the Song dynasty (960–1276). Zhengyi priests, who take pride in their highly literate tradition, insist on their distinction from other priests, often called 'ritual masters' (*fashi*) who perform a more vernacular liturgy (see **fachang**; **Lüshan jiao (Sannai jiao)**; **vernacular priests (Daoist/Buddhist)**). However, the connections between the two kinds of liturgies, and their performers, are always close, and vary from one place to the next. Studies on Daoist liturgy, prompted by more traditional folklore and performing arts research and by the opening of the countryside to fieldwork, have only begun since the 1990s to address the richness and complexity of these traditions (see **Minsu quyi (Min-su ch'ü-i)**).

In contrast to Quanzhen clerics (see **Daoism (Quanzhen order)**), Zhengyi priests do not usually live in a temple, although they are normally affiliated with one. They very rarely travel around the country, as they are members of families of hereditary priests and serve local communities. After the 1950s, when local communities ceased to invite them to perform rituals either because these were illegal or because the temples had been destroyed, the Zhengyi priests lived on as farmers or professionals. During the **Cultural Revolution**, many managed to hide and hang on to their liturgical manuscripts. Since the 1980s, some have begun to officiate anew, in the areas where rituals are more or less tolerated, and to train a new generation. The situation varies very much from one district to the next, because of pre-existing differences in traditional local practices, or local differences in persecution experienced in the recent past, or the ever sharper variations in the present-day application of religious policy in local areas. The number of Zhengyi priests is very difficult to estimate, but fieldwork suggests that they are quite numerous throughout the country, especially in the south, and in any case much higher than that of Quanzhen clerics.

The situation of the Zhengyi order within the Daoist Association, whose role is to certify clerics, is rather ambivalent. The Quanzhen dominance of the Daoist Association has ensured that Quanzhen ordinations have been organized first. Indeed, the question of the married Zhengyi priests has long tormented the Association. Finally, a Zhengyi ordination took place on Mount Longhu in 1991 for priests outside the mainland, and in 1995 for 191 ordinees for priests on the mainland. Zhengyi priests are now welcome to join the Association, even though many have not done so yet, either because of reluctance or because it has proved too complicated for them to establish a local branch of the Daoist Association. Another problem is the status of the Zhang Heavenly Master – the sixty-third holder of the title, Zhang Enpu (1904–69), fled to Taiwan in 1949, and his successor is not widely recognized in the PRC. Members of the Zhang family occupy important functions in the Daoist Association, notably the priest-scholar Zhang Jiyu, but none has yet claimed the title of Heavenly Master. Given the continued charisma of the Zhang family and the temples now restored on Mount Longhu, there is most certainly a bright future for them in Chinese culture.

VINCENT GOOSSAERT

Daoism among minority nationalities

Almost all of the various ethnic groups at the margins of the Chinese ecumene have had some contact with Daoism, and the cultures of some of them have been profoundly transformed by it. Generally, at present, Daoist influence is most profound and pervasive among the non-Han peoples of the south and southwest, while Tibetan Buddhist practices are widely influential among the peoples of the west and north. In their present form, Daoist teachings are thought to have been spread among the highland non-Han peoples of the south during the Southern Song dynasty (1127–1279), following the rise of new Taoist movements such as Tianxin zhengfa, Shenxiao, Qingwei and Jingming, most of which originated in south China.

Today, a particularly remarkable form of Daoism is found among the Mian-speaking **Yao** peoples of Guangxi and contiguous provinces. Mian-Yao have also migrated in recent centuries southwards into mainland Southeast Asia, and communities are found in northern Vietnam and northern Thailand. There, every male member of the community is ordained, at least ideally. Group ordinations are held, often for all the young men in the lineage. At the first level of ordination, called 'Hanging the Lamps' (*kwa-tang*), young men are given basic religious instruction, introduced to the gods of the pantheon, and are taught how to walk on the Bridge of the Seven Stars (of the Northern Dipper). They are given a religious name, provided with booklets for basic liturgy, and are subsequently entitled to perform some rituals.

There is a second degree of ordination. The ordination ceremony, called 'Ordination of the Master' (*tou-sai*), involves preparatory fasting and ordeals, such as climbing a sword ladder. Visits in a trance-like state to Plum Mountain (*Meishan*), the abode of the ancestors, and to the gate of the High Pavilion of Middle Heaven are followed by fire-walking and, finally, carrying a red-hot plough-share back to the house altar. Ordinates are given a seal and ordination certificate, and are henceforth qualified to perform a wide range of rituals. There are two additional levels of ordination available, 'Adding Duties' (*chia-tse*) and 'Enfeoffing Liturgies' (*pwang-ko*).

Women also participate. They attend ordinations in full ceremonial dress, and are granted seals, patents and religious names corresponding to those of their husbands. Both men and women receive command over spirit soldiers (*peng-ma*), the number of which depends on the degree of ordination.

Daoism among the Yao has been seen as representing a very conservative form of religious practice, exhibiting parallels with the communitarian Daoism that flourished in the earliest known Taoist communities and the collective fasts of medieval times. It may also be seen, however, as a response to the pressure of Han Chinese persecution of the Yao in recent centuries. The Yao themselves refer to their religion as the 'Plum Mountain Teaching' (*Meishanjiao*). Their liturgical texts, which also mention Lüshan, are all in Chinese, as are their ritual documents and charms (*fu*).

A more indigenized form of the Plum Mountain Teaching is found among the Zhuang in Guangxi, where Zhuang 'ritual masters' (*bouxsae*) combine the recitation of Chinese-language texts with those in 'old Zhuang script'. The Chinese-language texts are similar to those of the Yao but the texts in Zhuang often incorporate a great deal of pre-Daoist material, such as local legends and hagiographies of local saints. In the performance of rituals, song-forms and dance styles typical of the Tai-speaking south are encapsulated within a Chinese-style liturgical framework. Similar combinations of Chinese Daoist and indigenous elements are found in the religious practices of many non-Han peoples of southern China, such as among the Tibeto-Burman speaking Tujia in western Hunan and southern Sichuan. Given the intensification of assimilation pressures in recent centuries, Daoism often served as a form of protective colouring, allowing people to perpetuate the customs and the words of their ancestors under an acceptably Chinese guise.

Further reading

Holm, David (1994). 'The Redemption of Vows in Shanglin'. *Min-su ch'ü-i* [Folklore and Performance] 92: 853–909.

Lemoine, Jacques (1982). *Yao Ceremonial Paintings*. Bangkok: White Lotus.

Yoshiro, Shiratori (1975). *Yonin bunsho* [Yao documents]. Tokyo: Kodansha.

DAVID HOLM

Daoist monasteries/abbeys

(gong/guan)

Traditionally, among the great variety of Chinese temples, the terms *guan* (observatory) and *gong* (palace) define the category of Daoist monasteries.

Like their Buddhist equivalents (*si* or *yuan*), they house a monastic community governed by set rules. They may belong to a corporate clergy and are open to all ('ecumenical' status, *shifang*) or to a lineage, in which case they are passed on from master to disciple ('hereditary' status, *zisun*). In this regard, all monasteries are opposed to temples (*miao*), which belong to a lay community (most often territorial) and which may employ clerics as temple keepers. That said, the names of religious establishments usually endure while their status and function evolve over time: some *guan* or *gong* could happen to be privately owned, and even house no cleric, while some *miao* with a large clerical community might function as monasteries. Most *guan* were managed by the Quanzhen order, with a couple of exceptions in the Jiangnan area (such as the Xuanmiaoguan in Suzhou) where they were run by an alliance of hereditary Zhengyi families (see **Daoism (Quanzhen order)**; **Daoism (Zhengyi tradition)**).

Since the progressive reopening of temples, active *guan* are now controlled by the Daoist Association. In sharp contrast to temples, monasteries in general, including the major *guan*, have mostly been spared the brunt of the destruction that happened during the entire twentieth century – a destruction of which the **Cultural Revolution** was only the climax, that is still unstudied and little understood. Almost all 'ecumenical' *guan* of the early twentieth century have opened again, whereas a majority of the temples have been razed to the ground. Among the most important temples that were staffed by Daoists, few have been opened, and if reopened, only recently and as museums, not as places for religious activity (notable cases are the Dongyuemiao in Beijing and the Chenghuangmiao in Shanghai, though the latter has recently been seen to incorporate some Confucian rituals). One may explain this differentiated treatment by the fact that in pre-1949 society, monasteries were more isolated institutions, whereas large temples like those just mentioned played a key role in the self-organization of urban society (some say 'civil society').

Some *guan* have preserved both their architecture and their decoration (for example, those on Wudangshan); in most cases, statues and furniture had to be made anew. Almost all *guan* have lost their archives and libraries. Restoration is usually faithful, but some change in deities occurs. Buildings and statues from the Ming are not rare, but those from the Qing are common. The active *guan* are either in cities or clustered on one of many holy mountains throughout the country. From an architectural perspective, nothing fundamental differentiates Daoist from other temples. Nor does iconography in statues and murals: if the central deities (the Three Pure Ones, Laozi, Daoist patriarchs) are proper to *guan*, their style is the same as that of other religious works of art. The *guan* also house many popular gods in side halls. Beside sightseers, *guan* also attract many devotees. The Daoist laity is less formally organized than that of Buddhism, but people do come to pray, consult clerics or join in the festivals. In cities, the clerics are not allowed to perform services outside of the monastery, but families may request death rituals performed for them within the *guan*.

Further reading

Qiao, Yun (2002). *Taoist Buildings: Ancient Chinese Architecture (Zhongguo gujianzhu daxi)*. Princeton: Princeton Architectural Press.

VINCENT GOOSSAERT

Daoist music

The earliest reference to Daoist music is of the music of 'pacing the void' (*buxu*), said to have been a Daoist imitation of Buddhist hymns composed by Cao Zhi (192–232 BCE) in Yushan (*Yiyuanji*, cf. *Hôbôgirin*, s.v. Bombai: 96). However, no information is available on the nature of this music. The Daoist Kou Qianzhi (365–448) is said to have established the basis of Daoist music. He restructured the second-century Celestial Master sect (*Tianshidao*), established elaborate rites and created 'musical recitation from the clouds' (*yunzhong yinsong*), which incorporated singing into scripture performances which had hitherto been 'straight recitation' (*zhisong*). Building upon Kou's work, Lu Xiujing (406–77) compiled and edited over a thousand Daoist written documents into

systematic tomes, thus laying the foundation for Daoist ritual and music.

Daoism reached a peak in the Tang dynasty (618–907) when Emperor Xuanzong (712–56), a keen patron, actively promoted its music. He decreed **Daoist priests** and court musicians to compose Daoist music for the court; he further composed Daoist pieces and personally transmitted these to the Daoists. The significance of Daoist music in the later Song dynasty courts is seen in the emergence of the still extant collection of fifty Daoist chants, *Jade Sounds Ritual* (*Yuyin fashi*; *Zhengtong Daozang*, vol. 333), thought to have been published in the early twelfth century. The chants were notated in a type of contour notation which continues to defeat scholars' efforts at deciphering. Another extant collection of Daoist chants, compiled under the auspices of Ming Emperor Zhuli (1403–24), also contained music in the form of *gongche* notation (*Zhengtong daozang*, vol. 616).

An important development occurred between 1161 and 1189: Daoist Wang Chongyang established the Complete Perfection (Quanzhen) order in opposition to the early Celestial Masters sect, known by this time as the Orthodox Unity (Zhengyi) sect. These are still the two major sects of Daoism (see **Daoism (Quanzhen order)** and **Daoism (Zhengyi tradition)**). Today Quanzhen sect music is on the whole nationally homogeneous while music of the Zhengyi sect is strongly regional, usually closely linked to local musical genres.

Quanzhen Daoism, like monastic Buddhism, is a highly exalted monastic tradition. Quanzhen priests live a collective, celibate and strictly regulated life aimed at self-perfection. Music in Quanzhen Daoism is thus a tool for achieving this goal; its most important context is the daily rituals in which the vocal liturgy is accompanied only by ritual percussion instruments including hand-held gong (*dang*), cymbals (*cha*), bells (*ling*), drum (*gu*) and woodblock (*muyu*). This liturgical music is nationally unified and is known as 'melodies of the Ten Directions' (*shifang yun*). However, 'regional melodies' (*difang yun*) also exist in some areas; these are used in **Jiao** (offerings) or rituals performed for the dead (see **Gongde**). The collection of hymns nationally adopted by Daoist monasteries today is the *Orthodox Melodies of the Complete Perfection* (*Quanzhen zhengyun*). This volume of fifty-six hymn texts is said to have emerged around the seventeenth or eighteenth century. These same texts were reprinted around 1906, in an edition of the Daoist Canon (*Daozang jiyao*) printed by Erxian-an Monastery in Sichuan, with the addition of a type of percussion score known as *dangqingpu* (*dang* and *qing* being onomatopoeic sounds for the hand gong and cymbals respectively; Shi 1991: 2). This type of notation has since become the standard score used in all Daoist monasteries, although the melodies are still transmitted orally. (For a score of *Quanzhen zhengyun* in cipher notation, see Shi 1991.)

The Quanzhen sect exists mainly in northern and central China. Well-known monasteries are Baiyunguan in Beijing and Qingyanggong in Sichuan, and famous Daoist mountain complexes include Qingchengshan in Sichuan, Wudangshan in Hubei, Laoshan in Shandong, Huashan in Shaanxi and Qianshan in Liaoning. Unlike **Buddhist music**, which has a rich legacy of instrumental tunes, melodic instrumental music is largely absent from Quanzhen Daoism, although musical instruments are sometimes used to accompany vocal liturgy in offerings and rituals performed for the dead. In contrast, instrumental music plays an important role in the Zhengyi sect.

Zhengyi Daoism is a lay-based sect, also called 'Fire-dwelling' Daoism (*huoju dao*). Priests do not live in monasteries: they lead a normal family life and mainly perform rituals as a profession. This type of Daoism predominates in southern China, although *huoju* Daoists are also found in northern rural areas.

The music of popular folk Daoism is shared with local instrumental and/or theatrical genres. It is often closely related to the 'blowing-and-beating' (*guchui/chuida*) wind and percussion music of different regions. In the north, Zhengyi Daoists frequently perform *shengguan* (mouth-organ and reed pipe) music, which is closely related to regional folk genres which are in turn influenced by northern Buddhist music (see **Shanxi badatao**; **Xi'an guyue**). In Zhejiang and Jiangsu provinces, folk Daoist music is linked to Shifan instrumental music (see **Shifan (Shifan gu**, **Shifan luogu**)) and **Kunqu Xiqu** (sung drama/opera). In Yunnan, Dongjing music is also performed by folk Daoists, while in Fujian, the music of the local *kuilei* (string-

puppet) theatre and **Minnan nanyin** instrumental ensemble is borrowed by folk ritual specialists, both Daoist and Buddhist.

Daoist music, both instrumental and vocal, is differentiated by context. The instrumental labelled melodies (*qupai*) are divided into 'orthodox pieces' (*zhengqu*) and 'recreational pieces' (*shuaqu*). Its vocal liturgy also has two categories: 'yang melodies' (*yangdiao*) and 'yin melodies' (*yindiao*). The *zhengqu* and *yangdiao* are reserved for performances before the gods and in rituals of self-cultivation or celebratory contexts, while the *shuaqu* and *yindiao* are pieces performed for the souls and spirits in rituals for the dead or for entertaining the living.

The characteristics of Daoist music are revealed in the nature of the two sects. Quanzhen Daoism emphasizes spiritual enhancement and self-cultivation; its music is hence more refined and exalted. Zhengyi Daoism, which focuses more on providing rituals for the populace, draws on lively and popular folk music.

References and further reading

Cao, Benye (ed.) (1996 and currently). *Zhongguo chuantong yishi yinyue yanjiu jihua xilie congshu*. Taipei: Xinwenfeng chuban gongsi.

Demiéville, Paul (ed.) (1930 and currently). *Hôbôgirin: Dictionnaire encyclopédique du Bouddhisme d'après les sources chinoises et japonaises*. Tokyo: Maison Franco-Japonaise.

Jones, Stephen (1995). *Folk Music of China: Living Instrumental Traditions*. Oxford/New York: Oxford University Press. [2nd edn 1998, with CD].

—— (1995). 'Daoism and Instrumental Music of Jiangsu'. *Chime* 6: 117–46.

Lu, Cuikuan (1994). *Taiwan de daojiao yishi yü yinyue*. Taipei: Xueyi Chubanshe.

Pu, Hengqiang (1993). *Daojiao yü Zhongguo chuantong yinyue*. Taipei: Wenjin chubanshe.

Pu, Hengqiang and Cao, Benye (1993). *Wudangshan daojiao yinyue yanjiu*. Taipei: Taiwan Shangwu Yinshuguan.

Shi, Xinmin (1991). *Quanzhen zhengyun puji*. Beijing: Zhongguo wenlian chubanshe.

Tian, Qing (ed.) (1997). *Zhongguo zongjiao yinyue*. Beijing: Zongjiao wenhua chubanshe.

Wang, Chunwu and Gan, Shaocheng (eds) (1993). *Zhongguo daojiao yinyue*. Sichuan: Xinan jiaotong daxue chubanshe.

TAN HWEE-SAN

Daoist priests

(Daoshi)

Since 1980 and the partial relaxation of the government regulation of local religion, Daoist priests in contemporary China have performed communal rituals in tens of thousands of village temples, especially in south China. They have also performed rites of passage, exorcisms and minor rites for individuals in private homes. Nevertheless, severe and often arbitrary restrictions are still frequently imposed on their ritual practices. Daoist priests can be divided into two principal types – celibate monastic Quanzhen (Complete Perfection) initiates and 'hearth-dwelling' married Zhengyi (Orthodox Unity) priests, working out of their homes (primarily in south China) (see **Daoism (Quanzhen order)** and **Daoism (Zhengyi tradition)**). The former predominate in the north of China, and can be found in such famous historic Daoist monastic centres as the White Cloud Temple (Baiyunguan) in Beijing and in Shanghai, or in famous mountain monastic establishments such as Wudangshan, Louguanshan, Qingchengshan (Sichuan), Huashan and Laoshan (Qingdao). Some major Quanzhen monasteries can also be found in the south, such as the Luofushan in Guangdong and others in the New Territories of Hong Kong. Daily routines include meditation and recitation of scriptures. In addition to self-cultivation, Quanzhen Daoist priests perform a range of rituals for communities and individuals. A recent study by Li Yangzhen (2000) estimates the number of Quanzhen Daoist priests at over 7,000. Ordinations resumed in 1989. Four hundred Quanzhen monks and nuns were ordained at Qingchengshan in November 1995 (Lai 2003).

The second category of Daoist priests mostly claim some connection with the Zhengyi (Orthodox Unity) school, founded by the descendants of Zhang Daoling (now in their sixty-fourth generation), and based on the Longhushan (Dragon Tiger Mountain) temple complex in Shangqing, Jiangxi. Li Yangzhen (2000) estimates the number of Zhengyi priests at 20,000. Other sources claim that 4,000 Zhengyi Daoist priests are active in the Fujian areas of Putian, Quanzhou and Jinjiang alone. These numbers are only estimates, as many Daoist priests have not joined the official Daoist Association. Many have practiced unofficial ordinations of family members and acolytes for generations. A great many localized ritual traditions of Daoism have developed in south China. A major school of contemporary Daoist priests in south China are practitioners of forms of localized Lüshan (or Meishan) Daoism, building on the cult of the goddess Chen Jinggu, the 'Woman by the Side of the Waters' (see **Lüshan jiao (Sannai jiao)**). Daoist priests can also be found performing rituals among many of the national minorities of southwest China. Many work closely with spirit-mediums.

Most of the Zhengyi or Lüshan Daoist priests perform rituals in community temples or private homes for a fee. Their rituals are based on liturgical manuscripts and scriptures passed down within families or from master to disciple. They can perform a range of rituals of offering (**Jiao**), thanksgiving, propitiation, exorcism and rites of passage. These rites can vary in complexity from a few hours to several days or weeks, and can involve a single priest or a troupe of several priests and multiple acolytes. The priests usually construct a portable altar of the highest emanations of the Dao, the Three Pure Ones, and other representations of the gods of the Daoist heavens. Local gods from the vast localized pantheons of the hundreds of different local cultures of south China are sometimes incorporated into the altar in an apotheosized form. Daoist ritual remains central to most communal ritual in the tens of thousands of villages across south China. Training for priests in these local ritual traditions has been severely affected by the destruction of the Cultural Revolution, when many priests were imprisoned and vast quantities of scriptures and liturgical manuscripts were destroyed. Courageously, Daoist priests across China are reassembling their ritual repertoires, and attempting to reinvent their traditions in an ongoing negotiation with the forces of modernity.

Further reading

Dean, Kenneth (1993). *Taoist Ritual and Popular Cults in Southeast China*. Princeton: Princeton University Press.

Lai, Chi-tim (2003). 'Daoism in China Today, 1980–2000'. In Daniel Overmyer (ed.), *Religion in China Today*. Cambridge: Cambridge University Press, 107–21.

Li, Yangzheng (2000). *Dangdai daojiao* [Contemporary Daoism]. Beijing: Dongfang chubanshe.

Kohn, Livia (ed.) (2000). *Handbook of Daoism*. Leiden: E. J. Brill.

Overmyer, Daniel (ed.) (2002). *Ethnography in China Today*. Taipei: Yuan-Liou Publishing.

Schipper, Kristofer (1994). *The Taoist Body*. Berkeley: University of California Press.

KENNETH DEAN

Dashan

(a.k.a Mark Rowswell)

b. 1965, Ottawa, Canada

Xiaopin actor

Mark Rowswell graduated from the University of Toronto in 1988, and came to Beijing University for a three-year Chinese language and literature programme. Having worked briefly in the Canadian Embassy in Beijing, he started his Canadian business in 1995 to promote cultural and economic exchanges between China and Canada.

At the 1989 New Year Celebration National Television show that claimed millions of Chinese viewers, Rowswell played a young man named Xu Dashan in a **xiaopin** (skit) entitled *Yegui* (Back at Night). His near-perfect Mandarin and his charming personality left such an indelible impression upon the Chinese that they began to call him 'Dashan', without bothering to know his real name. Since then, he has become a beloved celebrity; his fans spanning from taxi drivers in Beijing to restaurant servers in Tibet. Today, Dashan is seen by hundreds of millions of Chinese with his television specials and through his weekly national radio programme that introduces Canadian music to the Chinese. He is married with a child, his wife being Chinese. Good-humouredly, he introduced himself as a Canadian 'hardware' with Chinese 'software'.

Following the steps of Norman Bethune, a Canadian doctor who died helping the Chinese fight the Japanese invasion during WWII, Dashan has become a bridge between the Chinese and the Westerners by embracing one of their most respected art forms and accepting their culture. He is 'the living proof that China and the West can find a middle ground'.

YUAN HAIWANG

dating

A culture of dating came late to Chinese society. For much of its history, marriages were arranged to suit parental interest. Individual preferences were seldom considered. In this milieu, children learned through cautionary tales of the disasters that befall people who ignore their parents in favour of their own desires. The moral was clear: obey your parents and live a more proper and satisfying life. By the 1980s, however, the ideas of arranged marriage had, especially in China's larger cities, gradually given way to individual choice. Urban parents continued to voice their preference, which children usually ignored. Without formal sanctions, parents could plead but could do little else. As one young woman noted: 'They have only one child, they cannot reject you for ever'.

In classic socialist China (1949–85) there was no true dating culture. Individuals seldom sought out the opposite sex for the exclusive purpose of fun and private enjoyment. In this era, it was deemed improper for unmarried individuals to be seen holding hands, much less kissing in public. Virginity was considered an ideal state for women and men. For most, pre-marital sexual play was considered obscene. Individuals, including those who were unofficially engaged, continued to adhere to the conventional ethos that required the denial of any involvement.

In this milieu, two forms or styles of association or 'dating' emerged. The formal style was organized around the idea of propriety in which people met with the aid of a go-between (e.g. a friend, a teacher or a dating service) to discuss family background and common interests and observe personality styles. If they agreed to meet again, they were considered all but engaged. The other dating style was informal. It was characterized by secrecy, denial and pragmatic considerations. In general, informal dating was conducted by individuals who were constrained by other factors (e.g. a prior marriage, avoiding local gossip). Intensely romantic entanglements often characterized informal dating, whereas the more formal dating was usually devoid of romantic excitement or aspirations. However, even the formal arrangements were not completely devoid of romantic fantasy. Unlike the Western ideal of romantic love, where individuals fall in love prior to marriage, Chinese couples appear to fall in love in reverse: Romantic anticipation followed rather than preceded marriage. Romantic infatuation may arise in either form of courtship and is characterized by emotional intensity, by a kind of anxiety, and expressions of romantic endearment. In short, the idealization of the other. The two styles differ only in the domain of public expression but not necessarily in the intensity of involvement. In the countryside, the two forms of dating continue to this day.

By the 1990s, informal dating, in China's large and mid-size cities, had moved away from secrecy to a new ethos of openness. Today, the urban youth regard dating as an opportunity to play, to seek pleasure and to delay assuming the responsibilities of marriage. A fully developed dating culture has arrived. The shift in public acceptance has been rapid. In the recent past the relationship between men and women was characterized by the expression 'the wall between us'; now it is distinguished by the expression the 'wall around us'. Young people use the public arena as a site in which to flaunt their exclusiveness and mutual involvement. In effect, they are proclaiming they are a couple. In the 1990s, China's single-child generation has completely embraced an orientation typically found in Western European countries: to associate with the opposite (or, in some cases, the same) sex for validation and erotic pleasure. In this milieu, virginity is no longer as important as it once was. Women talk about spontaneous affection, sexual enjoyment and the desire for erotic fulfilment. For example, young women often admit that

they would not want a boyfriend to have a condom as it would suggest that he had anticipated and thus planned something that should be based in spontaneous expression. For most singletons, it is given that people should marry for love.

The shift in dating styles has impacted the senior generation's dating style as well. Although those in their forties and fifties often met their spouse through a go-between, now divorced they often pursue a dating style characteristic of the junior generation. Clearly, there has been an enormous shift in the value placed on romance and personal expression. Today, China is characterized by several paths to finding a mate: use of a go-between, an informal or secretive style, and, in the 1990s, a more demonstrative, highly public, playful style. The later style is embraced primarily, but not exclusively, by China's singleton generation.

Further reading

Farrer, J. (2002). *Opening Up: Youth Sex Culture and Market Reform.* Chicago: University of Chicago Press.

Jankowiak, W. (1993). *Sex, Death and Hierarchy in a Chinese City.* New York: Columbia University Press.

WILLIAM JANKOWIAK

democracy and elections

Elections (*xuanxing*) and, to a much lesser extent, democracy (*minzhu zhuyi*) were elements of Chinese political discourse long before the first outpouring of democratic dissent in the late 1970s. Many of the political debates of late nineteenth- and early twentieth-century China revolved around the problem of democracy and the means by which democracy is actively assured: competitive elections. This may account for Mao's announcement on 1 March 1953 of the Electoral Law specifying that the lowest level congresses were to be directly elected. Consistent with the Leninist tradition of popular soviets or congresses, the nation's political and economic reforms were to proceed in concert with the 'separation of Party and government work', a proposal contained in the founding charters of the Party and later in the state constitution. Such separation required the creation of a new legal system to adjudicate the competing claims of civil and political authorities. However, over a lengthy interval of the 'people's democratic dictatorship', from the mid 1940s until the 1980s, in which figures like Deng Xiaoping reiterated the supremacy of this version of democracy as more advanced and substantial than the bourgeois democracies of the West, an independent judiciary was not instituted and the segregation of Party from government never occurred. Therefore, rule of law and a genuine people's democracy remain unfilled promises of the revolution and the legacy of China's 'democratic centralism' has been a skein of popular protests in 1975 (Tiananmen Square Incident), 1978–9 (Democracy Wall Protests), 1986–7 (national student protests against authoritarianism and for democracy) and 1989 (nationwide democracy protests), that registered the apparent limits of acceptance of this disavowal.

In the name of the 'people's democratic dictatorship', then, the Communist revolution liberated Chinese from fascism, semi-colonialism and warlordism, but rather than solving the problem of pluralist democracy forestalled it, projecting it indefinitely into the future through creative rhetorical exercises ('uninterrupted revolution', 'people's democracy', 'democratic centralism', 'socialist democracy with Chinese characteristics') and sporadic gestures in favour of democratic procedure ('Hundred Flowers', 'Four Big Freedoms', 'village elections'). Thus, democracy and elections define the Party's principal contradiction: the division between the CCP (one-party rule) and the masses (pluralism), a contradiction that has become increasingly antagonistic in the era of the economic and political reforms initiated in December of 1978 at the Third Plenum of the Eleventh Party Congress. For nearly twenty-five years the Chinese government has followed this path of 'reform and opening to the world' with near-religious fervour, but the results of this policy, both grand and grievous, have been staggering. One of the chief human consequences of this seemingly interminable reform period is mass disillusionment. Chinese society is more open and less impoverished, but its government struggles mightily with asserting

its legitimacy or having it affirmed by general acclaim.

The Chinese Communist Party, while refusing, nevertheless, to loosen its grip on political institutions, does avow a surface commitment to what it identifies as a 'multi-party system'. China has eight 'democratic parties' (*minzhu dangpai*), a number of which bear names derived from the earliest political organizations in Chinese history; they are: *Zhongguo guomindang geming weiyuanhui* (China National People's Party Revolutionary Committee); *Zhongguo minzhu tongmeng* (China Democratic League); *Zhongguo minzhu jianguo hui* (China Democratic National Construction Association); *Zhongguo minzhu cujin hui* (China Promoting Democracy Association); *Zhonggong nonggong minzhu dang* (China Peasants and Workers Democratic Party); *Zhongguo zhigong dang* (China Zhi Gong Party); *Jiu san xuehui* (September Third Society); and *Taiwan minzhu zizhi tongmeng* (Taiwan Democratic Self-Government League). These political parties have been officially acknowledged since 1948 when each responded to the call of the Communist Party leadership for a 'Chinese People's Political Consultative Conference' and was immediately subsumed within the supervisory authority of the CCP, with which each has since been fully complicit.

Single-party rule may serve as the unbending trunk of these pluralist branches, but democracy continues to pull at it, as evidenced in its persistence in Party discourse and the writings of loyal critics and dissidents. This was made clear in a speech by Jiang Zemin in the fall of 1997 in which, shamelessly purloining the core argument of Wei Jingsheng's 'The Fifth Modernization: Democracy', he asserted that 'without democracy there can be no modernization' and claimed further that 'we will ensure that our people hold democratic elections, make policy decisions democratically, carry out democratic management and supervision, and enjoy extensive rights and freedoms under the law'.

These noble sentiments were not mere cant. In 1979 the Party promulgated the Organic Law for Local People's Congresses and Local People's Governments that called for congresses of the nation's 50,000 townships to be elected every two years. In addition, 2,757 county congresses were to be directly elected every three years, with congresses of the twenty-nine provinces elected for five-year terms. The 1987 Organic Law on Villagers' Committees provided procedural safeguards for proper elections, but they are not widely carried out. In 1998 the National People's Congress announced that village committees were required by law to be democratically elected and these elections must take place every three years. Because the village committee alone is required to be elected by direct, competitive procedure, village heads may be democratically elected; however, township and county officials are not elected but appointed. Popular sovereignty is only apparent; representation is made more problematic by election law requiring that delegate representation of urban populations be four times greater than that of equivalent rural populations. Moreover, even with the increased involvement in village elections of non-governmental organizations like the Carter Center, the Ford Foundation and the International Republican Institution, observers report that only 10 per cent of these elections may be certified as democratic.

If 'democracy' means simply greater inclusiveness, then the opening by provincial people's congresses of legislative hearings to the public (as was done in the fall of 1999 in Guangzhou) stands as a significant democratic gesture. And by the same token, there is a modicum of democracy in Jiang Zemin's **Sange daibiao** (Three Represents) theory, announced in 2000: the Party represents the advanced productive forces (business people), the advanced cultural forces (intellectuals) and the masses (workers and peasants). And if 'democracy' means accountability and a margin of transparency within bureaucracy, then 'democratic methods' (*minzhu fangfa*) are now being tested at the lower levels of the People's Liberation Army, where vacant positions are announced; standards for appointments have been published; public recommendations have been written; open examinations have been held; and candidates for military office are made public.

At present, it is too soon to tell if these phenomena are best read as the tremors of shifting political ground, and perhaps little else, or whether they signal a deliberate movement towards establishing widespread franchise. These tremors represent more likely the urgings of a new generation of Party leaders concerned with addressing the widening political chasm between sovereign and people. It is also unclear if suffrage is actually desired by most Chinese or if they believe it to be a political experiment they are capable of undertaking. To be sure, Chinese have had many theories but no real practice of democracy. Some warn that the prosperity of the present under authoritarianism should be contrasted with the inevitable chaos consequent upon the dismantling of the Party-state in favour of pluralistic representation. Whether new forms of pluralist democracy can be developed either through substantive reform of the legal system or through the introduction of independent political parties is uncertain.

Between 1997 and 2003 political reflection has negotiated a number of positions on political reform that border on advocacy of democracy and elections, while also revealing the difficulties for intellectuals and Party members to advance themes suitable to resolving the political crisis China faces. It seems that China's ongoing dialectic of democracy and centralism demonstrates that the Party-state has yet to find a reliable method of encouraging democracy that would not also entail its own dissolution.

Further reading

Barmé, Geremie R. (1999). *In the Red: On Contemporary Chinese Culture*. New York: Columbia University Press.

Barmé, Geremie R. and Minford, John (eds) (1989). *Seeds of Fire: Chinese Voices of Conscience*. New York: Noonday Press.

Carter Center (1997). *The Carter Center Delegation to Observe Village Elections in China March 4–16, 1997*. Working Paper Series. Atlanta: Carter Center of Emory University.

Goodman, David S. G. (1981). *Beijing Street Voices: The Poetry and Politics of China's Democracy Movement*. Boston: Marion Boyars.

Han, Minzhu and Hua, Sheng (eds) (1990). *Cries for Democracy: Writings and Speeches from the 1989 Chinese Democracy Movement*. Princeton: Princeton University Press.

Nathan, Andrew J. (1985). *Chinese Democracy*. Berkeley: University of California Press.

Ogden, Suzanne (2002). *Inklings of Democracy in China*. Cambridge, MA: Harvard University Press.

Pan, Wei (1999). 'Yifazhi wei daoxiang, yi lizhi wei hexin de zhengzhi tizhi gaige' [Democracy or Rule of Law? – China's Political Future], unpublished manuscript.

Peerenboom, Randall (2002). *China's Long March toward Rule of Law*. Cambridge: Cambridge University Press.

Schell, Orville (1995). *Mandate of Heaven: The Legacy of Tiananmen Square and the Next Generation of China's Leaders*. New York: Touchstone.

White, Tyrell (ed.) (2001). *China Briefing: The Continuing Transformation*. Armonk, NY: M. E. Sharpe.

Xu, Ben (1999). *Disenchanted Democracy: Chinese Criticism after 1989*. Ann Arbor: University of Michigan Press.

LIONEL M. JENSEN

tradition of the 1930s and 1940s and had a tremendous impact on the development of Mandarin pop music. Despite her success in the PRC, she never visited the mainland. Deng remained loyal to the Republic and its army, and was honoured with many awards. She died of an asthma attack.

Further reading

Baranovitch, Nimrod (2003). *China's New Voices: Popular Music, Ethnicity, Gender, and Politics*. Berkeley: University of California Press, 10–13.

Gold, Thomas B. (1993). 'Go with your Feelings: Hong Kong and Taiwan Popular Culture in Greater China'. *China Quarterly* 136: 907–25.

Gu, Linxiu (1995). 'Teresa Teng Forever' (*Yongyuan de Deng Lijun*). *Sinorama* 20.7 (July): 6–19.

ANDREAS STEEN

Deng Lijun

(a.k.a. Teresa Teng)

b. 29 January 1953, Yunlin County, Taiwan; d. 8 May 1995, Thailand

Pop singer

Deng was the most successful Chinese female singers. Her songs are popular in Taiwan, Japan, Southeast Asia, the overseas communities and the PRC (www.teresa-teng.org.tw/). She was born into a military family, learned singing at the age of six in an army entertainment unit and won first prizes at song contests in 1964 and 1965. Four years later she began recording songs and acting in TV dramas. She released a very successful Japanese album in March 1974 and gave her first concerts in Hong Kong (1976) and in the USA and Canada (1979). Around that time her sentimental love songs spread via audio tapes to the mainland and started a Deng Lijun craze, reflected in the popular saying, 'Old Deng [Xiaoping] rules by day and Little Deng [Lijun] rules by night'. People cherished the sweetness in her voice, which allowed her to sing folksongs, romantic ditties and Western-style pop songs. She basically followed the Shanghai

department stores

Stores in traditional China were usually specialized. Iron and copper shops sold iron and copper tools; gold and silver shops sold gold and silver jewellery; pickle and sauce shops sold pickles and sauces; fabric shops sold fabrics. The modern, multi-storey department store selling 'a hundred different products' (*baihuo*) was a retail practice imported from the West during the Republican era, found mostly in major commercial cities, and most notably in Shanghai. During the Maoist era all department stores were nationalized and incorporated into the planned-economy network of severely restricted distribution. Though the department stores were better stocked than other commercial venues, people still had to use vouchers to purchase essential items (e.g. fabric, food, oil) and mobilize connections to purchase items in short supply (e.g. bicycles, radios, TVs). Salespeople during that era were notorious for rudeness towards consumers because of the stores' monopoly over retail. The reform era ushered in the era of privatization, commerce and consumption, and department stores mushroomed. Most people still shop at state-owned, more conservative and cheaper department stores. But joint-venture and foreign-owned luxury department stores have come to set the trends for a fashionable lifestyle. During the summer, people love strolling around in department stores and take advantage of their free air-conditioning. Because of fierce competition among department stores and between department stores and the throngs of *getihu* (private household) shops, all department stores regularly stage promotion campaigns (*huodong*) to attract customers. Beginning in the 1990s, **shopping malls** have also entered the fray, the most prominent of which is the Oriental Plaza in Beijing developed by the Hong Kong tycoon Li Ka-shing.

ADAM YUET CHAU

detective fiction

(zhentao xiaoshuo)

Detective fiction (*zhentan xiaoshuo*) presents a mystery, usually the investigation of a murder or other crime by the police. This genre is also called 'ratiocinative fiction' (*tuili xiashuo*). The works of Edgar Allan Poe (1809–49), the father of the detective story, and Arthur Conan Doyle (1859–1930) were translated into Chinese in the early twentieth century. Foreign films about Sherlock Holmes were shown in China in the 1980s. *Gong'an xiaoshuo* (crimecase fiction), traditional stories about clever magistrates who settle complicated criminal cases in imperial China, also belong to this category. In contemporary China, detective fiction may also be called *gong'an xiaoshuo*, with *an* using a different character. The term means 'public security fiction', because this type of story dominates magazines run by public security bureaux and other government organs. Serious magazines such as *Democracy and Legality* (*Minzhu yü fazhi*) also carry such detective stories, as do many popular literary magazines (e.g. *Pecks* or *Zhuomuniao*) for the purposes of education and profit. The state is wary that the genre reveals too much of the seamy side of society, but Chinese writers may create many stories as long as they are not excessively negative and almost always end with justice served. From corrupt officials to hooligans and rebellious teenagers, much of this popular literature is a combination of love, suspense and crime detection. Since

the late 1990s, some works, which would formerly belong to the category of 'detective fiction', have been positively relabelled 'anti-corruption fiction' (*fantan xiaoshuo*), as the many economic crimes exposed in these stories are committed by high-ranking officials. Many have been made into films or serial television dramas.

See also: corruption

Further reading

Kinkley, Jeffrey (1985). 'The Politics of Detective Fiction in Post-Mao China: Rebirth or Re-extinction?' *The Armchair Detective* 18.4 (Fall): 372–8.

—— (1993). 'Chinese Crime Fiction'. *Society* 30.4 (May/June): 51–62.

—— (2000). 'The Post-Colonial Detective in People's China'. In Edward Christian (ed.), *The Post-Colonial Detective*. New York: St Martin's Press.

HELEN XIAOYAN WU

development zones (urban)

'Development zones' (*fazhanqu*) are areas developed to attract foreign direct investment and economic development. A development zone may be called Special Economic Zone, Economic Development Zone, Technology Development Zone or Industrial Park. From 1980, when the Chinese government decided to establish 'special economic zones', to 2001, China had established and officially recognized about 200 development zones to attract investment from overseas and to promote economic development. Five Special Economic Zones established in the early 1980s were located in Shenzhen, Zhuhai, Shantou, Xiamen and Hainan. There are both national and regional development zones. National Development Zones currently include thirty-five Economic and Technological Development Zones, twelve Bonded Zones and thirteen Border Economic Cooperation Zones. In addition, more than 140 Regional Development Zones are spread across the country.

Economic development zones have played an important role in attracting foreign direct investment and restructuring the Chinese economy from a central planning system to a market-oriented system. The government provides incentives to foreign investors in the fields of land management, urban service, legal protection, and income and customs taxes. Multiple modes of ownership, including foreign ownership and joint venture between foreign-owned and domestic-owned firms, have been developed. A labour contracting system has replaced the government assignment system. Moreover, developmental zones have had important impacts on Chinese experiences of urban space. Millions of migrants, most of whom are from rural areas, work in development zones. Some special economic development zones like the Shenzhen Special Economic Zone have become tourist attractions.

REN HAI

dialects

Two levels of linguistic variation within Chinese are referred to as *fangyan*, usually translated 'dialect' but preferentially now following Victor Mair as 'topolect', 'language of a place'. At one level, linguists identify eight – sometimes seven – historically related language groups: Mandarin, Wu, Yue, Gan, Xiang, Kejia and Northern and Southern Min (sometimes combined). Mandarin,

also called Putonghua or 'common speech' in the PRC, is the official language and is spoken as a native language in north China. Shanghainese is said to be typical of the Wu dialects, which also include languages spoken in Suzhou, Hangzhou, Ningbo and other smaller areas. Yue includes the Cantonese spoken in Canton and Hong Kong (and in many overseas Chinese Chinatowns). Southern Min is spoken in Fujian province and across the straits in Taiwan (where it is also called Taiwanese, Hokkien and Ho'lo). Hakka (Kejia) is spoken throughout southern China and Greater China. These eight *fangyan* are not usually mutually intelligible but may be represented by the single Chinese writing system (with some exceptions).

Within each of these *fangyan* groups, additional variation exists. Villages separated by mountains and rivers may speak varieties that are noticeably different, though they may be mutually intelligible. The Mandarin *fangyan* are spoken as a mother tongue by approximately 70 per cent of the mainland population. Mandarin is increasingly regarded as the official language in Singapore, despite its residents being almost entirely speakers of southern dialects. Mandarin is the official language of Taiwan, though five-sixths of its population also speaks Taiwanese. Some *fangyan* have more speakers than well-known European languages; three – Mandarin, Wu and Yue – rank first, tenth and sixteenth in number of native speakers among all world languages. See Table 1.

Table 1 Linguistic variation

Dialect	Representative city or area	Percentage of Han in PRC (est.)	Population
Mandarin	Beijing	71.5	858,000,000
Wu	Shanghai	8.5	102,000,000
Yue	Canton (Guangzhou)	5	60,000,000
Xiang	Hunan	4.8	57,600,000
Kejia (Hakka)	Scattered in southern China and overseas China	3.7	44,400,000
Southern Min	Amoy, Taiwan	2.8	33,600,000
Gan	Jiangxi	2.4	28,800,000
Northern Min	Fuzhou	1.3	15,600,000
Total		100	1.2 billion Han (92% of PRC population

See also: Sino-Tibetan language speakers

Further reading

DeFrancis, John (1984). *The Chinese Language: Fact and Fantasy*. Honolulu: University of Hawai'i Press.

Mair, Victor H. (1991). 'What is a Chinese Dialect/Topolect? Reflections on Some Key Sino-English Linguistic Terms'. *Sino-Platonic Papers* 29 (September).

Norman, Jerry (1988). *Chinese*. Oxford: Oxford University Press.

Ramsey, S. Robert (1987). *The Languages of China*. Princeton: Princeton University Press.

SUSAN D. BLUM

dictionaries

Numerous comprehensive and specialized dictionaries have been published since 1980. The major ones are:

- (1986–90) *Hanyu Da Zidian* [Comprehensive Chinese Dictionary], 8 vols, Hubei Cishu and Sichuan Province Xinhua Bookstore. Good for single characters, with oracle bone and later variants.
- (1987–94) *Hanyu Da Cidian* (HDC) [Comprehensive Chinese Dictionary], 12 vols + Appendixes – Indexes vol., Shanghai: HDC; several supplementary dictionaries and a CD-ROM (1998). Good for Classical Chinese, older vernacular; also useful for Modern Chinese.
- (1991) Chen Xinwang, *Han-Ying Yulin* [A Dictionary of Chinese with English Translation]. Shanghai Jiaotong University Press. 34,643 idioms, proverbs and allusions, very large of its kind and useful for translating well-known expressions in Classical Chinese, inefficient indexes.
- (1995) *Han-Ying Cidian* [A Chinese–English Dictionary], rev. edn Beijing: Foreign Language Teaching and Research. Widely used since 1978, with about 18,000 single-character and over 80,000 word entries.
- (1996) *Xiandai Hanyu Cidian* [Modern Chinese Dictionary]. Beijing: Commercial; supplement (2002). Authoritative dictionary for Modern Chinese. See also *Xiandai Hanyu Da Cidian* [Comprehensive Modern Chinese Dictionary], Shanghai, 2001.
- (1999) *Cihai* [Sea of Words], 4 vols, one abridged vol. (2000), CD-ROM (2000), Shanghai Cishu. Combination of dictionary and encyclopedia.
- (2000) Wu Jingrong and Cheng Zhenqiu (eds) *Xin Shidai Han-Ying Da Cidian* [NewAge Chinese–English Dictionary). Beijing: Commercial. Nearly 120,000 entries, very large of its kind.
- (2000) *Yingyong Hanyu Cidian* [Applied Chinese Dictionary]. Beijing: Commercial, Practical, with parts of speech.
- (2000) *Yuhai* [Sea of the Language], 2 vols, Shanghai wenyi. Over 100,000 entries of adages, code words, idioms, proverbs, sayings and set expressions.

See also: Xinhua zidian, Xinhua cidian

HELEN XIAOYAN WU

dim sum

Dim sum (in Cantonese; *dianxin* in Mandarin) literally means 'to touch your heart'. These small morsels or snacks are associated with the Cantonese custom of *yum cha* (*yincha*: drinking tea) at tea, breakfast and lunch times. They are similar to hors d'oeuvres, the hot and cold delicacies served at French restaurants. Dim sum are colourful, fragrant, tasty and shapely, and they meet the needs of every eater in every season. The ingredients are of high quality and plentiful, the style is novel and there are many varieties such as egg custard tarts, mini spring rolls, cakes, steamed buns, green peppers with shrimp filling, meat balls, fried or steamed dumplings filled with everything from roast pork to Chinese leeks, and other delicacies. The wrapping of rice flour dumplings is so thin that the ingredients can almost be seen. Another favourite wrapping is the lotus leaf, filled with steamed glutinous rice and a filling. There is usually no ordering. Instead you choose from a wide assortment of snacks that the waiters or waitresses bring out on carts and trays. You may prefer not to take chicken's feet and duck's webbed feet in black bean sauce, but they are delicacies for the Chinese. It may take you several visits to different restaurants before you can taste all the varieties and determine your favourites. In big hotels in Hong Kong and the West, you may find Western variations.

Dim sum is often used for get-togethers. A film entitled *Dim Sum* (Wayne Wang, 1984) depicts three generations of a Chinese–American family living in San Francisco.

Further reading

Liley, Vicki (1999). *Dim Sum*. Hong Kong: Periplus.

HELEN XIAOYAN WU

Ding Fang

b. 1956, Wugong, Shaanxi

Oil painter

Ding Fang was admitted to the Nanjing Art Academy in 1978 where he would begin his master's in oil painting in 1983. He travelled widely during his studies visiting remote areas such as the Yellow Earth Plateau, Datong and the Taihang mountains. In 1984, he began the *City* (*Cheng*) series of paintings inspired by his encounters with the rugged landscapes and cultural ruins of northern China. His monumental abandoned earth-coloured cities yield the symbolic pulsating energy of bygone cultures in the series *Sword-Shaped Willpower* (*Jianxing de yizhi*, 1986–7). This trajectory suggests an escape from the present to find more eternal values in ancient culture and in the vigorous life depicted in his earlier pictures such as *Harvest* (*Shouhuo*, 1984).

Ding Fang participated in the Jiangsu Youth Art Week in 1986 and formed an art group called the 'Red Brigade' (*Hongse lu*), which held the

'Vanguard' (*Diyi feng*) exhibition in 1987. The Red Brigade Manifesto, written by him in 1987, explains his choice in the context of his tragic vision of human history, which is not so much a leap forward towards any greater purpose but an accumulation of ruins of grand dreams. Painting therefore takes on a religious overtone in this Sisyphean cycle of human endeavour. This sense of tragedy and religious fatalism becomes more overt and apocalyptic in the paintings completed when he lived in the artists' village next to the **Yuanming Yuan** – the Garden of Perfect Brightness (Beijing), such as The *Destruction of Sodom* (*Fenhuide suoduoma cheng*, 1993).

Further reading

(1994). *Ding Fang*. Nanning: Guangxi meishu chubanshe.

Andrews, Julia F. and Gao, Minglu (1995). 'The Avant-Garde's Challenge to Official Art'. In Debora, S. Davis (ed.), *Urban Spaces in Contemporary China: The Potential for Autonomy and Community in Post-Mao China*. Cambridge: Harvard University Press, 221–78.

Lü, Peng and Yi, Dan (1992). *Zhongguo xiandai yishushi* [A History of Modern Art in China]. Changsha: Hunan meishu chubanshe, 201–7.

EDUARDO WELSH

Ding Guan'gen

b. September 1929, Wuxi, Jiangsu

CCP propaganda chief (1992–2002)

Known most for policies that modernized the CCP's control over such cultural institutions as radio, film and television media organs, news agencies, publishing houses, artistic organizations and intellectual professional associations, Ding Guan'gen came from a distinctly technocratic background. Ding received a degree in railway transportation from Shanghai's Jiaotong University in 1951, entered the bureaucracy, and rose to minister of railways in 1985. He resigned in 1988, accepting responsibility for major train accidents that year, but was rewarded for his loyalty post-Tiananmen by assuming control over the CCP's propaganda portfolio.

As a member of the CCP's powerful Politburo and Secretariat, as head of the Leading Group for Propaganda and Ideology, and as director of the **Central Propaganda Department** from 1992 to 2002, Ding ensured that state media and cultural institutions would continue to be the ideological 'mouthpiece' of the Party. He also directed campaigns to promote popular support for the economic and political reform policies of leaders Deng Xiaoping, Jiang Zemin and Zhu Rongji, and as director of the 'central guidance committees' on **socialist spiritual civilization** and on cultural and ethical construction, he led crackdowns on pornography, intellectual piracy, 'bourgeois liberalism' and other reform-era phenomena deemed 'spiritual pollution'. Finally, Ding modernized traditional propaganda organs through the formation of radio, film, television and publishing groups with major multi-national media corporation partners.

See also: state control of media

STEVEN W. LEWIS

Ding Guangxun

(Bishop Ding)

b. 20 September 1915, Shanghai

Bishop, Protestant church leader, politician

Chairman of the **Three-Self Patriotic Movement (TSPM)**, president of the **China Christian Council** from late 1980 until early 1997 and president of **Jinling Union Theological Seminary** from 1953, Ding is also one of the vice chairmen of the Chinese People's Political Consultative Conference and a standing committee member of the National People's Congress.

Ding grew up in Shanghai and received a BA from St John's University in Shanghai 1937, followed by a BD from the same institution in 1942.

The same year he was ordained as an Anglican priest. In 1948 he moved to Geneva to serve as mission secretary for the World Student Christian Federation after working two years in Canada with student work.

After returning to China in 1951 he supported the TSPM and soon became one of its leading spokesmen. In 1955 he was consecrated bishop of the Anglican diocese of Zhejiang. Ding has played a decisive role in the development of Protestant Christianity in China after 1949, but has sometimes been criticized by more evangelical groups in the Church. He is one of the most well-known Chinese theologians. His theology emphasizes the unending love of God, the Cosmic Christ and the participation of Christians in society.

See also: Christianity (Protestantism)

Further reading

Ting, K. H. (1999). *Love Never Ends*, Nanjing: Yilin.

FREDERIK FÄLLMAN

Ding Yi

b. 1962, Shanghai

Painter

Graduating from the Shanghai Arts and Crafts Institute (1983) and the School of Fine Arts of Shanghai University (1990), Ding Yi is unique for an enduring and quasi-religious commitment exemplified in the monosyllabic abstraction of the *Cross (Shishi)* series, which he began in 1988. Using basic marks adopted for dividing a sheet of paper into many squares of equal size, Ding Yi chose to deny access to the pictorial surface of any element not inherent to the painting surface as a bi-dimensional unit defined by the primary elements of dots, lines, planes and colours. Flat and precise, Ding's early paintings were executed with the help of a ruler and adhesive stripes, resembling colour graphs. Later the square geometry was enriched by the introduction of diagonal and negative patterns of crosses, random juxtapositions of colours, and the use of freehand that added a coarse and random quality to the scientifically calculated character of his previous works. Recently Ding Yi has turned to tartans, juxtaposing their existing patterns and colours with his own.

Obsessive in their repetition, yet allowing for a myriad of variations, Ding's crosses are completely non-representational, offering complex compositions of brushstrokes and colours triumphing as a purely visual experience. They are the mark of timeless patience and enduring physical exertion. With nine solo shows to date, Ding Yi has been exhibiting in numerous venues at home and abroad, including the '**China Avant-Garde**' exhibition in Beijing (1989), the Venice Biennale (1993); the Biennale of Sydney (1998); 'Ding Yi: Fluorescence on Tartan' at the Chinese Art Archives Warehouse in Beijing (2000); and 'Appearance of Crosses' at the Galerie Waldburger in Berlin (2002).

Further reading

Dematté, Monica (1997). 'Theorization of Casualness'. In *Ding Yi* (exhibition catalogue). Shanghai: ShangART, 2–3.

Doran, Valerie C. (ed.) (1993). *China's New Art, Post-1989, with a Retrospective from 1979 to 1989* (exhibition catalogue). Hong Kong: Hanart T Z Gallery. (Reprinted in 2001 by Asia Art Archive, Hong Kong, 222–5.)

Li, Xu (1994). 'Shishi Ding Yi' [Appearance of Crosses of Ding Yi]. In *Ding Yi* (exhibition catalogue). Beijing: New Amsterdam Art Consulting, 1–2.

TANG DI

disabilities

The revised Chinese Constitution of 1982 states that 'the state and society help make arrangements for the work, livelihood and education of the blind, deaf-mutes and other handicapped citizens' (Article 45). Despite this very little was done until the mid 1980s, almost certainly at the instigation of Deng Pufang, the hemiplegic son of Deng Xiaoping. In 1984 the China Welfare Fund for the Disabled

was established, followed by the All China Federation for the Disabled in 1988. Deng Pufang is director of both organizations. Also in 1988, targets and services for people with a disability began to be included in the Five Year Plan. In 1994 a Co-ordination Committee for the Handicapped under the State Council was established and the Law on the Protection of Disabled People was passed.

The first national survey of disability was carried out in 1987, authorized by the State Council. It was found that China had 51,640,000 people with a disability, or approximately 5 per cent of the population. Eighteen per cent of all households contained someone with a disability. It has been suggested that the inclusion criteria were too broad and people were counted who did not necessarily perceive themselves to be disabled. Nonetheless, the numbers are huge and as China's population ages they will increase. The survey found that only 30 per cent of people with a disability were financially independent, most relying on family support. Only 2.65 per cent were reliant on government aid. Illiteracy is much higher among disabled people (70 per cent as opposed to the national level of 30 per cent). Half of those classified by the government as being 'in poverty' have a disability and 20 million people with a disability lack even the basic necessities of food and clothing. One matter of great concern is that some of the causes of disability are avoidable, for instance polio. The government is making great efforts, supported by international agencies, to immunize every child against polio. The national survey found there were 1.82 million people under the age of fourteen who were deaf, much of which is caused by the inappropriate prescription of antibiotics. Lack of iodine has led to completely avoidable goitre and cretinism in some of the remoter provinces, like Gansu. Some villages are reputed to have no adults of normal intelligence. Since the mid 1980s the government has taken enormous strides in the area of disability but the problems it faces remain serious.

See also: mental health; Shi Tiesheng

Further reading

Callaway, Alison (2002). *Deaf Children in China*. Gallaudet University Press.

Pearson, V. (1995). 'Health and Responsibility;
But Whose?' In Linda Wong and Stewart
MacPherson (eds), *Social Change and Social Policy in
Contemporary China*. Aldershot: Avebury Press.

Pearson, V., Wong, Y. C., and Pierini, J. (2002).
'The Structure and Content of Social Inclusion;
Voices of Young Adults with a Learning Disability in Guangzhou'. *Disability and Society* 17.4:
365–82.

Pierini, J., Pearson, V. and Wong, Y. C. (2001)
'Glorious Work; The Employment Situation of
Adults with a Learning Disability in Guang-
zhou'. *Disability and Society* 16. 2: 252–75.

Tian, E. C., Pearson, V., Wang, R. W. and
Phillips, M. R. (1994). 'A Brief History of
the Development of Rehabilitation Services
in China'. *British Journal of Psychiatry* 165,
Supplement 24: 19–27.

VERONICA PEARSON

divination and fortune-telling

Divination has been a prominent feature of
Chinese culture for at least three thousand years.
Until recently, the People's Republic of China
(PRC) has actively discouraged the practice, but
the 'Open Policy' inaugurated by the government in 1978 expanded significantly the state's
tolerance of so-called 'feudal superstitions'. The
result has been a flourishing of many types
of divination, including not only 'siting' or
'geomancy' (see **fengshui**) but also astrology,
physiognomy, dream interpretation, spirit-
writing, the use of 'divining blocks' (*beijiao* or
jiaobei), and various forms of horoscopic numer-
ology, including systems based on the trigrams
and hexagrams of the **Yijing** [Book of Changes].
Traditional almanacs (*huangli*, *lishu*, etc.), which
not only designate each day of the lunar year as
auspicious or inauspicious for certain activities
but also include other predictions based on
divination techniques, have become increasingly
popular, especially in south China, where,
generally speaking, religious beliefs are more
deeply seated than in the north.

Article 36 of the Chinese State Constitution
guarantees 'freedom of religious belief' and the
protection of 'normal' religious activity, but the state
continues to view fortune-telling as a 'feudal' superstition – abnormal, corrupt and exploitive, at least
when undertaken by private practitioners for money.
Indeed, 'feudal superstition' is invariably listed as one
of the 'six vices' relentlessly targeted by the Chinese
authorities, along with prostitution, gambling, selling of women and children, drug trafficking
and drug abuse and pornography. **Corruption**,
significantly, is in a different category.

Government reports periodically highlight stories
of 'feudal superstition' designed to underscore
their disruptive effects. One well-publicized case
involved a peasant named Zhang Jingui, from the
northeastern Chinese province of Heilongjiang,
whose wife had consulted a palmist to ask for
advice on their disintegrating marriage. According
to the *Heilongjiang Legal Daily*, the palm-reader told
Zhang's wife that cutting off her husband's penis
and allowing it to grow back would restore their
relationship to its previous harmonious state.
She promptly followed this advice, but oddly
enough the relationship didn't improve. Another
celebrated case involved a man named Yang
Jinjin, who was told by a fortune-teller that his
wife's long illness was caused by the presence of
his seventy-eight-year-old mother in their house.
Yang dutifully strangled his mother to save his
wife, who, as luck would have it, died a week later
from hepatitis.

Despite such negative press and the periodic
efforts of the state to suppress 'superstitious'
practices, divination continues to grow in popularity in the PRC. For instance, a national survey
conducted by the China Association for Science
and Technology in 2000 revealed that 35.5 per
cent of the Chinese people in the PRC believe in at
least one form of fortune-telling – an increase of
nearly 7 per cent from the 28.7 per cent figure in
1996. According to a recent Reuters story on
divination in China, the fortune-tellers thrive in
times of economic insecurity.

During the past two decades, a great deal of
valuable scholarly work has been done on virtually
all facets of Chinese divination, past and present.
Although most mainland authors persist in referring ritualistically to the Chinese mantic arts as

'superstition' or 'pseudo-science' (*wei kexue*), they have nonetheless investigated the subject of divination thoroughly and enthusiastically, producing a great many valuable articles, monographs, reference works and collectanea, and also making available to the scholarly community a wealth of new research materials – including recently uncovered archaeological artifacts and newly discovered written texts. At the same time, a number of authors such as Hong Pimo and Jiang Yuzhen have written books ostensibly criticizing divination but in fact pandering to popular interest in the practice.

Further reading

Smith, Richard J. (1991, 1993). *Fortune-tellers and Philosophers: Divination in Traditional Chinese Society.* Boulder, Colorado and Oxford, England: Westview Press.

—— (1992). Review of Hong Pimo and Jiang Yuzhen's *Zhongguo gudai suanming shu* (1990). *Journal of Asian Studies* 51.4 (November).

RICHARD J. SMITH

divorce

Until recent decades, divorce has been a taboo in Chinese society. For women especially, marriage is expected to be for life, as described in the old saying 'If a woman marries a chicken, she should stick with the chicken; if she marries a dog, she should stick with the dog' (*jiaji suiji jiagou suigou*). Thus, divorce has been viewed as a shameful event. Efforts have been made by the PRC to make divorces more accessible. The 1950 Marriage Law aimed to end 'feudal marriages' such as concubinages and was immediately followed by increased number of divorces. Similarly, the 1981 Marriage Law, which made marriage dissolution easier, was followed by a rise in the divorce rate. Divorces are granted by marriage registrars if both spouses have agreed to marriage dissolution, or through mediation or ruling by the court if one of the spouses files for divorce.

The number of couples seeking divorce has quadrupled from the late 1970s to the early twenty-first century. The official divorce rate in 2001 is 2 per 1,000 marriages and is still low by Western standards. However, the urban divorce rate is significantly higher and is estimated by some to be approaching 25 per cent. The rapid rise in the divorce rate is attributable to economic liberalization and a greater sense of individuality, and is greeted by some as a sign of progress as women have greater autonomy to break free from unhappy marriages. However, it also reflects a rise in infidelity and has alarmed those concerned with importation of Western values. Public opinion has changed slowly and greater stigma continues to be attached to divorced women than to divorced men, as evidenced by more men than women remarrying after divorce.

C. CINDY FAN

dizi

Musical instrument

The *di* or *dizi* is the name used today to refer to the Chinese transverse bamboo flute. It has six finger holes and, near the blowhole, an additional hole covered by a thin membrane which vibrates when the instrument is blown, resulting in a buzzy timbre.

There are essentially two main types of di, each one a prominent instrument in the accompanying ensemble of two different opera traditions. One is the *kundi* (also known as *qudi*), which leads the instrumental ensemble of the **Kunqu** opera native to the area around Shanghai. The other is the shorter and higher-pitched *bangdi*, which figures in the ensemble of the **Bangzi** opera in Henan. This northern version of the di is the one that is used today in the concert performances of 'national music' (*guoyue*) – music specifically composed for traditional Chinese instruments which arose after the 1940s and generally features a louder sound, tempered pitches and a virtuoso style of playing (see **national style**).

MERCEDES M. DUJUNCO

Document 19 (1982)

Document 19, a Chinese Communist Party (CCP) directive from the Central Committee to its CCP and government cadres promulgated in 1982, is a comprehensive religious policy that was part of Deng Xiaoping's 'reform and opening' (*gaige kaifang*). Document 19 resulted in the revival of many religious traditions in China through the gradual rehabilitation or release of many religious specialists of recognized religions (Buddhism, Daoism, Islam, Catholicism and Protestant Christianity) from prisons, the return of seized property to recognized religious organizations, and the re-opening of monasteries, convents and seminaries. Although it has been further refined and adjusted by succeeding CCP directives (such as Articles 144 and 145 from the PRC State Council, promulgated by Li Peng in 1994), it remains the most comprehensive official review of past CCP religious policy and the guiding strategy for contemporary CCP religious policy – the administrative co-optation of recognized religious organizations into various state structures, the role of religion in attaining CCP goals of modernization and the building of 'socialism with Chinese characteristics', and the official ambivalence towards foreign religious organizations and leaders. Document 19 contains an introductory explanation from the Central Committee and twelve sections that discuss: theoretical explanations of religion; an overview of religions in China; the past and present relationship between the CCP and religious organizations, including property issues, training of religious specialists, and special stances towards the religions of ethnic minorities; the proscription of illicit religious activities; and the role of religion in China's international relations. Document 19 is also central in understanding post-reform religious practices in the mainland because it highlights the idealized role of the state towards religion – while the freedom of religious belief is guaranteed in the PRC constitution, the freedom of religious practice is not, and must be carefully administered by the state to ensure the development and stability of Chinese society.

See also: religious policies of the state; Christianity (Protestantism)

Further reading

Luo, Zhufeng (1991). *Religion Under Socialism in China*. Maryknoll: Orbis Books.

MacInnis, Donald E. (1989). *Religion in China Today: Policy and Practice*. Maryknoll: Orbis Books. [Contains full English text of Document 19.]

ERIBERTO P. LOZADA JR

domestic space

Privacy has long been a luxury for most Chinese because of high population density and lack of adequate living space. Nevertheless, a distinction between domestic and public spaces has always existed. Traditionally, a gradation of publicness and privateness spans the typical household spatially from the main gate of the courtyard to the innermost bedchambers. Guests are received in the living room and only social intimates are allowed into the kitchen and the bedrooms. In rural areas where land is more plentiful, the ideal of the one-family enclosed courtyard house can be realized. In cramped urban homes, however, often one single room is used for living, dining and sleeping for the entire family. This lack of privacy does not stop people from hosting relatives and friends. During the Maoist era especially, people visited one another at home (*chuanmen*: 'going from door to door') a lot more because there was a paucity of public places for hanging out. The relative homogeneity of all the homes in terms of decor and furnishing also encouraged mutual visiting with an equalitarian ethos. The cluster-style, wall-enclosed 'work-unit'-assigned housing complexes are conducive to socializing in the public 'big courtyard' (*dayuan*). The housing revolution during the reform era, coupled with the success of the one-child policy, increased the per capita square-footage living space significantly in urban China. Following real estate developments, more and more families are moving 'out' into the city's peripheries and 'up' into high-rise apartment buildings. The social intimacy of the old neighbourhood and 'work-unit' complex is replaced by the anonymity of the elevator halls. Though much bigger and prettier now, the homes are increasingly becoming a private haven rather than a place to entertain and host guests. The hourly or live-in maid of rural origin has also become an important presence in urban domestic space, relieving the working couple of domestic duties of caretaking the elderly and children, cleaning, grocery shopping, cooking and laundry. Because of persistent Chinese cooking practices (i.e. stir-frying that produces a large quantity of oil vapours), the kitchen remains a space for chores separate and sealed off from the rest of the home (versus the American spatial practice of entertaining guests inside or from the kitchen).

See also: home refurbishing

Further reading

Fraser, David (2000). 'Inventing Oasis: Luxury Housing Advertisements and Reconfiguring Domestic Space in Shanghai'. In Deborah Davis (ed.), *The Consumer Revolution in Urban China*. Berkeley: University of California Press, 25–53.

ADAM YUET CHAU

domestic violence

In China, the term 'domestic violence' includes spousal, child, sibling and elderly abuse. The Marriage Law of 2001 specifically forbids domestic violence, an example of wishful thinking triumphing over reality. Physical discipline of children by parents is considered standard practice, not abuse. Wife abuse is the most common form of domestic violence. The National Survey on Domestic Violence Against Women was published in 2002. In it, 3,543 married men and women were interviewed. It was found that: (1) 71.9 per cent of respondents were beaten as children. They were more likely to be perpetrators (men) and victims (women) of spousal abuse in comparison with those not beaten as children; (2) 20.7 per cent of female respondents said their husbands beat them, while 16 per cent of men admitted to beating their wives; (3) when asked to define spousal abuse, respondents mentioned physical and sexual abuse, but did not included

emotional cruelty; and (4) respondents' rankings of the causes of wife abuse were as follows: patriarchal and feudal attitudes; alcohol abuse, gambling and extra-marital affairs; low education and the financial status of the couple; nagging wives; unequal social status between men and women in society, where the husband must discipline the wife for misbehaviour, or the husband has psychological problems because the wife's social status is higher than his own. China lacks a legislative framework that recognizes abuse and responds appropriately.

Further reading

Liu, Meng (2002). 'National Survey on Domestic Violence Against Women'. Unpublished report, No. 14. International Conference on Combating Violence against Women, Beijing.

LIU MENG AND VERONICA PEARSON

Dong, culture of

This minority nationality, also called Kam, lives mainly on the Hunan–Guangxi–Guizhou border area, their population being 2,514,014 (1990 census). The Dong speak a language belonging to the Zhuang-Dong branch of the Sino-Tibetan language family (see **Sino-Tibetan language speakers**). They lacked a writing system until 1958, when the Latin alphabet was adapted to the Dong language. Although this written language remains in use, most Dong use Chinese characters more readily.

The Dong are agricultural, their diet based on rice. Large Dong villages have about 700 households, although most are quite small, with only twenty to thirty. Houses are two-storeyed, with livestock and firewood kept on the lower floor. They are wooden and closely built, fire being a major hazard.

Characteristic features of the larger villages are splendidly designed high drum-towers, some of them a dozen storeys or so. These are used for festivities, performances or meetings. Some villages also have 'wind-and-rain bridges' (*fengyu qiao*), which are covered and supported by ornate pagoda-like structures at intervals. They serve as venues for social gatherings of various kinds, including dances or performances. The Dong have a form of drama, of nineteenth-century origin, and it remains fairly popular. The most famous item is *Julang and Nyangmui*, a tragic love story in which the lovers are themselves Dong. A landlord kills Julang because he lusts after Nyangmui, but she is later able to take revenge.

Further reading

Geary, D. N., Geary, R., Ou, Chaoquan, Long, Yaohon, Jiang, Daren and Wang, Jiying (2001). *The Kam People of China, Turning Nineteen?* Richmond, Surrey: Curzon.

COLIN MACKERRAS

Dong Wenhua

b. 1962, Dalian

Popular singer

Dong Wenhua is one of China's most distinguished singers of the last decade and a half, famous for her lyrical patriotic and propaganda songs, the best known of which include 'Spring Story' (*Chuntian de gushi*), a song praising Deng Xiaoping and his economic reforms, and 'The Great Wall is Long' (*Changcheng chang*), a song eulogizing the Great Wall and promoting patriotism.

Dong Wenhua is a member of the Song and Dance Troupe of the General Political Department of the Chinese People's Liberation Army (*Zhongguo renmin jiefangjun zongzhengbu gewutuan*) and a representative of a large group of singers who are closely associated with the Party-state and the army. Conforming to the orthodox official aesthetics of professionalism, discipline and solemnity, her performance style is highly choreographed and disciplined. She appears frequently in officially organized live and televised events all over the country, often in army uniform, and typically sings in the orthodox 'national/folksinging style' (*minzu/minge changfa*), a mixture of Chinese folk and Western bel canto singing that requires formal training.

Dong Wenhua has won many prizes since the mid 1980s, among which are included first prize for best MTV, awarded by China Music TV (Zhongguo yinyue dianshi), which she has won several times since this prize was first awarded in 1993. Her popularity in China, especially among those whose exposure to popular music is limited to **CCTV (Chinese Central Television)**, reflects the success of the state in maintaining a central position in contemporary popular culture.

NIMROD BARANOVITCH

Dongcun

(East Village)

Artist group

The actual name of Dongcun, or East Village, is Datou cun, a village situated in the eastern suburbs of Beijing. In the early 1990s, a group of young artists moved there either from other parts of the city, like **Zhang Huan**, who was then studying oil painting at the **Central Academy of Fine Arts**, or, like **Ma Liuming** and Zhu Min, from other parts of China to try their luck in the capital. They rented old peasant houses which functioned as their living quarters, studios and private showrooms. To help their public find the location of the shows and remember the name of the group, the artists decided to call themselves 'Dongcun', a geographical reference to their location that also established a cultural connection with New York's East Village, an international art hub considered to be the most significant space for the creation of cutting-edge experimental art. This group of artists was unknown to the public until late in 1993, when Zhang Huan's performance at the **China Art Gallery** (Zhongguo meishuguan) caused the cancellation of a group show. Most of the artists worked independently, but they also collaborated, as in the performance *Adding One Metre to an Anonymous Mountain* (1994), organized by Zhang Huan, in which seven naked men and two naked women artists stacked themselves on top of one another on a mountain top in suburban Beijing to underline the possibility of individual acts of will and self-empowerment, notwithstanding its meaninglessness. By the mid 1990s some of the artists had begun to move out of the village, and by the end of the decade most had relocated elsewhere.

See also: art exhibitions (experimental, 1990s); 798

Further reading

Qian Zhijian (1999). 'Performing Bodies: Zhang Huan, Ma Liuming and Performance Art in China'. *Art Journal* 58.2 (Summer): 60–81.

QIAN ZHIJIAN

Doyle, Christopher

(a.k.a. Du Kefeng)

b. 1952, Sydney

Cinematographer, photographer, film director

Christopher Doyle, known for his unique hand-held camerawork, is among the most important cinematographers in contemporary Chinese cinema.

Doyle worked as a seaman and in agriculture before studying art history at the University of Maryland and Chinese at the Chinese University of Hong Kong. In the early 1980s he worked as a cameraman and editor for a television station in Taiwan, before shooting *That Day on the Beach* (*Haitan de yitian*), a landmark work in New Taiwan Cinema directed by Edward **Yang**. In 1991, *Days of Being Wild* (*A fei zhengzhuan*) marked the beginning of a long and fruitful creative relationship between the cinematographer and Hong Kong director **Wong Kar-wai**, which has produced such films as *Chongking Express* (*Chongqing senlin*), *Fallen Angels* (*Duoluo tianshi*), *Ashes of Time* (*Dongxie xidu*), *Happy Together* (*Chunguang zhaxia*), and *In the Mood for Love* (*Huayang nianhua*).

Although best known for his signature camera work with Wong Kar-wai, Doyle has also worked with other important Chinese directors, including Stanley **Kwan** and Sylvia **Chang** from Hong Kong, **Lai Shengchuan** and Chen Guo-fu from Taiwan, and **Zhang Yuan**, **Chen Kaige** and **Zhang Yimou** from the PRC. Doyle's success in the Chinese film world has earned him several major international awards, bringing him to the attention of Hollywood, where he shot Gus Van Sant's remake of *Psycho* (2000), and more recently *Rabbit-Proof Fence* and *The Quiet American*.

Besides his work as a cinematographer, Doyle has acted in several films, most notably Peter **Chan**'s *Comrades* (*Tian mimi*), and has authored several books of essays and photos, including *A Cloud in Trousers* and *Don't Try for Me Argentina*. Doyle made his directorial debut in 1998 with *Away With Words* (*Santiao ren*), an experimental film about a young Japanese drifter, a gay Australian man and a Chinese fashion designer, whose paths cross in post-handover Hong Kong.

MICHAEL BERRY

Dragon Boat Festival

(Duanwujie)

For the Duanwu festival, people make glutinous rice rolls (*zongzi*) and hold dragon boat races. The traditional explanation of this festival is that these acts are performed in honour of the poet and minister (and patriot) Qu Yuan, who, unjustly accused and banished, committed suicide by leaping into the river on that day. It is also generally recognized that the festival has an exorcistic function, inasmuch as people hang prophylactic plants on their doors. More explicitly, the dragon boat races are meant to drive away the gods who bring epidemics (*wenshen*).

In Luokou, for example, in Ningdu county, Gannan, after two weeks of theatre in honour of the local gods, on the fourth day of the fifth moon the population organizes a procession through the village. At its head there is a wooden dragon, followed by flag-bearers and then the palanquin of the main god, Zhugong (Ancestor Zhu); next comes an orchestra and three persons carrying a paper boat and a basket. The dragon first, then Zhugong, enter each house in turn, the first to purify it, the second to be worshipped, and the people then place negative offerings in the paper boat and positive ones in the basket. The next day, in the late afternoon, when each house has been visited, a Daoist priest (see **Daoist priests**) leads the procession to the waterfront, downstream from the village, and there the paper boat and all its negativity are burned. The people explain – and the prayers recited by the Daoist confirm – that they are sending away the gods who bring pestilence.

A little to the south, in the county seat of Shicheng, each of the town's ten major temples had its own dragon boat, and three of these temples organized their own festivals at the beginning of the fifth moon. Already on the eighth day of the fourth moon, the temple dedicated to Houji had launched its boat. Holding peachwood branches in their hands, the people lined the shores of the river waiting for the boat to pass, and when it did, they used the branches to throw mosquitoes into the boat (the words for 'mosquito' and 'epidemic' are homophonous). On the last day of the fourth moon, everyone swept out their houses. On the first two days of the fifth moon, a dragon, whose head and tail were of wood, was carried from house to house to purify them: this was called 'sweeping the earth' (*saogan*). On the third day, it was time to 'sweep the water' (*saoshui*), which consisted in carrying the dragon, a paper boat and Houji in procession throughout the town. On the fifth day of the month the ten temples' dragon boats raced each other, and on the sixth day, after a one-day **Jiao**, the paper boat was carried to the river to be burned: this was called 'the dragon takes to the water'.

The examples could be multiplied, but let us rather note another, most curious phenomenon, also associated with Duanwu, to wit 'rock fights'. This phenomenon has been encountered recently in a village in Meixian county where the Wang and Xie lineages, separated by a river and generations of enmity, line up every year at Duanwu on either side of the river to throw stones at each other until the blood flows.

JOHN LAGERWEY

dried-food specialities

The Chinese began to dry foodstuffs for easy storage and transportation 1,500 years ago. Their dried foodstuffs (*ganhuo*) are abundant and of great variety. Bear's paw, bird's nest, shark's fin,

sea cucumber, abalone, fish maw and hedgehog hydnum, traditionally known as *shanzhenhaiwei* (treasures of mountains and sea), were delicacies for the privileged.

Other dried seafood includes a number of fishes and molluscs. Among dried meat and fowl specialities are Jinhua ham, Guangdong sausage and Nanjing pressed salted duck. Others include beef jerky, pork floss and dried parts of different animals. *Juecai* (rake) and *chongcao* (codyceps) are a few of the favourite vegetative products. Fungus products abound. Black 'wood-ears', tremella and the more expensive *niushejun* mushroom are on top of the list. There are hundreds of dried and candied fruits like dates, kumquat, raisin and longan. In a Bengdou Zhang chain store in Tianjin, one can find nuts, peas, beans and seeds of lotus, melon, pumpkin and sunflowers cooked in innumerable ways. Most of the nuts and fruits are snacks. The others are for cooking, but they must first be soaked and expanded.

Ganhuo has a huge market at home and abroad. In 2000, its sale amounted to 70 per cent of the total sales in Shanghai's supermarket chain stores. Meanwhile, Nanjing alone consumed 8,000 tons of chestnuts. New products like mushroom extract capsules are manufactured to satisfy customers' insatiable appetites. Most of the producers are law-abiding, but sporadic food inspections still find substandard marine and vegetative products.

YUAN HAIWANG

drinking games

In Chinese culture, 'solitary drinking' (*he menjiu*) is usually associated with depression, whereas wining and dining in a convivial social atmosphere, often denoted by the term *renao*, literally 'hot and noisy', is much preferred. Drinking games (*jiuling*) have long been part of this atmosphere. Literary games, including the spontaneous composition of poems, require excellent Classical Chinese and have consequently disappeared. Less refined games, however, like finger games, number games and other betting games, are still popular among students and the lower strata of society. A common game is 'finger-guessing' (*caiquan*), involving two drinkers shouting and shaking their hands. Each simultaneously stretches out a certain number of their fingers on one or both hands, representing the numbers one to ten. The one who shouts out a number that equals the number of fingers displayed by the other wins. The loser has to drink. Another game is to pour one glass after another of hard liquor or wine and then insist that the guests empty their glass in a single gulp (*ganbei*). This gives the host face; otherwise he will be looked down on. The host, in fact, may be secretly sipping tea when asked to drink. This may also be a ploy to get the guests 'to speak the truth over a drink' (*jiu hou tu zhenyan*). The host, or someone else present, will often provide encouraging words – *quanjiuci* or 'words that urge one to drink' – so that the guest will be carried away and unable to decline. The *quanjiuci* may be a **shunkouliu** (doggerel) like the following:

Ganqingshen, yikoumen.
Ganqinghao, hedezhao.
Ganqinghou, hebugou.

With deep feelings, you'll swallow it in one mouthful.
With good feelings, you'll have the drink.
With intense feelings, you've never drunk enough.

HELEN XIAOYAN WU

drugs and drug consumption

Opium (*yingsu* or *yapian*) has been imported for medicinal purposes since the seventh century, mainly by Arab maritime traders. Opium became popular as a panacea against illnesses such as dysentery and malaria and also as a general tonic. Its reputation for improving sexual intercourse and for curing venereal diseases and urological disorders furthered its popularity among men. Opium smoking owed its origins to the tobacco smoking culture of the late imperial period. Tobacco was first introduced during the 1570s and quickly integrated into the existing tea and alcohol cultures, despite official bans. Men, women and children of all social classes partook in the habit,

paving the way for opium, which was at first smoked as tobacco soaked in opium solution (*yapianyan*). Known as *madak* in seventeenth-century Java and Sumatra, the mixture developed sufficient popularity in southern China to be outlawed in 1729. The edict, however, explicitly allowed the trade in medicinal opium.

The smoking of pure opium can be traced to the early 1770s, with first detailed accounts of the concoction process and of recreational smoking dating to just before 1800. While *madak* smoking continued well into the 1800s, increasing numbers of smokers developed a taste for the unadulterated product – probably due to a drastic improvement in the quality of Patna opium. While the official Canton trade respected the ever stricter edicts (1796, 1800 and 1820), the illegal opium trade attracted contraband merchants from all continents. Spreading quickly throughout Chinese society, only the poorest would be unable to offer opium to their guests. The wealthy prepared opium in intricate rituals, accompanied by delicacies, while their smoking utensils were made of silver, ivory or precious wood. Among the less privileged, smoking was an occasion for social intercourse and leisurely conversation. Opium houses generally provided a pleasant environment, one of the few public spaces available in late imperial society.

After intellectuals and missionaries demonized opium as a symbol of moral decay and national backwardness, the Qing government banned poppy cultivation in 1906, while Britain agreed to cease all Indian exports within ten years. The Hague Convention (1912–14) and subsequent international agreements extended the anti-narcotic policy to other opiates. Ironically, the obsessive search for 'opium cures' fuelled the spread of other narcotics, in particular morphine. This 'modern' injectable narcotic was more effective than opium, while its price decreased dramatically until taxed in 1909. Pharmacies amplified their profits by adulterating morphine with sand, dross or animal matter, while dates and raisins could be added for flavour. International restrictions after 1914 were easily circumvented, especially since mass-produced morphine had become indispensable for the treatment of soldiers. Countries such as Japan and Switzerland profited from the confusion caused by the World War by smuggling 'medicinal' morphine to China and Manchuria.

The contraband traffic also spawned the proliferation of other narcotics, from heroin preparations to cocaine, codeine, noscapine, papaverine, thebaine and fully synthetic drugs. The Opium Suppression Act of 1929 and the Six-Year Opium Suppression Plan of 1934 were easily subverted since the new drugs were easy to conceal and because they were marketed as so-called opium replacement cures. These were easier to smoke than opium, no longer requiring any laborious preparation or paraphernalia. Red Pills (*hongwan*) typically consisted of heroin, strychnine or morphine, as well as caffeine or quinine, embedded in sugary starch and occasionally scented with rose or jasmine essence. Red Pills spread swiftly and even became an export item. When the relatively innocuous Red Pill was prohibited, heroin preparations such as the Golden Elixir (*jindan*), White Pills (*baiwan*) or White Powder (*baimian*) took its place. As a conceptual blend of Western medicine and Daoist alchemy, the new heroin products proved immensely popular. Other 'opium cures' available in Republican China, smoked or injected, were codeine, dionine, eukodol, novocaine, pantopon, papaverin and pavinol. Addiction to such replacement drugs constituted a serious obstacle to the government's suppression plans. Lack of hygienic understanding, furthermore, led to the spread of syphilis, pneumonia and septic infections. Cocaine and cannabis, meanwhile, enjoyed only marginal popularity, mainly within Shanghai's red light areas and among medical professionals.

Although the Republican legislation signalled a departure from uncompromising prohibition, emphasizing instead detoxification and moral reform, over-zealous implementation helped create a black market dominated by gangsters and disease. The government's most useful ally may have been the cigarette – exotic in appearance, yet filled with 'patriotic' Chinese tobacco. The Nanjing authorities' policy of utilizing the cigarette as an informal opium replacement tool was even more successfully applied after 1949. Both Nationalists and Communists regarded opium as a symbol of China's backwardness and foreign exploitation, and yet both managed profitable poppy cultivations during the civil war. After the creation of the People's Republic, the Communists were determined to eliminate all recreational use of opiates. Executions, mass campaigns and public immolations of impounded narcotics figured prominently. During the Korean War, the anti-drugs campaigns were curiously absent from the country's media. Even the printing of propaganda materials was prohibited, lest the image of Communist China as a 'drug-free' society was challenged abroad. Whatever the full truth, official campaigns and the provision of affordable alcohol and tobacco greatly decreased the demand for narcotics.

This began to change with the reform policies of Deng Xiaoping. Increased contact with the outside world and an upsurge in the heroin production in the Golden Triangle forced the authorities to resort to methods not seen since the early 1950s, with routine destruction of intercepted drugs and executions of smugglers and dealers. The current campaigns are, however, highly publicized, often citing the Opium War official Lin Zexu as a patriotic role model. Initially treated as a local problem affecting the southwest of Yunnan, heroin spread into the southern provinces along the international route from the Golden Triangle to Hong Kong and beyond. The well-documented case of Baoshan illustrates the pace of drug abuse in modern China: whereas in 1985 the city counted a mere handful of 'addicts', this figure had risen to more than 2,500 within five years. While in the southern border regions heroin continues to be trafficked, urban China is experiencing the proliferation of narcotics such as methamphetamine ('ice'). The spread of 'ice' was ironically a consequence of a Korean crackdown against drugs during the Seoul Winter Olympics of 1988. The Korean methamphetamine reappeared instantaneously in Taiwan, and found its way to Taiwanese businesses in Fujian. Equally worrying to the PRC as the loss of its 'clean' reputation abroad and the social problems connected with the abuse of drugs, is the fast proliferation of HIV/AIDS (see **HIV/ AIDS and STIs**). Drug consumption appears socially equally spread, although the ethnic composition of the border regions, which often act as contraband corridors, has meant that a disproportionate percentage of users belong to ethnic minority groups (Miao, Hui, Zhuang, Tai). The proliferation of drug use during the 1990s has, however, readjusted the ethnic ratio towards the majority of Han Chinese. The message of the day is prohibition and punishment, policies which in the past led to criminalization and contraband. At present, the authorities seem unprepared to experiment with more holistic approaches.

Further reading

Ch'en, Yung-fa (1995). 'The Blooming Poppy under the Red Sun: The Yan'an Way and the Opium Trade'. In Tony Saich and Hans van de Ven (eds), *New Perspectives on the Chinese Communist Revolution*. New York: Sharpe, 263–98.

Dikötter, Frank, Laamann, Lars and Zhou, Xun (2002). 'Narcotic Culture: A Social History of Drug Consumption in China'. *British Journal of Criminology* 42.2: 317–36.

Slack. E. R. (2000). *Opium, State and Society: China's Narco-Economy and the Guomindang, 1924–1937*. Honolulu: University of Hawai'i Press.

Yao, Jianguo (1991). 'Yunnan: China's Anti-Drug Outpost'. *Beijing Review* 26 (August): 20–5.

Zhou, Yongming (1999). *Anti-Drug Crusades in Twentieth-Century China: Nationalism, History, and State-Building*. Lanham, MD: Rowman and Littlefield.

LARS LAAMANN

drumming and blowing

(guchui, chuida)

Traditional ensemble music

'Drumming and blowing' (*guchui*) is the most common Chinese term for this genre of ensemble music, though in some regions it is also called 'blowing and hitting' (*chuida*). Although stringed instruments, such as plucked lutes (**pipa**, *sanxian*) and fiddles (*huqin*) may also be included in the ensemble, especially in those of the southern regional styles, percussion (drums, gongs and cymbals) and winds (shawms, reed pipes, bamboo flutes and mouth organs) are predominant. *Guchui* has a very long history. It appeared in the early Western Han dynasty (206 BC–AD 24). At that time, *guchui* was military music played for marching and processional activities. Subsequently, it was used as entertainment music in the palace. After the thirteenth century, Buddhist monks, **Daoist priests** and lay musicians started to play *guchui*. Nowadays, *guchui* ensembles are popular throughout China. *Guchui* can be divided into two sub-categories: *cuchui* (loud blowing) and *xichui* (soft blowing). Usually, the first category, led by shawm (*suona*) or double reed-pipe (*guanzi*), is used at outdoor performances; the second is a mellower sounding type, led by flutes (**dizi**), and used in indoor sitting performances. Musicians perform *guchui* in wedding and funeral processions, as well as at banquets, harvest celebrations or simply as entertainment. The most important genres of *guchui* in contemporary China are: Xi'an drum music (**Xi'an guyue**), 'Beijing music' (**Beijing yinyue**), 'Shanxi eight great suites' (**Shanxi badatao**), Central Hebei wind music (*Jizhong guanyue*), Shifan gong-drum music (see **Shifan (Shifan gu, Shifan luogu)**) of Jiangsu province, and Great Chaozhou Gong and Drum Music (Chaozhou daluogu) of eastern Guangdong province.

The musical materials of contemporary *guchui* repertory are adopted not only from traditional pieces of dynastic China, but also from folksongs, dance music sources, regional narrative song and opera. These are commonly divided into two parts: *qupai* and *luogu paizi*. *Qupai* (named songs/labelled melodies), written in *gongche* notation, are melodic pieces played mainly by wind instruments; *luogu paizi* (gong-drum sections) recorded in 'onomato-poeic notation' (*luogujing*), are played by percussion. In performance, pieces are commonly organized in extended suites, known as *taoshu* or *taoqu*. These are long forms constructed of different *qupai* and *luogu paizi*.

Suite organization is quite similar throughout the whole country, beginning with a slow, free-metred prelude, followed by a longer main section of many pieces successively performed at slow, moderate and fast tempos, and concluding with a short coda. In the suites of some regional genres, several *luogu paizi* sections are organized into a long movement called 'percussion movement' (*guduan*).

The texture of *guchui*, like traditional music in other ensembles, is heterophonic. Musicians decorate the same basic melody in different ways, according to the idiom of each instrument. Usually, the leading melodic instruments (*guanzi*, shawm or bamboo flute) play the basic melody. The mouth-organs play the same melody, together with the upper fifth (and sometimes octave) note above each pitch, and maintain constant motion. The role of other melodic instruments is to embellish the melody and make it richer and more colourful. The drum is the leading instrument in the percussion, while the gongs and cymbals are also very important. The theory of music and its role in ritual (*li* and *yue*) is a central idea in Confucian philosophy. Until today, *guchui* performance has been linked to ritual. Its repertory has been formulated into types according to programmatic functions. The sad compositions known as 'weeping pieces' (*kuqu*) are performed especially at **funerals**. A joyful repertory known as 'jubilant pieces' (*xiqu*) is played at weddings and birthday celebrations. Usually, ensembles of monks and priests play for funerals and lay musicians play for weddings. Among them, lay musicians belong to the lowest social class. The term for them is 'blowing-and-drumming men' (*chuigushou*). On the other hand, monks and priests are considered to be 'high status musicians'.

Further reading

Du, Yaxiong (2002). 'Ritual Music in the North China Village: The Continuing Confucian and Buddhist Heritage'. PhD diss., University of British Columbia.

Liang, Mingyue (1985). *Music of the Billion*. New York: Heinrichshofen.

Miao, Tianrui *et al.* (eds) (1985). *Zhongguo yinyue cidian* [Dictionary of Chinese Music]. Beijing: Renming yinyue chubanshe.

DU YAXIONG

Du Jinfang

b. 1932, Beijing

Theatre actor

Du Jinfang, is an outstanding **Jingju** (Peking opera) performer. She was a disciple of Master Mei Lanfang, and her exquisite performing skills are considered the best representation of Master Mei's performance-style (*Meipai*), which is duplicated in her make-up, body movements and gestures. Du's sweet and mellow voice complements her strong dancing and acting skills, which have been showcased in her performance of many of Mei's plays, such as *Guifei zuijiu*, *Bawang beiji* and *Yu Zhoufeng*. Her speciality is playing the *chinyi* and *huashen* roles (see **Xiqu role types**). She received the Mei Hwa Jiang, the highest award in the field of Peking opera. In the 1950s she joined the Jung Kao Xiqu Academic Experimental Troupe (now called Jing-juyan), working in conjunction with Yuan Shehai, Yu Kaizhi and Sun Yuehwa, among other outstanding actors. Her credits include *White Snake*, *Yu Shehwa*, *Tao Hwasan*, *Ye Zeuling*, *Bai Maonu*. Ms Du has achieved the highest performance level in the PRC.

CHANG HUI-MEI

Duan Jinchuan

b. 1962, Chengdu, Sichuan

Independent video documentary filmmaker

One of the pillars of the **New Documentary Movement**, Duan Jinchuan acknowledges the influence of US cinéma vérité filmmaker Frederick Wiseman; many of his rigorous, finely crafted pieces explore the relationship between institutions and individuals. In 1998, he co-founded a small company, China Memo Films (Beijing chuan linyue yingshi zixun youxian gongsi), with his colleague **Jiang Yue**.

Graduating from Beijing Broadcasting Institute in 1984, Duan then worked for Tibet TV Station before returning to Beijing in 1992. His Tibetan experience inspired such videos as *Highland Barley* (*Qingke*, 1986), *The Sacred Site of Asceticism* (*Qing puku xiuzhe de shengdi*, 1993, co-directed with Wen Pulin), and *The Ends of the Earth* (*Tianbian*, 1997), an epic-scale work which follows transhumant shepherds through the spectacular landscapes of the northern plateaus; his better-known work to date, *No 16 Barkhor South Street* (*Bakuo nanjie shiliuhao*, 1996: Grand Prix du Festival du Réel, Paris), elegantly conveys the intimate, politically charged, yet often humorous, interaction between citizens and the cadres of a Lhasa neighbourhood committee (*juweihui*).

Duan kept on filming the surface of everyday life by collaborating with **Zhang Yuan** on *The Square* (*Guangchang*, 1995), shot in 35 mm. With *Sunken National Treasures* (*Chen chuanjiu qinian de gushi*, 1999), he explores the comic foibles and grand absurdities of bureaucracy. *The Secret of My Success* (*Linqi da shetou*, 2002) focuses on the plight of a petty official in a village in rural northeast China – a jovial, ambitious, contradictory man who has to face local corruption, wayward women defying the **one-child policy** and possible retaliation if the law is not applied.

BÉRÉNICE REYNAUD

dumplings

(jiaozi)

Jiaozi is a popular dumpling-like food in north China, its stuffing made of vegetables, meat or both. The favourite stuffing is Chinese cabbage and ground pork, seasoned with green onion, ginger, soy and sesame oil. Use of vegetables is only limited by imagination, but the choice of meat confines to pork, mutton and beef, in that order.

Jiaozi was first recorded by the North Zhou Confucian Yan Zhitui 1,400 years ago. He mentioned a popular crescent-shaped wheaten food called *huntun*, which according to historians had existed 600 years earlier. Interestingly, *huntun* as the antecedent of *jiaozi* is still coexisting today with its descendent. *Huntun*, known as 'wonton' in North America, is boiled and served with the soup, while *jiaozi* can be boiled, steamed, and fried and served with a dab of vinegar sauce.

Jiaozi is significant to the Chinese New Year's Eve in north China as *niangao*, a cake of sweet rice to the south, both believed to bring good luck. With limited syllables in their language, the Chinese play heavily into homophones. Since *jiaozi* sounds the same as 'the juncture of the old and new years', having it then forebodes a happy beginning.

Like many other *jiachangcai*, *jiaozi* also becomes commercialized, available as frozen food in supermarkets, delivered home by food trucks and served in restaurants, the most famous of which is Defachang in Xi'an. It created a dinner of a hundred varieties of *jiaozi* in 1984. Its popularity is second only to that of the Terracotta Warriors.

YUAN HAIWANG

Duoduo

(né Li, Shizheng)

b. 1951, Beijing

Poet

Duoduo has been one of the most important Misty poets (*Menglongshi*) (see **Misty poetry**) of his generation, and one of the best Chinese poets writing both in and outside of China today. Duoduo's poetry career began in the early 1970s, during the **Cultural Revolution**, inspired by his private reading of Baudelaire and other Western authors. His early poems were full of intense, estranged and surreal images and visions, and thus created a strong shock effect, such as the opening lines from his *Wuti* (Untitled, 1973): 'Yige jieji de xue liujin le/yige jieji de jianshou haizai fashe [The blood of one class has drained away/the archers of another class are still loosing their arrows]'. These early poems, including *Zhi taiyang* (To the Sun, 1973) and *Jiaohui* (Instructions, 1976), all critiqued the Cultural Revolution and modern Chinese history from an insider's point of view and in a highly sophisticated and original style. Almost the last to gain public recognition among his Misty peers, Duoduo was awarded the first *Today* Poetry Prize with his unofficial collection of poetry, *Milestone* (*Licheng*), in 1988. After the Tiananmen incident in 1989, Duoduo went into exile and he currently resides in Holland. He has kept up a strong output of poetry and prose writing, which for the most part have been published in the exile Chinese literary journal *Today* (*Jintian*). Without doubt Duoduo is one of the most unforgettable voices ever heard in contemporary Chinese poetry.

Further reading

Duoduo (1989). Trans. Gregory Lee and John Cayley. *Looking Out From Death: From the Cultural Revolution to Tiananmen Square.* London: Bloomsbury.

Cayley, John (trans.) (1994). 'Underground Poetry in Beijing, 1970–1978'. In Henry Y. Zhao and John Cayley (eds), *Undersky Underground: Chinese Writing Today* 1. London: Wellsweep, 97–104.

Lee, Gregory (trans.) (1997). 'Selected Translations of Duo Duo (Part I)'. *Interpoetics: Poetry of Asia and the Pacific Rim* 1.1 (Summer).

—— (1998). 'Selected Translations of Duo Duo (Part II)'. *Interpoetics: Poetry of Asia and the Pacific Rim* 1. 2 (Spring).

Van Crevel, Maghiel (1996). *Language Shattered: Contemporary Chinese Poetry and Duoduo.* Leiden: CNWS Research School.

Zhao, Henry Y. H., Yanbing, Cheng and Rosenwald, John (eds) (2000). *Fissures: Chinese Writing Today.* Brookline, MA: Zephyr Press, 58–63. [Trans. Gregory Lee: 'It's Just Like Before', 'Five Years', 'Those Islands', 'Never a Dreamer' and 'Returning'.]

HUANG YIBING

Dushu

[Reading]

Intellectual periodical

Since the first issue was published on 10 April 1979, *Dushu* (*Reading*) has gradually become the most important book review monthly in mainland China. It belongs to the United Publishing House (Sanlian shudian), which was established in 1948 by merging three magazines: *Life* (*Shenghuo*), *Reading* (*Dushu*) and *Xinzhi* (*New Knowledge*), and is now well known for publishing the works of Chinese intellectuals and translations of modern Western thinkers.

With a format of 32 mo and a publishing capacity of 160 pages for each issue, *Dushu* usually accepts reviews which are less than 8,000 Chinese characters. Flagged with the faith that 'No Forbidden Zone in Reading' (*Dushu wu jinqu*), the title of the first article of the first issue, *Dushu* gathered a large numbers of intellectual writers, critics and humanities scholars around it and thus, in the early 1980s, formed a distinguishing style: humanistic, rhetorically lively and politically critical when the government's control temporarily loosened. In relevance with the feature, *Dushu* keeps a simple style of binding and layout designed by a famous painter Ding Cong (b. 1916).

From the later 1990s to now, *Dushu*, led by the two co-editors **Wang Hui** (b. 1959) and Huang Pin (b. 1958), who are both critical scholars, has evidently strengthened its theoretical colour while keeping the original features. Many books of social science, with more economic, social and even international affairs, were reviewed by the magazine. Now *Dushu* has an average impression of more than 100,000 copies, far more than other comparable magazines in China.

WANG XIAOMING

E

East Radio

Started on 28 October 1992, East Radio (ER) – the full name is Shanghai East Radio Broadcasting Station (http://www.eastradio.com/) – is the first provincial government broadcasting station in mainland China, which was separated from the existing provincial government broadcasting station and thus is in competition with the latter. Its broadcasting is therefore more active, various and interesting while involving a lot of very intense political propaganda.

ER owns four channels: News Round-up Programmes (*Xinwen yu zonghe jiemu*) at MW 792 KHz and FM 104.5 Hz; Music Programmes (*Yinyue jiemu*) at FM 101.7 Hz; Finance Programmes (*Jinrong jiemu*) at FM 97.7 Hz; and Children and Adolescent Programmes (*Shao er jiemu*) at FM 92.4 Hz. Broadcasts total ninety-two hours per day. Transmitted by the East Pearl Transmitter Tower (Dongfang mingzhu guangbo dianshita) located in Pudong, Shanghai, the highest such tower in Asia, ER's programmes cover not only Shanghai but also the whole of Zhejing and Jiangsu provinces and most of Anhui reaching a population of approximately 150 million.

Some well-known programmes have been developed in the recent ten years, such as *East Calling* (*Dong fang chuanhu*) and *Daily Requests* (*Tiantian dianbo*). A second music channel, run by ER, was established on the Shanghai **cable television** station.

ER established an Internet website (www.eastradio.com) in 1999, where one can listen online to all the programmes on the four channels.

ER also owns a traditional instruments orchestra, commonly regarded as of high quality.

WANG XIAOMING

economic thought

Political reforms after the **Cultural Revolution** and the economic necessities of 'opening up' (*kaifang*) China's economy have radically transformed both the theories of Chinese economic thought and its study, practice and influence as a profession.

Chinese economists have gradually abandoned Marxist historical-materialist and class-based economic theoretical analysis and the methods and models of Soviet-style central-planned economics. As reformist leaders Deng Xiaoping, Hu Yaobang and Zhao Ziyang in the 1980s, and Jiang Zemin and Zhu Rongji in the 1990s, liberalized the Chinese economy, arguing it was still in the 'initial stages of socialism' (*shehui zhuyi chuji jieduan*) and that they were developing 'socialism with Chinese characteristics' (*you zhongguo tese de shehui zhuyi*), senior economists Du Runsheng, Xue Muqiao and Ma Hong gained the freedom to explore Western neo-classical and neo-institutional economic theory. Popularly, many classic Western economic texts have been translated into Chinese, and biographies of such influential entrepreneurs as George Soros, Bill Gates and Jack Welch are common in bookstores.

Marketization has required the dismantling of independent planned-economy 'sectoral economics' (*bumen jing jixue*), each with their own unique quantitative analysis methods and standards, and the growth of broad-based 'market economics' (*shichang jingjixue*) with internationally accepted standards of data collection and analysis. Government ministries for specific industries and their large state enterprises have broken up into regulatory agencies, think tanks and cross-sectoral enterprise groups. At the same time, the colleges of the planned economy era that trained economists for these institutions have been forced to merge together as general curriculum universities. The evolution of the sectoral-specific state banks (e.g. the Bank of Agriculture, the Bank of Industry and Commerce) into general-lending institutions, and the rise of multi-purpose investment banks, development funds and stock market institutions, have also increased the demand for broadly trained economists.

Privatization has given economic thought more freedom in the reform era, providing the resources for the rise of fiscally autonomous think tanks and individual economists capable of sustaining themselves through income from public commentary. CCP leader Jiang Zemin's criticism of liberal economists Mao Yushi (director of the independent Unirule Institute) and Fan Gang (Economic Reform Foundation) in 1999 cut into their income from state media sources but did not silence them. Legal reforms and the downsizing of the bureaucracy have created competition among organs for government economic policy research and made individual economists drafters of economic legislation in the people's congresses. **Peking University**'s Li Yining was particularly influential in drafting the National People's Congress laws on bankruptcy, mergers and contracts. The rise of technocrats in the CCP has also increased the demand for sophisticated market economy analysis by think tanks under central organs, notably the State Council Development Research Institute and the Institute of Economics of the **Chinese Academy of Social Sciences**.

Decentralization has also seen the re-emergence of local economic think tanks as influential policy actors. The Shanghai Academy of Social Sciences' (SASS) World Economy Institute, under deputy-director Qin Benli, and its newspaper, the *World Economic Herald* (*Shijie jingji daobao*), became China's premier forum for economic theory and policy debates among scholars and government officials

until they were shuttered in 1989. The director of the SASS Economic Research Institute, Yuan Enzhen, served as a key macro-economics policy advisor in the 1990s to both the Shanghai Municipal Government and former Shanghai leaders in Beijing, including Premier Zhu Rongji.

Finally, the internationalization of China's economy has also transformed economic thought in China. Chinese economists with advanced training in liberal economics work with foreign governments (especially United Nations organizations), international investors (foreign banks and investment funds), and multi-lateral trade (WTO), monetary (International Monetary Fund) and lending (World Bank and Asian Development Bank) institutions. Internationalization has also meant the hiring of thousands of young economists trained overseas (especially the United States), with resulting pressure on Chinese universities and government agencies to offer salaries competitive with foreign academic institutions and the growing private consulting industry.

See also: Qin Hui

Further reading

Hamrin, C. and Zhou, S. (eds) (1995). *Decision-Making in Deng's China: Perspectives from Insiders*. Armonk and London: East Gate.

Hsu, R. (1991). *Economic Theories in China. 1979–1988*. Cambridge: Cambridge University Press.

Naughton, B. (2002). 'China's Economic Think Tanks: Their Changing Role in the State'. *China Quarterly* 171: 625–35.

STEVEN W. LEWIS

eggs

Chinese preserve chicken and duck eggs, sometimes geese and quail for a change. The typical preserved eggs are *xianjidan* (salt chicken eggs) and *xianyadan* (salt duck eggs), so named after the salt solution in which they are soaked, with or without spices. Boiled, they can be kept for a long time. Another Chinese favourite is *chajidan* (tea eggs) – boiled eggs stewed with tea leaves and other spices. Boiled and shelled eggs cooked in a pork stew are named *lujidan* (stewed eggs), which, after deep-frying, becomes *hupidan* (tiger-skin eggs). They can be eatable right away or are storable in cool temperature for some time. None except salt eggs are available on sale.

Duck eggs are seldom used in *jiachangcai* (home-style cooking) as they taste fishy. This makes *pidan* (skinned egg) a favourite alternative. *Pidan* is largely duck eggs mass produced with quick lime, soda, salt, black tea leaves, water and ashes of plants yielding oxidized calcium and potassium. Mixed together, they yield such chemicals as sodium hydroxide, potassium hydroxide, calcium carbonate and ions. Their combination results in the eggs' peculiar tea flavour and turns the yolk black and paste-like. The combination of amino acid and alkali osmosis gives the egg white a jelly-like texture covered with a crystal flowery pattern. For this reason, *pidan* is also known as *songhua* (pine flower).

To address concerns about food safety, traditional ingredients have been changed to produce lead-free *pidan* eggs. Medicinal *pidan* eggs with higher iodine, higher potassium, and lower sodium are welcomed by consumers.

YUAN HAIWANG

85 New Wave [Art] Movement

The '85 Movement' (*Bawu yundong*, *Bawu xinchao*) was an avant-garde art movement which flourished between 1985 and 1989. Gao Minglu coined the term '85 Art Movement' (*85 meishu yundong*) for a lecture given at the National Oil Painting Conference held by the National Artists Association on 14 April 1986, and published in *Meishujia tongxun*. After higher officials objected to this designation, the term *bawu meishu xinchao* ('85 Art New Wave') was briefly adopted as a less objectionable alternative, *xinchao* ('new wave') being considered less aggressive than *yundong* ('movement').

The 85 Movement was a group-movement because in only two years (1985 and 1986), seventy-nine self-organized avant-garde art groups, including more than 2,250 of the nation's young artists, emerged to organize exhibitions, hold conferences and write manifestos and articles about their art. A total of 149 exhibitions were organized by these groups within the two-year period. The movement continued to develop in 1987 towards a more provocative and conceptual direction, peaking in 1989 during the period of the **China Avant-Garde** exhibition.

Geographically, the avant-garde groups spread nationwide in twenty-nine provinces including some autonomous regions, such as Xinjiang, Inner Mongolia and Tibet. Most of the groups, however, were located on the eastern coast and centre regions of China, as areas more advanced in education and industrialization. Most groups from these areas were in favour of a conceptual approach, regardless of the kind of media employed. The two major conceptual approaches adopted were 'Rationalistic Painting' (*lixing huihua*), represented by the artworks and writings of the **Northern Art Group** (Beifang yishu qunti) from Harbin, the Red Brigade from Nanjing and the **Pond Society** (Chishe) from Hangzhou; and the Zen–Dada-like conceptual art, advocated by the **Xiamen Dada** Group from Fujian and the **Red Humour** (Hongse youmo) from Hangzhou. On the contrary, art groups located in the northwest and southwest, areas still vastly based on traditional peasant lifestyle and home of most of the ethnic minorities, were interested in a frank and militant expression of their intuitive feelings and favoured 'primitive' themes. The term 'currents of life' (*shengming zhi liu*) was used to define their approach. Among the groups, the most influential was the **Southwest Art Research Group** (Xinan yishu qunti), consisting of artists mostly from Yunnan and Sichuan provinces.

Further reading

Andrews, Julia F. and Gao, Minglu (1995). 'The Avant-Garde's Challenge to Official Art'. In Debora S. Davis (ed.), *Urban Spaces in Contemporary China: The Potential for Autonomy and Community in Post-Mao China*. Cambridge: Harvard University Press, 221–78.

Gao, Minglu (1986). 'Bawu meishu yundong' [85 Art Movement] *Meishujia tongxun* 5 (March): 15–23. (An English translation, 'The 1985 New Wave

Art Movement', was published in Valerie C. Doran (ed.) (1993) *China's New Art, Post-1989, with a Retrospective from 1979 to 1989*. Hong Kong: Hanart T Z Gallery, civ–cvii.

Gao, Minglu (ed.) (1991). *Zhongguo dangdai meishushi 1985–1986* [History of Contemporary Art 1985–1986]. Shanghai: Shanghai renmin chubanshe.

Lü, Peng and Yi, Dan (1992). *Zhongguo xiandai yishushi* [A History of Modern Art in China]. Changsha: Hunan meishu chubanshe.

GAO MINGLU

elite schools

(guizu xuexiao)

Guizu xuexiao or elite schools are non-public elementary, middle and high schools that have appeared in China since the 1980s. They are called elite schools because only rich families can afford their high tuition and other fees. The rise of elite schools is one more indicator of the economic growth of China and the enlarging gap between the rich and poor in today's China.

High expenses, however, are not the only difference between the elite schools and public schools. Many elite schools are boarding schools, whereas most public schools are not. High salaries ensure the quality of the teachers of the elite schools, whereas many public schools, particularly those in poor rural areas, often suffer from lack of qualified teachers. Elite schools usually attach particular importance to foreign language teaching by hiring native speakers as language teachers, whereas few public schools can afford this. Connections with foreign schools are used to attract students, and some graduates of the elite schools enter foreign universities directly. In general, however, the curriculum of the elite schools is not very different from that of the public schools – the elite schools, like the public schools, have to use officially approved textbooks.

Financially elite schools rely mainly on tuition money and investments made by businessmen and the families of their students. Though many elite schools start as money-making businesses, quite a few have been shut down because of financial problems. Elite schools are usually located in suburbs of large cities or rich areas. They are particularly popular in the Pearl River Delta.

HAN XIAORONG

empty-nest syndrome

Traditionally in Chinese families, adult children live with their elderly parents under the same roof. Chinese people start to experience empty-nest syndrome as a result of social change. Empty-nest syndrome is very peculiar in China in several aspects. First of all, women who experience this are relatively young. Since 1974, when the Chinese government enacted the one-child family policy, Chinese families experienced many changes. One of them is the dominance of the nuclear family in China. As the first generation of the one-child policy come to their adulthood, when they leave home their parents, especially mothers, are in their middle to late forties and early fifties. Women suffer from this earlier than in countries with more children. Second, women in this age group also suffer from a decrease in social status. Due to the economic reconstruction in China, many workers, especially female workers, are unemployed, or have an early retirement; most of them are between forty and fifty. This makes them feel useless and socially isolated. Third, they may be experiencing the menopause. Fourth, Chinese mothers usually devote their entire lives to their husbands and children. Their sense of success comes from that of their husbands and children (Liu and Cheung 2002). When the only child leaves home for university or marriage, they suddenly feel lonely, sad, useless and depressive. All these social, psychological and biological changes simultaneously worsen women's wellbeing, making life for them more challenging and tough.

Further reading

Liu, M. and Cheung, M. (2002). 'The Indigenization of Women's Social Work in China'. *Xinhua Digest* 2: 25–30.

LIU MENG

English-language dailies, periodicals and books

There has been an explosion of English-language publications in China since the country's economic reformation began. For several decades *China Daily* (*Zhongguo ribao*), run by central government as a propaganda tool, was the country's only English-language newspaper. Since the mid-to-late 1990s, however, every major city in China has come to have its own English-language newspaper. Most of these are dailies, such as the *Guangzhou Morning*, the *Shenzhen Daily* and the *Shanghai Daily*. The *China Daily* itself has also expanded to launch a weekend issue – the *Beijing Weekend*.

In addition to these English-language news-papers, there are also a range of English-language magazines, such as the *Beijing Review*, *Beijing Monthly* and *Shanghai Star*, and books, such as the Panda Books imprint, which offers translations of Chinese litera-ture into English. Rather than being used for pro-paganda purposes, these newer English-language publications seem aimed at making Chinese lit-erature, culture and society more accessible to a foreign audience.

In addition, many established Chinese-language newspapers have also now launched special English sections or editions, although these are aimed at an English-speaking Chinese rather than a foreign readership. At first these were intended primarily to help Chinese readers improve their English. Now they act more broadly as a window through which Chinese readers can learn about Western people and culture. One of the earliest and most influential of these is *Beijing Youth*. Another example is **Cankao xiaoxi** [Reference News], which began life offering digests of news from foreign news media translated into Chinese but has now launched an English-language version.

LILY CHEN

environment, perceptions of

Western visions of China's environment include streams meandering among soaring mist-cloaked peaks or bamboo forests filled with panda bears, exotic birds and the occasional Buddhist temple.

The world's third largest country in terms of area, China enjoys a diverse range of plant and animal life spread across a broad range of climates and geographic conditions. While the variety of cli-matic and geographical conditions are readily identifiable, China's beauty and diversity of species are becoming harder to find. China has suffered human-induced environmental degradation since the early dynastic era when emperors strove to conserve and rejuvenate over-exploited forests and to control flooding. In the contemporary era, environmental degradation has accelerated due to a combination of rapid economic growth and an immense and growing population. In an effort to alleviate environmental degradation, the Chinese state is striving to heighten public environmental awareness. However, the public seems more interested in improved material well-being.

As with people throughout the world, Chinese citizens strive for better and more plentiful food, longer and healthier lives, more education for their children and additional material goods. In general, the public views environmental protection as an un-affordable luxury. Furthermore, surveys of Chinese environmental awareness conducted in the 1990s found that most people recognize the importance of environmental protection, but believe environ-mental protection is a state responsibility. As a result, while maintaining clean private spaces, most people admit to polluting public areas, expecting the state to clean up. This attitude may be partially attributed to the Communist planned economic management system that minimized citizen responsibility for activities utside their own homes.

The state is convinced that environmental pro-tection is important to continued prosperity and growth. However, it is no longer able to afford the spiralling cost of environmental clean-ups. In search of other environmental protection options, the state has tried to awaken public respect for the environment by requiring schools, businesses and government officials to study environmentalism and environmental protection. The state has also encouraged activist green groups to form and the mass media to expose polluters and praise envir-onmentalists. These efforts have contributed to slowly increased environmental awareness among relatively well-educated and wealthy urbanites. However, in the countryside, home to 70 per cent of China's population, the emphasis remains on obtaining material benefits. The attitude of Chinese environmental protection officials illustrates the immense challenge to improving environmental awareness and protection in China. Even many environmental protection officials believe that China must sacrifice the environment by exploiting natural resources in order to satisfy the public's need and desire for material goods.

Ongoing efforts by the Chinese state will strengthen environmental awareness among Chinese citizens. However, if required to choose, for the foreseeable future the average citizen can be expected to favour a better living standard.

Further reading

China Quarterly 156 (December 1998). 'Special Issue: China's Environment'.

Elvin, Mark and Liu, Ts'ui-jung (1998). *Sediments of Time: Environment and Society in Chinese History.* Cambridge: Cambridge University Press.

Smil, Vaclav (1993). *China's Environment Crisis.* Armonk: M. E. Sharpe.

JONATHAN SCHWARTZ

environmental organizations

Environmental organizations here refer to non-governmental, non-profit and voluntary organizations devoted to environmental protection and sustainable development. Hundreds have been founded in the past eight years or so. They fall into five types. The first type register as 'social organizations' (*shehui tuanti*) or 'private, non-profit work units' (*minban feiqiye danwei*). Examples are Friends of Nature in Beijing and Green River in Sichuan. These are the closest to the Western understanding of non-governmental organizations (NGOs). The second type register as for-profit entities but operate as non-profit NGOs. This practice reflects a strategic adaptation to the regulatory framework in China, which put constraints on registering as NGOs. The Institute of Environment and Development and Global Village of Beijing, both based in Beijing, are prominent examples of this type of organization. The third type of environmental

organizations consist of unregistered voluntary groups. Although often loosely organized and without full-time staff or permanent office space, these organizations consider themselves as NGOs and usually aspire to register as such. Some organizations of this type depend on the Internet for most activities, so much so that they may be called web-based groups. Examples are Greener Beijing (gbj.grchina.net), the Tibetan Antelope Information Centre (www.taic.org), Green-Web (www.green-web.org) and Han Hai Sha (www. desert.org.cn). University-based student environmental associations make up the fourth type of environmental organization. As student associations, these may be set up on campus easily without having to follow the registration procedure required of 'social organizations'. According to one survey, there were 184 such student environmental organizations in China as of April 2001. Among the best-known student environmental associations are the Scientific Exploration and Outdoor Life Society of Beijing Forestry University (SENOL) and the Sichuan University Environmental Volunteer Association. The fifth type of environmental organizations have been called government-organized non-governmental organizations (GONGOs), because they are established and funded by the government. Some GONGOs, however, are becoming more and more independent both financially and administratively and are evolving into NGOs.

The rise of environmental organizations was a phenomenon of the 1990s while many more continue to be created into the new century. Especially instrumental in environmental education and the mobilization of community efforts for environmental protection, these organizations tend to emphasize cooperative rather than confrontational relationships with government agencies and business sectors. Many, however, face the challenges of funding and professionalization. So far, international organizations have been a major source of funding for many.

Further reading

Ho, Peter (2001). 'Greening Without Conflict? Environmentalism, NGOs and Civil Society in China'. *Development and Change* 32.5: 893–921.

Knup, Elizabeth (1997). 'Environmental NGOs in China: An Overview'. *China Environmental Series* 1. Washington, DC: Woodrow Wilson Center, 9–15.

Turner, Jennifer and Wu Fengshi (eds) (2002). *Green NGO and Environmental Journalist Forum: A Meeting of Environmentalists in Mainland China, Hong Kong, and Taiwan*. Washington, DC: Woodrow Wilson Center.

YANG GUOBIN

erhu

Musical instrument

Since the 1950s, *erhu* has been the name used to refer to most Chinese two-stringed wooden bowed lutes with a slender neck that bores through a hexagonal resonator covered with snakeskin and a bow with the horsehair permanently inserted in between the instrument's two strings. Before then, these and similar type instruments were generally called *huqin* ('barbarian stringed instrument'), in reference to their origin in areas beyond China's northern and western frontiers.

The erhu has traditionally figured in the performance of regional operatic, narrative and ensemble music. It was only in the twentieth century that it became a solo instrument. In the 1920s, composers such as Liu Tianhua (1895–1932) and Hua Yanjun (1893–1950, better known as Abing) began composing music that showcased the great level of expressiveness the instrument is capable of. Their music ushered in the **national style** (*guoyue*) that emerged after the 1940s and transformed the erhu into a virtuoso instrument. Modern erhu compositions essentially combined Chinese melodies with Western violin techniques. Left-hand techniques of fingering and positioning include pitch glides, trills and grace notes, while right-hand bowing techniques include tremolos and pizzicati.

See also: traditional music performers

MERCEDES M. DUJUNCO

Ershiyi shiji

[Twenty-First Century]

Intellectual journal

Ershiyi Shiji is a bimonthly interdisciplinary scholarly journal first founded in October of 1990 by a group of scholars, including **Jin Guantao**, of the Chinese Culture Research Institute of the Chinese University of Hong Kong. It orchestrates multiple voices in the global community of concerned scholars in the quest for the long-term development of Chinese culture.

Published in classic Chinese, this journal claims to be a forum to build bridges and promote communication across disciplines, schools of thought and ideological and political spectra among Chinese scholars and readers from all the Chinese communities in the world. Its editorial board membership includes leading scholars of Chinese culture such as Harvard Confucianist Tu Weiming, **Li Zehou**, a leading scholar of aesthetics from mainland China, and Ambrose King, a distinguished Hong Kong-based sociologist. Even Nobel Prize-winning scientists such as Li Yuanzhe, chemist and President of Academia Sinica in Taiwan, and Chenling Yang, a physicist, are on the board. Its current editor is Liu Qingfeng.

A brief glimpse of the table of content of its latest issue reveals a broad list of topics which include international relations, modern Chinese history and its relationship with the world history, politics and law, scientific and technological culture, economics, society and media, and finally book reviews, all related to Chinese culture. Contributors are encouraged to make original, thoughtful and readable submissions in all languages. The editor arranges a translation into classic Chinese if the accepted submission is in any other language rather than classic Chinese. Royalties are paid for any accepted submission, plus an issue of the journal.

JIA WENSHAN

ethnic costume

Ethnic costume, specifically that of China's fifty-five minorities, has seen significant reinvigoration under the impact of market forces. Prior to the

Maoist period, many minority groups, especially when isolated in rural areas, wore clothing particular to their ethnic traditions on a daily basis. This was especially true of minority women, and included hair and head pieces as well as modes of styling hair. During special occasions, such as ethnic festivals, more men's costumes would emerge, and women's costumes might be extremely elaborate, in some cases the products of years of handiwork. Handmade materials and handcrafted ornamentation was common, and included fabrics, dyes, embroidery, brocade, batik, metal jewellery and other forms. Except for specialist products such as silverwork and embroidery designs, it was uncommon for ethnic costume components to circulate widely through markets.

A significant proportion of such practices of customary dress persisted throughout the **Cultural Revolution**, albeit often in muted form. Then the 1980s inaugurated a boom in the production of costume components due in part to policies of cultural liberalization and also to the sharp rise in domestic and international tourism. The market presented two types of opportunities for minority groups to profit from costume. First, they could produce, develop and wear costumes in traditional or embellished style to attract visitors and audiences seeking ethnic tourism experiences. Costumes tended to be showcased and promoted as photogenic, especially at major tourist events such as village festivals. They also were key to cultural performances in urban venues such as ethnic theme parks, theatres, minority institutes, provincial trade fairs, television shows and nightclubs. Not only tourists but also media producers revelled in the visual potential of diverse costume styles. In response, a great deal of embellishment took place in the production of costumes for performance, including the intensification of colour through synthetic fabrics and dyes, and the use of other mechanically produced ornaments such as sequins and glitter.

Second, minorities and brokers developed a variety of means to transform costume components into commodities for sale. Sometimes minority women would bring their handiwork to market, and sometimes brokers would visit them in villages and buy their older pieces. This market in antique work coexisted with a demand for newly designed

merchandise. Often as their only vehicle for entry into the market, village women began making costume fragments for sale either as is or in the form of new products such as pillow covers and handbags. The success of these sales in turn gave rise to a range of production relations. A local villager would contract with other locals to produce items in a kind of cottage industry format. An outsider, sometimes a state agency, might establish similar contracts, or organize a small shop in a town where women, and sometimes men, would come to work for wages or doing piecework. In some cities, small-scale factories were established with professional designers and industrial materials added to the production process, with certain forms of specialized craft being sent back for skilled villagers to execute. Customers included international tourists as well as Han urbanites. With the solidification of these diversified production relations, intensified polarizations of gender and class also emerged.

By the later 1990s, the diversification of craft production had further extended. Developments included the incorporation into high fashion of ethnic designs or handicraft fragments by minority, Han and foreign designers. In the name of modernizing, minority performers elaborated syncretic styles that borrowed from mediated cosmopolitan cultures incorporating miniskirts, bare midriffs or bellbottoms into ethnic fashion. In tandem with the rise of modelling culture, runways and beauty contests showcased all these new developments.

Meanwhile, concerns have been voiced within and beyond China about the disappearance both of the actual older artifacts, which have been completely sold off in many villages, of the dress customs in the rural areas, and of the skills for making these traditional styles. Conservationists are working towards establishing archives and museum collections. Some seek to organize minority elders to pass on their skills and to ban the use and sale of antique crafts as commodities. International NGOs have initiated projects of poverty relief that rely on the production and maintenance of handicrafts. Concomitantly, some local governments in heavily touristed areas have sought to implement guidelines as to dress practices in the hopes that the quest for modernity will not discourage locals from continuing to look marketably ethnic.

Further reading

Corrigan, Gina (2001). *Miao Textiles from China.* Seattle: University of Washington Press.

Oakes, Tim (2002). *Dragonheads and Needlework: Textile Work and Cultural Heritage in a Guizhou County.* Hong Kong: Hong Kong Baptist University Centre for Urban and Regional Studies Occasional Paper Series 22 (June).

Schein, Louisa (2003). 'Minzu fuzhuang, wenhua ji fazhan' [Ethnic Clothing, Culture and Development]. In He Zhonghua (ed.), *Shehui xingbie, minzu, shequ fazhan yantaohui* [Proceedings of the Conference on Gender, Ethnicity and Social Development]. Guiyang: Guizhou minzu chubanshe.

Swain, Margaret Byrne (2001). 'Ethnic Doll Ethnics: Tourism Research in Southwest China'. In Valerie Smith and Maryann Brent (eds), *Hosts and Guests Revisited: Tourism Issues of the 21st Century.* Elmsford, NY: Cognizant Press, 217–31.

LOUISA SCHEIN

ethnic food

As in other cosmopolitan nations, clearly differentiated 'ethnic food' has been incorporated into Chinese urban life for centuries, but only some ethnicities' food is represented as desirable or adventurous. Mongolian, Korean and Japanese food, food represented by named and known societies, has been popular for a long time, especially in north China where going out to eat Mongolian barbecue or Korean dishes may punctuate an otherwise culinarily Chinese life. The food of some ethnic groups is scorned as inedible and disgusting, such as the yak-butter tea of Tibetans or the coarse grains and sweet potatoes of poor ethnic groups in the southwest. Ethnic food serves as a marker of ethnicity in ethnic theme parks, as in Xishuang Banna, in southern Yunnan. Certain food, such as the sour moss of the Banna Tai (Dai), is known as the prototypical food of various groups.

The ten Muslim ethnic groups in China follow the general Islamic proscriptions regarding pork. Muslim food – bread, noodles, grilled beef – is consumed as snack food by non-Muslims. In Greater China, especially Malaysia and Indonesia, one of the primary markers of difference between Chinese and Muslims is the consumption of pork and alcohol.

In Greater China, ethnic food may be consumed with greater frequency than in China itself. Many 'subethnic' or regional Chinese restaurants are popular in diasporic China, such as Hong Kong, Taiwan, Malaysia, Singapore, etc. These of course are Chinese, not ethnic. In those settings, foods of various international cuisines are also eaten. 'Foreign' – Euro-American – foods, especially those containing dairy products, are considered a different category from other Asian foods and from ethnic and regional Chinese foods. Villages and small towns in China are unlikely to have ethnic or foreign foods of any sort; options among foodways are a privilege that accompanies the growing affluence of China's middle class.

SUSAN D. BLUM

ethnic groups, history of

China reached its maximum territorial extent under the Qing dynasty (1644–1911) when China was ruled by the Manchus (population 10,682,262, 2000 census). The Manchus' heartland was incorporated into China when they ruled China, and in the eighteenth century they extended authority over ethnic areas like Mongolia (Outer and Inner), the mainly Muslim area in the far northwest, and Tibet.

The most important of many nineteenth-century Muslim rebellions was that of Yakub Beg from 1865 to 1877. Xinjiang (meaning 'new boundary') became a province in November 1884. Although Korean migration into the Manchu heartland had begun much earlier, the first major Korean migration to northeast China began in the 1860s (2000 census population of Koreans in China: 1,923,842).

Republican governments recognized five ethnic groups in China: the majority Han (2000 census population: 1,137,386,112), Manchus, Mongols (Chinese 2000 census population: 5,813,947), Muslims and Tibetans (Chinese 2000 census population of Tibetans: 5,416,021). A Turkic

Muslim conference held in Tashkent in 1921 revived the long-extinct ethnonym 'Uighur', and it became applied to the main Muslim ethnic group of Xinjiang (Chinese 2000 census Uighur population: 8,399,393). Republican policy placed overwhelming priority on national unity, granting minorities only secondary importance. Separatist rebellions persisted in Xinjiang throughout the Republican period, the most important being the founding of the East Turkestan Republic in 1944.

Mongolia declared independence of China at the end of 1911, and Tibet in February 1913. Republican Chinese governments refused to recognize either. In February 1929 Chiang Kai-shek's government set up the Mongolian and Tibetan Affairs Commission, equivalent to a ministry in status.

In Outer Mongolia, Soviet troops effected the establishment of an independent state, the Mongolian People's Republic being set up in 1924. Although Chiang Kai-shek refused to recognize this state until 1945, an independent Mongolia has proved permanent, though Inner Mongolia remains part of China. No Chinese government recognized Tibetan independence, even though this was the reality until PRC troops re-established authority in 1950. China's Manchu, Korean and most of its Mongolian areas fell under Japanese control from the early 1930s to 1945.

The PRC recognizes fifty-six ethnic groups in China, the majority Han and fifty-five 'minority nationalities' (*shaoshu minzu*). Like the Republicans, it places the highest priority on Chinese unity, and separatist rebellions such as those in Tibet (1987–9) and in Xinjiang in 1990 and 1997 received short shrift. Although PRC policy towards minorities is one of limited autonomy, the overall reality of the ethnic groups since 1949 has been towards national integration. Han immigration to the ethnic areas was not new in 1949, but has generally gathered momentum since then.

Further reading

Mackerras, C. (1994). *China's Minorities, Integration and Modernization in the Twentieth Century*. Hong Kong, Oxford, New York: Oxford University Press.

COLIN MACKERRAS

ethnic minority literary collections

Many minority groups in China have long and rich literary traditions, which mainly consist of epics, ballads, myths, legends, poems, anecdotes, words of wisdom, songs, and so forth. Most of these were created collectively and have been passed down orally from generation to generation. Only recently have efforts been made to write them down or have them published as literary collections. For example, in Tibet, it was discovered that a storyteller named Samzhub could sing 20 million words of the Tibetan religious epic *Gesser* despite the fact that he could not read. His words are being recorded by researchers. Samzhub is only one of many whose words have been recorded. In total, researchers have made 45,000 tapes and recorded 45 million words of various versions of *Gesser* told by Tibetan and Mongolian storytellers. Some of these stories have already been published.

Jangar, the heroic epic of the Mongols, was first published in Mongolian in the late 1950s, and was revised and republished in the 1980s. The hero epic of the Kirgiz in Xinjiang and Central Asia, *Manas*, has also been published. The Uigyurs are known for producing words of wisdom and stories of wit and humour. *Kutadgu Bilig* (*Bule zhihui* or *Wisdom of Royal Glory*), a long poem composed by Yusuf Khass-Hajib in the eleventh century, has attracted much academic attention, whereas stories about Afanti, a legendary figure who liked to make fun of the rich and powerful, have become popular among both adults and children throughout China. Oral traditions of some southern minority groups have also been collected, compiled and published, and these include Ashma of the Yi people and the Genesis of the Naxi people. A film based on the former became very popular nationally. The compilation, publication and translation of the literary collections of the minority groups ensure their preservation and help their spread among other ethnic groups.

Further reading

Afanti de gushi (1958). Shanghai: Shanghai wenhua.
—— (1959). Beijing: Zuojia.

Afanti de gushi (1963). Beijing: Zhongguo shaonian ertong.

——(1981). Beijing: Zhongguo minjian wenyi.

Ashma (1960). Kunming: Yunnan renmin.

——(1962, 1978). Beijing: Renmin wenxue.

Chuangshiji – Naxizu shishi (1962). Beijing: Renmin wenxue.

Chuangshiji – Naxizu minjian shishi (1978). Kunming: Yunnnan renmin.

Dongba jingdian xuanyi (1994). Trans. He Zhiwu. Kunming: Yunnan renmin.

Dongba wenhua cidian (1997). Trans. Li Guowen. Kunming: Yunnan jiaoyu chubanse.

Dongba xiangxing wenzi changyongci yizhu (1995). Trans. Zhao Jingxiu. Kunming: Yunnan renmin.

Fule zhihui (1979). Trans. Geng Shimin and Wei Zuiyi. Urumqi: Xinjiang renmin.

——(1986). Trans. Hao Guanzhong. Beijing: Minzu.

Gesa'er Wang Zhuan (1980–8). Multi-volumes. Trans. Wang Yinuan *et al*. Lanzhou: Gansu renmin.

——(1991). Trans. Wang Qinuan and Wang Xingxian. Lanzhou: Dunhuang wenyi.

——(1991). Trans. Xu Guoqiong and Wang Xiaosong. Beijing: Zhongguo zangxue.

——(2000). Trans. Liu Liqian. Beijing: Minzu.

Jiangge'er (1983). Trans. Sedaoerji. Beijing: Renmin wenxue.

——(1993). Trans. Heile and Ding Shihao. Urumqi: Xinjiang renmin.

Zhongguo shaoshu minzu yingxiong shishi – Manasi (1990, 1995). Trans. Lang Ying. Hangzhou: Zhejiang jiaoyu.

HAN XIAORONG

ethnicity, concepts of

While ethnicity has become a commonly used analytic concept in the study of societies around the world, it is quite new in China. The term *minzu* came into Chinese from Japanese around the turn of the twentieth century as increasing attention was paid to the relationships among groups within the new nation-state. *Minzu* is popularly shortened from the official term *shaoshu minzu*

'minority nationality'; it is translated as 'ethnic group', 'minority', 'minority nationality', 'ethnic minority'.

Ethnic groups are identified on the basis of four characteristics (common territory, common language, common economic life and common psychological characteristics (culture)). Actual cases violate these principles frequently, but at another level there is nonetheless faith in their guidance. As of the early twenty-first century, fifty-five ethnic minorities have been identified, though there are several other groups seeking official recognition. The **Han** constituted 92 per cent of the population in the 1991 census; minorities number approximately 104 million.

PRC policy has been influenced by the Soviet Union's nationalities policies and also by a theory known as cultural evolution, which holds that there is a single direction of historic change moving towards civilization, modernity and Communism, and that all groups can be located on this line. Each *minzu* is studied to determine its location, using marriage patterns, subsistence technologies, religion, housing and the presence or absence of writing systems. The Han Chinese are by definition most advanced, though some groups such as ethnic Koreans living in northeast China pose some challenge to the model by surpassing the Han in educational attainment.

Policies with regard to *minzu* revolve largely around the question of assimilation or tolerance. The officially stated goal is that all ethnic boundaries will dissolve at some unspecified future point, when Communism is attained, but those working with ethnic groups acknowledge that this is essentially irrelevant at present. There was a great deal of discrimination of *minzu* during the **Cultural Revolution**, with notorious humiliation of Tibetans and Hui. Since the Reforms, however, policies have tended to favour minorities and the percentage of people claiming *minzu* identity has increased. This is often explained as stemming from *minzu* exemption from the one-child policies, but may have roots as well in more profound questions of finding a place within the larger polity.

Political 'autonomy' for areas in which the population has traditionally been primarily *minzu* has been part of the Chinese constitution from the beginning. This has involved mostly the encouragement of ethnic cadres in governing their own areas.

A concept of 'subethnic' identity has sometimes been proposed to explain differences in groups usually considered Han, such as the Hakka (population est. 32 million). This opens up the possibility of creating multiple identities in China, a tendency deplored by a state focused on creating national unity.

Ethnic unity and harmony – encoded in the constitution, enshrined in street names (Minzu Tuanjie Lu, 'Nationality Unity Street') in most cities – is sometimes visible, but in some areas, such as Xinjiang, ethnic conflict has been increasing since the 1990s. About 17 million people in China are Muslims, in ten different ethnic groups. Ethnic consciousness among Muslims and other border groups is increasing (see **Islam in China**).

See also: Han; nationalism; representations of minorities

Further reading

Crossley, Pamela Kyle (1990). 'Thinking about Ethnicity in Early Modern China'. *Late Imperial China* 11: 1–34.

Dreyer, June Teufel (1976). *China's Forty Millions: Minority Nationalities and National Integration in the People's Republic of China*. Cambridge, MA: Harvard University Press.

Gladney, Dru C. (1990). *Muslim Chinese: Ethnic Nationalism in the People's Republic*. Cambridge, MA: Council on East Asian Studies, Harvard University.

Harrell, Stevan (ed.) (1995). *Cultural Encounters on China's Ethnic Frontiers*. Seattle: University of Washington Press.

SUSAN D. BLUM

ethnography

The direct study of society through observation and interview is usually called ethnography, or sometimes ethnology (*minzuxue*). In China this has been limited largely to study of ethnic minorities;

study of the Han has been considered part of sociology while in the United States it would often fall under anthropology. In the 1920s and 1930s, modelled in part on German folklore studies and on Western anthropology, a large number of studies of minority cultures were undertaken, especially in the southwest. In 1928 Academia Sinica's Institute of Social Science was established; it carries on studies of rural and urban Han and minority society in Taiwan in the Institute of Ethnology, under the Institute of History and Philology, as well as in the Institute of Sociology, founded in 2000.

Minzuxue was connected with radical social change; Cai Yuanpei, founder of Academia Sinica and organizer of Beijing University in its current form, was a reformer who sought to reinvigorate China through discovery of the strength of rural and minority cultures. One of the most famous Chinese ethnographers is Fei Xiaotong, who studied social anthropology with Bronislaw Malinowski at the London School of Economics. Fei conducted fieldwork on rural China, under the category of sociology. In 1952 anthropology and sociology were declared 'bourgeois sciences' and were abolished. Sociology was reinstated in 1979; anthropology has gradually been gaining acceptance.

During the 1950s and 1960s, for the purpose of classifying and identifying minorities, a process known as *minzu shibie*, hundreds of researchers were sent to the countryside to identify such groups and to study their languages. With the Cultural Revolution (1966–76), this was discontinued, and the more autocratic imposition of Han culture was implemented.

However, beginning in the 1970s, these programmes have gradually been restored, usually under the auspices of central or regional Nationalities Institutes (*minzu xueyuan*) or Academies of Social Sciences (central or regional). Since the late 1980s some anthropological studies of urban life have been undertaken. Vibrant programmes of social cultural anthropology have been established, mostly in the south, for instance at Zhongshan Daxue in Canton, Xiamen Daxue in Fujian, and Yunnan University in Kunming. **Peking University**'s Department of Anthropology includes both archaeology and ethnology (cultural anthropology). The Chinese University of Hong Kong has a Department of Anthropology with international connections to prominent scholars.

Ethnographic study in and of China focuses on minority culture, rural life, food in culture, religious practice, medical and botanical systems, tourism and identity, using direct observation as well as surveys.

See also: ethnicity, concepts of; Minsu quyi (Min-su ch'ü-i); research institutions for minority nationalities

Further reading

Guldin, Gregory Eliyu (ed.) (1990). *Anthropology in China: Defining the Discipline*. Armonk, NY: M. E. Sharpe.

—— (1994). *The Saga of Anthropology in China: From Malinowski to Moscow to Mao*. Armonk, NY: M. E. Sharpe.

SUSAN D. BLUM

etiquette

China has an etiquette system encompassing all its ethnic groups, each with a unique culture. Take Luoba nationality for example. Before treating guests to dinner, they take a bite first to demonstrate the innocence of their food.

In general, Chinese cultural etiquette has evolved largely from the Zhou (1034–221 BC) rituals related to eating. At its core is the respect for authority and parents. Therefore, seating is essential to a dinner. Gone are the elaborate rituals, but basic rules are still valid: the elderly and first-time guests are given priority, followed by children, whose ascendance in status is due to the one-child policy. Generally, Chinese dine at a round table or *baxianzhuo* (Table of the Eight Immortals). The seat facing the dining room's main entrance is the most important, with the degree of distinction lessening from left to right alternately.

Being early for home gatherings is welcome, but tardiness might be 'penalized' by an extra shot of wine. For drinking is a test of shrewdness. Sobriety with alcohol is a manly virtue. A dinner party could be raucous, each trying to get anyone but oneself drunk.

Monetary values used to be attached to gifts. Nowadays, however, gifts of sentiments become increasingly popular. A bottle of wine is good enough for a dinner invitation. As birthday gifts to the elderly, pears and angel-hair noodles symbolize longevity. Sending clocks is taboo, as the act sounds *songzhong*, a homophone of 'see to one's funeral'. Some of the other taboos include chopsticks straight up in a bowl of rice, as if it were offered to the dead. A little noise from eating soup may be tolerable, but smacking is repugnant.

Etiquette has regional flavours, too. Hooking up the middle and forefingers to tap on a tea table on the knuckles may be a gesture of thanks in Guangdong, but, with a slight twist, may signify 'I love you' in Beijing.

YUAN HAIWANG

evening newspapers and weekend editions

Evening newspapers, and more recently weekend editions, are noted for their less political content and focus on 'social news' emphasizing human-interest stories and issues close to people's everyday lives. In the post-Mao period, weekend editions in particular have exploited this degree of freedom from politics to great commercial advantage and set new agendas for the Chinese press.

In the late 1950s the Party launched several evening newspapers including the nationally recognized **Yangcheng Evening News** and Beijing Evening News, with a remit to provide readers with a broader range of news than the strictly politically oriented daily papers. Evening newspapers offered lighter, 'softer' news for an urban readership, although still retaining their political and propaganda responsibilities. In the 1980s and 1990s evening newspapers proliferated, numbering 128 titles by 1994 (Zhao 1998: 130).

In the 1980s, weekend editions, most notably the **Nanfang Weekend**, published in Guangzhou, pushed this manner of reporting much further. Weekend editions, even those launched by major

Party organ **newspapers**, did not carry the burden of political propaganda reporting that other newspapers, including evening papers, usually bore. They focused on longer feature articles about social issues from crime and corruption to education, health and consumerism, proving enormously popular with readers throughout the country. The leading weekend editions, such as the *Nanfang Weekend*, quickly accrued a lucrative circulation of millions. They were not only highly profitable but also showed other newspapers, who emulated them as far as possible within their politically defined remits, the kinds of stories readers liked to see. They showed a new way forward for a Chinese newspaper industry longing to loosen its politically defined chains.

See also: journalism; state control of media; Xinmin Evening News

Further reading

Zhao, Y. 1998. *Media, Market, and Democracy in China: Between the Party Line and the Bottom Line.* Chicago: University of Illinois.

KEVIN LATHAM

examinations for self-paced higher education

(zixue kaoshi)

In 1977, entrance examination for college enrolment resumed after a ten-year ban by the **Cultural Revolution (education)**. Universities already in dire need of accommodation, faculty and funding suddenly faced a relentless influx of talents of various ages who had been deprived of the opportunity to receive higher education for a decade. Beijing, hit the hardest by the predicament, adopted a resolution in July 1980 to allow its residents to pursue higher education through self-paced studies and get degrees by going through comparable procedures. In January 1981, programmes on offering exams for those who seek higher education through self-paced studies were piloted in Beijing, Tianjin, Shanghai, and later Liaoning province. In May 1985, the State Council set up the National Steering Committee on Exams for Those Who Seek Higher Education through Self-Paced Studies, which began to make the pilot programmes a standard practice throughout the country. By the year-end, examination systems for self-paced studies had been established all over the mainland.

Apparently this examination system proved to be an innovative solution to the country's unique problem. It helped pay off what the Cultural Revolution owed to the Chinese, and is still helping to fill the gap between a large population of prospective college students and an inadequate number of universities. Self-study examinations qualify students for a two-year non-degree diploma, a three-year associate degree and a four-year bachelor degree. Designated universities conducted examinations and confer degrees in accordance with the central and provincial governments' guidelines.

See also: Central Radio and Television University

HU MINGRONG

F

fachang

Daoist ritual

Fachang (method-arena) is a technical term used by the Daoists of northern Taiwan to refer to rituals of an exorcistic sort done by *fashi* (specialist in methods). It is used in opposition to *Daochang* (Way-arena) rituals like the **Jiao** (offering), which are performed by *Daoshi* (**Daoist priests**). The language, vestments and ritual actions of the *fachang* are all less formal and closer to everyday life than the Daochang. The first is as theatrical as the second is solemn, and it is based on a vernacular text and improvisation, while the Jiao is based on a fixed text written in classical Chinese. The first aims at the healing of ill individuals and is done in their homes, while the second is primarily for temple-based communities. These differences may all be traced to the fact that the *fachang* belongs to the regional **Lüshan jiao (Sannai jiao)** Daoist tradition, while the Daochang belongs to the national Zhengyi and Lingbao traditions. The Daoists of northern Taiwan generally learn both *men* (doors, traditions).

The *fachang* takes place in a ritual area marked off by portraits of Lüshan divinities, of which the *Sannai* (Three Ladies) are chief. As their representative, the master must in certain rituals play the part of a woman, as in the 'Presentation of the Memorial', when he walks graciously – even seductively – on his way to the site of presentation in the heavens. Each ritual in the six-hour sequence symbolizes one or another aspect of the war on the forces of evil that have caused the illness. In the 'Overturning of the Earth', for example, the master rolls himself up in a straw mat, then springs up with the turned-over mat to symbolize the burial of negative energies and the bringing to the surface of positive ones. In the 'Send-off of the Yin-Fire', the master first 'sweeps' up all negative (yin) energies with a lit torch, takes them into himself by swallowing the flame after each act of sweeping, then rushes to extinguish the torch outside the village. Throughout, by means of invocation and consecration, objects from daily life are transformed into magic ritual objects that can be used to attack evil and drive it out of the ill person's body, house and village. This, in addition to the role of improvisation in the *fachang*, is why the masters consider the exorcisms to be 'alive' and the Jiao to be 'dead'.

Further reading

Keupers, John (1977). 'A Description of the Fach'ang Ritual as Practiced by the Lü Shan Taoists of Northern Taiwan'. In Michael Saso and David W. Chappell (eds), *Buddhist and Taoist Studies* 1. Honolulu : University of Hawai'i Press, 82–92.

Lagerwey, J. (1987). 'Les têtes des démons tombent par milliers. Le fachang, rituel exorciste du nord de Taiwan'. *L'Homme* 101 (Jan.–Mar.): 101–16.

—— (1988). 'Les lignées taoistes du nord de Taïwan'. *Cahiers d'Extrême Asie* 4.

—— (1989). 'Les lignées taoistes du nord de Taïwan'. *Cahiers d'Extrême Asie* 5.

JOHN LAGERWEY

faith healing (Christian)

Faith healing is supernatural healing (*yibing*) from physical ailments, usually through intercessory prayer, charismatic rituals or individual psychological release through conversion. Practised in various forms by China's Protestants, faith healings are particularly common among rural populations, accounting for up to 90 per cent of all conversions to Christianity in rural areas. The practice of faith healing traces its roots in part to traditional Chinese religion, and in part to the charismatic practices introduced by American Pentecostal missionaries in the early twentieth century which fuelled much of Protestantism's growth in China before 1949.

The most common form of faith healing occurs through intercessory prayer. Church members often pray for those who are ill, petitioning God to heal them. Such prayer does not usually require any special healing charisma or ecclesial status, but can be practised by any believer or group of believers. In rural areas, church congregations often organize teams of members to visit the community's ill. They typically read Bible verses, sing hymns and pray for God to heal them. Intercessory prayer is often combined with other charismatic rituals such as the laying on of hands. Church members will place their hands on the infirm person's head and shoulders, praying simultaneously and aloud, creating an electric environment that comes alive with faith and the expectation of healing. These practices often result in an alleviation of symptoms in the ill person. Healing also often appears to occur from psychological release. Many converts claim that long-standing ailments such as perpetual migraines, digestion problems, partial blindness, fainting spells, and so forth, cease after conversion. In other cases, the afflicted convert responds as a result of the love and concern expressed by the church members, irrespective of any change in their physical illness.

Pursuant to the state's opposition to 'superstitious' practices, leaders in the official Protestant **Three-Self Patriotic Movement (TSPM)** and **China Christian Council** deride faith healings among China's Protestants as evidence of believers' 'low quality of faith' (see **wenhua shuiping**). The gulf between the official position and grassroots congregations is one of many sources of division between the Chinese Church's official bearers and the church body.

Further reading

Währisch-Oblau, C. (1999). 'Healing Prayers and Healing Testimonies in Mainland Chinese Churches: An Attempt at Intercultural Understanding'. *China Study Journal* 14. 2: 5–21.

JASON KINDOPP

Falun gong

Sectarian religion

As China 'marketized' its economy, opened to the outside world, and revised its national constitution in the interval between 1980 and 1986, there were several 'fevers' (*re*) or popular cultural enthusiasms that possessed urban residents (see **crazes**). Two of the more salient of these fevers were those of *wenhua* (culture) and Qigong (breath practice). Their contagiousness in two different political contexts a decade apart (1989 and 1999) would lead to appalling government repression, the effects of which continue to colour the international perception of China.

Falun gong (Dharma-Wheel Practice) or Falun dafa (Great Method of the Dharma Wheel) was introduced in 1991. It swiftly became the most prominent (and infamous) of a phalanx of Qigong movements – Zhong Gong, Qing Yang, Tian Tang Baolian, Guo Gong, Cibei Gong, Dayan gong – that emerged and prospered in this era of national 'Qigong frenzy' (see **Qigong (history)**). All are now banned by the Chinese government, following a nationwide crackdown in July 1999 on such groups for their propagation of *mixin* (superstition), and, more tellingly, their violation of the state's Law on Assembly, Procession and Demonstration. It is this combustible confluence of religion and politics and its widespread social appeal that makes Falun gong an especially productive site from which to observe the manifold changes of contemporary Chinese life.

By the late 1990s the nation's passion for self-healing emerged alongside an arc of cultural revival inscribed from city to countryside. The revival included the reconstruction of temples and lineage halls, the copying of scriptures, the conducting of exorcisms, the performance of divination, and the appearance of spirit-mediums. Falun gong boasted a following of more than 70 million in China and a grand total of 100 million scattered across thirty nations. The movement arose as a local healing sect based in breathing exercises, postures, visualizations and word magic. Its organizational identity was indissociable from the figure of Master Li Hongzhi, a former military musician and government cereals clerk from Jilin (Manchuria). Most notably, it is now an international *cause célèbre*, whose vicious persecution at the hands of the Chinese Communist Party stands in flagrant contravention of the very United Nations covenants governing civil and human rights that were endorsed by the government. Even though Falun gong's newfound global celebrity may assist in its preservation, it also distracts interpretive attention from a needed focus on the local forces that account for its popularity, for its political threat and for the government's heroic commitment to 'outlaw and extirpate' (*yuyi qudi*) it.

In response to the rising tide of popular interest in Qigong in the late 1980s, the China Qigong Scientific Research Association (Zhongguo qigong keyanhui), a quasi-official oversight body responsible for registering the thousands of Qigong associations, was founded and announced the political approval of this new mass activity that 'one in twenty Chinese, both young and old, strong and weak, now practises'. The research association's exuberance for the new scientific revolution of Qigong mirrored popular enthusiasms. This ecstatic interval witnessed an explosion of cheap publications, officially sponsored research, lectures, performances, seminars and the widespread dissemination of the multiple benefits of this newly restored 'traditional' Chinese therapy as purveyed by myriad Qigong masters (see **Qigong (masters)**) and itinerant spiritual guides. The Chinese government acted to monitor and to limit their popularity by requiring all Qigong organizations to register with the research association; for this registration each group was to return a substantial percentage of the tuition charged for the instruction of neophytes. However, the popularity of these practices extended far beyond the reach of official registry and official associations: virtually all Chinese were engaged in a range of physical cultivation exercises loosely organized under the rubric *yangsheng* (nourishing life exercises).

Yangsheng is a widespread and inextricable part of contemporary Chinese urban life. It has grown in popularity since the late 1980s, especially among the late middle-aged and elderly, as a reflexive response to the spiralling costs and decreased accessibility of both Western and traditional Chinese medical care. These practices are quite varied and all aim at longevity, including walking, *taiji quan* (see **martial arts**), respiratory and meditational regimens, badminton, croquet, and, above all, Qigong. Falun gong may be understood partially within this context of the therapeutic. Its initial reluctance to charge for the teaching broadened the reach of its message. However, even as the China Qigong Research Association recorded the increasing numbers of Qigong fellowships and observed the rapid growth of Falun gong, it obtained little reliable intelligence on the composition and organizational networks of such groups. With this popular fad abetted by official claims of scientific benefit, Qigong became a passionate, legitimate and very public spectacle – that is, until the number of the registered affiliate groups of the China Qigong Scientific Research Association exceeded government expectations and the claims by some (particularly Falun gong) of physical and mental health benefit metastasized into exclusivist theological postulates.

The literature of Falun gong describes a world of moral morass for which the practising self can escape through a regimen that assures mitigation of the karmic debt of avarice, commodity fetishism, competition, dipsomania, divorce, homosexuality and lust. In the eyes of *yangsheng* devotees, new age religion aficionados and the disaffected, there was much that Falun gong had to recommend – a comprehensive explanatory system for natural, social and political phenomena, energy, exuberance, group activity and, above all, the prospect of what the historian Peter Brown has termed 'clean power'. As quoted in *Zhuan Falun* [Revolution of the Dharma Wheel], Li Hongzhi stresses the darkness of the human state and fleshes out the powerful advantage afforded the practitioner of turning away from it to embrace the universe:

> Although great changes have taken place in human society, human moral values have declined tremendously... Human morality is deteriorating daily, and profits become the sole motivation. Yet changes in the universe do not occur according to changes in humankind... Only one who complies with this nature of the universe is a good person.
>
> (Li Hongzhi 2001: 16)

Self-help and transformation are incentives for 'practitioners' (*xiulian zhe*) or 'students' (*xueyuan*) who report that the required callisthenics of Falun gong refreshes and restores, offering them effective, invigorating alternatives to the materialist excesses of contemporary life. In a striking inversion of contemporary values, Li works the magic of contrast effect against the highly touted material accomplishment of the government's economic reforms:

> You know that with the reforms and openness, the economy has become flexible and policies are less restrictive. Many technologies have been introduced and people's living standard has improved... With the reforms bad things of different forms have also been imported... Human moral values have been distorted and changed. The standards that measure good and bad have all changed... Yet this universe's nature, *Zhen-Shan-Ren* (Truth, Goodness, Forbearance), remains unchanged as the sole criterion to differentiate good and bad persons.
>
> (*ibid.*: 361)

The dialectic of good and evil reflects the dynamic of suffering and self-healing at the core of Falun gong, and its continued appeal is due to its efficacy and to its minimal cost at a time when health care is entirely privatized and very expensive.

At the same time, the appeal of this teaching may have been more subtle, almost subliminal, for there is in its emphasis on rigorous individual cultivation that eventuates in alignment through the Master with the substance of the universe an odd recuperation of the collectivist, utopian bromides of the Cultural Revolution wherein citizens were exhorted to 'fight self' and through struggle and criticism to realize a more perfect national union with the Party. Moreover, in Li's dualistic portrait of a changing humankind and an unchanging nature of the universe, one might glimpse the outline of Lenin's dialectics of nature, according to which human culture was but a superstructural epiphenomenon of a basic, material nature.

For its practitioners, Falun gong is a way of life, a habit of mind that requires radical reconstruction of the person. It is conventionally defined as a spiritually based exercise and belief system based upon the rigorous cultivation of one's *xinxing* (mind/nature) in accord with the universal cosmic principles of *Zhen-Shan-Ren*, which in turn makes possible the ascendance of higher planes of consciousness, heightened moral awareness, ultimately enabling one to actualize the 'paranormal abilities' (*teyi gongneng*, residing in their 'third eye' or *tianmu*). A sustained commitment to the 'rectification of the dharma' ensures that, with time and steadfast effort, cultivation will make the practitioner a locus of spiritual power, a site for the radiant circulation of the dharma wheel, her body a microcosm of the universe. Although the psychosomatic regimen of breathing and meditation practices was first pontificated in 1991 and 1992 by Li Hongzhi, the scriptural texts (*jingwen*) assert that the teaching was privately taught for 'thousands of years' and only recently received or rediscovered by Li, who writes that it originally derived from 'Falun Xiulian Dafa, the Great Cultivation Way of the Dharma Wheel in the Buddha School'.

This is a vague precedent, to be sure, and one that conveys no clear descent from any of China's many traditions of Buddhism. The iconography of this system of beliefs – a yellow *wan* or Buddhist swastika set against a red circle (symbol of the rotating dharma wheel), surrounded by four smaller yellow cursive *wan* at the ordinal points, with four 'yin/yang' figures, red and blue and black and red between – and the rhetoric of its transmission suggests an ambiguous, amalgamate appropriation of varied concepts such as *wuwei* (non-intentional action), karma, *fashen* (law body), the figure of the Buddha, 'Buddha law', 'Buddha nature' and 'Buddha school', *de* (virtue) which when combined with Dao and the requisite exercises and breathing techniques constitute the syncretic mixture that is Falun gong. There are, then, diverse symbols and meanings coursing through the veins of this body of thought. In these respects, the teacher and his teaching resemble any of a long line of popular movements (Yellow Cliff, Triads, White Lotus, Boxers) founded upon a curious single revelation or exclusive mysterious transmission of doctrine put forward and interpreted by an inspired being (see **sectarian religion**). And like so many inventors of revelatory traditions before him, Li is an artifact of his own texts, an imagined, multiply projected product of his reported lectures and appearances, transmitted through the countless copies of *Zhuan Falun*, and the audio and video tapes of his teaching circulating in the expanding market of new age religion within which his self-initiating followers are enmeshed.

According to the catechistic literature of the movement, there are five principal exercises that promote self-cultivation in synch with the rotation of the dharma wheel (*falun*) each of which begins with a prescribed four-line, sixteen-character verse that is to be recited before the exercise. In the first collection of Li's teachings, *Zhongguo Falun gong* [China Falun gong] he explains that the 'Falun gong Practice System' (*Falungong shixing xitong*) is comprised of the following sequence: 'Buddha Showing One Thousand Hands' (*Fozhan qianshoufa*), a stretching exercise for hands and arms imitative of cosmic compression and rarefaction, meant to 'open all the energy channels and mobilize energy circulation in the body by stretching the body and relaxing it suddenly'; 'Falun Standing Posture' (*Falun zhuangfa*), 'a tranquil standing exercise composed of four wheel-embracing movements', the frequent practice of which 'will enable the body to open up and enhance energy potency'; 'Penetrating the Two Cosmic Extremes' (*Guantong liangjifa*), an exercise of simple up-and-down hand movements that purifies the body by 'mixing and exchanging energy from the cosmos'; and 'Falun Heavenly Circulation' (*Falun zhoutianfa*), slow movement exercise that 'rectifies the abnormal conditions of the human body' by circulating energy in the body over large areas; 'strengthening Divine Powers' (*Shentong jiachi*), performed in seated position, a meditation exercise aimed at strengthening 'supernormal powers [*teyi gongneng*] and energy potency'.

The description of these practices is redolent of the *neidan* or inner alchemy associated with the popular 'Daoist' cults of the early imperial era, even as the depiction of Li in the postures appropriate to each has him in Buddhist garb. If properly performed, these exercises yield both therapeutic and prophylactic effects: improved mental and physical health, and even resistance to illness, as dramatically recalled by Li in the numerous testimonies cited in the movement's scriptural texts, wherein pain is magisterially overcome through endurance and the binding of the suffering body of the believer to the law body of the Master and medicine is unnecessary. It is in the retelling of thaumaturgy, a testimonial genre found in Chan traditions, nineteenth-century martial arts fiction, medieval *biji* literature, and contemporary American televangelism, that the full force of prophylactic Falun gong is demonstrated:

> When I was teaching the *fa* [method] and the practice in Taiyuan, there was a practitioner over fifty years old ... She and her spouse ... walked into the middle of the street ... a car drove by very fast, and its rearview mirror caught the elderly lady's clothes and dragged her for more than 10 meters ... In the end she fell in the middle of the street ... The practitioner slowly got up from the ground and said, 'There's nothing wrong. You can leave' ... She came to the class and told me this story ... Our practitioners' *xinxing* [heart-natures] have indeed improved. She said to me: 'Teacher, I studied Falun Dafa today. If I hadn't studied Falun Dafa, I wouldn't have treated the accident this way.'
>
> (Li Hongzhi 2001: 164–5)

So pervasive and so convincing were the salubrious effects of this Falun gong phenomenon that Bill Moyers and David Eisenberg explained the scientific character of therapeutic Qigong as a new age Chinese alternative to Western biomedicine. This is one aspect of Falun gong that has become more prominent in the years since its proscription, promoted in the literature and virtual information disseminated by the official international organization, Minghui (Clear Wisdom).

Such foreign claims of efficacy were not lost on the Chinese Communist Party, which cautiously, then warmly, embraced Qigong as a traditional, and scientific, resource for the promotion of health and well-being between 1985 and 1993. Indeed, many of its members believed in the therapeutic benefits of practising *fa* as these were documented in two scientific surveys conducted in the fall of 1998 (*The Effect of Falun Gong on Healing Illnesses and Keeping Fit: A Sampling Survey of Practitioners from Beijing Zizhuyuan Assistance Centre*, and *Falun Gong Health Effect Survey of Ten Thousand Cases in Beijing*), wherein it was shown that 'Falun gong's disease healing rate is 99.1 per cent with a cure rate of 58.5 per cent; Improvement rate is 80.3 per cent in physical health and 96.5 per cent in mental health' (*Falun Gong Health Effect Survey*); thousands took up the teaching. And the engagement of a large percentage of Chinese officialdom in Falun gong could only have provided greater incentive for wider popular dissemination of the teachings and practices. Even Jiang Zemin allegedly believed in the curative efficacy of Zhong Gong massage.

Beginning in 1993, the Party signalled its apprehension by curtailing official recognition of Qigong groups and questioning the wisdom of popular devotion to the teachings of 'masters' like Zhang Hongbao (founder of Zhong Gong) and Li Hongzhi. As this apprehension gave way to restriction and then repression, many Qigong disciplines dissolved. But Falun gong was the beneficiary of their dissolution as disgruntled followers of other practices turned to Li's teaching. The membership, as has long been the case with sectarian groups and secret societies in Chinese history, is distinctly heterogeneous; there are among its ranks peasants, workers, deracinated youth, educated urban professionals, retirees, and the vast myriads of the health conscious who have turned to new age, native nourishing life exercises to keep fit in a society persuaded by the blandishments of global capitalism and changing with a rapidity too difficult to fathom.

From 1992 to 1993 Li made numerous public appearances at training sessions, seminars and conferences in the northeast and in Beijing. At these events thousands of Chinese (attendance ranging from 20,000 to 200,000 according to government estimates), captivated by Li's charismatic presence and compelled by his message of meaningful self-help and clean living through the activation of the innate impulses of truth, goodness

and forbearance were introduced to the rudiments of what he termed his 'spiritual teaching'. This teaching, as propounded under the name of the Falun gong Research Branch Society (Falun gong yanjiu fenhui) and consisting of his unique set of exercises, breathing techniques, visualizations and chants, gained ground on other Qigong movements. By Li's fortieth birthday (purportedly 13 May 1992, which happened to be the eighth day of the fourth lunar month, long identified by custom as the birthday of the Buddha), Falun dafa was officially recognized as a direct affiliate branch of the China Qigong Scientific Research Association. In 1993, Li was deemed a 'Direct-Affiliate Qigong Master' (*Zhishu qigongshi*), an official status he enjoyed until the following year when the first tensions developed between the China Qigong Scientific Research Association and Li's increasingly exclusivist claims for the greater scientific truth of Falun gong.

However, from the fall of 1994 and the winter of 1995, as Li battled with the government over official recognition of his practice, the Chinese press showed signs of scepticism as articles questioned the scientific validity of Falun gong's claims of health and well-being. Until this juncture, Li Hongzhi and his most prominent associates and guidance counsellors (*fudaoyuan*), Li Chang, Wang Zhiwen, Ye Hao and Yu Changxin, had successfully negotiated the narrow and troubling terrain between science and native tradition in the public representation of their teaching, avoiding any suggestion of superstition. Perhaps sensing an imminent attack on the 'pseudoscience' (*weikexue*) of Qigong, Li ceased offering instruction in the practice in 1995, the year that provincial authorities in Hangzhou moved to restrict membership in and dissemination of materials on Falun gong, but by this time the tide of popular commitment to the practice had risen above the levee of official constraint as millions of Chinese, and a surprisingly large number of government officials, had embraced Falun gong. The popularity of Qigong and of Falun gong among Party members complicated the government interdiction. In tandem, this movement and the government's response have pushed Chinese and international politics in new, very revealing directions. The Falun gong Research Branch Society continued to enjoy official recognition until 1996, when it withdrew from the China Qigong Research Association, and, in July of that year the movement's scriptural works, *Zhuan Falun* and *Zhongguo Falun gong*, were proscribed by the Chinese government.

Two years later (1997–8) Falun gong was on the verge of interdiction as the sect's serial efforts to register as a social organization with the National Minority Affairs Commission, the China Buddhist Federation and the United Front Department all failed. The Ministries of Civil Affairs and Public Security were not appeased by the formal abolition of the Falun dafa Research Branch Society nor by the fact that the entire national practice and teaching apparatus had been disarticulated and its many practitioners left to conduct their cultivation individually through the study of books and audio-visual materials. Li Hongzhi had left China to seek refuge in the United States, conducting seminars in Houston and New York. Li's departure did not mitigate enthusiasm for the practice, and even though the government no longer recognized Falun gong as a legitimate Qigong association it remained a very popular and a fearlessly independent movement.

These were the facts on the ground, as it were, prior to the spectacular incident that propelled Falun gong into international celebrity and concern; that is, by the spring of 1999, the relationship between the government and Falun gong was openly adversarial. Early on the morning of 25 April 1999, more than 10,000 (a curiously even and very powerful round number, *wan*, not disputed in any domestic or foreign report) Falun gong practitioners appeared implacably seated in orderly meditative lines on the pavement just outside the official residences of Communist Party luminaries in Zhongnanhai. For nearly nineteen hours they were assembled in lotus positions to appeal to the government's highest officials to reconsider their opposition to the practices of the discipline. The protesters, moved by Li Hongzhi, who had returned surreptitiously to China on 22 April 1999 for a forty-four-hour period, were particularly offended by what they believed was a savage discrediting of their practices, their salubrious effects and the scientific status of their claims of psychological and physical healing.

Scarcely two weeks prior to this grand assembly of meditative dissent, Professor He Zuoxiu of the Chinese Academy of Sciences engendered considerable disquiet among the sect's members. A physicist highly suspicious of the scientific evidence of Falun gong's benefits, Professor He first appeared on television in Beijing in 1998 and denounced Falun gong as a fraud. At the station the next day, sect members protested about his appearance and demanded a public retraction. Then on 11 April 1999, writing in an official Party publication from Tianjin, *Teenage Science-Technology Outlook*, he challenged the 'science' of Falun gong's health benefits, stating that one of the graduate students in his institute became deranged following practice of its exercises. Professor He's junk science criticism provoked another public reaction, a Falun gong protest in the streets of Tianjin on 22 April.

The unprecedented mass vigil in Beijing a week later precipitated political effects amazing in their violence and intensity, as though a seismic shock had shuddered through the very ground of the national government. From this mysteriously organized yet explicitly peaceful appeal, a fissure between state and society opened that has expanded and contracted with fluctuating volatility in subsequent years as thousands of Party members were compelled to resign their memberships in the sect and true believers of Li's teachings (even from Canada and the United States) have been beaten, jailed and executed. Hundreds were arrested, and in the ensuing weeks protests repeatedly broke out at many locations throughout China and the world. In fact, by the government's official tally, Falun gong followers had staged 307 domestic demonstrations in the period from late April to 22 July of 1999, when the Research Society of Falun dafa and its practice of Falun gong was condemned as 'an evil cult' (*xiejiao*) by the Ministry of Civil Affairs. And this was just the beginning, for practitioners from many parts of the country and from other nations obsessively returned to **Tiananmen Square**, where at this 'court of last resort', they lodged righteous appeals and signalled their unstinting commitment to the teaching and to Master Li, the most dramatic of these being the controversial 23 January 2001 self-immolation of several Falun gong practitioners. Every few months between the summer of 1999 and the spring of 2002, as few as one or two and as many as several hundred protesters made the pilgrimage to Tiananmen, unfurling banners bearing key symbols of the teaching, performing the callisthenics and chanting slogans. They were arrested, detained, beaten, tortured, interrogated, sentenced to labour camps, confined in psychiatric institutions, even executed.

The consequences of this colossal maltreatment of practitioners have been felt far beyond the many points of domestic Chinese repression, causing numerous complications in international relations, immigration, asylum and, in the summer of 2003, the filing of an amicus brief in support of a US District Court lawsuit in defence of the religious freedom guaranteed by Article 36 of the Chinese Constitution and against former General Secretary Jiang Zemin for genocide and crimes against humanity.

Perhaps because there has been so little visible evidence of broader dissent since the Tiananmen massacre, the protests by and incarceration of Falun gong practitioners have been carefully tracked by the Western media and are a constant source of inquiry among interested observers of religious freedom and human rights in China. Yet also, because Falun gong is a movement that has gathered immense momentum in the virtual environments of the Worldwide Web, where its sites such as Minghui.wang, Clearwisdom.net, Falundafa.org are strategically operated by invisible webmasters, interested parties outside the country can learn a great deal about the teaching and its ongoing political fate in China. These sites have also created new avenues for the purposive wanderings of followers through testimonials and the affirmation of forbearance under duress. On its homepage Clearwisdom.net keeps a running tab on the number of followers killed by the Chinese government (over 1,000 to date) and reports on illegal detentions, and in this fashion generates manifold compelling testimonies of the 'supernormal powers' (*teyi gongneng*) of its most tested practitioners while creating a virtual community of righteous conscience whose psychology of innocence steels them for the grand violence of their self-actualization. The galvanizing effects of persecution testimonies on collective action may be especially powerful for the many Chinese

practitioners who lived through the politically orchestrated truth telling of the *suku* (speak bitterness) campaigns of land reform. In this and many other homologies of group culture, rhetoric, personality cult and even organization, the Chinese Communist Party and the Falun gong display a curious filiation that may explain the escalating viciousness of their exaggerated claims and counterclaims.

Indeed, with the rigid maintenance of the Falun gong ban the Worldwide Web has emerged as a training ground for the practitioner while also serving as an international informational conduit. Graphic accounts of the experiences of survivors' detainments, arrests and incarcerations, demonstrate the devotion of followers to the principal tenet of Falun gong – *ren* or forbearance. The website testimonials of enduring persecution have become a critical tool of affirmation of faith in the method, but the ethical outcome of cultivation has been overcome by a disturbed, and disturbing, *résentiment*. As Li Hongzhi recently stated in arguing for the need of Falun gong followers, and not the United Nations, to bring an end to Chinese government repression:

> If human beings were to end the persecution, what a disgrace that would be to Dafa disciples! We wouldn't have validated the Fa, we wouldn't have established mighty virtue in the persecution, and our Dafa disciples wouldn't have blazed their own path.
>
> (Li Hongzhi 2003b)

However, this tragic tale of the mania of popular practice and government persecution discloses the workings of religio-genesis in contemporary China and also recalls the militant radicalization of village societies by the government in the late nineteenth century. The rhetorical war that each side has conducted with equal vigilance but grossly unequal force intensified in the early months of 2003, as Falun gong criticism of contemporary life went beyond the vague, moralistic denunciations against capital and material accumulation, and the Party itself assumed a prominent place in the occasional lectures that constitute Master Li's teaching in exile.

Purportedly speaking at the 'Mid-West Fa Conference' in Chicago on 22 June 2003, Li devoted several paragraphs to a serial recollection of government persecution of all Chinese, a denunciation of Jiang Zemin as 'the head of the evil beings that have persecuted us', and an exposition of SARS, not as epidemiology but as a pathology peculiarly drawn to evil:

> the fact that SARS managed to appear in Beijing, and even managed to break into Zhongnanhai and topple a few of the Politburo Standing Committee members, I'll tell you, this is not a simple matter of an infectious disease... that's because it's not human, and inside its human skin are wicked rotten spirits, it was those spirits talking.
>
> (Li Hongzhi 2003b)

Moreover, Li, with arresting frankness, castigated the Party, saying:

> The Party has never admitted any of its faults to the people... It's you, Party, that has caused your collapse while you have persecuted the people and the masses, and during your persecution you've been encouraging deceit, evil, strife, and corruption, and you've lost the people's hearts.
>
> (*ibid.*)

Li has not helped his followers by engaging Jiang Zemin in rhetorical confrontation referring to him as *mogui* (demon). His principal battle, and the one for which it seems many of his followers support him, is with corruption and the progression of immorality and evil, a hallmark of the Communist Party and a definitive quality of contemporary life. On this ground, which does not contract but expands with every day, Falun gong is a redoubtable adversary, and the record of the state's battle with it reveals the grand scope of China's legitimation crisis while demonstrating the real limits of change for both victor and victim.

Religio-genesis has long been an epiphenomenon of China's authoritarian politics, whether that of dynasties or national parties, because the exercise of political power often produced social disorder and human suffering conducive to the appearance of millenarian imaginings. And many a popular lay association, congregational folk practice, secret society or bandit group, when subject to government suppression, became increasingly militant and millenarian in defence of their existence and of their unique conception of collective faith. The most

infamous, and the most feared, of these coerced transmogrifications was reflexively identified by the imperial government as White Lotus (Bailian); it spawned an anti-establishment, Adventist eschatology of salvation that underwrote the millenarian rebellions of the eighteenth and nineteenth centuries, including the Boxer Rebellion.

As with earlier secret societies and popular religious sects, Falun gong must be recognized as a sophisticated but simple complex for the production and distribution of information and knowledge that educates and recruits. Traditionally, the membership of popular societies, congregational and charismatic, expanded and contracted along backroads, waterways and railroads. Secret handshakes, devotional tracts, talismans, amulets, graphs, marked the territory of such groups, much of whose ritual activity was effectively integrated into the quotidian but was punctuated by certain ceremonies centred at local temples and shrines. In a virtual age with myriad computer-literate followers at home and abroad of diverse and indeterminate motivation, Falun gong is, today, conducted along the endlessly self-replicating arteries of the Internet. And in a few scattered but spectacular events since 2000, movement followers have attempted to convey their practice's principles by the sabotage of state media.

These instances of resistance are particularly salient because they occur against a backdrop of Falun gong invisibility; however, there is little reason to conclude that the sect has been, or will be, eliminated. The government's own dubious yet appalling data from mental institutions:

> according to the doctors at the Beijing University of Medical Science, since 1992 the number of patients with psychiatric disorders caused by practising 'Falun Gong' [accounts for] 10.2 per cent of all patients... in the first half of this year [1999] the number rose further accounting for 42.1 per cent... Falun Gong practitioners now account for 30 per cent of all mental patients in China.
>
> (Human Rights Watch 2002b: 169 and Ji Shi 1999: 12)

attests more to the rapid social diffusion of Falun gong than it confirms the success of the government's repression. If one adds to these figures the government assertions of its confiscation and destruction of massive numbers of manuals, scriptural texts, video and audio tapes, then the facts of Falun gong's widespread dissemination are eloquent.

What these facts demonstrate is how the wide diffusion of the eclectic symbols and beliefs of indigenous religion could be drawn into the syncretic language of Falun gong. The government's *xiejiao* denunciations of the sect and its practitioners emphasize the aberrant or foreign quality of the teaching, yet it makes more sense to regard the undying enthusiasm for Falun gong as a unique fundamentalist product generated from within the complex situation of human longing, exacerbated by capitalism, but soothed by religion. Until the Chinese government finds a language appropriate to such an interpretation of popular behaviour, the inevitably violent struggle between religious diversity and political unity will persist.

In light of the last four years of oscillating opprobrium from the Chinese Communist Party and the Falun Dafa Information Centre, the repeated government calls for the elimination of the movement on the grounds of its danger to national security and public health, and the increasing incidence of anti-government rhetoric and envisioned apocalypse in the public statements of Li Hongzhi, it is likely that the Communist regime is repeating the colossal mistake of previous imperial governments which drove congregations, mutual aid groups, local brotherhoods and sectarian associations to rebellion through aggressive, paranoid persecution.

Bibliography

(1989). 'Fitness and Health through Qigong'. *Beijing Review* 32.17 (20–24 April).

(1998). *The Effect of Falun Gong on Healing Illnesses and Keeping Fit: A Sampling Survey of Practitioners from Beijing Zizhuyuan Assistance Centre*. Beijing (18 October). Available at http://www.unc. edu/foflg/falun/REPORTS/Survey2new.html [study conducted by six medical professionals from the General Hospital for Armed Police, the Stomatological Hospital of the Beijing Medical University, the People's University of China Hospital, the Beijing Hospital of Nuclear Industry, and the Dongshi Hospital for Women and Children].

(1998). *Falun Gong Health Effect Survey of Ten Thousand Cases in Beijing*. Available at http://www. falundafa-pa.net/survey/survey98-1_e.pdf [report of a study purportedly conducted in 1998 by a team of eleven scientists and physicians from China Union Medical University, Basic Science College, Chinese Traditional Medicine Research Institute, Beijing Medical University, The Chinese People's Military General Hospital 304, Beijing Hospital No. 2].

(2001). ' "Falun gong" and Fascists'. *Renmin ribao* (3 February).

Human Rights Watch (2002a). *Dangerous Meditation: China's Campaign against Falun gong*. New York: Human Rights Watch (7 February).

—— (2002b). *Dangerous Minds: Political Psychiatry in China Today and Its Origins in the Mao Era*. New York Human Rights Watch.

Human Rights Watch and the Geneva Initiative on Psychiatry (2002). *Dangerous Minds: Political Psychiatry in China Today and Its Origins in the Mao Era*. New York: Human Rights Watch (August).

Ji, Shi (1999). *Li Hongzhi and His 'Falun Gong' – Deceiving the Public and Ruining Lives*. Beijing: New Star Publishers.

Kang, Xiaoguang (2000). *Falun gong shibian quantoushi* [A Comprehensive View of the Falun gong Incident]. Hong Kong: Minbao chubanshe.

Li, Hongzhi (1999). *China Falun Gong*. New York: The Universe Publishing Company.

—— (2001). *Zhuan Falun: The Complete Teachings of Falun Gong*. Gloucester, MA: Fair Winds Press.

—— (2003a). *Fa-Lecture during the 2003 Lantern Festival at the US West Fa Conference*. (15 February). Available at http://www.clearwisdom.net/emh/articles/2003/2/27/32713.html

—— (2003b). *Teaching the Fa at the 2003 Midwest–US Fa Conference*, Chicago, Illinois (22 June). Available at http://www.clearwisdom.net/emh/articles/2003/7/8/37905.html

Further reading

Chen, Nancy (2003). 'Healing Cults and Anti-Cult Campaigns'. In Daniel Overmyer (ed.), *Religion in China Today*. Cambridge: Cambridge University Press, 199–214.

Eisenberg, David (1985). *Encounters with Qi*. New York: W.W. Norton.

Ownby, David (2000). 'Falun gong as a Cultural Revitalization Movement: An Historian Looks at Contemporary China'. Lecture delivered at Rice University, Houston, Texas, (20 October). Available at http://www.ruf.rice.edu/~tnchina/commentary/ownby1000.html

—— (2004). *Falun Gong and China's Future*. Lanham, MD: Rowman and Littlefield.

Palmer, David (2004). *'Qigong Fever': Body, Memory, and Power in Post-Mao China, 1949–1999*. London: Hurst.

Palmer, Susan and Ownby, David (2000). 'Falun dafa Practitioners: A Preliminary Research Report'. *Nova Religio* 4 (October): 133–7.

Penny, Benjamin (2002). 'Falun gong: Prophecy and Apocalypse'. *East Asian History* 23 (June).

Perry, Elizabeth J. (2002). *Challenging the Mandate of Heaven: Social Protest and State Power in China*. Armonk, NY: M. E. Sharpe.

Rahn, Patsy (2002). 'The Chemistry of a Conflict: The Chinese Government and the Falun gong'. *Terrorism and Political Violence* 14.4: 41–65.

Schechter, Daniel (2002). *Falun Gong's Challenge to China*. New York: Akashic Books.

ter Haar, Barend (2002). *Falun gong: Evaluation and Further References*. Available at http://www.let.leidenuniv.nl/bth/falun.htm

Tong, James (2002). 'An Organizational Analysis of the Falun gong: Structure, Communications, Financing'. *China Quarterly* 171: 636–60.

Wong, John and Liu, William T. (1999). *The Mystery of China's Falun Gong: Its Rise and its Sociological Implications*. Singapore: World Scientific Publishing.

LIONEL M. JENSEN

family planning

Family planning contradicts deep-rooted ideals among the Chinese, especially those in the countryside, who believe in large families and many sons. The concept of family planning was first advocated by some intellectuals after 1953, when the first census under the PRC reported a surprisingly large count of 588 million. Ma Yin Chu, then president of **Peking University**, was one of the supporters of family planning, arguing that rapid population growth slowed economic development. Mao, on the other hand, emphasized the productive contributions of the population rather than their consumption needs. His statements, 'of all things in the world, people are the most precious' and 'every mouth comes with two hands attached', among others, promoted pronatalist thoughts and behaviour. Family planning was labelled Malthusian and bourgeois, and accordingly Ma and others that advocated it were persecuted.

During the early 1960s, birth rates skyrocketed, alarming demographers and others. Yet the leftist political climate (e.g. the **Cultural Revolution**) rendered any large-scale attempts at family planning impossible. In the early 1970s, the total fertility rate (average number of children per woman) stood at 5.8. The notion that economic growth was seriously undermined by rapid population growth finally found acceptance among policy-makers, so that the 'late, sparse, few' (*wan xi shao*) campaign was introduced. It was a voluntary programme emphasizing late marriage, increasing birth parity, and fewer births in general. The programme was so successful that by the end of the decade the total fertility rate had declined to 2.8.

In 1979, however, policy-makers decided to launch a more aggressive birth-control programme, namely, the **one-child policy**. Their rationale was twofold. First, the economic reforms that began in the late 1970s aimed at boosting China's economic growth in order for the nation to catch up with the rest of the world. A further reduction of population growth would be conducive to achieving this goal. Second, the 1960s baby-boomers were reaching childbearing age during the 1980s. An aggressive birth-control policy was therefore seen as necessary to offset this demographic momentum. Thus, an incentive and penalty system was implemented and cadres throughout the administrative hierarchy, including those at neighbourhood and village levels, were mobilized to enforce the policy. Contraceptives are made widely and easily available; women violating the policy are under pressure for abortion and sterilization; and girl infanticide and underreporting are believed to be a response to the policy. The one-child policy is more relaxed in the countryside and among minorities. Currently, the total fertility rate for the nation as a whole is 1.8.

Further reading

Davis, Deborah and Harrell, Stevan (eds) (1993). *Chinese Families in the Post-Mao Era*. Berkeley: University of California Press.

Ten, H. Yuan (1991). *China's Strategic Demographic Initiative*. New York: Praeger.

Poston, Dudley L., Chang, Chiung-Fang, McKibben, Sherry L., Walther, Carol S. and Lee, Che-Fu (eds) (2004). *Fertility, Family Planning and Population Control in China*. London: Routledge.

White, Tyrene (1994). 'The Origins of China's Birth Planning Policy'. In Christina Gilmartin, Gail Hershatter, Lisa Rofel and Tyrene White (eds), *Engendering China: Women, Culture, and the State*. Cambridge: Harvard University Press, 250–78.

C. CINDY FAN

Fang Fang

b. 1955, Nanjing

Writer

Widely regarded as a writer of 'New Realism' (*Xin xieshi zhuyi*), Fang Fang's fiction is distinguished by a direct and fierce confrontation with reality. Fang Fang moved to Wuhan with her family when she was a child. After graduating from middle school, she did various manual jobs, including pulling carts, before entering Wuhan University, majoring in Chinese literature. Fang Fang became known when she was a college student after publishing several short stories about urban youth.

In 1987, with the publication of the novella *The Scenery* (*Fengjing*), Fang established her status as a key figure of the 'New Realism'. Told by a narrator who died as a baby, *The Scenery* portrays with stark realism the life of a coolie's nine children in a slum of Wuhan. In this setting, Fang Fang depicts ordinary people without any hint of optimism. The novella *Sunset* (*Luori*) focuses on a mother who treats her children badly while they wish her dead, both for understandable reasons. Fang Fang also deals with the life of intellectuals. *Nowhere to Escape* (*Wuchu duntao*) shows the crushing of an ambitious young university professor by the system; and *Lofty Clouds and Waters* (*Xingyun liushui*) concerns professors torn by a sense of duty and poverty. Her novel *Wuni-Lake Genealogy* (*Wunihu nianpu*, 1999) probes the complex psychology of Chinese intellectuals before and after the Anti-Rightist Campaign of 1957.

Further reading

Fang, Fang (1996). *Three Novellas by Fang Fang*. Contemporary Chinese Women Writers 5. Beijing: Panda Books.

—— (1997). 'Hints'. Trans. Ling Yuan. *Chinese Literature* (Summer).

—— (1997). 'Stakeout'. Trans. Zhang Siyang. *Chinese Literature* (Summer).

—— (1998). 'Predestined'. Trans. Zhang Siyang. *Chinese Literature* (Winter).

Wu, Lijuan (1997). 'Fang Fang, Reflecting Her Times'. Trans. Li Ziliang. *Chinese Literature* (Summer).

LEUNG LAIFONG

Fang Lijun

b. 1963, Handan, Hebei

Painter, woodcut artist

Heralded as leading representative of post-1989 **Cynical Realism** (*wanshi xianshizhuyi*) by art critic **Li Xianting**, the image of bald-shaved men set against a background of skies and oceans is one of the hallmarks of Fang Lijun's work.

Fang's work was included in the groundbreaking exhibition '**China Avant-Garde**' before his graduation in 1989 from the Department of Printmaking of the **Central Academy of Fine Arts** in Beijing (see also **art academies**). International recognition followed after his 1993 participation in the exhibitions 'China's New Art Post-1989' (Hong Kong), 'China Avant-Garde' (Berlin,

Rotterdam, Oxford and Odense) and the 45th Venice Biennale (see **China's New Art, Post-89 (Hong Kong, 1993) and China Avant-Garde (Berlin, 1993)**). His famous painting *Series 2 no. 2* (*Xilie er zhi er*, 1991–2) of a young bald-shaved man with a contorted facial expression somewhere between outspoken anger and utter boredom, captured the imagination of the West due to its perceived post-1989 rebellious mockery towards China's repressive political system. It featured on the cover of the *New York Times Magazine* in 1993.

His subsequent *Water* series (1992–) transcends the political agitation of Cynical Realism, taking his figures away from mundane reality into the psychological realm of water. While figures are depicted swimming and floating on cool silky water-surfaces, the apparent deep tranquillity of the water often harbours a certain menace. In other works the strong image of the back of a bald-shaved head, looming up out of nothing, gives the picture a powerful sense of suspense. Much of Fang's work (including monumental black-and-white woodcuts) bears traces and visual elements from the Cultural Revolution, a period which deeply marked Fang's world outlook.

Further reading

Chou, Yuting (1998). 'The Floating Body in the Art of Fang Lijun: An Artist's Comment on the Human Condition in Post-Cultural Revolution China'. *China Information* 13. 2/3 (Autumn/Winter): 85–114.

De Matté, Monica (1999). 'Fang Lijun'. In *La Biennale di Venezia, 48a Esposizione d'Arte, d'Apertutto, Aperto Over All*. Marsilio: La Biennale di Venezia, 198–9.

Fumichi, Yasuko and Nakamoto, Kazumi (eds) (1996). *Fang Lijun: Human Images in an Uncertain Age* (exhibition catalogue). Tokyo: The Japan Foundation Asia Centre.

Li, Luming (2001). *Fang Lijun*. Changsha: Hunan Fine Arts Publishing House.

Li, Xianting (1998). 'The "Shaved Head popi" created by Fang Lijun'. *SMA Cahiers* 13 (Amsterdam): 6–8.

CHOU YUTING

fashion designers

Since the end of the **Cultural Revolution**, mainland Chinese fashions have undergone a dramatic development as economic reforms have brought in Western concepts of clothing production and design. Although the majority of clothing is still designed anonymously and manufactured through joint ventures or state-run companies, such as the Shanghai Garment Group Ltd, an increasing number of individual designers and their companies are becoming recognized, often through the efforts of the China Garment Designers' Association.

Chen Xiang (b. 1969) graduated from the China Textile University in Shanghai and shortly after established his own label '3 Eux Et Elles'. The majority of his designs are highly commercial and are targeted at the growing number of fashion-conscious, unmarried, working women with some disposable income in the Shanghai and Nanjing regions.

Guo Pei (b. 1967), named one of China's top ten designers in 1997, initially worked for several fashion companies before becoming chief designer for the Beijing-based Tianma (Heavenly Horse) Clothing Company in 1989. Six years later, Guo moved to the Milano Fashion Company Ltd, a Taiwanese-American joint venture, again in Beijing. Whilst at Milano, she continued to design her own lines and this formed the basis for the establishment of her own company Meiguifang (Mayflower) in 1996. Although she offers a line of women's work outfits, she is best known for her more revealing casual wear, including signature loose-knit baggy crop-top jumpers paired with hipster shorts.

Sun Jian (b. 1967), a 1986 graduate of the Second Light Industrial Institute, began her fashion career in teaching design, but soon progressed to the post of chief designer at a number of organizations, including Aidekang (Ideal Couture Fashion Company Ltd), a Chinese-German joint venture in Beijing. By 1992, Sun had established her own company offering Chinese-inspired items under the label 'Sun Jian Fashion Studio'. Sun Yatsen-style jackets (see **Mao Zedong and Sun Yatsen suits**) and **qipao, cheongsam**-style evening dresses are prominent examples. Like many mainland designers, she combines couture popular with media personalities, with commercial commissions such as the Wangfujing Hotel Club and the Agricultural Bank.

Wu Haiyan, a graduate of the handicraft art department of the China Academy of Fine Arts in Hangzhou, held her first fashion show in 1990 and has since become one of the best-known faces in Chinese design. She has won prizes for her designs both in China and abroad and was one of the top ten designers in China in 1995 and 1997. She began working as chief designer for the Hangzhou Kaidisi Silks Company (see **silk industry**) in 1995 and has used silk in many of her subsequent designs known for their elegance and femininity. She holds senior positions at her alma mater and is also as chief designer at the China National Garments Group Company.

Ye Hong, a 1984 graduate of fashion design from the China Academy of Fine Art in Hangzhou, established her own company in Shanghai in 1991. Her designs range from couture, to ready-to-wear items for professional women, to commercial contracts for hotels, stores and fast-food chains.

See also: Shanghai Tang; Tang dress

Further reading

Roberts, Claire (1997). *Evolution and Revolution: Chinese Dress 1700s–1990s.* Sydney: Powerhouse Publishing, 97–102.

SARAH DAUNCEY

fashion designers – diaspora

The most internationally influential designers of Chinese descent to date have been those that are based in Europe and the USA. Although some have found inspiration in Western culture, many have returned to their Chinese heritage, bringing elements of Chinese design into their collections.

Amy Chan was born in Hong Kong and moved to New York when she was eleven. She studied buying and merchandizing at the Fashion Institute of Technology in New York City, but her interest soon shifted towards design. The first 'Amy Chan' collection was launched in 1994, but her most successful creations have been her bags, in rich textures such as Chinese silk brocade, leather, denim and suede in vivid colours, now sold in her Manhattan shop.

Andrew Gn, born in Singapore, was the first Asian designer to be appointed to a French couture house. Gn first studied at St Martin's College in London and went on to further study at the Parsons School of Design in New York and the Domus Academy in Milan. Gn was named as the ready-to-wear designer at Pierre Balmain in Paris where he concentrates on garments with clean lines and minimal detailing.

Han Feng (b. 1962) first studied painting at the China Academy of Fine Arts in Hangzhou and then moved to New York in 1985. Although she first worked as a Bloomingdale's sales assistant, she moved on to selling pleated scarves, and these have subsequently become her signature item since she began making clothing in 1993.

John Rocha, British Designer of the Year 1993, was born in Hong Kong in 1953 of Chinese-Portuguese parents. Following training at the London College of Fashion, he moved to Dublin, Ireland, having been inspired by Irish fabrics, particularly linens. His interest in Celtic traditions informs his softly tailored designs renowned for their simple lines and minimal decoration.

Anna Sui (b. 1955), a first-generation American from Detroit, studied at the Parsons School of Design in New York. She became a stylist for the fashion photographer Steven Meisel, and set up her own business in 1980. Sui's Soho boutique highlights her multicultural influences – punk rock, hippy, European chic and traditional Chinese style. She is best known for her Chinese-style dresses in contrasting fabrics such as gauze netting and velvet.

Vivienne Tam was born in Guangzhou and raised in Hong Kong. She studied at the Hong Kong Polytechnic University and has designed in London and New York, where she now owns a boutique. Her modern Chinese-themed garments have included stretch T-shirts decorated with Buddha designs, coiled dragons and lotus flowers. Even Mao makes an appearance in various guises. Traditional craftwork is incorporated through delicate embroidery, beading and local Chinese textiles.

Yeohlee Teng was born in Malaysia and went to the US aged eighteen. Another graduate of the Parsons School of Design, she is generally known by her first name. Although she is best known for coats, all her garments, which often come in monochromatic stretch velvet and satin and high-tech fibres, show strong shapes and forms, informed by traditional Chinese techniques rather than Chinese detailing.

SARAH DAUNCEY

fashion designers – Hong Kong

Although Hong Kong has been renowned for its Western-style tailoring since it came under British rule in 1841, it was not until the 1960s that it began to promote itself as an international fashion centre. Since the 1980s, local fashion designers have begun to make their names on the international stage.

Peter Lau (b. 1955), a graduate of textile technology at the Hong Kong Polytechnic, began working for clothing manufacturers in the mid 1970s. His own business was established in 1982; it now offers a label for special occasion wear, 'XCVIII Ninety-Eight', and a label for teenagers, 'China Doll'. Rebellious and anti-establishment, Wan was wary of the return to Chinese rule and this was reflected in his Autumn/Winter 97–8 collection, 'A Winter under the Red Flag', which saw bound and blindfolded models sporting short PRC flag-inspired outfits. Like many others, Lau has attempted to update the cheongsam (see **qipao, cheongsam**) with see-through materials and slits as high as the bustline.

William Tang (b. 1959) studied economics in Canada and fashion design at the London College of Fashion before returning to Hong Kong where he is also a television presenter/journalist. After working for international labels, he established his own company in 1985 offering 'William Tang', 'W by William Tang' and a teenage unisex label, 'W10'. Despite undertaking corporate-image design for Dragon Air and the new Hong Kong airport, he has earned the reputation of *enfant terrible*. He criticized as 'dated' the dress sense of Jiang Zemin's wife and was accused of promoting 'heroin chic' after his models came accessorized with syringes. Aspects of modern culture, such as **consumerism**

and the graffiti of Tsang Tso-choi, make frequent appearances in his designs.

Pacino Wan (b. 1964), a 1987 graduate of Hong Kong Polytechnic University's Swire School of Design, initially worked for local garment manufacturers and exporters before founding She & He Ltd in 1992. Designing under the labels 'Pacino Wan', 'Idees Et Silky' and 'Pacino La Grande Aventure Du Jean', he has become very much associated with women's street fashion. His 1996 show 'Say Goodbye to the Queen' made international headlines as models paraded down the catwalk with images of Queen Elizabeth II and the Queen Mother emblazoned on shift dresses. His humour has also focused on the trend to consumerism with quirky dresses made from instant noodle packages and pink rubber gloves.

There are several other notable up-and-coming designers. Ruby Li, a 1994 graduate of fashion design at the School of Design at Hong Kong Polytechnic, has developed her own line 'Ruby Li' that concentrates on combining unisex street clothing with tailored elegance. Grace Choi, 1995 winner of the Knitwear Group Prize at the Young Designers' Contest, owns a Hong Kong boutique that offers the labels 'Grace Choi' for custom-made and evening wear and 'Garex Ison' for executive-style knitwear and woven garments. Tommy Tsoi established the Kitterick Company Ltd in 1992, which is aimed at fashion-conscious young consumers. Teacher and designer Charmaine Leung has helped to promote the fashionability of the cheongsam among young women by combining this traditional style with street clothing such as trainers.

Further reading

Roberts, Claire (1997). *Evolution and Revolution: Chinese Dress 1700s–1990s*. Sydney: Powerhouse Publishing, 90–5.

SARAH DAUNCEY

fashion designers – Taiwan

Throughout the twentieth century, Taiwanese fashion had been heavily dominated by US and Japanese imports and domestic copies. Two designers, Lu Fong-chih and Wang Chen Tsai-hsieh, began to make an impact following the establishment of their own labels in 1978 and 1982 respectively; however, it was not until the 1990s that young local designers have become more prominent due, in part, to the promotional work of the Taiwan Taipei Fashion Designers' Association.

Carole Chang (Chang Yi-ping) was born in 1969 and studied fashion at the Ecole Bellecour Supemod in Lyon, France, from 1990 to 1992. Soon after her return to Taiwan she established her own label catering for women in their twenties and thirties, which were sold in her boutique, Hot Ice. A typical outfit emphasizes masculine lines through the use of straight-leg trousers and boldly patterned shirts, with female elements added in the form of a short overskirt. Chang has been outspoken in her attempts to combat the over-reliance on Western designer labels and has created garments that have a modern and individual feel.

Stephane Dou Teng-hwang (b. 1969), a 1991 graduate of fashion design and winner of the Taiwan Smirnoff Fashion Award, set up his own label, 'Stephane Dou', in 1996. Like many of his counterparts in Hong Kong and the mainland, Dou has consciously attempted to create garments that are distinctly local but take more modern elements from Western cutting-edge design. In collaboration with his partner Chang Lee Yu-gin and the Ta Ching Hwa Enterprise Company, a Taiwanese textile manufacturer, his collection at the Autumn–Winter 1996–7 Textile Design Show saw striking mix-and-match layered tops and skirts in hot pink, red and orange. Blocks of monochromatic colours are certainly a theme in his designs. More recent collections have ranged from utilitarian-style clothing in contrasting black, grey and white for both men and women, to more fitted feminine styles in peach, blue and burgundy.

Hu Ya-chuan (b. 1965) studied first in Taiwan and then at the Parsons School of Design in New York. Her own label was established in 1993 and this was followed shortly after with the opening of a boutique in the capital. Her collections have included distinctive cropped T-shirts combined with flowing ankle-length dresses in rich velvets, fusing Eastern and Western elements with the aim of attracting both those who buy international designer labels and those who are less fashion conscious.

Tim Yip would not claim to be a fashion designer as most of his work to date has been in the entertainment business dressing film and stage actors and pop stars, such as Wu Pai; however, his clothing designs have become highly influential in Asia. His career began in fashion photography and then he progressed into theatre and film costume design. Yip rocketed to international fame in 2001 with his Oscar-winning designs for the film *Crouching Tiger, Hidden Dragon* (see **Lee, Ang**) and has since made attempts to revitalize indigenous Taiwanese wear in an industry that has been heavily influenced by international fashions.

Further reading

Roberts, C. (1997). *Evolution and Revolution: Chinese Dress 1700s–1990s*. Sydney: Powerhouse Publishing, 95–7.

SARAH DAUNCEY

fashion shows and modelling

The rise of runway fashion modelling as a specialized profession in the West in the 1960s bypassed China. The emergence and development of the profession in the reform era was heralded as one of the signs of China's participation in cosmopolitan world culture.

The first post-Mao fashion show was held in Beijing in 1979 by Pierre Cardin. Fashion shows remained sporadic for the next fifteen years, with the largest ones organized by foreign designers, and only a handful of models nationwide were able to make a full-time profession out of it. Hindering the development of the profession was the dearth of famous Chinese brand-names and designers to hire them to showcase domestic products. Careers tended to last only a few years as the standards changed rapidly, particularly the height standard. Beijing's most influential agency, New Silk Road Models, was founded and held the first Chinese Supermodel Contest in 1991. While 1.70m was considered the minimum height requirement in the early 1980s, by 1995 the Chinese Supermodel

Contest had a minimum of 1.75m, and the average height of the participants was 1.785m. As the selection event for the prestigious Elite Model Look world competition, these biennial contests became a strategy in China's push to produce a 'super-model' of international reputation who would symbolize that 'Oriental beauty' had achieved global recognition. However, this goal remained elusive because of the limited opportunities for models to develop domestically, their tendency to be less educated and with poorer English than their Western rivals, and the general bias in international modelling towards European physiques and features. All of these aspects underwent gradual transformation so that by the turn of the new millennium Chinese models were getting more international exposure, but a Chinese 'supermodel' of global stature had yet to emerge.

Further reading

Brownell, Susan (1998). 'The Body and the Beautiful in Chinese Nationalism: Sportswomen and Fashion Models in the Reform Era'. *China Information* 13.2/3 (Autumn/Winter): 36–58.

—— (2001). 'Making Dream Bodies in Beijing: Athletes, Fashion Models, and Urban Mystique in China'. In Nancy Chen, Constance Clark, Suzanne Gottschang and Lyn Jeffery (eds), *China Urban: Ethnographies of Contemporary Culture*. Durham: Duke University Press.

Lan, C. (2000). *Zhongguo mote qishilu* [The Story of Chinese Models]. Shanghai: Shanghai renmin chubanshe.

SUSAN BROWNELL

fast food (Chinese and Western clones)

In contemporary China, there is a wide array of ready-to-eat food establishments that can be considered fast food: Western chain stores, Chinese imitations serving Western-style foods, Chinese fast-food restaurants serving Chinese foods, and street vendors serving Chinese food. With the cultural challenge of Western fast-food restaurants, there are claims that the origins of the fast-food industry in China can be found thousands of years ago in traditional foods, such as stuffed buns (*baozi*), **dumplings** (*jiaozi*) and fried breads (*youtiao*), and other foods that in the past could be bought on the streets of any market town. There are also roots for the idea of fast-food restaurants in the communal and work-unit canteens of Maoist China or the street vendors of Hong Kong (*dapaidang*). With the Deng era reforms, all sectors of the economy (including agriculture) experienced tremendous growth – resulting in increasing levels of individual consumption and an increased pace of life that promote fast-food consumption. Whatever the origin of the fast-food industry in China, 1984 marked the beginnings of the fast-food craze, with the first Western-style (industrialized production and preparation, self-service) fast-food restaurant, opened in the Xidan district, called the Yili Fast Food Restaurant, selling Western-style foods such as hamburgers, hot dogs and French fries. At the same time, Huaqing Snack Food Restaurant opened across from the Beijing railway station, making Chinese-style fast-food. Both early ventures used restaurant technology imported from abroad (Hong Kong and the United States) and distinguished themselves from other Chinese restaurants by using updated technology in food preparation. One early successful Chinese fast-food chain was California Beef Noodles (started up by a Taiwanese entrepreneur) that served Chinese-style noodle soups. With the arrival of Kentucky Fried Chicken (KFC) in 1987, more defining characteristics were added to the definition of a fast-food restaurant: high hygienic standards and standardization of quality and menus. With the success of fast-food restaurants, even established restaurants such as Quanjude (specializing in **Beijing Roast Duck**) started up fast-food outlets selling meals similar to their *haute cuisine* for mass consumption. In 2002, Chinese fast-food restaurants, especially Hong Kong chains like Café de Coral and Maxims, and Chinese fast-food restaurants serving Western-style foods have expanded out of major metropolitan areas to smaller cities and towns throughout the mainland as consumer spending continues to increase.

See also: fast food (Western); popular culture, mass culture

Further reading

Jing, Jun (ed.) (2000). *Feeding China's Little Emperors: Food, Children, and Social Change*. Stanford: Stanford University Press.

Watson, James L. (ed.) (1997). *Golden Arches East: McDonald's in East Asia*. Stanford: Stanford University Press.

ERIBERTO P. LOZADA JR

fast food (Western)

Although Western fast-food restaurants did not open in China until the late 1980s, their explosive growth during the 1990s has become a symbol of the rapidly changing Chinese popular culture and the explosive growth of the Chinese economy resulting from Deng Xiaoping's 'reform and opening' (*gaige kaifang*) policies. Kentucky Fried Chicken (KFC) was one of the first Western fast-food companies to open a restaurant in China in 1987, and with its success, many others followed suit, including McDonald's, Pizza Hut, Brownies (Canadian), Café de Coral (Hong Kong), Vie de France (Japan), Yoshinoya (Japan). The first American hamburger company to open fast-food restaurants in China was actually not McDonald's, Burger King or Wendy's, but Alfreds International Inc.'s Fast Lane Burger in 1990; McDonald's followed shortly with the opening of its first Chinese restaurant in Shenzhen in 1990. KFC is by far the most successful of Western fast-food restaurants in China: in 2002, there were over 600 KFC restaurants in China, compared to over 400 McDonald's, and according to an A. C. Nielsen survey released in 2001, KFC was the most popular international brand name (Coca-Cola was fourth, McDonald's was fifth). Western fast-food restaurants have been very successful in China for a number of factors: the increased amount of family income spent on children by families (including youth spending money), its symbolic representation of modernity and the United States, concerns over food safety and the high, standardized quality of food and the

restaurant environment, and its relative prestige and novelty compared to other food options (although this factor is gradually waning).

See also: fast food (Chinese and Western clones); popular culture, mass culture

Further reading

Watson, James L. (ed.) (1997). *Golden Arches East: McDonald's in East Asia*. Stanford: Stanford University Press.

Lozada, Eriberto P. (2000). 'Globalized Childhood? Kentucky Fried Chicken in Beijing'. In Jun Jing, (ed.), *Feeding China's Little Emperors: Food, Children, and Social Change*. Stanford: Stanford University Press, 114–34.

ERIBERTO P. LOZADA JR

Fei Dawei

b. 1954, Shanghai

Art critic, curator

Paris-based art critic and curator Fei Dawei is a veteran of the field who participated in the organization of many seminal events in the historical narrative of contemporary Chinese art. An art history graduate from the **Central Academy of Fine Arts** in Beijing (1985) (see **art academies**), he belongs to the first generation of art critics formed at the end of the Cultural Revolution and replacing the old generation of art historians and critics with a strong ideological formation. He participated in the organization of the February 1989 **China Avant-Garde** exhibition in the **China Art Gallery** in Beijing and was involved in one of the first participation of contemporary Chinese artists in a high-profile international exhibition 'Magiciens de la terre' at the Centre Georges Pompidou in Paris, also in 1989. His show 'Chine demain pour hier' (Pourrières, 1990) regrouped six Chinese artists recently relocated to the West and was the first event of such kind in Europe after the Tiananmen events. Numerous exhibitions followed, like 'Exceptional Passage' (Fukuoka, 1991), 'Asiana' (Venice Biennale, 1995) and 'In Between Limits' (Sonje Museum of Contemporary Art, 1997). He received the title of Chevalier des Arts et des Lettres from the French Ministry of Culture and has been artistic director of the Foundation Ullens since 2003. His publications include *Cai Guoqiang* (Fondation Cartier/ Thames and Hudson, 2001) and 'When We Look . . . ' (*Another Long March. Chinese Conceptual Art*, Breda: Foundament, 1997).

Further reading

Fei, Dawei (1989). 'China/Avant-Garde' (interviewed by Meng Mei). *Art Press* 141 (November): 8, 28–34.

—— (1997/8). 'An Aspect of Contemporary Chinese Art: In Between Limits' (comments on the exhibition). Available at http://www.shanghart.com/sh-texts02.htm

Qian, Zhijian (2000). 'The Changing Role of Critics in the 1990s'. In John Clark (ed.), *Chinese Art at the End of the Millennium*. Hong Kong: New Media, 25–8.

MARTINA KÖPPEL-YANG

feminism

Feminism in China has been intricately intertwined with both philosophy and political ideology. As early as the Zhou dynasty, men and women were associated respectively with notions of yang and yin in a philosophy that organized the world into polarized yet related entities. Confucianism promoted and legitimized patriarchal thought, which has remained dominant to the present day. Apart from isolated cases of great achievement, such as those by the heroine Fa Mu Lan (or Hua Mu Lan) depicted in a poem during the Northern dynasties (AD 420–589) and a spate of women poets in the sixteenth and seventeenth centuries, Chinese women have been constrained to the domestic sphere by rigid notions of virtue such as **good wife and mother** (*xianqi liangmu*). In Modern China – the period since 1842 – political change and new ideologies precipitated early forms of feminism. The Taiping Rebellion in the mid-nineteenth century and the collapse of the Qing dynasty in the early twentieth century, for example, both motivated discourses on gender equality, especially as a critique of the 'old (feudal) society'.

During the Maoist period (1949–76), the state went to great lengths to counter Confucian-based social and gender ideologies. It considered both proletarians and women as the oppressed under capitalism and thus championed them and their contributions to production. Mao's famous statement that 'women carry half of the heavens on their shoulders' summarizes a Marxist version of feminism and the socialist state's approach towards gender equality. The CCP sought in particular equality in labour force participation and encouraged women to work just like men. The term 'iron girls' was coined to describe strong, robust women capable of performing jobs commonly done by men, such as tractor drivers. The sameness, rather than difference, between men and women was emphasized. In fact, 'feminism' – a label connoting Western influence – was declared bourgeois; and feminist perspectives that address gender differences and identities were shunned. The **All-China Women's Federation**, for example, was the only national forum for women but it lacked autonomy and was largely an instrument for CCP's supervision of local women's associations. During the **Cultural Revolution** (1966–76), class struggle was re-emphasized as the key to resolving all social problems and in that context gender as a significant social category was rejected. Magazines such as *Women of China* were attacked and the Women's Federation was disbanded. It was not until the late 1970s that the Women's Federation was reconstituted at the national level. Thus, many Western feminist writers argue that class, rather than gender, was the Maoist state's main concern.

The Maoist version of gender equality did not change the fundamental ideology of patriarchy. Opportunities for the labour market, higher education, Party membership and administrative jobs continued to be biased towards men. While the state denied gender division of labour on the ideological level, women's responsibility for the home continued unquestioned and such work was uncompensated and devalued. Motherhood and childcare were largely ignored in political and public discourses.

Two parallel but seemingly opposing trends characterize the post-Mao period. First, increased numbers of Chinese women have begun to create their own ideas about feminine identity and a collective awareness of feminist perspectives has gradually come into being. Concerns over mistreatment of women and other gender issues have gained visibility in public discourse. Increasingly, Chinese intellectuals have accessed Western works and some have been influenced by Western feminist perspectives. Scholars at the Institute of Sociology of the **Chinese Academy of Social Sciences**, for example, have published many papers and books on **gender roles** and relations. The term 'gender' does not have a direct equivalent in the Chinese language, and among Chinese scholars it is commonly translated as 'social sex' (*shehui xingbei*), which emphasizes the social contexts in which gender identity is constructed. In terms of legislation, the enacting of the Marriage Law in 1981 and its recent revisions in 2001 expanded further the rights of women in relation to marriage, divorce and property (see **Marriage Law of the PRC (1 January 1981) and revisions (2001)**). In 1995, the United Nations Fourth World Conference on Women was held in Beijing, highlighting China's potential in improving women's status.

Despite the above changes, patriarchal ideology continues to be prevalent. The gender gaps in educational and occupational attainment remain large. The state has retreated from an explicit gender agenda and taken on a developmentalist role (see **two studies, two competitions**; **women's quality**; **women's work**). By doing so, it emphasizes policies for productivist goals, including those endorsing gendered practices that disadvantage women, rather than policies focusing on women's interests. The economic reforms that promote market forces have legitimized discriminatory practices in the labour market, such as sexist hiring policies, higher rates of layoffs for women workers, and earlier retirement age for women. The **one-child policy** legitimizes the state's surveillance of women's bodies, invades their privacy and penalizes fertility. The social vulnerability of mothers and daughters, the deterioration in the treatment of women, and the traditional preference for sons are further reinforced as most parents, especially those in urban areas, have only one chance to produce a son. Distorted sex ratios and systematic evidence of excessive deaths of girls depict escalation of female infanticide, especially in rural areas. In addition, the Household Responsibility System signifies changes in power dynamics in rural households. Rather than being part of a commune, women are now likely subordinate to men in the household as the husbands take on the role of the household head when negotiating with village authorities. Relaxation of migration restrictions (see **migration and settlement patterns**) has made it possible for peasants to work in cities, but married rural women are largely bound to the village, thus reinforcing the feminization of agriculture. The age-old inside–outside dichotomy and the notion that women belong to the domestic sphere have once again gained popularity. The 'iron girls', for example, have become a subject of merciless mockery; while *nüqiangren* – literally strong women and referring specifically to capable and/or professional women (see **nüqiangren, chiruanfan**) – are socially discouraged.

See also: women's studies

Further reading

Barlow, Tani (ed.) (1993). *Gender Politics in Modern China: Writing and Feminism*. Durham: Duke University Press.

—— (1997). 'Women at the Close of the Maoist Era in the Polemics of Li Xianjing and Her Associates'. In Lisa Lowe and David Lloyd (eds), *The Politics of Culture in the Shadow of Capital*. Durham: Duke University Press.

Gilmartin, Christina, Hershatter, Gail, Rofel, Lisa and White, Tyrene (eds) (1994). *Engendering China: Women, Culture, and the State*. Cambridge: Harvard University Press. [Part IV 'Becoming a Woman in the Post-Mao Era': Li, Ziyun, 'Women's Consciousness and Women's Writing'; Tani Barlow, 'Politics and Protocols of *Funü*: (Un)Making National Woman'; and Li, Xiaojiang, 'Economic Reform and the Awakening of Chinese Women's Collective Consciousness'.]

Liu, Lydia (1993). 'Invention and Intervention: The Making of a Female Tradition in Modern Chinese Literature'. In Ellen Widmer and David Der-Wei Wang (eds), *From May Fourth to June Fourth: Fiction and Film in Twentieth Century China*. Cambridge: Harvard University Press, 194–220.

C. CINDY FAN

Feng Boyi

b. 1961, Beijing

Art curator, critic

After his graduation in 1984 from the Department of History at Beijing Teachers' College (now Capital Normal University), Feng Boyi was assigned to work as an editor of *The Artists' Bulletin*, an internal publication sponsored by China Artists' Association, a government-controlled organization based in Beijing. In the early 1990s, Feng studied at the Art History Department of the **Central Academy of Fine Arts**, where he became involved in contemporary Chinese art. He was the editor of *The Black Book* (1994) and *The White Book* (1995), the first privately sponsored publication in China about contemporary art, published by **Ai Weiwei**. In 1996, he was one of the five organizers of 'Reality: Present and Future', the first show of contemporary art ever associated with the auction market (see **auctions (art and antiquities)**). His first independent curatorial work was 'Traces of Existence: A Private Show of Contemporary Chinese Art' (1998), where local Beijing artists **Wang Jianwei**, **Song Dong**, **Gu Dexin** and others, and returned artists from overseas, such as **Wang Gongxin**, **Lin Tianmiao** and Cai Qing, had their first chance to exhibit in a semi-public space. In 2000 during the Second Shanghai Biennial, Feng Boyi co-organized the controversial show 'Fuck Off', which was ordered to close the day after its opening because of the presence of the photographic works of real baby corpses by Zhu Yu, Sun Yuan and Peng Yu. Feng was also one of the organizers of the Guangzhou Triennial (2002) in Guangzhou.

Feng has published widely on contemporary Chinese art. He tends to showcase what he believes to be natural and truthful in the artist's presentation of issues related to existence, cultural power, fashion, postmodernism within the context of contemporary Chinese culture.

See also: 798

Further reading

(1998). *Traces of Existence* (exhibition catalogue). Beijing: n.p.

QIAN ZHIJIAN

Feng Jiali

b. 1963, Chongqing

Painter

Feng Jiali obtained her BFA in oil painting at the Sichuan Art Institute (1990) and a MFA from the Department of Oil Painting of the **Central Academy of Fine Arts** in Beijing (1993) (and see **art academies**). Her paintings are deliberate constructions of feminine excess and often display a 'silly' girlish atmosphere dominated by the colour pink. In her *Girl's Room Series*, begun in 1995, partially undressed girls are heavily made-up with pink foundation, creating the effect of a mask, and lie idly on beds and sofas covered with overly decorative motifs. A sensibility for textiles and their feminine connotations recurs often in Feng Jiali's paintings, where tactility is played out in the recurrent concern with patterning and textile designs. In *Colourful Quilt with Golden Pheasant* (1997), Feng paints a defiant contemporary girl reclining in the classic male-artist-arranged modelling position, her legs apart and her panties clearly on view. Yet the bold look and the conscious acceptance of the condition of intimacy in which she is represented transform the usual pin-up into an empowering description of contemporary feminine *ennui*. These girls, firmly situated in an explicitly feminine space, appear consciously detached from the active and productive roles assigned to them by society. And by excessive highlighting of the character normally associated with the idea of female spiritual 'lightness', Feng Jiali ironically mocks general stereotypes and transforms them into an occasion for self-empowerment.

She has taken part in numerous exhibitions, such as a solo exhibition at the Courtyard Gallery, Beijing (1999), 'Century-Woman' in Beijing (1998) and 'Die Hälfte des Himmels' (Half of the Sky) also in 1998 at the Frauenmusuem in Bonn, Germany.

Further reading

(1998). *Feng Jiali/The Pedigree of Painted Faces (Fen-mian puxi)*. Hong Kong: Xinshiji chubanshi.

Dal Lago, Francesca (1999) 'A Silent Revolution? Century – Woman, China Art Gallery, Beijing'. *ART AsiaPacific* 22 (January) [exhibition review].

Werner, Chris, Qiu Ping and Pitzen, Marianne (eds) (1998). *Die Hälfte des Himmels – Chinesische Künstlerinnen*. Bonn: Verlag Frauen Museum.

FRANCESCA DAL LAGO

Feng Jicai

b. 1942, Tianjin

Writer

Although born in Tianjin, Feng Jicai considers Cixi, Zhejiang, to be his 'old home' (*laojia*). Along with his wealthy parents he was singled out for abuse during the Great Proletarian **Cultural Revolution**. This decade-long event (1966–76) that Ba Jin once characterized as 'China's Holocaust' registered effects upon Feng that have endured and shaped his work as novelist, painter, screenwriter, literary critic, editor and cultural preservationist. He and his writing are synonymous with Tianjin, a port city whose complex history of colonialism, imperialist aggression and revolutionary resistance is displayed in its eclectic architecture.

He is the author of more than forty works: essays, novels, short stories, prose pieces (*sanwen*) – such as the 'Carriers of Taishan' (1983), which has been standard reading for grade school children for nearly twenty years – documentary literature and literary criticism. Feng is best known for his literary production of the 1980s and early 1990s, that

shortlived interval of 'enlightenment' (*qimeng*) and root-searching (*xungen*; see **Root-seeking school**) literature when Chinese writers encountered Modernism (*xiandai zhuyi*), and when narrative and the marvellous returned to acceptance.

Feng's earliest published work was a two-volume experiment in historical fiction on the early twentieth-century rebellion of the Righteous and Harmonious Fists (*Yihe quan*, i.e. Boxers) co-written with Li Dingxing in 1977. By 1979 this work had brought him to public attention in the early literary waves of **Scar literature** (*shanghen wenxue*) from the Cultural Revolution. The absurdist, xenophobic but anti-dynastic heroism of the Boxers and their tragic slaughter at the hands of the British and American occupying forces in Beijing offered Feng a canvas especially well suited to the complex critique of culture and politics. This critique was continued in his subsequent work, most notably *The Three-Inch Golden Lotus* (*Sancun jinlian*), a tale of footbinding situated in the final decades of Qing era Tianjin, but focused on the barbarism of celebrating self-mutilation as art. The tale unfolds across three generations of bound-footed women, their binders and their admirers.

The Three-Inch Golden Lotus, a novella, constituted one part of a trilogy titled *Curious Tales of a Strange World* that brought Feng considerable notoriety in China and beyond. Published in 1986 on the heels of the Anti-Spiritual Pollution Campaign (*Fandong jingshen wuran yundong*), the novella confuted socialist realism, restored narrative for narrative's sake, and urged readers to consider how the aesthetic of violence normalized in the Cultural Revolution made them complicit in their own destruction. The subject of footbinding is a keenly sensitive one in China's cultural memory, and is, according to Feng, 'a symbol of Chinese culture's corruption and bad tradition [that] lets people believe that the ugly is beautiful and man-made abnormal things should seem beautiful' (Barmé and Jaivin 1991: n.p.). *The Three-Inch Golden Lotus* is a fiercely clever and intensely political work that managed to elude censors because of the imagined quality of its history, emphasizing throughout the wholly fictitious quality of the tales: 'If you're looking for lies, then all becomes lies; If you're looking for truth, then all becomes truth; But when you're really into the story, you can't tell the difference between the two' (Feng Jicai 1994: 3). He seized upon this problematic and artistically productive gap between true and false to paint a national canvas of the efficacy of deceit.

As a political allegory there could be no better metaphor for the distortion of self-imposed constraint and the wider coercion of social mandate than the binding and unbinding of women's feet, which in Feng's hands served as microcosm for the viciousness and savagery paired with high art of the revolutionary cultural politics of 1960s China. Here, the many perverse details of human tragedy became the stuff of connoisseurship. The singular interweaving of the fabulous and factional recalled the *zhiguai* and *chuanqi* literature of Qing writers like Pu Songling (1640–1715), and offered through this resemblance the revolutionary promise of old-time storytelling resurrected in the first decade following the rejection of socialist realism. Feng forged history, sociology, cultural psychology and allegory into a narrative of dissent, thereby creating ground for the self-constitution of the meaningful against the canons of a national fiction.

By 1988, when the 'culture fever' of the mid 1980s gave way to heated debates over pseudo-modernism (*wei xiandai pai*), Feng departed momentarily from fiction writing to take up an experiment in what he termed **journalistic literature** (*jishi wenxue*), recording the many tortured tales of the lives of Chinese during the Cultural Revolution and serially published in the journal *Shiyue* (*October*), in 1991. This work, *The Decade of One Hundred People or Ten Years of Madness* (*Yibai geren de shinian*), is better understood as an ongoing project, the first twenty-four published accounts of which were culled from years of conversation engendered by Feng's solicitation by newspaper announcement of personal accounts of the Cultural Revolution. The consequent incomplete literary record offers numerous vignettes of revenge, violence, victimization, cruelty, each of which is followed, in the manner of Pu Songling, by a single epistrophe, such as: 'The worshipped destroy the worshippers by killing their souls', or 'In dehumanizing times, the highest expression of human nature is destroying oneself'. To date, there is no proper account of this era, but Feng's searing, honest record of wanton human destructiveness and its ongoing consequences is, like the Holocaust, destined to be forgotten if not actively remembered.

In recent years Feng has returned to painting watercolours of city (*Feng Jicai hua Tianjin*) and countryside, and has received the numerous honours befitting an accomplished writer, including election as Chairman of the Chinese Novel Study Society in 2001 (replacing **Wang Meng**). He serves as the president of the city's Municipal Federation of Literary and Art Circles and was honoured by Tianjin University with its establishment of the Feng Jicai Literature and Art Institute (Feng Jicai wenyi xueyuan). The last decade has been one of preservationist activism as Feng has undertaken the defence of the aesthetic and cultural integrity of his native city against the ravages of the bulldozers of development. His local success in this respect has led to a wider national initiative. In 2002 he formed a Chinese People's Artist Federation, calling for a national symposium on the protection of Chinese cultural heritage in folklore and folk art. This work is ongoing and expanding on a national scale so that the traditional cultural heritage of China's many peoples may be documented before it is extinguished.

Bibliography

Barmé, Geremie and Jaivin, Linda (eds) (1991). *New Ghosts, Old Dreams*. New York: Farrar, Strauss and Giroux.

Feng, Jicai (1985). *Chrysanthemums and Other Stories*. New York: Harcourt Brace and Company.

—— (1987). *The Miraculous Pigtail*. San Francisco: China Books and Periodicals.

—— (1991). *Paoda shuangdeng*. Beijing: Huayi chubanshe.

—— (1991). *Voices from the Whirlwind: An Oral History of the Chinese Cultural Revolution*. New York: Pantheon Books.

—— (1994). *The Three-Inch Golden Lotus*. Trans. David Wakefield. Honolulu: University of Hawai'i Press.

—— (1996). *Let One Hundred Flowers Bloom*. New York: Penguin Books.

—— (1996). *Ten Years of Madness: Oral Histories of China's Cultural Revolution*. San Francisco: China Books and Periodicals.

—— (1998). *Zhonghua sanwen zhen cang ben*. Beijing: Renmin wenxue.

Further reading

Braester, Yomi and Zhang, Enhua (2002). 'The Future of China's Memories: An Interview with Feng Jicai'. *Journal of Modern Literature in Chinese* 5.2: 131–48.

Gaenssbauer, Monika (2002). 'The Cultural Revolution in Feng Jicai's Fiction'. In Woei Lian Chong (ed.), *China's Great Proletarian Cultural Revolution: Master Narratives and Post-Mao Counter-narratives*. Lanham, MD: Rowman and Little-field, 319–44.

Wang, David (1988). 'Tai Hou-ying, Feng Chi-Ts'ai and Ah Cheng: Three Approaches to the Historical Novel'. *Asian Culture Quarterly* 16.2: 70–88.

LIONEL M. JENSEN

Feng Mengbo

b. 1966, Beijing

Painter, video artist

After graduating from the Design Department of the Beijing School of Arts and Crafts in 1985 and from the Printmaking Department of the Central Academy of Fine Arts in Beijing (1991), Feng became a prominent proponent of post-Maoist art and earned his reputation by subverting revolutionary icons. While still a student, Feng produced a series of three paintings entitled *Taxi! Taxi! – Mao Zedong (Lao Mao dadi)*, which showed the Chairman making a typical gesture of waving his hand, only instead of facing the Red Guards at Tiananmen Square he is hailing a cab. In 1994 Feng produced *Game Over: Long March*, a video game which features as the animated fighters Red Guards armed with Coca-Cola cans. In 1997, Feng created an interactive CD-ROM-based artwork entitled *Taking Mount Doom by Strategy*, based on the video game *Doom* and populated with figures from the Cultural Revolution model opera *Taking Tiger Mountain by Strategy*. Feng's recent works include the film *Q3* (1999), based on the video game *Quake III*

Arena, in which Feng plays a CNN reporter who joins a clone rebellion, and the installation *Q4* (2001), based on the same game. In these works Feng has moved beyond recycling Maoist images and associated himself with international video art, yet his art may be said to indirectly address China's postsocialist condition.

Further reading

Dal Lago, Francesca (2000). 'The Fiction of Everyday Life: Video Art in the PRC'. *ART AsiaPacific* 27: 53–7.

YOMI BRAESTER

Feng Xiaogang

b. 1959, Beijing

Film and television director/writer

Feng Xiaogang is presently the most successful commercial filmmaker in China. His comedies generate impressive profits at the box office. Feng learned filmmaking not through film school but in the production side of television. His early television series, such as **Stories from an Editorial Office** (1991) and **Beijingers in New York** (1992), won popular acclaim: the former as a social-political satire and the latter as a look at immigrant experience in the United States. After these directorial debuts, Feng attempted further social commentary in *Chicken Feathers on the Ground* (1994) and *The Dark Side of the Moon* (1997). Unfortunately, these television shows and other scheduled projects were either censored or banned.

Caught between official censorship and commercial necessity, after 1997 Feng turned his camera from social critique to urban comedies that found favour with city dwellers. These films focus on ordinary characters with extraordinary desires; comic structure or black humour drives the narratives. For instance, *Party A, Party B* (*Jiafang yifang*, 1997) shows how a three business partners create a variety of situations in which viewers can identify their own fantasies of pleasure and success. *Be There or Be Square* (*Bujian busan*, 1998) presents two Beijing natives pursuing their dream of America in

Los Angeles. *Sigh* (*Yisheng tanxi*, 2000), a tragic comedy that deals with an extramarital affair, exposes sexual relationships in contemporary urban China.

Feng's desire to make films that will be popular in both China and foreign markets led to his transnational project, *Big Shot's Funeral* (*Dawan'r*, 2002). A satirical comedy backed by Columbia Pictures Film Production Asia and featuring Chinese screen-star Ge You along with American actor Donald Sutherland, the film attempted to cross cultural and language barriers, but with questionable success.

See also: Shi Kang

Further reading

Keane, Michael (2001). 'By the Way, FUCK YOU! Feng Xiaogang's Disturbing Television Dramas'. *Continuum* 15.1: 57–66.

Keane, Michael and Tao, Dongfeng (1999). 'Interview with Feng Xiaogang'. *positions: east asia cultures critique* 7.1: 193–200.

Liu, Lydia H. (1999). 'Beijing Sojourners in New York: Postsocialism and the Question of Ideology in Global Media Culture'. *positions: east asia cultures critique* 7.3: 763–96.

Wang, Shujen (2003). 'Big Shot's Funeral: China, Sony, and the WTO'. *Asian Cinema* 14.2 (Fall/Winter): 145–54.

CUI SHUQIN

fengshui

(geomancy)

Fengshui is an ancient art form that deals with the placement of buildings or other structures so as to attain the most auspicious prospect. The present form of fengshui practice was probably started in the first century for the siting of graves (yin-residence) and houses (yang-residence). The fundamental element of fengshui is the live spirit or energy (*qi*/breath) circulating in the physical environment that can be captured and contained for the benefit of the inhabitants of the house, or the descendants of the deceased. Fengshui principles were widely practised by all sectors of the society even after the May Fourth Movement of 1919, when its practice was branded superstitious alongside other folk religions and practices. After 1949, it was regarded as one of the poisonous remnants of the old society and thus prohibited. In the meantime, fengshui practices continued to be widely observed in Hong Kong and Taiwan, fuelled by the economic prosperity of the 1980s. Similarly, with the economic liberalization of China since 1979, fengshui principles have again been applied, particularly in the business community. The academic world began to publish studies of the ancient art of fengshui in 1989, particularly the research of Wang Qiheng of Tianjin University. Scholarly publications by Wang and others attempted to rationalize fengshui practice and exonerate its principles as scientifically and environmentally sensitive.

With the rampant economic growth in the 1990s, business ventures invariably consulted the growing number of fengshui professionals for good fortune that would result from the proper arrangement of office interiors and the design of office or factory buildings, much like their counterparts in Taiwan and Hong Kong. Not only is fengshui practised in business circles and even among the cadres of more remote regions, but fengshui practitioners are constantly consulted by individuals to ensure the incumbent a successful career. The major effect of the return to popularity of fengshui practices can be seen in the proliferation of fengshui literature and self-made fengshui experts. Traditionally, the transmission of fengshui knowledge was through an apprenticeship system. With the forty-year break in fengshui practice between 1949 and 1989, direct transmission was broken and many fengshui practitioners learned the craft by reading old manuscripts. With increasing demand of fortune seekers, these practitioners are often asked to provide a way to alter the living and working environments of the inhabitant in order to ensure either more wealth, examination success, harmonious marital relationships, security in life or good health. Some may approach these practitioners for a brighter future, while others hope to ameliorate immediate difficulties. With experience, some fengshui practitioners go on to write books on fengshui principles together with examples of successful cases.

Some books list simple rules of thumb for fengshui placement, such as the orientation of the front door or furniture, while others start with first principles. With commercial activities increasing all over China, fengshui practitioners and literature will continue to be in great demand, and the proliferation of easy-to-use fengshui guides will allow more individuals to alter their living environment, usually just the furniture, in the hopes of a brighter future.

Further reading

Bruun, Ole (2003). *Fengshui in China: Geomantic Divination between State Orthodoxy and Popular Religion*. Honolulu: University of Hawai'i Press.

HO PUAY-PENG

Fifth Generation (film directors)

The 'Fifth Generation' is a group of directors whose films represent a particularly creative moment in the history of Chinese cinema, roughly spanning the 1980s and early 1990s. Educated after the **Cultural Revolution**, the 'Fifth Generation' includes such directors as **Chen Kaige**, **Huang Jianxin**, **Tian Zhuangzhuang**, **Wu Ziniu** and **Zhang Yimou**. According to George Semsel, the five generations correspond to historical periods: silent films; first sound films during the 1920s and 1930s; films from 1949 through the Cultural Revolution; films after the Cultural Revolution; and the fifth generation, films made by graduates of the **Beijing Film Academy** in the 1980s and 1990s. Another way of defining the different generations focuses on the filmmakers' aims: the first generation, described as May Fourth era filmmakers, were intellectuals concerned with social and cultural reform during the Republican era; the second generation, whose films are categorized as Socialist Realism (inspired by the Soviet Union), combined heroic celebration of the socialist state with condemnation of life in pre-revolutionary China; the third and fourth generations primarily focused on melodrama and produced films consistent with or reinforcing state ideology; and the fifth generation, whose films were made after the Cultural Revolution, continued the May Fourth tradition of social commentary and national critique, albeit from the vantage point of a very different historical moment.

'Fifth Generation' Chinese cinema has won international acclaim for films characterized by realism, powerful social commentary, spectacular visual imagery and high production values. These films reflect on Chinese history and engage in cultural critique. Remarkably, the 'Fifth Generation' films were funded by the state and passed by the state's film censors. By setting their films in the past or including dialogue explicitly endorsing the Communist Party, many of these films avoided political controversy. In Chen Kaige's **Yellow Earth** (*Huang tudi*), the dialogue and visual narrative present contradictory accounts, one praising the Communist Party, the other illustrating how the Party ultimately failed to ameliorate the lives of its converts, and stranded them in a society it was incapable of transforming. In *The Blue Kite* (*Lan fengzheng*), which has been banned in China, Tian Zhuangzhuang recounts life from the perspective of a child whose family is torn apart by continuously devastating political campaigns. Perhaps most daring, *The Black Cannon Incident* (*Heipao shijian*) by Huang Jianxin, the only filmmaker to set his films in the present and the future, satirizes bureaucracy, alienation and hopelessness in China of the 1980s and after. The reputation of these filmmakers has not fared as well in China as it has internationally. Some Chinese critics have accused them of pandering to a Western appetite for exoticism. Their films have had limited distribution in China, and since the violent suppression at Tiananmen Square in 1989, many critics consider this critical genre to be over. In spite of this, the 'Fifth Generation' directors continue to make films that occasionally provide a flicker of the depth achieved earlier.

See also: Hu Mei; Wang Xiao-yen; Zhang Jianya

Further reading

Browne, N., Pickowicz, P., Sobchack, V. and Yau, E. (eds) (1994). *New Chinese Cinemas*. Cambridge: Cambridge University Press.

Chow, Rey (1995). *Primitive Passions*. New York: Columbia University Press.

Huot, Claire (2000). 'Colorful Folk of the Landscape: Fifth Generation Filmmakers and Roots Searchers'. In *idem, China's New Cultural Scene: A Handbook of Changes*. Durham: Duke University, 91–125.

Ni, Zhen (2002). *Memoirs from the Beijing Film Academy: The Genesis of China's Fifth Generation*. Durham: Duke University Press.

Zhu, Ying (2003). *Chinese Cinema During the Era of Reform: The Ingenuity of the System*. New York: Praeger.

EMILY CHAO

film criticism

Since 1979, film criticism in China has developed in two distinct ways. The first began with introduction of Western film theory and methodology which offered alternatives to the Soviet-style socialist realism that had dominated intellectual discourse on film since the 1930s. Bazin's 'realism' and Kracauer's 'redemption of physical reality' helped film circles of the 1980s break through the traditional Chinese concept of film which had been dominated by a combination of dramatic conflict characteristic of Hollywood and Eisenstein's theory and practice of montage. The new concepts promoted the study of film as ontology and inspired a new generation of filmmakers after the **Cultural Revolution**. Later, film criticism broadened its theoretical scope to include the application of literary theory (structuralism, semiotics, psychoanalysis, feminism, neo-Marxism, postmodernism, post-colonialism and the like) to cinematic analysis, and also initiated a process of re-evaluating old films from the perspective of Cultural Studies. The second development in film criticism centred around a series of debates concerning the nature of film in Chinese society from which emerged an emphasis on film as an independent art form, thereby freeing film from its historical bondage to other literary, dramatic and theatrical modes, especially to the **Huaju** (spoken-drama) tradition. Such debates, which also underscored film's entertainment values over its political relevance, helped

create a significant number of exciting new films remarkably different from those made from the 1950s through the 1970s.

The most direct way to take the pulse of contemporary film criticism in China is to read journals on film as well as on literary and cultural studies published in the New Period. Among a number of periodicals on film, two stand out as serious journals of film criticism: *Contemporary Cinema* (*Dangdai dianying*) and *Film Art* (*Dianying yishu*). Besides film journals, there have appeared some collections of articles on film. The most comprehensive one is *A Collection of Chinese Film Theory* (*Zhongguo dianying lilun wenxuan*, Wenhua yishu chubanshe, 1992) edited by Luo Yijun, a two-volume anthology that brings together influential articles from the birth of Chinese film to the 1980s.

See also: Cheng Jihua; Chiao, Peggy; Dai Jinhua; Zhang Nuanxin

Further reading

Hu, Ke (1995). 'Contemporary Film Theory in China'. Trans. Ted Wang, Chris Berry and Chen Mei. *Screening the Past* 3: 65–73.

Li, Daoxin (2002). *Zhongguo dianying piping shi, 1897–2000* [A History of Chinese Film Criticism, 1897–2000]. Beijing: Zhongguo dianying chubanshe.

Semsel, George S., Xia, Hong and Hou, Jianping (eds) (1990). *Chinese Film Theory: A Guide to the New Era*. New York: Praeger.

—— (1993). *Film in Contemporary China: Critical Debates, 1979–1989*. New York: Praeger.

Zhang, Yingjun (2002). *Screening China: Critical Interventions, Cinematic Reconfigurations, and the Transnational Imaginary in Contemporary Chinese Cinema*. Ann Arbor: Center for Chinese Studies, University of Michigan.

DU WENWEI

film distribution

Film distribution in China has undergone significant changes since 1993. Before that year, the China Film Corporation (Zhongguo dianying gongsi) purchased all films produced in China and then distributed them to regional distribution companies. This system created a network in parallel with the administrative divisions of the municipalities and provinces. The state retained a monopoly on the purchase, marketing and allocation of films. Each film had to pass through different hierarchies of distribution companies to get from its producer to movie theatres. Under such a system, profits were not shared equitably among producers, distributors and movie theatres. In 1993, what is now the **State Administration for Radio, Film and Television**, which oversees China's film industry, passed a document known as 'Film Document No. 3' that promoted reform of the existing cinema industry. Film producers have now gained rights over distribution. Companies that combine film production and distribution, such as Beijing Forbidden City Company (Beijing zijincheng gongsi), have been established and are successful. Business ventures have also been made to link cinema chains directly to film producers. Examples include the East Cinema Chain (Dongfang yuanxian) that was created and organized by Shanghai Film Studio. In response, the original state-run distribution companies at different administrative levels in each region have formed single-level corporations in an attempt to continue to control the film distribution within their respective regions. As for profits, film distribution is being conducted in three different ways: profit-sharing distribution, right-purchasing distribution, and single-copy sales.

In the countryside, any company, any film projection team and any individual projectionist is now able to purchase 16 mm copies. Furthermore, each copy can be screened anywhere in the country. Increasing the quantity of distributed films has been promoted by the '2131 Goal' established by the government in 1998. The objective of the initiative is to send films to each and every village in China, with the ultimate goal of screening at least one film per month in every village by the beginning of the twenty-first century.

As for foreign films, the China Film Corporation still has the sole right to distribute them in China. The quantity of foreign films imported is determined by the Regulations for Film Control and Management (*Dianying guanli tiaoli*) which indicate that the screening time allocated by each projection entity for foreign films should not exceed one-third of its total screening time for all films.

Further reading

Wang, Shujen (2003). *Framing Piracy: Globalization and Film Distribution in Greater China*. Lanham, MD: Rowman and Littlefield.

Zhongguo dianying shichang [The Chinese Film Market, a monthly periodical published by the China Film Corporation under the supervision of SARFT].

DU WENWEI

folksongs (Han Chinese)

Over 93 per cent of the people in China belong to the **Han** nationality. Consequently, the Chinese culture generally referred to is the Han Chinese culture. The folksongs discussed here are also of the Han Chinese culture. The Han Chinese culture is broadly divided into two large geographic areas identified by the two major rivers, the Huanghe (Yellow River) in the north, and the Changjiang (Long River, or Yangzi River) in the south. Both rivers run from west to east and their basins are considered to be the cradles of Chinese civilization. The geography and environment along these rivers affect crop production, national habitat, living conditions, customs, language and music. The rugged Yellow River basin is cold, dry and windy. The main agricultural produce is wheat. Life is harsh. The melodies of northern folksongs are usually disjunctive, the vocal timbre tense, and the pitch range high. On the other hand, the Yangzi River basin has mild weather and plentiful rain. The main product is rice. Life is easier. The melodies of southern folksong in general tend to be conjunct and smooth. The vocal timbre is relaxed and the pitch range is lower.

Scholars follow a three-fold classification system for Han Chinese folksongs, namely: *haozi* (work songs), *shange* (mountain songs) and *xiaodiao* (lyric songs):

Haozi (work songs): *Haozi* literally means 'shouting' or 'calling' songs, an indication of its labour origin. The function of this type of songs is to relieve hardship during long hours of working or to coordinate a group of people who are working together. Most of these songs have a strong rhythm, limited melodic material, and frequent repetition of the same phrase (an ostinato pattern). Texts are rather limited. When singing as a group, a leader sings solo while the group answers in the same phrases again and again (call and response pattern).

Shange (mountain songs): The term *shange* (mountain songs) should be understood to mean songs sung in an open field, but not exclusively in a mountainous area. Some work songs with limited physical requirements are included in this category (i.e. herding songs). Mountain songs are freer in rhythm and high in pitch. Texts are improvised and nonsense syllables are abundant. Many mountain songs begin and end with a high and long call that has developed from outdoor shouting and calling. The favourite alternative singing style between two persons is a reflection of its use as a love duet between a man and a woman in the open field.

Xiaodiao (lyric songs): Literally 'little tunes', *xiaodiao* are folksongs in the most common sense. They are most numerous in numbers, and for the most part are for entertainment. Lyric songs' melodies are lyrical, rhythmically static, contain balanced phrases and have a clear form. Their texts are not improvised, and nonsense syllables, if present, are integrated. The most typical formal structure of this type of song is a four equal phrase construction labelled as *qi* (beginning), *cheng* (inheriting), *zhuan* (turning) and *he* (conclusion), terms and ideas borrowed from classical writing. Famous examples of lyric songs in this type of structures are 'Siji Ge' (Song of Four Seasons) and 'Meng Jiang Nu' (The Elder Daughter of the Meng Family), both from Jiangsu, and 'Liuyue Moli' (Jasmine Flowers in the Sixth Moon) from Taiwan. This form can also be clearly demonstrated in Stephen Foster's song: 'Old Folks at Home'.

Further reading

Han, Kuo-Huang (1989). 'Folk Songs of the Han Chinese: Characteristics and Classification'. *Asian Music* 20.2: 107–28.

Miao, Jing and Qiao, Jianzhong (1987). *Lun Hanzu minge jinshi secaique de huafen* [A Study of Similar Colour Area Division in Han Nationality Folk Songs]. Beijing: Wenhua Yishu.

Schimmelpenninck, Antoinet (1997). *Chinese Folk Songs and Folk Singers: Shang'ge Traditions in Southern Jiangsu*. Leiden: Chime Foundation.

Tuohy, Sue (1999). 'The Social Life of Genre: The Dynamics of Folksong in China'. *Asian Music* 30.2: 39–86.

Yang, Mu (1994). 'Academic Ignorance or Political Taboo? Some Issues in China's Study of its Folksong Culture'. *Ethnomusicology* 38.2: 303–20.

HAN KUO-HUANG

Fong, Allen

(né Fong Yuk-ping/Fang Yuping)

b. 1947, Hong Kong

Film and television director, actor

Allen Fong may be the director who has remained the most faithful to the ideals of the 'Hong Kong New Wave' of Western-educated film graduates – such as Ann **Hui**, **Tsui Hark** or **Yim Ho** – who first directed realistic dramas for television in the 1970s before changing the face of Hong Kong cinema.

After studying in the US (1971–5), Fong joined the public television station RTHK where his keen observation of the daily life of ordinary people in Hong Kong produced a series of outstanding works. His first feature film, *Father and Son* (*Fuzi qing*, 1981), was a semi-autobiographic rendering of the generation gap in working-class families torn between tradition and modernity. He then directed a couple of critically acclaimed, semi-improvised films. In *Ah Ying* (*Banbian ren*, 1982), a young fish vendor with dreams of becoming an actress is asked to play herself. In *Just Like Weather* (*Meiguo xin*, 1986), Fong films (and sometimes intervenes in) the 'road trip' of a young couple who try to resolve their problems by emigrating to the USA. *Dancing Bull* (*Wuniu*, 1991) is one of the first Hong Kong films to deal with the trauma of Tiananmen Square. In the 1990s, Fong went back to television, worked in theatre, taught video workshops in mainland China and directed *A Little Life – Opera* (*Yisheng yitaixi*, 1997), a narrative film shot in Fujian province about the loves and lives of an all-women opera troupe. In 2000, he made his first feature-length documentary, *Tibetan Tao* (*Zang Dao*), the unconventional report of a trip to Tibet with a Fujianese family.

BÉRÉNICE REYNAUD

football (soccer)

On 7 October 2001 every Chinese person with access to a TV was glued to the screen to witness the national soccer team beat Oman and clinch a berth in the 2002 World Cup. This historical first for China was hardly diminished by their three losses in Korea, especially for the Chinese supporters who hailed their team as heroes upon their return home. The interest shown by the fans and the massive media coverage are indicative of the popularity achieved by soccer in China.

The Chinese have been playing soccer for decades, but the sport has reached an unprecedented peak of vogue only recently. This spike in popularity has been aided by companies like Nike and Adidas, willing to open new markets in Asia for their products. Suddenly, by the mid 1990s, the faces – and the legs – of the best footballers from Europe and South America were pasted on billboards all over the region and were familiar to most metropolitan Chinese. Cable TV has also helped by broadcasting games from the top leagues in Europe.

As the national team level improved, so did the national league, promptly renamed C-League. The undisputed powerhouse in recent years has been Dalian Shide. Another late achievement for Chinese soccer was the exportation of a few C-leaguers to Europe, with Li Tie and Shun Jihai (both playing in the English Premier League) being the most representative players abroad. Soccer is now eagerly practised in schools, within Chinese companies and in the army. The sport has gained in popularity among girls as well, and the Chinese women's national team performed beyond all

expectations in the 1999 World Cup, only to lose against the US team in a controversial final.

Further reading

Jones, Robin (1999). 'The Emergence of Professional Sport – the Case of Soccer'. In James Riordan and Robin Jones (eds), *Sport and Physical Education in China*. New York: E. and F. N. Spon, 185–201.

CESARE POLENGHI

foreign community

During the Maoist era relatively few foreigners lived in China, and the sight of a foreigner remained a novelty even in the largest cities. Even in the 1980s foreign teachers and students at Chinese universities comprised the largest group of foreigners living in China. With the growth in foreign investment in the 1990s, employees of foreign firms formed a new foreign community centred in the cities of the booming coastal regions. By 2002, 80,000 foreign experts worked in Shanghai, 70 per cent as managers of the nearly 20,000 foreign enterprises in the city. In the same year, 167,000 foreign experts worked in Guangdong province, about 40 per cent of the national total. Increasing numbers of foreigners arrived in China with no employment contracts, competing with Chinese in the local labour market and bringing diversity to the foreign community. The numbers of foreign students continued to grow, mostly non-degree language students, with students from Japan and Korea numerically far in the lead. International schools, residential enclaves and entertainment facilities serviced this growing population. Japanese, Korean and Western expatriates formed largely separate communities with their own distinct educational and leisure facilities. In 2002, Shanghai had more than 300 restaurants run by expatriates. Young Chinese mingled with foreign residents in the cosmopolitan nightlife scenes in Shanghai and Beijing, and international dating and marriages were becoming commonplace, with 3,338 such marriages registered in Shanghai in 2000 (nine out of ten involving local brides and foreign grooms). The Shanghai government, in particular, saw a large foreign community as a requirement of a global metropolis and aimed at increasing the expatriate population to 5 per cent of the total metropolitan population in the near future.

Further reading

(2002). *2002 Statistical Abstracts of Shanghai*. Available at http:/tjj.sh.gov.cn/2002

Rusch, Beate (1997). 'The Shanghai "Zeitgeist Bookstore": A Case Study in the Practice of Intercultural Networking'. In R. D. Findeisen and R. H. Gassmann (eds), *Autumn Floods: Essays in Honour of Marian Galik*. Bern: Peter Lang.

Wagner, Rudolf (1995). 'The Role of the Foreign Community in the Chinese Public Sphere'. *China Quarterly* 142: 423–43.

JAMES FARRER

foreign enclaves (urban)

One effect of economic reforms since the late 1970s has been the re-emergence in many Chinese cities of areas that cater to the needs and desires of foreigners (*waiguoren*). Ranging in size from individual high-rises (e.g. near Jianguomenwai in Beijing) to clusters of gated communities (e.g. in Shanghai's Pudong district), these enclaves reinforce cultural segregation, reflect economic disparities and resurrect spatial, legal and ethnic distinctions that characterized many Chinese cities before 1949. As early as the eighteenth century, foreigners trading with China lived and worked in discrete 'factory' areas assigned to them by imperial authorities. Guangzhou, most notably, set a precedent that continued after 1842 when the Treaty of Nanjing that ended the first Opium War created six treaty ports along the coast between Shanghai and Hong Kong. In the late Qing, as economic activities by foreigners intensified and as a wider constellation of Chinese cities became treaty ports, the number of foreign enclaves, or concession areas (*zujie*), increased.

In contemporary Chinese cities smaller versions of these enclaves resurfaced in the late 1970s in two different guises: either as **hotels**, where foreigners

lived and conducted business with Chinese clients (e.g. Jianguo in Beijing, or White Swan in Guangzhou), or as compounds for 'foreign experts' (*zhuanjialou*) within universities. In the mid 1980s the government permitted more diversified business centres to be erected (e.g. Nanjing's Jinling fandian and Shanghai's Portman Centre), as well as low-rise 'villas', often on the outskirts of cities. These residences appealed not only to foreigners but also to Chinese investors abroad and upwardly mobile Chinese entrepreneurs. In the mid 1990s the central government briefly halted these projects because they had proliferated too rapidly and were thought to run counter to other avowed priorities to provide housing for the masses. However, in the late 1990s, both business centres and gated communities again attracted substantial investment, and they have again appealed to richer, domestic Chinese residents. Foreign enclaves, then, have become one of the measures of China's recent economic liberalization and globalization.

See also: housing; residential districts (urban); salon culture

Further reading

Davis, Deborah S. (ed.) (2000). *The Consumer Revolution in Urban China*. Berkeley: University of California Press.

Logan, John R. (ed.) (2002). *The New Chinese City: Globalization and Market Reform*. London: Blackwell.

JEFFREY W. CODY

foreign language acquisition and teaching

The 'English fever' of the 1980s continues. The international tongue suggests one's success and profit. Japanese is also popular. Xinhua News Agency reported in 2001 that China had over 3,000 foreign language institutions with the annual turnover exceeding 10 billion yuan (US$1.2 billion) or 1 per cent of the GDP. English skills have become a decisive factor related to one's income.

Those proficient in English reap an annual income of US$53,378 on average; it plays a favourable role in evaluating professional titles and promotions. Shanghai International Studies University (Shangwai) and Beijing Foreign Studies University (Beiwai: www.bfsu.edu.cn) are leading institutions with degree programmes in many languages which also accept **foreign students** for Chinese education. Private schools that specialize in **TOEFL and GRE**, IELT, CELPIP and GMAT preparation, are ubiquitous. Li Yang, founder of 'Crazy English', is perhaps China's most unorthodox but profitable English teacher and a pop-cult figure who pushes his audience to shout patriotic slogans in English. Radio and TV foreign language programmes, some of which are hosted by foreigners such as Canadian Mark Rosewell (see **Dashan**), are broadcast daily. The Internet offers another channel. The **translation industry** is booming and **English language dailies, periodicals and books** are numerous. Foreign words such as 'WTO' are common in speaking and writing (see **neologisms**). Since September 2001, children in Beijing have begun their study of English in grade three, while all other primary schools begin in grade four. Thanks to the 2008 **Olympics**, the Beijing municipal government has called on its officials to take a three-month English-language training programme, and taxi drivers and residents are urged to study English, too. Shanghai offers English classes from grade one on. English is even a compulsory subject in many kindergartens in big cities, where 'English corners' for people to speak English with each other are popular spots in major parks and on college campuses.

Further reading

Lii, Haibo (2002). 'The Profitable English Language'. *Beijing Review* 7 (November): 8.

HELEN XIAOYAN WU

Foreign Languages Press

Established on 1 July 1952, the Foreign Languages Press (FLP) is an international comprehensive publishing house editing, translating and publishing foreign-language books for readers abroad and textbooks and readings for readers at home. Under the jurisdiction of the China Foreign Languages Publication and Distribution Administration and abiding by the CCP's line, the FLP functions as the country's unified facility for foreign-language publication.

The broad scope of FLP's publications covers not only science and technology but almost all of the humanities. For half a century, it has published numerous government documents, political theories and works of Communist leaders in forty-three languages. Other achievements include translations of 600 first-class Chinese literary works. With the advent of reform and open-door policies in 1978, the FLP started to eye the foreign readers' market. Besides publishing on traditional topics, the FLP further widened its scope of publication to cover background information about China, traditional Chinese culture, economy, law, history, geography, medical and health care, children's readings and Chinese-language textbooks for foreign students.

While paying closer attention to the growing domestic market, because of China's entry into the WTO and the prospect of its hosting the 2008 **Olympics**, the FLP is opening up more foreign markets, distributing books in over a hundred countries and regions by copyright transfer and cooperative publishing. The practice is dubbed 'making imports drive exports'. FLP has a Chinese-language editorial department and various foreign-language translation departments. It has introduced collaboration between editors and translators to improve quality control and marketability.

HU MINGRONG

foreign students

The education of foreign students, who mostly came from socialist countries in the early years of the PRC, saw a rapid growth in the 1990s. According to the **Ministry of Education**, 350,000 foreign students were studying in China in 2001, which, for the first time, almost equalled the number of Chinese students studying abroad. They now come from all over the world and study in more than 360 universities majoring in some

200 specialties in the humanities, social sciences, natural and medical sciences and engineering and as Chinese language students, undergraduates, master and doctoral students, trainees and scholars of all kinds and participants in various fields of short-term training courses.

In 2001 alone, 52,000 foreign students from 166 countries went to China, of whom 3,500 were studying for more than one year and 2,100 were studying under the Chinese Government scholarships. Foreign students studying in Shanghai alone exceeded 6,300 in 2001, five times more than in the 1980s. This was the first time that the number of foreign students exceeded the number of Shanghai students going abroad. Foreign students can apply to study in China through exchanges between governments and universities, and by individual application. A certain level of **HSK** (Chinese Proficiency Test) is necessary in order to study subjects other than Chinese language. Top universities for foreign students are: Beijing Language and Culture University, **Peking University**, Fudan University, East China Normal University, Nankai University, Shanghai Normal University and **Qinghua University**. Some secondary and primary schools also admit foreign students. In November 2002, a group of universities held an unprecedented and highly successful overseas education exhibition to recruit German students to study in China. More such exhibitions are planned for the future.

Websites

www.cernet.edu.cn
www.csc.edu.cn
www.cscse.edu.cn

HELEN XIAOYAN WU

Fourth Generation (composers)

In many ways, the 'Fourth Generation' of Chinese composers is everything the 'Third Generation' – the so-called 'New Wave' (*Xinchao*) generation – was not. Although the 'New Wave' composers are considered part of a 'lost generation', whose education was postponed during the **Cultural Revolution** (1966–76), as composers, in fact, they were privileged. Not only did the 'New Wave' generation study at a time of pluralism, in the early 1980s, when economic and commercial concerns had yet to override everything else, but already, during their conservatory years, these composers were able to stage performances of their own works and to learn about developments in contemporary music largely ignored in previous decades. Most, in fact, had participated in propaganda music troupes during the Cultural Revolution and so had the opportunity to practise their skills at orchestration and composition even before entering university. They also had the opportunity to learn from China's popular musical traditions by being immersed in the countryside as 'sent-down youth' (see **xiafang, xiaxiang**).

The next, fourth generation of composers trained at the conservatories in the 1990s includes Zhou Xianglin (b. 1963), Yu Qiang (b. 1964) and Ding Ying (b.1969) in Shanghai, and Xiang Min (b. 1967), Hao Weiya (b. 1971) and Cao Jian (b. 1973) in Beijing. Their music reflects very different experiences from those of the 'New Wave' generation and often returns to some of the more conservative styles that had been evident before the latter. Xiang Min, for example, a student of Du Mingxin at the Central Conservatory in Beijing, is convinced that since audiences everywhere cannot understand **New Music** and since performers are also unwilling to play such music, it is preferable to compose in more conventional styles. The concern with audience response, typical of this generation, is at least partly economically minded. New Music alone simply does not pay the bills. Hence, many of these composers also write pop music (like Hao Weiya, Ding Ying and Zhou Xianglin) or take to scandalizing, experimental forms of music to attract fascinated crowds (like Yu Qiang).

Another distinct feature of this generation is an evident lack of interest in, and passion for, China's own tradition (with remarkable exceptions, such as Cao Jian). This sets their music apart both from that of the New Wave composers with their interest in the odd, the spooky and spectacular sounds from China's musical tradition as well as from older generations of composers with their love for **pentatonic romanticism**. To some of these composers the emphasis on **national style** (*minzuxing*) in Chinese music is considered entirely political and they are not interested in politics. Accordingly, like many of this generation, Hao Weiya, for example, made the required field trips to collect folk-material during his conservatory years, but his music does not reflect these experiences.

Further reading

Mittler, B. (1997). *Dangerous Tunes. The Politics of Chinese Music in Hong Kong, Taiwan and the People's Republic of China since 1949.* Wiesbaden: Harrassowitz.

Yu, Q. (1993). 'A New Generation'. *Chime* 6: 139. http://www.sinologic.com/newmusic/

BARBARA MITTLER

4 June [1989] esprit

(liusi qingjie)

Around early morning of 4 June 1989, the Chinese military fought their way into Tiananmen Square and repressed the seven-week-long 1989 Pro-democracy Movement. The repression resulted in hundreds of deaths, and many student activists and intellectuals fled abroad. The phrase '4 June esprit' (*liusi qingjie*) has been used ever since to refer to certain psychologies and activities derived from the repression. First, the repression antagonized the overseas Chinese communities. Each year on 4 June, overseas and Hong Kong Chinese hold protests, vigils and concerts that oppose the military repression and memorialize the dead. Second, the repression created an exile community with a common identity (the exited movement leaders, for example, call themselves the 'Tiananmen Square generation'). They continuously condemn the repression and demand rehabilitation, and strive to make the movement presently relevant. Third, the repression changed the image of the Chinese government in the West. Each year on 4 June, major media outlets in the West carry articles that discuss 4 June-related issues. Finally, the Chinese government has treated 4 June as a day of taboo since 1989. Each year around 4 June, the government carefully monitors the major university campuses and Tiananmen Square to prevent any commemorative activities from happening. At the repression's tenth anniversary, the government even sealed off Tiananmen Square and started a reno-vation project.

The magnitude of the '4 June esprit', however, has experienced a decline. In overseas and Hong Kong Chinese communities, commemorative activities continue, but fewer people are partici-pating. On China's university campuses, com-memorative activities have ceased in recent years. As China's economic reform further deepens, new concerns and identities have emerged.

ZHAO DINGXIN

funerals

With the cultural importance of the ancestors and geomancy (**fengshui**) – perhaps the defining characteristic of Chinese culture – funerals are a key component of Chinese rituals. Funerals are highly charged emotional events that delineate kinship and community relations, part of the cul-tural transformation of deceased people into ancestors. For **Han** Chinese (ethnic minority groups have a wide variety of funeral practices), there are two phases to Chinese funerals: what James L. Watson refers to as 'funerary rites' and 'rites of disposal'.

'Funerary rites' are the ritual practices that extend from the death of an individual to the body's removal from the community. There are ten distinct practices that structure the funerary rites: (1) the announcement of the death to the community, as in the ritual wailing of women; (2) the wearing of mourning clothes and other symbols of mourning worn; (3) the ritualized pre-paration of the corpse for burial, as in the 'pur-chasing of water' (*maishui*) to cleanse the body; (4) the transfer of goods to the deceased, as in the burning of paper objects or food offerings; (5) the preparation of a written memorial, such as the soul tablet; (6) the use of money in ritualized contexts; (7) the performance of music to mark transitions in the rites; (8) the sealing of the corpse in the coffin; (9) the transfer of the coffin out of the community, as in the funeral procession; and (10) the funerary banquet. Chinese funerary rites, however, reflect a diversity of beliefs and include localized or idiosyncratic practices within this structure. For example, families may organize a Catholic service, or employ Buddhist monks or **Daoist priests** (*Daoshi*) as part of the transition between events, and use a wide variety of sacrificial offerings.

'Rites of disposal', the second phase of funerary ritual, include a wide array of ritual practices. Cremation, the method preferred by the PRC government, is common in urban areas throughout China (see **tombs and cremation**). In south China, secondary burial is the traditional style. In secondary burial (*ercizang*), the deceased is first buried in a temporary grave. After three or four years, depending upon soil conditions, families exhume the body, clean the remaining flesh from the bones, and place them in a large urn inside the ancestor's final tomb. If they can afford it, descendants of the deceased build a permanent cement tomb to house their ancestor's remains.

Chinese funerals are a key social and political topic, and not only a familial or individual concern. James Watson has argued that a shared cultural emphasis on orthopraxy in funerary rites provides the base upon which Han Chinese identity is constructed. Orthopraxy is the 'proper performance of rites'. The proper conduct of funerary ritual as described above distinguishes Han Chinese from non-Han minority groups in China, and from other foreigners. In historical times, the Chinese elite and the imperial state sought to regulate and standardize the proper practice of funerary ritual, while largely disregarding the realm of belief. In contemporary China, the Communist state continues to intervene in funeral practices, seeking to reduce the cost and effort that families expend on such practices. Funerals are important on the cultural level because they are the first step in the transformation of a deceased person into an ancestor; if performed incorrectly, the individual might become a ghost, making life difficult for the descendants. Permanent tombs and continued veneration of the ancestors are important because of geomancy, whereby houses in the countryside are structured in relation to the placement of tombs and other geomantic considerations. In Chinese culture, good geomantic conditions result in good fortune for families, while bad geomancy results in misfortune. As a result,

funerals are public demonstrations of wealth, status and power by families, lineage segments and lineages. Tombs are maintained throughout the year, but especially during the **Qingming Festival**, when whole lineages gather together in a sign of strength to worship common ancestors. Once the most common ancestor has been venerated, lineage segments and families will proceed to the tombs of their own ancestors and 'sweep the graves' (*saomu*).

See also: ancestral halls/lineage temples; Ghost Festival; Gongde

Further reading

Watson, James L. (1993). 'Rites or Beliefs? The Construction of a Unified Culture in Late Imperial China'. In Lowell Dittmer and Samuel S. Kim (eds), *China's Quest for National Identity*. Ithaca: Cornell University Press: 80–103.

Watson, James L. and Rawski, Evelyn S. (eds) (1988). *Death Ritual in Late Imperial and Modern China*. Berkeley: University of California Press.

ERIBERTO P. LOZADA JR

fur fashion

A full mink coat may still be out of reach for most Chinese consumers, but furriers are expecting increasing market demand as the new trends in fur fashion begin to surface in the Chinese market. Fur is becoming a fashion fabric that promises to cater to the needs of increasingly wealthy consumers in China. At sector fairs in 2003, new fur-garment designs were seen everywhere, such as coats lined with fur and jeans jackets with fur trim. Following a global fashion trend, native materials are no longer confined to pricey full-fur garments, but are now widely used for accessories and combined with textiles. This new fur look fits well with China's booming fashion interests and search for flashy but affordable clothing.

In 2002, drawn by the huge potential buying power of China, a number of the world's leading fur merchants opened new offices in Beijing.

Experts in the industry say that the dramatic resurgence of fur as a hot international fashion trend presents special challenges and extraordinary business opportunities for Chinese furriers and manufacturers. The change is likely to lead China's fur industry into a new chapter of development.

China, according to Xu Chunchao, vice-president of China National Native Produce and Animal By-products Import and Export Corporation (China Tuhsu), has become the world's largest producer of pelts, owing to what soon may be the world's largest fur market. But the country is still only able to offer low-end and mid-range products. The level of Chinese technology in tanning, dressing and craftsmanship is relatively low, and most fur factories have made little progress in brand-building, according to experts. Since Chinese people are becoming more and more brand conscious, they still prefer foreign brands.

The fur industry is complex and the business chain is very long, involving work by fur farmers, processors, auction houses, designers and manufacturers. The fragmented sector is administered by several departments, including the Ministry of Agriculture and the All-China Federation of Industry and Commerce. China has been in the International Fur Trade Federation since 1986 only through the membership of China Tuhsu, a foreign trade company, while other countries are mainly represented by their national associations. Still, through efficient regulations, people in the industry aim at making China's mostly middle-sized and small enterprise fur industry global.

PAOLA ZAMPERINI

G

Gan Yang

b. 1952, Hangzhou

Intellectual

A leading Beijing-based intellectual activist during the 'culture fever' (*wenhuare*) of the 1980s, Gan Yang played an instrumental role in founding the book series, *Culture: China and the World* (*Wenhua: Zhongguo yü shijie*, 1985, CCCW). Gan's essays in the 1980s emphasized, among other things, the need for a thorough-going revaluation of Chinese tradition and modernity. His innovative mode of critical thinking generated much interest among Chinese intellectuals and students. As editor-in-chief of CCCW, Gan also directed massive translation and publishing projects that provided mainland Chinese readers with unprecedented access to influential Euro-American scholarship.

Gan Yang experienced the **Cultural Revolution** as a 'sent-down youth' in Heilongjiang during the late 1960s and early 1970s. He earned his doctorate in 1985 from the Institute for Modern Western Philosophy at **Peking University,** whereupon he became an assistant research fellow at the Philosophy Institute at the **Chinese Academy of Social Sciences.** The network of scholars that Gan drew around him at both these institutions provided most of the intellectual labour for the CCCW editorial committee's various publishing enterprises. Gan's active involvement in the 1989 Chinese student protest movement led to his sudden departure from mainland China on 4 June 1989. Since then, he has resided overseas and is currently based at the University of Hong Kong. Gan remains an influential voice in contemporary Chinese intellectual discourse. Since the late 1990s, his publications have explored the importance of public participation in democracy, with particular reference to the writings of Alexis de Tocqueville.

See also: postmodernism (houxiandai zhuyi) and 'post-ism' (houxue)

Further reading

Gan, Yang (2001). 'Debating Liberalism and Democracy in China in the 1990s'. Trans. Zhang Xudong. In Zhang Xudong (ed.), *Whither China? Intellectual Politics in Contemporary China*. Durham: Duke University Press, 79–101.

GLORIA DAVIES

Gao Minglu

b. 1949, Tianjin

Art critic, historian, and curator

Gao Minglu was a seminal figure of the **85 New Wave [Art] Movement**. After spending his middle school years during the Cultural Revolution in Inner Mongolia, he graduated from the Tianjin Academy of Fine Arts (1981) and received an MA in Art History from the Chinese Academy of Arts in Beijing (1984). From 1985 to 1991 he was an editor of *Meishu* [Fine Arts] magazine. After moving to the US in 1989, he obtained a PhD in Art History at Harvard University (2000). Gao Minglu now teaches Chinese art history at the State University of New York at Buffalo.

Following his ground-breaking exhibition **China Avant-Garde** (1989) of which he was chief curator, Gao organized 'Inside/Out: New Chinese Art' at the Asia Society Galleries in New York and MoMA in San Francisco (1998) – the first major showcase of contemporary Chinese art in North America. In 1999, he curated the Chinese section of 'Conceptual Art: Point of Origin 1950s–1980s' at the Queens Museum in New York. Recently he has organized the show 'Chinese Maximalism' for the Gallery of SUNY Buffalo in New York and the China Millennium Museum in Beijing (2003).

Inextricably linked with the definition and promotion of the avant-garde, Gao's activities have been incessantly dedicated to the critical and historical discussion of this central artistic phenomenon of the post-Mao era. In the 1989 exhibition, Gao provided a never-before-seen, anti-institutional selection of contemporary Chinese art from the reform period. In the 1998 'Inside/Out' show, which also included artists from Singapore, Hong Kong and Taiwan, his intent was to present this phenomenon to the Western public less as a fixed historical product and more as a transitional process that was responding to the fast changing pace of its country of origin. In most of his critical and scholarly production, Gao Minglu has sought to define the Chinese 'avant-garde' in ways that would set it apart from similar international movements and free it from the misunderstandings that often emerge from the use of the same, French-derived term.

Further reading

Dal Lago, Francesca (1998). 'Inside/Out: An Interview with Gao Minglu', *ART AsiaPacific* 20 (October).

Gao, Minglu (1986). ''85 Meishu yundong' [The '85 Art Movement]. *Meishujia tongxun* [Artists Communication] 3.

—— (1991). *Zhongguo dangdai meishushi, 1985-1986* [The History of Contemporary Chinese Art]. Shanghai: Shanghai renmin chubanshe.

—— (1998). 'Toward a Transnational Modernity – an Overview of the Exhibition' and 'From Elite to Small Man: Multi-Faces of a Transitional

Avant-Garde in Mainland China'. In *idem* (ed.), *Inside/Out: New Chinese Art*. Berkeley: University of California Press.

—— (2003). 'Post-Utopian Avant-Garde Art in China'. In Ales Erjavec (ed.), *Postmodernism and the Postsocialist Condition: Politicized Art under Late Socialism*. Berkeley: University of California Press.

—— and Andrews, Julia (1995). 'The Avant-Garde's Challenge to Official Art'. In Deborah Davis, *Urban Spaces in Contemporary China: The Potential for Autonomy and Community in Post-Mao China*. Cambridge: Cambridge University Press, 221–78.

FRANCESCA DAL LAGO

Gao Xingjian

b. 1940, Ganzhou

Playwright, novelist, artist

As playwright, writer and literary critic, Gao Xingjian has made multifaceted contributions to post-Mao culture. Graduating from Beijing Foreign Languages Institute in 1962, Gao began to publish only in 1978, the same year he began working as a French translator for the Chinese Writers' Association. In 1981, he was appointed scriptwriter at the **Beijing People's Art Theatre**. Between 1980 and 1982 he also published *Techniques of Modern Fiction* (*Xiandai xiaoshuo jiqiao*) in serial form, introducing modernist literary techniques to Chinese readers. The project caused a sensation and was so influential that it encouraged many artists and writers to experiment with new artistic forms, although the state deemed it necessary to launch a campaign against both modernism and Gao's works.

As a playwright Gao first attracted attention with *Alarm Signal* (*Juedui xinghao*, 1982), which articulates the psychological conflict of the protagonist, who must choose between the moral prescription against thieving and the threats made by outlaws pressuring him to steal. Despite these didactic elements, the play was considered a bold theatrical experiment. Staged in a small theatre, it broke down the fourth wall – the illusion of the stage – and the lack of a set forced the performers to use symbolic gestures.

Gao's second play (actually written before *Alarm Signal*), **Bus Stop** (*Chezhan*, 1983), is drawn from Beckett's *Waiting for Godot*: it too centres on futile waiting. Gao shares Beckett's existential concern with the meaning of life, yet at the same time he includes historical and cultural aspects specific to China: eventually the characters realize that they have waited ten years and the bus stop is in fact out of service. While Gao modifies Beckett's understanding of the impossibility of a final ending by including an optimistic vision of change, the play nevertheless seemed radically pessimistic in the early post-Mao era, when the optimistic outlook was invariably associated with the state propaganda machine.

Wild Man (*Yeren*, 1985) represents another new direction in Gao's stage writing. In addition to continuing the investigation into existential questions, the play introduces cultural and historical reflection. The play examines modernity in the form of science and progress from the perspective of the ecologist, contrasting contemporary society with an original harmony with nature as represented by ancient customs and attitudes. The scientific search for the wild man and the commercial exploitation of primitive forests imbue modernity with tragedy. Again Gao expands on the practice of modern Chinese **Huaju** (spoken drama) by synthesizing dialogue, dance and singing. The combination of styles and themes in this play already points to his later, more famous works. Gao's next play, *The Other Shore* (*Bi'an*), explores the conflict between individuality and collectivism. The play was so philosophical, anti-social and abstract that even though it was published in 1986, it was never staged while Gao lived in China.

In China, Gao is mainly known as a playwright and critic. But in 1988 he emigrated to France, where he has lived as an artist and won fame for his novel *Soul Mountain* (*Lingshan*, 1995; trans. Mabel Lee, HarperCollins, 2000). Written in the form of the picaresque novel, it represents a yearning to escape the official culture and 'go home', returning to a world of folk culture, myth and nature. In a dialectical metaphor of escape and return, the narrative perspective alternates between the first and second personal pronouns in different

chapters. If 'I' can be understood as signifying a search for the self, 'you' conveys a sense of a removed and self-conscious contemplation of the searching subject. Gao's second novel *One Man's Bible* (*Yigeren de shengjing*, 1998; trans. Mabel Lee, HarperCollins, 2002) examines the devastating impact of the **Cultural Revolution** through its invasion of personal space. Both the violation of the female body and ideological reforms are seen as examples of such violation. The use of bodily memories and the theme of privacy are critical techniques in the analysis of this period of collective cruelty. In 2000, Gao was awarded the Nobel Prize for Literature.

See also: avant-garde/experimental theatre; Xu Shuya

Further reading

Fung, Gilbert (ed. and trans.) (1999). *The Other Shore: Plays by Gao Xingjian*. Hong Kong: The Chinese University Press

Tam, Kwok-kan (ed.) (2001). *Soul of Chaos: Critical Perspectives on Gao Xingjian*. Hong Kong: The Chinese University Press.

Wang, Xinmin (ed.) (1997). *Zhongguo dangdai xiju shigang* [Compendium of Contemporary Chinese Drama]. Beijing: Shehuikexue wenxian chubanshe.

Yi, Sha (ed.) (2000). *On Gao Xingjian* (*Gao Xingjian pingshuo*). Hong Kong: Mirror Books.

—— (2002). *Modern Chinese Literature and Culture* 14.2 (Fall) [special issue on Gao Xingjian].

HE DONGHUI

Gaudy Art

(Yansu yishu)

Gaudy Art is a mid 1990s art movement appropriating the bright aesthetics of folk art and consumer culture. *Yansu* is a neologism (see **neologisms**) originally coined by art critic **Li Xianting** to translate 'kitsch', and later translated back as 'gaudy' to refer to the Chinese art phenomenon, the word being a composite of the words 'garish' (*yan*) and 'vulgar' (*su*). Gaudy art was first identified as a new trend in 1996 with the exhibitions 'Rouge Life' (*Yanzhuang shenghuo*), 'Model for the Masses' (*Dazhong yangban),* 'Brightly Coloured Peach and Plum Blossoms Among the Ruins' (*Kuilan zhi chu, yanruo taoli*) and 'The Damage from the Flooding of China' (*Fuhuade Shanghai*). Curated by Li Xianting, they featured works by **Wang Jinsong**, Qi Zhilong, Xu Yihui, Yang Wei, Feng Zhengjie and the Luo Brothers.

As a reaction to the 1989 movements, Gaudy Art reflected on society's loss of ideals and the superfluity of the artist: 'It demonstrates the powerlessness of art to impact on the pervasiveness of consumerism in today's reality' (Li Xianting). Not so much kitsch as a parody of it, it comments on the parasitical but meaningless reproduction of cultural signifiers and traditional motifs, turning the artist into a witty but marginalized commentator with little alternative but to knowingly become a part of the same game. A prominent example is Xu Yihui's *Art History* (*Yishushi*, 1999) in which he uses garish ceramic flower plate calligraphy to construct an altar eulogy to contemporary art 'shit', a pun on and homophone of the word 'history' (*shi*). Yu Bogong's silk sculpture of a turd with wings, *Shit with a Dream* (*Manhuai lixiang de dabian*), is another satirical excretion typical of this current.

Further reading

Liao, Wen and Li, Xianting (1999). *Oh La La Kitsch.* Wuhan. Hunan Fine Arts Publishing House.

EDUARDO WELSH

gay cinema and video

Long repressed as a 'perversion imported from the West' or a 'mental disorder', homosexuality (see **homosexuality and tongzhi culture**) could only be indirectly shown (**Xie Jin**'s *Stage Sisters/ Wutai jiemei*, 1965) or melodramatically represented (**Chen Kaige**'s *Farewell My Concubine/Bawang bieji*, 1993). Only a few recent independent/underground productions have started to articulate the voices and concerns of the queer community.

The first video documentary on the lives of homosexuals in mainland China was *Comrades* (*Tongzhi*, 1996), by Wang Feng and Gary Wu, who shortly after emigrated to the United States. Some heterosexually identified Sixth Generation directors (see **Sixth Generation (film directors)**) have produced challenging narrative images of homosexuality. **Zhang Yuan**'s *East Palace, West Palace* (*Donggong, Xigong*, 1996) is the highly stylized mise en scène of the encounter between a straight policeman and the young gay writer he arrests.

Liu Bingjian's *Men Men Women Women* (*Nan Nan Nü Nü*, 1999) casts a nonchalant, faux neo-realist look at the intertwining lives of five characters who turn out to be gay: a shy country youth, a repressed housewife and her best girlfriend, the editor of a queer fanzine and the anchor of gay radio station – the latter played by the film's screenwriter, Cui Zi'en, a **Beijing Film Academy** professor and a major figure in the independent film scene and the homosexual (*tongzhi*) movement. In 2001, a young female documentarist, Li Yu, completed *Fish and Elephant* (*Yu be daxiang*), 'the first Chinese lesbian underground feature', that was shown in more than seventy international film festivals. In 2001, Echo Y. Windy (Ying Weiwei) directed her first documentary video, *The Box* (*Hezi*), about a lesbian couple.

The first openly gay man to playfully represent homosexuality on film, Cui Zi'en, started directing digital features, *Enter the Clowns* (*Choujue dengchang*, 2001) and *The Old Testament* (*Jiuyue*, 2002). In December 2001, he organized the first gay and lesbian film festival in Beijing. Among the entries was *Lan Yu* (2001), a love story between two men, shot illegally in Beijing with independent Chinese financing by Hong Kong director Stanley **Kwan**.

Further reading

Berry, Chris, Martin, Fran and Yue, Audrey (eds) (2003). *Mobile Culture: New Media in Queer Asia.* Durham: Duke University Press.

Martin, Fran (2003). 'Perverse Utopia: Reading *The River*'. In *idem, Situating Sexualities. Queer Representation in Taiwanese Fiction, Film and Public*

Culture. Hong Kong: Hong Kong University Press, 163–84 [on Tsai Mingliang].

Song, Hwee Li (2002). 'Celluloid Comrades: Male Homosexuality in Chinese Cinema in the 1990s'. *China Information* 16.4: 68–88.

BÉRÉNICE REYNAUD

Ge Fei

(né Liu Yong)

b. 1964, Dantu, Jiangsu

Writer

Ge Fei is best known for his experiments with meta-fictional forms during the 1980s. Not a professional writer, he teaches composition, and narrative and film theory at **Qinghua University** in Beijing. Ge Fei became a central figure in **avant-garde/experimental literature** after the publication of his second story 'Lost Boat' (*Michuan*), using a meta-fictional style influenced by the Argentinean writer Borges. His next story, 'A Flock of Birds' (*Hese niaoqun*), is generally acknowledged to be one of the most intricate, psychoanalytical and esoteric stories of the late 1980s.

All of Ge Fei's stories feature an outside interrogator (doctor, policeman) which adds feelings of detachment and displacement to an already alienated authorial self. This highly self-conscious and stylistically ambitious fiction represents a self that doubts the nature of existence as much as the process of writing: memory, history, myth and reality all occupy the same indeterminate space. In his novel *Enemy* (*Diren*), a mysterious fire kills a man and for years to come causes terrorizing suspicion about who this enemy might be – in Ge Fei's later fiction, the doubting self also becomes a threatened self. Because of his disregard for causality and temporality, Ge Fei did not easily attract a large audience after the 1980s. Consequently his novel *Banner of Desire* (*Yuwang de qizhi*, 1996) abandoned his earlier radical experiments in narrative structure, although the work continues to describe the moral and ethical disintegration of society.

Further reading

Ge, Fei (1993). 'The Lost Boat'. Trans. Caroline Mason. In Henry Zhao (ed.), *The Lost Boat: Avant-Garde Fiction from China*. London: Wellsweep, 77–100.

—— (1998). 'Whistling', trans. Victor Mair; 'Green Yellow', trans. Eva Shan Chou; 'Remembering Mr. Wu You', trans. Howard Goldblatt. In Wang Jing (ed.), *China's Avant-Garde Fiction*. Durham: Duke University Press, 15–68.

Wang, Jing (1993). 'The Mirage of Chinese "Postmodernism": Ge Fei, Self-Positioning, and the Avant-Garde Showcase'. *positions: east asian cultures critique* 1.2: 349–88.

Yang, Xiaobin (2002). 'Ge Fei: Indeterminate History and Memory'. In *idem*, *The Chinese Postmodern: Trauma and Irony in Chinese Avant-Garde Fiction*. Ann Arbor: University of Michigan Press, 168–87.

Zhang, Xudong (1997). *Chinese Modernism in the Era of Reforms: Cultural Fever, Avant-Garde Fiction and the New Chinese Cinema*. Durham: Duke University Press.

BIRGIT LINDER

Ge Ganru

b. 8 July 1954, Shanghai

Composer

Ge Ganru was born into a family of scientists and began to play the violin in his teens. Between 1971 and 1974 he was sent to Chongming Island to do farm work. He took his violin and managed to study with Nian Kaili, a former concertmaster of the Shanghai Philharmonic. Ge worked hard during the day and practised his violin at night, which usually left him with only three or four hours of sleep. He was voted a 'model worker'. After Ge had founded an instrumental ensemble playing revolutionary songs and folk music for which he frequently wrote the arrangements, he was allowed to stay away from farm work for half a day for rehearsals. When in 1973 the Shanghai Conservatory started to admit students, Ge was selected and auditioned. He entered the violin class at the Conservatory in 1974. In 1977 he switched to the composition department and studied with Chen Gang (composer of the Butterfly Violin Concerto). After graduation, he received a scholarship to study at Columbia University with Chou Wen-chung and Mario Davidovsky (1983–92). He has since worked as a freelance composer in New York.

Ge Ganru is one of the first Chinese composers to begin to incorporate the sounds and techniques of **New Music**, which had been forgotten for years in China, in his compositions. Already in his earliest works, such as *Twelve Preludes* (1979), *Moment of Time* (1981) for piano, and *Chamber Symphony* (1982), dissonances dominate the harmonic framework. He also employs aleatory as well as twelve-tone and serial techniques.

Already in these compositions, Ge also takes up elements from Chinese musical tradition: frequent silences and the importance of single sounds are derived from *guqin*-zither-playing, for example. Apparently static but ever moving sound clusters dominate a number of his later compositions, too, such as the string quartet *Prose Poetry* (*Fu*, 1983) and the piano concerto *Resolute* (*Wu*, 1988). A particularly spectacular attempt at synthesis between Chinese musical practice and the structure of 'New Music' is his composition for amplified cello *Customs* (*Yi Feng*, 1982). This bruitish piece employs techniques derived from Chinese instruments such as *sanxian*, **pipa** and **erhu**. To incorporate the particular idiosyncrasies of these instruments into his music, he lowers the strings of the cello by one octave. The peculiar effects caused by the loose strings, a lot of playing behind the bridge and beating of the body of the cello, make this piece an exquisite example of how the holistic attitude to instrumental sound production in traditional Chinese music can be reinterpreted as 'New Music'.

Further reading

Kouwenhoven, Frank (1991). 'Mainland China's New Music (2): Madly Singing in the Mountains'. *Chime* 3: 51–2.

—— (1992). 'Mainland China's New Music (3): The Age of Pluralism'. *Chime* 5: 109–11.

Mittler, Barbara (1997). *Dangerous Tunes. The Politics of Chinese Music in Hong Kong, Taiwan and the People's Republic of China since 1949*. Wiesbaden: Harrassowitz, 173–7, 328–30.

Steinitz, Richard (1992). 'Ge Gan-ru'. In Brian Morton and Pamela Collins (eds), *Contemporary Composers*. Chicago: St James' Press, 320–2.

BARBARA MITTLER

Ge You

b. 1957, Beijing

Film actor

Ge You grew up in a movie studio where his father was an actor. A high school graduate, he worked briefly on a hog farm. Back in Beijing in 1979, he improvised a skit about pig farming for a job interview and joined a modern drama troupe affiliated with the All-China Federation of Trade Unions' Cultural Ensemble. In 1988, his performance in the film *A Mischievous Guy* (*Wanzhu*) brought him instant fame. His convincing performance as a salesman of great intelligence who nonetheless appeared slow-witted gained admiration from audiences and respect from critics, and he won 'Best Actor' at the Ninth Annual Golden Rooster Awards. In 1989, he received an award at the Third Annual Chinese Movie Performing Arts Association Awards for his depiction of a bandit chieftain in *Ballads of the Yellow River* (*Huanghe yao*) as knowing neither adequate polite letters nor martial arts, and being gentle and quiet in appearance but cunning and treacherous at heart. His year of proliferation was 1991, starring in *A Star Comedian* (*Xiju mingxing*), *Chinese New Year* (*Guonian*), *Warriors in the Blaze* (*Liehuo jingang*), *Following the Great Campaign* (*Juezhuan zhihou*), and **Stories from an Editorial Office** (*Bianjibu de gushi*), a TV comedy series about five editors of differing ages, genders and personalities who bond through their daily routines: Ge You won 'Best Actor' in the Tenth Annual Golden Eagle Awards for his leading role as the cynical, yet warmhearted junior editor in the office. His latest hits include *A Happy Funeral* (*Dawan*) co-starring with Donald Sutherland.

HU MINGRONG WITH YUAN HAIWANG

Geju

(sung plays)

This term, literally 'sung plays', refers both to dramas of the revolutionary movement that integrate folk-style tunes with partially Westernized musical accompaniments, and to Western-style opera, including those by Chinese composers. In contrasts to **Xiqu** (sung-drama) which groups indigenous musical dramatic traditions like Peking opera, Geju is seen as more squarely focused on singing, while the other Western import, **Huaju** (spoken drama), focuses on speech. An example of the revolutionary dramas is *The White-Haired Girl* (*Baimao nü*, 1945) by Ma Ke and others (see **He Jingzhi**). Written for a mixed ensemble of Chinese and European instruments, it combined local tunes with overseas orchestral, vocal and choral style. Such pieces are less often produced today.

Western opera was first performed commercially in China in Shanghai in 1874. Since then overseas opera companies have toured China regularly, and several professional Chinese troupes have been established. Initially, the technology and method of production of European drama was more influential than the music of specific operas. Western-style theatres were erected in major cities, and specialist composers and directors hired; indeed, some Xiqu troupe leaders now take Geju as a model in these respects. Chinese-composed Geju are generally close to European light opera in musical style, with a clear story and an alternation of spoken dialogue and songs for *bel canto* voices with orchestral accompaniment. Examples of Geju include *The Song of the Grassland* (*Caoyuan zhi ge*, 1955) by Luo Zongxian, and *The Hundredth Bride* (*Di yibai ge xinniang*, 1980) by Wang Shiguang and Cai Kexiang. Recently China's Third Generation composers (see **Third Generation (composers)**) have begun to challenge this model with more modernist and postmodernist works.

JONATHAN P. J. STOCK

gender roles

While sharing similar traditions with many other cultures that generally designate man as the bread-earner and woman the family caretaker, the Chinese have also viewed femininity and virility in terms of the complementary but also hierarchical pair of yin (negative) and yang (positive). Men were strong and women weak, men smart and women unintelligent, and so forth. The long history of Confucian indoctrination and imperial endorsement reinforced this notion of women's inferiority. Traditionally, a woman had to obey three men in her life: her father as a daughter, her husband as a wife, and her son when widowed.

Mao's New China and his proclamation that men and women were the same greatly elevated Chinese women's status. Women began to do what men traditionally did: piloting aircraft and participating in all levels of state affairs, while men, for their part, increasingly took housekeeping for granted as part of married life. With today's booming economy and more open society, China has provided more opportunities for androgyny: men wearing long hair and women short; men dressed like women and women like men. The number of women smoking and drinking is also on the rise. However, traditional notions of gender roles persist. An overwhelming majority of women that appear in children's literature, for example, assume the role of educators and caretakers, while the same percentage of men are portrayed as scientists. Similarly, in school, boys are engaged in more physically and mentally demanding tasks than their counterpart sex, whose activities tended to be of a more quiet and artistic nature.

China is a large country with diverse cultures, and notions of virility and femininity may differ. However, men's prowess versus women's gentleness are virtues of universal acceptance – a song that compares man to a mountain and woman to a river illustrates the point. Physically, girls view boys shorter than 1.70 metres as unattractive, while boys prefer girls with a good shape and fine complexion. Incidentally, young women in cities go to great lengths to avoid being tanned and many are obsessed with dieting. Generally, men and women in north China have a stouter and taller stature, while women in the lower Yangtze Delta and the Sichuan Basin are thought to best fit men's stereotype of femininity. Psychologically, women look to men as a safe haven that can provide them with financial and emotional security. Honesty and financial success, therefore, are still considered more important in a male than a sinewy body and handsome face. Interestingly, according to a recent study made by an advertisement company, Chinese men themselves resent such handsome sinewy male models. To a Chinese man, the power of control and the respect from others, what is known to them as 'face', are more important to virility than muscles.

See also: good wife and mother; language and gender; sexual attitudes; sexuality and behaviour

Further reading

Brownell, Susan and Wasserstrom, Jeffrey (eds) (2002). *Chinese Femininities, Chinese Masculinities: A Reader*. Berkeley: University of California Press.

Entwisle, Barbara and Henderson, Gail E. (eds) (2000). *Re-Drawing Boundaries: Work, Households and Gender in China*. Berkeley: University of California Press.

Evans, Harriet (1995). 'Defining Difference: The "Scientific" Construction of Sexuality and Gender in the PRC'. *Signs* 20.2 (Winter).

—— (1997). *Women and Sexuality in China: Female Sexuality and Gender Since 1949*. New York: Continuum.

Finnane, Antoine and McLaren, Anne (eds) (1999). *Dress, Sex, and Text in Chinese Culture*. Clayton: Monash Institute.

Louie, Kam (2002). *Theorising Chinese Masculinity: Society and Gender in China*. Cambridge: Cambridge University Press.

Louie, Kam and Low, Morris (eds) (2003). *Asian Masculinities: The Meaning and Practice of Manhood in China and Japan*. New York and London: RoutledgeCurzon.

Rofel, Lisa (1999). *Gendered Yearnings in China after Socialism*. Berkeley: University of California Press.

Smith, Christopher J. (2000). 'Gender Issues in the Transition out of Socialism'. In *idem*, *China in the Post-Utopian Age*. Boulder: Westview Press, 289–320.

Yang, Mayfair Mei Hui (ed.) (1999). *Spaces of Their Own: Woman's Public Sphere in Transnational China*. Minneapolis: University of Minnesota Press.

HU MINGRONG

Geng Jianyi

b. 1962, Zhengzhou, Henan

Painter, photographer, video and installation artist

A graduate of the Oil Painting Department of the Zhejiang (now China) Academy of Fine Arts in Hangzhou (1985) (see **art academies**), Geng Jianyi was an early member of the pioneering avant-garde group, the **Pond Society**, and a major protagonist of the experimental trends that marked the **85 New Wave [Art] Movement** during the second half of the 1980s. He is one of the most consistent, engaged and versatile artists on the contemporary scene, having produced an extremely varied array of works in different media. Geng Jianyi emerged on the national scene when his quadriptic, *The Second Situation* (1987) – portraying a blown-up black-and-white face that sneered with cynical laughter – became one of the icons of the seminal **China Avant-Garde** exhibition in 1989. With a body of work spanning a period of nearly twenty years and covering media as different as oil painting, video, photography, conceptual art and installation, Geng's *oeuvre* defies simple definition. Given the statement that he is 'interested in our awareness of what has happened, what is taking place, what will unfold; and our part in the process', Geng's body of work suggests a constant search for meaning beneath the surface of all kinds of appearances, be they social, visual or cultural. Geng is preoccupied with the workings of the social mechanisms of communication, interaction, memory and identity-formation. Some of his most interesting work has taken the form of performative tasks required of normal people, who are instructed to perform certain actions, such as filling forms or writing reports, and which question the significance of embedded social practices and state regulations. His more recent works, such as the photographic series *Watermarks*, have veered towards an approach focusing on the effects of immediate actions 'here-and-now' that seems inspired by Buddhist philosophical practices in their apparent minimal formal treatment paired with a meditative sensibility. Geng Jianyi lives and works in Hangzhou, where he has been recently hired in the New Media Programme of the China Academy of Fine Arts under the direction of **Zhang Peili**. His work has appeared in: 'China Avant-Garde' in Beijing (1989); 'China Avant-Garde' in Berlin (1993), 'China's New Art post-1989' in Hong Kong (1993) and the Venice Biennale (1993); 'Image and Phenomena' a video exhibition in Hangzhou (1996); 'Inside/Out: New Chinese Art' at the Asia Society in New York and the SFMoMA in San Francisco (1998); 'Living in Time' in Berlin (2001); and 'Paris-Pekin' in Paris (2002).

Further reading

Dreissen, Chris and van Mierlo, Heidi (eds) (1997). *Another Long March: Chinese Conceptual and Installation Art in the Nineties*. Breda: Fundament Foundation.

Gao, Minglu (1998). 'From Elite to Small Man: The Many Faces of a Transitional Avant-Garde in Mainland China'. In *idem* (ed.), *Inside/Out: New Chinese Art* (exhibition catalogue). Berkeley: University of California Press, 149–66.

Hou, Hanru (1996). 'Beyond the Cynical: China Avant-Garde in the 1990s'. *ART AsiaPacific* 3.1: 42–51.

van Dijk, Hans (1982). 'Painting in China after the Cultural Revolution: Style Developments and Theoretical Debates'. *China Information* 6.4 (Spring): 1–18.

Yang, Alice (1998). 'Beyond Nation and Tradition: Art in Post-Mao China'. In *idem, Why Asia? Contemporary Asian and Asian American Art*. New York: New York University Press, 107–18.

FRANCESCA DAL LAGO

geography of disease

There are certain diseases in China that show unique environmental characteristics. This particular focus is part of medical geography which studies the spatial variation of health and disease in any population *and* which searches for explanations for such geographical trends. To do this the epidemiological measurement of 'prevalence' has proven useful: it refers to the number of people in an area having a particular health problem during a defined period of time (e.g. one year). A bone illness that primarily affects children and young people, Kashin-Beck disease cuts a large swath across China. It is sometimes called 'big-bone disease', and areas of its high prevalence form a crescent running from the Tibetan plateau through China into eastern Siberia. The lack of normal levels of selenium in the soil is suspected of being a major factor in the aetiology of this disease. It is also thought that in Tibet it is related to the presence of fungi in damp stored barley, the staple diet. Once the seeds are contaminated the fungi spread through the new crop, and the cycle continues. *Keshan* disease is associated primarily with children between the ages of two and ten. Characterized by enlargement of the heart and fluid in the lungs, it is often fatal. Once again, the map of high prevalence of *Keshan* disease corresponds almost perfectly to the map of areas of low selenium in the soil.

But the biggest killer at the threshold of the new century is tuberculosis; epidemiologists say that at least a third of the population is infected with this debilitating affliction, including 6 million who have the active form of the disease. A quarter of a million Chinese die each year from pulmonary tuberculosis. One of the outstanding features of this contagious disease is that its prevalence appears to always be higher where people are concentrated in close proximity to each other. However, clearly this is not the only health problem that has to be dealt with. For example, lung cancer is increasing in China by 4.5 per cent each year, and a million are expected to die from the disease by 2025. Not unrelated to this trend is increasing cigarette consumption and the fact that close to 2 per cent of all cultivated land is devoted to tobacco production. On other fronts, while overall cancer rates are relatively low in China, stomach cancer is a major exception. Its yearly incidence (i.e. new cases) in China is just over 90 per 100,000 compared, for example, with 6.5 per 100,000 in the USA. It is thought that high rates of stomach cancer are related to the use of vegetables preserved through fermenting and salting. HIV/AIDS (see **HIV/ AIDS and STIs**) is a literal time-bomb: an official Chinese estimate in 2001 was 50,000 cases, whereas the WHO estimated twelve times as many and projects 10 million for 2010. In one area of Henan province, for example, close to 20 per cent of villagers had HIV, and among those who had sold blood to illegal traders over 40 per cent were infected. Another consequence of unsafe use of injections is the hepatitis epidemic in China which contributes to more than 200,000 deaths annually due to liver cancer, the highest number of all deaths related to cancer.

PETER M. FOGGIN

geography of health care

The geography of health care is a branch of the sub-discipline known as medical geography and includes the study of the spatial patterns and distributions of health care services in relation to the populations being served. This in turn can be of assistance in the planning of health care systems in various cultural settings. In China, the system of health care delivery has changed significantly since the inception of the economic reforms starting in the early 1980s.

Prior to this period total access to primary health care was guaranteed, both ideologically and practically, through the collective work units (at the rural brigade level or in the urban *danwei* or work unit). In rural areas the Cooperative Medical System (CMS) organized health care at three levels. The first tier involved the much-acclaimed **barefoot doctors** (health workers with minimal training) who provided primary care, including prescription medicines. For more serious cases they referred patients to the commune (township) health centres (the second tier), and ultimately to the county hospitals (the third tier).

After the agricultural reforms the CMS collapsed in most areas: the primary health care workers had decreased by at least a third by the early 1990s. Even at the township level the number of clinics decreased significantly. One study based on thirty 'poverty counties' observed that by 1993 only about half of all villages had functioning

health stations (Liu *et al.* 1999). By far the biggest negative impact of these changes was felt in rural areas. The gap between the health status of people in the city and those in the countryside widened considerably. For example, using one classic indicator of health status, Huang and Liu (1995) found that country-wide infant mortality rates (IMR) for rural areas had actually increased between 1990 and 1995, climbing from 30 to over 40 deaths per 1,000 live births (whereas in urban areas there was a slight decrease). When IMRs are calculated at regional levels they are much worse in the remote western provinces than in the more densely populated parts of China, and at the county level some areas have been found to have IMRs in excess of 100 deaths per 1,000 live births (Huang *et al.* 1997; Foggin *et al.* 2001). Clearly, although it is only one factor contributing to the health status of populations, the geographical variation of health care services available is one of the contributing factors.

There are two types of health care in China, both officially sanctioned and universally practised in varying proportions: traditional Chinese medicine and what is commonly referred to as 'Western medicine'. White (1999) has emphasized a peculiarly Chinese version of holistic, 'integrated medicine' (IM). Launched during the **Cultural Revolution**, it was intended to be a truly new and scientific synthesis of the best of both Chinese traditional and Western medicine. There are, however, wide geographical variations in the way IM is used and practised and, since the economic reforms, many urban health care institutions have reinstated the division of labour between 'traditional' and 'Western' medicine. An example of some of the problems observed in the still widespread but unregulated practice of IM is the often uninformed and massive use of easily obtained antibiotics, thus seriously diminishing their effectiveness not only in China but also around the world.

Further reading

Foggin, Peter, Armijo-Hussein, Nagib, Marigaux, Céline, Hui Zhu and Liu Zeyuan (2001). 'Risk Factors and Child Mortality among the Miao in

Yunnan, Southwest China'. *Social Science and Medicine* 53: 1683–96.

Huang, W., Yu, H., Wang, F. and Li, G. (1997). 'Infant Mortality among Various Nationalities in the Middle Part of Guizhou, China'. *Social Science and Medicine* 45: 1031–40.

Huang, Y. and Liu, Y. (1995). *Mortality Data of the Chinese Population*. Beijing: Chinese Population Press.

Liu, Xingzhu and Mills, Anne (2002). 'Financing Reforms of Public Health Services in China: Lessons for Other Nations'. *Social Science in Medicine* 54: 1691–8.

Liu, Yuanli, Hsiao, William C. and Eggleston, Karen (1999). 'Equity in Health and Health Care: The Chinese Experience'. *Social Science in Medicine* 49: 1349–56.

White, Sydney D. (1999). 'Deciphering "Integrated Chinese and Western Medicine" in the Rural Lijiang Basin: State Policy and Local Practice(s) in Socialist China. *Social Science and Medicine* 49: 1333–47.

PETER M. FOGGIN

Gezaixi

regional Xiqu (sung-drama/opera)

Gezaixi is a form of sung-drama or opera (**Xiqu**) performed in the dialect of the Minnan (southern Fujian), the language of the major Han Chinese ethnic group in Taiwan (see **dialects**). The Minnan brought the *jinge* (assorted folksongs) from Fujian to Taiwan and created short musical sketches for the purpose of entertainment. By the early twentieth century, these sketches had developed into the Gezaixi opera form. The hardship of the early settlers' lives in Taiwan made the crying tunes and the role of the 'lamenting female' (*kudan*) especially popular in Gezaixi. The genre has absorbed performance elements from many Chinese regional operas and ensembles, including **Jingju** (Peking opera), **Minju** (Fuzhou opera), *nanguan* (southern music; see **Minnan nanyin**), and *beiguan* (northern music). It was introduced to southern Fujian in the 1920s and has enjoyed considerable popularity there ever since. In Fujian,

the form is known as Xiangju (Xiang opera) in Zhangzhou, and Gezaixi in Xiamen.

Since 1949, Gezaixi as a regional opera has developed separately in Taiwan and China, resulting in differences in vocal and acting styles. The music in both areas, however, remains similar, with the *qizi* (seven-word) tune providing the major rhythmic and melodic structure. However, the performance of Gezaixi in China has been greatly influenced by Jingju (Peking opera) – actors sing in falsetto and with the natural voice only on occasion, and perform with more stylized movements, emphasizing an aesthetics of beauty and roundedness. In Taiwan, the performance conventions of those above-mentioned sketches based on rowdy folksongs persist. Performers sing in their natural voice and use less stylized gestures. Most of the leading roles, including the young males, are performed by females.

See also: Kejia daxi; music in Taiwan; performing arts in Taiwan

Further reading

Chang, Heui-Yuan Belinda (1997). 'A Theatre of Taiwaneseness: Politics, Ideologies, and Gezaixi'. *The Drama Review* 41.2 (T154): 111–29.

Tsai, Wen-ting (2001). 'Long-Lost Relatives – Taiwanese Opera on the Mainland'. Trans. David Mayer. *Sinorama Magazine* 11: 62–71.

Zeng, Yong-yi (1988). *Taiwan gezaixi de fazhan yü bianqian* [Development and Change in Taiwanese Opera]. Taipei: Lianjing.

UENG SUE-HAN

Ghost Festival

(Guijie)

The Ghost Festival (Guijie) takes place in the middle of the 'ghost month' (*guiyue*): the fifteenth day of the seventh month. In some parts of China, a 'ritual of universal salvation' (*pudu*) is performed in order to save the souls of the unfortunate dead (*guhun yegui*/solitary souls and marginal ghosts), lest they come back or linger and cause trouble (see **Gongde; Shuilu zhai**). In Minnan-speaking areas (i.e. Fujian), for example, every temple and every street celebrates the Pudu. This ritual does exist among the Hakka, but it is not a community festival: each family prepares, on its own, a sacrifice for the hungry ghosts. In Baisha (Shanghang, western Fujian), for example, people eat early that evening and then go to a crossroads to deposit a rice cake. Even more interesting, in Dongliu (Wuping, western Fujian), people write their own names and those of their ancestors on packages of paper money which they then burn outside the gate; at the same time, but off to one side, they burn money for the souls of the unfortunate dead. In the context of **Jiao** ('offering') celebrated for the souls of the unhappy dead by Buddhist monks in the ancestral halls of each lineage segment, the Cao of Caofang (Xuanhe, Liancheng, western Fujian) prepare, and later burn in front of the temple, the same type of package on which is written the names of their five ascendant generations. The same village had 'associations for those without sacrifices': accompanied by a master of Confucian rites (*lisheng*), their members went to one of twelve sites 'where there were many ghosts' in order to make sacrifice. In a village in Shangyou county (Gannan) the Li family hung up the portraits of their ancestors at the time of this festival, and no one would have dreamed of leaving the house: everyone feared his sacrificial money might be stolen by a visiting neighbour! The place of ancestors during the Ghost Festival is far more important among the Hakka than it is among Minnan- or Cantonese- speaking peoples.

JOHN LAGERWEY

Gong Li

b. 1965, Jinan, Shandong

Film actress

One of the world's most accomplished actresses, Gong Li has starred in twenty-two movies and won a number of national and international awards. She has been awarded a 'Berlinale Camera' and the title 'Officier des Arts et Lettres' for her contribution to cinema. She was president of the

international jury at the 2000 Berlin International Film Festival. For all her stardom, she is easy to approach, but said to be disdainful of the media's intrusions into her private life.

Gong Li entered the Central Dramatic Arts Academy in Beijing in 1985. In 1989 she became an actress in the academy's Modern Drama Research Institute. When she was a sophomore, Gong Li was handpicked by **Zhang Yimou** to play the leading role in *Red Sorghum* (*Hong gaoliang*). In this debut, she might be a little puerile, but appeared pleasantly pure and fresh, revealing her potential. Her reputation soared after *Red Sorghum* won the 1987 Golden Berlin Bear. In 1989–90, she starred in *Judou* and *Raise the Red Lantern* (*Da hong denglong gaogao gua*) in which she successfully depicted women repressed by their clans. Gong Li's performance reached new heights in *The Story of Qiu Ju* (*Qiu Ju da guansi*). Her vivid presentation of a dauntless country girl made an indelible impression on the audience, and for her efforts she was awarded 'Best Actress' at the Venice Film Festival. Others of her films include *Shanghai Triad* (*Yaoayao, yaodao waipo qiao*), *Farewell My Concubine* (*Bawang bie ji*), *Tempt ress Moon* (*Fengyue*), *The Emperor and the Assassin* (*Jingke ci qinwang*) and *Chinese Box* (*Zhongguo hezi*).

Further reading

Delamoir, Jeanette (1998). 'Woman as Spectacle in Zhang Yimou's "Theatre of Punishments"'. *Screening the Past* 5 (December).

Reyanud, Bérénice (1993). 'Glamour and Suffering: Gong Li and the History of Chinese Stars'. In Pam Cook and Philip Dodd (eds), *Women and Film: A Sight and Sound Reader*. Philadelphia: Temple University Press, 21–9.

HU MINGRONG WITH YUAN HAIWANG

Gongde

(merit offering)

Buddhist and Daoist ritual

Gongde (merit) is a structured set of rites performed by Buddhist or Daoist ritual specialists to deliver a soul from potential sufferings in purgatory or hell and transfer it either to Amitabha Buddha's Western Paradise or to a better rebirth. It may be performed as part of a funeral, or on any seventh day up to the forty-ninth day, and/or on the hundredth day, and on first and third anniversaries after death. Lasting from half a day to seven days, the length and scale of Gongde depend on the economic means of the family.

Gongde is a Buddhist concept whereby merit can be earned or cultivated by performing benevolent Buddhist-related deeds, which will constitute a person's store of benefits in the next life or the lives thereafter. Furthermore, merit can be transferred to another person, living or dead. Thus, paying Buddhist monks to perform a special set of rites, all of which contribute towards the accruement of merit, and transferring the merits to the dead can help pave the soul's way to a better rebirth. Gongde as a term to mean a private ritual performed to accrue merit and provide salvation for the soul is used primarily in Minnan (southern Fujian), Chaozhou and within the Chinese diaspora of these regions.

In urban Minnan, Gongde is performed by ordained Buddhist clerics in monasteries or temples. The last two decades have also seen the rise of a type of Buddhist lay women, known as *caigu* (vegetarian sisters), as Gongde ritual specialists. In townships and villages, Gongde is commonly performed either by lay male Buddhist ritual specialists known as *xianghua heshang* (incense-flower monks) or by lay **Daoist priests**, although not all Daoists perform Gongde.

Gongde performance alternates between two altars: the Buddha altar and the Soul altar. Several important rites form the basis of Gongde; the 'Purification' (*jingtan*), 'Penitence' (*baichan*), 'Offering' (*shanggong*) and a 'rite of universal salvation' (*yankou* or *mengshan*) to save 'hungry ghosts' (*egui*). The 'Penitence' is a major component of Gongde due to the length of its texts. For half- or one-day Gongde, the text frequently used is the three-volume *Cibei sanmei shuichan*; for Gongde lasting three days or more, the ten-volume *Lianghua bao-chan* is often performed. Additional rites include 'Turning the Wheel' (*qianzang*) to lead the soul out of hell, 'Bathing the Soul', the 'Rite of Pardon' (*fangshe*) and 'Smashing Hell' (*dacheng*), this last being the enactment of the story of Mulian saving his mother from her sufferings in hell. In contemporary Minnan, Gongde performed by the ordained Buddhists mainly adhere to the basic rites, while those performed by the 'vegetarian sisters' and lay Buddhist or Daoist ritualists may include some or all of the additional rites. Different interpretations of Gongde today constitute responses to socio-economic and political changes.

See also: Ghost Festival; Shuilu zhai

Further reading

Dean, Kenneth (1988). 'Funerals in Fujian'. *Cahiers d'Extrême-Asie* 4: 19–78.

Lagerwey, John (1987). *Taoist Ritual in Chinese Society and History*. New York: Macmillan; London: Collier Macmillan.

Tan, Hwee-San (2002). *Sounds for the Dead: Ritualists and Their Vocal Liturgical Music in the Buddhist Rite of Merit in Fujian, China*. PhD diss., SOAS, University of London.

TAN HWEE-SAN

good wife and mother

(*xianqi liangmu*)

Social concept

The Chinese traditional view of gender is rooted in Confucianism, which prescribes individuals' roles based on their positions relative to others. Accordingly, the Chinese woman is defined in relation to, and subordinate to, the males in the family – she is supposed to submit to her father before marriage (*zaijia cong fu*), to her husband during marriage (*chujia cong fu*) and to her son(s) during her old age (*laolai congzi*). The virtue of a woman is therefore measured by how well she plays the roles of wife and mother. In addition, women are believed to belong to the 'inside' and men the 'outside', referring respectively to activities within and outside the home. The notion of 'men till; women weave' had dominated historically the division of labour within the rural household. Women's interior domain is largely defined by their nurturing activities, and their identity is tied to their achievements in taking care of their husbands, reproduction and raising children. The old Chinese saying that 'it is a virtue for women not to have education and skills' (*nüzi wucai bian shi de*) further illustrates the ideological constraints that confine women to the domestic sphere.

During the Maoist period, traditional notions of women's roles were challenged and women were encouraged to contribute to both reproduction in the home and production outside the home. Though the CCP did little to change household division of labour, it organized collective services such as childcare so that women could participate in the labour force. Since the economic reforms of the late 1970s, it appears that the ideology that a woman should stay home and strive to become a good wife and mother has once again gained popularity. The state's retreat from the discourse of gender has paved the way for gendered practices, such as higher rates of layoff among women workers and gender discrimination in the labour market, that discourage women to work outside the home.

See also: gender roles

C. CINDY FAN

goudui

Social concept

Goudui refers to a practice among private entrepreneurs 'to thicken' the relationship with the state. *Goudui* originally referred to the making of liquor by mingling water with alcohol, and overlaps with the phrase *gouqian* – to add corn starch to thicken a soup. *Goudui* consists of a set of habitual and systematic activities initiated by private entrepreneurs to cultivate and please state officials and transform the relationship into a strategically cosy and congenial one. Activities include gift-giving, banqueting and a variety of night-life entertainment (karaoke, dancing, sauna, foot washing, massage) which often lead to erotic or sexual services paid for by the entrepreneurs. In terms of making connections, *goudui* is therefore similar to **Guanxi**, but it refers to a specific connection (between the

state and private enterprises) and more often involves prostitution. It emerged in the reform period and flourished in the consumer culture of the 1990s. It is also commonly practised among business partners. On the surface, the purpose of *goudui* is to gain favours from the state in order to benefit one's business, but the politics of *goudui* also feature psychological manoeuvring on the part of the entrepreneur to win the state's recognition of self-worth and of the novel and important role of the growing private sector after socialism. This male power play between state officials and entrepreneurs through the involvement of female bodies (prostitution) and the exclusion of women from equal participation reveals a male-centred construction of masculinity.

Further reading

Zhang, Everett (2001). 'Goudui and the State: Constructing Entrepreneurial Masculinity in Two Cosmopolitan Areas of Post-Socialist China'. In D. Hodgson (ed.), *Gendered Modernities: Ethnographic Perspectives*. New York: Palgrave. 235–65.

EVERETT ZHANG

Gu Cheng

b. 1956, Beijing; d. 1993

Poet

A major representative of **Misty poetry** (*Menglong shi*), Gu Cheng is known for his brilliant poetry and his controversial life. Gu Cheng worked as a swineherd in a remote part of Shandong province from 1969 to 1974. He began writing poems at the age of ten, but didn't establish himself as an influential poet until 1979 with the publication of the series *Nameless Flowers* (*Wuming de xiaohua*). In 1987 he was invited to Europe and one year later to New Zealand, where he served as a visiting lecturer at the University of Auckland. But he later resigned and moved to live in a virtual hermitage on a desolate island. After killing his poet wife (Xie Ye), he committed suicide on 8 October 1993.

Best known for his numerous Menglong poems in many collections (i.e. *The Moon in the Daylight* (*Baizhou de yueliang*), *Eyes of Darkness* (*Hei yanjing*) and *Allegorical Poems of Gu Cheng* (*Gu Cheng tonghua yuyan shixuan*)), Gu always aimed at artistic simplicity and poetic purity even at the sacrifice of clarity. He was at his best when he portrayed nature or created a world of fairy tale from a child's perspective. His short poems, such as 'This Generation' (*Yidairen*) and 'Far and Near' (*Yuan he jin*), have since become the most often quoted lines and the representative of his poetry. Gu also wrote essays and novels and even practised painting. His novel *Ying'er* was published posthumously in 1993.

Further reading

Brady, Anne-Marie (1997). 'Dead in Exile: The Life and Death of Gu Cheng and Xie Ye'. *China Information* 11.4 (Spring): 126–48.

Gu, Cheng (1998). 'Far and Near', 'Good-bye', 'In Sunset's Glow', 'In the Twinkling of the Eyes', 'The Origins of the Moon and Stars' and 'This Generation'. Trans. Gordon Osing and De-An Wu Swihart. *Salt Hill* 5.

Gu, Cheng and Lei, Mi (1995). *Ying'er, The Kingdom of Daughters*. Trans. Li Xia. Dortmund: Projekt Verlag.

Li, Xia (ed.) (1999). *Essays, Interviews, Recollections and Unpublished Material of Gu Cheng, Twentieth Century Poet: The Poetics of Death*. Lewiston: Mellon Press.

FU HONGCHU

Gu Dexin

b. 1962, Beijing

Installation, photography and computer design artist

A self-taught artist and founding member of the **New Measurement Group**, Gu Dexin's own signature style, physically and sexually charged, is the opposite of the radically depersonalized graphics created in his collective activities. His early installations, exhibited in the exhibitions **China Avant-Garde** (Beijing, 1989) and 'Les Magiciens de la Terre' (Paris, 1989), were reminiscent of disembowelled human organs and excrement created by burning and twisting discarded plastic materials. In a 1995 installation in a Venetian palace, a sumptuous hall was transformed into a mortuary with red plastic beads covering the entire floor and bloody chunks of beef decaying in transparent coffins.

The choice of perishable materials, such as meat, flowers and fruits, reflects Gu Dexin's deep-rooted pessimism towards human beliefs which he deems self-deceptive. Gu's works bear no title or simply adopt the time of the exhibition as their designation in order to emphasize the ephemeral nature of the work. In the exhibition 'Another Long March' held in Breda, Holland (1997), he displayed apples, bananas and strawberries – chosen for their direct sexual implications – which were left to decay or to be consumed by visitors and birds in an open courtyard for two months. In the same exhibition he also displayed a glass box containing a meatball, dried and darkened after hours of manipulation – a gesture subsequently memorialized in a large size, close-up photograph. In recent years, Gu Dexin has begun creating computer-generated figures with many breasts or genitals engaging in orgiastic acts. He has also begun producing short animated stories where human violence is mocked with an eerie humour.

Further reading

Doran, Valerie C. (ed.) (1993). *China's New Art, Post-1989, with a Retrospective from 1979 to 1989* (exhibition catalogue). Hong Kong: Hanart T Z Gallery. (Reprinted in 2001 by Asia Art Archive, Hong Kong, 152–4.)

Driessen, Chris and van Mierlo, Heidi (eds) (1997). *Another Long March: Chinese Conceptual and Installation Art in the Nineties* (exhibition catalogue). Breda: Fundament Foundation.

Noth, Jochen, Pöhlmann, Wolfger and Reschke, Kai (eds) (1994). *China Avant-Garde: Counter-Currents in Art and Culture*. Berlin and Hong Kong: Haus der Kulturen der Welt and Oxford University Press, 127.

TANG DI

Gu Wenda

b. 1955, Shanghai

Oil, traditional Chinese painter and installation artist

A talented and versatile artist, Gu Wenda's mid-1980s modern ink-wash paintings were generally taken as evidence of the vitality and viability of this traditional media (see **Modern Ink-Wash Painting**). Gu was drawn to the *shanshui* (landscape) painting tradition while studying woodcarving at the Shanghai College of Applied Art and subsequently when admitted to the *shanshui* (landscape) masterclass at the Zhejiang (China) Academy of Art, where he studied under the tutelage of Lu Yanshao (see **art academies**). Upon graduation in 1981, he turned to oil painting, only to effect a surprise return to *guohua* (traditional Chinese painting), producing powerful, enigmatic, monumental ink-wash paintings, such as *Contemplation of the World* (*Jingguan de shijie*, 1984) and *Crazy Door God* (*Fengkuang de menshen*, 1986). In the second half of the 1980s, Gu attended the workshop on soft sculpture and tapestry organized at the academy by Bulgarian artist Marin Varbanon, which was to have a lasting influence on his *oeuvre*. Gu's solo exhibition in Xi'an (1986) was considered a sensation. The most controversial works (including a pyramidal installation) had to be exhibited separately, for a restricted audience only. Gu's work in the 1980s was informed by cultural struggle. He was wary of becoming captive to Western modernism, but his reaction harboured a deeper distrust with respect to certainties and the authority of knowledge (including the written word).

Since moving to New York in 1987 – a transition marked by the changed phrasing of his name to Wenda Gu – he has been progressively active in the creation of controversial installations employing organic, human-derived products, such as used hygienic tampons, sent in by voluntary participants, for the project *2000 Natural Deaths* (1990) or powdered placenta, as in *Oedipus Refound* (1993). Most recently, his work revolves around the more innocuous material of human hair that he weaves together with glue, forming transparent tapestries and banners where often languages and scripts from across the world are brought together in a message emblematic of a future not ruled by racial or national boundaries. This ongoing series, for which Gu has created various national editions, is titled *United Nation* and is normally site-specific, i.e. created for a precise place with the hair of its inhabitants. It is striking that the formal sensibility and the colour palette allowed by the use of such material maintains the monochromatic visual qualities of traditional Chinese landscape painting, in which the artist was trained. Wenda Gu lives and works in New York City. He has shown his work in many important exhibitions: 'China Avant-Garde' in Beijing (1989); 'Silent Energy' at the Museum of Modern Art in Oxford (1995); 'China New Art, Post-1989' in Hong Kong (1993); the 2nd Johannesburg Biennale (1997); 'Inside/Out: New Chinese Art' in New York and San Francisco (1998); the 49th Venice Biennale (2001); and the important solo exhibition, 'From Middle Kingdom to Biological Millennium' in Texas, the Kansas Art City Institute, and the Maine College of Art (2003–4).

Further reading

Bessire, Mark (ed.) (2003). *Wenda Gu: Art from Middle Kingdom to Biological Millennium*. Cambridge, MA: MIT Press.

Gao, Minglu (1998). 'From Elite to Small Man: The Many Faces of a Transitional Avant-Garde in Mainland China'. In *idem* (ed.), *Inside Out: New Chinese Art* (exhibition catalogue). Berkeley: University of California Press.

—— (2003). 'Seeking a Model of Universalism: The United Nation Series and Other Works'. In Mark Bessire (ed.), *Wenda Gu: Art from Middle Kingdom to Biological Millennium*. Cambridge MA: MIT Press, 20–9.

Gu, Wenda (1990). *Gu Wenda, 2000 Natural Deaths: March 8–April 21, 1990. Curated by Peter Selz and Katherine Cook*. San Francisco: Hatley Martin Gallery, c. 1990.

—— (1993). *Oedipus Refound #2: The Enigma of Birth: Installation*. Oxford, England: Museum of Modern Art.

Hou, Hanru and Gao, Minglu (1998). 'Strategies of Survival in the Third Space: A Conversation on the Situation of Overseas Chinese Artists in the

1990s'. In Gao Minglu (ed.), *Inside Out: New Chinese Art* (exhibition catalogue). Berkeley: University of California Press.

EDUARDO WELSH AND FRANCESCA DAL LAGO

Gu Xiong

b. 1953, Chongqing, Sichuan

Painter, printmaker, installation artist

Gu's formal training was delayed by the **Cultural Revolution**. He earned his BFA in 1982 and MFA in 1985, both from the Sichuan Fine Arts Institute in Chongqing, where he continued to teach drawing, woodcut engraving and printing until 1989, residing one year at the Banff Centre for the Arts (1986–7). In the spring of 1989, Gu was involved in the censored 'No Return' art exhibition in Beijing, and in the aftermath of 4 June he emigrated to Canada. He commemorated his experience at Tiananmen in 'A Barricade of Bicycles', which shows a mound of bicycles, apparently flattened by a tank. In 1990 he settled in Vancouver, where he lives and teaches at the Emily Carr Institute and the University of British Columbia. Much of his work records his early experience as an immigrant, when he worked as a busboy to support himself. One series of prints shows a heap of kitchen utensils and another, crushed Coca-Cola cans; the objects reflect Gu's feeling at the time of being a dispensable worker. In his later work Gu documents his family life in playful portraits. Recently Gu has also picked up book illustration and realistic sketching, returning to the art form that sustained him during the Cultural Revolution, when he surreptitiously filled twenty-five sketchbooks as a sent-down youth. His life and art have been featured in Audrey Mehler's film *The Yellow Pear*.

YOMI BRAESTER

Guangdong Modern Dance Company

The Guangdong Modern Dance Company (Guangdong xiandai wudaotuan) pioneered China's first professional modern dance troupe. Within a decade it has become internationally renowned for its fascinating blend of contemporary dance vocabulary, Western music and ballet, and the rich dance heritage of China. It has won many prizes at home and abroad, including the three gold prizes consecutively at the biennial Paris International Dance Competitions. The company tours in Asia and Europe frequently. In 2001, it toured the USA for the third time and Canada for the first, during which the dancers' captivating performances were sold out. Domestically, it works to broaden the understanding of dance among the young people by touring regularly to universities, schools and remote villages. In June 2002, the troupe celebrated its tenth anniversary by performing award-winning works from the last decade and debuts works of young choreographers of the company, including the new four-act *Meng Bai* (Dreaming of Li Bai) to commemorate the 1,300th anniversary of the death of the poet (701–62). Some of the company's dance pieces include *The Pond*, in which the dancers give plausible renditions of the spirits of the true and false, beautiful and ugly; *Carnivore*, which is a horror story where everyone is corrupt and nothing is left unsullied by craven desire, and even death is no release; as well as *Sitting Still, Other Kinds, 180 Degrees, Sitting Still, I Want to Fly* and *Heart, Shape, Substance*.

See also: dance troupes; performing arts in Taiwan

HELEN XIAOYAN WU

Guangming ribao

[Enlightenment Daily]

Newspaper

Guangming ribao is the official newspaper for China's intellectuals who focus on science, education and culture. Launched in June 1949, the paper has its roots in a free-thinking and critically oriented tradition. It was originally the paper of the China Democratic League and in 1953 represented the eight minority 'democratic' parties in China. In 1957, the newspaper reported widely on the various forums critical of the Communist Party which followed Mao Zedong's exhortation to 'let one hundred flowers bloom'. As a result, the paper was severely criticized for its 'bourgeois tendencies' in the succeeding Anti-Rightist Movement (1958). Subsequently the paper joined the mainstream of Party publications.

In the 1980s, a period of flourishing intellectual debate, the *Guangming ribao* became a mouthpiece for the interests of intellectuals, focusing editorials on their political status and working and living conditions. In this period the paper returned, to some extent, to its critical roots, writing various editorials directly criticizing certain senior Party figures even though the paper remained under Party control. In 1994, the paper became a central Party organ under the direct supervision of the Central Party Propaganda Committee. In the early 2000s, the paper is still read widely in intellectual and academic circles, but has had some difficulty redefining its position in China's new commercially oriented newspaper market. It relies heavily upon obligatory subscriptions from Party and state work units such as schools, universities, and publishing and cultural organizations.

See also: newspapers

KEVIN LATHAM

Guanxi

Social concept

Guanxi (social relationship/social connections) refers to a whole complex of social practices, strategies and ethics of the exchange and reciprocity of gifts, favours and banquets. For most Chinese growing up in socialist China, the social practice of Guanxi is a taken-for-granted part of everyday life. *Guanxixue* (the art of Guanxi or Guanxiology) is what one needs to learn in order to conduct oneself appropriately in social relations, live up to obligations to one's circle of kin, friends, superiors and acquaintances, and also to enhance one's chances in life, obtain hard-to-find goods or get around the bureaucracy. Guanxi is about building a network of close social ties of obligation and mutual help, as well as a pragmatic reliance on social connections to obtain anything from imported colour TVs to

rare medicines to train tickets to access to good doctors to entry into a good school for one's children to obtaining raw materials for one's factory. It is thought to have developed after the initial revolutionary zeal of the 1950s, when universalistic values of socialism started to decline, and especially during the chaotic and scarce years of the **Cultural Revolution**. Studies show that in much of the countryside, Guanxi takes a different form. There are less incidences of explicit instrumental Guanxi, and instead one finds the total social phenomenon of the exchange and circulation of gifts and mutual aid in life-cycle rituals (which is called *renqing*) between families, with emphasis on proper social form and general social obligations.

It was not until China opened up to the outside (Western) world that China scholars from abroad, especially anthropologists and sociologists based in the USA and Western Europe, started to thematize Guanxi for academic scrutiny. From the perspective of Western observers coming from a capitalist individualistic market society, the pervasive reliance on one's Guanxi network and the drawing on social obligation and debt to get things accomplished provided a novel and sharp contrast. While Guanxi had evident roots in traditional Chinese culture, with its emphasis on proper Confucian ritual form, on kinship obligations, and on principles of *renqing* (human feeling) and reciprocity, in Taiwan, Guanxi practice was not as pervasive or central. This can be seen in the fact that in Taiwan, the phrase *Guanxixue* (the art of Guanxi) did not exist, and there was not an elaborated self-conscious discourse and vocabulary of Guanxi. Thus, scholars have emphasized not the continuity of an essential Chinese culture, but the importance of social institutions and historical process as the context for the production of Guanxi. Scholars of state socialist society in the former Soviet Union and Eastern Europe have observed similar forms of reliance on social reciprocity and social networks to get things accomplished, such as *blat* in Russia. Despite their considerable cultural differences with China, Soviet societies shared very similar social institutions and state socialist political-economic and bureaucratic orders.

In the mid 1990s, as the market economy provided more goods and social services obtainable with money, and many bureaucratic hurdles were removed, the need and uses for Guanxi for ordinary people underwent a change. Guanxi was less involved in obtaining consumer goods, but became important among entrepreneurs in gaining official approval to establish new business ventures, and in obtaining tax breaks, market information and wholesale supplies. Thus, Guanxi has increasingly moved into the intersection between the business and official worlds, where its ablest practitioners are found, and increasingly becomes synonymous with **corruption**.

Further reading

Bian, Yanji (1994). '*Guanxi* and the Allocation of Urban Jobs in China'. *China Quarterly* 140: 971–99.

Kipnis, Andrew (1997). *Producing Guanxi: Sentiment, Self, and Subculture in a North China Village.* Durham: Duke University Press.

Yan, Yunxiang (1994). *The Flow of Gifts: Reciprocity and Social Networks in a Chinese Village.* Stanford: Stanford University Press.

Yang, Mayfair Mei-hui (1996). *Gifts, Favors, and Banquets: The Art of Social Relationships in China.* Ithaca, N Y: Cornell University Press.

MAYFAIR MEI-HUI YANG

Guanyin

Deity

Guanyin, Guanzizai, or Guanshiyin – 'the One who looks at the World and [Hears] its Cries' – is the Chinese name for Avalokitesvara, the Indian bodhisattva of wisdom and compassion, the unfailing saviour of all living as well as dead beings. The reputation of this bodhisattva spread in China and gave birth to many legends about his miracles. Guanyin is part of the Pure Land eschatology of Amitabha's Western Paradise and is preponderant in the *Lotus Sutra* (ch. 24).

Until the Tang dynasty, Guanyin was represented as a young man, sometimes with a moustache. Since the late Tang and beginning of the Song, however, Guanyin has appeared as a female deity through several avatars, according to

different cults and traditions. The Chinese provided her with distinctive life stories, each anchored in a different part of China. In Xiangshan (Henan), she lived an embodied life as Princess Miaoshan and, after having sacrificed her arm and eyes to save her father, she revealed herself to be the thousand-armed thousand-eyed 'Dabei', the All-Compassionate One. This has formed the mainstream of her legends since the twelfth century. But she also appears as 'Mr Ma's Wife' (Malang fu), as 'Guanyin with Chained Bones' (Souku Guanyin) and as 'Guanyin with Fish-Basket' (Yulan Guanyin), an appealing fishmonger on Mount Nanwutai (Shaanxi), where she entered Nirvana.

In the Monastery of Upper Tianzhu, in Hangzhou, where the cult arrived after the revelation of a 'precious scroll' (*baozhuan*) to a monk called Pumin (stele erected in 1104), she is the 'White-Robed Guanyin' (Baiyi Guanyin). She is famous there for averting natural disasters (floods, plagues and locusts), but also for the oracles she transmits to pilgrims in dreams. Today this kind of temple incubation and divinatory or therapeutic dream sent by the goddess can still be observed in different places in China. All texts connected with 'White-Robed Guanyin' contain powerful mantras. These elements are connected with the tantric aspect of Avalokitesvara-Guanyin. Guanyin is also a goddess capable of granting children. Women who want to conceive a child ask for her help. In the seventeenth and eighteenth centuries she was represented as 'Guanyin who Gives Children' (Songzi Guanyin), a white-robed woman holding a baby in her arms. Finally, on the island of Putuoshan, the Chinese Potalaka, off the coast of Zhejiang, she is called 'Guanyin of the South Sea' (Nanhai Guanyin). Putuoshan is identified with Xiangshan. From the twelfth century, Guanyin is represented there with her two attendants, Sudhana (Shan Cai) and Dragon Princess (Long-nü), and also sometimes with a white parrot carrying a rosary. Putuoshan is still very active today as a **pilgrimage** site where she used to preach the Dharma. She still appears in visions to the faithful in the Cave of Tidal Sound or in the Purple Bamboo Grove.

Guanyin can choose to appear in many different forms in order to save human beings: she is the terrifying exorcizer Dashi, as well as a beautiful woman holding a willow branch and a vase of pure water or ambrosia. Her identity as the deity who answers all prayers is informed by these different myths and images. Her cult is celebrated on Miaoshan's birthday, the nineteenth day of the second month, and on the day of Guanyin's enlightenment, the nineteenth day of the sixth month (see **Buddhist calendar**), as well as on the occasion of the **Qingming Festival** and **Ghost Festival**, for the rescue of bad deaths.

Guanyin should also be viewed in connection with other female Chinese deities: Tianhou or Mazu (the Queen of Heaven; see **Mazu**), Bixia yuanjun (the Goddess of Azure Cloud) and Wusheng laomu (the Never-Born Mother). All of them had close bonds with different localities in their genesis, but came to enjoy a regional and even national cult following. They have their own mythology but also often claim to be related to Guanyin or to be her incarnation, like Chen Jinggu (Linshui furen) in Fujian (see **Lüshan jiao (Sannai jiao)**) whose mythology connects her with the episode of the building of the Loyang bridge by Guanyin. She would have been conceived through a drop of blood of the bodhisattva swallowed by her mother. Most of the time Guanyin is represented in the temples of these goddesses. They all embody different aspects of womanhood and 'motherliness' and also different religious and ritual traditions (Buddhist, Tantric or Daoist) syncretically. Women used to get together to recite Guanyin's sutra, and she may possess mediums to deliver oracles.

In Chinese mythology, the 'Horse-headed Guanyin' (Hayagriva; Matou Guanyin) is also connected with the breeding of silkworms. Interesting themes appear through the cult of Guanyin, like her sexual transformation and a display of a rich and, at first sight, paradoxical sexual symbolism: refusal of marriage and filial piety, virginity and motherliness, chastity and sexual promiscuity as a homeopathic therapy to free men of sexual desire by satisfying them 'once and for all' (Yulan Guanyin) in a kind of conversion by love, assumed or denied. The theme of the visualization, and of the care taken by the goddess to create her own miraculous image, or to have the faithful carve, paint icons or incubate dreams in front of them is also very important. This iconography as well as folk literature (precious scrolls), plays and novels (*Journey to the West*) also played an important role in the spread of the cult.

See also: temple fairs

Further reading

Dudbridge, Glen (1978). *The Legend of Miao-shan*. Oxford, Oxford Faculty of Oriental Studies Oriental Monographs 1. London: Ithaca Press.

Sangren, Steven (1983). 'Female Gender in Chinese Religious Symbols: Kuan-yin, Ma Tsu and the Eternal Mother', *Signs* 9: 4–25

——— (1987). *History and Magical Power in a Chinese Community*. Stanford: Stanford University Press.

Stein, R. A. (1986). 'Avalokitesvara/Kouan-yin, un exemple de transformation d'un dieu en déesse', *Cahiers d'Extrême-Asie* 2: 17–80

Yü, Chun-fang (2000). *Kuan-yin: The Chinese Transformation of Avalokitesvara*. New York: Columbia University Press.

BRIGITTE BERTHIER-BAPTANDIER

Guo Lusheng

(a.k.a. 'Indexfinger'/Shizhi)

b. 1948, Shandong

Poet

Guo Lusheng is a prominent poet and voice of the *zhiqing* generation (educated urban youth sent to the countryside) during and after the **Cultural Revolution**. After he had briefly joined the Red Guards, his poetry was denounced as bourgeois and he became an underground poet until he resurfaced under the pseudonym 'Indexfinger' after the Cultural Revolution.

His representative poems of the early period, notably 'This is Beijing at 4.08 p.m.' (*Zhe shi sidianlingbafenzhong de Beijing*), 'Three Songs on Fish' (*Yu'er sanbuqu*) and 'To Believe in the Future' (*Xiangxin weilai*), were, at the time, the only expressions of the traumatic experiences of the sent-down youth and still form a perceptive critique. After the Cultural Revolution, Guo Lusheng began a new period of creativity under his pseudonym. His earlier representative poems were published anew, while he also wrote for various magazines as part of the **Misty poetry** group. Diagnosed with schizophrenia in 1973, his illness unwittingly made him the first poet to make the disquiet of mental illness and institutionalization a topic of writing in the 1990s. Although his referential poetry is not great, Guo Lusheng's engagement exerted tremendous influence in literary circles. During the 1990s, as memories of the *zhiqing* generation become more public, he once again became an icon of a whole generation of displaced youths and consequently won the People's Literature Prize for Poetry in 2001.

See also: poetry; Third Generation (poets); xiafang, xiaxiang

BIRGIT LINDER

Guo Qihong

b. 1940, Chaozhou, Guangdong

Xiqu and Huaju playwright

Guo Qihong graduated in 1961 from Zhongshan University as a student of Wang Jisi, a renowned scholar of classical Chinese plays. After graduation, he was assigned to Beijing and worked as playwright in the China Pingju Troupe (Zhongguo pingju yuan), Beijing Jingju Troupe (Beijing jingju yuan), Northern Kunqu Troupe (Beifang kunqu yuan) and **Beijing People's Art Theatre** (Beijing renmin yishu juyuan) at different times. As a result, he has written about fifty plays in the forms of **Pingju** (Tangshan opera), **Kunqu Xiqu**, **Jingju** (Peking opera), **Huaju** (spoken drama) and television series.

His best works are his 'newly written historical plays' (*xinbian lishi xi*) (see **Xiqu**). *Reminiscence of the Southern Tang* (*Nantang yishi*) staged by Northern Kunqu Troupe in 1987 is about Li Yu, the famous emperor poet. *Sima Xiangru* produced by Shanghai Kunqu Troupe in 1995 retells the well-known love story between Sima Xiangru and Zhuo Wenjun. The spoken dramas *Li Bai* (1991) and *The Proud Son of Heaven* (*Tian zhi jiaozi*, 1995) for Beijing People's Art Theatre focus on the Tang poet Li Bai and the Wei-Jin poet Cao Zhi, respectively. These four

plays have earned the playwright, along with his troupes and leading actors, a significant number of awards at both national and municipal levels. Like most contemporary playwrights, Guo looks at well-known historical figures from new perspectives. At the same time his work remains faithful to the traditional cultural aura attending each personage. He has also joined some of the other playwrights in a new trend of adapting Western classics into Xiqu (sung-drama/opera). He wrote *Thebes* (*Tebai cheng*) for a large production by the Beijing Heibei Bangzi Troupe in 2002. Based on Aeschylus' *Seven against Thebes* and Sophocles' *Antigone*, the play sets the story in the Spring and Autumn period and combines Chinese poetry, costume and acting style with the concepts of Greek tragedy. Guo's plays have been praised by most critics for their literary quality in lyrics and content. His drama is not only for performance, but also for reading.

See also: Xiqu playwrights

DU WENWEI

Guo Shixing

b. 1952, Beijing

Playwright

The son of middle-class bank-workers and a descendent of a line of chess champions dating back to the Ming–Qing period, Guo Shixing authored the critically and commercially successful *Loafer* trilogy, consisting of three plays about the amateur obsessions of Beijing residents – goldfish, chess and birds – that were staged in Beijing between 1993 and 1997, all directed by **Lin Zhaohua**. *Fishmen* (*Yuren*) was written in 1989 during the Tiananmen demonstrations, but could not be produced because of the political climate. It opened at the **Beijing People's Art Theatre** in March 1997, the year after *Chessmen* (*Qiren*) was staged. *Birdmen* (*Niaoren*) was written in 1991 and staged in 1993, setting box-office records and running through 1995. A journalist by trade – formerly the theatre critic for the *Beijing Evening News* (*Beijing wanbao*) – the trilogy was Guo's first attempt at playwriting. He was hired as a resident playwright of the

Central Experimental Theatre in Beijing and went on to author other successful plays, including *Gossip Street* (*Huaihua yitiao jie*, 1998).

Further reading

Chen, Xiaoming. (2002) *Acting the Right Part: Political Theater and Popular Drama in Contemporary China*. Hawaii: University of Hawaii Press, 324–30.

Conceison, Claire (1998) 'The Occidental Other on the Chinese Stage: Cultural Cross-Examination in Guo Shixing's *Birdmen*'. *Asian Theatre Journal* 1: 87–101.

Guo, Shixing (1997). 'Birdmen: A Drama in Three Acts'. Trans. Jane Lai. In Martha Cheung and Jane Lai (eds), *An Anthology of Contemporary Drama in China*. New York: Oxford University Press, 295–350.

CLAIRE CONCEISON

Guo Wenjing

b. 1956, Chongqing, Sichuan

Composer

Guo Wenjing, a member of the musical 'New Wave' that has risen to prominence since the 1980s (see **Third Generation (composers)**), remains in Beijing and teaches composition at the Central Conservatory of Music. At age twelve, Guo learned to play the violin. Between 1970 and 1977, he was a member of the Chongqing Song and Dance Troupe, coming into close contact with the folk music of Sichuan. Guo belongs to the first group of students admitted to the Central Conservatory of Music when it reopened in 1978. His musical language is personal and rooted, consciously employing or avoiding European idioms. Guo's music can be visceral and energetic, remaining close to primal ritual functions.

With a prolific output that is performed worldwide, Guo differs from the rest of his classmates who emigrated (**Chen Yi**, **Zhou Long**, **Chen Qigang**, **Tan Dun**) after China opened its doors in the 1980s. Remaining in Beijing gives Guo access to the depth and range of Chinese contemporary culture and the best performers on traditional instruments. Guo's two chamber operas, *Wolf Cub Village* (1994), based on Lu Xun's novella *Diary of a Madman* (*Kuangren riji*), and *Night Banquet* (*Yeyan*, 1998), have been performed at major European and American festivals. Along with chamber and symphonic (both Western and Chinese orchestral) works and film music, Guo's work incorporates vocal styles and musical gestures from regional operas and folk idioms. *Buddhist Temple* (*Shanyuan*, 2002) is written for forty Chinese, Western and Middle-Eastern instruments.

Further reading

Kouwenhoven, Frank and Shimmelpenninck, A. (1997). 'Guo Wenjing, A Composer's Portrait: "The Strings Going *Hong Hong Hong* and the Percussion *Bong Kèèh* – That's My Voice!"' *Chime* 10/11 (Spring/ Autumn): 8–49.

JOANNA C. LEE

gymnastics

Gymnastics is a growth area for Chinese sporting success, particularly in men's events. China's version of the 'dream team' is the Chinese men's gymnastics squad that won the team gold at the 2000 Sydney Olympics, after taking silver in the two prior Summer Games. 'We have fought for this for forty years,' said the coach as the exuberant athletes raced around the stadium. Five members went on to take team gold at the next East Asian Games, and the Chinese men's team also took gold in gymnastics at the world university games held in Beijing in 2001.

Two decades of individual prowess in the field started with Li Ning, whose six medals (including three gold) for men's gymnastics were the most won by any athlete at the 1984 Los Angeles Olympics. In Atlanta in 1996, Li Xiaoshuang became China's first gymnastics all-around champion at the Olympic level. Chinese gymnasts earned both men's and women's all-round gold at the 2002 Asian Games. Although women's gymnastics has less depth for the future, the men's strength is expected to persist into the 2004 Olympics. Surveys show gymnastics is China's third most popular sport, after **football (soccer)** and **basketball**. Chinese are thought to have good body types for gymnastics; promising youngsters are funnelled into a training system that, even as other sports become more commercialized, remains state-run and highly centralized.

China's best-known female gymnast, sadly, is Sang Lan, left paralysed after breaking her neck at the 1998 Goodwill Games. Li Ning, meanwhile, has parlayed his happier celebrity into an entrepreneurial kingdom: his giant sports apparel company has been described as the Nike of China. And in anticipation of the 2008 Beijing Games, Li Xiaoshuang and his brother Li Dashuang have opened an agency called Omnipotent Stars to market Olympic athletes.

JUDY POLUMBAUM

Hai Bo

b. 1962, Changchun, Jilin

Photographer

After graduating from the Jilin Institute of Art in Changchun in 1984, Hai Bo moved to Beijing to advance his studies in the Printmaking Department of the **Central Academy of Fine Arts** (1984–9). Despite an initial career as a painter influenced by German expressionism, Hai Bo's interest in photography sprouted during his academy training as a result of a combined fascination with the power of time and visual memory that dated back to his early childhood during the **Cultural Revolution**. Based on a practical recollection of the past, Hai Bo's work fills in time gaps by juxtaposing old b/w portraits of relatives and friends with colour mirror images of the same taken in the present. In these works the confrontation of subjects and postures does not just stimulate chronological comparison, but captures the space separating past and present by indexing the issue of change. Representative of his painstaking research method is the series *They*, begun in 1997 and presented at the 49th Venice Biennale in 2001, as well as *I'm Chairman Mao's Red Guard* (1999) and *Three Sisters* (1999).

In 2000 he participated in the 3rd Shanghai Biennale and was awarded a prize in the second edition of the CCAA (Chinese Contemporary Art Awards). A new structural geometry appears in *Dusk* (1993–2002), consisting of three triptychs in which the artist combines intimate, b/w photo portraits of his grandmother (taken in 1993), his father (1998) and his son (2000) all within the image of a landscape familiar to his subjects. Here the correspondence with the past is embedded in the physical outline of a place connected to the history of the three people. Featured in the 1st Pingyao Photography Festival (2001), Hai Bo's work was also presented at 'Rencontres des Arles' (France, 2003).

Further reading

Exhibition catalogue (2001). *dApertutto Aperto Over All*. Venezia: La Biennale di Venezia/Marsilio.
—— (2003). *Photography Arles-Recontres Des Arles* (exhibition catalogue). Paris: Actes Sud, Le Mejan, 72–5.
Leanza, Beatrice (2003). 'Il cerchio invisibile: A caccia del Tempo e dell' Infinito – Fotografia di Hai Bo' (The Invisible Circle: Hunting Time and Infinity – Photographs by Hai Bo). In *GuangYIN/Tempi di Donne* (exhibition catalogue). Viterbo, Italy.
Smith, Karen (ed.) (2000). *Dangdai Zhongguo yishu jiangjin* (Contemporary Chinese Art Awards exhibition catalogue), 23–4.

BEATRICE LEANZA

hair

Hair do's and dont's have been a tricky subject in Chinese culture ever since the Manchu conquest in 1644. It has been observed by many writers and scholars that the transition from late imperial to modernity was, for many Chinese who lived at the turn of the twentieth century, marked, among other things, by radical changes in hairstyle. For men it meant getting rid of the queue, often under threat of death, while for women it often meant choosing to adopt it, as a marker of a student lifestyle. Later, in the 1920s and 1930s, while men adopted Western-style short crops, women chose the Hollywood-inspired bob. All this variety changed, of course, with the Communist revolution, and for many years, until at least the late 1980s, coloured ribbons tied to the end of pigtails was the biggest concession to female hair fashion. But with the economic changes of the late 1980s more women and men started to perm their hair, at least in the big cities. By the early 1990s, new hairstyles started to appear in the streets of Shanghai and Beijing, the most striking of which was the long unruly manes of rock-stars and artists. And for the past four years, the most striking hairdos are the bleached heads of Japanese inspiration that transform many Chinese urban youths in transnational visions of peroxide.

Clearly, China's huge population provides great potential for the beauty business. As the standard of living improves following market reforms, Chinese people are increasingly willing to pay high prices to have their hair done. Imported beauty products are more popular, since people are prepared to pay for quality and the profit margin is correspondingly higher. Decleor, a French cosmetics and skin care products enterprise, first ventured into the China market in 1996. Now, it has just opened its third beauty salon in Beijing at the China World Trade Centre. According to Decleor, although there are countless hair and beauty salons in Chinese cities, the market holds bright prospects because large professional operations are still few.

According to the Chinese Association of Hairstylists and Beauticians, beauty and hairdressing has been the fastest growing service sector in the mainland in recent years, with turnover leaping to 25 per cent per annum. As people are paying more attention to their overall appearance, the services offered by hair salons have extended from simple haircuts and shampooing to include treatment, styling, scalp treatment and hair planting. In addition, hair salons are also offering services in makeup, manicure, fitness training and body shaping.

These days there are over 1.2 million beauty and hairstyling operations in China, employing more than 6 million people and grossing Rmb24 billion a year.

Recently, Shanghai's avant-garde artists have also turned to hairy matters. Generation X Neo-Conceptualist Shi Yong (b. 1963) created 'image advertising' that comprised a series of fake ad campaigns soliciting the public to vote on Shi's hairstyle. New York-based artist **Gu Wenda** (b. 1955) is known as the 'hair artist', partially because of his hairstyle (a shaved crown flowing into a black mane well past his waist). But more to the point, he is best known for his ongoing succession of installations realized in different parts of the world and constructed of hair from around the world.

Further reading

Godley, Michael (1994). 'The End of the Queue: Hair as Symbol in Chinese History'. *East Asian History* 8 (Dec): 88–94.

Hiltebeitel, Alf and Miller, Barbara D. (eds) (1998). *Hair. Its Power and Meaning in Asian Cultures*. Albany: State University of New York Press.

Kuhn, Philip A. (1990). *Soulstealers. The Chinese Sorcery Scare of 1768*. Cambridge: Harvard University Press.

Sun, Lung-kee (1997). 'The Politics of Hair and the Issue of the Bob in Modern China'. *Fashion Theory* 1.4: 353–65.

PAOLA ZAMPERINI

Haizi

(né Zha Haisheng)

b. May 1964, Anqing; d. 26 March 1989, Shanghai

Poet

Haizi was a well-known poet who began writing as a campus poet in 1982. He entered **Peking University** at the age of fifteen and began writing lyrical and narrative poetry, short fiction and diaries. After graduation, he lived a hermetic life in the Beijing rural suburbs, marked by poetic ambition and mental illness until he committed suicide in 1989.

From the beginning Haizi stood out for his poetic genius and encyclopedic knowledge. He was a poet who lived his poetry and used his adolescent crisis-consciousness to search for a universal poetic truth. While **Misty poetry** (Menglongshi) and the Third Generation poets (see **Third Generation (poets)**) reflected the immediate situation of the time, it was Haizi's objective to create an epic of universal truth. Since the epic form has no tradition in China, he incorporated Western and Eastern religion, philosophy and art into his writing. His unfinished epic poem *The Sun* (*Taiyang*) comprises seven poetic dramas and a novel in verse, influenced by the Bible, Indian epics, Homer and Dante, Hölderlin, Shakespeare and Goethe. Although overly ambitious in its scope, it is a testimony to his keen instinct and original style. Haizi's mysterious death elevated him to almost mythological status. But it is the informed depth and accessibility of his poetry that remains a challenge to poets and constitutes an extraordinary part of Chinese literature.

See also: poetry; Xi Chuan

Further reading

Yeh, Michelle (2000). 'Death of the Poet'. In D. Wang and P. Chi (eds), *Chinese Literature in the Second Half of a Modern Century: A Critical Survey*. Bloomington: Indiana University Press.

BIRGIT LINDER

Hakka, culture of

The Hakka are a diasporic ethnic group, considered by most scholars and Chinese people to be a sub-group of the dominant **Han** Chinese who migrated southwards from central China starting in the fourth century. The seven counties of Meizhou prefecture in mountainous northern Guangdong is considered to be their homeland because of the area's high concentration of Hakka. Over 40 million Hakka, however, are scattered throughout China and Taiwan, and many more in over fifty countries, especially in Indonesia, Malaysia, Thailand, Mauritius, Canada and the United States. There are also distinct Hakka communities in the United Kingdom, France and Jamaica. Hakka (Mandarin, *Kejia*) literally means 'guest people', suggesting the ethnic group's marginality and frequent migration. Despite their marginalization, however, there have been many prominent Hakka individuals in Chinese history and contemporary society, including Qiu Fengjia (Qing political and educational leader), Hong Xiuquan (Taiping Rebellion leader), Sun Yat-sen (father of the Republican and Communist revolutions), Ye Jianying (PRC military and political leader), Lee Kuan-yew (leader of Singapore) and Han Suyin (writer), to name but a few.

Historically, the Hakka were marginal because they lacked prime agricultural land and lived for the most part in mountainous and other less desirable areas. Nonetheless, they are proud of their links to the culture of the Central Plains and especially to that of the Tang dynasty. Hakka culture is often delineated by the 'Hakka Spirit' (*Kejia jingshen*), which can be summarized by the following traits: hard work, self-reliance, independence, frugality and a pioneering spirit with a strong concept of roots. The Hakka are also known for greater gender equality – historically, Hakka women did not bind their feet, and were seen by both Hakka and non-Hakka as active participants in public life. The Hakka have a distinct dialect, with many colloquial words that cannot be expressed using Chinese characters and wide regional variations within the dialect itself. There is also a distinct Hakka cuisine, known for its combination of good taste and thriftiness – similar in some ways to Cantonese cuisine with its lack of spiciness, but largely prepared using more stir-fried techniques, heavier ingredients, preserved vegetables and tofu. Some well-known Hakka dishes include fatty pork with **preserved vegetables** (*meicai kourou*), tofu stuffed with pork (*niang doufu*), and meatball and fishball soups.

As 'guest people', another dominant characteristic of Hakka culture is their perpetual migration. The earliest usage of the term 'guest' (*ke*), used in opposition to those marked as 'native' (*zhu*), is found in a Tang dynasty census of 780. Since that time there has been constant friction between the

Hakka and other Han ethnic groups (such as the Cantonese), the so-called natives, who had settled in southern China earlier. Many Hakka cultural characteristics, therefore, reflect this history of conflict, including the importance of lineages in structuring Hakka social life and the architecture of some Hakka homes – the 'roundhouses' (*tulou*) in southern Fujian and the 'walled dragon houses' (*weilongwu*) in Meizhou, Guangdong – that resemble fortresses. Many of these walled structures can house over a thousand people, and have within their fortifications stables, granaries, ancestral temples and wells.

Hakka women are known for their independence and public role relative to the women of other sub-ethnic Han groups, and have become symbolic of both Hakka culture and modern gender relations. Luo Xianglin, the seminal, early twentieth-century historian of the Hakka, marked off Hakka women as a 'special characteristic' (*texing*) of Hakka culture, a tradition that has been continued by Hakka ethnic apologists. Because Hakka women did not practise footbinding, they have traditionally worked in farming, the marketing of agricultural products, and other paid labour outside the home. Although an object of derision by other Han Chinese groups in the past, when pejorative labels such as 'big feet' were used to describe Hakka women, contemporary opinion sees the absence of footbinding as a demonstration of the progressiveness of Hakka culture. In Hakka families, women create and manage family wealth, and there is no distinction in gender roles either in the management and cultivation of the family farm or in the management of household funds; Hakka men, however, still maintain a dominant position as the head of the household (*jiazhang*). The importance of women in Hakka culture is further indicated by the addition of an honorific – *ru ren* – on Hakka ancestral tablets; this title is based on a legend according to which a group of Hakka women, returning from work in the fields with farm implements on their shoulders, were mistaken as women soldiers by an invading Mongol army, who fled at the sight, resulting in the bestowal of this title on all Hakka women by the emperor. Relative gender parity is also reflected in Hakka 'mountain songs' (*shange*), an important element in Hakka culture. A highly stylized singing form, mountain songs, today

as in the past, usually involve two singers, a man and a woman, who take turns singing, each responding to the other. They are mostly love songs traditionally associated with courtship, but they also demonstrate that there has been less segregation between Hakka men and women in both work and play than among other Han Chinese ethnicities.

See also: Chaozhou-Hakka sixian; Kejia daxi

Further reading

Cohen, Myron (1976). *House United, House Divided: The Chinese Family in Taiwan*. New York: Columbia University Press.

Constable, Nicole (1994). *Christian Souls and Chinese Spirits: A Hakka Community in Hong Kong*. Berkeley: University of California Press.

—— (ed.) (1996). *Guest People: Hakka Identity in China and Abroad*. Seattle: University of Washington Press.

Johnson, Elizabeth L. (1988). 'Grieving for the Dead, Grieving for the Living: Funeral Laments of Hakka Women'. In James L. Watson and Evelyn S. Rawski (eds), *Death Ritual in Late Imperial and Modern China*. Berkeley: University of California Press, 135–63.

Lozada, Eriberto P. Jr. (2001). *God Aboveground: Catholic Church, Postsocialist State, and Transnational Processes in a Chinese Village*. Stanford: Stanford University Press [ethnography of a Hakka village].

ERIBERTO P. LOZADA JR

Han

Han Chinese are China's majority ethnic group, consisting of 92 per cent of the mainland's population. Regarded as descendants of the inhabitants of the Yellow River basin, they are traced to the earliest years of any identifiable Chinese culture, as in the Neolithic. In some scholarship, especially in which the goal is to trace a direct line of descent, the Han are identified with Shang culture. A popular image is of Han culture being an amalgamation of all other cultures into a single stream, absorbing them by the force of by its civilizing power. In many ways the notion Han is by implication equivalent to that of civilization.

The name Han is said to come from the Han dynasty (206 BCE–CE 220), which had its base in the Wei river valley near Xi'an. The term Han was not used frequently until the twentieth century; the precursor term is *Hua* or *Huaxia*. The Han speak any of the Sinitic languages, the assortment of loosely related though not mutually intelligible languages classified under the Sinitic branch of Sino-Tibetan (see **Sino-Tibetan language speakers**). There is not much Han consciousness; those who write about Han culture tend to do so only in contrast with ethnic minorities. Han culture is usually taken as the most advanced form of generalized Chinese culture, with emphasis on rationality, monogamy, education, writing, hierarchy, patriarchy, frugality, assiduousness, and other aspects of what is usually termed 'Confucian' culture. Food plays an important role in Han identity; pork is the central meat, and in contemporary China rice is the central grain (especially in the south). The Han are known to be largely free of food taboos.

Han people tend to be aware of themselves as Han principally in areas of contact with minorities, such as border areas. In those places, there may be mention of Han language, *hanhua*, in contrast to a much-spoken minority language. (A homophone, *hanhua*, means sinification, or sometimes Hanification, or becoming like the Han/Chinese.) Han culture is usually seen as charismatically pulling non-Han to the centre, with superior technology and social organization.

In the 1980s, the **Root-seeking school** (*xungen yishi*) sought an illustrious Han identity in the past, especially in the northwest around Xi'an. This is often connected to the idea of **nationalism**, with the Han serving as the core of the nation. Han are far from homogeneous, but this is glossed over in deference to the concept of national unity. Southern Chinese refer to themselves as *Tangren*, so that overseas Chinese 'Chinatowns' are usually called, in the local dialect version of the Mandarin, *Tangrenjie* (Streets of the People of the Tang Dynasty). 'Han' thus has a northern flavour.

See also: ethnicity, concepts of; River Elegy; writing systems

Further reading

Gladney, Dru C. (ed.) (1998). *Making Majorities: Constituting the Nation in Japan, Korea, China, Malaysia, Fiji, Turkey, and the United States.* Stanford: Stanford University Press.

SUSAN D. BLUM

Han Lei

b. 1967, Kaifeng, Henan

Photographer

Han Lei graduated from the Department of Bookbinding of the Central Academy of Craft and Design in Beijing in 1989. Even preceding his graduation, Han Lei's photographic work had been driven by his wanderlust and investigation of the human psyche. His first solo show, 'Alienation', opened at the Beijing Contemporary Art Gallery in 1995 with fifty idiosyncratic and estranged images of street life throughout China. This series of 35 mm black-and-white images carefully portray the isolated and disturbed spirits of their subjects – a back alley scene of a mentally handicapped person, lonely faces in the crowd, a silent stand-off between a German shepherd and a man – all are consistent in their haunting mood. 'Alienation' was a successful exhibition and the show went on to Germany and Finland; it was also compiled as a self-published catalogue under the same name.

In the late 1990s Han Lei began manipulating black-and-white photographs and negatives with dyes and paint to create impressionistic images of landscapes and portraits. *Fabricated Portraits* are circular prints of blurred out faces and figures from original and re-photographed found photographs that play on memory and disappearance. His *Fictional Landscape* series depict eerily romanticized scenes where nature and industry meet. Han Lei's project *Railways and People* was chosen for the 1998 Mother Jones International Fund for Documentary Photography Award (USA). His work has been exhibited in 'Disorientation – Photography and

Video in China Today' (Chambers Fine Art, New York) and in 'Contemporary Photography from Mainland China, Taiwan and Hong-Kong' (Hong Kong Arts Centre, 1994).

Further reading

Han, Lei (1995). *Alienation. 50 Photographs* (exhibition catalogue). Copyright Han Lei.

Zhang, Li (2001). *Disorientation. Photography and Video in China Today*. New York: Chambers Fine Art.

MATHIEU BORYSEVICZ

Han Shaogong

b. 1 January 1953, Changsha, Hunan

Writer

Han Shaogong is a writer primarily known for his 'root-searching' literature during the early 1980s. In 1985, he published an influential essay, 'The Roots of Literature' (*Wenxue de gen*), which gave the **Root-seeking school** (*Xungen pai*) its name and established him as its main representative. In the essay, Han calls for a literary inquiry into traditional Chinese culture so as to better understand China's modern literary and psychological heritage.

Unlike the 'root-seeker' **Ah Cheng**, Han did not identify with traditional Chinese culture. His quest to uncover ancient Chu culture was combined with the use of magical realism to portray the anxieties of a stagnant and superstitious culture in a style very much his own. In his representative short story, 'Daddy, Daddy, Daddy' (*Bababa*), the retarded Bing Zai is a symbolic figure of degeneration, and the only survivor of a mass suicide. Aunt Shu in 'Woman, Woman, Woman' (*Nününü*) is another prototype of the Chinese national psyche. After suffering a stroke, she undergoes a transformation in both character and physique that symbolizes the power of repression over the individual. Han caused another stir in the 1990s with his novel *Dictionary of Horsebridge* (*Maqiao cidian*, 1996). In it, he analyses 111 words that were used in Horsebridge village during the **Cultural Revolution** as though they were single events. Writing about the

politics, history, tradition, language and psychology of the village, he attempts to create a new literary consciousness about the Cultural Revolution, a hitherto uncharted field in Chinese literature.

Further reading

Han, Shaogong (1992). 'After the "Literature of the Wounded": Local Cultures, Roots, Maturity, and Fatigue'. In H. Martin and J. Kinkley (eds), *Modern Chinese Writers: Self-Portrayals*. Armonk, NY: M. E. Sharpe, 147–55.

—— (1995). *Homecoming? And Other Stories*. Trans. Martha Cheung. New York: Renditions Press.

—— (2003). *A Dictionary of Maqiao*. Trans. Julia Lovell. New York: Columbia University Press.

Lau, J (1993). 'Visitation of the Past in Han Shaogong's Post-1985 Fiction'. In E. Widmer and D. Wang (eds), *From May Fourth to June Fourth: Fiction and Film in Twentieth-Century China*. Cambridge: Harvard University Press.

Lee, Vivian (2002). 'Cultural Lexicology: *Maqiao Dictionary* by Han Shaogong'. *Modern Chinese Literature and Culture* 14.1 (Spring): 145–77.

BIRGIT LINDER

Hani, culture of

The Hani population of some 1.3 million dwell mainly between the Red and Lancang rivers in southern Yunnan province, including Xishuangbanna. The region is rich in minerals and plants which are to be developed and environmentally protected. The Hani are polytheists and practice ancestor-worship. They have a tradition of maintaining the family line by having a son's name begin with the last one or two words of his father's. The farmers are skilful at opening up new terraced fields which can stretch from the foot right to the top of the mountains. The staple food is rice and corn, plus self-produced fish. Deep-dried locusts and cooked chicken heads are considered the best to offer important guests. They have many traditional oral literary pieces, e.g. *Genesis* and *On the Floods* (see **ethnic minority literary collections**). In 1957 the government helped them create a written script using the Roman alphabet.

The major festivals of the Hani are: the Sheep Day, on which sacrifices are made; the June Festival, when people sing, dance, play on swings and hold wrestling contests; and the Hani New Year's Day, on the first day of the tenth month of the lunar calendar, when every village holds a big banquet in the centre of the main street. All the villagers gather and drink toasts by turns, wishing each other good luck and happiness. When evening falls, young people sing love songs and head for a world of their own, deep in the bamboo forests.

Further reading

Zhang, Xingrong (1997). 'A New Discovery: Traditional 8-Part Polyphonic Singing of the Hani of Yunnan'. *Chime* 10/11 (Spring/Autumn): 145–52.

HELEN XIAOYAN WU

hard liquor

China produces all sorts of alcoholic drinks, but primarily hard liquor, commonly called *baijiu* (white liquor) or *shaojiu* (burnt alcohol). Hard liquor is fermented from assorted grains such as rice, sorghum and wheat. The most famous brand names are: Maotai, Wuliangye, Jiugui [Drunkard], Xifeng, Fenjiu, Gujinggong, Jiannanchun, Yanghe Daqu, Guizhouchun, Luzhou Laojiao, Baiyunbian, Beijingchun, Kongfu [Confucius's Family] and Erguotou, a popular low-priced brand. The first two of these sell for about 300 to 500 yuan per 500 ml bottle. To satisfy alcohol drinkers but to minimize drunkenness, most hard liquor maintains a strength below 40 per cent, and hard liquor is almost always consumed with food. There are also medicinal forms which promote good health and virility. Ginseng liquor and snake liquor in fruity concoctions are two popularly taken as tonics.

Maotai, China's most famous hard liquor, is named after a town near Chishui (Red River) in southwestern Guizhou province. Dating back to the Song dynasty (960–1279), the liquor is made from sorghum and barley. It is fermented eight times and distilled seven times, and ranges between 38 and 55 proof. The entire process takes from one

to five years. The town of Maotai itself has become a tourist spot, hosting Maotai festivals and dominating the Museum of Liquor and Wine in nearby Zunyi, a city associated with Mao Zedong's rise to dominance over the CCP in 1935.

Wuliangye [Five-Grain Liquid], produced in the city of Yibin in southern Sichuan province, is another high-grade liquor and one of the most expensive brands. As the Chinese name suggests, Wuliangye is a spirit distilled from five types of grain: Chinese sorghum, glutinous rice, husked rice, wheat and corn. The raw and auxiliary materials are carefully chosen and proportionally prepared before they are steamed and mixed with yeast. Then they are fermented in sealed cellars and finally distilled into extracted liquor, which is then stored until blended. This liquor is distinguished by its mellowness, some say lusciousness, and lingering fragrance. Other varieties include: Wuliangshen, Wuliangchun, Wuhuye and Jianzhuang. Both Wuliangye and Maotai are the most common liquors served at state banquets and by Chinese consulates abroad, and are favourite gifts of China's political leaders when visiting foreign countries.

HELEN XIAOYAN WU

He Dun

b. 1958, Changsha, Hunan

Writer

A leading writer of 1990s new urban fiction, He Dun taught middle school art in his native Changsha in the 1980s before launching his own business in interior design. His lifestyle change from idealistic academic to materialistic entrepreneur followed the pattern of many in the early 1990s who chose to **xiahai** (take the plunge into the sea (of business)). With his changed lifestyle came an evolution of values and worldview; he decided to write so as to describe the attitudinal changes accompanying the commercialism of the 1990s, where individual choices abounded and personal ethics were re-examined. His realistic accounts of Changsha are closely based on personal experience, and delineate the moral fall-out accompanying urban business success stories.

He Dun first gained critical acclaim for his novellas *Hello, Younger Brother* (*Didi ni hao*), *Life is not a Crime* (*Shenghuo wuzui*), and *I Don't Care* (*Wo buxiangshi*), all published in 1993. He shows the value of material success in the 1990s to be as ephemeral as political or academic success proved to have been in the 1980s. His stories make striking references to fate and the rise of superstitious practices in the 1990s which are often directly related to the market economy. He Dun elaborates upon this in his novel *The Himalayas* (*Ximalaya shan*, 1998), where his protagonist searches unsuccessfully for spiritual ideals that are at odds with the decadent business environment of the city.

See also: Humanistic Spirit, 'Spirit of the Humanities'; Qiu Huadong

Further reading

Lu, Jie (2001). 'Cultural Invention and Cultural Intervention: Reading Chinese Urban Fiction in the Nineties'. *Modern Chinese Literature and Culture* 13.1 (Spring): 107–39.

Tang, Xiaobing (2000). *Chinese Modern: The Heroic and the Quotidian*. Durham: Duke University Press, 273–315.

ROBIN VISSER

He Jianjun

(a.k.a. He Yi)

b. 1960, Beijing

Film director

Among 'Sixth-Generation' directors (see **Sixth Generation (film directors)**), He Jianjun is the one most interested in exploring the dark side of human psyche. His movies are concerned with issues of repression and freedom, with the adjustment and survival of personality in a confined environment. Through stories of disturbed – and disturbing – individuals, his movies expand into a discourse about society at large. Not surprisingly, most of his movies have been banned in China.

He Jianjun graduated in 1990 from the **Beijing Film Academy** and started his career as assistant director to **Zhang Yimou** and **Tian Zhuangzhuang** before beginning to make short movies himself. His first full-length feature, *Red Beads* (*Xuan lian*, 1993), was inspired by the memory of a schoolmate who had become mentally unstable after reading the medical history of his unbalanced mother. It was shot in twelve days on a shoestring budget and won the Fipresci Award at the Rotterdam Film Festival. He's second feature, another independent production, also received an award at Rotterdam. *Postman* (*Youchai*, 1995) is the story of a young postman who – in a society that does not value individual privacy – cannot resist the temptation to read other people's letters and ends up interfering in other people's lives. The movie widened the exposure of social malaise by touching on taboo subjects like incest, loneliness and suicide. With his subsequent movies, He has continued the exploration of human weakness and obsession in the context of contemporary urban culture.

MARIA BARBIERI

He Jingzhi

(a.k.a. Ai Mo/Jing Zhi)

b. 1924, Yixian, Shangdong

Writer, poet

He Jingzhi finished his secondary school in 1937. In 1940 he entered the **Lu Xun Literary Institute** in Yan'an and joined the CCP. He then worked briefly in the Lun Xun Art Troupe before teaching in the College of Literature at the United University of North China in 1946. His writing career began in 1945 when he co-authored China's first realistic **Geju** (song-drama), *The White-Haired Girl* (*Baimao Nü*), with Ding Yi and Ma Ke. In 1961 his *Collection of Singing Heartily* (*Fangge ji*) was published. Poems like 'Back to Yan'an' (*Hui Yan'an*), 'Sing Heartily' (*Fang sheng ge chang*) and 'Songs at the San Men Gorge' (*Sanmen xiafangge*) made him 'the poet of the time'. The year 1963 saw the release of his 'Ode to **Lei Feng**' (*Lei Feng zhi ge*), which impacted a generation. *He Jingzhi's Selected Poems* (*He Jingzhi shixuan*, 1979) collects his best pieces over four decades.

Politically charged and timely, many of his poems may not endure. However they do reflect the poet's creativity, vigour and grandiosity. He could be lyrical and dainty as well, as in his 'Ode to the Beauty of Guilin's Landscape' (*Guilin shanshui ge*), the originality of which lies in his dexterous integration of folk and regional traditions with the borrowed style of free verse. A board member of the Chinese Writers' Association and the Chinese Dramatists' Association, He Jingzhi was Deputy and then Acting Minister of Culture from 1989 through 1992.

HU MINGRONG

He Jiping

Playwright

After graduating from the Central Academy of Theatre in Beijing in 1982, He Jiping was assigned to the **Beijing People's Art Theatre**, for which she wrote *Lucky Highrise* (*Haoyun daxia*) and *The World's Top Restaurant* (*Tianxia diyi lou*, 1987), a popular, award-winning comedy-drama based on a famous Peking Duck restaurant in late nineteenth and early twentieth century Beijing (see **Beijing Roast Duck**). In 1989 He moved to Hong Kong, where the film artist **Tsui Hark** (Xu Ke) invited her to work on the scripts for *Huang Feihong* (1991) and *Dragon Inn* (*Xin longmen kejian*, 1992). He worked on these and other films through the 1990s using pseudonyms. In 1997 she joined Du Guowei (Raymond To) as playwright-in-residence of the Hong Kong Repertory Theatre (www.hkrep.com), writing *Princess Deling and the Empress Cixi* (*Deling yü Cixi*, 1998); *A Brilliant Beginning* (*Kai shi da ji*, 1999), an adaptation of Lao She's satire of medical services in 1930s China; and *We Are One Family* (*Mingyue he zeng shi liang xiang*, 2001), about the competition between the proprietors, differing in age and background, of a Hong Kong noodle shop and a pizza parlour, respectively. In 2001 He Jiping also received considerable attention for a romantic script staged by celebrity performers, titled *A Red Boat in Misty Rain* (*Yanyu hongchuan*).

Further reading

He, Jiping. (2003). The World's Top Restaurant. In Chen, Xiaomei (ed.), *Reading the Right Text: An Anthology of Contemporary Chinese Drama*. Honolulu: University of Hawai'i Press.

EDWARD GUNN

He Ping

b. 1957, Beijing

Film director

He Ping is the filmmaker credited by international film critics as having reinvented the 'Western' genre in Chinese contemporary cinema. Having begun his career as an editor of documentaries, He joined the **Xi'an Film Studio**, where he directed his first feature film, *The Swordsman of Double-flag Town* (*Shuangqizhen daoke*, 1991). He won an award at the 43rd Berlin International Film Festival for this movie, which revolves around the adventures of a lonely swordsman looking for his bride in the barren land of the west region of the empire and is infused with a surreal atmosphere reminiscent of many Westerns. His talent as teller of passionate yet utopian stories was confirmed in his next feature, *Red Firecracker, Green Firecracker* (*Paoda shuangdeng*, released in 1995), which addressed the issue of sexuality and power through a tragic love story between the brave daughter of a rural landlord and a commoner. The movie won awards at the San Sebastian and Hawaii International Film festivals. He's subsequent movies have all been stories of intrepid and lonely medieval heroes in search of human interaction and spiritual awareness. Having chosen to remain within the structure of the state-owned studio system, He has managed to successfully combine the artistic ideals of the **Fifth Generation (film directors)** with the demands of the mass market. He was therefore one of the first contemporary filmmakers in China financed by Hollywood majors to direct big-budget yet completely locally made movies.

MARIA BARBIERI

He Qinglian

b. 1956, Hunan

Economist/journalist

He Qinglian is one of the most celebrated critics of China's economic and political system, arguing that reforms have been hijacked by officials and well-connected elites. He's sense of social justice was forged through her family's suffering during the **Cultural Revolution**. After earning a BA in history at Hunan Normal University and an MA in economics at Fudan University (1988), she moved to the special economic zone of Shenzhen. She worked in the city's propaganda department, then in a large company, and finally for the *Shenzhen Legal Daily*. He became disillusioned by what she saw in this city ostensibly at the forefront of progress. In 1997 she published *China's Pitfalls* (*Zhongguode xianjing*) in Hong Kong. It was released the following year in the PRC – with the most sensitive details removed – as *The Pitfalls of Modernization* (*Xiandaihuade xianjing*).

Chinese academics had written dry analyses on rent-seeking, but He coupled such charges with myriad cases of the 'marketization of power' – how officials misappropriate funds, accept bribes, extort small businesses and profit by re-selling goods bought at low state prices at higher market prices. To He, **corruption** is not a necessary evil and side-effect of reform, but the primary product of reform. *Pitfalls* sold 200,000 legal copies and countless more pirated editions. Senior officials originally encouraged *Pitfalls*, but the political winds changed and she came under attack. In mid 2000, after an essay on China's distorted social structure appeared, she was demoted, and authorities ordered the country's editors not to publish her work, though *We are Still Watching the Starry Sky* (*Women rengan zai yangwang xingkong*) was published in Guilin. In June 2001, facing possible arrest, she fled to the United States. She is presently teaching at the City University of New York.

Further reading

He, Qinglian (2003). 'A Listing Social Structure'. In Wang Chaohua (ed.), *One China, Many Paths*. London: Verso, 163–88.

SCOTT KENNEDY

He Qun

b. 1956, Beijing

Film director, screenwriter, art director

A 1982 graduate of the **Beijing Film Academy**, He Qun is a key member of the **Fifth Generation (film directors)**. After working as art director on several important films of the early 1980s, He turned to directing in 1988.

He Qun was a major creative force and artistic collaborator on several of the most important early films in the development of the Fifth Generation's cinematic style. As an art director, He contributed his skills to Zhang Junzhao's *One and Eight* (*Yige he bage*), a stunning war film that was among the first shots fired in the Fifth Generation's cinematic revolution, and **Chen Kaige**'s *The Big Parade* (*Da yuebing*), which traces the lives of a battalion of soldiers chosen to take part in a National Day parade.

Since his directorial debut *Mutiny* (*Huabian*) in 1988, He Qun has made nine additional films including *Westbound Convict Train* (*Xixing qiuche*), *Steel Meets Fire* (*Liehuo jingang*), *Conned Once Restaurant* (*Shang yidang*), *The Woman Who Disappeared* (*Xiaoshi de nuren*), *Women's Drug Rehab Centre* (*Nuzi jiedu suo*), *Strangers in Beijing* (*Hun zai Beijing*) and *The Flying Tigers* (*Feihu dui*). The beloved actor **Ge You** stars in several of these. He Qun has produced an eclectic and versatile body of work, which has featured everything from contemporary urban comedies to historical war epics. His masterpiece is his award-winning feature *Country Teachers* (*Fenghuang qin*, 1993), a moving portrait of the conflict between idealism and reality at a rural school. It won five major awards and evoked the most powerful performance in its lead actor Li Baotian's career.

MICHAEL BERRY

He Xin

b. 1949, Wenzhou, Zhejiang

Literary critic

A creature of the intellectual free-for-all of the 1980s, He Xin struck the pose of a renaissance man, writing tirelessly on literature, art, philosophy, economics and politics for the popular media. He was an early and acerbic critic of late-modernist trends in literature and art, warning of the dangers of Euro-American cultural decadence and the threat it posed to social coherence and political stability. He took particular delight in baiting the arrant media philosopher **Liu Xiaobo**.

The son of a failed Party cadre, He Xin followed an undistinguished academic career by concentrating his efforts on attracting the attention of Party and state leaders. Like many other thinkers and would-be courtiers during the 1980s, he petitioned Party elders regularly, submitting advice papers on a range of topics to anyone who cared to read them. His particular brand of cultural patriotism and anti-American opinion struck a chord with Party stalwarts like Wang Zhen and Li Peng.

A trenchant critic of pro-US intellectuals like **Li Tuo** (who, after a stint in the USA in the 1990s, became a born-again cultural patriot with a neo-Marxist inflection) and **Wang Meng** (novelist, Minister of Culture and reformist cultural critic) in the late 1980s, He Xin advocated **cultural purges** but cautioned that government extremism could create political martyrs. Some of his ideas were taken up by the authorities following 4 June during a time of political and intellectual poverty, and he also lectured widely at universities. He Xin's own career foundered, however, when he publicly claimed a greater influence on Party leaders than he really enjoyed.

An intellectual apparatchik in the baneful tradition of Hu Qiaomu, Yao Wenyuan, Zhang Chunqiao and Zeng Qinghong, He Xin's garrulous personal style and egomania led to his fall from favour in the early 1990s. The man who had played a crucial role in shaping the neo-patriotic discourse of the 1990s was later reduced to trading in antiquities. More populist and extreme voices, like those of Wang Shan (*China Through the Third Eye*) and the authors of *China Can Say No!*, would drown out the comparatively reasoned conservatism of writers like He Xin. Although he would continue to make occasional forays into the media, commenting on politics and culture, He was generally derided as a has-been contrarian. He launched a final salvo against the retiring premier, Zhu Rongji, on 1 March 2003, and announced on his website that he was withdrawing from public life.

GEREMIE R. BARMÉ

He Xuntian

b. 1953, Suining, Sichuan

Composer

He Xuntian's improbable career has seen him develop from a marginal member of China's 'New Tide' (*xinchao*, see **Third Generation (composers)**) musical avant-garde into one of the country's most commercially successful composers of popular music. Initially self-taught, He graduated from Sichuan Conservatory of Music, where he developed his own 'RD' (*renyilu duyingfa*) compositional method. He has won numerous awards both in China and abroad, including First Prize at the 1984 All-China Music Competition. Among his notable early works was *Sounds of Nature* for traditional Chinese instruments which employs extended techniques to evoke the sounds of the natural world. Other significant compositions include the symphonies *Four Dreams* and *Telepathy*, the chamber works *Imagine the Sound* and *Phonism*, and an orchestral piece based on folk materials, the *Daba River Capriccio*.

After joining the faculty of the Shanghai Conservatory of Music in 1992, He began a musical partnership with the singer Zhu Zheqin under the name of Dadawa. Their collaboration resulted in the massively successful CD *Sister Drum* (Sire Records, 1995), a New Age fantasy on Tibetan spiritualism and folk music that became the best-selling recording in Chinese history and garnered considerable attention in the West. A heavily stylized blend of ersatz Tibetan vocalisms and lush electronics, *Sister Drum* drew heavy criticism from Tibetans who felt it was a patronizing exercise in cultural exoticism that conveniently ignored China's controversial occupation of Tibet. In 2000, He Xuntian began work on the score of film maker **Zhang Yimou**'s major stage production of the opera (or folk musical), *Third SisterLiu* (*Liu Sanjie*), which was finally performed outdoors in the Guangxi Zhuang Autonomous Region in August 2003.

DENNIS REA

herbal medicine

Herbal medicine is the most popular form of 'traditional' health care in modern China. Bolstered by official government support since the mid 1950s, institutions of traditional medicine generate a great deal of health care knowledge and deliver modern medical services to at least 10 per cent of all clinic visitors in the PRC. The earliest materia medica (*bencao*) literature in China dates from the first century, and a vast systematic literature of herbal medicine has flourished since the sixteenth century. Since publishing returned to full activity in the 1980s, many popular 'self-health' publications have marketed information on the uses and benefits of herbal medicine. Although specialist Chinese medical physicians are often consulted for custom-made prescriptions, it is possible to buy medicinal herbs without a prescription in street markets, pharmacies and street-side clinics. Users generally decide for themselves when herbal medicine is needed, either to supplement biomedical treatment or in place of it. Those who prefer Chinese medicine explain that 'Western medicine cures the symptom, Chinese medicine cures the cause'. Herbal medicine is widely acknowledged to be especially effective for chronic complaints that are not well managed by biomedical means: digestive disorders, chronic pain, infertility and other functional disorders. People also realize that herbal treatments take a long time; they say, 'Chinese medicine is slow but it cures the root.' Herbal medicine is available as loose herbs, which must be decocted, or in patent medicines that can be taken as pills, tonics, compresses or lotions. Some herbal medicines are now exchanged as prestige gifts, and even the most Westernized consumers know a few helpful hints for maintaining everyday health through the use of Chinese medicine.

See also: Western-style Chinese medicine

JUDITH FARQUHAR

higher education through self-paced study

In 1977, entrance examinations for college enrolment resumed after a ten-year ban during the **Cultural Revolution**. Universities already in dire need of accommodation, faculty and funding suddenly faced a relentless influx of talent of various ages who had been deprived of the opportunity to receive higher education for a decade. Beijing, hit the hardest by the predicament, adopted a resolution in July 1980 to allow its residents to pursue higher education through self-paced study and receive degrees by going through comparable procedures. In January 1981, programmes offering exams for those seeking higher education through self-paced studies were piloted in Beijing, Tianjin, Shanghai and later Liaoning province. In May 1985, the State Council set up the National Steering Committee on Exams for Those Who Seek Higher Education through Self-Paced Studies, which began to make the pilot programmes standardized throughout the country. By the year-end, examination systems for self-paced studies had been established all over the mainland. Apparently, this examination system proved to be an innovative solution to the country's unique problem. It helped pay off what the Cultural Revolution owed to the Chinese, and is still helping to fill the gap between a large population of prospective college students and an inadequate number of universities.

Self-study examinations may qualify students for a two-year non-degree diploma, a three-year associate degree and a four-year bachelor's degree. Designated universities conduct examinations and confer degrees in accordance with guidelines set by the central and provincial governments.

HU MINGRONG

highways

(*gaosu gonglu*)

History and natural topography have greatly influenced the level of highway development in China. The density of highways in the eastern regions is five times that of western China. Accelerating the construction of the nation's highway network holds a major significance for vitalizing the country's overall economic development and promote commerce, trade and tourism in China's poorest areas. Highways in China are divided into five categories: national highways, provincial highways, county roads, township roads and roads for special purposes. The road network is further divided into five technical classes. Expressways, the highest standard, feature at least four lanes with a median strip separating traffic in opposite directions. Expressway construction only started in 1980s when the Ministry of Communication announced a plan for the construction of a 35,000 km national highway trunk network based on extensive expressways. The system will comprise five north–south and seven east–west expressways and connect inland provinces with coastal provinces and China's borders. Eight of the national trunk lines will cross into the western region. This system, which involves substantial investment, is bringing China to experience new ways of utilizing foreign capital. The first expressway in China was completed in 1990 between the industrial centre of Shenyang and the port of Dalian in Liaoning province. By 2000, the national expressway network in operation amounted to 16,314 km. Express delivery and door-to-door services are being developed. A number of goods-flow centres are being put into operation in cities. Warehousing facilities are being implemented along the major networks.

CLAUDE COMTOIS

historical and cultural cities

In 1982, in conjunction with China's Law of the PRC on the Protection of Cultural Relics, the State Council designated twenty-four 'historical and cultural cities'. The three criteria for such a designation were (1) the degree to which those cities possessed abundant and significant cultural relics; (2) how much the contemporary city reflected its traditional urban plan and context; and (3) whether the preservation of the city in general, and its historic districts in particular, would have a positive impact on, and provide useful guidelines for, other cities. In 1986 the Council determined that thirty-eight other cities met these criteria; thirty-seven more were added in 1994, and two more after 1999, totalling (as of early 2003) 101 cities.

Designation has not automatically led to protection. Because Chinese cities have faced extraordinary challenges in the past twenty years – e.g. population influx, infrastructural upgrades, real estate development, environmental transformation – the toll taken on historic and cultural resources within cities has been extraordinary. Furthermore, there is often a lack of public awareness about either the importance of heritage protection, or the extent to which Chinese governmental authorities truly consider such protection a priority. Although the central government provided US$18 million for protection projects in eighty cities between 1997 and 2002, demolition in the name of urban renewal continues to erode the historic fabric of many Chinese cities, thus calling into question governments' will or ability to remedy the situation. Therefore, designation carries a certain cachet of being 'historical' or 'cultural' which sometimes translates into tourism value, and such designation can also bring monetary benefit from the government, but it still remains unclear whether most Chinese people either know, or care, that their city is historic/cultural, or not.

Further reading

Chan, Jick Kong (1999). *The 99 Historic Cities of China*. Hong Kong: Historic City Books.

Ruan, Yisan (1995). *Planning and Conservation of Chinese Historic Cities*. Shanghai: Tongji University Press.

Wang, Jinghui, Ruan, Yisan and Wang, Lin (eds) (1999). *Lishi wenhua gecheng baohu lilun yu guihua* [Conservation Theory and Planning of Historic Cultural Cities]. Shanghai: Tongji University Press.

Wu, Liangyong (2000). *Rehabilitating the Old City of Beijing: A Project for the Ju'er Hutong Neighborhood*. Vancouver: University of British Columbia.

JEFFREY W. CODY

HIV/AIDS and STIs

In August 2001 the Chinese government stated that there were at least 600,000 people infected with HIV. It seems that China is now in the early stages of an epidemic. The first case was reported in 1985. China's United Nations HIV Theme Group, comprised of representatives of all UN agencies working on HIV issues in China, predicts that 20 million HIV infections will have occurred by the year 2010. The following risk activities relate to HIV transmission in China.

1   The spread of HIV by injection drug use, caused by needle-sharing practices, has been concentrated largely in the southern and western parts of China.
2   A lack of adequate screening of blood products and unsafe practices in taking blood has led to the transmission of HIV. Many (maybe as many as half a million) blood donors who sold their blood in the mid and late 1990s have been infected with HIV.
3   Non-sterile use of needles also has been a mode of spread in the practice of Western medicine. For example, an investigation in Hubei province in 1999 found that 88 per cent of injections made by village, district and epidemic prevention station medical workers were unsafe.
4   The heterosexual spread of HIV initially has been concentrated in the eastern coastal provinces of China but is now more widespread. There also has been a resurgence of other sexually transmitted infections (STIs), which renders individuals more susceptible to HIV. It was believed that STIs were virtually eradicated in China by the early 1970s, but with recent economic changes have come many social changes, including an increase in prostitution. The majority of sex workers have unprotected intercourse (see **sexuality and behaviour**).
5   Homosexuality is not illegal in China, but neither is it socially acceptable; therefore it is hard to predict HIV prevalence within this group (see **homosexuality and tongzhi culture**).

The epidemiology of HIV and AIDs seem to relate largely to the primary mode of transmission. Cases in Hainan province and through southeast China are mainly due to heterosexual transmission; in central China, particularly Henan province, due to unsafe blood practices; and in southwest China from intravenous drug use following the overland trafficking routes from the borders with Laos and Myanmar. Clearly there is more than one mode of spread within each region. Moreover, the large numbers of migrant workers and those living in poverty and relative poverty are much more vulnerable to HIV infection.

The Ministry of Health has demonstrated a steadily increasing commitment to addressing HIV issues. China has produced an Action Plan for Reducing and Preventing the Spread of HIV/AIDS (2001–5). This plan includes the closure of illegal blood and blood plasma collection stations and testing all clinical blood supplies for HIV; the training of all medical workers in HIV and STIs, including the prevention of HIV, and in treatment and management of HIV and HIV-related diseases; the provision of treatment and care in homes; the building of an HIV/AIDS and STI information network; and the provision of welfare assistance to people infected with HIV.

At present there is very little accurate information available as to the current extent of the disease, limited access to HIV testing, and a very limited knowledge among the general population and vulnerable groups as well as among many health workers. An HIV epidemic is likely to present a major challenge not only for those concerned with the health of the Chinese population, but also for those concerned with the financial situation of the country as a whole.

Further reading

Avert (2001) *HIV in China*. Available at http://www.avert.org/aidschina.htm

Seidman, Spencer (2001) *HIV/AIDS in China and its Implications for Tibetans and Other Minorities*. Available at http://itsa.ucsf.edu/~seidman/HIVC2.html (viewed on 17 October 2001).

Settle, Edmund (2003). *China AIDS Survey*. Available at http://www.casy.org/ pubpage.htm

State Council Office (2001). *China's Action Plan for Reducing and Preventing the Spread of HIV/AIDS (2001–5)*. Unofficial translation of State Council Office Document 2001–40, US Embassy-Beijing, environment, science and technology section, available at http://www.usembassy-china.org.cn/english/sandt/AIDS-actionplantranslation.htm

—— (2001) *Unsafe Injections: A Great Threat to China's Health*. Available at http://www.usembassy-china.org.cn/english/sandt/hivartic.html

US Department of Health and Human Services (2001). *Report of an HIV/AIDS Assessment in China* (30 July–10 August 2001 and 28–30 August 2001). National Center for HIV, STD and TB Prevention, Centers for Disease Control and Prevention.

MARION TORRANCE

holiday economy

(*jieri jingji*)

To pre-empt a perceived slowdown of the economy in the late 1990s, the Chinese government lengthened the National Day holiday to a week on 1 October 1999 and did the same to the International Labour Day on 1 May 2000. The move was designed to encourage the Chinese to spend their bank savings, the world's largest, so as to boost the economy. This was hence known as the 'holiday economy' (*jieri jingji*). As a result, the country is experiencing waves of travel mania each year. Statistics show that over 24 million Chinese travelled and spent about US$3.5 billion during the first week of May 2001 alone. Those who stayed behind were also kept busy shopping during the week. Retail sales in Beijing soared more than 40 per cent and even slightly more in Shanghai. Hotel reservations in popular tourist destinations like Guilin, Xiamen, Sanya and Zhangjiajie exceeded 80 per cent.

Opinions differ. Some argue that the 'holiday economy' may not help consumption because consumers tend to curtail spending after holiday sprees. While tourism-related businesses may reap profits, other sectors have to suffer. And with many people on vacation all at once, problems like traffic congestion, overbooking and overcrowding do increase. Complaints abound. Some are discouraged to 'purchase headaches' caused by such problems and poor services. Others have come to realize the inflexibility and inadequacy of universal weeklong holidays. They want to see the establishment of a paid vacation system that allows individuals to decide when to travel and to spend time with family.

YUAN HAIWANG

holidays (Western)

With their living standard improving, more and more Chinese have begun to celebrate Western holidays like Christmas, Mother's Day, Valentine's Day and Father's Day. A national survey revealed that a third of the sampled population thought that Chinese should celebrate Western holidays. Over half said that they did not care. The growing acceptance of Western holidays, however, does not translate into a desire for parting with traditional ones. The same survey showed that no one thought of Western holidays as more important than traditional ones. Comparing them with the Western holidays, of which few have much knowledge, most surveyed thought that the latter gave them a more relaxing alternative and an occasion for sentimental expression between friends and family members.

April Fool's Day and Halloween are occasionally celebrated by school and college students. Their enthusiasm for Valentine's Day is largely shared by white-collar workers and government employees. Most of the youngsters mistake Christmas Eve as party time and even carnival: flooding malls, shopping; bars, drinking; restaurants, feasting; and clubs, dancing and 'karaoke-ing'.

Mother's Day is endorsed by all levels of the government. The rest are left in the care of commerce. Western holidays are next to the Spring Festival (see **New Year Festival**) in adding to the Chinese **holiday economy**: Beijing residents spend no less on Valentine's Day than their Western peers. In some cities, hotels, cinemas and clubs vie with one another in promoting 'love chambers' or compartments to customers in disregard for their age, causing concern to parents and educators.

YUAN HAIWANG

home cooking

(*jiachangcai*)

Home cooking, as opposed to the expensive dishes and delicacies found in restaurants, forms the daily meals of average Chinese. It is low-cost, easy to cook and lacking in garnish. It might be a bowl of rice plus a dish of stir-fried potato with green pepper. As each family has an unwritten list of *jiachangcai* that make up its day-to-day diet, good planning is required. Cooking *jiachangcai* is therefore a learning process – from cookbooks, television programmes, family reunions and parties with friends. Traditionally, products of rice in south China or wheat in the north were the mainstay of a Chinese meal. Dishes were only subsidiary. This is changing as the living standard improves. Like all Chinese cuisines, home cooking now includes meat, seafood, vegetables and hybrid dishes where the ratio of vegetables to meat is roughly three to one.

Family preferences decide how a home-cooked meal is served. It may finish with an optional soup, such as a tomato egg drop, but rare are appetizers and desserts. *Jiachangcai*, like **dumplings** (*jiaozi*), may also have cultural significance related to special occasions or festivals. Each region has its own flavours – a Cantonese steamed fish or chicken without soy sauce may seem repulsive to people in northeast China. And numerous home-style dishes, such as cashew chicken and twice-cooked pork, have found their way onto the regular menus of restaurants. Driven by a booming and yet polarized economy, restaurants featuring *jiachangcai* are mushrooming, catering to those who cannot afford expensive restaurants or who want a lighter meal for a change.

YUAN HAIWANG

home refurbishing

(*zhuangxiu*)

The housing reforms of the 1980s and 1990s marked the end of the 'work unit' and the beginning of privately owned housing in urban China. The housing boom not only increased significantly the per capita square-footage of living space, but also spurred a complementary boom in the home furbishing industry. Most new housing units come as shell apartments (*maopeifang*, i.e. rough or no finish and with minimal internal partitions) because it is expected that the owners will want to arrange the space and design the interior themselves according to their individual taste and budget. This expectation is already a far cry from the spatial and decorative conformism found in *danwei* housing during the Maoist era. Most people treat their new apartments as permanent homes and subsequently

spend staggering sums of money on *zhuangxiu*, sometimes amounting to many years of the family's savings. While older people who are retired or nearly retired emphasize the bare essentials of comfort and function in furbishing their new homes (typically purchased from their work units at greatly subsidized prices), members of younger generations often pursue fashionable styles in interior decoration and furnishing (e.g. European or retro Chinese traditional). Home furbishing design companies and contractors enjoy good business, while typically male rural migrant workers execute the actual work. There is also a strong home furbishing Do-It-Yourself ethos, constituting a demand for a plethora of *zhuangxiu*-related magazines and books. The Swedish furniture company Ikea has become extremely popular. Gigantic home furnishing 'cities' and 'plazas' have sprung up in major cities, carrying everything from toilet bowls to hand drills, European-style leather sofas to faux Ming redwood beds.

Further reading

Tang, Xiaobing (1998). 'Decorating Culture: Notes on Interior Design, Interiority, and Interiorization'. *Public Culture* 10.3. Available at http://www.uchicago.edu/research/jnl-pub-cult/backissues/pc26/tang.html

ADAM YUET CHAU

homosexuality and tongzhi culture

In China, homosexuality has always conflicted with the traditional importance of marriage and posterity, but has rarely been regarded a crime. In the 1980s, homosexuals in the People's Republic developed their own subculture, referred to as '*tongzhi* culture' (*tongzhi wenhua*). *Tongzhi* literally means 'of the same intent'. In Chinese Communist discourse, it means 'comrade', and it was widely used as a form of address until after the **Cultural Revolution** (1966–76). Nowadays, the word *tongzhi* has been appropriated by homosexuals to mean 'gay'.

In the 1980s and early 1990s, homosexuals in big cities secretly met in parks and public restrooms, and sometimes in clandestine gay bars. They were occasionally arrested for 'indecent behaviour'. The rise of the Internet in the 1990s provided Chinese homosexuals with a convenient medium to communicate, and Chinese gay and lesbian websites have mushroomed ever since. These sites spread information about homosexuality throughout the Chinese-speaking world. As a result, some bars and clubs in big cities are now commonly known as 'gay places'. The Internet also forms a breeding ground for '*tongzhi* literature' (*tongzhi wenxue*). Gay novels often reflect on problems that a Chinese gay reader has to deal with in daily life: coming out, social pressure and relationship problems. Some stories have an erotic or pornographic character. Most authors are amateurs, but some have become celebrities among their Internet readership. One of the earliest and best-known stories in this genre is *A Story from Beijing* (*Beijing gushi*), that has been circulating on the Web since 1996. Hong Kong film director Stanley **Kwan** based his movie *Lanyu* (2001) on this novel. After the movie had won prestigious awards in Taiwan and Hong Kong, it immediately appeared in PRC video shops.

Many Chinese know about homosexuality through television and popular journals. The issue is no longer taboo. In the official guidelines for Chinese psychiatrists of April 2001, homosexuality is no longer listed as a mental disorder. In cities like Beijing and Shanghai, transvestites go to public places without being arrested. However, homosexuals in the PRC still feel heavily pressured by mainstream morality, and sometimes enter into heterosexual marriage to please their families. For the time being, heavy restrictions remain on free discussion of politically sensitive topics, such as gay rights and the government's attitude towards the growing problem of **HIV/AIDS and STIs**.

See also: gay cinema and video; lesbianism in literature; Wang Xiaobo

Further reading

Chinese Society for the Study of Sexual Minorities (estd 1 September 1997): www.csssm.org

Chou, Wah-shan (2000). *Tongzhi: Politics of Same-Sex Eroticism in Chinese Societies*. Binghampton, NY: Harrington Park Press.

Damm, Jens (2000). *Ku'er vs. tongzhi – Diskurse der Homosexualität. Über das Entstehen sexueller Identitäten im glokalisierten Taiwan und im postkolonialen Hongkong* [Discourses on Homosexual Identities in Taiwan and Hong Kong]. Bochum: Cathay Skripten.

Gil, Vincent (2002). 'The Cut Sleeve Revisited: A Contemporary Account of Male Homosexuality'. In Susan Blum and Lionel Jensen, *China Off Center: Mapping the Margins of the Middle Kingdom*. Honolulu: University of Hawai'i Press: 238–48.

Kam, Louie and Low, Morris (eds) (2003). *Asian Masculinities: The Meaning and Practice of Manhood in China and Japan*. London: Curzon Press.

Li, Yinhe (1998). *Tongxinglian yawenhua* [The Homosexual Subculture]. Beijing: Jinri Zhongguo chubanshe.

Xiaomingxiong [Shao, Mingxiong; a.k.a. Samshasha] (1984; rev. edn 1997). *Zhongguo tongxing'ai shilu* [A History of Homosexuality in China]. Hong Kong: Pink Triangle Press.

REMY CRISTINI

Hong Hao

b. 1965, Beijing

Printmaker, photographer

Hong Hao graduated from the Print-Making Department of Beijing's Central Academy of Fine Arts in 1989. In the early 1990s he began working on *Selected Scriptures*, a series of silkscreen prints that resemble a large open book. *Selected Scriptures* is a fictional encyclopedia that reinterprets the social/political history of the world and anticipates possible future scenarios through invented maps, diagrams and illustrated narratives. The works in the *Selected Scriptures* series comically question the legitimacy of historical accuracy and overtly criticize consumerism, imperialism and technology.

In 1997 Hong Hao began a series of photographs in which he himself poses as a pampered successful businessman in various luxurious settings. The photographs in this series function as mock advertisements replete with both English and Chinese captions. The works question the equation of success with material wealth and Westernization.

Hong Hao began to focus on the urban environment of Beijing as a subject matter in 1999. His photographs in the *Beijing Tour Guide* series show the artist posing heroically in traditional Chinese clothing and guiding Western tour groups through various historic sites around the city. In *Qingming shanghe tu* (Spring Festival on the River) and *Qianli jiangshan tu* (A Thousand Miles of Rivers and Mountains) the artist reinterprets these original Song dynasty paintings with colour photographs, showing street life in the respective capital cities of the day – Kaifeng in the twelfth century and Beijing in the twentieth century. Hong's horizontal scrolls are at one and the same time a dialogue with the original works and an exploration of the power structure through the architecture and daily life of disparate historical periods. Among other venues, Hong Hao has exhibited his work at the Max Protech Gallery in New York (1988), at Canvas International Art in Amsterdam (1999) and at the 2000 Shanghai Biennale (Shanghai Art Museum).

Further reading

Chaos, Y. Chen (2000). *Scenes from the Metropolis.* Beijing: Courtyard Gallery.

Kielstra, Martijn *et al.* (1999). *The Selected Scriptures of Hong Hao* (exhibition catalogue). Amsterdam: Canvas Foundation.

MATHIEU BORYSEVICZ

Hong Kong countdown clock

The Hong Kong countdown clock at **Tiananmen Square** operated from 19 December 1994 to 30 June 1997, the day marking Hong Kong's 'return' (*huigui*) to China. It also represents a new era in the history of public time-telling. For the first time in Chinese history, the second was used in public time-telling.

The clock was set up on 13 December 1994 and removed on 8 July 1997, and incorporated mechanical, electric and digital media. It was placed between two pillars in front of the museum building. It was a 16 metre high and 9.6 metre wide metal panel. On the top of the panel were the five golden-coloured stars of the national flag. Below the stars were four lines of Chinese characters. From top to bottom, it read: 'The Chinese Government [*Zhongguo zhengfu*]/resumes the exercise of sovereignty over Hong Kong [*dui Xianggang huifu xingshi zhuquan*]/counting-down time [*daojishi*]/to 1 July 1997 [*ju 1997 nian 7 yue 1 ri*]'. The next section below this included two lines indicating the days (*tian*) and seconds (*miao*) respectively. At the bottom were listed sponsors, including the magazine *China Brand-Names* (*Zhongguo mingpai*), the China Southern Aviation Engineering Company, the Linghua Food-Flavouring Group (Ji'ning, Shangdong) and the National Museum of Chinese Revolution. Below the list of sponsors, the panel indicated the first operational date of the clock: 19 December 1994.

Further reading

Wu, H. (1997). 'The Hong Kong Clock – Public Time-Telling and Political Time/Space' *Public Culture* 9: 329–54.

REN HAI

Hong Ying

(née Chen Hongying)

b. 1962, Chongqing, Sichuan

Writer

As a writer who commands a broad range of genres and themes, Hong Ying differs from the majority of contemporary women authors. Her difference lies first in her interest in avant-garde poetry, which she began writing in 1980; and second, in her interest in the genre of 'futuristic fiction' (*weilai xiaoshuo*) and autobiographical writing, though this only began after she emigrated to England in 1991. Her early attempts at prose fiction are mainly in the form of short stories and include fantasy constructions in which gender, racial and cultural issues are dealt with in a diversity of temporal and geographical sites. Her autobiography, *Daughter of Hunger* (*Ji'er de nu'er*, 1997), marks a departure from her early writing as well as from the tradition of fictional autobiography popularized by women writers in the

1990s. In contrast to many Chinese women writers, who identify themselves with the intelligentsia and examine female existence in an isolated psychological space, Hong situates the writer's genesis in the despair and psychological deprivation of the slums of her native Chongqing. The struggle for existence, the yearning for love and dignity, as well as the needs of survival, are blended together and integrated into the writer's search for self-identity. At the same time, the controlled and seemingly detached narration functions as a metaphor for the spiritual weariness that masks the setting's intense vitality. Hong's increasing mastery of many different materials, including photography, has made her a much more complicated as well as popular writer.

Further reading

Hong, Ying (1998). *Daughter of the River*. Trans. Howard Goldblatt. London: Bloomsbury Press.
—— (2002). *K: The Art of Love*. Trans. Henry Zhao and Nicky Harmon. London: Marion Boyars Press.
Sieber, Patricia (2001). 'Hong Ying'. In *idem* (ed.), *Red Is Not the Only Color: Contemporary Chinese Fiction on Love and Sex between Women, Collected Stories*. Lanham, MD: Rowman and Littlefield, 188–9.
Zhao, Henry (ed.) (1999). *A Lipstick Called Red Pepper: Fiction about Gay and Lesbian Love in China*. Bochum: Ruhr University Press [numerous stories].

HE DONGHUI

hospitals

Chinese hospitals are the pillars of the urban health care system and an important but not always accessible resource for rural residents with serious illnesses. Most of China's 16,732 hospitals were built after 1949 in accordance with Chinese Communist Party (CCP) health policies: to provide health care for all; to emphasize preventative care over curative care; and to unify Chinese medicine and biomedicine. The transition to a market economy in the reform era, however, has introduced new challenges to China's vast network

of hospitals and clinics and pushed them away from the egalitarian principles of the Maoist era.

At the founding of the People's Republic, China was confronted with dire public health conditions. One of the great achievements of Maoist-era health policy was to overcome this crisis by developing the infrastructure to bring basic health care services to both rural and urban areas. Rural health care delivery was structured around a three-tier network of institutions – village clinics, township health centres and county hospitals – whose services ranged from treating simple ailments at village clinics to providing a full spectrum of outpatient and inpatient services at the county hospital. In urban areas, a similar but more professionalized hierarchy of health care institutions was established – primary care street hospitals; secondary care district hospitals; and tertiary care municipal, provincial, and central ministry hospitals.

Reform era policies have raised the quality of health care but sacrificed accessibility. The government has made health care institutions responsible for their own profits and losses and at the same time tried to curtail skyrocketing **medical insurance** costs. Under these conditions, only the top-tier hospitals of the rural and urban systems possess the financial resources to compete aggressively for patients and grow hospital revenue. Hospital administrators have realized that cutting-edge medical equipment and the top drugs from the world's leading pharmaceutical producers bring both the highest marginal returns and the greatest number of patients. As a result, large hospitals are flourishing while lower-tier health institutions languish. At the same time, rural residents and uninsured urban residents are increasingly unable to defray ballooning medical costs. Thus, while health care delivery to remote rural areas has stagnated or even regressed in the reform era, some urban areas have CT and MRI densities per hospital bed that exceed those of the USA or Europe. Although policy-makers are implementing major reforms of the health insurance system and eager to reinvigorate the lower tiers of the urban and rural health care system, the current trend towards uneven resource distribution is not likely to abate soon.

Another important achievement of the Maoist era was the development of a health care infrastructure for Chinese medicine. Since 1949, China has built over 2,500 hospitals of Chinese medicine, accounting for about 15 per cent of all hospitals. Chinese medicine hospitals also offer a wide range of biomedical diagnostic and therapeutic procedures. China's general hospitals, although dedicated to biomedicine practice, also have designated departments of Chinese medicine.

Further reading

Hsiao, William *et al.* (1997). *Financing Health Care: Issues and Options for China*. Washington, DC: World Bank.

ERIC I. KARCHMER

hotels

The Chinese have always travelled. Officials take up posts in distant places; traders accompany their goods on short or long-distance journeys; pilgrims travel to famous religious sites; others travel to visit friends or relatives or to find work; and still others are tourists pursuing exoticism or simply a different space and time. When they have no friends or relatives to stay with at the destination, people stay at some kind of serviced accommodation such as hotels or guesthouses. The imperial government ran an extensive guesthouse system to cater for all government travellers including officials, clerks and messengers. Privately run inns catered for private travellers. Travelling monks stayed at temples. Major pilgrimage sites had dormitories. All of these establishments also provided important complementary services such as food, drink (tea and wine), hot baths and sometimes even sensual pleasure (prostitutes and sing-song girls). Western-style hotels came to China during the Republican period (1912–49), but had a presence only in Shanghai and other foreign concessions. The state-run guesthouse system persisted through the high socialist era until today. There were only state-run guesthouses during the Maoist era because all privately owned inns and hotels were nationalized. The restriction on private citizens' travel also drastically reduced the need for hotels. The ability to travel and stay at guesthouses (*zhaodaisuo*) was a privilege available mostly to cadres. Just as in imperial times, differently ranked cadres received

different grades of rooms and services. The very few foreign visitors were mostly foreign dignitaries who were received at designated guesthouses (e.g. Beijing's Friendship Hotel). The reform era opened the hotel field dramatically. Foreign and overseas tourists swarmed in and luxury hotels sprang up in major cities. The five-star hotel-accreditation system was introduced. Chinese people who became rich during the reform era and executives of larger companies also became customers of luxury hotels. People travel for business and pleasure like never before in Chinese history, and the number of hotels of all grades will only increase at a faster speed, making hotels one of the most visible institutions in China's urban landscape.

ADAM YUET CHAU

hotpots

(huoguo)

Huoguo (hotpots) refers either to the utensil or the dish prepared with it. Made of red copper, a typical *huoguo* is a vessel with a shaft running through as a hearth and airway. A grate in the hearth holds the charcoal and drops the ashes to the base, where a door controls air intake. First recorded around the year 220, *huoguo* was a wintry royal delicacy of the Qing dynasty (1644–1911). By the early 1900s, numerous styles had evolved. Today, charcoal is being replaced by electricity and natural gas, and a *huoguo* may be as simple as a pot of iron or steel. The method of cooking is the instant boiling (*shuan*) of meat, vegetables, seafood and other foodstuffs. Instant-boiled mutton slices (*Shuanyangrou*) is a northern Chinese favourite, known for its dipping sauce made of scallion, garlic, vinegar, sesame oil and chillies. A chain restaurant, Xiaofeiyang, offers an equally savoury alternative without sauces.

'Chongqing hotpot', a nationally popular Sichuan specialty, used to be fishermen's **home cooking** (*jiachangcai*). A certain Ma family introduced it to restaurants in 1926. Spicy and rich in its selection of meat and vegetables, it is celebrated for its culture: men and women, old and young, associating in countless *huoguo* shops all year round, dripping with sweat and glowing with amusement. To accommodate different tastes, a chef named

Yan Wenjun invented 'Yuanyang hotpot' in 1983, a pot split into a spicy compartment and a mild one. Other hotpot cuisines include the northeastern specialty 'Pork with pickled vegetable hotpot' (*Suancaibairouguo*), the Cantonese seafood hotpot (*Dabianlu*) and the Taiwanese ginger chicken (*Jiangmuji*). Vegetarian and medicinal food hotpot recipes are increasingly popular.

YUAN HAIWANG

Hou Baolin

b. 1917, Beijing; d. 1993, Beijing

Xiangsheng (comic dialogue) actor

Hou Baolin began learning **xiangsheng** at sixteen and became an actor at twenty-three. A master of humour for half a century, Hou brought new life to the art and was known to every Chinese. Replacing the vulgarism and obscenity prevalent in old *xiangsheng* with wholesome jocular entertainment, Hou provided his audience with aesthetic ecstasy. In fact, the success of his performances was due to his ardent pursuit of aesthetic and professional perfection. He had acquired a characteristic style of his own through years of practice: jocular without being vulgar and humorous without being cunning. His lively and witty skits were amusing as well as enlightening.

Hou not only wrote *xiangsheng* scripts but also collaborated with Professor Wu Xiaozhen on research into this art form. With six months of schooling, Hou became qualified as **Peking University**'s home professor and published prolifically. His success was partly due to his natural gift but largely to his hard work. He taught himself and read widely: jesting, comedy, history and miscellaneous classics. He also adapted from foreign resources. He believed that a funny face alone could not make a great comedian. Instead, one must know how to learn from others and be blessed with talent, diligence and a good teacher, one that was knowing rather than renowned. His most popular performances included 'An Anachronous Battle' (*Guangong zhan Qinqiong*), 'Change of Trades' (*Gaihang*) and 'Yin, Yang and the Five Elements' (*Yinyang wuxing*).

HU MINGRONG

Hou Dejian

b. 1956, Taiwan

Rock musician

Throughout the 1980s, rock musician, political activist, and all-around *cause célèbre* Hou Dejian was the embodiment of China's post-1949 split personality. The Taiwan-born singer-songwriter emerged from the island's so-called 'coffeehouse folk' movement, which flowered under the relatively benign regime of Chiang Ching-Kuo in the 1970s. He was soon catapulted onto a larger stage with the release of his huge 1979 hit, 'Descendants of the Dragon', a ringing statement of pan-Chinese nationalism that made Hou a lightning rod for the contentious issue of Chinese reunification.

> In the ancient East there is a dragon;
> China is its name.
> In the ancient East there lives a people,
> The dragon's heirs every one.
> Under the claws of this mighty dragon I grew up
> And its descendant I have become.
> Like it or not –
> Once and forever, a descendant of the dragon.
> ('Descendants of the Dragon')

Hou created headlines and reversed a trend when he defected to the mainland in 1983 to reassert his Chinese roots. Welcomed at first by the PRC government, who viewed him as a useful propaganda tool, Hou became a popular performer and important influence on the nascent Chinese rock music scene (see **rock music, rock bands**). He eventually grew disenchanted with Communist rule and in 1989 acted as a highly visible spokesperson for pro-democracy demonstrators in **Tiananmen Square**. The following year PRC authorities forcibly repatriated him to Taiwan, where he was arrested and briefly detained. Hou remains active in music and has composed soundtracks to films ranging from Hong Kong martial arts thrillers to the dark 1993 Taiwanese drama *Moonlight Boy* (*Yueguang shaonian*).

Further reading

Jaivin, Linda (1996). 'Hou Dejian and the Rise of Pop Music in Taiwan in the Seventies'. *Chime* 9 (Autumn): 118–23.

DENNIS REA

Hou Hsiao-hsien

b. 1947, Meixian, Guangdong

Film director, actor, producer

Born to a Hakka family in Meixian, Guangdong province (see **Hakka, culture of**), Hou Hsiao-hsien helped pioneer Taiwan's New Cinema movement (see **cinema in Taiwan**) and remains one of Asia's premier film artists today. His family moved with the post-war flow of mainlanders to Taiwan. Despite his father's service as an education administrator, Hou became a gangland 'enforcer' in his late teenage years. Figuring greatly in his films are love for his adopted homeland, and especially for the simple village life of his youth; Taiwan's transition to a modern urban culture; Taiwan's complex mix of languages, politics and sub-cultures; and a fascination with the gangster underground as an alternative to established authority.

Hou graduated in film from the National Taiwan College of the Arts in 1972. Following a series of light comedies, Hou's contribution to the three-part film *Sandwich Man* (1983) helped signal the beginning of a new era in Taiwan film. With *A Time to Live, A Time to Die* (*Tongnian wangshi*), which won the Critics' Award at Cannes, Hou introduced a slow-paced, lyrical but realistic style that captured the essence of Taiwan's disappearing village lifestyle, nostalgically seen through his own childhood experience. *Dust in the Wind* (1986), by contrast, illustrated the pressures of modernization on the island's rural youth forced to move to the cities during a period of rapid economic development.

As development brought a loosening of the Nationalist Party's ruling grip, Hou's *A City of Sadness* (*Beiqing chengshi*, 1989) led to the first public acknowledgement of government massacre of intellectuals that commenced on 28 February 1947. The first Chinese-language film to win at the Venice Film Festival, *A City of Sadness*, was a political event in its own right, describing the impact of the transfer of colonial control from Japan to mainland China on a single family comprised of businessmen, gangsters and intellectuals. Two films completed Hou's so-called *Taiwan Trilogy*. *The Puppet Master* (1993), a semi-documentary life of Taiwan's famous puppeteer Li Tianlu during Japanese rule; and *Good Men, Good Women* (1995), a complex narrative and profound consideration of historical morality as experienced by two women born into widely divergent roles – one a real-life patriot, the other a fictional gangster girlfriend-turned-actress, representing Taiwan in two different generations. Hou's most recent major films are *Flowers of Shanghai* (1998) and *Millennium Mambo* (2001). Hou's film career has also taken him into acting (*Taipei Story*, 1984, dir. Edward **Yang**) and producing (*Raise the Red Lantern*, 1991, dir. **Zhang Yimou**).

Further reading

Browne, Nick (1996). 'Hou Hsiao-hsien's *Puppetmaster*. The Poetics of Landscape'. *Asian Cinema* 8.1 (Spring): 28–38.

Li, Tuo (1993). 'Narratives of History in the Cinematography of Hou Xiaoxian'. *positions: east asia cultures critique* 1.3 (Winter): 805–15.

Neri, Corrado (2003). 'A Time to Live, A Time to Die: A Time to Grow'. In Chris Berry (ed.), *Chinese Films in Focus: 25 New Takes*. London: BFI, 160–6.

Reynaud, Bérénice (2002). *A City of Sadness*. London: British Film Institute.

Udden, James (2002). 'Hou Hsiao-hsien and the Question of a Chinese Style'. *Asian Cinema* 13.2 (Fall/Winter): 54–75.

Xu, Gang Gary (2003). 'Flowers of Shanghai: Visualising Ellipses and (Colonial) Absences'. In Chris Berry (ed.), *Chinese Films in Focus: 25 New Takes*. London: BFI, 104–10.

JEROME SILBERGELD

house churches

House churches are an important phenomenon in Chinese **Christianity (Protestantism)** and their members form a large part of the Christians in the PRC today. Other commonly used names are 'unregistered churches' – in contrast to the registered ones belonging to the **Three-Self Patriotic Movement (TSPM)** – and 'underground churches'.

Several wholly Chinese denominations were formed both before 1949 (e.g. the **Little Flock**) and after, and these groups refused to join the TSPM. They were persecuted but survived as free groups, often referred to as 'house churches'. In the late

1970s when religion was once again allowed after the **Cultural Revolution**, people met in homes to worship since most churches were either still closed, being used for other purposes or had been demolished. This was another basis for the emergence of house churches. There are also house meetings within the TSPM that are often called 'meeting points' (*juhuidian*). Here a grey zone exists where some 'meeting points' are only loosely affiliated with the local TSPM. In some places as well, new church buildings have been erected by unregistered groups and have been allowed to remain.

House churches grew quickly during the 1990s, often formed by iterant evangelists (see **itinerant evangelists (Protestant)**) who travel around China and start new congregations. Henan and Zhejiang provinces supposedly have millions of house church members. A problem for both house churches and the TSPM is the appearance of a number of pseudo-Christian sects, the result of a shortage of well-educated pastors to take care of the fast-growing numbers of believers. Despite their differences, house churches and registered churches share a basic theology and faith, both evangelical and Bible-centred. Nonetheless, persecutions and denunciations of house church leaders by the TSPM in the 1950s led to a mistrust of registered church leaders and their faith which has long disturbed relations between them.

In the 1990s, local level cooperation between house churches and the TSPM improved somewhat, but after the suppression of **Falun gong** in 1999, new laws against cults and sects were passed that have also been used to harass the house churches. In 1998, leaders from several large house churches assembled to formulate a statement about their faith, their view of the TSPM and their relation to the CCP and the state. They stressed their identity as law-abiding citizens of the PRC but decried state control over religion. They also recognized the idea of 'three-self' but not the TSPM as a government-controlled organ. A draft for new regulations for registering churches appeared in December 2001, but the process has been stalled as the draft suggests that it is no longer necessary to register through the TSPM.

See also: Jesus Family; patriotic covenants

Further reading

Lambert, T. (1999). *China's Christian Millions: The Costly Revival.* London: Monarch Books

FREDERIK FÄLLMAN

housing

Before 1949 housing was largely owned by private individuals or families. After the establishment of Mao's socialist regime, however, almost all residential structures in the cities were nationalized. Each housing unit was divided into several sections and allocated to different families by the city government. In the relatively mixed, neighbourhood-based communities, the police and residents' committees (*juweihui*), led directly by the district government, became the primary agents of social regulation and community services. Meanwhile, the majority of urban Chinese workers and state employees were provided with state-subsidized public housing by their work units (*danwei*). Located within or adjacent to the site of the *danwei*, these undifferentiated, military barrack-like apartment blocks were usually divided into separate compounds to prevent outsiders from trespassing freely. The social composition within the compound tended to be homogeneous since the heads of the households often belonged to the same work unit. In this type of community, basic services and social control are provided primarily by the work unit that serves simultaneously as the employer, landlord and the source of local authority.

The public housing system, which was firmly in place for nearly forty years, had many problems. There was a serious housing shortage and overcrowding throughout Chinese cities. It was common for several families to share a kitchen and bathroom and for a family of three generations to live in a one-bedroom unit. The extremely low rent and heavy reliance on government subsidies resulted in poor housing maintenance and substandard living conditions. There was also disparity in housing access between work units and among employees within the same work units.

Beginning in the late 1980s, the central state launched urban housing reform, which sought to privatize existing public housing and eventually to commercialize the entire housing market. But it was not until the early and mid 1990s that housing reform was carried out nationwide and became a centrepiece of China's economic development strategies. Under the new policy, families living in public housing are encouraged to buy back the apartments from their work unit at a rate significantly lower than market value. The state urges urban residents to discard their old socialist welfare mentality and embrace the new trend of private home ownership. As this popular state slogan advocates: 'Housing is a now consumer product, no longer a welfare product.' By the end of the 1990s, most public housing in all Chinese cities had been privatized, although there is a great deal of local variation in the ownership form.

At the same time, there has been rapid growth in the development of commercial housing for sale to individuals, mostly China's emerging middle-class people. The newly constructed, gated residential compounds are usually detached from the work-unit system and are run by private 'property management firms' (*wuye guanli gongsi*) and protected by security guards. Ordinary working-class people cannot afford such new commercial housing. These new communities have become an important measure of one's socioeconomic status and have transformed the urban Chinese social landscape into a highly stratified one.

See also: hukou

Further reading

Dutton, Michael (1998). *Streetlife China*. Cambridge: Cambridge University Press, 40–61, 214–21 [on the work unit in the reform period].

Lu, Xiaobo and Perry, Elizabeth (eds) (1997). *Danwei: The Changing Chinese Workplace in Historical and Comparative Perspective*. Armonk, NY: M. E. Sharpe.

LI ZHANG

HSK

(Chinese Proficiency Test)

HSK, the acronym for *Hanyu shuiping kaoshi* (Chinese Proficiency Test), is a standardized test developed by the HSK Centre of the Beijing Language and Culture University to assess the Chinese-language proficiency of non-native speakers, including foreigners, overseas Chinese and national minorities. There are three HSK tests: HSK Basic (or *Jichu* HSK, levels 1–3); HSK Elementary and Intermediate (or *Chu-zhongji* HSK, levels 3–5 and levels 6–8 respectively), which is the regular type of test if not otherwise specified; and HSK Advanced (*Gaoji* HSK, levels 9–11), including an oral test. The highest level in HSK Basic overlaps the lowest level in HSK Elementary–Intermediate.

Those who pass the different levels of one of the three HSK tests will be issued the corresponding HSK Certificate from the State HSK Commission under the Ministry of Education. All **foreign students** who apply for an undergraduate programme must reach minimum Level 3. Level 6, however, is necessary for the Arts, and Level 9 for all graduate studies. Otherwise, foreign students must first take Chinese language courses. The regular HSK test dates back to 1988 in Beijing. By the end of 2002, 540,000 people from 120 countries had taken HSK tests in China and abroad. There are currently forty-four testing centres in twenty-seven cities in China, including Hong Kong and Macao, and almost sixty testing centres in twenty-four countries in Asia, Europe and the Americas. In 2002, 14,000 people from around the world took the HSK test.

HELEN XIAOYAN WU

Hu Mage

b. 1973, Wufeng, Hubei

Folk-rock musician

Originally named Hu Qunfeng, Hu Mage joined the 'floating population' in Beijing after graduating from the Department of Geography at Middle China Normal University in 1995. The rural background and life as a sojourner in the metropolis later became the hallmark of his songwriting.

Hu's first album, *Everyone Has a Wooden Bench, Mine Will Not Be Brought to the Twentieth-First Century* (*Renren dou you ge xiaobandeng, wode bu dairu ershiyi shiji*), was recorded by himself with a wooden guitar and a four-track machine in August 1998, officially distributed by Modern Sky Records (see **New Sound Movement, Modern Sky Records**) in March 1999. Although Hu's music can roughly be categorized as indie folk-rock, it is distinguished from any existing Chinese music with its DIY production, the irregular use of fingering and rhythm, the freely incorporated singing and narration in Hubei dialect, the good-humoured account of the daily ironies in a sojourner's life, and the expressiveness of its extraordinarily repetitive refrains.

Hu carried out his ideals of recording life and exploring new sonic possibilities further in his second album, *Kill Seven with One Slap* (*Yi bazhang dasi qige*), finished in August 1999 and released online by his own company, Pythagorean Records (Gougu changpian, 2001). Designed as a two-scene drama, it consists of nearly thirty episodes, often a parody of Chinese sociopolitical life, accompanied by sounds from altered guitar, kitchen utensils, faked voices and other samplings. Hu Mage also earned fame as a DV filmmaker with the short film *Life is Very Boring, Fortunately We Have High-heeled Shoes* (*Shenghuo hen wuqu, xinghao you gaogenxie*), which premiered at the First Unrestricted New Image Festival in Beijing (December 2000), the festival in which Ying Weiwei's *The Box* (*Hezi*, 2001), the first video documentary on lesbian life produced in China, had its first showing (see **gay cinema and video**).

BAO YING

Hu Mei

b. 1958, Beijing

Film director/producer

A 1982 graduate of the **Beijing Film Academy**, Hu Mei is a 'Fifth Generation' film director (see **Fifth Generation (film directors)**) as well as an important women's director. Hu's film career began when she was assigned the position of assistant director at the August First Film Studio, one of the major state-owned film production centres. Her debut, *Army Nurse* (*Nü'er lou*, 1985), is one of the important women's films, addressing

issues of gender and female directorship. The film asserts a female voice through voice-over narration and employs a female perspective in structuring its point of view. Nonetheless, the protagonist finds herself trapped as the woman's voice collides with official discourse and female desires conflict with social role. Hu's second film, *Far from War* (*Yuanli zhanzheng de niandai*, 1987), explores the dislocation felt by an old former revolutionary as current socio-cultural norms begin to contradict his lifelong political ideals.

Following these psychological studies of gender and emotion, Hu Mei immersed herself in commercial projects and entertaining films. In addition to a number of commercial features, such as *The Gunslinger Without a Gun* (*Wuqiang qiangshou*, 1988) and *Urban Gunslinger* (*Dushi qiangshou*, 1992), her interests expanded to include directing and producing television series. Recently, Hu was invited to direct a film about an Austrian woman (Fanny Ehner) who married a Chinese man she met in Vienna in 1931, moved to China, and continued to live in rural Zhejiang after her husband is deported (*On the Other Side of the Bridge/Fengni de weixiao*, 2002).

Further reading

Berry, Chris (1988). 'Interview with Hu Mei.' *Camera Obscura: A Journal of Feminism and Film Theory* 18 (September): 32–42.

Cui, Shuqin (2003). 'Desire in Difference: Female Voice and Point of View in Hu Mei's *Army Nurse.*' In *idem*, *Women Through the Lens: Gender and Nation in a Century of Chinese Cinema*. Honolulu: University of Hawai'i Press.

CUI SHUQIN

Hu Shuli

b. 1953, Beijing

Journalist, publisher

Hu Shuli is a media pioneer who has pushed the boundaries of media ownership, reporting and legal rights. Though not her original plan, after farming and serving as a nurse's assistant during the **Cultural Revolution**, Hu followed in her mother's and grandfather's footsteps by entering the journalism programme of People's University in 1978. From 1982 to 1998 she reported for *Workers' Daily* and *China Business Times*; the latter gave her greater leeway to pursue important stories and interviews. Two fellowships in the United States in 1987 and 1994 strengthened her commitment to independent reporting.

In 1998, with financial support from the private Stock Exchange Executive Council, she founded *Business and Finance Review* (*Caijing*), a glossy bi-weekly magazine dedicated to uncovering the unethical, illegal and nonsensical behaviour of Chinese companies, banks, investment houses, accountants and regulators. In one celebrated report in October 2000, *Caijing* revealed the price-fixing and inside-trading rampant among China's largest investment funds – the schemers had met naked at a Shanghai bathhouse to ensure none of them would record the conversation. *Caijing* has vigorously defended itself against several lawsuits brought by companies unaccustomed to such aggressive reporting. Despite these pressures, Hu has not been cowed. In words reminiscent of Qin Benli, editor of the 1980s reformist *World Economic Herald* (*Shijie jingji daobao*), Hu says, 'We know where the line is, and we walk right up to it.' Some claim *Caijing* endures only with the support of a patron, but Hu denies having any political backers.

SCOTT KENNEDY

Hu Xuehua

(Sherwood Hu)

b. 30 November 1961, Shanghai

Huaju (spoken-drama) director, filmmaker

Hu Xuehua was one of the youngest **Huaju** directors to participate in the creation of seminal, experimental productions during the 1980s. The son of Huaju director Hu Weimin, his training as a **Jingju** (Peking opera) actor (1976–79) is unusual for a Huaju artist and has informed his later work. After majoring in theatre at the Beijing Arts Academy, Hu became a resident director at the Airforce Theatre in 1983, where he worked on the highly controversial premiere production of Wang Peigong and Wang Gui's **WM (W[o]m[en]** (literally *We* or *Us*). The subject matter and radical,

confrontational staging of this production led to it being banned in Beijing. In spite of this, Hu was invited to mount a second production, at the Shanghai People's Art Theatre in 1985, which was equally controversial.

In 1987 Hu worked with legendary Huaju director/theorist **Huang Zuolin** on the premiere of Sun Huizhu's **China Dream** (*Zhongguo meng*), using approaches and techniques inspired by Peking opera to evoke the ambivalent feelings of a young Chinese woman who emigrates to the US. Criticized politically but praised artistically, this production ran for two years, a remarkable record. In 1987 Hu moved to the USA, received an MFA at SUNY Buffalo and a PhD at the University of Hawai'i, and studied at the New York Public Theater with Joseph Papp. His later work as a filmmaker includes two award-winning Hollywood–Shanghai joint productions, *Warrior Lanling* (1995) and *Lani Loa – The Passage* (1998).

ELIZABETH WICHMANN-WALCZAK

Huaju

(spoken drama)

Huaju (spoken drama) is the Chinese term used to categorize modern Western-style theatre that was imported early in the twentieth century. Adopted by Chinese intellectuals living overseas, in hopes of addressing social problems faced by post-Qing China, Huaju contributed to the New Culture Movement and the May Fourth Enlightenment as a whole, offering a new form of theatre radically different from classical **Xiqu** (sung-drama/opera). Huaju was performed in vernacular Chinese and thus accessible to the masses, and had immediate political application. The first spoken drama written and staged by Chinese citizens was *Black Slave's Cry to Heaven* (*Heinu yutianlu*) – an adaptation of the Chinese translation of Harriet Beecher Stowe's novel *Uncle Tom's Cabin* – presented by the Spring Willow Society in Tokyo in 1907. The earliest spoken dramas in China were staged by the Spring Society in Shanghai and other dramatic societies such as the Progress Troupe, Creation Society and People's Drama Society, and were primarily adaptations of translated works by foreign playwrights. Seminal figures in early Chinese spoken drama include Hu Shi, Hong Shen, Ouyang Yuqian, Tian Han, Cao Yu and Guo Moruo, who created native plays that borrowed from Western playwrights but were original works addressing local and national Chinese concerns.

During the War of Resistance against Japan (1937–45), drama troupes were mobilized into the countryside to spread nation-building propaganda, and Huaju continued to be utilized ideologically after the Communist government was established in 1949 to promote the precepts of the Chinese Communist Party. State-run spoken drama training institutes were established, and in the early 1950s state theatres with resident companies such as the **Beijing People's Art Theatre**, China Youth Art Theatre and Shanghai People's Art Theatre were created. During this period, Soviet artists came to China to train actors at the newly established venues in the techniques of Stanislavsky and the Moscow Art Theatre. During the **Cultural Revolution** (1966–76) spoken drama was removed from the national stage and only Jiang Qing's eight model operas were performed. When performances of Huaju resumed in the late 1970s and early 1980s, there was a combination of restagings of the Chinese and foreign plays of earlier periods, as well as the beginnings of **avant-garde/experimental theatre** influenced by similar movements that had occurred earlier in Europe and elsewhere. In addition to proscenium stagings at state-run theatre companies, **Little Theatre** performances proliferated and some independent productions were staged. In addition to adaptations of foreign works, many foreign directors and designers collaborated with Chinese artists on spoken drama projects in China, the most celebrated of which was Arthur Miller and **Ying Ruocheng**'s production of Miller's *Death of a Salesman* at the Beijing People's Art Theatre in 1983 (see **Western theatre**).

One of the most famous original Chinese spoken dramas of the twentieth century is Lao She's epic *Teahouse* (*Chaguan*), whose content spans several decades of Chinese political movements and whose production history bridges several periods in the development of Huaju. It premiered in Beijing in 1958 (directed by **Jiao Juyin**), was restaged in 1979, toured Europe in 1980, and was revived with

a new cast and new interpretation by director **Lin Zhaohua** in 2000. During the 1990s, such experimental restagings of Chinese and foreign classics – along with 'salon' theatre, environmental theatre, international casting, bilingual productions, performance art, and intra-cultural as well as inter-cultural experiments – were all in evidence on the mainland and were often preceded by efforts in the more progressive independent theatre communities of Taiwan and Hong Kong (see **performing arts in Taiwan**).

Anthologies

Chen, Xiaomei (ed.) (2003). *Reading the Right Text: An Anthology of Contemporary Chinese Drama*. Honolulu: University of Hawai'i Press.

Yan, Haiping (ed.) (1998). *Theater and Society: An Anthology of Contemporary Chinese Drama*. Armonk: East Gate Books.

Yu, Shiao-ling (1996). *Chinese Drama After the Cultural Revolution, 1979–1989: An Anthology*. New York: Mellen Press.

Further reading

Chen, Xiaomei (2002). *Acting the Right Part: Political Theater and Popular Drama in Contemporary China*. Honolulu: University of Hawai'i Press.

—— (2003). 'Performing the Nation: Modern Spoken Drama'. In Joshua Mostow (ed.) and Kirk Denton (ed. China section), *Columbia Companion to Modern East Asian Literatures*. New York: Columbia University Press, 437–45.

Wang, W., Rong, B. and Zhang, Y. (eds) (1998). *Zhongguo huajushi* [A History of Chinese Spoken Drama]. Beijing: Culture and Art Press.

CLAIRE CONCEISON

Hualang

[Art Gallery Magazine, Guangzhou, 1980–]

Art journal

When launched in the 1980s as a bimonthly by the Lingnan Fine Art Publishing in Guangzhou, *Hualang* would become one of the three most comprehensive art periodicals in China along with **Meishu** [*Art*] in Beijing and **Jiangsu huakan** [*Jiangsu Pictorial*] in Nanjing. In 1994, following the appointment of the renowned critic and curator Huang Zhuan as senior editor, *Hualang* underwent the first drastic change in its editorial line. Beginning with the September–October issue (no. 46), it begun to focus solely on contemporary art with an eye on current trends in and outside China. Great emphasis was given to avant-garde artists who were internationally acclaimed yet little known in China, as well as to emerging young Chinese artists in its 'Reports from Artists' Studios'. Extensive coverage was provided on exhibitions and new art practices such as installation, video and performance and on important issues concerning cultural identity and the postmodernist constructs of art making. Sensing the market influences that had begun to affect the production of Chinese art, *Hualang* introduced a column on art sponsorship, investment and collection. After the resignation of Huang Zhuan at the end of 1996, *Hualang* tried to maintain its cutting-edge quality, but with the reshuffling of its editorial board and the release of other more radical and better-designed art periodicals in the late 1990s, it switched its editorial orientation for the second time in October 2001. Now *Hualang* specializes in art collection and connoisseurship.

TANG DI

Huang Chunming

(Hwang Ch'un-ming)

b. 1939, Taiwan

Writer

Restless and rebellious as a youth, Huang Chunming obtained a degree from the third college he attended and found success among the press literary supplements and literary magazines promoting 'homeland literature' for his stories about the neglected, oppressed, and humiliated poor folk of Taiwan. A major figure of the homeland literature movement (see **literature in Taiwan**), his fiction attracted readers both for its social conscience and its deft humour and satire. With the launching of the New Cinema movement

in the early-1980s (see **cinema in Taiwan**) several of his stories were adapted into films, beginning with *Sandwich Man* (*Erzi de da wanou*, 1983). This portmanteau film features three of Huang's stories, most famously 'The Bitter Taste of Apples' (*Pingguo de ziwei*), depicting economic boom through a peasant family catapulted into middle-class status after the father is injured by a US military vehicle and showered with compensation. The novella *Sayonara, Goodbye* (*Shayonala, zaijian*, 1973), was adapted into a film (1985), satirizing the attitudes of Japanese businessmen, while the lyrical 'Days for Watching the Sea', also called 'Flower in the Rainy Night' (*Kanhai de rizi*, 1967) was filmed in 1983. Social concern continued with *Two Painters* (*Liangge youqijiang*, filmed in 1990) and a collection of stories titled *Set Free* (*Fangsheng*, 1999).

Further reading

Huang, Chunming (2001). *The Taste of Apples*. Trans. Howard Goldblatt. New York: Columbia University Press [includes: 'The Fish', 'The Drowning of an Old Cat', 'His Son's Big Doll', 'The Gong', 'Ringworms', 'The Taste of Apples', 'Xiaoqi's Cap', 'The Two Sign Painters' and 'Sayonara · Zaijian']

EDWARD GUNN

Huang Jianxin

b. 1954, Xi'an

Film director

Huang Jianxin entered film as a scriptwriter after studying Chinese literature at Xi'an's Northwest University in the 1970s. Associated by age with the so-called 'Fifth Generation' directors (see **Fifth Generation (film directors)**), who received their initial administrative support from the director of the **Xi'an Film Studio**, Wu Tianming, Huang's style differed from the others by focusing on contemporary urban settings and situations and by its satirical comedy. The primary concern of Huang's films is the pervasiveness of bureaucratism and the intrusion of the Party's paranoid political style into the modern workplace.

Huang's first and finest film as director, *Black Cannon Incident* (1985), presented an intellectual anti-hero around whom all of China's bureaucratic errors could be committed. This became such a popular success with audiences that a rare sequel was filmed the next year (*Dislocation*, 1986) in which the popularity of this ironic figure was made the theme of the film. In 1988, a distinctly more grim but powerful film was made, **Transmigration (a.k.a. Samsara)**, in which Party corruption was depicted as poisoning an entire post-Mao generation of China's youth. Subsequent films reverted to Huang's satirical style, including *Stand Up, Don't Bend Over* (1992), *Back to Back, Face to Face* (1994), and *Signal Left, Turn Right* (1995). Huang's one international success has been the erotic *Wooden Man's Bride* (1993), whose formal beauty was poorly matched by its derivative character.

Further reading

Kaldis, Nicolas (1999). 'Huang Jianxin's *Cuowei* and/as Aesthetic Cognition'. *positions: east asia cultures critique* 7.2 (Fall): 421–58.

McGrath, Jason (2003). '*Black Cannon Incident*: Countering the Counter-espionage Fantasy'. In Chris Berry (ed.), *Chinese Films in Focus: 25 New Takes*. London: BFI, 8–14.

Pickowicz, Paul (1994). 'Huang Jianxin and the Notion of Postsocialism'. In Nick Browne, Paul G. Pickowicz, Vivian Sobchack and Esther Yau (eds), *New Chinese Cinemas: Forms, Identities, Politics*. Cambridge: Cambridge University Press, 57–87.

JEROME SILBERGELD

Huang Shuqin

b. 1940, Guangdong

Film director

Daughter of famed stage director **Huang Zuolin**, Huang Shuqin graduated from the **Beijing Film Academy** in 1964, but received no assignments until she co-directed *Lianxin Dam* (*Lianxin ba*, 1977). Beginning with *The Modern Generation* (*Dangdai ren*, 1981), she received regular assignments as a director

for Shanghai Film Studios, completing award-winning films such as the adaptation of **Wang Meng**'s 1953 novel, *Forever Young* (*Qingchun wansui*, 1983) and *Childhood Friends* (*Tongnian de pengyou*, 1984). She first received international attention outside socialist countries with *Woman, Demon, Human* (*Renguiqing*, 1987), an account of an innovative female performer of male roles in the traditional theatre (**Xiqu**). Huang directed *La Peinture* (a.k.a. *A Soul Haunted by Painting*; *Huahun*, 1994), based on the life of Pan Yuliang, who was sold into prostitution as a young girl and struggled to become a pioneering woman artist, never, however, to overcome persecution. Although Huang has continued to direct films, she became best known in the 1990s for directing acclaimed telenovellas such as the adaptations of **Qian Zhongshu**'s masterpiece, *Fortress Besieged* (*Weicheng*, 1990) and the topical *Moral Debts* (*Niezhai*, 1995), which depicts children searching for the parents who abandoned them, in Shanghai.

Further reading

Xiao, Li (1992). 'Huang Shuqin: A Woman Film Director'. *Chinese Literature* 2: 178–81.

EDWARD GUNN

Huang Xiang

(né Wu Gang)

b. 1941, Hunan

Poet

Huang Xiang appeared as a lone wolf on the contemporary Chinese poetic scene. Born to a KMT general and having grown up in Guizhou, Huang Xiang had lived almost his entire life in post-1949 China as a social outcast and was several times imprisoned because of his various political and literary activities.

Huang Xiang wrote some of his major political poems in the late 1960s. His poem 'The Beast' (*Yeshou*, 1968) describes a beast that was hunted by the era as well as the beast's stubborn will, sticking his remaining bone into the throat of his era.

Echoing some of the Russian Osip Mandelstam's late poems written during the Stalin era, 'The Beast' testifies to the terrible reality of the **Cultural Revolution** as well as to an equally strong individualistic defiance of history. His long poem *Symphony of the God of Fire (Huoshen jiaoxiangshi)*, written in 1969, was posted in Beijing during the 'Beijing Spring' of 1978. Huang Xiang's late poetry became more philosophical, mainly propagating a neo-Nietzchean life-philosophy, as in his long poetic-philosophical manifesto *The Beasty Figure Who Will Never Get Drunk (Kuangyin buzui de shouxing)*. In the mid-1990s Huang Xiang moved to the USA. Huang Xiang, who never officially published any collection of poetry in China and was nearly forgotten by the public for a time, is now considered to be a major forerunner of the underground poetry and **Misty poetry** movements of the late 1970s and early 1980s.

Further reading

Emerson, Andrew G. (2001). 'The Guizhou Undercurrent'. *Modern Chinese Literature and Culture* 13.2 (Fall): 111–33.

Garside, Roger (1981). *Coming Alive: China After Mao.* New York: McGraw Hill, 285–98. [includes four poems]

Huang, Xiang (2000). *Nine Poems.* Trans. Andrew G. Emerson. Ohio State University MCLC Resource Center Publication. Online. Available at http://mclc.osu.edu/rc/pubs/huangxiang.htm

HUANG YIBING

Huang Yongping

b. 1954, Xiamen, Fujian

Artist

Huang Yongping was one of the first and most influential Chinese artists to gain international notoriety. After graduating from the Zhejiang Academy of Fine Arts, Hangzhou in 1982 he founded the group **Xiamen Dada**. This avant-garde movement claimed to take inspiration from both Chan Buddhism and Western Dadaism.

Since the political upheavals of 1989, Huang Yongping has made Paris his home. Much of his work since comments on cultural conflict and cultural imperialism. Influenced as much by Duchamp as by Daoism and the **Yijing**, his artwork functions as philosophical statements that reflect various social and political phenomena of the post-colonial era. His work often involves an explicit collision of Western and Eastern iconography in an attempt to negotiate confounded cultural space in the era of globalization. Huang's large-scale, often site-specific installations employ traditional Chinese objects and themes and occasionally live animals and insects. *Le Pont et le théâtre du monde* (1993–5) is an elaborate cage that contains over 700 different snakes, lizards and insects. As a Hugo Boss Prize recipient in 1998, Huang suspended metal mesh bags containing black widow spiders throughout the space. Huang's work has been included in many major exhibitions, including 'Chinese Hand-Laundry' at the New Museum of Contemporary Art (New York 1993); the French Pavilion at the 1999 Venice Biennale, where he was chosen to officially represent France; 'Global Conceptualism: Points of Origin 1950s–1980s' at the Queens Museum of Art; 'Cities on the Move' in 1998 and 1999, and 'Inside/Out: New Chinese Art' at the P.S.1 Contemporary Art Center and Asia Society galleries in 1999. At the 2003 Venice Biennale Huang presented a documentary piece, *Bat Project I&II*, which reconstructs the artist's two attempts to recreate a life-size model of the US EP-3 spy plane that was forced to land on Hainan Island in April 2001 after colliding with a Chinese fighter jet. The installation piece, scheduled to be exhibited in Shenzhen (2001) and Guangzhou (2002), was in both cases denied permission due to the official involvement of both Chinese and American authorities in Guangzhou.

Further reading

Borysevicz, Mathieu (1999). 'Huang Yongping in Venice'. In John Clark (ed.), *Chinese Art at the End of the Millennium.* Hong Kong: New Media Limited, 210–12.

Fei, Dawei (ed.) (2003). *Huang Yongping's Work 'Bat Project II'.* Orsieres: Guy and Myriam Ullens Foundation.

Hou, Hanru (1994). 'Departure Lounge Art, Chinese Artists Abroad'. *Art and Asia Pacific* 1: 2.
—— (1998). *Huang Yong Ping* (exhibition catalogue). Fondation de Appel: Amsterdam.
Jouanno, Evelyne (1999). 'Huang Yong Ping'. *Flash Art* (June).
Köppel-Yang, Martina (2000). 'A Transcultural Roulette's Game: Huang Yongping's *Roulette Series* and Recent Related Works'. In Wu Hong (ed.), *Chinese Art at the Crossroads: Between Past and Future, Between East and West*. Hong Kong: *New Art Media*, 314–28.
—— (2003). 'A Bat's Life, or Big Brother is Watching You'. *Yishu – Journal of Contemporary Chinese Art* 1.2.

MATHIEU BORYSEVICZ

Huang Zongluo

b. 1926, Beijing

Huaju (spoken drama) actor

Huang Zongluo was an actor in the **Beijing People**'s **Art Theatre** (Beijing renmin yishu juyuan) before he retired a few years ago. He played leading roles in almost a hundred stage productions and films and his best-known work includes *Tea House* (*Chaguan, huaju*), *The Thirty-cent Note* (*Sanjiaoqian guobi*), *To Live* (*Huozhe*, film) and *Looking for Fun* (*Zhao le*, film). He won national and international prizes for his excellent acting skills. Together with his brother Huang Zongjiang (a playwright and a critic) and sister Huang Zongying (a celebrated film actress and prose writer), the Huangs contributed greatly to modern Chinese drama and cinema.

Educated at Northern University (Huabei daxue), Yen Ching University and the Central Academy of Drama (Zhongyang xiju xueyuan), Huang joined the Beijing People's Art Theatre in the 1950s. Following general director **Jiao Juyin**'s emphasis on character portrayal, Huang worked out his own creative process. Whenever he needed to perform a new role, he would always try to find a 'model' in everyday life. He regarded this as a necessary approach to his future stage work. He then wrote an 'autobiography' of the role he would play. By using expressive details, such as hand gestures, body movements and specific facial expressions, Huang not only explored the characters' inner world, but also managed to bring out the characters' feelings and emotions. Huang was also good at creating small comic roles.

LI RURU

Huang Zuolin

b. 24 October 1906, Tianjin; d. 1 June 1994, Shanghai

Playwright, director, administrator, theorist

Often referred to in theatre circles as simply Zuolin, Huang directed more than a hundred stage plays and films during his career and has trained countless actors. He is most renowned for his efforts to combine the acting techniques of Stanislavsky, Brecht and the **Jingju** (Peking opera) actor Mei Lanfang into a unique Chinese theatre aesthetic. From traditional Chinese aesthetics he adopted the term *xieyi* to describe his ideal concept of theatre. *Xieyi* has been translated variously as 'intrinsicalism', 'essentialism' and 'imagism' by Huang himself, and as 'suggestive' by the scholar Chen Xiaomei, but is best left in its original language, as Huang insisted in his later years. A top administrator at the Shanghai People's Art Theatre since 1951, Huang delivered a famous lecture in 1959 explaining Brecht's drama theory and also directed the latter's *Mother Courage and Her Children* (1959, Shanghai) and *Galileo* (1978, Beijing). In 1962, he gave a speech 'On the Concept of the Theatre' (*Mantan xiju guan*) in Guangzhou which was published in *People's Daily* on 25 April 1962. Active as a director and adviser up until his death in 1994, Huang is widely considered to be the most significant theatrical figure in Shanghai during the twentieth century.

Further reading

Drama Division of Shanghai Arts Research Institute (ed.) (1990). *Zuolin yanjiu* [Research on Zuolin]. Beijing: China Theatre Press.
Fei, Faye Chunfang. (1991). 'Huang Zuolin: China's Man of the Theatre'. PhD diss., City University of New York.

Huang, Zuolin (1990). *Wo yü xieyi xiju guan* [My Concept of the Theatre as 'Xieyi']. Beijing: China Theatre Press.

—— (1999). 'On Mei Lanfang and Chinese Traditional Theater.' In Faye Chunfang Fei (ed./trans.), *Chinese Theories of Theater and Performance from Confucius to the Present*. Ann Arbor: University of Michigan Press, 154–8.

Quah, Sy Ren (2000). 'Searching for Alternative Aesthetics in the Chinese Theatre: The Odyssey of Huang Zuolin and Gao Xingjian'. *Asian Culture* 24 (June): 44–66.

CLAIRE CONCEISON

Huangmeixi

(Hubei–Anhui–Jiangxi sung-drama/opera)

Huangmeixi is a local regional style of traditional drama found in Anhui, Hubei, Jiangxi, Jiangsu and other provinces. It began as a small-scale folk form of theatre in the villages along the Anhui–Hubei–Jiangxi borders, the place and time of first performance probably being Huangmei in Hubei during the nineteenth century. It did not reach the cities until the 1920s. The PRC sponsored Huangmeixi, quickly setting up some thirty professional troupes. In 1983 there were about fifty professional troupes, the number rising by 1990 to fifty-three, in addition to four schools. There are also many village folk troupes, which perform during festival times (see **temple fairs**). Since the 1980s, various levels of central and local government have invested considerable amounts of money in maintaining and enhancing the vitality of Huangmeixi against the challenges of modernization, which have tended to reduce its popularity, especially among urban people and youth. This money has gone into propaganda campaigns that have included competitions and festivals.

Initially, only percussion accompanied Huangmeixi singing. However, the orchestra adopted instruments from other parts of China, and even the West. The singing voice is natural, and the music is soft, melodious and hence accessible. The costumes are colourful and the performance techniques marked by their soft and emotional expressiveness. Several

Huangmeixi items have been recorded or filmed. Under the PRC, many traditional and modern themes have been incorporated into the Huangmeixi. One particularly well-known item is based directly on the novel *Honglou meng* (The Dream of the Red Chamber).

Further reading

Anhuisheng wenxue yishu yanjiusuo (1983). *Huangmeixi xinqiang jieshao*. Hefei: Anhui renmin chubanshe.

Qi, Mingcong and Qi, Kebin (1988). *Zenyang yanchang Huangmeixi*. Hefei: Anhui wenyi chubanshe.

Shi, Bailin (1993). *Huangmeixi yinyue gailun*. Beijing: Renmin yinyue chubanshe.

Shi, Jinan and Zhu, Yufen (1985). *Huangmeixi yilin*. Beijing: Zhongguo guangbo dianshi chubanshe.

COLIN MACKERRAS

Hui, Ann

(Hui On-wah/Xu Anhua)

b. 1947, Liaoning

Film director, producer

The only woman and one of the most respected figures of the 'Hong Kong New Wave' of the late 1970s, Ann Hui has used her versatile talents to create a distinct, original voice. Her recurrent theme is the dialectic between personal relationships and a larger, societal or historical situation, which she has been able to explore within the context of genre cinema. Starting with a near-masterpiece, *The Secret* (*Feng Jie*, 1979), she has periodically revisited the ghost story, with a humorous twist in *The Spooky Bunch* (*Zhuang Dao Zheng*, 1980) or a darker touch in *Visible Secret* (*Youling Ren Jian*, 2001). She made two violent political thrillers – *The Story of Woo Viet* (*Hu Yu de Gushi*, 1981) and *Boat People* (*Touben Nuhai*, 1982) – as well as a two-part, highly stylish **martial arts** film, *Romance of Book and Sword* (*Shujian Enchou Lu*, 1987), one of the first Hong Kong co-productions with the PRC.

She adapted two books by the 1930s Shanghai writer Eileen Chang (Zhang Aileen) – *Love in a Fallen City* (*Qingcheng zhi Lian*, 1984) and *Eighteen Springs* (*Ban Sheng Huan*, 1997) – and directed woman-centred dramas: *Starry is the Night* (*Jingye Xingguang Canlan*, 1988) and *Song of the Exile* (*Ketu Qiuhen*, 1990). Going beyond genre films, she powerfully explored complex political or personal dilemmas in *Summer Snow* (*Nüren sishi*, 1995), *Ordinary Heroes* (*Qian Yan Wu*, 1998) and *July Rhapsody* (*Nanren sishi*, 2002). Some of her best works were the realistic dramas she directed for television in the 1970s. She has also made a few documentaries.

See also: Chang, Sylvia; Fong, Allen

Further reading

Erens, Patricia Brett (2000). 'The Film Work of Ann Hui'. In Poshek Fu and David Desser (eds), *The Cinema of Hong Kong: History, Arts, Identity*. Cambridge: Cambridge University Press, 176–95.

Ho, Elaine Yee Lin (2001). 'Women on the Edges of Hong Kong Modernity: The Films of Ann Hui'. In Esther Yau (ed.), *At Full Speed: Hong Kong Cinema in a Borderless World*. Minneapolis: University of Minnesota Press, 177–206.

Law, K. (ed.) (1999). *Hong Kong New Wave – Twenty Years After*. Hong Kong: Provisional Urban Council.

Stringer, Julian (2003). 'Boat People: Second Thoughts on Text and Context'. In Chris Berry (ed.), *Chinese Films in Focus: 25 New Takes*. London: BFI, 15–22.

BÉRÉNICE REYNAUD

Huju

(Shanghai sung-drama, opera)

Huju (Shanghai opera) is the only traditional music drama originating in Shanghai, where several other regional dramas have also been popular. It originated from folk songs popularized during the late Qing period in the rural areas along Wusong and Huangpu rivers, which flow through Shanghai. Influenced by *tanci* and other forms of musical storytelling (see **quyi**), these folksongs developed into *shentan*, the early form of the drama, involving two or a few more actors. Performance of *shentan* began in the city of Shanghai around 1900. As the theatrical form gradually matured, it was renamed *shenqu* in 1914 and Huju around 1941. Shanghai was also the heartland of film and spoken drama, which influenced Huju significantly in content and form from the 1920s to the 1940s. Unlike the majority of other regional dramas, Huju has staged many productions of modern and contemporary themes with common people as their leading characters. It adopted divisions of acts and recognized the role of the playwright and director at a much earlier time. In the 1950s and 1960s, Huju was a champion in performing modern plays. The two revolutionary model **Jingju** (Peking opera), *Red Lantern* and *Shajiabang* – the most influential ones among the eight model plays created during the **Cultural Revolution** – were actually both adapted from Huju plays. Huju has also been popular in southern Jiangsu and the Hangzhou area of Zhejiang province.

Since the late 1970s, Huju classics from its early period to the 1960s have been revived. The representative plays include *A Bida Returns to Her Mother's Home* (*A Bida hui niangjia*), *Blue Sky and Yellow Spring* (*Biluo huangquan*), *Thunderstorm* (*Leiyü*), *Arhat Money* (*Luohan qian*), *Sparks of Prairie Fire* (*Xingxing zhi huo*) and *Kindling Fire in Reed Marshes* (*Ludang huozhong*). At the same time, a significant number of new plays have been written and staged, such as *Death of Zhang Zhixin* (*Zhang Zhixin zhi si*), *The Bitter Experience of an Actor* (*Yige mingxing de zaoyu*), *Two Sisters* (*Jiemei lai*), *Bright Moon Shines in Mother's Heart* (*Mingyue zhao muxin*), *Grow Together through Thick and Thin* (*Fengyu tongling ren*), *Dream Realized Today* (*Jinri mengyuan*), *My Heart Holds Your Hand* (*Wo xin wo ni shou*), *Shanghai Teacher* (*Shanghai laoshi*) and *Song Qingling in Shanghai* (*Song Qingling zai Shanghai*).

Huju has produced three generations of great performers since the 1930s. The first generation is represented by Ding Shi'e, Yang Feifei, Wang Pansheng, Shao Binsun, Shi Xiaoying, Xiao Aiqin and Xie Hongyuan, who had been active on stage until the early 1980s. The second generation is exemplified by Ma Lili, Mao Shanyu, Wang Huazhong, Chen Yu and others who have been prominent actors and actresses in the New

Period. Since the late 1990s, a third generation of well-known performers has gradually emerged.

Currently, there are about nine professional Huju troupes and several non-professional troupes performing in the city and its neighbouring regions. Shanghai Huju Troupe, ranked as a national-level troupe, is composed of two performing companies named the No. 1 Huju Company (Huju yituan) and the Youth Huju Company (Qingnian hujutuan). The other seven local professional troupes are Shanghai changning hujutuan, Shanghai Baoshan hujutuan, Shanghai Dashijie hujutuan, Shanghai Chongmingxian hujutuan, Taicangshi hujutuan, Wuxianshi huju tuan and Wujiangshi Wuzhongqu hujutuan.

The performing venues are mainly theatres that sometimes transport suburban audiences into the city, public squares in various communities, and auditoriums in cultural palaces. Some well-known productions have been adapted into Huju opera films and TV series for large audiences (see **Xiqu on television**).

Further reading

Stock, Jonathan P. J. (2003). *Huju: Traditional Opera in Modern Shanghai*. Oxford: Oxford University Press.

DU WENWEI

hukou

(residential permits)

Geographic and social mobility are relatively recent phenomena in China. It is thought that roughly 10 per cent of China's citizens constitute a floating population of mostly rural people migrating to cities in search of work (see **migration and settlement patterns**). However, most remain impoverished because they find themselves outside the official urban household registration system that involves a kind of resident's permit called the *hukou*. The *hukou* system, which was adopted into law in 1958, was originally set up to avoid overwhelming the cities of China with uncontrolled immigration. Under this system all Chinese received a document that classified them as either 'rural' or 'urban'. In order

to receive state benefits – education, health care, subsidized staple foods and work permits – one had to be an officially registered person in the city or rural county of birth. Since the end of the Mao era, however, the *hukou* system is seen by some as an obstacle to the development of China's cities and bureaucratically very difficult to administer. On the other hand, many of the more privileged urbanites see it as their entitlement and a protection of their living standard in the face of massive and potentially destabilizing urban growth. For example, millions of city dwellers depend on the *hukou* to ensure their benefits in old age. Nonetheless, officially the system is being gradually phased out as urban populations tend more and more to be influenced by the 'socialist-market economy' in China's cities.

See also: housing; residential districts (urban)

Further reading

Dutton, Michael (1998). *Streetlife China*. Cambridge: Cambridge University Press, 77–159.

PETER M. FOGGIN

human rights

For much of the post-1949 period human rights was a taboo subject in the PRC, or dismissed as a bourgeois slogan irrelevant to a socialist society. Towards the late 1970s, however, as a result of both domestic changes and China's increasing incorporation in the world community, human rights surfaced in political debate. Participants in the Democracy Wall movement of 1978–9 were the first to challenge the official view of the class nature of rights, which led some establishment intellectuals to begin elaborating on a Marxist conception of human rights. China's position on human rights gradually became more affirmative during the 1980s; it became a member of the UN Human Rights Commission in 1982 and signed several conventions.

Calls for human rights were heard again in the much larger democracy movement of 1989. The crushing of the movement provoked strong criticism from the West, and human rights now became an important and contested issue in China's international relations. To counter the criticism the political leadership launched its own human rights policy, mainly in the form of official White Papers, and encouraged academic research on the topic.

This official blessing has resulted in an impressive number of academic works. The majority of these are still confined, however, within a Marxist theoretical framework that builds upon a historical and relativistic approach according to which the level of economic development determines the understanding and realization of human rights in a given society. Many argue furthermore that the right to subsistence is more important to the Chinese people than civil and political rights. But some works have appeared that propose a more liberal understanding of human rights, stressing the importance of civil and political rights and affirming their universality.

In contrast to other Asian countries, there are few references in either the official or the academic discourse to cultural distinctiveness or attempts to ground human rights claims in traditional values. Xia Yong is one of the few scholars to have attempted to relate Confucian ideas to the concept of human rights. Although official spokespersons often refer to 'national conditions' (*guoqing*) when defending China's position on human rights, their emphasis is more on economic constraints than on cultural distinctiveness. It is important to note that the idea of Asian values never became a cornerstone in the official Chinese human rights policy. Chinese intellectuals and dissidents are generally very critical of Asian values and the view that universal human rights would be foreign and inapplicable to China. For example, Liu Junning, a prominent liberal, has argued that Asian values only serve to defend and justify the power of despotic and authoritarian political leaders.

See also: 4 June [1989] esprit; liberalism; New Confucianism; socio-political values

Further reading

Angle, Stephen C. (2002). *Human Rights and Chinese Thought. A Cross-Cultural Inquiry.* Cambridge: Cambridge University Press.

Angle, Stephen C. and Svensson, Marina (2001). *The Chinese Human Rights Reader.* New York: M. E. Sharpe.

De Bary, Theodore W. (1998). *Asian Values and Human Rights: A Confucian Communitarian Perspective.* Cambridge: Harvard University Press.

Svensson, Marina (2002). *Debating Human Rights in China: A Conceptual and Political History.* Lanham, MD: Rowman and Littlefield.

MARINA SVENSSON

Humanistic Spirit, 'Spirit of the Humanities'

(*Renwen jingshen*)

Intellectual debate

The 'Spirit of the Humanities' debate is an umbrella term for a variety of cultural topics that engaged the literary elite in the mid 1990s. While the '**cultural discussion**' (*wenhua taolun*) of the mid 1980s focused on theoretical questions first posed in the West regarding subjectivity and enlightenment, the 1990s debates delved into China's literary and intellectual heritage in order to salvage a lost 'spirit'. The debate originated in a dialogue among Shanghai scholars published in *Shanghai wenxue* [Shanghai Literature] in 1993. It was continued in the journal **Dushu** [Reading] which serialized discussions over several months in 1994, causing instant controversy. That same year the **Chinese Academy of Social Sciences** sponsored a discussion on the 'Spirit of the Humanities' in preparation for a 1995 national meeting on the subject.

Zhang Rulun, Wang Xiaoming, Zhu Xueqin, Chen Sihe, Li Tiangang, Yuan Jin, Gao Ruiquan and **Xu Jilin**, young professors in Shanghai, identified and criticized the loss of the humanistic spirit in contemporary Chinese intellectual life. A spiritual poverty, they asserted, was manifest by a money-grubbing trend recently pervasive among intellectuals, as a phenomenon associated with China's globalization. In the long run, the poverty was due to official domination of humanities fields since the mid-twentieth century, or even earlier, to China's loss of tradition a century ago. The discussions concluded with an urgent call for re-establishing a faith in intellectual pursuits, or in a new role of criticism. In response, Wu Xuan, Wang Gan, Fei Zhenzhong and Wang Binbin in Nanjing agreed to rebuild a Chinese humanistic spirit and yet looked forward to the opportunities provided in the new global situation. As they held, this rebuilding requires intellectuals to play a role in the new order, such as the currently blooming mass culture, to rediscover their vitality and creativity, rather than high-mindedly seeking to return to a May-Fourth style elitism.

One focal point in the debates was how to evaluate the rise of mass culture in the 1990s. Critics such as **Wang Xiaoming** and Chen Sihe (see **minjian**) harshly assessed the contemporary cultural climate and considered works by the novelists **Wang Shuo** and **Jia Pingwa** and the films of director **Zhang Yimou** to epitomize the current spiritual depravity in their failure to address 'ultimate concerns' (*zhongji guanhuai*). Works

by **Zhang Chengzhi**, **Shi Tiesheng** and **Zhang Wei**, by contrast, were seen to exemplify the 'Humanistic Spirit'. In response, Wang Shuo and others published articles defending their artistic and occupational choices in the new market economy. Critics such as **Wang Meng**, **Zhang Yiwu** and Chen Xiaoming celebrated the 'postmodern sensibilities' exhibited in the criticized works (see **postmodernism (houxiandai zhuyi) and 'post-ism' (houxue)**).

Further reading

Wang Xiaoming (ed.) (1996). *Renwen jingshen xinsi lu* [Thoughts on the 'Humanistic Spirit']. Shanghai: Wenhui chubanshe.

Xu, Ben. (1999). *Disenchanted Democracy: Chinese Cultural Criticism after 1989*. Ann Arbor: University of Michigan.

CHEN JIANHUA AND ROBIN VISSER

'I Have Nothing'

(Yiwu suoyou)

Rock song

Composed by **Cui Jian**, the song had its debut on 9 May 1986, when it was performed at a state-organized concert in the People's Workers' Stadium, commemorating the Year of World Peace. The 'Concert of 100 Singers' (*Baiming gexing yanchanghui*) was broadcast on television nationwide and the song immediately reached a massive audience. In the uniform of a PLA soldier, Cui's appearance was provoking, while his lyrics appealed to many young Chinese, who found their own feelings thus expressed. They can either be understood as a pure love song, depicting a penniless singer who tries to persuade his lover to go with him, or as a political statement, directed against the PRC's reform policy.

The song was widely discussed and even printed with a comment in the **People's Daily** (16 July 1988), when Cui and ADO released it that year. Framed in a musical structure of tension and release, the song combines Western rock with Chinese instrumentation, featuring the *suona* (Chinese oboe) and a distorted electric guitar as solo instruments. It turned into a student hymn in summer of 1989. Since then it has been covered by many other singers, appeared on wedding parties and found its way into karaoke bars and literary anthologies.

Further reading

Baranovitch, Nimrod (2003). *China's New Voices: Popular Music, Ethnicity, Gender, and Politics*. Berkeley: University of California Press, 31–6.

Jones, Andrew (1992). *Like a Knife. Ideology and Genre in Contemporary Chinese Popular Music*. Ithaca: Cornell University.

Steen, Andreas (1996). *Der Lang Marsch des Rock 'n' Roll. Pop- und Rockmusik in der Volksrepublik China*. Hamburg: Lit-Verlag.

ANDREAS STEEN

In the Heat of the Sun

[Yangguang canlan de rizi, 1995]

Film

Adapted from **Wang Shuo**'s novella *Fierce as Beasts* (*Dongwu xiongmeng*) by the actor **Jiang Wen**, *In the Heat of the Sun* presents the highly subjective account of a callous boy's infatuation and coming of age. Set during the **Cultural Revolution**, the narrator endows this period with nostalgia for his jejune idealization of both the nation and the young dancer he admired, his ability to manipulate society and his self-affirming participation in a youth gang. In these ways, the film refuses the historical condemnation of the Cultural Revolution. At the same time, however, the narrator calls into question his own memory, and the film concludes with his violent disillusionment and ostracism from the very subculture that had sustained him in his youth.

Further reading

Braester, Yomi (2001). 'Memory at a Standstill: 'Street-Smart History' in Jiang Wen's *In the Heat of the Sun*'. *Screen* 42.4 (Winter): 350–62.

EDWARD GUNN

Indo-European language speakers

Indo-European language speakers native to China are represented principally by Tajiks and Russians. The mother tongue of most Tajiks is Tajik, a language of Indo-Iranian group, but a number speak Uighur, a Turkic language. Tajik spoken in China lacks a writing system. Tajik speakers inhabit southwest Xinjiang and are distributed over approximately five counties with a total population of about 30,000. As a minority nationality, the Tajik people in China can be traced back to the Tang dynasty. Their economy is based on farming and animal husbandry; families maintain a patriarchal system, and their religion is Islam.

Russian speakers, of which there are only about 3,000 in China, live scattered in Xinjiang, Inner Mongolia and Heilongjiang. They migrated from Russia in the nineteenth century and around the October Revolution in the early twentieth century. The Russian language in China is closely related to southern Russian in Russia, but it shows characteristics of pronunciation (accent) and vocabulary resulting from the influence of surrounding languages such as Chinese, Uighur and Mongolian. The writing system employs the Cyrillic alphabet. The people's lifestyle and convention is similar to that in Russia and their religion is the Orthodox Eastern Church. Many Russian speakers have relatives abroad, mainly in Russia, Australia and Canada, and a number of them have migrated abroad in the previous decades. The number of Russian speakers has thus decreased.

YANG LAN

instant food

The Chinese were first exposed to instant food in 1960s. It was largely instant noodles. Today, China has a large variety of instant foods. Customarily, the Chinese regard wheaten and rice foods as *zhushi* (the main part of a meal) and the rest as *fushi* (auxiliary part of a meal). Therefore, apart from instant noodles, rice, porridge and all kinds of instant frozen breads and dumplings, there are also instant meats, vegetables and tofu products packaged in cans or vacuumed plastic bags.

Instant noodles claim a 60 per cent share of the Chinese instant food market. In 2000, there were 158 instant noodle factories with a total annual output of 360 tons. A study found that the market still had large room for development: while individual Japanese were eating an average of forty-four packages of instant noodles annually, the Chinese were consuming only fifteen packages per person. Competition has since ensued. The Japanese instant noodle inventor Nissin Food Products Co., Ltd, vowed to beat the Taiwanese brand names Kangshifu [Master Kang] and Tongyi [Unification], which, together with seven other mainland companies, were enjoying the lion's share of the Chinese instant noodle market. The battle was joined by Chunqi Food Co., Ltd, from Shanghai. It has been marketing aggressively a series of Chinese instant foods, covering the whole range of a traditional Chinese meal – from main and auxiliary foods to stews and soups. It also focuses on instant medicinal foods and instant sauces, with which a dish can be made in an instant even by 'dummies'.

YUAN HAIWANG

Institute of Linguistics

(Yuyan yanjiusuo)

The Institute of Linguistics of the **Chinese Academy of Social Sciences** is the premier organization for research in Chinese, Chinese dialects, and applied and theoretical linguistics. Since its establishment in 1950, the Institute has engaged many of China's most renowned linguistic scholars, including Luo Changpei, Lü Shuxiang,

Ding Shengshu, Lu Zhiwei and Fu Maoji. The Institute's research mission covers both modern and historical linguistics, in the fields of phonetics, phonology, syntax, grammatology, etymology and lexicography. It is also charged with investigating developments and trends in linguistic theory and research methodology outside of China. Its scholars and lexicographers have compiled some of China's most authoritative **dictionaries** and linguistic reference works, including *Xiandai Hanyu cidian* [Dictionary of Modern Chinese], *Zhongguo wenfa yaolüe* [Essentials of Chinese Grammar], *Xiandai Hanyu babaici* [Eight Hundred Words in Modern Chinese], *Gujin ziyin duizhao shouce* [A Comparative Handbook of Modern and Ancient Chinese Character Readings], *Hanyu fangyan diaocha shouce* [Handbook for the Investigation of Chinese Dialects] and *Language Atlas of China*. China's most influential linguistics journals are also published there, including *Zhongguo yuwen* [Chinese Language], *Fangyan* [Dialect] and *Dangdai yuyanxue* [Modern Linguistics]. The Institute houses the Linguistics Department of the Graduate School of the Chinese Academy of Social Sciences, in which students may do advanced study and research in the fields of Chinese lexicography and applied and theoretical linguistics, leading to both master's and PhD degrees. The Chinese Linguistics Association and China's Association for Chinese Dialectology are also headquartered in the Institute.

RICHARD VANNESS SIMMONS

intellectual property

'Intellectual property' or IP (*zhishi chanquan*) is central to the development of China's cultural and media industries. Existing widespread IP non-compliance can be attributed to a number of factors. First, the legacy of a Confucian tradition that viewed imitation as flattery meant that ideas were to be shared. Second, the nationalization of creative workers as 'engineers of the soul' meant that privately owned monopolies or exclusive rights were deemed bourgeois. Third, the sheer scale of China's population has made effective intellectual property rights (IPR) education difficult. It has therefore been difficult for the Chinese government to change

public perceptions and to monitor the illegal pirating of cultural works, particularly in south China. Indeed, the popularity of pirated versions of software, including CDs and VCDs, has substantially reduced the price of licensed software.

The Chinese government has regularly made a show of appropriating and destroying illegal material primarily to satisfy the demands of foreign investors and governments. In fact, it was only in the wake of the Agreement on Trade-related Aspects of Intellectual Property Rights (TRIPS) in 1994 and China's moves to secure WTO membership (see **World Trade Organization (WTO) debate**) that the issues of rights came to national policy attention. The control of print products – and CDs and DVDs – is now increasingly monitored under a new intellectual property regime. Further, the notion of copyright (*banquan*) is considered central to the multiple rights distribution of film and television products, superseding the dominant system that saw broadcasters such as **CCTV (Chinese Central Television)** holding exclusive rights, with smaller stations bartering 'programme packages' amongst themselves.

Further reading

http://www.ncac.gov.cn/
http://www.ncac.gov.cn/cn/fagui/newcopyright-law. htm
Feng, P. (1997). *Intellectual Property in China*. Hong Kong: Sweet and Maxwell.

MICHAEL KEANE

intellectuals and academics

Since the late 1970s China's intellectuals have presented themselves in public as university-based academics, first fighting to establish some social autonomy from the Maoist state, then trying to reform it, and currently trying to find a social place between the Party-state and institutions of a globalized economy. Their identity has increasingly moved from state cadres to academic professionals, while their social role has shifted from administrators and propagandists to experts and public critics. These changes have been marked by a series of dominant debates from 'liberation of thought' to **New Authoritarianism**, to bitter fights between **New Left** advocates and 'liberals' (see **liberalism**). At the same time, these changes and debates have been connected by the broad acceptance of some fundamental assumptions: that democracy is good, that nationalism is natural, that commercialization is unavoidable, and that professionalization is the sensible solution for intellectuals. In all of these debates foreign theory (largely from Europe and the USA) has been accepted by nearly all intellectuals as authoritative in illuminating Chinese conditions and for suggesting the shape of Chinese solutions.

The post-Mao period: recovery

China's intellectuals began the reform period by trying to reclaim their status as intellectual cadres and custodians of public morals that had been promised to them under the Mao period and stolen from them in the **Cultural Revolution**. China's universities, which had been subservient to the State Plan under Mao and closed in the late 1960s, opened again. Purged professors and leading Party intellectuals returned to their former positions. Theorists like Wang Ruoshui and **Li Zehou**, journalists like Liu Binyan, and writers such as **Wang Meng**, who had all been active before the Cultural Revolution returned to pursue a 'liberation of thought' that rejected the ultra-leftism of late Maoism. This soon moved to a reconsideration of Marxism and Maoism and the 1980s opened with public debates on **Marxist Humanism** and efforts by the CCP to revise Party orthodoxy. Li Zehou, the philosopher at CASS, and Su Shaozhi, director of the Institute of Marxism–Leninism at CASS, were leaders in this effort at internal reform.

The 1980s: reform

The 1980s was the decade of the generalist public intellectual in Chinese politics. Leading speakers drew their authority from their Party position, general studies, and ability to manipulate Party ideology to address the issues of economic and political reform under Deng Xiaoping. There was

still a single public sphere dominated by the media outlets of the Party-state, but it was becoming more open to dissident voices.

Intellectuals increasingly sought the formal protection of university appointment, strengthened by the example of Western universities from which increasing numbers of foreign scholars came to visit China and to which thousands of Chinese students went to undertake advanced studies. With this came a broad acceptance that the Cultural Revolution had demonstrated the failings of socialist and Chinese theory and that the economic development and democratic societies of the West confirmed the superiority of Western theory as a tool of social analysis that could be applied to China's case. From Li Zehou using Kant to undermine the Hegelian assumptions of CCP ideology and Fang Lizhi using Einstein to discredit the scientism of Engels in the 1980s, this instrumental use of foreign theory to address Chinese issues has dominated Chinese academic and public debates into the new century.

Arguments over democracy and neo-authoritarianism dominated intellectual debates in the 1980s, beginning with Wei Jingsheng's famous call in 1979 on Beijing's Democracy Wall. By mid-decade Wang Huning and Xiao Gongqin articulated the neo-authoritarian response that asserted that a strong authoritarian state was needed to monitor economic reform while over-early democratization would lead to instability. Reform and democracy won intellectual hearts in the late 1980s, but the popular protests and military repression of 1989 dashed these hopes. Into the gap crept nationalist rhetoric – to buttress the insecure Party and as something that intellectuals could safely talk about. **He Xin**, widely despised as a government toady, enjoyed a brief fame in the early 1990s, but his strident **nationalism** has since become a major popular trend in China.

The 1990s: globalization

The 1990s was the decade of the academic in public debates in China. This reflected not only the increasing independence of intellectuals from the grasp of Party power, but at the same time the fragmentation of the public sphere under the deluge of globalized media outlets (most notably **satellite television** and the Internet) along with the concomitant marginalization of intellectuals from the halls of power. In the 1980s, intellectuals read the Party media and tried to publish in them; in the 1990s they turned elsewhere. Key outlets for academic and public debate in China since the mid 1990s have been the popular intellectual journals, ranging from **Dushu** [Reading] to *Zhanlue yu guanli* [Strategy and Management], to book series, and the Internet, where such journals cum websites as **Ershiyi shiji** [Twenty-first Century] draw Chinese intellectuals from around China and across the world.

The underlying assumptions about democracy and nationalism continued through the 1990s. China's intellectuals also came to believe that commercialization was inevitable as China's economic reforms and opening to world markets continued, and they came to see professionalization as the most sensible way to protect their public role as experts. **Liu Dong**'s efforts, as a professor of comparative literature at Beijing University, to edit China's first contemporary peer-review academic journal, *Zhongguo xueshu* [China Scholarship], is a notable example of this.

These four assumptions (democracy, nationalism, commercialization and professionalization) are shared by the three major intellectual stands among China's academics today: the 'New Left', the 'liberals' and the 'New Confucians' (see **New Confucianism**). Among New Left theorists and writers, the best-known internationally is **Wang Hui**, at CASS, but also prominent are **Gan Yang** in Hong Kong, **Zhang Yiwu** at Beijing University, and **Cui Zhiyuan**, first at MIT and later in Singapore. This stand takes a dim view of the social costs of neo-liberal economic policies to working people in China. Some, such as Cui, look back with frank admiration to some of the social policies of Mao Zedong. The 'liberals' in contrast excoriate the excesses of the Mao period and seek to adapt institutions and values of the liberal West to Chinese conditions. More radial liberals, such as Liu Junning (now an expatriate in the West) promote the neo-liberal, laissez-faire doctrines congenial to American conservatives. More moderate liberals, such as **Qin Hui** at Qinghua University, Beijing, and **Xu Jilin** at East China Normal University

in Shanghai, promote something closer to social democracy that seeks to limit both the power of the state and of the market. Finally, New Confucianism, also known as *Guoxue* (**National Studies**), has found a niche at Beijing University and other institutions and in the hearts of some intellectuals as a supplement to the Western-oriented theory of both New Left and liberal intellectuals. At its worst, such National Studies are a sop to an unreformed authoritarian state, while more sensitive interpreters (often Chinese scholars outside China), such as Du Weiming, make a case for integrating norms and concepts from China's varied traditions into contemporary discourse.

Further reading

Davies, G. (2001). *Voicing Concerns: Critical Voices from China*. Lanham, MD: Rowman and Littlefield.

Fewsmith, J. (2001). *China Since Tiananmen: The Politics of Transition*. New York: Cambridge University Press.

Goldman, Merle (1994). *Sowing the Seeds of Democracy in China*. Cambridge: Harvard University Press.

Gu, Edward X. (1999). 'Cultural Intellectuals and the Politics of the Cultural Public Space in Communist China (1979–1989): A Case Study of Three Intellectual Groups'. *Journal of Asian Studies* 58.2 (May): 389–431.

Gu, Edward X. and Goldman, Merle (eds) (2004). *Chinese Intellectuals Between State and Market*. London: Routledge.

Li, Shitao (ed.) (1999). *Zhishifenzi lichang* [Intellectual Positions], 3 vols. Changchun: Shidai wenyi chubanshe.

Wang, Chaohua (2004). 'Introduction: Minds of the Nineties'. In *idem* (ed.), *One China, Many Paths*. London: Verso, 9–45.

Zhang, Xudong (2001). 'The Making of the Post-Tiananmen Intellectual Field: A Critical Overview'. In *idem* (ed.), *Whither China: Intellectual Politics in Contemporary China*. Durham: Duke University Press, 1–75.

Zheng, Yongnian (1999). *Discovering Chinese Nationalism in China*. New York: Cambridge University Press.

TIMOTHY CHEEK

Internet (content)

Internet content in China is in many ways similar to Internet content elsewhere. There are **Internet portals**, chat-rooms, noticeboards, e-auction and e-commerce sites for **Internet shopping** as well as websites for businesses, news organizations, universities, research projects, government departments and so on. However, the Chinese government is constantly faced with a difficult dilemma. As with other media, it is keen to keep Internet content under state and Party control as far as possible (see **state control of media**). Yet at the same time, it is keen to promote the development of the Internet for all the commercial, educational and cultural potential that it has for the betterment of the country, its economy and its people.

Control of Internet content has generally been erratic, retrospective and often through unpublished rules. It also depends to a large degree on systems of self-censorship and perceived surveillance by Internet content providers (ICPs) who fear the consequences of upsetting those in power. In October 2000, a State Council decree established that ICPs should be able to supply the authorities, on demand, with the full content as well as records of all visitors to their sites for the preceding two-month period. This followed a number of well-publicized cases of political security breaches. One pro-democracy activist, for instance, was arrested in 1998 after sending tens of thousands of Chinese email addresses to a pro-democracy newsletter in the United States. Others have included activists who have posted details about the events of 1989, Tibetan independence and so on. A few well-publicized arrests have therefore served as a potent warning to others who might contemplate similar action.

In the early 2000s, the Chinese government has become more adept at blocking key foreign news websites such as CNN, the BBC or US and European newspapers. However, it is still impossible for the government to block all such sites and there have always been notable loopholes. Moderately competent Internet users who are so inclined have always also been able to find ways around such blocking, for instance by entering banned websites through an anonymous gateway site.

The blocking of foreign news and politically motivated sites is a significant issue, not least because it is a government preoccupation. However, it is also easily blown out of proportion. It should be remembered also that the vast majority of Chinese Internet users do not have sufficiently good English, or other languages, to be able to read foreign sites. Similarly most of them show little interest in such sites and according to user surveys show increasing satisfaction with the content that is available. At the same time, it is not generally difficult to find politically sensitive comments or jokes on noticeboards or in chat rooms – at times even on sites such as that of the **People's Daily** or **CCTV (Chinese Central Television)**.

In the midst of concern over the control of Internet content in China, it is easy to forget the plethora of new sources of information that the Internet has made available to Chinese users. Leaving foreign sites aside, the massive proliferation of Chinese sources of news, comment, cultural debate, economic and business information, to mention just a few, has been astounding. Chinese citizens can now readily read news from sources all over the country, they have greater access than ever to government information and advice including reports, statistics, official documents or decrees, and they can communicate effortlessly using email with people throughout the country and the world. The Internet may not be the bringer of freedom, democracy and civil society to China, but it is radically transforming flows of information throughout the country and among its citizens.

The most popular websites in China are portals, and recent Internet user surveys have consistently shown that users' primary concerns in using the Internet are to gather information (46.1 per cent) or for leisure and entertainment purposes (31.1 per cent) (CNNIC 2002). Three-quarters of those seeking information are looking for news and the most widely used online service is email.

See also: Internet (history and structure)

Further reading

Chase, Michael and Mulvenon, James (2002). *You've Got Dissent. Chinese Dissident Use of the Internet* and *Beijing's Counter-Strategies*. Santa Monica: Rand.

CNNIC (2002). *Statistical Report of the Development of the Internet in China (2002/1)*. Beijing: China Internet Network Information Centre (CNNIC).

Fravel, M. T. (2000). 'Online and on China: Research Sources in the Information Age'. *China Quarterly* 163: 821–42.

Harwit, E. and Clark, D. (2001). 'Shaping the Internet in China: Evolution of Political Control over Network Infrastructure and Content'. *Asian Survey* 41.3: 377–408.

Tsui, Lokman (2003). 'The Panopticon as the Antithesis of a Space of Freedom: Control and Regulation of the Internet in China'. *China Information* 17.2: 65–82.

Yang, Guobin (2003). 'The Internet and Civil Society in China: A Preliminary Assessment'. *Journal of Contemporary China* 12.36 (August): 453–75.

KEVIN LATHAM

Internet (history and structure)

By the end of 2001, official statistics put the number of Internet users in China at 33.7 million, showing an accelerating growth rate of 27 per cent over the preceding six-month period (CNNIC 2002). Although this represents less than 3 per cent of the country's population it reveals a massive growth in Internet use since the mid 1990s. In 1994, there were only 1,600 users in the entire country. These figures reflect the way in which the Internet in China has developed from being a largely specialist research- and education-oriented network in its early years, to being an increasingly popular medium of mass information, entertainment and commerce.

The Internet in China dates back to 1987 when two education- and research-oriented computer networks, the China Academic Network (CANET) and the Institute of High Energy Physics (IHEP) network, were established. In 1990 these were joined by the China Research Network (CRNET) and in 1996 these three networks combined to form the China Science and Technology Network

(CSTNET) under the supervision of the Chinese Academy of Sciences (CAS).

By the year 2000 China's Internet was made up of eight principal interconnecting networks: China Science and Technology Network (CSTNET) under the jurisdiction of the Chinese Academy of Sciences (CAS); CHINANET under the Ministry of Information Industries (MII); China Education and Research Network (CERNET) under the State Education Commission (SEC); China Golden Bridge Network (CHINAGBN); UNINET under telecoms operator China Unicom and the MII; China Network Communications Network (CNCNET) under telecoms and broadband operator China Netcom; China International Economics and Trade Network (CIETNET) under the Ministry of Foreign Trade and Economic Cooperation (MOFTEC); and China Mobile Network (CMNET) again under the MII and mobile telecoms operator China Mobile. To these should be added the military's China Great Wall Network (CGWNET) and China Satellite Network (CSNET) still being completed in early 2002.

The SEC launched its own educational network, CERNET, in 1993 with the aim of linking up first the nation's universities and eventually also middle and primary schools. However, shortly after that the development of the Internet became increasingly embroiled in issues of commercial and interministerial rivalry.

A key issue that dictated the development of the structure and functioning of the Internet is that of funding and ownership. A clear contrast has emerged between the ownership and control of the infrastructure and Internet service provision on the one hand and Internet content on the other. Importantly, much of the infrastructural development was funded by central government and in the early years the lines were predominantly owned by the dominant telecoms operator China Telecom who leased out use of the lines to the fledgling networks. However, as the Internet developed, ownership of the growing number of networks was increasingly in the hands of ministries and their subsidiary telecoms operators.

In 1993 the Ministry of Post and Telecommunications (MPT), which merged with its rival the Ministry of Electronic Industries (MEI) in 1998 to become the MII, set up its own packet-data network

Table 2 China's Internet networks

Network	Established	Operator and/or ministerial interest	International bandwidth (Mbps), December 2002
CHINANET	1993 as CHINAPAC renamed 1995	Initially MPT then MII through China Telecom	6,032
CNCNET	1999	MR, SARFT, CAS, Shanghai Municipality through China Netcom	465
UNINET	1999/2000	MEI then MII through China Unicom	418
CERNET	1994	SEC	257.5
CMNET	1999/2000	MII through China Mobile	200
CHINAGBN	1996	MEI then MII through Jitong Communications	168
CSTNET	1987 (CANET and IHEP Network) 1990 (CRNET) combined in 1996 as CSTNET	CAS	55
CIETNET	1999/2000	MOFTEC	2

Source: CNNIC 2002.

initially called CHINAPAC but which later become the dominant network CHINANET run by China Telecom.

At about the same time the MEI set up its own company called China Jitong Communications which was involved in various telecoms and Internet infrastructure projects including the Golden Bridge Network (CHINAGBN) which was set up in 1996. CHINAGBN was initially intended to serve financial institutions and enhance flow of information for them across the country, but it soon also provided Internet connectivity to other users also. The MEI had other Internet interests through its other subsidiary telecoms provider China Unicom which set up China UNINET.

The establishment of the MII, however, did not end inter-ministerial rivalry as MOFTEC launched its CIETNET in 2000, the same year that China Netcom was set up by a conglomerate of interests including the Ministry of Railways (MR) and the **State Administration for Radio, Film and Television** (SARFT). By the end of 2001, these combined networks gave China an international bandwidth (a measure of network capacity) of

7,597.5 Megabits per second (Mbps) distributed among the various networks as in Table 2.

Internet service providers (ISPs), offering Internet access to businesses and the general public first emerged in 1995. Initially ISPs, running under licence from the network operators, were predominantly owned and run by regional branches of China Telecom in the major cities and more advanced provinces such as Beijing, Shanghai, Guangdong and Zhejiang although there were also a small number of independent operators.

The dominance of the local telecoms administrators among ISPs was only enhanced, however, by the high set-up costs, low revenues and high line rental fees. In 1999 as much as 80 per cent of ISP expenditure went on line leasing from China Telecom (Harwit and Clark 2001: 390). Although user numbers were starting to grow steadily and sharply, their still relatively small numbers could not offset such high running costs and only ISPs with deep-pocketed backers, such as the local telecoms operators, survived.

By contrast Internet content provision has flourished in the private sector although following the so-called global 'dotcom downturn' of 2000–1, many content providers have struggled to survive on advertising revenues alone and branched out into other areas.

See also: Internet (content); Internet shopping; Internet portals

Further reading

CNNIC (2002). *Statistical Report of the Development of the Internet in China (2002/1)*. Beijing: China Internet Network Information Centre (CNNIC).

Harwit, E. and Clark, D. (2001). 'Shaping the Internet in China: Evolution of Political Control over Network Infrastructure and Content'. *Asian Survey* 41.3: 377–408.

Hughes, Christopher and Wacker, Gudrun (eds) (2003). *China and the Internet: Politics of the Digital Leap Forward*. London: Curzon.

Liu, Kang (2004). 'The Internet in China: Emergent Cultural Formations and Contradictions'. In *idem, Globalization and Cultural Trends in China*. Honolulu: University of Hawai'i Press, 127–61.

KEVIN LATHAM

Internet portals

Official Internet user surveys have consistently shown that the primary use of the Internet in China is to search for information. Chinese Internet portals therefore have a central position in Chinese Internet use. Chinese portals, rather than foreign ones (including Chinese language versions of foreign portals), are the most popular offering email, chatrooms, mobile phone short messaging services, newsgroups, notice boards and **Internet shopping** in addition to the standard news, information and search engine facilities.

The most well-known national portals are Nasdaq-listed Sina.com, Sohu.com and Netease (163.net). Although there are government owned news portals such as Xinhuanet.com, and People. com.cn (the site of the **People's Daily** newspaper), many portals such as Sina.com and Sohu.com are private or cooperative companies. However, there are also hundreds of other private and

government-backed smaller portals and portal-style news websites, many aiming at local or regionally specific audiences.

Many news organizations such as newspapers, radio and television stations, which initially launched their own websites in the late 1990s, found them a significant drain on resources. As a result, many joined together to run combined portal-style news websites, such as Beijing's Dragon News Network run jointly by six Beijing newspapers as well as radio and television stations in the capital.

Initially, Chinese portals existed in certain regulatory grey areas, as private companies have been traditionally banned from news provision and for a short while portals supplied their own news and even provided links to foreign news websites. However, in November 2000 the government required portals to source their news only from officially authorized sources such as the **Xinhua News Agency**.

Portals have relied heavily on advertising revenue for their income but following a sharp downturn in the early 2000s, portals have sought alternative forms of funding, such as Internet shopping, commercial e-business solutions and pay email services.

KEVIN LATHAM

Internet shopping

Internet shopping has offered new opportunities for Chinese businesses and consumers but the full development of electronic commerce in China is hampered by a number of key structural obstacles. Although the Internet was launched in China in 1987 and saw large-scale user growth from the mid-1990s onwards (see **Internet (history and structure)**), substantive online shopping was not feasible until the end of the decade and into the 2000s. Chinese Internet users saw great shopping potential in the new technology early on. However, by the end of 2001, they had become more experienced and more realistic, with less than a third claiming to have made a purchase online in the year (CNNIC 2002).

Internet shopping has great potential in China considering the size of the country and the size of the market. Yet up to 2002, few e-commerce businesses had actually made a profit. Indeed, many online start-up companies went out of business between 2000 and 2002 as Internet fever cooled. Internet shopping has been helped by a steady growth in the use of debit and credit cards in China (around 385 million in early 2002). However, credit limits remain low, Chinese surfers have real concerns about online security and are wary of being sold substandard or damaged goods. The most popular form of payment remains cash on delivery. The post office in China is gradually adapting to the delivery needs of e-commerce but long delivery times and damage to goods remained problems in 2002. Consequently, the most vibrant growth in online shopping has been in the areas of books, music and video – items that are relatively cheap, easy to deliver and indestructible. They also cater to the interests of Chinese Internet users who are predominantly young, low-income earners or students.

Further reading

CNNIC (2002). *Statistical Report of the Development of the Internet in China (2002/1)*. Beijing: China Internet Network Information Centre (CNNIC).

KEVIN LATHAM

iron rice bowl

Political concept

During the heyday of China's socialist system, jobs in state-owned enterprises (SOEs) were highly secure and so were the goods and services that came with them. While wages were low, employment in SOEs was for life and the work unit (*danwei*) provided housing, medical care, education and certain foods to workers and their families essentially for free. The term 'iron rice bowl' (*tiefanwan*) is a shorthand reference to the indestructible nature of those jobs and, more generally, to socialism's promise to look after the livelihood of its workers. During the Communist period public sector workers came to view the 'iron rice bowl' as an entitlement.

The system of lifetime employment in SOEs continues today but there is no longer a consensus within the government that it is sustainable. Because most SOEs do not turn a profit but instead cost the Chinese government money, in 1997 the Communist Party committed itself to the elimination of all but the most indispensable of these enterprises. This task has become more urgent since China's accession to the World Trade Organization in December 2001, which is certain to open up the country to the unforgiving forces of global capitalism. Massive lay-offs from SOEs have been occurring for several years and have led workers to accuse the government of 'smashing the iron rice bowl': that is, of reneging on its socialist contract with the people. In the eyes of many unemployed workers, then, the destruction of the 'iron rice bowl' has robbed the government of its legitimacy.

Further reading

Hughes, Neil (2002). *China's Economic Challenge: Smashing the Iron Rice Bowl*. New York: M. E. Sharpe.

TIMOTHY WESTON

Islam and women

The active historical contribution of women to Chinese Islam has developed differently in various regions. As early as the seventeenth century, *nüxue* (women's religious schools) were created by Muslims in central China; the southwest province of Yunnan followed suit in the eighteenth century. Male Islamic scholars constituted the earliest teachers, replaced in the eighteenth century by suitably trained women. By the end of the eighteenth century, women's religious schools in central China (Henan province) became *nüsi* (women's mosques), with resident women *ahong* (religious leaders) taking charge of all religious affairs.

In the Republican Period (1911–49), Muslim scholars began to link progress in women's status and education with the significance of women's mosques. Mosques and schools for women developed quickly. Some modern women's schools in

Beijing and elsewhere catered both for Muslim women's secular and religious education, with a few girls' primary schools set up in the northwest region of Qinghai, Gansu and Ningxia. The number of women's mosques continuously increased until 1958. All women's mosques were closed in 1966, but even during the **Cultural Revolution** (1966–76) a few women *ahong* still performed their religious duties.

Since the 1980s, Hui Muslim women have come to occupy a prominent role in the reconstruction and organization of religious life, whether in relation to administration, political representation, education, training or mosque restoration. Although most women's mosques and schools are still linked to (men's) mosques, their administrative committees consist predominantly of women. Women *ahong* fulfil multiple functions, responsible for teaching, ritual and prayer guidance, for sermons, counselling, and also for political representation. Female administrators manage mainly the daily affairs of women's mosques but can also be found on committees managing affairs of men's mosques. Independent women's mosques, a growing trend in central China since the 1990s, are legally registered sites of religious activity, enjoying thus equal social position with (men's) mosques. Outstanding women *ahong* and female administrators may become elected members of local branches of the Islamic association as well as of the People's Congress. Women determine independently all activities and affairs of women's mosques, including training of young *ahong* and provision of adult education. Traditional mosque-based Persian language education (*jingtang jiaoyu*) and modern Arabic-centred Islamic education coexist in many Muslim communities, as is the case in southwest China. Elsewhere, as in northwest China, girls' Arabic language schools are the preferred educational model since the 1980s.

In daily life, the dress of Hui Muslim women in central China is largely indistinguishable from that of other Chinese women. Wherever Muslims live widely dispersed, observation of religious dress is mostly confined to older women, or is worn during worship in the women's mosque. However, due to greater contact with international Islam through pilgrimages and visits, due to **Islamic Brotherhood (Yihewani)** reform of religious education and fundamentalist teaching, religious dress, as in other countries, is becoming for some women a visible symbol of distinctive Islamic identity. In the close-knit northwest (Ningxia, Qinghai and Gansu) Muslim communities, women of Hui, Salar, Dongxiang and Baoan nationalities wear a headdress (*gaitou*) or a scarf, the colour varying with age.

Where there is no history of women's own religious organization and leadership, as in the western province of Xinjiang, Uyghur, Kazakh, Tajik and women from other Muslim minorities adhere to a more prescriptive Islamic praxis of hijab and domestic confinement, in stark contrast to their Chinese-speaking Muslim sisters in the rest of China.

See also: Islam in China

Further reading

Jaschok, Maria and Shui, Jingjun (2000). *The History of Women's Mosques in Chinese Islam*. Richmond: Curzon.

MARIA JASCHOK AND SHUI JINGJUN

Islam in China

Islam, which entered China in the seventh century, is one of five religions recognized by the People's Republic of China. It has a membership of between 18 and 25 million adherents.

After more than a thousand years of dissemination and development, Islam mixed with Chinese traditional and indigenous cultures to become a Chinese Islamic religion which is tightly bound to ethnicity. Nearly all Muslims are members of the ten designated ethnic minority groups: Hui, Uyghur, Kazakh, Tartar, Khalkhas, Tajik, Uzbek, Dongxiang, Salar and Baoan. A few Muslims are members of Zangzu (Tibetan) or Han nationality.

Although present throughout China, most Muslims live in compact communities in the autonomous regions of Xinjiang and Ningxia; in the provinces of Gansu, Qinghai, Henan, Hebei, Shangdong, Shaanxi, Shanxi, Anhui, Yunnan, Liaoning; and in the cities of Beijing and Tianjin.

As with other sanctioned religions, Islam is subject to the comprehensive **religious policies of the state**. Historically, mosques and full-time Islamic professionals increased in number between 1949 and 1957, and religious activities were vigorous; between 1958 and 1965, mosque-building was curtailed and activities came to a standstill. All mosques in China were closed in 1966 as the **Cultural Revolution** began, and religious life closed down or went underground. However, some female *ahong* (religious leaders) held prayer services and kept collective faith alive. Since the 1980s, Islamic organizations but also Islamic scholarship and education have entered a new, active era. During the 1990s, many Muslim communities have given special attention to Islamic education, and modern **Islamic schools** have been founded. At the same time, more liberal policy and greater affluence have seen restoration and enlargement of mosques; also, more new mosques are being built. Construction funds for mosques come in the main from individual donations. Only a few ancient mosques (such as the Beijing Ox Street Mosque), classified as cultural relics, receive subsidies from the Heritage Department or the Religious Affairs Bureau.

In 1979, serious scholarly study of Islamic religion in China was conducted by senior research scholars from the Chinese Academy of Social Science and from provincial academies, from universities as well as from the China Islamic Association and provincial Islamic associations. Studies focus on the history of Chinese Islam and on the diversity of Muslim ethnic cultures. Numerous academic conferences, scholarly research papers and books, authored by both Chinese and foreign scholars, testify to a reinvigorated academic culture. Moreover, religious professionals, such as *ahong*, and ordinary Muslims are contributing to satisfy popular interest in Islamic culture and Islamic study. This grassroots movement, commenced in the 1990s, accounts for the creation of Muslim magazines, of compiled and printed booklets carrying Islamic news, and of new translations from Arabic to Chinese. Many of these initiatives are carried by local communities and individual Muslims, and are a force not to be ignored in the re-awakening of Islam.

The China Islamic Association, created in 1953, carries out government religious policy, oversees publication of religious literature, collects and collates historical Islamic documents, salvages cultural relics and conducts research into Islamic history and belief. The Association also organizes annual pilgrimages to Mecca. In 1955, the Association set up a national Islamic College in Beijing for the training of religious professionals and founded a bi-monthly magazine for Muslims in China in 1957. With the beginning of the Cultural Revolution in 1966, these activities ceased and were reactivated only in 1979. Provinces, cities, autonomous regional prefectures and counties with large Muslim populations set up local Islamic associations in the course of the 1980s, as did Taiwanese and Hong Kong Muslims.

See also: Islam and women; Islamic orders; Islamic mosques; Islamic worship

Further reading

Allés, É. (2000). *Musulmans de Chine: Une anthropologie des Hui du Henan*. Paris: Éditions de L'École Pratique des Hautes Études en Sciences Sociales.

Dillon, M. (1996). *China's Muslim*. Oxford: Oxford University Press.

Gladney, D. (1991). *Muslim Chinese: Ethnic Nationalism in the People's Republic*. Cambridge: Harvard University Press.

—— (2003). *Dislocating China: Muslims, Minorities, and Other Subaltern Subjects*. Chicago: University of Chicago Press.

—— (2003). 'Islam in China: Accommodation or Separatism?' In Daniel Overmyer (ed.), *Religion in China Today*. Cambridge: Cambridge University Press, 145–61.

Jaschok, M. and Shui, J. J. (2000). *The History of Women's Mosques in Chinese Islam*. Richmond: Curzon.

Li, X. H., Feng, J. Y., Qing, H. B. and Sha, Q. Z. (1998). *Zhongguo Yisilanjiaoshi*. Beijing: Zhongguo shehuikexue chubanshe.

Lipman, J. (1997). *Familiar Strangers: A History of Muslims in Northwest China*. Seattle: University of Washington Press.

Mi, S. J. and You, G. (eds) (2000). *Zhongguo Yisilanjiao jianshi*. Beijing: Zongjiao wenhua chubanshe.

SHUI JINGJUN AND MARIA JASCHOK

Islamic art (Arabic–Chinese hybrid designs)

Chinese Islamic art incorporates Arabic calligraphy, architecture and Islamic music, each expressive of Muslim religious life. Hybrid Arabic–Chinese calligraphy is referred to as 'Arabic- character painting' (*jingzihua*), and by non-Han Muslims in Xinjiang as 'Chinese style' (*zhongguoti*). Borrowing from Arabic writing and blended perfectly with the techniques of Chinese calligraphy and aesthetics, a distinctive artistic genre of *jingzihua* calligraphy and painting has been created. The unique art works of Arabic-character painting carry poetic names, such as 'seawater welcomes the sun' (*haishui chaoyang*), and 'golden dragon climbs the jade pillar' (*jinlongpanyuzhu*).

Diversity of design results from the use of different art media and techniques employing fine brushwork, freehand brushwork, seal character brushwork, and from application of regular and cursive script, resulting in vertical scrolls, horizontal hanging scrolls, couplet scrolls, fan-shaped screens or paintings. The content of 'Arabic-character painting' is inspired by the Koran, hadiths and other religious texts. Calligraphy tools are usually made by the calligrapher: this can be a hard brush made from plant stems and tree roots, or a soft brush made from cloth, yarn or flax.

Islamic music comprises ritual eulogies praying to Allah and praising the Prophet Muhammad, chants for reciting the Koran, and other poems or songs which express belief and religious devoutness in prayers, rituals and religious festivals. These chants tend to have no instrumental accompaniment; cadence and modulation induce a worshipful and stirring mood. In women's mosques, the tradition of 'religious songs' (*jingge*) is being revived, their tunes closely related to popular local Han folksongs.

See also: Islamic mosques; Islam and women

Further reading

Dillon, M. (1996). *China's Muslims*. Oxford: Oxford University Press.

SHUI JINGJUN AND MARIA JASCHOK

Islamic Brotherhood (Yihewani)

Yihewani (*al-Ikhwan*, Muslim Brotherhood), an Islamic order founded in China at the end of the nineteenth century, is also known as Xinxingpai or Xinpai. Haji (pilgrim) Ma Wanfu, founder of this new school, was influenced by the fundamentalist Wahhabi movement, which called for the return to 'the ancients' and emerged as a force during the mid eighteenth century. Basic principles held by Yihewani are: strict adherence to the Koran and Hadiths; unswerving implementation of the five basic Muslim duties ('Pillars of Faith'); reform of those rites which violate Islamic principles; expulsion of Han Chinese cultural accretions (such as wearing Chinese mourning apparel); rejection of heresy; rejection of Sufi mysticism and Sufi claims to spiritual authority; strict enforcement of a religious dress code for Muslim women with its insistence on *gaitou* (Islamic head-dress which covers hair and neck).

As a modernizer, Haji Ma Wanfu found it difficult initially to attract a following in a conservative culture. It was only during the 1940s, and with local warlord support, that the Yihewani expanded its influence into the provinces of Qinghai, Ningxia and Gansu. Although some followers separated after the 1930s from Yihewani core beliefs and became known as Sailaifiye (*al-Sailaifiye*) Muslims, Yihewani membership has continued to increase. The shift of loyalty from the Gedimu order to Yihewani took place on the whole without creating divisive tensions in the Muslim communities (see **Islamic orders**). Because the Yihewani order encourages modern Islamic education and has developed new curricula, reforming religious rites easily comprehensible to followers, many Muslims have recognized a basic affinity with Yihewani, and continue to identify themselves with its doctrines and rites.

See also: Islamic menhuan; Islamic mosques

Further reading

Dillon, M. (1996). *China's Muslims*. Oxford: Oxford University Press.

Gladney, D. (1991). *Muslim Chinese: Ethnic Nationalism in the People's Republic.* Cambridge, MA: Harvard University Press.

SHUI JINGJUN AND MARIA JASCHOK

Islamic menhuan

(Sufi groups)

The Sufi descent groups, of which adherents can be found among Hui, Dongxiang, Salar and Baoan ethnic minorities in northwest, northeast and southwest China, are called *menhuan* (*al-Tariqah*). The provinces of Hebei and Henan have only a small Sufi following. The *menhuan* is a socio-religious institution based upon the family of the saint – the first *jiaozhu* ('master of the teaching', i.e. founder) and his successors and followers. The order has over thirty *menhuan* schools and branches in China. As in other Islamic schools, *menhuan* worshippers follow the Koran and Hadith (oral sayings), and practise the five basic religious rites (Pillars).

Special duties of all *menhuan* believers are: to revere the founder of their *menhuan*; to believe that their revered *jiaozhu* will lead his followers to heaven; to obey the *jiaozhu*'s *kouhuan* (words of authoritative import) and instructions absolutely; to build *gongbei* – the *jiaozhu*'s tomb which forms the centre of a site designed for worship and congregation. Members bestow homage and perform special rites, such as reciting the Koran, chanting *dhikr* (whereby the believer calls to Allah, affirms core precepts of faith, and praises Allah and His prophet) and meditating on the mysteries of God.

For most *menhuan* orders, only a descendant of *jiaozhu* can succeed to a leadership position. The absolute authority and comprehensive privileges of a *jiaozhu*, including of property and appointments, were abolished only in the religious reform movement of 1958. Like other Islamic orders, since the 1980s, affairs of mosques have been directed by elected democratic administrative committees.

See also: Islamic orders; Islamic tombs; Islamic Brotherhood (Yihewani)

Further reading

Dillon, M. (1999). *China's Muslim Hui Community.* Richmond: Curzon.
Murata, S. (2000). *Chinese Gleams of Sufi Light.* Albany, NY: State University of New York Press.

SHUI JINGJUN

Islamic mosques

Since the Yuan dynasty (1276–1368), Chinese Muslims have referred to mosques as *qingzhensi* (temple of purity and truth) – centres for worship, education and varied religious activities. In central China, varying degrees of Chinese and Arabic influence on the exterior and interior of mosques have their origin in history and in Muslim cultural diversity. However, common to most Chinese mosques is the *siheyuan* structure, a compound with buildings framing a courtyard. Main features include main gate, prayer hall, minaret, classrooms (*jiangtang*) and ablution facilities. Courtyards are beautified with flowers and trees, and steles tell of mosque history.

Some mosques are palatial in size, boasting pavilions, steles, stone carvings, gardens and even ponds with Chinese-style bridges. Prayer halls in the more affluent mosques impress with painted pillars, carved beams and decorative patterns, often playing on both indigenous and Arabic cultural motifs. Their influence can be seen in decorations on the *yaotian* (arch inside the prayer hall, in the direction of Mecca), on eaves and ceilings, or on the *xuanyutai* (platform for sermons in the corner of the prayer hall). Stone tablets carry Chinese, Arabic and Persian writing; and scrolls featuring couplets hang from pillars supporting spacious halls. Where the local congregation is poor and donations minimal, mosques are in contrast simple and crude, little better than a common family house. Whereas the interior of mosques in its Arabic style reflects Islamic cultural origins, most mosque exteriors, built during the Qing dynasty (1644–1911) or earlier, share in the predominant stylistic idiom of their locale. Since the 1980s, mosques rebuilt or built anew in both Gedimu and Yihewani traditions show up predominantly Arabic architecture and Islamic aesthetic, and thus illustrate a radical departure from previous concessions to Chinese host culture.

The structure of women's mosques is similar to (men's) mosques, although comparatively smaller as of more limited socio-religious function. Certain differences need noting: women's mosques have no minaret, no *yaodian* and *xuanyutai* in the prayer hall and most women's mosques are built in Chinese-style architecture. Only after the 1980s have some new or rebuilt women's mosques adapted to Arabic conventions.

The mosque and its congregation constitutes an independent *jiaofang* (parish; also called *fang*). An *ahong* (religious leader), invited to the position by the mosque administrative committee, is responsible for leading prayer, training *hailifan* (Islamic students), giving religious lectures, holding weddings and funerals. Women *ahong* are not permitted to perform wedding and funeral rites; some female *ahong* wash the female corpse before burial.

Mosque affairs, such as appointing an *ahong*, ensuring religious education, managing welfare and finances, are overseen in men's and women's mosques by several elected, Muslim dignitaries. Called *shetou*, *xuedong* or *xianglao*, after 1958 these elders were organized into a mosque administrative committee. Similarly, whereas before 1958 the mosques of **Islamic menhuan** (Sufi groups) were controlled by *jiaozhu* (succession by inheritance), and in many traditions strict hierarchy subordinated smaller to larger mosques, after the movement for religious reform mosques were placed on an equal and independent footing – religiously, socially or politically. Most women's mosques, however, continued to be subordinate to (men's) mosques in economic and financial affairs. However, since 1993, when mandatory registration allowed registered women's mosques independent status, the trend for autonomy among women's mosques has been on the rise.

See also: Islam and women; Islamic art (Arabic–Chinese hybrid designs)

Further reading

Dillon, M. (1996). *China's Muslim*. Oxford: Oxford University Press.

Ma, Q. C. and Ding, H. (1998). *Zhongguo Yisilan wenhuade leixing yü minzu tese*. Beijing: Zhongyan minzu daxue chubanshe.

Qiu, Y. L. and Yu, Z. S. (1992). *Zhongguo Yisilanjiao jianzhu*. Beijing: Zhongguo jianzhu gongye chubanshe.

SHUI JINGJUN AND MARIA JASCHOK

Islamic orders

The structure of Islamic orders in the PRC has remained congruent with that of the Republican period (1911–49). The majority of Chinese Muslims belong to the Sunni schools, which include followers of Gedimu, Yihewani, Islamic *menhuan*, Xidaotang, Salafiyyah and Yichan (Ishan) orders.

Gedimu, the oldest and largest school of the Sunnis, is also called Laojiao (Laopai) and has adherents throughout China. Gedimu places emphasis on basic beliefs and the five primary duties (Pillars) of all Muslims, respects Islamic orthodoxy and traditions, and strictly observes religious rites and tradition. The strong Confucian accretions have been modified since the 1990s, moving this tradition closer to other Islamic orders.

Xidaotang, also known as Hanxuepai (Chinese Islamic School), was founded in the early twentieth century, and most of its following is concentrated in Lintan county, Gansu province. Basic beliefs and practices of this school are similar to others, but it is more deeply permeated by the writings of Chinese Islamic scholars of the Ming and Qing periods. Xidaotang religious rites resemble the Gedimu school, but the organizational system is more akin to a Sufi *menhuan*. Before the early 1950s, Xidaotang functioned as both an Islamic school and an economic entity, but in the PRC it has only a religious function.

Salafiyyah, also called Santaipai because worshippers raise their hands three times in prayers, was founded in 1930s but developed only in the 1950s. This school, similar to the Islamic Brotherhood, is influenced by Wahhabi fundamentalism and follows the 'ancient way' in a strict interpretation of the Koran and Hadith (oral teachings). The growing number of adherents, a development particularly notable since the 1990s, are located in

Qinghai province – in Linxia, Lanzhou, Tianshui, Xian, Zhangjiachuan and other cities.

Yichan (Ishan), practised among Xinjiang minorities, shares similarities with Sufi *menhuan*. But their religious practices and rites have come to intermingle more closely with other local religious traditions.

Further reading

Dillon, M. (1996). *China's Muslims*. Oxford: Oxford University Press.

Gladney, D. (1991) *Muslim Chinese: Ethnic Nationalism in the People's Republic*. Cambridge, MA: Harvard University Press.

Wang, J. P. (1996). *Concord and Conflict*. Stockholm: Lund Studies in African and Asian Religions.

SHUI JINGJUN

Islamic schools

(Madrasa)

Islamic college education (*Jingxueyuan*, madrasa) in China is sponsored by both private Islamic sources and government funding. Organized by the China Islamic Association and provincial branches of Islamic Associations, the altogether nine *Jingxueyuan* receive operating funds from the Chinese government, supplemented by grants from mosques and/or individuals. The central *Jingxueyuan* in Beijing was established by the China Islamic Association in 1955, closed in 1966 and reopened in 1982 – to male students only. Its objective is to train patriotic religious professionals who will occupy authoritative positions after graduation. In the course of the 1980s, several regional Islamic colleges were set up in Urumqi, Yinchuan, Lanzhou, Zhengzhou, Xining, Kunming, Shenyang, and a second *Jingxueyuan* in Beijing. College curricula, apart from teaching the scriptures and the history of Islam, also contain Arabic language, Chinese language as well as politics, Chinese history and world history.

Islamic education, sponsored by mosques or by individuals, can be divided into three categories. Traditional Islamic education (*jingtang jiaoyu*) was started in the sixteenth century for training male

and female *ahong* (religious leaders) and continues into the present. Since the 1980s, educational reform has led to an 'Arabic-based curriculum' (*ayuxuexiao*) or a 'mixed Chinese–Arabic curriculum' (*zhongaxuexiao*), registered with government education departments. The content of study is closely modelled on that of Islamic colleges. Such schools are located within mosques or adjacent sites, less commonly in privately built schools. Part-time religious education is thought most suitable to address the needs of women, children and the elderly.

See also: Islam and women

Further reading

Wang, J. P. (1996). *Concord and Conflict*. Stockholm: Lund Studies in Africa and Asian Religions.

Jaschok, M. and Shui, J. J. (2000). *The History of Women's Mosques in Chinese Islam*. Richmond: Curzon.

SHUI JINGJUN AND MARIA JASCHOK

Islamic tombs

Muslims distinguish five types of burial sites: *Gumu*, tombs of ancient Islamic scholars and historic figures; *Gongbei* (*qubba* in Arabic), the burial chamber of the *jiaozhu* (founder/leader) of an Islamic *menhuan* (Sufi order); *Mazha*, Sufi tombs in Xinjiang; *Huimingongmu* or Muslim graveyards; and family graveyards. Muslims are buried with the head of the deceased oriented to the north, with the face turned to the right in the direction of Mecca.

Most *gumu* – also known locally as *Huihuifen* (Muslim tombs), *Babamu* and *Shaihaifen* (tombs of prestigious elders, scholars, teachers) – commemorate famous Islamic scholars and Muslim historical figures since the Tang dynasty. The ancient tombs built (or rebuilt) by Muslims in inland China are on the whole plain and without ornamentation. They also lack large plots of land, a feature of more modern times. Ordinary Muslim burial places are even simpler, with only a common gravestone to mark the grave. Nearly all inscriptions on tombstones are in Arabic or

Persian. Only a few well-known tombs, usually built on the order of Chinese emperors, are situated in parks, like Chinese mausoleums, with an adjacent hall for prayer, a mosque, pavilions and stone carvings. Many of these famous tombs and graveyards are located in Guangzhou, Quanzhou, Fuzhou, Hangzhou, Yangzhou, Nanjing, Kunming and Hainan Island.

The tomb forms the centre of the *Gongbei*, the burial sites of *menhuan* founders and famous Sufi scholars, and most tombs feature a dome in the Arabic style. An attached building is in Chinese style, and includes a prayer chamber, meditation room, living room, bedrooms and a tower. A *Gongbei* is not only a place of memorial, but also an important centre of religious activity.

In Xinjiang, the tombs of famous Islamic scholars, persons of renown and members of the elite are called *Mazah*. The architecture is palatial and, as with *Gongbei*, an array of buildings provide a communal site to congregate, study and worship.

Muslim graveyards in the PRC are called *Hui-mingongmu* or, colloquially, *Yidi*. Most are located in the vicinity of Muslim communities in the cities or towns. Family graveyards, by contrast, are located in the countryside. In either case, only followers of Islam are given the right in the PRC to maintain their own burial sites.

See also: Islamic orders

Further reading

Dillon, M. (1999). *China's Muslim Hui Community: Migration, Settlement and Sects*. Richmond: Curzon.

SHUI JINGJUN

Islamic worship

Lived Muslim praxis emphasizes halal food, daily prayer and ritual highlights, such as saints' days, naming rites, wedding ceremonies and funeral rites. Festivals common to all Chinese Muslims are Kaizhaijie (Id al-Fitr), the Festival of Fast-Breaking, and Zaishengjie (Id al-Adha). All Muslim communities hold grand ceremonies on Kaizhaijie, also known as Da'erde ('most important festival').

Muslim men worship in mosques, and women wherever they are permitted. In areas where women's mosques exist, they are as crowded as the men's. Before prayer, Muslims give alms (Sadaqah al-Fitr, also known as *maiziqian*) in support of the poor. After prayer, worshippers exchange *seliamu* (blessings) and families partake in *youxing* (Islamic food). Some believers go to the ancestral grave, chanting the Koran and mourning the dead. Muslim minorities in Xinjiang give special attention to Zaishengjie.

Shengji is a feast-day observing the Prophet's birthday and day of death. All Chinese Muslims honour the occasion except for **Islamic Brotherhood (Yihewani)** and Sailaifiye Muslims. Muslim women observe Nüshengji (*Fatima taitaijie*), with prayer at their mosque to commemorate Fatima, the Prophet's daughter (see **Islam and women**).

Three important religious rites are observed in the life of every Chinese Muslim: baby naming, weddings and funeral rites. The ritual of naming a new-born is known as *Qijingming*, presided over by an *ahong* (religious leader). Boys are given names of great Islamic prophets, while the names of girls are commonly derived from female members of the Prophet Muhammed's family.

The wedding ceremony is also performed by an *ahong*, chanting the Koran and pronouncing in both Arabic and Chinese on the legitimacy of the wedding. While the ritual is unvaried, bridal dress, banquet and ornamentation reflect changing times and regional tastes. Similarly, funeral rites, known as *Zhenazi* (*Janazah*), are similar in the various **Islamic orders**, but mourning, filial dress and prescribed mourning periods reveal diversity. Like Han Chinese, Gedimu Muslims cover their head, waist and shoes with white cotton cloth, crying loudly and chanting the Koran to mourn the deceased (after seven days, forty days, one hundred days and one year). Islamic Brotherhood and Sailaifiye Muslims only wear white prayer caps at the funeral and do not observe the mourning period. Since the 1990s, some Gedimu Muslims have chosen to mourn in a manner more akin to the Islamic Brotherhood.

Special *qingzhen* (Islamic) plates marked in Arabic and carrying pictures of a traditional ablution kettle (*tangping*) are seen on windows or above the gate of Halal restaurants and food stalls offering

Islamic goods (*qingzhenshipin*). Deep-fried dough cake (*youxiang*) is a common religious food made and eaten during Islamic banquets (*jingtangxi*), religious festivals, weddings and funerals. But Muslims in different regions have their own distinctive foods, such as *zhuafan* (made of mutton, carrots and rice) popular in Xinjiang.

See also: Islam in China

Further reading

Dillon, M. (1999). *China's Muslim Hui Community: Migration, Settlement and Sects*. Richmond: Curzon.

Ma, Q. C. and Ding, H. (1998). *Zhongguo Yisilan wenhuade leixing yü minzu tese*. Beijing: Zhongyan minzu daxue chubanshe.

SHUI JINGJUN

itinerant evangelists (Protestant)

Itinerant evangelists have been the primary agency by which **Christianity (Protestantism)** has spread since about 1980. Travelling evangelists, who bring the gospel to a community and stay a few days or weeks before moving on, represent both the **Three-Self Patriotic Movement (TSPM)** and house church sectors of Protestantism (see **house churches**), although much more the latter, because the former operates under restrictions limiting the range of travel of local TSPM evangelists. House church and quasi-Christian sectarian evangelists observe no such limitations and, while vulnerable to harassment or arrest, are also quite effective.

Itinerant evangelism dates back to the earliest missionaries of the nineteenth century. In the first few decades of the twentieth century, Chinese evangelists such as Dora Yu (Yu Cidu, 1873–1931), Ding Limei (1871–1936), **Wang Mingdao** (1900–91), John Sung (Song Shangjie, 1901–44) were important figures on the Christian scene, travelling to cities and towns more than the countryside. Today's evangelists draw somewhat on this tradition, but are also different in several aspects. They work more often in the countryside and villages, where control is more lax than in cities. Young people, especially young women, often in their mid-teens, are common among their ranks. They often have only minimal formal education. Typically the message they present is Pentecostal, with faith healing (see **faith healing (Christian)**) prominent, and some preach a distorted – in the opinion of some orthodox believers, heretical – message. Some evangelists represent well-organized house church groups, while others are entrepreneurial and operate individualistically. Itinerant evangelism is one of the most important and interesting features of the Protestant movement today.

DANIEL BAYS

J

jazz

Although jazz has been slow to take root in China, by the late 1990s a significant number of Chinese musicians had adopted the genre, an international jazz festival had been established in Beijing, and numerous jazz clubs were thriving in China, Taiwan and Hong Kong.

Appropriately, China's first encounter with jazz came during Shanghai's 'Jazz Age' of the 1920s and 1930s, when visiting jazz stars such as trumpeter Buck Clayton performed for largely expatriate audiences in the city's foreign concessions. Local musicians soon embraced the imported genre, most famously the Peace Hotel Jazz Band that played in the hotel's opulent ballroom. Filtered through jazz-influenced musicians such as Jin Huaizu (a.k.a. Jimmy King) and the prolific composer Li Jinhui, echoes of jazz were audible in much of the popular and film music of the day. After the 1949 revolution, Shanghai's jazz musicians were stigmatized as purveyors of a decadent foreign art form and silenced by an insular Communist regime. Jazz remained virtually non-existent in China until its revival during the cultural thaw of the post-Mao era, when the now elderly Peace Hotel Jazz Band resumed playing to packed houses in the expensively refurbished hotel ballroom.

Jazz gained a small but enthusiastic following in the 1980s and 1990s, fuelled by the increasing availability of jazz recordings from abroad and public exposure to expatriate and touring jazz musicians. Perhaps the first noteworthy jazz statement from a new generation of Chinese musicians was pianist Gao Ping's recording *Jazz in China* (1988); though only marginally 'jazz' by most standards, this early effort was nevertheless significant for its emphasis on improvisation. In 1993, German expatriate Udo Hoffmann staged the inaugural Beijing International Jazz Festival. Though not the first event of its kind in the Chinese cultural area – a distinction held by the Macau Jazz Festival, now more than twenty years old – the Beijing International Jazz Festival has grown into a major annual event featuring leading international performers. The festival has provided a showcase for Chinese jazz musicians, as well as opportunities to study and play informally with visiting artists, and has inspired similar events in other Chinese cities. Concurrently, jazz clubs have opened in Chinese cities from Beijing to Chengdu.

The most influential modern Chinese jazz musician is Liu Yuan, a virtuoso saxophonist who first came to prominence as a member of the band of Chinese rock icon **Cui Jian**. A vigorous and assured improviser in a conservative bebop vein, Liu Yuan appears regularly at festivals and smaller venues and has performed alongside such visiting jazz luminaries as Wynton Marsalis. Other notable Chinese jazz musicians at the turn of the millennium include pianist Liang Heping, saxophonist Jin Hao and Hong Kong-based guitarist Eugene Pao. Worldwide, Chinese musicians such as Wu Man, Min Xiao-fen, **Liu Suola** and **Wang Yong** are actively exploring cross-cultural improvised music. In the jazz motherland of the United States, critically acclaimed Chinese-American jazz musicians – including Fred Ho, Jason Hwang, Jon Jang and Francis Wong – are pioneering the integration of Chinese instruments and musical concepts into the open structures of jazz.

Further reading

http://www.dennisrea.com/chinatour.html

Rea, Dennis (1997). 'China Witnesses a Sudden Vogue for Jazz: The Land Tour and the Emergence of Jazz in China'. *Chime* 10/11 (Spring/Autumn): 129–38.

DENNIS REA

Jesus Family

Protestant sect

The Jesus Family (Yesu jiating) is a charismatic, communal indigenous Protestant sect that emerged during the Protestant revival of the early decades of the twentieth century, along with the **Little Flock** and the **True Jesus Church**. The Jesus Family (JF) was formally established in 1927 by Jing Dianying (1890–1953), who had been drawn to monastic Buddhism and a White Lotus sect before embracing a Pentecostal strain of Protestant Christianity. Jing was strongly influenced by the communal lifestyle of the early disciples described in the book of Acts, and moulded the Jesus Family on that model. The group practised charismatic Pentecostal rituals, emphasizing gifts of the Holy Spirit such as speaking in tongues and divine revelations in trance, and cohered around highly millenarian beliefs, upholding the imminent return of Christ. Attracting mostly poorly educated and socially marginalized converts, Jing formed members into small communities of up to a few hundred adherents. The groups practised a communal lifestyle, living and working together and holding property in common under the direction of a family 'head' (*jiazhang*). Communities also constructed rigid boundaries, requiring members to several relations with the families outside the group. By the late 1940s, the JF had formed more than a hundred 'families' with about 10,000 members.

After 1949, leaders of the **Three-Self Patriotic Movement (TSPM)** initially extolled the Jesus Family as a paradigm of Christian Communism. JF leaders were also early signators of the Christian Manifesto (see **patriotic covenants**). Nevertheless, the group came under attack in 1952. Jing Dianying was arrested, and TSPM

officials were dispatched to disband all JF communities. The JF has revived somewhat in the reform era, mostly in Shandong and Shaanxi provinces. The group remains formally banned, however, and is subject to government repression.

JASON KINDOPP

Ji Xianlin

b. 1911, Qingping, Shandong

Scholar, writer

Ji Xianlin began his career in the early 1930s with a series of studies of Western literature. After completing his education in Germany, Ji returned to China in 1946 to become head of the Department of Oriental Languages at **Peking University** and one of the leading experts in Indian studies. His autobiography, *Miscellaneous Memories of the Cowshed* (*Niupeng zayi*, 1988), deals with Ji's experiences during the **Cultural Revolution**. At Peking University, where the Cultural Revolution originated, the ideological struggle on the campus was extremely fierce, and as head of a department, Ji was taken to be a typical representative of the old ruling class. The most dramatic and shocking part in his memoir takes place between late 1967 and the spring of 1968 when, after a sudden change in the balance of power, Ji was beaten, put under house arrest and deprived of all rights.

THOMAS ZIMMER

Jia Pingwa

b. 1953, Shangzhou, Shaanxi

Writer

A writer of prose and poetry and editor of the literary magazine *Meiwen* [Belles Lettres], Jia Pingwa has published many short-story collections and three well-known novels: *Turbulence* (*Fucao*, 1988), *The Abandoned City* (*Feidu*, 1993) and *The Earthen Gate* (*Tumen*, 1996). His writings are set predominantly in the countryside, where Jia grew up, and express traditional beliefs and values, but also reflect the emergence of new ideas that disturb and put traditions in question. Some of his short stories exhibit ideals of generosity and bravery, while also portraying a complex reality where human beings live in tragic and conflicting situations despite their aspirations to harmony. *The Abandoned City* shifts the plot to the city (Jia lived for several years in Xi'an) and describes the decadent life and sexual obsession of an intellectual who confronts various forms of disillusionment and perversity. While officially banned, the novel remained available in small bookstores and was widely read and debated. *The Earthen Gate* provides a more subtle analysis of the effects of urbanization, and the invasion of opportunistic values associated with the city, on rural mentalities.

Further reading

Jia, Pingwa (1991). *Turbulence*. Trans. Howard Goldblatt. Baton Rouge: Louisiana State University Press.

—— (1997). *La Capitale déchue*. Trans. Geneviève Imbot-Bichet. Paris: Stock.

—— (2000). *Le Village englouti*. Trans. Geneviève Imbot-Bichet. Paris: Stock.

ANNIE CURIEN

Jia Youfu

b. 1942, Suning, Hebei

Traditional Chinese painter

Jia is famous for cloudy, atmospheric and monumental 'traditional landscape paintings' (*shanshui*). Born to a peasant family and growing up at a time generally hostile to traditional artistic practices, Jia studied with some of *Zhongguohua* (traditional Chinese painting)'s most important living exponents, beginning with Zhu Lian and Xue Yulu. Admitted to the **Central Academy of Fine Arts** in 1960, he was taught by Li Keran, Ye Qianyu, Li Kuchan and He Haixia. Graduating in 1965, Jia was assigned to teach at the Stage Design Department of the Central Academy of Drama. There he weathered the **Cultural Revolution**, painting in his spare time. Transferred to the Central Academy in 1977, he

subsequently became professor of traditional landscape painting.

Jia Youfu's oeuvre emerges from a combination of traditional ink-wash aesthetics and personal experience. *Mifu Paying Respects to a Rock* (*Mifu baishi*, 1991) is a typical poetic image in traditional style about the Song dynasty calligrapher. Jia, however, is best known for his monumental paintings of the Taihang mountains, a life-long destination. The fruit of this long relationship are paintings exploring the atmospheric moods of Taihang's majestic scenery in which the intense light and vast expanses of poured-ink clouds dwarf any human presence. In *Taihang Mountains: The Great Monument* (*Taihang fengbei*, 1984) the mountains are transmuted into large, coarse and forbidding textured strokes where the sheer faces of the rock are made to symbolize its inhabitants' rugged spirit of resistance. In other paintings the mountains are textured with finely peppered strokes that surreally metamorphose into tranquil, dormant human figures.

Further reading

Andrews, Julia F. and Shen, Kuyi (1998). 'Transformations of Tradition, 1980 to the Present. Chinese Painting in the Post-Mao Era'. In Julia F. Andrews and Shen Kuyi (eds), *A Century in Crisis: Tradition and Modernity in the Art of Twentieth-Century China*. New York: Guggenheim Museum.

Jia, Youfu (1992). *Jia Youfu Zhongguohuaji* [The Collected Paintings of Jia Youfu]. Beijing: Jinri Zhongguo chubanshe.

EDUARDO WELSH

Jia Zhangke

b. 1970, Fenyang, Shanxi

Film director

Jia Zhangke is known as the filmmaker of contemporary Chinese castaways, people caught between the backwardness of the countryside and the modernity of urban culture. He left his native town at eighteen in order to study painting in the provincial capital of Taiyuan. In 1993, Jia entered the **Beijing Film Academy** and graduated in

1997. He was one of the founding members of the Youth Experimental Film Group in 1996. However, he subsequently returned to Fenyang to film his movies that, despite their 'local' characteristics, address issues of a more global, even universal nature. Jia very soon established himself as one of the major independent filmmakers in China. His first short (a video), *Xiao Shan Going Home* (*Xiao Shan huijia*, 1995), won the Hong Kong Independent Short Film and Video Award. The award secured the necessary financing for his first full-length feature, *Little Wu* or *Pickpocket* (*Xiao Wu*, 1997), the story of a youngster unable to cope with the dramatic changes happening in China. The film was shot with non-professional actors and won a NETPAC prize at the Berlin International Film Festival in 1998. Jia's talent for describing the change from a revolutionary to a market culture was confirmed in *Platform* (*Zhantai*, 2000), a story that begins in 1979 and ends in 1990 and represents the coming of age of the director. His most recent film, *Unknown Pleasures* (*Ren Xiaoyao*, 2002), locates its young protagonists between a hedonistic present and a thoroughly commercialized future. In line with his interest in contemporary society, Jia is also involved in the production of documentaries (e.g. *In Public*, 2001, about a small mining town in Inner Mongolia).

See also: New Documentary Movement

Further reading

Berry, Michael (2003). 'Cultural Fallout'. *Film Comment* (March/April): 61–4.

MARIA BARBIERI

Jiang He

(né Yu Youze)

b. 1949, Beijing

Poet

Jiang He was an important member of the group of Misty poets (see **Misty poetry**) who were loosely associated with the literary journal *Today* (*Jintian*) in the late 1970s and early 1980s. Jiang He began writing poetry in the 1970s in Baiyang dian as

a 'sent-down youth' from Beijing. But he gained his fame with sequences of civic-style poems, including 'The Monument' (*Jinian bei*, 1977) and 'Motherland, O Motherland' (*Zuguo, ah zuguo*, 1978). Many of his early works were published in *Today*, but very soon were accepted in official magazines and became tremendously influential with a larger audience in the early 1980s.

Along with his fellow Misty poet **Yang Lian**, Jiang He is regarded as the main founder of the 'modern epic' (*xiandai shishi*) movement of the mid 1980s. In his mature work, Jiang attempted to create a new kind of poetic fusion, rejoining and synthesizing East and West, modernism and tradition. He published two collections of poetry: *Beginning From Here* (*Cong zheli kaishi*, 1986) and what is regarded as the best illustration of his poetic ideals, *The Sun and Its Reflections* (*Taiyang he tade fan'guang*, 1987). Jiang He gradually faded from the Chinese poetic scene, particularly after his move to the USA in the late 1980s. Nevertheless, he remains a key figure in the renaissance of contemporary Chinese poetry.

HUANG YIBING

Jiang Weiguo

(a.k.a. David W. Jiang)

b. 1943, Shanghai

Theatre director, actor

Dean of the School of Drama at the Hong Kong Academy for Performing Arts, David Jiang has been actively involved in intercultural theatre since his first trip abroad in 1989. Graduating from the Acting Department of the Shanghai Theatre Academy in 1964, Jiang was assigned to work in Anhui province. After four years in the countryside, Jiang settled down to hone his skills in the Anhui Provincial Spoken Drama Company. As an actor, playwright and director, Jiang then worked and taught in Shanghai, New York, Leeds, Taipei and Hong Kong. He also completed a doctoral degree in the UK in 1997.

Jiang's best-known work as a director includes a **Huangmeixi** (Hubei opera) version of *Much Ado*

About Nothing (Anhui, 1986), *Macbeth* (UK, 1994), *Paravda* (by Howard Brenton and David Hare, Taiwan 1998), *Man from Wuling* (*Wuling ren* by Zhang Xiaofeng, USA, 1999), *Miss X* (*X Xiaojie* by Yao Yiwei, Taiwan 2000), *An Ordinary Day* (by Dario Fo and Franca Rame, China, 2001) and *Family* (*Jia* by Cao Yu, Hong Kong 2002). Drawing upon a background in the Stanislavsky system, which he received while pursuing his BA, an understanding of traditional Chinese theatre and its aesthetic concepts, and experience collaborating with various Euro-American counterparts, Jiang is known for the diversity of his directing styles, using strong visual imagery to deliver his reading of the text.

LI RURU

Jiang Wen

b. 1963, Beijing

Actor/film director and producer

A talented actor and sophisticated director, Jiang Wen is well known both in China and abroad. He graduated from the Central Academy of Drama in Beijing with a degree in performing arts (1984). Jiang Wen has since established a superstar screen persona through the many films he has co-starred in, directed or produced. Jiang Wen has played various roles in his career, and each has presented a distinct identity. He first established his reputation playing the 'rightist' in Xie Fei's *Hibiscus Town*, (*Furong zhen*, 1985). Then, as the legendary hero in **Zhang Yimou**'s *Red Sorghum* (*Hong gaoliang*, 1987), Jiang gained international recognition. The roles of bookseller in Zhang Yimou's *Keep Cool* (*Youhua haohao shuo*, 1997) and emperor in Zhou Xiaowen's *The Emperor's Shadow* (*Qin Song*, 1996) demonstrated his versatility, while his performance in the television series **Beijingers in New York** made him immensely popular in China.

Jiang Wen has also directed two impressive feature films. His directoral debut, **In the Heat of the Sun** (*Yangguang canlan de rizi*, 1995), is a coming-of-age story that examines the **Cultural Revolution** from the personal perspective of a teenager, re-staging a revolutionary past when radical adolescents seized centre-stage from authoritarian adults. His second feature, *Devils on the Doorstep* (*Guizi laile*, 1999), in which he also plays the lead, revisits the conflict between China and Japan in the Second World War in a confrontation between Chinese villagers and two prisoners-of-war. The film satirically reveals the Chinese treating their enemies as victims only to have their kindnesses repaid with the slaughter of innocents. Jiang Wen also plays the protagonist in Lu Chuan's directing debut, *Xun Qiang* (2002), in addition to being the film's producer.

Further reading

Cui, Shuqin (2001). 'Working From the Margins and Outside the System: Independent Film Directors in Contemporary China'. *Post Script* 20: 77–93.

Hajari, Nisid (2000). 'Devils' Advocate'. *TIME asia* 155 (22 May). Available at http://www.time.com/time/asia/magazine/2000/0522/cinema.jiangwen.html

CUI SHUQIN

Jiang Yue

b. 1962, Beijing

Video documentary filmmaker

A graduate of the China Drama Institute, Jiang Yue has asserted himself as one of the major voices of the **New Documentary Movement** since making independent work in 1991. In the early 1990s, Jiang spent a few years in Tibet where he shot *Tibetan Theatre Troupe of Lama Priests* (*Lama zangxituan*, 1991), *Bakhor* (*Bakuo jie*, 1992), *The Residents of Lhasa's Potala Square* (*Xue jumin*, 1992) and *Catholics in Tibet* (*Tianzhu zai xizang*, 1992). Back in Beijing, he directed *The Other Shore* (*Bi'an*, 1995), a meandering, fascinating, heart-wrenching meditation on artistic endeavour and failure. Begun as a documentation of avant-garde theatre director **Mou Sen**'s rehearsals of **Gao Xingjian**'s play by the same name, Jiang ends up focusing on what happens *after* the performance is over, when the fourteen young students in the workshop find themselves unemployed and fight to keep their illusions and artistic drive in a society that marginalizes them. *A River Stilled* (*Bei tingzhi de he*, 1999), by contrast, is an intimate, sympathetic gaze at the lives of workers involved in building the Three Gorges Dam on the Yangtze River. Jiang reached artistic maturity with *This Happy Life* (*Xingfu shenghuo*, 2002), a powerful yet tender exploration of masculinity, in which he interweaves and compares the psyches of two railway workers in Hunan as they confront loss, emotional longing, unemployment and the constant challenge posed by women and children. In 1998, Jiang Yue opened a small production company, China Memo Films, with fellow documentary filmmaker **Duan Jinchuan**.

BÉRÉNICE REYNAUD

Jiangnan sizhu

(Jiangnan Silk and Bamboo ensemble)

Traditional music genre/ensemble

Jiangnan sizhu is the **Silk and Bamboo** (*sizhu*) music tradition indigenous to the region commonly known as Jiangnan (South of the River) – the area along the south bank of the lower Changjiang (Yangzi River) that includes parts of the provinces of Zhejiang, Jiangsu and Anhui, and the cities of Shanghai, Suzhou, Wuxi, Hangzhou and Nanjing. Native musicians have traditionally referred to this wind-and-string ensemble music simply as 'sizhu', but it has been common among musicologists and performers alike since the 1950s to prefix the term with the place name Jiangnan in order to distinguish it from other regional sizhu traditions such as **Chaozhou-Hakka sixian**, **Minnan nanyin** and Guangdong yinyue (see **Cantonese music**).

Jiangnan sizhu ensembles typically consist of a core group of wind and string instruments that include the **dizi** (bamboo transverse flute), *xiao* (end-blown bamboo flute), *sheng* (mouth-organ), **erhu** (two-stringed fiddle), **pipa** (four-stringed plucked lute), *sanxian* (three-stringed plucked lute) and *yangqin* (hammered dulcimer), accompanied by small percussion instruments such as a clapper and a small drum or woodblock. The melodic instruments may be doubled and may also be supplemented by

other string instruments such as the **zheng** (board zither), *ruan* or *qinqin* (both plucked lutes) and two-stringed bowed lutes of various sizes, as well as a pair of small concussion bells.

The dizi assumes the lead role, in that it often plays the opening measures of a piece, after which the rest of the melodic instruments join in. All the instrumentalists play the same melody, but each one renders it slightly differently according to the idiomatic techniques characteristic of the individual instrument. For example, a bowed instrument such as the erhu will tend to play more elongated or held notes, while a plucked instrument such as the pipa or sanxian will fill in that space with repeated notes or tremolos as the dizi or xiao flutes play trills. The effect is that of a seamless, flowing melody. Thus, although in theory Jiangnan sizhu is often described as having a heterophonic texture, in practice it is actually contrapuntal, because of the individuality and relative independence of the instrumental parts in spite of the ensemble's collective adherence to the melodic structure of a particular piece.

Jiangnan sizhu repertory is relatively small and concentrates on a corpus of eight pieces traditionally known as 'Badaqu' (Eight Great Pieces). The pieces are mainly derived from three 'stock tunes' (*qupai*): 'Lao liuban' (Old Six-Beat), also known as 'Baban' or 'Eight-Beat'; 'Sanliu' (Three-Six); and 'Sihe' (Four United). Each of these stock tunes (or fixed melodies) is the source of several other pieces that are generated using a technique known to insiders as *fangman jiahua* (slowing down and adding flowers). It involves slowing down the tempo of the original melody and adding other notes in between its structural notes. This practice has resulted in several different melodic variants, in which on occasion the relationship with the original tune or with each other is not readily apparent.

In the early twentieth century, members of some Jiangnan sizhu clubs in Shanghai spearheaded the efforts to develop traditional musical instruments, adapt solo pieces for ensemble, and perform new compositions. These practices served as precursors to *guoyue* (national music), which emerged after the 1940s (see **modern Chinese orchestra**). After a period of suppression during the Cultural Revolution, public performances of Jiangnan sizhu resumed in the early 1980s with the reopening of music clubs, the traditional venue for performances of this type of music. Since then, the number of performance groups has increased; Jiangnan sizhu festivals have been held on a regular basis; and new pieces for the ensemble have been composed.

Further reading

Wiztleben, J. Lawrence (1995). *'Silk and Bamboo' Music in Shanghai: The Jiangnan Sizhu Instrumental Ensemble Tradition*. Kent: Kent State University Press.

MERCEDES M. DUJUNCO

1990s its style seemed less glamourous than other more recent periodicals with their sharper pitch and clearer-cut graphic images, *Jiangsu huakan* remains one of the most longstanding publications that have witnessed and encouraged the growth of contemporary Chinese art. In July 2003, it changed its name to *Huakan*.

Further reading

Lü, Peng and Yi, Dan (1992). *Zhongguo xiandai yishu shi* [A History of Modern Art in China]. Changsha: Hunan meishu chubanshe, 114–20.

TANG DI

Jiangsu huakan

[Jiangsu Art Monthly, Nanjing, 1974–]

Founded in the early 1970s as a bi-monthly publication aimed at popularizing the totalitarian art canon of the time, *Jiangsu huakan* became a specialized contemporary art monthly in 1985, a year that saw the emergence of new art expressions facilitated by the relaxed political climate and manifested in a vast range of art practices and critical debates. This nationwide phenomenon known as the **85 New Wave [Art] Movement** was actively followed by *Jiangsu huakan*, which in the July issue of 1985 published a provocative essay by **Li Xiaoshan** questioning the limitations, and the future, of 'traditional Chinese painting' (*Zhongguohua*). The article stirred a series of heated debates dealing with the innovation/tradition issue that put traditional academic education under scrutiny. In 1989 the abrupt end of the exhibition '**China Avant-Garde**' brought about the closure of **Zhongguo meishubao** [Fine Art in China], a Beijing weekly that provided the theoretical backbone for the exhibition. After this episode, *Jiangsu huakan* became the most important continuously published arena for Chinese and Western contemporary art thinking and practices. It played a significant role in the development of **New Literati Painting** (*Xin wenren hua*), and includes detailed reports on major national and international events such as the Venice Biennale and Documenta. Although in the late

Jiao

(offering)

Daoist ritual

Daoist rituals form a central part of festivals on the anniversaries of the local gods (see **temple fairs**). These rites are now being performed with increasing frequency and complexity in contemporary China, particularly in the south. A Jiao ritual can take many forms, depending on the specific Daoist ritual tradition of each locale. Most share certain basic features, however, such as the laying out of a sacred space, often marked by talismans, and the construction of a portable altar with images of the highest emanations of the Dao, the Three Pure Ones, and other Daoist deities. Within this over-coded and symbolically charged space, a series of rites unfold. First the deities are invited to the altar, and presented with pure offerings of incense, tea, wine and fruit, along with symbolic gifts of great value. Scriptures are recited, in a re-revelation of cosmic symbols of power which is said to generate merit for the community. The principal Daoist master performs mudras, recites words of power, and visualizes an audience with the high gods, before whom he presents a memorial, requesting blessings for the community. Finally, the gods are sent off and the sacred space is deconstructed. The rites can last from one day to several weeks. Local musical traditions complement more broadly used

Daoist hymns. The entire ritual is accompanied by music and percussion, and features dance, elaborate ritual vestments and intricate ritual artifacts. In certain ways, these rites mimic imperial court audiences, but at the same time they may include elements of humour and farce. Divination is frequently integrated into the performance. Depending on local traditions, the rites may take place in a closed temple before community representatives (usually selected by divination) or in open altars. Community offerings are blessed by the Daoist priests before being consumed in great feasts at the conclusion of the festivities.

See also: Daoist music; Gongde

Further reading

Dean, Kenneth (1993). *Taoist Ritual and Popular Cults of Southeast China*. Princeton: Princeton University Press.

Lagerwey, John (1987). *Taoist Ritual in Chinese Society and History*. New York: Macmillan.

KENNETH DEAN

Jiao Juyin

b. 1905, Tianjin; d. 1975

Theatre director

Jiao Juyin was a leading practitioner of the Stanislavsky system in China and a longtime director of the **Beijing People's Art Theatre**. His accomplishments in these two areas represent his most important contribution to Chinese **Huaju** (spoken drama).

Jiao's 'theory of mental images' (*xinxiang xue*) was the director's adaptation and application of the Stanislavsky system. The theory calls for the actors to form images of the characters in their mind before performing them on the stage. Jiao's method of training actors was divided into three stages: experiencing life, developing mental images, and creating stage images, with mental images serving as a bridge between real life and theatrical performance, moving, as Jiao said, from external to internal, and from internal to external.

Like many Chinese dramatists of his time, Jiao also participated in the 'nationalization of spoken drama' (*huaju minzuhua*) in order to give this imported dramatic form a Chinese character. Jiao's lifelong pursuit was to create a Chinese system of performance by integrating the artistic techniques and aesthetic principles of Chinese opera with the realistic Western drama, and both his theoretical writings and stage productions were directed towards this goal. The Beijing People's Art Theatre – which was modelled after the Moscow Art Theatre – provided Jiao with a testing ground for his experiments, and became the pre-eminent national company of spoken drama under his guidance.

In 1979, Jiao Juyin was posthumously rehabilitated and buried in the Babaoshan Cemetery in Beijing.

YU SHIAO-LING

Jin Guantao

b. 1947, Hangzhou

Scholar, writer, social critic

Jin Guantao is now a Senior Research Fellow of the Institute of Chinese Studies and the Director of the Research Centre for Contemporary Chinese Culture at the Chinese University of Hong Kong. He was trained as a scientist, but became interested in the humanities and social sciences during the **Cultural Revolution**. In the late 1970s and early 1980s, he and his wife, Liu Qingfeng, published many articles on history and philosophy and also some on literary works. The most influential of these were a history article entitled 'Traditional Society in China: An Ultrastable Structure' (1980) and a novel called *Open Love Letters* (1980). In the article, they applied cybernetics and systems theory to historical studies and argued that, in feudal China, the peasant economy, bureaucratic polity and Confucian ideology were closely integrated into an ultra-stable structure. This structure developed a self-correcting mechanism to maintain its integration. It tolerated no deviation of any of these three sub-systems from its normal function. Because of this, traditional society in China was stable, stagnate and long-lasting. The article was later expanded into a book, *The Cycle of Growth and Decline – On the Ultrastable Structure of Chinese Society*, which further elaborated on the analysis and argument. The novel expressed their concerns about and reflections on life, love, society, history and the fate of Chinese nation while they were living in the countryside during the Cultural Revolution as 'sent-down youths' (see **xiafang, xiaxiang**). It is more philosophical dialogue than story.

In 1984 Jin and his wife began to edit and publish the first book series of the reform era: *Towards the Future* (*Zou xiang weilai*). This ambitious project was designed to introduce a younger generation to recent developments in the fields of the natural sciences, social sciences, humanities, art and literature. By 1989, before it was banned, about eighty books were published in the series. Their writings and academic activities greatly shaped intellectual life in the 1980s. After 1989, they left the mainland and worked at Hong Kong Chinese University. There they launched a journal, **Ershiyi shiji** [Twenty-First Century], which quickly became a major forum for intellectual debate, attracting much attention on the mainland and abroad. They have authored more than a dozen books and numerous articles on history, philosophy, literature, science, and on various social issues.

Further reading

Chen, Fong-ching and Jin, Guantao (1997). *From Youthful Manuscripts to River Elegy: The Chinese Popular Cultural Movement and Political Transformation, 1979–1989*. Hong Kong: Chinese University of Hong Kong Press.

Jin, Guantao (2001). 'Interpreting Modern Chinese History through the Theory of Ultrastable Systems'. Trans. Gloria Davies. In Gloria Davies (ed.), *Voicing Concerns: Contemporary Chinese Critical Inquiry*. Lanham, MD: Rowman and Littlefield, 157–83.

Wang, Jing (1996). *High Culture Fever: Politics, Aesthetics, and Ideology in Deng's China*. Berkeley: University of California Press, 56–64.

LIU CHANG

Jin Xiang

b. 20 April 1935, Nanjing

Composer

Between 1954 and 1959 Jin Xiang studied composition at the Central Conservatory of Music in Beijing under Chen Peixun (Chan Pui-fang). He was branded a 'rightist' and sent to work in Tibet, where he led a local ensemble, and then on to Urumqi in Xinjiang where he served as conductor from 1973 to 1979. Only after the **Cultural Revolution** was he able to return to Beijing. He was conductor and composer-in-residence at the Beijing Symphony Orchestra (1979–84) and at the same time retrained in composition, and especially techniques of New Music. Until 1989, he was director of the Composition Research Centre at the Chinese Conservatory in Beijing. In 1990 he left for the University of Washington in Seattle to continue his studies in composition, and in 1992 spent a year as a visiting scholar at the Juilliard School of Music. He has since returned to China to compose and teach.

Jin Xiang's style is characterized by a particular sensibility for musical colouring. His opera *The Savage Land* (*Yuanye*, 1987) features a Chinese-style *verismo*, reminiscent of Russian opera but at the same time permuted by distinctly Chinese elements which include flutes used in the manner of a Chinese **dizi** and whole-tone-passages in typical *shuochang* (storytelling) rhythms (see **quyi**). His *Chamber Concerto for Fourteen Instruments* (1983) is – again typically Chinese – a study in the reduction of motivic material. Beginning with his stay in the United States, Jin has become ever more eclectic and begun to introduce more and more colours other than the Chinese in his pieces. *Goddess* (*Nüwa*, 1990), for example – for voices, orchestra and synthesizer – is conceived as a collage, juxtaposing elements of African drumming, Jewish chant, laughter and exuberant shouts.

Further reading

Jin, Xiang (1991). *Zuoqujia de kun'gan* [A Composer's Difficulties]. Beijing: Zhongguo wenyi.

Kouwenhoven, Frank (1991). 'Mainland China's New Music (2): Madly Singing in the Mountains'. *Chime* 3: 42–75 (esp. 64).

—— (1992). 'Mainland China's New Music (3): The Age of Pluralism'. *Chime* 5: 76–134 (esp. 118–19).

Luo, Zhongrong (ed.) (1996). *Xiandai yinyue xinshang cidian* [Dictionary for the Appreciation of Contemporary Music]. Beijing: Gaodeng jiaoyu, 280–3.

Mittler, Barbara (1997). *Dangerous Tunes. The Politics of Chinese Music in Hong Kong, Taiwan and the People's Republic of China since 1949*. Wiesbaden: Harrassowitz.

BARBARA MITTLER

Jin Xing

b. 1967, Shenyang

Dancer, choreographer

Jin Xing is a modern dancer and choreographer. Coming from a minority Korean military family, Jin Xing joined a dance troupe run by the army in Shenyang at age nine. By 1987, Jin Xing had emerged as China's top male dancer, winning a national competition and then going to New York for four years of study. In 1996, one year after undergoing a sex-change operation, she founded the Jin Xing Dance Theatre in Beijing and became Artistic Director of a company of sixteen freelance dancers. This was China's first independent modern dance company, but it later disbanded. She is now based in Shanghai.

Jin Xing's works are startlingly original and provocative, and often explore issues of love and identity. One of her most celebrated pieces is *The Imperial Concubine Has Been Drunk for Ages* (*Guifei zui jiu*), which is based on a traditional **Jingju** (Peking opera), *The Drunken Imperial Concubine* (*Guifei zui jiu*). A pun in her title revolves around the word *jiu*, which in the opera title means 'wine' but in the dance piece means 'for a long time'. In this innovative work, Jin Xing brings out popular unease with position between the rich traditions and a fast forward-moving postmodern industrial society. In November 2002, Jin Xing and the British pianist Joanna

MacGregor presented a newly created performance called *Cross Border – Crossing the Line* (*Cong dong dao xi*), a multimedia production of dance, live music and video art representing the noise and chaos of post-industrial society. The work was performed in Beijing, Shanghai, Guangzhou and Chongqing.

Further reading

Sylvie Levey *et al.* (dirs). *Colonel Jin Xing* [documentary film, 52 min.].

LI RURU

Jin Yong

(né Zha Liangyong; a.k.a Louis Cha)

b. February 1924, Haining

Writer, publisher, political commentator

Jin Yong is a Hong Kong-based novelist, publisher, and political figure whose martial arts adventures (*Wuxia xiaoshuo*) are perhaps the most widely read of all twentieth-century Chinese fiction (see **martial arts fiction**). Jin Yong serialized his first martial arts novel *Book and Sword* (*Shujian enchou lu*) in 1955. His own newspaper, *Ming Pao Daily*, established in 1959, succeeded on the strength of Jin Yong's fiction, his incisive daily editorials, and the paper's critical coverage of mainland politics during the **Cultural Revolution**. It became the foundation of a publishing empire that included overseas affiliates and *Ming Pao Monthly*, an influential digest for the diasporic intelligentsia. After completing *The Deer and the Cauldron* (*Luding ji*) in 1972, Jin Yong spent ten years revising his 36-volume *Complete Works*. Though once banned in both Taiwan (for the author's early associations with the left) and the mainland (for his criticism of the CCP), the novels circulated widely in contraband editions, and are now universally available in authorized form, as well as repeatedly adapted into television serials, **martial arts films**, comic books and video games. They are increasingly credited with transcending the limitations of formula fiction and comprising a significant chapter in the history of modern Chinese fiction. Jin Yong himself became a supporter of mainland policies during the reform era and a player in Hong Kong's 1997 return to Chinese sovereignty; and through the 1990s he continued to be a prominent public figure and cultural spokesperson.

Further reading

Cha, L. (2000–02). *The Deer and the Cauldron*. Trans. John Minford (3 vols). Hong Kong: Oxford University Press.

JOHN CHRISTOPHER HAMM

Jin Zhaojun

b. 1958, Beijing

Music critic

Jin Zhaojun is of China's most prominent music critics, most notably for his numerous articles on Chinese and Western popular music. His articles have been published in various newspapers and magazines, among them **People's Daily** (*Renmin ribao*), *People's Music* (*Renmin yinyue*), and *China's Broadway* (*Zhongguo bailaohui*). Jin has also published a monograph on Chinese popular music entitled *Under the Naked Sun: My Personal Experience of Chinese Popular Music* (*Guangtianhuari xia de liuxing: qinli Zhongguo liuxingyinyue*).

Born in 1958 of Manchu origin, Jin Zhaojun graduated in 1982 from the Chinese Department at Beijing's Teachers' College. In 1986 he became an editor of *People's Music* and in 2002 was promoted to run its editorial department. His articles on popular Chinese music constitute an indispensable source for anyone aiming to study the subject. They approach music in a multifaceted way, combining sensitive analysis of the aesthetic, socio-political and economic aspects of music, with critical comments from the point of view of a concerned Chinese intellectual. Although often writing for the most official of newspapers and magazines, he has been able to maintain and articulate independent and original views which are evident, for example, in many sympathetic articles on rock music, a style officially banned in

China until the late 1990s. In addition to his work as a music critic, Jin has also been active in planning and organizing large-scale artistic events and television programmes.

Further reading

Baranovitch, Nimrod (2003). *China's New Voices: Popular Music, Ethnicity, Gender, and Politics*. Berkeley: University of California Press.

NIMROD BARANOVITCH

Jingju

('Capital [sung]-drama', a.k.a. 'Peking Opera')

Also called Jingxi (capital theatre) and Guoju (national drama) and commonly rendered as 'Peking opera' in English, Jingju is a regional form of **Xiqu** (sung-drama/opera) that developed in Beijing beginning in the late eighteenth century and has been the predominant form in China since the mid nineteenth century. Jingju's extensive body of plays, broad range of subject matter, lavish costumes, falsetto voices for youthful roles, and wealth of acrobatic and martial techniques have greatly influenced other forms of Xiqu. Jingju follows *banqiangti* musical structure, belonging to the *pihuang* musical system (see **Xiqu musical structure**); its instrumental music is led melodically by a small, high-pitched two-string spike fiddle (*jinghu*) and features extensive percussion. Two primary styles developed in the early twentieth century and have re-emerged since the **Cultural Revolution**: the more conservative and traditionally pure Jingpai ([Bei]jing style) or Beipai (Bei[jing] style), and the more commercially and artistically experimental Haipai ([Shang]hai style).

More than any other form of Xiqu, Jingju has been the focus of attention of the PRC government. Beginning in the 1940s, with the creation of *Driven up Mount Liang* (*Bi shang Liangshan*) inspired by Mao Zedong's *1942 Yan'an Talks*, the CCP has intimately concerned itself with the lives and works of Jingju artists. Party attention to Jingju reached its peak during the Cultural Revolution, when all but revolutionary modern Xiqu plays were banned, and of these, only selected Jingju plays were designated as 'model works' (*yangbanxi*).

After the Cultural Revolution, Xiqu and especially Jingju experienced a brief resurgence of tradition. Once-banned plays and the older actors who had starred in them drew large audiences. But the novelty wore off, and shrinking and aging audiences, coupled with progressive reduction in state support during the 1980s and 1990s, produced a crisis situation in Jingju, prompting economic and artistic efforts at amelioration. Troupes have been reduced in size or disbanded; the 248 Jingju troupes in 1978 were reduced to 213 by 1984 and 126 by 1990, and some further reduction clearly continued throughout the 1990s as well. Many troupes have opened 'extra income enterprises' such as restaurants and hotels, and are booking high-priced performances targeted to foreigners. Other economic measures include outreach efforts aimed at building audiences among elementary and secondary school students, and attempts to tie income to productivity.

Some artistic efforts to increase audiences have involved realistic acting and staging techniques borrowed from **Huaju** (spoken drama). Others have used elements from other forms of Xiqu and Chinese performing arts, such as the 'face-changing' (*bianlian*) technique from **Chuanju** (Sichuan opera) and a vast array of musical influences. The latter also include elements from Western concert and other more recent musical styles, and the use of Western musical instruments has been common since the early 1970s. Further creative efforts include the expansion of traditional modes of performance. For instance, the *chou* or comic male Xiqu role type is traditionally a supporting character, but a number of new plays featuring *chou* in the leading role have been created, such as *A Pig Butcher Places First in the Imperial Examinations* (*Tufu zhuangyuan*) and *The Seventh-Rank Sesame Seed-Sized Official* (*Qi pin zhi ma guan*). New plays have also been developed for targeted audiences. The Shanghai Jingju Company (Shanghai jingjuyuan) has been creating plays for targeted audiences since the early 1980s. The award-winning **Cao Cao and Yang Xiu** (*Cao Cao yü Yang Xiu*), created for urban intellectual audiences, is among the most successful.

See also: Du Jinfang; Xiqu playwrights; Xiqu role types

Further reading

Wichmann, Elizabeth (1990). 'Tradition and Innovation in Contemporary Beijing Opera Performance'. *The Drama Review* 34.1: 146–78.

Wichmann-Walczak, Elizabeth (2000). ' "Reform" at the Shanghai Jingju Company and Its Impact on Creative Authority and Repertory'. *The Drama Review* 44.4: 96–119.

ELIZABETH WICHMANN-WALCZAK

Jinling Union Theological Seminary

Jinling Union Theological Seminary in Nanjing is the only national Protestant seminary in the PRC. It was founded in the early twentieth century as the Theological College (Shenxueyuan) of Jinling University. The seminary got its present name in 1952 after uniting with several other eastern Chinese seminaries. It is the only Protestant seminary in China to confer degrees to its students, the highest being a Master of Theology.

Bishop **Ding Guangxun** has been President of the seminary since 1953. During the **Cultural Revolution** the seminary was closed and did not re-open until 1981. The seminary normally has approximately 170 students, but also has a great number of students enrolled in correspondence courses in theology. These students are mainly local evangelists from all over China who are not able to study full-time in Nanjing or at a local seminary. Many students graduating in the mid 1980s later became leaders in regional Christian councils and in local seminaries around China. Jinling Seminary is the centre for theological development in China, and many of the most well-known Chinese theologians have worked or still work there, e.g. Zhao Zichen, Wang Weifan and Chen Zemin. The seminary also publishes a theological journal, *Nanjing Theological Review* (*Jinling Shenxue zhi*).

FREDERIK FÄLLMAN

journalism

Due to the political significance of communication and propaganda in the PRC, journalists have long occupied a critical position between the Party-state and the populace. They play a crucial role in publicly legitimating the CCP even while often being privately critical of its overbearing hold on news production. The CCP holds strongly to the principle that all media function as the 'mouthpiece' of the Party and government (see **state control of media**), although what this entails in practice has changed markedly since the early 1980s. Journalists, most notably in print media, have found numerous ways to circumvent political dogma and offer the public lively, popular and commercially viable copy (see **newspapers**; **evening newspapers and weekend editions**; **Nanfang Weekend**).

Even though all areas of media production have been affected by commercialization and the development of market forces, the Chinese government still regards news production as the most political, and therefore the most sensitive, sector of the media. Journalists therefore feel the pressure of political control more strongly than others. This pressure is exerted through a system of self-censorship and retrospective criticism that operates largely through a hierarchy of editors, each responsible to the one above them. Television journalism is subject to the heaviest control, but even here journalists have found ways of reporting social scandals, **corruption**, crime and other 'negative' news once strictly controlled by the Party.

Traditionally, journalist recruitment has focused on journalism or Chinese literature graduates. There are numerous renowned schools of journalism throughout the country, most notably at Fudan University in Shanghai and the People's University in Beijing. Journalism education still somewhat anachronistically revolves around the central tenets of 'socialist news' production emphasizing the 'Party mouthpiece' principle. However, many courses also include critical and pragmatic reference to commercial and Western models of news production. Furthermore, news organizations are increasingly recruiting young graduates from other non-specialist degree courses at the country's top universities which stress intelligence, creativity and enthusiasm over political and technical training.

The development of the Internet has had a number of effects on journalistic practice. First, subject to certain controls, it has given journalists access to a vast array of new sources, often including leading foreign news websites (see **Internet (content)**; **Internet portals**; **Internet (history and structure)**). Second, it has demanded new forms of journalism specifically tailored to online reporting. Finally, the Internet is attributed with enhancing the feedback effect of journalists on those in power. For example, Internet reporting of an explosion in a school used for manufacturing fireworks in 2001 is widely considered to have spurred a more open and responsible acknowledgement of the disaster than would have occurred in the past.

Chinese journalists generally have a strong sense of ethics and professionalism associated with their understanding of their crucial position of responsibility in society. However, with the commercialization of the media various forms of paid journalism have emerged, and although widely condemned, the practice nonetheless continues. Journalists played a key role in the political demonstrations of 1989 through both their participation in and their reporting of events. Journalists from many leading news organizations, including central Party propaganda organs, joined marches in Beijing, and prior to the implementation of martial law, the student demonstrations, including student demands and negotiations with the government, were openly reported on national television and in the press. However, after the political clampdown of June that year, journalists once again found their work heavily monitored, and moves towards greater press freedom in the 1990s have been focused in more commercially oriented directions.

Further reading

De Burgh, Hugo (2004). *Chinese Journalist: Mediating Information in the World's Most Populous Country*. London: Routledge.

Latham, Kevin (2000). 'Nothing but the Truth: News Media, Power and Hegemony in South China'. *China Quarterly* 163: 633–54.

Lee, Chin-chuan (ed.) (1990). *Voices of China; The Interplay of Politics and Journalism*. New York: Guilford Press.

KEVIN LATHAM

journalistic literature

(Jishi wenxue)

Journalistic literature is a literary genre that first appeared in popular magazines and literary journals in the late 1970s. The genre is close to, but differentiated from, 'reportage' (*baogao wenxue*). On the one hand, works in this genre are, or are supposed to be, based on journalistic investigation, especially interviews and research, but, on the other, their authors do not always use the true names of real people and are less bound by the facts. In other words, the genre actually allows more fictional description and the use of other literary devices than *baogao wenxue*. Although the term *jishi wenxue* literally means 'fact-recording literature', much writing in this genre cannot be taken as a true record. Even in the case of writings about historical figures identified by their real names, one has to be sceptical about the reliability of the stories being presented, because such writings typically do not provide sources. A wide range of topics is covered in *jishi wenxue*, including crime, official corruption, sexual culture, the floating population, unemployment, historical events, and the private lives of celebrities. The genre is popular with both authors and readers because it allows social and historical commentary in addition to popular tabloid entertainment. As the genre is as sensitive to public issues as it is commercially motivated, the emergence and popularity of the genre reflects a broadening of ways in which social commentaries are made possible in post-Mao China, as well as the pervasive trend towards commercialization of literary and intellectual endeavour.

Further reading

Zhao, Yuezhi (2002). 'The Rich, the Laid Off, and the Criminal in Tabloid Tales: Read All About It'. In Perry Link, Richard P. Madsen and Paul G. Pickowicz (eds), *Popular China: Unofficial Culture in a Globalizing Society*. Lanham, MD: Rowman and Littlefield, 111–36.

XU XIAOQUN

K

Ke Yunlu

(né Bao Guolu and Yang Xueke)

b. Beijing

Writers

Ke Yunlu is the pen name of a husband–wife writing team that received widespread attention in the post-Mao era with novels that explored the effects of reform on daily life. Their nom de plume combines characters of their real names. The high-school sweethearts at Beijing 101 High, an elite boarding school for the children of government officials before the **Cultural Revolution**, were both sent to Shanxi province for re-education in 1968, when they started writing together in the remote village. Their first novel, *New Star* (*Xinxing*, 1986), portrays a rural county leader during Deng Xiaoping's economic reform era in the early 1980s, while their second, *Nights and Days* (*Ye yü zhou*, 1986), based on similar themes, brought them national fame. Their later work engages the themes of spirituality, philosophy and science. The publication of *Great Qigong Master* (*Da Qigongshi*) in 1989 documents a person's search for mystical knowledge and received widespread popular acclaim. During the bans on Qigong practices, the book was withdrawn from publication, though old copies were widely circulated. Their novel *The New Age* (1991) offered interpretations of Laozi's *Dao-dejing* [Book of the Way and its Power] and the Bible. Ke Yunlu has also served as editor(s) of the *International Qigong Daily*. In all their writing, whether about rural change, the search for spirituality, or alternative healing, their examination of belief has raised key questions for many Chinese about the meaning of life in late socialism.

Further reading

Ke, Yunlu and Zhang, Xianglian (1985). *Prize Winning Stories from China 1980–1981*. San Francisco: China Books and Periodicals.

Li, Liyan and Chaoji, Huangyan (1997). *Dui 'Ke Yunlu xinji bingxue' yü 'Zhongguo qigong jiuda jishu' di piping*. Beijing: Zhongguo shehui chibanshe.

NANCY N. CHEN

Kejia daxi

(Hakka Grand Opera)

Kejia daxi is a form of **Xiqu** (sung drama/opera) performed in the language of the Hakka ethnic group on Taiwan. The genre developed from the 'mountain songs' (*shange*) and 'tea-harvesting song skits' (*caichaxi*) that pervaded Hakka life and work among the tea gardens in the mountainous areas of southern China. Kejia daxi is also known as Kejia gezaixi, for its process of development and performance structure parallel **Gezaixi**, the opera created by the Minnan-speaking majority on Taiwan. Kejia daxi absorbed its major performance elements and repertory from **Jingju** (Peking opera) and other regional operas. Several full-fledged Kejia daxi troupes had been formed by the 1920s.

Kejia daxi is distinguished from other regional operas by its music. The convention persists of singing duets in 'tea-harvesting song skits'. Performers continue to sing in the vocal style of the traditional Hakka folksong performances, using their natural register. Two major song styles, *shangezi* and *pingban*, provide the basic melodic structures and rhythmic patterns to which lyrics can be fitted. With rising endnotes in each lyrical line and greater intervals between notes, the *shangezi* is employed in scenes involving heightened emotions or strong declarations. The *pingban*, on the other hand, is characterized by a regular beat and more level notes, ideal for descriptive and sentimental narration. Songs with set melodies and lyrics are also be used for particular scenes. Kejia daxi is performed outdoors at **temple fairs** in Hakka communities, and indoors in performance centres for theatre festivals. There are currently about twelve Kejia daxi troupes in Taiwan.

See also: music in Taiwan; performing arts in Taiwan

Further reading

Chang, Chiung-fang (2000). 'Opera, Anyone? Hakka Traditions in Transition'. Trans. David Mayer. *Sinorama Magazine* 6: 94–100.

Qiu, Hui-ling (2000). *Chashan quweiyang: Taiwan kejiaxi* [Resonance in the Mountains: Hakka Opera in Taiwan]. Taipei: Shangzhou (BWE).

UENG SU-HAN

Kong Jiesheng

b. 1951, Guangzhou

Writer, broadcaster

Kong Jiesheng is a dissident writer. He emerged on the post-Mao literary scene in 1979 with his fiction on the damage done by the **Cultural Revolution** to overseas Chinese, factory workers and sent-down youths. His fiction is known for its lyricism and a distinct 'southern' flavour with its skilful use of the Cantonese dialect (see **dialects**).

Kong grew up in an intellectual family. In 1968, he was sent to Gaoyao county as an educated youth, and from 1970 to 1974 to a Production and Construction Corps on Hainan Island. In 1979 Kong became known nationwide with his sensational and controversial story, 'On the Other Side of the Stream' (*Zai xiaohe neibian*), which reveals a family tragedy through two youths in exile. His 1982 novella *The Southern Shore* (*Nanfang de an*) depicts the alienation of educated youths after returning to the city (Guangzhou), and their search for a new identity and destiny. Another novella, *An Ordinary Woman Worker* (*Putong nügong*, 1983) deals with the constant struggle of a determined single mother in face of social prejudice. The destruction of human talents and the destruction of nature form two parallel lines in his novella *The Big Jungle* (*Da linmang*, 1984). Kong escaped from China after the 4 June Massacre and now works for the Radio Free Asia in Washington, DC.

Further reading

Leung, Laifong (1994). 'Kong Jiesheng: A Cantonese Writer'. In *idem* (ed.), *Morning Sun: Interviews with Chinese Writers of the Lost Generation*. New York: M. E. Sharpe, 65–79.

LEUNG LAIFONG

Kong-Tai style

The pervasive influence of the 'Kong-Tai style' has been of immense importance in the cultural amalgam of Greater China (the mainland, Hong Kong, Taiwan and international Chinese communities). The expression itself is a shorthand for the introduction into China of Hong Kong and Taiwan advertising and pop culture from the late 1970s onward. But the commercial impact of Kong-Tai should not be seen simply as part-and-parcel of an overall influx of capital, the conversion of China into an avaricious consumer society and the vulgarization of social mores. The process of cultural osmosis that has existed since the late 1970s is complex and multi-faceted, and Kong-Tai has in many ways provided the mainland the means for bridging the gaps with both its own past and its possible future.

After the Communist takeover of 1949, Kong-Tai culture had initially survived in isolated offshore centres, which increasingly from the 1960s–70s onwards were transformed into wealthy consumer societies. Hong Kong and Taiwan developed the popular written and performance culture that had once been a feature of mainland urban life, in particular of Shanghai and Beijing during the Republican period. Commercial styles of film, music, essay writing and journalism flourished in these offshore Chinese cultures and provided indigenous forms of modern pop culture that infiltrated the mainland from as early as the late 1970s, when the first Kong-Tai films were screened inland.

From the 1980s, the Kong-Tai style, with its evocation of hip, modernized Shanghai decadence, worldly *petit-bourgeois* patina and consumer sheen, profoundly influenced the face of mainland culture. Writers on the mainland generally had only a marginal interest in it, rarely taking it seriously, however, even when debates within elite culture have been sparked by issues related to commercialization. Mainland critics have generally been blinded by their own linguistic bias, chauvinistic prejudice or lack of resources to appreciate the transformative significance of these formerly peripheral worlds.

Many of the early advertisements for consumer items were often imported from or inspired by Kong-Tai and Japan, the leading entrepôt cultures for the mainland. In the 1980s, as ideological justifications for the new commercial culture were found, advertising producers and outlets proliferated. Advertising companies, many of which were spawned by state-run film and television organizations, first flourished in southern cities like Guangzhou. Due to ease of access these ad agencies came more directly under the sway of Hong Kong archetypes, and thereby set the standards of quality and innovation for inland provinces and the north.

Kong-Tai had become cultural trendsetters because they were perceived of as being modern, integrated urban environments, their communications more developed and their consumer cultures more sophisticated than those of the out-of-touch northern capital of Beijing. Satellite TV boomed in the boondocks, and throughout the 1990s access to it increasingly allowed audiences to feel that they were part of a virtual global village even while they imbued narrowly defined nationalist ideology.

The consumer age also led to a new style of campaign, not a repetition of the theatrical political movements of the past, *yundong*, but ever-new waves of media-generated and media-enhanced frenzies and crazes (*re, xianxiang, chao*, as they are variously called). These crazes included the rise and fall of a broad spectrum of ready-made fashions, from the re-consumption of Chairman Mao that began in the late 1980s, to the hula hoop fever of 1992, as well as the media-fired cultural debates of 1993–6, and the contretemps between neo-liberals and the new left wing in the late 1990s. Manufacturing *re*, literally 'fevers', became the focus of many publicists, be they official (the Party, for example, attempted to engender a 'fever for the study of Deng Xiaoping's works' in 1993, and new 'patriotic fevers' at various times) or private. The style of these Party-PR campaigns was imitative of Kong-Tai commercial culture, and much of the language used for the promotions, whether it be in the political or in the cultural realm, was taken from the Kong-Tai media, sometimes with a further input from the neo-Chinese state propaganda of Singapore. The Kong-Tai style has also had a major impact on the public face of the Party. This is obvious in regard to the updated political paraphernalia of congresses and meetings, the new style of political slogans (now cannily recycled as 'public service announcements') and banners, as well as language, within every realm of the media and the Chinese Internet.

GEREMIE R. BARMÉ

Koreans, culture of

The Koreans of China are virtually the same, culturally and linguistically, as the Koreans of Korea. Their architecture, female clothing and diet remain basically the same as in Korea, despite changes brought about by Han and modernization influences.

Immigration began in the seventeenth century, but the first major wave was in the 1860s, with others following later. Although there was major emigration also back to Korea, especially after the victory against Japan in 1945, the PRC censuses show numbers rising from 1,120,405 in 1953 to 1,920,597 in 1990. The overwhelming majority live in the northeastern provinces, especially Jilin, which borders Korea and is the site of the most important of Korean autonomous places, the Yanbian Korean Autonomous Prefecture, established in September 1952.

The Koreans are the most literate and educated of China's nationalities. In 1998, 99.97 per cent of school-age children in Yanbian were in primary schools, with 99.98 per cent of them entering a higher grade. Not only is Korean-language education widespread at primary level, but it also exists at secondary level, complete with the appropriate textbooks at both levels. In Yanbian public life, Korean is used alongside Chinese. Buddhism was never as strong in Yanbian as in Korea and is now all but dead. Christian missionaries were once influential, and there are still both Protestant and Catholic Christians among Chinese Koreans, although the Catholics are not in communion with Rome.

The Korean arts feature elegant dancing, females dominating. Korean musical instruments like the zither-like *kayagum* are popular among the Chinese Koreans. There is a tradition of drama and novels. Since the late 1970s, Korean writers have produced good plays and novels in Korean, illustrating contemporary life, including the new family, gender and generation relations. The novels have attracted interest among Koreans outside China.

COLIN MACKERRAS

Kunqu

(Xigu (sung-drama/opera) genre)

Considered the oldest living theatre in China with a history of over 600 years, Kunqu has influenced most regional music-dramas, including **Jingju** (Peking opera). It originated in the regions of Kunshan (hence its name) and Suzhou. Later it became the major medium for performing

Chuanqi plays in the Ming and Qing periods. Its popularity peaked from the mid-Ming dynasty to the early-Qing dynasty and declined in the middle of the nineteenth century. The form nearly became extinct by 1949. A new production of *Fifteen Strings of Cash (Shiwu guan)* in 1956 saved the genre. It was made into an opera film whose influence reached the entire country. Since then, Kunqu has been professionally studied and performed (except during the **Cultural Revolution**) by four generations of excellent performers who are currently distributed among seven troupes: Shanghai Kunqu Troupe (Shanghai kunqutuan), Kunqu Troupe of Jiangsu Province (Jiangsusheng kunjuyuan), Su and Kun Opera Troupe of Jiangsu Province (Jiangsusheng sukun jutuan), Northern Kunqu Troupe (Beifang kunqu juyuan), Beijing and Kun Operas Artistic Troupe of Zhejiang Province (Zhejiang jingkun yishu juyuan), Kunqu Learning and Performing Troupe of Yongjia, Zhejiang Province (Zhejiang Yongjia kunqu chuanxisuo), and Hunan Kunqu Troupe (Hunan kunjutuan). In addition to these professional troupes, about fifteen non-professional Kunqu societies have been revived or newly established since the late 1970s. In 1986, the Ministry of Culture set up a special committee to revive this rich theatrical genre by instituting a policy of 'protecting, inheriting, innovating and developing [Kunqu]'. The first national Kunqu festival was held from 31 March to 6 April 2000 in Kunshan and Suzhou, with the seven troupes performing the best of their respective repertoires to audiences totalling more than 40,000 people. On 18 May 2001, UNESCO proclaimed Kunqu a 'masterpiece of the oral and intangible heritage of humanity'. Kunqu was among the first nineteen cultural spaces or forms of cultural expression around the world to be recognized by the organization. Kunqu is now treated as a Chinese national treasure.

Plays that have been staged and performed since the late 1970s fall into three categories: adaptations or excerpts from masterpieces of the Ming-Qing Chuanqi or Naxi plays; newly written plays with historical themes; and plays with non-traditional themes and innovative performing styles. The first category represents the revival and inheritance of the traditional Kunqu repertoire. Well-known stage productions in this category include: *Peony Pavilion*

(*Mudan ting*), *Peach Blossom Fan* (*Taohua shan*), *The Palace of Eternal Regret* (*Changsheng dian*), *The Story of the Lute* (*Pipa ji*), *Money Slave* (*Kanqian nu*), *The Story of the Top Scholar* (*Huakui ji*), *The Story of Western Garden* (*Xiyuan ji*), *Top Scholar Zhang Xie* (*Zhang Xie zhuan-guan*) and *The Story of Thorn Hairpin* (*Jingcha ji*). The second category reflects the recent achievements in producing new Kunqu plays whose subject matter is mainly historical. Representative plays of this kind are *Ban Zhao: Woman Historian of the Han Dynasty* (*Ban Zhao*), *In Love with Sima Xiangru* (*Sima Xiangru*) and *Things of the Past Southern Tang* (*Nan Tang yishi*). The third category refers to modern productions of experimental themes and theatrical styles. *Concubine Yang Travels to Japan* (*Guifei dongdu*) is a new play based on a legend concerning a historical figure which also incorporates Japanese theatrical styles; *Fighting Upward to Mount Ling* (*Shang Lingshan*) is a fairy tale told in a non-traditional performing style utilizing modern technology and contemporary forms of entertainment, with the aim of attracting young audiences.

The influence of Kunqu has reached beyond mainland China. While there are no formal Kunqu troupes of the same stature in Taiwan and Hong Kong, Kunqu societies have been particularly active among intellectual circles. Since the 1980s, they have been inviting actors, experts and scholars of Kunqu from China to lecture and perform. Among the most noted recent theatrical events in the West were Peter Sellars' radical adaptation of and Chen Shizheng's unabridged version of *The Peony Pavilion*. The former was staged in Europe and America in 1998 and 1999 and incorporated components and acting styles of Kunqu and Western drama and opera. The latter was first commissioned for the Summer 1999 Lincoln Center Theatre Festival and later toured parts of Europe. The Western public is now becoming aware of the existence of this living theatre that is much older than Peking opera.

Further reading

Swatek, Catherine (2003). *The Peony Pavilion Onstage: Four Centuries in the Career of a Chinese Drama*. Ann Arbor: University of Michigan Press.

Wu, Xinlei *et al.* (eds) (2002). *Zhongguo kunju da cidian* [Encyclopedia of China's Kunqu]. Nanjing: Nanjing daxue chubanshe.

DU WENWEI

Kwan, Stanley

(né Kwan Gum-pang/Guan Jinpeng)

b. 10 September 1957, Hong Kong

Film director, producer

Emerging from the Hong Kong 'New Wave', Stanley Kwan titled his first film *Women* (*Nüren xin*, 1985), the first of many films focusing on women's issues which have earned him the sobriquet, 'Hong Kong's George Cukor'. Like Cukor, but more explicitly, Kwan has also revealed himself to be a gay director, committed to exploring male as well as female identities in the ex-colony of the British crown. His internationally acclaimed feature films include *Rouge* (*Yanzhi kou*), winner of seven Hong Kong Film Awards in 1987; *Centre Stage* (a.k.a. *Actress*; *Ruan Lingyu*), which won him 'Best Director' at the 1992 Chicago Film Festival; and *Red Rose, White Rose* (*Hong meigui yü bai meigui*), which won a 'Best Actress' for Joan **Chen** at the Taiwan Golden Horse Awards in 1994.

His first gay film, *Hold You Tight* (*Yu kuaile yu duolou*, 1998), also won multiple awards in Hong Kong and Taiwan, in addition to the Frameline Award conferred on Kwan at the 23rd San Francisco International Lesbian and Gay Film Festival (1999). His recent gay film, *Lan Yu*, was a mainland collaboration adapted from the web novel *Beijing Story* (*Beijing gushi*; see **web literature**), and was selected for the Cannes Film Festival in 2001. It garnered four Golden Horse Awards, including 'Best Director'. Kwan's credits also include documentaries such as *Yang + Yin: Gender in Chinese Cinema* (*Nansheng nüxiang: Zhongguo dianying zhi xingbie*, 1996), dealing with the queer dimension of Chinese cinema, and *Still Love You After All This* (*Nianni ruxi*, 1997), a reflection on Hong Kong on the verge of becoming part of China.

See also: homosexuality and tongzhi culture

Further reading

Chow, Rey (2001). 'A Souvenir of Love'. In Esther Yau (ed.), *At Full Speed: Hong Kong Cinema in a Borderless World*. Minneapolis: University of Minnesota Press, 209–29 [on *Rouge*].

Reynaud, Bérénice (2003). 'Centre Stage: A Shadow in Reverse'. In Chris Berry (ed.), *Chinese Films in Focus: 25 New Takes*. London: BFI, 31–8.

Stokes, Lisa and Hoover, Michael (2000). 'Resisting the Stage: Imaging/Imagining Ruan Lingyu in Stanley Kwan's *Actress*'. *Asian Cinema* 11. 2 (Fall/Winter): 92–8.

Yau, Ching (1999). 'Bisexuality and Duality in Hold You Tight'. In *Cindossier: The 35th Golden Horse Award-winning Films*. Taipei: National Film Archive, 116–22.

WANG YIMAN

L

Lai Shengchuan

(a.k.a. Stan Lai)

b. 1954, Washington, DC

Theatre and film director, playwright

Lai grew up in the USA and in Taiwan. After earning a PhD in Theatre Arts from the University of California at Berkeley in 1983, he returned to Taiwan, where he established in 1984 the **Performance Workshop Theatre** (Biaoyan guangzuofang) troupe and has held various academic positions. Together with talented actors such as Ding Naizheng, Jin Shijie and Li Liqun, Lai produced *Anlian/Taohuayuan* (1986, English title: *Peach Blossom Land*), in which two theatre troupes vie for the same stage: the juxtaposed rehearsals of a play about an aging mainlander and a dramatization of the fifth-century tale about a lost Utopia provide poignant commentary on contemporary Taiwan. The prize-winning play has been restaged twice and made into a film (1992). Lai continued to collaborate with Christopher **Doyle** as Director of Cinematography in his second film, *Red Lotus Society* (*Feixia Ada*, 1994), a 'a fairy-tale film of the modern city'. Meanwhile, Lai has written and produced a large number of successful original and adapted plays. Especially popular were three **xiangsheng** (cross-talk) shows, which use the comic dialogue form typical of northern China to convey social and political criticism pertinent to Taiwan of the 1990s. More recently, *I Me He Him* (*Wo he wo he ta he ta*, 1998) continued to explore the fraught relation between Taiwan, Hong Kong and the mainland. Since 1998, Lai has also directed in the PRC and has established a branch of the Performance Workshop in Beijing.

Further reading

Kowallis, Jon (1997). 'The Diaspora in Postmodern Taiwan and Hong Kong Film: Framing Stan Lai's *The Peach Blossom Land* and Allen Fong's *Ah Ying*'. In Sheldon Lu (ed.), *Transnational Chinese Cinema: Identity, Nationhood, Gender*. Honolulu: University of Hawai'i Press.

Lai, Stan (1994). 'Specifying the Universal'. *TDR: The Drama Review: A Journal of Performance Studies* 38.2: 33–7.

YOMI BRAESTER

Lam Bun-ching

b. 1954, Macao

Composer

Lam Bun-ching, composer, pianist and conductor, challenges cultural boundaries by combining Chinese and Western idioms with a distinctive voice. She studied piano in Hong Kong before receiving a PhD in Music Composition from the University of California in 1981. Lam has garnered a number of prestigious awards, including the Rome Prize in 1991.

Lam's musical idioms, atonality, chromaticism and minimalism, are inspired by avant-garde composers such as Schoenberg, Takemitsu, Cage and Berio. Her *Three Dada Songs* for soprano, flute, piano and cello (1985) show her satirical quotation and allusion to the stalwarts. Her style weaves colour, texture and movement in a process she compares with action painting wherein the flow of time is captured by the musical equivalent of drops and splashes of paint.

Lam's modernism with a distinctive Asian sensibility is well demonstrated in the composition for voices and electronic sampler, *EO-9066* (1992), titled after an executive order calling for the internment of Japanese-Americans during WWII. This personal response to the events is built around whistling sounds and decomposed vocables that gradually evolve into the word *shikataganai* ('it cannot be helped', in Japanese) in a fashion reminiscent of Takemitsu's *Vocalism A.1* (1956). Some pieces in her ongoing *Spring* cycle employ successive notes instead of chords which create the effect of energizing silence in the manner of John Cage. At the same time, her frequent preference for sparse melodic lines over harmonic successions denotes her Chinese roots. Her contemporary chamber opera *Wenji: Eighteen Songs of a Nomad Flute*, which premiered at Asia Society in New York in 2002, is based on the story of poet/musician Cai Wenji, a scholar's daughter in the Eastern Han dynasty (25–220 CE), who becomes a prize of war, and is torn, in the clash between the Mongolian (Xiongnu) and Chinese worlds. It is accompanied by a mixed orchestra of Chinese and Western instruments and sung in Chinese and English, with the latter language being reserved for the 'barbarian' Mongols.

See also: New Music; Xu Ying

ISABELLE DUCHESNE

Lamb, Samuel

(né Lin Xiangao)

b. 1924, Macao

Protestant pastor

Samuel Lamb founded the 1,600-member Damazhan church in Guangzhou, China's most famous autonomous house church (see **house churches**). During the 1940s, Lin was an associate

of theologically conservative pastor **Wang Mingdao**. Lin was arrested in 1958 for refusing to join the **Three-Self Patriotic Movement (TSPM)**, and remained imprisoned until 1978. He founded the Damazhan church in 1979, which grew to several hundred members by the early 1980s. Throughout the 1980s and 1990s, police arrested or detained Lin several times, raided his church, confiscated materials and harassed Damazhan members, threatening them with losing their jobs and pensions if they continued to attend the church. In spite of these intimidations, Lin has persistently refused to register his church with the government and submit to TSPM control, and his church remains filled to capacity. Lin's resistance derives from his conservative theological beliefs, which posit a strict separation of church and state. Lin's success in resistance is due in part to his high profile abroad. American evangelist Billy Graham has preached at Damazhan, and Lin received a letter of support from US President Ronald Reagan.

See also: Christianity (Protestantism)

Further reading

Anderson, K. (1991). *Bold as a Lamb*. Grand Rapids, MI: Zondervan.

JASON KINDOPP

language and gender

Language and gender are mutually influential. On the one hand, speakers of different sexes use language differently to fit their communicative and socializing needs; on the other hand, language helps create and reinforce gender differences. Speakers of different sexes can be said to have different sets of expectations and different means of accessing language. In Chinese, female speakers generally have more restrictions than their male counterparts. For example, female speakers traditionally are not expected to utter profanity in public places, nor are they expected to speak loudly or too directly (though many such expectations have changed in mainland China since the **Cultural Revolution**).

One way in which language varies is in the association of different linguistic forms with different sexes. Men and women can usually be distinguished by phonological properties such as high and low pitch levels, but equally important is the distribution of vocabulary. Exclamations such as *ai you!* and *ai ya!* are almost exclusively associated with femininity, as are utterance-final particles such as *ou, hou, ma*, especially when accompanied by vowel-lengthening. The Chinese pronoun *renjia*, when uttered by men, merely refers to third persons; when used by a woman, however, it may refer to others or, under special circumstances such as whining to a lover, to herself. Also, since females are generally perceived to be more emotional, it is perhaps no surprise that most female-exclusive lexical items tend to express the passions; thus expressions indicating disgust, such as *taoyan!* ('disgusting, come on!'), are mostly used by females. In interactive discourse strategies, Chinese female speakers tend to be more cooperative with their interlocutors, frequently using feedback tokens such as *en, ao* ('oh'), *zhende* ('really?!'), *dui* ('right') and the like in conversation.

Another way in which language discriminates between the genders is in the reference forms for men and women. Male dominance is evident in many aspects of the Chinese language. Linguistic elements referring to men usually precede those referring to women, as exemplified in words such as *nannü laoshao* ('male-female old-young', or 'everyone') and *fuqi* ('husband-wife', or 'spouse'). Professional titles are often prefixed with *nü*, as in *nü yisheng* ('female doctor') when referring to females, whereas the same titles for males do not require any special marking. Such linguistic properties indicate some of the social realities of the Chinese language.

Speakers can also change language. Women are generally considered more sensitive to language use and better innovators of linguistic forms. A case in point is the so-called 'feminine Mandarin accent' (*nü guoyin*), which refers to the substitution of j, q, and x sounds with z, c, and s sounds, respectively, in words such as *gaoxing* > *gaosing* ('happy'). Such changes have been led by female speakers in Beijing since the 1920s. There is evidence that the feminine Mandarin accent now appears to be spreading beyond the female speech community. Another example is the **women's script** (*nüshu*), a system of written characters similar to the Han Chinese and developed and used exclusively by women in Hunan.

TAO HONGYIN

Lantern Festival

Also known as the Festival of First Origin and the First Moon Festival, the celebration of the first full moon of the Chinese New Year, on the fifteenth day of the first month, is one of the most ancient observances in the Chinese ritual calendar. Scholars have linked its origins to ancient fire worship, fertility rites, veneration of the primordial forces of Daoism, and the introduction of Buddhism, among other things. The date has long been marked by displays of lanterns, lion and dragon dances, competitive riddle-telling and eating of special foods. Today, the festival combines elements of religious, civic and political rituals and, of course, commercialization. In rural areas, the festival is often the highlight of the **New Year Festival**, with parades of lanterns that mark the reincorporation of households into their community. There is considerable regional variation; one distinctive local practice is found in parts of north China, where villagers construct a maze of lanterns, and simultaneously perform rituals ranging from simple secular dancing to elaborate Daoist liturgies (see **Jiao**). The festival is also promoted as a tourist event, in Harbin, for example, where it coincides with exhibitions of ice sculpture. Some legends associated with the festival have romantic themes, and Chinese businesses have sought to present it as a kind of indigenous version of Valentine's Day. The festival also has a political component, with government officials using it as an opportunity to meet with the public. For example, in recent years senior national leaders have joined leading intellectuals for a 'sing-along' in the Great Hall of the People. With its multiple levels of meaning encompassed within a single calendrical event, the Lantern Festival provides a rich example of the reinvention and transformation of tradition in contemporary Chinese popular culture.

Further reading

Johnson, David (2002). 'A "Lantern Festival" Ritual in Southwest Shanxi'. In Daniel Overmyer with Shin-yi Chao (eds), *Ethnography in China Today*. Taipei: Yuan-Liou Publishing, 287–95.

MICHAEL SZONYI

laosanjie

(old three classes)

Laosanjie, literally the 'old three classes', is a generational concept referring to the middle school (junior and senior high) graduates in China's urban areas in the three years of 1966, 1967 and 1968. Members of this generation were born around 1949, the year when the People's Republic of China was founded. They were the initiators of and main participants in the Red Guard Movement (1966–8) and the 'Up to the Mountains and Down to the Villages Campaign' (*Shangshan xiaxiang yundong*, 1967–79), two movements that together spanned the entirety of the Great Proletarian **Cultural Revolution** (1966–76). Because of its historical experience, this generation overlaps with the 'Red Guard generation', 'Cultural Revolution generation', and 'educated-youth generation', and all four terms are often used in interchangeable ways, though in current Chinese-language publications, *laosanjie* and 'educated youth' are used more often than others, especially by those who belong to this generation.

No one knows exactly how and when the term *laosanjie* came into use. What *is* clear is that it became popularized as part of a powerful nostalgic wave that swept across the generation in the 1990s. The triggering event was a museum exhibit that opened on 25 November 1990 in Beijing, entitled 'Our Spiritual Attachment to the Black Soil – A Retrospective Exhibit about the Educated Youth of Beidahuang', that traced the history of the 'sent-down' movement in the northernmost part of China. From then on, all kinds of social occasions and events involving this generation began to appear across the country. TV documentaries were produced, and hundreds of books were published containing reminiscences of the past or featuring old photos, diaries, letters and poems. An influential book of this kind is Jin Dalu's *Hardship and Heroism – Life Trajectories of Members of the Three Old Classes* (*Kunan yü fengliu – laosanjie ren de daolu*) published in Shanghai in 1994. In 1998, Jilin People's Press launched a book series featuring the autobiographies of well-known *laosanjie* writers, including Chen Jiangong, Lu Xing'er, Xiao Fuxing, Ye Xin, **Zhang Kangkang**. The conditions of contemporary life contributed to the rise of nostalgia in this generation. While the more successful individuals of the *laosanjie* felt compelled to reassert and prove themselves, the less fortunate ones felt neglected and wronged during a time of rapid economic transformation. According to the published estimates of some Chinese scholars, when state-owned enterprises began to lay off employees on a large scale in the 1990s, members of the *laosanjie* were among the hardest hit. Under these conditions, *laosanjie* and their reminiscences entered China's cultural discourse as social and moral critique.

See also: xiafang, xiaxiang

Further reading

Chen, Yixin (1999) 'Lost in Revolution and Reform: The Socioeconomic Pains of China's Red Guards Generation, 1966–96'. *Journal of Contemporary China* 8.21: 219–39.

Rosen, Stanley (2000). 'Foreword'. In Jiang Yarong and David Ashley, *Mao's Children in the New China: Voices from the Red Guard Generation*. London: Routledge.

Yang, Guobin (2003). 'China's Zhiqing Generation: Nostalgia, Identity, and Cultural Resistance in the 1990s'. *Modern China* 29.4: 267–96.

YANG GUOBIN

Law, Clara

(née Law Cheuk-yiu/Luo Zhuoyao)

b. 1957, Macao

Film director

After graduating from the National Film School in London (1985), Law returned to Hong Kong to become one of the most influential 'second wave' directors (together with **Wong Kar-wai** and others).

Her first Hong Kong film, *The Other Half & the Other Half* (*Wo ai taikongren*, 1988), also marked the beginning of her collaboration with husband Allen **Fong** (Fang Yuping). The film's subject matter, the effect of emigrating to Canada on two Hong Kong yuppies, set the tone for many of Law's later films, including *Farewell China* (*Ai zai taxiang de jijie*, 1990), which follows a young Chinese woman's descent into madness in New York, and *A Floating Life* (1996), about a Hong Kong immigrant family's adjustment to suburban Australia amidst generational conflict. While Law has expressed admiration for Yasujiro Ozu's ascetic style, much of her own work tends to involve complex scenes. In *The Reincarnation of Golden Lotus* (*Pan Jinlian zhi qianshi jinsheng*, 1989), an adaptation of popular writer Li Bihua's novel of the same title, Law portrays the karmic reappearance of a sixteenth-century novel's heroine in modern-day Hong Kong. The fantastic story provides an opportunity to comment on Hong Kong's contemporary identity crisis. *Temptation of a Monk* (*Youseng*, 1993), possibly the director's best-known film, includes a Fellini-like bacchanal and culminates in a showdown between a female assassin and a general-turned-monk. Law showed her versatility again in *The Goddess* of 1967, a psychological drama set in Australia, to which Law had emigrated. Among her other films: *Fruit Punch* (*Yes! Yi zu*, 1991), *Autumn Moon* (*Qiuyue*, 1992), and *The Great Conqueror's Concubine* (*Xichu bawang*, 1994).

Further reading

Braester, Yomi (1998). 'Modern Identity and Karmic Retribution in Clara Law's *Reincarnation of Golden Lotus*'. *Asian Cinema* 10.1: 58–61.

Louie, Kam (2003). '*Floating Life*: Nostalgia for the Confucian Way in Sydney'. In Chris Berry (ed.), *Chinese Films in Focus: 25 New Takes*. London: BFI, 97–103.

Millard, Katherine (2001). 'An Interview with Clara Law'. *Senses of Cinema* 13 (April–May).

YOMI BRAESTER

lawyers

Once reviled as lackeys of the capitalist class, lawyers have not only come to enjoy high socio-economic status, but are viewed as central to developing China's market economy and the rule of law. At the beginning of the Reform Era, China had fewer than 3,000 lawyers, all employed by the state. Two decades later, over 110,000 lawyers worked in 10,000 law firms, most of which were private, primarily partnerships and cooperatives. As indicative of a new profession, although the number of law schools jumped to over a hundred in the 1990s, few lawyers attended law school; the largest segment only had a junior college degree in law.

Lawyers have both fed and taken advantage of a growing litigiousness among the populace, as lawsuits have become more common in the context of a weakening system of informal mediation in the workplace and neighbourhood. There has been an explosion of cases in contracts, intellectual property rights, consumer protection, foreign investment and trade, and family law. The legal profession, however, faces major problems. Criminal defence lawyers have difficulty seeing state evidence before trial, are often not allowed to fully question witnesses, and are themselves beaten or arrested. Verdicts are commonly politically directed. Not surprisingly, few criminal defendants have counsel. Lawyers also often use bribes and connections to obtain favourable rulings. And although there were over a hundred foreign law firms operating in China at the turn of the century, they are confined to foreign-related legal issues and cannot represent clients in court or administrative hearings.

See also: legal culture; People's Mediation Committees

Further reading

Alford, W. (2002). 'Of Lawyers Lost and Found: Searching for Legal Professionalism in the People's Republic of China'. In A. Rosett, L. Cheng and M. Y. K. Woo (eds), *East Asian Law: Universal Norms and Local Cultures*. London: RoutledgeCurzon.

SCOTT KENNEDY

Lee, Ang

(Li, An)

b. 1954, Taipei

Film director/producer

Born in Taiwan, Ang Lee moved to the United States to study in 1978. He is the best-known Chinese filmmaker in the world, working in both Asia and America. His films have won numerous international and local awards, beginning with *Dim Lake* (1983) and *Fine Line* (1985). His feature films are: *Pushing Hands* (*Tuishou*, 1992), *The Wedding Banquet* (*Xiyan*, 1993), *Eat Drink Man Woman* (*Yinshi nannu*, 1994), *Sense and Sensibility* (1995), *The Ice Storm* (1997), *Ride with the Devil* (1999), *Crouching Tiger Hidden Dragon* (*Wohu canglong*, 2000), which won four Oscars, including best foreign film, and *The Hulk* (2003).

Crouching Tiger Hidden Dragon is a martial arts extravaganza that features global Chinese stars: **Chow Yun-fat**, Michelle **Yeoh**, **Zhang Ziyi**, Zhang Zhen and Zheng Peipei. Adapted from the novels of Wang Dulu (1909–77), it tells the story of the legendary swordsman Li Mubai, whose famous sword, Green Destiny, is stolen by the wayward daughter of a Manchu aristocrat, Xiao Long (Little Dragon). The plot has two strands: retrieving the sword and avenging the murder of Li's master, and romance between Li and a woman warrior, Xiulian, and between Xiao Long and her outlaw lover, Xiao Hu (Little Tiger). The plot is punctuated by spectacular combat sequences, choreographed by Yuan Woping.

See also: martial arts films

Further reading

Berry, Chris (2003). 'Wedding Banquet: A Family (Melodrama) Affair'. In *idem* (ed.), *Chinese Films in Focus: 25 New Takes*. London: BFI, 183–90.

Chan, Felicia (2003). 'Crouching Tiger, Hidden Dragon: Cultural Migrancy and Translatability'. In Chris Berry (ed.), *Chinese Films in Focus: 25 New Takes*. London: BFI, 56–64.

Sunshine, Linda (ed.) (2000). *Crouching Tiger, Hidden Dragon: Portrait of the Ang Lee Film*. New York: Newmarket Press.

MARY FARQUHAR

legal culture

Legal culture consists of values and norms concerning the content and operation of law. Reflecting as it does embedded values about socio-economic and political relationships, legal culture constitutes the cognitive environment for legal behaviour. Chinese legal culture draws on a reservoir of Chinese tradition derived from Confucianism and its emphasis on authority and hierarchy in social organization. Popular legal culture in China reflects the rich diversity of Chinese society and varies considerably across the many contours of class, gender, occupation and education. Official legal culture, on the other hand, reflects the official norms of the governing regime concerning the role of law. Influenced by ideals of revolutionary transformation drawn from Marxism–Leninism and Maoism, official legal culture in China tends to emphasize governance by a political authority that remains largely immune to challenge. During the first thirty years of the PRC, law and regulation served primarily as instruments for enforcing policies of the Party/state. Norms and processes for accountability were challenged as bourgeois artifacts deemed inappropriate to China's conditions. Official legal culture also reflects conclusions that legal limits on government authority might limit improperly the strong state that is needed for China's development. By the turn of the twenty-first century, even after twenty years of legal reform, the supremacy for the Party/state remains a salient feature in the legal system. Thus, the patrimonialism of Confucianized Marxism–Leninism Mao Zedong Thought combines with the sovereignty of Party/state supremacy to establish a powerful modality of governance in the PRC. Patrimonial sovereignty is thus a typology by which regulators are accountable only to their bureaucratic and political superiors, and as a result have few obligations to heed the subjects of rule in the process or substance of regulation. Under the dynamic of patrimonial sovereignty, political leaders and administrative agencies have responsibility *for* society but are not responsible *to* it. This is not an immutable legal culture, however. As the legal reform process progressed through the 1980s and 1990s, increased reliance was placed on legal professionals, an emerging elite whose privilege is based on specialized ability to interpret the policy expressions of law and regulation. Many of these specialists have been trained abroad, in principles of government accountability in law and regulation, raising the possibility of significant changes in official legal culture.

PITMAN POTTER

Lei Feng

b. 1940; d. 1962

Political icon

Lei Feng is perhaps the most enduring icon of model behaviour of modern China. Lei became an orphan after the Japanese killed his father and his mother committed suicide. The CCP saved him and brought him up. He joined the Army and became a Party member. Diligent study of the works of Mao Zedong taught him to live a life of frugality, to eschew selfishness and to devote himself to the people. In his diary, he expressed his desire to be 'a revolutionary screw that never rusts'.

This diary became the object of study in 1963 after Mao called on the nation to learn from him. Photographs of Lei in action turned up, movies and comic strips were made about his life, and posters bearing his image were produced in staggering quantities. He became a fixture in propaganda and education, a true icon of desired obedient behaviour. Lei's model status was based on his many good but unspectacular deeds: he sent his savings to a fellow soldier's parents, stricken by a flood; he washed his buddies' feet after a march, and even darned their socks while they were asleep. Unlike most other models, Lei was not martyred, but killed in an ordinary accident.

After the 1989 Tiananmen massacre, Lei returned in propaganda posters. This time around, Lei was presented as a much more stern and forbidding figure than before. Despite his more aggressive posture, Lei's model behaviour was seriously out of sync with the social realities of the early 1990s. In a society in which money, market and mobility were increasingly valued, people could gain little by following his example of self-sacrifice. Many Chinese have long considered

Lei a joke, and have mocked the emulation campaigns.

In 2000, Lei's image suddenly turned up in places reserved for **advertising**. He urged passers-by to surf a website devoted to health information. Lei's billboard reappearance testifies to his lasting influence to make people's behaviour conform to some norm. At the same time, it indicates to what extent propaganda, as a form of political advertising, and commercial marketing techniques have intersected.

See also: Party advertising and self-promotion; poster art and artists; posters and education; socialist spiritual civilization

Further reading

Farquhar, Judith (2002). *Appetites – Food and Sex in Post-Socialist China*. Durham: Duke University Press.

http://www.leifeng.org [Lei Feng Memorial Hall]

STEFAN LANDSBERGER

leisure culture

Poker, chess and **mahjong**, along with early morning exercises and singing parties in city parks, were among the very few Chinese pastimes for decades. 'Decadent tunes' from Taiwan and Hong Kong slipping into a newly opened China in late 1970s set off the history of its pop music. A dancing craze soon seized the country, followed by the enthusiasm for karaoke, assisted first by analogue tapes and later by digital CDs. Leisure culture diversified in 1990s as the economic reform considerably improved the Chinese living standard. Elderly people began to publicly display their skills in *yangge*, a traditional Chinese folk dance, while a burgeoning middle class, though still a small minority, took the lead in new leisure trends: golfing, bowling, parachuting, fishing, climbing, piloting, bungee jumping, and even participating in Hashing, an eccentric international running game. Flourishing everywhere were massage bathhouses, indoor swimming pools, dance clubs, gymnasiums, beauty parlours, teahouses, cafés and all kinds of bars. Video, CD, DVD and cable TV became standard household entertainment.

The Chinese government's decision to substantially extend paid holidays consecutively in 2000 and 2001 created a **holiday economy**. Travelling at home and abroad is now a new fad. Average Chinese enjoy *nongjiale* (an experience of packaged rural life), while the wealthier flood vacation resorts: the city of Zhuhai (Guangdong) alone entertained 8 million visitors in 2001, eight times the city's total population. Despite periodic crackdowns, vices like drug use and unlicensed prostitution have found their way (back) into the leisure culture.

Further reading

Hansson, Anders (ed.) (2002). *The Chinese at Play*. London: Kegan Paul.

YUAN HAIWANG

Leng Lin

b. 1965, Nanjing

Art critic, curator

Graduating from the Art History Department of the **Central Academy of Fine Arts** in Beijing (1988), Leng Lin was an editor, from 1988 to 1990, of *Wenyi yanjiu*, a bi-monthly magazine sponsored by the Chinese Art Research Institute. In 1993, he obtained his MA degree in Art History, again from the Central Academy, and got a job as an assistant researcher at the Institute of Literature Studies of the **Chinese Academy of Social Sciences** in Beijing. In the mid 1990s, Leng started writing broadly on Chinese contemporary art and in particular on the younger generation of oil painters and installation artists. In the meantime he organized several exhibitions of recent works by young artists, two of which – 'Shishuo xinyü' [A New Account of Tales of the World] (1995) and 'Shi wo' [It's Me] (1998) – attracted great attention. Leng has also promoted contemporary Chinese art on the art market, organizing with other artists, critics and curators auctions that feature emerging artists.

Leng Lin's writing focuses mainly on emerging artists of the 1990s and especially those art-school graduates who have had few opportunities to show their work in public exhibitions. In much of his writing, Leng promotes the notion of 'selfhood', which is a significant issue in the works of artists like Liu Ye, **Hong Hao**, **Zhang Xiaogang** and **Zhang Huan**. He believes that the pursuit of social ideals in art before the 1980s has been replaced by the self-conscious expression of individualist values in the art of the 1990s.

Further reading

Leng, Lin, (2000). '*Shi wo*/It's Me'. In John Clark (ed.), *Chinese Art at the End of the Millennium*. Hong Kong: New Media, 142–4.

—— (2000). 'Hong Lei and Wu Xiaojun'. In John Clark (ed.), *Chinese Art at the End of the Millennium*. Hong Kong: New Media, 204–6.

Wu, Hung (2000). *Cancelled: Exhibiting Experimental Art in China*, Chicago: The Smart Museum of Art.

QIAN ZHIJIAN

lesbianism in literature

Since market reform began in China in the early 1980s, the era has brought many tumultuous changes, including dramatic transformations in sex culture. While most Western studies of postsocialist Chinese sexuality have thus far focused on dominant heterosexual practices and narratives, researchers have also been quick to recognize that cosmopolitan gay and lesbian identities have sprung up in many mainland Chinese metropolises. Indeed, the lives and subcultures of lesbians and gays in postsocialist China are now intently probed, not only by sociologists and anthropologists, but also by local and foreign journalists.[i] What has perhaps been neglected by the growing social sciences literature and media reportage on the mainland Chinese lesbian and gay scene is the fact that same-sex sexuality has been at the centre of the oeuvres of some serious fiction writers in the People's Republic since the 1980s.

Two cases in point are **Lin Bai** (b. 1958) and **Chen Ran** (b. 1962). Lin's short stories, novellas and novels are noted for their sensitive treatment of female sexuality. They have long been acknowledged by Chinese literary critics such as Chen Xiaoming, **Dai Jinhua** and **Xu Kun** as fine examples of Chinese feminist writing. Although Lin's daring exploration of female sexuality is not limited to the desire between women, lesbian desire is one of the recurring themes in her works. Years before cosmopolitan queer activists (such as the Beijing-based female painter and actress Shi Tou) became vocal about lesbian issues in the media, Lin's fiction had already challenged homophobia as a form of internalized social discrimination. For example, Duomi, the protagonist of Lin's autobiographical novel, *One Person's War* (*Yige ren de zhanzheng*, 1993), experiences instinctual urges as a child to explore the sensations of her own private parts and does so by enlisting another girl's assistance. As Duomi grows up, however, she learns to consider intimacy with other women as abnormal and comes to identify her childhood same-sex play as shameful. Even though Lin does not explicitly criticize homophobia as socially constructed, her depiction of a protagonist who constrains her own spontaneous polymorphous desire because of society's prejudices against homosexuals sets the stage for future critiques of heteronormativity and lesbian self-denial.

Chen Ran, like Lin, is one of the most discussed authors in Chinese literary critics' debate over 'female writing' (*nüxing xiezuo*) and 'individualistic writing' (*gerenhua xiezuo*) between the mid and late 1990s. Her representations of female sexuality, including female–female love, have frequently invited comparison with Lin's despite the fact that the two writers actually have rather different styles. Whereas Lin's language is lyrical, metaphoric and highly evocative of sensory experiences, Chen's tends to be quirky, eccentric and parodic. Ideologically, the two writers are also different. Contrary to Lin's morbid fascination with internalized homophobia, Chen adamantly defends the rights of minorities, including sexual minorities. Her opposition to heterosexual hegemony has been articulated most directly in her essay 'Gender-Transcendent Consciousness and My Creative Writing' (*Chao xingbie yishi yü wode chuangzuo*, 1994), and in her short story 'Breaking Through' (*Pokai*, 1995). Her only full-length novel to date, *Private Life*

(*Siren shenghuo*, 1994), also explores bisexuality in depth. She is, in addition, a candid sympathizer of a group of lesbian-identified young women in Beijing who started the underground lesbian newsletter *Sky* (*Tiankong*; chief editor Shi Tou) in March 1999. In Chen's case, then, there is only a thin line between literary experimentation and social activism. Her pursuit of artistic freedom constantly gets translated into a passionate concern about individual freedom, and vice versa.

Despite their differences, one might see that Lin and Chen both champion the aesthetics of the liminal, giving seductive shapes to an existential ambiguity that refuses to be neatly boxed into identity categories. The recurring motifs of Lin's work are irreducible personal difference, self-doubts and self-denial. Paradoxically, as can be seen in *One Person's War*, a salient performative lesbian identity is called into being precisely by her main character's repeated utterances to negate that identity. By contrast, Chen imagines a restless romantic longing that is unrestrained by conventional gender definitions, that subverts dominant postsocialist ideals of femininity and heterosexual courtship. Her desired fluidity disintegrates both gender and sexual identities. Paradoxically, the two writers' hesitation to affix identity labels to the gender and sexual dissidents of their creation seems to resonate with a national mood – in that their examinations of liminal states of being aptly articulate the general discomfort with identity in a globalizing China, as the nation moves away from the memories of Mao and yearns to become cosmopolitan, yet resists foregone (i.e. globally dominant) conclusions of what it means to be cosmopolitan.

Significantly, as women writers' fictional representations of female homoeroticism proliferate, there is also in general a broadening social realm in which pluralistic interpretations of such works are becoming possible. The growing pluralism unsettles the dominance of traditional moralism, on the one hand, and the voyeuristic fantasies encouraged by the new consumer economy, on the other. Although thus far literary scholars in the mainland academic establishment have turned out far more feminist analyses than specifically queer readings of women's homoerotic fiction, China may be now poised at a point where specifically lesbian or queer critical analyses will enter the academic establishment from the margins.

Further reading

Aizhi (2001). Transcript of the programme *Let's Talk* on Hunan Satellite Television in December 2000 when Shi Tou and the gay film critic and novelist Cui Zi'en came out in the show, available at http://www.aizhi.org.hnws.htm

Farquhar, Judith (2002). *Appetites: Food and Sex in Post-Socialist China*. Durham, NC: Duke University Press.

Farrer, James (2001). *Opening Up: Youth Sex Culture and Market Reform in Shanghai*. Chicago: University of Chicago Press.

Rofel, Lisa (1999). 'Qualities of Desire: Imagining Gay Identities in China'. *GLQ: A Journal of Lesbian and Gay Studies* 5.4: 451–74.

Sang, Tze-lan (2003). *The Emerging Lesbian: Female Same-Sex Desire in Modern China*. Chicago: University of Chicago Press.

Sieber, Patricia (ed.) (2001). *Red Is Not the Only Color: Contemporary Chinese Fiction on Love and Sex between Women, Collected Stories*. Lanham, MD: Rowman and Littlefield.

Xiandai wenming huabao [Modern Civilization Pictorial] (2002). Special issue on lesbians and gays (January).

SANG TZE-LAN

Leung Ping-kwan

(Liang Bingjun; a.k.a. Ye Si)

b. 1948, Guangdong

Poet, writer, professor

After receiving a bilingual education in Hong Kong, Leung Ping-kwan received a PhD in the USA. He is Professor of Chinese at Lingnan University in Hong Kong. He is a poet, writer and critic, interested in all aspects of culture, including photography and cinema. His first publications were translations of foreign literature in the 1970s. In both his poems and his stories, Leung expresses his doubts, hesitations, wanderings and sensitive

curiosity, all through objective landscapes as well as through the ordinary things of daily life. One of his books of poetry is entitled *Dongxi* (which can be translated as either 'Things' or 'East–West', 2000). *Islands and Continents (Dao yü dalu*, 1987) figures the many moods of the protagonist, who travels in his memories through the years and to various places, including mainland China, the USA and, of course, Hong Kong. His contributions as a researcher of Hong Kong culture are considered of major importance; see especially his book *Hong Kong Culture (Xianggang wenhua*, 1995). Because Leung often feels that life and its cultural expression in Hong Kong are too narrow, he likes to collaborate with artists in experimental ways: for example, with the photographer Lee Ka-sing, he published *Foodscape (Shishi diyu zhi*) in 1997.

Further reading

Leung, Ping-kwan (1992). *City at the End of Time (Xingxiang Xianggang)*. Trans. Gordon T. Osing. Hong Kong: Twilight Books Company, University of Hong Kong [bilingual edition of poems].

—— (2001). *Iles et continents*. Trans. Annie Curien. Paris: Gallimard.

—— (2002). *Travelling with a Bitter Melon (Dai yimei kugua luxing)*. Trans. Martha P. Y. Cheung. Hong Kong: Asia 2000 [bilingual edition of poetry].

ANNIE CURIEN

Li, culture of

Approximately 1.2 million Li live in seven counties and two cities along the Wanquan River and among the Wuzhi mountains in the island province of Hainan. The region is abundant in minerals and tropical crops. The Li are closely related to the Zhuang, Bouyei, Dong and Tai (Dai) ethnic groups (see **Zhuang, culture of**; **Bouyei (Buyi), culture of**; **Dong, culture of**; **Tai (Dai), culture of**), whose languages the Li language resembles. Though a Roman script for the Li's spoken language was introduced, Han Chinese characters are common. The Li dwell in boat-shaped thatched bamboo houses. They farm and fish, and like to eat roast meat or pickled meat mixed with rice and wild herbs. Arica is a favourite, especially among women because the juice dyes their lips red. The Li are heavy smokers and drinkers, but they are also known for their knowledge of herbal medicine and their effective remedies for snakebite and rabies. They make their own clothes of cotton and flax, spinning, weaving, dyeing and sewing. They keep a calendar according to a twelve-day cycle, with each day named after an animal, similar to the twelve earthly branches used by the Han Chinese. On 3 March, the Li celebrate the 'Love Festival' to honour their ancestral couple, an occasion for offering sacrifices and holding singing, dancing and sports competitions. Of course, young people also try to find love on that day. As the Chinese government wants Hainan Island to develop tourism, the Li are making use of their location and traditions as well as tropical resources to attract large groups of tourists and investors from home and abroad.

HELEN XIAOYAN WU

Li Hong

b. 1967, Beijing

Video documentarist

The first woman in the **New Documentary Movement**, Li Hong brings a unique delicate sensitivity to her work. She deals with intimate psychological details, excerpting silent tragedies from the mundane, which may explain why her total output is still relatively modest. Li studied at the Beijing Broadcasting Institute (1986–90). Her first and most famous piece, *Out of Phoenixbridge* (*Hui dao Fenghuangqiao*, 1997), adopts a first-person, confidential tone to recount her encounter with four young women from the small village of Phoenixbridge in Anhui province who have come to Beijing to work as domestic workers or street vendors for minimum wages. Gradually the piece refocuses on one of the women, follows her back to the village and takes a melancholy look at the social, familial and psychological forces that may drive a young girl, once full of hopes, into leaving home.

Dancing with Myself (*He ziji tiaowu*, 2002) is made of small snippets of life that Li captures almost on the sly, but always with the warm collaboration of her subjects. In a public park, a beautiful laid-off waitress teaches dance to an odd group of 'ordinary people'; in a hospital boiler room, a middle-aged man speaks of his sexual longings, while a pigeon lands by him; in the kitchen of a cramped working-class apartment, a young woman, whose husband is in jail, raises her son alone, while bickering with a vengeful sister-in-law.

BÉRÉNICE REYNAUD

Li Jie

(né Lu Weimin)

b. 1955, Shanghai

Literary critic

Li Jie is one of the most original and fearless voices in contemporary criticism. Li Jie graduated with a BA in Chinese literature from Shanghai Normal University in 1982, and then studied under Qian Gurong, a famed scholar of modern Chinese literature and a strong advocate of 'literary humanism' (*wenxue shi renxue*) at East China Normal University in Shanghai. He received an MA from this university in 1987 and taught there until 1998, when he was dismissed for political reasons. Li Jie now resides in New York and works as an independent writer, editor and Chinese teacher.

In the 1980s, Li Jie was an untiring defender of **avant-garde/experimental literature** (*xianfeng xiaoshuo*). With passion and conviction, he wrote a series of influential essays touting its stylistic innovations as well as its uninhibited display of human desires. In the 1990s, Li Jie became a maverick cultural critic. His prolific writings were published in the five-volume set *A Collection of Li Jie's Writings on Thought and Culture* (*Li Jie sixiang wenhua wenji*, 1998). This well-received collection shows Li Jie as a phenomenal thinker and critic, his razor-sharp pen traversing literature, history, aesthetics, philosophy, the cult of Mao, and 'Redology' (*Hongxue*: the study of the novel *Dream of the Red Chamber*), all the while exposing various myths and untruths that shackle the individual spirit.

Li Jie is a rare combination of classical humanist and postmodern radical.

DIAN LI

Li Longyun

b. 1948, Beijing

Huaju (spoken-drama) playwright

A notable Chinese playwright since the 1980s, Li was born and grew up in the south district of Beijing. Just as other city students of his generation, he joined in the construction of rural villages during the **Cultural Revolution**. After spending ten years in northeast China (Manchuria), he was admitted to the Chinese Department in Heilongjiang University in 1978. His first play, *There Used to be Such a Small Courtyard* (*Youzhe yang yige xiaoyuan*) aroused national attention when it debuted in 1979. Because of this piece, Li was able to enrol in the Chinese Department as a graduate student that same year. Upon graduation he entered the **Beijing People's Art Theatre** as a professional playwright in 1982. In his most influential plays, 'Small-Well' Lane (*Xiaojing hutong*) and *Wasteland and Man* (*Huangyuan yü ren*), Li sought a poetic style in realistic spoken drama (**Huaju**). 'Small-Well' Lane, which was praised as a sequel to Lao She's *Teahouse*, describes the daily life of the common inhabitants of 'Small-Well' Lane from the eve of Liberation through the early 1980s, without any focus on plot or character. *Wasteland and Man* was Li's introspective recollection of over ten years of life in northeast China and a tragedy arising between the young intellectuals and their instructor in the ways of rural life. By blurring theatrical space–time and creating poetic beauty out of a wasteland, this piece revealed the universality that transcends the particularistic backdrop of the Cultural Revolution. Li's other major plays are: *The Yuanmingyuan is Near Here* (*Zheli bu yuan shi Yuanmingyuan*), *Under Zheng Hongqi* (*Zheng Hongqi xia*), *A Myriad of Twinkling Lights* (*Wanjia denghuo*), and *Jiao wo yishengge, wo hui leiluo ruyu* (shortened to *Jiao wo yishengge* on its second run, English translation 'When You Call Me Big Brother').

LI JIWEN

Li Qingxi

b. 1951, Shanghai

Literary critic

Active especially in the 1980s, Li Qingxi is a critic and writer known for his challenge to the literary principles and practices promoted in China between the 1950s and 1970s. Li Qingxi went to work in the 'great northern wilderness' after finishing his junior secondary education. He graduated from the Department of Chinese Language and Literature of the University of Heilongjiang in 1982. He has had experience working both as a cadre and an editor, and is now engaged in literary writing and criticism in Hangzhou.

The Modernity of Literature (*Wenxue de dangdaixing*), a collection of critical articles, represents his work in literary criticism. In the context of a long-standing opposition to Western modernism in the PRC, these articles, of which most were published in the mid 1980s, inspired people to rethink the virtues of Western modernist literature and theory, especially the work of Joyce, Eliot, Hemingway, the New Critics and the structuralists. He emphasizes the independent awareness of critics and the stylistic quality of critical writing. Another characteristic of Li's criticism is its emphasis on traditional Chinese literary theory and technique. Li's own literary writing encompasses different genres, including poems and fiction. He likes *biji xiaoshuo*, a traditional genre of literary sketches. His serial fiction, *Notes of the World* (*Renjian biji*), to which Li tried to apply modern narrative techniques, attracted an audience in the 1980s.

YANG LAN

Li Rui

b. 1949, Beijing

Writer

A writer of the **Root-seeking school** (*Xungen pai*), Li Rui began publishing fiction in 1974 when he was a 'sent-down youth' (*zhiqing*) in the area of the Luliang mountains in Shanxi province. He did not make his name, however, until the publication of *Deep Earth* (*Houtu*, 1988), a collection of eighteen short stories. In a concise style, Li blends his sympathy with a careful depiction of the helplessness and stagnation of peasant life against an austere landscape. Li's first novel, *Silver City* (*Old Site*; *Jiuzhi*, 1993), is a gripping family saga based on his father's experience as an underground Communist, and the latter's tragic death in a cadre school. Li's preoccupation with peasant life continued in his second and third novels, *No-Wind Tree* (*Wufeng zhishu*, 1996) and *No Clouds for Ten Thousand Miles* (*Wanli wuyun*, 1998). In both novels, Li uses peasants as first-person narrators, letting them speak their minds and feelings, creating a polyphonic effect. The skilful use of dialect further adds an authentic flavour. Because Li sets his rural stories in the area of the Luliang mountains, some critics associate him with the 'Potato School' (*Shanyaodan pai*), which began in the mid 1940s and flourished in the 1950s with writers such as Zhao Shuli (1906–70) and Ma Feng (1922–). Actually, Li's peasant tales are more concerned with the gloomy aspects of rural China than with the optimistic depiction of socialist construction characteristic of this school.

See also: xiafang, xiaxiang

Further reading

Li, Rui (1997). *Silver City*. Trans. Howard Goldblatt. New York: Henry Holt.

—— (1995). 'Sham Marriage'. Trans. Schaeffer and Wang. In Howard Goldblatt (ed.), *Chairman Mao Would Not Be Amused: Fiction from Today's China*. New York: Grove, 90–8.

—— (1990). 'Electing a Thief'. Trans. J. Kinkley. In Helen Siu (ed.), *Furrows: Peasants, Intellectuals, and the State: Stories and Histories From Modern China*. Stanford: Stanford University Press, 201–11.

LEUNG LAIFONG

Li Shan

b. 1942, Lanxi, Heilongjiang

Painter

A prominent representative of the art current known as **Political Pop**, Li Shan graduated in 1968 from the Shanghai Drama Institute and was subsequently hired as a member of the faculty. Li Shan rose to fame in the early 1990s for his remakes of Mao portraits in which contrasting photorealist headshots of Mao's face are juxtaposed against a monochrome background, most often painted in a garish hue of blue, pink or green. The lack of depth and the surface quality of his paintings directly mimic the graphic effect of posters. The series, which was begun in the late 1980s, is entitled *Rouge* and applies the colour pink or fuchsia to some detail in every image – a colour normally associated with folk art such as New Year's prints or with the make-up of actors in Chinese opera, signifying a low cultural status or a frivolous character. The artist's declared intent is to 'vulgarize' an image normally considered to be the epitome of high political status by smearing it with a colour immediately recognizable as 'low' and suggesting 'queer' undertones in the image of China's strong man. Li Shan has declared that his use of Mao's image is an attempt to provide 'a comment on his own personal history, not on the history of China'. His interventions are in fact a comment on his own personal memories of the time when Mao's portrait was a ubiquitous reality.

Among many exhibitions, Li Shan participated in the **China Avant-Garde** in Beijing (1989); the 45th Venice Biennale (1993); the 22nd Sao Paulo International Biennial (1994) and 'Inside/Out, New Chinese Art' at the Asia Society in New York and MoMA in San Francisco (1998–9). He lives and works in Shanghai.

Further reading

Dal Lago, Francesca (1999). 'Personal Mao: Reshaping an Icon in Contemporary Chinese Art'. *Art Journal* 2 (Summer): 46–59.

Doran, Valerie C. (ed.) (1993). *China's New Art, Post-1989*. Hong Kong: Hanart T Z Gallery.

Gao, Minglu (ed.) (1998). *Inside Out – New Chinese Art*. Berkley: University of California Press.

FRANCESCA DAL LAGO

Li Shaobai

b. 1931, Taihe, Anhui

Film historian, theorist

Li started work in film distribution in Chongqing in 1950, after a year in the PLA. He published his first film criticism in 1951 and moved to the publicity department of the Film Distribution Corporation in Beijing in 1954. In 1957 he joined the research section of the China Filmmakers' Association. Li began work in 1958, with Cheng Jihua and Xing Zuwen, on the *History of the Development of Chinese Film* (*Zhongguo dianying fazhan shi*). Published in 1963 as a two-volume study of film in China before 1949, the book was the object of **Cultural Revolution** criticism. Li was assigned to the China Art Research Institute (Zhongguo yishu yanjiuyuan) in 1973, where he took charge of the establishment of a specialist film institute and a film department in the graduate programme. He remained at the institute in Beijing until his retirement. His articles appeared in *Film Art* (*Dianying yishu*) and *Contemporary Film* (*Dangdai dianying*). Li's books include *Film History and Theory* (*Dianying lishi yu lilun*, 1991) and *Filmic Explorations: Film History and Theory* (*Yingxin tanze: dianying lishi yu lilun*, 2000), both of which collect his articles from journals and elsewhere. His writings on theory tended to evince a Marxist orthodoxy. In his historical studies on films of the 1930s, however, a more concrete and careful analysis of contemporary materials informed his conclusions. This work in particular influenced younger generations of film researchers, many of whom he supervised at the China Art Research Institute.

See also: film criticism; Cheng Jihua

Further reading

Semsel, George (1999). 'Cheng Jihua and Li Shaobai, Pioneers in Chinese Film Studies:

Interview II'. *Asian Cinema* 10.2 (Spring/ Summer): 90–5.

PAUL CLARK

Li Shenzhi

b. 1923, Wuxi, Jiangsu

Journalist, liberal intellectual

Li Shenzhi joined the Chinese Communist Party in 1942 and worked at the *Xinhua Daily*, the official newspaper of the Chinese Communist Party, as a news reporter and editor. From 1949 until he was purged as a Rightist in 1958, he was the head of the International Department of the **Xinhua News Agency** and the chief editor *of Cankao ziliao* and **Cankao xiaoxi** – daily newspapers providing foreign news and information for Party and government officials, the former being circulated only among the top Party leaders. During this period, he also served as Zhou Enlai's secretary and advisor on foreign affairs. In 1956 he advocated 'great democracy (*da minzhu*)' that would expand people's political rights and allow them a voice in important decisions that concerned the interests of the whole nation. However, his views were criticized by Mao Zedong as heretical, and he himself was purged as a Rightist during the Anti-Rightist campaign. He was rehabilitated in 1978 when Deng Xiaoping wanted him to serve as his advisor on his trip to the United States. Between 1983 and 1993, Li was the Vice President of the **Chinese Academy of Social Sciences**. He encouraged intellectuals to study the new problems that had surfaced in the course of economic reform and also advocated immediate political reform to ensure the continuity and success of the economic and social transformations. He was sympathetic to the 1989 democratic movement and wrote articles and gave speeches criticizing the government crackdown. After his retirement in 1993, Li has continued to devote himself to political critique and theoretical reflection and has written several widely circulated articles discussing the urgency and necessity of political reform.

LIU CHANG

Li Tuo

b. 1939, Hohhot, Inner Mongolia

Writer, critic

Writer of fiction and film and television scripts, critic, theorist, editor of scholarly works and popular magazines – even these creative accomplishments fail to capture what Li Tuo is: a life-long 'man of letters'. Versed in both classical poetry and the street humour of Beijing, he may cite Bazin or Barthes in a piece of high theory only to dissect the glamour of McDonald's or fashion advertising. An industrial worker for twenty-some years, he is still proud of his working-class roots while enjoying Steven Spielberg and John **Woo**. The rich experiences of modern China have produced this self-taught intellectual, undisciplined by academic norms, with finicky taste and a rugged stomach.

Representative of his early theoretical contributions is the essay 'The Modernization of the Film Language' (1979), co-authored with **Zhang Nuanxin**. It was the pioneering piece in a six-year discussion of Chinese cinema and film theory which had a significant impact on the **Fifth Generation** of directors. In fiction writing he is best known for the narrative innovation of 'Granny Qi' (*Qi nainai*) and 'The Fall' (*Chuizhi luoti*). He has mentored young writers like **Yu Hua** and **Su Tong** and edited several influential volumes of fiction. The past decade saw him rewriting the complex history of Maoism as a form of discursive practice that is embodied in the works of Ding Ling and **Wang Zengqi**. While responsible for two book series on popular cultural studies, he also launched *Horizons* (*Shijie*) in 2000, the theoretical flagship of the **New Left**.

Further reading

Li, Tuo (1993). 'The New Vitality in Modern Chinese'. In W. Larson and Anne Wedell-Wedellsborg (eds), *Inside Out: Modern and Post-modernism in Chinese Literary Culture*. Aarhus, Denmark: Aarhus University Press, 65–77.

—— (2000). 'Resistance to Modernity – Reflections on China's Literary Criticism in the 1980s'. Trans. Marshall McArthur and Han Chen. In Pang-yuan Chi and David Wang (eds), *Chinese*

Literature in the Second Half of the Twentieth Century: A Critical Survey. Bloomington: Indiana University Press, 137–45.

YUE GANG

Li Xianting

b. 1949, Jilin

Art critic, curator

Li Xianting graduated from the Department of Traditional Chinese Ink Painting at the **Central Academy of Fine Arts** in Beijing (1978). Between 1978 and 1980 he was one of the editors of the magazine **Meishu** [Fine Arts], through which he became one of the first outspoken supporters of the **Stars** group. In the years 1985–9 he co-founded and edited the tabloid newspaper **Zhongguo meishubao** [Fine Arts in China], the first to be dedicated solely to contemporary experimental art. In 1989 he participated to the organization of **China Avant-Garde** in Beijing with **Gao Minglu**. After the 1989 events and the progressive harassment he received from the authorities, Li quit all positions and began to work as a freelance critic and curator. He is responsible for coining the names of the art currents **Political Pop** and **Cynical Realism**. In 1993, together with **Chang Tsong-zung**, he curated the exhibition 'China New Art Post '89' in Hong Kong (see **China's New Art, Post-89 (Hong Kong, 1993) and China Avant-Garde (Berlin, 1993)**) and helped organize the first large-scale participation of Chinese artists at the Venice Biennale in the same year. Since the second half of the 1990s, Li has been curating several exhibitions, mostly in Beijing, that attempt to scrutinize and interpret the incessantly emerging new artistic trends produced by the tumultuous transformations that are criss-crossing Chinese society. These exhibitions include: 'Model from the Masses' and 'Gaudy Life', with **Liao Wen**, at the Beijing Art Museum and Wan Fung Art Gallery in Beijing (1996); 'Oh La La Kitsch', also with Liao Wen, at the Teda Contemporary Art Museum in Tianjin (1999); and 'Prayer Beads and Brush Strokes' in Beijing (2003). Li Xianting (affectionately called Lao Li by most of his friends) lives and works in Tongxian on the outskirts of Beijing.

Further reading

Li, Xianting (1980). 'Guanyu "Xingxing' meizhan"'
[On the 'Stars' Exhibition]. *Meishu* [Fine Arts]
(8–9 March).
—— (1993). 'Major Trends in the Development of
Contemporary Chinese Art'. In Valerie C.
Doran (ed.), *China's New Art, Post-1989* (exhibition
catalogue). Hong Kong: Hanart T Z Gallery,
x–xxii.
—— (1994). 'The Imprisoned Heart: Ideology in
an Age of Consumption'. *ART and AsiaPacific* 1.2
(April): 25–30.
—— (2000). *Zhongyaode bu shi yishu* [What Matters is
Not Art]. Nanjing: Jiangsu meishu chubanshe.
—— (2001). 'The Pluralistic Look of Chinese
Contemporary Art since the mid-1990s'. In John
Clark (ed.), *Chinese Art at the End of the Millennium*.
Hong Kong: New Media, 72–80.
—— (2001). 'Some More Thoughts on the *raison
d'être* of Gaudy Art'. In John Clark (ed.), *Chinese
Art at the End of the Millennium*. Hong Kong: New
Media, 81–8.
—— (ed.) (2003). *Curator's Notes on Prayer Beads and
Brush Strokes*. Beijing: Beijing Tokyo Art Projects.

FRANCESCA DAL LAGO

Li Xiaoshan

b. 1957, Nanjing

Art critic

A daring art critic mainly preoccupied with the
future of *Zhongguohua* (traditional Chinese painting),
Li Xiaoshan's provocative article, 'My Opinion
about Contemporary Chinese Painting' (*Dangdai
zhongguohua zhi wojian*, 1985) raised a roar in the art
world for its nihilistic evaluation of the old generation of established painters and the statement
that traditional Chinese painting had reached a
dead end and belonged in museums. A follow-up
article, 'The Preconditions for the Existence of
Chinese Painting' (*Zhongguohua cunzai de qianti*),
challenged the possibility of a conscious effort at
innovation, stating that tradition could be continued but that all artificially imposed efforts to
modernize it were misguided. A heated nationwide

debate ensued, and numerous conferences were
organized on the theme. A collection of the resulting articles were published in a volume bearing the
title of his original essay. Li's *A History of Modern
Chinese Painting* (*Zhongguo xiandai huihuashi*, 1986),
written with Zhang Shaoxia, though too often
defined by notions of historical determinism, was
remarkable for its daring tones, such as the open
condemnation of the Soviet choice in art during
the 1950s.

Li's writing on art is unusually frank and overtly
critical. He has a knack for picking weak points in
current discourse and prodding them mercilessly,
unafraid of offending peers and elders alike. In the
1990s he continued to write on *Zhongguohua*, often
entering in open disagreement with other critics for
their lack of apparent appreciation of tradition and
their indifference to *Zhongguohua*'s most fundamental values such as ink and brushwork.

Further reading

Li, Xiaoshan (1985). '*Dangdai zhongguohua zhi wo jian*'
[My Opinion on Contemporary Chinese Paint-
ing]. *Jiangsu huakan* 7.
Li, Xiaoshan and Zhang, Zhaoxia (1986). *Zhongguo
xiandai huihuashi* [A History of Modern Chinese
Painting]. Nanjing: Jiangsu meishu chubanshe.
Welsh, Eduardo (1999). 'Negotiating Culture. The
Discourse of Art and Position of the Artist in
1980s China'. Unpublished PhD diss. The
School of Oriental and African Languages,
93–101 (translation, 197–202).
Zhang, Xuecheng (ed.) (1990). *Dangdai zhongguohua
zhi wo jian taolunji* [My Opinion on Contemporary
Chinese Painting. Collected Essays]. Nanjing:
Jiangsu meishu chubanshe.

EDUARDO WELSH

Li Yongbin

b. 1963, Beijing

Video artist

A self-taught artist, Li Yongbin explored different
visual terrains before coming to video-making in
1995 with *Come Round*, a private work that records

the inexorable disappearance at dawn of his late mother's face projected on a tree. In 1996 he participated in the video exhibition 'Image and Phenomena' in Hangzhou with *Face I*, a one-channel one-angle piece, motionless and unedited – elements that characterize most of his video oeuvre to date. In this work his own face is portrayed with a hypnotic but intense gaze and with features blurred by the superimposition of the slide-projection of an old woman's face.

The portrayal of an unsettled identity has always been Li's main concern, but this has never been so powerfully manifested as in his *Face* series (1996–2002), each showing a face, most often the artist's, being either replaced by another (*Face IX, X*), or distorted by rippling water (*Face II*), or consumed by melting heat (*Face III*), or pieced together through broken mirrors but never fully recovered (*Face VIII*). The face comes and goes like an apparition (*Face V, VII*), sinks into a pool (*Face VI*) or reveals itself only to vanish within the city seen through a window (*Face IV*). These works, simple yet strong, silent yet eloquent, poetic yet disturbing, were exhibited in 'Another Long March' at Breda in 1997 and at the Melbourne Biennial in 1999. In 2000, the Palais des Beaux-Arts in Brussels hosted Li Yongbing's solo show. Recently, Li has begun a new series, entitled *Sun*, of which the first work was exhibited in Beijing in 2002.

Further reading

Driessen, Chris and van Mierlo, Heidi (eds) (1997). *Another Long March: Chinese Conceptual and Installation Art in the Nineties* (exhibition catalogue). Breda: Fundament Foundation.

Li, Yongbin (2000). 'An Ever-lasting Memory'. *Gargarin* 1.2 and 16. Belgium: GAGAvzw.

Tang, Di (2000). 'Who Am I? Face': Li Yongbin's Reflection on Mankind'. In *Li Yongbin* (exhibition catalogue). Brussels: Palais des Beaux-Arts. (Also in Wu Hung (ed.) (2001). *Chinese Art at the Crossroads: Between Past and Future, Between East and West*. Hong Kong: New Art Media, 339–43.)

TANG DI

Li Yongping

b. 1947, Malaysia

Taiwan writer

Li Yongping was born in Malaysia, but subsequently moved to Taiwan for schooling. After coming to Washington University in St Louis for graduate school, Li returned to Taiwan to teach Chinese literature and focus on writing. Like fellow modernist **Wang Wenxing**, Li's fiction often lacks a clear linear plot, and seeks to push the expressive potential of the Chinese language to its limits.

Li's first major novel was *The Jiling Chronicles* (*Jiling chunqiu*, 1986). The novel revolves around the ways in which various inhabitants of a remote village respond to a rape and a resulting suicide, which take place before the novel actually begins. This act of sexual violence provides the narrative pivot around which the rest of the novel is structured. The reader is presented with a Roshomon-style, kaleidoscopic view of mutually intersecting narrative lines, each of which provides an additional perspective on the rape and the cycles of retribution which follow. Li's next two novels were *The Eagle Haidong Qing* (*Haidong qing*, 1992) and *Zhu Ling's Adventures in Wonderland* (*Zhu Ling manyou xianjing*, 1998). Totalling almost 1,500 pages, these two novels have overlapping characters and themes. The protagonists include Jin Wu, a Chinese literature professor who has returned to Taiwan after a stay in the United States, and Zhu Ling, the young girl with whom he develops an intimate friendship. Against a backdrop of rampant paedophilia and social corruption, Jin Wu sees Zhu Ling as a unique point of purity in an otherwise decadent social landscape. In this way, Li reflects on Taiwan's socio-political status and its conflicted relationship with the mainland.

Further reading

Li, Yongping (2003). *The Jiling Chronicles*. Trans. Howard Goldblatt and Sylvia Li-Chun Lin. New York: Columbia University Press.

Rojas, Carlos (1998). 'Paternities and Expatriatisms: Li Yongping's *Zhu Ling Manyou Xianjing* and the Politics of Rupture'. *Tamkang Review* 29.2: 22–44.

CARLOS ROJAS

Li Yuru

(neé Li Shuzhen)

b. 1923, Beijing

Xiqu (sung-drama/opera) actress

Jingju (Peking opera) actress Li Yuru is one of the few living masters of the *dan* role, or female character type. Her best known repertoire includes *The Red Plum-Blossom Pavilion* (*Hongmei ge*, 1959), *Marriage Associated with the Chest* (*Gui zhong yuan*, 1958), *Princes Baihua* (*Baihua gongzhu*, 1960) and *The Royal Concubine Mei* (*Mei Fei*, 1961). She started writing in the 1980s, and has published: *Hatred and Raven Hair* (*Qingsi hen* 1983), a full-length Jingju play; *A Little Woman* (*Xiao nüren* 1996), a novel; and many columns in the **Xinmin Evening News** (*Xinmin wanbao*) and the *Wenhui Daily* (*Wenhui bao*).

In Jingju, women's roles were traditionally played by female impersonators. Li Yuru and her generation played an important part in the development of the genre as they transformed the *dan* into a role also played by females. When Li Yuru was nine, her family, which was descended from Manchu nobility, was living in dire poverty and sent her to study Jingju at the Chinese Theatre School (Zhonghua xiqu zhuanke xuexiao). She became a star at fourteen, and since that time a seventy-year stage career has continued through wars, political campaigns, the Cultural Revolution and the current radical economic reforms. On the basis of the solid and strict training she received as a child, and as a disciple of the greatest female impersonators (Mei Lanfang, Xun Huisheng, Cheng Yanqiu, Furongcao and Xiao Cuihua), Li has profound knowledge of different acting and singing schools. She specializes in both singing and acting, and has also formed her own repertoire and style. In 1979, she married Cao Yu, the most important playwright in twentieth-century Chinese spoken drama, and this brought new directions to her Jingju career.

LI RURU

Li Zehou

b. 1930, Hankou

Philosopher, intellectual

Li Zehou is arguably the most distinguished and influential modernist philosopher of the last fifty years and one of the very few intellectual figures whose work has acquired an audience outside China. His significance for contemporary Chinese is, like that of most exiled intellectuals, complex. This is a reflection of the troubling distance between present-day hedonistic excess and the 1980s **culture fever** in which his work first held sway over the Chinese imagination, as well as the complexity of Li's philosophy, variously characterized as neo-traditional, instrumentalist, romantic, historical materialist, Neo-Kantian, post-Marxist, Marxist–Confucian. He, like **Liu Zaifu**, advanced exceptionally creative readings of art, literature, philosophy in the creative urgency of the 1980s when it seemed that aesthetics offered the greatest prospect of redemption from China's post-Cultural Revolution morass.

Working within the conceptual dyadic framework of subjectivity and objectivity peculiar to historical materialism, but selectively drawing inspiration from the works of Kant, Hegel, Heidegger, Lukács, the Frankfurt School, Lacan, Piaget and Habermas, Li deepened the problematic of the self in post-revolutionary modernism, raising his neologism 'subjectality' (*zhutixing*) to a level of respectability and debate. With *zhutixing* he put forward a new conception of human nature, infusing the passive subject of the audience (*duifang*) of Mao's lectures on art at Yan'an with an assertive, sensuous, moral purpose, as he explained in a recent interview translated by John Zijiang Ding:

> It does not have the Western sense of 'subjectivity' (*zhuguan*). I feel rather we should use a new term 'subjectality' – even though there is no such word in the English – that means that a human person has the capacity of an active entity. *Zhutixing* is not a concept of epistemology; instead it implies that a human being is considered as a form of material, biological, and objective existence and an active capability in relation to the environment.

(Ding and Li Zehou 2002)

In refuting the passivity of the subject, as well as the Diamat Marxist status of its consciousness as mere mechanical reflection of the material world, Li engineered a revolution in the name of beauty and against state ideology that grounded human, as opposed to Promethean, agency in the conscious, historically conditioned, environmentally subsumed subject.

Born in Hankou but raised in Changsha, Hunan, Li graduated from **Peking University**'s philosophy department in 1954 and immediately assumed an appointment in the Institute of Philosophy at the **Chinese Academy of Sciences** in 1955, playing a prominent role in the founding of the journal *Zhexue yanjiu* [Studies in Philosophy]. He quickly entered the national currents of intellectual discourse in the aesthetic debates over socialist realism of 1956, publishing 'Lun meigan, mei he yishu' [On Aesthetic Feeling, Beauty, and Art] in *Zhexue yanjiu*, in which Li first put forward his key cultural-psychological concept of 'sedimentation' (*jidian*). For this essay, published in a tense atmosphere of literary politics dominated by attacks on the aesthetic theories of Zhu Guangqian by Cai Yi, he was branded a 'rightist' and, along with so many other intellectuals identified with Hu Feng's critique of establishment literature, consigned to a work camp in Hebei.

During this lengthy detention that continued through the Great Leap Forward and for two decades afterwards, Li wrote on an array of topics in aesthetics, history, philosophy and politics, including the *Studies on the Thought of Kang Youwei* (*Kang Youwei sixiang yanjiu*), *Literary Chats on Exile* (*Menwai wentan*), *Vertebrates and Prehistoric Humanity* (*Gu jizhu dongwu yu gu renlei*). With each publication he laid the foundation for 'a pragmatic philosophy of subjectality' (*zhutixing shijian zhexue*) that would release human agency from bondage to Maoist chiliasm and scientific determinism. However, it was not until 1979–81 that this radical re-conception of the subject achieved national notoriety and scholarly distinction with the publication of *Pipan zhexue de pipan: Kande shuping* [A Critique of Critical Philosophy: A Review of Kant], a work he laboured to complete while undergoing another labour detention at a 'May Seventh Cadre School' during the Cultural Revolution.

In this book he argued that a proper understanding of the dialectical mechanisms of Marx's epistemology was to be found in the 1844 Manuscripts, especially the discussion of estranged labour and species being, and, more importantly, in a return to Kant's three *Critiques*, where one finds the most effective articulation of subjectivity, will and moral duty. This 'return to Kant' was an 1980s phenomenon and extended, as well, to Japan, where Kojin Karatani's *Transcritique: On Kant and Marx* (trans. Sabu Kohso. Cambridge: MIT Press, 2003) read Kant's first *Critique* to disclose the ethical foundations of socialism. The greatest interpretive advantage of Kant's *Critique of Pure Reason* was its assertion, in Li's words, 'that human knowledge is the result of the interactions of sensibility and understanding', and further, according to Kant, these interactions 'perhaps spring from a common, but to us unknown, root'. The perennial Kantian dilemma of ought/is occasioned by the 'thing in itself' is overcome in a single, materialist gesture as Li asserts that this common root is the primary practice of tool-making and tool-using by the human subject whose transcendental aesthetic and analytic are encased in the cultural-psychological formation (*wenhua xinli jiegou*), the locus of human reasoning. In essence Li, by his own admission, was giving Kant's philosophy 'a materialistic foundation' by recovering Marx's emphatic definition of humanity as *homo faber*, or what Li calls *renhua ziran* (humanized nature).

Understanding as he did that the greatest challenge to the modern subject was meaningful context, Li worked from his dynamic conception of a sensuous moral reasoning in action to narrate the evolution of the cultural sedimentation that formed the contemporary subject. *The Path of Beauty* (*Meide licheng*, 1981), a survey intellectual history of cultural production from the Neolithic to the Qing dynasty, is his best-known work which takes art as an evolving transcript of the psychological condition of the subject's being in the world. His activist reconception of the aesthetic of human feeling and material form recalled the work of Suzanne Langer and was an attempt to bring Chinese thought into dialogue with world philosophy on terms that were Chinese, while also giving the experience of the Chinese subject a historicized, activist role through the neologism of sedimentation.

Because of this creative reinvention of an activist self grounded in material moral being and beyond politics, Li was one of the most inspirational intellectual figures of China's 'enlightenment' (*qimeng*) period of 1984–9, who argued that enlightenment had begun in the 1890s but was extinguished by the dense fervour of national political parties and the fever of national salvation. At this critical second juncture of enlightenment with its unusual receptiveness to Western philosophy, especially aesthetics, Li made much of this fortuitous East/West confluence in his oft-quoted *xiti zhong yong* (Western substance, Chinese application), offering a myth of humans as agents of craft to a generation looking beyond the meaningless, overpoliticized bromides of state ideology. In *The Path of Beauty* and the subsequent *Four Lectures on Aesthetics* (*Meixue sijiang*) Li advanced a uniquely creative but not altogether consistent fusion of continental rationalism, medieval aesthetics, Marxism and traditional Chinese moral philosophy, insisting that science and technology were things of beauty, to be admired by the aesthete as products of human moral striving that might bring about the reconciliation of heaven and man (*tianren heyi*).

The political urgency of his revolutionary overcoming of the traditional subject was not overcome in the violent government repression of democracy activists in 1989, for throughout the 1990s Li's conception of human agency as relatively independent of, but always acting on, the material world, became even more relevant. Yet for this original philosophical contribution, he was spurned. After the Beijing Massacre of 1989, his works were proscribed and Li was made the focus of yet another state-driven criticism campaign against 'bourgeois liberalism' that ran until 1992 when he ultimately bade farewell to the Communist Party and his allegiance to the state in a famous essay (written with Liu Zaifu) *Gaobie geming* [Farewell to the Revolution]. He was prohibited from leaving the country until 1992, at which time, with the assistance of Professor Howard Goldblatt and the Chiang Ching-kuo Foundation, Li (along his colleague Liu Zaifu and his daughter) was brought to the University of Colorado at Boulder, where he owns a home and has nominally resided ever since, occasionally assuming teaching and research appointments at Swarthmore, Colorado College, and the City University of Hong Kong. Most recently he returned to China and for the 2003–4

academic year served as an Honorary Professor at the City University of Hong Kong.

He continues to work in the space between Western and Chinese philosophy and recently published *Lunyu jindu* [A Contemporary Reading of the Selected Sayings (of Kongzi)], an effort to draw the classical text into modern philosophical discourse through interpretive and aphoristic annotation and *Meide sijiang* [Four Lectures on Beauty]. For his use of the four-character phrase, 'reconciliation of heaven and man' (*tianren heyi*), of Song-Ming Neo-Confucian metaphysics to describe the optimal future architecture of human practice, many consider him to be a 'Confucian' and his work a conservative twenty-first-century recuperation of this ethos; thus it is that many New Confucians (see **New Confucianism**) count him among their number, in spite of his conceptual indebtedness to laws of economic development and his valorization of technology.

His work, with its fluid formulations of humanizing nature and naturalizing humanity and his repeated emphasis on the 'Chinese mind', does resemble the essentialist, value orientation advocacy of the New Confucians with their insistence on Confucianism's facilitation of the Chinese modern. In this way, by cauterizing the self-inflicted nationalist wounds of fifty years of socialist experimentation, Li's aesthetic reconstruction of affirmative human agency offers yet another philosophical means of reconciling past and present, West and China, while neglecting to consider how the pragmatic rationality (*shiyong lixing*) of the nation's productive forces of subjectality may be exercised at the grievous expense of the world we inhabit, leaving us buried in the sediment of our industrial humanization of nature.

Bibliography

Li, Zehou (1979). *Pipan zhexue de pipan: Kande shuping* [A Critique of Critical Philosophy: A Review of Kant]. Beijing: Renmin chubanshe.
—— (1981). *Meide licheng* [The Path of Beauty]. Beijing: Renmin chubanshe.
—— (1985). *Li Zehou zhexue meixue wenxuan* [The Collected Essays on Philosophy and Aesthetics of Li Zehou]. Changsha: Hunan renmin chubanshe.

—— (1987). *Zou wo ziji de lu* [Taking My Own Path]. Beijing: Sanlian shudian.

—— (1988). *Huaxia meixue* [Chinese Aesthetics]. Hong Kong: Sanlian shudian.

—— (1988). 'Ting Li Zehou, Liu Shu-hsien tan *He Shang*' [Listening to Li Zehou and Liu Shu-hsien discussing *River Elegy*]. *Jiushi niandai* 227 (December): 88–91.

—— (1990). *Wode zhexue tigang* [An Outline of My Philosophy]. Taipei: Fengyun shidai chuban gongsi.

—— (1998). *Meide sijiang* [Four Lectures on Beauty]. Hong Kong: Sanlin.

—— (1998). *Lunyu jindu* [A Contemporary Reading of the Selected Sayings (of Kongzi)] Hong Kong: Tiandi tushu youxian gongsi.

Further reading

Ban, Wang (1997). *The Sublime Figure of History: Aesthetics and Politics in Twentieth-Century China.* Stanford: Stanford University Press.

Cheek, Timothy (ed.) (1999). '*Subjectality': Li Zehou and his Critical Analysis of Chinese Thought.* Special issue of *Philosophy East and West* 49.2 (April): 113–84.

Ding, John Zijiang and Li, Zehou (2002). 'Chinese Aesthetics from a Post-Marxist and Confucian Perspective'. In Cheng Chung-ying and Nicholas Bunnin (eds), *Contemporary Chinese Philosophy*. London: Blackwell, 246–59.

Gu, Xin (1996). 'Subjectivity, Modernity, and Chinese Hegelian Marxism: A Study of Li Zehou's Philosophical Ideas from a Comparative Perspective'. *Philosophy East and West* 46.2 (April): 205–45.

Jing, Wan (1996). *High Culture Fever: Politics, Aesthetics and Ideology in Deng's China.* Berkeley: University of California Press.

Liu, Kang (2000). *Aesthetics and Marxism: Chinese Aesthetic Marxists and their Western Contemporaries.* Durham: Duke University Press.

Woei, Lien Chong (2002). 'Philosophy in an Age of Crisis. Three Thinkers in Post-Cultural Revolution China: Li Zehou, Liu Xiaobo and Liu Xiaofeng,'. In *idem* (ed.), *China's Great Proletarian Cultural Revolution: Master Narratives and Post-Mao Counternarratives.* Lanham, MD: Rowman and Littlefield, 215–54.

LIONEL M. JENSEN

Liao Wen

b. 1961, Beijing

Curator, art critic

Graduating from the Department of Chinese Language and Literature of Beijing Normal University in 1984, Liao Wen became editor of the weekly newspaper **Zhongguo meishubao** [Fine Arts in China] in 1986 and an independent critic after the newspaper's closure in 1989. While working as an assistant to exhibitions curated by **Li Xianting** which mainly involved male artists, she began questioning women's role in the art world. The search for female expressions in art practice resulted in two exhibitions that she curated in Beijing: 'Woman's Approach to Chinese Contemporary Art' (1995) and 'Woman and Flower' (1997). In the companion essays, Liao Wen analysed the gender issue concerning women artists. She considered the direct importation of a woman's subtle and intimate feelings into artwork to be a 'silent subversion' and 'undercurrent of turmoil' which reflects, in Liao's view, the awakening of a female consciousness unfiltered and uncontaminated by public *language* codes set by men. Between 1996 and 1997 she published a book, *Feminism as a Method* (*Nüxingzhuyi zuowei fangshi*). In 1998, as curator of the TEDA Contemporary Art Museum in Tianjin, she organized its inaugural exhibition, 'Personal Touch' (*Liangxing pingtai*). In 1999, with funding from the Asian Cultural Council, Liao Wen spent six months in the USA, where she visited numerous women artists, and in 2000 she published a collection of her interviews, *No More Good Girls – Interviews with American Feminist Artists* (*Bu zai you hao nühai le – Meiguo nüxing zhuyi yishujia fangtanlu*).

See also: feminism; language and gender; Lin Tianmiao

Further reading

Liao, Wen (1995). 'Jingji de dianfu, qianxing de shandong: Zhongguo dangdai yishu zhong de nüxing fangshi' [The Silent Subversion, the Turmoil Beneath – Woman's Approach to Chinese Contemporary Art]. In *Woman's*

Approach to Chinese Contemporary Art (exhibition catalogue). Beijing: Beijing Art Museum.

Liao, Wen (1998). *Nüxing zhuyi zuowei fangshi* [Feminism as a Method]. Changchun: Jilin Fine Arts Publishing.

—— (2000). *Buzai you hao nühai le – meiguo nüxing zhuyi yishujia fangtan lu* [No More Good Girls. Interviews with American Feminist Artists]. Taipei: Artist Publishing.

TANG DI

liberalism

The liberalism currently active in the Chinese intellectual arena was embryonic in the late 1970s, intertwined with democratic and populist appeals. As it rapidly developed in the early 1990s in parallel with the country's accelerating globalization, liberalism shifted from the calls for freedom and democracy of the 1980s to an alternative democracy associated with the market economy. Despite their growing influence, however, liberals did not speak publicly until the middle of the decade.

From the outset there were two types of 1990s liberalism – an 'economic liberalism' and a 'political liberalism'. The former, represented by Lin Yifu, Fan Gang, Zhang Shuguang and others, advocated the speedy and thorough development of the marketing economy as prelude to political reform. The latter, represented by **Li Shenzhi** and Liu Junning, stressed the necessity of an urgent reform of democratic constitution in addition to solving the problem of **human rights**. These advocates, albeit with differences, were influenced by Western classical liberalism, especially that of Friedrich A. Hayek.

In the late 1990s, a heated debate occurred between the liberals and those representing the so-called **New Left**. After that, liberalism became more popular and more diversified, and there emerged the 'New Liberalism' of **Xu Jilin**, Wang Dingding and others. Grounded in John Rawls' *A Theory of Justice*, they tried to combine liberalism with republicanism, and held that China needed to realize not only freedom and democracy but also economic justice. Theories of and debates over liberalism were published in newspapers and magazines such as *Twentieth-First Century* (**Ershiyi shiji**, Hong Kong), *Res publica* (*Gonggong luncong*, Beijing), *The Open Times* (*Kaifang shidai*, Canton) and **Nanfang Weekend** (*Nanfang zhoumo*, Canton).

See also: intellectuals and academics

Further reading

Fewsmith, Joseph (2001). *China Since Tiananmen: The Politics of Transition*. Cambridge: Cambridge University Press, 122–31.

Zhu, Xueqin (2004). 'For a Chinese Liberalism'. In Wang Chaohua (ed.), *One China, Many Paths*. London: Verso, 86–107.

CHEN JIANHUA

Lin, Brigitte

(neé Lin Qingxin/Lam Ching Ha, a.k.a. Venus Lin)

b. 1954, Taipei, Taiwan

Film actress

Brigitte Lin started her career playing romantic heroines before reaching international fame through her transgender parts in **martial arts films**. She had made more than a hundred films in Taiwan and Hong Kong before her marriage in 1994. Lin first appeared as a troubled teenager in Song Cunshou's *Outside the Window* (*Chuanwai*, 1972), and was soon working in Hong Kong. In Patrick Tam Kar-ming's *Love Massacre* (*Aisha*, 1981), she still wears flowery dresses, but wields a knife against a killer. Ann **Hui** cast her as a liberated woman in *Starry is the Night* (*Jinye xingguang canlan*, 1988), and **Yim Ho** gave her the part of writer Eileen Chang (Zhang, Ailing) in his fictionalized biopic, *Red Dust* (*Gungun hongchen*, 1990).

In 1986, **Tsui Hark** dressed her in men's clothes for *Peking Opera Blues* (*Dao ma dan*). An icon was born. Lin was mesmerizing as the castrated villain, Asia the Invincible, in parts II and III of the *Swordsman* (*Xiao'ao jianghu*) produced by Tsui in 1992 and 1993. Other martial arts movies followed, notably Ronny Yu Yan-tai's *The Bride with White*

Hair (*Baifa monü zhuan*) series in 1992 and 1993. Her most fascinating, enigmatic parts are in two movies directed by **Wong Kar-wai** in 1994: the dual gender-switching role of Yin and Yang in *Ashes of Time* (*Dongxie* xidu) and the drug-runner with a blonde wig in *Chungking Express* (*Chongqing senlin*).

See also: cinema in Taiwan

BÉRÉNICE REYNAUD

Lin Bai

b. 1958, Beiliu, Guangxi

Writer

Lin Bai made a name for herself in the late 1980s as an experimental writer known for intense intro-spection and a daring exploration of female experience. Although she began writing as a poet in 1977 and continues to publish poetry, she is pri-marily known as a fiction writer whose work bears strong autobiographical features. Many of her novels and novellas are based on her childhood growing up in the 1960s in the small southwestern town of Beiliu. Combining intense emotional energy and a vivid sense of place, these stories spring from personal memory, which the author explores as a fresh source of literary inspiration against a background of drab mass culture and the falsehood of collective history. Some of her fiction explores strong friendship between women with homoerotic overtones.

Her novel, *One Person's Battle* (*Yigeren de zhanzheng*), stirred up considerable controversy when published in 1994. Based on her own life as a young writer moving from an outlying provincial town to the cultural centre of Beijing, the novel is noted for its highly individualized treatment of a woman's pro-fessional and private life. Its frank portrayal of female bodily experience marked a new depth in the exploration of forbidden territory in the post-Mao cultural scene. Her other works include the novels *Bullet through an Apple* (*Zidan chuanguo pingguo*) and *Glass Beetle* (*Boli chung*), and the novellas *Water in a Glass* (*Pingzhong zhi shui*) and *Chair in the Corridor* (*Huilang zhi yi*).

HU YING

Lin Tianmiao

b. 1961, Taiyuan, Shanxi

Installation artist

Graduating from the Fine Art Department of Capital Normal University in 1984, Lin spent nearly ten years in New York before establishing herself in Beijing in 1994. The following year, in a solo show at her home, she presented *The Prolifera-tion of Thread Winding* (*Chan de kuosan*), in which she used, for the first time, cotton thread. It involved a bed pierced through the middle by myriads of needles, each holding the loose end of a ball of thread. These balls, in turn, spread in the thousands on the floor like a bride's gown, while a monitor, placed at the pillow's height, recorded the perpetual winding of thread, a labour recalling certain moments Lin spent with her mother as a child. Taking these childhood memories as the point of departure, Lin created a striking contrast between the white, soft and spreading quality of the thread and the black, sharp and piercing quality of the needle, and made a strong statement with respect to a woman's role. She has continued her research with thread. In the monotonous and enslaving process of winding (thread), hundreds of objects – from kitchenware and utensils to trees and bicycles – are transformed into something deprived of their original function. When presented as installations, their dialectic quality is reinforced by the theatri-cality of display. Her work has been shown in exhibitions worldwide, including the 5th Istanbul Biennial, 'Another Long March' (Breda), 'Crack in the Continent' (Tokyo, 1997) and 'Inside/Out' (New York, 1998). Lin's recent works include the surgical treatment of portrait photographs with thread, balls, knots and plaits of thread.

Further reading

Dal Lago, Francesca (1998). 'Against the Tide' *ART AsiaPacific* 17 (January): 100.

Gao, Minglu (ed.) (1998). *Inside Out New Chinese Art*. Berkeley: University of California Press.

Pollack, Barbara (2004). 'Chinese Photography: Beyond Stereotypes'. *Artnews* 103.2 (February): 98–103.

Smith, Karen (2001). 'Lin Tianmiao'. In Wu Hong (ed.), *Chinese Art at the Crossroads*. Hong Kong: New Art Media Limited, 310–13.

Werner, Chris, Qiu, Ping and Pitzen, Marianne (eds) (1998). *Die Hälfte des Himmels – Chinesische Künstlerinnen*, Bonn: Verlag Frauen Museum, 76–9.

TANG DI

Lin Zhaohua

b. 1 July 1936, Tianjin

Theatre director (Huaju and Xiqu)

Lin Zhaohua is renowned for his pioneering experimental work in **Huaju** (spoken drama). Vice President of the prestigious **Beijing People's Art Theatre** (BPAT) from 1984 until 1998, Lin remains a major artistic voice. He was a leading figure in the 'exploration' theatre movement in the 1980s, introducing a variety of non-illusionistic styles and techniques in defiance of socialist realism, the established rule for Huaju. Lin's experimental productions of **Gao Xingjian**'s *Absolute Signal*, **Bus Stop**, and **Wild Man** and of **Liu Jingyun**'s *Second Uncle Doggie's Nirvana* earned him national acclaim. Lin's production of *Absolute Signal* was staged in a small rehearsal room at BPAT in 1982 and initiated the **Little Theatre** movement of the post-Mao era. In 1989, Lin established one of the earliest independent theatre groups, popularly called the 'Lin Zhaohua Studio'.

Over a distinguished thirty-year career, Lin has directed an extraordinary body of work covering a broad range of styles, from naturalism to the avant-garde: **Guo Shixing**'s three plays, *Bird Man*, *Chess Man* and *Fish Man*, and a famed revival of Lao She's *Teahouse*. His avant-garde work, continuing to spark controversy, includes *Orphan of China*, *Hamlet*, *Emperor Romulus*, *Faust*, *Chess Man*, *Three Sisters*, *Waiting for Godot* and *Richard III*, with his most frequent collaborator the stage designer Yi Liming. Lin's eclectic approach encompasses a mix of realistic and anti-illusionistic techniques: the aesthetics of **Xiqu** (sung drama/opera) and other indigenous performance forms; anti-realistic Western techniques, expressionism, symbolism, and Theatre of the Absurd; non-naturalistic acting and staging; new dynamics in the actor–audience relationship; a synthesis of the real and abstract.

In addition to spoken drama, Lin has also directed traditional Xiqu, such as **Jingju** (Peking opera) and Huiju (the ancestor of Jingju; see **Huju**). Like his spoken-drama works, these works carried an experimental character. His Jingju works include: *Shanhua*, *Turandot*, *The Hunchback Prime-Minister, Parts I–VI (Zaixiang Liuluoguo, 1–6)* and *Huiju hujia shibapai*. Among these, the six parts of *The Hunchback Prime-Minister* were well received both at the box office and in art circles, and as a result have been staged every year since 2000 during the Chinese **New Year Festival**.

Further reading

Lin, Kehuan (ed.) (1992). *Lin Zhaohua daoyan yishu* [Lin Zhaohua's Art of Direction]. Harbin: Northern Literature Arts Press.

BETTINA S. ENTELL

literacy (and illiteracy)

The PRC has given a great deal of attention to eradicating illiteracy. Many campaigns have been directed towards this objective, including one beginning in 1994. Some census figures indicate the progress made. The 1964 census showed 38.1 per cent of all people aged twelve and over were illiterate or semi-literate, by which was meant knowing few or no written words. By 1982, the rate had dropped to 23.5 per cent. However, the 1990 census changed the age boundary from twelve to fifteen (and older), in which case the rate of illiteracy or semi-literacy in the entire population had now fallen from 22.81 per cent in 1982 to 15.88 per cent in 1990. The figure for the 2000 census among people aged fifteen and older was 6.72 per cent.

The improvement between 1990 and 2000 is due to the 1994 literacy campaign and to the deaths of old people, who show comparatively high rates of illiteracy. Yet some have suggested that the figures are too low, for example arguing that many older people claimed literacy falsely.

The United Nations Development Programme (UNDP) had a figure of adult literacy in China in 1990 of only 73.3 per cent (UNDP 1993: 136), moving up to 83.5 per cent in 1999 (UNDP 2001). In other words, illiteracy and semi-literacy was 26.7 per cent in 1990 and 16.5 per cent in 1999, both figures very much higher than those given in the Chinese census, but decreasing at about the same rate. The UNDP (2001) defines literacy as 'the percentage of people aged fifteen and above who can, with understanding, both read and write a short, simple statement on their everyday life'. This certainly reflects a considerably higher demand than the census, which regards illiteracy and semi-literacy as knowing few or no written words.

Furthermore, there are inequalities in literacy. For instance, about 70 per cent of illiterates or semi-literates in China are female. Rates are comparatively high in the border areas, other than in the northeast, and among most ethnic minorities (but see **Koreans, culture of**). A serious problem is the 'new illiterates'. The term refers to young people who leave school because of good employment opportunities, which means that it is a problem particular to the current period of reform. In March 1990, the Chinese representative at a UNESCO Conference on Education held in Bangkok disclosed that there were altogether 2.7 million 'new illiterates', accounting for 3 to 4 per cent of all school-age children. This is more than half the number who throw off illiteracy every year. The announcement of the 1994 literacy campaign revealed that about 1 million 'new illiterates' were being added every year.

Further reading

Hayhoe, R. (ed.) (1992). *Education and Modernization: The Chinese Experience*. Oxford: Pergamon Press.

United Nations Development Programme (UNDP) (1993). *Human Development Report, 1993*. New York, Oxford: Oxford University Press.

—— (2001). *Human Development Report 2001: Making New Technologies Work for Human Development*. New York, Oxford: Oxford University Press.

COLIN MACKERRAS

literary awards

China's main literary prizes are named after famous twentieth-century writers: Lu Xun (Zhou Shuren, 1881–1936), Mao Dun (Shen Yanbing, 1896–1981), Lao She (Shu Qingchun, 1898–1966), Bing Xin (Xie Wanying, 1900–99), Chen Bochui (1906–97) and Cao Yu (Wan Jiabao, 1910–96). The Lu Xun Literary Prize (LXLP) and the Mao Dun Literary Prize (MDLP) are awarded by the Chinese Writers' Association (CWA) approximately every four years. By 2001, the LXPL had been awarded twice to one hundred works. It also awards seven additional prizes for short stories, novellas, reportage literature, **poetry**, prose and essays, literary criticism, and the Rainbow Prize for National Excellent Literary Translations. By 2000, the MDLP had been awarded five times to twenty novels. Controversies over the fairness of both contests have delayed the presentation of the awards. In addition, the CWA runs annual nationwide competitions in short stories, novellas, reportage literature and new poetry, respectively. The Lao She Literary Prize granted the literary prize (to four short-story writers) for the first time in 2000, and to seventeen literary works in October 2002. The Bing Xin Prize is mainly for children's literature, as is the Chen Bochui Prize. Other awards include: the Cao Yu Drama Literature Prize; the China Drama Literature Prize, which had been awarded twice by May 2002; the Plum Blossom Prize for Chinese Drama; the Xu Chi (1914–96) Reportage Literature Prize; and the Song Qingling (Mme Soong Ching-ling, 1890–1981) Literary Prize. Finally, there are many regional and other awards granted by **literary periodicals**.

See also: Alai; Liu Heng; Liu Xinwu; Shi Tiesheng; Tie Ning; Wang Anyi; Zhang Jie

[Note: the latest prize for Zhang Jie is the Lao She Literary Prize for her novel, *No Words (Wuzi)*, awarded in October 2003.]

HELEN XIAOYAN WU

literary periodicals

In comparison with Japan, France and even Russia, mainland China has a large number of literary periodicals. If we include academic journals of literary research as well as magazines of popular fiction, literary periodicals in 2001 numbered 346 while the number of all kinds of periodicals was 8,726.

Literary periodicals are often, though by no means exclusively, run by national literary associations, especially the Chinese Writers' Association, which is actually a ministry of the government, and the many provincial writers' associations, such as the Shanghai Writers' Association. The CWA, for example, runs *People's Literature* (*Renmin wenxue*: monthly, Beijing, established in October of 1949) and *Magazine of Poems* (*Shikan*: monthly, Beijing, established in January of 1957). Furthermore, almost every important literary publishing house has a literary periodical. Examples include: *October* (*Shiyue*: bimonthly, Beijing, established in August of 1978), *Prose* (*Sanwen*: monthly, Tianjing, established in January of 1980) and *Master* (*Dajia*: bimonthly, Kunming, established in January of 1994).

Most literary periodicals are of 32 mo and can be classified into two kinds: monthlies, with approximately 100,000 characters/issue, that include short stories, verse, prose and reviews; and bimonthlies, with approximately 250,000 characters/issue, that include not only the writings in short forms, but also novelettes, long reviews and even novels. Among the former, the best known are: *Shanghai Literature* (*Shanghai wenxue*: Shanghai, established in January of 1953), *Writer* (*Zuojia*: Changchun, established in July of 1983) and *Beijing Literature* (*Beijing wenxue*: Beijing, established in October of 1980). Among the latter, the most influential are: *Harvest* (*Shouhuo*: Shanghai, established in July of 1957), *Zhong Mountain* (**Zhongshan**: Nanjing, established in January of 1979), *Flower City* (*Huacheng*: Guangzhou, established in April of 1979), *The Present Age* (*Dangdai*: Beijing, established in June of 1979) and *Frontiers* (**Tianya**: Haikou, established in June of 1980).

Since the early 1990s, most literary periodicals have been in trouble because government financial support at all levels has been heavily reduced if not cut completely (while government oversight has not). As a result, the market of the literature periodicals has been greatly narrowed. Today a monthly usually prints fewer than 5,000 copies/issue, though the number may have been as high as 100,000 in the early 1980s. Only several periodicals can still attract a large number of subscribers: *Harvest*, for example, has more than 100,000 subscribers, while *Frontiers* has only 30,000. The magazines of popular fiction are exceptions, and here the market seems to be getting better and better. Strictly speaking, there are only five journals of literary criticism today, among which *Critique of Contemporary Writers* (*Dangdai zuojia pinglun*: bimonthly, Shenyang, established in January of 1984) is the best, although it produces only about 4,000 copies/issue.

See also: state control of media

Further reading

Kong, Shuyu (2002). 'Between a Rock and a Hard Place: Chinese Literary Journals in the Cultural Marketplace'. *Modern Chinese Literature and Culture* 14.1 (Spring): 93–144.

WANG XIAOMING

literature in dialect

Together with local opera and radio, the film industry adopted both Mandarin and local (sub-national) languages, but by the early 1970s in Taiwan and Hong Kong investment in these productions had all but vanished, while in the People's Republic the state put an end to the use of local languages in all but local radio and stage performances. In Hong Kong, however, investment in commercial broadcast television also fostered local language in print media as well as in broadcasting and film, distinguishing them from the press, which was dominated by editors from northern regions committed to standard Chinese. Although standard Chinese has remained the style of much of the print media in Hong Kong, the broadcast media writers did foster a distinctive youth culture writing in Cantonese. On Taiwan the New Cinema of the early 1980s revived the use of Taiwanese Southern-Min dialect film and fostered its use in poetry and fiction. In particular, Taiwan promoted the use of multiple dialects and multiple languages in film and later in television, an aesthetic that was also adopted in many Hong Kong films, suitable for texts devoted to a de-centred vision of cultural displacement among its characters. In the People's Republic, the use of local languages was adopted largely in stories of the historic past and in officially promoted themes that lent themselves to productions in local languages, such as accounts of entrepreneurs of the past or of urban renewal and relocation. The wave of Cantonese-language popular culture entering from Hong Kong also de-centred Mandarin writing styles, prompting both fiction and television productions in a variety of local languages. Film and television directors were also drawn to the use of local and multiple languages promoted in Taiwan and Hong Kong productions.

See also: dialects

EDWARD GUNN

literature in Taiwan

The 1980s, a decade which lingered between the aftermath of the Nativist Literature debate of 1977 and the lifting of martial law in 1987, saw the emergence of the 'trilogy' (*daho xiaoshuo*) in Taiwanese literature. Li Qiao's *Cold Night: A Trilogy* (*Hanye sanbuqu*, 1981) is the pioneering work in this regard. It is a family saga that recounts the story of Hakka people who endure the hardships of working the mountainous land under Japanese colonial rule. The 1990s witnessed two other outstanding achievements in the trilogy form. One is Bai Dongfan's *The Waves Sifting the Sand* (*Langtaosha*, 1991), which tells the story of three families of Minnan and Hakka origin who are forced to live in the 'diaspora' and struggle to survive in America, Japan and the Philippines during WWII. The other is Shi Shuqing's *Hong Kong: A Trilogy* (*Xianggang sanbuqu*, 1993–7), in which the female protagonist, a prostitute from a small village in Guangdong, builds up a prosperous family in high-class Hong Kong society through her connections with English and Chinese lovers, who are compared to the island city that has persisted under both English and Chinese

rules. The themes of postcolonialism and feminism are intricately interwoven in the narrative. The emergence of the trilogy is a prominent marker of the preoccupation with the theme of historical revisionism that still inspires the fictional imagination at the beginning of the twenty-first century.

It is also worth noting that although political fiction had existed before the lifting of martial law, it is in the post-martial law period that women writers such as Shi Shuqing and Li Ang, as well as aboriginal writers, have begun to participate actively in political discourse through their writing. Chen Yingzhen, one of the major supporters of nativism during the 1970s, continued in the 1980s to write works of anti-imperialism such as the short-story series *Washington Building* (*Huashengdun dalou*, 1978–82) and the article, 'Irony of Ironies: On "Associations of Third World Literature"' (*Fanfeng de fanfeng: ping 'disan shijie wenxue de lianxiang'*, 1984). In her short-story series, men usually lose their sense of self-identity in the pursuit of worldly success in international corporations, whereas women, serving as mediators between the material world and the spiritual world (represented by the homeland), are those through whom the 'truth' of the stories is revealed: the colonized need to return to the homeland in order to find their true selves.

Chen, who created a postcolonial fable of China (and Taiwan) versus the West in the short stories, would find followers among the next generation of writers, such as Shi Shuqing, Li Ang and Lin Yaode, despite the fact that since the 1980s the nativist movement has taken on a radicalism that opposes China's cultural as well as political sovereignty. In Li Ang's *Lost Garden* (*Miyuan*, 1991), the problem of political identity is mixed up with that of gender identity: the violence of colonial governments experienced by native Taiwanese is constantly equated to male sexual violence experienced by the female body. When the female protagonist manages to buy back her father's garden with her husband's money, the message seems to be that the colonized in their struggle to survive will learn to gain favour, and even to benefit from the established colonial order. In Lin Yaode's *1947 Lilium Formosanum* (*1947 Gaosha baihe*, 1990) Taiwan Island is seen as a stage on which different colonial peoples (the Dutch, the Japanese) play distinct roles in shaping the Taiwanese consciousness experienced by the aboriginal people, the real natives of the island. The message is that cultural hybridity will become a source of strength and will distinguish the colonized from their oppressors, while the colonized, having lost their sense of identity, will in the long run discover the true meaning of their existence, which is symbolized by the bearskin sack that the old chief passes on to his grandson, who has been wandering like a lost dog in the cities.

Whereas the writers mentioned above intend to reconstruct Taiwanese history through a postcolonial point of view, there are other writers who demonstrate their concern with national history through metafictional techniques that have marked them off as an aesthetically distinguished group. They explore the relationship between fictional reality and the reality of the world outside of fiction, while putting into relief the impossibility of arriving at truth either in fiction or in the real world. Another characteristic element of their stories is the intention of challenging the grand récit of national narratives with personal accounts (the petit récit) told by the characters. In Zhang Dachun's 'The General's Tombstone' (*Jiangjun bei*, 1986), an old general, suffering from Alzheimer's disease, is totally unable to grasp present reality and lives in his own imaginative world of the past and the future. All the main characters, who try to reconstruct the old general's life, appear with versions that contradict each other. In the end, not even the general himself is sure whether he was as great as people say. The conclusion seems to be that history is a lie. In **Zhu Tianwen**'s *Notes of a Desolate Man* (*Huangren shouji*, 1994), the gay narrator, who keeps random accounts of his relationships with eight men, indulges in his own meandering thoughts and turns the narrative into a disorganized pastiche of eruptive language, sensual pleasure, philosophical rumination and an encyclopedic itemization of knowledge. There are scarcely the minimum elements of a story, and even the concept of the novel as a genre is questioned. At the same time a homosexual erotic utopia is constructed as a challenge to the heterosexual order of life. In Zhu Tianxin's 'Ancient City' (*Gudu*, 1997), the woman narrator is a first-generation Taiwanese mainlander who has lost faith in the Nationalist

government together with what it has taught about modern Chinese history for decades. She uses the Taipei of the Japanese occupation, when there were no environmental problems, as a critique of the present Taipei under the Democratic Progressive Party government. Resorting to personal memory to tell her own version of Taiwanese history, she challenges the authority of the mainstream version of history, namely the newly emergent DPP version of history, which has tried to de-legitimize personal accounts of history such as hers.

The nativist trends of the 1980s and 1990s also witnessed the emergence of political poetry, which took as its themes Taiwanese colonial history and identity issues. Liu Kexiang's 'Posthumous Sons' (*Yifuzi*, 1983) highlights the multiple languages used in Taiwan – Classical Chinese, Japanese, the Minnan dialect, and Mandarin – to reflect the multicultural reality of Taiwan and her groping struggle for a sense of self-identity. Chen Li's 'No Cacuminal Sounds Movement' (*Bu juanshe yundong*, 1995) proudly points out that the Taiwanese pronunciation of Mandarin is marked off by its lack of cacuminal or retroflex sounds, and this speech habit is a result of cultural difference and historical development. The renowned poet Yang Mu (a.k.a. Yeh Shan), who started to write poetry in the 1950s, also wrote political poems during the 1980s. 'Someone Asks Me About Justice and Righteousness' (*Youren wenwuo gongli he zhengyi de wenti*, 1984) is a narrative poem about a man whose father is a mainland soldier who emigrated to Taiwan after the war and married a Taiwanese, his mother. Abandoned by his father when he was a child, he feels deprived and discriminated against all through his adult life. On the other hand, Yang Mu also continues to write in the neo-classical mode embraced by poets in the 1960s. There are invocations to past laureates such as Samuel Taylor Coleridge in 'Frost at Midnight' (*Shuangye zuo*, 1985), Xie Tiao (464–99) in 'Variations on a Passenger's Mood' (*Kexin bianzou*, 1992), and the author of *Sir Gawain and the Green Knight* in 'An Unoccupied Seat' (*Quezuo*, 1998). The female poet Xia Yu has been a conspicuous presence since the 1980s. Her witty language and originality of thought often make her poems pleasant surprises. Works such as 'Poet's

Day' (*Shirenjie*, 1982) and 'The Ripest, Rankest, and Juiciest Summer Ever' (*Zuishou zuilan de xiatian*, 1999) are marked by everyday language closely connected with popular culture.

See also: Bai Xianyong; cinema in Taiwan; Li Yongping; music in Taiwan; performing arts in Taiwan; Ouyang Zi; Qiong Yao; Wang Wenxing; Wang Zhenhe; Wu He

Further reading

Chou, Ying-hsiung and Liu, Chi-hui (ed.) (2000). *Wenxueshi, houzhimin yü houxiandai* [Literary History, Postcolonialism, and Postmodernism]. Taipei: Maitian Chubanshe.

Peng, Hsiao-yen (2000). *Lishi henduo loudong: cong Zhang Wuo-jun dao Li Ang* [There Are Many Loopholes in History: From Zhang Wuo-jun to Li Ang]. Taipei: Institute of Chinese Literature and Philosophy, Academia Sinica.

—— (2001). 'Literature and Historical Reconstruction: A Post-Martial Law Phenomenon'. In *Weiquan tizhi de bianqian: jieyanhou de Taiwan* [The Change of an Authoritarian Regime: Taiwan in the Post-Martial Law Era]. Taipei: Institute of Taiwanese History, Academia Sinica, 471–95.

Wang, David Der-wei (2002). *Kuashiji fenghua: dangdai xiaoshuo ershi jia* [Turn of the Century Splendour: Twenty Contemporary Fiction Writers). Taipei: Maitian chubanshe.

Yeh, Michelle and Malmqvist, N. G. D. (eds) (2001). *Frontier Taiwan: An Anthology of Modern Chinese Poetry*. New York: Columbia University Press.

PENG HSIAO-YEN

little emperors

social concept

The term 'little emperors' (*xiaohuangdi*) has been coined to describe the spoiled children raised since the implementation of the **one-child policy** in 1979. Unlike previous generations, the 'onlies' (or, 'singletons') have no siblings to share and compete with and are easily the undivided focus of the so-called '4–2–1 indulgence': four

grandparents and two parents indulging one child. In urban areas, in particular, where the one-child policy is most strictly enforced and where income has risen most sharply, parents are showering their only children with love and money. Thus, the one-child generation has expanded the market for not only brand-named toys and clothes but also imported baby foods that are believed to be highly nutritious.

Many of the parents of the only children were born and raised during the **Cultural Revolution** (1966–76) and had themselves lost their childhood, which reinforced their desire to live their dreams through their children. When the hopes of the family are entrusted to a single child, some parents are driven to raise overachievers by pushing them in academic performance and in extracurricular classes. Thus, the 'onlies' experience a 'pressure–pleasure paradox' whereby they are simultaneously being pushed and spoiled by the same parents. Recent research shows that the spoiled-child syndrome is not as bad as expected, but that still there are differences between only children and children with siblings. The 'onlies' have higher academic achievements and are taller and heavier. They display a stronger sense of self-respect and confidence, but are more egocentric and inconsiderate. It is also likely that they will be less able and willing to care for the elderly, thus potentially breaking a Chinese tradition that children support parents in their old age.

Further reading

Jun, Jing (ed.) (2000). *Feeding China's Little Emperors: Food, Children, and Social Change*. Stanford: Stanford University Press.

C. CINDY FAN

Little Flock

Protestant sect

The Little Flock (*Xiaoqun*, also known as the Assembly Hall, or *Juhuisuo*) is an indigenous Protestant sect that emerged in the early decades of the twentieth century, along with the **Jesus**

Family and the **True Jesus Church**. The group was founded by a group of Chinese Protestants who combined the premillennialist doctrines of the Brethren sect, charismatic practices in the Holiness tradition, and a strong antagonism towards foreign mission organizations. Led by the charismatic Ni Tuoshen (Watchman Nee, 1903–72), the Little Flock organized a nationwide network of highly associational 'assemblies' which was headquartered in Shanghai. By the mid 1940s, the group claimed a membership of over 70,000, organized into some 700 assemblies.

The strongly anti-Communist Ni was jailed as a counter-revolutionary in 1952, and he remained imprisoned until his death in 1972. Officials in the **Three-Self Patriotic Movement (TSPM)** repeatedly denounced the Little Flock, resulting in the arrest of many of its leaders. One of the group's lieutenants, Li Changshou (Witness Lee), migrated to Taiwan, where he established a splinter group, the Local Church (see **Local Church (and 'shouters')**), based in part on Little Flock traditions and in part on Li's own subjective doctrines. He later migrated to Anaheim, California, where the church's global headquarters remain today. Local Church missionaries returned to the mainland after 1978, primarily targeting Little Flock congregations. Although the state quickly banned the Local Church, dubbing it the 'shouter sect' (*huhan pai*) after its charismatic worship practices, the group expanded rapidly, attracting over 200,000 adherents by the mid 1980s. Together, the traditional Little Flock and the Local Church claim over 800,000 adherents today.

Further reading

Deng, Zhaoming (2001). 'Indigenous Chinese Pentecostal Denominations'. *China Study Journal* 16.3: 5–22.

JASON KINDOPP

Little Theatre

(*Xiao juchang*)

'Little Theatre' in China, often characterized by experimentation and avant-garde work, refers to **Huaju** (spoken drama) staged in small theatres or non-theatre spaces with 50–400 seats. Following early twentieth-century Little Theatre movements in the West, it was first introduced into China in the 1920s and was called *aimei de xiju*, a transliteration of 'amateur theatre'. The movement became widespread during the May Fourth Period, but soon subsided during the struggles between the CCP and KMT. 'Little Theatre' (*xiao juchang*, or *hei xiazi/*'black box') was resurrected in August 1982 when **Gao Xingjian**'s *Absolute Signal*, directed by Lin Zhaohua, was staged in a small rehearsal hall at the **Beijing People's Art Theatre**. In late 1982, the Shanghai Youth Art Theatre presented *Mother's Song*, directed by Hu Weimin, in its small rehearsal room. The popular success of both plays led to the rise of 'Little Theatre' performances. By the mid 1980s, Huaju troupes in China's major cities were staging productions in newly created 'Little Theatre' spaces.

'Little Theatre' has been flourishing since the 1990s, with nationwide festivals generating hundreds of productions. This is a direct reflection of socio-economic change during China's transformation from a planned to market economy. Previously, Soviet-style 1,200–1,500 seat theatres were the standard. Responding to financial pressures brought on by diminishing state subsidies, 'Little Theatre' has lower production costs and serves the needs of an audience with greater individuality and a larger choice of entertainment venues. The intimacy of 'Little Theatre' is changing performance and staging techniques by engendering direct actor–audience communication and encouraging audience participation.

See also: Zhang Xian

Further reading

Tian, Benxiang (ed.) (1996). *Xin shiqi xiju lunshu* [Discourse on Theatre of the New Era] Beijing: Cultural Art Press.

Yu, Shiaoling S. (ed.) (1996). *Chinese Drama After the Cultural Revolution, 1979–1989: An Anthology.* New York: Edwin Mellen Press.

LIN WEI-YÜ AND BETTINA S. ENTELL

Chinese Studies (*Haiwai Zhongguo yanjiu congshu*); director of the 'Women and Gender Studies Project' sponsored by the Ford Foundation, and director of the 'China Scholarship Forum' at the National Library.

CHEN JIANHUA

Liu Dong

b. 1951

Cultural critic

In 1966, Liu Dong's schooling was stopped when the Cultural Revolution began. In 1970 he began to attend a middle school, yet in the following year he was assigned to work in a foundry factory as a 'child labourer' of sixteen. In these years, Liu Dong studied the high-school and university courses by himself. From 1977 he entered **Nanjing University**, majoring in philosophy. After graduation in 1982 he taught at Zhejiang and Nanjing Universities. In 1985 Liu Dong started his graduate study at the **Chinese Academy of Social Sciences** and obtained the PhD degree in Chinese Aesthetics in 1990. Afterwards he worked in the Academy. In 2000 he was appointed a professor at **Peking University**. His research interests have focused on comparative aesthetics and world sinology (the study of China). He has written *The Western Aesthetics of Ugliness* (*Xifang de chouxue*, 1986), *Descriptions of the Floating World* (*Fushihui*, 1996), *Self-Selected Essays of Liu Dong* (*Liu Dong zixuan ji*, 1997), and *Theory and Heart-Mind* (*Lilun yü xinzhi*, 2001). His publications also include book-length translations of Max Weber, Wittgenstein, Kant and Rousseau.

In the 1990s, Liu Dong was one of the most active organizers of 'non-official scholarship' (***minjian*** *xueshu*) in China. In 1991, along with Yan Buke, Liang Zhiping, and **Chen Pingyuan**, he lobbied for the **Research Institute for National Studies** (Guoxue yanjiusuo, originally called the Institute of Chinese Culture), a non-official academic organization that has aimed at reviving Chinese scholarly and historiographic tradition through solid and independent studies. Currently, Liu Dong is editor of the journal *China Scholarship* (*Zhongguo xueshu*) and the *Serial of Overseas*

Liu Heng

(né Liu Guangjun)

b. 1954, Beijing

Writer

Liu Heng, a novelist, short-story writer and scriptwriter, is the most important representative of 'new realistic writing' (*xin xieshi*), which emerged in the middle of the 1980s. Originally a blue-collar worker, Liu Heng first came to public notice with his short story 'Dogshit Food' (*Gouri de liangshi*, 1985). The realistic depiction of scatological and psychological details of rural life has since become a hallmark of new realism in China. His fictional characters come from all walks of life, but most of his stories fashion a drama of depraved existence. In his later novels he evinces challenging characterizations of human vulnerability: *Black Snow* (*Hei de xue*) provides an interesting perception of an ex-convict's life in a changing Beijing; *Green River Daydreams* (*Canghe bairimeng*) is a remarkable portrayal of the manifold psychological intrigues of a feudal family at the turn of the last century.

Liu Heng's film scripts also have become central pieces in Chinese movie history. His novella *Fuxi Fuxi* was turned into the notable film *Judou*; *Black Snow* was rewritten as the movie *Ben mingnian*. He also wrote the scripts for *Qiuju Goes to Court* (*Qiuju da guansi*) and *White Snow* (*Bai de xue*), almost all the above directed by **Zhang Yimou**. Liu Heng is also noted for the extremely popular TV series, *The Happy Life of Garrulous Zhang Damin* (*Pinzui Zhang Damin de xingfu shenghuo*), a twenty-part series about an ordinary family trying to survive in a changing Beijing.

Further reading

Linder, B. (1999). 'Alienation and the Motif of the Unlived Life in Liu Heng's Fiction'. *Journal of Modern Literature in Chinese* 2.2: 119–48.

Liu, Heng (1993). *Black Snow*. Trans. Howard Goldblatt. New York: Atlantic Monthly Press.

—— (1995). 'Dogshit Food'. Trans. Sabina Knight. In Joseph S. M. Lau and Howard Goldblatt (eds), *Columbia Anthology of Modern Chinese Literature*, 416–28.

Visser, Robin (2002). 'Privacy and its Ill Effects in Post-Mao Urban Fiction'. In Bonnie S. McDougall and Anders Hansson (eds), *Chinese Concepts of Privacy*. Leiden: Brill, 171–94.

BIRGIT LINDER

Liu Huan

b. 1963, Tianjin

Pop singer, professor

Liu Huan is one of China's pioneers of popular music. Since his unofficial public debut in 1985, he has become a major pop star. Liu Huan graduated in 1985 from the French Department of the Institute of International Relations in Beijing. He is a professor of the History of Western Music at the Foreign Economic and Trade University in Beijing; singing is a sideline. A singing contest at the French Embassy launched his career.

Liu Huan's steady stream of theme songs for popular television series made him a household name. He has sustained his popularity for over a decade, and is considered the top pop singer of the 1990s. He is best known for the theme songs for **Beijingers in New York** (*Beijingren zai Niuyue*), 'Sunrise East, Rain West' (*Dongbian richu, xibian yu*), 'The Third Legion' (*Disan juntuan*), *Hu Xueyan*, and 'Heroes' Song' (*Haohan ge*). Liu also sang the theme song for the 11th Asian Games, entitled 'The Strong Wind of Asia' (*Yazhou xiongfeng*), and has sung at other international sporting events. He has won both popular and critical acclaim with his songs, including the

National Top Ten Young Composers Appraisal awards for composition and performance in 1990. The theme song for *Beijingers in New York* held the top spot on the radio charts for ten weeks, and won the award for Best Annual Film and TV Music. In 1999, he was recognized by the CCTV–MTV music awards as Best Male Artist.

MARGARET BAPTIST WAN

Liu Jingyun

(a.k.a. Jing Yun)

b. 1938, Hebei

Spoken-drama playwright, theatre director and administrator

Liu Jingyun was one of the most influential playwrights in China during the 1980s. He was educated at **Peking University** in the Chinese Department. After 1963, he became a high school teacher and local official in the suburbs of Beijing and he continued to write until 1982, when he entered the **Beijing People's Art Theatre** as a professional playwright. **Uncle Doggie's Nirvana** (*Gou'er ye niepan*, 1986) is his representative work, sketching the many transitions arising in China's rural villages, and is considered one of the 'great harvests' of contemporary **Huaju** (spoken drama). Liu excels at combining historical context and modern theatrical narration, making his plays both educational and entertaining. His other celebrated works, *Ruan Lingyu* and *Boundless Love* (*Fonyue wobian*) are contemporary takes on the true stories of two great Chinese artists – Ruan Lingyuan (1910–35) and Li Yu (1610–80). Liu was nominated for the vice presidency of the Beijing People's Art Theatre in 1992 and led the reform of its artistic guiding principles, which were now to publicize the main themes of art and advocate variety and innovation. In Liu's term of office, the policy was confirmed that the Beijing People's Art Theatre should perform not only famous classics but also experimental plays. Liu's other well-known play is entitled *The Man Who Carries a Stele on His Back* (*Beibei* ren). Liu is currently the president of the Beijing People's Art Theatre.

LI JIWEN

Liu Miaomiao

b. 1962, Ningxia

Film director

In 1978, Liu enrolled in the **Beijing Film Academy** at age sixteen. The youngest graduate from the directing class, she was assigned a position in the Xiaoxiang Film Studio in Hunan, where she has remained since 1982. *Women on the Long March* (*Mati shengsui*, 1987) is an important early work that focuses on eight female Red Army soldiers who struggle to survive as they try to join up with the main force. Although the film takes the Long March as its subject, a female perspective and nondramatic approach subordinate the narrative to a consideration of women's issues. After this serious experiment, Liu became involved in television and commercial film production. Memories of her childhood and her close attachment to relatives in rural China inspired a second serious work, *The Gossiper* (*Zazuizi*, 1992). The film centres on the figure of a lonely child and explores the alienation between adults and children. After her treatment of broadly humanistic themes from a personal and gendered perspective, Liu next turned to the genre of family melodrama. *The Family Feud* (*Jiachou*, 1994) unveils the inner conflicts of a family running a pawnshop. Viewers learn how the female maid is forced to become the master's concubine, how the son rebels against his father's will, and how the servant inherits the family business and abuses the old master to death. Liu's career has alternated between a quest to express an artistic vision and the need to attract financial support by appealing to mainstream tastes.

Further reading

Liu, Miaomiao (1996). 'Xiantan wode congying shengya' [Comments on My Career in Film Directing]. In Yang Yuanying (ed.) (1996), *Tamen de shengyin: Zhongguo nüdaoyan de zisu* [Their Voices: Chinese Women Directors' Self-expression]. Hebei: Zhongguo shehui, 241–9.

Shen, Yun. 'Interview with Liu Miaomiao'. In Yang Yuanying (ed.) (1996), *Tamen de shengyin: Zhongguo nüdaoyan de zisu* [Their Voices: Chinese Women Directors' Self-expression]. Hebei: Zhongguo shehui, 250–70.

Yun, Duo (1994). 'Liu Miaomiao – A Fervent Director'. *China Screen* 3: 22–3.

CUI SHUQIN

Liu Shuyong

b. 1962, Linqu, Shandong

Photographer, exhibition organizer

Liu Shuyong obtained his BA degree in Chinese literature at Nankai University in Tianjin (1993). In the same year he was assigned to teach as an Assistant Professor at the Central Institute of Finance and Banking in Beijing, where he is now Associate Professor. With the help of a friend, he began learning photography in 1988 and by the following year was working on a series of photographs under the title *Dwarfs*. From 1990 to 1991, with the help of his assistant, Liu finished his project *Ruins*, a series of pictures that focus on ruins in cities, like Beijing, that are experiencing rapid transformation. In 1993, he worked on several projects, including *The Death of a Beijing Man, What Are the Mainland Chinese Busy With?* and *Sex in China*. In 1994, he started working on his year-long project *Ping'anyu*, named after his home village, which is about the changes in a small village in northern China. In 2001, he was the organizer of 'Self', a group show of younger-generation photographers, including **Lu Zhirong** (a.k.a. Rong Rong), Mo Yi and **Hong Hao**.

Focusing on ordinary people – workers, peasants, and teachers – Liu is concerned with extraordinary themes – death, sex, ruins, social crisis – through a representation of non-dramatic, everyday-life-like images. In his *Death of a Beijing Man* (1993), in which a picture of a young man is seen over an altar-like table in an old dark room, the implication seems obvious: how and why did a young man like this die?

Further reading

Dislocation (1996). *Dislocation* vol. 7, 'New Beijing Photography'. Publisher unknown.

QIAN ZHIJIAN

Liu Suola

b. 1955, Beijing

Musician, writer

Born into a family of high-rank Communist officials, Liu Suola (or Sola) received a good art education and got access to Western modernism at early age. A composer by training, she graduated from the Central Conservatory of Music in 1983 and wrote music for film, theatre and television. However, she made her nationwide fame with the novella *You Have No Choice* (*Ni biewu xuanze*, 1985), which won the Chinese National Novella Award and presaged, together with **Xu Xing**'s 'Variations Without a Theme' (*Wu zhuti bianzou*), a 'new wave' of modernist literature. Liu's publications in the mid 1980s, including 'In Search of the King of Singers' (*Xunzhao gewang*) and *Blue Sky, Green Sea* (*Lantian lühai*), were avant-garde in their anti-social, anti-tradition consciousness, reflecting the idealism and frustrations of rebellious urban youth in post-Cultural Revolution China.

Liu left China in 1988 and has developed her artistic life overseas, mainly in London and New York. After a short break from writing, she published *Chaos and All That* (*Hundun jia ligeleng*, 1994), *Stories in Daji's family* (*Daji jia de xiaogushi*, 2000), and the bestseller *Liu Suola on the Move* (*Xingzou de Liu Suola*, 2001). Her music work was transformed into a kind of 'world music' as she sought to combine Chinese opera, folk, blues, jazz and African-American storytelling. Her first album released in USA, *Blues in the East* (1994), remained for many weeks in the top ten of the New World Music chart. *China Collage* (1996), *Haunts* (1998), and *Spring Snowfall* (2000) were also acclaimed. She has set up her own recording company, Also Productions, and has been working on the New Folk Project to bring Chinese musicians together with musicians from other countries.

Further reading

Liu, Suola (1994). *Chaos and All That*. Trans. Richard King. Honolulu: University of Hawai'i Press.

——(2001). *Xingzou de Liu Suola* [Liu Suola on the Move] Beijing: Kunlun chubanshe (with CD).

LILY XIAO HONG LEE WITH YING BAO

Liu Wei

b. 1965, Beijing

Painter

Liu Wei was born into a family of army officers and became one of the most successful protagonists of the art current known as **Cynical Realism (Popi)** which emerged in the early 1990s. Graduating from the Print Department of the **Central Academy of Fine Arts** in Beijing (1989), Liu's signature style deforms the faces and bodies of figures presented in anecdotes of everyday life which in his early paintings belong to the immediate experience of the artist himself. The actual appearance of members of his family or group of close friends in these paintings is distorted through a strong textural processing of the faces and the unnatural positions of the bodies. This practice transforms 'normal' individuals into surreal 'types' that assume an iconic, universal demeanour of malaise.

In *New Generation* (1990), for example, Liu portrays two baby boys (himself and his brother) against the backdrop of a huge Mao portrait for a photo-taking ritual. While the Chairman's face towers over the composition, it is only present as a portrait on the wall used to frame the artist's self-portrait. The tension produced by the juxtaposition of the highly iconic portrait of Mao and the restlessness of the children illustrates a shift, whereby the Chairman has become a memory while a new generation is making its way to the centre of the picture. Liu Wei has taken part in numerous shows: the Venice Biennale (1993, 1995), 'China's New Art Post-89' in Hong Kong (1993) (see **China's New Art, Post-89 (Hong Kong, 1993) and China Avant-Garde (Berlin, 1993)**); 'China!' in

Bonn (1996); 'Inside/Out' at the Asia Society in New York and MoMA in San Francisco (1998–9). He lives and works in Beijing.

Further reading

Doran, Valerie C. (ed.) (1993). *China's New Art, Post-1989*. Hong Kong: Hanart T Z Gallery.

Gao, Minglu, (ed.) (1998). *Inside Out – New Chinese Art*, Berkeley, Los Angeles: University of California Press.

Pong, Melanie *et al.* (eds) (1995). *L'altra Faccia, Tre Artisti Cinesi a Venezia*. Milano: Zanzibar. [Catalogue published on the occasion of the 46th Venice Biennale].

Singapore Art Museum (1997). *Quotation Marks, Chinese Contemporary Paintings*. Singapore: Singapore Art Museum.

FRANCESCA DAL LAGO

Liu Wenxi

b. 1933, Shengxian, Zhejiang

Artist, illustrator of bank-notes

In 1953, Liu Wenxu enrolled in the Zhejiang Academy of Fine Arts, from which he graduated in 1958. After graduation, he moved to Xi'an to teach in the Xi'an Academy of Fine Arts. In 1984, he became a professor. Among other positions, Liu holds the vice-chairmanship of the Shaanxi chapter of the Chinese Artists' Association. He has also served as the deputy mayor of Yan'an, and as a delegate to the National People's Congress.

The people and the scenery of northern Shaanxi have inspired many of Liu's works. At the same time, Liu is considered to be one of the artists who most frequently have portrayed Mao Zedong. The Great Leader features in no fewer than fifty-six of Liu's oil paintings. In Liu's treatment of Mao, two themes dominate. One is the events that took place during the period when the CCP was based in Yan'an. Another revolves around the close relations Mao had with the masses in that liberated area. In recognition of Liu's eminence as a Mao portraitist, the People's Bank of China commissioned him in

the late 1990s to design a portrait of Mao Zedong for a new set of currency. The currency went into circulation in 1999 to mark the fiftieth anniversary of the founding of the PRC. Mao's head graces the 100-yuan note, the 50, the 20 and the 10 of this, the fifth, set of bank notes that have been released since 1949.

STEFAN LANDSBERGER

Liu Xiaobo

b. 1955, Changchun, Jilin

Literary critic

Liu studied and taught in the Literature Department of Beijing Normal University, receiving his doctoral degree in 1988. He first drew national attention criticizing the **Root-seeking school** (*Xungen pai*) in literature and those promoting the value of cultural traditions in the humanities. He developed his arguments in 'Unavoidable Reflections' (*Wufa huibide fansi*, 1986), and thereafter in books based on the philosophy of Nietzsche, among them *Aesthetics and Freedom* (*Shenmei yü ren de ziyou*, 1989) and *A Critique of Choice: Dialogues with Li Zehou* (*Xuanzhe de pipan: yü Li Zehou duihuya*, 1988). Opposing the leading aesthetician, **Li Zehou**, Liu argued that great art was inevitably achieved by abandoning existing values. Thus, the need for individual freedoms outweighs the value of harmony with a given cultural order. In 1989, while visiting Columbia University, he returned to Beijing to join the demonstrations at Tiananmen Square and was arrested for counter-revolutionary activities. After his release, he again was arrested in 1996 for co-authoring a petition on behalf of democratic reforms that called for the impeachment of Jiang Zemin for violating the existing constitution. Released in 1999, he became a columnist for journals based outside China, while his work remains banned inside the country.

Further reading

Barmé, Geremie R. (1990). 'Confession, Redemption and Death: Liu Xiaobo and the Protest Movement of 1989.' In George Hicks (ed.),

The Broken Mirror: China after Tiananmen. Essex: Longman.

Mok, Ka-ho (1998). *Intellectuals and the State in Post-Mao China*. New York: St Martin's Press.

Solomon, Jon (2002). 'The Sovereign Police and Knowledgeable Bodies: Liu Xiaobo's Exilic Critique of Politics and Knowledge'. *positions: east asia cultures critique* 10.2 (Fall): 399–430.

EDWARD GUNN

Liu Xiaodong

b. 1963, Jincheng, Liaoning

Painter

Liu Xiaodong graduated in 1988 from the Oil Painting Department of the **Central Academy of Fine Arts** in Beijing where he is currently part of the faculty. His work is characterized by a realistic narrative, which seems unconcerned with the ongoing aesthetic changes and the rapid succession of theoretic constructs that has been affecting the Chinese art world since the mid 1990s.

Liu's paintings are well-structured figurative compositions executed with a rich communicative palette and energetic brushstrokes able to capture subtle psychological details. His subjects are mainly friends or acquaintances cast in idle postures, with bored, vacant or derisive expressions and pictured in situations that are the product of the artist's recollection and personal experiences. In dealing with such topics, he offers a peculiar sensibility and an on-the-spot immediacy intensified and offset by a certain masculine distance. Yet these compositions also possess an almost melancholic turn. Since his first solo show was held in Beijing in 1990, he has taken part in many exhibitions in China and abroad, including 'Representing the People' that toured the UK in 1998 and the 3rd Shanghai Biennale in 2000. A retrospective of his work, 'Liu Xiaodong 1990–2000', was organized at the Museum of the Central Academy of Fine Arts in the same year. In Liu's recent works, the sympathetic representation of peasants living on the borderline between urban and rural spaces reflects his deep concerns about the growing social inequalities affecting Chinese society since the end of the twentieth century.

Further reading

Jose, Nicolas (2001). 'At Home: Liu Xiaodong and Yu Hong'. *Art AsiaPacific* 30: 42–9.

Ying, Yi (2000). *Liu Xiaodong*. Changsha: Hubei Fine Art Publishing.

—— (2000). 'Liu Xiaodong'. In John Clark (ed.), *Chinese Art at the End of the Millennium*. Hong Kong: New Art Media Limited, 213–14.

TANG DI

Liu Xiaoqing

b. 1951, Sichuan

Actress, producer

Liu Xiaoqing was among the most important actresses of the 1980s, starring in more than twenty major feature films. After working as a farm labourer, a propaganda worker in the People's Liberation Army and a stage actress with the Chengdu Army Drama Troupe, Liu Xiaoqing turned to film in 1976 with a high-profile role in *Great Wall of the South China Sea (Nanhai changcheng)*. She followed with several other films, including *Comrade, Thank You (Tongzhi, ganxie ni)*, *Spring Song (Chunge)*, *Little Flower (Xiaohua)* and *Oh, What a Family! (Qiao zhe yi jiazi)*, for which she won a Best Supporting Actress award. In 1980 Liu joined the Beijing Film Studio where she delivered powerful performances in such films as *Savage Land (Yuan ye*, 1981), playing Jinzi, a woman driven by desire and lust. Although the film was not shown until 1987, upon its release Liu took home the Best Actress trophy at the Hundred Flowers Awards. She also starred in **Xie Jin**'s powerful melodrama about the Cultural Revolution, *Hibiscus Town (Furong zhen)*, for which she won another Best Actress title at the Golden Rooster Awards. Liu Xiaoqing is also known for her work in several traditional costume dramas, including veteran director Li Hanxiang's *Reign Behind a Curtain (Chuilian tingzheng)* and **Tian Zhuangzhuang**'s *The Imperial Eunuch, Li Lianying (Da taijian Li Lianying)*. *Li Lianying* proved to be a star vehicle for Liu and her former beau **Jiang Wen**, with whom she had also starred in *Chuntao: A Woman for Two* (*Chuntao*).

Liu starred in a handful of television mini-series in the 1990s, while her visibility on screen decreased as she became increasingly involved in investment and the business world. Liu Xiaoqing's transformation from glamorous movie star to successful businesswoman fuelled an insatiable interest in her personal and professional life, and she has become the subject of numerous books and the target of tabloid newspapers. Part of this transformation included an interest in film production, her most notable production credit being Jiang Wen's hit film **In the Heat of the Sun** (*Yangguang canlan de rizi*, 1995). In 2002 Liu Xiaoqing was imprisoned on charges of tax evasion and fraud. In the wake of her arrest, Liu once again became the subject of a new flurry of tabloid books published under such titles as *End of the Road for a Star* (*Mingxing molu*) and *I Sent Liu Xiaoqing to the Courthouse* (*Wo ba Liu Xiaoqing song shang fating*). Liu herself is also the author of several books, including *My Way* (*Wo de lu*) and *Me During the Past Eight Years* (*Wo zhe ba nian*).

MICHAEL BERRY

Liu Xinwu

b. 1942, Chengdu

Writer

A pioneer of **Scar literature**, Liu Xinwu is known for his preoccupation with social criticism, particularly the legacies of Mao. He was a middle school teacher for fifteen years in Beijing before he gained overnight fame with the publication of 'The Class Teacher' (*Banzhuren*, 1977). It was the first story to expose the failure of education during the **Cultural Revolution** as embodied in the hooligan Song Baoqi and the dogmatic Xie Huimin. 'Save the children' is the key theme. In a succession of stories from 1978 to 1980, Liu called for: the return of love in 'The Place of Love' (*Aiqing de weizhi*); individuality in 'Every Leaf' (*Mei yipian luoye*); faith in 'Wake up, Brother!' (*Xinglai ba, didi*); and freedom of choice in 'Black Walls' (*Heiqiang*). His novella *A Gift* (*Ruyi*), which reveals the damage

done to human relations by class struggle through the humane behaviour of an honest servant, is a probing study of human nature which moves beyond political protest.

Liu's stories on urban problems are more successful. His novella *The Overpass* (*Liti jiaochaqiao*) vividly depicts psychological suppression in an unbearably crowded environment. His novel, *The Bell Drum Tower* (*Zhonggu lou*), which won the Mao Dun Literary Prize, shows the multifaceted life of ordinary Beijing people, who live in an old-style compound. The novel, *The Wind Blows Past* (*Feng Guo'er*) satirizes the philistinism of literary circles through a rivalry over the possession of a manuscript left by a supposedly deceased writer in a plane crash.

See also: Cultural Revolution (education)

LEUNG LAIFONG

Liu Yichang

(né Liu Tongyi)

b. 1918, Shanghai

Writer

Liu studied at Saint John's University in Shanghai. He is a writer, editor and translator, who has published novels and short stories, as well as essays and articles in newspapers and magazines. He began his career as a journalist in Chongqing during WWII. He moved to Hong Kong in 1948. In 1985, he founded *Hong Kong Literature* (*Xianggang wenxue*), a monthly magazine in which he acted as director until his retirement in 2000. His best-known novel, *The Drunkard* (*Jiutu*, 1963), describes the quest of a man, half writer half journalist, to come to terms with Hong Kong's complex and moving reality. This, and many other stories written by him, are evocative of the speedy, noisy, impersonal but also challenging and open place that Hong Kong is, revealing the coexistence of many worlds, and expressing confusion between past and present, Chinese and Western culture, even things and spirits, as in *Bust-up* (*Chaojia*, 1980). His role in introducing Western literature and art in

Hong Kong Literature, and before that in other magazines, has been essential to Hong Kong culture. The movie *In the Mood for Love* by **Wong Kar-wai** is based on his *Intersection* (*Duidao*, 1972).

Further reading

Liu, Yichang (1995). 'The Cockroach'. Trans. D. E. Pollard. In D. E. Pollard (trans.) *The Cockroach and Other Stories*. Hong Kong: Chinese University of Hong Kong.

Larson, Wendy (1993). 'Liu Yichang's *Jiutu*: Literature, Gender, and Fantasy in Contemporary Hong Kong'. *Modern Chinese Literature* 7.1: 89–104.

ANNIE CURIEN

Liu Zaifu

b. 1941, Nan'an, Fujian

Literary, culture critic

Liu graduated from Xiamen University in 1963 with a degree in Chinese literature and immediately joined the **Chinese Academy of Social Sciences** in Beijing. Years and a great number of jarring political campaigns later, he became the director of the Academy's Literature Research Unit. He also served as editor in chief of *Wenxue pinglun* [Literary Review] and suffered the political excesses of the **Cultural Revolution**, the Anti-Spiritual Pollution Campaign (1983–4) and the **Campaign against Bourgeois Liberalization** (1986–7), the last of which precipitated his departure from China and compromised, perhaps fatally, a wider dissemination of his message of national rejuvenation through literary reform. Over the last decade he has generated a great many works: essays (*Shuyuan sixu*), prose (*Du canghai*), commentary (*Fangzhu zhu shen*), aphorism (*Duyu tianya*), and scholarly dialogue (with **Li Zehou** in *Gaobie geming*, and with **Gao Xingjian** in *Lun Gao Xingjian zhuangtai*) while becoming a literary citizen of the world, nominally residing in Boulder, Colorado, where he shares a house with his daughter, Liulian, but also at the University of Chicago, the University of Colorado, and the University of Stockholm and the City University of Hong Kong, where he is serving as Honorary Professor in 2004.

Although a Party member for most of his life, Liu was a Marxist of curious stripe, one devoted to a proper accounting of the Chinese Communist Party's deviance from its original revolutionary message. His creative reading of Chinese 'Marxoid' thought, in which he recuperated the revolutionary agency of the subject, as well as his call to Party intellectuals to assume a *zishen yishi* (self-critical attitude) constituted an immanent critique of contemporary politics and art, especially the violent excesses of the Cultural Revolution. This eccentricity earned him government harassment throughout the mid 1980s, and by the time of the 'anti-bourgelib' crackdown in 1986, his residence had been ransacked and Liu was placed under house arrest. He was expelled from the Communist Party in 1987. Still, it wasn't until the government savagery at Tiananmen (after which Liu was placed on the government's most wanted list), and another six months of political refuge in peasants' homes in the south before Liu Zaifu left China and delivered his valedictory in 'Farewell to the Ancestors' (*Gaobie zhushen*).

Liu is now an expatriate, itinerant Marxist cultural critic and romantic modernist writer who came to prominence as the 'phenomenon' (*Liu Zaifu xianxiang*) of a literary cult in a precious, abbreviated interval of the middle decade. This was the period of *qimeng* (enlightenment) and *wenhua re* (**culture fever**), when intellectual enthusiasts focused on the problem of the 'subject' with a vigour provoked by the unexpected aesthetic intervention of the translations of Barthes, Croce, Jauss, Heidegger, Lukács, Marcuse and the *1844 Manuscripts* of Marx. Indeed, in this heady interval of literary experiment and political liberalization, Liu's literary criticism, with its obsessive emphasis on aesthetic subjectivity (*zhuti*) as a site of resistance to state administered ideology, inspired a new generation of writers to rebel against the sterile, exhausted socialist realism of Party-approved literature. His reputation was made from a string of influential meditations on literature and the prospect of authentic recovery of the aesthetic subject that appeared between 1984 and 1986, most notably *Xingge zuhe lun* [On the Composition of Literary Personality], which defined the subjectivity of the writer as a unique position of moral authority whose intrinsic duty was to engineer his society's 'return to humanity'.

Since 1989, Liu, along with other exiled former Party members and intellectuals who constitute the 1980s intellectual diaspora – Su Xiaozhi, Liu Binyan, **Bei Dao** and Gao Xingjian (who remains Liu's close friend) – has lived and travelled abroad. From this culturally disadvantageous vantage, he has continued to write and lecture on the full variety of themes of subjectivity, literature and human character, that brought him disfavour and persecution at home in large part because his conception of national responsibility moves him to conceive of China's political crises as solvable only through the inspired intervention of the intellectual – a May Fourth era inheritance. But, unlike his predecessors, Liu is cannily aware of his complicity in his own domination.

Referring to China's deported literary pantheon Liu recently claimed that 'displacement and exile has set our minds free'; however, the emancipatory impulse to resurrect the true, revolutionary subject through a dialectical process of self-negation (*wuwo*) cannot be satisfied under such circumstances. Free to speculate, but not to effect change in the morally authoritative subjectivity of their countrymen, so it is that Liu and his cohort bear the scars of *youhuan yishi* (anxiety and crisis consciousness) and remain in a state of perpetual longing for home (*xiangjia*). Exile has removed him from the very audience his writing aims to provoke, so that with time, his message for Chinese has become, ipso facto, harmless. In the contemporary moment of Chinese fiction, with its post-adolescent narcissism and mindless devotion to the commercial gods of self-gratification, as exemplified in the stupendous popular success of *Beijing Wawa* and *Shanghai Baobei*, Liu Zaifu's cry for cultural self-interrogation as a basis for a 'human revolution' seems cloyingly self-indulgent. Subjectivity is no longer a site for literary experiment, much less a harbinger of liberation. Rather, it is a reservoir for hedonistic accumulation.

For more than a decade Liu has been barred from returning to China, although recently he has visited the country and even been offered a teaching appointment at Xiamen University. However, with his work readily published from the literary émigré nexus of Taiwan and Hong Kong,

he has conducted an ongoing confessional literary tour, lecturing and writing on the predicament of the Chinese intellectual, specifically his/her incapacity to politicize aesthetics for social good and, recently going so far as to affirm a vision of a repressed common humanity shared with Daisaku Ikeda, President of Japan's fundamentalist Sokka Gakai Institute. Thus, he remains, at heart, a romantic or a frustrated utopian, whose valorizing of the subject, once radical, is now passé, perhaps because it was never effectively detached from the Promethean premises of revolutionary literature wherein the intellectual was the sole conductor of the symphony of the larger public's education in the recovery of their original human nature (*huigui*).

With these last years of exile and of the receding of the waters of zealous self-criticism and literary experiment, Liu Zaifu sits on the distant island of Chinese consciousness devoting his scholarly energies to the literature of exile. Yet his message of national rescue through cultural regeneration is perhaps more important today than it was two decades ago when his writings on the aesthetic of subjectivity made him a national celebrity. In today's China it seems very clear that art can no longer influence the world, but it is Liu's unreasonable, but necessary, contention that the intellectual cannot stop believing in art's capacity to effect politics, national identity and fate. In the political struggles of Chinese literary figures to exhort resistance through writing and declamation, the heart is all too often only half a prophet, and so it is that the responsibility for political and cultural reform through art has passed with the twentieth century in China and, thus, it is likely that Liu Zaifu will be for ever an exile. However, it is his nation's loss that his message of self and cultural transformation is no longer audible amidst the din of rapacious commercialism and urban hedonism.

Bibliography

Li, Zehou and Liu, Zaifu (1997). *Gaobie geming* [Farewell to Revolution]. Hong Kong: Tiandi tushu youxian gongsi chubanshe.

Liu, Zaifu (1986). *Xingge zuhe lun* [On the Composition of Literary Personality]. Shanghai: Shanghai wenyi chubanshe.

—— (1993). *Piaoliu shouji* [Wandering Notes]. Hong Kong: Tiandi tushu youxian gongsi.

—— (1994). *Fangzhu zhushen* [Deporting the Gods]. Hong Kong: Tiandi tushu youxian gongsi.

—— (1999). *Du canghai: Liu Zaifu san wen* [Reading the Blue Sea: The Prose of Liu Zaifu]. Anhui: Anhui wenyi chubanshe.

—— (1999). *Duyu tianya* [Soliloquy (for) the Far Corners of the Earth]. Hong Kong: Tiandi tushu youxian gongsi.

—— (2000). *Lun Gao Xingjian zhuangtai* [On the Condition of Gao Xingjian]. Hong Kong: Minbao chubanshe.

Liu, Zaifu and Yang, Chunshi (2002). *Shuyuan sixu* [Thoughts in the Garden of Letters]. Hong Kong: Tiandi tushu youxian gongsi.

Further reading

Barmé, Geremie R. (1999). *In the Red: On Contemporary Chinese Culture*. New York: Columbia University Press.

Lee, Mabel (1996). 'Walking Out of Other People's Prisons: Liu Zaifu and Gao Xingjian on Chinese Literature in the 1990s'. *Journal of Asian and African Studies* 5.1: 98–112.

Liu, Kang (1993). 'Subjectivity, Marxism, and Cultural Theory in China'. In Liu Kang and Xiaobing Tang (eds), *Politics, Ideology and Literary Discourse in Modern China*. Durham: Duke University Press, 23–55.

Wang, Jing (1996). *High Culture Fever: Politics, Aesthetics, and Ideology in Deng's China*. Berkeley: University of California Press, 201–6 and passim.

LIONEL M. JENSEN

Institute. After graduation in 1991, he got a job as a photo-journalist for *Workers' Daily*, and was assigned to the cover the coal-mining industry, which he did for more than a year. In 1993 Liu established the Topic Photo Group and began work on the series *Countrymen*, in which he explored the exoticism of ethnic minorities regions and set the stage for his later tripartite project re-examining 'China's People, Myths and History' – the *Three Realms* series. This was initiated in 1995 together with the publication of a private printed serial entitled *New Photo* in cooperation with Rong Rong (**Lu Zhirong**) and Jin Yongquan and dedicated to conceptual photography.

In 1997 Liu left the job at the newspaper for a freelance career, continuing his artistic projects, which soon came to include the *Peking Opera* series. First shown in a solo show at the Taipei Photo Gallery in 1998, these works are 'simulated theatrical stills' (Wu Hong) inspired by the old photo-compositions of 1920s–30s Shanghai and recounted in traditional opera stories like *The Legend of the White Snake* (*Baishezhuan*). The vintage flavour suggested by a brownish-antique finish, the static and dramatized postures, and the placement of the subjects on a prearranged studio-stage with a weightless painted backdrop recall a nostalgia for a recent past, while the nudity and uninhibited poses load the works with the texture of contemporary kitsch. Liu Zheng's sophisticated style and unique technique has won him a part in major art events like the exhibition of 'Contemporary Chinese Photography' at the Neuer Berliner Kunstverein in Berlin (1997), the Tachikawa Art Festival in Tokyo and New York (1999), the 50th Venice Biennale (2003) and the ICP Triennale, ICP, New York (2003).

Liu Zheng

b. 1969, Wuqiang county, Hebei

Photographer

Soon after his family moved to Datong in 1987, Liu Zheng headed to Beijing to major in optical engineering at the Beijing Technological

Further reading

Goodman, Jonathan (2000). 'Human, Demonic and Divine in the Photographs of Liu Zheng'. *Art on Paper* 4.3 (January–February).

Li, Jiangshu (2003). 'Liu Zheng he ta de gainian sheyin' [Liu Zheng and His Conceptual Photography]. *Yishu dangdai* [Art Today] 2.6: 90–3.

Photographers International (2001). 'The Chinese: Liu Zheng Monograph', special edition. *Photographers International* 58.

Wu, Hong (1999). *Transience. Chinese Experimental Art at the End of the Twentieth Century*. Chicago: University of Chicago Press.

Wu, Hung (2001). 'Photographing Deformity: Liu Zheng and His Photo Series "My Countrymen"'. *Public Culture* 3.13: 399–427.

BEATRICE LEANZA

Liu Zijian

b. 1956, Shashi, Hubei

Abstract ink-wash painter

Ever since his graduation in 1983 from the Department of Chinese Painting at the Hubei Academy of Fine Arts, Liu Zijian has been experimenting with abstract ink-painting (see **Modern Ink-Wash Painting**). His early works, *Net* and *Wall* (1986), were shown at the Hubei Youth Art Festival (1986) and revealed his intention to focus more on 'inkwork' than on traditional 'brushwork'. In 1988, he accomplished his *Abstract Ink Painting* series, one of which was reproduced in **Jiangsu huakan**, a magazine that was actively promoting contemporary art. His *Escape* was shown at 'China Avant-Garde' (1989), the largest exhibition of contemporary art in China in the 1980s. His *Floating Spirits, 1989* was exhibited at 'I Don't Want To Play Cards with Cézanne: Avant-Garde Art from China' (1991) at the Asia-Pacific Museum in the USA. In 1992, Liu was transferred from the Hubei Academy of Fine Arts to South China Normal University, where he became an Assistant Professor of Fine Arts. In the second half of the 1990s, his abstract ink paintings were frequently shown at important international exhibitions: 'An Exhibition of Modern Chinese Ink Painting' at the Taiwan Art Museum (1994); 'Returning Home: An Exhibition of Contemporary Chinese Experimental Ink Painting' at the San Francisco Museum of Modern Art (1996) and 'China: 5000 Years' (1998) at the Guggenheim Museum in New York.

Like many artists of abstract ink painting, Liu Zijian tends to deconstruct traditional Chinese ink painting by borrowing elements from Western abstract painting. But unlike others who rely more or less on the brushwork, Liu prefers unconventional tools like grids and a broad paintbrush, and techniques like rubbing and printing, in order to create what he calls ' a floating ink world' on paper. Liu Zijian is currently Associate Professor of Fine Arts at the Art College of Shenzhen University, Guangdong.

Further reading

(1993–7). *Ershi shiji mo Zhongguo shuimo hua zoushi* I, II, III [Trends in Chinese Ink-Wash Painting at the End of Twentieth Century, v. 1-3]. Tianjin: Yangliuqing chubanshe.

QIAN ZHIJIAN

Liushou nüshi

[Women Who Are Left Behind]

Spoken drama

Written by Le Meiqin and directed by Yu Luosheng, this prize-winning experimental play recounts the lives and emotions of a young woman and a young man whose spouses have gone abroad to seek a new life. Waiting in anxiety for news from her husband in America, Nai Qing, a physician, encounters Jia Dong, a taxi driver, whose wife has gone to Japan and has become a well-known Ah Xiu of the red-light district in the Ginza. Nai Qing's knowledge of her husband cohabiting with another man's wife in America draws her close to Jia Dong, who is in a similar situation. Before long, they fall in love. After an emotional struggle for her conscience and the abortion of Jia Dong's baby, the play ends with Nai Qing's decision to leave Jia Dong and join her husband in America. When the play premiered in a **Little Theatre** in Shanghai in 1991, it touched the hearts of many Shanghai residents, tens of thousands of whom had gone abroad since the beginning of reform, often leaving loved ones behind. The realistic portrayal of the moral bewilderment, psychological predicament and final transcendence with respect to the issue of infidelity struck a sympathetic chord. The play quickly became popular and was even adapted for film.

FU HONGCHU

Further reading

(1986). *Liyuanxi zonghengtan*. Quanzhou: Fujiansheng liyuanxishi yanjutuan.
(1998). *Haixia liang'an liyuanxi xueshu yantao huilun wenji*. Taipei: Guoli zhongzheng wenhua zhongxin.

JONATHAN P. J. STOCK

Liyuanxi

(Pear Garden Opera)

A significant regional opera tradition originating in Quanzhou, Fujian, Liyuanxi is named after an eighth-century court training school for actors, the Pear Garden. Its scripts have been traced back to the mid sixteenth century, and some of its tunes may well date back even earlier, which makes it one of China's most long-established drama traditions. The music of Liyuanxi is distinctive in several respects from that of many other regional styles, including the notable use of a small, foot-held drum called *nangu* and several instruments of the exact design used in Fujian's mellow **Minnan nanyin** ensemble tradition: **pipa** (lute), *xiao* (endblown flute), *erxian* (fiddle) and *sanxian* (lute). A **dizi** (transverse flute) can also be heard on occasion, and a small amount of other percussion is found. Further melody instruments occur less often. The tunes of Liyuanxi are also largely shared with Minnan nanyin, although performance practice has now diverged, the operatic performance being generally faster than the ensemble. The movements of Liyuanxi are also unusual, being modelled on those of local puppet theatre.

Like many regional traditions, aspects of Liyuanxi were modernized and reformed from the 1940s on. Some performers transferred to other, more contemporaneous traditions, while specialist directors were brought into Liyuanxi. Today, performance focuses on historical tales, among which the romance *Chen San and Wu Niang* (*Chen San Wu Niang*) is considered particularly representative. The opening of Taiwan to touring mainland ensembles has provided a new market for master performers of Liyuanxi.

See also: Wang Renjie

Local Church (and 'shouters')

Protestant sect

The 'Local Church', which is sometimes called by its adherents 'churches in the Lord's recovery', is a movement partially derived from ideas of Watchman Nee (Ni Tuoshen, 1903–72) and his movement, called by some the **Little Flock**. A cardinal principle of Nee from the 1920s on was the desire to supersede denominationalism, which he despised as a pernicious Western creation, and to have just one church – the 'local church' – in each city or locality. When Nee was imprisoned in the 1950s, the legacy of his movement was elaborated by his followers, including a former lieutenant, Witness Lee (Li Changshou), in Taiwan and then in North America.

The Little Flock remnants in China which had survived the years of persecution linked up around 1980 with missionary representatives of the Local Church movement based outside China. The result was a spectrum of groups, to greater or lesser degrees standing in the tradition of Nee's old movement, mixed with the newer doctrines of Witness Lee. In the 1980s, some of the groups, especially those in Zhejiang province, engaged in loud verbal behaviours during worship, and were dubbed the 'shouters' (*huhanpai*). Several cases of violent disruption among Protestants were associated with their activities in the 1980s. These elements, rightly or wrongly, were denounced by the government and by the **Three-Self Patriotic Movement (TSPM)** as sectarian and illegitimate, and have been persecuted on and off ever since. In the early 2000s, the 'shouters' were still on the list of 'evil cults' pursued by the authorities. During 2002, some foreign representatives of the Local Church reportedly announced an end to relationships with the 'shouters'. Thus the links between them are uncertain at the present.

DANIEL BAYS

local religion

Rural society in China is intensely local in orientation, and as a result, villages or clusters of villages often maintain characteristic traditions of religious practice. Religion celebrates local tradition by preserving idiosyncratic festivals, and benefits the community by ensuring divine blessing. In addition, the religious resources of local society are also employed in the religious lives of families and individuals. Although suppressed during the first three decades of the People's Republic, local religion began to revive during the late 1970s.

Local religion can be focused on material resources, such as shrines and temples, or a tradition of performance, such as religious opera or sectarian ritual. During the early twentieth century, most villages had at least one temple, even if only small shrines to the tutelary deity, and the calendar of local festivals revolved around the worship of temple gods. However, the prominence of village temples also made them easy targets; many were destroyed in the political campaigns and warfare of the early twentieth century, and most of those which remained were appropriated or razed during the 1950s and 1960s.

Especially before 1949, ritual practice was often the responsibility of local religious specialists. The Jiangnan region supported tens of thousands of Buddhist monks, and even poorer villages of north China often had a monk or Daoist priest (see **Daoist priests**) residing nearby. In other cases, lay villagers acted as specialists, performing elaborate rituals on important days in the liturgical calendar, such as the New Year, as well as on days of local significance, such as the birthdays of temple deities. The form of these festivals was shaped by local custom. In rural Shanxi province, local festivals were operatic rituals called *sai*, which were performed either by professionals or by villagers. Elsewhere in north China, ritual performance consisted of scripture recitation by

sectarians. After 1949, the official definition of religion was construed so as to exclude local religious specialists, who were branded as exploitative. Even ritual performed by peasants themselves was banned as feudal superstition, and by the mid 1960s, local religious practice almost completely ceased.

After 1979, local religion began a period of cautious revival. Often, this was specifically a restoration of pre-1949 local religious customs. Areas along the southeast coast have reconstituted temple cults and rebuilt extensive temple networks, even reaching out to Taiwan or overseas communities for funding. Villages in north China have revived operatic and sectarian ritual, often after great efforts to retrain specialists. As often, local religion has been created along more general lines, without specific regard for earlier village customs.

At the same time, although official policy is not always enforced with great diligence, it has shaped the revival of local religion. Many groups, such as **Yiguan Dao**, Protestant **house churches**, and especially **Falun gong**, are regarded as a continuing threat, and must remain underground. Other groups have fended off criticism by portraying their practices as orthodox Buddhism or Daoism, or else not as religion at all, but simply 'folk culture'. In addition, local religion is a significant tourist attraction, as with sanctioned minority festivals, such as the Tai (Dai) Water Splashing Festival, and invented traditions like the Chrysanthemum Festival celebrated in towns along the Hong Kong border.

See also: sectarian religion; spirit-mediums; temple fairs

Further reading

Chau, Adam Yuet (2001). 'The Dragon King Valley: Popular Religion, Socialist State, and Agrarian Society in Shaanbei, North China'. PhD diss., Stanford University.

Dean, Kenneth (2001). 'China's Second Government: Regional Religious Systems in Southeast China'. In Wang Ch'iu-kui, Chuang Ying-chang and Cheng Chung-min (eds), *Shehui, minzu yü wenhua zhanyan huoji yantaohui lunwenji*. Taipei: Hanxue yanjiu zhongxin, 77–107.

—— (2003). 'Local Communal Religion in Contemporary South-east China'. In Daniel Overmyer (ed.), *Religion in China Today*. Cambridge: Cambridge University Press, 32–52.

Fan, Lizhu (2003). 'The Cult of the Silkworm Mother as a Core of Local Community Religion in a North China Village: Field Study in Zhiwuying, Baoding, Hebei'. In Daniel Overmyer (ed.), *Religion in China Today*. Cambridge: Cambridge University Press, 53–66.

Flower, John and Leonard, Pamela (1998). 'Defining Cultural Life in the Chinese Countryside: The Case of the Chuan Zhu Temple'. In Eduard Vermeer, Frank N. Pieke and Woei Lien Chong (eds), *Cooperative and Collective in China's Rural Development: Between State and Private Interests*. Armonk, NY: M. E. Sharpe, 273–90.

Judd, Ellen (1996). 'Ritual Opera and the Bonds of Authority: Transformation and Transcendence'. In Bell Yung, Evelyn Sakakida Rawski and Rubie S. Watson (eds), *Harmony and Counterpoint – Ritual Music in a Chinese Context*. Stanford: Stanford University Press, 226–48.

Liu, Tik-sang (2003). 'Nameless but Active Religion: An Anthropologist's View of Local Religion in Hong Kong and Macau'. In Daniel Overmyer (ed.), *Religion in China Today*. Cambridge: Cambridge University Press, 67–88.

Yang, Mayfair Mei-hui (2000). 'Putting Global Capitalism in Its Place: Economic Hybridity, Bataille, and Ritual Expenditure'. *Current Anthropology* 41.4: 477–509.

THOMAS DUBOIS

Long Yingtai

(a.k.a. Lung Ying-tai / S. Ying Tai Walther)

b. 1952, Tainan, Taiwan

Writer

Long Yingtai became the founding director of the Taipei Cultural Affairs Bureau in late 1999. A famous Taiwan writer, literary and social critic, she sometimes writes under the pen name of Hu Meili. She earned her PhD in English from Kansas State University and had lived in the USA and Europe for twenty years before serving the Taipei municipality. She has taught at various universities abroad and in Taiwan. 'Chinese, Why Aren't You Angry?' and many essays collected in *Wildfire* (*Yehuoji*, 1985) sharply criticized deep-rooted malpractices in society and had a great influence on Taiwan. Her work became known on the mainland in the 1990s. She has estimated that before 1995, she spent 20 per cent of her writing time for European readers and 80 per cent for Taiwan readers. Since 1995, however, she has been devoting 20 per cent of her writing to European readers, 40 per cent to Taiwanese and 40 per cent to mainlanders. Her long experience abroad made her think that nothing could surprise her, until, that is, she met 'lovely' Shanghai men, who cook and clean the floor and even wash their wives' underwear. Her humour in 'Ah, Shanghai Men' led to a warm welcome in Shanghai in 2001. She believes that intellectuals play different roles under democratic and authoritarian regimes, finding it ironic that intellectuals in the latter cannot function well, yet devote themselves to changing society. Her articles about Beijingers and Singaporeans aroused many arguments.

HELEN XIAOYAN WU

lotteries

(caijuan, caipiao)

Playing the lottery (*caijuan / caipiao*) is a popular recreational activity in contemporary China. Lottery selling has become a multi-billion dollar business in recent years: $6 billion were generated through selling paper tickets in 2001. The Chinese government banned gambling when it came to power in 1949. Although the government considered gambling illegal, it decided to sell lotteries to raise funds for social welfare projects in the 1980s. Rather than calling the lottery gambling, Chinese leaders refer to it as 'competitive guessing' (*bocai*). The first lottery, a half-million-yuan welfare lottery approved by the Ministry of Civil Affairs, was on sale in Shijiazhuang on 27 July

1987. The top prize was 5,000 yuan. Since then, the lottery industry has been growing rapidly.

Currently, lotteries cover four major categories: welfare, the elderly, education and sports. Types of lotteries include traditional, instant win and computerized lotteries. The most recent category of lottery, soccer lottery, was launched by the State Sports General Administration in 2001. Although the current limit for the top prize in each lottery category is 5 million yuan, its increase is under consideration. Hundreds of lottery ticket outlets are established in major cities (for example, over 500 outlets in Chengdu). In addition to paper lottery tickets, lottery sales also use newly available media like the Internet and the wireless phone. The lottery industry nationwide produces at least dozens of millionaires each year. In Sichuan in the period from August 1999 to February 2000, for example, lottery games created more than forty millionaires.

REN HAI

like Lou himself and taking Alfred Hitchcock's *Vertigo* as its point of departure, *Suzhou River*'s complex plot used mistaken identity, betrayal and voyeuristic surveillance as themes by which to critique the money-orientation and disaffection of China's post-Mao youth culture and – contra Hitchcock – to urge a romantic leap of faith.

Lou Ye's most recent film is *Purple Butterfly* (*Zi hudie*, 1993), starring **Zhang Ziyi**, and takes up the subject of love, collaboration, and resistance in the years before the outbreak of war between China and Japan in 1937.

Further reading

Berry, Chris (2000). 'Suzhou River' [review]. *Cineyama* 49: 20–1.

Silbergeld, Jerome (2002). 'Hitchcock with a Chinese Face: Lou Ye's *Suzhou River*'. *Persimmon* 3.2 (Summer): 70–3.

JEROME SILBERGELD

Lou Ye

b. 1965, Shanghai

Film director

Lou Ye graduated from the **Beijing Film Academy** in 1989 and represents the first generation of modern Chinese filmmakers educated equally in Western and Chinese film traditions. He also studied film at New York University and lists Casavettes, Antonioni and Fellini as major influences. After his prize-winning first film, *Weekend Lovers* (*Zhoumo qingren*, 1995), Lou produced a television series, *Super City* (1995), the first digital film project in China, in which members of his Beijing Film Academy class were invited to direct ten episodes. His own contribution to the series developed into his digitally produced film, *Suzhou River* (1999), which epitomized the globalization of Chinese filmmaking in its European financing and German post-production. Lou's third feature – coming after *Girl in Danger* (*Weiqing shaonü*, 1995) – was awarded Best Film at the Paris and Rotterdam film festivals, along with directorial and acting awards. Narrated and purportedly filmed by a fictional videographer

Lü Peng

b. 1956, Chongqing, Sichuan

Art historian, critic

A prolific writer, Lü made his mark in the contemporary art world with the publication of *The History of Modern Chinese Art, 1979 to 1989* (*Zhongguo xiandai yishushi 1979–1989*, 1992), co-written with Yi Dan. This work was premised on redefining 'tradition' as the struggle against the fait accompli. As such, it championed avant-garde experiments as the only valid choice for Chinese artists. Lü's career had been unusual: he had graduated in 1981 in political science and law at Sichuan Normal University and only later became involved in art. His ideas were dominated by Western modernism and art theory, which he helped introduce to the Chinese public through numerous essays and translations, and which were mostly elaborated in his *Modern Art and the Critique of Culture* (*Xiandai yishu yü wenhua pipan*, 1992).

In the 1990s, he shifted his effort to the building of a Chinese art market. In 1991 he founded the magazine *Art and Market* (*Yishu yü shichang*), which aimed to provide collectors with data on artists, including the analysis of art-related investments. In 1992 he organized the 'First 1990s Art Biennale' in Guangzhou. This was created as a conscious competitor to the Chinese Artists' Association's National Art Exhibitions and was to be financed by investors rather than official patronage. It would be regulated by legal documents rather than official bureaucracy and a board of art critics would act as selection committee, instead of the politically nominated board typical of the Artists' Association's exhibitions. But Lü also continued to write extensively in the 1990s. In 2002, he again beat out other critics in the race to sum up the decade with the publication of *1990s Art China 1990–1999* (*Zhongguo dangdai yishushi*).

Further reading

Lü, Peng (1992). *Zhongguo xiandai yishushi* [A History of Modern Art in China]. Changsha: Hunan meishu chubanshe.

—— (2000). *Zhongguo dangdai yishushi, 1990–1999/ 1990s Art China*. Changsha: Hunan meishu chubanshe.

Qian, Zhijian (2000). 'The Changing Role of Critics in the 1990s'. In John Clark (ed.). *Chinese Art at the End of the Millennium*. Hong Kong: New Art Media, 25–8.

EDUARDO WELSH

Lü Shengzhong

b. 1952, Dayujishancun, Shandong

Paper-cut installation artist

When Lü Shengzhong obtained a master's degree in folk art from the **Central Academy of Fine Arts**, he was already a veteran artist in developing a new genre of *nianhua* (woodcut prints) popular in the countryside as a New Year decoration. He remained as member of the faculty at the Central Academy. The folk heritage proves to be an inestimable source of inspiration for Lü. In the solo show 'Lü Shengzhong's Paper-Cut Art' at the **China Art Gallery** (1988), he designed a spiritual labyrinth extending to the gallery floor with hundreds of paper-cut footprints, bearing men's faces, wavering along the path. Together with this work, entitled *Hesitant Steps* (*Chichu*), Lü also presented thousands of foetus-like humanoid cut-outs in red paper (*xiao hongren*). They swam away, confronting or leaving behind the shadow of their self – the hollow and 'negative' silhouette on the paper. Symbols of the human soul, these red effigies were going to follow Lü's footsteps in his search for the essence of life and art. In 1990, he transformed his studio inside the art academy into a *Séance Room* (*Zhaohun tang*) with myriad *xiao hongren* suspended in and covering the entire space. That year he also started his journey by train, sowing the red souls along the Chinese rails in *Vagrant Séance* (*Zhaohun youfang*, 1990–2) and as far as Germany, in *Red Train* (1992). Lü has had eighteen solo shows to date in and outside China. His soul-reaching installations and collages have been exhibited in numerous venues, including the 1995 Gwangju Biennale and the 'De Wann' in Venray Asylum, Holland (2002).

Further reading

Lü, Shengzhong (1990). *Lü Shengzhong zuopin* [The Works of Lü Shengzhong]. Changsha: Hunan Fine Arts Publishing.

—— (1996). *Mianhun ji* [Searching for Soul]. Changsha: Hunan Fine Arts Publishing.

Weiqing (ed.) (2000). *First Encounter Lü Shengzhong New York* (exhibition catalogue). New York: Chambers Fine Art.

TANG DI

Lu Xinhua

b. 1954, Shandong

Writer, businessman

Lu Xinhua became a household name after he published his first story 'The Scar' (also translated as 'The Wound') in *Wenhui Daily* (11 August 1978), when he was a freshman at Fudan University in

Shanghai. He grew up in Shandong province where his father was an officer in the army. After graduating from middle school in 1968, he returned to his native place, Rugao county, as a 'sent-down youth' (*zhiqing*), joined the army in 1973, was discharged in 1977, and became a worker in Nantong briefly before he entered university, majoring in Chinese literature.

'The Scar' deals with a female Red Guard, Wang Xiaohua, who breaks off relations with her mother after the latter has been denounced as a 'traitor'. She returns home from the countryside nine years later only to find her mother dead with a scar on the forehead. As the first work to deal with family tragedies inflicted by the **Cultural Revolution**, it aroused a great sensation. Similar works quickly followed, making Lu the founder of **Scar literature**. Lu continued to write stories, but none attracted such attention. He went on to study in the United States and obtained a Master's degree. After working many years in there, he published a novella, *Details* (*Xijie*, 1998), which concerns the life of Chinese students studying abroad. It aroused some attention largely owing to the curiosity about what he had done during those years of silence.

See also: xiafang, xiaxiang

LEUNG LAIFONG

Lu Xuechang

b. 1964, Beijing

Film director

Lu Xuechang's movies are defined less by their style than by the common subject – the coming of age of contemporary urban youth. As with many fellow filmmakers of the so-called 'Sixth Generation' (see **Sixth Generation (film directors)**), Lu is concerned with the changing values and lifestyle of contemporary society. However, despite showing the confused and dangerous side of modernity, his movies maintain an idealistic, almost optimistic, point of view. While the leading characters of his movies are anti-heroic, Lu is not afraid to use also

traditional, positive heroes to lead the characters in the search for awareness.

Lu studied painting for four years at the **Central Academy of Fine Arts** before entering the Directing Department of the **Beijing Film Academy**, where he graduated in 1990. After joining the Beijing Film Studio he directed several short films before shooting his controversial first full-length feature, *The Making of Steel* (*Zhanda chengren*, 1998), the story of a young boy's coming of age during the **Cultural Revolution** (see **Tian Zhuangzhuang**). The movie, exploring the meaning of heroism in rapidly modernizing China through the relationship between the young worker and an older train driver, was severely censored and revised many times before being approved for distribution. Lu's second feature, *A Lingering Face* (*Feichang xiari*, 2000), based on the real event of a woman's rape and the witness to the crime, despite being more commercial in style, maintained the true-to-life qualities of all his work. His third and most recent film is *Cala, My Dog!* (*Kala shitiaogou*, 2003), produced by **Feng Xiaogang** and starring **Ge You**, is about a worker fighting the system.

MARIA BARBIERI

Lu Xun Literary Institute

Before adopting its present name of Lu Xun Literary Institute in 1984, the institute went through several stages after its founding in 1950 as the Central Literary Research Institute (Zhongyang wenxue yanjiusuo). As an institution under the **Ministry of Culture**, its mandate is to teach literature and train literary officials and writers according to the Party line. Cultural officials and promising writers from various provinces are recruited for systematic training. The prominent writer Ding Ling (1904–86) was its first director. Well-known literary figures and professors of literature are invited to give lectures. From 1986 to the late 1990s, the literary critic He Zhenbang was in charge of the curriculum.

In 1954, the Central Literary Research Institute was renamed the Literary Institute (Wenxue jiangxisuo) and put under the leadership of the Chinese Writers' Association. In 1958, it was closed down, largely because of the interference of the Anti-Rightist Campaign of 1957. After Mao's death in 1976, and with the relaxation of political control under the new leadership, it opened again in March 1980. Writers recruited into this class include Gu Hua, Jiang Zilong, **Kong Jiesheng**, and **Wang Anyi**. To cope with the increasing number of literary magazines, in 1982 and 1983, editors and literary critics were recruited for training. Beginning in late 1983, acceptance was based on examination scores rather than through recommendation. Between 1988 and 1995, a collaborative programme was established with Beijing Normal and Central China Universities.

LEUNG LAIFONG

Lu Yushun

b.1962, Harbin

Traditional Chinese painter

Lu Yushun, a contemporary painter of modern ink-wash paintings, is also a member of the Chinese Artists' Association. Lu graduated from Harbin Teachers' College in 1983, and then pursued graduate studies in the Ink-painting Department at the **Central Academy of Fine Arts** in Beijing. In 1996, he was appointed Dean of the Fine Arts Faculty at Harbin Teachers' College, and became the chairman of Heilongjiang Province Artists' Association. He received awards from the 1st International Ink-painting Exhibition in Beijing (1988) and from the 8th National Art Exhibition, and has participated in numerous other art exhibitions, at home and abroad, especially in those Asian countries which have been traditionally linked to Chinese culture.

Lu Yushun is best known for striking red landscapes, painted on large, hanging scrolls along a distinctive central axis, often set against a black background that demonstrates an extremely sophisticate use of the ink. His landscapes are also painted on album leaves and fans, and are inspired by poetic verses. His compositions do not consider perspective; the likenesses of objects are deliberately crude. The glacial aloofness of his compositions displays an awareness of patterning practices and familiarity with Western abstract art. Lu Yushun has participated in the annual exhibitions of **New Literati Painting** since 1989, and in 1993–4 he attended a special graduate seminar that was organized for the adherents of this movement.

Further reading

Olivová, Lucie (2001). *Contemporary Chinese Ink Painting: Tradition and Experiment*. Prague: The National Gallery, 40–8.

LUCIE OLIVOVÁ

Lu Zhirong

(a.k.a. Rong Rong)

b.1968, Zhangzhou, Fujian

Photographer

Despite an early interest in painting, Lu Zhirong quickly pursued the photographic medium as his form of artistic expression. After several failed attempts at enrolling in art school and a series of odd jobs, including a position as a passport photographer, in 1993 Rong moved to **Dongcun** (East Village), a budding artistic community on the outskirts of Beijing. It was shortly after this move that Lu Zhirong changed his name and has since been known as Rong Rong. He documented the vibrant, experimental artistic activities of this art-community in his series *Artists in Exile*. Some of his best-known works are documents of performances by the artists **Zhang Huan** and **Ma Liuming**. In 1995, after several artists were arrested and quarrels erupted over copyright issues of Rong's photography, he left the community. The documentary photographs of East Village were featured in Rong's inaugural photography exhibition, 'The Witness of Contemporary Art in China', at the Tokyo Gallery, Japan (1995).

In 1996, Rong established RR Photo Studio. Shocked by the programmatic destruction of Beijing's historical *hutong* (alleyways) and courtyard homes, Rong created a series of untitled works sometimes referred to as the *Ruins* series. Like his previous work, *Ruins* is a personal response to

Rong's living environment, featuring partially destroyed homes bearing haunting evidence of past inhabitants. This is often achieved through re-photographing photographs and posters left behind among the rubble. Rong held a solo exhibition at the French Embassy in Beijing in 1997 and at the Galerie H. S. Steinek in Vienna in 1998. His photographs were also included in 'Contemporary Photo Art from the People's Republic of China' (Neuer Berliner Kunstverein, Berlin and other venues in Germany).

See also: 798; Zhang Hai'er; Zhuang Hui

Further reading

Pollack, Barbara (2004). 'Chinese Photography: Beyond Stereotypes'. *Artnews* 103.2 (February): 98–103.

Schmid, Andreas (1997). *Zeitgenössische Fotokunst aus der Volksrepublic China.* Heidelberg: Edition Braus, 66–9.

Wu, Hung (1999). *Transience – Chinese Experimental Art at the End of the Twentieth Century.* Chicago: University of Chicago Press.

——— (2002). 'Ruins as Autobiography: Chinese Photographer Rong Rong'. *Persimmon* 2.3 (Winter): 36–47.

MATHIEU BORYSEVICZ

Luo Dayou

b. 1954, Taiwan

Folk singer/songwriter

In the winter of 1976, a young painter named Li Shuangjie, who had just returned to Taiwan, broke a bottle of Coca-Cola at a concert and yelled, right in front of the audience, 'Sing our own songs!' A contemporary folksong movement was thus started, of which the Taiwanese troubadour, Luo Dayou, became one of its main protagonists. The driving cultural force behind his music was as Taiwanese as Chinese. In the 1980s, Luo Dayou moved his base to Hong Kong and started his Music Factory label. In his music Luo Dayou shows a strong sense of social

and political engagement. He is above all an intellectual songwriter who constantly asks what 'Chineseness' is. He distances himself as much from essentialist interpretations of culture based on blood, race or soil as he remains critical of current processes of globalization-cum-Westernization. However, by insisting on the notion of 'Chineseness' and by juxtapositioning it with Westernization (for example, his song 'Orphans of Asia' (*Yaxiya de gu'er*): 'The West wind is singing sad songs in the East'), he at times reifies rather than challenges dominant binaries.

After retreating to Taiwan in the 1990s, in 2002 Luo Dayou established the Music Factory in Beijing, a place from which he was banned for most of his professional career. At a press conference held at a Confucian temple, he told reporters of his confidence that Beijing would become the capital of global Chinese music. His highly relevant and eloquent critique of the current imbalances in the global flows of popular culture, however, seems to have inspired Luo Dayou to an uncritical celebration of Beijing as the capital of Chinese culture and the power centre of Chinese transnationalism.

JEROEN DE KLOET

Luo Huaizhen

b. 1956, Huaiyin, Jiangsu

Xiqu (sung-drama/opera) playwright

Luo Huaizhen's career as a playwright in the **Xiqu** genres started in the mid 1980s in Shanghai. Prior to writing plays, he had performed on the Huaiju (Huai opera) stage in his home town in the late 1970s. His first published **Jingju** (Peking opera) play was *The Story of an Ancient Actor* (1984), after which he received a short-term professional training at Shanghai Academy of Theatre. Since then he has, on average, written one play a year. All of them, except the first, have been staged in one or more of the regional forms of Xiqu. His most successful plays include *Wind and Moon by the Qinhuai River* (*Fengyue Qinhuai*, **Yueju (Zhejiang opera)**), *Golden Dragon and Mayfly* (*Jinlong yü fuyou*, Huaiju),

The Hegemon King of Western Chu (Xichu bangwang, Huaiju), Xi Shi Returns to the Kingdom of Yue (Xi Shi gui Yue, Jingju), Magic Lotus Lantern (Baolian deng, Jingju), and Ban Zhao (**Kunqu**). In addition to Yueju, Huaiju, Jingju and Kunqu, Luo has also written plays for Hanju (Hubei opera), Yueju (Cantonese opera; see **Yueju (Guangdong, Guanxi opera)**), and even for musicals (yinyueju).

Luo's plays are all set in imperial China and can be divided into two categories: those that portray historical or literary female figures such as Xi Shi, Ban Zhao, Li Qingzhao and Liu Rushi; and those that invent new allegorical tales set in the past. The former is best represented by Xi Shi Returns to the Kingdom of Yue, which goes against the traditional portrayal of Xi Shi – who had long been honoured for her sexual sacrifice to save the kingdom of Yue – and poses the poignant question: 'What if Xi Shi had been pregnant with the child of the King of Wu?' In Luo's play, the King of Yue cannot tolerate the birth of the child and makes Xi Shi kill her own child and commit suicide. Like most of his tragedies, the play questions the validity of traditional Chinese ethics and some of its virtues. The second category is illustrated by Golden Dragon and Mayfly, in which Luo uses the concepts of Greek and Shakespearean tragedies to portray a prince who abandons his wife in order to save his father's kingdom. Later, because of both a flaw in his personality and the obscurity of several characters' identities, the prince kills his faithful general, castrates his own son and compels his daughter-in-law to become his concubine, leading to the deaths of everyone in his family except for his grandson, who is likely to start the same vicious cycle all over again. It is a political fable questioning the validity of male authority over women and exploring the interrelations between the private and the public. With this and other Huaiju plays, Luo helped initiate a Huaiju revival called 'Metropolitan New Huaiju' (Dushi xinhuaiju) which turned the genre into a major regional style in Shanghai and the lower Yangtze River area. It has even reached the Beijing stage, and is attracting audiences from all walks of life, from young college students to old peasants in the countryside.

DU WENWEI

Luo Zhongli

b.1948, Chongqing, Sichuan

Oil painter

Arguably the most important representative of the **Native Soil Painting** trend, Luo Zhongli caught people's imagination with the painting Father (Fuqin 1980), which won the top award at the 'Second Youth Art Exhibition'. Luo's monumental portrait (240 cm x 165 cm) of a peasant was intentionally painted on a scale reserved for state leaders and filled with details revealing life's hardships (including a mole of bitter fate). Critics objected to this lack of idealization, observing that were it not for the biro behind his ear he would be indistinguishable from a peasant of the 'old society'. Luo exacerbated the problem by writing a self-defence in the magazine **Meishu** [Fine Arts], describing his intent to shout on behalf of the poor, honest (laoshe) peasant he saw on a New Year's Eve who had been assigned to guard the faeces of the communal latrines from being pilfered by neighbouring work units. Father punctured the stereotype of the 'new society' peasant, but was also welcomed as a eulogy to the common peasant who created China's wealth.

A steel-factory worker, Luo was admitted to the Sichuan Academy of Arts oil painting department in 1979. Graduating in 1982, he went on to take a master's degree at the Royal Belgian Academy in Antwerp. Upon his return, Luo continued to paint countryside scenes based on daily life in the Liangshan mountains. He was eventually appointed dean of the Sichuan Academy of Art.

Further reading

Andrews, Julia F. (1994). Painters and Politics in the People's Republic of China 1949–1979. Berkeley: University of California Press, 377–405.

Galikowski, Maria (1998). Art and Politics in China, 1949–1984. Hong Kong: Chinese University Press, 193–207.

Wang, Yuejin (1993). 'Anxiety of Portraiture: Quest for/Questioning Ancestral Icons in Post Mao China'. In Liu Kang and Tang Xiaobing (eds),

Politics, Ideology and Discourse in Modern China. Durham: Duke University Press, 243–72.

EDUARDO WELSH

luogu

(gongs and drums)

Traditional music ensemble

Literally 'gongs and drums', *luogu* is a general term for the Chinese percussion ensemble that may include gongs, drums, cymbals, bells, clappers, woodblocks, etc. Historical records indicate that gongs and cymbals were introduced into China with Buddhism from India and Central Asia by way of the Silk Road during the Southern and Northern dynasties (420–589 CE). Due to the loud sound and non-melodic nature of these instruments, scholars seldom paid attention to them and not much was written about them in the past. But the common people loved these instruments and made good use of them. Nowadays, the *luogu* ensemble can be seen and heard in parades, folk dances, theatres and especially in the accompaniment to the lion dance and dragon dance in the Chinese New Year and other seasonal festivals. In the traditional operas (**Xiqu**), the *luogu* performs the prelude to attract attention, accompanies actions, punctuates singing, and concludes the show.

The size of a *luogu* ensemble ranges from two or three to a dozen musicians. The instrumentation and style vary according to the function and location. The major instruments are *gu* (drums), *luo* (gongs) and *bo* (cymbals). The drummer is always the leader. Also, melodic instruments can be a part of the ensemble. The most commonly melodic instrument used is the *suona* (a double reed oboe probably originating in the Middle East) whose piercing sound penetrates the dense sound of the percussion.

Traditionally *luogu* is taught through oral patterns. Each instrument is represented by one or two oral sounds. The combination of sound and rhythm make up *luogu* patterns called *luogujing*, somewhat similar to bols in Indian tabla music. However, written notation with characters and symbols was introduced in the mid-twentieth century for teaching purposes. This practice is especially popular in schools and social clubs.

Further reading

Han, Kuo-Huang and Campbell, Patricia S. (1996). *The Lion's Roar: Chinese Luogu Percussion Ensemble* (2nd edition). Danbury, CT: World Music Press.

Yang, Mu (1994). 'The Use of Chinese Luogujing in Classroom Music'. *The International Journal of Music Education* 23: 17–23.

HAN KUO-HUANG

Lüshan jiao (Sannai jiao)

Regional religious tradition

The 'Religious Teaching of Mount Lü' (*Lüshan jiao*), or 'Religious Teaching of the Three Ladies' (*Sannai jiao*), is a Daoist ritual tradition of southern China (Fujian, southern Zhejiang and Taiwan) whose origins are still unclear. Very active today, it is related to the cult of Chen Jinggu (767–90), who was enfeoffed as 'Linshui furen' or 'Shunyi furen', and is one of the most important cults of this region. According to her myths as a goddess, she was an avatar of **Guanyin**, born from a drop of blood of this bodhisattva, and caused the demons of the Kingdom of Min (909–45) in Fujian to submit to her power. The Master of Lüshan is the Perfected Lord Xu (Xu Xun), founder of the 'Way of Filial Piety' (Xiaodao) based at the Wanshou Palace north of Nanchang, Jiangxi. Connections also can be found between this tradition and the rituals of the Yao and Zhuang (see **Yao, culture of**; **Zhuang, culture of**; **Daoism among minority nationalities**), and it is also present among the Hakka (see **Hakka, culture of**). In the field, the Lüshan jiao is often opposed to the Maoshan ritual tradition and related to the Wang laomu religion.

The Lüshan jiao, shamanistic in its essence, is complementary and very much connected with the tradition of the **Daoist (Zhengyi tradition)** masters, even if it remains specific. It is a healing, exorcistic, martial tradition and also reveals certain features derived from Tantric Buddhism. The rituals are performed by 'Masters of Ritual Methods' (*fashi*) (see **vernacular priests (Daoist/ Buddhist)**), who work closely together with **spirit-mediums**, especially in Taiwan and the Penghu Islands.

The Masters perform rituals as the head of celestial troops, the soldiers of the five directions, while invoking the 'Three Ladies' (*sannai*): Chen Jinggu and her two disciples, Lin Jiuniang and Li Sanniang, who, like herself, had suffered a bad death. Though the Masters are men, in performance they wear the ritual red skirt of Chen Jinggu and a crown or headdress with the words 'Three Ladies' painted on it (or a martial one). They also wear red turbans, which is the reason they are called 'red head' (*hongtou*) Masters, especially in Taiwan. Their ritual instruments include: a divine pewter or buffalo horn; a wooden seal on which are carved the seven stars of the Dipper; a hempen whip with a serpent handle to frighten demons; and a curved root of bamboo, also called a whip, used to 'recall souls' (*tiaohun*); a bell, sometimes with a vajra handle; and a small gong.

A whole pantheon comes with these beliefs, and the Masters of Lüshan possess ritual paintings that represent it. They are initiated by receiving a 'register' (*lu*) listing the spirits that submit to their banners that they lead in performance. The magical treasures of the Masters include, in addition to ritual texts, a body of written 'talismans' (*fu*) for exorcism, curing and protection which are transmitted from generation to generation. These appear sometimes to be true scriptural rituals. The Masters of Lüshan are equally celebrated for their 'hand-seals' (mudras), reputed to be very efficacious and associated with secret mantras, which recall the practices of the magical 'arts of thunder' (*leifa*) performed by **Daoist priests**.

The ritual substrata of the Lüshan are mainly rites of healing and of exorcism often performed along with a 'substitute' (*tishen*; often a spirit-medium), the **fachang** ritual, and *xietu*, an 'exorcism of earth evils' and of the White Tiger. They also perform a 'transformation of the destiny' (*gaiyun*) ritual, a Dipper (*beidou*) ritual, and rites for 'calling the souls' of the living or dead

(*shoujing/tiaohun*). The rituals performed for women, called 'cultivating flowers' (*caihua*), and for children, called 'crossing the passes' (*guoguan*), are closely related to the cultic worship of Chen Jinggu. Finally, they have a shamanistic voyage rite called 'crossing the roads and the passes' (*guo luguan*).

The Masters perform community rites during pilgrimages and gods' festivals (see **temple fairs**), such as 'presenting or dividing incense' (*jinxiang fenxiang*), which is related to incense-burner (local temple) communities. They take part in the seasonal rites of passage. A ritual for rain and the re-establishment of cosmic harmony had been performed by Chen Jinggu herself, who died on one such occasion while pregnant, which is why she is obligated to protect women (especially during childbirth) and children. In certain parts of Taiwan and Fujian, Masters also carry out the **Jiao** or Daoist 'offering' ritual. The *liandu* ritual, a kind of posthumous rite of passage, and the *chaodu* death ritual have been adopted by some Lüshan Masters on occasion, though they are more often concerned with rituals for the living.

Further reading

Baptandier, B. (1994). 'Le talisman de l'empereur de jade. Construction d'un objet d'écriture'. *L'Homme* 129: 59–92.

—— (1996a). 'Le rituel d'ouverture des passes. Un concept de l'enfance'. *L'Homme* 137: 119–42. [Also as 'Kaiguan ritual and the Construction of the Child's Identity'. In *Popular Beliefs and Chinese Culture/Minjian xinyang yu zhongguo wenhua*. Taipei: Centre for Chinese Studies Research Series 4.]

—— (1996b). 'The Lady Linshui: How a Woman became a Goddess'. In R. Weller and M. Shahar (eds). *Unruly Gods. Divinity and Society in China*. Honolulu: University of Hawai'i.

—— (1997). 'Penser par substitut. Le rituel du corps de remplacement'. In J. Galinier and R. Jamous (eds), *Penser et agir par substituts. Le corps en perspective*. Nanterre: Ateliers 18, 29–48.

—— (2002). 'Lushan Puppet Theatre in Fujian'. In Daniel L. Overmyer (ed.). *Ethnography in China*

Today: A Critical Assessment of Methods and Results. Taipei: Yuan-liou, 243–56.

—— (2003). 'Façonner la divinité en soi. A la recherche d'un lieu d'énonciation'. In Alison Marshall (ed.), *Negotiating Transcendence/Négocier la transcendance*. Special issue of *Ethnologies* 25.1.

Berthier, B. (1987). 'Enfant de divination, voyageur du destin'. *L'Homme* 101: 86–101.

—— (1988). *La Dame du Bord de l'Eau*. Nanterre: Société d'ethnologie.

BRIGITTE BERTHIER-BAPTANDIER

M

Ma Ke

b. October 1930, Hebei

Theatre director

Ma Ke is one of the most influential and prolific **Xiqu** (sung-drama/opera) directors working in the post-**Cultural Revolution** era. Trained as a **Jingju** (Peking opera) actor at the Voice of China Theatre School (Xiasheng jushe) in Xi'an, Ma specialized in the martial-male (*wusheng*) and comic-male (*chou*) role types, gained extensive stage experience, and graduated in 1949. He then acted for two years in a People's Liberation Army 'Little Sister Theatre Troupe' (*Meimei jutuan*), and in 1951 became one of the core members of the newly formed East China Jingju Troupe (Huadong jingjutuan), later to become the Shanghai Jingju Company (Shanghai jingjuyuan), where Ma continues to be based.

Ma was one of the first actors to direct Jingju. In 1954 the master actor Zhou Xinfang wanted to experiment with working under a director, and chose Ma to serve as the director for his new production, *Wen Tianxiang* (the eponymous Song dynasty official). Zhou then arranged for Ma to study directing at the Shanghai Xiju Academy (Shanghai xiju xueyuan), a **Huaju** (spoken drama) training academy where he was introduced to the Stanislavsky system of acting by teachers from the Soviet Union. Ma then directed the modern Jingju *Red Thunderstorm* (*Hongse fengbao*) in 1958; it exerted a seminal influence on succeeding modern Jingju production.

Ma has directed over eighty productions of newly written historical and contemporary plays, primarily in the Jingju form but also in many other forms of Xiqu as well as **Geju** (song-drama) and Huaju (spoken drama). Among his major achievements are the Jingju productions *Cave of the Coiled Webs* (***Pansi dong***, 1986), **Cao Cao and Yang Xiu** (*Cao Cao yü Yang Xiu*, 1988) and *Dream of the King of Qi* (*Qiwang meng*, 1996), based on Shakespeare's *King Lear*. Since the early 1990s, Ma has also co-directed several productions in Europe, collaborating with Swedish theatre artist Peter Oskarson.

ELIZABETH WICHMANN-WALCZAK

Ma Lihua

b. 1953, Jinan, Shandong

Writer

A prolific author on modern Tibet, Ma volunteered to work in Tibet upon college graduation in 1976 and has since called it her home. A long-time editor of *Xizang wenxue* [Tibetan Literature] and currently the vice-chair of the Writers' Association of Tibet, she has played a critical role in promoting a new cadre of modern Tibetan literature-in-Chinese.

Ma began her creative career as a lyrical poet celebrating the natural splendour and the enduring human spirit of the snow land. She later added to her humanistic idealism a pronounced cultural-relativist strand and produced three volumes of essays documenting her field trips to rural Tibet and her reflections on Tibetan culture and society, all now collected in *Traversing Tibet* (*Zouguo Xizang*,

1994). The first of the trio has been translated into English as *Glimpses of Northern Tibet*. But her romanticism and relativism proved untenable as she had to confront the question of how the 'enlightened' intellectual can romanticize the 'primitive' Tibet when many rural Tibetans are struggling for survival and in dire need of modern education, health care, and economic development.

The second half of the 1990s saw her publication of a volume on modern Tibetan literature and another on the history of the scientific research of the Tibetan Plateau. She now oversees the Internet *Xizangwang* (TibetWeb) that fosters public awareness of Tibetan culture and society. Her life and work embody much of the ambivalence of Chinese intellectuals who work in Tibet.

YUE GANG

Ma Liuming

b. 1969, Huangshi, Hubei

Performance artist

Despite a traditional training in the Department of Oil Painting at the Hubei Academy of Fine Arts, Ma experimented with performance even before graduation in 1991. In 1988, in response to the socio-political pressures of the **Campaign against Bourgeois Liberalization** (1987), Ma realized *Suicide Project*, which involved wrapping and restraining his body in a white cloth, in collaboration with Wei Guanqing in Wuhan. In 1993 he moved to Beijing where he joined the artists' colony at **Dongcun** (East Village), and became involved in the underground avant-garde movement as the community's youngest member. That year he realized his first solo piece, *Dialogue with Gilbert and George*. Inspired by a visit of this eponymous artist duo to China, Ma inserted his hand in a crack in the ceiling while standing on a table placed at the centre of a room as blood dripped down his arm and body. The same year, 1993, was also the year of the birth of his transgendered artistic persona, 'Fen-Ma Liuming', in which a character (*fen*), meaning 'incense' but also connoting 'separation', is prefixed to his male name to create an alter-ego that will feature in his

performances, paintings and sculptures. This androgynous persona becomes the neutral ground where issues of sexual identity, the territory between self and others, and the coexistence of contrasting elements (a yin/yang poetics) are acted out. The body is reclaimed as uniquely 'political and critical' (Yuko Hasegawa) in reaction to the levelling directions imposed by traditional Communist ideology.

Through 1996 Ma Liuming's works were predominantly narrative and symbolic. In *Fen-Ma Liuming Lunch I–II* (1994), for example, Ma connected the act of cooking food to that of consuming sex (by sucking his own, tube-extended penis), hinting at a possible, interiorized fusion of collective and individual selves. After that performance he was imprisoned for two months, and the Dongcun artistic community dispersed. From 1997, his site-specific series of performances, entitled *Fen-Ma Liuming at/in . . .*, reached a turning point with a performance in Breda in which he let the audience interact by posing in various alienated stances next to him in front of a mirror. Ma has performed in several venues in Asia, Europe and the USA, and has been featured in group shows with photos and videos derived from his performance, including 'Degenderism' at the Setagaya Art Museum, in Tokyo (1997), 'Inside Out: New Chinese Art' at the P.S.1 Contemporary Art Centre in New York (1998), 'Aperto Over All' at the 48th Venice Biennale (1999) and 'Egofugal: the 7th International Istanbul Biennale' in Turkey (2001).

Further reading

Dematté, Monica (1999). 'Ma Liuming'. In *La Biennale di Venezia, 48a Esposizione d'Arte, d'Apertutto, Aperto Over All*. Venice: La Biennale di Venezia/Marsilio, 304–7.

Dreissen, Chris and van Mierlo, Heidi (eds) (1997). *Another Long March: Chinese Conceptual and Installation Art in the Nineties*. Breda: Fundament Foundation.

Gysen-Hsieh, Beatrice Peini (n.d.). 'Mihu xunzong: Shitan Ma Liuming yishu xinglu de xueni hongzhao' [Meddled Traces: Exploring the Footprints of Art Voyager Ma Liuming]. Unpubl. article provided by the artist.

Hasegawa, Yuko (2002). 'Ma Liuming: The Politics of Non-differentiation'. Unpubl. ms.

Qian, Zhijian (1999). 'Performing Bodies: Zhang Huan, Ma Liuming and Performance Art in China'. *Art Journal* 58.2 (Summer): 60–81.

BEATRICE LEANZA

Ma Xiaoqing

b. 1968, Shanghai

Film actress

Born into an intellectual's family, Ma Xiaoqing started her film career as a child star. She was selected by famous director **Xie Jin** to play the part of a Red Army child, Xiangzhu, in the film *Ah, Yaolan* (1979) at age eleven. Later she acted in *Bitter Fruit* (*Kuguo*, 1981), *Midnight* (*Ziye*, 1981), *The Letter Without Words* (*Meiyou zi de xin*, 1981), and *Be Head Over Heels in Love* (*Yiwang qingshen*, 1984). In 1986, Ma enrolled in Shanghai Theatrical Arts Academy (Shanghai xiju xueyuan), but soon found herself incompatible with the system and withdrew, heading to Beijing to develop her career. In 1987, Ma played the part of Liu Meiping, a lovely and confused urban girl, in *The Trouble Shooters* (*Wanzhu*), which was adapted from a **Wang Shuo** novella. Considered a turning point in Ma's acting career, her vivid and natural performance won acclaim from both critics and audiences. In 1988, she played the part of Xiao Shaobing in *The Female Detective Bao Gaiding* (*Nüshentan Bao Gaiding*), which resulted in a 'Hundred Flowers Award' nomination for best supporting actress. In 1989, Ma played a lively country girl Ding Shuihua in *Do You Love Me?* (*Ni ai wo ma?*) – Ma's first leading role. In that year, Ma also played Shi Xiangyun in a movie version of *Dream of the Red Chamber, Parts 3, 4, 5, 6* (*Hongloumeng III, IV, V, VI*). In the 1990s, Ma acted in the films *Someone is in Love with Me* (*Youren pianpian aishang wo*, 1900), *Street Knighthood* (*Malu qishi*, 1990), *Good Morning, Beijing!* (*Beijing nizao*, 1990, directed by the renowned woman director **Zhang Nuanxin**), *War of Divorce* (*Lihun dazhan*, 1992) and *The Woman from the Lake of Scented Souls* (*Xianghunnü*). In 1997, Ma acted as the chief nurse in *I Have a Father, Too* (*Wo yeyou baba*), a film about children afflicted with leukaemia

fighting for life which won her the best supporting actress award at the 1998 'Golden Rooster' awards. Her most recent appearances include *Weekend Lover* (*Zhoumo qingren*, 1995), *Frozen* (*Jidu hanlen*, 1997) and *The Unusual Summer Day* (*Feichang xiari*, 1999). Most of Ma's films are comedies. She is known for playing childishly unconventional and rebellious girls, such as the daughter in the TV series **Beijingers in New York**.

Further reading

www.filmsea.com
www.gzmovie.com
http://ycwb.com

LU HONGWEI

Ma Yuan

b. 1953, Jinzhou

Writer

Hailed as the pioneer of the **avant-garde/experimental literature** that emerged in the mid 1980s, Ma Yuan also writes poetry under the pen-name Lu Gao. Upon graduating from college in 1982 he was assigned to work in Tibet. When he left Tibet for health reasons in 1989, he left his creativity behind, too. He has since worked on various other projects, especially a long documentary film featuring one hundred Chinese writers. But he is yet to produce much more in fiction or poetry.

Ma's path-breaking story is 'Xugou' (*A Fiction*). He employs the technique of circular narrative and embedded storytelling to subvert conventional rules defining autobiography and fiction, reality and illusion. Central to all his fiction is the use of his own name to identify the author, the narrator and a fictional character, sometimes all at once. He attributes much of his inspiration to his encounters with the Tibetan world and its unique understanding of time, life and meaning. Despite his acclaimed avant-gardism, Ma writes in accessible language and plausible details for distinctive characters. More controversial is his exoticization of Tibet and eroticization of women, especially

Tibetan women. In recycling the myth of the Shangri-la he is rather conventional. But for a bohemian author intent on taking politics out of his writing, the Shangri-la stands to reverse the previous portrayal of Tibet as a living hell, and the eroticization of Tibetan women is meant to transgress the Confucian code of sexual propriety and expose its concurrent sexual hypocrisy.

Further reading

Huot, Claire (2000). 'Literary Experiments: Six Files'. In *idem*, *China's New Cultural Scene: A Handbook of Changes*. Durham: Duke University Press, 7–48.

Ma, Yuan (1993). 'Fabrications'. Trans. J. Q. Sun. In Henry Zhao (ed.), *The Lost Boat: Avant-Garde Fiction from China*. London: Wellsweep, 101–44.

—— (1998). 'More Ways Than One to Make a Kite' (trans. Zhu Hong) and 'A Wandering Spirit' (trans. Caroline Mason). In Wang Jing (ed.), *China's Avant-Garde Fiction: An Anthology*. Durham: Duke University Press, 246–83.

Yang, Xiaobin (2002). 'Narratorial Parabasis and *Mise-en-Abime*: Ma Yuan as a Model'. In *idem* (ed.), *The Chinese Postmodern: Trauma and Irony in Chinese Avant-Garde Fiction*. Ann Arbor: University of Michigan Press, 153–67.

YUE GANG

mahjong

Game

Mahjong (*majiang*; also *maque* [sparrow]) is a popular game normally played by four people using dice and 144 tiles which have numbers and suits – the winds, dragons, Chinese characters, bamboo and circles. At the beginning of the game, the tiles are arranged face down in a square 'court' which has four walls, each eighteen tiles long and two tiles high. The walls, which are jokingly called the Great Wall, are built indiscriminately. The player taking the last wall breaks the square by extracting two tiles. From this point the players start making sets and sequences of tiles by taking fresh tiles in turn (thirteen in all) and discarding unwanted tiles into the

court. Points are given according to the value of the tiles and of the various sets and sequences. In the past centuries Mahjong was introduced to Japan, America and other countries, where rules are modified. There are many mahjong clubs in and outside of China, e.g. the Beijing Mahjong Club, and one can also play online in different languages. Due to variations in play and scoring from place to place or even from house to house, people who do not often play together may have to agree on the rules beforehand. The Shanghainese, Cantonese and Taiwanese versions are well known.

Many Chinese are mahjong addicts, but many also, especially in the PRC, look down on mahjong as gambling associated with the criminal underworld: Edward **Yang**'s film *Mahjong* (1995) is about corrupt expatriates and the low life among Taipei gangs. In fact, mahjong was discouraged after 1949 in the PRC, and even forbidden during the **Cultural Revolution** (1966–76) because of its association with a decadent life. It was still frowned upon during the 1980s, when people had to play indoors. In Shanghai's community centres, where neighbours like to play mahjong, one can still see the 'No gambling' (*buxu dubo*) signs displayed. Interestingly, with the popularity of computer games, mahjong has not declined, especially among senior citizens. Probably for the purpose of distinguishing mahjong from gambling, the PRC government recognized it as a competitive athletic sport (*tiyu jingji xiangmu*), and in September 1998, the **State Sports General Administration (Sports Bureau)** announced the 'Chinese Mahjong Competition Rules (for Trial Implementation)' (*Zhongguo majiang jingsai guize, shixing*). National and regional contests have been held according to the official rules. The game is often a social event with wining and dining, and games may last for days. A *shunkouliu* (doggerel verse) satirises cadres:

Zui xing fende shi kai qiecuo (majiang) hui,
Zui xiaosade shi zoujin yezhonghui.

The most exciting thing is to hold a discussion
    [playing mahjong] meeting;
The most natural and unrestrained thing to do is
    go to a nightclub.

What they do at those places is vividly described in examples (2) and (4) under the entry **shunkouliu**.

Further reading

Papineau, E. (2000). 'Mah-jong, a Game with Attitude: Expression of an Alternative Culture'. Trans. M. Black. *China Perspectives* 28: 29–42.

HELEN XIAOYAN WU

Malqinhu

(Malaqinhu)

b. 1930, Inner Mongolia

Writer

A Mongolian writer and veteran CCP official, Malqinhu is renowned for imbuing his portrayal of the Mongolian ethnic minority with the Party's ideology. Malqinhu published his first story in 1951 and quickly rose to fame as one of the first notable minority writers in the PRC. During the 1980s, Malqinhu acted as editor-in-chief of *Minzu wenxue* [Minority Literature] and *Zuojia chubanshe* [Writers' Press] in Beijing. He was appointed general secretary of the Chinese Writers' Association in 1989.

Malqinhu was among the first PRC writers to set his fiction in the vast Mongolian grassland. In perfect keeping with CCP socialist propaganda, his 1950s and 1960s grassland stories often depict Mongolia's 'new life' as a liberation from the 'old life' of slavery. While sharing a humanist sentiment with **Scar literature** in exposing the horrible crimes of the 'Gang of Four' (see **Cultural Revolution**), Malqinhu's fiction in the early 1980s attempted to rehabilitate the Party's political and ideological legitimacy. In his short story 'Walking in the Deep Snow' (*Taguo shenshen de jixue*), Malqinhu portrays a Mongolian official who ignores her own political trauma while sparing no effort in uniting with the herdsmen and correcting the Party's mistakes. Malqinhu also won the National Excellent Short Story Prize for 'The Story of a Living Buddha' (*Huofo de gushi*, 1980), which criticizes certain Buddhist practices as superstitious and inhuman. Besides its ideological significance, the rich Mongolian local colour in his works may also explain why they have been translated into more than ten languages.

See also: Buddhism in Inner Mongolia; Mongols, culture of

Further reading

Malqinhu (1990). 'Love that Burns on a Summer's Night'. Trans. Simone Jouhnstone. In *Love that Burns on a Summer Night*. Beijing: Panda Books, 231–313.

ZHANG YULONG

Manchus, culture of

About 10 million Manchus mainly live in northeast China, in Liaoning, Jilin and Heilongjiang provinces. Since the Qing dynasty (1644–1911), which was ruled by the Manchus, large numbers moved to the Han regions south of the Great Wall and have been largely assimilated into the Han Chinese culture. They have their own spoken and written languages, but most now generally speak **baihua/Guoyu** and write Han characters. Some of the Manchu legacies still around are: (1) the **qipao, cheongsam**, a close-fitting dress flared at the base with a rolled-up hem reaching to the ankle. It has long become the national costume of Chinese women; (2) *Man-Han quanxi* [the complete banquet of the Manchu and the Han] was revived when wining and dining at public expense became epidemic in the 1980s and was made famous in **Tsui Hark**'s film *The Chinese Feast (Man Han quanxi*, 1995). Although the 108 dishes and 44 courses of **dim sum** – which take three days to consume – hardly fit present-day society, various dishes popular in the Qing palace are still prepared today in the restaurants of big hotels; and (3) *saqima*, a common sweet snack. Besides the royal families in history, the Manchus have produced many celebrities, e.g. the linguist Luo Changpei (1899–1958); the founder of the Cheng school of Peking Opera, Cheng Yanqiu (1904–58); and the writer Lao She (1899–1966). Their works or performances are still heavily studied. Tan Jie is a contemporary Manchu author whose lengthy works of reportage literature, *The Heavenly Way (Tiandao), Thick Soil (Houtu)* and *Holy Hands (Shengshou)*, and a prose collection,

Children of the Great Liao River (Daliaohe de er'nümen), are well known.

Further reading

Crossley, Pamela Kyle (1997). *The Manchus.* (The Peoples of Asia series.) Oxford: Blackwell.

HELEN XIAOYAN WU

Mao A'min

b. 1963, Shanghai

Pop singer

Mao A'min is monumental in Chinese pop music. She had a talent for singing when young. She began her singing career with the Shanghai Chemical Workers Performance Troupe and from 1985 with the Front Singing and Dancing Ensemble of the People's Liberation Army, Nanjing Military Area Command. In June of that year, she won the first prize at the First Young Vocalist Contest of Jiangsu province. A month later, she received a third place at the National Young Vocalist Contest. Her unique style of sub-soprano became her hallmark.

In 1987, at the International Music Festival in Belgrade, Mao won the third place with 'A Leaf's Feelings Towards the Root' (*Lüye dui gen de qingyi*). This achievement secured her a stardom enjoyed by few other pop singers. In 1989, Mao transferred to the Singing and Dancing Ensemble of the PLA General Political Department. The theme song of the early Chinese TV series *Yearnings (Kewang)* (see **Yearnings, Aspirations**) brought her singing career to new heights. She was selected as one of the top ten film, TV and singing stars in 1992. Her albums include *Pursuing (Zhuixun)*, *A Stray Girl (Milu de nühai)* and *The Experienced (Guolai ren)*. For personal reasons, Mao lived in Britain, the United States and Australia between 1995 and 1998. Her bond with her Chinese audience, however, has pulled her home, and she staged her official comeback on 27 February 2002 in the Great Hall of the People in Beijing.

Further reading

Baranovitch, Nimrod (2003). *China's New Voices: Popular Music, Ethnicity, Gender, and Politics, 1978– 1997.* Berkeley: University of California Press, 146–8.

HU MINGRONG

Mao Lizi

(né Zhang Zhunli)

b. 1950, Shanxi

Oil painter

Mao Lizi is a partially self-taught painter and member of the 'rusticated youth' generation (see **Cultural Revolution (education)**; **xiafang, xiaxiang**). He worked as a set designer for the Chinese Air Force and was a member of the **Stars** group. In the mid 1980s he attended a specialization course in oil painting at the **Central Academy of Fine Arts** in Beijing, graduating in 1987. In 1990, he received a grant from the French government and was a Visiting Professor at the Ecole Nationale des Beaux Arts in Paris.

Mao Lizi's trademark images are hyper-realistic, blown-up details of apparently insignificant places magnified visually and metaphorically through the artistic process. In a 1976 triptych exhibited for the Stars exhibition – *Hesitating, Ten Years of Chaos* and *New Life* – he focuses on street details to reflect upon the dispiritedness that had washed over an entire generation at the end of the euphoric period of the **Cultural Revolution**. By depicting with photographic verisimilitude, respectively: a detail from a cement pavement marked by circular footsteps and cigarette butts; a wall with washed-out slogans and children's graffiti; and a wall where a new plant emerges from a crack, Mao captures the destruction of a whole era and the sense of loss suffered by its protagonists, questioning hopes for a new beginning. Selected exhibitions of Mao's work include: 'Stars' in Beijing (1979 and 1980); the 5th National Exhibition in Beijing (1984); 'The Stars: Ten Years' in Hong Kong and Taipei (1989); 'Reckoning with the Past' at the Fruitmarket Gallery in Edinburgh (1996); 'Chinese

Contemporary Painting' at the Hefner Gallery in New York (1987).

Further reading

Andrews, Julia and Shen, Kuiyi (eds) (1998). *A Century in Crisis* (exhibition catalogue). New York: The Solomon R. Guggenheim Museum, 237.

Cohen, Joan Lebold (1987). *The New Chinese Painting, 1949–1986*. New York: Harry N. Abrams.

Hui, Ching-shuen (ed.) (1989). *The Stars: Ten Years* (exhibition catalogue). Hong Kong: Hanart T Z Gallery, 2.

Lü, Peng and Yi, Dan (eds) (1992). *Zhongguo xiandai yishushi 1979–1989* [A History of Modern Art in China, 1979–89]. Changsha: Hunan meishu chubanshe, 77.

FRANCESCA DAL LAGO

Mao restaurants

(Maojia Fanden/Maojia Caiguan)

In 1987, Maojia Fanden (Mao Restaurant) was opened in Shaoshan, Mao Zedong's native place in Hunan province, to serve dishes called *Maojiacai* that Mao used to enjoy. Since Shaoshan had become a pilgrimage spot for millions of people including national leaders, the restaurant too became famous and in 1995 obtained a patent right from the government to monopolize the brand name 'Maojia'. In 1999, it became incorporated and opened branch restaurants in Beijing and Shanghai. In 1993, a new restaurant, Maojia Caiguan, was opened in Shaoshan to celebrate the hundredth anniversary of Mao's birth, and soon numerous other small restaurants serving Mao dishes appeared. In Beijing, sixty restaurants serving Mao dishes were reported in 1999. *Maojiacai* is similar to Hunanese **home cooking** (*jiachangcai*), which has also become famous through media attention. Nowadays, many restaurants invent and modify spicy dishes under the name of Mao. The popularity of Mao restaurants is understood in connection with the Mao cult that has surged in the middle of post-socialist changes (see **Neo-Maoism and Mao Fever**).

KIM KWANG-OK

Mao Yan

b. 1968, Xiangtan, Hunan

Painter

A virtuoso portrait painter, his fascination with technique is apparent from his remarkable untitled early self-portrait imitating Rembrandt's portrait of himself as a young man. Opting for the subtler, classical and tranquil techniques of painting, he seemed to unearth fresh possibilities, imbuing the stillness of his subjects with contemporary edginess. Graduated from the **Central Academy of Fine Arts** in 1991, he was assigned to teach at the Nanjing Academy of Art. Mao shot to national attention soon afterwards at the 1992 Guangzhou Biennial with his humorous portrait of the art critic **Li Xiaoshan** and a screaming doll sidekick. His later portraits tend to tone down both the range of colours and the subject's expressiveness. Mao's preference to work from photographs keeps the subject at a controllable distance, as if he is not so interested in his or her personality or individuality, but in interacting with the process of painting human beings. Such speculation is borne out in titles such as *The Nature of Portraiture* (1998). Despite his seemingly unfashionable choice, the timeless approach of Mao's hermitic exploration seems to slip him to the forefront of contemporary Chinese art. Mao Yan's paintings have been shown at, among other venues, the 1996 Shanghai Biennial and the exhibition 'One Hundred Years of Chinese Portraiture' in Beijing (1997).

Further reading

Li, Xianting (1997). 'The Boundary between Language and Craft – In Reference to the Works of Mao Yan and Zhou Chunya (*Yüyuan yü shouyi de jiexian*). In *The Nature of Portraiture* (exhibition catalogue). Beijing: Gallery of the Central Academy of Fine Arts.

EDUARDO WELSH

Mao Zedong and Sun Yatsen suits

Inspired by military uniform, the fitted jacket with rounded collar and Western trousers of the Sun Yatsen suit (*zhongshanzhuang*) emerged as an important fashion for young revolutionaries in the 1920s. Mao Zedong adapted the style for the Communist revolution, a variant that also drew inspiration from the trousers, tunics and black cotton shoes of Chinese peasants. The Mao suit (*maozhuang*) thus symbolized revolutionary tradition, militarization of society, and revolutionary asceticism. It dominated the sartorial landscape of the 1960s and reached its height in the Cultural Revolution. Subtle differences in the Mao suit differentiated the population: peasants and workers wore indigo blue Mao jackets; People's Liberation Army soldiers donned khaki green; and Party cadres sported grey barathea – thus ensuring, paradoxically, that uniformity maintained hierarchical difference even while advocating egalitarian ideals.

The Mao jacket is associated with the redefinition of femininity through a masculinization of society as well as with the rejection of bourgeois norms that objectify the female body. In the post-Maoist period and subsequent promotion of consumer culture, leaders and urban populations replaced Mao suits with Western styles. With the **Neo-Maoism and Mao Fever** of the early 1990s, the Mao suit emerged again as desired youth fashion. At this time, its appeal derived from kitsch-based consumerism and contestation over the memory and legacy of Mao Zedong.

See also: Tang dress

Further reading

Barmé, Geremie R. (1996). *Shades of Mao, The Posthumous Cult of the Great Leader*. Armonk and London: M. E. Sharpe.

Chen, Tina Mai (1999). 'Dressing for the Party: Clothing, Citizenship, and Gender-Formation in Mao's China'. *Fashion Theory* 5.2: 143–72.

TINA MAI CHEN

marriage

For most of Chinese history, marriage was arranged by parents. This tradition has its roots in the strong belief that marriage is a family affair and should involve households of similar socioeconomic statuses (*mengdang hudui* or 'matching doors').

Pragmatism is central to the mate-selection process, which tends to emphasize the matching and trade-off of attributes between prospective spouses. Though the 1950 Marriage Law outlawed arranged marriage, even today it is still customary for 'introducers' (*jieshao ren*) or 'matchmakers' (*meiren*) to facilitate the mate-selection process, especially in the countryside.

In rural China, in particular, marriage is governed by patrilocal exogamy, whereby the daughter moves out from the natal family and joins the husband's family. This tradition is in part a by-product of the notion that marriage requires and legitimizes the transfer of a woman's membership and labour. To the natal family, the daughter's labour is forever lost, as described by the old Chinese saying, 'daughters married out are like spilled water'. This discourages the natal family from investing in the education of girls relative to their male siblings. A brideprice is usually offered by the husband's family as a practical and symbolic compensation to the natal family for raising the daughter. Parents of sons are eager to recruit the labour of daughters-in-law, and this in part accounts for the prevalence of early marriage. The natal family is also eager to arrange for the marriage of a daughter as early as possible, lest she become too old to get married and continue to be a burden to the family. Thus, the dowry tradition is considered a gift to the husband's family for taking up the responsibility for the daughter. Even today, in rural China, girls are expected to be married young. After the daughter reaches twenty years old, parents are eager to see to it that arrangements be made to find her a husband.

The Confucian ideology that governs gender roles stresses the importance of marriage to women. The notion that a woman's well-being or happiness (*xingfu*) depends on her marriage has been one of the major cornerstones of gender roles and relations in China. Marriage has always been considered an inevitable and indispensable life-event, hence the old saying 'when boys and girls reach adulthood they should get married' (*nanda danghun nüda dangjia*). The centrality of marriage to women's well-being is perhaps most prominent in the countryside. While peasant men may improve their social and economic mobility by joining the military, going to school, and becoming cadres, most peasant women have few alternatives other than marriage for escaping poverty and achieving upward mobility. Though the majority of marriage migration takes place to nearby villages, increased volumes of long-distance marriage migration from inland China to coastal provinces show that spatial hypergamy is gaining prominence.

Further reading

Croll, Elizabeth (1984). 'The Exchange of Women and Property: Marriage in Post Revolutionary China'. In R. Hirschorn (ed.), *Women and Property – Women As Property*. London: Croom Helm, 44–61.

—— (1987). 'New Peasant Family Forms in Rural China'. *The Journal of Peasant Studies* 14.4: 469–99.

Fan, C. Cindy and Ling, Li (2002). 'Marriage and Migration in Transitional China: A Field Study of Gaozhou, Western Guangdong'. *Environment and Planning A* 34.4: 619–38.

Fan, C. Cindy and Youqin, Huang (1998). 'Waves of Rural Brides: Female Marriage Migration in China'. *Annals of the Association of American Geographers* 88.2.2: 27–51.

Hildebrand, Margaret (1999). 'Beleaguered Husbands: Representations of Marital Breakdown in Some Recent Chinese Fiction'. *Tamkang Review* 30.2 (Winter).

Ruan, Xinbang, Luo, Peilin and He, Yuying (eds) (2003). *Marriage, Gender and Sex in a Contemporary Chinese Village*. Armonk, NY: M. E. Sharpe.

Xu, Xiaoqun (1996). 'The Discourse of Love, Marriage, and Sexuality in Post-Mao China; or, A Reading of the New Journalistic Literature on Women'. *positions: east asia cultures critique* 4.2 (Fall).

Yan, Yunxiang (2003). *Private Life under Socialism: Love, Intimacy, and Family Changes in a Chinese Village, 1949–1999*. Stanford: Stanford University Press.

C. CINDY FAN

Marriage Law of the PRC (1 January 1981) and revisions (2001)

One of the major steps the PRC took to counter age-old forces that undermine women's status is the Marriage Law of 1950. It outlawed arranged marriages, concubinage, footbinding and child marriages, and provided greater access to divorce for women. The 1981 Marriage Law reinstated much of the 1950 law while extending some of its provisions. The minimum marriage age was raised by two years to twenty-two for men and twenty for women, in order to encourage late marriage and delay childbirth, both deemed necessary for slowing population growth. Restrictions on divorce were further relaxed so that it could be granted even if only one spouse felt it was necessary. Like its predecessor, the 1981 law was followed by a rise in divorce. Moreover, the principle of equality between the sexes was emphasized in language that reinforced men's and women's equal status in the home and their shared responsibility in caring for parents and children.

On 28 April 2001, the National People's Congress approved a set of revisions to the 1981 Marriage Law. These revisions were deemed necessary because social and economic changes in the reform era had rendered the old law inadequate, especially in areas of adultery, domestic violence, divorce, property rights and elderly care. The 2001 revisions specify that adultery and domestic violence are illegal and that the violating party can be prosecuted and has legal responsibility to compensate the other party. This is a response to policy-makers' concern over increasing cases of infidelity, husbands having mistresses ('**bao ernai**') and domestic dispute, especially in the most developed parts of China. These are widely interpreted as symptoms of spiritual pollution (see **socialist spiritual civilization**) and as such must be controlled. Most importantly, the revisions introduce the concept of fault in divorce, especially when adultery, domestic violence, abuse or abandonment is involved. This is an extension of the previous laws' philosophy of protecting the rights of women and children, as they are most often the victims in the above situations.

Addressing the increasing material wealth and re-emergence of private property in the reform era, the 2001 revisions provide elaborate definitions about joint and individual property within marriage, prenuptial agreement, and property allocation after divorce. In addition, the revisions specify the social and financial responsibility of children towards their parents and that of grandchildren towards their grandparents. By doing so, the government assigns elderly care to the household in light of the nation's demographic changes – a shrinking number of children (see **little emperors**) and an expanding proportion of the elderly. As a whole, the 2001 revisions articulate more fully than previous laws the legal rights and responsibilities of spouses, children and parents.

Further reading

Croll, Elizabeth (1984). 'The Exchange of Women and Property: Marriage in Post Revolutionary China'. In R. Hirschorn (ed.), *Women and Property – Women as Property*. London: Croom Helm: 44–61.

Ma, Yuan (ed.) (2001). *Xin hunyinfa yinan shijie* [Explanations of Difficulties in the New Marriage Law]. Beijing: Renmin fayuan chubanshe.

Smith, Christopher J. (2000). 'Gender Issues in the Transition Out of Socialism'. In *idem, China in the Post-Utopian Age*. Boulder, Colorado: Westview Press, 289–320.

C. CINDY FAN

martial arts

(wushu)

The history of martial arts since the **Cultural Revolution** is intrinsically tied to policies initiated in 1949. Until about 1979, the overall objective was to convert the martial arts into a performance art and a national sport (hereafter referred to as 'modern wushu') in the hopes of attaining international recognition. Since 1979, there has been a concerted effort to rescue elements of traditional culture, and from 1990 to the present, the critical issue for the PRC has been to establish its cultural legitimacy in the eyes of the international community.

During the ten years of the Cultural Revolution, the practice of martial arts was strictly forbidden, and those who were caught were severely punished. The practice of martial arts, even in the countryside and small villages, stopped completely, while many historical records of traditional martial arts were destroyed. In 1979, in an effort to save the tradition, the Physical Culture and Sports Commission issued a document entitled 'Circular for Unearthing and Establishing Our Wushu Heritage'. Some of the first traditional martial arts that benefited were *bagua zhang*, *xingyi quan* and *taiji quan*. However, private schools were still not free to operate.

It was not until the mid 1980s, however, that a collection of extant pieces of traditional martial art forms were put together. In June of 1984, a 'Report on the Meeting for the Discovery of the National Wushu Heritage' was issued in Chengde. The material collected was substantially incomplete because so much had been lost in the previous thirty years, and because of the reluctance on the part of remaining old masters to contribute. This first report included written records and videotapes of demonstrations. A second report was issued in Beijing in March of 1986. The material collected was also insufficient for much the same reason – so much (including entire arts) had been lost or was being withheld. During the mid 1980s, Chinese masters living abroad were solicited to 'come home' so as to document their systems. Few did, and those that did were reluctant to be involved in the process of extensive documentation. Many were, in fact, discretely teaching their arts abroad. In the 1990s, therefore, officials were sent abroad in search of the 'old *shifu*' (teachers) who left China before the active destruction of tradition within the PRC.

In 1982 a traditional curriculum was adopted at the Shaolin Monastery. This was a result of the changes in policy towards tradition, and a growing international interest in traditional Chinese martial arts, fuelled largely by the entertainment industry. In the 1920s Liu Ting had been appointed to teach martial arts to the Shaolin monks. Sixty years later, in the early 1980s, his grandson Liu Baoshan was now employed to resurrect the traditional martial arts at Shaolin. His students were newly recruited 'monks' with previous 'modern wushu' expertise. This has resulted in a martial arts that is composed of some traditional forms augmented with standardized basics influenced by 'modern wushu'.

By the late 1980s and early 1990s it was finally acknowledged that combat effectiveness is very much part of, if not entirely, the essence of Chinese martial arts. In 1994 Wang Xin, director of the Propaganda Department of the Zhengzhou

Municipal Committee of CCP, said so much in an inscription commemorating a textbook on Shaolin wushu, as did the Abbot of Shaolin, Shi Yongxin, in a foreword for the same series of textbooks in 1996. Excessive gymnastics have been removed from the compulsory forms in wushu sports competitions, while the International Wushu Federation has begun featuring competitive full-contact free fighting called Sanshou. Traditional terms such as *leitai* for the fighting platform are back in use. All this signals a growing interest in both tradition and combat effectiveness, but if the intent has been to restore authenticity, the result has been a spectator combat sport. It is clear that what is being promoted is something other than the old traditions.

Throughout the 1990s and today, the government has orchestrated touring shows by PRC Shaolin monks. Monks have been sent abroad to open schools in both Europe and North America. A major public relations effort with a deluge of articles featuring Shaolin monks and their martial arts has been launched in the media. Today, it is obvious that the PRC still maintains its control over what is (and is not) incorporated into Chinese martial arts, making their practice more reflective of mid-twentieth-century politics and twenty-first-century public relations than tradition. In the period of reform, the PRC has continued to discourage independent traditional martial art organizations, while desperately trying to undo the self-inflicted damage and reconstruct 'tradition'. In March 2002, after international criticism of opportunistic commercialization, the State Administration of Religions 'explained' that what the delegation sent by the Shaolin Temple of Mt Songshan was offering was purely a 'cultural performance'. In order to further its political objectives, however, the state feels it is critical to appear as the legitimate and sole representative of Chinese traditional culture in the eyes of the rest of the world.

Baguazhang

As part of the dramatic initiative to restore the martial arts traditions that began in January 1979, Baguazhang was the first such tradition to be investigated in detail. In 1980, Kang Gewu began working on a doctoral dissertation on the origins of Baguazhang, and in 1981, the Baguazhang Research Institute was established under the auspices of the Beijing Municipality Martial Arts Association, becoming the first research institute devoted to the study a single martial arts tradition. That same year, in a public demonstration of the change in official policy, the PRC allowed Bagua practitioners to move the remains of their famed nineteenth-century founder, Dong Haichuan (the site of his tomb had been turned into farmland during the Cultural Revolution), to a public cemetery in Beijing. The original headstone was now placed over a new grave, and a shrine detailing the Baguazhang lineage was built.

It is generally believed by researchers in the PRC that the founder of Baguazhang is Dong Haichuan (1813–82). The thesis is that Dong's martial arts training and skills were based on Shaolin lohan quan, which he apparently taught to his closest and longest student, Yin Fu. At one point Dong became a member of a Daoist sect, incorporated aspects of the sect's exercises into his Shaolin martial arts, and created what later became known as Bagua quan. Dong had many students, most of whom had previous training in other martial arts, a fact that is used to explain the great technical diversity among the many lineages that exists today. However there are dissenting opinions. Some traditional practitioners in Taiwan believed that Bagua quan evolved out of Shaolin lohan quan and Daoist practices and were integrated into a system over a number of generations prior to Dong's time. In either case, it appears that Bagua quan is a much more extensive system than what is currently practised in the PRC, and like other such systems, its lineages are no longer intact in the PRC.

The art derived from Yin Fu's lineage has many similarities with older Shaolin lohan martial arts, especially in the use of bare hand techniques and weapons. Some of these weapons include: the staff (*gun*), single and double straight swords (*jian*), spear, the long-handled crescent-shaped knife (*yanyue dao*), the three-section staff (*sanjie gun*), double 'tiger hooks' (*hutou shuanggou*), the horse knife (*madao*), dagger, iron fan (*tie shanzi*), and a 'bolo-like' weapon called *liuxing chui*. Among the most striking features of Baguazhang are the practices of walking in circles and of evasive body turning. Despite the lingering questions about the survival of Baguazhang as a complete system in the PRC, it is currently being transmitted by Ma Chuanxu of the Beijing Baguazhang Research Association and by other teachers at various sports universities.

Shaolin wushu

Despite claims by the PRC that 'real' traditional Shaolin martial arts are still flourishing at Shaolin Monastery, what is presently practised there is but a small sampling of the original, combined with modern wushu and elements of surviving lay traditions. Systems that, like Shaolin, comprised a large body of forms suffered the most damage from thirty years of government suppression, the previous war with Japan, and the sorry state of affairs at the collapse of the last dynasty.

For well over a thousand years martial arts have been researched, systematized, developed and taught at Shaolin Monastery. Shaolin training was a complex combination of para-religious health practices, exercises, lethal combat-oriented military methods and non-lethal self-defence methods. Because of its fame, Shaolin Monastery attracted some of the most accomplished warriors and martial artists in China's history. There are records that indicate that Shaolin Monastery in Henan province had been given the legal right to maintain a defensive force since the Tang dynasty. The early years of the Yuan dynasty were the most influential period for the development of wushu at Shaolin, and are linked to Abbot Fu Yu (1203–75.) Fu Yu established the precedent of inviting accomplished martial art experts as teachers for the monks in charge of defending the monastery.

Shaolin martial arts were noted for their pragmatic effectiveness, variety and extensiveness. Tradition holds that during the Yuan dynasty, the Shaolin martial art curriculum included 273 forms. Its barehanded martial methods include: (1) long-armed techniques, exemplified by the two hallmark forms, Da/Xiao Hong Changquan (Greater and Lesser Hong Long Fist); and (2) advanced close-combat methods, exemplified by the Shenlong shi'erbu wuxing quan, the twelve famous forms of the 'Five Shaped Fist' style. Internal energy development known as *neigong* is practised ('Yi Jinjing' and '108 Qigong'). Literally dozens of weapons are trained with, and several staff weapons are central

to the curriculum: the *Meimao gun* (eyebrow staff), *Fangbisn chan* (convenient shovel alarm staff), *Yueya cha* (crescent-moon tooth-fork alarm staff) and the *Lujing dang*, which is an alarm staff with a spade at both ends.

Taijiquan

Taijiquan is a martial art that is characterized by forms executed in a slow, continuous manner. The art is composed of single- and two-person routines, as well as a signature two-person training method called 'pushing hands' – an exercise which develops a sensitivity in detecting weaknesses in an opponent and instantly attacking. The art has developed into five principal branches. The mother style, called Chen (after Chen Wangting (1600–80), a military official, and alleged founder of the art) emphasizes 'silk-reeling energy' and uses fast powerful movements in addition to the more characteristic slow flowing movements. Although there has been a tradition of crediting the art solely to Daoist sources, research strongly points to the martial arts associated with the Shaolin Monastery and/or military training methods of the sixteenth and seventeenth centuries as being the more likely principal source of its techniques. Taijiquan has a number of striking similarities with Shaolin forms like 'Greater and Lesser Hongchangquan'. Taijiquan training, moreover, once included the use of a number of military weapons: single and double broadsword (*dao*), spear (*qiang*), single and double straight sword (*jian*), long staff (*gun*), halberd (*ji*), iron fan (*tei shanzi*), long-handled crescent-shaped knife (*yanyue dao*) and the two-section staff (*saozi gun*). Due to years of neglect and suppression, forms employing some of these weapons no longer exist. During the 1950s, the basics of Taijiquan in the PRC were standardized, and a new, simplified 'twenty-four-sections' routine was added. In the 1970s, a more advanced form made up of forty-eight sections was also developed. In 1992, as part of the effort to recover traditional martial arts, a history of Chen Taijiqaun was compiled by the Culture and History Committee of Wen County, and was published by the Chinese People's Political Consultative Conference. However, Tang Hao (1897–1959), a wushu historian and member of the Physical Culture and Sports Commission of the PRC, was one of the first researchers to look carefully into its history.

Xingyiquan

Xingyiquan is an aggressive Chinese martial art that is believed to have had its origins in Shanxi province in the early 1600s. Its early development is credited to Ji Jike (a.k.a. Ji Longfeng), but the art as it is practised today appears to have been most significantly developed by Li Laoneng. Despite the general suppression of traditional martial arts in the PRC, the art has survived in Shanxi relatively intact. As a result of the PRC policy change of 'unearthing martial arts' in 1979, the restoration of Xingyiquan traditions began in 1982–3. Since then it has been taught at various sports universities, including the Beijing Sports University. The basic strategy used by Xingyi boxers involves aggressively forcing the opponent backwards while delivering powerful attacks from the centre. Xingyi boxers generally move linearly, stepping forward or at an angle towards the opponent in straight lines. The feet, the head and the lead hand are usually held on the same vertical plane, so the practitioner moves directly into the opponent, striking with power generated through use of the entire body, not just the arms. The heart of Xingyi is 'five fist forms' called *wuxing*. These are short forms, each designed to generate a different kind of energy, or attacking power, depicted by the Chinese five elements of metal, wood, water, fire and earth. Advanced training methods also include 'twelve animal forms' based on the *wuxing*.

RIK ZAK

martial arts fiction

(wuxia xiaoshuo)

Martial arts fiction (*wuxia xiaoshuo*, literally 'fiction of war and chivalry') has been one of the most widely read thematic subgenres of mass-distributed popular fiction in modern and contemporary China, and the one most often perceived as expressing a uniquely Chinese sensibility. *Wuxia xiaoshuo* has been closely tied with similar material in other media, most notably **martial arts films**, and its themes, characters and imagery are well-nigh ubiquitous in Chinese popular culture.

Representations of martial prowess and the chivalric ideals of the figures known as 'knights-errant' (*xia*) can be traced back to Sima Qian's *Records of the Historian* (*Shi ji*, first century BC) and recur throughout Chinese literary history, most notably in Tang dynasty classical tales and in the Ming vernacular novel *Tales of the Water Margin* (*Shuihu zhuan*). In its modern form as vernacular fiction produced for a mass reading public, *wuxia xiaoshuo* took shape in Shanghai and other urban centres in the 1920s and 1930s, its characteristics and popularity interwoven both with the nascent film industry's treatment of related material and with nationalistic revivals of China's traditional **martial arts**.

Banned on the mainland after the founding of the PRC, *wuxia xiaoshuo* experienced a revival in Hong Kong, Taiwan and among overseas Chinese communities beginning in the latter half of the 1950s. The leaders of what came to be called 'new school' (*xinpai*) *wuxia xiaoshuo* in Hong Kong were Liang Yusheng (pen name of Chen Wentong, b. 1922) and **Jin Yong** (Zha Liangyong, b. 1924). Their novels, serialized in newspapers and then republished in book form, offered readers elaborate tales of heroism, revenge, chivalry and romance in historical or semi-historical settings, blending elements of traditional vernacular narrative with themes from contemporary adventure fiction and film and leavening the whole with patriotism and the evocation of a mythicized cultural heritage.

On Taiwan, where martial law restricted the circulation of both Republican-era novels and contemporary *wuxia xiaoshuo* from Hong Kong, an indigenous 'new school' arose, including such authors as Wolong Sheng and Sima Ling. The most prominent of the Taiwan authors was Gu Long (Xiong Yaohua, 1936–85), whose accelerated plotting, cinematic imagery, aphoristic prose and dehistoricized settings are sometimes credited with establishing a truly 'modern' *wuxia xiaoshuo* and blazing a trail for such successors as Wen Rui'an.

Wuxia xiaoshuo from Hong Kong and Taiwan flooded the mainland in the 1980s, and many new authors, both popular and middlebrow, tried their hand at the genre. Hong Kong's Huang Yi gained popularity in the 1990s. In general, however, film, television, comic books and video games replaced full-length fiction as the favoured media for new martial arts adventure, and readers increasingly came to regard the works of the 1960s through 1980s as the 'classics'. The last decade of the twentieth century also saw increasing critical and scholarly attention to the genre as a whole and to the works of Jin Yong in particular.

Further reading

Chen, Pingyuan (1992). *Qiangu wenren xiake meng: wuxia xiaoshuo leixing yanjiu* [The Scholars' Age-Old Dream of the Knight-Errant: A Generic Study of Chivalric Fiction]. Beijing: Renmin wenxue chubanshe.

Hamm, J. C. (2001). 'Local Heroes: Guangdong School *wuxia* Fiction and Hong Kong's Imagining of China'. *Twentieth-Century China* 27.1: 71–96.

Liu, J. (1967). *The Chinese Knight-Errant*. London: Routledge and Kegan Paul.

JOHN CHRISTOPHER HAMM

martial arts films

The genre of martial arts films has cultural origins in an earlier tradition of 'knights errant' novels (see **martial arts fiction**), opera and street performance, and was represented in the earliest days of Chinese cinema by such films as *Burning of Red Lotus Monastery* (1928). However, for its advocacy of superstition and glorification of such anti-social figures as roving swordsmen, the film genre was banned in 1930. It fared little better under the early People's Republic, when state film studios produced increasingly stylized portrayals of popular struggle and the heroism of the masses, leaving no room for the romanticized secrecy or individuality of martial artists.

The martial arts genre came into prominence with the explosion of films produced in Hong Kong during the 1960s and 1970s. Throughout these two decades, major studios, most notably the Shaw Brothers studios, fed a growing kung-fu craze with classic films such as *The Drunken Master* and

Enter the Dragon, launching the careers of Jackie **Chan**, Sammo Hung, David Chiang and international superstar Bruce Lee. These films established many of the conventions defining the genre, which remained within a few stylized storylines. Plots such as the revenge tale, the patriotic hero (usually set against the backdrop of the Manchu or Japanese invasions), and the gangster story tended towards the gory, while more mythic or religious themes were fanciful, with actors suspended by wires performing stupendous feats. Hong Kong remained the unquestioned centre of the genre, providing inspiration for a smaller industry in Taiwan. Hong Kong director King Hu (Hu Jinquan) worked briefly in Taiwan, but for the most part the flow of talent went in the reverse direction, as with the director Zhang Che (Chang Cheh), who left Taiwan for a career in Hong Kong.

As state-sponsored wushu training developed during the late 1970s, the People's Republic began to make a contribution to the genre in the form of martial arts prodigies who were featured in Hong Kong productions. The first of the major productions was *Shaolin Temple*, starring a sixteen-year-old Jet Li (Li Lianjie). This film sparked a national interest in Shaolin wushu (see **martial arts**), prompting the reopening of the Shaolin Temple in Henan, as well as a brief period during the early 1980s in which Mainland studios produced their own films in the genre, such as *The South Shaolin Master*.

During the 1980s and 1990s, martial arts films began expanding beyond traditional conventions, partially in order to capture emerging international markets. Martial arts choreography and storylines were incorporated into other genres, such as the science fiction films of **Tsui Hark** and the action films of director John **Woo**. Martial artists such as Jet Li and Jackie Chan both starred in English-language films, alongside Hollywood stars, while behind the camera long-time director Yuen Wo Ping added his distinctive choreography to the Hollywood blockbuster, *The Matrix*.

The Hong Kong industry also courted the burgeoning mainland market by adding more Chinese-style *wushu* to its films, and building up patriotic themes, as in features such as *Once Upon a Time in China*. At the same time, low-budget, Mandarin language serials produced in Hong Kong and

Taiwan proved immensely popular and soon became stock programming on PRC television. During the 1990s, the internationalization of the martial arts genre came to focus on cooperation within 'Greater China', particularly after the 1997 return of Hong Kong to the PRC. The culmination of this process was Ang **Lee**'s *Crouching Tiger, Hidden Dragon*, which conspicuously combined talent from the PRC, Taiwan, Hong Kong and overseas Chinese.

Further reading

Farquhar, Mary (2003). '*A Touch of Zen*: Action in Martial Arts Movies'. In Chris Berry (ed.), *Chinese Films in Focus: 25 New Takes*. London: BFI, 167–74.

THOMAS DUBOIS

Marxist Humanism

Marxist Humanism is an intellectual strand within the Marxian tradition that is critical of Stalinist variants of socialism and looks to the early writings of Marx, such as the Paris Manuscripts of 1844, as a source for humanitarian values and ethical principles. In 1983, during ceremonies marking the centennial of Marx's death, some Chinese intellectuals utilized General Secretary Hu Yaobang's call for emancipating the mind to focus attention on themes like individual freedom, subjectivity and human nature. Drawing inspiration from the early Marx, as had Soviet and European Marxists in the wake of de-Stalinization two and a half decades earlier, Wang Ruoshui, Zhou Yang, Ru Xin, Su Shaozhi and others criticized the cult of personality, arbitrary exercise of power, and lack of democracy in Stalinist/Maoist systems as manifestations of alienation and of the subordination of individual rights to collectivist goals. By arguing that the theme of socialist humanism and the subject-centred view of history was the essence of Marxist philosophy, these intellectuals made a case for political democratization, constitutional guarantees of basic human rights, and the personal freedom and dignity of the individual. This critical and humanist version of Marxism undermined the

concept of class dictatorship and questioned both the achievements of Chinese socialism and the CCP's monopoly of power. Consequently, it found little favour with the political leadership and came to be repudiated as a form of 'bourgeois individualism'.

Further reading

Brugger, B. and Kelly, D. (1990). *Chinese Marxism in the Post-Mao Era*. Stanford: Stanford University Press.

Hua, S. (1995). *Scientism and Humanism*. Albany: SUNY Press.

Liu, Kang (1993), 'Subjectivity, Marxism, and Cultural Theory in China'. In Tang Xiaobing and Liu Kang (eds), *Politics, Ideology and Literary Discourse in Modern China: Theoretical Interventions and Cultural Critique*. Durham: Duke University Press, 169–209.

Wang, Jing (1996). *High Culture Fever: Politics, Aesthetics, and Ideology in Deng's China*. Berkeley: University of California Press, ch. 1 (esp. 25–31).

KALPANA MISRA

mass movements

(qunzhong yundong)

Mao Zedong (1893–1976) favoured 'mass mobilization' as a government mechanism. As a result mass movements were incessant during his rule, by far the most important being the **Cultural Revolution**. Other than mass participation, these movements' main features were: they were organized by Mao himself for his own purposes; they scapegoated enemies; and they centred on an ideological point or set of points of concern to Mao.

After Mao's death, the idea of the mass movements declined in favour. The post-Mao leadership's interest lies in economic development within a stable society, based on law and order. While much attention is still given to the 'masses', and there are numerous mass organizations with a wide range of functions, such organizations are subject to CCP leadership and regulation. In the period of reform, the CCP, in fact, has opposed mass action.

Even when such action supports government policy, as the demonstrations denouncing the American bombing of China's Belgrade Embassy in May 1999, the CCP moves to stop mass action, fearing it can spin out of control. Yet there have been a few ideological movements. Other than the **Campaign against Bourgeois Liberalization** (1987), the most important one was that against 'spiritual pollution'. Launched by the CCP Central Committee in October 1983, it aimed to defend the concept of the 'spiritual civilization' and oppose such unhealthy phenomena as excessive commercialization in the arts, literature and the theatre. However, it was over by the end of 1983.

COLIN MACKERRAS

massage

Massage, the physical manipulation of the surface of the body to relieve illness or discomfort, is one of the unique therapeutic methods of Chinese medicine. Although widely accepted as a popular means of health maintenance, massage is a marginalized practice within the **herbal medicine**-dominated field of Chinese medicine. In the early 1980s, Chinese medicine colleges responded to this problem by forming independent departments of **acupuncture and moxibustion** and massage. In spite of this new institutional support for students and faculty, most massage doctors treat a limited range of orthopaedic and soft tissue problems, usually in departments of massage or Chinese medicine orthopaedics at Chinese-medicine **hospitals**. Other important branches of massage, such as internal medicine and paediatric massage, are relatively neglected because herbal medicine physicians dominate these respective hospital departments. Most massage doctors insist that skilful hand technique and proper application of Chinese medicine theory are the keys to clinical efficacy. Contemporary orthopaedic massage has also successfully integrated biomedical anatomy into its practice. Internal medicine and paediatric massage share a strong theoretical foundation with acupuncture, but each has its own unique hand techniques and innovative use of acupoints.

Outside of China's health care institutions, massage thrives in different forms. Many massage doctors run lucrative private consultation services. Blind masseurs, excluded from the medical establishment, employ their own unique skills in a growing number of private clinics. Less skilled practitioners operate in new niche markets, such as foot massage and head massage. And countless individuals incorporate massage in their own daily health maintenance regimens.

ERIC I. KARCHMER

Mazu

Deity

Like all Chinese deities, the goddess Mazu was originally a human, born in 960, the first year of the Northern Song dynasty, in Xianlianggang, a fishing town in Putian county, Fujian. She led an exemplary life helping drowning sailors, died unmarried in 987, and ascended to heaven on nearby Meizhou Island. In the following centuries, as her reputation grew, several imperial courts bestowed official titles on the goddess, and expanded her temple and built other official Mazu temples. Mazu started out as a minor local deity worshipped by poor fisherman, and was transformed into one of the two most important female deities in the imperial religious pantheon overseen by the Board of Rites. Thousands of Mazu temples were built along coastal China, from Manchuria in the north to Guangdong province in the south, and waves of emigration brought Mazu to Taiwan, southeast Asia and Japan. While for commoners she stood for the safety of seafarers, female fertility and divine intervention in times of personal and familial adversity, her cult was also standardized and appropriated by the imperial state as a civilizing force and as a symbol of the coastal pacification of pirates, smugglers and rebels.

While the Mazu cult declined in socialist China due to anti-religious political sentiment and state action, today in Taiwan Mazu is the largest deity cult, her temples are the most numerous of all deities, and popular estimates are that 70 per cent of Taiwanese worship her in some form. Many

Mazu temples sponsor annual festivals to celebrate her birthday on the twenty-sixth of the third lunar month (see **temple fairs**) and make pilgrimages to senior Mazu temples (see **processions (religious)**). The most prominent temples, such as the Chaotiangong temple in Beigang, Zhenlangong temple in Dajia and Tianhougong temple in Tainan, compete for historical precedence, fame, political influence, worshippers and lucrative donations. Since 1987, Mazu temples on Taiwan have increasingly led pilgrimages across the politically fraught Taiwan Straits to their ancestral temple on Meizhou Island, and have donated large sums to help build or rebuild Mazu temples in Fujian province and other places in China.

See also: Guanyin

Further reading

Huang, Mei-yin (1993). 'Mazu's Incense and the Construction of the Authority of the Spirits'. *Journal of History* 4.63: 43–6.

Sangren, Steven (1993). 'Power and Transcendence in the Ma Tsu Pilgrimages of Taiwan'. *American Ethnologist* 20.3: 564–82.

Watson, James L. (1985). 'Standardizing the Gods: The Promotion of T'ien Hou ("Empress of Heaven") along the South China Coast, 960–1960'. In David Johnson, Andrew J. Nathan and Evelyn S. Rawski (eds), *Popular Culture in Late Imperial China*. Berkeley: University of California Press, 292–324.

MAYFAIR MEI-HUI YANG

medical doctors

Categories of medical doctors include senior Western medicine doctors, assistant doctors and village doctors, as well as doctors of Chinese medicine, and a new official classification for doctors who practiced 'integrated Chinese and Western medicine'. The training of physicians in China had suffered from the suspension of enrolment during the early years of the **Cultural Revolution** and the shortening of the curriculum to three years in the first half of the 1970s. After 1978, the length

of study has been generally five or six years for medical colleges, and three years for secondary medical schools. Colleges of Chinese medicine also offer five- or six-year courses, but graduates can study for postgraduate degrees in Western medicine (and vice versa), and with appropriate training they can practise whatever type of medicine they choose and prescribe Western drugs. Since the 1980s, higher medical education has increasingly emphasized postgraduate studies and research. Secondary medical schools, which recruit junior middle school graduates, train intermediate medical personnel, offering specialisms in Western and Chinese medicine. Many of the village doctors are former **barefoot doctors** who have passed certifying examinations instituted since the late 1970s and early 1980s, giving them qualifications equivalent to graduates of secondary medical schools.

The number of medical doctors has increased steadily in the post-Mao period. In 1975, there were 649,100 Western medicine doctors (both senior and assistant) in official health institutions, and the number had risen to 1,582,700 by 1996. The rate of growth for doctors of Chinese medicine has been slower, increasing from 228,600 to 347,800 in the same period. The contingent of intermediate medical doctors, which include assistant doctors and village doctors, has also grown; in 1989, there were 320,671 assistant doctors, 95,097 secondary doctors of Chinese medicine, and 753,686 village doctors. The distribution of doctors, however, reveals the urban–rural disparity as most of them, especially the senior Western medicine doctors, practise in urban areas. The increased professionalization of medicine, the specialization of services and the renewed emphasis on medical technology have also affected the availability of, and access to, physician care. These changes, as well as post-Mao modernization policies, have enabled medical doctors to move into leadership positions in the organization and management of medical practice.

The government's decision to permit for-profit medicine in the mid 1980s led to the emergence of 'individual household doctors' who set up their own clinics or hospitals. Such private practice takes many forms and appears at every level of the health system, ranging from small village clinics to storefront medical offices in towns and cities. By the end of 1994, there were seventy-four private hospitals. The privatization and commodification of care assumes greater significance as economic changes open up new entrepreneurial opportunities and the state continues to scale back the national health care system.

See also: hospitals; medical insurance; public health care

Further reading

Chen, H. (ed.) (1984). *Modern Chinese Medicine v.3: Chinese Health Care*. Lancaster: MTP Press.

Farquhar, J. (1996). 'Market Magic: Getting Rich and Getting Personal in Medicine after Mao'. *American Ethnologist* 23: 239–57.

Henderson, G., Akin, J., Zhiming, L., Shuigao, J., Haijiang, M. and Keyou, G. (1994). 'Equity and the Utilization of Health Services: Report of an Eight Province Survey in China'. *Social Science and Medicine* 39: 687–700.

White, S. (1998). 'From "Barefoot Doctor" to "Village Doctor" in Tiger Spring Village: A Case Study of Health Care Transformation in Socialist China'. *Human Organization* 57: 480–90.

YIP KA-CHE

medical foods

Food and medicine are a continuum both in popular practice and in the systematic work of 'traditional' Chinese pharmaceutics. Though the medicines used in the indigenous materia medica number more than 5,000 and include many more plant, mineral and animal substances than are used in cooking, the logic that governs the theory and practice of prescriptions is very similar to that of cuisine. Herbal decoctions, for example, are referred to as 'soups', and a major classification system for materia medica is in terms of the five 'flavours'. Conversely, food is widely thought of as efficacious in affecting bodily states far beyond simple nutrition. Foods that 'drive out heat' or 'boost qi', for example, are routinely used in family cooking and noted in everyday health advice. In the self-health movement that gained ground in the 1980s and 1990s, nutritional practices have played a major

role. An interesting neo-tradition of 'medicinal meals' has emerged with its own cookbooks, technical manuals and restaurant specialties. A soup oriented towards boosting qi and preserving strength for aging men, for example, might include ginseng, astragalus, schisandra, chrysanthemum, fennel, hawthorn and Asian cornelian cherry alongside the meat and vegetables that are its base. There are numerous popularly published materials on modifying diet to prevent or treat heart disease, diabetes, cancer, arthritis and other chronic illnesses. All these sources rely heavily on medical knowledge, classifying readily available foods according to the same technical systems that allow Chinese doctors to prescribe complex drug decoctions responding to a patient's every symptom. Perhaps more marked in southern China than in the north, there is a great interest among eaters in both the immediate and long-term health effects of commonly consumed foods.

JUDITH FARQUHAR

medical insurance

Health care in China has been largely segmented between urban and rural populations. Among the urban population, for over four decades since the early 1950s, there were two major programmes: the Labour Insurance Programme (LIP) and the Government Insurance Programme (GIP). LIP was an employer-based programme, primarily for urban employees and retirees, covering around one-third of the urban residents or 10 per cent of the total population. GIP was a government-financed programme mainly for people working in public sectors, including about 2 per cent of the total population. Along with China's market-oriented economic reform, both GIP and LIP were critically challenged by some fundamental problems: low coverage, poor risk pooling and the lack of accountability for economic efficiency. This led to a fundamental reform of the old system beginning in 1996 with a community-based insurance programme, mandating the participation of all community-wide employers and employees with their joint premium contributions through the Individual Savings Accounts and Social

Pooling Account. In 2002, most of the large cities have started to implement the new programme, currently covering about 80 million employees.

In contrast, rural residents, accounting for over 70 per cent of the total population, have never been eligible for the publicly financed insurance programmes. The rural population must either pay out of pocket for health care, or join the so-called 'cooperative medical plans' (CMP) operated with the voluntary contributions of the local residents at the village or township level. CMPs were once popular back in the 1960s and 1970s, covering the majority of the rural population, but mostly collapsed in the early 1980s when the rural collective economy was replaced by the individual household responsibility system. Currently, it is estimated that CMPs cover no more than 10 per cent of the rural population. Given the current Chinese economy and population size, it is unlikely that the uninsured status of the rural population would change with public financing in a foreseen period. Looking ahead, the significant urban–rural differential in health insurance seems to be one of the most challenging issues facing Chinese policy-makers in the twenty-first century.

GORDON LIU

Mei Shaojing

b. 1948, Sichuan

Poet

Uniquely combining the purity of folksongs and the complexity of the postmodern sensibility, Mei Shaojing is one of the New Era (*Xinshiqi*) poets who began writing during the **Cultural Revolution** and emerged as a new tide swept poetic conventions in the 1980s. Growing up in Beijing, Mei was sent to Yan'an in 1969 and worked as a farmer, factory worker and literary magazine editor until she entered the **Lu Xun Literary Institute** in 1984. Since 1971 she has published four collections of poetry and a large amount of prose, and has won multiple literary prizes. Many of her poems have been translated into other languages.

One of the best 'rural poets' (*xiangtu shiren*) of the PRC, Mei is renowned for her portrayal of rural life

and creative use of the folk tradition. Her prize-winning collection, *She's That Mei* (*Ta jiushi nage Mei*, 1986), is regarded as a poetic representation of the life and soul of the yellow earth. Although many of her poems are inspired by her experience in the countryside, Mei's poetry is not limited to pastoral themes. Simultaneously simple and poignant, her poems capture the essence of human conditions in most ordinary images and with unadorned language, as seen in the following lines:

> Life is a water jar
> filled with clear and sweet thoughts –
> it's pouring out tears and sweats
> to make my throat choke.
> ('What is Life'/*Rizi shi shenmo*, 1984)

QIU PEIPEI

Meishu

[Fine Arts]

Art journal

Meishu, first published in 1951 as *Renmin meishu* [The People's Art], was relaunched under its present name in 1954. It is sponsored by the China Artists' Association, which is controlled by the Propaganda Department of the Chinese Communist Party. Cancelled for ten years during the **Cultural Revolution**, it began to publish again in 1978. In the early 1980s, with He Rong as chief editor, *Meishu* welcomed art school graduates to form its new generation of editors: Li Xianting, **Gao Minglu**, Tang Qingnian and Wang Xiaojian, all of whom later played a central role in the **85 New Wave [Art] Movement**. In the mid 1980s, Shao Dazhen, an art historian and critic from the **Central Academy of Fine Arts**, was appointed as the chief editor. A graduate from Soviet art schools in the 1950s, Shao was nonetheless an open-minded scholar who was tolerant of the new ideas being expressed in the magazine, although he still had to comply with government censorship. With the efforts of young editors, Gao Minglu in particular, *Meishu* became the most important art magazine in the 1980s, enthusiastically promoting Western art from classical to early modern, from

Impressionism, Post-Impressionism and Expressionism to Cubism, Dadaism, Abstract Art and Happenings, and from Dali and Picasso to Beuys. *Meishu* was also one of the major sponsors of **China Avant-Garde** (1989), the first show of non-official art held since 1949. Soon after the 4 June Incident of 1989, Shao Dazhen was replaced by Hua Xia, a Leftist art critic who reversed the policies of his predecessor. With the support of Wang Qi, head of the China Artists' Association and an early chief editor of *Meishu*, Hua Xia transformed *Meishu* into a 'Leftist' magazine that only published articles and images complying with the official political viewpoint and/or highly commercial trends.

QIAN ZHIJIAN

Meishu sichao

[Trends in Aesthetics]

Art journal

A bi-monthly journal of art criticism established in Wuhan in November 1984 by the Hubei branch of the Chinese Artists' Association, *Meishi sichao* was closed down for political reasons in December 1987. Its stated purpose was to 'master the changes in art theory at home and abroad, introduce and promote enterprising contemporary artists, and diagnose and advise on art's social maladies'. It advocated destroying the regionalism of art criticism and emphasized openness in critical discussion. The chief editor was art theorist Peng De, with Zhou Shaohua and Lu Muxun as deputy editors.

Meishu sichao was a lively publication where artists and theorists shared equal status and could hold theoretical debates on their own terms. While providing space for critics to write about specific critical approaches, it also allowed artists to articulate the theoretical side of their work with little editorial restraint, so that some articles would become semi-metaphorical forays in theory, criticism and creative writing. Directed towards peers rather than the general public, it published important articles by leading artists of the **85 New Wave [Art] Movement** such as **Wang Guangyi**, **Gu Wenda**, **Huang Yongping**, Wu Shanzhuan and Mao Xuhui. The sixth issue of

1987 was remarkable for its collection of articles produced by the editors of all the main art magazines of the time: **Meishu** [Fine Arts], **Zhongguo meishubao** [Fine Arts in China], **Jiangsu huakan** [Jiangsu Pictorial] and *Xin meishu* [New Art]. It became an important forum for focusing on the domestic development of art and criticism and was arguably the most important periodical in terms of debating new ideas.

EDUARDO WELSH

memorization

The large amount of memorization required of students in China has been a point of controversy on and off for the past century. The structural importance of testing in the education system, the number of characters that must be memorized to write Chinese, a moral culture that emphasizes the emulation of models from the past (including the memorization of sayings (*chengyü*) and poems), and a political system that is more comfortable with students regurgitating pre-approved statements than questioning have all been described as reasons behind this over-reliance on memorization.

During the 1990s, educational reformers again focused their critical attention on the pitfalls of too much memorization. They argued that it stifled students' capacities for creativity and self-organization, and lamented that China would inevitably fall behind other nations economically if reforms were not implemented. Embracing parts of this critique, in 1999 the State Council announced that 'quality education' principles (*suzhi jiaoyu*, sometimes also translated as 'competence education') should serve as guides for all levels of education in the twenty-first century. How these principles will change the place of memorization in Chinese education remains to be seen.

See also: university entrance examinations

Further reading

Kipnis, A. (2001). 'The Disturbing Educational Discipline of "Peasants"'. *The China Journal* 46: 1–24.

Unger, J. (1982). *Education Under Mao: Class and Competition in Canton Schools, 1960–1980*. New York: Columbia University Press.

ANDREW KIPNIS

Meng Jinghui

b. 1966, Beijing

Theatre director

The work of celebrated avant-garde director Meng Jinghui is integral to the renewed popularity of **Huaju** (spoken drama). Meng is a resident director of the National Theatre Company of China in Beijing. He is also artistic director of the independent PlayPlay Studio, a collaborative group organized in the mid 1990s.

Meng's signature work, *Si Fan*, juxtaposed a traditional Ming dynasty *kunshan* opera with stories from Boccaccio's *Decameron*, and caused a sensation in 1993. His adaptations of foreign and newly written Chinese plays include: *The Balcony, Put Down Your Whip – Woyzeck, Gossip Street, Accidental Death of an Anarchist, Rhinoceros in Love, Bootleg Faust* and *The Bedbug*. Meng's *I Love XXX* and *Love Ants* were produced, like all his plays, in connection with his work unit, the Central Experimental Theatre, but authorities 'banned' his controversial *Comrade Ah Q* while still in rehearsal. Meng's first feature film is *Chicken Poets* (*Xiang jimao yiyang fei*, 2002).

While exploring larger social issues and politically sensitive subjects, Meng's productions are comedies infused with playful, animated energy, cajoling and provoking the audience. His style is characterized by a mix of politics and popular culture, and of dark and humorous elements. He juxtaposes disparate styles, periods and cultures, including classical references, current events and pop culture – TV, film and the latest slang. Recurrent elements include mime, dance, music, poetry and prose, a vignette structure with a chorus of actors playing multiple roles, improvisation and spontaneity, sound and movement rhythm games, vocal 'sound parts' and gibberish, a rock band and multi-media. The 'Meng style' is so popular that other directors imitate his unconventional techniques. Frequent collaborators are his wife, writer Liao Yimei, and musician Zhang Guangtian.

Further reading

Melvin, Sheila (2001). 'Chinese Welcome a Break from Old-Style Drama'. *New York Times* (10 June).

Meng, Jinghui (ed.) (2000). *Xianfeng xiju dang an* [Avant-Garde Theatre Files]. Beijing: Writers' Press.

BETTINA S. ENTELL

menstruation

Like anywhere else, menstruation in China is a deeply personal and yet evocative topic with multiple associations that vary widely by geographical region, age, gender, class, education, personal circumstances and many other factors. As an indicator of a woman's reproductive capacity, it was the object of careful observation and manipulation in traditional China where the continuation of the family line by providing descendants was women's primary social function. Consequently, the maturing and aging of the female body was conceptualized in stages of seven years, with the onset of menstruation occurring at the age of fourteen (or 2×7) and menopause at forty-nine (or 7×7). The Chinese term for menstruation, *yuejing* ('monthly period'), expresses its direct associations with the moon – and thereby implicitly with the yin aspect of the yin–yang dualism, femininity, fluidity and ocean tides, as well as with cyclical regularity.

While menstruation is still not a popular topic for polite dinner-table conversations, modern sex education classes ensure that young girls now approach the onset of menstruation openly as a natural and positive event, marking their entry into adulthood. Traditionally, Chinese women have observed a wide range of precautions during their menstrual period, such as not washing their hair or ingesting cold drinks and cooling foods, avoiding wet feet and cold water in general, and refraining from strenuous physical exercise. These practices have become less prevalent in mainland China since the Cultural Revolution and the concurrent stress on gender equality, but are still widely observed in Taiwan and other more conservative places. Particularly for middle-aged women, menstruation is regarded as a time of increased debility during which exposure to cold or exertion can cause severe health problems.

The treatment of menstrual conditions, ranging from headaches and cramps to abdominal lumps, amenorrhea and infertility, is one of the most popular reasons why women consult practitioners of traditional Chinese medicine and ingest herbal decoctions. A careful diagnosis analyses the timing, duration, volume, colour and consistency of the menses, as well as secondary symptoms. This provides a traditional Chinese physician with a window into the patient's general health, reflecting such pathologies as general blood depletion, imbalance between yin and yang, cold in the uterus, or a lack of circulation and impeded flow of bodily fluids. Menstrual blood is also of central significance for women's reproductive functions: The cessation of the menses during pregnancy and lactation is explained in medical theory as due to the fact that menstrual blood provides nourishment for the foetus during pregnancy and, after delivery, ascends to transform into breast milk. Thus, Chinese physicians have for centuries defined the gendered female body by the maxim, 'in women, blood is the ruler'.

In conclusion, the recurring loss of blood during menstruation is seen as predisposing women to chronic depletion and systemic vulnerability, often necessitating the ingestion of a jujube decoction and other tonics. But it is also interpreted positively as a necessary elimination of bodily waste products. Ultimately, the regular cycles of movement within the female body symbolize the generative power of the female body.

SABINE WILMS

mental health

It is estimated that there are 66.3 million people suffering from various forms of mental disorder in China (Murray and Lopez 1996a, 1996b). The majority of patients in psychiatric hospitals have schizophrenia or other psychotic disorders. Depression, bi-polar disorder and obsessive-compulsive disorder tend to go undiagnosed and untreated.

These sources estimate that mental illness and **suicide** are the most important category of disease for China and impinge more heavily on women than on men. Higher prevalence rates are reported amongst women for schizophrenia (unusual) and depression (similar to trends elsewhere). China is the only major country in the world where the suicide rate for women exceeds that for men. Treatment, where it exists, is almost exclusively based on Western psychotropic medication. ECT is used rarely but usually without anaesthetic.

There are three government ministries primarily responsible for the provision of mental health care in China: Public Health, Civil Affairs and Public Security. Public Security is in charge of the forensic psychiatric system (twenty hospitals, with 5,000 beds) with most provinces supposed to have one forensic hospital (usually in the provincial capital). Civil Affairs provides beds for veterans and the poor (known as the 'three have-nots': no family, no job, no means of support) and runs 200 hospitals with 30,000 beds. Public Health has traditionally sought the 'better' patients, i.e. those who are acutely ill and whose work units or families are able to pay the fees. They run 482 hospitals and provide 95,000 beds. The three ministries account for over 92 per cent of all psychiatric beds. The rest are provided by other ministries' (e.g. railways and mines) psychiatric units in urban general hospitals (that have never really caught on in China although they are the preferred way of providing in-patient care in other countries) and a small number of privately run institutions. There are approximately 1.2 psychiatric beds per 10,000 of the population.

In 1987 the government published a document entitled *Some Opinions about Strengthening Mental Health Work* that pointed out that 80 per cent of people requiring psychiatric treatment did not receive it and that only 5 per cent needing treatment were hospitalized. Psychiatric hospitals received only 50 per cent of the funding that the government gave to general hospitals of the same grade. It identified inadequate staff training, low pay, poor promotion prospects and little support or respect from the general public as significant deterrents to development.

Funding drives the provision of psychiatric care in China. Many people assume that because China is a socialist country medical care is provided free. This has never been true (see **medical insurance**). The economic reforms led to the collapse of the commune-based rural health insurance system. People in urban areas, especially women, are now infrequently covered by comprehensive health insurance. Meanwhile the government has withdrawn much of its funding for hospitals and told them that they must be self-sufficient. Hospitals have been forced to run businesses (e.g. factories, restaurants) to support themselves, and have raised hospital fees to an extent that there is now serious under-occupation of psychiatric hospital beds because families cannot afford them. Civil Affairs and Public Health hospitals are now in competition for patients who can afford to pay, and the former have lost their traditional emphasis on the poor.

Community-based treatment and rehabilitation would seem to be an answer to some of these problems. However, Shanghai is the only major city that has developed and sustained an integrated system of community care despite the fact that there is a well-articulated model consisting of 'guardianship networks', workstations, factory-based vocational rehabilitation programmes and 'home beds'. The mentally ill have never been allowed to participate in the Civil Affairs-run welfare factories that are reserved for people with sensory, motor or learning disabilities. Community services, such as they are, are technically co-ordinated at all levels of local administration by cadres from Public Health, Civil Affairs, Public Security and the Federation for the Disabled. Efforts have been made to change this moribund situation, through lobbying by the China Rehabilitation Research Association for People with Mental Disabilities under the All China Federation for the Disabled. The *Eighth Five Year Plan for the Psychiatrically Disabled, 1991–1995* (the first to include psychiatric illness) specified the development of community-based pilot projects in thirty-two rural and thirty-two urban sites. This was a valiant effort but largely scuppered by insufficient central and local funding.

In effect families do most of the caring for people with mental illness in China, with little help from formal or informal systems. They make the decisions about whether treatment is to be sought and how much of the family income is to be invested in it. They experience the stigma of the condition along with the patient and usually do their utmost to hide the illness from outsiders so that the marriage prospects of siblings are not badly affected.

Chinese authorities have been accused of using the psychiatric system to punish political dissidents, including the **Falun gong**. The World Psychiatric Association has expressed deep concern and the comparison with Russia is frequently made. Chinese psychiatrists are resentful at these accusations, saying that those few political dissidents in psychiatric hospitals are there because they are mentally ill and need treatment. In private conversations they point out that psychiatric beds are an expensive and scarce resource in China. Why would they waste them on people who do not need them when so many alternatives are available?

See also: disabilities; hospitals

Further reading

Lee, S and Kleinman, A. (2002). 'Psychiatry in its Political and Professional Contexts'. *Journal of the American Academy of Psychiatry and Law*, 30: 120–5.

Murray, C. J. L. and Lopez, A. D. (1996a). *The Global Burden of Disease: A Comprehensive Assessment of Mortality and Disability from Disease, Injuries and Risk Factors in 1990 and Projected to 2020*. Cambridge, MA: Harvard University Press.

—— (1996b). *Global Health Statistics: A Compendium of Incidence, Prevalence and Mortality Estimates for over 200 Conditions*. Cambridge, MA: Harvard University Press.

Pearson, V. (1995). *Mental Health Care in China; State Policies, Professional Services and Family Responsibilities*. London: Gaskell Press.

Phillips, M. R. (1998). 'The Transformation of China's Mental Health Services'. *The China Journal*, 39: 1–36.

VERONICA PEARSON

Miao, culture of

The Miao number approximately 8 million and are mainly found in Guizhou, Yunnan, Hunan, Guangxi, Guangdong and Sichuan provinces, with some in Hainan and Hubei. They live harmoniously with the Tujia, Boyei, Dong, Zhuang, Li and **Han** Chinese (see **Tujia, culture of; Boyei (Buyi), culture of; Dong, culture of; Zhuang, culture of; Li, culture of**). Much of their areas is hilly, mountainous or drained by several big rivers. Their houses are usually built of wood. They like to eat various sour foods like pickles, sour fish and meat, and they like wine. The Miao women excel in embroidery, weaving, batik and paper-cutting. The head ornaments and decorations they wear are often made of silver, symbolizing nobility and beauty. A Roman script was introduced for their spoken language in 1956. They have a rich oral literature. Folksongs, from a few lines to over 15,000, are very popular. The *lusheng*, made of bamboo pipe, is their favourite wind instrument with a reed, so are *lusheng* dances which focus on footwork. Their culture is diversified. Different Miao communities celebrate various festivals. Even the same festivals may fall on different dates. The Miao New Year's Day is celebrated on 'Rabbit Day' or 'Ox Day' on the lunar calendar, including beating drums, horse-racing and bull-fighting. Of the multi-ethnic autonomous prefectures and counties, Miaos account for a larger percentage in the leadership due to their larger population. Some autonomous counties were established in the 1980s and 1990s. The railways between Guiyang and Kunming, and between Hunan and Guizhou, have boosted the development of the Miao and other ethnic groups along the routes.

Further reading

Enwall, Joakim (1995). *The Myth Becomes Reality: History and Development of the Miao Written Language*, 2 vols. Stockholm East Asia Monographs, 5–6. Stockholm: Institute of Oriental Languages, University of Stockholm.

Schein, Louisa (2000). *Minority Rules: The Miao and the Feminine in China's Cultural Politics*. Durham: Duke University Press.

HELEN XIAOYAN WU

Mid-Autumn Festival

(Zhongqiujie)

The Mid-Autumn Festival is generally thought to have long since become an entirely folklorized event: people eat 'moon cakes', share a family meal, and then go outdoors to 'gaze at the moon' (*shangyue*). The reality is very different: in the Hong Kong New Territories, for example, it is the day of all days to consult the *mann mae phox* ('women who consult the rice') and speak with the dead. In 1985 in Quanzhou, just after nightfall, people began to gather in the street near the site of a former temple to Chen Jinggu to 'listen to the incense' (*tingxiang*). Each person lit sticks of incense, planted them in the cracks in the brick wall in the alley where a small altar replaced the destroyed temple, and then stood silently in the street to wait for the chance word of a passer-by that could be used to divine the future. In 1990, in Fuzhou, I was told to go to a famous temple in nearby Fuqing dedicated to the Nine Immortals – nine brothers who, having turned into carp, ascended to heaven: the temple is, every Mid-Autumn Day, a privileged moment to come in 'search of a dream' (*qiumeng*). Clearly, the Mid-Autumn Festival is a key moment for entering into contact with the invisible world of spirits.

This festival clearly has religious dimension, particularly in the south, where it is associated with a specifically feminine mode of worship of the moon. In the Hakka county of Renhua (Shaoguan, Yuebei), starting on the first day of the month, the women gather in an inner courtyard – the men may not even watch – to 'worship the Big Sister of the moon'. Under the direction of an elder, they invite the Lady of the lunar palace by means of songs that she herself once taught when she descended to earth during the Tang dynasty. The song of invitation begins thus:

Enjoy the moon high in the sky, up in the clouds,
Up in the clouds on high, in a thousand-room [palace];
Contract the lunar contract, contract with the Yin world,
Contract with the Yin world where Chang'e wraps;
Chang'e wraps the clouds up in the clear sky above.

When the Big Sister arrives, she is asked to designate the woman who, this year, will be her 'replacement body' (*tishen*). She obliges by causing chopsticks held by two young women to write in the rice in a winnowing basket. Once her representative has been named, the latter answers, by means not of words – speech is forbidden – but of gestures, whatever questions the women wish to ask about their lives and future. After fifteen days of songs and divination, on the evening of the sixteenth day of the month, the women thank the Lady of the Chang'e palace and send her back to the moon. Zhang Zhaohua adds this remark: 'In northern Guangdong, there is a popular saying which states, "The men amuse themselves during the first month; in the eighth, it is the women who have fun."'

Men, however, are not entirely excluded from this festival: throughout western Fujian, one encounters tales of divinatory practices – by dream, by the 'god of the winnowing basket' and the 'god of the carrying stick' – which involve men every bit as much as women. In Yangjiang (along the coast, in southwestern Guangdong), by the light of the moon, the men gather on the rice-drying arena to 'invite Huagang', a 'warrior god'. Some of the men stretch out full length on the ground, as if asleep: they are the potential 'substitute bodies' of the god. The others, having planted incense sticks at the four 'entry gates' of the arena, run around the supine men, singing, 'Master Huaguang, show yourself. A troupe of players, many people, wish to perform martial arts, and have prepared money and gold.' Among the sleepers, some begin to tremble – those who do not thus show themselves incapable of trance – and then slowly stand up, somnambulate, and finally begin to leap and assuming the postures of the **martial arts**. Men may also invite the 'god of the table' or the 'mother of bullfrogs' – some even leap into a pond – while the women, closeted inside the house, invite the Seventh Lady, who can divine the future by inspecting the flowering tree of each of the women in the other world.

In general, the Hakka, even where the Mid-Autumn Festival no longer involves any rituals, celebrate a 'meal of cohesion' on that day whose only equal is that of New Year's Eve. Even today, the young folk who have gone to work in the cities invariably come home for a week, often to participate in the annual village festival, sometimes called a **Jiao** ('sacrifice', 'offering'), but in some areas known as *chansha*, a term no one is sure how to write but which may mean 'to make confession before the god of the earth'. Both are community rituals addressed to the divine protection of the village – sacred rituals in which Daoists, dressed as women, play the sacred theatre of Chen Jinggu (see **Lüshan jiao (Sannai jiao)**).

What is the relationship between the first and eighth months, that they are both characterized by major community festivals? According to Suzuki, 'The rituals of thanksgiving for a good year begin in the eighth month and fulfil thereby the vows made the day of the **Lantern Festival** when prayers for good fortune were made.' A Taoist master in Zhangping (Longyan) told me that they did locally three kinds of *jiao*: those for the Lantern Festival, which involve the sacrifice of a pig and the dispatch to heaven of a document (*pang*) bearing the names of all the faithful; those of the first day of the seventh month, 'for peace'; and those of Mid-Autumn, for the birthday of the god of the earth. An observer of customs in Taiwan, Wu Yingtao, confirms that the fifteenth day of the eighth moon is at once the birthday of the goddess of the moon, Taiyin niangniang (Lady of the Great Yin), and of the god of the earth: 'On that day, every family must worship its ancestors, as well as the god of the earth.' Thus is concentrated on that single day in the middle of autumn everything that belongs to the yin principle – the moon, the god of the earth, the dead – just as all that is yang is honoured in the first month.

JOHN LAGERWEY

migration and settlement patterns

The household registration law (*hukou*) enacted by the Chinese socialist state in 1958 played the primary role in blocking population movement, especially rural-to-urban labour migration in Mao's era. Government officials believed that it was necessary to keep the rural population on the farmlands so that they would continue to produce food for those working in industry and would not burden the existing urban infrastructure. Restricting people's spatial mobility was also seen as key to maintaining social control and political stability. As a result, spontaneous labour migration was largely absent in China from the 1950s to the 1970s. During this period, however, a very different kind of state-directed, politically motivated, 'reversed' migration took place. Many skilled urban workers and professionals were urged by the Maoist state to relocate to economically underdeveloped regions, while millions of urban youth were sent down to the countryside to be 're-educated' by the peasants (see **xiafang, xiaxiang**).

With rapid commercialization, a booming urban economy, the influx of foreign capital, and relaxed state migration policy, there have been several large waves of mass labour migration in the post-Mao reform era. Over 100 million Chinese farmers have poured into the cities to look for jobs and small business opportunities. This large mobile population is known as 'the floating population' (*liudong renkou*); and its members are often called 'peasant workers' (*mingong*), or 'working brothers' (*dagongzai*) and 'working sisters' (*dagongmei*). The vast majority of these rural transients are temporary or seasonal menial workers who have nothing but their labour to sell; the rest of them are small independent entrepreneurs in family-based businesses. Migrants today are required to register with local authorities and obtain temporary resident status, but they are treated as second-class citizens and can be driven out of the city whenever officials deem necessary. While most rural migrants move from place to place frequently in response to the unpredictable job market demand, some have also formed their own unofficial settlements on the outskirts of Chinese cities based on their common local place of origin. Such settlements are usually named by urbanites as 'villages' after the provincial origin of the migrants living there. The largest and best-developed one is the so-called 'Zhejiangcun' in Beijing, created by migrant entrepreneurs and merchants from rural Wenzhou in Zhejiang province. Not only did Wenzhou migrants build their own housing and permanent market buildings for garment production and trade but they also developed a sense of group solidarity and a nascent community leadership. At its peak, there were about 100,000 migrants living and working in this settlement. Yet authorities and urbanites often regard such unofficial migrant communities as hotbeds for crime and a threat to state regulatory power. As a result, there have been periodical government campaigns to clean out migrant settlements in the cities, but migrants persistently come back to stay and resume their economic activities after each political tornado ends.

Further reading

Gaetano, Arianne and Jacka, Tamara (eds) (2004). *On the Move: Women and Rural–Urban Migration in Contemporary China*. New York: Columbia University Press.

Li, Zhang (2001). *Strangers in the City: Reconfigurations of Space, Power, and Social Networks within China's Floating Population*. Stanford, CA: Stanford University Press.

Solinger, Dorothy (1999). *Contesting Citizenship in Urban China: Peasant Migrants, the State, and the Logic of the Market*. Berkeley: University of California Press.

—— (2002). 'The Floating Population in the Cities: Markets, Migration, and the Prospects of Citizenship'. In Susan Blum and Lionel Jensen (eds), *China Off Center: Mapping the Margins of the Middle Kingdom*. Honolulu: University of Hawai'i Press, 273–88.

Williams, Philip F. (1998–9). 'Migrant Laborer Subcultures in Recent Chinese Literature: A Communicative Perspective'. *Intercultural Communication Studies* 8. 2: 153–61.

LI ZHANG

Ministry of Culture

The Ministry of Culture of the PRC reports directly to the State Council, with corresponding agencies in cities and provinces. Sun Jiazheng is the Minister. Major duties of the ministry are studying and drafting policies and regulations; making strategic plans; overseeing literary and artistic creation and production; administering community and ethnic cultural undertakings; supervising public libraries, museums and Internet cafés; coordinating the work of excavating, preserving and protecting cultural relics; promoting cultural exchange programmes and cooperative activities with Chinese territories and foreign countries.

To carry out these and housekeeping duties, the Ministry of Culture is divided into thirteen departments, including those of Policies and Regulations, Planning and Finance, Personnel, Art, Education and Technology, Cultural Market, Cultural Industry, Community Cultural Services, and Cultural Liaison. The State Bureau of Cultural Relics reports to the ministry, its head being a member of the ministerial leadership. The bureau's functions are to excavate, study and protect cultural relics; provide public services and educational programmes; report historical cultural sites to the United Nations for preservation; and administer foreign affairs relating to cultural relics and promote cooperation and exchanges.

The Ministry of Culture has fifty-five research and operative institutions under its direct supervision, such as the Art Studies Institute of China, Centre of Cultural Exchange of China, Chinese Orchestra, Central Academy of Art, and Literature and Art Publishing House. The ministry has built three Internet portals and six websites, including China Culture Information Net, Digital Library, and Management of Chinese Community Cultural Activities.

HU MINGRONG

Ministry of Education

Named National Council of Education before 1999, the Ministry of Education PRC is one of the State Council's cabinet level departments responsible for the nation's K-12 and post-secondary education as well as language programmes. The ministry has under its direct jurisdiction branch offices at all levels of governments. After the Central Government adopted the policy of *kejiao xingguo* (building up the nation with science and technology), the Ministry of Education has been playing a more and more important role in Chinese society.

The Ministry of Education PRC exercises a wide range of responsibilities. It studies and formulates educational policies; makes strategic plans for reform and development; administers education funds; and establishes and enforces standards of school setups, teaching programmes, research projects, faculty management, enrolment, and degree conference. The ministry also coordinates and supervises all education-related international exchange and cooperation programmes. In addition, it drafts guidelines and policies with regard to the nation's linguistic issues.

Since the Central Government started the campaign to develop the western regions of the country and made education prerequisite to its success, the Ministry of Education has taken the following measures: speeding up the development of core curricula in the western regions; locating partners from developed regions to help their K-12 schools; improving classes taken by ethnic residents; enhancing school personnel's qualities; building distance education systems; improving institutions of higher education; attracting more talent; and promoting exchange programmes so that education leaders in the western regions can be exposed to new ideas.

HU MINGRONG

Ministry of Information Industry

The Ministry of Information Industry (MII; *Xinxi chanyebu*) is the regulatory watchdog for China's electronic communications industries. Formed in 1998, this super-ministry absorbed the functions of the Ministry of Posts and Telecommunications (MPT), the Ministry of Electronic Industries (MEI), and the network management responsibilities of the Ministry of Radio Film and Television (MRFT). The formation of the MII is seen as a response to the convergence (*ronghe*) of telecommunications, broadcasting and information technology and the need to develop national strategies, policies and technical standards. It oversees telecommunications and information service licences and fees, multimedia and broadband developments, broadcasting networks and spectrum allocation, satellite orbit positioning, as well as monitoring the development of China's Internet and the commercial applications of wireless, fixed line and satellite networks.

While the MII is responsible for licensing Internet Service Providers (ISPs), control of content is subject to regulation by the State Information Office. Likewise television content is monitored by the **State Administration for Radio, Film and Television** (SARFT).

The MII is also responsible for overseeing the development of China's National Information Infrastructure (CNII), a process that involves a delicate balance between the need to protect domestic information and communication technology industries from foreign control, and the need to attract foreign investment in high-tech value-added services industries. To the extent that this process necessitates integration in the world trading system, the MII is more constrained by the regulatory architecture of the World Trade Organization than the SARFT, which primarily administers and licenses domestic television industries.

Further reading

http://www.mii.gov.cn/

Ure, J. and Liang, Xiong-Jian (2000). 'Convergence and China's national Information Infrastructure'. In M. Hukill, R. Ono, and C. Vallath (eds). *Electronic Communication Convergence: Policy Challenges in Asia*. New Delhi: Sage.

MICHAEL KEANE

minjian

(popular space)

Political cultural concept

The Shanghai literary critic Chen Sihe's concept of *minjian* began to appear in two essays, published in 1994, entitled 'The Ups and Downs of Popular Space' (*Minjian de fuchen*) and 'The Origins of Popular Space' (*Minjian de huanyuan*). Instantly these essays evoked discussion among literary critics and university students in Shanghai, and the concept of *minjian* has since drawn attention both home and abroad. The essays exalt the floriate of Chinese literature since the 1980s as a revival of the humanities and creative energy. In this literary renaissance, asserts Chen, there has been an autonomous drive in

which one may detect the 'hidden structure' of the 'popular space'. He also describes how the contemporary 'popular space' was rooted in Chinese literature at the turn of the twentieth century and its political and cultural vicissitudes in later decades.

As Chen defines it, 'popular space' is close to Habermas's theory of the 'public sphere' as they both resist the power of the nation-state. Yet the Chinese popular space is primarily a 'cultural space', discursively engaged with the process of Chinese modernization, and different from the 'public sphere' of seventeenth- and eighteenth-century Europe, where bourgeois liberals institutionally handled their political and economic affairs interests. In the triangular relation between the Chinese 'popular space', the nation-state and the intellectual class, 'popular space' has always been oppressed by the state, whose power has been concentrated through a series of national crises, and by intellectuals, whose primary goal has been to serve the state. However, the 'popular space' has never disappeared; instead it has shown energy and vitality, with a capacity to enrich itself by drawing upon diverse resources, whether from the feudalist (traditional), urban or peasant cultures. In one form or another, whether visible or not, it has persistently engaged or negotiated with these oppressive forces.

See also: popular culture, mass culture

Further reading

Litzinger, Ralph (2001). 'A Government from Below: The State, the Popular, and the Illusion of Autonomy'. *positions: east asia cultures critique* 9.1 (Spring): 253–66.

Wang, Jing (2001). 'Guest Editor's Introduction'. *positions: east asia cultures critique* 9.1 (Spring): 1–27.

CHEN JIANHUA

Minju

(Fujian sung-drama/opera)

Minju (Min opera) is one of the main opera genres in Fujian. The gradual integration over three centuries of opera styles produced a new genre by the twentieth century, Fuzhouxi (Fuzhou theatre) – known today as Minju. For all its borrowing, including traces of classical drama, Minju, which is sung in the Fuzhou dialect, is rich in local flavour.

The music of Minju may be divided into four main components: the *douqiang* (lingering melody); light-hearted folk melodies known as *Yangge* (Yang songs); *Jianghu diao* or 'melodies from the rivers and lakes'; and *xiao diao* or short folk melodies. In Minju, male and female roles sing in their natural voice, unlike many other opera genres. The seven-piece orchestra is divided into two sections: *ruanpan* or 'the soft split' (dialectal), featuring mostly **Silk and Bamboo** instruments and including fiddles such as the *yehu*, made of coconut, and several oboe-like *suona*; and *yin pan* or 'the hard split', mostly gongs and drums.

Minju's five types of roles are the *sheng* (male), *dan* (female), *chou* (clown), *jing* (painted face) and *mo* (another male part). Among the traditional repertory of over a thousand plays, *The Hairpin* (*Chaitoufeng*), a play depicting the tragic love of the poet Lu You for his cousin, and *Honeymoon on a Fishing Boat* (*Yuchuan huazhu*) are particularly popular. Modern plays include *Xin chahua*, an updated version of *La Dame aux Camélias* in period costume, and *Song of a Fisherman at Sea* (*Haishang yuge*).

Early twentieth-century Minju actors were usually trained as singers or courtesans before re-converting into an opera career. Such is the case of Zheng Lianzou (b. 1910), one of Minju's 'Four Great Female Role[-Players]', nicknamed 'The Mei Lanfang of Fujian', who trained many generations and toured in Indonesia. The art was diffused through commercial recordings in the 1920s and 1930s and famous actors ensured the transition with the Communist regime.

Like **Bangzi**, Minju maintains an active presence in the countryside, where performing tours by the professional companies are partly sponsored by individuals (including overseas Chinese), families or groups for special occasions. However, audiences have been steadily dwindling since the 1980s due to the disaffection of the public because of the high price of tickets and the diversification of leisure. Though there are fewer young talents, three to four companies still perform periodically in Fuzhou.

ISABELLE DUCHESNE

Minnan nanyin

Regional traditional music ensemble genre

Minnan nanyin (southern Min music) is a regional **Silk and Bamboo** (*sizhu yinyue*) chamber ensemble tradition found along the China coast. When the Minnan or southern Hokkien people migrated to southeast Asia, they brought *nanyin*, 'the southern sound', to Taiwan, the Philippines, Singapore, Malaysia, Indonesia, and later to Hong Kong.

Nanyin is played at birthdays, weddings, house-warming events, grand openings, memorial services, holiday celebrations and Buddhist and Daoist festivals (see **Jiao**; **Gongde**). It also accompanies the centuries-old **Liyuanxi** (Pear Garden Theatre), *budaixi* (hand-held puppetry) and *kueilei xi* (marionette). The nanyin repertoire includes *zhi* (finger) instrumental suites with singing, *pu* (notation) instrumental suites, and *sanqu* (individual songs). Instruments include the core *shangsi guan* (upper four pipes), *paiban* (clappers), *dongxiao* (end-blown flute), **pipa** (pear-shaped lute), *erxian* (two-stringed fiddle) and *sanxian* (three-stringed lute).

Beginning in the 1980s, the government sponsored nanyin training in Xiamen and Quanzhou and competitions to revive this traditional art form. Free public performances were given because they appealed to visiting *huaqiao* (overseas Chinese), who regard this music as their *xiangyin* (homeland sound). In Minnan, *huaqiao* often invest in businesses and donate generously to rebuilding schools, temples, hospitals, homes for elders. Nanyin has now moved into *chalou* (teahouses), where customers pay to listen. Amateurs are gradually replacing professionals. Few instructors use *gongchi pu* (notation), while many use the popular Arabic-numbered *jianpu* (simple notation) to teach students. Some dedicated individuals and organizations promote this music through the publication of new handbooks, compilations, articles, compact discs, video compact discs (DVDs), public concerts and educational programmes.

Further reading

Chen, Bingji (1985). *Fujian nanyin jiqi zhipu*. Beijing: Zhongguo wenlian chuban gongsi.

Lu, Chuikuan (1982). *Quanzhouxian guan* [*nanguan*] *yanjiu*. Taipei: Xueyi chubanshe.

Lu, Chuikuan (1983). *Nanguan jipufa gailun*. Taipei: Xueyi chubanshe.

—— (1986). *Taiwan de nanguan*. Taipei: Yueyun chubanshe.

Quanzhou duiwai wenhua jiaoliu xiehui, Quanzhoushi wenhuaju (1988): *Quanzhou nanyin yishu*. Fuzhou: Haixia wenyi chubanshe.

Wang, Yaohua (2000). *Fujian chuantong yinyue*. Fuzhou: Fujian renmin chubanshe.

—— (2002). *Fujian nanyin*. Beijing: Renmin yinyue chubanshe.

Yeh, Nora (1985). *Nan Guan Music in Taiwan: A Little Known Classical Tradition*. University Microfilm International Dissertation Information Service.

NORA YEH

minority pop musicians: the new generation

The popular music scene in China of the last decade boasts several famous young musicians of ethnic minority origin who live in Beijing and compose and perform songs in both Chinese and minority languages which highlight their different ethnicity. With their minority songs this group of musicians join a long tradition that has existed in the PRC at least since 1949. The CCP has always encouraged the production and popularization of songs about minority regions and peoples as part of its general effort to advance the integration of China's ethnic minorities within the general Chinese culture. These songs have typically incorporated elements from minority music and language, described the local scenery and customs of minority people, and with the massive support of the government became an important component of mainstream culture. Yet despite the obvious continuity, in the context of the general political liberalization and the resurgence of ethnicity in the reform era, these minority musicians have also challenged this tradition in important ways.

The old-style minority songs have typically called for loyalty to the state and unity among China's different nationalities. They also tended to exoticize minorities, idealize their lives, and depict them through the eyes of the Han majority. These characteristics derived in part from the highly politicized climate during the Maoist era and in part from the fact that many of the songs were created by Han Chinese. The new songs, by contrast, lack the orthodox official calls for loyalty and unity and express more diverse messages which in some cases go as far as to problematize the position and the orthodox representation of ethnic minority people in China.

The most prominent representative of the new generation of minority pop musicians is **Teng Ge'er**, a Mongol born in Inner Mongolia. Though in many of his songs he perpetuates the stereotypical exotic images of Mongolia, he has also expressed discontent over the loss of Mongolian identity and land, and longing for the times when the Mongols dominated China. Another representative is Askar (Chin.: Aisika'er), a Uighur born in 1964 in Xinjiang, who calls both himself and his heavy metal band Grey Wolf, after the famous symbol of pan-Turkic nationalism. Many of Askar's songs express discontent over the position of Uighurs in China and the situation in Xinjiang, and are widely interpreted by Uighurs as calls for Uighur independence or autonomy. His famous songs include 'Daolang', 'Laopo' [Wife] and 'Zhufu' [Blessing]. Other famous minority musicians and groups of the new generation include Lolo (Yi), Han Hong (half Tibetan and half Han), Siqingerile (Mongol), Shanying [Mountain Eagle] and Yiren zhizao [A Product of the Yi People] (two groups of Yi musicians), and Afanti (a group of predominantly Uighur musicians).

With their biographies and artistic activity, the above-mentioned musicians reflect and shape two coexistent and contradictory trends that relate to China's minorities in the reform era: the first is an enhanced sense of ethnic identity and nationalism among China's minorities, and the second is an increased integration of minorities and minority cultures in the general Chinese cultural sphere.

See also: representations of minorities

Further reading

Baranovitch, Nimrod (2003). *China's New Voices: Popular Music, Ethnicity, Gender, and Politics*. Berkeley: University of California Press.

Harris, Rachel (2002). 'Cassettes, Bazaars, and Saving the Nation: The Uyghur Music Industry in Xinjiang, China'. In Timothy Craig and Richard King (eds), *Global Goes Local: Popular Culture in Asia*. Vancouver, BC: University of British Columbia Press, 265–82.

NIMROD BARANOVITCH

minority presses

(minzu chubanshe)

Minzu chubanshe are presses in China that mainly publish books in minority languages and books about minority groups. There is a state-level *minzu chubanshe* in Beijing and many provincial level *minzu chubanshe* in the autonomous regions and frontier provinces. There are even some prefectural-level *minzu chubanshe*, such as Mudanjiang Chaoxian minzu chubanshe in Heilongjiang province and Dehong minzu chubanshe in Yunnan province. All of these are official presses under the control of different levels of government.

The minority presses in Beijing were established in 1953 and put under the control of the State Ethnic Affairs Commission. One of the original official missions of the press was to publish Marxist classics, works of the Chinese Communist leaders, and important documents of the Chinese Communist Party and government in minority languages. The *minzu chubanshe* in Beijing publishes books mainly in six languages: Chinese, Mongolian, Tibetan, Uighur, Khazak and Korean. Since its founding, the press has published over 20,000 different books. It also publishes several periodicals in these six languages, including *Minority Nationality Pictorial* (*Minzu huabao*), *Minority Nationality Solidarity* (*Minzu tuanjie*) and *Minority Nationality Literature* (*Minzu wenxue*). Provincial and prefectural-level minority presses also publish books about local minority groups in Chinese and in the languages of these groups. As a result of the increasing influence of the market economy, however, some minority presses have begun to publish books that do not have much to do with minority groups, and the original political mission of the minority presses may gradually fade away.

See also: Sino-Tibetan language speakers; Turkic language speakers

HAN XIAORONG

Minsu quyi (Min-su ch'ü-i)

[Journal of Chinese Ritual, Theatre and Folklore]

Minsu quyi was founded in November 1980, its original goal being to publish essays and field reports introducing Taiwanese folk culture. Wang Ch'iu-kuei became editor-in-chief in 1989, and has worked to transform the journal into a scholarly publication now internationally known for publishing research about Chinese ritual and ritual theatre. Since 1991, the journal's scope has expanded to include mainland China and examine a broad range of cultural phenomena, particularly religion and ritual. Professor Wang also edited a number of important special issues containing detailed ethnographic reports of rituals and theatrical performances, especially Nuo dramas and Mulian dramas. *Minsu quyi* also took the lead in organizing a series of international conferences, as well as publishing conference papers.

During the 1990s, *Minsu quyi* took its place at the forefront of researching what Kenneth Dean has termed the 'renaissance' of Chinese local culture, most notably by publishing the 81-volume *Minsu quyi congshu* (*Monograph Series of Studies in Chinese Ritual, Theatre and Folklore*), which consists of ethnographic reports about actual performances of ritual dramas in rural China, as well as rare editions of scripts. Most of the data covers provinces in south China, particularly Anhui, Fujian, Guizhou, Hunan, Jiangsu, Jiangxi, Sichuan, Yunnan and Zhejiang. The importance of the *Monograph Series* is clearly attested to by the growing attention it has begun to command throughout the scholarly community worldwide.

Beginning in 2000, *Minsu quyi* took new steps to increase its status as an academic publication. Professor C. K. Wang turned the management of the journal over to a new team of editors, including Professors Wang An-ch'i, Wang Sung-shan, Wang Ying-fen and myself. *Minsu quyi* began to be published as a quarterly in 2002, and all submissions are now subject to a rigorous peer review process involving at least two referees. Moreover, the cover design and format have been modified, and the final issue of each calendar year contains an author index.

The results of these changes may be seen in the two most recent issues of the journal (137 and 138), a special double issue about the ways in which religious beliefs, rituals and dramatic performances both reflected yet also shaped the development of local society. Topics covered in these two issues include: the history of local cults to nature spirits among the ancient Ba people of southwest China; the cult of a Zen Buddhist master (*Dingguang gufo*) as practised among the inhabitants of ten Hakka and She minority villages in southwestern Fujian; the cult and festival of the Queen Mother of the West in Gansu province; cults to the ghosts of Taiwanese girls who did not conform to traditional gender norms due to their dying before getting married; the cult of silkworm deities in northern Zhejiang during the late imperial era; the role dramatic performances play in the perpetuation of cult worship of the Cattle King in southwestern Shanxi; the cult of a fox spirit and its spirit-medium at a popular Buddhist temple located in northern Shaanxi; the interaction between the state, lineages and religious networks in Fujian; the links between local elites and popular temples in northern Taiwan during the Qing dynasty (1644–1911); and the religious aspects of one of the most important rebellions that occurred in Taiwan during the Qing dynasty, the Dai Chaochun Incident (1862–8).

At present, *Minsu quyi* continues to receive a constant flow of submissions, including historical studies and field reports written in Chinese and English on regional theatre, music, folklore, religion and ritual.

PAUL R. KATZ

Misty poetry

(Menglongshi)

Also translated 'obscure poetry,' *Menglongshi* was one of the most controversial phenomena on the Chinese literary scene in the post-Mao era. From the late 1970s to the early 1980s, a group of young poets who had experienced suffering and disillusionment during the **Cultural Revolution** wrote poems that were distinctively different from the socialist realist style prevailing during the Mao era. Symbolically subtle and thematically iconoclastic and polysemous, these poems are novel in images and bold in self-expression. Although the term *menglongshi* has been generally used to refer to them, it does not properly characterize their diversified poetry. *Menglongshi* was first used by Zhang Ming in 1980 to criticize the newly rising poetic style as obscure and inappropriate; similar criticism had appeared the year before which condemned the poetry as indulging in individualism and betraying the social responsibilities of intellectuals. Defence of the *menglong* poetry came immediately from different generations of Chinese intellectuals, including articles by Sun Shaozhen, Xie Mian, Xu Jingya and Ai Qing. The supporters saw in *menglongshi* a strong call for humanism and an insuppressible pursuit of individual freedom, both direct reactions to the Cultural Revolution. They also applauded the refreshing aesthetic principles asserted by these poets, who opposed the didactic and political literary theories that governed Chinese poetry in earlier decades. The rise of *menglongshi* and the five-year debate over it exerted considerable impact on the intellectual discourse in the PRC and gave new direction to freestyle poetry. The best-known *menglong* poets include **Bei Dao**, **Shu Ting**, **Gu Cheng**, **Jiang He**, **Yang Lian** and Meng Ke.

Further reading

Chen, Xiaomei (1991). 'Misunderstanding Western Modernism: The Menglong Movement in Post-Mao China'. *Representations* 35 (Summer): 143–63.

Yeh, Michelle (2003). 'Misty Poetry'. In Joshua Mostow (ed.) and Kirk A. Denton (China section, ed.), *Columbia Companion to Modern East Asian Literatures*. New York: Columbia University Press, 520–6.

QIU PEIPEI

Mo Wuping

b. 1958, Hengyang, Hunan; d. 1993

Composer

Mo Wuping enrolled in the Central Conservatory of Music in 1983. He studied composition with Luo Zhongrong, with whom he formed a strong friendship, and who guided him in the systematic study of contemporary Western composers. In 1987 Mo's *Shui Diao Ge Tou* won an Honourable Mention in China's first art-song composition contest. In 1988 he went to Hong Kong to attend an international modern music festival, and his second string quartet, *Sacrificial Rites in the Village*, won second prize in a composition competition for young Asian composers. In the next year, the quartet received its European debut in Amsterdam and the score was published in Beijing.

Mo went to France in 1990 to study at the École Normale de Musique de Paris. During his first year in Paris, Mo experienced severe financial difficulties and suffered from depression. He managed to complete *Fan I*, written for nine players and male voice. The piece was commissioned by the Dutch Nieuw Ensemble and premiered by that group with Mo himself as vocalist; the score was published by Éditions du Visige in Paris in 1992. Mo returned to China in January 1993 where he was diagnosed with liver cancer. He died at home in June 1993. Mo's music is known for its drama, rich timbre and exquisite melody. His works were compiled and edited by his widow, Li Shuqin, a musicologist, and were published in Beijing in 1994.

JIN PING

Mo Yan

(né Guan Moye)

b. 1956, Gaomi county, Shandong

Writer

Mo Yan emerged in the mid 1980s as one of the most important writers of contemporary China. He has been associated with the **Root-seeking school** (*Xungen pai*), an avant-garde group, but Mo's writing defies clear-cut classification.

Influenced by magical realism of Latin American writers, especially Marquez, Mo Yan combines the supernatural and surrealism with nostalgia to explore human cruelty, bureaucratic corruption and individual heroism. Mo Yan enlisted in the People's Liberation Army in 1976 and was admitted to the literature department in the PLA College of Literature in 1984. He completed graduate work at the **Lu Xun Literary Institute** and resigned from the Cultural Affairs Department of the PLA in 1999. He first published in 1981 and is best known for his 1986 novel, *Red Sorghum* (*Hong gaoliang*), which is a first-person account of a grandson's visit to his ancestral home and his retelling of its history during the Japanese invasion. Mo Yan's depictions of rural life and his examination of the transmission of local history reveals an interest in putting the political events of twentieth-century China into a larger historical and cultural context. Ultimately, this family saga addresses the need to understand the deeply imbedded cultural and historical influences on human society. The novel was made into a film with the same title by **Zhang Yimou** in 1987. *Garlic Ballads* (*Tiantang suantai zhige*) and *Republic of Wine* (*Jiu guo*) complete what is considered to be a trilogy of nativist stories that centre on northeastern local culture. His collection of short stories from the 1980s and 1990s, *Shifu, You'll Do Anything for a Laugh* (*Shifu yue lai yue youmo*), deals with corruption, greed and the supernatural.

Further reading

Feuerwerker, Yi-tsi Mei (1998). 'The Post-Modern Search for Roots: Han Shaogong, Mo Yan, and Wang Anyi'. In *idem* (ed.), *Ideology, Power, Text: Self-Representation and the Peasant 'Other' in Modern Chinese Literature*. Stanford: Stanford University Press.

Lu, Tonglin (1993). '*Red Sorghum*: Limits of Transgression'. In X. Tang and L. Kang (eds), *Politics, Ideology, and Literary Discourse in Modern China: Theoretical Interventions and Cultural Critique*. Durham: Duke University Press.

Mo, Yan (1993). *Red Sorghum*. Trans. H. Goldblatt. New York: Viking.

—— (1996). *The Garlic Ballads*. Trans. H. Goldblatt. New York: Penguin.

Mo, Yan (2001). *Shifu, You'll Do Anything for a Laugh.* Trans. H. Goldblatt and S. Li-Chun Lin. New York: Arcade.

—— (2001). *Republic of Wine.* Trans. H. Goldblatt. London: Penguin.

—— (2004). *Big Breasts and Wide Hips.* Trans. H. Goldblatt. Arcade Books.

Wang, David Der-wei (1993). 'Imaginary Nostalgia: Shen Congwen, Song Zelai, Mo Yan, and Li Yongping'. In Ellen Widmer and David Wang (eds), *From May Fourth to June Fourth: Fiction and Film in Twentieth-Century China.* Cambridge: Harvard University Press.

Yue, Gang (1999). 'From Cannibalism to Carnivorism: Mo Yan's *Liquorland*'. In *idem, The Mouth that Begs: Hunger, Cannibalism, and the Politics of Eating in Modern China.* Durham: Duke University Press.

Zhong, Xueping (2000). '*Zazhong gaoliang* and the Male Search for Masculinity'. In *idem, Masculinity Besieged? Issues of Modernity and Male Subjectivity in Chinese Literature of the Late Twentieth Century.* Durham: Duke University Press.

MEGAN M. FERRY

modern Chinese orchestra

The name 'modern Chinese orchestra' is a convenient descriptive term to denote a musical organization that has various names in different places: *Minzu yuetuan* or *Minyue tuan* (national or folk orchestra) in mainland China, *Guoyue tuan* (national orchestra) in Taiwan, *Zhongyue tuan* (Chinese orchestra) in Hong Kong, and *Huayue tuan* (Chinese orchestra) in Singapore. All these names refer to the same type of orchestra made up of Chinese instruments, but partially formed according to Western orchestral principles that was developed in the twentieth century to represent both traditional and modern Chinese taste and identity. As a result of modernization at the turn of the twentieth century, Western music was introduced to the Chinese public through Christian churches, Western-style military bands and the newly established school system. Intellectuals who were trained in the new music system began to think and hear music in terms of Western intonation and harmony, and came to prefer the standardization of musical instruments as well as large orchestras.

Using the traditional **Jiangnan sizhu (Silk and Bamboo** ensemble of the lower Yangzi River valley) as a base, the first attempt at such an orchestra took place in Nanjing in 1935. It was the Central Broadcasting Company's orchestra and only performed on air. The first appearance of such an orchestra on stage in concert form took place in Chongqing in 1942. This was the same orchestra that was moved to Chongqing due to the Sino-Japanese War. The orchestra continued its mission on Taiwan after moving there in 1949. One important step in the formation of the orchestra was the 'improvement' of Chinese musical instruments according to Western standards of tuning, range and efficiency. Medium and large instruments were made to accommodate the lower pitch range for Western harmony. From the 1950s on, this new type of orchestra went through numerous transformations in China and Taiwan until it finally reached the form we see and hear today.

Principally based upon the Western classical symphony orchestra that is categorized into strings, woodwinds, brass and percussion, the modern Chinese orchestra is also divided into four sections, namely bowed strings, plucked strings, winds and percussion. The bowed string section that consists of several sizes of **erhu** (fiddle) type of instruments is the equivalent to the violin family of the West. The plucked string section is unique due to the many lute type of instruments popular in China, for instance the **pipa** (lute). *Yangqin* (hammered dulcimer) and **zheng** (zither), both stringed instruments, are part of this section even though they are played differently. Or they are considered to be independent. The wind section consists of *di* (flute), *sheng* (mouth-organ), *suona* (oboe), etc. The percussion consists of many gongs, cymbals and drums (see **luogu**). In recent practice, some Western instruments such as timpani and harp, have been included. In fact, cello and double bass have replaced the larger-sized Chinese fiddles for their better intonation and volume. The high bowed string is subdivided into two sections and the first erhu player is the concertmaster. Finally, a conductor is essential. This type of orchestra can be encountered in all urban areas including overseas Chinese communities. Unlike traditional folk ensembles whose function is for gatherings of musical friends or to accompany seasonal activities, the modern Chinese orchestra is for concert performance, just like its counterpart in the West.

See also: traditional music; traditional music composers; traditional music performers

Further reading

Han Kuo-Huang (1979). 'The Modern Chinese Orchestra'. *Asian Music* 11.1: 1–40.

Thrasher, Alan R. (2000). *Chinese Musical Instruments.* Hong Kong: Oxford University Press.

—— (2002). 'The Introduction of Western Music in Modern Times'. In Robert C. Provine, Yoshihiko Tokumaru and J. Lawrence Witzleben (eds), *The Garland Encyclopedia of World Music*, vol. 7: 373–8.

Witzleben, J. Lawrence (1995). *Silk and Bamboo Music in Shanghai.* Kent: Kent State University Press.

HAN KUO-HUANG

Modern Ink-Wash Painting

(Xiandai shuimo)

Xiandai shuimo is also known as *Chouxiang shuimo* (Abstract Ink-Wash Painting) and *Shiyan shuimo* (Experimental Ink-Wash Painting) in the writings of different critics. It's an artistic phenomenon that emerged in the mid 1990s when artists like **Liu Zijian**, Zhang Yu, Chen Tiejun, Wang Tiande and Wang Chuan, who had been trained in traditional Chinese painting (*Guohua*), turned to experimenting with abstract ink painting. Important events for this group of artists include: 'Zhangli de shiyan: '94 Bianxian xing shuimohua zhan' [An Experiment in Tension: An Exhibition of Expressive Ink Painting, 1994] and ''95 Zhangli yü biaoxian: Xuimo zhan' [Tension and Expression: An Exhibition of Ink-Wash Painting, 1995], both at the **China Art Gallery** (Zhonggou meishuguan); a symposium on contemporary Chinese ink painting held at Huanan Normal University in Guangzhou in 1996; and the publication of *Trends*

in Modern Chinese Ink-Wash Painting at the End of the Twentieth Century volumes I, II and III (1993, 1994, 1996) and *Experimental Ink-Wash Painting in China of the 1990s* (1998).

The phenomenon of Modern Ink-Wash Painting appeared when art historians and critics, such as Lang Shaojun among others, were strongly advocating 'brushwork as the central issue' in Chinese painting at a time when young artists and critics were enthusiastic about contemporary Western art forms such as performance, installation and video art. Most of the *Xiandai shuimo* artists, however, reject the idea of brushwork as the fundamental element for their work and have absorbed, to a great extent, elements from modern Western art. But in the meantime, they maintain many elements from traditional Chinese painting, therefore exploring an artistic space located between those of the traditionalists and their more radical contemporaries.

See also: New Literati Painting

Further reading

(1993, 1994, 1996). *Ershishijimo Zhongguo xiandai shuimo yishu zoushi* [Trends in Modern Chinese Ink-Wash Painting at the End of the Twentieth Century], vols 1–3. Tianjin: Yangliuqing chupanshe.

(1998). *Experimental Ink Painting in China of the 1990s.* Hong Kong: World Chinese Arts Publication Company.

Zhang, Yu and Zou, Jianping (eds) (1998). *Zhongguo dangdai shuimohua* [Contemporary Chinese Ink-Wash Painting]. Changsha: Hunan meishu chupanshe.

QIAN ZHIJIAN

Mongols, culture of

It is well known that the area occupied by 'cultural Mongolia' extends well beyond the borders of the PRC. In China, however, where there are almost three times as many Mongolians as in Outer Mongolia, most live in the Inner Mongolia

Autonomous Region (IMAR) and in nearby provinces such as Xinjiang and Qinghai. However, wherever they live they constitute a minority, particularly in the IMAR itself, where they make up only a tenth of the population even though the territory bears their name, the vast majority being **Han** Chinese. This formerly nomadic and now semi-nomadic people share many features of nomadic pastoralists in general, but in unique ways. Their relationship to livestock is extremely important and they most often speak of the five animals in a set order: the horse, cattle, the camel, sheep and goats. The horse is the most valued and signifies mobility and status; horse-racing at the occasion of special holidays is a very important activity – young children are often used as riders to permit horses to race with a lighter load. Nevertheless, many younger Mongols are finding that the motorcycle can go just as fast, and in some cases is less trouble to maintain. Oxen are still used for seasonal migrations, but more often than not a truck is borrowed to move all the household goods, including the *ger* (yurt) that is so characteristic of this culture. Almost every rural Mongolian family herds sheep, and these are a major source for their meat-oriented diet. After a sheep is killed, everything but the bones is consumed with great pleasure. This could explain at least partially how Mongols seem to be healthy even though they eat almost no vegetables. It is recognized that goats are problematic for the environment, but in certain areas their presence is encouraged by the high market value of the Kashmir wool that they can produce.

The Mongolian yurt usually faces the southeast (winds come from the northwest). Its walls are made from thin birch willows that are formed into a collapsible lattice and are usually held together by pieces of leather. The entire surface is covered with felt and held in place by ropes. The ceiling is an umbrella-like structure that is also easy to dismantle. In its centre is a hole through which passes a chimney from the inevitable cast-iron stove which burns dried dung. There are important customs relating to the use of this mobile dwelling. For example, one should never step on the threshold (this would symbolize stepping on the neck of the owner); one goes in towards the left and always leaves from the right side. In most places in Inner Mongolia there is a small bed placed opposite

the entrance, a place to stack quilts, pillows and clothing. Often there is a shelf with a picture of a deceased parent as well as religious objects (see **Buddhism in Inner Mongolia**). On one side of the entrance are various tools used for the production of various milk products such as butter and a very hard cheese. Even when families move to an urban area they will often choose to live in a 'yurt-suburb' at the edge of town.

Further reading

Bulag, Uradyn Erden (1998). *Nationalism and Hybridity in Mongolia.* Oxford: Clarendon Press.

—— (2002). *The Mongols at China's Edge: History and the Politics of National Unity.* Lanham, MD: Rowman and Littlefield.

Foggin, Peter M., Foggin, J. Marc and Shiirev-Adiya, C. (2000). 'Animal and Human Health among Semi-Nomadic Herders of Central Mongolia'. *Nomadic Peoples* 4: 148–68.

Pegg, Carole (2001). *Mongolian Music, Dance and Oral Narrative: Performing Diverse Identities.* Seattle: University of Washington Press.

Sechin, Jagchid and Hyer, Paul (1979). *Mongolia's Culture and Society.* Boulder: Westview Press.

Sneath, David (2000). *Pastoral Mongolian Society and the Chinese State.* Oxford: Oxford University Press.

Williams, Dee Mach (2002). *Beyond Great Walls: Environment, Identity and Development on Chinese Grasslands of Inner Mongolia.* Stanford: Stanford University Press.

PETER M. FOGGIN

monuments and public sculpture

Since the late 1970s, the urban landscape of Beijing, blighted by shoddy buildings that have increasingly dwarfed the scant remains of the old city, has been further scarred by public sculptures rendered in cement, steel, aluminium and glass. The first example of post-Mao public art was firmly in the tradition of high monumental socialism. *Great Achievements* was an 8.7-metre group sculpture set up at the northern or front entrance of the Mao

Mausoleum in **Tiananmen Square** that celebrates the achievements of the Chinese people under the late Great Leader. At the back, or south, of the mausoleum two similar sculptures bracket the exit, and are entitled *Carry the Cause of our Revolution through to the End*.

Most post 1976 monumental art has been less ideologically charged, with statues and structures celebrating Chinese heroes, martyrs, cultural paragons and legendary figures dotting the landscape. And then there are the tortured noodles of steel, the blobs of aluminium and uncarved blocks of iron that pass for modern public art, crowding as they do the urban scene in the company of kitsch statues bearing titles like *Reading*, *Flight*, *Hope*, *The Future*, that are generally sculpted in some blancmange-like material that soon turns grey-black in the polluted air.

Ironically, what are honoured as age-old buildings are often recent reconstructions. While the Liuhe Pagoda in Hangzhou and the Zhenhai Lou in Guangzhou date back to the Qing dynasty, as does the famous pagoda in the revolutionary base at Yan'an in southern Shaanxi, the Yellow Crane Pagoda at Wuhan is a modern cement-and-tile confection. It is a replacement structure built on the site of the ruined original that celebrates a famous poem by the Tang dynasty writer Li Bo bidding farewell to Meng Haoran. The new monstrosity (abutted by a gargantuan bell tower) even contains a mini-museum dedicated to Mao.

The China Millennium Monument, called the 'Century Altar' (*Shijitan*) in Chinese, started falling down the minute the clock struck midnight on 31 December 1999. Every inch of the ungainly structure located north of the city's Western Train Terminus has some symbolic meaning. After Party chief Jiang Zemin led official celebrations ushering in the new century far from Tiananmen and the centre of the city, the monument was closed for extensive repairs. Eventually reopened, and although ugly but not pointless (its featured steel poker points to some uncertain future, and looks like a clumsy reprise of a Russian Constructivist design from the 1920s), it does feature a small art museum that in 2002–3 put on foreign-curated exhibitions featuring Hedda Morrison's famous photographs of old Beiping, and even Indian bronze statues. The Monument itself stands next to

two extraordinary buildings that symbolize army might: the Stalinesque wedding-cake edifice of the Military Museum, one of the 'ten grand buildings' of the late 1950s, and the post-Stalinist marble-faced headquarters of the PLA, completed in 2000. Jiang Zemin's final monument was the approval of the National Grand Theatre for the centre of the capital. The ovoid titanium and glass structure is situated on the western flank of the Great Hall of the People and will appear to float in a lake, palpable evidence of Jiang's devotion to music (he was known to entertain foreign dignitaries with renditions of 'O, solo mio' and Elvis Presley songs at the drop of a cap).

The most fleeting public artwork was the 'Goddess of Democracy' (whose aspect seemed inspired by the Shanxi Communist martyr Liu Hulan posing as the Statue of Liberty) set up in Tiananmen Square in late May 1989 and destroyed by army soldiers on the morning of 4 June. The greatest monument to the afflatus of Chinese socialism, meanwhile, is the Three Gorges Dam that straddles the Yangtze River.

See also: architectural styles; Tiananmen Square

Further reading

Flath, James (2002). 'Managing Historical Capital in Shandong: Museum, Monument, and Memory in Provincial China'. *The Public Historian* 24.2: 41–59.

Hung, Chang-tai (2001). 'Revolutionary History in Stone: The Making of a Chinese National Monument'. *China Quarterly* 166 (June): 457–73.

Wu, Hung (1991). 'Tiananmen Square: A Political History of Monuments'. *Representations* 35 (Summer): 84–117.

GEREMIE R. BARMÉ

morality

Morality (*daode*) has been regarded as at least partially the government's responsibility since China's historical records began. Warring States rulers were enjoined to serve as moral models, like parents, and Song emperors commissioned recitation of moral treatises in each town. Education and morality were seen as inseparable; the goal of studying classical texts was as much moral as practical. Since the end of imperial China the relationship between morality and politics – and education – has been by turns direct and indirect. One of the principal goals of the Communist Revolution was moral education, with its height in the Socialist Education Campaign (1963) and the **Cultural Revolution** (1966–76). Campaigns pushing Chinese to be more selfless, to become better socialists, etc., employed moral exemplars, revolutionary heroes with peasants' practicality and simplicity.

Not all morality is explicitly encoded: there is a moral dimension to the idea of progress, with history teleologically moving toward a better, more civilized world in which individual 'quality' (*suzhi*) is ever higher. (This is aided by eugenic campaigns for 'fewer births, later births, better births'.) Sometimes morality is used to serve political ends, eliciting performative affirmation of willingness to say the proper words (*biaoxian*) and acknowledge authority.

Since Mao's death, distrust of and cynicism about simple moral messages have grown, though the government has nonetheless embarked periodically on such campaigns (anti-spiritual pollution, 1983; anti-bourgeois liberalization, 1987). With the Reforms, a unitary moral line has failed to emerge, though many more personal moral lines, including those of various religions, have been pursued privately. Burning moral questions now involve **Guanxi** and reciprocity (who owes what to whom for what), rectitude and **corruption**, the nature of money, the role of the individual vis-à-vis the family and society, and sexual practices. Cynical mockery of the earlier exhortation, 'Serve the People' (*Wei renmin fuwu*), is visible in the variant 'Serve the People's Money' (*Wei renminbi fuwu*), acknowledging the common motive of commerce which had been forbidden during the first years of the People's Republic. Nevertheless, in some films and literature, tension between modern cynicism and traditional morality is depicted, often with peasants and minorities playing the role of the moral agent. Television dramas often situate the moral world in the past. Indeed, tradition plays the role of morality, despite fifty years of treating the past as 'feudal' and to be discarded. Nostalgia for the simple moral messages of the Cultural Revolution can also be observed. A kind of post-morality is visible in the works of some authors, such as **Wang Shuo**, who lampoon all moral postures. Tensions between capitalism and socialism, urban and rural life, modernity and tradition, the foreign and the domestic, male and female, old and young, collective and private good, honesty and cleverness, kin and strangers, egalitarianism and hierarchy are all evident in contests that dare not quite call themselves moral.

See also: consumerism; Campaign against Bourgeois Liberalization; socialist spiritual civilization; shunkouliu; socio-political values; sexual attitudes; sexuality and behaviour; xiahai

SUSAN D. BLUM

Mormons

The first attempt by the Mormons (officially, The Church of Jesus Christ of Latter-Day Saints) to enter China in 1853 was a failure. Arriving in Hong Kong during the Taiping Rebellion with no language preparation or understanding of the culture, the three missionaries had no success converting Chinese or Westerners. They stayed for about eight weeks before returning to the United States. On 9 January 1921, David O. McKay, an apostle of the church on a world tour to evaluate areas for possible missions, stopped in Peking and dedicated China for the preaching of the gospel. However, the turbulent times of the 1920s, 1930s and 1940s made missionary work impractical. The end of World War II brought another apostle to China, and on 14 July 1949 Matthew Cowley officially opened the Chinese mission of the church. Internal tension in China and the Korean War prompted the United States consul general in Hong Kong to advise all American dependents to leave. The mission moved to Hawaii and then to California and worked with Chinese Americans. There was little success. As hostilities ceased in Korea, again an apostle was sent to Asia. Joseph Fielding Smith created the Southern Far East Mission, 17 August 1955. It included Hong Kong, Taiwan, the Philippines, Guam, South and Southeast Asia and the People's Republic of China. Headquarters were established in Hong Kong. People were more receptive and the church grew. On 4 June 1956, four missionaries were sent to Taiwan where they were hosted by an American family serving in the US military. The church grew as people in Taiwan were exploring new ideas brought in from the West. Translating church materials has been a challenge, but the standard scriptures and texts are available. By 2001 there were 21,084 members meeting in forty-one congregations in Hong Kong. They make up 0.3 per cent of the population, accounting for one in 331 residents. In Taiwan there are 35,506 members in eighty-one congregations (0.01 per cent or one in 667).

In 1979, as Deng Xiaoping opened China to the world, a song and dance performance group from the church's Brigham Young University performed before 17,000 people in four major cities. Other BYU groups followed. This resulted in the development of relationships between the church, its leaders and several Chinese entities. The church's Polynesian Cultural Centre in Hawaii became a model for several minority folk villages. The BYU China Teachers' Programme, started in 1988, has grown, and in 2003 seventy people were employed. To date over 600 teachers have served in China and trained some 10,000 students. The teachers are not allowed to preach or teach about their religious beliefs, but are to perform humanitarian service. Other church members in business, education or government service increased in number after 1979 and lived in various cities across China. The government has allowed expatriate congregations and several small groups of church members to meet for services in China since the 1980s. Chinese who joined the Mormon Church while studying or working abroad have faced challenges upon their return. Since the 1989 Tiananmen Square incident, the government has forbidden Chinese citizens from attending services conducted by expatriates. The church has worked hard to develop the trust of government officials and avoid any underground teachings or distribution of religious materials. The church looks forward to the day when it can be more active in sharing its message, but for now is practising patience and placing its efforts in Hong Kong and Taiwan.

Other Christian groups have influenced China's educational, health care and orphanage systems.

The impact of the Mormon effort has been more on a personal level attempting to make individuals better human beings, better family members and citizens.

Further reading

Britsch, R. L. (1998). *From the East: The History of the Latter-Day Saints in Asia, 1851–1996*. Salt Lake City: Deseret Books.

RICHARD B. STAMPS

Mou Sen

b. 22 January 1963, Liaoning

Theatre and film director

Mou Sen is considered one of China's most avant-garde theatre and documentary film directors. He attended the Beijing Teachers' University, majoring in Chinese literary criticism. At the university, which offered no formal theatre training, he directed several student productions. After graduation he volunteered to work as resident director for the Tibet Theatre Company. In 1987 he returned to Beijing and established the Frog Experimental Theatre, the first independent theatre company in China since 1949. There he directed Ionesco's *Rhinoceros*, Stravinsky's *A Soldier's Story* and Eugene O'Neill's *Great God Brown*. In 1989 he became a student of **Lin Zhaohua**, the deputy director of the **Beijing People's Art Theatre**, and together they created the Experimental Studio Theatre Laboratory. At the Laboratory they collaborated on experimental stagings of *Hamlet* and *The Beijing People*, a play by Chinese playwright Cao Yu.

He returned to Tibet in 1991 to set up the Tibet Theatre Studio, and in that same year received a grant from the United States Information Agency to visit the United States to conduct a series of interviews with American theatre artists. In 1993 he organized an actor-training programme for actors at the **Beijing Film Academy**. That same year he changed the name of his theatre company to the Workshop Theatre (Xiju chejian). The company has produced a number of experimental performances including *The Other Shore* (*Bi'an*), *File O* (*Ling Dang'an*) and *Things Related to AIDS* (*Yu aizibing you guande*).

File O, his most famous work, based on a poem by contemporary Chinese poet **Yu Jian**, is a complex blend of first-person narrative, symbolic imagery, poetry and documentary film footage. It was first performed at the Kunsten Festival des Arts in Brussels (May 1994) and has since toured Europe, Canada and the United States.

See also: Jiang Yue; Meng Jinghui

Further reading

Salter, Denis (1996). 'China's Theatre of Dissent: A Conversation with Mou Sen and Wu Wenguang'. *Asian Theatre Journal* 13.2 (Fall): 218–28.

CARLA KIRKWOOD

Mui, Anita

(neé Mui, Yimfong)

b. 1963, Hong Kong; d. 2004

Pop singer

Whereas **Deng Lijun** can be considered the queen of Mandapop, her Hong Kong counterpart Anita Mui might well be considered the – younger – queen of Cantopop. Unlike Deng, who was immortalized by her girlish sweetness, Anita shot to fame by being tough, hardworking and independent. She always made it clear that she started earning money by performing in parks, streets and fairgrounds with her mother from when she was five. Anita Mui became a public icon in Hong Kong, setting an example of what an undereducated girl can become in the prospering 1980s. Her career reached new heights in 1985 with the album *Bad Girl* (*Huai nühai*), a title emblematic of the performing identity of Anita Mui: daring, independent and, above all, refusing to conform.

Her controversial lifestyle that frequently made the headlines in the tabloids of Hong Kong (alleging, for example, her involvement in Triads), the changes in image and music style as well as her glamorous live performances all account for the vast creative spectrum of Anita Mui. Her occasional provocations inspired audiences and shocked governments. The song 'Bad Girl' was forbidden on the mainland, and a tour in 1995 was cut short after she insisted on performing it live. Anita Mui, frequently referred to as the 'Madonna of Asia', was also active in movies, like most Hong Kong pop stars, for which she received critical acclaim (see her performance as the ghost in *Rouge* (1987) and most recently in *July Rhapsody* (2002) with Jackie Cheung). The pop music of Hong Kong is often considered inauthentic, overtly commercial and fake. Anita Mui forces us to give a more subtle reading that gives due credit to both the agency of the artists, given her constant reinvention of the self, as well as the political potential of pop. Unfortunately, she succumbed to cancer in 2004 at the age of forty.

Further reading

Witzleben, Larry (1999). 'Cantopop and Mandopop in Pre-Postcolonial Hong Kong: Identity Negotiations in the Performances of Anita Mui Yim-Fong'. *Popular Music* 18.2 (Fall): 241–57.

JEROEN DE KLOET

Museum of Modern Chinese Literature

The National Museum of Modern Chinese Literature is the largest state-level literature museum in China. Set up in 1985 at the initiative of noted writer Ba Jin and opened to the public in May 2000 in Beijing, the museum gives an in-depth account of the evolution of modern Chinese literature from the late Qing through the 1970s, with a focus on pre-1949 literature. In an area of 15,000 square metres, the museum holds about 300,000 manuscripts, translations, letters, diaries, photos, audio and videotapes, relics, books, magazines and newspaper clippings. In addition to an archive and a research library, the museum has three permanent displays. The first is a chronological presentation of the most significant events in China's literature since the late Qing, including single authors and their central works as well as various literary circles. The second highlights the accomplishment of several distinguished writers like Lu Xun (1881–1936), Lao She (1899–1966), and Bing Xin (1900–99), while the third represents literary collections and other items of interest that have been donated by famous Chinese writers over the past fifteen years. It also features reproduced studies and personal items of various writers. Although the museum's original mission to highlight the horrors of the **Cultural Revolution** has not been met, it still holds one of the largest and finest literature collections in the country and is a central place of research for those interested in pre-1949 Chinese literature.

See also: museums

BIRGIT LINDER

museums

As important cultural institutions, Chinese museums are managed by the State Bureau of Cultural Relics. Since the first museum appeared in China in 1868, there are currently more than 1,400 museums, most of which have been established since the 1980s. Museums (*bowuguan*) are officially defined as non-profit organizations that function to educate the public through the exhibition, collection, preservation and research of artifacts or specimens. There are three major types of museums: (1) social history museums, which include history, revolutionary history, ethnology, folklore, memorial and art museums; (2) natural science museums, which include natural history, and science and technology museums; and (3) general museums.

A history of Chinese museums can be traced back to 478 BC when Confucius's clothes, hats, musical instruments and carts were on display in his former residence. The first modern museum, however, was the Sikowei Museum in Shanghai, a natural history museum established by the Frenchman Pierre Heude in 1868. The first modern museum established by a private Chinese person was the Nantong Museum in Jiangsu, a natural history museum, by Zhang Qian in 1905. The incorporation of museums into the nation-building process taking place in Republican China began with the establishment of the first national museum, the National Historical Museum in Beijing, in 1912. Republican China witnessed the establishment of such important museums as the Palace Museum (established in Beijing in 1925 and moved to Taipei in 1948) and the Central Museum (1933). The total number and types of museums reached a peak in the 1930s: 129 museums were founded, including art, history and natural history museums. Because of the series of wars from 1937 to 1948, however, only thirteen of these museums had survived by 1949.

In the PRC, the Great Leap Forward (1957–9) witnessed a significant development of museums. The number of museums rose from seventy-two in 1957 to 480 in 1959. Three important museums were founded: the National Museum of Chinese History, focusing on the ancient Chinese civilization; the National Museum of Chinese Revolution, focusing on the history of the Chinese Communist Party; and the Military Museum of the Chinese Revolution, devoted to the history of revolutionary wars and that of the People's Liberation Army. As a result of the numerous archaeological discoveries in recent decades, the National Museum of Chinese History has received the best, most important and most representative artifacts from all over the country. It also provides a general framework for displaying ancient history. Since the 1980s, the development of museums has been rapid. The total number of museums has reached 1,400. Almost every city has at least one museum. The Chinese Society of Museums was established in 1982 to coordinate professional activities. In addition, relevant laws are formulated, including Procedures for the Provincial Museums (1979), the Cultural Relics Preservation Act (1982), and Procedures for the Collections Management in Museums (1986).

See also: monuments and public sculpture; restoration districts (urban)

Further reading

Mitter, Rana (2000). 'Behind the Scenes at the Museum: Nationalism, History, and Memory in the Beijing War of Resistance Museum'. *China Quarterly* 161 (March): 279–93.

Ren, Hai (1998). 'Economies of Culture: Theme Parks, Museums, and Capital Accumulation in China, Hong Kong, and Taiwam'. PhD diss., University of Washington.

REN HAI

music conservatories

There are nine major conservatories in China: the Central Conservatory of Music in Beijing, the Chinese Conservatory of Music in Beijing, the Shanghai Conservatory of Music, the Shenyang Conservatory of Music, the Sichuan Conservatory of Music in Chengdu, the Tianjin Conservatory of Music, the Wuhan Conservatory of Music, the Xi'an Conservatory of Music, and the Xinghai Conservatory of Music in Guangzhou. The majority were founded in the 1950s, and were closely modelled after the conservatories in the Soviet Union. Since 1980 there has been more Western influence because of the large number of Western musicians visiting China and the many Chinese students studying in the West who have returned to teach.

Unlike many music departments in the universities, which are generally small in size and lack both faculty and funds, conservatories are the principal institutions responsible for training professional musicians and music scholars. Their curricula consist of Western music courses balanced with a significant proportion of Chinese music courses. Most conservatories offer bachelor's and master's degrees in composition, musicology, conducting, Chinese instrument performance, orchestral instrument performance, piano, voice, and music education. Some conservatories, such as the Central and the Shanghai Conservatories, also offer doctoral degrees. All conservatories have preparatory music schools affiliated with them. While the Central Conservatory, the only one to receive government funds, and the Shanghai Conservatory recruit students nationwide, other conservatories attract mostly local students. Since 1990 the enrolment of students from Hong Kong,

Taiwan and foreign countries has been growing steadily.

See also: musicology

JIN PING

music in Taiwan

Taiwan's musical scene is a lively mix of traditional, popular, classical and hybrid genres. Over the course of a day, traditional drums and *suona*, Western classical and a variety of popular musics are all likely to stream into one's sonic environment. During any given week in Taipei, performance venues such as the National Concert Hall, Novel Hall, Sun Yatsen Memorial Hall and the Red House Theatre, to name a few, stage a wide range of performances. Complementing this scene are numerous pubs scattered throughout the city where one may hear aboriginal singers, Taiwanese folk singers, Hakka rock, jazz and many other pop music varieties performed by local, expatriate and touring artists. A host of other musical activities occur beyond the domain of these publicly advertised events and outside the capital city. In addition, music plays an important role in religious life from the daily chanting of Buddhist and Taoist clergy to the performance of Taiwanese opera, hand-puppet theatre and instrumental genres at temple festivals and other ritual events. The richness of the music scene is partly explained by the diversity of the island's peoples coupled with Taiwan's rather complex settlement and colonial histories.

Aboriginal music

Taiwan's original inhabitants are not Han Chinese. Numerous culturally and linguistically distinct tribes of Malayo-Polynesian (Austronesian) peoples lived throughout the island prior to the migration, which began in earnest in the 1600s, of settlers from southeastern China. The aborigines remained the dominant population until the nineteenth century. Their ultimate origination point is much debated. One theory conjectures southeast Asia while another asserts mainland China. Based on linguistic evidence, yet another theory posits that Taiwan itself was the origination point of all Austronesian-speaking peoples, who now inhabit a huge area spanning from Madagascar through Indonesia to New Zealand (Aotearoa), Hawai'i and to Easter Island (Rapanui). Taiwan's government currently recognizes ten mountain tribes whose home villages are located mainly in the interior mountains and along the eastern coast. These tribes are the Amis, Atayal, Bunun, Paiwan, Puyuma, Rukai, Saisiyat, Shao, Tsou and Yami (also called Tao). Currently, all tribes combined comprise less than 2 per cent of Taiwan's population.

The traditional cultures of most tribes are endangered. Commercially released collections of field recordings made during the 1990s confirm that traditional songs and instrumental music are now largely the province of the senior generation. Lyric content ranges from the narration of daily activities such as hunting, fishing and farming to songs used for important rites and rituals, including weddings, funerals, music for exorcism and prayers for a good harvest. Vital knowledge such as legends, origin tales and concepts of nature are contained in various forms of musical expression. In the past, tribal members grew up surrounded by musical expression, and most were practised singers by the time they reached adulthood. The living patterns that closely integrated life and song have been significantly disrupted. Years of outward migration to urban centres combined with an educational system – which until very recently aimed at assimilation in **Han** Chinese culture – has taken a heavy toll on the transmission of traditional knowledge, including native languages and musical repertoires.

Presently, annual festivals draw tribal members who live in areas beyond their village, home for several days of singing, dancing and general celebration. It is in this context that young people learn to perform the communal singing and dancing that are an integral part of these gatherings. Typically, participants sing, hold hands and move in long lines, which often form concentric circles, as they dance to simple repeated patterns. Jingling ankle bracelets and small bells, which they attach to their colourful costumes, add rhythmic accompaniment to the unison or multi-part singing. Many of these events are now open to outsiders. One of the best known is the Amis harvest festival, which is held in July or August each year in Hualian and Taidong counties along the east coast.

Aboriginal music gained both domestic and international attention in the mid 1990s when the voices of Amis singers Difang Duarna (Kuo Ying-nan) and his wife Ignay (Kuo Shin-chu) were used as the basis for the mega hit 'Return to Innocence', which was originally released in 1993 by the European musician Michael Cretu. How Cretu, who works under the name 'Enigma', came to possess the recording of the Kuos' singing is a long and sordid tale; suffice to say that Cretu used the Kuos' voices without their knowledge or consent. Though more than half of 'Return to Innocence' featured the Kuos, Enigma failed to credit their contribution. When the song was used as a theme song for the 1996 Atlanta Olympic games, people in Taiwan were both belatedly awakened to the unique beauty of aboriginal song and angered by the unfair use of the Kuos' intellectual property. With the financial backing of the Taiwan-based Magic Stone Company, the Kuos sued Cretu, EMI/Capitol and the International Olympic Committee, among others, in the United States. The case was settled out of court in June 1999.

Kuo Ying-nan passed away at the age of eighty-two on 28 March 2002 and his wife died just twenty-one days later at the age of seventy-nine. In the six years between the use of their music for the Olympics and their deaths, the Kuos were frequently invited to perform in Taipei and throughout the island. They were especially favoured guests of politicians who wished to identify themselves with aboriginal Taiwan. Magic Stone produced two CDs featuring Difang and a small group of elderly Amis singers. The music of both CDs combines the original Amis tracks, which were recorded a cappella (as is the Amis tradition), with 'new-age style' music. The new age music for the *Circle of Life* (1998) was created in Belgium, while various composers from Malaysia, Hong Kong, mainland China, Japan and Taiwan contributed music for the *Across the Yellow Earth* (1999).

The attention paid to the Kuos in the wake of the 'Enigma affair', coupled with a renewed interest in aboriginal culture, paved the way for numerous aboriginal singers to launch recording careers beginning in the mid 1990s. The most commercially successful of these has been A-mei (Zhang Huimei), who is the daughter of a Puyuma tribal chief. A-mei has released more than fifteen recordings and is famous in Taiwan, mainland China, and throughout the Mandarin-listening world. Her vocal style is somewhat 'sultry', and the overall sound of her music is similar to mainstream American pop and includes elements of rock, blues and hip-hop. She sings predominately in Mandarin, but has also recorded in English and Japanese. A-mei occasionally draws on her Puyuma musical heritage as in her first hit single 'Jiemei' [Sisters], which was released in 1996 on a CD of the same name. In this song, she and her mother converse in Puyuma and her mother sings a traditional tune. The aboriginal group Power Station (Dongli huoche) broke into Taiwan's pop music mainstream about a year after A-mei and also enjoys considerable popularity in China. Power Station is frontlined by two young men from the Paiwan tribe. Their music only occasionally includes uniquely aboriginal elements.

The music of both Samingad (Ji Xiaojun) and Pur-dur (Chen Jiannian) retains close ties to their Puyuma heritage. Samingad won the 'Best New Artist' award for her first CD, *Voices of the Sun, Wind and the Grassland* (1999), at the 2000 Golden Melody Competition (Taiwan's equivalent of the Grammies). Pur-dur, who happens to be Samingad's uncle, won in both the 'Best Male Vocalist' and 'Best Song Writer' categories for his first album *Ho-hi-yan Ocean* (1999). Samingad sings in both Puyuma and Mandarin, and frequently utilizes traditional Puyuma melodies. Pur-dur sings to simple guitar accompaniment primarily in Mandarin, though he sometimes includes Puyuma text and melodies. Biung's (Wang Hongen) exclusive singing in his native Bunun won him the Golden Melody Award in the 'Best Non-Mandarin Singer' category in 2002. Other aboriginal singers from various tribes have released CDs, including: Jiang Jinxing (Kuo Ying-nan's son); Panai; Beiyuan Shanmao (North Aboriginal Mountain Cats); A-mei mei (a female duo which includes A-mei's sister, Saya, and their cousin, Raya); and Feiyu Yunbao (Flying Fish, Cloud Leopard). An aboriginal singer of particular note is Hu Defu (Kimbo), who first achieved island-wide recognition in the 1970s during the campus folksong movement for his rendition of the song, 'Beautiful Formosa'

(*Meilidao*). Hu still occasionally performs at pubs in Taipei, though he makes his home with his Puyuma family in Taidong county.

Han Chinese traditional musics: Holo

The Holo, also referred to as Hokkien or 'Taiwanese' in English, are those people whose ancestors came to Taiwan from southern Fujian province before 1945 and whose native language is derived from the southern Fujian dialect. Holo comprise about 75 per cent of Taiwan's population. There are numerous varieties of traditional Holo music actively practiced in Taiwan. Folksongs have been passed down from generation to generation, mainly by amateur musicians. Though originally sung to accompany work or to entertain oneself or a small group, some folksongs were used as subtle protest songs by opposition supporters during the years of the KMT-imposed martial law (1947–87). They continue to be heard during election campaigns, and some have been recorded by famous singers of Taiwanese popular songs. In some cases, the songs have no specific political association and may serve simply to invoke a nostalgic mood. Though folksongs traditionally existed in many variant forms, over the last several decades, particularly following the publication of Lü Chüan-sheng's influential choral arrangements, the melodic forms of many songs have become more or less standardized.

Native scholars classify most Holo music into either the southern style, called *nanguan* (southern pipe), or the northern style, called *beiguan* (northern pipe). These two styles comprise a wide variety of genres including instrumental music, solo singing with accompaniment, and operatic forms. One genre that has received a great deal of scholarly attention is the sizhu (**Silk and Bamboo**; and see **Jiangnan sizhu**) ensemble referred to as *nanguan*, a slow-moving, delicate music whose ensemble is comprised of bowed and plucked string instruments, an end-blown flute and wooden clappers, and often includes a solo singer (see **Minnan nanyin**). Believed to have first arrived in Taiwan in the 1600s, *nanguan* was traditionally the province of the educated elite due partly to its refined sound and use of notation. *Nanguan* musicians form clubs that meet either in community centres, in the homes of club members or in temples. Besides playing at club meetings, these groups may perform during biannual rites that commemorate patron gods and deceased club members, as part of temple festivals or for public concerts. Only about a dozen nanguan ensembles currently remain active in Taiwan, and a number of these have had in recent times to rely on government patronage.

The most commonly encountered form of *beiguan* music is a raucous ensemble comprised of the several *suona* (double-reed instrument with a wooden body and flared metal bell) and gongs and drums (see **luogu**) whose players ride on trucks during funeral processions. This form of ensemble also plays an important role in temple festivals and other celebratory events and may be regularly heard throughout the island. *Beiguan* music provides the basis for a number of other genres, including the popular hand-puppet theatre (*budaixi*) and a dying opera form called *luantan*.

Han Chinese traditional music: Hakka

Hakka people migrated to Taiwan mostly from Guangdong province beginning in the mid 1600s. Hailing from different areas of Guangdong province and migrating at different times, Taiwan's Hakka belong to two culturally distinct groups, the northern and the southern. The earliest arrivals settled in Taiwan's southern counties of Kaohsiung and Pingdong and tended to maintain fairly closed communities. The later arrivals initially settled in the central and northern counties of Miaoli, Xinzhu and Taoyuan and were generally more open to cultural exchanges with other groups than their southern counterparts. All Hakka combined currently comprise about 11 per cent of Taiwan's population.

The most representative examples of traditional Hakka music are mountain songs (*shange*) and *bayin* ensemble music. Realizing that fewer and fewer young people were learning to sing Hakka songs, a number of efforts to ensure their survival were made starting in the 1960s: a Hakka Song Research Association was established in 1962 and several magazines dedicated to printing song notation and essays about the songs were founded around the same time. The 1960s and 1970s saw the release of numerous recordings of Hakka mountain songs

sung by accomplished folk singers and by winners of newly established Hakka song competitions.

The *bayin* (eight sounds) ensemble takes its name from the ancient Chinese system that classifies instruments according to eight essential elements: metal, stone, silk, bamboo, skin, earth, gourd and wood. Though the ensemble includes several types of string instruments, the predominance of percussion and *suona* places *bayin* in the loud *chuida* (blowing and beating) category of traditional Chinese ensembles. In Taiwan, Hakka *bayin* groups are either professional or amateur and are hired to play for auspicious events such as weddings, birthdays and temple festivals, and recently, for funerals as well. Most ensembles have between four and eight players, but as many as ten additional *suona* players may be added for special occasions.

Mountain songs have inspired the creations of the Hakka rock group, the Labour Exchange Band (Jiaogong Yuedui), which artfully combines traditional and traditionally inspired tunes with Western harmonies and rhythmic patterns. The band's instrumentation includes *suona*, **erhu** (two-stringed bowed lute), *yueqin* (plucked short-necked lute), guitar and both traditional and Western percussion. The band is politically active and is particularly well known for its opposition to the Meinung Dam construction project. The band's first CD, *Let Us Sing Mountain Songs* (1999), earned awards for the 'Best Production of a Non-mainstream Album' and the 'Best Songwriter for a Non-mainstream Group' at the Golden Melody Award competition in 2000. In the 2002 competition, their second album, *The Night March of the Chrysanthemums* (2001), won in the 'Best Band' category. The group has toured abroad, including appearances in 2001 at the Brugge Festival and the Gent Folk Festival in Belgium and the Respect World and Ethnic Music Festival in Prague.

Han Chinese traditional musics: other

Emigrés arriving in the late 1940s brought a variety of musics from all over China to Taiwan. A number of Chinese opera forms, solo instrumental traditions and narrative song genres were among the arts that the mainlander refugees hoped to keep alive in exile. The **modern Chinese orchestra**, which employs instruments derived from China's own instrumentarium and is modelled after the Western symphony orchestra, has been one of the most successful of the post 1949 arrivals. This genre, termed *guoyue* (national music), typically uses Chinese folk tunes or newly written 'oriental-sounding' melodies with Western-influenced harmony and orchestrational style. There are currently four professional *guoyue* orchestras active in Taiwan: the Taipei Municipal Chinese Classical Orchestra, the National Chinese Orchestra, the Kaohsiung Chinese Orchestra and the Chinese Orchestra of the Broadcasting Corporation of China. Legalization of cross-Straits travel in the late 1980s, and the ensuing cultural exchanges, has brought renewed life to some traditions, though others, such as **Jingju** (Peking opera), are sadly fading away.

Popular music

The commission of a Taiwanese theme song, 'Weeping Peach Blossoms', for the local showing of a Shanghai film in 1932 is typically cited as the germinal event in Taiwan's popular music history. The sorrowful movie and song told the story of star-crossed lovers from different social classes. Melancholy love songs have dominated Taiwan's popular music scene ever since. Neither the Japanese colonial regime nor Chiang Kai-shek's authoritarian Nationalist Party tolerated songs with overt social or political criticism. Songs of love provided a relatively safe expressive outlet. Taiwanese frequently point to the primacy of sad songs as the product of a people that have been long governed by outsiders.

Numerous local recording companies were established in the mid 1930s. Local composers (such as Deng Yuxian and Wang Yunfeng) and lyricists (such as Zhou Tianwang, Zhan Tianma and Li Linqiu) created numerous songs that are still sung today. Following the outbreak of war with China in 1937, the Japanese initiated a policy that restricted the use of the Chinese language, including local dialects, and until Japan's defeat in 1945, artistic creation was preferably conducted in Japanese. The inaugural period of Taiwanese pop music came to an abrupt end. The withdrawal of Japan did not, unfortunately, bring an improvement in creative conditions. The devastated post-war economy combined with Nationalist-imposed restrictions on

and disparagement of local culture forced many talented artists to abandon creative endeavour. The need for Taiwanese-language songs was partly filled by translations of Japanese songs that could be produced far more cheaply than original works.

When the mainlander refugees arrived in the late 1940s, the sounds of Mandarin popular music quickly filled Taiwan's airwaves. Shanghai and Hong Kong-style Mandarin pop dominated the scene through the 1960s. Televised variety shows became a key venue for the promotion of locally produced Mandarin songs. The first generation of local Mandarin singers included Bao Nana, Xie Lei and Qing Shan. The music of the enormously popular Teresa Teng (**Deng Lijun**) dominated the Mandarin song market in the 1970s and 1980s and spread, albeit surreptitiously, to the Chinese mainland. With the US military presence during the Vietnam War, American soldiers and pop music also filled island nightspots, and during the 1960s American pop music was favoured by upwardly mobile young people. The elder generation and the less well educated, however, continued to favour locally produced music.

The Campus Folksong Movement emerged following a series of diplomatic setbacks for the ROC in the late 1970s and represented a new direction for the island's pop music. With anti-Western sentiment running high, university students shunned American pop. Inspired by the phrase 'sing our own songs', they composed songs in Mandarin that they sang to simple guitar accompaniment. Following in this spirit, medical student turned songwriter and singer **Luo Dayou** became a pioneer in musically criticizing social realities in the early 1980s. His early songs, such as 'Small Town Lugang' and 'Super Citizen', departed significantly from the melancholy and apolitical songs of previous decades.

The work of creative artists quickly began to flow following the lifting of martial law in July 1987. Released in 1989 by a consortium working under the name **Blacklist Studio** (or Workshop), *Songs of Madness* was perhaps the most significant work of this new era. Combining rock, hip-hop and lyric elements with uniquely local sounds, this CD brought new life to Taiwanese-language music. Song content ranged from vivid depictions of everyday life in Taiwan to sharp criticism of the

Nationalist regime as in the song, 'Democracy Bumpkin'. One of the group's key artists, Chen Mingzhang, went on to create a body of his own works and remains one of the island's most important and visionary musicians.

The 1990s witnessed a musical renaissance as artists drew their creative materials from Taiwan's own cultural heritage, particularly from the traditions practised by uneducated folk musicians. The rise to fame of Lin Qiang (Lim Giong), Wu Bai and China Blue, Bobby Chen (Chen Sheng), and Zhu Yuexin (Joy Topper), among other artists who often sing in Taiwanese, gave birth to 'New Taiwanese Music'. Zhu, in particular, excelled at ridiculing the continuing lack of clarity surrounding Taiwan's political and cultural identity in his pastiche-like compositions. Also significant is the 'Queen of Taiwanese Music', Jiang Hui (Jody), who brought new life to 'wine songs' and other kinds of melancholy Taiwanese songs. She continues to produce top-selling CDs. The last several years, however, have witnessed a sharp decline in the production of inspired pop music. Rampant piracy, aided by the proliferation of MP3 technology and a general economic downturn, has resulted in many companies being unwilling to back any but the most formulaically mainstream singers. In addition, opposition to Nationalist rule, which inspired the creation of many ingenious works, dissipated following the election of President Chen Shui-bian in early 2000. Youthful love songs reign once again, although labels such as Taiwan Colours Music, Crystal Records and a few other indies, continue to support the production of alternative and unique music.

Western classical idiom

Though traditional music holds an important place in contemporary society, Western classical music enjoys a higher status; and many more people are trained in Western than in Chinese music. The study of Western music began in earnest during the Japanese colonial period, when the most promising young musicians travelled to Japan for advanced training. Since the end of WWII, the USA and Western Europe have been the preferred sites for overseas study. However, many students receive their training in Taiwan's own universities and institutes.

The most important state-subsidized symphony orchestras include the National Symphony Orchestra, the Taipei Symphony Orchestra and the semi-professional, Kaohsiung City Symphony Orchestra. There are also privately operated professional orchestras, including the Taipei Sinfonietta and Philharmonic Orchestra (founded in 1985) and the Evergreen Symphony Orchestra, established in 2002 with the stated goal of cultivating Formosan musicians and promoting Formosan music which is rarely appreciated beyond the island.

Taiwan has produced a number of art music composers whose works tend to be a confluence of Western and local musical elements. Hsu Tsang-hui (1929–2001) was an important pioneer who was active as both a composer and music scholar. He earned his advanced degree in France, founded the Music Creative Group, which aimed to stimulate local music composition in the 1960s, and was one of the founders of the Asian Composers' League in 1973. Hsu conducted extensive research on Taiwan's traditional music and was a key in the development of ethnomusicology in Taiwan. Other composers known regionally and internationally include: Lü Chüan-sheng (b. 1916); Hsiao Tyzen (b. 1938) who identifies himself as a Taiwanese-American; Ma Shui-long (b. 1939); Li Tai-hsiang (b. 1941), who is of Amis heritage; Pan Huang-lung (b. 1945); and Chin Hsi-wen (b. 1957).

Further reading

Guy, Nancy (2001). 'How Does "Made in Taiwan" Sound?: Popular Music and Strategizing the Sounds of a Multicultural Nation'. *Perfect Beat* 5.3: 1–17.

—— (2002). 'Trafficking in Taiwan Aboriginal Voices'. In Sjoerd R. Jaarsma (ed.), *Handle with Care: Ownership and Control of Ethnographic Materials.* Pittsburgh: University of Pittsburgh Press, 195–210.

Hsu, Tsang-houei, Lu, Chuikuan, and Zeng, Rongxing (2002). *Taiwan chuantong yinyuezhi mei* [The Beauty of Taiwan's Traditional Music]. Taipei: Morning Star Publishing.

Li, Ping-hui (1991). 'The Dynamics of a Musical Tradition: Contextual Adaptations in the Music of Taiwanese Beiguan Wind and Percussion Ensemble'. PhD diss., University of Pittsburgh.

Loh, I-to (1982). 'Tribal Music of Taiwan: With Special Reference to the Ami and Puyuma Styles'. PhD diss., University of California, Los Angeles.

Yun, Eugenia (1994). 'A Place on the Pop Map'. *Free China Review* 44.6: 4–19.

Wang, Ying-fen (2002). 'Ensembles: *Nanguan*'. *Garland Encyclopedia of World Music, East Asia*. New York: Routledge, 205–9.

Yeh, Yueh-yu (1995). 'A National Score: Popular Music and Taiwanese Cinema'. PhD diss., University of Southern California.

NANCY GUY

musicology

The terms 'musicology' and 'ethnomusicology' in Chinese usage are not as separated as in the West. Because most Chinese music researchers, as far as this article's scope is concerned, study their own music, they are musicologists from their point of view (as insiders), but ethnomusicologists in the eyes of their Western colleagues (as outsiders). In the following, the term 'musicology' is preferred.

After repeated defeats by foreign powers in the late nineteenth century, there were attempts to modernize the country by introducing Western technology and ideas, including the methodologies of modern music research. Wang Quangqi (1892–1936), a student of the Berlin School under Curt Sachs and Erich von Hornbostel in the 1920s, was the first to apply its musicological methods to the study of Chinese music. His ultimate goal in studying music, as in so many other areas, was to create a new national music comparable to the West. Similarly, the sporadic collection of folksongs and teaching of folk music were all for the purpose of improving traditional music and creating new music, not for musical analysis or research. During the Sino-Japanese War and the civil wars of the 1930s and 1940s, both Nationalists and Communists emphasized collecting folk music for patriotic purposes, inspiring **mass movements** by way of folk or folk-like music. Nevertheless, several prominent modern musicologists emerged in the 1940s, including Yang Yinliu (1899–1984).

It was not until the 1950s that institutionalized music research began with the establishment of the National Music Research Division at the Central Conservatory of Music (founded in 1950). After several changes of name and a period of closure during the **Cultural Revolution**, it was reopened in 1973 as the Music Research Institute of the Chinese Academy of the Arts. Yang Yinliu subsequently became the director of the Institute. To this date, it remains the leading music research institute in China. Other prominent directors/musicologists were Huang Xiangpeng (1927–97) and Qiao Jianzhong (b. 1941). Since the 1950s, in fact, all major conservatories have established music research institutes and offer musicology degrees. With very few exceptions, all of the research is concerned with Chinese music, which includes music of the Han majority and that of the fifty-five ethnic minorities. A major event in the history of modern Chinese musicology was the 'First National Symposium of Ethnomusicology', held in Nanjing in 1980. It was the first time the term 'ethnomusicology' was 'officially' employed by scholars, though some questioned its use. It also marked the beginning of the influx of post-war musicological ideas and research from the West. By now, however, musicology/ethnomusicology has become a firmly established discipline with many promising scholars and a purpose that is purely academic and scholarly.

In addition to the above-mentioned Yang Yinliu, whose major contribution is to ancient music history and music theory, other musicologists of the 1940s and 1950s include Shen Zhibai (ancient history), Yin Falu (ancient history) and Li Chunyi (music archaeology). Since the 1970s, a large number of musicologists have emerged: Huang Xiangpeng (music archaeology, theory), Yang Kuanmin (folksong), Qiao Jianzhong and Miao Jin (geography of music), Du Yaxiong (minority music and methodology), Mao Jizhen and Tian Liantao (minority music), Shen Qia (methodology), Wu Zhao (**qin**, music archaeology), Gao Houyong, Yuan Jinfang and Wang Yaohua (music genres), Ye Dong, Chen Yinshi and He Changlin (cultural studies), Wang Yuhe and Liang Maochun (modern history), among many others.

The journals published by research institutes now belong to the highest level of music scholarship. These include: *Musicology in China* (Music Research Institute of the Chinese Academy of the Arts, Beijing), *Music Study* (Beijing), *Journal of the Central Conservatory of Music* (Beijing), *Chinese Music* (China Conservatory, Beijing), *The Art of Music* (Shanghai Conservatory), *Huang Zhong* (Wuhan Conservatory), *Jiao Xiang* (Xi'an Conservatory), *Explorations in Music* (Sichuan Conservatory), *Journal of Xinghai Conservatory* (Guangzhou). A journal published in Los Angeles, *Journal of Music in China* (Music in China, Inc.), specializes in translating into English major research articles from the above journals.

Further reading

Shen, Qia (1999). 'Ethnomusicology in China'. *Journal of Music in China* 1 (October): 7–36.

Tang, Yating (2000). 'Influences of Western Ethnomusicology on China: A Historical Re-evaluation'. *Journal of Music in China* 2.1 (April): 53–72.

Wong, Isabel K. F. (1991). 'From Reaction to Synthesis: Chinese Musicology in the Twentieth Century'. In Bruno Nettl and Philip V. Bohlman (eds), *Comparative Musicology and Anthropology of Music: Essays on the History of Ethnomusicology*. Chicago: University of Chicago Press: 37–55.

HAN KUO-HUANG

N

Nanfang Weekend

[Nanfang zhoumo]

Newspaper

The *Nanfang Weekend* is the weekend edition of the *Nanfang Daily* newspaper published by the Nanfang Daily News Group based in Guangzhou. The *Nanfang Daily* is the Party organ newspaper of the Guangdong Province Party Propaganda Committee and therefore has little leeway to avoid political propaganda reporting relating to politicians' speeches, Party meetings and so on. The *Nanfang Weekend*, however, emerged as a force in the media in the early 1990s, offering a solution to the problem facing all newspaper editors as to how to fulfil their political obligations to the Party on the one hand while producing lively, interesting copy on the other. An effectual division of labour between the daily and the weekend edition was the way out of this double bind. The *Nanfang Weekend* was thereby able to focus on often sensationalist human interest stories dealing with crime, corruption scandals, revelations about past leaders such as Mao Zedong, and the negative social consequences of the reform period, such as unemployment, worker exploitation and so on. The paper was an immediate success in Guangdong and soon grew to a national circulation of several million, making it one of the most popular and widely read newspapers in China in the 1990s. It was soon copied nationally by other newspapers, as the number of weekend editions rose from fewer than twenty in 1990 to more than 400 in 1994.

See also: evening newspapers and weekend editions; journalism; newspapers; state control of media; Yangcheng Evening News

Further reading

Zhao, Y. (1998). *Media, Market, and Democracy in China: Between the Party Line and the Bottom Line.* Chicago: University of Illinois.

KEVIN LATHAM

Nanjing University

Established in 1902, Nanjing University is one of the major institutions of higher learning in China and is known for its academic excellence. The University's 36 departments and 55 undergraduate programmes, 106 master's programmes, 55 doctoral programmes and 43 post-doctoral programmes are organized into ten schools in such areas as humanities, law, international business, foreign languages and international studies, natural sciences, chemistry and chemical engineering, technology, geosciences, life sciences, and medicine. At present the University has an enrolment of over 13,000 national and international students. The faculty members include scientists of national and international renown. Over a hundred of those who have studied or taught at the University have been members of the Chinese Academy of Sciences. The University's library houses more than 4 million volumes. With over 110 research institutes and interdisciplinary research centres – including a Centre for Chinese and

American Studies, co-founded with the Johns Hopkins University, and a Sino-German Economic Law Institute, co-founded with Göttingen University – Nanjing University leads China's universities in the number of entries in such authoritative research literature indexes as SCI, ISR and ISTP. In recent years the University has received over 2,000 students and visiting scholars from more than fifty countries and regions and has hosted sixty international academic conferences.

The University's School of Foreign Studies is where translation is taught and studied. Its English, French, Russian, German, Spanish and Japanese programmes offer translation tracks in their BA and MA degree choices. The English and French programmes also offer PhD degrees in translation. The School has a translation studies centre and a centre for corpus-based bilingual lexicography. In the past decade, its faculty has been commissioned to undertake over thirty research projects, including several major ones in translation studies.

KE PING

National Studies

(Guoxue)

Academic discipline

The term 'National Studies' was revived in the early 1990s. Charged with a new meaning, it was initially circulated among young academics in Beijing, closely tied to the **Research Institute for National Studies** (Guoxue yanjiusuo), a non-official organization initiated by **Liu Dong**, Yan Buke, Liang Zhiping and **Chen Pingyuan**. These younger academics in various fields of Chinese humanities advocated 'National Studies' in order to raise a voice for cultural values, and specifically for the tradition of Chinese scholarship and evidential historicism; such a voice was motivated, in part, as a response to the rapidly changing society and culture under the impetus of globalization, and was imbued with anxiety for intellectual and national identity.

The Institute was joined by many scholars, such as **Wang Hui**, Li Ling, Chen Lai, Ge Zhaoguang and Wang Shouchang. They met regularly and held a series of forums; in discussing scholarly

issues they strictly abided by rules that favour solid and independent research, professional discipline and free discussion. 'National Studies' became known as a public space where a new mode of scholarship arose, with the characteristics of autonomous operation, open-mindedness and scholarly professionalism. From the mid 1990s regular meetings were rarely held, although the Institute still existed under the direction of Liu Dong. Recently, its activities have been incorporated into the China Scholarship Forum sponsored by Beijing Library.

CHEN JIANHUA

national style

(minzuxing)

'New Music'

The history of Chinese **New Music**, which began in the first decades of the twentieth century, has been dominated by the constant worry over 'national style'. It is not easy for a Chinese composer to simply opt for 'being himself' and write in an individual style, as Messiaen once suggested to his last student, the Chinese **Chen Qigang**. Foreign music critics, as well as critics within China, will often judge Chinese compositions deficient if they do not contain 'national flavour' (*minzu fengge*). A foreigner, Alexander Tcherepnin, with his 1934 competition for 'Piano Pieces in Chinese Style', was perhaps the first to explicitly ask Chinese composers to write their music in a 'national style', but, to the present day, the question of what constitutes this particular style and how it should be perpetuated determines discussions of Chinese New Music both within China and abroad.

There are many options for writing music with 'Chinese flavour'. In Hong Kong as well as in the PRC and Taiwan, the style of **pentatonic romanticism** is dominant. It has been used by Chinese composers since the early days of New Chinese Music in the 1910s and 1920s and is still being used in the post-war period (e.g. Chen Gang's and He Zhanhao's *Butterfly Violin Concerto* 1959). This style makes use of Chinese raw material, such as the pentatonic melodies from folksongs (see **folksongs (Han Chinese)**) or **Xiqu** (opera), and stylizes them by transferring them onto Western instruments and by pressing them into a Western system of notation. Chinese folksong and operatic singing, however, are characterized by a changing, irregular metre. They also make use of notation for elaborate ornamentation and tonal inflection which is difficult to adapt to the Western five-staff system. These idiosyncrasies are therefore lost in stylized composition.

In a more radical mode, composers attempt to capture precisely these just-mentioned elements of Chinese melody. This alternative approach to 'national style' occurs frequently in pieces composed since the early 1980s, but it was also once in vogue in the 1940s, when Sang Tong wrote the piano piece 'In that Place, Far Far Away' (*Zai na yaoyuan de difang*), which he later renounced. It is polytonal and constantly changes the metre, just as Sang attempted to capture the rhythmic as well as the tonal idiosyncrasies of Chinese folksong. Chinese composers today have become even more radical in their translation of these idiosyncrasies into sound, allowing for microtonal inflections and aleatory rhythms.

Apart from Chinese melody, Chinese instrumental techniques, too, have been used frequently by Chinese composers to mark their 'Chineseness'. Again, the stylizing approach simply transfers Chinese instrumental technique onto a Western instrument, while the more radical approach, found particularly among composers of the 'New Wave' of the late 1970s and 1980s (see **Third Generation (composers)**), changes the Western instrument into one that is essentially Chinese (e.g. **Qu Xiaosong**'s *Mong Dong*, for bass and chamber ensemble, 1984).

Yet another approach to 'Chineseness' is to draw from Chinese myths and literature (e.g. **Chen Yi**'s *Chinese Myths Cantata*, 1996). In terms of musical language, compositions which fall into this category appear in a great variety of styles, ranging from eighteenth-century classicism to the electronic sounds of the avant-garde. Another commonly used method is the translation of Chinese philosophical ideas into sound. Chinese composers, not just John Cage, take up on the ideas of the **Yijing** [Book of Changes] and design entire compositional systems on these (see **Zhao Xiaosheng**). The

emphasis on single sounds (derived from the aesthetics of **qin** playing) and on silence is derived from the teachings of Daoism, where the greatest sound is said to be 'rare, unhearable', the best instrument being a *guqin* without strings. This approach is epitomized in **Tan Dun**'s *Circle* (1992), where a bar of complete silence is marked with a crescendo and a decrescendo. Silence is perhaps one of the most powerful and frequently heard elements in much New Chinese Music today; perhaps it will substitute for 'pentatonic romanticism' as the dominant style of new Chinese music in the twenty-first century.

Further reading

Mittler, Barbara (1997). *Dangerous Tunes. The Politics of Chinese Music in Hong Kong, Taiwan and the People's Republic of China since 1949*. Wiesbaden: Harrassowitz, ch. 4.

—— (2004, in press). 'Zwischen Tradition und Moderne: Von den alten Wurzeln neuer chinesischer Musik'. *MusikTexte*.

Utz, Christian (2002). *Neue Musik und Interkulturalität. Von John Cage bis Tan Dun*. Stuttgart: Steiner.

BARBARA MITTLER

nationalism

Nationalism, which is in essence pride in the nation and resentment against those perceived as attacking or harming its interests, has exercised a crucial influence in Chinese politics since the beginning of the twentieth century. On the whole, Chinese Marxists have appealed not to nationalism but to 'patriotism' (*aiguozhuyi*). Marx stressed class, not nation, believing that the working classes of all nations should unite against exploiters. Yet most scholars have seen nationalism in many PRC policies and actions.

Since the early 1990s, nationalism has tended to replace Marxism. Fewer ordinary people, and even CCP members, believe in Marxist ideologies, but retain strong confidence in China. This nationalism is of two kinds: proactive and reactive. The first derives from pride in China's remarkable economic performance since the late 1970s, and on such major events as the resumption of Chinese sovereignty over Hong Kong (1997) and Macau (1999). Such developments have made Chinese leaders and people feel that their country is again taken seriously on the world stage. Reactive nationalism is based on perceived attempts by Western countries, especially the United States, and Japan to counter Chinese interests. Several specific events illustrate this rising nationalism, but the most important of them was the series of hostile demonstrations that followed the bombing of the Chinese Embassy in Belgrade in May 1999 during the intervention of the North Atlantic Treaty Organization powers in Serbia over Kosovo. Few PRC Chinese accepted NATO claims that the bombing was accidental.

In addition to specific incidents, trends in the 1990s sparked Chinese nationalism, including constant criticism, especially from the United States, over **human rights** and China's policy on Tibet and Taiwan. Human rights had taken centre-stage in American policy on China since troops suppressed independence demonstrations in Tibet from 1987 to 1989 and especially the student movement of April to June 1989. A Chinese diplomatic effort from November 1991 to defend China's record on human rights on the grounds that communal, not individual, rights mattered most, brought little success. In 1996, several books appeared with the theme that China could 'say no'. They justified a China that stood up for its position on human rights, Taiwan, Tibet and other issues. In one of them (Peng *et al.* 1996: 127–72), a typical chapter is entitled 'Taiwan: The Fifty-first American State?' – the rhetorical question indicating the nationalist tone. One specialist sees nationalism as both popular and official, the first being the stronger of the two. He considers that nationalism is 'due to external stimulation', not to China's rapid development (Zheng 1999: 159), the implication being that it is unlikely to lead to chauvinism.

See also: Olympics; Zhongguo keyi shuo bu

Further reading

Gries, Peter Hays (2004). *China's New Nationalism: Politics, Pride, and Diplomacy*. Berkeley: University of California Press.

Guo, Yingjie (2004). *Cultural Nationalism in Contemporary China: The Search for National Identity Under Reform*. London: Routledge.

Peng, Q., Yang, M. and Xu, D. (1996). *Zhongguo weishenma shuo bu* [Why Does China Say No?]. Beijing: New World Press.

Unger, J. (ed.) (1996). *Chinese Nationalism*. Armonk, NY: M. E. Sharpe.

Zheng, Y. (1999). *Discovering Chinese Nationalism in China: Modernization, Identity, and International Relations*. Cambridge: Cambridge University Press.

COLIN MACKERRAS

Native Soil Painting

(Xiangtu ziranzhuyi huihua)

Native Soil Painting is an artistic current that emerged in the early 1980s and focused on the depiction of the countryside and national ethnic minorities. It was initiated by young artists, who had been 'sent down' to the countryside during the **Cultural Revolution** and looked back on the rugged life of the period with a degree of nostalgia. Sharing a humanist tendency with **Scar art**, it sought to honour the real, ordinary heroes of daily life rather than the glorified characters of the Cultural Revolution. The 'red, bright and shining' (*hongguangliang*) pictorial conventions of the Cultural Revolution were to be replaced in these paintings by the 'small, bitter and old' (*xiaokujiu*) of the so-called backward regions. The current reached its highest level with the early works of **Luo Zhongli** and **Chen Danqing**, but later became more mannerist, losing its immediacy and spontaneity.

The portrayal of similar subject-matter was perpetuated by the *xiaxiang* (going down to the countryside) curriculae in art academies whereby students were sent off to sketch and experience down-to-earth life, an educational inheritance of the French *plein-air* tradition adopted to serve socialist artistic purposes. In such way artists had an opportunity to travel to distant areas, coming into contact with different lifestyles and the remnants of China's ancient culture. This prompted a root-seeking fever evident in the fascination with the Loess Plateau (Huangtu gaoyuan) culture in the works of **Ding Fang** and Shang Yang or in Shen Qin's imaginative reconstruction, *Master and Disciple Dialogue* (*Shitu duihua*, 1985). China's minorities also supplied a romantic, unfettered contrast to Chinese urban existence in the early works of Ai Xuan and **Zhang Xiaogang**, and were the subject of Zeng Xiaofeng's quasi-anthropological sketchbook diaries. The mystical appeal of Tibetan culture was apparent in the 'Tibet Five Men Exhibition' (*Xizang wuren huazhan*, Beijing, 1986).

See also: xiafang, xiaxiang

Further reading

Andrews, Julia F. (1994). *Painters and Politics in the People's Republic of China 1949–1979*. Berkeley: University of California Press, 377–405.

Galikowski, Maria (1998). *Art and Politics in China, 1949–1984*. Hong Kong: Chinese University Press, 199–207.

Li, Xianting (1993). 'Major Trends in the Development of Contemporary Chinese Art'. In Valerie C. Doran (ed.), *China's New Art, Post-1989, with a Retrospective from 1979 to 1989*. Hong Kong: Hanart T Z Gallery, x–xxvi.

Lü, Peng and Yi, Dan (1992). *Zhongguo xiandai yishu shi* [A History of Modern Art in China]. Changsha: Hunan meishu chubanshe, 27–57.

EDUARDO WELSH

Naxi, culture of

A small group (with a population of over 200,000) inhabiting the mountainous border between Sichuan and Yunnan provinces, the Naxi people have been strongly influenced both politically and culturally by their more powerful neighbours – the Han Chinese and Tibetans. Tibetan influence in the Naxi area can be traced back to the Tang dynasty, and Lamaism was brought to the Naxi area in the Ming dynasty. The influence of Han Chinese culture also reached a high point during the Ming dynasty, when the local powerful families began to promote Confucian learning. This led to the rise of generations of Naxi scholars who are expert in both Naxi and Chinese culture. A good

example is the twentieth-century Naxi scholar Fang Guoyu, who became a nationally renowned expert on Naxi history and culture, as well as history of Yunnan and China. In the modern period, Western influence also reached the Naxi area, and there appeared Christians among the Naxi people.

External cultural influence and native tradition have coexisted peacefully with each other in the Naxi area. One of the most unique native cultural elements is the polytheistic Dongba religion. The Dongba, which literally means shamans, have created and preserved about 20,000 scriptures written in Naxi hieroglyphs first created about a thousand years ago. Another native element of the Naxi culture is the matriarchy that still exists in some Naxi areas: descent is traced along the female line, children live with their mother, women are the centre of the family, control family property and enjoy high social status. Some of these women do not live with their husbands, while their *A-zhu*, or lovers, usually visit at night and return to their mother's home in the morning.

Further reading

Chao, Emily (1996). 'Hegemony, Agency, and Representing the Past: The Invention of Dongba Culture Among the Naxi of Southwest China'. In Melissa Brown (ed.), *Negotiating Ethnicities in China and Taiwan*. Berkeley: University of California, 208–239.

McKhann, Charles (1995). 'The Naxi and the Nationalities Question'. In Steven Harrell (ed.), *Cultural Encounters on China's Ethnic Frontiers*. Seattle: University of Washington Press, 39–62.

Mueggler, Erik (2001). *The Age of Wild Ghosts: Memory, Violence, and Place in Southwest China*. Berkeley: University of California Press.

Rees, Helen (2000). *Echoes of History: Naxi Music in Modern China*. Oxford University Press.

HAN XIAORONG

Neo-Conservatism

'Neo-Conservatism' is a major trend in the spectrum of political thought that emerged in China after 1989. It is a product of the political climate of the 1990s and also a reflection on and reaction to political and cultural radicalism that was prevalent in the 1980s. Some of its basic ideas can be found in the so-called **New Authoritarianism**. Neo-Conservatism takes radicalism as its foil and criticizes various radical propositions for ignoring China's reality and for trying to transform the country by totally rejecting the existing order and authorities. In this view, the democracy movement of 1989 becomes another example of romantic radicalism. Interestingly, the failure of the Reform Movement of 1898 is attributed to the radicalism of Kang Youwei rather than to the obstructionism of the Empress Dowager Cixi. Similarly, the 'New Authoritarian' Zhang Binjiu had argued in the 1980s that the necessity of separating economic from political reform explained if not quite justified Yuan Shikai's assassination of the democrat Song Jiaoren in 1915.

In 1990, Xiao Gongqin, who held the above-mentioned interpretation of 1898 and offered Yan Fu (1853–1921) as a model, became the first person to label this trend of thought 'Neo-Conservatism' and to elaborate its main arguments. Neo-Conservatism holds that modernization is a gradual process (incrementalism), and that, during this process, traditional values, the existing order and an authoritarian government are necessary to maintain social stability and ensure a successful social transformation. On the other hand, Neo-Conservatism distinguishes itself from traditional conservatism and fundamentalism by emphasizing that the legitimacy of the existing (political and ideological) authorities is secured only through supporting and promoting reform and modern transformation. As far as China's reform is concerned, Neo-Conservatism advocates the strengthening of government authority, especially the central authority, so as to direct the reform and speed up economic development, and also to ensure stability and fairness while combating rampant corruption and crime and the decentralization produced by the economic reforms of the 1980s. Neo-Conservatism is also characterized by a state-centred **nationalism** and a retreat from the cultural cosmopolitanism of the 1980s, two characteristics it shares with the advocates of postmodernism (see **postmodernism (houxiandai zhuyi) and 'post-ism' (houxue)**), **National**

Studies and **New Confucianism**. The leading proponents of the Neo-Conservative trend in political thought include Chen Yuan (b. 1945, son of Party elder Chen Yun), **He Xin**, Wang Huning, **Wang Xiaodong**, Yang Ping and Xiao Gongqin. However, it has been criticized by Liberal and **New Left** intellectuals as trying to defend authoritarianism and obstruct democratization.

Further reading

(1996). *Chinese Law and Government* 29 (March/April) [includes translations of several of the important statements of Neo-Conservatism]

Fewsmith, Joseph (2001). *China Since Tiananmen: The Politics of Transition.* Cambridge: Cambridge University Press, 75–100.

Li, Youzhou (1997). 'Will Neo-Conservatism Dominate Post-Deng China?' *China Strategic Review* 2.2: 31–40.

LIU CHANG

Neo-Maoism and Mao Fever

The Tiananmen crisis and collapse of the Soviet bloc prompted a leftist resurgence within the Chinese government in the early 1990s. The apparent vindication of Mao's concerns about capitalist restoration received extensive attention, and terms like 'class struggle' and 'dictatorship of the proletariat' resurfaced in speeches and editorials. Hardliners like Deng Liqun asserted that economic liberalization and Open Door policies were creating a new class of private entrepreneurs and cadre capitalists in Chinese society. Reaffirmation of reform by the Fourteenth Party Congress (1992) dealt a setback to leftists in the Party and government. However, widespread dissatisfaction with rising inequality, official corruption and declining social mores elicited a new nostalgia for the Mao era among a younger generation of intellectuals and the public. Mao's revolutionary vision and leadership were favourably reassessed by academics. In the popular imagination, Mao's incorruptible and non-nepotistic image posed a stark contrast to the self-serving bureaucrats of the reform era. 'Mao Fever' was manifested in a lucrative market for Mao memorabilia and the popularity of Maoist themes for restaurants and business establishments. The fad waned subsequently, but rising nationalist sentiment through the decade contributed to enhanced appreciation of Mao as a 'great patriot and national hero' who had liberated China from backwardness and imperialism.

See also: political icons (and art); Political Pop

Further reading

Barmé, Geremie R. (1996). *Shades of Mao: The Posthumous Cult of the Great Leader*. Armonk, NY: M. E. Sharpe.

Friedman, Edward (1994). 'Democracy and "Mao Fever"'. *Journal of Contemporary China* 6 (Summer): 84–95.

Hitchcock, Peter (2001). 'Mao to the Market'. In Zhang Xudong (ed.), *Whither China? Intellectual Politics in Contemporary China*. Durham: Duke University Press, 263–84.

Misra, Kalpana (2001). 'Curing the Sickness and Saving the Party: Neo-Maoism and Neo Conservatism in the 1990s'. In S. Hua (ed.), *Chinese Political Culture*. Armonk: M. E. Sharpe.

KALPANA MISRA

neologisms

Neologisms are newly coined words or old words used with new connotations. They arise as a response to new circumstances. Based on the statistics of the **State Working Commission on Language**, over 8,000 neologisms have been in use since 1978. Foreign words, in translation, transliteration or in a combination of both, are a big source of Chinese neologisms. The coolest neologism for young people is perhaps '*ku*' (cool) itself. The hottest neologism in politics in late 2002 was perhaps '**Sange daibiao**' (Three Represents). When the Chinese authorities want to whip up enthusiasm for a new policy or criticize an event, new neologisms suddenly spring up and old ones disappear. For example, since *geti jingji* (individual economy) was allowed in the late 1970s, *getihu*

(self-employed households or individuals) flourished. Linguistically, it is unnecessary to create new words, as the concept of small-scale private economy and being self-employed was not new; however, it was politically wise to use two neologisms as their older synonyms had been associated with derogatory things like 'a capitalist tail' and 'capitalist roaders'. Many *getihu* now became *dakuan* (cash gods) through *daomai* (speculative resale), and were called *daoye* (speculators), who often relied on officials to get rich. Soon officials themselves became *guandao(ye)* (official-speculators) by abusing power to obtain goods at the government-fixed price and then by re-selling them at the market price. A political slogan in the 1989 democracy movement was 'Down with *guandao*', but since the movement failed, *guandao* became entirely replaced by *jingji fanzui* (economic crimes) that anyone might commit, not primarily officials. During the era of *zhishi jingji* (knowledge economy), *fanfu changlian* (opposing corruption and promoting honesty) thus became urgent.

See also: goudui

Further reading

Micic, Peter (1999/2000). 'Pop 'n' Rock Loan Words and Neologisms in the PRC'. *Chime* 14/15: 103–23.

HELEN XIAOYAN WU

New Authoritarianism

(Xin quanweizhuyi)

The political ideas associated with the 'New Authoritarianism' emerged in the mid 1980s, when urban social problems produced by the economic reforms in China had already become palpable. The advocates of New Authoritarianism argued that a strong, authoritarian government was indispensable both to maintain political order and social stability and to further the economic reform necessary to begin to establish a liberal democracy. They drew their lessons from the modernization experience of developing countries, especially from that in East Asia, arguing that modernization in a non-Western developing country like China could not follow the Western model. Rather, economic modernization and political modernization should be carried out in two separate stages, with economic development taking precedence over political democratization and led by a reform-oriented authoritarian government. Thus, authoritarian governments were responsible for providing the favourable conditions for sustained economic development, which meant, first of all, a stable social and political order. Thus economic reform and modernization could avoid being interrupted by frequent social and political turmoil, eventually giving rise to a strong middle class, which would then press for political democracy. The leading proponents of the New Authoritarianism were Wu Jiaxiang, Zhang Bingjiu, Wang Huning and Xiao Gongqin, while the latter two also exemplify the transition from the New Authoritarianism to **Neo-Conservatism**. The New Authoritarians positioned themselves between the 'Old Left' and the radical reformers (i.e. Liberals), who maintained the necessity of political reform to accompany or even precede economic reform. Though they shared a set of basic principles, there were some differences among them, especially on economic issues. People usually divided this political trend into two schools: the Northern school in Beijing and the Southern school in Shanghai. Wu and Zhang belonged to the former, and Xiao to the latter. New Authoritarianism stimulated a heated debate in 1988 and early 1989. Though the debate was silenced after 1989, some of its basic ideas were inherited by a new ideological and political trend of the 1990s, Neo-Conservatism.

Further reading

Ma, Shuyun (1990–1). 'The Rise and Fall of Neo-Authoritarianism in China'. *China Information* 5.3 (Winter): 1–18.

Qi, Mo (ed.) (1991). *Xinquanwei zhuyi: Dui Zhongguo dalu weilai minyun de lunzheng* [New Authoritarianism: Debates on the Fate of the Chinese Mainland]. Taipei: Tangshan chubanshe.

Sautman, Barry (1992). 'Sirens of the Strongman: New-Authoritarianism in Recent Chinese Political Theory.' *China Quarterly* 129 (March): 72–102.

LIU CHANG

New Confucianism

(Xinrujia)

The term *xinrujia* or *xinruxue*, loosely translated as 'New Confucianism', is increasingly understood as an intellectual and cultural phenomenon of the last twenty-five years, one that has garnered considerable attention in Western academic and media circles, yet is remote from the real religious and life experience of Chinese. It is cited by foreign pundits and Communist Party officials as a significant determining factor in China's rapid and largely successful economic transformation. Followers and advocates, who have grown in number in the past decade, are principally found in academic institutions in Beijing, Hong Kong, Taipei and the United States. The increasingly self-proclaimed existence of these *dangdai xinrujia* (contemporary New Confucians) is evidence of a revolution in cultural politics and emergent global intellectual affinities generated by the search of a deracinated intelligentsia for moral justification and the accidental advent of the Chinese economic miracle. By turns considered a matter of cultural identity, religion, philosophy and social ethos, in its vast range of contemporary cultural reference, 'New Confucianism', not unlike its predecessor 'Confucianism', is everything and yet no-thing.

Regardless of the manifold forms it assumes, *xinruxue*, its adherents would concur, is grounded in a mythopoeic conception of the moral self as the conscience of community and cosmos; 'its primary purpose', according to Tu Wei-ming, 'is individual and communal self-realization with a view toward Heaven'. Beyond this commonality, there are distinct, and sometimes rivalrous schools of thought that lay claim to affinitive genealogical descent from the *daoxue* (learning of the path) fellowship of Zhu Xi (1130–1200), or the *lixue* (learning of principle) teachings of Cheng Yichuan (1033–1107), or the *xinxue* (learning of the mind) of Wang Yangming (1472–1529). As a whole, the present generation of *ru* (Confucian) scholars see themselves as the 'third wave' or 'third era' of legitimate succession from the heralded twin points of imperial-era Confucianism – the Han (206 BCE–CE 221) and Song/Ming (960–1644) dynasties.

Arguably any Confucianism put forward with good faith at any time after the revolution must be 'new'; there have certainly been currents of *ru* advocacy running in the broader tumultuous stream of Chinese culture in the twentieth century and indeed in previous centuries. Nevertheless, today's New Confucianism is a distinct product of China's economic reforms, particularly the capitalist triumphalism of the Deng Xiaoping era. In this guise it is the principal cultural precipitant of this economic transformation. It operates as an ideology that unites the diverse contemporary constituencies of the meta-national entity that is 'cultural China' (*wenhua Zhongguo*) while explaining, in a mild chauvinist temper, the rapid economic expansion of China and the heralded 'mini dragons' of Hong Kong, Singapore, South Korea and Taiwan.

In the creative convulsion of the 1980s **cultural discussion** (*wenhua taolun*), *Ruxue* or 'Confucianism' returned to respectability alongside the Qigong revival, and the literary experiments in 'roots searching' (*xungen*), as China opened to the outside world while looking inward in search of cultural resources that might offer moral solace and regenerate indigenous models for community in the wake of spiritual crisis (*jingshen weiji*). So, alongside the searing retrospective self-reflection of **Scar literature** (*shangwen*), the conscious disarrangement of sense in **Misty poetry** (*menglongshi*) that announced the aesthetic coming to terms with the domestic trauma of the **Cultural Revolution**, Confucian revivalism first took its place as a discrete movement to reassess cultural identity, and quickly metamorphosed into a state-supported research institute in Beijing, the China Confucius Research Institute (Zhonghua Kongzi yanjiusuo). And, of the manifold cultural exuberances of this anxious era, New Confucianism, perhaps because of its alignment with the Party-state, was one of the few that survived the massacre at Tiananmen and the subsequent **Campaign against Bourgeois Liberalization**. It endured and became a discourse with multiple constituencies, as scholars in China who had long worked on the subject in isolation or self-censorship learned of a larger academic dialogue in Hong Kong, Japan, Singapore, Taiwan and the United States over the restitution of Confucian studies.

The recent frenzy of reinvention follows a longer interval of multiple forms of conceptual invention. The term *xinruxue* may be traced to He Lin (1902–92), the Chinese idealist who, writing in the early 1940s, saw in the unfolding (*kaizhan*) of a 'new' Confucianism (specifically, the *xin xinxue* or 'new learning of the mind' of Wang Yangming), a cultural path for China's reconciliation of subjective and objective spirit in a manner parallel to that sketched out by Hegel's phenomenology for Europe. His vision was blocked by decades of oscillating violence against 'revisionism', bourgeois sentiment and tradition, most spectacularly the prolonged national campaign of the 1970s to criticize Lin Biao and Kongzi (*piLin piKong*), wherein everything that was wrong with China was placed at the feet of Confucianism.

He Lin's was not the first mid-century affirmation of a 'New Confucianism', as there were others, just beyond these paroxysms of mainland political excess and from a slightly different angle, who had also directed their attention to the revival of *ruxue*. 'A Respectful Declaration on Behalf of Chinese Culture to the World' (*Wei Zhongguo wenhua jinggao shijie renshi xuanyan*), written in 1957 by the four great thinkers outside China – Zhang Junmai (Carsun Chang, 1887–1969), Tang Junyi (1909–78), Mou Zongsan (1909–95) and Xu Fuguan (1903–82) – and published the following year on New Year's Day in Hong Kong and Taiwan, asserted a revitalization of the conservative intellectual alternative of *xinrujia*, but was in fact a dilatory extension of the late 1934 movement to bring about 'cultural construction on a Chinese basis' (*Zhongguo benwei de wenhua jianshe*), offering a new language of affirmative cultural conception but without a movement or school. Although Mou and Xiong Shili (1885–1968) may be credited with the invention of a line of *xinru* transmission, it was Xu Fuguan and Xiong Shili in particular who were responsible for the instruction of a younger generation of Chinese scholars who took up the cause of new Confucian studies with fervour.

The aetiology of the New Confucian movement is complex but, owing to the documentary industry of scholars like Fang Keli and Li Jinquan, an arc of this most recent revival can be inscribed through several salient points in the intellectual landscape:

- 1978, the recuperation of *ruxue* at a post-Cultural Revolution symposium on Confucian studies convened in October of 1978 at Shandong University, not far from the purported birthplace of Kongzi (Confucius);
- 1980, the establishment of the Kongzi yanjiu zhongxin (Kongzi Research Centre) in Qufu;
- 1982, the First International Conference on Zhu Xi at which the most eminent Confucian studies scholars from Taiwan, Hong Kong, and China (Cai Renhou, Feng Youlan, Li Zehou, Liang Shuming, Liu Shuxian, Qian Mu, Xu Fuguan, Yu Yingshi) were gathered for the first time, and the earliest retrospective articulation of Mou Zongsan's three generations theory (*sange niandai*) of *ru* doctrine was proposed;
- 1984, the 2,535 anniversary of the birth of Kongzi and the first massive public celebration of rites to the 'first teacher' (*xianshi*);
- 1985, the official visit of Tu Wei-ming, at Deng Xiaoping's behest, to Beijing, the founding of the China Confucius Research Institute (Zhonghua Kongzi yanjiusuo), and the convening of the first national symposium on Kongzi in Beijing, when New Confucianism and the study of Kongzi turned scientific with projected research in Confucian studies organized into Five Year Plans;
- 1986, the national conference on the future of Chinese philosophy and the initiation of a domestic scholarly programme to study modern New Confucian thought, as well as the publication in Qufu of a new journal, *Kongzi yanjiu* [Confucius Research];
- 1987, the joint international conference (China and Singapore) on Confucianism as the cultural force behind East Asian economic development;
- 1989, 2,540 anniversary of Kongzi's birth coextensive with the national symposium on Confucianism;

- 1994, 2,545 Kongzi birth anniversary and second international conference on Confucianism hosted in Beijing by the International Confucian Association;
- 1998, third international conference on Confucianism held in Beijing at which Confucianism and its contributions to human rights and ecology were addressed.

Owing to the co-emergence of the revival of Confucianism (*fuxing ruxue*) and Asian regional hypergrowth, many have concluded that this coincidence indicates causation. Chief among them are the 'Confucian scholars' Tu Wei-ming and Liu Shuxian, the sinologist Yu Yingshi, and eminent Communist Party officials. One very critical aspect of the intellectual context for these claims is Max Weber's influential argument that late Qing Confucianism exhibited an ethic of accommodation with the world that inhibited the growth of capitalism and its modern rationality. The capitalist Confucians contend that Confucianism properly understood, that is New Confucianism, is as world-transforming as Puritanism, but without its otherworldly, transcendent yearnings. This particular brand of New Confucianism is only one of a growing number of post-Cultural Revolution era *xinruxue* manifestations, wherein the urge for a secure native identity by Chinese both at home and abroad was paramount.

Consequently, 'Confucianism', *qua* the traditional values of social hierarchy and familial tranquillity, exerts considerable influence over academic commentary on the political and economic reforms that have brought China unforeseen prosperity, as seen in recent works by Peter Berger, André Gunder-Frank, Samuel Huntington and David Landes. This common reading may be taken as the popular afterlife of an interpretative phenomenon that, having achieved conceptual assent in the West, has been regenerated in China, Singapore, Taiwan and Hong Kong as an ideology of sensible capitalist development under the watchful eye of Kongzi (Confucius) and managed by authoritarian governments. Nothing confirms this creative misreading as effectively as a **People's Daily** op-ed piece that appeared in 1996 and declaimed the harmony of Confucianism and China's market Leninism, asserting that

'Confucianism's rule of virtues and code of ethics and authority' were 'the soul of the modern enterprise culture and the key to gaining market share and attracting customers'. This coincided with international symposia on Confucianism convened by Chinese officials, such as Gu Mu and Li Ruihuan who also provided funds for research into New Confucianism because of its advocacy of 'harmony making for prosperity'.

The faith of this form of New Confucianism is likely to remain prominent in explaining the eminence of Asia in the twenty-first century, given the widespread acceptance of the facticity of Confucianism and of its principal explanatory role in the sophisticated accumulation of Asian capital and Chinese modernization. China's capitalist achievement, or for 'harmony above all', or of the 'pervasiveness of the Confucian mentality in contemporary East Asia', occludes a necessary, broader vision of the nation's definitive religious pluralism. In this way, the scholars of New Confucianism, whether in Boston, Hong Kong, Beijing or Taipei, commit the grievous error of Han era orthodoxy: aligning themselves and their readers with the official country, as Kristofer Schipper has pointed out, against 'the real country, the local structures being expressed in regional and unofficial forms of religion'. In this way, all talk about a spiritual Confucianism or of Confucian humanism and any of the other manifestations of essentialist cultural self-definition, leaves New Confucianism especially vulnerable to the ardent populist critique of Dai Zhen (1723–77), who inveighed against followers of Song-Ming Confucianism for 'slaying the people with principle'.

Further reading

(1994). *Dangdai Ruxue zhi ziwo zhuanhua* [The Subjective Turn in New Confucianism]. Taipei: Zhongyang yanjiuyuan.

(1997). *Zhongguo Ruxue baike quanshu* [Encyclopedia of Confucianism in China]. Beijing: Zhongguo da baike quanshu chubanshe.

Bresciani, Umberto (2001). *Reinventing Confucianism: The New Confucian Movement*. Taipei: Ricci Institute for Chinese Studies.

Cai, Shangsi (1986). *Kongzi sixiang tixi* [The System of Kongzi's Thought]. Shanghai: Shanghai renmin chubanshe.

Dirlik, Arif (1995). 'Confucius in the Borderlands: Global Capitalism and the Reinvention of Confucianism'. *boundary 2* 22.3: 229–73.

Fang, Keli and Li, Jinquan (eds) (1989). *Xiandai xin Ruxue yanjiu lunji* [Collected Essays on New Confucianism Studies]. Beijing: Zhongguo shehuo kexue chubanshe.

Feng, Zusheng (ed.) (1989). *Dangdai xin Rujia* [Contemporary New Confucianism]. Beijing: Sanlian.

—— (1999). *Guoji Ruxue yanjiu* [International Confucianism Studies]. Beijing: Zhongguo shehui kexue chubanshe.

He, Lin (1995). *Rujia sixiang de xinkaizhan: He Lin xinruxue lunzhu jiyao* [The New Unfolding of New Confucian Thought: He Lin's Key Works on New Confucianism]. Beijing: Zhongguo guangbo dianshi chubanshe.

Jensen, Lionel M. (2000). 'Human Rights, Chinese Rites, and the Limits of History'. *The Historian* 62.2 (Winter): 378–85.

Liu, Shuxian [Shu-hsien] (2000). 'Lun dangdai xin Rujia de zhuanxing yu zhanwang,' *Zhexue zazhi* 31.

Makeham, John (ed.) (2003). *New Confucianism: A Critical Examination*. London: Palgrave/Macmillan.

Neville, Robert (2000). *Boston Confucianism: Portable Tradition in the Late-Modern World*. Albany: State University of New York Press.

Tu, Wei-ming (1991). 'The Search for Roots in Industrial East Asia: The Case of the Confucian Revival'. In Martin E. Marty and R. Scott Appleby (eds), *Fundamentalisms Observed*. Chicago: University of Chicago Press, 740–81.

—— (ed.) (1991). *The Triadic Concord: Confucian Ethics, Industrial Asia, and Max Weber*. Singapore: Institute of East Asian Philosophies.

—— (ed.) (1994). *The Living Tree: The Changing Meaning of Being Chinese Today*. Stanford: Stanford University Press.

Xu, Yuanhe (1994). *Ruxue yü dongfang wenhua* [Confucianism and Eastern Culture]. Beijing: Renmin chubanshe.

Yu, Yingshi (1986). 'Zhongguo jinshi zongjiao lunli yu shangren jingshen'. [Modern China's

Religion and Ethics and the Spirit of Merchants]. *Zhishi fenzi* 2.2: 3–45.

Yu, Yingshi (1998). *Xiandai Ruxue lun* [On Contemporary Confucian Studies]. Shanghai: Shanghai renmin chubanshe.

LIONEL M. JENSEN

new cookbooks, recipes

Since the 1980s, changes in China's economic and social life have also impacted its cookbooks and recipes. Take *People's Recipes* (*Dazhong caipu*), published by the Chinese Light Industry Press in the mid 1960s, for example. Cabbages and carrots predominate, as they did the national diet. Its 264 recipes, which were meant to add spice to a harsh life, could barely be detached from it: a typical recipe might be simply cabbage boiled with salt, lard and scallion. In the late 1990s, the press not only revised the cookbook, but also dished out an 18,000-recipe series, *People's Dinner Tables* (*Dazhong canzhuo*), including the cookbooks *Meat Delicacies* (*Meiwei roucai*), *Delicious Vegetables* (*Shuangkou shucai*) and *Savoury Seafood* (*Xianxiang yuxia*).

As people aspire to a healthier life, the market for new cookbooks of medicinal foods and recipes conducive to weight loss and beauty is growing rapidly. A 500-page *Latest Practical Healer Food Recipes for the Contemporary Family* (*Zuixin shiyong xiandaijiating yaoshanshipu*) sells for $280. Other bestsellers include ethnic recipes; ancient recipes, particularly of royal families; recipes from natural food sources; and ones prompted by new cooking devices like microwaves and rotisseries. The quality and format of cookbooks have also improved – a new trend is to accompany recipes with photo samples. Digitized recipes are available on CD-ROMs, VCDs and the Web, while television programmes offer cooking shows like *Daily Meals* (*Tiantian yinshi*). Though weeds and game are appealing food sources, cookbooks usually shun recipes that make use of protected flora and fauna, which may occasionally be found illicitly in restaurants.

YUAN HAIWANG

New Documentary Movement

The New Documentary Movement (*Xin jilu yundong*) began in the early 1990s with a group of independent filmmakers who hoped to reveal a social reality different from that presented in the official or commercial media. To do so, they turned their cameras to the lower strata (*diceng*) of Chinese society as well as to people living an alternative lifestyle, two social groups whose voices had been suppressed or ignored in 'special-topic films' (*zhuantipian*) produced by the state-owned television networks.

Provoked and informed by the democratic movements of the late 1980s, especially that of 4 June 1989, the New Documentary Movement emerged in response to the accelerated changes experienced throughout the 1990s. Some of the artists involved had experience in working for the state-run television networks, where access to film equipment made it possible to work on their own projects in their spare time. Later, the advent of digital video cameras and cheaper editing technology made independent production easier, increasing the number of works and fostering a more intimate cinematic gaze. Stylistically, the majority of these new documentaries tilt heavily towards the tropes of 'direct cinema' and cinéma vérité: an absence of omniscient voiceover commentary, and minimum use of script, synchronized sound recording, and so forth. The work of Frederick Wiseman has been identified as a major inspiration.

While some of the videomakers associated with this informal movement started making documentaries while stationed in Tibet in the early 1990s (e.g. **Duan Jinchuan** and **Jiang Yue**), the work that brought international recognition to the New Documentary Movement was **Wu Wenguang**'s *Bumming in Beijing: The Last Dreamers* (*Liulang Beijing:zuihou de mengxiangzhe*, 1990), a 165-minute-long video documenting the lives of five marginalized young artists in Beijing. Other important works include Kang Jianning's *Yin Yang* (*Yinyang*, 1997), which relates the quiet hardships and contradictions encountered by a **fengshui** (geomancy) master in a poor village in the Ningxia Autonomous Region, and **Li Hong**'s *Out of Phoenixbridge* (*Hui dao fenghuangqiao*, 1997), the first 'New Documentary' directed by a woman. This is an intimate and sympathetic portrait of the hopes and disillusionments of several peasant girls who have left their home to try and make their livings in Beijing. Apart from these better-known filmmakers, mostly based in Beijing, an increasingly large group of amateur documentary-makers have begun to appear all over China in this newly found territory for personal expression. This is made possible by the popularity and affordability of handheld digital video cameras. Because of the increasing number of such filmmakers, more complete, varied and colourful representations of Chinese life are now appearing on screen, including Yang Lina's *Home Video* (about her parents' divorce), Li Lin's *Three Five People* (about HIV-infected drug addicts in Chengdu), Chen Weijin's *To Live is Better Than to Die* (about HIV infection in Wenhou, Hebei), Du Haibin's *Along the Railway* (about homelessness in Shaanxi) and Wang Bing's *West of the Tracks* (about the collapse of a state-owned enterprise in Shenyang).

See also: Tiananmen Square (1991); Wang Jianwei

Further reading

Berry, Chris (1998). 'Chinese Documentary at Home in the World'. *Documentary Box* (31 January). Available at http://www.city.yamagata.yamagata. jp/yidff/docbox/11/box11-3-e.html

—— (2002). 'Facing Reality: Chinese Documentary, Chinese Postsocialism.' In Wu Hung (ed.), *The First Guangzhou Triennial: Reinterpretation: A Decade of Experimental Chinese Art (1990-2000)*. Guangzhou: Guangzhou Museum of Art/Chicago: Art Media Resources, 121–31.

Lu, Xinyu (2003). *Jilu Zhongguo: dangdai Zhongguo de Xin jilu yundong* [Documenting China: The New Documentary Movement in Contemporary China]. Beijing: Sanlian chubanshe.

Reynaud, Bérénice (1996). 'New Visions/New China: Video – Art, Documentation, and the Chinese Modernity Question.' In Michael Renov and Erika Suderburg (eds), *Resolutions: Contemporary Video Practices*. Minneapolis: University of Minnesota Press, 229–57.

—— (2003). 'Dancing with Myself, Drifting with My Camera: The Emotional Vagabonds of China's New Documentary'. *Senses of Cinema* 28 (September/October). Available at http://www. sensesofcinema.com/contents/03/28/chinas_ new_documentary.html

Wu, Wenguang (2002). 'Just on the Road: A Description of the Individual Way of Recording Images in the 1990s.' In Wu Hung (ed.), *The First Guangzhou Triennial: Reinterpretation: A Decade of Experimental Chinese Art (1990–2000)*. Guangzhou: Guangzhou Museum of Art/Chicago: Art Media Resources, 132–8.

WANG QI

New Left

(Xinzuopai)

The 'New Left' was invented as a label to stigmatize the group's alleged ideological complicity with the state and was rejected by most of those so labelled. It is 'new' because it is independent from the old left of the Communist Party. It is 'leftist' because it questions the new dogma of the 'free market' as the centrepiece of modernity. Not strictly a 'faction' or 'school of thought' (*pai*), it has evolved into an amalgam of loosely associated intellectuals and groups articulating alternative visions that move beyond the rigid dichotomy of *laissez-faire* capitalism and state socialism. Its brief history, especially through its entanglement with **liberalism**, defines and reflects much of the intellectual reconfiguration in post 1989 China.

The phrase was first applied to a small circle of fiction writers – **Zhang Chengzhi**, **Zhang Wei** and **Han Shaogong** – for their attribution of the growing socioeconomic inequities and moral decline in China to the market reforms. The phrase was publicly circulated after **Cui Zhiyuan** called for a second intellectual liberation and institutional innovation in 1994. Meanwhile, Wang Shaoguang and Hu Angang raised the question of 'state capacity', calling for an increase in the central government's share of revenues to strengthen its power of redistribution and to counter growing social and regional economic disparities. With the then current experience of the former state socialist countries in mind, these intellectuals went against the grain of neo-liberal economics that had been elevated to orthodoxy during the Reagan–Thatcher era and were now being emulated by liberal thinkers and policy-makers in China and the rest of the world (see **economic thought**).

In the cultural arena, an aggregate of questions emerging under the guise of 'Western theory' were also placed under rubric of the 'New Left', most prominently, 'Western Marxism' (*Xima*) and what was called 'post-ism' (*Houxue*). The former drew on the Frankfurt School, Wallerstein's world-systems and S. Amin's dependency theories, and especially the views of Anglophone cultural theorists best represented by Frederic Jameson; the latter transplanted poststructuralism, postmodernism and postcolonial cultural politics. With much divergence and some overlap, 'Western Marxism' and 'post-ism' stand largely as avant-garde academic discourses with a foreign flavour, yet bearing varying populist and nativist banners. In response to the changing global geopolitics of the post-Cold War era, a myriad of nationalist sentiments arose around the same time, from serious questioning of US hegemony and cultural imperialism to the 'China-can-say-no' hype. Extremist views of all kinds were attached to the 'New Left' for no substantive reasons other than the appearance of a shared oppositional rhetoric.

Of all 'New Leftist' intellectuals in the PRC, **Wang Hui** has been a central figure. His systematic rethinking of modernity in relation to contemporary issues of China has helped develop a more comprehensive and sophisticated leftist discourse. **Dushu** [Reading], co-edited by Wang Hui since 1996, and **Tianya** [Frontier], where Wang published his cornerstone essay, stand as the two major venues for 'New Leftist' voices, though both remain open to authors of differing viewpoints. *Shijie* [Horizons], a new theoretical journal co-edited by **Li Tuo**, has joined the cause. Once disassociated from state power, leftist ideas are poised to regain ideological legitimacy and historical relevance.

See also: literary periodicals; nationalism; Neo-Conservatism; postmodernism (houxiandai zhuyi) and 'post-ism' (houxue)

Further reading

Chen, Jianhua (1998). 'Local and Global in Narrative Contestation: Liberalism and the New Left in Late 1990s China'. *Journal of Asian Pacific Communication* 9.1/2: 113–29.

Hu, Angang (2004). 'Equity and Efficiency'. In Wang Chaohua (ed.), *One China, Many Paths*. London: Verso, 219–33.

Xu, Jilin, Liu, Qing, Luo, Gang and Xue, Yi (2001). 'In Search of a "Third Way": A Conversation regarding "Liberalism" and the "New Left Wing"'. Trans. Geremie R. Barmé. In Gloria Davies (ed.), *Voicing Concerns: Contemporary Chinese Critical Inquiry*. Lanham, MD: Rowman and Littlefield, 199–226.

YUE GANG

New Literati Painting

(Xin wenren hua)

The New Literati movement asserted itself during the decade 1987–97 as yet another, considerably respected and exacting orientation in the broad field of **Modern Ink-Wash Painting** (*Xiandai shuimohua*), distinguished by a masterly technique and a high level of artistry. The movement was conceived in 1986 by postgraduate students in the Ink-Painting Department of the **Central Academy of Fine Arts** in Beijing, notably Bian Pingshan (b. 1958), Ji Youchen (b. 1945) and Wang Heping (b. 1949). On the one hand, they stressed the technical aspects of a painting; on the other, a mutual loyalty within the newly formed group, which was originally called 'Nanfang beifang Zhongguohua' (Southern and Northern Traditional Chinese Painting), underlining the fact that their style and approach were widely practised. After exhibitions in Tianjin, Fuzhou and Guilin, they were joined in 1988 by artists based in Nanjing, e.g. Zhu Daoping (b. 1953) and Chang Jin (b. 1951). Other prominent adherents were **Chen Ping** (b. 1960), Chen Xiangxun (b. 1956), Li Laoshi (1957–96), **Lu Yushun** (b. 1962), Shen Shaojun (b. 1956), **Tian Liming** (b. 1955), Wang Mengqi (b. 1947), Xu Lele (b. 1953), Yu Shui (b. 1955), Zhu Xinjian

(b. 1953), among others – more than fifty artists altogether.

Since 1989, Chen Shouxiang (b. 1944) of the Chinese Art Research Institute took over the organization of yearly exhibitions (1989, 1990 and 1997 in Beijing; 1991 in Linyi, Shandong; 1992 in Lanzhou; 1993 in Fuzhou; 1994 in Nanjing; 1995 in Shanghai; 1996 in Hangzhou). Chen made up the appellation 'New Literati' (*Xin wenren*), not for any theoretical reasons but by borrowing the catchy title of a book he was compiling. Thus, the link between this movement and the true 'literati' of the past is somewhat vague, and not very essential. Due to the scarce opportunities of this generation of painters to view and study old paintings (until recently, even good reproductions were hard to come by in China), it is rather doubtful that ancient masters could truly be their inspiration. Rather, the New Literati followed the painters older than themselves by two generations who had continued the classical style even after 1949 and the devastating **Cultural Revolution**. Thanks to them, traditional painting survived and has remained quite strong in artistic terms. On the whole, however, it had received a severe blow and has remained in the shadow of the progressive, Western-oriented trends of most artists and critics. The New Literati claimed the legacy of classical Chinese painting despite their connection to fine-art academies, where ink painting was slighted, and despite the general search for a Western and Chinese synthesis over the last two decades. The New Literati, in fact, have even gone so far as to reject Western influence, and have stressed perfect brushwork, rather than precise drawing. Such attitudes clearly distinguish and separate them from most other contemporary art-currents in China. Nonetheless, while the idea of recovering the qualities and character of classical painting was not a new one, among such efforts, the New Literati have received the widest response by far among contemporary Chinese artists, and their artistic concepts have demonstrated an astonishing ability to reflect and evolve in light of contemporary aesthetic perceptions. Although, after a decade of activity, their adherents have rejected any collective programme and even its name, most of them have maintained the aesthetic approach in their individual work.

Further reading

Andrews, Julia F. and Shen, Kuiyi (1998). 'Chinese Painting in the Post-Mao Era'. In *idem* (eds), *A Century in Crisis: Tradition and Modernity in the Art of Twentieth-Century China*. New York: Solomon R. Guggenheim Museum.

Chen Shouxiang (1999) *Xin wenren hua yishu: wenxin wanxiang* [The Art of New Literati: Ten Thousand Images of the Literati Mind]. Changchun: Jilin meishu chubanshe.

Dal Lago, Francesca (1998). '"New Literati Painting" at the China Art Gallery, Beijing'. *ART AsiaPacific* 19 (July): 32–4.

Olivová, Lucie (2001). 'The Heritage of the New Literati Painting'. In *idem* (ed.), *Contemporary Chinese Ink Painting: Tradition and Experiment*. Prague: National Gallery, 79–88.

LUCIE OLIVOVÁ

New Measurement Group

(Xin Kedu, 1989–95)

artist group in Beijing

Founded in 1988 and reorganized in late 1989, after a reshuffling of the original 'New Analyst Group' (Jie Xi), the 'New Measurement Group' (Xin Kedu) made its first appearance at the groundbreaking **China Avant-Garde** exhibition at the **China Art Gallery** in Beijing. Xin Kedu was formed by three of the artists belonging to the former group: **Gu Dexin** (b. 1962), Wang Luyan (b. 1956) and Chen Shaoping (b. 1947). They would continue in the spirit of artistic self-denial that brought together the New Analysts: meeting on a regular basis, the three would adopt rules agreed upon by majority with the goal of regulating every aspect of artistic creation, from the type of drawing tools to working procedures. This resulted in erasure of all individual trace in the end product. Between 1990 and 1995, the group produced five books that bear witness to the process through which objects, human behaviours and situations are transformed in pure graphs. Entitled *Analyst I–V* (*Jie Xi I–V*), the five books were exhibited at various venues in and outside China, including the exhibition 'China's New Art Post 1989' at the Hong Kong Arts Centre in 1993 and 'Des del País del Centre' at the Centre d'Art Santa Mónica in Barcelona in 1995. In the autumn of 1995, in view of the conflicts created between its radical founding principles – i.e. to deconstruct the legitimacy of the collective institutional system by creating an institution of its own – and the unavoidable sanctioning process of the artistic system, the group called its final meeting and decided to destroy all documents and drawings heretofore produced as a final 'measurement' required to terminate its mission.

Further reading

(1995). *Des del País del Centre: avantguardes artístiques xineses* (exhibition catalogue). Barcelona: Generalitat de Catalunya, Departament de Cultura 45.

Lü, Peng and Yi, Dan (1992). *A History of Modern Art in China*. Changsha: Hunan Fine Art Publishing, 346–69.

TANG DI

New Music

China's traditional music is played on the **pipa**, **erhu** and *guqin* (see **qin**). It is based on musical and rhythmic patterns that are transmitted orally; it is a music which does not know the concept of a 'composer'. The exclusive reign of this type of Chinese music ended around the turn of the last century, with the arrival of foreign missionaries, foreign armies and foreign merchants who brought to nineteenth-century China the musical fare of their own culture. In the wake of this foreign invasion, a new type of 'Chinese music' arose. It makes use of violins, organs, pianos and clarinets. It is performed according to strict notation. It is linked with the name of a particular composer. This music was, if anything, both a new type and concept of music to China. But it was soon to be assimilated into the Chinese musical universe to such an extent that a song like 'Frère Jacques' would be considered a 'Chinese folksong'.

China's New Music appears at the same time as New Music in the West – at the beginning of the twentieth century. Stylistically, however, it comes in very different guise: New Music from China includes works written in many different idioms: classicist, romanticist or modernist. Thus, New Music from China is not called such because it employs techniques also known in New Music in the West, but simply because it uses Western instrumental and compositional techniques which were new to China at the beginning of the twentieth century.

It is politics that has caused the diversity of styles in China's New Music. European modernism has not fared well in modern China. Music, like all other artistic products, was supposed to 'serve the masses' – at least since Mao formulated this dictum in his 1942 Yan'an Talks. Therefore, the sounds of modernism have been suppressed: during the anti-Rightist campaigns, in the **Cultural Revolution** and also during the Spiritual Pollution Campaigns of the 1980s and 1990s (see **socialist spiritual civilization**). Chinese politicians prefer the more mellow sounds of **pentatonic romanticism**, created by many a Chinese composer to the present day.

See also: Fourth Generation (composers); Third Generation (composers); traditional music

Further reading

Kouwenhoven, Frank (1990). 'Mainland China's New Music (1): Out of the Desert'. *Chime* 2: 58–93.

—— (1991). 'Mainland China's New Music (2): Madly Singing in the Mountains'. *Chime* 3: 42–75.

—— (1992). 'Mainland China's New Music (3): The Age of Pluralism'. *Chime* 5: 76–134.

Liu, Ching-chih and Wu, Ganbo (eds) (1994). *History of New Music in China: The Development of Chinese Music*. Hong Kong: University of Hong Kong.

Liu, Jingzhi (Liu Ching-chih) (1998). *Zhongguo xin yinyue shilun* [Essays on China's New Music], 2 vols. Taipei: Shaowen.

Mittler, Barbara (1997). *Dangerous Tunes. The Politics of Chinese Music in Hong Kong, Taiwan and the People's Republic of China since 1949*. Wiesbaden: Harrassowitz.

Utz, Christian (nd). *Database of Contemporary Music in Taiwan*. Available at http://www.t0.or.at/~utz/Taiwan

BARBARA MITTLER

New Sound Movement, Modern Sky Records

Beijing's New Sound Movement (*Xinsheng yundong*) is associated with rock musicians who grew up in the 1970s. It began around 1997, initially supported by the independent record company Modern Sky (MS; Modeng tiankong). The movement is both a marketing strategy and the product of young musicians who are less influenced by CCP policy than by the growing quantity of (illegally) imported international music products. MS was founded by Shen Lihui (b. 1970), a musician and art designer in 1997, when the first bands appeared in concerts. In December, his Brit-pop inspired band, Sober (Qingxing), released the first album on the new label. The company founded the sublabel Badhead in late 1998 and since then has grown into an influential enterprise. New bands were first introduced via compilation-CDs. In 1999 MS started to publish its own music magazine, which includes a CD of new releases. The package created a new standard for commercial music marketing.

MS concentrates on the promotion of Third Generation internationalized music, and does not focus on one particular music style, but on creativity in sound and design, e.g. heavy underground sounds, pop-punk and folk-styles. The lyrics of the 'New Sound' generation vary from having fun to individual problems, alienation and bizarre reflections on urban society, while the movement combines postmodern avant-garde culture with music and art/design.

See also: rock music, rock bands

Further reading

Kloet, Jeroen de (2001). *Red Sonic Trajectories. Popular Music and Youth in Urban China*. Enschede: Ipskamp.

Steen, Andreas (2000). 'Sound, Protest and Business – Modern Sky Co. and the New Ideology of Chinese Rock'. *Berliner China Hefte* 19 (October), 40–64 (http://parapluie.de/archiv/china/rock/original_aus.html).

Yan, Yun (1999). *Beijing xinshen – New Sound of Beijing*. Changsha: A Sonic China Project.

ANDREAS STEEN

New Year Festival

(guonian, chunjie)

The 'Spring Festival' (*chunjie*), as the 'Chinese New Year' is properly known, includes throughout China two separate focal points, namely *guonian* (crossing into the new year) and *yuanxiao jie* (the festival of the primal evening) on the fifteenth day of the first lunar month, corresponding to the day of the 'upper (heavenly) prime' (*Shangyuan*): that is, the birthday of the Officer of Heaven (Tianguan). The first focal point is essentially domestic in character, a parenthesis in time bounded by the departure to and return from heaven of the stove god (*zaojun*; the return usually occurs by the fifth day of the new year). On New Year's Eve (*chuxi*), usually after year-end visits to the local 'altar of the god of the earth' (*shetan*) and village temples, the family gathers for its 'meal of cohesion' (*tuanyuan fan*), and the auspicious 'parallel phrases' (*duilian*) on the door-posts are replaced. On New Year's Day (*nian chuyi*), 'well-wishing' (*bainian*) begins with worship of the gods, first the god of the earth, then the gods housed in temples. Only after the gods have been honoured can the visits to family and friends begin.

The 'domestic New Year' is also the time when those families that have portraits of their ancestors hang them up above the domestic altar and when lineages worship together in the ancestral hall (*citang*) (see **ancestral halls/lineage temples**). Often, there will be a special ritual called *shangpu*, or 'entering(the names of the sons born in the previous year) in the "lineage register"' (*zupu*). This latter act, which is public and surrounded by ritual precautions, is followed by an all-male banquet during which 'lanterns are hung up (in the ancestral hall)' (*shangdeng*).

The 'public New Year' consists in dragon and lion dances, as well as in lantern processions and competitions; it is also one of the main moments for the celebration of the Daoist community sacrifice (**Jiao**). Dances and processions, usually organized by lineage or lineage segment (*fang*), are an occasion for the expression of rivalry between the component parts of local society, and they often occur in the context of the Jiao. We need to realize that the words for 'lantern' and 'boy' are homophonous (*ding*) in Hakka and other dialects to understand that the first phase of the New Year's celebrations in fact prepares the second, and that both phases reach their culminating point in the **Lantern Festival**. If, then, the Spring Festival is a predominantly lineage festival, it is very important to see that lineage fecundity and strength are thought of as blessings of the gods, from the local earth god all the way up to the Officer of Heaven. That is why the first half of the first month is also so frequently the time for Jiao, and it is also the reason the segments of the long dragon are assembled in front of the local temple.

JOHN LAGERWEY

New Year's movies

(Hesuipian)

Hesuipian are a film-marketing phenomenon that became prominent around 1997, when the Chinese film industry faced increasing competition from Hollywood movies and Hong Kong action movies. Aiming at the 'golden season' from Christmas to the Chinese **New Year Festival**, *Hesuipian* often feature light-hearted comedy and action, and are therefore criticized by some critics as focusing too much on ticket sales and ignoring artistic quality. However, the majority of Chinese audiences – film critics and taxi drivers alike – welcomed *Hesuipian* as a necessary boost to the slump in the film market. The number of *Hesuipian* has been growing, and their style has become increasingly diversified.

From his first big hit, **Parties A and B** (*Jiafang yifang*, 1997), director **Feng Xiaogang**'s name has

become synonymous with *Hesuipian*. His *Be There or Be Square* (*Bu jian bu san*, 1998), *Sorry, Baby* (*Mei wan mei lao*, 1999) and *Big Shot's Funeral* (*Da wan'r*, 2001) continued to lead the box office each year. Concealing social criticism in gritty humour and witty shtick is the defining feature of Feng's *Hesuipian*. Produced by Columbia Pictures Film Production Asia, Huayi Brothers and the China Film Group, *Big Shot's Funeral* portrays how deeply commercialism has permeated all corners of Chinese society: the funeral of a legendary Hollywood director is turned into a sale by his Chinese colleagues for making big advertising bucks. Feng's popularity lies fundamentally in the absurdity that mirrors real life as exemplified in this black comedy, and the success of his films contributes to the prosperity of *Hesuipian*.

Further reading

Kong, Shuyu (2003). 'Big Shot from Beijing: Feng Xiaogang's *He Sui Pian* and Contemporary Chinese Commercial Film'. *Asian Cinema* 14. 2 (Spring/Summer): 175–87.

Xu, Ying and Xu, Zhongquan (2002). ' A "New" Phenomenon of Chinese Cinema: Happy-New-Year Comic Movie'. *Asian Cinema* (Spring/Summer): 112–27.

QIU PEIPEI

newspapers

Newspapers are a crucial part of contemporary Chinese cultural life, selling hundreds of millions of copies every day. Newspapers have been at the forefront of media change as newspaper journalists have had greater leeway to test the limits set by the Party and the state than their counterparts in television. In the post-Mao reform era, the newspaper market has undergone a massive transformation through the proliferation of new titles, new formats and new styles of reporting.

Although court bulletins and monthly journals can be traced back to at least the eighth century (e.g. *Di Bao*) or even to the Han dynasty (206 BC to AD 220), it was only in the nineteenth century that China's newspaper industry really took off, largely driven by foreign missionaries and businessmen.

Perhaps the most famous of these was *Shen Bao* (a.k.a. *Shanghai Gazette*), launched in 1872. Most titles, despite foreign involvement, were nonetheless published in Chinese and they soon became closely associated with politics, particularly becoming the public voice of political reformers at the end of the century. Following the May Fourth movement of 1919, many politically and socially motivated progressive journals came into circulation throughout China, including those of the Communist Party, founded in 1921, that would later develop into the nationally recognized papers of the People's Republic. During the Mao period Chinese newspapers became one of the main vehicles used by the Communist Party to promulgate policies and deliver political education to the people, and the **People's Daily** became the key to understanding the latest policies and political trends.

The 1980s saw a massive growth in the number of newspaper titles in China, most of them local publications. Between 1979 and 1986 the number grew from 186 to 1,574, a growth rate of nearly 200 new titles per year. By 1989 this had risen further to 1,618 and by 1996 there were 2,235 titles, a twelve-fold increase since 1979. This massive proliferation in newspapers meant that the Party could no longer fully subsidize production as it had in the past, and newspapers found themselves exposed to the commercial pressures of the market for effectively the first time since 1949.

The combined pressures of Party control on the one hand and the market on the other have led newspapers to seek out new and innovative ways of pleasing readers and meeting readership demands for livelier, interesting and socially relevant content. One way to do this has been to launch **evening newspapers and weekend editions** that are more easily able to circumvent Party news. Many newspaper groups have also launched tabloid-style, 'metropolitan', non-Party-organ newspapers that adopt a slightly more sensationalist and populist approach to news production. These newspapers are strongly driven by commercial motives, stretching the limits of Party control as far as possible in order to sell more newspapers in a highly competitive market. Unlike large Party-organ newspapers, tabloids, evening papers and weekend editions generally rely almost entirely on street sales and advertising for their revenue.

Newspaper content is usually more than 80 per cent domestic news, although Chinese readers have a great interest in foreign issues as well. However, apart from major national papers like the *People's Daily*, very few have their own overseas correspondents or stringers and rely principally on news agencies for overseas news. In recent years, many of the leading urban papers have increased the size of their papers with pull-out supplements on entertainment, lifestyle and sports news.

The government divides newspapers into the following categories: (1) national newspapers (such as the *People's Daily*); (2) Party-organ newspapers (see below); (3) specialist professional newspapers; (4) industry newspapers; (5) evening newspapers (e.g. **Yangcheng Evening News**); (6) digest newspapers; (7) interest group newspapers (e.g. for workers, soldiers, youth, women, the elderly and so on); (8) lifestyle papers; and (9) army newspapers.

Although all Chinese newspapers must be owned by state or Party organizations (see **state control of media**), there is an important, though subtle, distinction to be made between Party-organ and non-Party-organ newspapers. Party-organ newspapers are those which come under the direct jurisdiction of Party propaganda committees at whichever is the appropriate level. For instance, the *Nanfang Daily* is the Party organ of the Guangdong Province Party Propaganda Committee (see **Nanfang Weekend**). The *People's Daily* is the organ of the Central Committee of the CCP. A Party-organ newspaper comes under the direct control of the propaganda committee, which is able to take a more forceful part in the daily management and content of the newspaper than it can for non-Party organs. Party organs have a greater obligation to publish political news – such as meetings, leaders' visits, mass campaign mobilization propaganda and so on – while non-Party papers can more easily avoid, or place in less conspicuous positions, such items which are not popular with readers.

However, even non-Party organs cannot avoid strong central directives on major issues such as the events of 1989, **Falun gong** or Tibetan independence, and they cannot publish anything critical of the Party. Newspapers are supervised at the central level by the Ministry of Press and Publications. At the local level their output is usually monitored by local Party propaganda committees. The system of content control depends on self-censorship and post hoc chastisement for breaches of codes and regulations. Such regulations are often vaguely defined which leaves a degree of flexibility in the system. This means that editors can (and do) regularly try to push the understandings of certain codes to publish what they consider more lively copy. However, this flexibility also means that censors have various tools at their disposal – such as accusations of breaching the interests of the Party or national security that can cover a plethora of activities – that enable them to tighten up on media production at critical moments. In this way there is a constant game of give and take going on between more adventurous journalists and Party officials.

Further reading

Latham, K. (2000). 'Nothing but the Truth: News Media, Power and Hegemony in South China.' *China Quarterly* 163: 633–54.

Lee, C.C. (ed.) 1990. *Voices of China; The Interplay of Politics and Journalism*. New York: Guilford Press.

Zhang, X. (1997). 'Zhongguo baoye: jixu zou baotuan zhi lu' [China's Newspaper Industry: Continuing Down the Road of Corporatization]. In J. M. Weng, X. Zhang, Z. Zhang and K. M. Qu (eds). *1996–7 nian Zhongguo fazhan zhuangkuang yü qushi* [China's Development Situation and Trends 1996–7]. Beijing: China Society Publishing House.

Zhao, Y. (1998). *Media, Market, and Democracy in China: Between the Party Line and the Bottom Line*. Chicago: University of Illinois Press.

KEVIN LATHAM

Nie Hualing

b. 1925, Hubei

Writer

Nie Hualing is a renowned Chinese-American woman writer. She was educated in Wuhan and Sichuan. After she graduated from the Department of English Literature of the National Central University in 1948, she went to Taiwan and

became an editor for a semi-monthly, *Freedom China* (*Ziyou Zhongguo*), which was later closed down by Chiang Kai-shek's government. Then she became an associate professor at Taiwan University and Tunghai University. In 1964 she went to the USA. In 1967 together with Paul Engle, an American poet who later became her husband, she founded the International Writing Programme at the University of Iowa. Under this programme several hundred writers from more than seventy countries were invited to Iowa for literary activities. In 1976, 300 writers from all over the world nominated Nie Hualing and Paul Engle for the Nobel Prize for Peace. Twenty-two of her books have been published in different regions and countries, including stories, novellas, novels and essays. *Mulberry and Peach* (*Sangqing yü taohong*) is the most popular. Somewhat experimentally, it depicts a Chinese woman's struggle for her life in mainland China, Taiwan and the United States. Nie Hualing's prizes include an American Book Award and an Award for Distinguished Service to Literature and the Arts by fifty governors of the United States in 1981.

Further reading

Nie, Hualing (1998). *Two Women of China – Mulberry and Peach*. Trans. Jane Parish Yang with Linda Lappin. New York: Feminist Press at the City University of New York.

Yu, Shiao-ling (1993). 'The Themes of Exile and Identity Crisis in Nie Hualing's Fiction'. In Hsin-sheng C. Kao (ed.), *Nativism Overseas: Contemporary Chinese Woman Writers*. Albany: SUNY Press, 127–56.

WANG XIAOLU

night markets

(yeshi)

Night markets mushroomed throughout China in 1980s due to the economic reform. While 'market' had been synonymous with 'capitalist decadence', the new policy unleashed the suppressed business instinct of the Chinese. Pedlars and stall-keepers sprang up everywhere. Local governments organized them in centralized locations, allowing them to open late into the night so that people could enjoy themselves after work. At a time when entertainment options were few, a night market was a big attraction, particularly with the resurfacing of traditional foods that had vanished for more than a decade. Available also were cheap fashions marketed by *daoyer*, a *neologism* for 'greedy resellers'.

Things changed after 2000. Night markets began to close because of economic progress and the ensuing social changes. Air-conditioning was no longer a luxury. Video, CDs, DVDs and cable TV became standard home entertainment. TGI Fridays, Starbucks, KFC and McDonald's were in walking distance. Internet cafés, teahouses, bars, cinemas, concert halls, dance clubs and indigenous Chinese food chains opened late or continuously (see **fast food (Chinese and Western clones)**). The night market as a way of night life has been definitely marginalized by other options, but the idea of the night market is far from dead. It still thrives in such forms as Curio Yeshi in Beijing, Cultural Yeshi in Yichang, and Upholstery Yeshi in Chongqing. Traditional night markets that feature local eateries, moreover, are still alive in historical cities like Kaifeng and tourist spots like Xi'an and Xinjing. The night market off Wangfujing Street in Beijing has become an established tradition. And then there is the night market at Longshan Temple in Taipei!

YUAN HAIWANG

1982 Constitution of the PRC

China's constitutional law framework is based on the 1982 Constitution, as revised in 1993 and 1999. As with all Chinese constitutions, the 1982 document set forth the jurisdictional and organizational principles for organs of government, including the authority of government ministries, the National People's Congress, the Supreme People's Court and Procuracy. The 1982 Constitution was an effort to repudiate fully and finally the **Cultural Revolution** legacies evident in the constitutions of 1973 and 1978. Thus, the 1982 Constitution echoed principles from the 1954

Constitution on such matters as the independence of judicial organs from administrative (but not Party) interference; the authority of the National People's Congress to enact and interpret legislation; and the role of the State Council in setting and carrying out government programmes and policies. While the role of the Communist Party of China (CPC) is scarcely mentioned in the text of the Constitution itself, the references to the Four Basic Principles in the Preamble and in Drafting Committee Chair Peng Zhen's explanatory speech make clear the centrality of CPC leadership over interpretation and implementation of the Constitution. This was made particularly clear in 1989, when an effort to challenge the declaration of martial law on constitutional grounds was rejected as the 'use of law for an unlawful purpose'. The 1982 Constitution has been revised to account for policy changes made by the CPC leadership. The 1993 constitutional revisions specified the importance of the socialist market economy. The 1999 revisions to the Constitution strengthened the role of private property. However, the central leadership role of the Communist Party of China has been retained throughout.

PITMAN POTTER

Ning Ying

b. 1959, Beijing

Filmmaker

Ning Ying is an independent female filmmaker and screenwriter who has become the main representative of 'new realist film' (*xin xianshi zhuyi*) that combines technique with realistic storytelling. Ning Ying entered the Beijing Film Academy in 1978 and is a graduate of the Fifth Generation class of 1982 (see **Fifth Generation (film directors)**). From 1982 to 1986 she studied film in Italy and was Bernardo Bertolucci's assistant director for *The Last Emperor*. After first assisting other directors, she made her debut, a comedy feature called *Somebody Loves Just Me* (*You ren pianpian aishang wo*), in 1990. Ning Ying is best known for her *Beijing* trilogy: *Zhao le* (*For Fun*, 1992), *Minjing gushi* (*On the Beat*, 1995) and *Xiari nuan yangyang* (*I Love Beijing*, 2000). *For Fun* is a piece about retirees trying to set up a Peking opera group; *On the Beat* is a police movie in which policeman Yang is ordered to exterminate all the domesticated dogs and discovers that the social system is the enemy; *I Love Beijing* follows the life and loves of a young taxi driver. Her semi-documentary storytelling, use of mostly amateur actors, and appropriate technique draw a realistic image of the contemporary Beijing of ordinary people. Her combination of social criticism and wit has become a hallmark of Ning Ying's art as a filmmaker, screenwriter and editor and makes her a rather unique 'Fifth Generation' director.

Further reading

White, Jerry (1997). 'The Films of Ning Ying: China Unfolding in Miniature'. *Cineaction* 42.1: 2–9.

BIRGIT LINDER

non-governmental organizations

Non-governmental organizations (NGOs) refer to private, non-profit, self-governing and voluntary organizations. Two broad types of organizations in China fall roughly within this definition, namely, 'social organizations' (*shehui tuanti*) and 'private non-profit work units' (*minban feiqiye danwei*) as defined by the administrative regulations promulgated by China's State Council in 1998. Official statistics in China show that, as of 1999, there were 165,000 social organizations and 700,000 private non-profit work units in urban China. Numerous such organizations exist in rural areas in more or less organized forms, but there are no statistics on their number.

China Development Brief, a non-governmental research institution based in Beijing, published a special report in 2001 with a descriptive list of 250 Chinese NGOs. These encompass sixteen categories: (1) arts and culture; (2) advocacy and services for people with disabilities; (3) broad-based charitable organizations; (4) civil society development; (5) disaster response and relief; (6) ethnic minority culture and development; (7) education: (8) environment and natural resource management; (9) government, law and rights; (10) health; (11) HIV/AIDS; (12) rural development

and poverty alleviation; (13) urban community welfare and services for older people; (14) volunteer placement; (15) welfare of children and young people; and (16) women's rights, welfare and development.

There is no consensus among scholars as to the nature and functions of NGOs in China. Overall, however, NGOs may be distinguished from the traditional 'mass organizations' (*qunzhong tuanti*). While 'mass organizations' function more as the organizational branches of the Party and the government (see **mass movements**), NGOs are relatively more independent both financially and administratively. They are able to pursue their own interests and agendas to a greater extent. As such, NGOs represent a recent phenomenon in China. Their development reflects the need in China for a 'third sector' to deal with issues and problems that the government and the market are unable or unwilling to confront. In response to the rise of NGOs in China, **Qinghua University** set up an NGO Research Centre in October 1998 dedicated to the study of this new phenomenon.

Further reading

Gold, Thomas (1998). 'Bases for Civil Society in Reform China'. In Kjeld Erik Brodsgaard and David Strand (ed.), *Reconstructing Twentieth-Century China: State Control, Civil Society, and National Identity*. Oxford: Clarendon Press.

Saich, Tony (2000). 'Negotiating the State: The Development of Social Organizations in China'. *China Quarterly* 161: 124–41.

Young, Nick (ed.) (2001). *250 NGOs in China: A Report from China Development Briefing*. Beijing: China Development Briefing.

YANG GUOBIN

noodles

The Chinese used to call all wheaten food *bing*, a word exclusively referring to crepes or **pancakes** in modern times. Around 25–220 AD, *zhubing* (boiled bing) and later *tangbing* (soup bing) emerged in central north China. It acquired its current name *mian* in the Tang dynasty (618–917) and started spreading throughout the territory from the mid-fourteenth century. By the Qing dynasty (1644–1911), Beijing's noodle specialty *zhajiangmian* (noodles with fried sesame bean sauce), Yangzhou's *qundaimian* (petticoat noodles), known for its generous soup, and Fujian's *bazhenmian* (eight-treasure noodles) – famous for its multiple flavours – had already gained national reputation.

Originally, noodles were pancake-shaped. Not until the Song dynasty (960–1279) were they judged aesthetically by their length and diameter. The current Guinness record is held by Li Enhai and Li Entao, father and son. The noodles they pulled out of a kilogram of dough, if connected, would have stretched 300,000 metres. This is the famous *shoulamian* (stretched noodles). There are numerous other types of noodles known for their diverse flavours instead of length: to name a few, *dalumian* (noodles with gravy), *chaomian* (stir-fried noodles), *rousimian* (sliced-meat noodles), *niuroumian* (beef noodles), *yangchunmian* (noodles with clear savoury soup) and *chaoxianlengmian* (Korean cold noodles). Each region has its renowned specialties. While Sichuan takes pride in its spicy noodles (*dandanmian*), Shanxi boasts its noodles chopped from dough held above the chef's head and directed into a boiling pot by the knife's momentum (*daoxiaomian*).

Added to the list should be *fangbianmian* (convenient noodles), an **instant food** quickly gaining popularity in the land of noodles.

YUAN HAIWANG

Northern Art Group

(Beifang yishu qunti)

Artist group

The foremost exponents of the 'rational' (*lixing*) trend in the **85 New Wave [Art] Movement**. Influenced by German philosophy, particularly Hegel, Kant and Nietzsche, these artists sought utopian values that transcended the sentimental humanism popular at the time. Their art was an attempt to raise new ideals following the disillusionment of the **Cultural Revolution**. As such, they were less concerned with the values of

art itself than with problems of culture and human existence. The name Northern Art Group derived from their belief that Eastern and Western cultures were in the process of disintegrating and yielding to a new rational, sublime and healthy cultural power – that of 'Northern civilization' (*Beifang wenming*). Their ideas were elaborated in numerous articles, of which 'The Spirit of the "Northern Art Group"' is considered their manifesto.

The group was established in Heilongjiang in 1984 by fifteen youths, including **Wang Guangyi**, Shu Qun, Ren Jian and Liu Yan. They began by publishing art works and articles, and in September 1985 held a conference in Harbin to review 'Northern art' and assess its prospects. Their first exhibition, 'Beifang yishu qunti shuangnianzhan' (Northern Art Group Biennial), followed only in February 1987 (Changchun). Their paintings were characterized by a cold and solemn atmosphere, tinged with religious overtones, from which human beings are generally absent unless in highly abstract form. Prominent examples are the works of Wang Guangyi, Shu Qun's series *Absolute Principle* (*Juedui yuanze*, 1985) and Ren Jian's *Primeval Chaos* (*Yuanhua*, 1987).

Further reading

Andrews, Julia F. and Gao, Minglu (1995). 'The Avant-Garde's Challenge to Official Art'. In Debora S. Davis (ed.), *Urban Spaces in Contemporary China: The Potential for Autonomy and Community in Post-Mao China*. Cambridge: Harvard University Press, 221–78

Lü, Peng and Yi, Dan (1992). *Zhongguo xiandai yishushi* [A History of Modern Art in China]. Changsha: Hunan meishu chubanshe, 157–72.

Shu, Qun (1985). '"Beifang yishu qunti" de jingshen' [The Spirit of the 'Northern Art Group'] *Zhongguo meishubao* 18.

EDUARDO WELSH

nouveaux riches

Under Mao, people were poorer but more equal and less insecure economically. China now ranks among those countries with extreme inequality of wealth. The international income disparity Gini index of Chinese people's income has soared from 0.33 in 1980 through the threshold 0.4 in 1994 to over 0.45 in 2002 (*China Daily*, 13 May 2002, p. 4). According to a government survey in 2000, some directors in Sichuan's state-owned enterprises earned up to 200 times more than their workers. Successful capitalists in south-eastern areas are definitely rich. But how rich is rich? A **shunkouliu** (doggerel) says:

Wanyuanhu bu suan fu,
Shi-wan-yuan gang qibu,
Bai-wan-yuan hai mahu,
Qian-wan-yuan cai suan fu.

With ten thousand yuan, you're not rich;
With a hundred thousand yuan, you're a starter;
With a million yuan, you're only so so;
With ten million yuan, you're rich.

By that unofficial definition, the total number of the nouveaux riches, who are private entrepreneurs and government officials, may be tens of million of people. 'To get rich is glorious' (*zhifu guangrong*), a saying attributed to Deng Xiaoping, is everyone's dream. The policy 'To let some people get rich first' (*Rang yibufen ren xian fuqilai*) and the get-rich-quick mentality have brought with them serious **corruption**. Another *shunkouliu* exposes the wealth–power exchange methods of the nouveaux riches:

Yong wo shouzhong de qian,
Qu mai Gongchandang de quan,
Zai yong Gongchandang de quan,
Wei wo zhuan gengduo de qian.

Using the money in my hands,
I go to buy the Communist Party's power;
I then use the power from the Communist Party,
To make more money for myself.

HELEN XIAOYAN WU

nüqiangren, chiruanfan

(career women, kept husbands)

In contemporary China, there has been a move towards granting women greater independence and status, so that they are no longer entirely reliant upon men for their position in society or for financial security. Women, indeed, are to be found employed in virtually every trade and profession, from factory and construction workers to politics, local and national government, business, the armed forces and the police. The phrase *nüqiangren* (strong women, career women) has been coined to describe those women who have achieved success in the traditionally male-dominated professions such as politics, business, science and technology. The Vice Premier Minister Ms Wu Yi is highly respected in China as a proud representative of the modern class of *nüqiangren*. *Chiruanfan* (eater of soft rice), on the other hand, is a phrase used with contempt to describe 'kept husbands' – often men who are simply in a lower position, or who earn a lower salary than their wives. The general contempt in which such men are regarded has itself created a new kind of social problem in China. Women with high degrees, successful careers or well-paying jobs can often find it difficult to find a husband, especially in big cities, because a prospective husband knows that he will be held in contempt by others because his status or position would be comparatively lower than that of such a wife. In lists of the kind of woman to avoid when seeking a marriage partner, therefore, the *nüqiangren* often comes out at the top.

LILY CHEN

Olympics

There may be no better window on the complexity of China's postmodern era (*houxin shiqi*) than that offered by its two successive bids (1993 and 2001) to host the International Olympic Games. Long before the international media frenzy and national celebratory commotion generated in 2002 by the signing of Yao Ming to a National Basketball Association contract with the Houston Rockets, most Chinese were well aware that sport, while a significant reflection of national character, is a business, the globalization of which in the 1990s drew China into a popular cultural media that transcends the nation-state. The Olympics bids were advanced in a decade of new-found as well as government-sponsored nationalism, a great deal of which was fostered through the symbolic abduction of the United States as national enemy; it was the era of China's long march to post-Tiananmen respect as Hong Kong and Macao were both 'returned to the motherland', and as China applied for admission to the World Trade Organization (WTO), lobbied for most favoured nation (MFN) status and permanent normal trade relations (PNTR) with the United States, and sought to stage the first Olympics of the second millennium.

The CCP recovery strategy depended upon world recognition of China's legitimacy in each of these three areas as it went all out to recover the international respect China had lost in the internationally televised slaughter of innocent citizens. The domestic ideological thrust of the Jiang Zemin regime was **socialist spiritual civilization**, a critical feature of which was **nationalism**

(*aiguo zhuyi*). As Zhang Xudong observed, 'for this occasion, which combined sports and politics, economics, and aspirations for recognition, nationalism found its most popular channel of expression in the 1990s'.

Nationalism and recognition were integral to both of these bids and, although certain members of the International Olympic Committee (IOC) were concerned that there was danger in giving the 2000 games to Beijing, they did not, and the United States did not, comprehend the volume of popular support for the government's campaign. In the wake of the success of Beijing's hosting of the Eleventh Asian Games in 1990 and the reassertion by Deng in 1992 of the correctness of 'socialism with Chinese characteristics', China aggressively bid to host the 2000 games. The nation was captivated by the effort, because throughout the 1990s national pride was implicated in all of China's international relations but none more intensively than in its effort to be selected the host city of the summer Olympic games. The government's domestic and international lobbying for the games resembled state-choreographed jingoism, with **CCTV (Chinese Central Television)** televising rallies of thousands of enthusiasts at the Temple of Heaven and as many as 50,000 supporters bussed to the Great Wall. (The orchestration of these nationalistic performances would later be regarded as a warm-up for the staged protests in May 1999 at the US Embassy in Beijing, in which students were bussed in from their campuses on the outskirts of the city to fulminate against US imperialism and the bombing of the Chinese Embassy in Belgrade.)

Under the official banner, 'A More Open China Awaits the 2000 Olympics', the sprint up to the final vote in Monte Carlo was fierce, as the Olympic bid committee, led by Zhang Baifa, Vice-Mayor of Beijing, executed strategic political moves such as the loan of terracotta warriors from the tomb of Qin Shihuangdi to the Olympic Museum in Lausanne and the nomination of Juan Antonio Samaranch, the IOC President, for the 1993 Nobel Peace Prize, in an attempt to pull away from the other finalists (Berlin, Istanbul, Manchester and Sydney). Arguments in favour of China's bid ranged from the nativist culturalism of the antiquity of Chinese civilization, to the demographic immensity of its 1.2 billion population, to the gigantism of its economic growth. Political positioning by competing site countries, long a feature of IOC culture, was quite energetic as the US House of Representatives and the European Parliament in Strasbourg passed resolutions decrying China's deplorable human rights record and urging the IOC to reject that nation's bid.

By most accounts, the politicking in 1993 for the 2000 games was more intense than usual, with wild claims of corruption in the IOC (most of these later confirmed when the international Olympic scandal was revealed in 1999) and anecdotal stories of the Chinese government's offer to pay for all costs of the participating nations including roundtrip transit to Beijing. Then, quite unexpectedly, on 14 September 1993, Wei Jingsheng, the former electrician of the Beijing Zoo and renowned democracy advocate imprisoned in 1979, was set free. Also released were two prominent democracy activists, Zhai Wenmin and Wu Xuecan, both jailed since 1989 for their involvement in the Tiananmen protests – a dramatic yet risky sign of humanitarian goodwill intended to influence the deliberations of the IOC just over a week before their announcement.

In the end, all argument and effort and even threat – Zhang Baifa commented on Australian television that 'they've passed a resolution objecting to our Olympic bid; on the other hand, we could boycott the US in the 1996 Olympic Games in Atlanta' – was to no avail as Sydney was selected over Beijing by two votes (45 to 43). In October, **Tiananmen Square** was overrun by college students, amassed to lend their voices in support of the government's failed bid. In the eyes of the diverse domestic constituencies favouring China's hosting of the games, the United States and Britain were the parties responsible for the defeat, preventing China from receiving what it considered a much-deserved international respect for its economic achievements. Indeed, quite a number of the nation's students and young intellectuals, most notably Zhang Xiaobo and Song Qiang, were especially provoked to a maniacal xenophobia by this event, as they revealed in their 1996 anti-Western diatribes, *Zhongguo keyi shuo bu* [China Can Say No] and *Zhongguo haineng shuo bu* [China Can Still Say No], charging the United States in particular with engineering the rejection of China's bid and blocking its entrance into the WTO.

This same conflictual confluence of native pride and international turmoil was visible in China's 2001 follow-up bid for the 2008 Olympics, which, considering the closeness of the 1993 vote and the greater distance in time from the Tiananmen Massacre, made China the 'front runner' in the race against its competitors Istanbul, Osaka, Paris and Toronto. But China's strategic advantage was undermined by its domestic political complexity: rivalrous factionalism, profound urban/rural tensions, division between centre and regions, and a general crisis of popular faith in the government – a consequence of the recession of the state and its ideology, the growing space between rich and poor, unbridled **corruption** (local, regional, and national), the lack of effective channels for legal redress of grievances, the slowing growth of the national economy, and rising unemployment. Yet in this instance national pride trumped the play of these many contentious issues, especially because most Chinese perceived opposition to their attainment of proper international recognition. Consider this denial of recognition in light of centuries of Chinese humiliation at the hands of Western powers, and one will appreciate the febrile intensity with which many citizens of China awaited the IOC announcement.

Thus, most Chinese reacted enthusiastically to the official announcement on 13 July 2001 that Beijing received 56 votes and had been selected to host the 2008 summer games. It represented perhaps the most important in a series of events in which China's pride as a nation on a par with the other prominent nations of the world had been incontrovertibly established: the ceding of Hong Kong (1997) and Macao (1999), the spring 2000 United States Congress vote granting permanent normal trade relations to China, the imminent admission of China into the World Trade Organization, and ultimately the selection of Beijing as the site for the 2008 summer Olympics. As a Beijing university teacher put it in the first moments following the IOC's decision, 'The world has recognized us'.

Nonetheless, in the spring and summer of 2001, there was considerable reason to reject Beijing's bid, optimistically shrouded in the motto 'New Beijing: Great Olympics', in favour of Paris, which had finished ahead of it in the preliminary review. In February of that year, at about the same time that the IOC's site selection committee was conducting its final review of Beijing, the Chinese government detained six academics and business-people, native Chinese who were either citizens or residents of the United States, on charges of espionage. One of them, Li Shaomin, was arrested on 25 February in Shenzhen but was not seen again until he appeared before Beijing's Number 1 Intermediate People's Court on charges of espionage twelve hours after the IOC decision had been made. He was immediately convicted and deported. Another, Gao Zhan, a Chinese sociologist and a permanent legal resident of the United States, was also detained in February, but not permitted to see a lawyer until 12 July, just over twenty-four hours before the IOC vote.

There were other more striking human rights concerns, all brought to the forefront by domestic and foreign critics of the Beijing bid. In the first six months of 2001, the Chinese government executed nearly 1,800 people and sentenced another 2,690 to death under the aegis of another of its reiterative 'Hard Strike Campaigns' (*yanda yundong*) against criminals convicted of murder, robbery, drug offences (drug dealing and distribution as well as drug use), corruption and violent crime. In late June 2001, twenty-five such unfortunates were executed in Kunming in Yunnan Provincial Stadium, while at least a dozen were killed for similar crimes in Guangzhou on 9 July. Again, within mere weeks of the announcement of the IOC's decision, fourteen members of the **Falun gong**

spiritualist movement died while incarcerated in a state labour camp. Critics further alleged, as they had in 1993, that of all the finalists, China least exemplified the defining charter of the international Olympic movement of the democratic honouring of diversity and brotherhood in sport. In international competitions in the late 1990s, a great number of Chinese athletes were found in flagrant violation of amateur athletics rules, particularly the use of performance-enhancing drugs. In fact, in a surprise announcement just days before the opening of the 2000 games in Sydney, forty athletes and officials were dismissed from the Chinese national team (including all but one of the fabled world-record-setting runners trained by Ma Junren), after testing positive for erthyropoietin (EPO), a banned substance capable of accelerating the production of red blood cells.

Most, if not all, of these issues were raised in the world media, as well as vociferously protested by Tibetans in Moscow for the IOC vote, as well as other groups in Hong Kong and the United States. Moreover, some IOC members and a few journalists cited the negative example of South Africa in support of rejecting the Chinese bid for the 2008 games. When South Africa made a bid to host the games in the 1980s, the IOC insisted that it could not be considered as long as apartheid was a foundation of the state. China, these critics pointed out, was an authoritarian state that practised human slavery as well, though certainly not on the order or in the manner of 1980s South Africa. What was good for South Africa, a rogue nation, was good for China, another rogue nation.

George Orwell once wrote in a savage critique of socialism that 'some brothers are more equal than others'. Herein lies the difference between the South African and the Chinese bids. International commerce is the foundation of this inequality: many foreign corporations (US and European) were divesting their holdings in South Africa at the time of that nation's bid, while today such corporations are investing in China with legendary largesse. Corporate Olympic sponsors certainly must savour the prospect of an even deeper exploration of a market with which they have become familiar in the ten years since the last IOC consideration of Beijing's eligibility. And the Olympics and the multinational committee that governs it, as the world learned in 1999–2000 IOC bribery scandals, are about money, both legal and illegal.

A cynical gloss of the IOC decision and of the Chinese bid may be read in this way. The hopeful reading has it that the hosting of the Olympic Games permits the International Olympic Committee and the Chinese Communist Party to reform themselves in spectacular, very public ways that may very well precipitate even greater fundamental changes. To be sure, China and the IOC stand to gain much international respect from a successful hosting of the Olympics and it is possible that neither is quite aware of what their pursuit of this objective will demand of them. What is certain is that both have been tarnished by corruption, and the practices of both have fallen demonstrably short of their foundational ideals. When the IOC proclaimed that the 'Olympic Games in Beijing would leave China and sport a unique legacy', it was commenting allusively on the mutual entailment of its and China's political fates, something confirmed by IOC Vice-President Dick Pound when he opined that:

> human rights problems remain an issue but it is more of a challenge and an opportunity for the Olympic movement to make a contribution to some of its own goals – which is to put sport at the service of mankind everywhere and maybe bring about some change.
>
> (Reuters 2001)

Also, China is the third of the East Asian nations to be honoured by selection of a capital city to host the Olympics. Japan (Tokyo) hosted them in 1964 and South Korea (Seoul) in 1988. Both of these selections came in critical phases in the domestic political and economic development of these countries. Japan and South Korea laboured assiduously to display their astonishing domestic accomplishments before the world and in the years following the Olympics even more was obtained: in 1968 Japan became the third largest industrialized nation and in 1993 South Korea had become a democracy. Juan Antonio Samaranch, among others, was cannily aware of such parallels and, citing South Korea's present vigorous multiparty democracy, said, 'There is a unanimous feeling in international politics that the

change in the country [Korea] came through the 1988 Olympics. Maybe it [China] would undergo a similar development as South Korea by winning the Olympics' (Reuters 2001). This is no small matter, particularly because China's political and economic history since the Tiananmen Massacre has very closely resembled that of South Korea from 1972 to 1987, and it is increasingly evident that the Chinese state is modelling itself after Japan.

Mindful of the challenges China faces, challenges that are unlikely to be resolved but made more prominent, the government casts its cash ($23 billion) like the feverish roll of dice towards the transformation of virtually every aspect of Beijing's urban infrastructure, so that national pride in the achievements of socialism with Chinese characteristics may be brilliantly displayed on the international stage. It is inevitable that China will continue to be affected by the more complete integration into the world represented by the Olympics; however, the costs of it 'joining the world on the cosmopolitan tide', of resolving the exigencies of nation and world may well be more prohibitive than either Party or people can fathom.

See also: posters and education; World Trade Organization (WTO) debate

Further reading

Barmé, Geremie R. (1999). *In the Red: On Contemporary Chinese Culture*. New York: Columbia University Press.

Brownell, Susan (1995) *Training the Body for China: Sports in the Moral Order of the People's Republic*. Chicago: University of Chicago Press.

——(2001). 'Making Dream Bodies in Beijing: Athletes, Fashion Models, and Urban Mystique in China'. In Nancy N. Chen, Constance D. Clark, Suzanne Z. Gottschang and Lyn Jeffery (eds), *China Urban: Ethnographies of Contemporary Culture*. Durham, NC: Duke University Press, 123–42.

Reuters (2001) *Beijing Wins Olympics for China*. Available at http://www.rediff.com/sports/2001/jul/13oly1.htm

Tong, Lam (2000). 'Identity and Diversity: The Complexities and Contradictions of Chinese Nationalism'. In Timothy B. Weston and Lionel M. Jensen (eds), *China Beyond the Headlines*. Lanham, MD: Rowman and Littlefield, 147–70.

Zhang, Xudong (2001). 'The Making of the Post-Tiananmen Intellectual Field: A Critical Overview'. In Zhang Xudong (ed.), *Whither China? Intellectual Politics in Contemporary China*. Durham, NC: Duke University Press, 1–75.

LIONEL M. JENSEN

one-child policy

The government formally introduced the policy in 1980 in order to reduce population growth and has pushed it vigorously since then. With slight modifications, the policy remains in force as the twenty-first century dawns. The censuses of 1982, 1990 and 2000 showed the PRC population in millions respectively at: 1,008.2, 1,133.7 and 1,265.8. The two last figures represent average annual growth rates since the preceding census of 1.56 and 1.13 per cent. The census number of those aged fourteen and under fell from 312.9 million in 1990 to 289.8 million in 2000. The policy has thus had the desired effect of reducing population growth.

It has also had unwanted and highly negative side effects, the main one being population imbalance. The 2000 census preliminary results showed a sex ratio of 117 males for every 100 females. This was a very big rise since 1990, when the census had a sex ratio of 106.6. Selective abortion and infanticide of females are clearly very significant problems.

The minority nationalities are exempt from the one-child policy. In general, the nearer an ethnic minority is to sensitive borders and the more remote from the eastern seaboard, the more relaxed is the family planning policy. However, the local governments of autonomous regions have almost all imposed restrictions on the number of children couples may have.

Further reading

Croll, Elisabeth, Davin, Delia and Kane, Penny (eds) (1985). *China's One-Child Family Policy*. New York: St Martin's Press.

Peng, X. with Guo, Z. (eds) (2000). *The Changing Population of China*. Oxford, UK and Malden, USA: Blackwell.

COLIN MACKERRAS

one country, two systems

(yiguo, liangzhi)

Political policy

Since the PRC was established, it has sought to unify China by extending its sovereignty over Taiwan and other islands governed by the Republic of China (ROC). To allay anxieties that unification would subject Taiwan to rule imposed by the CCP-led government of the mainland, the PRC proposed that after Taiwan is united with the 'motherland' as one country (*yi guo*), two systems (*liang zhio*) of governance and economics would coexist: the PRC's and Taiwan's. The PRC professes no interest in determining how Taiwan is administered after unification so long as it and other islands governed by the ROC do not exist as a separate state. The PRC's 'one China' principle asserts that there is only one Chinese state, that Taiwan is a part of it, and that the sole legal government of China is that of the PRC.

By 1949, the CCP had wrested control of the mainland territories of China from the ROC government after years of civil war. The ROC leadership took refuge on Taiwan where it claimed to be the legitimate government of China, denounced the PRC as illegitimate, and vowed to unify China. Until 1979, the United States recognized the ROC claims. Then, the USA established diplomatic relations with the PRC, severing official and military ties to the ROC that had deterred the PRC from attacking Taiwan. In 1981, following this transition, the PRC expected the ROC to be sufficiently vulnerable that it would agree to negotiate about unification. Ye Jianying announced that the PRC would grant Taiwan a 'high degree of autonomy', permit it to maintain its own armed forces and regulate its 'local affairs' while maintaining its socio-economic system, as well as 'economic and cultural relations with foreign countries' (Ye 1981). This formula, which Deng Xiaoping characterized in 1982 as 'one country, two systems', was adapted by the PRC when it asserted control over Hong Kong in 1997 and Macao in 1999. The PRC has reiterated this formula repeatedly in efforts to entice Taiwan's population to unify.

The ROC has not been willing to renounce all claims of sovereignty. In 1991, the ROC acknowledged it was no longer the government of China. By that time, the authoritarianism of the ROC had given way to democracy, and there was no popular will to compete with the PRC for sovereignty over the mainland. The ROC also affirmed that the PRC legitimately governs the mainland, but insisted the ROC retains sovereignty over Taiwan. Although it has not officially forsaken the goal of unification, the ROC has rejected the 'one country, two systems' approach because it is unwilling to be subsumed by the PRC. Taiwan's populace is divided. Some seek unification, most are sceptical about the merits of the 'one country, two systems' formula, and some advocate that Taiwan, not the ROC, be designated a sovereign state forever autonomous of China.

Further reading

Ye, Jianying (30 September 1981). *Taiwan's Return to Motherland and Peaceful Reunification.* Available at http://www.china.org.cn/english/7945.htm
http://taiwansecurity.org [a compendium of official documents, press coverage and analysis of relations between the PRC and ROC].

ALAN M. WACHMAN

Operators, The

[Wanzhu, 1988]

Film

The Operators, an Emei Film Studio release, is one of several films from the late 1980s based on **Wang Shuo**'s fiction. The screenplay is by Wang and director Mi Jiashan. The title is also translated as *The Trouble-Shooters.* Disaffected 'operators'

Yu Guan (played by Zhang Guoli), Yang Zhong (**Ge You**) and Ma Qing (Liang Tian) run the 'Three T Company' (three substitutes company), which takes on its clients' worries, troubles and responsibilities. They keep a doctor's date with his girlfriend, take abuse meant for a woman's husband, and assume a man's filial duty to his elderly mother. A failed writer named Bao Kang (Li Geng) hires them to give him an award. The awards ceremony includes a fashion show during which workers, peasants, KMT and CCP soldiers, Peking Opera characters, capitalists, Red Guards and female body-builders meet on the runway, eye one another warily and then dance together in reconciliation. This playfulness turns wistful as Bao Kang sues the company; a professor of ethics denounces Yu Guan and his partners on television; the old woman in their care jumps to her death from a hospital window; and Yu Guan's father and girlfriend push him to change his ways. The film's irreverent satire skewers the pieties of the revolutionary generation and the hypocrisy of intellectuals. The last shot is of a line outside the Three T offices. In a time of collapsing ideologies, when nothing is real and everything is for sale, there is demand for the company's services.

THOMAS MORAN

Ouyang Zi

(née Hong Zhihui)

b. 1939, Hiroshima, Japan

Writer

Born in Japan, Ouyang Zi moved (back) to Taiwan with her family after World War II and began writing in 1957 when she went to study English at the National Taiwan University. She and her classmates **Bai Xianyong**, **Wang Wenxing** and Chen Ruoxi together founded *Modern Literature,* a literary bimonthly, where she published a series of critical essays and short stories under her pen name. In 1962, she went to study at the University of Iowa and later at the University of Illinois. After obtaining her MA in 1964, she moved to reside with her husband in Austin, Texas.

Ouyang Zi is both a literary critic and a writer. Well known among her critical works is *Swallows before the Houses of Wang and Xie* (*Wang Xie tangqian de yanzi*), where she closely analyses the short stories in Bai Xianyong's *Tales of Taipei Characters* (*Taibei ren*) in psychoanalytical and New Critical terms. As a writer, she wrote her first collection of short stories, *The Girl with the Long Hair* (*Na changtoufa de nuhai*), in 1967. In 1971, another collection, *Autumn Leaves* (*Qiuye*), was published. Much influenced by the New Criticism, she pays special attention to the images, symbols and structures of her writings. Keen on examining human nature and dissecting human psychology, Ouyang Zi is good at portraying characters' emotional vicissitudes and at analysing their psychology.

Further reading

Ouyang, Zi (1975). 'Vase' and 'Perfect Mother'. Trans. Chu Limin. In Chi Pang-yuan, John J. Deeney, Ho Hsin, Wu Hsi Chen and Yü Kwang Chung (ed.), *An Anthology of Contemporary Chinese Literature*, vol. 2. Taipei: National Institute for Compilation and Translation, 345–56 and 357–74.

FU HONGCHU

P

Pan Hong

b. 1954, Shanghai

Actress

Pan Hong is a popular film and television actress who reached the peak of her popularity in the mid 1980s. After graduating from the Shanghai Institute of Performing Arts in 1976, Pan Hong entered the Shanghai Film Studio as an actress before moving to the Emei Film Studio in 1980. Her early films include *Bitter Laughter* (*Kunaoren de xiao*), *Du Shiniang* and *Cold Night* (*Hanye*). She delivered powerhouse performances in *At Middle Age* (*Ren dao zhongnian*) and *The Well* (*Jing*), which won her Best Actress honours at the 1983 and 1988 Golden Rooster Awards, respectively. An actress of great talent and versatility, Pan Hong is able to handle such diverse parts as the lead role of Empress Wanrong – opposite **Jiang Wen**'s Puyi – in *The Last Empress* (*Modai huanghou*, 1987) and the psychological complexities of a woman tortured by her own untold secrets in **Xie Jin**'s adaptation of a **Bai Xianyong** short story, *The Last Aristocrats* (*Zuihou de guizu*, 1989), which was also among the first PRC films ever shot entirely on location abroad.

In the 1990s Pan Hong starred in several television mini-series, such as *Qianqiu jiaguo meng*, and while she remained active in film, turned increasingly towards comedic vehicles. She acted opposite Hong Kong action star Liu Qingyun in the satiric comedy *Shanghai Fever* (*Gu feng*, 1993), which offered a new take on the economic boom of the 1990s. Her performance as a woman with a knack for numbers earned Pan Hong dual Best Actress honours at both the Golden Rooster and Hundred Flowers Awards. The success of *Shanghai Fever* inspired Zhang Min's hit comedy, *Stocks, Oh, Stocks!* (*Gu a gu*, 2002), which also featured Pan Hong in the lead role.

MICHAEL BERRY

Pan Jinlian (1985)

Xiqu (sung-drama/opera)

Pan Jinlian, a **Chuanju** (Sichuan opera) by **Wei Minglun**, is a reworking of the story about this most notorious immoral woman in Chinese literature. Wei Minglun transforms Pan from an adulteress and murderer in classical fiction to a victim of male-dominated society. Her search for happiness pits her against traditional morality and seals her tragic fate. The opera also calls attention to the conditions of Chinese women in contemporary society through a re-examination of Pan Jinlian's case. In the final trial scene, Pan is condemned to die despite the intervention of a sympathetic woman judge of the People's Court. The implication of this ending is clear: the lot of Chinese women has not improved much since Pan Jinlian's time.

In additions to its exploration of women's conditions, *Pan Jinlian* breaks new ground in technical innovation. Action leaps across time and cultural barriers; characters include personages drawn from history, contemporary society and literary works.

The author uses these 'characters outside the play' as commentators on the dramatic action, and by looking at this old story from different perspectives, Wei casts it in a new light and invests it with new meanings. Wei calls his play 'theatre of the absurd' because of its disregard for temporal and spatial boundaries. However, this 'absurdist' Sichuan opera is not an expression of existential philosophy; rather, it seeks to demonstrate the close relationship between the individual and society. Its sensitive political content and 'absurd' form have made *Pan Jinlian* very controversial in China since it was first performed in 1985.

Further reading

Braester, Yomi (2003). 'Rewriting Tradition, Misreading History: Twentieth-Century (Sub)versions of Pan Jinlian's Story'. In *idem*, *Witness Against History: Literature, Film, and Public Discourse in Twentieth-Century China*. Stanford: Stanford University Press, 56–80.

Wei, Minglun (1996). 'Pan Jinlian: The Story of One Woman and Four Men (An Absurdist Sichuan Opera)'. In Yu Shiao-ling (ed.), *Chinese Drama after the Cultural Revolution, 1979–1989*. Lewiston: Edwin Mellen Press, 97–158.

—— (1999). 'I Am Dreaming a Very Absurd Dream: Thoughts on *Pan Jinlian*'. In Faye Chunfang Fei (ed. and trans.), *Chinese Theories of Theater and Performance from Confucius to the Present*. Ann Arbor: University of Michigan Press, ch. 11.

YU SHIAO-LING

Pan Ying

b. 1962, Beijing

Artist

An ethnic Manchu, Pan Ying graduated from the Art Institute of the People's Liberation Army (1983), specializing in traditional Chinese painting. She is now on the staff at the Fine Arts Department of the **Central University for Nationalities** in Beijing.

In her most mature works Pan repaints with the traditional *gongbi* technique strips and ribbons of white material arranged in endless monochrome combinations that spiral and intersect on the surface of the painting. Using a traditionally high artistic idiom, therefore, Pan Ying provides a cooler description of practices generally classified as belonging to 'handicrafts' and thus disregarded as 'low'. Still the representation of what for centuries was classified as menial is replayed with elegant minimalist effects, reminiscent of drawing and etching that bestow the coiling movement of the thread with an abstract formal beauty. Pan Ying has participated in many exhibitions both nationally and internationally, including: 'Century – Woman' in Beijing (1998); 'Die Hälfte des Himmels' (Half of the Sky) at the Frauenmuseum in Bonn (1998); and 'On This Side of the Sky: UNESCO Salutes Women' in Art in Paris (2003).

Further reading

(1997). *Between Ego and Society: Exhibition of Contemporary Women Artists of China* (exhibition pamphlet). Chicago: Artemisia Gallery.

(1998). *Century Woman* (exhibition catalogue). Hong Kong: Shijie huaren yishu chubanshe.

Dal Lago, Francesca (1999). 'A Silent Revolution? Century – Woman, China Art Gallery, Beijing' (exhibition review). *ART AsiaPacific* 22 (January).

Dewar, Susan (1996). 'Beijing Report' (review of 'China Exposition '95'). *ART AsiaPacific* 3.1: 101–2.

FRANCESCA DAL LAGO

pancakes

Chinese make wheaten food by steaming, boiling and baking. Varieties are in the thousands. Originally, the term *bing* referred to all of them, but now exclusively to crepes and pancakes. Lots of Chinese pancakes have their cultural references. *Zhima shaobing* (sesame cake), first introduced from Central Asia during the Tang dynasty, frequents breakfast tables in Beijing, Tianjin and Xi'an. *Tuotuomu*, a namesake of the Arabic *turml'* (food), constitutes the famed *yangrou paomu* (bing crumps in mutton soup), another Xi'an specialty. The well-known *laopobing* (wife's cake) was said to originate from a baker's wife. The *Shangdong jianbing*, a crisp crepe served with scallion, was allegedly the creation of a pretty girl trying to save her poor love despised by her snobbish stepmother. Confining the lad to a study, the stepmother provided him with nothing but stationery, as he had modestly requested, hoping that starvation would make him quit. But instead she found him well sustained by the girl's crepes and scallions passing for paper and pen. Behind *yuebing* (moon cake), a food for the **Mid-Autumn Festival**, was a lass ascending to the moon. *Yuebing* is a big business in China and in other Asian countries, including Taiwan and Hong Kong, with the Guangdong style the most popular. *Laobing*, a cake baked on a thick iron pan called cheng, served with fried egg, is a favourite *jiachangcai* (see **home cooking**) in north China. *Congyoubing* (cake baked with scallion and lard) proves even more appealing. A few more bing samples are Jiangsu's *huangqiao shaobing*, Shanghai's *xiekehuang* and Tianjin's *jianbing guozi*.

See also: noodles

YUAN HAIWANG

parent–child relationships

Traditionally, fathers have believed that their role, as a counterpoint to the role of mothers was decidedly not to encourage or tolerate emotional indulgence and promote dependency. They assumed instead the role of stern disciplinarian (Fei 1939; Ho 1987). Chinese fathers were not, however, without compassion or love for their children. Most Chinese fathers, in fact, felt a warm deep sentiment towards their children, though the articulation of that sentiment was restrained by their traditional parenting role and its expectations (Solomon 1971). In some cases, a father supplied strict discipline as a complement to a mother's overindulgence (Solomon 1971). It was a posture that occasionally produced resentment and acute anxiety for the child later in life (Solomon 1971: 39–61). It was assumed as well that the sexual

division in parenting roles contributed to producing a more responsible and ethical person overall.

The sex-linked parenting roles, moreover, were sustained by the different roles men and women occupied within the social structure. On the one hand, by controlling the distribution of the family inheritance, a father could effect his own special, if not psychological, dependency on the part of the child. On the other, a mother's parenting style was seen to derive as much from her being considered an 'outsider' as from the 'natural' attachment fostered by childbirth and early child care: given her reduced importance and status in her husband's family, the mother needed both a friend and an ally (Wolf 1972). In this way, the different access to, and use of, economic and psychological 'resources' contributed to the establishment and elaboration of the two complementary parenting styles: the father as disciplinary provider, the mother as intimate nurturer.

The 'traditional' Chinese conception of the parenting process assumes that, within the domestic sphere, men perform an instrumental or competence-directed role, whereas women perform the more expressive or empathetic role. The typology is an accurate representation of how the Chinese peasant views parent–child relations. It is also strikingly similar to the parenting style found in Taiwan (Ho 1987). However, in contemporary China, the emergence of a new urban infrastructure has fostered a supportive environment for the expression of warmer sentiments and closer interaction between father and child. This new attitude is now readily found in casual conversation and reflective comments, and stresses the importance of intimate father–child interaction. As such, it challenges the traditional father–child role, a role and style of interaction that had been seen already by fathers of the previous generation as no longer satisfying or necessary. Although urban Chinese continue to publicly value sons over daughters, I have found that parents are also very happy with the birth of daughters. In fact, even in those families that unreservedly wished for a son, parents rapidly adjust and come to value their daughter. Sons, moreover, are increasingly regarded as unreliable in fulfilling family obligations. They are seen as easily lost to their wife and her family, while daughters are thought of as more considerate and faithful in continuing to visit their natal home. Sons, therefore, are now viewed as less of an asset than before.

Chinese have a clear sense of gender-specific duties. This sense is patterned by the setting, timing and manner of parental interaction with the child. A child's age and sex affects the frequency and style of parental interaction. There are several developmental stages of parent–child interaction: early infancy, late infancy (*ying'er*), and early childhood (*er'tong*). During the infant stages the mother is the more involved parent, whereas the father becomes more involved when the child reaches the childhood stage (three to six years old). This is especially so if the father is highly educated.

There are also gender differences in parent–child caretaking styles. For example, women typically hold a child close to their body, while men hold the child away from their body. Mothers are also more patient and will wait twice as long before picking up a recalcitrant child. When walking together, however, women rarely walk ahead of a child, while men do. The style of conversation also differs between mothers and fathers. If a mother holds the child she rarely talks to it, but as soon as she starts walking, she breaks into a continuous mode of verbal coaching and patter (this pattern is less so in southwest China). The mother cares for a sick child, dresses the child for school, and scolds the child when he or she misbehaves. The father remains somewhat aloof and only takes on the disciplinary role when something serious occurs. As a child enters late childhood, parents become sensitive about touching a child in public. This is especially so for father–daughter relations but not mother–son interaction. Chinese fathers also indicate they are more demanding with their son than their daughter. They interact with their daughters more openly, more warmly and less critically. Moreover, fathers tend to speak less harshly to their daughter. Whenever fathers discuss their children, it is common to stress 'how wonderful little girls are'. This is a new occurrence, and as such it constitutes an enormous shift in a patrilineal tradition that valued sons and grandsons over daughters and granddaughters.

The socialist transformation of cultural meanings has had a corresponding impact on men's conception of themselves as husbands and fathers.

Young fathers continue to assume a firm and somewhat formal posture towards their sons, while paradoxically insisting they do not want to be as formal and reserved as their fathers had been with them. Although many contemporary Chinese fathers wish to become a close friend with their child, as opposed to striking the more traditional note of the stern moral authority ever ready to criticize shortcomings, they remain uncertain and confused as how to express this desire (Jankowiak 1993). Warmth and immediacy of affection are not easily achieved. It is easier for them to accomplish this with a daughter than with a son. Significantly, fathers are more ambivalent than mothers in balancing their obligations as both spouse and parent. This ambivalence is profoundly articulated by many college-educated fathers who voice concerns that their child loves its mother more than them. Although the male desire to become more emotionally involved is far from achieved, it is a desire frequently heard in intimate conversation among close friends. As such, it has enormous implications for the quality of future parent–child relations and the development of a new Chinese person.

See also: little emperors

Further reading

Farrer, J. (2002). *Opening Up: Youth Sex Culture and Market Reform*. Chicago: University Chicago Press.

Fei, Xiaotong (1939). *Peasant Life in China*. Chicago: University Chicago Press.

Jankowiak, W. (1993). *Sex, Death and Hierarchy in a Chinese City*. New York: Columbia University Press.

Ho, D. (1987). 'Fatherhood in Chinese Society'. In M. Lamb (ed.), *The Father's Role: Cross-Cultural Perspective*. Hilldale: Lawrence Erlbaum.

Solomon, R. (1971). *Mao's Revolution and Chinese Political Culture*. Berkeley: University of California Press.

Wolf, M. (1972). 'Uterine Families and the Women's Community'. In M. Wolf (ed.), *Women and the Family in Rural Taiwan*. Stanford: Stanford University Press.

WILLIAM JANKOWIAK

parks and squares

Squares, faux-public spaces, were constructed in cities throughout China after the 1949 revolution in imitation of Red Square in Moscow for the holding of officially orchestrated mass parades, reviews and political rallies (although they later came to be used by anti-government protesters). They were not supposed to be places of leisure or entertainment, except on state-ordained holidays when the skies overhead would fill with extravagant firework displays. Public parks, created on the basis of Western and Japanese models from the early twentieth century, were provided for individual and family diversion, and education. On holidays they are also used as entertainment sites, or for improving moral or patriotic displays.

After the **Cultural Revolution**, older parks, like the Beihai Park in central Beijing, were reopened to the public; and from the mid 1980s places like the Altar of the Earth (Ditan) and similar sites were allowed once more to hold fairs (*miaohui*), as were many temples (see **temple fairs**). New parks have proliferated in recent decades. Many of these incorporate designs that imitate the private demesnes of the old scholar-gentry. The famous Ming-Qing gardens in the Lower Yangtze region, in particular those in Suzhou and Hangzhou, with their craggy scholar rocks, writhen trees, intricate stone walkways, pavilions, loggia, ponds, lakes and poetic mini-landscapes, provide inspiration to those who craft their parks out of modern materials. Concrete balustrades, bumpy ill-mowed lawns, clumps of trees, topiary and Taihu stones mark the people's parks, and they are often also crowded with game stalls, souvenir stands and fair rides.

Older parks converted for public use during the Republic (1912–49), like the former imperial Summer Hunting Villa in Chengde, or the **Yuanming yuan** in northwest Beijing, have also inspired contemporary park designers. Lakes and ponds in parks, be they new or old, are popular for boating (and theme-boats – dragon-headed skiffs, duck-, swan- or goose-headed vessels – often course through the waters with snap-happy visitors disporting themselves to the music of the latest Cantopop songs that blare from ubiquitous loudspeakers). And, finally, despite the rise of club and bar culture in the cities, for the less upwardly mobile the public park remains a place for trysts, be they hetero- or homosexual.

See also: Tiananmen Square

Further reading

Kraus, Richard (1999). 'Public Monuments and Private Pleasures in the Parks of Nanjing: A Tango in the Ruins of the Ming Emperor's Palace'. In Deborah Davis (ed.), *China's Consumer Revolution*. Berkeley: University of California Press.

GEREMIE R. BARMÉ

Parties A and B

[Jiafang yifang, 1997]

Film

Written and directed by **Feng Xiaogang**, this comic feature film is said to be based on **Wang Shuo**'s story 'You Are Not an Ordinary Person' (*Ni bushi yige suren*). Using a tourist project called 'Dreams Come True for a Day' (*Haomeng yiri you*), the film puts together seven stories, each characterized by a specific comic situation: a melon pedlar wants to be General Patten, a cook likes to have a taste of being tortured and executed, a wife-abuser requests to be ill treated, a nouveau-riche wishes to live a life of poverty, and a film star desires to be an ordinary person without fame, and so forth. Funny, mischievous, boisterous and absurd at times, the film tries to mock people with pretentious manners, educate men with male chauvinistic attitudes and praise those who selflessly help others.

Awarded 'best film' at the 21st Hundred-Flowers Film Festival and the first in a series of **New Year movies** (*Hesuipian*) made in China, Feng's *Parties A and B* was a huge success at the box office. In its first four days, it earned a record 2.5 million yuan in Beijing and Shanghai alone, in sharp contrast to the generally poor audience for Chinese domestic films. Breaking with the didactic film tradition, it was the first successful attempt by Chinese filmmakers to make a Chinese movie more entertaining than instructive and to pay more attention to commercial success than either moral enhancement or artistic accomplishment.

FU HONGCHU

Party advertising and self-promotion

As Victor Klemperer noted in his classic study of totalitarian language, *The Language of the Third Reich*, political sloganeering and propaganda ('public enlightenment') campaigns have a symbiotic relationship with the language of advertising. While Maoist-era political jargon reflected a more militaristic and hyperbolic age, feeding off hoary Chinese traditions (enumeration was particular common) and shaped by the unique linguistic flair of Mao, Deng–Jiang–Hu era politics rarely rings with the clarion call of agit-prop. This is an age when droning Party pronouncements contrast with increasingly glitzy 'public service' announcements. The spiritual civilization campaigns launched periodically since 1986, the media mobilizations to study the political speeches or 'theoretical' writings of the leaders, the slogans promoting social stability, public safety, urban order and patriotic zeal cleave to the methods of commercial advertisement, but while they are often as jingoistic as before, they generally lack memorable jingles.

The Party promotes itself not simply as the 'ruling political organization', an expression used to sheath the apparatus of rule in a cloak of constitutional formality (see **1982 Constitution of the PRC**), but also as the final or ultimate historical choice of the Chinese people. Moreover, its multifaceted propaganda-cum-public-relations organizations increasingly represent it through a statist-corporate voice that offers basic definitions of group morality and ethics, consensus, coherence and community in ways more familiar to us from international corporate advertising practice than Maoist hyper-propaganda. Not only does the Party manipulate routine public pronouncements and orchestrated news reporting to achieve this end: it pursues its goals also through a range of national media entertainments and promotions. It achieves

this through the Party Propaganda Department (that's Propaganda), the government instrumentalities devoted to public enlightenment like the **Ministry of Culture** and **State Administration for Radio, Film and Television**, as well as a myriad of subordinate organizations: Party **newspapers, CCTV (Chinese Central Television)**, Central People's Radio (see **radio (stations and content)**), and so on. At other times, the Party's messages are conveyed through non-Party organs and allied mass media that are directed at one level or another by in-house Party committees. Such committees function both as surrogates for Party authority and as representatives if not mediators for non-Party interests. As a result, they are enmeshed in a complex of relationships that range from the purely propagandistic-ideological to the corporate-promotional.

It was not until the 1990s that, for want of better terminology, 'politico-tainment' or 'Partimercials' appeared. Party culture, even when packaged for television ratings, was not necessarily all that popular and, since it has been in competition with more commercial (and in many cases foreign) programmes, inducements have had to be found to keep viewers watching. Taking the lead from the 'opposition', quiz shows and newspaper competitions were introduced that tested the skills of participants in memorizing, for example, official Party history, not to mention facts and figures related to new Party policies.

The conscious development of Party and state 'institutional advertising' (*gongguan guanggao*) and 'public service announcements' (*gongyi guanggao*), as they are now called, has been a gradual process pursued by what were now called Party PR *gongguan* specialists. But the awareness of these modified forms of propaganda has been heightened by the general development of commercial culture. With the establishment of Spiritual Civilization Propaganda Offices at provincial and municipal level from 1996, the use of a new commercial standard in state propaganda became evident. When in 1996 the Party launched its latest 'spiritual civilization' offensive which featured moralizing slogans exhorting people throughout the country to comply with road rules and to speak politely, huge computer-enhanced images, neon slogan boards and advertising displays were erected throughout

Beijing and provincial cities to help deliver the message (see **socialist spiritual civilization**).

Similarly, the creation of 'corporate identities' for venerable state institutions developed apace from the mid 1980s onward, and became something of a fad from 1993. The influence of the **Kong-Tai style** of mercantile environment in all of this was fundamental. Many state bodies like the Bank of China, China Travel, publishing organizations like Joint Publishers, Commercial Press and Chung-hwa Books, as well as various other state or pseudo-private groups engaged in business in Hong Kong, were the first to construct a corporate facade, which was then introduced to their head and branch offices on the mainland. Also by the mid 1990s, a corps of journalists, editors and designers now existed within the mainland media that constantly negotiated a working relationship between the esoteric communications favoured by traditional staid propagandists, on the one hand, and the more newsworthy style of partial disclosure and pseudo-honesty that fitted in with the modernized urban style of contemporary mainland life, on the other.

Through broad-based appeals to national symbols and patriotic indoctrination – increasingly delivered via a mass media that has appropriated elements of avant-garde art, culture and global advertising styles – the ideological promotion of the Party continues to claim a competitive stake on the public's attention and continues to shape socio-cultural norms (see **socio-political values**). It is often considered that commodity culture and the market have fatally undermined the primacy of Party rule in China. This is supposedly a process that has been accelerated by the opening up of greater public spaces and discursive realms, as well as being the result of international political and economic pressures, and the tripartite dialogue within the Chinese world – Sino-Kong-Tai. It is argued that Party control has thus been weakened, or at least diversified, and its ideology gradually undermined to the point of becoming little more than a window-dressing disguising a basic nationalistic political and economic agenda. Nonetheless, the Party as an organization has also benefited greatly from many of these various pressures, including advertising culture. The Party retains its dominant role, and through competition

in the marketplace its symbolic world has been enriched.

Further reading

Barmé, Geremie R. (1999). *In The Red: On Contemporary Chinese Culture*. New York: Columbia University Press, 115–22, 235–54.

Lewis, Steven (ed.) (2002). *China's Public Advertising Culture: Spiritual Civilization, Local Development, Privatization and Public Service*. Baker Institute, Rice University: Transnational China Project (online). Available at http://www.ruf.rice.edu/tnchina/index.html

GEREMIE R. BARMÉ

Party-building

(dangjian)

'Party-building' (*dangjian*) refers to the Chinese Communist Party's adaptation, ideologically and structurally, to the requirements of a new grand mission, which only the central leadership has the prerogative to decide. Party-building entails new guidelines on the role of the Party, and adjustments or alterations in organizations, membership competence and style of Party leadership.

The current Party-building, which began at the Twelfth Party Congress in 1982, is perhaps the most significant in the history of the CCP, because it aimed at nothing less than a transformation of the character of the CCP. Deng Xiaoping proclaimed that the new mission of the Party was the 'four modernizations' – in industry, agriculture, defence, and science and technology. Deng and associates desired rapid economic growth by whatever means. Hence, practices that were commonly associated with capitalism, such as the market mechanism, private business and foreign investment, all became acceptable. Accordingly, the most important skill of a Party member was leadership in economic development, and the chief qualification of a Party member was an advanced education, preferably in science and engineering. Organizationally, there would be a separation of functions between the Party and the government, with the Party's being mainly a monitor of policy execution. Formally, the Party's past practice of controlling every aspect of life and work was terminated.

The most noteworthy achievements of Party-building so far are, first, in the educational upgrade of Party members. In 1982, approximately less than a quarter of Party members had a high school education or more; by 1997, the proportion had risen to half. Second, the Party became more inclusive of social groups than ever before, admitting private businessmen into the Party. But the main character of the CCP – as an organization of functionaries – has remained unchanged. Among general cadres, 70 per cent are Party members; and the proportion of Party members has risen to 90 per cent for those above the county level. In sum, to most existing and prospective Party members, the CCP is the channel to political patronage.

At one and the same time, Party-building exposed broad divisions within the Party, especially between the interior and the coastal provinces, and between the countryside and the city. Those in the southeastern (coastal) provinces tend to support Deng's reform, while those in the interior are opposed to it. With the exception of Tibet, most ethnic minorities, especially the Muslim population, also support reforms. A high proportion (said to be as high as 70 per cent) of Party organizations in rural areas have ceased to function, and a large number of Party members, especially in the countryside, are perplexed, disillusioned and alienated. In sum, Party-building has yet to produce a unified modern organization, with its ranks dominated by development specialists as Deng had wished.

Further reading

Chi, His-sheng (1991). *Politics of Disillusionment: The Chinese Communist Party under Deng Xiaoping, 1978–1989*. New York: M. E. Sharpe.

ALAN P. L. LIU

patriotic covenants

Patriotic covenants are mandatory pledges of support for CCP rule by all of the patriotic religious organizations. The practice of signing patriotic covenants was inaugurated during the early 1950s in an attempt to rally popular support for the new regime. Numerous covenants were formulated. Some were intended for the entire population, seeking popular pledges of support for Chairman Mao, the Communist Party, the Central People's Government, and the People's Liberation Army. Others were formulated to elicit support from target populations, such as religious groups. For example, leaders of the **Three-Self Patriotic Movement (TSPM)** drew up a 'Christian Manifesto' in May 1950 which called on China's Protestants to recognize 'the evils that have been wrought in China by imperialism' and that 'imperialism has made use of Christianity', and called on grassroots congregations to 'purge imperialistic influences from within Christianity itself' (Founding Group of the Three-Self Movement 1951). Activists within the TSPM launched a nationwide campaign to obtain the signatures of all of China's Protestants endorsing the Manifesto.

In the reform period, patriotic covenants have been enshrined in the state's regulations on religion and incorporated as core principles of the patriotic religious organizations. The State Council's *Document 6* (1991) requires religious professionals to 'accept Party leadership' and to 'constantly educate their religious staff in patriotism, socialism, and the policy on current developments' (see **religious policies of the state**). The constitutions of the patriotic religious organizations mirror these sentiments. For example, the TSPM's constitution reads:

> The purpose of the TSPM is to unite all Protestants in China under the leadership of the Chinese Communist Party and the People's Government, to love our socialist motherland, [and] to abide by our country's constitution, laws, regulations, and policies.

Further reading

(2000). Constitution of the National Committee of the Three-Self Patriotic Movement of the Protestant Churches in China (2 January 1997). *Chinese Law and Government* 33.6: 37.

Founding Group of the Three-Self Movement (1951). 'Direction of Endeavor for Chinese

Christianity in the Construction of New China'. In F. Jones (ed.) (1963), *Documents of the Three-Self Movement: Source Materials for the Study of the Protestant Church in Communist China*. New York: National Council of the Churches of Christ in the USA, 19–20.

JASON KINDOPP

Pearl River Economic Radio

Pearl River Economic Radio (PRER), launched on 15 December 1986, was at the forefront of the practitioner-led media reform of the 1980s that saw the introduction of livelier formats and a content that was depoliticized and had greater immediate relevance to everyday life. It clearly showed the commercial potential for depoliticized media production and is an example of how the market has changed Chinese media over the last two decades.

The station was born when Guangdong People's Radio found its audience stripped away by the livelier, more relaxed and lifestyle-oriented radio stations broadcasting in Hong Kong and picked up, across the border, by the residents of the Pearl River Delta. The station obtained permission to re-launch its Cantonese-language station as PRER, which proved enormously popular with Guangdong audiences even in the face of stiff competition from Hong Kong broadcasters. The new pioneering format emulated the Hong Kong style, prioritizing what audiences wanted over government propaganda demands. Subsequently, the station was copied by other mainland radio stations, both in the Pearl River Delta region and throughout the country. The example of PRER also demonstrates the rather unique position of Guangdong. The province has always had greater exposure to foreign media, particularly from and through Hong Kong, and has also been used as a laboratory for experimenting with more liberal media formats by the Chinese authorities.

See also: Nanfang Weekend; Yangcheng Evening News; radio (stations and content); satellite television

Further reading

Zhao, Y. (1998). *Media, Market, and Democracy in China: Between the Party Line and the Bottom Line*. Chicago: University of Illinois Press.

KEVIN LATHAM

Peking University

(Beijing daxue)

Peking University, or Beida, was founded in 1898 during the Hundred Days Reform. It was then known as the Imperial University (Jingshi daxuetang), which clearly indicates that it was in the service of the Qing dynasty. Liang Qichao and the other reformers who designed the university envisioned it as a Western-style school, but it was a decidedly transitional institution. A mix of progressive thinking and old-style values and practices characterized the culture of the university during its first decade.

After the 1911 Revolution the school's name was changed to National Beijing University. Yan Fu, the noted intellectual and translator, introduced important changes during his short tenure as chancellor, but it was only after Cai Yuanpei filled that office in 1917 that Beida evolved into a dynamic and nationally influential centre of political and cultural progressivism and serious scholarly research. During his administration Cai became China's best-known champion of academic freedom and the university the leader of the New Culture and May Fourth Movements. The future Chinese Communist Party also got its start at Beida at this time in the form of an extra-curricular society dedicated to the academic study of Marxism. The university remained a vibrant centre of political activism and intellectual trail-blazing into the 1930s. During the war with Japan Beida removed to Kunming in southern China, where its faculty and students joined with those from Qinghua and Nankai universities to form Southwest Associated University, or Lianda. Lianda helped keep Chinese intellectual life alive and gave substance to the idea that scholars had a vital contribution to make to the preservation and construction of the Chinese nation.

After the Communist Revolution, under the leadership of Chancellor Ma Yinchu, Beida continued to stand out as a centre of liberalism. In 1957 the university played a leading role in the Hundred Flowers movement. During the anti-rightist crackdown that followed over eight hundred people at Beida were labelled rightists, the highest number for any Chinese university. Instead of destroying Beida because of its 'rightism', however, Communist Party leaders learned to use the university's symbolic power to further their own ends. In 1966 it was selected as the starting place for the **Cultural Revolution**; under Kang Sheng's direction, Nie Yuanzi, a professor in the philosophy department, hung the big-character poster that marked the beginning of that decade-long 'period of chaos'. In subsequent years revolutionary developments at Beida received extensive coverage in the national media and the university became an important pilgrimage site for Red Guards visiting the capital.

Following the Cultural Revolution Beida was restored as a working institution. The atmosphere once more became quite liberal, and by the middle of the 1980s the university was a leader of the new tendency towards political and cultural questioning then sweeping the country. Beida played host to a series of freethinking public discussions organized by students who belonged to 'democracy salons' (see **salon culture**), and in spring 1989 it played an important role in the massive demonstrations that rocked Beijing and the rest of China. After the government crushed those demonstrations it carried out a crackdown at Beida that succeeded in silencing its opponents. In the mid 1990s Beijing University was a relatively calm and increasingly apolitical place. Many students who felt stifled by life under the Communist Party bided their time until they could go abroad to study; others threw themselves headlong into the pursuit of lucrative and high status careers. By 1998, when Beida celebrated the one-hundredth anniversary of its founding, the extremely politicized atmosphere that obtained there in the preceding decades had dramatically receded, and life had become more normalized.

Further reading

Israel, John (1999). *Lianda: A Chinese University in War and Revolution*. Stanford: Stanford University Press.

Weston, Timothy (2003). *The Power of Position: Beijing University, Intellectuals, and Chinese Political Culture, 1898–1929*. Berkeley: University of California Press.

TIMOTHY WESTON

Peng Xiaolian

b. 1953, Shanghai

Film director/writer

One of the female graduates of the **Beijing Film Academy** class of 1982, Peng Xiaolian shares the collective label of the **Fifth Generation (film directors)** but is interested in different narratives and forms. Her directing career began at the Shanghai Film Studio with a children's film, *Me and My Classmates* (1985). A director and a writer, she has scripted most of her films.

Peng is best known for her second feature film, *Women's Story* (*Nüren de gushi*, 1987). The film follows three peasant women who step out from their village and traditional roles to pursue wealth and freedom in the city. Seen from a woman's perspective, the film communicates a strong sense of gender consciousness. The difficulty in finding a language that speaks for female experience prevents the film from achieving a female subjectivity. Indeed, the rise of gender consciousness coupled with the lack of feminine aesthetics is a problem central to women's film production.

In 1989, Peng Xiaolian came to the United States on a scholarship to pursue an MFA degree at New York University. After returning to China, she continued to make films in Shanghai, including *Once Upon a Time in Shanghai* (*Shanghai wangshi*, 1999) and a children's animation, *Keke's Umbrella* (2000). A new project explores how a teenage girl growing up in a single-parent household pretends to be normal although everything around her strikes her as abnormal. Peng Xiaolian also scripted and directed *Jiazhuang mei ganjue*, 2002.

See also: animation; children's feature film

Further reading

Berry, Chris (1988). 'Interview with Peng Xiao-lian'. *Camera Obscura: A Journal of Feminism and Film Theory* 18 (September): 26–31.

Cui, Shuqin (2003). 'Feminism with Chinese Characteristics?' In *idem, Women Through the Lens: Gender and Nation in a Century of Chinese Cinema.* Honolulu: University of Hawai'i Press.

CUI SHUQIN

pentatonic romanticism

Pentatonic romanticism is a musical style that couples pentatonic melodies (melodies based on a five-tone scale without semitones) evocative of Chinese folk music with harmonic structures reminiscent of late nineteenth-century Western art music. Compositions written in this style are often composed for Western-style chamber, symphonic and vocal ensembles. Prominent among composers of pentatonic romanticism are the Hong-Kong based composers Ling Shengshi (1915–91) Huang Yauti (b. 1912), Wong Yokyee (b. 1924) and Shi Kumpor (b. 1932).

Pentatonic romanticism must be understood in its historical and social context. Under a variety of political circumstances and social conditions, composers from mainland China, Taiwan and Hong Kong have sought to create distinctly Chinese concert music – often by combining Western and Chinese musical techniques or ideas. In some cases the 'Chineseness' of a composition is found in programmatic or extramusical references. In other cases a Chinese musical identity is conveyed by the use of Chinese instruments. Pentatonic romanticism, however, represents a distinct stylistic response by mainly Hong Kong composers to the need for a national voice on local and international concert stages. Moreover, it is a response that consciously locates a national identity in the sound structures themselves. This compositional approach uses Western instrumentation and harmonies, but relies primarily on pentatonic melodies to communicate a sense of Chineseness.

Further reading

Mittler, Barbara (1996). 'Mirrors and Double Mirrors: The Politics of Identity in New Music from Hong Kong and Taiwan' *Chime* 9: 46–56.

JAMES DALE WILSON

People's Daily

[Renmin ribao]

The *People's Daily* is the official organ newspaper of the Chinese Communist Party's (CCP's) Central Committee. Along with the **Xinhua News Agency**, **CCTV (Chinese Central Television)** and China People's Radio, the newspaper is one of the principal mouthpieces of the CCP. Founded on 15 June 1948 as the organ of the North China Bureau of the CCP, after liberation it soon became the most influential newspaper in China. Its overseas edition has long been one of the key indicators of CCP policy for political scientists throughout the world.

In the Mao period, the paper was often used as the vehicle for launching new mass mobilization campaigns through its editorials. Newspapers throughout the country were required to republish these pieces, which were often the focus of political study meetings throughout the country. The paper became the best indication of contemporary Party thinking and future policy directions.

In the post-Mao period, the symbolic significance and mouthpiece function of the paper remain unchanged. However, in a commercialized and highly competitive market for **newspapers**, the character of its readership has narrowed. The paper is no longer required reading for almost the entire population, most of whom would prefer to read other titles. It is impossible to buy on the streets of some of China's major cities and relies principally on work unit subscriptions for its estimated 4 million circulation. Its editorials and articles are nonetheless still often carried by other Party organ newspapers and are distributed through Xinhua. A key editorial on 26 April 1989 written by Party officials described the student demonstrations at the time as 'counter-revolutionary turmoil' presaging sterner attitudes to come. Nonetheless, journalists from the newspaper were active participants in the demonstrations supporting the students.

See also: evening newspapers and weekend editions; newspapers; radio (stations and content); state control of media

KEVIN LATHAM

People's Mediation Committees

The powerful economic, political and social forces transforming Chinese culture and society in the reform era are also changing the ways Chinese solve disputes. Established in the early years of the PRC as a means to carry socialist policies into the countryside through a merging of revolutionary organizations and traditional dispute resolution norms, the People's Mediation Committees have re-emerged after the break-up of the communes in the 1960s and the chaos of the **Cultural Revolution** as the primary means to resolve minor disputes within families, workplaces, villages and urban neighbourhoods. Never meant to preclude the use of administrative and judicial courts or to deal with criminal matters, mediation committees and their volunteer members (mainly retired cadres) often provide a low-cost, timely, easily understandable and informal way to solve a range of civil conflicts.

Reforms are gradually establishing a code of civil law and court institutions, including the training of legal professionals, which the Chinese people can use to resolve disputes over complex legal issues, particularly contracts involving corporations and international investors and trade partners. And local, national and international arbitration commissions are also an increasingly common alternative to courts in economic matters. With the standardization of training and record-keeping practices through 1989 legislation, however, mediation committees survive as a popular means for solving small, local disputes.

See also: lawyers

Further reading

Lubman, S. (1999). *Bird in a Cage: Legal Reform in China after Mao.* Palo Alto: Stanford University Press: ch. 8.

STEVEN W. LEWIS

Performance Workshop Theatre

(Biaoyian guangzuofang)

The Performance Workshop Theatre was one of the most important **Little Theatre** groups in the mid 1980s and later developed into the leading theatre company in Taiwan. The Performance Workshop was founded in 1984 by **Lai Shengchuan** (Stan Lai) who was, and is, the major playwright and artistic director. Lai himself is an innovative stage and screen director, as well as a playwright and theatre professor. He received his PhD in Dramatic Art from UC Berkeley in 1983 and currently is the dean of the Theatre School at the Taipei National University of the Arts.

The distinguishing features of the Performance Workshop's work are methods of collective improvisation method, a satiric/comedic style and political subject matter. Their first work, *The Night We Became Hsiang-Sheng Comedians* (*Nayiye, women shou xiangsheng*, 1985), successfully integrated collective improvisational methods learned from the West, the traditional Chinese performing art form of **xiangsheng** (cross-talk or comic dialogue) and contemporary Taiwan/China political subject matter. The production was a great success, and not only succeeded in reviving *xiangsheng* but brought new audiences to Taiwan theatre. The Performance Workshop later developed a series of *xiangsheng* in repertoire, including: *Look Who's Cross-talking Tonight* (*Zheyiye, shuilai shou xiangsheng?* 1989), *The Complete History of Chinese Thought* (*Youyiye, tamen shou xiangsheng*, 1997) and *Millennium Teahouse* (*Qianxiye, women shou xiangsheng*, 2000). As well as in-house productions, the Performance Workshop also introduced numerous contemporary Western plays into Taiwan, such as Tony Kushner's *Angels in America, Part I* (1996), Dario Fo's *Accidental Death of an Anarchist* (1995) and *Can't Pay, Won't Pay* (1998). Other works include *Secret Love for the Peach*

Blossom Spring (1986/1991/1999) and *Red Sky* (1994). In 2000, the Performance Workshop established OFF PW as a platform for young directors, as well as Stan Lai himself, to stage alternative and experimental works. The Performance Workshop is the only Taiwanese theatre group with a branch in China which has regularly performed there for several years. Their works have proved to be well received by young Chinese people.

LIN WEI-YÜ

performing arts in Taiwan

Dance

After 1980, dance development in Taiwan can roughly divide into three major genres: modern dance, ballet and Chinese folk dance. Among these, only modern dance is considered mainstream because of the lack of strong Chinese folk dance and ballet traditions in Taiwan. Ballet, though popular as a training system, is less so as a performing genre. As for Chinese folk dance, it is most often presented in small-scale commercial studios for children, and only a handful of Chinese folk dance groups concentrate on more sophisticated choreography.

Modern dance

Modern dance in Taiwan has been influenced by American modern dance styles, such as those of Martha Graham, Merce Cunningham, Alvin Ailey, Paul Taylor and Contact Improvisation. Since the 1970s, Taiwanese dance talent has often gone to Western countries to study at different modern dance schools, particularly those in the USA. Among them, Martha Graham's technique has proven the most popular and influential in the development of Taiwanese modern dance, especially from the 1970s to the mid 1980s.

Lin Hwai-min, the founder of the Cloud Gate Dance Theatre (Yunmen wuji, 1973), was the most important contributor to the establishment of a Taiwanese modern dance. Lin introduced Graham's dance technique and dramatic-dance style to Taiwan, but also outlined, along with the

famous musician Shr Wei-lyau, a new direction: 'Chinese compose, Chinese choreograph, Chinese dance, [all] for Chinese audiences' (*Zhongguoren zuoqu, zhongguoren bianwu, zhongguoren tiao gei zhongguoren kan*). This directive led Cloud Gate to undertake a fusion of dance techniques and theatrical concepts from East and West. His choreography has roots in Asian myth, folklore, literature and aesthetics. Lin's movement vocabulary is drawn from Taiji and **Jingju** (Peking opera), as well as from modern dance and ballet, all of which are routine training for the dancers. In 1978, Lin choreographed a historical piece, *Xin Chuan*, which described the history and hardships of the early Chinese immigrants to Taiwan. Another major modern dance group is the Neo-Classic Dance Company, founded by Liu Feng-shueh. Liu's dance focuses on exploring the dynamic interaction between action, time and space, as well as fusing Chinese traditional elements with modern dance and Taiwanese aboriginal culture with Western performing arts.

Generally speaking, modern dance from the 1970s to the mid 1980s tended to adapt traditional Chinese literature and ancient philosophical concepts as sources for their choreography. From the second half of the 1980s to the early 1990s, and particularly after Martial Law was lifted in 1987, radical socio-political changes unleashed both freedom and chaos in cultural expression. Meanwhile, a younger generation of dance talent, with different training and new interests, returned to Taiwan from abroad. The dominance of Martha Graham waned, and diversity came to characterize modern dance. The founding of Contact Improvisation by choreographer Ku Ming-Shen in the early 1990s, for example, was a revolutionary event, introducing shapeless body movement and welcoming the participation of non-trained dancers. In fact, with the exception of Cloud Gate, most of the modern dance companies performing today were established in the post Martial Law period. These new groups practise various dance techniques and styles and have generated numerous influential works. In contrast to Cloud Gate and Neo-Classic's close relationship with Chinese culture, these groups also reveal an alienation from Chinese culture and a strong identification with that of Taiwan.

Since the mid 1990s, we can mark a new trend towards the development of unique movement systems. The interest of modern dance groups has shifted from probing social problems to the expression of individuality and spiritual mental states through more purified dance movements with less dramatic elements. Most of these groups have developed their systems by mixing ballet or modern dance technique with Asian systems of physical movement, such as Taiji, Qigong, yoga and traditional Taiwanese folk performances. They are also inspired by traditional Asian philosophical concepts as found in meditation, Buddhism, Taoism and the Asian myths. The important groups at this time include: Cloud Gate Dance Theatre, Taipei Dance Circle, Tao and Dancers, Taigu Tales Dance Theatre, Dance Forum Taipei, Ku and Dancers, Legend Lin Dance Theatre and Hsiao Ching-wen Dance Theatre.

Ballet

Ballet has long been used as a form of basic training for most professional dancers in Taiwan, but currently only about five companies regularly present concerts, and most of these were formed from the late 1980s to the mid 1990s. Among them, the Taipei Ballet Company, the Capital Ballet-Taipei, and Taipei Shinei Balei Wutuan are the most active. Most works focus on modern ballet with the addition of a Taiwanese flavour.

Chinese folk dance

Chinese folk dance includes the folk dances introduced from mainland China as well as local Taiwanese folk dances. The Chinese folk dance in Taiwan today has absorbed ballet and modern dance techniques, as well as ideas from modern dance choreography. There are about ten Chinese folk dance companies in Taiwan: among them, the Taipei Folk Dance Theatre and the Lan Yang Dancers are the most active and senior. Taipei Folk is certainly the most productive and the only professional Chinese folk dance group in Taiwan and aims to create a new Chinese folk dance by adapting both Chinese and Taiwanese styles. Lan Yang was formed by Father Gian Carlo Michelini to keep Chinese folk dance alive in Taiwan. The group emphasizes dance training and education

rather than performance, and the dancers often go on to professional careers with Chinese folk dance or modern dance companies.

Theatre

Modern theatre

Modern theatre, called **Huaju** or 'spoken drama' in China, was brought to Taiwan during the Japanese colonial period (1895–1945). When the KMT (Nationalist Party) withdrew to Taiwan from China in 1949, Chinese spoken drama came along with the military. Before 1980, Taiwan's spoken drama was presented in an outdated quasi-realistic theatrical style, and was more or less political propaganda. Departing from the old spoken drama, the development of a Taiwanese modern theatre began with the **Little Theatre** movement in the 1980s. Most Little Theatres share certain commonalities: they are non-profit, suffer from poor financial conditions, are basically anti-system, experimental or avant-garde, and are dominated by young amateur performers/writers/directors.

The Little Theatre movement began in the late 1970s, when a group of young people began performing experimental theatre in small theatres and non-theatre spaces. They had invited a psychology scholar, Wu Jing-jyi, director of the La MaMa Theatre in New York, to lead and train the group. This group named themselves the Lanling Theatre Workshop and presented several experimental theatrical pieces in 1980. Their works met with success, which encouraged others to form their own Little Theatre groups, including **Performance Workshop Theatre**, Fangyuan juchang, Xiaowu juchang and the Pin-Fong Acting Troupe. The works of this first generation showed the intention of searching for a way of combining contemporary Western theatre with Chinese tradition. However, their successful productions showed a marked tendency towards popularization.

From the mid 1980s to the early 1990s, many of the first-generation groups folded, a few developed into larger-size theatres, and a second generation appeared and developed into a major force. Numerous Little Theatre groups, many short-lived, were formed at this time. A distinct feature of the second generation is a development of avant-garde theatre with stronger political themes embodying the rebelliousness and anti-systemic attitude of the post Martial Law period. These groups refused to receive funding from the government in order to avoid becoming a propaganda tool. Their work challenged social and political taboos and was highly critical of the government. Additionally, in contrast to the first generation, the second generation conscientiously avoided popularization. While staging productions in the theatre, they also performed in non-theatre spaces, such as in the streets, mountains, underground passageways, coffee shops, restaurants and public squares. The important Little Theatre groups in this period were: Huangxu juchang, Rive-Gauche, U-Theatre, 425 Environmental Theatre and Linjiedian juxianglu.

After the early 1990s, modern theatre began to diversify, like modern dance. Although Little Theatre groups still occupied an overwhelming proportion of the modern theatre, they no longer dominated the latter's development as before. Several groups from the first and second generation evolved into professional and semi-professional large-size theatres and some newly formed large groups also appeared. These companies gradually won the most audiences and dominated the theatre market because of their commercialization. The important larger theatre groups are the Performance Workshop Theatre, Pin-Fong Acting Troupe, Godot Theatre Company and Greenray Theatre. Among these, Godot Theatre Company has developed into a professional musical theatre company. Their repertoire includes: *Black Comedy*, *Kiss Me Nana*, *The Angel Never Sleeps*, *Look Up the Golden Sun* and *Communicating Door*. Countless Little Theatre groups were also established in this period, but most were short-lived. Unlike the second generation, almost all groups now receive government or semi-official subsidies. However, they have retained their rebellious, anti-system attitudes, in keeping with an alternative theatre. Yet because of the democratization of Taiwan and the improvement in the political environment, the third-generation Little Theatre lost their political target, if not their interest in politics; thus, their works are less, or even non, political. The new issues now concern the individual, individuals vs groups, homosexuality,

feminism and local community issues. There are also a number of groups that stress experimental, artistic innovation over ideologies. The important groups in this generation are Taiwan Walker, Assignment Theatre, Shakespeare's Wild Sisters Group and U-Theatre.

Foreign influences have also been important during this period. Translated Western plays are often staged by both Little Theatre and large theatre groups, not to mention drama clubs and university theatre departments. Meanwhile, through visits by Asian theatre artists and participation in Asian theatre festivals, the modern theatre from other regions in Asia has begun to influence modern theatre in Taiwan. Influences include the Little Theatre and Butoh from Japan, the People's Theatre from the Philippines, avant-garde theatre from Hong Kong, and spoken drama from mainland China.

Another important feature in this period has been the development of community theatre. Before the 1990s, most modern theatre was concentrated in Taipei City. In 1990s, groups began to be formed outside of Taipei regions. Calling themselves community theatre, they share many characteristics with the Little Theatre – small size, rebelliousness, experimental productions – but their works often focus on regional issues – local histories, lives and social problems – and use local dialects. The important groups are Tainan Jen Theatre Troupe, Taitung Drama Theatre and Spring Wind Art Theatre.

Finally, a significant development in modern theatre on Taiwan has been the founding of the Creative Society (Chung-cho-she) in Taipei in 1997 by a group consisting of Taipei's theatre elite: playwrights, directors, theatre scholars, performing arts educators and theatre players, all from a single generation. Most of them had experienced the era of political reforms, were involved in the Little Theatre movement in the mid 1980s, and had studied abroad. Their motive in coming together was to experiment with new theatrical possibilities through collaboration and coordination. Because of the de-emphasis on play-writing during the avant-garde theatre movement in the late 1980s and 1990s, the Creative Society insists on producing good original scripts so as to raise the quality of Taiwan's modern plays. Furthermore, they insist on not limiting themselves to any theatrical style and refuse to let their work be influenced by the market. The Creative Society made their debut with *Metamorphosis* in 1997. And because of the fine quality of their productions, the following works have been well received by audiences: *KiKi Wanders Around the World* (1998), *Launch Theatre Institute on Line* (1998), *Kiss of Death* (1999), *I Want You, I Want You* (2000), *No Comment* (2001).

Traditional theatre

Traditional theatre in Taiwan can be divided into three types: large-scale theatre, small-scale theatre and puppet theatre. The large-scale theatre includes **Jingju** (Peking opera), **Yueju (Zhejiang opera)**, Nanguan (southern music; see **Minnan nanyin**), Beiguan (northern music) and **Gezaixi** (Taiwanese opera). With the retirement or death of old performers, Nanguan and Beiguan are in decline, while Jingju and Gezaixi remain popular. Before the 1990s, there were five national opera troupes and five conservatory schools, but these was gradually reduced to one troupe by 1995 – the National Kuo-Kuang Chinese Opera Company (combining Jingju and Yueju) – and one conservatory by 1999 – the National Taiwan Junior College of Performing Arts (now called the National Fu Hsing Chinese Opera School). Generally speaking, Taiwan's Jingju preserves the old style popular during the 1920s and 1930s in China. On the other hand, since the late 1970s, a few Jingju performers have begun reforming Jingju through the use of modern theatrical elements. The important groups involved in reform are Yayin xiaoji and the Contemporary Legend Theatre, both private companies. However, because of the radical social changes since 1980, a lack of talent, new repertoire or new audiences, and competition from mainland troupes, Taiwan's Jingju has experienced a serious decline. From the late 1980s, the Taiwanese government began to allow performing arts groups from China to tour Taiwan, bringing some great performers and a more abundant repertoire. They have attracted large audiences and dominated the stage, whereas the market for Taiwan Jingju has shrunk considerably.

Among large-scale theatre, Gezaixi is considered the only genre originating in Taiwan. Gezaixi evolved from a small-scale theatre (*gezai*), which had only three role types: young male, young female and clown (see **Xiqu role types**). Originally using folksongs to tell simple stories, *gezai* gradually evolved into the large-scale Gezaixi by absorbing music, role types and the elements of movement from other regional ensemble and opera genres: Nanguan, Beiguan, Jingju and Sipinxi. The end result was a larger performance with a complete set of stock characters and the staging of more complicated stories. There have been many venues and/or occasions for the performance of Gezaixi: *yetai* (outdoors), *neitai* (indoors), radio, movie, TV and the theatre stage. At present there are about fifty ongoing professional Gezaixi troupes. *Yetai* Gezaixi (outdoor Gezaixi) once combined entertainment and religious functions, but now it mostly serves purely religious purposes. It is normally staged within, in front of or near temples. Although Gezaixi has declined seriously since the 1970s due to movies, TV and other new forms of entertainment, it is this religious function that has allowed Gezaixi to survive in the present day. *Neitai* Gezaixi (indoor Gezaixi) was staged in indoor theatres from the 1920s to the 1960s for entertainment purposes only. 'Radio and movie Gezaixi' developed during the 1950s, and boomed in the 1960s, but quickly died out by the end of the 1960s. 'TV Gezaixi' developed in the early 1960s, and thrived from the 1970s to the mid 1980s. However, because of new entertainment options and the development of pop culture, 'TV Gezaixi' also disappeared in the 1990s. In the face of these trends, there has been a more positive development visible since the 1980s: the staging of Gezaixi in modern theatre buildings. The aim here has been to produce highly artistic plays, with good scripts, thoughtful topics, profound meanings, humour, refined performances and advanced stage techniques. This type of Gezaixi is called *jingzhi* Gezaixi (Refined Gezaixi), and its troupes, consisting of both professional and amateur performers, are almost all sponsored by the government: Yang Lihua Gezaixituan, Hsin-Chuan Taiwanese Opera Troupe and Ho Lo Taiwanese Opera Troupe.

Small-scale theatre includes Cheguxi, Hakka tea-harvest drama, *bendi* Gezai (original Gezai; the basis of Gezaixi), and Fashixi (Daoist ritual-master theatre). These are chiefly performed during religious and seasonal occasions, such as temple festivals, gods' birthdays, and at planting and harvest time (see **temple fairs**). In the present day, small-scale theatre is often practised in local communities, or in elementary and junior high schools as a way to continue Taiwanese folk traditions.

There are three major types of puppet theatre in Taiwan: marionette theatre (Kuilaixi), **shadow puppet theatre** (Piyinxi), and palm puppet theatre (Budaixi). Puppetry is the most sacred of performances, often used in driving evil spirits away and always on religious occasions. There are only two professional marionette theatre troupes left: Xinfuxuan and Fulongxuan, both from I-Lan county. Shadow puppetry is also in decline and only three troupes remain: Donghua, Fuxingge and Huazhouyuan. On the other hand, palm puppetry is still extremely popular. The traditional palm puppet theatre performed on a small, wood-framed raised stage near a temple. Traditional palm puppetry uses Nanguan, Beiguan, Jingju and Gezaixi music to sing stories. The palm puppet troupes – Iwanjan and Hsiao Hsiyuan – are important groups for preserving live, traditional-style palm puppetry. There are also *yetai*, *neitai*, radio and TV palm puppet theatres in Taiwan, though *neitai* and radio are now rare.

From the 1970s, the Huang Jungxun Puppets Broadcasting Production Company, a family troupe formed by puppeteer Huang Jungxun and now lasting four generations, began to produce TV palm puppetry. They called their kind of theatre Jinguangxi (special effects theatre) or Jianxiaxi (martial theatre) in which gods, demons and supernatural and military roles were primary, and in which complex plots, fantastic fighting and splendid special effects were the main focus of the show. They didn't use traditional music and percussion, but created their own modern popular music instead. The Huang TV Palm Puppet Show was a tremendous success, so much so that his family purchased a TV channel explicitly for presenting it. Other palm puppet troupes immediately imitated Jinguangxi, but found a cooler response. At present, Huang's family remains very popular, and his TV palm puppetry forms the mainstream of Taiwanese puppet theatre. However, the success

of TV palm puppet is exceptional among all traditional theatres in Taiwan; all other genres have experienced a sharp decline in popularity for many years.

See also: music in Taiwan

Further reading

Li, Xiao-ti (1995). 'Xili Qiankunda'. *Performing Arts Review* (July): 30–6.

Li, Xiaoyang (1995). 'Chule yonggan, dadan, youmeiyou yuanchang?' *Performing Arts Review* (July): 50–8.

Lin, Maoxian (1995). 'Lijing cangshang bjiansang'. *Performing Arts Review* (July): 23–9.

Ping, Heng (ed.) (1995). *Wudao xinshang* [Appreciate Dance]. Taipei: Sanming.

Wu, Quancheng (ed.) (1996). *Taiwan xiandai juchang yiantaohui luwenji: 1986–1995 Taiwan xiaojuchang.* [A Compilation of Taiwan's Modern Theatre Symposium: Taiwan's Little Theatre, 1986–1995]. Taipei: Wenjianhui.

Yang, Mengyu (1998). *Baowu: Lin Hwai-min Yunmen chuanqi.* [The Legends of Lin Hwai-min and Yunmen] Taipei: Tianxia yuanjian.

Zhong, Mingde (1999). *Taiwan xiaojuchang yundongshi.* [The Little Theatre Movement of Taiwan (1980-89): In Search of Alternative Aesthetics and Politics]. Taipei: Yangzhi.

http://creative.microtheatre.org.tw/
http://www.cloudgate.org.tw/index.htm
http://www.cyberstage.com.tw/

LIN WEI-YÜ

pets

The literal translation of the Chinese term for pet is 'thing to dote on'. For centuries, the imperial family doted on its pet dogs, and China cultivated special breeds, notably the Pekinese. After the founding of the People's Republic, pets officially became bourgeois and unsanitary. As a result of dog-killing campaigns in the 1950s, virtually no dogs remained in the cities by the 1960s, except in the northeast and southeast, where they were raised for food. The post-Mao economic reforms and the growth of a Chinese middle class led to a marked change in views and policies towards pets. By the 1990s, pet dogs were reappearing in large numbers in the cities, many imported over the border from Russia. Today, about one in six households in Beijing keeps a pet – about half are dogs, with cats, birds and goldfish also popular, and family crickets, pigs and even rats not unusual.

Localities still control the dog population through tight regulations and high fees, as well as high fines for transgressing the rules. In major cities, a dog licence costs hundreds of dollars, and owners must pay additional annual fees. Beijing restricts dog-walking to after daytime business hours, and owners cannot keep animals over a certain size. Health checks and vaccinations also are required. The pet boom has spawned associated services and industries, from veterinarians and pet hospitals to shelters and hotlines, from import and manufacture of pet food to provision of fancy fish tanks, dog kennels, pet toys and pet clothes. Shanghai boasts the first animal crematorium.

JUDY POLUMBAUM

pharmacies

It's not possible to fully understand China's pharmacies without considering them within the larger context of how market reforms have impacted China's health care services and pharmaceutical industry. Although China has a rapidly growing retail pharmacy industry, the majority of China's pharmacies are associated with **hospitals** and clinics. Market reforms have left China's health care institutions responsible for their own profits and losses. As a result, drug sales have become the major source of revenue for China's health care institutions, constituting 50 per cent or more of total hospital income. Imported, joint venture and locally manufactured drugs all vie for a share of this lucrative market; joint venture products have been particularly successful. Pharmacies are at the nexus of the economic well-being of China's pharmaceutical industry, health care institutes and doctors.

China's pharmacies are also distinguished by their diversity of products, which span the spectrum from innovative new pharmaceuticals to **herbal medicine** products that have been part of China's material medica for more than two millennia. Larger hospitals generally separate these products into four different pharmacies: biomedical pharmaceuticals, 'Chinese medicine raw herbs' (*yinpian*), 'Chinese medicine patent drugs' (*zhongchengyao*) and hospital preparations (not available elsewhere). In retail pharmacies, these distinctions are blurred. All retail pharmacies carry a wide range of biomedical pharmaceuticals and a growing number of *zhongchengyao*. Other pharmacies, some with long histories of commercial operations, also feature Chinese medicine *yinpian*. Beijing's Tongrentang Pharmacy, established in 1669, is a famous example of the latter; it served as the official pharmacy of the Qing court.

ERIC I. KARCHMER

physical education

China pays great attention to physical education (PE). The State Council's 'Regulations on Physical Education in Educational Institutions' (1990) defines PE as a programme to build students' physical health; to increase their knowledge of physical training; to build character and moral strength; and to cultivate prospective athletes. To promote PE, China has made great efforts to upgrade its PE teachers. PE teachers in K-12 must have at least an associate PE degree. China now has twenty specialized PE colleges, sixty PE programmes in comprehensive universities, and over 200 PE teacher training schools. A total of 300,000 PE teachers have been licensed.

PE in China takes the form of class teaching, extra-curricular activities, after-school training, and sports competitions, of which class teaching is fundamental. PE is a compulsory course from primary school until one's sophomore year of college. Failure in PE disqualifies a high school senior from enrolling in college. Extra-curricular activities are part of PE, which include bodybuilding, dancing and recreational sports. Elementary and secondary school students are required to do morning and recess exercises. Talented students receive systematic training in spare-time sports schools, which number in the thousands throughout the country and have turned out a great number of outstanding athletes. Sports competitions are organized on a regular basis: the National School Games are held every three years and the National University Games every four years. Research in physical education with modern technology is conducted regularly and systematically.

Further reading

Jones, Robin (1999). 'Sport and Physical Education in School and University'. In James Riordan and Robin Jones (eds), *Sport and Physical Education in China*. New York: E. and F. N. Spon, 90–119.

HU MINGRONG

physical fitness and sports clubs

The Mandarin Chinese word *tiyu*, commonly translated as physical culture, physical education or sports, was a Japanese invention of the mid to late nineteenth century. Western notions of physical fitness arrived in China via Japan, mainly in association with plans for developing national military strength, an association that continued into the PRC. It gained iconical status from a slogan penned by Chairman Mao in 1952: 'Develop physical culture and sports, strengthen the people's physiques'. The central government attempted to organize all fitness activities through its various organs, such as schools, factories, neighbourhood associations and state-supported sports teams. Not until the reform era did the link between physical fitness and national military strength come into question. In the late 1980s, the first fitness clubs appeared that offered access to any individual who paid an admission fee. Although they increased rapidly in large cities, they were too expensive for the vast majority of the populace. Until the late 1990s, the patrons of the upscale fitness clubs located in luxury hotels or multi-functional recreational clubs tended to be the **nouveaux riches** or state officials making dubious use of state funds.

The commercialization of physical fitness caused a shift away from the collective, militarized notion

of *tiyu* towards an individual, recreational notion of 'fitness' (*jianshen*) pursued for personal health and enjoyment. The change in language was officially reflected in the 1995 Sports Law, which dropped the old 'mass physical culture' (*qunzhong tiyu*) for the new 'fitness for all' (*quanmin jianshen*).

Further reading

Reekie, Shirley (1999). 'Mass Fitness'. In James Riordan and Robin Jones (eds), *Sport and Physical Education in China*. New York: E. and F. N. Spon, 243–54.

SUSAN BROWNELL

pilgrimage

Traditional pilgrimage practices, having all but ceased to exist during the **Cultural Revolution**, re-emerged in the 1980s. In addition, new forms of pilgrimage to sites associated with CCP history and the revolution that appeared following the Communist victory on the mainland in 1949 continue to be popular. **Sacred mountains** associated with Buddhism and Daoism are the primary focus of traditional pilgrimage. Pilgrimage to cities or city temples, common in West Asia, or to rivers and water sites as in India, are relatively rare in China. There are numerous Buddhist and Daoist pilgrimage mountains throughout China. The 'Five Marchmounts' (*Wuyue*), five peaks prominent as sacred sites for over two millennia, are the best-known pilgrimage destinations in China, replete with Buddhist, Daoist, Confucian and, previously, imperial sites of practice. The 'Four Great Mountains' (*Sida mingshan*) are primary destinations for Buddhists. However, few pilgrimage mountains are exclusively Buddhist or Daoist, and most pilgrimage practices are common regardless of religious association.

There is no single term for traditional pilgrimage, and the practice is generally described as 'paying respect to the mountain and presenting incense' (*qiaoshan jinxiang*). Incense plays a central role in pilgrimage. Incense sticks are burnt not only in the temples, but also along trails, beside rocks, springs and trees, on peaks and in caves. A pilgrim is an 'incense guest' (*xiangke*), and a significant source of income for temples at pilgrimage sites is the sale of incense. Many identify themselves as pilgrims by wearing yellow 'incense bags' around their necks. Motives are not easy to ascertain, but a frequently heard expression of purpose is 'to invite fortune and ensure good health'. Another motive is to accumulate merit in preparation for a post-mortem existence or on behalf of deceased relatives. 'Flesh bodies', the preserved corpses of monks believed to have self-mummified, are enshrined on many Buddhist mountains. Many pilgrims regard a wake in proximity to such relics on festival days as conducive to good fortune. Much pilgrimage is also an occasion for light-hearted tourism, the purchase of trinkets, taking pictures, and eating together, generally as part of large pilgrimage groups. This aspect of pilgrimage has generated a flourishing and somewhat aggressive tourist industry: hotels, restaurants, souvenir shops and charter bus companies. Begging, often noted with resentment in pre-modern travel narratives, and outlawed for several decades during the Cultural Revolution, has made a vigorous recovery at most pilgrimage sites.

As in many modern states, pilgrimage as an exercise in nationalism has also emerged in China. Monuments (see **monuments and public sculpture**) and sometimes **museums** mark sites of famous battles with the Japanese or with the Nationalists along the course of the Long March. These in several instances are conveniently located near traditional pilgrimage sites, either supplanting them or benefiting from a shared flow of pilgrims. Tourist agencies have emerged to offer packaged tours to these sites. In Beijing, thousands visit **Tiananmen Square**, the Mao mausoleum and the Imperial Palace every day. In a creative use of history, the reconstructed Hangzhou tomb of Yue Fei, the great Song dynasty general, revered for his adamant loyalty, receives more visitors than almost any other site in this tourist town. Though no incense is burned and few if any can be seen bowing, the structures and use of space in such sites generally reproduce those of traditional Buddhist and Daoist sacred sites. The distinction between pilgrimage and **tourism** is, and has long been, a fuzzy one.

See also: Daoist monasteries/abbeys; Guanyin; Mazu; processions (religious); religion, recent history of

Further reading

Naquin, Susan and Yu, Chun-fang (eds) (1992). *Pilgrims and Sacred Sites in China*. Berkeley: University of California Press.

WILLIAM POWELL

Pingju

(Tangshan, Hebei sung-drama, opera)

Pingju (Ping opera) is a regional form that emerged around 1910 in the Tangshan area, Hebei province, where it was particularly popular among coal miners and peasants. It incorporates musical elements from narrative song form (*Lianhua lao* or 'Lotus Song'; see **quyi**), folk dance (*bengbeng* or 'to caper'), **shadow puppet theatre** (Luanzhou yingxi), and Hebei opera (**Bangzi**). Among the forerunners of Pingju are Tangshan laozi (Tangshan narrative song) or Pingqiang bangzi (clapper opera with Ping melodies). The form's folk roots and colloquial language facilitated its spreading throughout most of northern China, and then to other parts of the country. Pingju's music features a range of dialogue and declamatory styles, arias (*changqiang*), airs for melodic instruments and percussion (*qupai*), and folk melodies. The arias, accompanied notably by the *banhu* (two-string fiddle), are sung in melodic and rhythmic modes (*banqiang*) like most northern opera genres (see **Xiqu musical structure**).

The first decades of Pingju's history were dominated by actresses performing both male and female roles. Some collaborated with left-wing playwrights in Shanghai in 1935–6, such as the actress Bai Yushuang ('Empress of Pingju') with Ouyang Yuqian in a modern adaptation of the classic story of Wu Song and **Pan Jinlian**. In the 1950s, Communist authorities saw in Pingju the prospect of promoting plays conveying the appropriate ideology by highlighting the positive image of the common folk and of female heroines, and the inevitability of justice. Pingju's strong appeal before the **Cultural Revolution**, evidenced by films such as *Flowers as Matchmakers* (*Hua wei mei*, 1963) featuring the famous actress Xin Fengxia (1925–98), continued through the 1980s with a new crop of contemporary plays and actors. Pingju's accessibility and adaptability explain its continuing success and resilience in a vastly changed country.

ISABELLE DUCHESNE

pipa

Traditional musical instrument

The pipa is a four-stringed, pear-shaped, fretted plucked lute from Central Asia that had appeared in China by the seventh century AD. Its body is made out of hollowed out teak covered with a soundboard of *wutong* wood (*Firmiana platanifolia*). Four strings traditionally made of silk (now often of steel) stretch from a string attachment and bridge located near the base of the resonator to their individual tuning pegs which are inserted two on each side of the head. A varying number of frets consisting of horizontal bamboo strips (*pin*) glued to the soundboard run from the midsection to the upper body and give way to frets consisting of triangular blocks (*xiang*) made of ivory, cow horn or plastic on the neck of the instrument. With four *xiang* and ten to thirteen *pin*, a traditional pipa was capable of playing in only two or three modalities. Since the late 1940s, more *pin* have been added, resulting in a total of twenty-four frets that allowed for equal-tempered tuning, increasing the instrument's harmonic and transpositional capabilities.

The term pipa is onomatopoeic, representing a downward and an upward stroke respectively by the thumb and index finger of the right hand on a string. All five fingers are used quite extensively for plucking. In performance, the instrument is typically set on the left thigh of the seated player, who holds it upright with the instrument's neck and head close to his left ear. An exception can be found with the pipa used in the **Minnan nanyin** ensemble wherein the instrument is held at a horizontal angle.

The pipa has long been employed in narrative song (**quyi**) and **string ensemble** traditions and as a solo instrument. It provides the main accompaniment in oral narrative genres such as Suzhou tanci, Beifang quyi pipa and Sichuan qingyin pipa. Both traditional ensemble and solo pipa pieces are part of repertories associated with five different schools of pipa-playing based in the Jiangnan area with Shanghai as the centre. Since the 1950s, additional contexts for performance have been created. The expanded musical and expressive capabilities of the modern pipa lend it to the performance of Western-style compositions as well as new chamber music arrangements of traditional pieces using both Chinese and Western instruments. In the **modern Chinese orchestra**, which performs *guoyue* (national music), there is a pipa section.

See also: traditional music; traditional music composers; traditional music performers

MERCEDES M. DUJUNCO

poetry

Reflecting China's rapidly changing political, social and cultural topography at the end of the twentieth century, poetry too has experienced a dazzling and fast-paced transformation in both thematic concern and aesthetic orientation. The function of poetry in cultural life and the role of the poet in society have become increasingly problematic and polemical, an indication of the continuing internal crisis – since the 1910s – of vernacular poetry as a viable literary genre. On the other hand, through endless self-generated controversy and debate, poetry manages to hold on to, at least partially, its avant-garde status in literature and its former glory as a harbinger for cultural change. What is at stake is no less than the possibility of poetry in a commerce-dominated society, not to mention its relevance in China's agenda of modernization.

The resurgence of socialist realism poetry at the end of 1970s and the beginning of the 1980s led the way for the resurrection of poetry in the wake of the **Cultural Revolution**, during which poetry had been reduced to mere slogan-ism and a mechanical hymn to the Communist Party and Chairman Mao. The poetry of realism was written by a group of 'returning poets', established poets who had been silenced in numerous political campaigns since 1949. They returned to poetry with a vengeance to write about their personal suffering and to expose rampant corruption and injustice. Their poetry of 'truth' resonated with the public and reclaimed a lost audience. But the complicity of socialist realism with the Maoist ideology forestalled the potential of the 'returning poets' so that they were unable to completely break with the power that created them. It was the **Misty poetry** (*Menglongshi*) that provided a real alternative to the official poetry of propaganda.

Led by **Bei Dao**, **Gu Cheng**, **Shu Ting** or the so-called *Today* (*Jintian*) group (see **literary periodicals**), Misty poets burst onto the scene almost at the same time as the 'returning poets', but they quickly replaced the latter as the dominant voices of discontent and nonconformity. Bei Dao's well-known statement 'I – do – not – believe!' strikes at the heart of the discredited Maoist ideology and summarized the sentiments of a generation. The uniform concern of Misty poetry was the restoration of personal space and the freedom to live a life of dignity and fulfilment without political consequences. More far-reaching was Misty poetry's creation of a poetic language with novel metaphors, unusual image combinations, and elliptical syntax that stood in sharp contrast to poetry of realism. Through the example of working against its immediate predecessor, Misty poetry led contemporary poetry into an exhilarating journey of stylistic innovations.

By the mid 1980s, Misty poetry was pronounced 'dead' as a genre by younger poets. This was not so much a denial of the legacy of Misty poetry as the declaration of an open season for poetic experimentalism. In 1986, two newspapers listed almost a hundred self-described schools of poetry featuring several hundred new poets and created an exciting national cultural event. Although many of the schools were without substance, their existence (however brief) helped to create an atmosphere of uninhibited experimentation in style and language that is still the spirit of poetry today.

In the 1990s, an all-consuming debate between 'intellectual poetry' (*zhishifenzishi*) and 'street poetry'

(*minjianshi*) continued to energize poetry (see **minjian**). The former, which includes the 'cultural epics' (*wenhua shishi*) by **Yang Lian, Jiang He** and **Haizi**, all of whom produced major works in the 1980s, and the metaphysical poetry by **Duoduo**, Wang Jiaxin and **Xi Chuan**, maintain a close relationship with Misty poetry in its sense of social mission and humanistic thrust. The latter, which includes the poetry of Han Dong, **Yu Jian**, Li Yawei and Yi Sha (see **Tamen**), underplays the importance of personal voice and resorts to narrative or dramatization to produce parody and humour. In the early 2000s, more extreme positions of anti-hero, anti-allegory and anti-image have become common among the 'New Generation' (*Xinshengdai*) poets. In contrast, some women poets, including **Zhai Yongming**, Yi Lei and Tang Yaping, have moderated their position on 'personalization' (*gerenhua*) and 'impersonalization' (*daiyan*), making the body both a physical sign and an allegorical text. As China's market economy takes root and power relations continue to shift from the centre to the periphery, contemporary poetry will thrive in a state of 'beautiful disorder' and sustain its momentum with its culture of experimentation.

Further reading

Li, Xinyu (2000). *Zhongguo daidai shige yishu yanbian shi*. Hangzhou: Zhejiang daxue chubanshe.

McDougall, Bonnie and Kam, Louie (1997). 'Poetry: The Challenge of Modernity'. In *idem*, *The Literature of China in the Twentieth Century*. New York: Columbia University Press, 421–40.

van Crevel, Maghiel (1998). *Language Shattered: Contemporary Chinese Poetry and Duo Duo*. Leiden: Research School CNWS.

DIAN LI

political culture in Shanghai

Shanghai is China's First City. Shanghai in the past and present holds the key to China's transformation to a modern society. It is the first and probably the only Chinese city that wholeheartedly embraced Western ideas, practices and institutions.

Western powers seized and built the city after 1843, when the Manchu dynasty signed yet another so-called unequal treaty with the Western powers.

In Shanghai, the Chinese first experienced all the amenities of a modern city, such as electricity, gas, running water, cable car and, later, automobile. It was in Shanghai that modern press, periodicals, publishing houses, motion pictures, theatres and other Western performing arts made their debut. Shanghai gave birth to China's first classes of capitalists and modern literary intellectuals. As a result of all this, Shanghai became the centre of the constitutional monarchy movement of 1900–10. After the founding of the Republic of China in 1911, Shanghai took the lead in the federalist movement in the early 1920s. Reformers from interior provinces, where conservatism was deeply entrenched, used Shanghai to propagate their causes. Periodical literature from Shanghai contributed significantly to the intellectual revolution of the May Fourth movement in 1919. To prominent Chinese and Westerners, Shanghai and its surrounding region were the ideal place to build a new Chinese republic.

From 1949 to 1976, Mao terminated Shanghai's links with the West, confiscated Shanghai's industrial and human resources, and then scattered these in the interior. But Mao had exploited the residuals of Shanghai's former avant-gardism by launching his **Cultural Revolution** in Shanghai between 1966 and 1969. Ultimately, Mao left behind an inward-looking and dilapidated Shanghai. Since the early 1980s, however, Shanghai steadily regained its pre-Communist status as the centre of libertarian ideas. Reformers across the nation used Shanghai media to advocate views such as the obsoleteness of Marxism, the supremacy of the Party Congress instead of the Party centre (head of the CCP and the Politiburo), the redefinition of the Party character as a ruling rather than a revolutionary party (so as to base the Party's legitimacy on performance), and the illegality of military interference in the political process. It is noteworthy that after the Democracy Wall movement in 1979, the most prominent Chinese newspaper calling for a market economy and democracy was the Shanghai journal *World Economic Herald* (*Shijie jingji daobao*).

After his celebrated southern excursion in 1992 (see **Southern Excursion Talks (Deng Xiaoping, 1992)**), Deng Xiaoping copied Mao's practice of using Shanghai's former cultural status for his own political purposes. First, Beijing invested substantially in the Pudong district of Shanghai, hoping to turn it into the fifth 'tiger' in Asia (after Hong Kong, Taiwan, South Korea and Singapore). Second, Deng Xiaoping and Jiang Zemin designated Shanghai as the national model in transforming state-owned enterprises into modern corporations and accomplishing Deng's idea of a **socialist spiritual civilization**. Shanghai may finally realize its historic role as 'the leading sheep' (*daitouyang*) of Chinese modernization.

Further reading

Yang, Mayfair Mei, Hui (1997). 'Mass Media and Transnational Subjectivity in Shanghai: Notes on (Re)cosmopolitanism in a Chinese Metropolis'. In Aiwha Ong and Donald Nonini (eds), *Ungrounded Empires: The Cultural Politics of Modern Chinese Transnationalism*. New York: Routledge, 287–319.

Yeung, Y. M. and Sung, Yun-wing (eds) (1996). *Shanghai. Transformation and Modernization under China's Open Policy*. Hong Kong: The Chinese University Press.

ALAN P. L. LIU

political culture in Singapore

Singapore is a multiethnic society, with political influence institutionally from the West and culturally from the East. On a 250-square-mile island between the Indian Ocean and the South China Sea, Singapore is among the richest countries in the world. Its success is largely attributed to the 'Singaporean Spirit'. Pragmatism is an important component of the spirit. Singapore believes that only economic success can maximize its national security and democratize its political system. Pragmatism allows Singapore to enjoy a market economy with a socialistic distribution system. Ethnic harmony and religious tolerance are other traits of the spirit. As immigrants from China, Malaysia and South Asia, Singaporeans have had few ethnic conflicts since independence due to a clever ethnic policy. It allows each ethnic group to maintain its way of life while encouraging its identification with Singapore as 'one country, one nation, and one fate'. Singapore has all the major religions in the world: Buddhism, Daoism, Islam, Hinduism and Christianity. All coexist peacefully. As early as 1949, a religious federation was founded to include leaders of all beliefs. In 1974, the federation drafted a 'Joint Prayer' to be used in all religious ceremonies. Conversion is approached with an open mind. In fact, 60 per cent of the Christians are converts.

Conservatism, however, is a hallmark of the 'Singaporean Spirit'. Singapore takes pride in its so-called 'oriental democracy', characterized by maintenance of a one-party system, an emphasis on political stability and social order, clean government and good citizenship, and giving priority to economic development. Singapore has re-established Confucianism as a norm of public behaviour and a guiding principle for the government in order to combat the problems of modernization, which it has not succeeded in avoiding: altruism is giving way to selfishness; the family is slowly in disarray; emigration is on the rise; crime and drug abuse are resurgent; and consumerism and hedonism are encroaching upon lofty aspirations. Confucian teachings have been invested with new meanings: 'loyalty' is interpreted as identification with the country's interests; 'filial piety' as respect for the elderly; 'benevolence' humaneness; 'courtesy' politeness; 'virtue' as social morality; 'honesty' as immunity from corruption; and 'sense of shame' as knowledge of right and wrong. Meanwhile, Singapore strives to establish a new value system that all Singaporeans can call their own – a system that values the country, the family, compassion, harmony and tolerance. Apparently, 'nation' and 'family' are the gist of the Singaporean socio-political values. Singaporean conservatism is also reflected in the literary trend of 'returning to tradition'. Chinese literature is the mainstream literary creation in Singapore. Early Singaporean Chinese literature was part of the literary movement in China. In 1956, however, a campaign to build a 'patriotic popular literature' was initiated,

meant to educate Singaporean Chinese to play a greater role in Singapore's national liberation. It ended with Singapore's independence in 1965. Post-independence Chinese literature in Singapore identifies itself with the Singaporean nation politically, but culturally still with the Chinese literary tradition. Literature is also expected to save the younger generation from being Westernized.

The 'Singaporean Spirit' advocates authority and discipline. The paradox that 'Singapore is a democracy without freedom' rings true in the sense that with all the ingredients of a democracy, Singapore has been continuously ruled by one party. The odd marriage of democracy with authoritarianism is mainly due to Singapore's Chinese cultural heritage. Chinese immigrants amount to 70 per cent of the population, Confucius' socio-political ethics that celebrate patriarchy and hierarchy have greatly influenced Singapore's socio-political value system. Singapore's patriarchal rule is characterized by the government's absolute authority and its parental benevolence. It disciplines speeches and religious activities deemed detrimental to national interests, advocates individual obedience to the collectivist society and yet, at the same time, also holds the government accountable for the people (if not to the people). Singapore believes in the rule by the crème de la crème of the society with an iron hand. Law enforcement includes flogging. The ruling government must be devoid of corruption. As soon as the People's Action Party came to power, it began to fight corruption through legal means. The success in keeping Singapore's government clean is largely credited to the establishment of the independent Corrupt Practices Investigation Bureau. Appointed by the president and responsible directly to the prime minister, the bureau is almighty. Personal feelings have no place in its operation. All perpetrators will be dealt with whatever their rank or merit.

Rigid law enforcement, however, does not preempt change. But changes have always been carefully managed so that no chaos will result. Stability is always the priority. A good example is Singapore's transition in political leadership. The process is long and gradual, but smooth and peaceful. In 1980s, the triune system of party, government and military was restructured. The amended constitution required that the president, who used to be chosen by the parliament, be elected directly by the people.

The 'Singaporean Spirit' is nurtured through education. Lacking natural resources, Singapore attaches great importance to people. Its investment in education is next only to national defence. The educated are expected to make productive use of information and knowledge. Singapore sees the development of information technology as its short-cut to global competitiveness. Since it launched the IT 2000 master plan in 1991, Singapore has been working diligently to become an 'intelligent island'. Libraries, as the hub of information and knowl-edge, are expected to play a pivotal role. The National Library serves as the central agency for the Singapore Integrated Library Automated Service (SILAS), linking libraries at home and abroad.

Further reading

Guan, Shijie (1995). *The Studies of Exchanges among Cultures*. Beijing: Beijing University Press.

Lee, Kuan Yew (2000). *From Third World to First: The Singapore Story, 1965–2000*. New York: HarperCollins.

Mauzy, Diane. (2002). *Singapore Politics under the People's Action Party*. London: Routledge.

Tao, Hung-chao (1989). *Confucianism and Economic Development: An Oriental Alternative*. Washington, DC: Washington Institute Press.

Tremewan, Chris (1994). *The Political Economy of Social Control in Singapore*. New York: St Martin's Press.

Wei, Hong (2000). *The Singaporean Spirit*. Beijing: Changjiang [Yangzi] Literary Press.

HU MINGRONG

political icons (and art)

Political figures, artists, intellectuals and unruly elements have readily used emblems, icons and cultural paraphernalia both to express themselves and to claim, or generate, cultural capital.

Sometimes the commercial sector has treated Party icons as considerably less than sacrosanct, but in ways that were anything but hostile. Indeed, this commercialization of Party icons has played on the fact that many people feel comfortable with the icons – and it is this sense of familiarity, driven home through the new commercialization, that indirectly reinforces of political legitimacy.

Since the Cultural Revolution the Great Wall has been promoted as an ancient artifact and symbol of Chinese resilience. Although the present wall is a late-dynastic creation, it has been used to epitomize variously the solidarity of the masses and the strength of the People's Liberation Army. The creators of the 1988 tele-series **River Elegy** used the wall as a metaphor for China's inward-looking, landlocked recidivism, while for neo-patriots in the 1990s it was emblematic of continuity, strength and diversity in unity. The artist **Xu Bing** decided to beat the problem, literally, by making rubbings of the wall into avant-garde art. Xu is also famous for having created – with the help of dedicated artisans – a majestic artwork out of hand-carved nonsense characters. His *Book of Heaven* is a gibberish testament to the semiotic turn popular among some practitioners of contemporary Chinese art during the 1980s.

Others have preferred more embodied icons. In the early months of Red Guard agitation in 1966, the Monkey King (Sun Wukong, or Houwang) – the much-loved upstart hero of the Wu Cheng'en's novel *Journey to the West (Xiyou ji)* – was used as a symbol of rebellion, and in the reform era the lovable rascal has been a popular figure among manufacturers and consumers alike. Mao Zedong, the politician who authorized the contemporary valence of the Monkey King, having famously compared himself to the fictional char-acter, has also been transmogrified into a public icon that has repeatedly been re-branded since his demise in 1976. After taxidermy successfully solved the problem of the Great Leader's physical remains, a sanitized version of Mao was claimed by the Party-state as a patriot and statesman. But his is an unquiet ghost that appeals to different con-stituencies. In the new, mass Mao cult of the early 1990s, his image featured in a plethora of popular and garish guises (on T-shirts, in talismans, on cigarette lighters, and so on); meanwhile, from the

1980s non-official artists found in his image a daunting inspiration (**Li Shan**), a lingering spectre that had to be exorcized (**Wang Keping**, **Zhang Hongtu**, *et al.*) or playfully celebrated (**Wang Guangyi** and **Yu Youhan**), and their remade images of the Chairman readily found an international audience, and buyers.

See also: advertising; cars and taxis; Neo-Maoism and Mao Fever; Party advertising and self-promotion; Political Pop; poster art and artists; Sheng Qi

Further reading

Dal Lago, Francesca (1999). 'Personal Mao: Reshaping an Icon in Contemporary Chinese Art'. *Art Journal* 58 (Summer).
—— (2002). 'Images, Words and Violence: Cultural Revolution Influences on Chinese Avant-Garde Art'. In Wu Hong (ed.), *Chinese Art at the Crossroads: Between Past and Future*. Hong Kong: New Art Media.

GEREMIE R. BARMÉ

political jokes

Chinese political jokes are language-related, which means satire and irony may be lost in translation. Instead of pulling political leaders' legs, they are subtle, impersonal, and are common in **xiang-sheng** (comic dialogue) and **shunkouliu** (doggerel). Political jokes often centre around **corruption**, e.g. Mao said, 'Revolution is not a dinner party' (*Geming bushi qingke chifan*), but for many cadres 'Revolution is not entertaining guests, but eating dinner [at public expense or at the cost of the **nouveaux riches**]' (*Geming bushi qingke jiushi chifan*). Cadres are supposed to 'serve the people' (*wei renmin fuwu*), but many 'serve the people's currency' (*wei renminbi fuwu*). Deng Xiaoping's 'four basic principles' (*si xiang jiben yuanze*) are Marxism–Leninism–Mao Zedong Thought, the Communist Leadership, the socialist road and the people's democratic dictatorship. But some cadres had their own version: 'Eat a lot, but don't drink too much; take gifts, but don't accept bribes; love the new, but

don't hate the old; be romantic, but don't be obscene' (*Dachi bu dahe; shouli bu shouhui; xixin bu yanjiu; fengliu bu xialiu*). Beijingers are particularly good at making implicit political jokes about current affairs. For example, a bus conductor, seeing the crowd at a bus stop, shouts, 'Don't push! Let comrades from Shanghai get on first' which pokes fun at many Shanghai-related top leaders (Jiang Zemin and Zhu Rongji served as Shanghai mayors; the Gang of Four was Shanghai-related).

See also: political language; political culture in Shanghai

HELEN XIAOYAN WU

political language

Contemporary Chinese cultural expression enjoys a linguistic richness and variety unprecedented under Party rule. Written styles are enriched by classical Chinese, late-dynastic vernacular, Republican-era writings, Kong-Tai usage (see **Kong-Tai style**), Maoist diction, regional argots and all manner of foreign influences. After the years of politically induced linguistic paucity during the **Cultural Revolution** era, this efflorescence of language was gradual. But politics never expunged linguistic variety. Although books were burnt or banned, many young and older people still managed to read illicit works in secret, or they enjoyed books that were reprinted as part of the arcane political purges of the 1970s, in particular the anti-Confucius campaign.

Most words of the Cultural Revolution era are marked off with quotation marks, a punctuated cordon sanitaire that says look but do not accept. The sixty-sixes and ninety-nines that are still used for ironic or negative effect were a European import, but they came into their own during the Cultural Revolution when much of the pre-1966 world was consigned to imprisonment within quotations. While the laudable sayings or quotations from theoretical paragons like Mao, Marx, Engels, Lenin and Stalin were printed in bold type, all that was condemned appeared between quotation marks that questioned the very 'truth' and 'value' of their existence.

While the sarcastic quote mark is still widely used, much Maoist-era language has fallen from daily use. The verb *gao* (originally meaning 'do' or 'screw' in Mao's patois) remains, but for many years the educated have often replaced it with the more conventional word *zuo* (do, make). Although in retrospect many feel that *gao geming* (making revolution) is just what they did. Most persistent are the evaluative terms that colour official pronouncements, leaders' speeches and every civic campaign. There is no neutrality in the political realm, things are black-and-white, and there is a rich connotative language to depict it. These 'descriptive-evaluative' words, as the Russian philosopher Mikhael Epstein calls them in his work on totalitarian language, are terms that combine both descriptive and evaluative meanings; they communicate not only information but also a particular ideological message, or concealed judgments that take the form of words. This kind of language, which reached an apogee during Mao's last decades, is marked by an ability to employ ideologically laden words to weaken opposing sides while taking advantage of the resulting confusion.

The Chinese language has a rich and venerable lexicon of words that were converted under both Nationalist and Communist rule to act as 'descriptive-evaluative' words. It is a lexicon that was, according to tradition, first formulated by Confucius when he edited the history of the State of Lu, the *Spring and Autumn Annals*, judiciously choosing expressions to describe political actions in moral terms. Classical scholars talk of Confucius creating a 'Spring and Autumn writing style' (*chunqiu bifa*) which relied on a vocabulary of *baobianci*, or judgmental words, to praise (*bao*) or censure (*bian*) every political act and event contained in the annals of Lu. In modern usage, all activities beneficial to the Party-state are represented by words with positive connotations or *baoyici*, while those that are deleterious in nature are condemned with negative verbs, nouns and adjectives, or *biianyici*.

Even now, the style of denunciation and modes of criticism current in mainland Chinese culture readily echo habits of mind and language inculcated by decades of Party rule. Even in an environment of increased free speech and media openness, the rhetorical style of totalitarianism

(that is, a style that attempts a total embrace of all aspects of life and thought) and constant moral evaluation and judgment, and its refusal to allow for critical self-reflection, retains its appeal. Nonetheless, the militaristic style of language and enunciation has gradually given way to a more civil tone. TV and radio presenters speak with a less strident tone, although when necessary they can still don Mao suits and intone official condemnations with steely resolve as in the past.

GEREMIE R. BARMÉ

Political Pop
Artistic trend

'Political Pop' is a critical art term I coined and used for the first time in a 1991 article 'Apathy and Deconstructive Consciousness in Post-1989 Art'. It describes a social current emerged in the 1990s to contrast the arrival of Western consumer culture to China and often defined as 'Mao Fever', which transformed the 'holiness of politics' of the Mao era into a satirical popular trend, characterized by pop music arrangements of famous songs of the Mao period or the application of Mao's portrait on lighters and other paraphernalia (see **Neo-Maoism and Mao Fever**). The earliest artists expressing themselves in such style had participated in the **85 New Wave [Art] Movement** and subsequently abandoned their metaphysical concerns to adopt a deconstructive approach defined by the use of Pop Art techniques.

The language of 'Political Pop' characteristically combines political symbols of the Mao era, most often Mao portraits, and symbols of Western consumer culture to create a feeling of irony and absurdity. Similar trends have emerged in many post-socialist societies, such as the phenomenon of Sots Art in Russia. In later periods, this artistic trend spread to many kinds of art forms, including film and television. Like 'Mao Fever', 'Political Pop' reflects a complex psychological effect stemming from the inability to find release from the so-called 'Mao complex' created though years of hammering indoctrination. By acknowledging political reality, 'Political Pop' satirizes and neutralizes it as form of breaking through from an overly saturated political mentality. Artists whose work is mostly associated with this trend or who have occasionally used this approach in their oeuvre include **Feng Mengbo**, **Li Shan**, **Yu Youhan**, **Wang Guangyi**, **Wang Xingwei**, Wang Ziwei, **Zhang Hongtu**, among others.

Further reading

Dal Lago, Francesca (1993). 'Il realismo critico della giovane arte cinese' [The Critical Realism of Young Chinese Art]. In *Punti Cardinali dell'Arte, Catalogo della XLV Esposizione Internazionale* d'Arte. Venezia: Edizioni La Biennale di Venezia, 538.

—— (1999). 'Personal Mao: Reshaping an Icon in Contemporary Chinese Art', *The Art Journal* (Summer): 75–87.

—— (2001). 'Images, Words and Violence : Cultural Revolutionary Influences on Chinese Avant-Garde Art'. In Wu Hong (ed.), *Chinese Art at the Crossroads: Between Past and Future.* Hong Kong: New Art Media, 32–9.

Li, Xianting (1992). 'Hou 89 yishu zhong de wuliaogang he jiegou yishi' [Apathy and Deconstructive Consciousness in Post-1989 Art], *Yishu chaoliu* 1 [Art Currents, Taiwan].

—— (1993). 'Major Trends in the Development of Contemporary Chinese Art'. In Valerie C. Doran (ed.), *China's New Art, Post-1989* (exhibition catalogue). Hong Kong: Hanart T Z Gallery, x–xxii.

—— (1994). 'The Imprisoned Heart, Ideology in an Age of Consumption'. *ART AsiaPacific* (April): 25–30.

LI XIANTING (TRANS. FRANCESCA DAL LAGO)

political slogans

China is a country of slogans, which are ubiquitous. What is in a political slogan? Everything, though some may not appear obvious at first sight. For instance: (1) 'Practice is the sole criterion to test truth' (*Shijian shi jianyan zhenli de weiyi biaozhun*) was not a philosophical proposition, but an ideological weapon used by reformers against conservatives, who were using whatever Mao said to serve their own interests; (2) 'Building socialism with Chinese characteristics' (*Jianshe you Zhongguo tese de shehuizhuyi*) seems vague, but whatever it means, it can be used to break through many dogmatic taboos as long as it is still 'socialism' and 'Chinese'; (3) 'To give birth to only one child is good' (*Zhi sheng yige hao*) is not about women's health, but a fundamental statement of the **one-child policy** controlling population growth; (4) 'Oppose hegemony; maintain world peace' (*Fandui baquanzhuyi, weihu shijie heping*) is dialectical, meaning China can say 'No' to the USA, but, meanwhile, peace is important for China to obtain Western technology; and (5) 'Grasping opportunities and developing ourselves' (*Zhuazhu jiyu, fazhan ziji*) sounds realistic and diplomatic, but implies that whatever others are saying about and doing to China now, China will have a better say when it is developed. Linguistically, Chinese political slogans are not necessarily short, as electioneering slogans in the West. They can be sentences with or without a subject, as shown in (1) and (2); they can be parallel phrases or sentences without a subject, like (4) and (5); and they can be rhetorical, but empty in content, such as (3).

See also: neologisms; Party advertising and self-promotion; political language

HELEN XIAOYAN WU

Pond Society

(Chishe)

Artist group

Formed by former students of the China Academy of Fine Arts (see **art academies**), the Pond Society removed art from a narrow academic context to explore public interaction. Established in May 1986 by **Zhang Peili**, **Geng Jianyi** and Song Ling, its first activity, *Work No. 1, Yang Taiji Series*, consisted of large newspaper cut-out figures pasted on the wall outside the Academy. Their aims found perfect expression in Geng Jianyi's installation *Waterworks* (*Zilai shuichang*, 1988). Zhang Peili's *Plan for the Realization of a Dialogue and Its Observation* (*Duijiang huodong xieyishu*, 1987) and *Brown*

Leather Book (*Hepishu*, 1988), both mailings, developed as a reaction to public apathy towards the Pond Society activities. They explored social interaction through themes of conformity, manipulation and the ominous connotations of health (*jiankang*) and sterility.

Many of these social concerns were already discernable in the '1985 New Space Exhibition' (*Xin kongjian*, 1985), which also featured Wang Qiang and Bao Jianfei. The exhibited works adopted a cold, ambiguous and questioning attitude towards modern life – habitually reduced to images glorifying industrialization. Wang Qiang sculpted a headless, handless musical conductor. Zhang Peili's *Midsummer Swimmers* (*Zhongxia de yongzhe*), painted in clean intense blues, suggested an environment de-humanized to the point of sterility, whereas his *End Note* (*Xiuzhi yinfu*) denies the usual fanfare celebration of progress. Geng Jianyi's *Haircut 3, Yet Another Bald Head* (*Lifa sanhao – 1985 nian xiajide you yige guangtou*) has an underlying reference to the rebelliousness of having one's head shaved, an attitude also present in the congealed smile of his *The Second State* (*Di'er zhuangtai*, 1987).

Further reading

Lü, Peng and Yi, Dan (1992). *Zhongguo xiandai yishushi* [A History of Modern Art in China]. Changsha: Hunan meishu chubanshe, 208–25.

EDUARDO WELSH

pop music in Hong Kong

Hong Kong's indigenous popular music industry became a commercial force in the early 1970s, when the city became affluent and urban youths (post-1949 baby-boomers) developed a sense of local pride.

Popular music from Taiwan (in Mandarin) and Western-imported pop and rock dominated Hong Kong's radio programming in the 1960s. However, the 1970s generation, rather than treating Hong Kong as a transitory place, claimed it as their home. The city's entertainment industry developed at the same time, not only in popular television ratings (especially serial dramas), but also in the

popular film and music markets in Asia and overseas Chinese communities.

While English-language pop had been imported for many decades (the Beatles visited Hong Kong on their 1964 world tour), indigenous pop began only in the early 1970s with local star Sam Hui. Hui had originally been a singer for Lotus, a post-Beatles local band singing in English. When Hui and his brother Michael produced and starred in their own television shows, their original songs in Cantonese reached the population at large. Other singers and songwriters followed suit, leading to the first generation of Cantopop stars, among them Alan **Tam**, Leslie **Cheung** and Anita **Mui**. Most Cantopop stars moved easily from one entertainment media to another. As the Hong Kong film industry grew, these stars became ever more valuable as cross-genre celebrities.

The musical styles of 1980s Cantopop, however, closely followed the Japanese scene. A large number of Alan Tam's and Anita Mui's hits were covers of Japanese chart-toppers. Most Cantopop songs are romantic ballads; few have strong and vigorous dance beats. In the early 1990s, a new generation of pop singers took the scene by storm, including the heavily marketed Four Heavenly Kings (Andy Lau (b. 1961), Jacky Cheung (b. 1961), Leon Lai (b. 1966, Beijing) and Aaron Kwok (b. 1965)) competing among themselves for fans and awards, and each following the same combination of film, television and singing. Most of their fans were teenage girls, falling in love less with their idols' singing ability (with the possible exception of Jacky Cheung) than with their image.

By the mid 1990s, Faye **Wong** captured many new fans, with a more cutting-edge style and delivery, encouraging original composition. Between 1991 and 2001, a few rap groups were also popular, performing lyrics ranging from socially challenging, confrontational hip-hop to sugary 'bubble-rap'. The first rap duo, **Softhard Wizards**, began their careers as radio disc-jockeys. In 1999, underground rap group LMF's first hit was banned on the radio because of obscenities in the lyrics. However, LMF has since signed with a major label, and their lyrics became tame.

When China re-opened its doors to outside influences in the late 1970s, Hong Kong's popular music took a foothold in the mainland market.

Many of Hong Kong's pop artists travel to China to perform in stadium shows and appear on national television. Their appearances also include popular films, which made them household names in China. The year 1997 was clearly a watershed that marked Hong Kong's position *vis-à-vis* China, and popular music has proven to be a lucrative niche in the post-1997 period, influencing the burgeoning music markets of China and Taiwan.

See also: Beyond; Kong-Tai style

JOANNA C. LEE

popular culture, mass culture

(tongsu wenhua, dazhong wenhua)

Social concept

Tongsu wenhua (popular culture) emerged in the late 1970s, developed in the 1980s, and was transformed in the 1990s, when it came to include commercialized and industrialized 'mass culture'. From 1979 through the mid 1980s, *tongsu wenhua* was shaped by Hong Kong and Taiwan-style (popular) culture (*Gangtai liuxing wenhua*), particularly film and music (see **Kong-Tai style**). A high 'culture fever' (*wenhua re*) in the mid 1980s created an 'elite culture' (*jingying wenhua*), which promoted 'enlightenment' and critiqued traditional Chinese culture. Differing from this elite culture, *tongsu wenhua* included tabloid newspapers, mass-circulation monthlies, cartoon books, pop music and **martial** arts films and **martial arts fiction**. Since 1992, when Deng Xiaoping delivered his **Southern Excursion Talks** (see **Southern Excursion Talks (Deng Xiaoping, 1992)**), *tongsu wenhua* has been gradually transformed into a commercialized mass culture, or 'consumer culture' (*xiaofei wenhua*). The transformation has blurred the boundaries between the 'high' and the 'low', between the elite and the masses, between official (state) and non-official (society), and between cultural and commodity production.

The recent development of 'popular culture' can be traced back to past revolutionary practices. The Chinese Communist Party had incorporated many elements of regional, folk and traditional culture into an official popular culture. Mao Zedong's 'Talks at the Yan'an Conference on Literature and Art' in May 1942 institutionalized the concept of the 'people' (*renmin*). Since then, cultural production has aimed at 'serving the people', a departure from the goal of the revolutionary intellectuals who were based in the major cities (Shanghai and Beijing) during the 1920s. However, during the **Cultural Revolution**, Jiang Qing (Mao's wife) played an important role in guiding the development of revolutionary popular culture. As a former film star in Shanghai who never liked folksong or folk music, regarding it as naive, vulgar and low, she openly voiced her contempt for kitschy folk plays. Jiang believed in the blending of Peking opera (**Jingju**) with Western orchestral music and mixing folk dance with Western ballet. As a result of her influence, ethnic and folk entertainment was never a focus in the official discourse of cultural production during the Cultural Revolution. Instead, 'model plays' (*Yangbanxi*), focusing on the representation of heroic characters, dominated the cultural scene (see **Xiqu**). The representation of such models (i.e. workers, peasants and soldiers) as the basis of cultural production continued until the 1980s when state-run cultural institutions began to seriously consider consumer reception of their products.

Since the late 1980s, cultural production has begun to reject the hero or model principle to focus on the stories of 'ordinary folks' (*laobaixing*). Some successful examples include **Wang Shuo**'s novels, **Ai Jing**'s songs, **CCTV (Chinese Central Television)**'s programme *Living Space* (*Shenghuo gongjian*) and **Feng Xiaogang**'s television series and **New Year's movies**. As the representation of the ordinary person becomes the norm in the popular culture industry, *tongsu wenhua* is no longer the top-down revolutionary 'culture of the masses' (*qunzhong wenhua*), but a commercial 'mass culture' (*dazhong wenhua*) from below.

See also: advertising; beauty magazines; bestsellers; book publishing; consumerism; minjian; rock music, rock bands

Further reading

Cheng, Fong-ching (2001). 'The Popular Culture Movement of the 1980s'. In Gloria Davies (ed.), *Voicing Concerns: Contemporary Chinese Critical Inquiry*. Lanham, MD: Rowman and Littlefield, 71–86.

Chen, Fong-ching and Jin, Guantao (1997). *From Youthful Manuscripts to River Elegy: The Chinese Popular Cultural Movement and Political Transformation, 1979–1989*. Hong Kong: Chinese University of Hong Kong Press.

Dai, Jinhua (1999). 'Invisible Writing: The Politics of Chinese Mass Culture in the 1990s'. *Modern Chinese Literature and Culture* 11.2 (Spring): 31–60.

Huang, Huilin (ed.) (1999). *Dangdai Zhongguo dazhong wenhua yanjiu* [Studies on Mass Culture in Contemporary China]. Beijing: Beijing shifan daxue.

Kaikonen, Marja (1995). 'From Knights to Nudes: Chinese Popular Literature since Mao'. *Stockholm Journal of East Asian Studies* 5: 85–110.

—— (1999). 'Stories and Legends: China's Largest Contemporary Popular Literature Journals'. In Michel Hockx (ed.), *The Literary Field of Twentieth Century China*. Honolulu: University of Hawai'i Press, 134–60.

Link, Perry, Madsen, Richard and Pickowicz, Paul G. (1989). *Unofficial China: Popular Culture and Thought in the People's Republic*. Boulder: Westview Press.

—— (2002). *Popular China: Unofficial Culture in a Globalizing Society*. Lanham, MD: Rowman and Littlefield.

Liu, Kang (2000). 'Popular Culture and Culture of the Masses in Contemporary China'. In Zhang Xudong and Arif Dirlik (eds), *Postmodernism and China*. Durham: Duke University Press, 123–44.

Lu, Sheldon (2002). 'Popular Culture: Toward an Historical and Dialectical Method'. In *idem* (ed.), *China, Transnational Visuality, Global Postmodernity*. Stanford: Stanford University Press, 185–212.

Wang, Jing (2001). 'The State Question in Chinese Popular Cultural Studies'. *Inter-Asia Cultural Studies* 2.1: 35–52.

Wu, Dingbo and Murphy, Patrick (eds) (1994). *Handbook of Chinese Popular Culture*. Westport: Greenwood Press.

Zha, Jianying (1995). *China Pop: How Soap Operas, Tabloids, and Bestsellers are Transforming a Culture*. New York: The New Press.

REN HAI

poster art and artists

In the twenty-first century, propaganda posters are fighting an up-hill battle to reach the people. The Party's posters no longer serve as important sources of information, and must compete with a flood of messages and images put out by a plethora of media. People generally consider posters old-fashioned, or too tainted by their earlier political usage, even though their subject matter has been brought in line with the rapidly changing times, social circumstances and popular taste. The declining number of poster titles published yearly indicates the loss of credibility and appeal. The introduction of state-of-the-art printing techniques and the use of thick glossy paper of good quality, or even plastic sheeting, has updated the look and the feel of the posters considerably, but this has not resulted in greater sales. A diversified market approach, which directs different types of propaganda contents at specific social groups, has largely failed. Only primary and secondary school students are still specifically targeted with educational propaganda (see **posters and education**), stressing elements of **socialist spiritual civilization** and patriotism. With popular interest in politics low, many ignore the Party's utterances and appear to be more worried about the size of their pay packets and the question whether they'll still be employed in the future.

The decline in the relevance of propaganda posters started in the early 1980s. Under Deng Xiaoping, alternative modes of creation were allowed, replacing the dominant style of Socialist Realism. The Open Door policy enabled artists and designers to reacquaint themselves with various artistic trends and developments abroad. The introduction of **advertising** in the print and broadcast media, and of many foreign television programmes, inspired artists and designers to borrow or emulate design techniques from the

West and from Taiwan, Hong Kong and Japan. As a result, propaganda poster themes became less heroic and militant, and more impressionistic. Slogans no longer called for mobilization but for economic reform, and had a less strident and aggressive tone. Abstract images replaced realism and more subdued colours replaced the bold hues. Westernized elements of modernity crept in, and female representations increasingly favoured a Eurasian rather than Chinese look.

In an attempt to give propaganda posters an aura of modernity, photography and photo-montage were introduced in the late 1980s. Photography was not favoured for propaganda purposes before, as it was considered a mere craft, without artistic potential. The popularity of the two techniques was related to developments external to the art world. First, photography had become one of the many new status symbols and one of the essential activities in urban life under reform. Once photography thus had entered the cultural mainstream, consumers demanded photographic images to replace the idealized and often simplistic realism that had prevailed before. The manipulation of photographic images was greatly facilitated by the proliferation of personal computers. Electronic manipulation of (parts of) photographs did away with old-fashioned methods of manual clipping and pasting, leading to more sophisticated results. Advertising companies led the way in applying these advanced techniques, which inevitably impacted on propaganda poster design.

But whether modernized in form and content or not, the Reform-era posters all lack conviction and strength. One of the main reasons is that they are designed to gently nudge people into the desired direction of thought and behaviour, and not to rouse the target group(s) into action. Another explanation can be found in the quality of the artwork. Artists and designers are no longer seen as the Party's 'spin doctors', a role they played during the heyday of poster production, and have lost considerable occupational status. The artists of old all have retired; the prolific designer He Qiongwen (b. 1925), for example, designed his last, unpublished, poster in 1991. Truly gifted young designers and artists now have more opportunities to market their works, and no longer feel compelled to work for the Party. A commercial art sector has come into being that is not dominated by the Party-state, and advertising agencies can offer higher incomes and more artistic freedom. As a result, the propaganda departments are left with artistic talent that can be considered capable, but second-string.

Propaganda posters continue to be part of the government's communication strategy, but television has become *the* medium to present propaganda by broadcasting highly sophisticated, extremely well-made forms of political advertising (see **Party advertising and self-promotion**). These political messages support general propaganda themes, stressing the central, and historically inevitable role of the Party in China's development or ethnic unity. In subtle ways, the Chinese are thus confronted with a type of propaganda that is very difficult to identify as such at first sight.

Further reading

Donald, Stephanie and Evans, Harriet (eds) (1999). *Picturing Power in the People's Republic of China: Posters of the Cultural Revolution.* Lanham, MD: Rowman and Littlefield.

Landsberger, Stefan R. (1995, 1998, 2001). *Chinese Propaganda Posters – From Revolution to Modernization.* Amsterdam/Armonk: Pepin Press/M. E. Sharpe.

—— (nd) *Stefan Landsberger's Chinese Propaganda Poster Pages.* Available at http://www.iisg.nl/~landsberger/

STEFAN LANDSBERGER

posters and education

Propaganda posters are increasingly targeted at children and adolescents. Such posters, usually produced in sets, are designed specifically for use in classrooms, or are directly aimed at young people outside of school. These groups are considered more impressionable, and more receptive to the messages the posters contain. They are also seen to be less inclined to reject them as 'mere propaganda', as the posters must now compete with a flood of other voices and images. In posters published in the early 2000s, the influence of the many

Japanese cartoons shown on Chinese television can be easily recognized: youngsters are depicted with the typically Westernized round eyes and spiky hairdos made popular in manga. The important themes that emerge in these materials convey patriotism and other elements of **socialist spiritual civilization**. They are partly derived from the 'Five Loves' (*wu'ai*, i.e. love the nation, the people, labour, science and socialism) that have been part of the moral education curriculum since 1989.

The issues of loving the nation, the collective and labour are visualized in a number of recurring themes. Loving the nation usually involves images of the flag of the PRC and/or the Constitution. Loving the nation also entails maintaining unity and friendship within the multi-ethnic composition of the population. Loving the collective is often visualized in the form of cleaning up, or tied in with activities aimed at protecting, the environment. Images of street-sweeping, window-cleaning and tree-planting ceremonies are often used to instil this sentiment.

The calls to honour teachers, authority figures and the elderly in general are standard elements in the various educational poster series and evoke a strong Boy Scout ethos. Youngsters are often shown assisting the elderly while shopping or while crossing the street. An interesting subset is the attention paid to (obedience to) the police. This often comes in the form of children reporting (petty) crime, or returning found goods.

The posters urging to love education and/or science continue to feature Mao Zedong's call to 'Study hard, make progress every day' (*Haohao xuexi, tiantian xiangshang*) that used to define prowess at school in the revolutionary era. Exhortations to study hard by other leaders, including Deng Xiaoping and Jiang Zemin, are also invoked. The precept of love for education usually shows a boy and a girl in a classroom situation. Love of science often situates a boy and a girl in front of high-rise buildings, freeways, rocket launches and other *Star Wars* imagery. Sometimes the image of Albert Einstein is visible in the background, as an icon of intellectual excellence. By the late 1990s, the ardent love for science and education also has been invoked as an antidote to the possible attraction that the forbidden teachings of the

Falun gong and other organizations may have on youngsters.

CCP-leaders since 1992 have increasingly stressed patriotism (*aiguo zhuyi*), 'loving the state', defined as loving the socialist system and the leadership of the Party. As a result, patriotism has by and large replaced the political and class struggle content that dominated propaganda posters in the pre-reform era. Love for the Mother Country in these images is largely related to the success of the modernization process. It is stressed time and again that the results of modernization have made the world once again stand in awe of China. Further concrete factors that have contributed to intense patriotic feelings include the successful resumption of sovereignty of Hong Kong (1997) and Macao (1999), the commemoration of the fiftieth anniversary of the founding of the PRC (1999), the organization of the 2008 Olympic Games, and the accession to the World Trade Organization (the latter two events both took place in 2001). The qualification of the national **football (soccer)** squad for the World Championships (which were organized by Japan and South Korea in 2002) initially did contribute to patriotic feelings. However, the goalless team failed to present a convincing performance.

The newfound Chinese self-confidence is expressed by a desire to stand up for what China sees as its legitimate rights. Patriotism is a theme that has not only found its way onto posters, but is also expressed in the various rituals that have become part of the daily activities of many young Chinese. These include singing patriotic songs and, in primary and secondary schools across the nation, singing the national anthem and taking part in flag-raising ceremonies. Raising the flag has not only become part of the school curriculum, but can also be witnessed daily at sunrise in front of the rostrum of **Tiananmen Square** since 1991.

See also: nationalism; Olympics; World Trade Organization (WTO) debate

Further reading

Landsberger, Stefan R. (2001). 'Learning by What Example? Educational Propaganda in

Twenty-First-Century China'. *Critical Asian Studies* 4: 541–71.

Tyl, Dominique (2002). 'The Formation of New Citizens in China's Secondary Schools'. *China Perspectives* 39: 4–16.

STEFAN LANDSBERGER

postmodernism (houxiandai zhuyi) and 'post-ism' (houxue)

Postmodernism as a rubric covering various critical methodologies (deconstruction, post-structuralism, post-colonialism, New Historicism, and so forth) was assimilated by intellectual and academic circles during and after the mid 1980s, largely through the translated work and public lectures of contemporary Western critical theorists such as Frederic Jameson, Jürgen Habermas and Jean-François Lyotard. Postmodernism as a distinctive and distinctly Chinese form of cultural discourse, however, did not emerge until the 1990s and very much shares in the de-politicized, nativist mood of the post-Tiananmen period. The results of a forum on Chinese postmodernism published in the January 1993 issue of *Wenyi yanjiu* [Literary and Art Research] and articles on Edward Said's *Orientalism* and *Culture and Imperialism* by Zhang Kuan, Qian Jun and Pan Shaomei published in the September 1993 issue of **Dushu** [Reading] adumbrated the issues around which Chinese postmodernism would take shape – the valorization of Chinese popular culture, a corresponding hostility to modernity, enlightenment and democracy as proxies for Western hegemony, and an obsession with Chinese and national identity, these last two summed up in the title of the 1994 'manifesto', 'From "Modernity" to "Chineseness"' (*Cong 'xiandaixing' dao 'Zhonghuaxing'*) by Zhang Fa, Zhang Yiwu and Wang Yichuan. In 1994 **Zhang Yiwu** and Wang Ning, young academics at **Peking University**, both claimed, in different terms, that in the 1990s China (too) had entered a 'new post-era' (*hou xin shiqi*) linked, on the one hand, to global postmodernity, and freed, on the other, from Western historicity and meta-narratives. While Wang Ning elaborated his postmodern criticism in the context of Chinese literature, Zhang Yiwu extended its use

in broadly cultural terms, praising the recent flowering of **popular culture** in urban China for its democratic power (and see **minjian**), while denouncing Chinese modernity in the twentieth century as created and represented by the May Fourth iconoclasts. Zhang asserted, however, that China needed to explore postmodern space in her own language and resist current postmodern discourses as forms of Western cultural hegemony.

In 1995, the term 'post-ism' or 'post-studies' (*houxue*) was coined by Zhao Yiheng in an article, '"Post-Isms" and Chinese New Conservatism', published in the Hong Kong journal **Ershiyi shiji** ([Twenty-First Century] 27: 4–15). The 'post-isms', wrote Zhao, were shaped by theories borrowed from the West, and while they performed a critical role in the contemporary West, when translated into China as means of articulating her social and political reality, they paradoxically served the conservative aim of subverting the revolutionary radicalism that had dominated past decades. His article aroused a heated debate, which was joined by Xu Ben, Liu Kang and others in future issues of the same journal. In his own critique of the ideology of the various 'post-isms', for example, Xu Ben also emphasized its conformity with the **nationalism** and political censorship of the 1990s.

See also: Neo-Conservatism; New Left

Further reading

Wang, Hui and Yu, Guoliang (eds) (1998). *90 niandai de 'houxue' lunzheng* ['Post-ism' in the Nineties]. Hong Kong: Chinese University Press.

Williams, Philip F. (1998/1999). 'The Rage for Postism and a Chinese Scholar's Dissent'. *Academic Questions* 12.1 (Winter): 43–53.

Xu, Ben (1999). 'The Postmodern–Postcolonial Stimulus and the Rise of Chinese Post-ist Theory'. In *idem, Disenchanted Democracy: Chinese Cultural Criticism after 1989*. Ann Arbor: University of Michigan Press, 88–128.

—— (2001). 'Postmodern–Postcolonial Criticism and Pro-Democracy Enlightenment'. *Modern China* 27.1 (January).

Zhang, Longxi (1998). 'Postmodernism and the Return of the Native'. In *idem, Mighty Opposites: From Dichotomies to Differences in the Comparative Study of China*. Stanford: Stanford University Press, 184–212.

[See also the special issue of *New Literary History* 28.1 (1997), entitled 'Cultural Studies: China and the West', and the special issue of *Boundary 2* 24.3 (1997), reprinted in Zhang Xudong and Arif Dirlik (2000), *Postmodernism and China*. Durham: Duke University Press.]

CHEN JIANHUA

Power versus Law

(Quan yü fa)

Huaju (spoken drama)

Written by Xing Yixun and premiered at the China Youth Art Theatre in 1979, *Power versus Law* (*Quan yü fa*) was one of the most popular **Huaju** (spoken dramas) of the late 1970s, when artists and audiences were excited by the fresh possibilities offered by the theatre – and permitted by the new post-Mao political regime – for denouncing the **Cultural Revolution**. Seen today as a typical example of an anti-'Gang of Four' play, *Power versus Law* depicts a new Party Secretary, Luo Fang, and his efforts to protect the innocent and punish the guilty. Luo wins the trust of Ding Mu, an accountant who has been coerced into cooking the books so as to hide the fact that state funds have been diverted from their original purpose of helping refugees after a natural disaster to building a luxurious house for a Party official named Cao Da. Encouraged by Luo, Ding succeeds in exposing Cao. Set in 1978, the play raised a timely issue: do those in power have the right to abuse their power and take reprisals against those who challenge them? The critique of privilege and corruption was cleverly balanced by the creation of a positive Party official, who thereby affirmed the legitimacy of the Party, although to some viewers his character seemed too good to be true. At the very least, however, Luo Fang embodied hope for a better and more just future, and the play satisfied both audiences, who sought catharsis in theatre, and

the censors, eager to see that the new theatre in post-Mao China adhered to a socialist realist orientation.

Further reading

Xing, Yixun (1980). 'Power versus Law'. *Chinese Literature* 6: 31–91.

CHEN XIAOMEI

preserved vegetables

Vegetable preservation dates back to *Qimin yaoshu* [Agricultural Techniques in Qi], China's first encyclopedia of agriculture (531–50 AD). There is hardly a place in the country that does not produce preserved vegetables. Each has its own traditions and flavours. The most famous are: Beijing's rutabaga (*shuigeda*), Tianjin's garlic cabbage (*jindongcai*), Baoding's potherb mustard (*chunbulao*) and Sichuan's preserved mustard (*zhacai*), king of Chinese preserved vegetables.

Chinese preserve their vegetables by soaking them in brine or applying salt after they are deprived of moisture. Another method, called *pao*, is to sour vegetables with lactobacillus or organic acid such as vinegar. Sichuan spicy pickled cabbages (*paocai*) is one of the most popular. Yet another big family of preserved vegetables is 'vegetables preserved with soy' (*jiangcai*). There is a northern school of *jiangcai*, represented by the famous Liubiju, Tianyuan and Dahulu brands in Beijing and a southern school, represented by the brand names of Sanhe and Simei in Yangzhou. The northern tastes a little salty, while the southern is sweeter. Everything can go into the soy jars: turnips, melons, lettuce, garlic bolt and lotus root, as well as peanuts, almonds and walnut meat.

With the availability of non-seasonal vegetables and refrigerators, very few families now preserve vegetables on a large scale. Mass production of preserved vegetables is, however, a multimillion-dollar business – Liubiju, maker of *jiangcai*, has an annual output of 5,000 tons. Today, people eat preserved vegetables for a change. Before the 1980s, by contrast, 'corn bread with preserved vegetables' (*wotou xiancai*) was the hallmark of a harsh life.

YUAN HAIWANG

prisons

Prisons, understood here specifically as spaces of confinement in which convicted criminals are detained for the duration of their custodial sentence, did not appear in China until the beginning of the twentieth century. After the disaster of the Boxer rebellion in 1900, punishments were limited to the death penalty, imprisonment or fines. The movement for prison reform that appeared at the end of the Qing gathered momentum after the fall of the empire in 1911: Beijing Number One Prison, one of the first model prisons built to the highest international standards in China, opened its doors in 1912. Dozens of similar penal institutions followed, as local and central authorities actively pursued an extensive programme of prison building guided by the belief that criminals could be educated and reformed in the therapeutic space of the prison (*jianyu*). By the 1930s, over 25,000 prisoners were detained on any one day in China's modern prisons, not counting detention houses and county gaols (this was comparable to the prison population of a large European country like France or England). Republican prisons were theoretically accountable to the public and practically scrutinized by a variety of competing elements – charitable associations, judicial inspectors, local journalists and foreign observers.

After 1949, however, China became a hermetically closed universe in which information on labour camps was a state secret. The CCP shared the faith of previous regimes in the power of institutions to mould a socially cohesive polity, but the transformation of the penal system into a political tool magnified the worst problems of the prison. While Republican penologists had envisaged indeterminate sentences and forced agricultural labour, these ideas were never fully implemented due to administrative impediments and legal constraints. Under the CCP, millions ended up in labour camps in the countryside for indeterminate periods until deemed by the Party to

have been re-educated: they formed the backbone of the 'reform through labour' system referred to as the *laogai*. The brutal treatment of political and common prisoners, the gradual destruction of human beings, the widespread use of torture and physical violence in 'thought reform' are some of the most disturbing aspects of the *laogai* system, which has administered the lives of 20 to 30 million convicts since 1949.

Since the mid 1990s, the authorities have attempted to streamline the penal system, and labour camps and prison factories are again called 'prisons', as the cycle of penal reform has come full circle, and government authorities themselves have accepted the failure of the *laogai* to either reform prisoners or contribute to the economic output of the country. Profit became the main criterion by which prison activity was evaluated in the 1980s, as penal authorities were forced to make the prisons financially self-sustaining, often at the expense of the inmates' education and rehabilitation. Food remains a central concern – in the wave of 'economic reforms' the amount allocated even to prison personnel declined between the mid 1980s and 1990s, leading to the theft of provisions intended for prisoners. Without sufficient funds for medical care, moreover, health problems have become endemic. Explosions in the prison population – which regularly follow the 'hard-strike campaigns' (*yanda*) against crime since 1983 – have caused prison congestion in many parts of the country. On the whole, prisoners have not benefited from the 'economic reforms' initiated by Deng Xiaoping since 1979.

FRANK DIKÖTTER

private universities

(minban daxue)

Minban daxue, or non-governmental universities, first emerged in China in the early 1980s, a product and integral part of the reform programme. Today, there are *minban daxue* in almost every province of China. There are two major categories of *minban daxue*: those that can grant academic degrees and those that cannot. In 2002, there were only 105 *minban daxue* in the first category. Students who study at those that cannot grant academic degrees have to take government-sponsored examinations in order to get a degree. *Minban daxue* are quite different from the private universities that existed in China before 1949 in their subjection to tight government control. The government maintains the right to approve the founding of a *minban daxue*. Before 1949, there were many church-affiliated private universities in China. Today, the government will not permit any religious group to get involved in the founding of a *minban daxue*. The government also decides what kind of students a *minban daxue* can admit, what programmes they can offer, and finally, whether or not it can grant degrees to its students. What makes the *minban daxue* non-governmental or private is mainly the fact that they do not receive money from the government.

Generally speaking, *minban daxue* are much smaller in size than public universities. Most of their students are those who fail to get into a public university. Most faculty members are temporary or part-time: many of them are retired professors or professors of public universities who want to earn extra income. Their campuses and buildings are less fancy than those of public universities, and their programmes are limited to technical and professional studies at the undergraduate level. Despite these obvious deficiencies, the rise of *minban daxue* signals, at least nominally, the end of the total government control over higher education, and the future of *minban daxue* looks bright.

Further reading

Deng, Peng (1997). *Private Education in Modern China*. New York: Praeger.

HAN XIAORONG

processions (religious)

Impregnated with local culture and displaying an extensive palette of popular traditions and arts, processions in China are, or were, inherent constituents of local identity. Our focus here is processions of a religious nature, which play a vital role for cults and in temple fairs, most often celebrated on the birthday of a protective god. National day and political parades will be left to one side, although in the 1940s and 1950s the latter did make use of traditional processional elements, one example being the renowned 'rice-sprout song' playlets (*yangge*), as political instruments to promote socialism. The private nature of processions for weddings (see **weddings (rural)**; **weddings (urban)**) and **funerals** makes them significant primarily for affines and kin and they therefore fall outside our ambit, which centres on processions organized by communities of cults.

The vernacular terms referring to 'processions' vary depending on local traditions, ritual functions, or the simultaneous performance of other rituals, such as the Daoist **Jiao** (offering ritual). Among the most common denominations we find *youshen*, *chuxun*, *raojing*, *youxing*, *chuzhen*, *gexiang*, *yingshen* and *jinxiang*. The written sources also refer to processions in different ways, sometimes using analytical terms or the generic name of the festival (*shehui*, [*yingshen*] *saihui*, *miaohui*).

As the favoured collective ritual of Chinese popular religion, processions are assigned a variety of symbolic functions. Generally speaking, they connect sacred places together, in an ostentatious manner, allowing people to assume a ritual role and revitalize the bonds both among themselves and directly between the human and the supernatural worlds. Three main kinds can be distinguished.

1   *Territorial processions*, which carry gods on a tour of inspection through a delimited inner territory, along a progressive route or departing every day from a symbolic centre. Exorcistic in nature, their goal is eventually to bring prosperity and fertility to the inhabitants.

2   *Pilgrimages*, through which temple communities regularly revive the ties of ritual kinship connecting them to an original temple or god, or which aim to visit a famous cult place. Both forms strengthen the supernatural power of the god.

3   *Processions inviting a god* from a renowned temple or directly from the supernatural realm to sojourn in the community – generally during

a temple festival – and, at the end, walking the god back, though with less pomp (see **temple fairs**).

A fourth category could be constituted by *processional convolutions*, not only around a temple or sacred site, but also on a ground transformed into a labyrinth or representing a gigantic talisman or a propitious Chinese character. This delimited microcosmic scale results in slightly different components here.

Three periods during the year are habitually chosen all over China as the time for cyclical temple fairs and processions, which are held for one or several days, though not necessarily every year. These periods fall closely in step with agricultural life: right after the Lunar New Year, a time of renewal; the fourth and fifth lunar months, critical when it comes to crops, threats from insects, epidemics and water; and in the autumn after the harvest.

Different from carnivals, participation in Chinese processions is not spontaneous but channelled into a delegation strictly representing a community and its families and almost exclusively composed of male individuals. The scale of a procession ranges from one delegation – sent by a village, urban neighbourhood, lineage, patronymic group, corporation or any other association that constitutes a cult community – to an alliance of several such communities, sometimes comprising over one hundred delegations, as in Saikang (Tainan, Taiwan). A delegation includes (1) at the rear, generally the place of honour, a palanquin carrying the statue(s) of the god(s) and the incense-burner – the emblem of the community – preceded by bearers of an umbrella and different banners, as well as a group of percussionists (see **luogu**) and **spirit-mediums** mortifying themselves at appropriate times; and (2) at the front, one or several processional troupes performing **martial arts**, dances, songs and music, or floats. The head of the cortège often emulates the official retinues of imperial times, including a squad bearing banners, lamps, boards and other insignia of authority.

Processions offer the observer an insight into the system of beliefs, representations and values, as a coherent and synthetic whole, in which popular religion resides. They also exteriorize and activate, within a delimited time and space, the social organization and networks that are not controlled by the state apparatus, despite certain links with it. This is the main reason why they are not appreciated by officials. The organization of inter-communal processions with territorial implications– very complex in nature – generates different types of partnerships: a rotation or a simultaneous sharing of responsibilities. Ceremonial exchange is the motor of such events and also reveals the local power structure, which tends to be egalitarian, hierarchical or embedded (i.e. supportive of another delegation). The entrepreneurial knowledge and endeavour that processions activate are simply enormous and so are the expenses, which boost the local economy for a time. Processions can also be put on hold by locals in periods of crisis or when proscribed by the government, as was broadly the case in Communist China during the period of collectivism and the **Cultural Revolution**. Manifesting the flexibility of popular religion, a revival, albeit in altered forms, occurred in the late 1980s and 1990s, especially in the southeastern, the lower Yangzi, and Huabei regions, though in other areas as well (Hunan). However, the repression in the late 1990s and early 2000s of the – unrelated – **Falun gong** movement provided the pretext for new, severe restrictions, which betray a clear political fear on the part of the government. More than anywhere else in the Chinese world, these complex traditions have been maintained in Taiwan, where they have been able to thrive.

Apart from official policy, the factors of change affecting processions vary in nature. We note that increased wealth in the community is translated into more lavish expenditure. Urbanization and industrialization do not necessarily occasion socio-religious anomie. In Taiwan, by contrast, where processions flourish, television coverage and tourism are starting to have corrosive effects.

See also: local religion

Further reading

Allio, F. (1998). 'Procession et identité', *Cahiers d'extrême-Asie* 10: 1–18.

Sangren, S. (1987). *History and Magical Power in a Chinese Community*. Stanford: Stanford University Press.

FIORELLA ALLIO

Project Hope

Project Hope is a broad-based educational charity initiated and organized by the China Youth Development Foundation (CYDF), a subsidiary of the Communist Youth League, in October 1989. In accordance with government guidelines for raising money for education, its main purpose is to raise money from all sectors of society to fund a Project Hope Foundation whereby students otherwise too poor to attend or remain in school can do so, and the physical conditions of their education can be improved. The foundation focuses on remote and poor areas, especially in western China. Its goal is to improve the standards and conditions of elementary education in those areas and to help all students stay in school, thereby also fulfilling the government policy of Nine Years' Compulsory Education. Since 1989, the foundation has helped 23 million students enter or return to school, and about 8,000 Hope Schools have been built (the CYDF plans to provide on-line education to these schools). Donations, totalling $1.8 billion by 2001, have come from individuals and groups, and from home and abroad, including businesses and Chinese communities in the USA. Disbursement of the money is controlled by the Project Hope Office in every province and major city. A Project Hope Grant may go directly to a student, school or area. Project Hope is the largest broad-based charity in China and is the most influential social programme for education in the PRC. Unfortunately, the Project has also been accused of corruption. In March of 2002, a lengthy piece of investigative journalism in **Nanfeng Weekend** documenting the misuse of funds was pulled at the last minute under pressure from the Ministry of Propaganda.

See also: literacy (and illiteracy); village schools

WANG XIAOLU

Project 211

'Project 211' stands for the resolution of the **Ministry of Education** embodying the Chinese government's commitment to strengthening the top hundred universities and certain key disciplinary areas as a national priority for the twenty-first century. This project is the largest key programme for the reform of higher education since 1949 in the PRC. Begun in 1993, investment had reached 15 billion yuan by the end of August 2000. Of this 1.5 billion came from local governments and other channels and departments. So far, ninety-eight top universities and 602 key disciplines have been approved for participation. Since the central and local governments and various departments have joined hands to increase funding for the universities and disciplines, the manpower, material resources and financial resources have been better allocated within the designated universities.

WANG XIAOLU

Pu'an jiao

(Teachings of Pu'an)

Regional religious tradition

The Pu'an jiao is a ritual tradition known to exist in west-central Fujian and much of southern Jiangxi. Whether it is to be found elsewhere as well is not yet known. Nor is it known whether this tradition really goes back to the monk Pu'an whom practitioners worship as their 'founding master' (*zushi*). Pu'an (1115–69), whose lay name is Yu Yinsu, was a native of the district of Yichun (central Jiangxi, near the Hunan border) who is said to have achieved awakening during an interview with the Linji monk Mu'anzhong on Mt Wei in Hunan. Later, as abbot of the Cihuasi near his home village, he became famous for his miracles and exorcisms. Incorporated into the Linji lineage, Pu'an is the author of 'discussions' (*yülu*), which have been preserved in the Buddhist canon. His image in the Yuan-era *Soushen daquan* shows him with a bald pate and tufts of hair over both ears.

This iconography corresponds to tales told of Pu'an in west-central Fujian which recount that he was a Taoist who converted to Buddhism, but who wished to retain a trace of his Taoist origins by keeping these tufts (which resemble those of the Taoist exorcist par excellence, Zhang Daoling). Rituals performed by Pu'an specialists include communal **Jiao**, exorcisms, and funeral rituals (**Gongde**). Their texts, like their ritual implements and paintings, belong essentially to the Tantric tradition, albeit with a heavy admixture of Daoist elements of both national (see **Daoism (Zhengyi tradition)**) and local (see **Lüshan jiao (Sannai jiao)**) origin. Most practitioners identify themselves as 'half-Buddhist, half-Taoist', but some consider their identity to be Buddhist.

See also: vernacular priests (Daoist/Buddhist)

Further reading

Lagerwey, John (2001). 'Popular Ritual Specialists in West Central Fujian'. *Shehui, minzu yu wenhua zhanyan guoji yantao hui lunwen ji*. Taipei: Hanxue yanjiu zhongxin. 435–507.

JOHN LAGERWEY

public health care

China's economic and administrative reforms since the late 1970s have led to important changes in the system of public health care. In the countryside, township (former commune) health centres assume a larger share of administrative and financial responsibilities. At the village (former brigade) level, the cooperative medical system has generally disintegrated, and some village clinics are run as fee-for-service businesses. While the state health care system at the provincial, municipal and county levels remains essentially unchanged – each still maintains its functional public health departments and hospitals (including hospitals of Chinese medicine) and other specialized care institutions – the trend has been to encourage wider use of enterprise hospitals by the public and the cooperation of medical institutions from different

administrative units. Other developments include a rise in private practice, an increase in fees for treatment and drugs, as well as the growth of specific patient-requested services, such as special hospital rooms or enhanced nursing care. The government maintains and funds organized public health activities, including immunization programmes and maternal and child care, while anti-epidemic stations at the provincial, municipal and county levels work to prevent and control communicable diseases through environmental and food sanitation monitoring. The decentralization of the health system and the reduction of public subsidies to lower-level agencies have aggravated the uneven distribution of resources between the urban and rural sectors, and the rising cost of health care, especially with the expansion of private practice, has increased the burden on low-income families.

See also: hospitals; medical doctors; medical insurance; mental health

Further reading

Huang, S. (1988). 'Transforming China's Collective Health Care System'. *Social Science and Medicine* 27: 879–88.
Liu, X. and Wang, J. (1991). 'An Introduction to China's Health Care System'. *Journal of Public Health Policy* 12: 104–15.

YIP KA-CHE

public libraries

China has public libraries, university libraries, scientific research libraries, school libraries, and libraries affiliated with government organizations, army units, trade unions, enterprises, and local communities, with 6 billion books and about 400,000 employees. While these other libraries belong to their respective affiliated institutions, public libraries – the National Library of China being the largest – are under the auspices of the **Ministry of Culture**.

The uniqueness of the Chinese public library system lies in the Ministry's effort to build a digital network connecting the 27,000 public libraries to the 72,000 public art and cultural centres, museums, cinemas and theatres throughout the country. Led by the National Library of China, the 'Project for Information Sharing', which is to be completed by 2005, has already made great progress. Its library system provides free access to 10.78 million bibliographical records and 60 million audio and video documents. This project is built upon a networking backbone that so far provides over 200 cities with Internet connectivity and a cable and satellite television network targeting 350 million television sets.

Public libraries fall into three tiers: the national, the municipal or provincial, and the district or county. Development is by no means even. Generally, the higher the tier, the better funded the library is. However, this is not always the case. The Xicheng District Library of Beijing, for example, with its 10,000-square-metre premises, has a collection of 400,000 monographs, a computer lab, a music collection with lab, a state-of-the-art reading room that accommodates sight-impaired patrons, a special collection of multimedia tour guides and travelogues, and a German Self-Teaching Centre, which is a joint venture with the Beijing campus of the Goethe Institute. From collection development to circulation, the library is fully automated. By 1999, the library had created an online database with bibliographical records of its entire current and back holdings.

Chinese libraries in the main have made remarkable progress. Besides a library system now serving multiple functions, libraries have also been upgraded with better facilities and modern technology. The establishment of China Digital Library Corporation Ltd and the organization of China's first international digital library conference in 2002 in Beijing marked the country's maturity in digital library development. At the same time, library management reforms are in full swing, and library services have become more proactive and value-added. Librarians are increasingly aware of their new role as information creators and providers. Library and information education has progressed, as has library research – librarians have authored over 1,000 professional monographs and written 60,000 papers published in over fifty core library journals. The China Society of Library Science, set up in 1979, has been pivotal in this effort. More and more libraries have developed exchanges with their counterparts abroad and now participate in activities organized by the International Federation of Library Associations and the American Library Association.

Further reading

Lin, Sharon Chien (1998). *Libraries and Librarianship in China. Guides to Asian Librarianship*. Westport: Greenwood Press.

HU MINGRONG AND YUAN HAIWANG

Q

qi guanyan

(henpecked husbands)

Qi guanyan, literally 'my wife controls me strictly,' is a pun on the Chinese word for bronchitis. Although dating back to the Republican era, the term became popular in the 1980s as a description of a man whose wife controls his everyday activities, social relations and expenditures. As a joke about gender relations in the early reform era, the discourse of *qi guanyan* represented a perceived crisis of masculinity among urban males during the transition to a market economy. Because of socialist policies of roughly equal pay and employment opportunities for men and women, urban Chinese men contributed more time to housework and childcare than men in most other societies, probably contributing to the reputation of Chinese men as overly domesticated and willing to be controlled by their wives. Under socialist living conditions neither men nor women had much time or money for leisure outside the home. In contrast, reform-era men increasingly were expected to succeed at making money through business activities. A wife's complaints about everyday household chores were now seen as incompatible with the new image of entrepreneurial masculinity. The successful new man was expected to spend more time outside the home, including business entertainment, leading to more complaining and suspicion from his spouse and consequently his own complaining of *qi guanyan*, itself a display of masculinity. Many Chinese commentators argued that *qi guanyan* was a desired condition among Chinese husbands, since it demonstrated the concern and love of the wife for her husband and family.

Further reading

Parish, William and Farrer, James (2000). 'Gender and the Family'. In William Parish and Wenfang Tang (eds), *The Changing Social Contract: Chinese Urban Life During Reform*. New York: Cambridge University Press, 232–72.

Zhong, Xueping (2000). *Masculinity Besieged? Issues of Modernity and Male Subjectivity in Chinese Literature of the Late Twentieth Century*. Durham: Duke University Press.

JAMES FARRER

Qian Liqun

b. 1939, Chongqing

Literary historian

Qian Liqun is a leading proponent of May Fourth humanism in post-Mao literary and cultural criticism. After graduating from the People's University in 1960, Qian worked in Guizhou. He returned to Beijing in 1978 when he was accepted as a graduate student at **Peking University**. As he himself explains it, the political discrimination and social exclusion that he suffered during the **Cultural Revolution** motivated his interest in Lu Xun's form of criticism.

Qian has made a signal contribution to the study of modern Chinese literature through his comprehensive studies of Lu Xun and his brother, Zhou Zuoren. Because Zhou, in particular, had served as the Minister of Education during the Japanese occupation, he had been a taboo subject for literary historians for decades. Zhou's involvement in establishing the disciplines of literary and cultural criticism and his efforts at cultural reconstruction were deliberately ignored. Qian's comparative studies of Zhou Zuoren and Lu Xun have provided the cultural/historical context that had been missing for years. Qian's interest in these figures, moreover, is not restricted to literary history. There are connections between what Qian has written about Lu Xun and his own commitment to, and views about, the place of literature in the education of the whole person. In the 1990s, therefore, Qian increasingly turned his attention to lay audiences in a series of lectures on Lu Xun and Zhou Zuoren, as well as editing anthologies of modern Chinese literature for middle-school students.

HE DONGHUI

Qian Zhongshu

b. 1910; d. 1998

Literary critic

Son of the distinguished literary scholar Qian Jibo, Qian was educated at **Qinghua University**, Oxford and the University of Paris. He returned to China in 1938, after the outbreak of the War of Resistance against Japan. Qian held a series of teaching positions until he was assigned to the Chinese Academy of Sciences (later **Chinese Academy of Social Sciences**) after 1949. A polyglot with a photographic memory, Qian was China's most erudite literary critic. His scholarship consisted of broad but detailed comparative studies of poetics, beginning with Chinese theatre, then the poetic tradition in *On the Art of Poetry* (*Tan yi lu*, 1948), and early Chinese literature in the four-volume *Limited Views* (*Guan zui bian*, 1979). Wit and an eye for paradox filled his literary criticism, and these also characterized his familiar essays and fiction, including the novel for which he is best remembered, *Fortress Besieged* (*Weicheng*, 1947), set

during the war with Japan. Celebrated as a satire of the educated elite of modern China, the novel also reaches to psychological and existential dimensions in its depiction of a young couple. Both his fiction and scholarship consistently distanced themselves from the trends and expectations of his times.

See also: Huang Shuqin; Yang Jiang

Further reading

Hsia, C. T. (1971). *A History of Modern Chinese Fiction*. New Haven: Yale University Press, 432–43.

Huters, Theodore (1982). *Qian Zhongshu*. Boston: Twayne.

Linsley, Robert (2002). 'Qian Zhongshu and the Late, Late Modern'. *Yishu: Journal of Contemporary Chinese Art* 1.1 (Spring): 60–7.

Qian, Zhongshu (1998). *Limited Views: Essays on Ideas and Letters*. Trans. and ed. Ronald Egan. Cambridge: Harvard University Press.

—— (2001). *Cat: A Translation and Critical Introduction*. Hong Kong: Sanlian.

—— (2004). *Fortress Besieged*. Trans. Jeanne Kelly and Nathan Mao. New York: New Directions.

Tian, Huilan *et al.* (eds) (1990). *Qian Zhonshu Yang Jiang yanjiu ziliaoji* [Collection of Research Material on Qian Zhongshu and Yang Jiang]. Wuhan: Huazhong shifan daxue.

EDWARD GUNN

Qigong (history)

In the 1980s and 1990s, traditional breathing, gymnastic and meditation techniques were highly popular in China, in what was described by media chroniclers as 'Qigong fever' (*Qigong re*, see **crazes**). At its peak, the Qigong or 'breath training' movement attracted over 100 million practitioners. The Qigong boom declined in the late 1990s and most Qigong organizations were dismantled after the crackdown on **Falun gong**.

Prior to 1949, body cultivation techniques were widely practised in monastic, medical, literati and sectarian circles, but there existed no self-conscious movement aiming to unite all practitioners. Although the term Qigong had appeared in a handful of books in the first half of the twentieth century and earlier, the term was seldom used and it had not acquired its modern meaning. It was only after 1949 that Qigong became a generally used term, including in a single category all Chinese gymnastic, meditation, visualization and breathing techniques, to which, over the years, were added martial, performance, trance, divination, charismatic healing and talismanic techniques, as well as the study of paranormal phenomena, UFOs, the *Book of Changes* (**Yijing**) and so forth.

Modern Qigong was founded by Party cadre Liu Guizhen in southern Hebei in the late 1940s. After recovering from various illnesses by learning a breathing technique from a traditional master, he reported on the efficacy of the method to his superiors, who charged him with conducting clinical research. He and his colleagues chose the term Qigong to designate the methods. In the 1950s, Qigong was recognized as a discipline of Chinese medicine and specialized clinics and sanatoria were established in many cities. The practice was denounced as 'feudal superstition' and driven underground during the Cultural Revolution. By the end of the 1970s, however, there was a new explosion of Qigong activities. Already, artist and self-healed cancer victim Guo Lin had been teaching Qigong in Beijing parks since the early 1970s, turning the institutional Qigong of the 1950s into a mass activity practised in public spaces. Guo Lin's 'New Qigong Therapy', hailed as a cure for cancer, and other methods quickly spread to all parts of China. In 1978, Gu Hansen of the Shanghai Nuclear Research Institute announced that he had discovered the material basis of 'External Qi' (*waiqi*), a form of energy which is said to be sent by Qigong masters towards their patients. Gu's experiments were considered by many to be a scientific discovery of historical significance.

While Qigong spread in China's parks and laboratories, the mass media became gripped by the strange phenomenon of children reading with their ears, leading to widespread media debate on 'extraordinary functions of the human body' (*teyi gongneng*). Most fascinating was the possibility of a link between Qigong and extraordinary functions: that Qigong exercises could lead to the practitioner acquiring paranormal powers.

Qigong came to be seen no longer as a mere branch of Chinese medicine, but as a scientific discipline in its own right, specialized in investigating the powers of External Qi, which could be controlled and projected by the mind. In early 1986, the semi-official China Qigong Science Commission was founded on a triumphant note, as Professor Qian Xuesen proclaimed the new scientific revolution.

A flourishing Qigong subculture emerged, with its associations, its magazines, its conferences, its healing and cultural activities. A space was thus opened within which traditional masters could practise their healing arts and create organized groups under the guise of Qigong. Millions of adepts congregated in parks and public spaces every morning to practise exercise routines disseminated by the groups. The most popular routines in the early 1980s involved entering the trance of 'spontaneous movements', a phenomenon comparable to possession states. Throughout the 1980s, Qigong became a legitimized outlet for the resurgence, reconfiguration and 'modernization' of religious beliefs and practices. The interplay and interpenetration of these popular networks and official institutions gave form to the new Qigong circles.

A young Qigong master, **Yan Xin**, raised Qigong fever to a frenzy in early 1987 when researchers at Qinghua University publicized results of experiments showing that his External Qi had changed the molecular structure of water at a distance of 2,000 km. Yan Xin began a series of public lectures in large auditoriums and sports stadiums across the country. Entitled 'Force Field Experimental Lectures' (*Daigong baogao*), they drew audiences of up to 20,000, lasted up to ten hours without interruption, and became the scene of trance reactions and miraculous healings.

However, opposition to Qigong grew within the scientific community. The media reported cases of Qigong quackery and of practitioners unable to come out of trance, starving themselves to death while fasting, or displaying psychotic behaviour. Many researchers claimed that External Qi was merely psychological suggestion. Anti-Qigong articles appeared in the press throughout 1995, attacking it as pseudo-science, superstition, and a dangerous cult. The Qigong movement began to flounder.

During this period, one Qigong master, Li Hongzhi, began to distance himself from Qigong, claiming that his method of Falun gong was not a Qigong method but the highest Law of the universe. His teachings went beyond health concerns to a rejection of the corrupt moral order, attracting millions of disillusioned practitioners of other Qigong methods. An increasingly characteristic feature of Falun gong was its militant defence against any form of criticism through systematic protests against media and government agencies, culminating in the 10,000-person protest around the Party headquarters in Beijing on 25 April 1999. This led to the state's crackdown on Falun gong, which was followed by the banning or dismantling of most other large Qigong organizations.

See also: culture-bound syndromes

Further reading

Chen, Nancy (1995). 'Urban Spaces and Experiences of Qigong'. In Deborah Davis, Richard Kraus, Barry Naughton and Elisabeth J. Perry (eds), *Urban Spaces in Contemporary China*. Washington and Cambridge: Woodrow Wilson Center Press and Cambridge University Press.

—— (2003). *Breathing Spaces: Qigong, Psychiatry, and Healing in China*. New York: Columbia University Press.

—— (2003). 'Healing Sects and Anti-Cult Campaigns'. In Daniel Overmyer (ed.), *Religion in China Today*. Cambridge: Cambridge University Press, 199–214.

Eisenberg, D. (1985). *Encounters with Qi: Exploring Chinese Medicine*. New York: Norton. [An American doctor's experiences while researching Qigong in China.]

Hsu, Elizabeth (1999). *The Transmission of Chinese Medicine*. Cambridge: Cambridge University Press. [Contains an ethnographic description of a Qigong master's transmission of his skills to a disciple.]

Kartchmer, Eric (2002). 'Magic, Science, and Qigong in Contemporary China'. In Susan D. Blum and Lionel Jensen (eds), *China Off Center: Mapping the Margins of the Middle Kingdom*. Honolulu: University of Hawai'i Press, 311–22.

Ots, T. (1994). 'The Silenced Body – The Expressive *Leib*: on the Dialectic of Mind and Life in Chinese Cathartic Healing'. In T. Csordas (ed.), *Embodiment and Experience. The Existential Ground of Culture and Self*. Cambridge: Cambridge University Press. [Contains ethnographic data on practitioners of spontaneous Qigong.]

Palmer, David (2004). *'Qigong Fever': Body, Memory, and Power in Post-Mao China, 1949–1999*. London: Hurst.

Zhu, Xiaoyang and Penny, Benjamin (eds) (1994). 'The Qigong Boom'. *Sociology and Anthropology* 27.1. [Special issue. Contains translations of Chinese documents and press articles on the Qigong phenomenon.]

DAVID A. PALMER

Qigong (masters)

A significant characteristic of the post-Mao Qigong boom is the resurgence of Qigong masters. Until the Republican era, Qigong masters had been labelled as a 'low class' or 'superstitious' profession. But in the 1950s, Qigong masters were invited by the government to work as health professionals. This change was largely due to the work of Liu Guizhen (1920–83), a Communist Party cadre. Liu and his team worked on applying Qigong practice on health improvement in Beidai He Rehabilitation Centre and gained positive results. The government established more Qigong treatment centres where numbers of Qigong masters had worked. During the Cultural Revolution era, Qigong practice was once again labelled as 'superstitious', hence Qigong clinics were shut down.

From the 1970s to 1980s, Qigong masters gradually resurfaced as healers. Former cancer patient Guo Lin (1909–84) began teaching 'Guo Lin's New Qigong' (*Guo Lin xin qigong*) in parks to thousands of people diagnosed with cancer since 1971. After being promoted by the media in 1975, Guo was invited to give lectures in universities and hospitals nationwide. By the mid 1980s, more Qigong masters had become popular through teaching and healing. Among the best known are Yang Meijun (b. 1903), a master of 'Wild Geese' (*Dayangong*); Zhao Jinxiang (b. 1936), creator of the

'Crane style' (*Hexiangzhuang*); Ma Litang (1930–88), creator or the 'Nurturing Qi' (*Yangqi gong*); Pang Ming (b. 1940), creator of 'Intelligent Qigong' (*Zhineng gong*); and Zhang Mingwu (1920–90), creator of 'Methods of Self-Healing through Qigong' (*Qigong zikong liaofa*). By the end of the 1980s, several million copies of various Qigong manuals were in circulation. Qigong masters provided conferences in working units and treatment in hospitals and began to form organizations.

Between 1985 and 1995, some 2,000 Qigong masters registered organizations at the government agency. Many of them were not only healers but were also perceived as superbeings and spiritual leaders. They had gained popularity by launching qi-emitting conferences and claiming paranormal abilities, such as **Yan Xin** (b. 1949), who was the first to launch qi-emitting conferences where the audience were induced into trance, and Zhang Xiangyu (b. 1943), founder of the 'Qigong of the Great Nature' (*Daziran gong*), who claimed to have been possessed and to be able to communicate with spirits through 'messengers'. Many Qigong masters were also successful business people through selling books, audio or video tapes as well as qi-emitting merchandise. For example: **Ke Yunlu** and Ji Yi were both writers turned Qigong masters who made a living by writing Qigong books; Zhang Hongbao's (b. 1954) Chinese Qigong organization (Zhonggong) had more than one hundred service centres, selling qi-emitting merchandise and Qigong services. By 1995, Qigong practice had become a very profitable business that had outgrown government control. Since the summer of 2000, however, the government has forbidden Qigong masters to have organizations or private businesses.

See also: Qigong (history)

Further reading

Wu, Hao (ed.) (1993). *Zhongguo dangdai qigong quanshu* [Encyclopedia of Contemporary Chinese Qigong]. Beijing: Renmin tiyu chubanshe.

MENG QING

qin

Traditional musical instrument

The qin, also called *guqin* (ancient qin), is a seven-stringed long zither without frets or bridge. The Western term 'lute', which has been applied by Robert H. van Gulik, is misleading because lute and zither belong to two separate families of musical instruments and are different in construction and playing technique. The convex top of the qin is made of *wutong* wood (*sterculia plantamiolia*) and the flat bottom of *zi* wood (*catalpa kaempferi*), symbolic of heaven and earth, respectively. The two sound holes on the underside are called *longchi* (dragon pond) and *fengzhao* (phoenix pool). Many other parts of the instrument also have literary names. The entire wooden body is painted with lacquer. Thirteen ivory or mother-of-pearl studs are inlaid on the outer side of the surface as position marks. The strings are made of silk or silk-wrapped steel. The player plucks the strings with the right-hand fingers and stops the strings with the left-hand fingers. The three sounds produced – open, stopped and harmonics – represent earth, man and heaven, respectively.

The qin is one of the oldest and most respected musical instruments in Chinese culture. Its history goes back three thousand years. It was the instrument par excellence of the ancient elite class, referred to in classical literature, and seen in landscape paintings again and again. It was also regarded as one of four types of knowledge necessary to the literati, the others being *qi* (chess), *su* (calligraphy) and *hua* (brush painting). In fact, the name embodies beauty and perfection and is frequently used as a girl's name.

Low pitched and quiet in sound, the qin is primarily a solo instrument. Other than playing in a ritual orchestra for its cultural rather than musical significance, it is only accompanied by the *xiao* (bamboo flute) or voice (often that of the same player). In recent years there has been a revival of interest in the qin. The instrument can be seen in many museums, while many old qin, dating back several hundred years, are still playable.

See also: traditional music performers; Wu Zhao

Further reading

Bell, Yung (1998). 'Music of *Qin*: From the Scholar's Studio to the Concert Stage'. *ACMR Reports* 11 (Fall): 1–14.

Liang, David Ming-Yueh (1972). *The Chinese Ch'in: Its History and Music*. San Francisco: Chinese Music Association and San Francisco Conservatory of Music.

Thrasher, Alan R. (2001). *Chinese Musical Instruments*. Hong Kong: Oxford University Press.

van Gulik, R. H. (1940, 1969). *The Lore of the Chinese Lute: An Essay in the Ideology of the Ch'in*. Tokyo: Sophia University in cooperation with the Charles E. Tuttle Company, Rutland, Vermont.

Wu, Zhao (2002). *Guqin jichu jiaoxue* [Guqin Teaching Fundamentals]. 5 VCDs. Beijing: Renmin yinyue yinxiang chubanshe (ISRC CN-M26-01-319-00V.J6).

HAN KUO-HUANG

Qin Hui

b. 1952

Historian, social critic

Qin Hui is now a professor at **Qinghua University**. He graduated from Lanzhou University (1981), where he majored in Chinese history, and then taught at several universities before being recruited by Qinghua. Qin started his academic career as a historian, specializing in peasant studies and the socio-economic history of imperial China. In the 1990s, his academic interests shifted to contemporary issues. He organized and directed a series of field studies in rural China, discussing the various problems emerging from the recent reforms, and edited a book series: *A Series of Peasant Studies*. His work greatly promoted peasant studies in China and he is considered one of its most authoritative scholars. Since the mid 1990s, Qin has also paid great attention to urban reform and has done many comparative studies of economic reform in China, Eastern Europe and Russia. In his writing, he has criticized those economists who have used 'neo-institutional' economics (see **economic thought**) to justify the corruption

that has resulted from the reform and privatization of state-owned enterprises, emphasizing that in contemporary China, the most urgent and important issue with respect to the transformation of state ownership and to the definition of property rights is to uphold social fairness and justice, rather than to reduce as efficiently as possible the so-called transaction costs. His critical views have made him a prominent spokesman for, and defender of, public interests. His current research focuses on the history and reality of rural China, the comparative study of reform, and issues of globalization and China's modernization.

Further reading

Qin, Hui (2004). 'Dividing the Big Family Assets'. In Wang Chaohua (ed.), *One China, Many Paths*. London: Verso: 128–59.

LIU CHANG

Qinghua University

Qinghua University is one of the two most prestigious universities in the PRC, the other being **Peking University**. With part of the 'Boxer Indemnity', it was established in 1911 as Tsinghua hsueh-t'ang, a preparatory school for students who would be sent by the government to study in the USA. In 1925 the school was renamed Tsinghua School and a university section was also instituted. The name 'National Tsinghua University' was adopted in 1928, and a Research Institute was set up in 1929. The scholars Wang Guowei, Liang Qichao, Chen Yinque and Zhao Yuanren (the 'Four Tutors') helped lay the foundation of a research tradition that sought to combine the academic styles of East and West. During World War II, Qinghua became part of Xinan Lianda (Southwest Associated University) in Kunming, along with Peking and Nankai Universities. Subsequently, it moved back to Beijing. After 1949, Qinghua University was remoulded into a polytechnic institution, focusing on engineering, as part of a nationwide 'restructuring of universities and colleges' undertaken in 1952.

Since 1978, it has re-established departments in the sciences, economics and management, and the humanities. As of the end of 2000, there were 7,100 faculty and staff working for the 8 colleges and 43 departments, 44 research institutes, 9 engineering research centres, 163 laboratories and 16 postdoctoral research centres, including 15 national key laboratories. Altogether there were 37 bachelor's, 107 master's and 64 doctoral programmes, and student enrolment had reached 20,000.

WANG XIAOLU

Qingming Festival

(Qingmingjie)

Qingming is usually described as a festival of the dead, which takes place fifteen days after the spring equinox. Among the **Hakka**, however, this festival can last as long as a month, because tombs are scattered across the surrounding hills and must be swept according to generational order. For the first sacrificial visit, to the tomb of the founding ancestor (*kaiji zu*), each segment of the lineage must send representatives; as the sweeping comes ever closer to the present generation, successive visits concern ever smaller groups. Each time, after the grasses have been cleared from the tomb and the offerings set out, a cock is killed and its blood poured over 'sacrificial money', which is then placed according to a fixed pattern on the outer, horseshoe-shaped 'rim' of the tomb. For this reason, Qingming is more popularly referred to by its characteristic act, that of 'hanging paper money [on the tomb]' (*guazhi*). This stretched-out manner of celebrating Qingming means that it is a privileged occasion for the exhibition of lineage segmentation, as well as for learning lineage history, for in many areas the young boys are given a few coins every time they succeed in recognizing a tomb and telling the inherited tales of its inhabitant.

See also: ancestral halls/lineage temples

JOHN LAGERWEY

Qiong Yao

b. 1938, Hengyang, Hunan

Writer

Qiong Yao is Taiwan's most famous writer of love stories. She is also a playwright and lyricist. Qiong Yao was drawn to literature at an early age, and her maiden work debuted in Shanghai when she was only nine. By sixteen she had already published over 200 articles, one of which, 'Outside the Window' (*Chuangwai*), established her fame. When she was barely twenty, Qiong accomplished her first novel, titled *Many Enchanting Nights* (*Jidu xiyang hong*), set during the Anti-Japanese War. Qiong took up writing as a career after she failed her college entrance examinations. She finished a 200,000-word novel every four or five months. All her novels, over forty in all, were published by Crown, her husband's printing house. They include *Romance in the Rain* (*Yanyu mengmeng*), *Misty Moon* (*Yue menglong, niao menglong*) and *My Heart in a Million Knots* (*Xin you qian qian jie*).

Qiong's love stories have enjoyed wide readership, and were especially popular among young readers in the 1960s and 1970s in Taiwan and in the 1980s in China. There, Qiong Yao's popularity continued even into the late 1990s due to the adaptation of her novels as TV series. *Princess Pearl* (*Huanzhu gege*) was particularly successful. It is a representation of life inside and outside a royal compound revolving around the story of two pairs of young lovers. Qiong's depiction of the princess Little Sparrow, however, triggered controversy as many critics were appalled at the misguided valorization of an 'uncouth ruffian' as the courageous and righteous heroine.

Further reading

Lang, Miriam (2003). 'Taiwanese Romance: San Mao and Qiong Yao'. In Joshua Mostow (ed.) and Kirk Denton (ed. China Section), *Columbia Companion to Modern East Asian Literatures*. New York: Columbia University Press, 515–19.

HU MINGRONG

qipao, cheongsam

The silk dress with frog-button closures and high collar known as the *qipao* or *cheongsam* assumed the status of the Chinese national dress during the twentieth century. Derived from the Manchu banner gown, the *qipao* in the early twentieth century was a loose-fitting gown worn by emancipated female students, who adopted it as an indigenous alternative to Western school uniforms, thus associating the *qipao* with demands for gender equality. During the Nanjing decade (1927–37), the *qipao* gained in popularity, but was linked to a fitted sleek image. Promoted through Shanghai calendar posters and associated with Western fashions, including high heels, make-up and permanent waves, the *qipao* redefined 1930s Chinese modernity as 'cosmopolitan'. Through the circulation of such images abroad, the *qipao* became identified internationally as the typical Chinese dress, while also producing a sexualized and feminized representation of China. In 1950s Hong Kong, local beauty pageants promoted the *cheongsam* as the signifier of Hong Kong cultural identity, strengthening its popularity. The Miss Asia contest (since 1988), in which wearing a *qipao* is a required segment, has furthered the *qipao* as national dress. (The PRC had outlawed the *qipao* during the **Cultural Revolution** decade as signifier of bourgeois decadence.)

Intrinsically related to understandings of cultural identity, modernity, and femininity in China, the *qipao* functions as a contested symbol of 'Chineseness' and femininity throughout greater China. Moreover, in the 1990s, with global fashion often focused on Asia, with designers like Vivienne Tam (see **fashion designers – Hong Kong**), and with the packaging of Shanghai nostalgia by **Shanghai Tang**, the *qipao* emerged as an international fashion item.

Further reading

Clark, Hazel (2001). *The Cheongsam (Images of Asia)*. Oxford: Oxford University Press.

TINA MAI CHEN

Qiu Huadong

b. 1969, Changji, Xinjiang

Writer

A leading writer of new urban fiction in the 1990s, Qiu Huadong capitalizes upon his experience as a Beijing journalist with extensive social networks to write contemporary fiction with a strong ethnographic dimension. Qiu studied Chinese literature at Wuhan University from 1988 to 1992, and moved to Beijing after graduation to work as the cultural-affairs reporter for the business journal *China Commercial Times* (*Zhonghua gongshang shibao*). Since first publishing poetry at age sixteen, Qiu has published over twenty works, including three novels, collections of short stories, novellas, poetry and essays, and an Internet novella (see **web literature**). His works have been translated into English, Japanese and German.

His novel *City Tank* (*Chengshi zhanche*, 1997) focuses on a wide variety of artists attempting to survive in an increasingly commercial Beijing, illuminating the choices confronting artists in a post-revolutionary consumer society. Another novel, *Fly Eyes* (*Yingyan*, 1998), describes young urban professionals. Many of his characters change careers in the early 1990s from artists or teachers to business professionals. In recollecting their past idealism, those who are satiated with their materialistic lifestyle attempt to live more simply but perish in their attempt to seek spiritual value in contemporary society, whereas the 'survivors' live prosaic, middle-class lives.

See also: He Dun; Humanistic Spirit, 'Spirit of the Humanities'; xiahai

Further reading

Visser, Robin (2000). 'The Urban Subject in the Literary Imagination of Twentieth Century China'. PhD diss., Columbia University, 159–84, 265–80.

ROBIN VISSER

Qiu Zhijie

b. 1969, Fujian

Artist

Beijing artist Qiu Zhijie majored in printmaking at Zhejiang Academy of Fine Arts in Hangzhou (BFA, 1992). An internationally acclaimed artist, curator and art critic, Qiu is best known for his calligraphy, photography and video-installations. Like **Xu Bing**, **Gu Wenda** and **Song Dong**, Qiu's early works explore the centrality of the text in relation to social orthodoxy. In the long-term performance *Assignment No. 1: Copying 'Orchid Pavilion Preface' a Thousand Times* (1986–97), Qiu repeatedly copied Wang Xizhi's classic text on a single piece of paper, resulting in a mass of illegible ink. In his environmental installation project, *A Quiz of Memories Before the Spring Festival 1994*, Qiu obfuscated names on grave markers during the 'tomb-sweeping' festival, resulting in chaos for the living and dead (see **Qingming Festival**). Qiu's recent work examines cultural practices that circumscribe the dissemination of art, displacing the conceptual art dominating mid 1990s experimental art. In 2002 he co-curated *The Long March – A Walking Visual Display*, 'marching' contemporary art by Chinese and international artists into local communities along the historic route to examine notions of cultural and historical reciprocity.

Further reading

Gao, Minglu (ed.) (1991). *Inside Out: New Chinese Art*. New York: San Francisco Museum of Modern Art and Asia Society Galleries, New York [for *Assignment No. 1*].

Wu, Hung (2000). *Exhibiting Experimental Art in China*. Chicago: Smart Museum of Art/University of Chicago Press. [Co-curated the exhibitions 'Post-Sense Sensibility: Distorted Bodies and Delusion' (1999) and 'Home? Contemporary Art Proposals' (2000).]

—— (2000). *Transience: Chinese Experimental Art at the End of the Twentieth Century*. Chicago: Smart Museum of Art/University of Chicago Press.

ROBIN VISSER

Qu Xiaosong

b. 1952, Guiyang, Guizhou province

Composer

Qu Xiaosong is one of the most avant-garde of the New Wave composers. He teaches composition at the Shanghai Conservatory of Music, after returning to China from an American sojourn (1989–99). During the **Cultural Revolution**, Qu was sent to the mountainous countryside as a farmer for four years. He taught himself to play the violin in 1972, and a year later joined the Guiyang Beijing Opera Troupe as a violist. When the Central Conservatory reopened in 1978, Qu, along with **Chen Yi**, **Zhou Long**, **Tan Dun** and **Chen Qigang**, was accepted in the composition class. While at the Conservatory, Qu studied with Du Mingxin and graduated in 1983. In 1989, at the invitation of Columbia University's Center for US–China Arts Exchange, Qu moved to New York, where his international fame grew.

Early works, such as *Mong Dong*, were experiments with sound. Qu has an affinity for nature, intent on returning the concept of Chinese music to its most pristine form. His stage work, *Life on a String* (*Ming ruo qinxian*, 1998), is sung in the Sichuan dialect, because Qu appreciates the dialect's latent musicality, similar to his native Guizhou. His *Ji* [Silence] series explores the minutest sonic shades. *Ji No. 4 'Kou'* (2001) was scored for a septet, but the volume of any performance of this work is intentionally low. Qu is a very theatrical composer, sometimes performing as vocalist and conductor himself in Europe, America and Asia.

Further reading

Kouwenhoven, Frank (1995). 'Operas by Qu Xiaosong and Guo Wenjing'. *Chime* 8 (Spring): 158–61.

—— (1997). 'New Chinese Operas by Qu Xiaosong, Tan Dun, and Guo Wenjing'. *Chime* 11/12 (Spring/Autumn): 111–22.

Saunders, Glen (1996). 'A Chinese Composer's Views on Greek Drama and Buddhism. Qu Xiaosong's Opera *The Death of Oedipus*'. *Chime* 9 (Autumn): 46–56.

JOANNA C. LEE

quyi

(song-arts)

Performed narrative arts known as *quyi* (song-arts), or *shuochang yishu* (telling and singing arts) vie with importance in Chinese oral literature with **Xiqu** (sung-drama/opera) and folksongs. As a professional art dramatizing tales in instalments, *quyi* have survived in China for over a millennium, producing numerous local forms in the vernacular.

The three broad types of *quyi* are distinguished by the proportion of speech to song. The spoken genres include the long serialized tales known as *pingshu* (book telling) in northern and central China and *pinghua* or 'storytelling' in the southeast (see **Suzhou pingtan**), as well as shorter forms like **xiangsheng** (comic dialogues) filled with plays on words and repartees. Sung forms, such as the *dagushu* (long stories for drum) and *danxian* (ballads for one string instrument), constitute a second type. A third one stretches the musical and rhythmic qualities of language far beyond ordinary speech. These are the *kuaibanshu* (clappertale) forms in rhymed prose in which the storyteller stresses the intonations and rhythm of the words in a quasi-melodic 'rap' accompanied by bamboo clappers. The latter type also may juxtapose speech and song as in *tanci*, a form of chantefables that alternates the singing of accompanied ballads with dialogue and narration.

Unlike traditional theatre, the performance of *quyi* requires very few artists (usually between one and three), little make-up and no scenery. Storytellers may use accessories like a fan or a piece of wood for emphasis or to represent an object in the story. They may also accompany themselves with a drum and clappers or string instruments such as the *sanxian* (three-string lute), *yangqin* (hammered dulcimer) or **pipa** (pear-shaped lute). With this economy of means comes the requirement that the storyteller be able to embody several characters and display a panoply of narrative and mimicry techniques. The classic repertoire often shares stock stories with classic novels and drama, such as *The Romance of Three Kingdoms* (*Sanguo yanyi*), *Tales of the Water Margin* (*Shuihu zhuan*) and *The Journey to the West* (*Xiyou ji*). Extra episodes are often added to embroider the exploits and foibles of heroes, whose characters come through all the more vividly. Some of the contemporary repertoire directly takes to a socialist lifestyle, while others, such as Ma Sangli's sketches about factory meetings and hospital care, satirize the absurdities of modern life. National (non-Han) minorities possess their own genres and repertoire, such as the Tibetan *Epic of Gesar*.

In the 1950s, the Communist regime, realizing the potential of *quyi* as a vehicle for reinforcing their cultural policy, began to support storytelling through public institutions and programmes. Artists, now salaried, performed in 'storyteller houses' (*shuochang*) or **teahouses**, where a modest cover charge replaced the traditional contribution for 'storytelling and tea' (*shuocha qian*). 'Cultural workers' collected and revised traditional works in accordance with the new ideology, in effect censoring works considered feudal, superstitious or erotic. Some entirely new creations are immensely popular. For example, **Hou Baolin**'s comic sketch on local cultures, 'Theatre and Dialects' (*Xiqu yü fangyan*) achieves its comic effect by imitating local dialects and the idiosyncrasies of regional operas. The radical reorientation of society since the 1980s, however, has deprived most storytellers of their government support and does not augur well for a living art form more suited to the conviviality of the past. With the exception of *xiangsheng* and *pingtan*, *quyi* tend to have become museum pieces for special events before an audience of workers, students or tourists.

See also: string ensemble

Further reading

(1983). *Zhongguo da baike quanshu, xiqu quyi* [Encyclopedia of China: Drama and Quyi]. Shanghai: Zhongguo da baike quanshu chubanshe.

Bordahl, Vibeke (1999). *The Eternal Storyteller: Oral Literature in Modern China*. Nordic Institute of Asian Studies. Richmond, UK: Curzon Press.

Bordahl, Vibeke and Ross, Jette (2002). *Chinese Storytellers: Life and Art in the Yangzhou Tradition*. Boston: Cheng and Tsui.

ISABELLE DUCHESNE

R

radio (stations and content)

Although in recent years television has become the dominant medium in China, the political and historical significance of radio should not be overlooked. Not only was radio the most direct form of mass communication between the state or Party and the Chinese populace for the first three and a half decades of Communist rule, but in the post-Mao reform era, radio has also been at the forefront of changes to media content and format in the face of rapid commercialization since the early 1980s (see **Pearl River Economic Radio**).

In 1949 there were forty-nine government-operated radio stations in China, of which seventeen were new. At the same time, the Communist authorities temporarily permitted a further thirty-three privately owned stations to continue to operate. However, by 1953 these were taken over by Party-led people's broadcasting stations. The dominant national broadcaster was Central People's Radio (CPR – formerly Yan'an Xinhua Radio) broadcasting fifteen and a half hours daily with 50 per cent news, 25 per cent public education and 25 per cent culture and entertainment. An important feature of radio at this time was that it was received not only through wireless receivers but also through wired radio, which penetrated almost any area of public space, from paddy fields to dormitories, all the time delivering the messages the Party wanted the population to hear. Designated monitors were even assigned in work units throughout the country to muster up audiences and ensure that crucial broadcasts were heard.

In the 1980s, as with television, the restriction that had limited broadcasting to central and provincial levels was removed, opening up the field to city and county levels. By the end of 1992, the number of radio stations in China had grown to 812. At the same time, radio was coming under increasing commercial pressure to be profitable, and the proliferation of stations, many with multiple channels, also introduced competition into the radio industry. Apart from Pearl River Economic Radio (PRER), which fought against Hong Kong broadcasters, other stations throughout the country were looking for ways to engage their audiences more fully.

One such station is Shanghai's Oriental Radio, affiliated to **Shanghai Oriental Television** under the auspices of the Shanghai Radio and Television Bureau. Financially independent, the station has been forced to pay its way by attracting, and keeping, audiences. Like PRER, Oriental Radio, launched in 1992, endeavoured to get closer to its audiences with new livelier, friendlier formats, including music, talk shows and phone-ins. It is possible to see these shows as a step towards greater participation in an emerging public sphere. However, they can conversely be seen as a necessary safety valve for releasing people's tensions and frustrations in a controllable and relatively harmless way. Phone-ins with invited guests, who are likely to be Party officials, can also serve as a useful tool for keeping the Party in touch with the people and their contemporary concerns.

See also: East Radio; state control of media

Further reading

Chang, Won Ho (1989). *Mass Media in China: the History and the Future*. Ames: Iowa State University Press.

Hamm, Charles (1991). 'Music and Radio in the People's Republic of China'. *Asian Music* 22.2 (Spring/ Summer): 1–41.

Zhao, Yuezhi (1998). *Media, Market, and Democracy in China: Between the Party Line and the Bottom Line*. Chicago: University of Illinois.

KEVIN LATHAM

radio and TV hotlines (rexian) and call-in shows

Radio and TV hotlines, which offer listeners and viewers the chance to debate 'hot' issues of the day, live and on air, began life in China in the 1980s. The phenomenon first began to appear on the business channels (*jingji tai*) of major broadcast stations, since these channels concentrated on business and economics rather than politics and current affairs and so enjoyed greater freedom from direct political control. The hotlines initially had two main functions: playing songs chosen by the audience, and helping listeners and viewers trace missing people. Gradually they developed, involving audiences more and more in live discussions of hot social issues ranging from marriage, relationships, children and parents, to drugs and anticorruption campaigns.

In China now almost all radio and broadcast stations, at national, provincial and local level, have radio hotlines. In the main, the content of what is discussed on these hotlines is still controlled by the Chinese government. In line with other media, they promote the Chinese Communist Party line on social reform, and are used for airing approved social problems such as consumer protection, environmental protection and local government corruption. Discussion of issues considered harmful to the image of China, such as the unification of Taiwan or the spread of cults such as **Falun gong**, is forbidden.

The top national hotlines, however, such as *Focus* (*Jiaodian fangtan*) and *Today's Hotline* run by the Guangdong People's Broadcast Station, enjoy greater freedom. *Today's Hotline* is particularly well known for its critical stance and is one of the most popular programmes in China.

LILY CHEN

recreational associations

Sports and fitness activities were governed by the State Sports Commission from the top down from 1955 until 1984, when the central government first called for the 'societization' (*shehuihua*) or grassroots development of sports through corporate and private sponsorship. Recreational associations rapidly emerged outside the Sports Commission system, funded by wealthy peasants and private entrepreneurs, families, villages, occupational groups and corporations. Defined as apolitical, they were relatively free of government control and were among the first voluntary associations to proliferate across the landscape of the emerging grassroots democracy. They did not directly challenge the political system, but exerted subtle influence that brought about social change by working around it. Competitive bodybuilding became the first sport to develop outside the state-supported sports system, and over time it contributed to greater openness concerning the display and aesthetic appreciation of the human body, resulting in the first officially sanctioned public appearance of bikini-clad women bodybuilders in 1986. In 1988, China's first post-1949 **football (soccer)** fan club received official approval; as the majority of members were young, male and working class (or unemployed), this amounted to the organization of a working-class voice that was publicly expressed in the popular media. In the new millennium, as the singular role of the work unit in social life began to dissipate, recreational associations played a central role in organizing a social life between strangers in the new 'communities' (*shequ*), consisting of residence complexes (*xiaoqu*) not attached to any single work unit (*danwei*) (see **residential districts (urban)**).

SUSAN BROWNELL

Red Humour

(Hongse youmo)

Artist group

An art group that uses humour to subvert the power of language, script and presentation, the Red Humour group was established in February 1986 by Wu Shanzhuan, Zhang Haizhou, Lü Haizhou, Luo Xianyue, Song Chenghua, Ni Haifeng, Huang Jian, all students from the education department of the Zhejiang Academy of Fine Arts. They were initially interested in the aesthetic quality of printed Chinese characters, which they explored in the '70% Red, 25% Black, 5% White' exhibition (Zhejiang Academy of Art, May–June 1986). The exhibition drew great interest because of the absurd contrasts created by the re-contextualization of phrases from varied sources such as market language, colloquialisms, advertising, news, religion and philosophy. While visually reminiscent of the **Cultural Revolution** 'big-character posters' (*dazibao*), the resulting disjuncture of language created an amusing atmosphere of 'serious absurdity', and the space was pervaded by a Chan-inspired irreverence towards authority and the significance of human endeavour. Though the group's existence ended after their graduation in 1986, the spirit of the group was perpetuated by some of its members. Ni Haifeng continued doing works with Chan connotations, covering buildings and objects with mystical numbers and inscriptions. He now lives in Amsterdam. Red Humour became the 'trade mark' of Wu Shanzhuan, who parodied the cultural values of art: selling shrimps at the 'China Avant-Garde' exhibition (1989) and setting up stalls of typical Chinese cultural icons such as toy pandas at various international venues. Water and the 'no water today' slogan are recurrent themes in his work. Wu Shanzhuan lives in Germany where he often collaborates in artworks with his partner, Inga Svala Thorsdottir. He has taken part in major international exhibitions such as the 1995 'Des del País del Centre: avantguardes artístiques xineses' at the Centre d'Art Santa Mónica in Barcelona (1995) and 'Inside/Out: New Chinese Art' at the Asia Society, New York, and San Francisco MoMA (1998–9).

Further reading

Andrews, Julia F. and Gao, Minglu (1995). 'The Avant-Garde's Challenge to Official Art'. In Debora S. Davis (ed.), *Urban Spaces in Contemporary China: The Potential for Autonomy and Community in Post-Mao China*. Cambridge: Harvard University Press, 221–78.

Lü, Peng and Yi, Dan (1992). *Zhongguo xiandai yishushi* [A History of Modern Art in China]. Changsha: Hunan meishu chubanshe, 295–9.

Wu, Shanzhuan (1987). 'Women de huihua' [Our Paintings]. *Meishu sichao* 1: 22–4.

EDUARDO WELSH

reform (ideological justifications)

The late 1970s marked the beginning of sweeping economic, cultural and social changes in China. Given the crucial defining role of ideology in Chinese society, the post-Mao reformist leadership was well aware that the retreat from Maoism and the reorientation of policy towards rapid and sustained economic and technological modernization needed to be justified in theoretical terms. The ideological reorientation and intellectual evolution that it initiated aimed at rejecting ultra leftist orthodoxy in favour of an interpretation that both rationalized the new policies of liberalization and provided a critique of past errors like the Anti-Rightist campaign, Great Leap Forward, Cultural Revolution and Mao's cult of personality.

The discussions on 'practice as a criterion of truth' launched in 1978 were meant to justify a more flexible and utilitarian orientation in policy-making and obviate the need to seek legitimacy from the canon of Marxism–Leninism–Mao Zedong Thought. Additional debates on the source of knowledge, stages of socialism and feudal culture attempted to trace the philosophical and social roots of leftist radicalism and repudiate its disruptive emphasis on class conflict and continuous revolution. The new Party line of the decreased salience of classes and class struggle in Chinese society legitimized the elite bureaucrat and intellectual agents of change and at the same time permitted the rehabilitation of millions of people who had been persecuted during the political campaigns of the Maoist era.

In the short term, the ideological offensive was quite successful in discrediting past policies and theoretical orientations as well as providing a wide measure of popular support for the post-Mao coalition. In the longer term, the intellectual evolution that had been set in motion proved difficult to control and restrict within the limits prescribed by the leadership. The debates on epistemology became a fertile breeding ground for scepticism and doubts about the validity and relevance of Marxism, which would be emphasized prominently in the 1980s by Liu Zaifu, Jin Guantao and others. Furthermore, the extolling of scientific methods and practical verification undermined the Party elite's hitherto unassailable monopoly over truth and provided critics, like the astrophysicist Fang Lizhi, an avenue to press for complete intellectual autonomy and refute the 'guiding role' of any 'supreme principles', including those of Marxist philosophy. The shift in focus from social classes to the individual subject in the emerging intellectual discourse of alienation, subjectivity and practical philosophy (see **Marxist Humanism**) strengthened the positions of those who advocated moving China in the direction of a market economy, rule of law and a pluralist democratic system. For Chinese intellectuals the ideological reorientation encouraged in the immediate post-Mao era marked the beginning of a period of creativity, intellectual liberation and reconstruction prompted by critical questioning of orthodoxy and a new interest in other non-Marxist intellectual traditions. However, for the political elite whose goals were far more limited, these ideological developments were threatening and destabilizing, and ended up undermining rather than enhancing its legitimacy and claims to power.

Further reading

Misra, K. (1998). *From Post-Maoism to Post-Marxism: The Erosion of Official Ideology in Deng's China.* New York: Routledge

KALPANA MISRA

religion, recent history of

The recent history of Chinese religion can be said to begin at the end of the nineteenth century with the emergence of a concerted ideological critique of religion. This critique gradually intensified over the next several decades, and was accompanied by increasingly violent and physically destructive attacks on all manner of religion. These attacks began to abate only in 1978 with the implosion of the **Cultural Revolution** and the government's relaxation of its hard-line on religion. Though universally devastated by these events, most of the religions that could be found in China at the end of the nineteenth century have since shown an unforeseen resiliency in their re-emergence at the end of the twentieth. Though much of the modern religious landscape of China will appear familiar to those knowledgeable about pre-twentieth-century China – temples, incense, ancestor shrines, pilgrimage, monks, fortune-tellers, healers, etc. – there is little of Chinese religion that has been left untouched by the events of the twentieth century, and much that has significantly changed.

China has undergone many anti-religious campaigns in its past, but none so pervasive and debilitating as those in the twentieth century. This is accounted for by a unique constellation of factors. Among these were anti-Manchu animosities that conflated much traditional religion with the imperial system, the political power and single-minded intensity of the anti-religion forces over a period of almost one hundred years, the capacity of the nation-state to penetrate more deeply into all aspects of Chinese life, and the vastly improved technologies of communication and violence of the modern period. Abetting these tendencies from abroad were the Meiji Restoration in Japan and the ascendancy of Marxism, particularly in neighbouring Russia. The emergence of Japan and Russia as dominant powers, moreover, was perceived to be rooted in notions of scientific modernity.

By the beginning of the twentieth century, an influential majority of Chinese intellectuals, though an infinitesimal minority of the total Chinese population in whose name they spoke, sought to account for China's humiliating defeats in the face of Western and Japanese imperialist aggression by blaming not only the Manchu monarchy but also religion, which was regarded as indistinguishable from pre-scientific, traditional or feudal society. Influenced by Western theories of Social Darwinism, these intellectuals saw the monarchy and religion as two of the primary forces enervating the Chinese people and inhibiting China's evolution into a modern state, characterized by science and nationalism. Thus, the overthrow of the monarchy in 1911 opened the door to an attack on its perceived accomplice, religion. Among the earliest casualties of these campaigns was **local religion**. In routing the Manchus and seeking to erase the symbols of their presence in cities throughout China, officials of the Republican government set about destroying temples patronized by the Manchus and their Chinese subjects, such as those of the City and Earth gods. Government bureaus and taxation replaced local religious associations that had effectively structured and managed most of the social and economic infrastructure of rural China. Labelling local religion 'superstitious' (*mixin*), a neologism imported from Japan and applied initially by the Catholic missionaries, celebrations associated with lunar New Year (see **New Year Festival**) were prohibited in many regions, images of gods were removed from temples, and scores of smaller shrines destroyed – all this well before the Cultural Revolution. Geomancers, healers and diviners avoided the initial attack on local religion, largely due to the itinerant nature of their professions (see **fengshui**; **divination and fortune-telling**). Their itinerancy, however, tended to bring these quasi-religious professionals into contact and often affiliation with supra-village sectarian movements (see **sectarian religion**). As a result, the Nationalists generally viewed them as anti-government, and their demise began with the military suppression of these sectarian movements in the late 1920s.

The large traditional text-based religious institutions suffered initially as well. As part of the rhetoric of nationalism, **Christianity (Protestantism)**, **Catholicism** and even Buddhism were intermittently attacked as 'foreign.' Daoism, often indistinguishable from forms of popular religion in the eyes of the intellectuals, suffered the same fate as local temples. Ultimately, however, many of these groups, through the

formation of national associations, were better able to defend themselves and garner support among national and local authorities, thus gaining a temporary reprieve as 'true religions'. Those not so organized or influential were suppressed as 'superstitious'. Many of these largely anti-religious tendencies were instituted as government policy in the Nationalist-sponsored 'Standards for Preserving and Abandoning Gods and Shrines' in 1928.

During this period a number of local transformations of what had been foreign religions began to emerge among Christians. The Assembly Hall Movement of Watchman Nee (see **Little Flock**; **Local Church (and 'shouters')**), a separatist Trinitarian movement, and the **True Jesus Church**, a separatist Pentecostal movement, were both founded by local charismatic figures (and see **Jesus Family**). Separatist Christian movements are not a new phenomenon in China, as demonstrated by the Taiping movement in the nineteenth century.

By the mid 1930s, the anti-religious rhetoric was shifting from Social Darwinism to Marxist, promising the eventual disappearance not only of religion but of the state as well. With the Communist victory in 1949, the so-called 'true religions', though still criticized, enjoyed a modicum of freedom under the umbrella of the **Three-Self Patriotic Movement (TSPM)**, namely self-governing, self-propagation and self-supporting. Numerous documents and public statements authored by members of the Party elite, while maintaining the position that religion would 'wither away', asserted that this would happen naturally with education and the expected prosperity of Communist reform. Force would not and should not be used. At the same time, the new government continued the policy of suppressing groups and individuals it labelled as 'superstitious', often quite violently (see **Yiguan Dao**).

The attack intensified in 1966 with the onset of the Cultural Revolution. The government formally dissolved the distinction between legitimate 'true' religion and illegitimate 'superstitious' religion, declaring the practice of religion in any form whatsoever illegal. The Red Guards took it upon themselves to enforce this policy, often with a viciousness far exceeding the intentions of their elders. Groups that up until this time had been minimally affected, such as Muslims and Tibetan Buddhists, suffered along with the traditional targets of state animosity (see **Islam in China**). Great numbers of religious monuments were painstakingly dismantled or burned, relics smashed and practitioners harassed, in many cases to their deaths. Those religious buildings that survived destruction did so through conversion to factories or schools, and through the intervention of the PLA or highly positioned members of the Communist Party such as Zhou Enlai. The anti-religious movements peaked in the mid 1970s.

With the end of the Cultural Revolution in 1978 and the repeal of many of the more stridently anti-religious policies, religions began a cautious reappearance, still largely without formal government approval. By the late 1980s, some ten years after the 'opening up', an increasingly pragmatic approach began to emerge. While not officially reversing its position on religion, the government began to overlook religious activities it had attempted to suppress before.

The Buddhists quickly reconstructed themselves on the ruins of the past, becoming the wealthiest and most conspicuous form of religion in contemporary China (see **Buddhist monasteries (Chinese)**). The government allows one Catholic church building and one Protestant church building for religious activity in any given area. Beijing is, for example, divided into a number of districts with one Protestant church building serving each district. In each church, the membership tends to be dominated by one of the older denominations, and the style of worship on Sunday morning will reflect, for example, the Anglican, Baptist, Methodist or Lutheran past. The state management of religion has been the responsibility of thousands of officials working in the **Religious Affairs Bureau (State Administration for Religious Affairs)** in cities throughout China, and is brokered in many cases by large pan-China confederations of religious groups such as the Buddhist Association, the Daoist Association, the Islamic Federation, the Chinese Church of Christ and the Patriotic Catholic Church. These non-governmental confederations are delegated, in effect, the responsibility for determining which groups are legitimate and which are not. Much of the criteria determining legitimacy is based of the principles of the Three-Self Movement. Most **house churches** are evangelical Christians and do not wish to be associated with the Three-Self Movement, which they regard as heretical. Hence, they have been labelled 'underground' (*dixia*) religion. The government actively attacks groups it characterizes as 'evil cults' (*xiejiao*), understood as particularly harmful forms of 'superstition'. This label has been applied to some of the house churches and to the **Falun gong**. Since the beginning of the twenty-first century the government has granted tacit though unofficial approval to some healers, geomancers and diviners, and they again operate with a modicum of freedom, though largely in rural areas. Foreign-based missionary groups and churches, such as the **Mormons** and the Roman Catholic Church (as opposed the Patriotic Catholic Church), have explicitly been denied legal status into the twenty-first century and are effectively underground.

See also: Daoism (Daojiao), recent history of; Daoism (Quanzhen order); Daoism (Zhengyi tradition); pilgrimage; processions (religious); religious policies of the state; spirit-mediums

Further reading

Duara, Prasanjit (1996). *Rescuing History from the Nation*. Chicago: University of Chicago Press.
Kipnis, Andrew (2001). 'The Flourishing of Religion in Post-Mao China and the Anthropological Category of Religion'. *Australian Journal of Anthropology* 12.1: 32–46.

WILLIAM POWELL

Religious Affairs Bureau (State Administration for Religious Affairs)

Formerly known as the Religious Affairs Bureau, the State Administration for Religious Affairs or SARA (Guojia zongjiaoju) is the government bureau charged with implementing the state's religion policies and enforcing official regulations.

Headquartered in Beijing, SARA is administered by the State Council and its policies dictated by the United Front Work Department of the Party. It has branches from the national level on down to the municipal and district levels. Its institutionalization at lower levels varies widely. Offices in provincial capitals, major cities and sensitive regions are well staffed and highly bureaucratized. In many small cities, villages and most rural areas, however, SARA has a minimal presence, and it is not uncommon for its entire portfolio to be managed by a single cadre with other responsibilities.

SARA is responsible for registering venues for religious activities and conducting annual inspections of them. It also retains 'administrative control' over all religious organizations (see **religious policies of the state**). In practice, this means that religious organizations may not act as autonomous legal entities, but must go through SARA to reclaim properties, obtain permits from other ministries, and so forth. SARA is also charged with authorizing religious professionals. In practice, SARA cadres often tap politically loyal figures within religious circles, or SARA may even appoint its own cadres to leadership positions within the patriotic religious organizations. SARA is also responsible for monitoring religious activities to ensure that their content, locale and leaders are in conformity with official regulations.

SARA's political orientation has become increasingly conservative since the appointment of Ye Xiaowen as its director in 1995. Formerly an official in the Communist Youth League, Ye attracted the attention of Party leaders by writing treatises which advocated enhanced Party-state control over religion. Shortly after his appointment, Ye Xiaowen instructed an assembly of cadres at the annual SARA conference that the government's objective is not merely 'registration for its own sake', but is to assume 'control over places for religious activities as well as over all religious activities themselves'. Ye's remarks were published in the *People's Consultative Conference News* on 1 February 1996 in a section entitled 'Religion and the Nation' under the title 'Stress Three Matters' (see *Tripod* 16.92: 45–50 for a translation).

Further reading

Ye, Xiaowen (1996). 'China's Current Religious Question: Once Again, an Inquiry into the Five Characteristics of Religion' (22 March). *Selection of Reports of the Party School of the Central Committee of the Chinese Communist Party, no. 5*. [Reprinted in *Chinese Law and Government* 33.2 (2000): 75–100].

JASON KINDOPP

religious policies of the state

The CCP's policy towards religion in the reform period has offered limited protection for individuals' right to believe in and practise religion, while regulating religious activities and controlling religious organization. Within this broad framework, various branches of the government and Party at all levels have issued regulations governing religion, forming a comprehensive web of restrictions on religious sites, professionals, activities and foreign involvement.

China's top leaders set the government's broader policy orientation towards religion. The initial reform-era policy platform sought to reverse the radical anti-religion policies of the late Mao era and to establish a framework for accommodating certain religious beliefs and practices while preserving control over religious organization. The regime's authoritative statement on religion was issued in the CCP Central Committee's **Document 19 (1982)**, which affirmed that as a complex social phenomenon, religion would endure for a long time under socialism. The document recognized five world religions (Buddhism, Daoism, Catholicism, Islam and Protestantism), and laid out a policy of permitting 'normal' religious activities within venues under the supervision of resurrected Mao-era 'patriotic' religious organizations (see **patriotic covenants**; **Three-Self Patriotic Movement (TSPM)**). The document also unveiled a strategy to co-opt religious elites and utilize them to retain control over religious groups.

The rapid growth of religious activity throughout the 1980s, culminating with the spring 1989 violence and the demise of Communism in Eastern Europe, triggered a conservative backlash in religion policy. In February 1991, the CCP Central Committee and the State Council jointly issued *Document 6*, which promulgated new rules and restrictions on the registration of religious venues and professionals, and also called on provinces and municipalities to issue their own regulations. Continued religious growth and increasing resistance to official manipulation prompted a new focus on compelling religious groups to refashion their doctrines and identities into conformity with CCP rule. This new emphasis was promulgated in a November 1993 speech by President Jiang Zemin, in which he called on authorities to 'take active steps to guide religions in a direction compatible with socialist society'. Jiang reaffirmed all of these components of religion policy in a speech at a major conference on religion in December 2001, in which he underscored the state's policy of containing religion's influence in society, actively guiding religion's development into conformity with CCP rule, and suppressing religious elements that resisted state control.

To achieve the state's policy objectives, government and Party branches from the national level down to the municipal and district levels have issued regulations on religion. Broadly, regulations require venues for religious activity to register with the government and to submit to annual inspection. All religious clergy must receive government authorization before conducting religious activities. All religious activities must be presided over by a government-authorized professional, and must occur within registered venues. Religious groups must submit all religious materials to the government for inspection. The production of any religious materials requires prior government authorization. Foreigners are forbidden from establishing religious organizations, recruiting adherents or conducting any other missionary activities. Members of the CCP are prohibited from believing in religion, or participating in any religious activities. Regulations typically offer vaguely worded but ominous penalties for violations.

Further reading

Chen, Weiwei (1993). 'Jiang, Li Peng Meet Delegates'. *Beijing Xinhua Domestic Service* (FBIS-CHI-93-214).

Katz, Paul (2003). 'Religion and the State in Post-war Taiwan'. In Daniel Overmyer (ed.), *Religion in China Today*. Cambridge: Cambridge University Press, 89–106.

Potter, Pitman (2003). 'Belief in Control: Regulation of Religion in China'. In Daniel Overmyer (ed.), *Religion in China Today*. Cambridge: Cambridge University Press, 11–31.

Spiegel, M. and Tong, J. (2000). 'Documents on Religion in China: Central Government Policy'. *Chinese Law and Government* 33.2.

JASON KINDOPP

representations of minorities

Ethnic minorities are best known to people in China through portrayals in a variety of domains. The most widespread domain is the lower-denomination currency, depicting ethnic groups in stylized clothing and headdresses on bills from ten yuan down to one mao. The next most common representation is in song and dance performances. Each area, and the central government, has a 'song and dance troupe' (*gewutuan*). In the southwest especially, the 'minority song and dance troupes' (*minzu gewutuan*) have frequent performances of songs and dances styled after actual minority ritual (but usually jazzed up and made more homogeneous), usually portraying one after another of the fifty-six ethnic groups. Since the 1980s, minority **theme parks** – with housing, costumes and other artifacts built to resemble minority areas – have been popular, with the most famous in Shenzhen.

Colourful representations of minorities are found on postage stamps, postcards and murals in some peripheral areas. Minorities are also a favourite theme in film, art and literature. For instance, the film **Sacrificed Youth** shows Tai culture (see **Tai (Dai), culture of**) as an appealing natural antidote to the stultifying restrictions of **Han** (Chinese) culture. The Yunnan school of painting depicts in bright oils certain themes such as graceful minority nude women. In literature there is a romantic view of minorities, as in **Bai Hua**'s *Remote Country of Women*. A growing set of folktales and stories written by minorities in Chinese has been published.

The basic ideas portrayed are several-fold: the minorities represent China's past, with the Han representing the present and future. Minorities are seen as primitive, backward, quaint, in some ways innocent yet in other ways immoral (with 'free' sexual encounters). Depictions often equate minorities with women, with children or with nature. On the evolutionary scale within which all of Chinese social science operates, the minorities are behind the Han.

See also: ethnicity, concepts of; minority pop musicians: the new generation; Tian Zhuangzhuang

Further reading

Blum, Susan D. (2001). *Portraits of 'Primitives': Ordering Human Kinds in the Chinese Nation.* Lanham, MD: Rowman and Littlefield.

Clark, Paul (1987). 'Ethnic Minorities in Chinese Films: Cinema and the Exotic'. *East–West Film Journal* 1.2 (June): 15–31.

Gladney, Dru (1994). 'Representing Nationality in China: Refiguring Majority/Minority Identities'. *Journal of Asian Studies* 53.1 (February): 92–123.

Kuoshu, Harry H. (2000). 'Othering the National Minorities: Exoticism and Self-Reflexivity'. In *idem, Lightness of Being in China: Adaptation and Discursive Figuration in Cinema and Theater.* New York: Peter Lang Publishing, 95–122.

Oakes, Tim (1998). *Tourism and Modernity in China.* London: Routledge.

Schein, Louisa (2000). *Minority Rules: The Miao and the Feminine in China's Cultural Politics.* Durham, NC: Duke University Press.

Zhang, Yingjin (1997). 'From "Minority Film" to "Minority Discourse": Questions of Nationhood and Ethnicity in Chinese Cinema'. In Sheldon Lu (ed.), *Transnational Chinese Cinema: Identity, Nationhood, Gender.* Honolulu: University of Hawai'i Press.

SUSAN D. BLUM

reproductive health

Reproductive health in contemporary China must be understood in the context of eugenics and birth control. Like population control, eugenics was a taboo subject until the late 1970s when the PRC was about to announce its **one-child policy**. In 1979, the desire to avoid unnecessary births with genetic diseases was formally articulated and linked with the political claim of the 'four modernizations'. It was followed in 1980 by the revision of the Marriage Law that prohibited marriages between, or with, people who have genetic diseases or mental illnesses (see **Marriage Law of the PRC (1 January 1981) and revisions (2001)**). Since 1981, some but not many studies of the effect of birth control on reproductive health have been incorporated into China's Five-Year Economic Plans. After having practised birth control for about two decades, China passed the Law of the Health of Mothers and Infants (*Muyin baorenfa*) in 1994, indicating explicitly that where marriage is recognized, forced abortion is allowed.

Although the law also offers a legal basis of women's right to reproductive health – marriage and pregnancy consultation, prenatal screening and neonatal health – it should also be examined in regard to social context since reform. Originally called the Eugenics Law, it allows for the abortion of a couple's *unwanted* children, especially in rural areas where hospitals may offer services, such as sonograms, to confirm the sex of a foetus. The sex ratio of newborns in China rose from 108.47 males for every 100 females in 1981 to 113 males for every 100 females in 1996. The ratio increases to 130 males for every 100 females with a third child. Also in rural areas, where many women suffer problems brought on by birth control technologies such as intra-uterine devices, medical facilities are still in severe shortage, and the law actually fails to grant them benefits as claimed.

Other related problems include a rising number of unmarried teenage mothers and prostitution. Since economic reform, a large population of women have also moved to the larger cities seeking jobs, yet the law fails to take care of them if they become pregnant when underage or lacking proper registration. The law also fails to deal with actual reproductive health risks such as **HIV/AIDS and**

STIs, which are rising in coastal cities where prostitution has followed a booming economy (see **sexuality and behaviour**). In short, although China has devised laws, their application in solving the practical problems with respect to women's reproductive health is another matter, as pointed out at the UN Conference on Women hosted by the PRC in 1995.

KUO WEN-HUA

Research Institute for National Studies

(Guoxue yanjiuyuan)

The Research Institute for National Studies is a transdisciplinary entity, originally founded as the Research Centre of Traditional Chinese Culture (Zhongguo chuantong wenhua yanjiu zhongxin) by **Peking University** in 1992. In 2001, it was renamed. Placed under the patronage of well-known scholars like Ji Xianlin and Zhang Dainian, it has been financially supported by well-known personalities, such as the writers Nan Huaijin and **Jin Yong**. The Institute bases itself on the resources of four departments of Peking University (Philosophy, History, Literature and Archaeology) in order to foster transdisciplinarity in the academic world of Chinese studies and promote traditional culture to a broader audience.

Between 1995 and 1998, such educational and social roles were realized through the production of **television programmes**. A weekly series in 150 episodes, *The Light of Chinese Civilization* (*Zhonghua wenming zhi guang*), enjoyed a nationwide broadcast and reached a large audience. Collections of books have been published as well, in order to highlight key features of Chinese culture or civilization. On the academic front, the Institute publishes a bi-annual review, *Studies in Sinology* (*Guoxue yanjiu*), and organizes symposia (in 1998 an international meeting on sinological research was held) and scholarly exchanges (in 1997 fifty students and professors from Taiwan came to Peking University). It has also created the first transdisciplinary doctoral programme.

See also: Academy of Chinese Culture; Liu Dong; National Studies

SÉBASTIEN BILLIOUD

research institutions for minority nationalities

Research institutions about minority nationalities are mainly scattered in the capital and the frontier provinces. These research institutions can be classified into three categories. The first category includes the institutions affiliated with the social science academy system. In the **Chinese Academy of Social Sciences** in Beijing, there are two institutes that conduct research on the minority nationalities. One is the Institute of Nationality Studies, which is one of the oldest and largest institutes in the academy. It was founded in the 1950s, and many of its researchers participated in large-scale field investigations into the history and society of China's minority nationalities in the 1950s. It once boasted more than three hundred researchers and staff, but today the number has been greatly reduced. Presently the institute consists of several departments: of ethnology, of history of minority nationalities, of languages of minority nationalities, of the economy of the minority areas, of Marxist theories of ethnicity, of global ethnic studies, and of visual anthropology. The other institute in the CASS is the Institute of the Literature of Minority Nationalities, which is much younger and smaller than the Institute of Nationality Studies. There are similar institutes in the provincial-level academies in the frontier provinces, where the minority nationalities live.

The second category consists of the research institutes directly affiliated with the central and local governments. In the State Ethnic Affairs Commission, there is an Institute of Ethnic Studies, which conducts research on policies towards minority nationalities. There is also the China National Centre for Tibetan Studies in Beijing, which is under the direct control of the central government. There are institutes that conduct similar policy research in the provincial governments of the frontier area.

The last category is formed by the research institutes affiliated with the universities, particularly the universities for minority nationalities and the universities in the frontier provinces. In the **Central University for Nationalities** in Beijing, for example, there are more than a dozen institutes that conduct research on various aspects of the minority nationalities. In Yunnan University, Xinjiang University and Inner Mongolia University, there are renowned institutes that conduct research on local minority groups.

HAN XIAORONG

residential districts (urban)

The history of residential districts – planned (often gated) enclaves of urban housing – in Chinese cities parallels the modern development of Chinese society. Yet the idea that the urban residential landscape should consist primarily of enclaves dates back at least to the Tang dynasty, whose capital Chang'an was divided into walled compounds (*fang*). In the Qing dynasty, Beijing's neighbourhoods of one-storey courtyard housing within *hutong* (see **streets**) were also organized according to the military units ('banners') whose members inhabited them. Western influences after the mid nineteenth century included the development of multi-storey attached houses and apartments, sometimes laid out in planned 'neighbourhood units', designed to particular standards to accommodate residents of different social classes. After the organization of society into productive entities called 'work units' (*danwei*) in 1949, 'new villages' (*xincun*) for workers took a more utilitarian and egalitarian form, inspired by the Soviet Union. In the absence of capital and a land market, most inner-city housing was left un-redeveloped while the 'new villages' were built on vacant land at the cities' edge, usually by and near the residents' 'work unit'. Since Reform, the commercialization of housing has led to the revival of strictly 'residential-housing estates' (*xiaoqu*) of increased density and varying standards – reflected at one extreme by the recent development of enclaves of luxury villas. The emergence of land markets in the early 1990s has also prompted the

replacement of old inner-city neighbourhoods with new 'estates'.

See also: domestic space; home refurbishing; nouveaux riches

Further reading

Lü, Junhua, Rowe, Peter G. and Zhang, Jie (eds) (2001). *Modern Urban Housing in China, 1840–2000*. Munich: Prestel.

DANIEL B. ABRAMSON

restoration districts (urban)

In the aftermath of the Cultural Revolution, many Chinese 'work units' that had jurisdiction over historic neighbourhoods in urban areas were unsure about when, where and how they should either rehabilitate or restore (*xiufu*) them. Until the mid 1990s, with few policy guidelines coming from above, city administrators were often in a state of stasis. Some opted for inertia, unsure whether (or how) to stem the tide of degradation. Facing intense property development pressures, historic architecture often suffered. This was especially the case with vernacular, less monumentally significant buildings. Other decision-makers, however, began to assert greater initiative by examining alternatives to the demolition of historic neighbourhoods. In some cases (e.g. Shanghai's Bund in the late 1980s) the restoration of internationally famous districts seems to have been met with general approval and monetary profit. In other cases, such as the restoration of Sunwen Street in Zhongshan (Guangdong), which began in the early 1990s, the decision to upgrade or restore early twentieth-century shophouses (*yangfang*) was more adventurous and uncertain. Quanzhou (Fujian) is another case where rehabilitation/restoration has been a challenging venture. By the mid 1990s many urban politicians had begun to realize how profitable it could be for their cities to earmark certain districts for restoration, thereby creating tourist attractions, distinctive shopping areas, innovative public places and attractive pedestrian areas. Therefore, as of 2003 one can find such pockets of restored historic architecture throughout Chinese cities. The rationales vary from cultural, economic and political to a combination of these. Until recently, most residents suffered these changes without possessing any power to influence the decisions that have affected their districts. However, a few recent cases (e.g. certain neighbourhoods in Beijing, Guangzhou and Quanzhou) demonstrate that the exclusively top-down approach to restoration/rehabilitation may be changing.

Further reading

Abramson, Daniel, Leaf, Michael and Students of Plan 545 (2000). *Urban Development and Redevelopment in Quanzhou, China: A Field Study Report.* (Asian Urban Research Network, Working Paper 26.) Vancouver: UBC Centre for Human Settlements.

Balderstone, Susan, Qian, Fengqi and Zhang, Bing (2002). 'Shanghai Reincarnated'. In William S. Logan (ed.), *The Disappearing 'Asian' City: Protecting Asia's Urban Heritage in a Globalizing World.* Hong Kong: Oxford University Press, 21–34.

Gaubatz, Piper (1999). 'China's Urban Transformation: Patterns and Processes of Morphological Change in Beijing, Shanghai and Guangzhou'. *Urban Studies* 36: 1495–521.

JEFFREY W. CODY

development. In Shanghai, for example, Nanjing Road remains the downtown core retail shopping area with major outlets of leading world-class retailers from Japan, Europe and the United States. High-rise construction of commercial and some residential space proceeds apace as the use of core urban land assumes a value similar to that found in all market economies. The cities then begin to resemble Western cities with taller buildings nearer the city centre (see **skyscrapers**). Yet retail activities also follow consumers in China's growing cities and are springing up outside the older traditional cores in peripheral and suburban areas. Construction of complexes containing four and five-star **hotels** have led to additional multiple retail centres in various parts of the larger cities to serve the increasingly affluent (see **shopping malls**). In the south, the relatively new but rapidly growing city of Shenzhen has witnessed the appearance of major retail outlets associated with European and North American chains, including a Sam's Club located near large new high-rise apartment complexes for the growing wealthy class. China's cities are thus being made over both in the older downtowns, which are being rebuilt piecemeal, often upwards, and especially towards their peripheries with improved transportation (see **ring roads**) and a greater abundance of land available for new development.

See also: urban planning/renewal

CLIFTON W. PANNELL

retail and business districts (urban)

The urban and retail business districts of China's cities are undergoing dynamic and rapid change. Rising income in step with China's overall rapid economic growth, coupled with greater openness and involvement with the global economy, are leading to rising demand for consumer goods. This dynamic growth and intensified economic activity in turn are having a dramatic impact on land use, spatial structure and the appearance of downtown core areas, as well as leading to a substantial expansion of major retail outlets in peripheral areas of large cities in response to the increased mobility of affluent urbanites and rapid suburban

revivals and other 're-' words

The **Cultural Revolution** era (early 1960s to late 1970s) began with a promise of *renewal*, a *reanimation* of the *revolutionary* impetus, and opposition to *revisionism*, that is backsliding in all its manifestations, whether it be political, cultural or social, that would lead to a *restoration* of bourgeois society and the power of capital. To create a truly new world the old had to be smashed and *repudiated*. However, during this haphazard process, apart from the destruction of human life and much of the material heritage of the nation, the old order proved to be *recalcitrant*.

The post-Mao era was ushered in with a wave of *rehabilitations* and *revivals*. Long-forgotten cultural figures and artistic works made a fitful and then a clamorous *return* to the scene. Books, films, art works, people, historical incidents and eventually entire eras were *regurgitated* by the memory hole that had been created by the denunciations and cultural purges not only during the Cultural Revolution era, but in the years following the founding of the People's Republic itself. Along with this *resurrection* and *rectification* of the past, quotidian life was also *regenerated*. Chinese cuisine in particular, long impoverished by policy-induced shortages and dour revolutionary sobriety, has once more become the gourmand's *redoubt*.

Much of the cultural *resurgence* of the 1980s and 1990s was fed by the wellsprings of socialist culture, as well as the cultures of the Republican era (1911–49) and before. Along with these *revivals*, old debates were *rehearsed* as a younger generation vied for cultural authority and a niche in the booming marketplace. The *reviviscence* of the past also allowed for the flourishing of *retro* fashions, and old-new styles in clothing, writing and art quoted freely from the past while adding their own contemporary inflections. The 1990s was not only a decade of *resuscitation* in China, for elements of *renascence* touched countries throughout the former socialist bloc of Europe, and the motherland of *revolution* itself, the Soviet Union/Russia. As the millennium approached, Party General Secretary Jiang Zemin went so far as to hail in one of his crudely written classical Chinese poems the Deng–Jiang era as being one of '*restoration*' or *zhongxing*. He employed an expression dating from imperial times that signified an attempt by court officials to *revive* the flagging fortunes of an endangered dynasty. While many aspects of traditional social practice remained outlawed, other things that could serve a utilitarian function were sanctioned, including the *revival* of veneration for state Confucianism.

China is a place where the change of dynasties or the ascension of new rulers often allows for unexpected comebacks and *rehabilitations*, and the present age is no different. No one can predict what the future will bring, although amidst the shock of the new there will always be a place for the *reassuring* familiarity of the old.

GEREMIE R. BARMÉ

ring roads

A ring road is a circulation axis permitting high-speed traffic around a city to avoid interfering with inner-city traffic. A number of Chinese cities have adopted a road network comprising several high-speed ring roads and radial roads. Networks of ring roads in China exhibit similar characteristics. The first ring road is the main traffic artery around the urban centre area. It passes through a series of commercial belts and is marked by high traffic volume. The second ring road stretches along the site of the city proper or the former city walls, as in Beijing. The third ring road links the emerging secondary centres with large-scale retail and service businesses. The fourth ring road is designed for freight transport linking the new industrial regions with rail, port and airport terminals. Beyond, ring roads are linking satellite towns across the countryside. In order to maintain high traffic flow, many of these ring roads are fly-overs at busy road junctions. Ring roads are connected together by trunk roads radiating outwards to ensure smooth traffic dispersion. The system of ring roads and radial roads is copied from the Soviet model of transport planning. Ring roads permit the adaptation of old cities to the traffic demands of an expanding and modernizing economy. They reduce bottlenecks off main trunk roads and funnel traffic away from the city centre. With increasing levels of motorization, Chinese ring road networks will serve as the backbone for urban expansion in concentric circles.

CLAUDE COMTOIS

River Elegy

[Heshang]

Television serial

River Elegy (*Heshang*) was a six-part television documentary series broadcast in 1988 that presented a damning critique of Chinese culture and led to heated social, intellectual and political debate about the relationship between China and the West. Reminiscent of intellectual debates of the May Fourth era earlier in the century and picking up on issues at the centre of China's 'Culture Fever' of the 1980s, the programme criticized Chinese people's submission to a feudalistic culture represented metonymically by the Yellow River and the Great Wall. The producers of the programme, a group of university intellectuals and television professionals led by scriptwriters **Su Xiaokang** and Wang Luxiang, suggested through a lyrical narrative superimposed upon beautiful photography that China's introversion over the millennia had left the country isolated and backward compared to the more 'scientific' West.

The programme indirectly hinted at the failure not only of Chinese culture to modernize but also of Chinese socialism to bring about such a modernization. The programme therefore inevitably drew a storm of criticism from Party traditionalists and hard-liners who questioned the historical and factual accuracy of the programme's content as well as its negative, demeaning and unhelpful attitude. With large audiences nationwide and openly voiced support and criticism from various circles, the programme was notable in its own right. However, following the events of May and June 1989, the year after the programme was broadcast, when students led demonstrations against Party corruption and lack of democracy, it gathered an even greater significance both in China and overseas as a retrospectively identified precursor to these events.

Further reading

(1992). *Chinese Sociology and Anthropology* 25.1 (Fall). Special issue on *River Elegy*.

Ma, Shu-yun (1996). 'The Role of Power Struggle and Economic Changes in the "Heshang phenomenon" in China'. *Modern Asian Studies* 30.1 (Feb.): 29–50.

Su, X. and Wang, L. (1991). *Deathsong of the River: A Reader's Guide to the Chinese TV Series 'Heshang'*. Trans. R. W. Bodman and P. P. Wang. Ithaca: Cornell.

Wakeman, Frederic E., Jr (1989). 'All the Rage in China'. *New York Review of Books* (March 2): 19–21.

Wang, Jing (1996). 'Heshang and the Paradoxes of the Chinese Enlightenment'. In *idem, High Culture Fever: Politics, Aesthetics, and Ideology in Deng's China*. Berkeley: University of California Press, 118–36.

KEVIN LATHAM

rock music, rock bands

The history of Chinese rock music (*yaogun yinyue*) began in the early 1980s. Since then, the number of bands and musicians has increased as much as the variety of music styles performed. The centre of Chinese rock is Beijing and today, due to the reform policy and market economy, the genre is supported by several music publishing companies (*yinxiang gongsi*), whose number climbed from one in 1978 to 300 in the mid 1990s. By 1993, rock music had lost its former underground status and transformed into a still subversive but tolerated genre within the PRC's mainstream popular culture. The following overview will provide an outline of its four major periods.

The first Chinese rock band was founded at Beijing's Foreign Language School No. 2 in 1980. Its name, Wan-Li-Ma-Wang, derived from the family names of the four band members, who played songs by the Beatles, Rolling Stones and the like. Three years later a band called Dalu (Mainland) appeared, made up of Chinese and foreign musicians that also played Western titles. The first important Chinese rock bands were founded in 1983–4, including Tumbler (Budaoweng), that mainly performed popular Japanese songs and is said to have been the first band to use electronic instruments. Musicians like **Zang Tianshuo**, **Wang Yong**, Sun Guoqing, Li Li and Ding Wu started here. A second band, Seven-Ply Board (Qiheban), was organized by professional musicians from the Beijing Philharmonic Orchestra, such as **Cui Jian**, and a group of folk musicians, among them Liu Yuan. Its repertoire consisted of popular Western songs. Within the following four years and amid the political **Campaign against Bourgeois Liberalization**, other musicians enlarged the scene and, together with those already mentioned, organized new bands, e.g. White Angel (Bai Tianshi, 1987), Mayday (Wuyuetian, 1987), Black Panther (Heibao, 1987), Tang Dynasty (Tang Chao, 1988) and Cui Jian and ADO (1987). Apart from organizing 'parties' and performing in small bars and foreign hotels, it was only Cui Jian who was known to a larger audience. In 1988 he released the PRC's first rock album.

In terms of creativity and authenticity, Chinese critics often regard the second period (1989–93) as the heyday of Chinese rock music, before the genre became commercialized. It began with Cui's nationwide beneficial concert tour for the Asian Olympics (cancelled after the fourth concert, 12 May 1990) and Beijing's 'Concert of Modern Music' (*Xiandai yinyue yanchanghui*), featuring six bands on 17 February 1990: ADO, Tang Dynasty, Breathing (Huxi), Brothers (Baobei xiongdi), '1989' and the first women's rock band, **Cobra** (Yanjingshe). The concert is remembered as a milestone in the PRC's rock history which made Beijing's new rock culture publicly known. Meanwhile, a set of new bands emerged: while such groups as Red Army (Hongse budui), Self-Education (Ziwo jiaoyu), Acupuncture Point (Xuewei) and Wa-Minority (Wazu) recorded only a few songs, others were more successful, e.g. Face (Miankong), Again (Lunhui), Compass (Zhinanzhen), Overload (Chaodai) and Cobra.

At this point the Taiwanese record company Rock Records & Tapes (Gunshi changpian) recognized the market potential of Chinese rock and signed contracts with some of the bands. In 1992 it released a compilation under the name *China Fire* (*Zhongguo huo*) and one successful album by the heavy-metal band Tang Dynasty, featuring a distorted version of the 'Internationale'. One particular feature of this period was the musicians' aim to create rock with 'Chinese characteristics'. Some incorporated traditional instruments and/or ancient lyrics or, in case of folk rock singer Zheng Jun, features of national minorities. Another example is Hou Muren, who arranged the album *Red Rock* (*Hongse yaogun*, 1992), which includes revolutionary classics such as 'Socialism is Good' (*Shehui zhuyi hao*). By 1993, many of the bands had their songs released in compilations or on solo CDs.

The third period (1994–7) saw a new professionalism, both in creativity and in marketing. It began with three outstanding albums, released by Rock Records & Tapes in June 1994: the spherical rock sounds of Dou Wei (ex-member of Black Panther), the folk rock of Zhang Chu, and He Yong's (ex-member of Mayday) *Garbage Dump* (*Laji chang*), which was also the title of the PRC's first punk song. Their stylistic innovation was denoted as 'New Music' (*Xin yinyue*) and underscored the diversity of Beijing's rock circle in the mid 1990s. At this point the community split into different scenes and styles. Bands like Thin Man (Shouren) continued to play heavy rock, while others such as Black Panther turned to pop rock, a genre that is also popular with Zang Tianshuo, Point Zero (Lingdian), Baojia Rd. No. 43 (Baojiajie 43 hao) and the female vocalist Tian Zhen.

A stylistic fragmentation became visible in 1997, when the fourth period started with the emergence of the New Sound Movement (see **New Sound Movement, Modern Sky Records**). Newly founded independent record companies began promoting young pop-rock and pop-punk bands such as Catcher in the Rye (Maitian shouwangzhe), The Flowers (Hua'er), New Pants (Xin kuzi) and the experimental underground music of 'NO', The Fly (Cangying), Wooden Horse (Mum), **Tongue** (Shetou), Confucius Says (Zi Yue) (see **Yaoshi-Ziyue**) and the electronic individualist Chen Dili. This spectrum of sounds was enlarged by the female folkstyle singer Ai Jing and the singer **Hu Mage**, who accompanies himself on acoustic guitar, by the rap music of Li Xiaolong, and by fashionable bands such as Sober (Qingxing), Supermarket (Chaoji shichang) and The Dada (Dada). Hardcore punk is played by Bored Contingent (Wuliao yuedui) as well as by the bands Anarchy Jerks, Brain Failure, Reflector, 69 and the all-female band Hang on the Box.

Today, Beijing's rock community consists of three generations who perform everything from heavy metal to pop rock, folksong to digital hardcore, grunge and blues rock to punk (for punk, see http://www.studio-ito.net/scream/twisted.html). While the genres are promoted by both national and international record companies and via the Internet, the musicians engage themselves in ideological debates over the meaning and authenticity of Chinese rock. Topics such as social responsibility, Chinese characteristics and/or internationalization are frequently discussed in the media. Bands are formed and split apart; some are more successful than others and manage to participate in big concerts inside and outside the capital. Considering the rock scenes that have already emerged in cities like Shanghai, Chengdu and Canton, one cannot speak of Chinese rock as such, but rather of a heterogeneous field.

See also: Beyond; Jin Zhaojun; Tat Ming Pair; Wang Lei

Further reading

Baranovitch, Nimrod (2003). *China's New Voices: Popular Music, Ethnicity, Gender, and Politics, 1978–1997.* Berkeley: University of California Press.

de Kloet, Jeroen (2001). *Red Sonic Trajectories. Popular Music and Youth in Urban China.* Enschede: Ipskamp.

—— (2003). 'Marx or Market: Chinese Rock and the Sound of Fury'. In Jenny Lau (ed.), *Multiple Modernities: Cinemas and Popular Media in Transcultural East Asia.* Philadelphia: Temple University Press, 28–52.

Efird, Robert (2001). 'Rock in a Hard Place: Music and the Market in Nineties Beijing'. In Nancy Chen, Constance Clark, Suzanne Gottschang and Lyn Jeffery (eds), *China Urban: Ethnographies of Contemporary Culture.* Durham: Duke University Press.

Huang, Liaoyuan (ed.) (1997). *Shinian Zhongguo liuxing yinyue jishi* [Ten Years: A Chronic of Chinese Popular Music, 1986–1996]. Beijing: Zhongguo dianying chubanshe.

Jones, Andrew (1992). *Like a Knife. Ideology and Genre in Contemporary Chinese Popular Music.* Ithaca: Cornell University.

Steen, Andreas (1996). *Der Lang Marsch des Rock 'n' Roll. Pop- und Rockmusik in der Volksrepublik China.* Hamburg: Lit-Verlag.

http://www.yaogun.com/

ANDREAS STEEN

Root-seeking school

(Xungen pai)

Literary movement

The 'Root-seeking school' denotes a group of fiction writers who explored native cultural traits to come to a new understanding of present culture during the 1980s. Instrumental in the development of the 'Root-seeking school' were **Gao Xingjian**'s pamphlet, 'A Preliminary Inquiry into the Techniques of Modern Fiction' (*Xiandai xiaoshuo jiqiao chutan*), and **Han Shaogong**'s seminal article, 'The Roots of Literature' (*Wenxue de gen*), which gave the school its name. The former included a first introduction to the magical realism of Borges and Marquez; the latter called for a redefinition of self-consciousness rooted in traditional but non-standard culture.

Most *xungen* authors investigate local cultures to gain insights into the vices and virtues of their present culture. This writing makes a symbolic connection between individual life, race and humanity and between man and culture. Some use ancient Chu culture (Han Shaogong) or Shandong (**Mo Yan**) to depict instinct and degeneration. Others extract the virtues of Daoism (**Ah Cheng**) or Confucianism (Shandong group) or depict the life of the northern plains and Muslim culture (Zhang Chengzhi), Wu culture (Li Kangyu), and ancient Tibetan culture (**Tashi Dawa**).

The use of magical realism and the affirmation of literary subjectivity is a serious departure from the previous realistic mode of writing and it gave direction to the Chinese modernist impetus in the years to follow. Many of the works produced by these authors have allowed Chinese literature a re-entry into world literature and cinema, notably Mo Yan's famous novel (and movie) *Red Sorghum* (*Honggaoliang jiazu*).

See also: Chen Kaige; Wang Anyi; Zhang Yimou

Further reading

Feuerwerker, Y. (1998). 'The Post-Modern "Search for Roots" in Han Shaogong, Mo Yan, and Wang Anyi'. In *idem* (ed.), *Ideology, Power,*

Text: *Self-Representation and the Peasant 'Other' in Modern Chinese Literature*. Stanford: Stanford University Press.

Huot, C. (2000). 'Colorful Folk of the Landscape: Fifth Generation Filmmakers and Roots Searchers'. In *idem, China's New Cultural Scene: A Handbook of Changes*. Durham: Duke University Press.

Kong, H. (1997). 'The Spirit of "Native-Soil" in the Fictional World of Duanmu Hongliang and Mo Yan'. *China Information* 11.4 (Spring): 58–67.

Li, Q. (2000). 'Searching for Roots: Anticultural Return in Mainland Chinese Literature of the 1980s'. In P. Chi and D. Wang (eds), *Chinese Literature in the Second Half of the Twentieth Century: A Critical Survey*. Bloomington: Indiana University Press.

BIRGIT LINDER

Rupture writers

(Duanlie, 1998–2000)

The Rupture movement was a controversial cultural and artistic declaration representing the iconoclastic literary views of a new generation of Chinese writers in the late 1990s. The principal participants and organizers were the Nanjing-based writers Zhu Wen and Han Dong. Zhu Wen (b. 1967), a 1989 graduate of Southeast University, quit his job in the sciences in 1994 to pursue a fulltime career in literature. He has published several volumes of poetry, stories and novels, including *I Love US Dollars* (*Wo ai meiyuan*), *Because of Loneliness* (*Yinwei gudu*) and *What is Garbage, What is Love?* (*Shenme shi laji, shenme shi ai*). He has also served as screenwriter for several 'Sixth Generation' films (see **Sixth Generation (film directors)**) and made his own directorial debut in 2001 with the powerful film **Seafood** (*Haoxian*). Han Dong (b. 1961) is a 1982 graduate of the Philosophy Department of Shandong University. After graduation he taught Marxism at several universities before resigning in 1992. Highly regarded as a poet and

novelist, Han Dong's body of works includes *Our Bodies* (*Women de shenti*) and *Lucky Tiger* (*Jixiang de laohu*).

In May 1998 Zhu Wen and Han Dong sent out a questionnaire to several dozen contemporary Chinese writers which marked the origin of the Rupture movement. Fifty-five writers responded to Zhu Wen's carefully posed questions about such issues as the legitimacy of state-sponsored cultural entities, like the Chinese Writers' Association system and major national **literary awards**, as well as questions about the influence of academics, literary critics, foreign sinologists and iconic modern Chinese writers on their work. The startling results included such figures as: 69 per cent who felt that there are no contemporary Chinese writers who have had a profound influence on their work (avant-garde writer **Ma Yuan** was one of the few Chinese they acknowledged); 98.2 per cent who felt that contemporary Chinese literary criticism has not had any major impact on their work; 81 per cent who felt that the opinions of sinologists were not important or to be valued; 91 per cent who felt that Lu Xun has not served as a guide for contemporary Chinese literature; and 94.6 per cent who do not acknowledge the authority of the Mao Dun and Lu Xun Literary Awards.

The questionnaire and a complete list of the answers given by the fifty-five participating writers were printed in several literary magazines. The outcome represented nothing short of a collective proclamation of a cultural break with tradition – a 'rupture' wherein young writers articulated their dissatisfaction with the existing literary structure, which they felt no longer relevant to their life and work. The radical views of the group caused an academic and media controversy, with some critics even labelling the entire movement as nothing but a savvy literary marketing ploy. In March of 1999, Haitian Publishing House published a six-volume *Rupture Series* edited by Han Dong, whose purpose was to introduce unpublished, fresh literary voices. The series included authors Chu Chen, Wu Chenjun, Gu Qian, He Yi, Jin Haishu and Hai Lihong, all of whom were among the initial participants in the 'rupture' questionnaire.

Further reading

Wang, Jifang (2000). *Duanlie: Shijimo de wenxue gushi – ziyou zuojia fangtanlu* [Rupture: A Literary Tale from the Fin-de-siècle – Interviews with Independent Writers]. Nanjing: Jiangsu wenyi chubanshe.

MICHAEL BERRY

S

sacred mountains

Though it is often said that all mountains in China are sacred, certain mountains have taken on a particularly sacred significance if numbers of pilgrims and temples are considered. The latter include the sets of mountains known as the 'Five Marchmounts' (*Wuyue*) and the 'Four Great [Buddhist] Mountains' (*Sida mingshan*). Though some are exclusively Buddhist or Daoist, most have an eclectic occupancy – Buddhist, Daoist and local cult. Mountains are considered 'sacred' through association with gods, ghosts, ancestors, immortals, buddhas or sages. Throughout much of Chinese history, mountains have been regarded as assembly points of the dead: ghosts or demons if fearful, gods if powerful, though not necessarily beneficent. It was such understandings that are responsible for most mountains being characterized as sacred. They were the physical refuges, places of judgment or residences of these post-mortem beings. With some exceptions, one need not go to the high point on the mountain to address a transcendent deity, as is common in many other cultures. The gods, ghosts and their demon attendants could be encountered throughout the mountain domains, and this was cause for either great caution or eager anticipation when entering mountains. The Chinese term most commonly characterizing mountains as sacred is 'numinous power' (*ling*). According to a popular expression, a mountain is not sacred or powerful because of its height, but because of the god (*shen*) or gods dwelling on it. Indeed, the central peak on Mt Putuo, one of the 'Four Great [Buddhist] Mountains', is only

300 metres above sea level. The presence of the bodhisattva, **Guanyin**, presumably accounts for its sacredness. Mountainous *ling* is seen as marked by the presence of springs and caves, as well as of unusually shaped rocks, trees, waterfalls and distinctive landforms and orientations considered significant according to Chinese geomancy (**fengshui**). Medicinal herbs, roots and minerals gain much of their efficacy through 'growing' in and on such mountains (see **herbal medicine**). The sale of these drugs to visitors is a lucrative enterprise on sacred mountains.

In the pre-modern and contemporary periods, most of the gods regarded as inhabiting such mountains in earlier periods are understood as having been subdued by bodhisattvas or perfected Daoist masters and transformed into devotees and protectors. Accounts of mythic battles between these Buddhist and Daoist agents of order and the untamed denizens of mountains are a common feature of traditional and contemporary guidebooks. These civilizing heroes and their human agents further transfigured *ling*-filled mountains by projecting onto them images drawn from Buddhist and Daoist sacred texts, pacifying them and making their power more accessible to the devout. These spatial projections of text can be seen in the arrangement and location of temples, the identification and naming of numinous objects and shapes, and the location of ritual or austerity sites. Monks and recluses take up residence on a mountain to access its power for their own transformations, and pilgrims, also hoping to benefit from that power, visit these mountains as acts of piety, which is called, 'paying respects to the mountain and presenting incense' (*jinshan qiaoxiang*) (see **pilgrimage**). Many seek visions of the resident deity. Gentry scholars have built retreats and academies on many of the sacred mountains and composed or edited mountain gazetteers (*shanzhi*), gathering together maps, literary compositions and information on history, flora, fauna and religious structures associated with a particular mountain. These gazetteers, which add one more layer of lustre to the mountain, continue to be reproduced today.

Further reading

Einarsen, John (ed.) (1995). *The Sacred Mountains of Asia*. Berkeley: Shambhala Publications.

Naquin, Susan and Yu, Chun-fang (eds) (1992). *Pilgrims and Sacred Sites in China*. Berkeley: University of California Press.

Yinguang, Fashi (ed.) (1979). *Sida mingshan zhi* [Gazetteer of the Four Sacred Mountains of Buddhism], 4 vols. Taipei: Fojiao chubanshe.

WILLIAM POWELL

Sacrificed Youth

[Qingchunji, 1985]

Film

Sacrificed Youth is a feature film by director **Zhang Nuanxin**, based on a novella by Zhang Manling. During the **Cultural Revolution**, seventeen-year-old Li Chun, daughter of urban intellectuals, is sent to a mountainous village in a Tai (Dai) minority region in Yunnan. Assigned to a family that includes 'Dadie' (Father), 'Yiya' (Grandmother) and 'Dage' (Elder Brother), Li joins a brigade of women who chop bamboo. Envious of the Tai uninhibitedness and sensuality, Li eventually discards her **Han** clothing and demeanour to 'go native'. Trouble arises when she befriends a male Chinese intellectual, named Ren Jia, and rejects the love of her 'Dage'. To avoid the ensuing hostilities, Li leaves the village. Eventually permitted to return to the city, she comes back to the village upon learning of floods that have killed both her Tai family and her Chinese friend.

Sacrificed Youth is filmed in an intimate documentary style, using non-professional actors and a first-person voice-over narrative. It recounts Li's thoughts on two planes. The first contrasts her Han 'civilized' but repressed self with the idealized primal and unfettered Tai 'other'. Although charmed by the youthful sensuality of Dai culture, Li is also aware of its shortcomings – poverty, ignorance, seasons passed in back-breaking labour, in contrast to Han culture that privileges age and wisdom.

The second relates Li's past self – bonded with a nurturing environment – to a self-reliant but alienated present/future self. It is a tribute to a lost state of grace, a condition once known but no longer attainable, in which the pre-sexual individual was content within the warm maternal embrace.

See also: representations of minorities

CYNTHIA Y. NING

Saifu (Sai Fu) and Mailisi (Mai Lisi)

Mongolian film directors

Saifu and Mailisi are two film directors, a husband and wife of Mongolian origin, famous for their films on Mongolian life and history, some of which have won numerous domestic and international prizes. Their most celebrated film is *The Proud Son of Heaven: Genghis Khan* (*Yidaitianjiao Chengjisihan*), a film depicting the life of the founder of the Mongolian empire with a special emphasis on his childhood and his relationship with his mother. This film earned Saifu and Mailisi the Golden Rooster Award for best directors in 1997. Their most recent film is *Heavenly Grassland* (*Tianshang caoyu*, 2002).

Saifu and Mailisi were born in Inner Mongolia in 1954 and 1956 and graduated from Jilin University and Inner Mongolia Normal University, respectively. Both also studied at the prestigious **Beijing Film Academy** and are currently affiliated with the Inner Mongolia Film Studio, of which Saifu is the president. Saifu and Mailisi's films highlight Mongolian identity and therefore represent a general trend that began in China in the early to mid 1990s, in which minority artists have started to play a greater and more independent role in the construction and representation of their ethnicity in the national cultural sphere. Nevertheless, their work reflects at one and the same time the influence of Chinese cinema and the control that the state exerts on film production. The former is evident in many Chinese-style martial arts scenes which pervade their films, while the latter manifests itself in the financial aid and prizes which they have been awarded by the government, as well as in the fact that their films studiously avoid sensitive issues, such as the conflicts and wars between the Mongols and Han Chinese.

See also: Mongols, culture of; minority pop musicians: the new generation

NIMROD BARANOVITCH

salon culture

The 'foreign salon' (*yang shalong*) – a Chinese term I coined in 1987 – has played an estimable role in the cultural life of Beijing (and later other cities) from the late 1970s. Salons of various descriptions held in the apartments of journalists, 'foreign experts', diplomats and business people (and latterly in the homes of ex-pat Chinese and mainland returnees, including in particular US-based academics) were also crucial in helping non-official culture go international from the 1980s onwards. Film festival organizers and overseas critics (those in Hong Kong, Taiwan and Japan played a key initial role, as did individuals and organizations in a range of Western countries) often felt themselves not only to be expressing artistic discrimination by their support for the fringe-dwellers of the Chinese arts scene, but also felt that they were exercising a morally worthy function by promoting nascent artists.

There are those who celebrated this internationalization of Chinese avant-garde art in the 1990s, the collapse of boundaries and the cross-cultural movement of bodies. However, perhaps amidst the laudable moves towards an artistic global dialogue in the late twentieth and early twenty-first centuries, we can also detect a reconfiguration of the presumed bourgeois civilizing mission of an earlier age. A century after the zenith of Western empires, some international cultural brokers appear to have the 'courage' to shoulder once more the 'White Man's Burden'.

The line of reasoning pursued by both indigenous cultural figures and their supporters was that international recognition would force the authorities to tolerate innovative cultural figures, and thereby contribute to a liberalization of cultural production in general. Trading on their international success, many of the independents play their Western supporters and mainland opponents against each other to create an alternative system of counter-cultural hierarchy that, although less restricted and paternalistic than official culture, represents a new kind of orthodoxy, one that fits neatly into the chain of production and consumption for global festival culture. Among writers, artists and film-makers who have 'made it' internationally, one can often detect a strain of resentment and neo-patriotic ire directed at their patrons. This sentiment is often only vocalized in the Chinese media, or privately among their fellow cultural practitioners.

For the avant-garde scout who is active in the 'salon' (salons can be manifest in dinner parties, dances, private exhibitions, as well as binges of all descriptions), the collector of radical chic who is in search of the authentic dissenting. Other, there is something enticingly self-reaffirming in the embrace of the non-official artist. In the alignment of the cultural adventurer/investor with the progressive Chinese artist there is, to quote Tom Wolfe, a 'feeling that he is a fellow soldier, or at least an aide-de-camp or an honorary cong guerrilla in the vanguard march through the land of the philistines' ('The Apache Dance', in *idem*, *The Purple Decades*. Harmondsworth, Middlesex: Penguin Books, 1984, 345). This process of identification and validation through discovery is part of a 'particularly modern need and a peculiarly modern kind of salvation'. One can assuage a guilt about one's wealth, for 'avant-garde art . . . takes the Mammon and the Moloch out of money', while also allowing the individual to engage in a fight against a repressive socialist state that fails to recognize the artist's worth, and the tussle with the bourgeois West in tempting it to embrace the talents of an Eastern *terra incognita*.

The academic salons of the new century feature mavens of Cultural Studies and neo-Marxist connoisseurs in Euramerica (be they ethnically Chinese or not) who make a claim for an intellectual-moral high ground from which they presume to judge and police cultural exchanges.

GEREMIE R. BARMÉ

Sang Ye

b. 1954, Beijing

Journalist

Sang Ye, along with the novelist and later TV personality **Zhang Xinxin**, became famous for their oral history interviews with 'the cadre in the street' in the mid 1980s. Their interviews, like **Dai Qing**'s, were in part inspired by the work of US oral historian Studs Terkel, and were edited into publishable form according to the censorship guidelines of the day. The interviews first appeared in literary journals throughout the country, creating a 'buzz' that fired the book sales for *Beijing Man* (*Beijingren*, also known as *Chinese Profiles or Chinese Lives*) in 1985. The profiles were the first relatively candid interviews with everyday people ever published in the People's Republic, and they sparked a wave of similar volumes, as well as a literature of 'true confessions' that has seen many bestselling books since. Sang Ye produced a number of other oral histories, the most important of which only appeared in Hong Kong (1949, 1989, 1999) due to mainland censorship. A resident of Australia since 1989, he is also known as an essayist, freelance curator and an expert on the **Cultural Revolution** era.

Further reading

Barmé, Geremie and Sang, Ye (1997). 'The Great Firewall of China', *Wired* 5.6 (June): 138–51, 182 [about the Internet].

Sang, Ye (1999). 'Beam Me Up'. Trans. Geremie Barmé. *Humanities Research* 2: 71–8.

—— (2001). 'Rising High: A Beijing Builder Tells Her Story'. Trans. Jonathan Hutt with Geremie Barmé. *Persimmon* 1.3 (Winter): 30–6. [interview].

Zhang, Xinxin and Sang, Ye (1987). *Chinese Lives*. Trans. W. J. F. Jenner and Delia David. London: Macmillan.

GEREMIE R. BARMÉ

Sange daibiao

(Three Represents)

Political slogan

Jiang Zemin's 'Three Represents' (*sange daibiao*) was first put forward in a speech in early 2000:

> As long as our Party unswervingly *represents* the development trend of advanced productive forces, the orientation of advanced culture, and the fundamental interests of the overwhelming majority of the people in China, it can remain invincible, win wholehearted support of the people of all ethnic groups, and lead the people to make steady progress.

The 'Three Represents' was further elaborated at the Party's eightieth anniversary in July 2001 and adopted as an Amendment to the Constitution of the Party at the end of the 16th National Party Conference in November 2002. While insisting that workers, farmers, intellectuals and cadres are the backbone of the Party, Jiang said that it is also necessary to accept other outstanding people into the Party, including entrepreneurs from the private sector and personnel employed by foreign-funded enterprises. This new idea, which moves away from the former Constitution that the Party is the 'vanguard of the working class', is not without dissent from hard-line veteran revolutionaries (see **Party-building**). Organized conferences and workshops from the highest-level Party School to the grassroots have been held and all sorts of speeches have been given in support of Jiang's 'important thought'. It sounds a theoretical legacy, and the new leadership of Hu Jintao (b. 1942) must pursue China's modernization programme guided by the 'Three Represents'.

Further reading

Jiang, Zemin (1 July 2001). *Speech at the Rally in Celebration of the 80th Anniversary of the Founding of the Communist Party of China*. Beijing: New Star Publishers, 26–42.

HELEN XIAOYAN WU

Sanyi jiao

(The teaching of the Three-in-One)

Sectarian religion

The syncretic sectarian religious movement known as the Three-in-One (Confucianism, Daoism and Buddhism) was founded by Lin Zhao'en (1517–98) in Putian, Fujian. After his death, Lin was apotheosized as the 'Lord of the Three-in-One'. His disciples developed his cult and his religious movement in a series of splinter groups. His image is worshipped in over a thousand temples in the Xinghua region (Putian and Xianyou counties) of coastal Fujian, and in temples in Taiwan and Southeast Asia as well. The Three-in-One requires initiation into the 'Heart Method' of personal spiritual self-cultivation, which is still widely practised in Xinghua today. This religious movement has also developed a parallel rival ritual tradition to that of local Daoist and Buddhist traditions, and troupes of Scripture Master ritualists often perform communal offerings (**Jiao**) and requiem services (**Gongde**), along with individual rites. The movement has popularized a mix of Confucian self-cultivation, Daoist inner alchemy and Buddhist illumination. The primary emphasis is still on Confucian morality, but inner cultivation and ritual practice now also play a major role in Three-in-One activities. In some communities in the Xinghua region, the Three-in-One temple has become the primary village temple, and thus the centre of collective life. Annual **pilgrimage**s are made to the cult centre, the Zongkongtang, in Putian, Fujian.

See also: Lüshan jiao (Sannai jiao); sectarian religion; Yiguan Dao

Further reading

Dean, Kenneth (1998). *Lord of the Three in One: The Spread of a Cult in Southeast China*. Princeton: Princeton University Press.

KENNETH DEAN

satellite dishes

Satellite dishes have become a commonplace feature of China's urban landscapes. Dishes, often 2–3 metres in diameter, are scattered over the roofs of China's large buildings serving variously telecommunications and television reception purposes. Direct-to-home **satellite television** reception is not allowed in China, and satellite television dishes can only be installed with special permits. Nonetheless, legal loopholes and difficulties over control and implementation of regulations saw millions of illegal devices erected in the early 1990s.

In 1990 a government regulation permitted educational, scientific, financial and media organizations, as well as hotels for foreign guests, to install satellite dishes under licence for business purposes. Importantly, individual households were not specifically excluded in the regulations, and the lure of quick, easy profits saw many businesses exploit the loophole and offer satellite dish installation services. The number of illegal satellite dishes is inevitably hard to measure with accuracy, but estimates in the mid 1990s put their number at around 30 million. In the late 1990s, regulations have specifically banned individual dishes, but the difficulties of implementation remain.

See also: cable television

Further reading

Chan, J. M. (1994). 'Media Internationalization in China: Processes and Tensions'. *Journal of Communication* 44.3: 70–88.

Zhao, Y. (1998). *Media, Market, and Democracy in China: Between the Party Line and the Bottom Line*. Chicago: University of Illinois.

KEVIN LATHAM

satellite television

Satellite television has played a crucial role in the development of Chinese television since the mid 1990s. The significance of satellite television has to be seen against the backdrop of a commercializing television industry and a fragmenting audience. Even though direct-to-home reception is still banned and satellite channels are only legally received through cable television relays, they are watched daily by hundreds of millions of viewers throughout the country. The development of satellite television has therefore been closely linked to the development of **cable television**. In 2001 there were thirty-one provincial satellite television stations and twenty-seven of these were set up after 1995.

Through setting up satellite television stations, local or regional level television operators have been able to compete at a national level in a way that, prior to cable television, they could never have done. Before the multiple channels that came with cable provision, the only nationally received television station was **CCTV (Chinese Central Television)**, which competed locally with county-, city- or provincial-level stations. Satellite television, in conjunction with cable networks, changed this as local television channels from other regions suddenly became available to viewers for the first time. China's television market was truly opened up to nationwide competition. The arrival of new channels from other parts of China also served to highlight regional differences and identities to increasingly fragmented television audiences while also deflecting their attention away from the national broadcaster. Although CCTV generally remains the dominant television station, its audience share has been markedly reduced with the proliferation of satellite channels.

Satellite television therefore played a crucial role in the development of the television industry by enhancing competition at all levels and opening up new sources of funding. The expansion of the real and potential audience (which in some cases is more than 90 per cent of the population) has enabled stations to raise their advertising revenues and increase investment in both infrastructure and programme production. In the case of Hunan's provincial television station, one of the best-known satellite television stations in China, it also made possible a lucrative initial public offering on the Shanghai stock exchange, as Hunan Broadcast and Television Media Group, at the end of 1998.

Foreign satellite channels remain heavily restricted in China. In early 2002, there were twenty-one approved channels including many recognized names such as CNN, HBO, CNBC, BBC World, MTV, National Geographic, Star Movies and the Discovery Channel. However, the channels were legally received only in three-star hotels. The exception has been Phoenix Satellite Television, the Mandarin-language entertainment channel partly owned by Rupert Murdoch's Hong Kong-based Star TV, which has been transmitted through various cable networks, to varying degrees, since the mid 1990s. Offering a light entertainment diet centred around drama series, the channel has achieved great popularity in many areas where it is available. In late 2001, the Chinese authorities approved two foreign satellite channels for direct transmission into Chinese homes in Guangdong. These were AOL Time Warner's China Entertainment Television (CETV), a repackaged version of an old unsuccessful Hong Kong-based no-news Mandarin satellite channel, and News Corporation's Xingkong [Star Sky] Satellite, a newly launched Mandarin entertainment channel from the Star TV Group.

KEVIN LATHAM

Scar art

A current of the late 1970s, Scar art represented a coming to terms with the calamitous consequences of **Cultural Revolution** fanaticism. Named after the short story 'Scar' (*Shanghen*, 1978) by Lu Xinhua, it shared many affinities with its literary namesake. One of the most outstanding works in the genre, the cartoon strip *Maple* (*Feng*, 1979) by Chen Yiming, Liu Yulian and Li Bin, was based on a short story – a tale of two young lovers whose lives are destroyed through supporting opposing Red Guard factions. Focusing on sentimentality and tragedy, such works avoided the accusations and vilification of Cultural Revolution art. They interpreted historical events through a humanist, emotional viewpoint, and were said to portray 'emotional reality' (*qinggan xianshi*). Some of the ambivalence of Scar art derived from artists' own involvement in the Cultural Revolution. A work such as *Why?* (*Weishenmo*, 1979) by Gao Xiaohua is full of self-reflection and mixed sentiments: pain and anguish over the past, confusion over the present, nostalgia for past certainties. A sub-genre, exemplified by Wang Hai's *Spring* (*Chun*, 1979) and Wang Chuan's *Good Bye Little Road* (*Zaijianba, xiaolu,* 1980), developed around the experience of urban youths 'sent-down' to the countryside (see **xiafang, xiaxiang**). He Duoling's *Awakened Spring* (*Chunfeng yijing suxing*, 1982), influenced by the sentimental realism of Andrew Wyeth, is notable as an image of hope renewed. His *Youth* (*Qingchun*, 1984) won a bronze award at the Sixth National Art Exhibition.

See also: Scar literature

Further reading

Galikowski, Maria (1998). *Art and Politics in China 1949–1984*. Hong Kong: Chinese University Press, 193–9.

Lü, Peng and Yi, Dan (1992). *Zhongguo xiandai yishushi* [A History of Modern Art in China], Changsha: Hunan meishu chubanshe, 22–9.

EDUARDO WELSH

Scar literature

The first new genre of fiction to emerge after the **Cultural Revolution**, 'Scar literature' or 'wound literature' (*shanghen wenxue*) lasted from the end of 1977 to 1979. It was new only in terms of its themes, and few of its writers or works survived the immediate need for fictional denunciations of the recent past. The keynote for the new literature was struck with the publication of 'Class Teacher' (*Ban zhuren*), a short story by Liu Xinwu, which appeared in *People's Literature* in November 1977. It condemned the educational and cultural policies of the previous decade. It was followed by Lu Xinhua's 'The Scar' (*Shanghen*, 1978), a short story about the personal tragedies caused by the excesses of the Cultural Revolution. These stories

dwell on the mental or physical scars left by the previous decade of radical politics. The analysis of the causes of the radicalism was superficial, and the stories generally lacked any depth, subtlety or artistic maturity. Nonetheless, Liu Xinwu and Lu Xinhua became overnight celebrities, and while many critics wrote in their defence, nothing critical was published. Within the next two years, hundreds of hastily written 'Scar' stories, poems and plays were published, 'exposing' the 'dark side' of socialist society. By the early 1980s, however, this highly emotional genre gave way to a more reflective, problem-oriented 'reform literature' (*gaige wenxue*).

Further reading

Braester, Yomi (2003). 'Disjointed Time, Split Voices: Retrieving Historical Experience in Scar Literature'. In *idem, Witness Against History: Literature, Film, and Public Discourse in Twentieth-Century China*. Stanford: Stanford University Press, 146–57.

Knight, Deirdre Sabina (2003). 'Scar Literature and the Memory of Trauma'. In Joshua Mostow (ed.) and Kirk A. Denton (ed. China section), *Columbia Companion to Modern East Asian Literatures*. New York: Columbia University Press, 527–32.

KAM LOUIE

Seafood

[Haixian, 2001]

Film

One of the first Chinese digital features, *Seafood* brilliantly recounts, with an arresting mixture of cynicism and humour, the shifting power relationships between a suicidal prostitute and a corrupt policeman. *Seafood* is the first film directed by Zhu Wen, one of the **Rupture writers** who became involved with the Sixth-Generation filmmakers (see **Sixth Generation (film directors)**) when he wrote Zhang Ming's *In Expectation* (*Wushan yunyu*, 1995; banned in China after receiving a prize at the Pusan Film Festival) and then collaborated on the screenplay for **Zhang Yuan**'s *Seventeen Years*

(*Guonian huijia*, 1999), the director's first 'legal' film, which was produced in collaboration with the studio system. The two executive producers of *Seafood* were Yu Lik-wai – a Hong Kong filmmaker who has collaborated with **Jia Zhangke** as his DP and producer since *Xiao Wu* (1998) – and the video documentary maker **Wu Wenguang**. Both men are enthusiastic advocates of the use of digital media in independent/underground productions (see **New Documentary Movement**).

In the resort town of Beidaihe, desolate in winter, Xiaomei, a beautiful prostitute contemplating suicide after a failed love affair, is physically and sexually abused by a policeman intent on 'saving' her. Zhu Wen inserts some unexpected twists in the plot, with a double ending – one in the snow fields surrounding Beidaihe, another in a seafood restaurant where Xiaomei and a hooker friend attempt to swap a fake bill obtained illicitly in the brothel, and so on. Zhu's masterful exploration of the *sexual impasse*, and his imaginative use of violence and vulgarity, turn *Seafood* into an idiosyncratic masterpiece.

BÉRÉNICE REYNAUD

sectarian religion

Sectarianism is the general name given to a broad tradition of lay religious teachings, also referred to as the 'White Lotus'. This tradition developed out of Buddhist devotional societies of the Song dynasty, and grew to encompass elements of Daoism and Confucianism, under the belief that these three teachings were each expressions of the same truth. The ultimate source of this truth is a deity called the Eternal Venerable Mother, who over the ages has sent a series of divine teachers to reveal specific elements of it to humankind. This process will culminate in a final apocalypse, after which the faithful will ascend to a millennial kingdom presided over by the Maitreya Buddha. Owing to this apocalyptic element, sectarian teachings have served as the inspiration for millenarian rebellion, and were strictly banned throughout most of the Ming and Qing dynasties. However, this policy proved difficult to enforce, especially in rural areas, not merely because

sectarian teachings satisfied popular longing for a future paradise, but also because these lay teachings were often stable centres of **local religion**, and performed important ceremonies such as healing, exorcism and funerals. During the early twentieth century, restrictions against sectarianism were relaxed, and many teachings began to take on new prominence. Some schools, such as the temperance-based Zaili jiao, formed national organizations in emulation of reformed Buddhism, while others, such as the **Yiguan Dao**, became active in Japanese occupation-era politics.

After 1949, the newly formed People's Republic again banned sectarian teachings, and used its unprecedented presence in rural society to enforce this policy locally. The first strike was a highly successful 1951 campaign against the Yiguan Dao, which was accused of having supported the Japanese occupation. Throughout the 1960s and 1970s, 'White Lotus sectarians' were touted in political campaigns as a universal villain, and accused of using 'superstition' to enslave the masses. Under this pressure, even apolitical sectarian groups such as the Zaili jiao disbanded, and local organizations disappeared from public life.

The loosening of religious policy in the late 1970s allowed a limited revival of sectarianism. Although lay religious organizations remain technically illegal, many local officials allow them to operate so long as these groups maintain a low profile and restrict their ritual activities to personal devotion. Sectarian groups in the cities participate in public religious life, such as temple festivals, under the acceptable guise of 'folk Buddhism'. The more significant revival has been in the rural areas, where the sectarian tradition is more deeply entrenched. As local religion revived during the early 1980s, village sectarian groups were faced with the challenge of retraining ritual specialists, and recovering a liturgical tradition that had been suppressed for decades. Those groups with strong local networks were able to pool resources and overcome these problems. However, even with the loosening of policy, certain teachings, such as the Yiguan Dao, remain strictly outlawed, and actions such as spiritualism, spirit writing or making apocalyptic predictions will bring swift attention from local officials. This vigilance increased with the 1999 movement against **Falun gong**, which was portrayed as a modern-day variation of sectarian heresy.

See also: religion, recent history of

THOMAS DUBOIS

Sensationalism, Shock Art

Artistic trend

Sensationalism, or Shock Art, appeared in embryo form as an alienated mutation of body art, in the first performances by **Zhang Huan** held at the **Yuanming Yuan** artist community since 1993. Zhang used his own body to inflict and signify pain, as in *65 Kg* of June 1994. This kind of extreme art, which broke out in the second half of the 1990s, aimed at subverting the audience's notions of art and standards of morality by exploring the material borders of the horrific. Artists began to use the corpses of human adults and infants, specimens and dead animals as their main vehicle of expression, using pain and the viewing of disturbing body parts as a media with which to 'cause sensation by creating paralysis' (Berghius).

Shock Art reached something of a group-specific consensus with the underground show 'Post-Sense Sensibility: Alien Bodies and Delusion', organized by curator **Wu Meichun** and artist **Qiu Zhijie** in Beijing in 1999, and then with a fringe exhibition organized at the margins of the Shanghai Biennale entitled 'Fuck Off' in 2000. Works of Shock Art were later presented in a documentary for the 5th Lyon Biennale and broadcast on BBC 4 in a much-discussed report, entitled *Swinging Beijing*, on 29 December 2002. Among the most shocking works were those by artist-duo Sun Yuan and Peng Yu, often using foetuses, as in *Siamese Twins* (2000), in which they transfused their own blood into the fused corpses of two babies, or as in *Oil of the Human Being* (2000) in which Peng Yu incubated a deceased child's body with the same oil used to drain off the blood of corpses in a morgue. Zhu Yu's *Pocket Theology* (1999) showed a human arm, hung from a hook in the centre of the exhibition hall, holding a rope that ran down to cover

the entire floor. For *Skin Graft* (2000), Zhu sewed a piece of his own flesh onto the body of a dead pig. Xiao Yu used lab specimens of a premature baby, mice, ducks and rabbits to make up animal aberrations as in the three-piece series *Ruan* (1999), *Wu* (2000) and *Jiu* (2000), where he addresses the issues of contemporary clone-inflated environment and technological culture. Among other artists that adopt the same trend, albeit in a less provocative yet still disturbing fashion are: **Gu Dexin**, who used pigs' hearts and brains in his installations of 1996 and 1998, Zhang Hanzi, Qin Ga, Jin Feng ('Unusual & Usual', Yuangong Modern Art Museum, Shanghai, 2000) and Feng Weidong.

Further reading

(2001). *Bu hezuo fangshi* [Uncooperative Method] (exhibition catalogue). Shanghai: Eastlink Gallery.

Berghuis, J. Thomas (2001). 'Flesh Art: Performance and Body Art in Post-Mao China'. *Chinese-art.com Online Magazine* 4.5.

Dao, Zi (2001). 'The Confusion of the Body'. *Chinese-art.com Online Magazine* 4.5.

Erickson, Britta (2001). 'From the Edge of Beyond: Artists Probe the Mundane and the Horrific'. *Chinese-art.com Online Magazine* 4.3.

Liao, Wen (2001). 'Racing through Forbidden Territory: "Sex" in the Works of China's Female Artists'. *Chinese-art.com Online Magazine* 4.3.

Qiu, Zhijie and Wu, Meichun (1999). *Post-Sense Sensibility: Alien Bodies and Delusion* (exhibition catalogue). Beijing: Shaoyaoju.

Yi, Ying (2001). 'Mundane and Profound'. *Chinese-art.com Online Magazine* 4.3.

BEATRICE LEANZA

serial picture books

(lianhuanhua)

Commonly called comic books, *lianhuanhua* are more accurately translated as 'serial picture books' because they adapt stories from other genres. The form is to be distinguished from both *manhua* (cartoons) and *lianhuan manhua* (serial cartoons or comic books) that are original works and descend from the Japanese *manga* tradition. The form is also to be distinguished from *tuhuashu* (picture books) for very young children. *Lianhuanhua* popularize favourite stories as part of China's visual mass media.

Modern *lianhuanhua* have a dual audience. They originated as **children's literature** early in the twentieth century. They are still considered a commercial staple of this field across Chinese-speaking countries where they are colloquially known as *shaorenshu* (children's books). But they are also considered mass literature, especially in the PRC. The form is accessible (told through images), cheap (mass-produced in small booklets), and visual, critiqued as a revolutionary art form and the subject of national awards and regional exhibitions. The popularity of this form made *lianhuanhua* a perfect medium for political propaganda among China's masses. Banned in the Cultural Revolution, *lianhuanhua* made a comeback in the contemporary period where whole shops and stalls sell old and new favourites. In the contemporary period, however, *lianhuanhua* are being superseded by technological visual forms of mass communication such as television, film, the Internet and the VCD/DVD.

See also: animation

Further reading

Andrews, Julia F. (1997). 'Literature in Line: Picture Stories in the People's Republic of China'. *Inks: Cartoon and Comic Art Studies* 4.3 (November): 17–32.

Farquhar, Mary Ann (1999). 'Picture Books and Popularization'. In Mary Ann Farquhar (ed.), *Children's Literature in China*. New York: M. E. Sharpe.

Lent, John and Ying, Xu (2003). 'Chinese Women Cartoonists: Historical and Contemporary Perspectives'. *International Journal of Comic Art* 5.2: 351–366.

—— (2003). 'Timeless Humor: Liao Bingxiong and Fang Cheng, Masters of A Fading Chinese Cartoon Tradition'. *Persimmon* 3.3 (Winter).

Available at http://www.persimmon-mag.com/winter2003/feature0.htm

Shen, Kuiyi (1997). 'Comics, Picture Books, and Cartoonists in Republican China'. *Inks: Cartoon and Comic Art Studies* 4. 3 (November): 2–16.

http://www.cartoonwin.com [Katong zhi chuang, Shanghai]

MARY FARQUHAR

798

Artist community/district

One of several factories (including 706, 707, 761 and 797) that eventually split off from 718, 798 is a factory complex constructed in the 1950s in Dashanzi, Chaoyang district, in northeastern Beijing to produce military technology. By the 1990s, the shine on this former jewel of socialist high-tech had faded, and like so many State-Owned Enterprises, it had closed its doors and disbanded thousands of workers. This 'hollowing-out', however, was followed by an 'in-migration' of artists and other members of the 'creative class' seeking large spaces, cheap rents, relative privacy and/or the charm of the Bauhaus structures of 718's original East German architects. In 1995, the **Central Academy of Fine Arts** rented 706 to store its monumental sculpture, and the school's dean, **Sui Jianguo**, later moved his own sculpture and installation studio there. By the end of 2001, 798 and vicinity housed the offices of fashion magazine publisher Hong Huang; Robert Bernell's bookstore and publishing house Timezone 8 (see **chinese-art.com**); an elegant studio of writer/musician **Liu Suola**; the Beijing Tokyo Art Project (BTAP: Beijing Dongjing yishu gongcheng), a gallery directed by Tabata Yukihito of the Tokyo Art Gallery; and the working spaces of various artists including **Mao Lizi**, Cang Xin and performance artist Huang Rui. Over the next two years, 798 became home to the offices of graphic and interior designers, publicists and small ad agencies; to designer cafés, nightclubs, restaurants, boutiques and fashion-show venues; and to the studio/homes of dozens of artists, including **Zhao Bandi**. Numerous domestic and international art exhibitions have contributed to the success of 798, beginning with 'Beijing Afloat', curated by **Feng Boyi** at BTAP in October 2002. 'Reconstruction 798' and 'Operation Ink Freedom' inaugurated, respectively, the 798 Space Gallery and the 25,000 Li Cultural Transmission Centre in April 2003. Fourteen different exhibitions were presented under the guise of the Beijing Biennale in September 2003, including, most significantly, 'Tui-Transfiguration', an exhibition of the photographs of Rong Rong (see **Lu Zhirong**) and Inri curated by Wu Hong at Daoyaolu Workshop B, and 'Left Hand – Right Hand', an exhibition of Chinese and East German artists curated by Feng Boyi at the 798 Space Gallery and Daoyaolu Workshop A, reviving the collaboration that built the original 718 factory complex. Several exhibitions have also given space to emerging artists, and the entire district was showcased in the 'First Beijing Dashanzi Art Festival' in April and May 2004. Increasingly 798 has taken on the commercial profile of New York's SoHo, though a more germane comparison has been made with the warehouses along the Suzhou River or with the former textile mill at 50 Moganshan Road, both in Shanghai (see Carol Lu, 'From Underground to Public', in Huang Rui (2004), 84–7). In either case, 798 is a far cry from **Dongcun** (East Village) and other avant-garde artist communities of the late 1980s and early 1990s, and serves as a kind of palimpsest of China's economic reform; it will be interesting to watch as its new residents battle the plans of the government to turn Dashanzi into an electronics city.

Further reading

Huang, Rui (ed.) (2004). *Beijing 798: Reflections on Art, Architecture and Society in China.* Beijing: Timezone 8/Thinking Hands.

EDWARD L. DAVIS

sex shops and products

All sorts of sex products in the name of health care are for sale in shops and on the Internet. Gone are the days of puritanical socialism when people could not even find open display of bras in stores and had to present their identification indicating 'Married' for contraception. Now lovemaking devices are widely available in department stores, university campus shops, speciality boutiques, not to mention pharmacies and health-supply stores, as sex is considered a physiological phenomenon. Among them are the Adam and Eve Health Care Centre (Yadang xiawa baojian zhongxin) at 143 Zhaodengyu Road, Beijing, which is reportedly the first sex shop in China. Founded in 1993 as a state-owned enterprise, it has set up a branch at Beijing's Xinjiekou area and has over a hundred employees, including doctors, pharmacists and psychologists, and a production base. Following the name 'Adam and Eve', three brothers surnamed Wu in Wenzhou, Zhejiang province, established their own Adam and Eve Health Care Products Company Limited (Yadang Xiawa baojianpin youxian gongsi), the Adam and Eve Sex Health Care Store (Yadang Xiawa xing baojianpin shangdian) which has a branch and over ten chain stores in Shanghai. There are also other sex shops with similar names, like the Shanghai Adam and Eve Adult Toys Shop (Shanghai Yadang Xiawa chengnianren shangdian). Countless sex shops with other names have sprung up, too. Products such as prickly clitoral stimulators, garish plastic vaginas, physiotherapeutic rings, aphrodisiacs, vibrators, condoms and disinfectants are all for sale in shops, some of which have online businesses. Shop assistants, many in clinical white coats, are handy for help. All companies claim that they will not reveal anything sensitive on the mail order parcel out of respect for clients' privacy. Condom vending machines have been installed in urban areas. Condoms are even found on the bathroom counter in Shanghai's ordinary hotels for the Chinese. The measure seems more to prevent STIs (see **HIV/ AIDS and STIs**) than to implement the **one-child policy**, as seldom as would a company send a married couple on a business trip. Over 300 companies produced 2.4 billion condoms in 2001 of various brands, but only 50 per cent of the products were considered of good quality. As a prescription drug, Viagra is sold at hospitals and designated shops, but fake Viagra found in sex health shops may indicate that Western products are catching up with *zhuangyang* (invigorating the *yang* or male sexual potency) and *buyin* (nourishing the *yin* or female body) tonics sold at traditional Chinese medicine shops. The government has approved joint-venture sex product manufacturing. Locally made Durex, Jissbon and other foreign brand names have been brought to the Chinese and exported abroad. One of the Wu brothers has a joint-venture company with Japan called Ailü (Love Partner), where 90 per cent of the products are for international markets. Another Wenzhou company boasts its products on www.mmhy.net/english/aboutus.htm called 'China Loves Sex Toys Online', and the Chinese name 'Lameisi' literally means 'Spicy Girls Think [of Sex]'. All these toys demonstrate how far China has gone in its sexual behaviour (see **sexuality and behaviour**). In 2003, the authorities lifted the long outdated ban on condom advertisements amid concern at the HIV/AIDS situation.

Further reading

McMillan, M. (1999). 'China's Eden'. *China in Focus* 7: 8–10. [Note: the Chinese website provided at the end of this article has been changed to www.adam-eve.com.cn]

HELEN XIAOYAN WU

sexual attitudes

The erotic has always held much ambivalence for Chinese writers and commoners alike. Sexuality was regarded as a natural, pleasurable act, while also deemed a dangerous and potentially contaminating activity. From a naturalistic point of view, sex was conceptualized as an exchange of body fluids necessary to restore health as well as reproduce. For men, an orgasm was viewed as potentially harmful in that it resulted in the loss of bodily fluids and thus a depletion of their *yang* energy. However, if a man could prolong an orgasm or not have one at all he would obtain valuable female energy (*yin* essence), while not giving up much of his own. Sexual intercourse was deemed, therefore, hazardous as the loss of too much yang essence (or semen) could result in a weakened body vulnerable to illness.

It was during the Republican period that contemporary Chinese understanding of human sexuality shifted from a cosmology based in metaphysical images of competing essences (yin and yang) to one that was anchored in an emergent, albeit often erroneous, biological discourse. This transformation has its roots in Qing intellectual history and thus was already under way prior to Western contact. The shift in thinking about human sexuality found ready currency in the production of numerous 'how-to' books which had an audience wanting greater clarification and eager to adopt a modern, and thus cosmopolitan, outlook on the erotic and its place in daily life. One way this was accomplished was through reading 'childbirth manuals, gynaecological treaties, books of medical remedies, family handbooks, marriage guides, and primers on sexual hygiene' (Dikötter 1995: 14). These medical and popular texts helped shape the average urban (though not necessarily rural) Chinese understanding of male and female sexual behaviour.

Chinese intellectuals who were concerned with improving the overall quality of urban life started to map out new sexual itineraries which resulted in the orgasm becoming the symbol of marital intimacy and conjugal satisfaction. In this new urban milieu, the kiss, which was regarded in some quarters as a primary index of marital intimacy, became a lively and popular topic for debate 'in vernacular newspapers, with some hospitals warning patients who suffered from high blood pressure or weak constitution [to refrain] from kissing' (Dikötter 1995: 48). Masturbation was considered to be a bad habit acquired by a weak mind, like addiction to cigarettes and alcohol, and would erode the memory. After the 1920s, however, there were a few authors calling for a greater tolerance towards masturbation and the need for a hygienic sexual outlet (Dikötter 1995).

Chinese society, excluding the socialist era (1949–85), has historically been more tolerant of extramarital sex for men. However, until the late 1980s, Chinese culture did not sanction the pursuit of sexual variety. From the greater part of post 1949 history, male identity, unlike that found before, was not coterminous with sexual promiscuity. Although some Chinese men fantasized about having love affairs, and some kept an active correspondence with women living in different cities, and a few daring married men had a 'lover', these 'relationships' were conducted with the utmost discretion. The cultural mores, even in the early 1980s, simply did not sanction this kind of behaviour.

The strength of this attitude can be found, paradoxically, in the results from the 1987 nation-wide sex survey, which found that in 24 to 40 per cent of all Shanghai divorce cases women listed extramarital affairs as the primary reason for seeking a divorce (Liu *et al.* 1997: 359). The increase in extramarital sex also corresponds with increasing reports of sexual disharmony among married couples. This suggests that sexual pleasure is regarded as a fundamental aspect or right of married life (Liu *et al.* 1997: 35). It also suggests, however, that many Chinese men are less committed to sexual monogamy than they were in the previous decade.

During the post 1949 period and through the 1980s, the idea of chastity was an ideal state applied equally to females and males. Sexual intercourse took place usually after a couple had agreed to marry. For example, 62 per cent of all married couples in the 1987 survey had their first sexual intercourse on their wedding night (Liu *et al.* 1997: 243). Other sexual surveys also reported that male sexual satisfaction varied by social class (Liu *et al.* 1997). Zha Bo and Geng Wenxiu's sex survey found that 'most females did not experience an orgasm due primarily to the short duration [of foreplay]' (1992: 18). It is consistent with my own findings (Jankowiak 1993). It is also consistent with Kinsey's finding that people with higher education tended to change sexual positions more often. By the late 1990s, however, this percentage was significantly lower due to the increased tolerance of premarital sex. The singleton generation (born after 1979) has fundamentally altered China's moral code (see **little emperors**). Today, sexuality is no longer regarded as a tacit agreement to marry but instead is perceived to be simply a pleasurable experience that may or may not result in marriage. Sexual pleasure is regarded as a fundamental aspect of married life. It is also not unusual for men to have a mistress or a girlfriend (see **bao ernai**), or to visit prostitutes. And in

China's largest cities, it is easier for women to participate in extramarital affairs than at any time in its history.

A popular Chinese proverb from the Republican era asserted that women's sexual appetite increases with age: 'Women in their thirties are tigers and in their forties are wolves.' If this proverb was an accurate representation of behaviour, then one explanation for women's relative lack of interest in sexual intercourse in the socialist era may lie in the negative impact of Communist revolutionary ideology, which de-emphasized the body as a site of sensual enjoyment. As a consequence, many men as well as women were raised to regard sexual intercourse as a necessary, albeit perfunctory, activity. The return to a consumer economy appears to have stimulated a renewed appetite for physical pleasure and erotic experimentation. This is especially so among China's singleton population, whose sexual behaviour resembles that of their American counterpart. Contemporary researchers are finding that the pursuit of sexual adventure is now commonplace. This is fuelled in part by the increase in urban prostitution, mistresses and extramarital affairs (Farrer 2002). Today, the erotic is considered natural, healthy and vital to the enjoyment of life. For example, masturbation is no longer considered harmful; rather, like all things sexual, it is now deemed a healthy activity (see **sexuality and behaviour**).

There has been an enormous variation in China's attitudes towards homosexuality (see **homosexuality and tongzhi culture**). In Imperial China it was common for an emperor to have male and female concubines. During the Qing (1644–1911), however, this attitude was replaced with a more puritanical view that regarded extramarital sex – with women or men – as unacceptable. In this milieu, male (but not female) homosexuality was regarded as a threat to patriarchal authority (Wasserstrom and Brownell 2002). This mindset has continued throughout much of the twentieth century. By the 1990s, homosexuality was tacitly tolerated, albeit with misgivings. There are known homosexual (gay and lesbian) bars in China's largest cities. In this and in every other way, the Chinese attitude towards the erotic is strikingly similar to that found in Western European cultures.

Further reading

Dikötter, F. (1995). *Sex, Culture and Modernity in China*. London: Hurst.

Farrer, J. (2002). *Opening Up: Youth Sex Culture and Market Reform*. Chicago: University of Chicago Press.

Jankowiak, W. (1993). *Sex, Death and Hierarchy in a Chinese City*. New York: Columbia University Press.

Kinsey, A. C., Pomeroy, W. B. and Martin, C. E. (1953). *Sexual Behavior in the Human Female*. Philadelphia: W. B. Saunders.

Liu, Dalin, Ng, Man Lun, Zhou, Li Ping and Haeberle, Erwin (1997). *Sexual Behavior in Modern China*. New York: Continuum.

Parish, W. (2002). 'Open-Door Sexuality'. *The University of Chicago Magazine* 95: 1–4.

Wasserstrom, J. and Brownell, Susan (2002). *Masculinities and Femininities*. Berkeley: University of California Press.

Zha, Bo and Geng, Wenxiu (1992). 'Sexuality in Urban China'. *The Australian Journal of Chinese Affairs* 28 (July): 1–20.

WILLIAM JANKOWIAK

sexuality and behaviour

Chinese have long been perceived as prudish about sex, a judgment at odds with the culture's rich textual history of erotica and pornography, but very strictly in keeping with the administered sexual Puritanism of the Chinese Communist Party. Although the Chinese revolution was led by early twentieth-century advocates of free love, it produced revolutionary masses poorly informed about sex and tethered to conventional domestic arrangements brokered by lineage heads, parents or cadres. However, since the 1980s and particularly in Chinese cities, this post-revolutionary sexual repressiveness has given way to sexual licence, as young people experiment with public displays of affection, public trysts, premarital sex, same-sex alliances and self-gratification, while sex education lags troublingly behind sexual awareness. The magnitude of these cultural effects is so great as to constitute a revolution in national attitude and habit.

In contemporary China, as in the broad stream of global media in which the country wades, sex has a distinct and expanding currency. All of the nation's urban centres have hostess bars, massage parlours, 'barber shops', karaoke lounges, singles' bars, while out in the rural points of transit between Yunnan and Myanmar, or in the exotic sites of tourism in minority nationality autonomous regions, commercial sex availability is public and polymorphous. Cash is king and sex is its servant, an attitude ironically bound up with local politics. In 1999, the mayor of Shenyang, Mu Suixin, encouraged the development of prostitution in order to combat unemployment of laid-off workers of state-owned enterprises as well as the migrant labour force of an economically depressed countryside. His 30 per cent tax on Shenyang's new sex trade has been a boon to the city's economy (luxuriously fed by the nightwork of the city's more than 5,000 'places of entertainment') and has inspired other mayors and regional officials to mimic the practice.

In certain locales, such as the hyper-urbanized enclaves of the south and southeast coast (Hainan, Guangzhou, Hong Kong, Shanghai, Shenzhen and other Special Economic Zones) and the northern capital, Beijing, sex is both inescapable and profitable. A cultural revolution of sexual commodities is visible everywhere: risqué clothing styles, brazenly displayed tattoos, pin-up calendars, women's fashion magazines, supermodel contests, pornographic books, magazines and videotapes, notices for private clinics treating sexually transmitted diseases, national anti-HIV/AIDS campaigns, prostitution, sex slavery, condom promotion, breast enhancement advertisements, along with a proliferation of visual images of the body, clad and scantily clad, strewn throughout the commercial blandishments of the new urban streetscape.

There are other ways to assess the changing and more open character of China's sexual climate from novel sex education programmes in schools, to radical legal guarantees of reproductive freedom, to the scientific study of sexual relations, to the commercial pathology of sex work and, unfortunately, the grisly epidemiology of sexually transmitted disease. In the Haidian district of western Beijing, not far from Peking and Qinghua universities, sex education books have been introduced into the middle school classroom, and in Jilin province in northeast China in 2002, the provincial government passed a law ensuring the right of single women of legal marriageable age to bear a child.

The prominence of the changes of sexual attitude in official public life became widely evident since the late 1980s with a newfound scientific pursuit of sexual knowledge and sexual practice that culminated in the first national survey, the 'Sex Civilization Survey', which was conducted from February 1989 to April 1990. Since then seminars and conferences on sexuality and contemporary sexual problems have been convened as the subject of sex and **reproductive health** has become professionalized. Now there are a number of centres for sex research in Beijing, Heilongjiang, Shanghai, Shaoguan and Shenzhen and increasing numbers of scientists with degrees in sexology. One of the most celebrated of these sexologists, one of the authors of the national sex survey, Liu Dalin, startled government officials in Shanghai when in November of 2000 he opened China's first sex museum.

The most commonly discussed and the most salient of these indices of behavioural change is the astonishing growth in prostitution in the era since the reforms. According to the World Health Organization, China has the largest commercial sex workforce in the world, with an estimated 10 million men and women so employed – more than 300,000 in the city of Beijing alone. Yet commercial sex availability is not simply an urban problem, and its rapid expansion cannot be explained as a sudden escalation of public desire. The burgeoning market for commercial sex is evident in the perverse plurality of its offerings as displayed in the voluminous records of police blotters. There have been hundreds of thousands of arrests of men and women in the official 'Hard Strike Campaigns', numerous national scandals involving children in the sex trade, solicitations of underage sex (under fourteen years of age), involuntary sexual servitude, and kidnapping.

In 2001, Yunnan's provincial government uncovered a prostitution ring operating in Kunming that was composed of high-school girls, some as young as thirteen and many of whom had been introduced to the flesh trade by older teenagers. The girls admitted that they prostituted themselves voluntarily because of the glamour and the inordinate compensation in wealth and power they received from their clients. However, one learns from the research of Pan Suiming, a scholar who has conducted fieldwork among urban prostitutes, from streetwalkers to call girls, that the work may seem glamorous but it is certainly not easy and often not as remunerative as one might presume looking at the figures indicating that commercial sex work generates between 6 and 12 per cent of China's annual GDP. According to Pan, a woman working an average 'barber shop' solicitation post every day will be engaged by one client every four days.

In recent years escort services and the like have become more common manifestations of sex work as the government's 'Regulations on the Management of Places of Entertainment' attempt to restrict the otherwise unabashed traffic in flesh. Escort or 'leisure' services of the 'Mayflower Madam' sort have sprung up, so that enterprising women can find work as 'swim companions' or 'theatre companions' of this new pornography lite. Private agencies in larger cities offer employment for $40–70 a month for women who can work as housekeepers, yet the women (and girls) who have answered such ads have been coerced into commercial sex trafficking. In this light it makes little sense to assess the sexual revolution in terms of sex or individual empowerment. Rather, it is better to recognize China's sex industry as a capitalist pathology consequent upon economic scarcity and social jeopardy than to see it as voluntary election; and given the mutual entailment of commercial sex and official sponsorship of the entertainment industry through hotels, restaurants and so forth, it is unlikely that national campaigns to prosecute prostitutes and their clients will turn back the tide of vice in which many cities are awash.

For more than a decade prostitution and sexual transhumance has been rampant in the sites of illicit transit of drugs and people, such as Ruili in the southwest where young women in their early teens from Burma and even Nepal offer themselves for an entire day's pleasure for a few dollars; there the incidence of HIV/AIDS can be read on the small, emaciated bodies of transit point traffickers. It is also at these flesh conduits and truck stops that a high percentage of migrant sex workers and the lowest echelon of prostitution is found, along with intravenous drug use and an elevated transmissibility of sexually transmitted disease (see **HIV/ AIDS and STIs**).

Today sex and sexuality are front-and-centre, boldly displayed in billboards, magazines, on film and television, and in forms of dress, but because it is still not easily spoken of, sex stands on the edge of Chinese social life. A more liberal sexual attitude is found among high school and college-age youth (something documented in the Sex Civilization Survey). In 2000 UNESCO reported that studies conducted in Beijing and Shanghai disclosed that 50 to 85 per cent of women interviewed at premarital checkups had experienced sexual intercourse. The sexual liberation of Chinese youth is stridently proclaimed throughout the pulp fiction that passes as the standard of contemporary literary craft read by China's GenX and GenY adults. Works such as Wei Hui's *Shanghai Baby* (*Shanghai Baobei*), Hong Ying's *Summer of Betrayal* (*Luowudai*) and Mianmian's *La la la* (see **Beauties' Literature**) are populated with pseudo-biographical figures of prominent sexual bearing and interests whose self-gratification is paramount and whose identity is indissociable from sex. Of course, this addictive conjuncture of sex and commerce may not represent the actual lives of its readers, but the salience of the effects of this pulp is gauged by its overweening popularity.

In the countryside, the sexual atmosphere is less thick yet perhaps more real, in that there sex is more immediately about life choices and is not so easily commoditized as a product of natural desire. Since 2002 the government has moved to interdict the growth of strip shows in the rural towns of Shanxi, Hebei and Zhejiang. Like the age of marriage, the incidence of first sexual intercourse occurs three years earlier among village couples than urban ones. The ideal of romantic love and its presumption of sexual parity are communicated to rural China via film, television and the frequent movement of family members to regional capitals for both legitimate and illegitimate work. The chief consequence of this infusion of sexual knowledge is a refunctioning of traditional marriage practices so that the union of the rural couple may be predicated on love, but accomplished through a deliberative process involving family and friends.

Population density and crowded living conditions make it difficult for such comparatively permissive attitudes to be realized across the nation, although a more mobile rural population and the omnipresence of television have made the practices of China's sexual revolution familiar. Most Chinese, including urban residents, still rely upon a go-between (*zhongjianren*), usually friends rather than official matchmakers, to negotiate the early phases of **dating**, and **marriage** is still arranged in much of rural China, with women moving to live with their husband's families. At the same time the countryside in the provinces of Guizhou, Sichuan and Yunnan is the site of the new sexual predation on girls and young women who are abducted and either sold into sexual slavery or bought by men in search of a wife. (This phenomenon was the focus of government attention from the mid 1980s to early 1990s, when an investigation led to the shutting down of a national kidnapping and slavery racket operating in Shandong and Jiangxi (see Xie and Tan 1989)). Highly publicized figures from the 2000 'Hard Strike Campaign' revealed that women drawn into the dark commerce of sexual enslavement by aggressive brokers and kidnappers were conveyed like currency along the backroads of China's drug trade to Burma and Thailand, on to Malaysia and Singapore, and sometimes as far as Italy, Mexico and the United States – integers in the global calculation of sex. One of the kingpins of such a trade operated out of Guangxi (where he was executed in 2002), abducting and selling more than a hundred women for as much – or as little – as $125 to $375 per person.

In most parts of the country intimacy is still regulated by customs of restraint and repression, but there are signs of the advancing incidence of premarital sex. Yet, as Harriet Evans has noted in fieldwork on women and the sexual culture of Beijing, although extramarital and premarital sex are increasing, choosing not to marry or to have a male lover is considered abnormal. Even with the sexual liberation of the 1990s it is common for patrons of Beijing singles' bars to register with the house if they are actively seeking a marriage partner. On matters of sex, attitudes and behaviour have changed perhaps forever; however, at this juncture it is not clear whether such change will be especially advantageous to the nation and its women, who have long held up more than half of the sky while receiving recognition for far less.

Further reading

Blum, Susan D. and Jensen, Lionel M. (eds) (2002). *China Off Center: Mapping the Margins of the Middle Kingdom*. Honolulu: University of Hawai'i Press.

Dutton, Michael (1998). *Streetlife China*. Cambridge: Cambridge University Press.

Evans, Harriet (1997). *Women and Sexuality in China: Dominant Discourses of Female Sexuality and Gender since 1949*. New York: Continuum Books.

Farquhar, Judith (2002). *Appetites: Food and Sex in Postsocialist China*. Durham, NC: Duke University Press.

Farrer, James (2002). *Opening Up: Youth Sex Culture and Market Reform in Shanghai*. Chicago: University of Chicago Press.

Hyde, Sandra (2001). 'Sex Tourism Practices on the Periphery: Eroticizing Ethnicity and Pathologizing Sex on the Lancang'. In Nancy N. Chen, Constance D. Clark, Suzanne Z. Gottschang and Lyn Jeffery (eds), *China Urban: Ethnographies of Contemporary Culture*. Durham, NC: Duke University Press, 142–62.

Liu, Dalin, Ng, Man Lun, Zhou, Li Ping and Haeberle, Edwin J. (eds) (1997). *Sexual Behavior in Modern China*. New York: Continuum Books.

O'Connell Davidson, J. (2001). *Children in the Sex Trade in China*. Stockholm: Save the Children Sweden.

Pan, Suiming (2000). *Shengcun yu tiyan: dui yige dixia 'hongdengqu' de zhui zong kaocha* [Subsistence and Experience: An Investigation into an Underground Red Light District]. Beijing: Zhongguo renmin daxue xing shehuixue yanjiusuo.

Ruan, Fangfu (1991). *Sex in China: Studies in Sexology in Chinese Culture*. New York: Plenum Press.

Wasserstrom, Jeffrey N. and Brownell, Susan (eds) (2002). *Chinese Femininities/Chinese Masculinities: A Reader*. Berkeley: University of California Press.

Xie, Zhihong and Tan, Lusheng (1989). *Gulao de zui'e: funüji* [An Age-Old Evil: A True Account of the Countrywide Abduction and Sale of Women]. Zhejiang wenyi chubanshe.

Zha, Jianying (1995). *China Pop: How Soap Operas, Tabloids, and Bestsellers are Transforming a Culture*. New York: The New Press.

LIONEL M. JENSEN

Sha Yexin

b. 1939, Nanjing

Theatre director

The Director of Shanghai People's Art Theatre from 1985 to 1993, Sha Yexin is known for blending sharp social criticism with artistic innovation, both testing the limits of and enriching post-Mao theatrical expression.

Sha disrupted the media-promoted optimism about post-Mao Chinese society with his play *If I Were Real* (*Jiaru wo shi zhende*, 1979), that satirizes the Party bureaucracy. The plot is based on a news report: someone pretends to be the son of a high-ranking official to secure a job transfer from a farm to the city. Sha accentuates the tragic aspect of the fact that his protagonist is arrested for assuming a false identity yet was compelled to do so by circumstances beyond his control. Moreover, the other people involved in the plot go free. Sha uses Gogol's *The Inspector General* as a framing text to add a historical dimension to the phenomenon. He also repeatedly interrupts the action to highlight the artificiality of the staging in a Brechtian manner, thus expanding the theme to something larger than the play itself. The play gave rise to heated debates on the positioning of post-Mao China and the use of an anti-hero as the protagonist. Because of the controversy, the audience for the play was restricted after three months. Sha's noted theatrical experiments also include his socio-psychological play *In Search of the Manly Man* (*Xunzhao nanzihan*, 1984) and the absurdist *Jesus, Confucius, and John Lennon* (*Yesu, Kong zi, Pi-tou-shi Lienong*, 1988).

Further reading

Chen, Xiaomei (2002). *Acting the Right Part: Political Theatre and Popular Drama in Contemporary China.* Honolulu: University of Hawai'i Press.

Sha, Yexin (1983). 'If I Were Real'. In Edward Gunn (ed.), *Twentieth Century Chinese Drama: An Anthology.* Bloomington: University of Indiana Press, 468–74.

—— (1995). 'Jesus, Confucius, and John Lennon'. *Renditions* 43 (Spring).

—— (2003). 'Jiang Qing and Her Husbands'. Trans. Kirk Denton. In Chen Xiaomei (ed.), *Reading the Right Part: An Anthology of Contemporary Chinese Drama.* Honolulu: University of Hawai'i Press, 282–335.

Vittinghoff, Natascha (2002). 'China's Generation X: Rusticated Red Guards in Controversial Contemporary Plays'. In Woei Lian Chong (ed.), *China's Great Proletarian Cultural Revolution: Master Narratives and Post-Mao Counternarratives.* Lanham, MD: Rowman and Littlefield, 285–318.

Wang, Xinmin (1997). *Zhongguo dangdai xiju shigang* [Compendium of Contemporary Chinese Drama]. Beijing: Shehuikexue wenxian chubanshe.

HE DONGHUI

shadow puppet theatre

The most enduring myth concerning the origin of the Chinese shadow theatre was first suggested by a Song dynasty scholar. Emperor Wudi of the Han dynasty was so distraught after the death of a favourite consort, Lady Li, that he hired a Daoist adept to conjure up her spirit. Whereupon the Daoist lit candles, made offerings and produced the likeness of the consort behind a gauze curtain. Besides Gao's attribution, however, there is no evidence that the séance had anything directly to do with the origins of any continuous tradition of the shadow theatre.

The origin of the shadow theatre may have been influenced by the use of paintings to tell *bianwen* (transformation) stories, and the light displays of the Tang dynasty. It was not until the Song dynasty that the shadow theatre not only existed for certain, but was also highly developed. Sources on the shadow theatre during the Yuan and Ming dynasties are scarce. By the Qing, however, this particular form of theatre had developed to a height of sophistication the world had never seen. The shadow theatre suffered a decline during the first part of the twentieth century. But like many other cultural activities, it enjoyed a revival during the 1950s and early 1960s, mainly under government auspices, but was then banned during the Cultural Revolution from 1966 to 1976. Government-sponsored troupes created during the 1950s performed animal fable stories with cartoon-like characters aimed at entertaining while inculcating young audiences. Traditional shadow theatre made a comeback during the 1980s, but an estimated 85 per cent of the revived troupes were no longer in existence by the end of the 1990s.

The more prevalent traditional style Chinese shadow theatre is basically a type of **Xiqu** (sung-drama/opera), very similar to the genre with human actors. Many of the role types, music and musical instruments used demonstrate a mutual influence. Considerably cheaper to hire than human actor troupes, the shadow theatre gained immense popularity for public liturgical festivities (birthdays of deities, local and national festivals) in poorer rural areas, as well as for celebrations within private homes (birthdays, **funerals**, **weddings**, the building of new houses and establishment of new businesses). Although the shadow theatre served mostly secular purposes when it originated in the entertainment quarters of the Song capitals, it came to be performed mainly for the gods during festive celebrations by the Yuan dynasty. The same traditional-style shadow opera troupes are still being hired to serve mainly liturgical purposes in rural villages. Its rapid decline in popularity can be attributed as much to the incursion of television and other modern entertainments as it is to attrition in the desire to please the deities during special occasions.

Shadow figures of almost all Chinese shadow traditions use coloured translucent parchment. Aside from some large composite figures of deities, all the figures have detachable heads. Before performance, the heads to be used for the play are attached to appropriate bodies and hung on two lines perpendicular to the sides of the screen backstage. All the limbs and body of the individual figures are articulated. A flexible central rod is attached to the collar of the shadow figure, and two others to each of the hands. The shadow master manipulates the parchment figures behind a paper or cloth screen, which is illuminated by dint of an oil lamp/lamps or electrical light/s, accompanied invariably by an orchestra. In some shadow theatre traditions, the shadow master does all the manipulation, singing and dialogues in solo, while in others one person will be in charge of manipulation, with the possible aid of an assistant, with another or others performing the vocal parts. Also, depending on the degree of sophistication, hand-copied scripts are used in some traditions while others rely solely on memory.

A troupe usually consists of four to nine performers, and has one or two trunks of shadow figures. The trunk usually belongs to the shadow master of the troupe. A trunk typically contains numerous labelled folders of shadow figures of humans, supernatural beings, animals and scenery. The size of the figures in different traditions may range from over a metre to barely 30 cm high. Unlike operas with human actors, the shadow theatre 'stage' is frequently ornately decorated with scenic pieces of palaces, inner gardens, tables, chairs and so forth. Celestials ride on clouds, and fantastic beasts and supernatural weapons really perform magical feats. Some figures have a movable piece on the face so that it can be flipped and change into a demon or into a face with blood streaming down. Traditional-style troupes are by far more popular and they tend to thrive in remote villages.

The government-sponsored modern-style troupes located in some cities use considerably larger screens and figures. The figures are often made with celluloid rather than parchment, with more pieces per figure. These troupes also use boxes of fluorescent lights to create brighter and more even lighting, and often add innovative special effects. When performing modern animal fables, they use pre-recorded music with narrations and dialogues in Mandarin. Several manipulators usually perform at the same time creating more intricate articulation of the figures. Modern-style troupes had their heyday during the 1950s and early 1960s.

Three regional museums are dedicated to the preservation of this art form: the Puppet and Shadow Theatre Museum (Mu'ou piyingxi bowuguan) in Xiaoyi, Shanxi; the Puppet Museum in Taipei; and the Shadow Figure Museum in Gaoxiong, Taiwan.

See also: shadow puppet theatre (troupes and traditions)

Further reading

Chin, Chen-an (1993). 'The Arts of the Lanchou Shadow Show'. In *idem, The Mainstay of the Chinese Shadow Show – The Lanchou Shadow Show*. Taipei: The Student Book Co., 75–166.

Fan, Pen Chen (2004). *Visions of the Masses: Chinese Shadow Plays*. Ithaca: Cornell University Press. [Videotape of a traditional shadow play, *The Temple of Guanyin*, with English and Chinese subtitles can be obtained at a nominal charge from fanpenchen@hotmail.com]

—— (forthcoming). *The Chinese Shadow Theatre and Popular Religion and Women Warriors*. Honolulu: McGill and Queens Universities Press and the University of Hawaii Press.

Jiang, Yuxiang, *Zhongguo yingxi yü minsu* [The Chinese Shadow Theatre and Local Customs]. Taipei: Suxiang chubanshe, 1999.

Ruizendaal, Robin (1995). 'The Quanzhou Marionette Theatre: A Fieldwork Report (1986–1995)'. *China Information* 10.1: 1–18.

—— (2000). 'Ritual Text and Performance in the Marionette Theater of Southern Fujian and Taiwan'. In Jan A. M. Meyer and Peter M. Engelfriet (eds), *Linked Faiths: Essays on Chinese Religion and Traditional Culture in Honor of Kristofer Schipper*. Leiden: E. J. Brill, 336–60.

FAN PEN CHEN

shadow puppet theatre (troupes and traditions)

Eight distinct shadow traditions of varying styles can be discerned today. Playscripts are used in Wanwanqiang Shadows and Laoqiang Shadows of Shaanxi; the Luanzhou Shadows of Beijing, Hebei and northeastern China; the Chengdu Shadows of Sichuan: and the Parchment Monkey Shadows of Taiwan. The eight traditions with their local variations are as follows.

1   *The Qin and Jin shadow tradition*: Agonqiang Shadows (Shaanxi), Wanwanqiang Shadows (Shaanxi), four styles of Daoist Shadows (Shaanxi); Laoqiang Shadows (Shaanxi), Xianbanqiang Shadows (Shaanxi), Ankang yuediao Shadows (Shaanxi); Lingbao Shadows (Henan), Eastern Henan Shadows (Henan), Xinyang Shadows (Henan); Piqiang Shadows (Shanxi), Wanwanqiang Shadows (Shanxi); Eastern Gansu Shadows (Gansu), Southern Gansu Shadows (Gansu); Qinghai Shadows (Sichuan), Northern Sichuan Shadows or Weinan Shadows (Sichuan).

2   *The Luanzhou shadow tradition*: Gargantuan Shadows (Hebei), Luanzhou Shadows [Beijing Eastside Shadows (Hebei), Leting Shadows (Hebei) or Eastern Hebei Shadows (Hebei), Beijing Westside Shadows (Hebei), Zhozhou Shadows (Hebei), Prayer Mat Shadows (Hebei), Flowing-from-the-mouth/Memory Shadows (Hebei), Beijing Shadows (Hebei), Southern Hebei Cattle Parchment Shadows (Hebei); Luanzhou Shadows (or Northeastern Shadows) (Lianing, Jilin, Heilongjiang).

3   *The Shandong shadow tradition*: Shandong Shadows.

4   *The Hangzhou shadow tradition*: Zhejiang Shadows, Shanghai Shadows.

5   *The shadow traditions of Sichuan, Hubei and Yunnan*: Hubei Shadows (Hubei), Tongbo Shadows (Henan), Luoshan Shadows (Henan), Chengdu Shadows (Sichuan), Tengchong Shadows (Yunnan).

6   *The Hunan and Jiangxi shadow tradition*: Hunan Shadows.

7   *The Chaozhou shadow tradition*: Parchment Monkey Shadows (Taiwan), Parchment Monkey Shadows or Paper Screen Shadows (Guangdong).

8   *The modern tradition*: children's stories, revolutionary tales, rewritten traditional plays.

Members of rural troupes are all farmers who perform to supplement their income. They generally follow inherited traditional styles. While the owner of a trunk of shadow figures (usually the master puppeteer) is considered to be the head/director of a troupe, his assistant and the musicians of the orchestra may change depending on availability. When a show is booked, the director will contact other performers and form a troupe. Many village musicians perform for several different troupes, including human actors' opera troupes. The film *To Live* (*Huozhe*), directed by **Zhang Yimou**, features the Wanwanqiang Shadows of Shaanxi. The most renowned troupes are located in Huaxian, Shaanxi.

Starting from the 1950s, government-sponsored puppet troupes in cities such as Changsha (Hunan) Beijing, Shanghai, Tangshan (Hebei), Xi'an (Shaanxi), Chengdu (Sichuan), Lufeng (Guangdong) and Harbin (Heilongjiang) began to perform animal fable stories as well as plays with revolutionary content and a few rewritten plays from traditional repertoires. These modern-style troupes were revived after the Cultural Revolution. But as government funds for the performing arts dwindled in the 1980s, some, such as the one in Shanghai, ceased to exist; while others, such as the one in Lufeng, only perform when they are hired to put on shows abroad. The Tangshan Shadow Play Theatre is the most successful troupe of this kind. It draws most of its income from commissions abroad and performing at village festivals.

The following troupes, listed by province or municipality, are still active. Private troupes are usually identified locally by the name of the master puppeteer/director, who owns the trunks:

Shaanxi: Sun Jingfa at Lintong; Wei Zhengye (Guanghuashe), Pan Jingle (Guangyishe), Yang Xinlu (Guangqingshe), Dong Jinrui (Guangmingshe) and Jiang Zhanhe (Zhenhuashe) at Huaxian; Chen Zenli, Zhang Ximin (Jindian piyingshe), Wei Xingbao (Gexinshe) and Zhang Bimin, Wang Zhenzhong (Baimao piyingshe) at Huayinxian; Cheng Youcai and Wang Tiande (Tiandeshe) at Liquanxian; Wang Yunfei at Qishanxian; Provincial Folk Art Theatre and Li Shijie (Deqingshe) at Xi'an; He Bao'an at Yangxian; Ma Tianhu at Fengxiangxian; Meng Mingshe at Xingpingxian; Duan Manwong (Shadi piyingshe) and Wang Jinfa (Xizhai piyingshe) at Dalixian; Huan Ziwa (Minleshe) at Fupingxian; Li Youcai (Qizhenban) at Fufengxian.

Shanxi: Wu Haitang at Biducun, Xiaoyi; Xiaoyi Shadow Theatre Troupe at Xiaoyi.

Hebei: Tangshan Shadow Play Theatre at Tangshan; Luannan Shadow Play Theatre at Luannan; Lu Fuzeng at Ershengmiaocun, Fengrunxian.

Heilongjiang: Han Feizi and Gao Jinhua at Shuangchengshi; Ha'erbin Ertong yishu juyuan piying jutuan at Harbin.

Shangdong: Li Xingtang at Jinan.

Henan: Suo Xinyou at Xichecun, Yinzhuangzhen, Lingbao.

Gansu: Zhu Tingyu, Wujiamencun, Sanchaxiang, Zhangxian.

Sichuan: Xiong Weisheng at Santaixian (recently deceased); Wang Wenkun at Liquancun, Baotaixiang, Langzhong (recently deceased); He Zhengtong at Mawangxiang, Nanbu; Shen Xiao in Chengdu.

Shanghai: Tang Baoliang at Qixianzhen, Fengxianxiang.

Zhejiang: Jijiaban at Haining.

Guangdong: Lufeng Shadow Theatre Troupe at Lufengshi; Zhuo You'er at Huanlincun, Nantangzhen, Lufeng (recently deceased).

Yunnan: Liu Yongzhou at Tengchong.

Taiwan: The troupes Donghua, Hexing, Fude, Yongxingle and Fuxingge at Gaoxiongxian.

See also: shadow puppet theatre

FAN PEN CHEN

Shandong guchui

Regional traditional ensemble music genre

Shandong guchui is a local **drumming and blowing** instrumental genre which is popular in the southwestern corner of Shandong province, surrounding the counties of Heze and Jijing. Its modern name is 'drumming and blowing music of southwestern Lu' (*Lu xinan guchui*). Lu was the ancient name for the province. The local people call these professional or semi-professional ensembles, which are composed of members of the same

family, 'drum music bands' (*guyue ban*). Usually, the genre is used in ceremonies for **weddings** and **funerals**.

The repertory includes traditional 'labelled melodies' (*qupai*) of the Yuan (1271–1368) and Ming (1368–1644) dynasties, melodies of folksongs and opera-mimicry (*kaxi*), and performances given by musicians who use double-reed instruments to imitate vocal music from local operas. There are three performing styles according to different leading instruments in the genre:

1 The leading instrument of the first style is shawm (*suona*), in a band of bamboo flutes, mouth-organs, cymbals, gongs and drums. This style can be divided into two types: (a) the band led by a single shawm is called *dan dadi*; (b) the band led by two shawms is called *dui dadi*, meaning paired *suona*.

2 The leading instruments of the second style are the cylindrical double reeds (*shuangguan*). The band includes shawm, bamboo flute, mouth-organ, a small gong called *dangzi*, and a temple block called 'wooden fish' (*muyu*).

3 The leading instrument of the third performing style is the bamboo flute. This band includes mouth-organ, small cymbals and wooden clappers called **Bangzi**.

Adding a 'tassel' (*suizi*) is the famous technique of this genre. The 'tassel' is a flamboyant improvisatory ostinato section employing short phrases, which revolve around several pivotal pitches. A 'tassel' is used at the end of a piece to create a climactic and humorous atmosphere. The most famous pieces of the genre are 'One Hundred Birds Paying Respect to Phoenix' (*Bainiao chaofeng*) and 'A Flower' (*Yizhi hua*).

Further reading

Du, Yaxiong (1999). *Zhongguo minzu qiyue gailun* [An Outline of Chinese Instrumental Music]. Changsha: Hunan renmin chubanshe.

Miao, Tianrui, Ji, Liankang and Guo, Naian (eds) (1985). *Zhongguo yinyue cidian* [Dictionary of Chinese Music]. Beijing: Renmin yinyue chubanshe.

DU YAXIONG

Shang Changrong

b. 15 July 1940, Beijing

Xiqu (sung drama/opera) actor

Shang Changrong is the most famous currently active performer of the *jing* or painted-face Xiqu role type in **Jingju** (Peking opera) (see **Xiqu role types**). The son of Shang Xiaoyun, one of the 'Four Great *Dan* [female role type]' Jingju performers of the twentieth century, Shang Changrong trained in Jingju performance at home, and was on stage by age five. In 1950 he entered the school attached to his father's troupe, where he studied painted-face performance and gained extensive stage experience. In 1960 Shang became the personal disciple of the master painted-face performer Hou Xirui; Shang is the principal inheritor of Hou's 'performance style' (*liupai*), which is the foundation of his own creative work.

Shang was one of the original actors in the model revolutionary modern Jingju, *Taking Tiger Mountain by Strategy* (*Zhi qu wei Hushan*). His first major original work after the **Cultural Revolution** was in the newly written historical play *Zhang Fei Honours Virtue* (*Zhang Fei jingxian*), which won numerous awards and was made into a popular television film. One of his most famous and influential achievements is the celebrated Jingju play **Cao Cao and Yang Xiu** (*Cao Cao yü Yang Xiu*, 1988). Shang discovered the script, convinced the Shanghai Jingju Company (Shanghai jingjuyuan) to produce it, and created what is widely recognized as one of the all-time finest characterizations of the historical figure Cao Cao. His most recent major work is in the newly written historical play *A Great Occasion in the Zhen Guan Years* (*Zhen Guan shengshi*), which received major national prizes in 2000 and 2001 and, like *Cao Cao and Yang Xiu*, has toured widely in and outside of mainland China. Shang has received innumerable national honours, including multiple Plum Blossom Awards (*Meihua jiang*). His work has already been recognized by many authorities as constituting its own, original 'performance style'.

ELIZABETH WICHMANN-WALCZAK

Shang Yang (1996)

Huaju (spoken drama)

Shang Yang, a newly written historical drama (*lishiju*), takes its name from the main character, a renowned political reformer of the Warring States period (fourth century BC). Arriving at the state of Qin from the state of Wei, Shang Yang tries to persuade King Xiao to adopt Legalism, leading to heated debates within the court, but ultimately leading to the implementation of reforms despite resistance from conservative elements of the court. When a younger king assumes the throne, he orders Shang Yang arrested for treason. Shang Yang flees with his mother, but ultimately cannot be saved because of strict penal codes he himself implemented. He is drawn and quartered, but remains an enduring symbol of brave reform in feudal China. The play, written by Yao Yuan and featuring Yin Zhusheng in the role of Shang Yang, was first staged in 1996 by the Shanghai Dramatic Arts Centre and won several national and regional awards. The original staging ran for thirty-five performances and was performed in several subsequent runs. Featured in the Singapore Arts Festival in the summer of 2001, *Shang Yang* also travelled to Hong Kong in October of the same year.

See also: Huaju

CLAIRE CONCEISON

Shanghai Oriental Television

Shanghai Oriental Television (SOTV) was launched on 18 January 1993 by Shanghai's Radio, Film and Television Bureau, as part of a move to open up competition in the local television industry. The station has a strong local focus with emphasis on social and educational issues; however, its significance in the local television industry is due to the flotation of 'non-political' subsidiary companies (which control advertising) on the stock exchange in 1994. This move, which raised around 800 million yuan in a matter of months, made it the first Chinese television station to raise funds on private capital markets. This figure favourably compared to the total revenue for Shanghai's television industry (400 million yuan) in 1994. By 1998 the station's advertising revenue had reached 500 million yuan. In this way, the station provided a massive injection of new funding for the Shanghai television industry and paved the way for Hunan's provincial satellite television station under the name of the Hunan Television and Broadcasting Media Company Ltd (Hunan guangdian meiti youxian gongsi), which made a highly publicized and successful initial public offering in December 1998.

At the end of 1995, the station launched a joint venture with Shanghai Scientific Education Film Studios which has now become one of the country's leading science education and cartoon filmmaking units (see **animation**). In May 2001, along with Shanghai's other television stations and leading media organizations, SOTV was incorporated into the newly formed cross-media Shanghai Culture and Broadcasting Group (Shanghai wenguang jituan). In 2001, the station employed around 600 people, operating two channels that broadcast an average of thirty-seven hours per day, of which seven hours consisted of programming in-house.

KEVIN LATHAM

Shanghai Tang

Clothing company

Shanghai Tang was founded in 1994 by Hong Kong-born and British-educated businessman, David Wing-Cheung Tang. The name Shanghai Tang is said to be derived from the Chinese translation of the highly recognizable river embankment in Shanghai known as the Waitan (The Bund). Shanghai Tang's first line, 'Imperial Tailors', specialized in affordable Chinese haute couture produced by Shanghaiese tailors. Ready-to-wear collections have also subsequently been added. Although these are, for the most part, bulk-made in mainland China, Shanghai Tang is attempting to overturn the perception that 'made in China' means mass-produced, poor-quality

goods through the use of internationally renowned designers.

The style of the clothing and accessories could be described as 'East meets West', whereby traditional Chinese cultural elements and 1920–30s throwbacks are interwoven with distinctly twenty-first-century styles. Classics include velvet Mao jackets (see **Mao Zedong and Sun Yatsen suits**) and silk cheongsams (see **qipao, cheongsam**) in often flashy and unconventional colours. Shanghai Tang's offerings have also now expanded to include other goods that range from home furnishings decorated with Chinese motifs to popular novelty gifts such as Mao mugs and watches. Despite the fact that its market still remains firmly planted in Asia, where the new face of Shanghai Tang is one of China's top film actresses, **Gong Li**, its custom base in the West is expanding with boutiques opening around the world. Shanghai Tang goods have already become identified with fashionable celebrities and items have even featured on the popular American television series *Sex and the City*.

See also: fashion designers; silk industry

SARAH DAUNCEY

Shanxi badatao

Regional traditional ensemble music genre

Shanxi badatao is a local **drumming and blowing** instrumental genre which is popular in northern part of Shanxi province, around the counties of Wutai and Dingxiang. Because the repertory includes eight suites, this genre is called 'eight great suites' (*badatao*). The eight suites are: 'Blue Sky' (*Qingtian*), 'Dressing Table' (*Banzhang tai*), 'Turning the Winch' (*Tui luzhou*), 'A Building with Twelve Floors' (*Shi'er ceng luo*), 'Swearing' (*Dama yulang*), 'Admonition' (*Zhenyan*), 'Gander' (*E lang*) and 'Golden Cup' (*Quan jinbei*). A suite includes a prelude and three sections: slow, mid-tempo and fast. The slow section is called the 'main piece' (*zhengqu*), having two or more long labelled melodies. The second section is usually the variation of the opening and concluding phrases of the main piece. The third, called the 'supporting piece' (*peiqu*), is a semi-improvised section.

The badatao repertory includes sixty-one melodies originating from traditional instrumental pieces, folksongs, opera music and religious music. A band playing this genre is called 'eight-tone association' (**Bayinhui**) and usually includes two cylindrical double reeds, one shawm, one bamboo flute, two mouth-organs, and percussion (drums, gongs and cymbals). The genre is traditionally used for **funerals** and calendrical rituals, such as the **New Year Festival**, the **Qingming Festival**, the **Ghost Festival** in the fifteenth of the seventh lunar month, and at the ancestral offering ceremonies at the beginning of the tenth month. At the beginning of twentieth century, local Buddhist monks and **Daoist priests** learned the genre from the 'eight-tone associations' and currently use this genre in their religious ceremonies.

See also: Buddhist music; Daoist music

Further reading

Miao, Tianrui, Ji, Liankang and Guo, Naian (eds) (1985). *Zhongguo yinyue cidian* [Dictionary of Chinese Music]. Beijing: Renming yinyue chubanshe.

DU YAXIONG

Shen Xiaomei

b. 20 December 1937, Shanghai

Xiqu (spoken drama/opera) actress

Shen Xiaomei is a personal student of the master **Jingju** actor Mei Lanfang. During the 1980s and early 1990s, Shen was a prolific and respected performer of plays created by Mei and a versatile and successful creator of new performances in Mei's 'performance style' (*liupai*), making her one the most influential creative artists in the *dan* Xiqu role type (see **Xiqu role types**). Since the mid 1990s she has prominently promoted Jingju education in elementary and secondary schools, leading efforts to build new audiences for the form.

Shen was privately tutored in Jingju and **Kunqu**, and in 1953 became the personal disciple

of Mei Lanfang, who placed her with the Jiangsu Province Jingju Company (Jiangsusheng jingju yuan) in 1956. For the next ten years, she gave between 150 and 350 performances per year in tours travelling as far as Vienna, where she received the top performance prize at the Seventh International Young People's Arts Festival in 1959.

Shen taught at the Jiangsu Province Xiqu Academy (Jiangsusheng xiqu xueyuan) during the **Cultural Revolution**, returning to professional performance in 1981. Her major achievements during the following decade include *The Decorated Candles* (*Baozhu ji*), for which she received the 'Hundred Flowers Award' (*Baihua jiang*) for best performer in a newly created play (1983), and *Mirror of Honour and Disgrace* (*Rongru jian*), for which she received numerous awards in 1986. Shen taught Jingju performance at universities in the USA and Canada on several occasions during the 1980s and 1990s, and has headed the Jiangsu Province Committee for the Promotion of Jingju in Education since its inception. She has received innumerable national honours, including multiple 'Plum-Blossom Awards' (*Meihua jiang*), and has been recognized as a 'Living Treasure'.

See also: Xiqu

ELIZABETH WICHMANN-WALCZAK

Sheng Qi

b. 1965, Hefei, Anhui

Performance artist, painter

Even before graduating from Beijing's Central Academy of Art and Design in 1988, Sheng was among the founders of Concept 21, a pioneering performance art group (together with Zhao Jianhai, Kang Mu, Zheng Yuke and Xi Jianjun). Since 1986, they have staged performances that used landmarks such as the Great Wall and the Summer Palace as backdrops. From 1990 to 1992, Sheng worked in Italy, and in 1993 he entered Central St Martin's College of Art and Design in London, receiving an MFA in 1998. In 1999, he returned to Beijing, where he is teaching at the Central Academy of Art and Design. Sheng's recent art has taken up many of his earlier concerns. His first works were based on the idea of using the human body as a tool, and in a performance soon after 4 June 1989, Sheng chopped off the little finger on his left hand. Photographs of Sheng's mutilated hand appear in many of his works, sometimes in conjunction with his frequent use of the AIDS ribbon. Sheng has revived Concept 21 in a number of performance pieces and virtual performances envisioned through digital collages. Wearing only an Armed Police jacket and gloves, donning the AIDS ribbon, his face covered in a red cloth and his genitalia wrapped in gauze, he is placed in improbable locations, such as Beijing landmarks and the Tibetan countryside. Some works, such as *Ambush from All Directions* (1999) are overtly political, while others, such as *Yang Guifei on the Road* (2002), juxtapose symbols of Chinese tradition and modernization.

See also: political icons (and art)

YOMI BRAESTER

Sheng Zongliang

(a.k.a. Bright Sheng)

b. 1955, Shanghai

Composer

Bright Sheng, one of the most prominent composers of the post-Cultural Revolution generation, left China in 1982. He defines himself as an American-Chinese composer, and his music combines culture and music from the East and West. He was appointed a MacArthur Fellow in 2002. Sheng started piano study at the age of four. During the Cultural Revolution he worked as a pianist and percussionist in a folk music and dance troupe in Qinghai province for seven years, near the Tibetan border, where he also studied and collected folk music. In 1978, when universities reopened, he was one of the first students accepted by the Shanghai Conservatory of Music. Leaving China for New York City in 1982, Sheng studied at Queens College and Columbia University, where he graduated with a DMA in 1993. Among his mentors and

teachers were Leonard Bernstein, George Perle and Chou Wen-chung. Bela Bartok – ethnomusicologist, composer and teacher – also inspired Sheng.

The orchestral piece *H'un (Lacerations): In Memoriam 1966–76* (1988) launched Sheng's career in the United States and worldwide. A work created for the Lyric Opera of Chicago when Sheng served as composer-in-residence was *The Story of Majnun* (1992). *The Silver River* (1997, revised in 2000) was a multicultural music theatre collaboration. Sheng's first full-length opera, *Madame Mao* (2003), was commissioned by the Santa Fe Opera. Since 1995 Sheng has held a composition professorship at the University of Michigan, Ann Arbor. He also conducts.

JOANNA C. LEE

Shi Guangnan

b. 1940, Chongqing; d. 1990, Beijing

Composer

Shi Guangnan is one of the most important composers of the 1970s and 1980s, best known for pioneering 'popular' music in China. After graduating from Tianjin Conservatory of Music in 1964, Shi Guangnan served as a composer at Tianjin Opera House until he was transferred to the Central Philharmonic Society in Beijing in 1978. He served as Vice-Chairman of the Chinese Musicians' Association in the mid 1980s. After his death, he was honoured with the title 'People's Musician', the highest honour for a musician in China, and a commemorative concert in Beijing in 2000.

In his twenty-year career in the wake of the **Cultural Revolution**, Shi Guangnan defined 'popular' music as a genre distinct from strident propaganda songs on the one hand and rock music on the other. Shi's melodic style is reminiscent of 'easy listening'. While the lyrics are ideologically safe, they are evocative portraits of an idealized China rather than abstract paeans to socialism. Shi's success is partly due to his songs' ability to express popular sentiment, such as his early work 'Premier Zhou, Where are You?' (*Zhou Zongli, nin* *zai nali*), commemorating the beloved premier. Shi composed over a hundred pieces of music, including the popular songs 'In the Fields of Hope' (*Zai xiwang de tianye shang*), 'Beat the Drums, Sing the Song' (*Daqi shougu, changqi ge*), 'When Grapes are Ripe in Tulufan' (*Tulufan de putao shoule)* and 'A Toast' (*Zhu jiu ge*). *Qu Yuan* and *Shangshi* – Shi's attempts to imitate Western-style opera – met with less success.

MARGARET BAPTIST WAN

Shi Hui

b. 1955, Shanghai

Sculptor

Shi Hui graduated from the China Academy of Fine Arts in Hangzhou (1982) (see **art academies**). In the second half of the 1980s, and like the artist **Gu Wenda**, she attended the workshop organized by Bulgarian tapestry (soft sculpture) artist Marin Varbanov, at the same school. During this period she was introduced to experimental practices with fibre and other soft material, which have since become her trademark. Shi Hui's soft sculptures, often made by weaving and mixing white paper or fibre, defy gravity with their overwrought constructions intertwining webs of spiky white elements. These piles of thread and mesh create the feeling of something both monumental and very light, suggesting a three-dimensional lace, but maintaining a strong sense of weight and physical presence. Shi Hui has stated:

> During my artistic work ... I have become aware of the fact the dialogue between artist and material is the simplest and purest form of expression in art. I especially prefer fibres because they bear both natural plant life and the will to be used by nature and man. Be it fibrous hemp threads, very elastic cotton threads, white paper mesh or rough bamboo sticks, they all reflect the movement of life.

Shi Hui's work has been shown at: 'Alors la Chine?' at the Centre Pompidou in Paris (2003); 'Imaginaire Féminin: 5th International Exhibition of Sculptures and Installations, Open 2002'

in Venice; 'Living in Time' in Berlin (2001); 'Century – Woman' in Beijing (1998); 'Die Hälfte des Himmels' (Half of the Sky) at the Frauenmuseum in Bonn (1998); 'Pulp Matters: Works on Paper' at Art Beatus in Vancouver (1997).

Further reading

(1997). *Between Ego and Society: Exhibition of Contemporary Women Artists of China* (exhibition pamphlet). Chicago: Artemisia Gallery.

Liao, Wen (1998). 'Tumultuous History of China's Feminist Values and Art'. *Chinese Type Contemporary Art Online Magazine* 1.2 (January). Available at http://www.chinese-art.com/volume1issue2/

Xu, Hong (1995). 'Dialogue: The Awakening of Chinese Women's Consciousness'. *ART Asia-Pacific* 2.2 (April): 44–51.

Xu, Jiang and Shi, Hui (1995). *Chess–Paper–Art: Selected Works by Xu Jiang/Shi Hui*. Hangzhou: China National Art Academy Press.

FRANCESCA DAL LAGO

Shi Kang

b. 1968, Beijing

Writer, screenwriter

Shi Kang is a popular contemporary Beijing-based novelist who embodies a new breed of post-**Wang Shuo** rebelliousness and iconoclasm. Shi Kang burst onto the Chinese literary scene in 1999 with a fresh, highly readable narrative style that seemed to carry on the literary mantle of popular writers Wang Shuo and Wang Xiaobo, after the former gave up writing and the latter passed away. He is best known for his popular *Youth* trilogy, which consists of the novels *Smashed and Broken* (*Zhili pocui*), *Wobbling Along* (*Huanghuang youyou*) and *Completely Muddled* (*Yichang hutu*), which were published between 1999 and 2001. Filled with local colour from the author's home of Beijing, the three novels established Shi Kang's unique first-person narrative voice and his signature novelistic structure of dividing books into hundreds of short chapters which always begin with the number zero. In 2002

Shi Kang published *Passion and Blindness* (*Jiqing yü mimang*), a contemporary urban love story, which is also the author's first novel written in the third person.

Also a prolific screenwriter, Shi Kang was a co-writer of **Feng Xiaogang**'s 2002 Spring Festival comedy smash, *Big Shot's Funeral* (*Da wan*), which starred PRC comic hero **Ge You** opposite Donald Sutherland (see **New Year's movies**). Shi also adapted the screenplay from his own *Passion and Blindness* for a forthcoming film by Taiwan director Lee Gang (Ang **Lee**'s brother). Shi Kang is among the first PRC writers to promote himself through the Internet, where he ran Shikang.com, a website where his entire body of literary work was made available for downloading at no cost.

MICHAEL BERRY

Shi Tiesheng

b. 1951, Beijing

Writer

Shi Tiesheng was sent to Guanjia village near Yan'an as an 'educated youth' (*zhiqing*) in 1969, returning home in 1972 suffering from an illness that left him with a permanent disability and prevented him from working. Shi Tiesheng turned to writing fiction. His first major short story was the award-winning 'My Faraway Qingpingwan' (*Wo yaoyuan de Qingpingwan*, 1983). The story looks back at the narrator's time in northern Shaanxi as an educated youth. It recalls with affection the simple and natural world he left behind, its harsh beauty and the strengths and kindness of its impoverished inhabitants.

Shi Tiesheng's main contribution to contemporary fiction is his description of the disabled (see **disabilities**). Whereas other writers tend to use the disabled as symbols of either China's degeneration or the shortcomings of individuals, Shi Tiesheng's disabled characters show compassion for others and steadfastly pursue meaning in life. Shi's most complex story on this theme is 'Strings of Life' (*Ming ruo qinxian*), about two blind banjo players, a master and his apprentice. The old musician was told by his own master that when

he has worn out a thousand banjo strings, he can tear open the banjo's casing and find inside a prescription for medicine that will restore his sight. After the old man breaks his thousandth string, he discovers that the piece of paper carrying the 'prescription' is blank. Realizing that this was how his master had 'encouraged' him to face the hardships of life, he does the same for his own student.

Further reading

Shi, Tiesheng (1984). 'My Faraway Qingping Wan'. Trans. Shen Zhen. *Chinese Literature* (Spring): 61–76.

—— (1991). *Strings of Life*. Beijing: Panda Books.

KAM LOUIE

Shi Yukun

b. 1943, Jiangsi

Xiqu (spoken-drama/opera) director

Shi Yukun is an accomplished director working primarily in **Jingju** (Peking opera), but also in several other regional **Xiqu** (sung-drama/opera) forms as well as television, completing over forty projects by the end of the twentieth century.

Shi began studying Jingju performance at age seven with his father, and entered the China Xiqu Academy (Zhongguo xiqu xuexiao) in 1960, training in the martial male (*wusheng*) Xiqu role type (see **Xiqu role types**). He has been with the Jiangsu Province Jingju Company (Jiangsusheng jingjuyuan) since 1960, as an actor until 1975 and as a director since then, entering the Shanghai Xiju Academy (Shanghai xiju xueyuan, a **Huaju** training institution) for directorial training in 1978. He has received numerous directing awards and is a 'First Level' director within China's national artist ranking system. Among his most notable Jingju directing achievements are *The Decorated Candles* (*Bao zhu ji*), which received a 'cultural award' (*wenhua jiang*) from the Ministry of Culture in 1983; *Mirror of Honour and Disgrace* (*Rong ru jian*), which received numerous awards at the Jiangsu Province Festival of New Plays in 1986; and *Luotuo*

Xiangzi, based on Lao She's novel of the same name (usually translated as *Rickshaw Boy* or *Camel Xiangzi*), which won the Gold Prize at the Second National Jingju Festival in December–January 1998–9 and was recognized as one of the three finest new Jingju plays at the Sixth China Art Festival in 2000. *Luotuo* was praised for the depth of character development achieved by the performers as well as for the innovative use of many Jingju conventions.

See also: Xiqu playwrights

MEGAN EVANS AND ELIZABETH
WICHMANN-WALCZAK

Shifan (Shifan gu, Shifan luogu)

Traditional music genre

Shifan includes Shifan gu and Shifan luogu, two traditional **drumming and blowing** genres which flourished in the cities of Suzhou and Wuxi in the southern part of Jiangsu province. According to a late seventeenth-century book, *Banqiao zaji*, [Miscellaneous Notes on the Broad Bridge], written by Yu Huai (b. 1616), the two genres were already popular in the area during the Ming dynasty (1368–1644). Usually, local folk musicians, **Daoist priests** and Buddhist monks perform these two genres at **funerals**, **weddings** and birthday parties.

The two Shifan are in fact closely related. Both of their ensembles are almost the same as the basic ensemble which accompanies **Kunqu** opera. They include: **dizi** (bamboo flute), *sheng* (mouth-organ), *xiao* (bamboo recorder), *sanxian* and **pipa** (plucked lutes), banghu and **erhu** (two-stringed fiddles), gongs, drums and cymbals in different sizes (see **luogu**). Shifan gu is also called *fanyin* (pure music) or Sunan chuida (blowing and beating music from southern Jiangsu). The leading instruments are dizi and drum. The repertoire of this genre can be divided into two categories: wind and string instrumental pieces, and solo drum pieces. A suite is composed of more than ten pieces, including one, two or three drum solos. Shifan luogu is also called *shiyangjin* (ten pieces of brocade) because of its colourful instrumentation, which includes: *dichui luogu* (type led by a flute), *shengchui luogu* (type led by a mouth-organ), *cuxi sizhu luogu* (type played by gruff-and-sharp **Silk and Bamboo** instruments) and *qing luogu* (type played only by percussion). Among them, the last is the most famous, and its formal structure is a cycle of variations and pre-composed labelled percussion pieces.

See also: Buddhist music; Daoist music

Further reading

Jones, Stephen (1995). *Folk Music of China: Living Instrumental Traditions*. Oxford: Clarendon.

Liang, Mingyue (1985). *Music of the Billion*. New York: Heinrichshofen.

DU YAXIONG

shopping malls

Years of socialist transformation and economic impoverishment left China with a few large but under-stocked department stores. Most were housed in pre-1949 multi-storey buildings. Friendship Stores, built originally to cater to Soviet experts and a handful of foreigners, also provided limited goods to high-level cadres as part of a system of 'privileged supply' (*tegong*) developed during the Yan'an days of wartime rationing. They were off-limits to the masses.

While shopping provided little respite during the days of high socialism, there were educational sites that emulated Soviet models called 'cultural palaces' (*wenhuagong*). These glum arcades were indoor venues for mass edification, and many of the men and women who later became prominent cultural figures were initially trained in these ersatz entertainment centres. With the end of mass enlightenment under socialism, the shopping centre or the mall would take over the diversionary and educative functions of these old cultural palaces. The rhythms of political movements and mass mobilization campaigns have been replaced with the hectoring sales pitch of merchants, the promise of astronomical reductions, and the lure of great bargains.

While new shopping centres have mushroomed, old shopping areas have not been spared the attentions of the developers. Yuyuan in Shanghai, with its famous garden and teahouse in the centre of a lake in the old city, blossomed into a labyrinthine shopping complex, while in Beijing the Wangfujing Boulevard (formerly known as Morrison Street, (Molisun jie), named in honour of the Australian-born journalist and political advisor George E. Morrison, d. 1920, who had lived there) underwent a radical makeover to mark the fiftieth anniversary of the People's Republic in 1999. The trees that lined the avenue were felled and many buildings (excluding a few like the No. 1 Department Store) were razed to give rise to gargantuan and characterless shopping centres and malls, including a bland new Dong'an Market (formerly the East Wind Market, and before that a charming shopping centre beloved of old Beijing/Beiping residents). In a symbolic gesture showing that the business of the self-styled socialist state is commerce, the street was transformed and it now competes with similar renovated mall complexes at Xidan, Dongsi and numerous other locations around the city. As Beijing's oldest shopping avenue, the pedestrian mall of Wangfujing has been 'twinned' with the Champs Elysées in Paris. Like many other shopping complexes it too features outlets for homogeneous global favourites like KFC, Delifrance and Starbucks.

The shopping flaneur – ready to snap up the latest fashion for self-adornment and aggrandizement – has replaced the old-style ruffians and street-smart wisecrackers of **Wang Shuo**'s fictional world. China has its own mallrats, and it also has the charisma to attract international wannabe flaneurs whose actual world is the maze of merchandise. While Walter Benjamin (creator of the unfinished 'Arcades Project') is popular among the theoretically driven connoisseurs of the Chinese street, in real life consuming commodities is not so much an act of everyday resistance to the Party-state as an endorsement of capital and the allure of material goods.

GEREMIE R. BARMÉ

Shu Ting

(née Gong Peiyu)

b. 1952, Futian

Poet

Shu Ting is an important and influential poet especially in the years immediately after the **Cultural Revolution**. Her love poems in particular enjoyed a large readership in the early 1980s. Shu spent three years working in the countryside and eight years in a light-bulb factory before becoming a professional writer in 1980. Shu's first published poem, 'To the Oak Tree' (*Zhi xiangshu*, 1978), appeared in *Today* (*Jintian*), an underground journal run by the dissident poet **Bei Dao**. Since then her name has become entwined with Bei Dao and his associates, known as the Misty poets (*Menglong shiren*; see **Misty poetry**). Like most of these poets, Shu rejects the formulaic and slogan-like language as well as the stereotypical feelings that characterize much of socialist realistic poetry. She digs into the predicament of human existence, for example 'On the Assembly Line' (*Liushuixian*), and at the same time attempts to give voice to personalized feelings.

For the most part, Shu Ting is read as a 'female' poet in the sense of being a poet who explores sexual difference. 'To the Oak Tree' in particular describes an awakening of sexual consciousness expressed in the search for the ideal male figure. Shu's construction of this imaginative figure is the first contemporary projection of self-identity by a Chinese woman writer. It is revisionist and subversive of the desexualized image of male and female revolutionaries represented in the didactic works of the Mao era (see **sexual attitudes**). 'To the Oak Tree' marks a transition from Maoist politics to a burgeoning interest in the variety of human experience in the post-Mao era.

Further reading

Chen, Xiaomei (1995). *Occidentalism: A Theory of Counter-Discourse in Post-Mao China*. New York: Oxford University Press.

Kubin, Wolfgang (1988). 'Writing with your Body: Literature as a Wound – Remarks on the Poetry of Shu Ting'. *Modern Chinese Literature* 4.1/2: 149–62.

Shu, Ting (1994). *Selected Poems. An Authorized Collection*. Trans. Eva Hung. Hong Kong: Renditions.

—— (1995). *Mist of My Heart: Selected Poems of Shu Ting*. Trans. Gordon Osing and De-an Wu Swihart. Beijing: Panda Books.

HE DONGHUI

shuhao

(book numbers)

A *shuhao* (literally book number) is a registration number required to publish any book in China. *Shuhao* are allocated by the Ministry of Press and Publications (MPP) to recognized publishers as a means of controlling book publishing in a country where it is still considered a politically sensitive industry. Without a book number it is illegal to publish. In the post-Mao reform era, the commercialization of book publishing has also led publishers to realize how lucrative can be the publication of controversial titles, making the authorities all the more enthusiastic in their efforts to control book numbers. Publishing houses must still be state-owned enterprises in China although the country's recent entry to the World Trade Organization has seen some relaxation on the rules pertaining to Sino-foreign joint ventures.

Book numbers, which are also required for printed publications other than books such as calendars, posters and so on, have long been the focus of illicit trading and exchanges among publishers. *Shuhao* are allocated in blocks to publishers according to their expected production. The rigid system of allocation, however, inevitably leads to some publishers having excess book numbers in some years while others experience a shortfall. Publishers with surplus book numbers have then found it convenient, and occasionally lucrative, to sell off their extra numbers to others. The MPP has tried with difficulty to control this trade over the years.

See also: bestsellers; book publishing; state control of media

KEVIN LATHAM

shuilu zhai

Buddhist ritual

For the past millennium the *shuilu zhai* (Purificatory Feast/Fast of Water and Land), or *shuilu fahui* (Ritual Assembly for the Creatures of Water and Land), has been one of the most conspicuous rites of the Chinese Buddhist repertoire. Like the Daoist **Jiao** (offering ritual), to which it bears a resemblance, Buddhist clergy have routinely performed the *shuilu* on major nodes of the Chinese festival year as a means for renewing relationships between the human community and the cosmos, and on an ad hoc basis in times of crisis for pacifying disruptive forces. Today it is most widely contracted for mortuary purposes, from whence comes its characterization as the '*tour de force* of Buddhist rites for the dead'.

Typically the *shuilu* takes seven days to complete, although a three-day version also circulated in earlier periods. The performance involves a massive outlay of human and material resources, with multiple layers of ritual activity taking place concurrently at several different altar sites. The core protocol of the *shuilu*, staged in the central 'inner altar' (*neitan*), devolves around the two phases of 'offering to the upper assembly' of supramundane or enlightened Buddhist deities and saints (*sheng*) and 'offering to the lower assembly' of afflicted beings (*fan*) who inhabit the six mundane realms of cyclic rebirth (samsara). During the latter phase, the 'lower' denizens of cyclic rebirth (including local Chinese gods (*shen*), 'dispossessed souls' (*guhun*) and the liminoids of purgatory (*wanghun/ling*)) are purified through bestowal of the Buddhist precepts and escorted into the presence of the supramundane Buddhist deities in the 'inner altar'. There the two assemblies affirm their mutual commitment to the Buddhist Three Jewels in a massive fête of food and Dharma. Thus the *shuilu* plays out as a 'grand purificatory feast' (*dazhai*) and rite of 'universal salvation' (*pudu*), its reference to 'waters' (*shui*) and 'land' (*lu*) deriving from the claim to assemble and deliver, *en masse*, creatures who inhabit the most trying domains of samsara.

Like most Buddhist rites, the *shuilu* locates its religious efficacy in the absolute primacy of the 'Three Jewels' (Buddha, Dharma, Sangha) and traditional Buddhist cosmological and soteriological norms. But within the course of the liturgy itself, this power also serves to mediate second-order relations between human clients and local gods or the dead, concerns that are often considered to be the domain of Chinese **local religion** (see also **temple fairs**). Through a deliberate appropriation of non-Buddhist idioms, the lore of gods, ghosts and ancestors is reinscribed within a master Buddhist framework of ritual and ideology, while the salvific technologies of the latter are exported to the broader field of Chinese religious concerns.

Buddhists trace the *shuilu*'s genesis to Emperor Wu (r. 502–49) of the Liang dynasty, although this attribution is most certainly apocryphal, given the absence of any verifiable evidence of the its existence prior to the end of the ninth century. While its precise origins remain obscure, by the end of the Northern Song (960–1,127) the *shuilu* became a well-established part of the Buddhist ritual topography, with dedicated *shuilu* halls and troupes operating in most major monasteries across the realm. Contemporary practitioners of the *shuilu* in the PRC, Taiwan, Hong Kong and Singapore uniformly follow the version of the rite developed by the late-Ming reformer Yunqi Zhuhong (1535–1615). However, this situation is of rather recent historical vintage, Zhuhong's version having eclipsed earlier traditions through active promotion in the national ordination system sponsored by the Qing imperial court (1644–1911).

The enthusiasm for science and modernity that heralded the collapse of the imperial system in 1911 brought troubled times for the *shuilu*, especially among critics who saw the rite as a holdover of debilitating feudal regimes and superstitions of the past (see **religion, recent history of**). Repulsed by the image of Buddhist monks reduced to the role of funeral-monger, the Republican era Buddhist modernizer Taixu (1890–1947) rejected the *shuilu* as a debasement of the Buddha's 'original' spirit of rational insight and self-cultivation. Although the *shuilu* continued to be performed in Taiwan, Hong Kong, Malaysia and Singapore, it suffered the severest setback under the proscriptions on public religious activity enacted by the PRC, its practice reaching the brink of extinction during the **Cultural Revolution**. With the subsequent opening of China and relaxation of religious policies in the late 1970s, interest in the *shuilu* has come back strongly. The initial impetus for this resurgence has come mainly from returning overseas Chinese who sponsor the rite for kin who have died during their absence, although the recent boom in China's economy has fuelled an increase in local patrons. In both instances, the motives are similar to those that have inspired performances of the *shuilu* for the past thousand years, namely as a traditionally sanctioned means to heal the traumas of dislocation, death and loss. For the monks, it has once again become an important source of revenue, providing resources to rebuild institutions devastated by the Cultural Revolution.

See also: Gongde

Further reading

Davis, E. L. (2001). 'Appendix: *Huanglu jiao* and *Shuilu zhai*'. In *idem*, *Society and the Supernatural in Song China*. Honolulu: University of Hawai'i Press.

Stevenson, D. (2001). 'Text, Image, and Transformation in the History of the *Shuilu fahui*, The Buddhist Rite for Deliverance of Creatures of Water and Land'. In M. Weidner (ed.), *Cultural Intersections in Later Chinese Buddhism*. Honolulu: University of Hawai'i Press.

Strickmann, M. (1996). 'Les banquets des esprits'. In *idem*, *Mantras et mandarins: Le bouddhisme tantrique en Chine*. Paris: Gallimard.

Welch, H. (1967). 'Rites for the Dead'. In *idem*, *The Practice of Chinese Buddhism, 1900–1950*. Cambridge: Harvard University Press.

DANIEL B. STEVENSON

shunkouliu

(doggerel verse)

Shunkouliu are anonymous doggerel verses. They are also called *minyao* or folk rhymes. They are especially of the topical and political types, and reflect ordinary people's opinions. To a certain extent, they are similar to political cartoons in the West. Numerous *shounkouliu* have been created to satirize **corruption** in an entertaining way. E.g.

1

Lian yu Bu Lian

Bu lian gongzuo lian wuchi,
Bu lian xianqi lian xiaomi.
Bu lian maowu lian bieshu,
Bu lian jiejian lian shechi.

Love and Don't Love

They don't love work but a dance floor.
They don't love their good wives but their young mistresses.
They don't love their thatched huts but villas.
They don't love thrift but luxury.

2

Da majiang santian-wutian bu shui,
He Maotai sanping-wuping bu zui,
Gan zhengshi sannian-wunian bu hui.

He can play **mahjong** for three to five days without sleep,
And drink three to five bottles of Maotai liquor without a hangover,
But he can't do anything properly in three to five years.

3

Gaoji ganbu youlong-xifeng,
Zhongji ganbu zuofeng bu zheng,
Putong ganbu liumang cheng xing.

High-ranking cadres amuse themselves with men and women,
Intermediate-ranking cadres are dishonest and immoral in their ways,
Ordinary cadres have become by second nature hooligans.

4

Dang guan bu pa hejiu nan,
Wanzhan-qianbei zhi dengxian;
Yuanyang huoguo teng xilang,
Haixian shaokao zou yuwan;
Sangna anmo zhoushen nuan,
Majiang zhuo qian wugeng han;
Geng xi xiaojie bai ru xue,
Sanpei guo hou jin kai yan.

An official doesn't fear the hardship of drinking;
And thinks nothing of endless cups and glasses.
The steaming 'lover's hot pot' simmers;
There're also seafood and barbecued fish balls.
Sauna and massage make him warm all over,
And he plays mahjong till it gets cold just before dawn.
What makes him happier is that the girl has snow-white skin;
He's all smiles after Ms Three Accompanies has done whatever he wanted.

Shunkouliu (1) depicts the **xiaomi** (mistress) phenomenon; (2) and (3) mock the Party style and high-level mistress scandals and corruption cases, such as Cheng Kejie; (4) is especially popular as it is an imitation of Mao's poem, 'Long March', praising the Red Army which had endured extreme hardship. Now many cadres have abused their power to have a good time, including using 'Ms Three Accompanies' (*sanpei nülang*, see **bao ernai**). The government is ambivalent towards *shunkouliu*, but has no recourse. Many in fact have been legally published and are a hit, as those quoted here. A few of them have been included in **xiangsheng** (cross-talk) and comedies. There are many variations of the published ones. With the wide use of **cellular phones**, new *shunkouliu* and variations of the well-known ones spread more quickly.

See also: drinking games; neologisms; political jokes

Further reading

Link, P. and Zhou, K. (2002). 'Shunkouliu: Popular Satirical Sayings and Popular Thought'. In P. Link, R. Madsen and P. Pickowicz (eds), *Popular China: Unofficial Culture in a Globalizing Society*. Lanham, MD and Oxford: Rowman and Littlefield, 89–109.

HELEN XIAOYAN WU

Silk and Bamboo

(Sizhu)

Traditional music genre/ensemble

The phrase 'Silk and Bamboo' is a direct translation of the term *sizhu*, which refers to any one of the various regional Chinese musical ensembles composed of a combination of mellow-sounding string and wind instruments. In the ancient Chinese system of instrument classification called *bayin* (eight sounds), which divides musical instruments according to the type of material producing their sound, string instruments fall under the category of *si* (silk) and wind instruments under *zhu* (bamboo). The term *sizhu* has appeared in poetry for a long time, but its common use by Chinese scholars to refer to a particular instrumental genre dates only from the 1950s.

Sizhu instrumentation varies in number and in kind, depending upon the region. An ensemble may have as few as two instruments – one string and one wind instrument – or as many as ten or more. The string instruments typically include bowed and plucked lutes, such as **erhu**, *yehu* and/or other similar types of two-stringed fiddles; plucked lutes such as **pipa**, *sanxian* (in two sizes), *yeqin* and *ruan*; and plucked as well as hammered zithers such as **zheng** and *yangqin* (see **qin**). The wind instruments may include either one or both of the transverse and end-blown bamboo flutes (**dizi** and *xiao* respectively) and/or a *sheng* mouth-organ. A few small percussion instruments may also be played for rhythmic accompaniment. These often consist of a woodblock, one or two small drums, a clapper and, sometimes, a pair of small concussion bells (see **luogu**).

Sizhu music is a form of chamber music that is often performed within the confines of a music club or a private home for self-entertainment. Its practice is typically accompanied by the adoption of Confucian aesthetic values and behaviour by its performers. These include performing this music strictly as amateurs without thought of monetary compensation; emphasis on simplicity, refinement and moderation in the rendering of the music as manifested by the judicious use of melodic ornaments, even rhythms, a restrained tempo and fine tone production; and, last but not least, communality and equality in the distribution and interaction of the various instrumental parts by means of heterophony which heightens the timbral differences. There are several Chinese regional sizhu traditions, most of them in the south, and aside from instrumentation they also vary from each other in terms of historical development and performance conventions. The major genres include **Jiangnan sizhu**, **Chaozhou-Hakka sixian**, **Minnan nanyin** and **Guangdong yinyue**.

MERCEDES M. DUJUNCO

silk industry

In recent years, China, with strong support from the government, has become the biggest silk producer in the world, but only in terms of total output and output of raw materials. According to the Foreign Economy Department and the Cocoon and Silk Office of the State Economic and Trade Commission, China's silk industry has to foster its own brands in order to develop. China can satisfy the needs of the international market in quantity, but not in quality and variety and it has a very limited influence on global prices, even if its output of silk can meet 70–80 per cent of the demand on the world market.

At present, China's silk industry depends heavily on export (about 80 per cent of China's silk products are sold on foreign markets). The main concern among Chinese officials is now the disastrous effects the silk industry may face if and when exports drop, as domestic demand still remains limited. Thanks to joint ventures in the late 1980s and early 1990s with silk giants such as Mantero S.R.L., the industry has already made breakthroughs in technological development in resistance against crushing, shrinking and colour fading, as well in producing printed silk. Most Western companies are totally dependent on Chinese silk producers for raw silk and have been trading it for technology hardware (such as computerized looms) and advanced training. At the same time, Western and especially Italian companies are wary of disclosing their entire know-how to Chinese silk factories and feel threatened by the awareness that China will become a strong silk power by employing these high technologies. However, there are difficulties for the silk industry at present, such as lowering prices for cocoon silk on the domestic market, a decrease in exports, the cancellation of quota controls, and stricter technological requirements from European and American markets.

PAOLA ZAMPERINI

simplified characters

(jiantizi)

Chinese characters have been evolving throughout recorded history, roughly from the 'oracle bone script' (*jiaguwen*), through the 'great seal script' (*dazhuan*), 'small seal script' (*xiaozhuan*), and 'clerks' script characters' (*lishu*), to the 'regular script' (*kaishu*). Various cursive calligraphic styles, moreover, further abbreviated the strokes in the 'regular script', which has lasted for about two thousand years and is still in use today. Due to the push towards modernization a century ago, the Chinese language has undergone many reforms – the importation of Western punctuation marks, the romanization of Chinese characters, the use of the written vernacular (*baihua*) instead of Literary Chinese. In 1935, the Nationalist Government proposed 324 simplified characters which in fact had been in use for centuries, but this was the first time attention had been drawn to standardization.

The PRC government wasted no time in reforming the written Chinese language. Following 'The First List of Variant Characters Arranged' (*Diyipi yitizi zhengli biao*), set by the Script Reform Commission of China (SRCC) in 1955, it stated that all publications would have to stop using the variants beginning in 1956, except for classical works. In 1956, the State Council announced the 'Chinese Character Simplification Scheme' (*Hanzi jianhua fang'an*), which contained 515 simplified characters. In 1964, the SRCC published 'The Complete List of Simplified Characters' (*Jianhuazi zongbiao*), containing 2,238 simplified characters and fourteen simplified components. In 1986, the **State Working Commission on Language** (Guojia Yüwei) promulgated a new edition of the list, returning five characters to their complex forms and giving more detailed explanations of some characters in use. Meanwhile, the State Council officially abolished a 'Second Chinese Character Simplification Scheme (Draft)', which had been published in 1977 and used briefly.

Some scholars suggest that it is more accurate to translate *jiantizi* as 'simple form of characters' ('simple form' or 'simple characters', for short) instead of 'simplified characters' which correspond to *jianhuazi*. It is also more accurate to translate *fantizi* as the 'complex form of characters' ('complex form' or 'complex characters', for short) rather than 'traditional characters'. The reason lies in the fact, according to many historical linguists, that over 80 per cent of the so-called 'simplified characters' are as 'traditional' as the complex forms, and many have an even longer history.

In the age of information technology, many people assume that switching between the simple and complex forms would be easy. It is largely true, but proofreading and corrections are still essential, because (1) simple and complex characters do not correspond one to one; (2) the variants (*yitizi*) are often not recognized by the software that is designed according to the PRC's national standard (*guojia biaozhun*; *guobiao* or GB for short); and (3) 'The Correspondence List of the New and Old Script Codes' (*Xinjiu zixing duizhao biao*), a list always included in standard **dictionaries**, is ignored by most people, including writers and teachers of Chinese. It is no wonder Chinese software users are frustrated switching between the two forms of characters, as are Chinese teachers who may not find a corresponding character in the three sections of 'The Complete List of Simplified Characters'. It is interesting to note that Singapore introduced its own list of simplified characters, which, except for about forty characters, is the same as that introduced in China. The differing characters were later changed according to the GB of the PRC.

See also: Chinese as a foreign language; writing reform movements; writing systems; Xinhua zidian, Xinhua cidian

HELEN XIAOYAN WU

Sino-Tibetan language speakers

The Sino-Tibetan language family is a high-level grouping of languages, at the same level as Indo-European, with over a billion speakers worldwide. On the basis of historical reconstruction of vocabulary, the nearly 300 languages in this family are believed to be historically ('genetically') related. This family is divided into the Sinitic and Tibeto-Burman groups. Scholars differ as to whether other languages in the region, especially the Tai-Kadai (Zhuang-Dong) languages and the Miao-Yao (Hmong-Mien) languages, should be included within this family. Scholars outside China tend to exclude them, while scholars within China tend to include them. Many languages, such as Bai, have not been fully studied, and their classification is uncertain.

Tibeto-Burman speakers number approximately 60 million, in China and in many bordering nations, especially mainland Southeast Asia and north India. The best-known of these languages within China is Tibetan, with around 4 million speakers and a well-preserved literary collection; the best-known Burmese languages are called Loloish, of which Yi is a prominent example, with nearly 7 million speakers.

In China itself, most people are speakers of Sino-Tibetan. Virtually all Han Chinese, constituting 92 per cent of the population, are native speakers of Sinitic languages. The remaining 8 per cent of the population considered ethnic minorities speak an assortment of languages, many – but not all – of

them Sino-Tibetan. Sixteen or seventeen of China's fifty-five officially identified ethnic minorities speak Tibeto-Burman languages. Other minorities in China speak languages classified as Altaic (including Turkic, Tungusic and Mongolian), Mon-Khmer (Austroasiatic), Tai-Kadai, Miao-Yao and Indo-European; Taiwan's aboriginal peoples speak Austronesian (Malayo-Polynesian) languages. The linguistic complexity of the region is cross-cut by national boundaries, with many speakers of various languages straddling national borders.

Recent efforts to link Sino-Tibetan to broader linguistic groupings include a proposed Sino-Caucasian, a larger grouping called Eurasiatic, similar to the somewhat controversial construct of the macro-family Nostratic, which aims to reconstruct a common ancestor to Indo-European, Altaic, Afro-Asiatic and other language families.

See also: dialects; ethnicity, concepts of; Han

Further reading

Matisoff, James A. (1991). 'Sino-Tibetan Linguistics: Present State and Future Prospects'. *Annual Review of Anthropology* 20: 469–504.
Ramsey, S. Robert (1987). *The Languages of China*. Princeton: Princeton University Press.

SUSAN D. BLUM

Sixth Generation (film directors)

The Sixth Generation of directors denotes the group of mostly independent filmmakers who began directing after 1989. They are sometimes also called the 'urban generation' because of their focus on city culture. Generally acknowledged as the founder of the Sixth-Generation style is **Zhang Yuan**, whose third feature **Beijing Bastards** (*Beijing zazhong*) – with its marginal characters, semi-underground life style, low budget, non-professional actors and improvised script – became the representative piece of new urban cinema in the early 1990s.

The often improvised style and focus on social issues created a cinema verité with a very different atmosphere from the national epics of the **Fifth**

Generation (film directors). Themes such as homosexuality, substance abuse, drifting youths, small crooks or divorce often made it difficult to pass through censorship, and consequently, most of these films were shown to overseas audiences first and remained unavailable to the general public in China. Central directors and films are: Wang Xiaoshuai's *Frozen* (*Dongchun de rizi*), *Seventeen-Year-Old Bicycle* (*Shiqisui de danche*) and, most recently *Drifters* (2003), produced by Peggy **Chiao**; **He Jianjun**'s *Postman* (*Youchai*); **Lu Xuechang**'s *The Making of Steel* (*Zhangda chengren*); and Wang Chao's *Orphan of Anyang* (*Anyang gu'er*). **Wang Quan'an**'s *Lunar Eclipse* (*Yue shi*) and **Lou Ye**'s *Suzhou River* (*Suzhou he*) tend towards the mystical and added art film to urban realism. **Jia Zhangke**'s two features, *Little Wu* (*Xiao Wu*) and *Platform* (*Zhantai*), remain two of the most important films for their pointed but stylish look at friendship, love, family and post-Mao society.

See also: New Documentary Movement; Tang Danian

Further reading

Cornelius, Sheila (2002). *New Chinese Cinema: Challenging Representations*. London: Wallflower Press.

Cui, Shuqin (2001). 'Working from the Margins: Urban Cinema and Independent Directors in Contemporary China'. *Post Script* 20.2/3 (Winter/Spring): 77–92.

Dai, Jinhua (2002). Trans. Wang Yiman. 'A Scene in the Fog: Reading the Sixth Generation Films'. In Jing Wang and Tani Barlow (eds), *Cinema and Desire: Feminist Marxism and Cultural Politics in the work of Dai Jinhua*. London: Verso, 71–98.

Lau, Jenny Kwok Wah (2003). 'Globalization and Youthful Subculture: The Chinese Sixth Generation Films at the Dawn of the New Century'. In *idem* (ed.), *Multiple Modernities: Cinemas and Popular Media in Transcultural East Asia*. Philadelphia: Temple University, 13–27.

Teo, Stephen (2003). 'There is No Sixth Generation: Director Li Yang on *Blind Shaft* and His Place in Chinese Cinema'. *Sense of Cinema* 27 (July/August). Online journal, available at http://www.sensesofcinema.com [interview with Li Yang].

Wedell-Wedellsbord, A. (1995). 'Chinese Literature and Film in the 1990s'. In R. Benewick and P. Wingrove (eds), *China in the 1990s*. Basingstoke: Macmillan.

Zhang, Yingjin (1998). 'Chinese Cinema and Transnational Cultural Politics: Reflections on Film Festivals, Film Productions, and Film Studies'. *Journal of Modern Literature in Chinese* 2.1: 105–32.

BIRGIT LINDER

skyscrapers

The 1990s' urge to be the tallest follows the 1950s' impetus to be the largest. When the Soviet Union was the standard for political and cultural expression, Red Square next to the Kremlin in Moscow, the largest parade ground of its kind in the world, was the model to be emulated and exceeded. **Tiananmen Square**, the creation of which in the 1950s saw the destruction of the formal entrance to the Imperial City, was built as the largest space for Party-orchestrated spectacle in the world. It was; and so it remains. At the time, plans were even mooted to raze the imperial palace and construct a 'Chairman's Office' complex that would compete with the Kremlin. It was the late 1950s, however, and China was experiencing the worst man-made famine in history. Moderation, and economic good sense, prevailed. Mao and his fellow leaders resigned themselves to ruling from nearby Zhongnanhai, a former sequestered imperial lake palace that had housed local government offices during the Republican era.

Since the 1970s, an urge for altitude has swept the nation, and in the 1990s the competition between and within cities produced ever more extravagant skyscrapers. They are touted as the 'triumph of modern [read "international commercial"] civilization' by investors and developers. As a new wave of reforms hit Shanghai, first the Oriental Pearl TV Tower (1995) was erected on Pudong, the eastern bank of the Huangpu River, facing 'old Shanghai' and the Bund to become the third tallest tower in the world (outclassing similar aspirant towers in Beijing and Tianjin). The low-lying façade of the treaty port buildings of the Bund became a floodlight-drenched themescape that is in stark contrast to the vertiginous po-mo skyline of Pudong.

In 1998 the Jin Mao Tower, a super-tall structure of eighty-eight storeys, was completed. Arguably the most graceful of all the high-rise buildings of the reformist era, the Jin Mao is the tallest building in China and third tallest in the world after the Petronas Towers in Kuala Lumpur and the Sears Tower in Chicago. Like most of the other new gargantuan skyscrapers in China's cities, Jin Mao was designed by an international architectural firm and built by a foreign construction company. Although vaunted as palaces of commerce, such buildings can readily put on a political turn, and in November 2002 the façade of Jin Mao was emblazoned with the slogan 'Celebrate the 16th Congress of the Chinese Communist Party'. However, it is destined to be outclassed by the tallest building in the world, the 101-storey Shanghai World Financial Centre built at the heart of the Lujiazui Finance and Trade Zone in Pudong and projected for completion in 2007 (construction by a Japanese firm having been delayed for many years supposedly as a result of the Asian financial downturn of the late 1990s). The building is of symbolic significance for a city that aims to rival Tokyo and New York as an international financial centre. Meanwhile, the urban wannabes of Beijing have been plotting their own gigantism, and an even higher skyscraper is planned for the capital that will outdo both the finest of China's south and the new World Trade Center towers in New York.

In the 1990s, Shanghai saw the construction of some forty-one skyscrapers (buildings exceeding 500 feet or 152 metres in height), in comparison to a handful in Beijing and other Chinese cities, although Hong Kong has constantly added to its man-made mountains of skyscrapers. While one skyscraper was built in China over the decade 1970–80, and fourteen in the first ten years of the reforms, during the 1990s fifty-two skyscrapers were constructed. The buildings feature in numerous TV shows and ads, in movies and in literature, where the 'white-collar worker' has become both a leading protagonist and a ready consumer of new cultural products. China's vertical building boom is expected to wane during the decade to come for reasons of economy, market saturation and, of course, terror.

GEREMIE R. BARMÉ

smoking

Chinese Communist leader Mao Zedong was a lifelong smoker, often photographed with a cigarette; and Deng Xiaoping, architect of China's post-Mao economic reforms, also was a chain-smoker, but reportedly gave up smoking some years before his death. Today, none of the top leadership smokes in public, and bans on smoking in meeting rooms extend to the Great Hall of the People in Beijing. Yet smoking still looms large on the social and economic landscape.

China is the world's largest producer and consumer of tobacco. The state tobacco monopoly generates approximately 10 per cent of state revenues. Two out of three Chinese adult men smoke, and nationwide there are more than 300 million male smokers and just 20 million female ones, but rates among women as well as youth are rising. The human toll of smoking is correspondingly huge: approximately 700,000 Chinese die each year of smoking-related illness, and that figure is expected to reach 3 million annually by 2025.

Chinese smokers spend an average of 15 per cent of their income on cigarettes. Foreign cigarettes are priced high due to import taxes and constitute only a small part of Chinese consumption, although smuggling and counterfeiting are widespread. China does not limit imports, but Chinese brands still take 70 per cent of market share. To date, the Chinese government has strictly limited foreign investment in the domestic industry, although China's admission to the World Trade Organization makes additional concessions to foreign tobacco interests likely in the future, while also giving Chinese tobacco leaves and cigarettes more outlets in the global marketplace. Since the mid 1990s, the national legislature and many localities have placed broad curbs on tobacco advertising as well as restrictions on smoking in public places, but implementation is highly variable.

JUDY POLUMBAUM

socialist spiritual civilization

Political concept

In line with the social changes under Reform, the Party-state has attempted to formulate new values and concepts that aim to raise the ideological awareness of the Chinese. The most important element in this learning process is the building of a system of 'socialist spiritual civilization' (SSC). Deng Xiaoping first raised the concept in 1980, and it subsequently has become one of the main planks of Jiang Zemin's political programme.

SSC should reflect and match the improved material conditions in large sections of society, and at the same time should guide people in the social transformation taking place. SSC was to create a superior moral civilization that would raise the people's political consciousness and morality by fostering revolutionary ideals and discipline without giving in to 'bourgeois liberalizing influences'. Many old ideals had to be redefined and given new meaning; they had to be represented in a new and fresh manner in order to be applicable in this 'New Era'. Moreover, SSC had to serve as a brake on the severe social dislocation and the various negative social aspects of nihilism, commercialism, hedonism and consumerism that arose in the course of modernization.

Marxism–Leninism, Mao Zedong Thought remained at the core of SSC. To update this core and to provide the modernization process with a semblance of a theoretical basis, Jiang added Deng Xiaoping Theory in September 1997. Moreover, Jiang set out to leave his own ideological footprints in 2000. Important elements of Jiang Theory are the so-called 'Three Represents' (**Sange daibiao**), which attempt to replace ideology with loyalty to the CCP without doing away with it altogether.

As part of SSC, the Party-state has taken important steps to harness Chinese history to the project. In pre-Reform China, the notion that Chinese history basically was at the root of all that was wrong, and responsible for everything that was feudal or backward, was widespread. Now, the past is reappraised and presented as the foundation from which the reforms in the present logically have sprouted. Similarly, China's historical development inexorably had to result in the founding of the CCP and the leading role it plays in society. Moreover, by appropriating history in this manner, the Party can truly present itself as the sole heir to the Chinese tradition.

To bring about this reappraisal, many important icons and personages of the non-Communist past have been brought into play to instil feelings of national pride. Huangdi, the Yellow Emperor, for example, the foundation figure of all Chinese history and civilization, is no longer seen as an element of folklore, as a metaphysical figure that needs to be criticized, but is in fact lauded as the unifier of the nation. The most remarkable of the rehabilitees (see **revivals and other 're-' words**) is probably Confucius, who became the focal point of mass criticism in 1974 (see **Confucius (recent interpretations)**). In 2000, however, it was officially admitted that efforts during the **Cultural Revolution** to erase Confucius' influence had proven unsuccessful.

The rehabilitation of Confucius is even more significant when we look at its wider consequences in the international arena. It enables China to join the ranks of neighbour states that invoke Confucian culture to strengthen their position versus the decadent and potentially dangerous influences of Europe and the United States. This gives more credibility to the Chinese desire to strengthen its position in the region. Moreover, the economic successes of Japan, South Korea and Singapore have not led to the same social dislocation to which China has fallen victim. The influence of values such as self-control, stability and conformity is seen as one of the major reasons behind the social cohesion in these countries. It testifies to certain redeeming qualities in the Sage's teachings that may find application as a way to fill China's moral and ethical void. Hundreds of Chinese public schools have started offering classes in Confucianism since the late 1990s, attracting some 2 million students.

SSC has failed to manifest itself as a new superior moral civilization, if only because the CCP itself lacks a clear moral framework. Moreover, the use of CCP-defined socialism as the controlling and sanctioning ideology to guide SSC has turned it into a self-defeating process. Instead of acting as a facilitator, the CCP has turned into a stumbling block for the type of modernization that more and more Chinese want. Over the years, the values of collectivism and altruism have been replaced by private and material desires, which require instant gratification. Party rule and tight control, in particular in the cultural and the political arenas, are considered impediments to the realization of these desires.

STEFAN LANDSBERGER

socio-political values

China's transition from a Stalinist to a 'socialist market economy' has greatly impacted the Chinese socio-political values. Since the 1980s, China has been seized by a series of crazes: from 'knowledge', 'diploma', 'college' and 'going abroad', to 'doing business', 'purchasing stocks', 'investing in real properties' and 'maximizing income sources'.

The transition is marked by the coexistence of mixed values. The dominant traditional values of patriarchy, egalitarianism and contempt for profit-making are declining. Western values are making inroads: 44.2 per cent of a survey sample chose Bill Gates as their hero while only 13 per cent picked Paul Kortchagine, a USSR Communist model popular among elder Chinese. Law is increasingly important in everyday life. Cases of litigation have risen exponentially. Hatred for wealth is replaced by envy. The Leninist idea of 'All individuals are only gear wheels in a great mechanics' is yielding to that of self-realization through talent. Belief in money's omnipotence is pervasive, so much so that corruption runs rampant despite risks of harsh punishment. Consumers are often victimized by profiteers. While emphasis on love improves the quality of marriage, divorce, extramarital affairs and prostitution are also on the rise.

Meanwhile, new socio-political values are stemming from the economic reform, characterized by

Deng Xiaoping's maxim: 'Any cat, black or white, that catches mice is good.' When asked whether they preferred socialism or capitalism, 52 per cent of the samples surveyed did not care. Even the CCP begins to represent the Chinese interests across the board instead of a few segments.

See also: consumerism; morality; reform (ideological justifications); 'socialist spiritual civilization'; xiahai

YUAN HAIWANG

Softhard Wizards

(Ruanying tianshi)

Singer/songwriters

Forerunners of indigenous Wulitou (Nonsense) Culture in Hong Kong, Softhard Wizards are the most alternative singer-songwriters in Cantonese pop music. The two Wizards, Jan Lamb and Eric Kwok (born in Hong Kong in 1967 and 1966, respectively), were originally disc-jockeys of Commercial Radio Hong Kong. Starting their careers as traffic reporters in the 1980s, Softhard Wizards soon developed their unique styles – addressing serious topics with funny presentations – to attract audiences. *The Nursing-Home Hour* (*Laorenyuan shijian*, 1992–5) was their hottest radio programme, and they released three albums between 1991 and 1993.

Featuring their own lyrics and occasional melodies, Softhard Wizards' albums continued their humorous approach to social issues, including fashion, drugs, sex and idol worship. Technically rapping most of the time instead of singing, Softhard Wizards neither encouraged nor criticized the issues they targeted, but rather assumed the role of spectators and reporters. Inspirationally, their popularity confirms the suitability for Hong Kong of the indirect approach. Softhard Wizards terminated their musical collaboration in 1995, but remained quasi-attached as broadcasters. Lamb continued to release solo albums intermittently, yet probably reflecting the maturation of the Wizards, his more recent songs were more alienated from the masses than before.

See also: rock music, rock bands

SIMON SHEN

Song Dong

b. 1966, Beijing

Performance, installation artist

While studying academic painting at Capital Normal University (BFA, 1989), Beijing artist Song Dong was strongly influenced by the **85 New Wave [Art] Movement**. An internationally acclaimed avant-garde artist, his performance, installation and video art resists commercialism by portraying a private spiritual world discrete from an external material one. In *Breathing* (1996), he created a patch of ice in **Tiananmen Square** using only his breath, and in *Water Writing Diary* (1995–present) he produces an ephemeral record written in water on a rock similar to his *Printing on Water* (1996), performed in a river near Lhasa.

Song's challenge to the hegemony of academy art includes organizing a seven-city exhibition, 'Wildlife: An Experimental Art Project Held Outside Conventional Exhibition Spaces and Devoid of Conventional Exhibition Forms' (5 March 1997–5 March 1998). His contribution, *Displacing Central Axes*, subverts Beijing's symbolic ascendancy over its subjects. He first mapped out the respective central axes of Beijing and his home, took photos along each axis, and created two long narrow compositions. Finally he transposed the photograph of one axis onto the other in reality, resulting in a complex inversion of public and private space. He and his wife, **Yin Xiuzhen**, produce similar effects in their installations utilizing relics collected from Beijing construction sites from which families were forcibly relocated.

Further reading

Gao, Minglu (ed.) (1999). *Inside Out: New Chinese Art*. San Francisco/New York: San Francisco Museum of Modern Art and Asia Society Galleries, New York [for *Printing on Water* and *Water Writing Diary*].

Song, Dong and Yin, Xiuzhen (2002). *Chopsticks/Kuaizi*. New York: Chambers Fine Art.

Wu, Hung (2000). *Exhibiting Experimental Art in China*. Chicago: Smart Museum of Art/University of Chicago Press [for *Father and Son in the Ancestral Temple* and *Wildlife*].

—— (2000). *Transience: Chinese Experimental Art at the End of the Twentieth Century*. Chicago: Smart Museum of Art/University of Chicago Press [for *Breathing*].

ROBIN VISSER

Song Yonghong

b. 1966, Quyang, Hebei

Painter

After graduating from the Department of Printmaking at the China Academy of Fine Arts in 1988, Song Yonghong moved to Beijing where he took part in two landmark exhibitions, **China Avant-Garde** (1989) at the **China Art Gallery** and 'The New Generation' (1991) at the Museum of Chinese History (see **Yin Ji'nan**).

Bringing the techniques of etching to oil painting, Song's canvases are inhabited by people, objects and scenes executed with sharp edges and solid colours. They either lack or possess well-defined and heavy shadows. Such treatment, together with the puppet-like movements of the characters – often portrayed as lost in sexual desires – communicates a strong sense of disorientation. 'Anxiety' is the perfect word to describe Song Yonghong's oeuvre. This quality has never abandoned Song's visual domain since the time of 'Burning Reality', his first solo show held in 1995 at Hanart T Z Gallery (see **Chang Tsong-zung**) in Hong Kong, and has returned even more acutely in his recent series, *The Bath of Consolation* (*Weijie zhi yu*), which was also the title of a solo exhibition organized at the Museum of the Central Academy of Fine Arts in 2001. Using a reduced palette of mainly blue, pink and dark grey, Song portrays a series of lonely souls caught in the act of bathing. Unlike his earlier paintings, there is no cynical derision in the description of the figures of softened contours sculpted out of a dark background. They appear soiled rather than cleaned by drops of a substance too thick and sticky to be called water.

Further reading

Doran, Valerie C. (ed.) (1993). *China's New Art, Post-1989, with a Retrospective from 1979 to 1989* (exhibition catalogue). Hong Kong: Hanart T Z Gallery, 168–73. [Reprinted in 2001 by Asia Art Archive, Hong Kong.]

Li, Xianting (1995). 'The Immediacy of the Burning Reality'. In *Song Yonghong. Burning Reality* (exhibition catalogue). Hong Kong: Hanart T Z Gallery.

Song, Yonghong (2001). 'Yishu Suibi' [Random Notes on Art]. In *Weijie zhi yu* [*The Bath of Consolation*] (exhibition catalogue). Beijing: Other Shore Arts, Inc.

TANG DI

Southern Excursion Talks (Deng Xiaoping, 1992)

A relatively new political phenomenon in post-Mao China has been the high frequency of visits by national leaders to the provinces. In some instances, these so-called inspection trips have led to major policy decisions. From 18 January through 21 February 1992, Deng Xiaoping journeyed to the southern cities of Wuchang, Shenzhen, Zhuhai and Shanghai, delivering talks on economic and political matters. Unlike trips by other leaders, Deng's southern tour (*nanxun*) soon assumed an extraordinary importance in Chinese economic and political developments.

Deng called on political leaders of all levels, particularly those in the provinces, to break free of socialist ideological strictures and boldly adopt measures associated with capitalism – market mechanisms, stocks and stock exchanges, foreign investments. According to Deng, what counted were increases in production, productivity, living standards and national strength. Deng encouraged Chinese officials to emulate Singapore, which had succeeded in creating a dynamic economy along with a stable political and social order (see **political culture in Singapore**). For these reasons, Deng wished to see the Party install young reformers in leading positions.

The timing of Deng's trip seems to have been associated with the turnaround in the political situation in Eastern Europe and particularly with the collapse of the conservative coup in Russia. And with the pro-democracy movement of April–June 1989 still fresh in his mind, Deng apparently decided that to ensure the survival of the CCP there was no alternative but to carry the reforms even further. The domestic situation in China was worrisome, as the conservatives in Beijing had launched a propaganda campaign in 1990–1 to discredit the reforms. Deng was determined that the new Party leadership that would emerge in the Fourteenth Party Congress later that year would be overwhelmingly reformist.

Deng's southern tour produced two immediate results. First, Deng's designated successor, Jiang Zemin, was emboldened to act more decisively than he had before and implemented a series of experiments with the introduction of stocks, the reduction of price controls, the closure of inefficient state enterprises, and the installation of a civil service system. Second, Shanghai became the new growth centre of China, for what Deng had wanted for all of China was where Shanghai had excelled in the pre-Communist era (see **political culture in Shanghai**).

Deng and his successors also wished to gain symbolically from the trips. The regular inspection tours were a substitute for democracy, by signifying that the post-Mao Communist Party had moved closer to the people, in contrast to Mao's aloofness and isolation. Second, Deng's southern excursion reflects the fact that the political centre of China, for all ages, lies in a paramount leader, not in a national consensus derived from a constitutional and representative process.

See also: xiahai

Further reading

Daily Report-Supplement: China (1992). 'Deng Xiaoping's Southern Trip'. *FBIS-CHI-92-063-S* (1 April 1992): 1–18.

MacFarquhar, R. (1992). 'Deng's Last Campaign'. *The New York Review of Books* (12 December): 22–8.

ALAN P. L. LIU

Southwest Art Research Group

(Xinan yishu yanjiuqunti)

A mid 1980s group from Yunnan and Sichuan who reacted against the sentimental beauty of **Native Soil Painting**. Stating that art should move souls rather than eyes, they ditched representation of generic figures in favour of depicting personal experience. Their passionate and subjective approach, known as 'stream of life' (*sheng huozhiliu* or *shengmingzhiliu*), was a countercurrent of 'rational painting' in the **85 New Wave [Art] Movement**. Notable works include Mao Xuhui's intense, frank exploration of the self and private space in his series *Figures in a Concrete Room* (*Shuini fangjianli de renti*, 1986), *Private Space* (*Siren kongjian*, 1987) and *Patriarch* (*Jiazhang*, 1989–2000). Also **Zhang Xiaogang**'s poetic allegories of life and death and Ye Yongqing's paintings on themes of nature, urban life and escapism. Portraying a personal, psychological realism, their works reflected on the existence of the soul and the instinct to live: an attitude that questioned the values of civilization and explored the individual's need for self-preservation.

The group grew from a core of artists which held the 'New Figurative [*Xin juxiang*] Painting Exhibition' in June 1985. One of the earliest self-funded and initiated exhibitions, it brought the art of southwest China first to Shanghai, and subsequently to Nanjing. Following the nationwide trend, they established themselves formally as the Southwest Art Research Association in August 1986 with a membership of thirteen. The group held several slide shows and conferences in Shanghai and Kunming in 1986, co-organized the large-scale 1988 Southwest Modern Art Exhibition, Chengdu, and featured prominently in the 1989 **China Avant-Garde** exhibition.

Further reading

Gao, Minglu *et al.* (1991). *Zhongguo dangdai meishushi 1985–1986* [The History of Contemporary Chinese Art 1985–1986]. Shanghai: Shanghai renmin chubanshe, 241–60.

'Southwest Modern Art Exhibition' (1988) (exhibition catalogue). Special issue of *Huajia* [Painter] 9 (Hunan meishu chubanshe).

van Dijk, Hans (1992). 'Painting in China after the Cultural Revolution: Style Developments and Theoretical Debates (Part II: 1985–1991)'. *China Information* 4.4 (Spring): 1–17.

EDUARDO WELSH

spirit-mediums

Mediums possessed by the local gods played a prominent role in the religious life of China into the twentieth century. These mediums channel the commands of the gods to their supplicants. Some also channel the dead. Some mediums write out messages or medical prescriptions from the gods with a planchette on sand or some other medium. Many are illiterate, but nonetheless compose powerful talismans. To demonstrate the power of the possessing god, these mediums cut themselves with swords, skewers or other weapons, displaying an uncanny imperviousness to pain. They also perform extraordinary feats, such as falling into trance, leaping and shouting, climbing sword ladders, walking across fire, and so forth. They still frequent temple festivals in Taiwan, in the Chinese communities of Southeast Asia, and in southern China. In south China these mediums are referred to as 'divination lads' or 'children of the gods'. After going into trance, they often go barefoot, loosen their hair and don a child's apron. Such activities have been declared illegal and branded as prime examples of 'feudal superstition' by Republican and CCP governments, and they are still illegal under the most recent, comparatively relaxed regulations on lawful religious practice in China (see **religious policies of the state**). Despite these bans, in the past twenty years performances by spirit-mediums have become fairly common in many parts of China, particularly in the southeast coast of Fujian, where mediums frequently enter into trance on the festivals of the local gods (see **temple fairs**). They are carried on sedan chairs in processions, skewer or cut themselves, climb sword ladders, and consult with the gods or the dead to solve urgent social or familial problems. Young mediums are beginning to emerge, but in most areas the traditions of training and transmission have been interrupted. In a few areas, all young village boys are given training in the chanting of invocations, collective dance and ritual performance inside temples to prepare for a role as either a spirit-medium or an altar-lad assistant. Chinese spirit-mediums should be distinguished from shamans of the Siberian kind, who go on long spirit journeys. Some journeys to the underworld have been reported by a class of mediums working with **Daoist priests** involved in death rituals, but the majority of mediums in China are possessed by local gods or dead relatives, and act out communication between the unseen and the visible.

Further reading

Davis, Edward (2001). *Society and the Supernatural in Song China*. Honolulu: University of Hawai'i Press.

Dean, Kenneth and Zheng, Zhenman (1994). 'Group Initiation and Exorcistic Dance in the Xinghua region'. *Min-su ch'ü-i* [Studies in Ritual, Folklore and Theatre] 91: 567–640.

KENNETH DEAN

sports arenas

Until the reform era introduced financial and cultural concerns, major sports events were occasions for the display of state power. In Beijing, the Workers' Stadium was built in preparation for the First National Games of the PRC in 1959 and subsequent National Games were held there. Economic reform, however, brought about a change in the management of stadiums and gymnasiums: No longer subsidized by the state, they support themselves through renting space to shops, selling advertising signage, running hotels

and taxi fleets, and charging admission. The Asian Games Village was constructed in the north of the city for the 1990 Asian Games and has since become a major tourist site charging admission. No longer commemorating only the power of the central state, the natatorium was funded by a wealthy Hong Kong developer, Henry Fok, with his name prominently displayed. Another new concern was that stadium architecture should possess 'Chinese characteristics', such as the dragons and cauldron added to the Workers' Stadium for the 1990 Asian Games, and the sloping roofs at the Asian Games Village. Plans for the 2008 Beijing Olympic Games have budgeted US$2 billion for the construction and renovation of thirty-two venues in Beijing, five elsewhere, and an Olympic village in northern Beijing near the Asian Games Village on a site that had been reserved by city planners for that purpose because of its good **fengshui**.

See also: architectural styles; Olympics

SUSAN BROWNELL

Stars

Artist group

The 'Stars' were the earliest Chinese artistic group that broke through the unified state-politics-centred format of 'Revolutionary Realism' to pursue a free, modern and politically truthful artistic spirit. On 27 September 1979 on the eastern side of the **China Art Gallery** (Zhongguo meishuguan) in Beijing, the Stars organized the first street exhibition, which was closed by the police few hours later. After a march of protest, the exhibition was hosted between 23 November and 2 December at the Huafang Studio in Beihai Park with a total public attendance estimated at 200,000 people. A second exhibition took place a year later between 24 August and 7 September at the China Art Gallery. The name 'Stars' was explained by artist Ma Desheng: 'Every artist is a star...We called our group "The Stars" in order to emphasize our individuality. This was directed at the drab uniformity of the Cultural Revolution.' Stylistically they sponsored a kind of incessant creativity typical of the work of Pablo Picasso, while promoting at the level of content a humanistic spirit such as that expressed by the work of the German artist Kaethe Kollwitz. In particular their work explored the spiritual hardships caused by the period of the **Cultural Revolution**. This created a heated reaction both at a social level and within artistic circles. Representative artists of the group include, among others, **Wang Keping**, Ma Desheng, **Mao Lizi**, Huang Rui, Li Shuang, Yang Yiping and Bo Yun.

Further reading

Hui Ching-shuen, Janny (ed.) (1989). *The Stars: 10 Years* (exhibition catalogue). Hong Kong: Hanart T Z Gallery.

Li, Xianting (1980). 'Guangyu "Xingxing" meizhan' [On the 'Stars' Exhibition], *Meishu* (8–9 March).

Lü, Peng and Yi, Dan (1992). '"Xingxing" shijian yu lishi' [The 'Stars' Incident and History]. In *Zhongguo xiandai yishu shi* [A History of Modern Art in China], Changsha: Hunan meishu chubanshe, 69–83.

van Dijk, Hans (1994). 'The Fine Arts after the Cultural Revolution: Stylistic Development and Theoretical Debate'. In Jochen Noth, Wolfger Pöhlmann and Kai Reschke (eds), *China Avant-Garde: Counter-Currents in Art and Culture*. Oxford: Oxford University Press, 14–39.

LI XIANTING (TRANS. FRANCESCA DAL LAGO)

State Administration for Radio, Film and Television

The State Administration for Radio, Film and Television (SARFT) is the central government body that oversees these three sectors of the media. It is responsible for a wide range of projects and activities that come under the general remit of promoting development, organizing and funding research, granting licences and permissions when required, drafting laws and statutes as well as regulating and policing radio, film and television production and transmission throughout the country. SARFT has a split identity in two ways. On the one hand it is an organ of both the Party and the State, and on the other it is responsible not only for the regulation and supervision of film and broadcasting but it also has responsibilities itself for the production of propaganda. It is directly in charge of Chinese Central Television (CCTV), China People's Radio (CPR) and China Radio International (CRI).

Formerly the Ministry of Radio, Film and Television, SARFT has branch offices at all levels of government down to the township level which supervise the broadcasting and film industries within their local jurisdiction. The branch offices have some degree of autonomy – for instance, in the daily running of **cable television** networks but are always responsible to the levels above them.

With the development of cable television networks, usually under the immediate control of branch offices of SARFT, broadband and increasing attention to 'three networks convergence' (i.e. computers, television and telecoms), in recent years the Administration has found itself periodically in competition with the more powerful **Ministry of Information Industry** (MII), responsible for computer and telecoms networks (and see **Internet (history and structure)**). This competition is not only for control over emerging networks but significantly, with the enormous commercial value of China's media, also over emerging markets.

See also: CCTV (Chinese Central Television); film distribution; Pearl River Economic Radio; satellite television

KEVIN LATHAM

state control of media

All media in China have the designated function of supporting, promoting and serving the Party and the government as their 'mouthpiece' and vehicle for propaganda. However, despite the Party's insistent and unbending retention of this principle, in the post-Mao era it has been at times openly questioned by media professionals and academics and gradually subverted by a depoliticization of some areas of media production on the one hand, and by the commercialization of media on the other.

Until the late 1990s all media organizations had to be state owned, run and controlled. However, the opening up of the media to commercial market forces from the early 1980s onwards has put media practitioners in a difficult position, sandwiched between government or Party control and the obligations and restrictions that this entails on the one hand, and commercial pressures for more popular, lively, varied and relevant media products on the other. These often opposing pressures have seen Chinese media production develop characteristics of its own that seek to satisfy both sets of demands.

So, for example, the newspaper industry has seen the emergence of hundreds of new **evening newspapers and weekend editions** since the beginning of the 1990s (see **newspapers**; **Nanfang Weekend**; **Yangcheng Evening News**). Radio stations have been forced to find more competitive styles of presentation (see **radio (stations and content)**; **Pearl River Economic Radio**), and the television industry has come to split its production into political and non-political realms. The former, most notably news, remains firmly under Party control, while the latter – for instance the production of television dramas or game shows – has even been opened up to private companies.

With economic reform in the 1980s came a more relaxed attitude to the media than had been seen under Mao. It was also a period of flourishing intellectual debate and optimism. Several very senior journalists and media executives, as well as academics, for the first time openly questioned the sacred link between Party and media and called for greater freedom of the press. These were themes revisited by students and others in the demonstrations of 1989. However, following the events of June that year, a shaken and nervous Communist Party reverted to more conservative understandings of media production. The reformist energies from this time on were channelled more into commercialization than liberation.

Among media professionals, in industry journals, in speeches and at conferences, the Party–media link has once again been tentatively challenged at the end of the 1990s and early 2000s. However, whatever the official stance, of equal or greater significance are the concrete changes that are happening in media practice. Slowly, Chinese media continue to transform themselves, to respond to market demands, to explore new avenues of production and to push the limits of Party control. This is made possible by, on the one hand, the system of self-censorship that implements Party control, and, on the other, by the fact that the individuals in key positions – such as senior editors and managers – are in fact those responsible to both the Party *and* the market. Furthermore, the presupposition upon which the mouthpiece principle is formulated – that the only source of information available is the Party – has become increasingly anachronistic as telecommunications, the Internet, foreign travel and foreign travellers open up the Chinese population to news from other sources.

See also: journalism; newspapers; Party advertising and self-promotion; People's Daily; Xinhua News Agency

Further reading

Keane, Michael (2001). 'Television Regulation: Creative Compliance, and the Myth of Civil Society in China'. *Media, Culture and Society* 23: 791–806.

Latham, K. (2000). 'Nothing but the Truth: News Media, Power and Hegemony in South China'. *China Quarterly* 163: 633–54.

Shoenhals, Michael (1993). 'Media Censorship in the People's Republic of China'. In S. Whitfield (ed.), *After the Event: Human Rights and Their Future in China*. London: Wellsweep.

Weber, Ian (2002). 'Reconfiguring Chinese Propaganda and Control Modalities: A Case Study of Shanghai's Television System'. *Journal of Contemporary China* 11.30 (February): 53–75.

Zhao, Y. (1998). *Media, Market, and Democracy in China: Between the Party Line and the Bottom Line.* Chicago: University of Illinois Press.

KEVIN LATHAM

state policies on minority cultures

The PRC's basic policy on minority cultures is to promote and support them, provided they do not threaten the socialist state or risk separatism. The Law on Regional National Autonomy (see **autonomous regions, prefectures, counties and banners**) bans discrimination against minorities or their cultures, but also forbids acts that undermine unity or instigate division. The policy defends the use of the local language in government, education and law (and see **bilingual education**). Publication in ethnic languages is encouraged as well, official statistics showing that the number of newly published books in ethnic languages rose from 1,385 titles and 11.24 million copies in 1989 to 1,473 titles and 18.96 million copies in 1999 (see **ethnic minority literary collections**; **minority presses**). However, policy also requires the spread of Modern Standard Chinese (*putonghua*) and, with the exception of a few minorities like the Uighurs, Tibetans and Koreans, the local languages are seriously losing out to Chinese.

The state has invested heavily in collecting and preserving the traditional arts of the minorities, and in setting up cultural institutions such as professional song-and-dance and drama troupes and museums showcasing the minority arts. As China modernizes, these professionalized traditional arts are losing hold in most places, including among the minorities. Many of the troupes perform more for tourists than for local people. The number of personnel in professional ethnic song-and-dance troupes in the minority areas fell from 4,908 in 1994 to 3,897 in 1999.

See also: Tibetan theatre

Further reading

Mackerras, C. (1995). *China's Minority Cultures, Identities and Integration Since 1912.* New York: St Martin's Press; Melbourne: Longman.

COLIN MACKERRAS

State Press and Publication Administration (State Copyright Bureau)

State Press and Publication Administration (SPPA), directly under the State Council, oversees China's publication activities and deals with its copyright issues. Since 1954, press and publication have been regulated by SPPA. In January 1987, SPPA was first established wearing concurrently the hat of the State Copyright Bureau. It has corresponding administrations, named 'bureaus', in provinces and cities.

On 25 June 1998, as a result of a reform of government institutions, SPPA was reorganized, with its responsibilities reallocated: import of audio/video products going to the Ministry of Culture and import of programmes used for radio and television broadcasting to the **State Administration for Radio, Film and Television**. SPPA began to take on the duties of supervising printing and planning for processing and publishing ancient books. Jobs such as overseeing China's ISBN (**shuhao**), issuing IDs to journalists and identifying works whose copyrights have been violated were delegated to non-profit organizations directly under SPPA and related community agencies.

SPPA has eight departments of 140 staff whose responsibilities include drafting codes and ordinances related to press and publication, drawing up development plans, examining and approving new publishing houses, monitoring publication activities, supervising the publication and replication of audio and video products, organizing and offering consultation to projects that publish and distribute the important government documents and works of state leaders, cracking down on copyright violation, engaging domestic publication circles in negotiations over bilateral and multilateral international copyright treaties, and managing exchange and cooperation programmes with foreign countries.

HU MINGRONG

State Sports General Administration (Sports Bureau)

In 1952 the State Physical Culture and Sports Commission (Guojia tiyu yundong weiyuanhui) was established as the ministry-level organ responsible for sports and physical education, following the Soviet model. In 2000, its status was changed to that of a bureau (*zongju*), although its functions have remained unchanged. The Sports Bureau system consists of a hierarchical structure of sports training centres: at the base of the pyramid are the local (county, township and city) sports commissions; above them are the provincial and municipal sports commissions; at the top is the State Sports Bureau, which is headquartered on Tiyuguan Road to the east of the Temple of Heaven in Beijing, and which manages the National Team Training Centre there. The organs at each level control the training centres under their jurisdiction. The Sports Commission was a leading organ in the post-Mao economic reforms because the 'mechanism of competition', which had to be reinstated into other spheres of life, had remained an integral part of sports. It was a leader in the practice of contracting projects to individual managers (*chengbao*), and China's success in international competitions was heralded as an example of the benefits of competition, which should be studied by factories, the arts world, and others. As China emerged as a world sports power, the influence of the State Sports Bureau continued to increase, and Beijing's hosting of the 2008 Olympic Games provided an even greater platform to exert influence over Chinese popular culture.

See also: Olympics; physical education; physical fitness and sports clubs; sports arenas; swimming and diving

Further reading

Riordan, James and Jones, Robin (eds) (1999). *Sport and Physical Education in China*. New York: E. and F. N. Spon.

Wu, Shaozu *et al.* (eds) (1999). *Zhonghua renmin gongheguo tiyushi* [History of Sport in the PRC]. Beijing: Zhongguo shuji.

SUSAN BROWNELL

State Working Commission on Language

(Guojia yüyan wenzi gongzuo weiyuanhui)

The State Working Commission on Language (Guojia yüwei, for short), which adopted the name on 26 December 1985, is the successor to the former Script Reform Commission of China (Zhongguo wenzi gaige weiyuanhui, 1954–85) under the State Council. It formulates and enforces language laws, regulations and policies; conducts research on the standardization of Chinese characters and Chinese language information processing; and promotes the use of the romanization system (*Hanyu pinyin*), modern standard Chinese (*Putonghua*) and **simplified characters**. It works closely with relevant organizations under the Ministry of Education such as the Research Institute of Applied Linguistics (Yuyan wenzi yingyong yanjiusuo) and the Putonghua Training and Testing Centre (Putonghua peixun ceshi zhongxin), which holds nationwide Putonghua Contests and runs the Putonghua Proficiency Test and the Language Press (Yuwen chubanshe) with its main publications: *Language and Characters Newspaper* (*Yuyan wenzibao*), *Language Planning* (*Yuwen jianshe*), *Applied Linguistics* (*Yuyan wenzi yingyong*) and *The World of Language* (*Yuwen shijie*). Its Chinese website is www.china-language.gov.cn

See also: neologisms

HELEN XIAOYAN WU

Stories from an Editorial Office

[Bianji bu de gushi, 1991]

Television serial

Stories from an Editorial Office was produced by the Beijing Television Arts Centre and directed by Zhao Baogang and Jin Yan, and is widely regarded as China's first television sit-com. *Stories* was the most talked-about television programme of the immediate post-Tiananmen period, at least until the broadcast of **Beijingers in New York** in late 1993. The 'stories' revolve around circulation difficulties at the lifestyle magazine *Guide for Living* (*Renjian zhinan*) at a time when the Chinese print media was moving from state subsidies to commercial self-reliance. The humour emerges as the editorial team of veteran journalists and youthful tyros seek out new ploys to rebuild their readership.

Despite widespread condemnation by conservative critics for its alleged vulgarity and excessive materialism, *Stories* earned the official 'Fly to the Sky' award (*Feitianjiang*) for its portrayal of reform issues. It also garnered the coveted 'Golden Eagle' award (*Jinying jiang*), which is adjudicated by viewers' votes rather than critics. A fast-paced script, laced with rich Beijing street slang and self-mocking black humour, parodied many Maoist values. The unusual aspect of *Stories* was that journalists were portrayed as enterprising rather than mere cogs in the wheels of the propaganda machine. The distinctive self-mockery (*kan*) that made *Stories* so successful was the work of a team of writers that included **Wang Shuo** and **Feng Xiaogang**. *Stories* provided a splendid vehicle for the comic skills of **Ge You** (one of China's favourite film actors), Lü Liping and Hou Yaohua, a son of the legendary **xiangsheng** artist **Hou Baolin**.

Further reading

Huot, Claire (2000). *China's New Cultural Scene: A Handbook of Changes*. Durham: Duke University Press, 50–5.

Keane, M. (2002). 'Television Drama in China: Engineering Souls for the Market'. In R. King and T. Craig (eds), *Global Goes Local: Popular Culture in Asia*. Victoria: University of British Colombia Press.

MICHAEL KEANE

Stories of Mulberry Village

[Sangshuping jishi 1988]

Huaju (spoken-drama)

Based on Zhu Xiaoping's three related novellas about hardship and struggles in a village in northern China, *Stories of Mulberry Village* was written by Zhen Zidu, Yang Jian and Zhu Xiaoping and produced by the Central Academy of Drama (Zhongyang xiju xueyuan). The production attracted great attention in Chinese theatre circles.

The play is set during the **Cultural Revolution** in a small village enclosed by huge mountains where the barren land cracks when the weather is dry and becomes muddy when wet, and the wooden-wheeled carts are the only transportation. The play includes no central storyline but three intertwined narratives. (1) Li Jindou, the Party secretary and symbol of patriarchal tradition, tries his utmost to flatter and even to bribe the cadres sent by the government in order to keep more grain for his villagers. At one and the same time, however, he manipulates every aspect of the village's life. His widowed daughter-in-law refuses to remarry his younger son and is finally driven to commit suicide by throwing herself into an old well. Her real sweetheart, a labourer from outside, is beaten up and not allowed to return. (2) With Li's help, Fulin's parents have sold their twelve-year-old daughter through a child marriage to gain enough money for getting a wife for their only son (Fulin), a strong young man with mental problems. Provoked by the village youth, Fulin strips his wife in public and chases her around to boast his possession of her. (3) Wang Zhike is the only man who does not share the same surname with the rest of the village. By accusing him of being a murderer and putting him in prison, Li and other villagers manage to get hold of his two rooms in a shabby cave dwelling. The whole village relies on one ox to plough the land, but it has to be killed because a 'revolutionary committee' has been organized and cadres need the meat to celebrate their victory. The play offers audiences a living fossilized image of Chinese peasants' fate on the yellow earth, and the particular tragedy depicted here was caused by feudalism, ultra-leftism and the direst kind of poverty.

The play was directed by Xu Xiaozhong, the Moscow-trained director, teacher and president of the College at the time, as an example of his own ideal of creating a 'new vocabulary' for Chinese spoken drama. He attempted to combine the realistic drama with the aesthetic principles of the traditional Chinese theatre. In fact, the whole company went to the village twice in order to experience real life there. While on the stage, chorus, tableaux and dances rarely seen in spoken drama were used. The scenes of stripping Qingnü, the young peasant's wife, catching adulterers and slaughtering an ox were all presented with rich imagery on stage.

Further reading

Chen, Zidu, Yang, Jian and Zhu, Xiaoping (1994). 'Selection of Scenes from *Stories of Mulberry Village*'. Trans. Sun Zhongshu, Ed. Richard Schechner. *The Drama Review* 142 (Summer): 113–30.

—— (1998). *Sangshuping Chronicles*. Trans. Cai Rong. In Yan Haiping (ed.), *Theatre and Society: An Anthology of Contemporary Chinese Drama*. New York: M. E. Sharpe.

Fei, Faye C. and Sun, William H. (1994). '*Stories of Mulberry Village* and the End of Modern Chinese Theatre'. *The Drama Review* 142 (Summer): 131–7.

Pan, Ping (1999). 'Triumphant Dancing in Chains: Two Productions of Chinese *Huaju* plays in the Late 1980s'. *Asian Theatre Journal* 16.1 (Spring): 107–20.

Xu, Xiaozhong (1994). 'A Report on the *Stories of Mulberry Village* Experiment'. *The Drama Review* 142 (Summer): 106–12.

LI RURU

streets

The streets of contemporary Chinese cities can essentially be categorized according to three types that have roots in imperial history. First are avenues (*dajie*) that originated in the planning of ancient administrative centres, where they usually formed a grid oriented to the cardinal points of the compass. They are predominantly broad, tree-lined and laid out at large intervals between expansive residential, industrial or administrative compounds and concentrated markets, with little street-front activity. Often they include generous bicycle lanes, separated by medians from the automobile lanes. Historically, they served as governmental processional space, and such modern avenues as Chang'an jie in Beijing continue to play this role. A second type of main street, characteristic especially of south China, is the commercial street lined with shophouses, which in many of those cities with migrant ties to Southeast Asia includes arcade-sidewalks. Finally, there are the residential lanes (*xiang, hutong* or *long*) which provide direct access to individual dwellings, though most housing built since 1949 has taken the form of residential districts (*xiaoqu*) of apartment blocks. Reform-era transformations have focused on increasing commercial space and accommodating heavier traffic (see **transportation patterns (urban)**; **urban planning/renewal**), usually by widening existing streets (which pedestrians increasingly cross via overpasses), but also by driving new streets through old blocks. Two new street types are the dedicated pedestrian street (e.g. Nanjing Road in Shanghai and Wangfujing in Beijing, see **shopping malls**) and the consciously historic 'tourist street' (*luyoujie*) which are often the core of historic restoration districts (see **restoration districts (urban)**).

Further reading

Heng, Chye Kiang (1999). *Cities of Aristocrats and Bureaucrats: The Development of Medieval Chinese Cityscapes*. Honolulu: University of Hawai'i Press.

Yang, Dongping (1995). *Chengshi jifeng: Beijing he Shanghai de wenhua jingshen* [Urban Monsoon: The Cultural Spirit of Beijing and Shanghai]. Shanghai: Dongfang Chubanshe.

DANIEL B. ABRAMSON

string ensemble

(Xiansuo)

Traditional music genre

In the strictest sense of the term, *Xiansuo* refers to the instrumental accompaniment for northern sung-narratives (**quyi**) and vocal music derived from regional opera. This is often played on the *sanxian* (long-necked three-stringed plucked lute), but the **erhu** (formerly referred to as *huqin*), **pipa** and/or **zheng** (zither) are also used. Before the eighteenth century, there had developed an ensemble with these four string instruments at the core, and it became identified with the performance of a chamber music repertory called *Xiansuo shisantao* (Thirteen Suites for Strings), which was favoured by the Manchu and Mongol aristocracy who made up the Qing-dynasty literati in Beijing. The nineteenth-century handbook, *Xiansuo beikao*, written and compiled by Rong Zhai, a Mongol nobleman, includes notes on and a score of the thirteen suites, and shows some of the melodies to be similar or related to pieces in the southern pipa repertories of the Jiangsu and Zhejiang schools. According to this source, in practice the string ensemble was occasionally augmented by a secondary ensemble of reed and bamboo instruments, such as the *xiao* and **dizi** bamboo flutes and the *sheng* mouth-organ, thus leading it to resemble a sizhu (**Silk and Bamboo**) ensemble to some extent. The handbook also mentions that this music was known to the blind street musicians of Beijing, and one of them in particular, Zhao Debi, excelled in performing all thirteen suites on the sanxian. With the fall of the Qing in 1911, the northern *xiansuo* tradition has since ceased to exist and hardly any musician today knows the entire repertory. However, some of the pieces survive in the active repertoires of two major contemporary string ensemble genres, Henan bantou and Chaozhou xiyue, and their related solo zheng traditions.

Henan bantou (also known as Zhongzhou guyue) is typically performed as a prelude to the local singing narrative tradition of Henan province called Henan quzi. It can be performed by a string ensemble or by just one person on either pipa or zheng. Henan bantou pieces formerly had texts and could be sung prior to the performance of Henan quzi or completely independent from them. There also used to be the practice of composing poems especially for *bantou* melodies, but perhaps because of their high literary style and content, the resulting textualized *bantou* did not catch on and gradually declined. By contrast, the purely instrumental *bantou* music continues to be performed today.

Chaozhou xiyue is a genre of music performed on a more intimate and scaled-down version of the **Chaozhou-Hakka sixian** (also known as *xianshi*) ensemble that consists of a zheng, a pipa and a small sanxian. As with *xianshi*, Chaozhou xiyue is performed within the context of Chaozhou amateur music clubs for entertainment, often following the performance of a succession of *xianshi* pieces in the form of *taoqu* (sets of variations based on a melody), by which time it is already late in the evening. Musicians will then switch to the softer and mellower-sounding Chaozhou xiyue, performing short stock melodies (*qupai*) from the Hakka sixian repertoire in the highly refined style associated with that regional music tradition.

MERCEDES M. DUJUNCO

student movements

College students have played a highly visible and important role in Chinese politics during the twentieth century. Student activism began in the late Qing period, but it was the May Fourth Movement of 1919 that created the standard by which later student movements would be judged. The two central themes defined the 1919 movement – an ardent nationalism and a quest for social and individual emancipation – have dominated virtually all subsequent student movements. The two themes have not always coexisted comfortably, however, for nationalism tends to engender support for the building up the power of the state, the very entity that students and intellectuals have viewed as an obstacle to the emancipation of individuals or groups within society.

The student movements of the 1980s, which culminated in the massive and widely publicized protests in the spring of 1989, generally focused on the expansion of individual and group rights within a society dominated by the Communist Party. For example, some of the ideals for which students in the 1980s fought included: freedom of speech, freedom of the press, increased political representation, and equality under the law. Not surprisingly, given this set of goals, the student movements of that decade usually came into conflict with the authorities, a point that was underscored, tragically, by the bloody state-led crackdown on 4 June 1989.

The mood and behaviour of Chinese college students has changed significantly since 1989, and might be described as having swung from an emphasis on emancipation to a focus on **nationalism** in the 1990s. In addition, the most recent generation of Chinese students is far more materialistic, careerist and apolitical than the one that came before it. Nevertheless, students at China's top universities still tend to be well informed and deeply concerned about political and social issues even if, as a rule, they are less quick to challenge the authority of the state or to blame the Communist Party for all that ails Chinese society. Indeed, today's students often display strong support for the Communist Party as China's representative on the world stage, and as such they are generally more critical of those whom they perceive as China's geopolitical opponents – first and foremost the United States.

As far as the Communist Party is concerned, a nationalistic generation of students is preferable to one focused on liberation. Still, the Chinese government dislikes spontaneous activism of any sort and looks on highly emotional outpourings by students, even if they are fuelled by patriotic sentiment, with great alarm. From the perspective of the Party, it may well be better to act tough on the international stage than to appear weak and risk incurring the wrath of student activists yearning for a strong China of which they can feel proud. The current generation of Chinese students is thus encouraging their government to adopt hard-line stances in international affairs.

See also: Olympics; Peking University

TIMOTHY WESTON

study abroad

Overseas education is an important experience shared by a large part of the political and cultural elite in China. The first Chinese students were sent abroad in the late nineteenth century, the largest overseas student migration in the world at the time, when more than 10,000 students went to Japan. Since then, and particularly from the 1920s and 1930s, the USA and Western European countries, as well as the USSR, became increasingly attractive. Russia and the socialist countries were the main centres of overseas study during the early years of the PRC. Since the re-establishment in 1979 of a formal programme to send students abroad, approximately 400,000 Chinese have left the mainland to study in the USA, with lesser numbers going to Japan, Canada, Australia and Western Europe. Since the late 1990s, approximately 25,000 students per year study abroad. Although returned students have continuously played an important role in the cultural, political and economical modernization process of China, the returnees, as in the past, often come under attack for their alleged loss of political loyalty and patriotic spirit. And the fact that returnees are often unable to attain what they believe to be adequate positions in their country, among other reasons, has led to the 'brain drain' phenomenon by – 2002, only 140,000 of the students sent since 1979 had returned. Since China joined the WTO, reform-minded government officials have increased efforts to attract these students to come home.

NATASCHA VITTINGHOFF

Su Cong

Composer

Although overshadowed by **Tan Dun**, **Zhou Long** and other of his peers among China's 'New Tide' (*xinchao*) musical avant-garde (see **Third Generation (composers)**), Su Cong holds the unusual distinction of having won an Oscar, a Grammy, a Golden Globe and other international awards for his contribution to the soundtrack of Bernardo Bertolucci's epic *The Last Emperor*

(1987). Su studied composition in Beijing and in Germany, where he attended the München Musik Hochschule and the Ludwigsburg Film Academy. Throughout his career he has pursued an interest in multimedia, composing music for ballet, film, opera and 'media opera', in addition to chamber and symphonic pieces. His affinity for cinema led to the inclusion of his folk-influenced work *Paper Emperor* in the original score for the Bertolucci film. Su's subsequent international awards were widely celebrated in China but are deceptive, as he contributed less than two minutes of music to the soundtrack of *Merry Christmas Mister Lawrence* which was largely written by Japanese composer Ryûichi Sakamoto and US rock musician David Byrne.

He remains active as a composer of concert works incorporating everything from full orchestra to drums and electric guitar, and continues to compose film soundtracks, including the score for **Ning Ying**'s *On the Beat* (*Minjing gushi*, 1995). Su works frequently in Germany, where he has held the post of professor of composition at the Film Academy in Baden-Württemberg. Among his major compositions are the ballet *Distance to Eternity*, the opera *The Franklin Expedition*, and the multimedia chamber opera *When the Sun Is Rising*.

DENNIS REA

Su Shuyang

b. 1938, Baoding, Hebei

Huaju (spoken drama) playwright

Su Shuyang entered the Department of History of China's People's University in 1956. He became an overnight success with his first play, entitled *The Story of Loyal Heart* (*Danxinbu*, 1978). As a representative work in a new genre known as 'anti-"Gang of Four" plays', it depicts a Chinese-medicine doctor, Fang Lingxuan, who strives to invent a new medicine to cure heart disease in the face of sabotage by followers of the 'Gang of Four'. The play ends with the initial success of the experimental medicine, but the happy moment turns sad with the heartbreaking news of the death

of Premier Zhou Enlai. The play continued the Maoist socialist realist artistic tradition, while critiquing the Maoist ideology of the **Cultural Revolution**.

Su's second play, entitled *Neighbours* (*Zuolin youshe*, 1980), further developed the form and content of socialist realist drama by depicting the lives of ordinary people – workers, teachers, Party officials and doctors – who reside in a traditional courtyard home in Beijing. One central character is a retired worker who takes care of the sick, the old and those in need of help, such as a former 'rightist' wrongly accused of having attacked the Party in the late 1950s. In setting, style and language, *Neighbours* worked in the genre of the Beijing-flavoured play, pioneered by Lao She, whose dramas were celebrated for their depiction of Beijing life.

Su's play *Taiping Lake* (*Taipinghu*) further experimented with the Beijing-flavoured play by representing on stage Lao She's own life. It depicts the playwright's last day, on 24 August 1966. After having been brutally beaten by the Red Guards, Lao She wanders around Taiping Lake for a day and night, meditating on the paradoxes of his past devotion to the Party and the present anti-Party charges against him. Puzzled, he engages in conversations with the living – those who still fondly remember his famous works such as *Dragon Beard Ditch* and *Tea House* – and with the dead – his own characters, such as Madman Cheng in *Dragon Beard Ditch*, and Wang Lifa in *Tea House*, the teahouse owner who committed suicide to protest against the miserable old society. *Taiping Lake* also restages scenes from both *Dragon Beard Ditch* and *Tea House* to underscore the dramatic ironies presented by the playwright's life and death in relation to the fate of his dramatic characters. When Madman Cheng from *Dragon Beard Ditch* says to Lao She that he is defenceless against the brutality of others and can only hide, he interrupts: 'Madman Cheng, you should not hide! It is not right for them to beat an honest person like you.' But Madman Cheng insists that he can do nothing, since his character has been written this way. Lao She then promises to change his play, in order that an honest man will not be beaten for nothing! Just as it is too late to rewrite his play, so it is too late to reverse that history in which

Lao She helped create the façade of a happy socialist society.

CHEN XIAOMEI

Su Tong

b. 1963, Suzhou

Writer

Educated in the Chinese Department of Beijing Normal University, Su Tong began publishing short stories before his graduation in 1984, after which he was assigned to Nanjing, where he eventually became editor-in-chief of the literary magazine **Zhongshan**. His novella *On the Run in 1934* (*1934 nian taowang*, 1987) attracted critical attention as an avant-garde rewriting of history. A succeeding novella, *Wives and Concubines* (*Qiqie chengchun*, 1990), also set in the early twentieth century, contained depictions of sexuality and irrationality that attracted popular attention and was adapted into the film *Raise the Red Lantern* (*Dahong denglong gaogao gua*, 1991), directed by **Zhang Yimou**. Su Tong's rising reputation for depicting historical situations saturated with illicit sexuality, bold female characters and unrelieved depravity was confirmed in his first novel *Rice* (*Mi*, 1990), about the rise and fall of a Yangtze River gangster, and in 'Hongfen', the story of two Shanghai prostitutes and their lover at the time of Liberation in 1949–50 which was twice adapted into film: by Li Shaohong as *Blush* (*Hongfen*, 1994) and by **Huang Shuqin** as *Rouged Beauties* (*Hongfen jiaren*, 1995). Critics have been taken with Su's stories of south China as a locus of decadence, centred on his mythical Mapel Village (Fenzgyangshucun). Su also wrote several novels during the 1990s, among them *North of the City* (*Chengbei didai*, 1994) and *Empress Wu Zetian* (*Wu Zetian*, 1994), which continued to develop his fascination with historical topics.

Further reading

Knight, Deirdre Sabina (1998). 'Decadence, Revolution and Self-Determination in Su Tong's Fiction'. *Modern Chinese Literature* 10.1/2: 91–122.

Su, Tong (1996). *Raise the Red Lantern: Three Novellas*. Trans. Michael S. Duke. Harmondsworth: Penguin.

—— (1996). *Rice*. Trans. Howard Goldblatt. Harmondsworth: Penguin (rep. edn).

Xu, Jian (2000). '*Blush* from Novella to Film: The Possibility of Critical Art in Commodity Culture'. *Modern Chinese Literature and Culture* 12.1 (Spring): 115–63.

EDWARD GUNN

Su Xiaokang

b. 1949

Journalist/cultural critic

The son of a Communist Party journalist, Su also turned to journalism as a youth active during the **Cultural Revolution**, and later was sent to study at the Beijing College of Broadcasting. His report on a flood in 1984 introduced his reflections on the disasters of political thought, leading to such popular pieces as 'Memorandum on Freedom' (*Ziyou beiwanglu*, 1987). Taking up an assignment to write a television documentary on the Yellow River, he developed this material into the controversial series **Heshang** (*Deathsong of the River*, 1988). Drawing from the cultural criticism of the 1980s to argue that China's cultural heritage was to blame for the devastation of Maoism and the Cultural Revolution, the television series also provided a scathing indictment of the failures of the post-Mao reform movement at a time when the economy was facing a crisis. Su and many of those involved in the series were subsequently accused of counter-revolutionary activity in the Democracy Movement of 1989. Su, along with others, went into exile, co-authoring a collection of essays re-examining some of the arguments in *Heshang*, titled *Distress of the Dragon* (*Long de beichuang*, 1989).

Further reading

Su, Xiaokang (2001). *A Memoir of Misfortune*. Trans. Zhu Hong. New York: Knopf.

EDWARD GUNN

Su Xinping

b. 1960, Jining, Inner Mongolia

Printmaker

After graduating from the Painting Department of the Tianjing Institute of Fine Arts in 1983, Su Xingping started his career as a teacher in the Department of Fine Arts of the Inner Mongolia Teachers' College, an experience that inspired his earliest lithographic works of nostalgic and quiet scenes of vast grasslands and unchanging people. Growing in a period when art was still commissioned as propaganda, Su wanted to keep a distance from politicized art, directing his attention on individual images extracted from his private feelings about life and time. Having moved to printmaking, with a degree from the **Central Academy of Fine Arts** (see **art academies**) in Beijing (1989), he began to work with intimate black-and-white depictions of social transformations during the decade of open policy promoted by Deng Xiaoping, expressing his deepest concern for the issues of isolation and lack of communication among people emerging in the new course.

By means of a smooth and controlled technique he completed *Dialogue* in 1990, a subject repeated also in 1998. This work reflects the artist's position in the art trends of the early 1990s, when **Cynical Realism** was saturating art with feelings of solitary spiritualism, loss of cultural identity and restricted freedom (in whatever sense). Challenged by the increasing pressure posed by the accelerated economic growth, Su's works of the mid and late 1990s present an in-depth critique to the related psychological concerns, as in the *Sea of Desire* series. Here he depicts the dissatisfaction and unattainable character of desires in a fast-developing society approaching an open market model of pluralism. Su was nominated as candidate for the UNESCO Award for the Promotion of the Arts in 1993. Su has exhibited worldwide, featuring in shows like 'Faces and Bodies of the Middle Kingdom' at the Galerie Rudolfinum in Prague (1997) and 'Inside Out: New Chinese Art' at the Asia Society Galleries in New York (1998).

Further reading

(1997). 'Su Xinping Lithograph – Supplement au No. 203'. *Art et Metiers du Livre* (May/June).

Kesner, Ladislav (1997). 'Faces and Bodies of the Middle Kingdom'. In *Chinese Art of the 90s: Faces and Bodies of the Middle Kingdom* (exhibition catalogue). Galerie Rudolfinum, Prague.

Smith, Karen (1998). 'Su Xinping at Red Gate Gallery'. *Asian Art News* (Jan./Feb.).

BEATRICE LEANZA

Sui Jianguo

b. 1956, Qingdao, Shandong

Sculptor, installation artist

Sui Jianguo graduated in 1980 from the Shandong Art Institute. He fostered his early artistic interests volunteering to run a Cultural House for factory workers during the decade of the **Cultural Revolution**. Subsequently awarded with a master's degree in sculpture from the **Central Academy of Fine Arts** in Beijing in 1989 (see **art academies**). Sui has always balanced a 'bold experimental approach to materials, with his own subdued, personal introspection' (Wu Hung 1999). Since his first sculptural series such as *Balancer* (1988) and *Hygiene* (1989), the mixing of media stands out as a kind of metaphor he first used to delve into the past as a follower of the Native Soil Movement (see **Native Soil Painting**) and then as an intellectual engaged in the social and political debate on developing China with an aspiration for technical perfection. In his monumental installations, stone, granite, wood and fabric coexist with steel and iron, creating a tension between passive and active forces, as for example in the piece *Earthly Force* (1990–2) first exhibited in 1995, where a group of granite boulders are embraced by a net of steel rods. In 1996 Sui Jianguo teamed up with Yu Fan and **Zhang Wang** in the Three Men United Studio, which led to the realization of two big installations, *Property Development* and *Women/Site* (both in 1996).

In the late 1990s, Sui began to insert historical quotations into his works, producing the series of aluminium Mao jackets *Uniform* (1997) and *A Study of Folds* series (1998–9), where the backdrops of post-colonialism and cultural-vacuum issues are invoked by moulding together the aesthetic models of ancient Greece and the Socialist Realism, via the Mao suit. Sui's works have featured in many exhibitions such as 'China's New Art Post 89' at the Hong Kong Arts Centre in Hong Kong (1993), 'Between Heaven and Hearth: New Classical Movements in the Art of Today' at the Museum of Modern Art, Ostend (2001), and 'Open 2001: 4th International Sculpture and Installation Exhibition' in Venice (2001).

Further reading

Desde el Pais del Centre (1995). *Avantguardes Artistiques Xineses* (1995). Barcelona: Centre d'Art Santa Mónica.

Dewar, Susan (1995). 'Sui Jianguo and the Sculptural Dilemma'. *Asia-Pacific Sculpture News* 1.1 (Winter): 28–30.

Feng, Boyi (2002) *Fushihui (Beijing Afloat)* (exhibition catalogue). Beijing: Beijing Tokyo Art Projects.

Wu, Hung (1999). *Transience: Chinese Experimental Art at the End of the Twentieth Century.* Chicago: David and Alfred Smart Museum of Art, University of Chicago, 66–71, 188–9.

BEATRICE LEANZA

suicide

Suicide is a major public health problem for China that is only gradually being recognized. During the period from 1995 to 1999, there were an estimated 287,000 suicides each year, which makes suicide the fifth most important cause of death in the country. Unlike other countries, the female rate is 25 per cent higher than the male rate – primarily because of the large number of suicides of young rural women – and rural rates are three times higher than urban rates. Among young adults between fifteen and thirty-four years of age, suicide is the leading cause of death, accounting for 19 per cent of all deaths. A national study, conducted from 1998 to 2000, that investigated a representative sample of 519 suicides, found that 84 per cent lived in rural villages, 35 per cent never attended school, 62 per cent died by ingesting pesticides or rat poison, 55 per cent had relatives, friends or associates who had shown suicidal behaviour, 63 per cent suffered from a mental illness, and only 7 per cent had ever seen a mental health professional. Financial difficulties, marital conflict and serious illness are the most common negative life events experienced by persons who die by suicide.

The relatively high rate of suicide in China (23 per 100,000), and the unique pattern and characteristics of suicides may be related both to the rapid social changes that have occurred since the economic reforms begun in 1978 and to the low social status of rural women; but the suicide rate in China has been relatively stable over the last fifteen years, and gender inequality is a problem experienced in many developing countries that do not have high female suicide rates, so other explanations also need to be considered. The ready availability of pesticides and rat poisons in rural homes in China, combined with an environment in which there are no strong social or religious prohibitions against suicide make self-poisoning an appealing alternative for persons who are experiencing acute or chronic stress. Of attempted suicides in China, 75 per cent a rate similar to that found in other countries, occur in women; but it appears that a much higher proportion of the attempted suicides in China are impulsive acts following acute interpersonal conflicts. Moreover, the lethality of the poisons used in rural suicide attempts and the lack of well-trained medical personnel in the countryside result in high mortality rates among persons who impulsively ingest these poisons but actually have a low intent to die. This may be one of the main reasons for the higher suicide rate in rural areas and the relatively high rate among females.

Government figures on suicide have been available since 1987, but it is only since the late

1990s that the public have become aware of the magnitude of the problem. Preventive efforts have lagged far behind those of other countries, but there is now increasing momentum to develop a national suicide prevention plan. To be effective, this plan must coordinate the activities of the wide range of agencies and organizations which are needed to develop and test methods to (1) monitor rates of suicide and attempted suicide; (2) identify high-risk individuals or groups; (3) control access to potent poisons, particularly pesticides; (4) provide basic mental health services to rural areas; (5) develop social support networks that give persons experiencing interpersonal crises alternative methods of dealing with their problems; and (6) educate the public about suicide and other mental health issues.

See also: medical insurance; mental health; public health care

Further reading

Pearson V., Phillips, M. R., He, F. S. and Ji, H. Y. (2002). 'Attempted Suicide among Young Rural Women in the People's Republic of China; Possibilities for Prevention'. *Suicide and Life Threatening Behaviour* 32.4: 359–69.

Phillips, M. R., Liu, H. Q. and Zhang, Y. P. (1999). 'Suicide and Social Change in China'. *Culture, Medicine and Psychiatry* 23: 25–50.

Phillips, M. R., Li, X. Y. and Zhang, Y. P. (2002). 'Suicide Rates in China: 1995–1999'. *The Lancet* 359: 835–40.

Phillips, M. R., Yang, G. H., Zhang, Y. P., Wang, L. J., Ji, H. Y. and Zhao, M. G. (2002). 'Risk Factors for Suicide in China: A National Case-Control Psychological Autopsy Study'. *The Lancet* 360: 1728–36.

World Health Organization, Department of Mental Health and Substance Dependence (2001). *Report on Workshop on Suicide Prevention in China* (Beijing, China, 22–24 March). Geneva: WHO.

MICHAEL R. PHILLIPS

Sun Ganlu

b. 1957, Shanghai

Writer

Sun Ganlu first drew critical attention with his short story, 'A Visit to Dreamworld' (*Fangwen mengjing*, 1986). A key representative of **avant-garde/ experimental literature** (*xianfeng xiaoshuo*), Sun's mid 1980s experimentation pushed the limits of fiction, which he wrote as a series of poetic lines unconnected by narrative progression. In his poem-story, *The Postman's Letters* (*Xinshi zhi han*, 1987), inspired by his job as a postman, Suin observed the faith people invest in an interlocutor. Over fifty lines start with 'A letter is …' (*xin shi*…), a play on the multiple meanings of the word *xin*, which also means 'belief' or 'trust'. Sun Ganlu wrote his first novel, *Breathing* (*Huxi*), during his second creative stage from 1989 to 1991. The depressing aftermath of the Tiananmen crackdown informs the narrative, which takes place in Shanghai in the early 1990s. History, memory and gender are prominent themes, and the events are described enigmatically by lush metaphors and random associations. The *modus operandi* is not action but progression towards philosophical and psychological resolution of the protagonist's identity.

Sun's works since the mid 1990s invoke Shanghai's clan history and cultural heritage. Sun depicts Shanghai allegorically as the traditional city gives way to the pressures of global capitalism. His recent novel, *This Place is That Place* (*Cidi shi taxiang*, 2002), is a provocative retrospective on how Shanghai's twentieth-century vicissitudes inform its contemporary ethos.

Further reading

Sun, Ganlu (1997). *Respirer: Roman*. Trans. Nadine Perront. Arles: Philippe Picquier.

—— (1998). 'I Am a Young Drunkard'. Trans. Kristina Torgeson. In Wang Jing (ed.), *China's Avant-Garde Fiction*. Durham: Duke University Press, 235–45.

Visser, Robin (2000). 'The Urban Subject in the Literary Imagination of Twentieth Century

China'. PhD diss., Columbia University, 215–31. [Analysis of *Huxi*.]

ROBIN VISSER

Sun Zhou

b. 1954, Shandong

Cinematographer, film director, actor

Sun began his film career as the cinematographer for the Shandong Agricultural Film Studio which propelled him to the **Beijing Film Academy** and a degree in directing. His early work for the Shandong Provincial Television Station included the prize-winning series *Wu Song*, *Wreath on the Soldier's Tomb* and *A Blizzard Comes Tonight*. The first feature film he directed (*Add Sugar to Your Coffee*, 1987) was nominated for China's Golden Rooster Award, but it was *Heartstrings* (1992) that earned him international acclaim, winning awards both domestically and overseas (Hawaii and Montreal Film Festivals). Thereafter, he suffered a frustrating eight-year drought, when none of his scripts cleared the Film Bureau and he supported himself by making commercials. In 1994, he was scholar-in-residence at the Stuttgart Film College in Germany, and in 1997 was lured back to the Chinese film world with a supporting role in **Chen Kaige**'s *The Emperor and the Assassin*. On the set, actress **Gong Li** persuaded him to develop and direct a film specifically for her. The result was *Breaking the Silence* (*Piaoliang Mama*, 2000), featuring Gong as the single mother of a deaf child in a China moving from state control to private enterprise. Nearly a quarter of the director's cut was excised for political content, leaving only the mother–son story. The film showed in Berlin, won Best Actress in Montreal, the NETPAC award in Hawaii, and numerous awards domestically. Sun's recent opus, *Zhou Yu de huoche* (2002), again showcases Gong Li.

Further reading

Chen, Lora (2000). '*Breaking the Silence*: Sun Zhou' (review). *Cineyama* 50 (Winter).

CYNTHIA Y. NING

Suzhou pingtan

Pingtan, a genre of musical storytelling (see **quyi**), originated in Suzhou at the end of the Ming dynasty and employs the Suzhou dialect as its linguistic medium. It enjoyed its golden age during the first sixty years of the twentieth century in Shanghai as well as in the southern part of Jiangsu and northern part of Zhejiang provinces. It has two forms: *tanci* and *pinghua*. A *tanci* performance can be solo, duo or trio, telling a story through prose narration and lyric singing and accompanied by a plucked instrument, either **pipa** or *sanxian*; a *pinghua* performance is usually staged by one storyteller without singing. In both forms, the stories are generally traditional romances, and the storytellers sit at table but may move around as they impersonate characters in the narration. Stage props mainly consist of a folding fan that can be used to symbolize anything.

While its traditional repertoire was banned during the **Cultural Revolution**, *pingtan* still enjoyed a special status as a preferred medium for singing poems by Mao Zedong, making *pingtan*'s musical component known and appreciated throughout China, despite the dialectal barrier. Since the late 1970s, the traditional repertoire has been revived. With competition from new forms of entertainment, *pingtan* artists are now trying various means to reach and attract audiences. There are now around thirty-five *pingtan* troupes in the region, performing both in traditional and non-traditional venues: *pingtan* theatres (*shuchang*), teahouses and restaurants, professional gala performances (*huishu*), *pingtan* societies (*shuhui*) and radio and television broadcasts. The format of the performance varies in each of these venues. In *shuchang*, each show usually begins with a *kaipian*, an independent aria sung to open the show and to warm up the audience, and is followed by an episode from the previous day's performance. A run of performances lasts anywhere from a week to half a month, after which a new run begins with a couple of different performers. The audiences are mainly dedicated fans and old people. A programme in a restaurant, however, would contain more singing pieces and offer more episodes independent of one another because the audiences are always different. A *huishu* performance is usually held in a large theatre on a festive or commemorative occasion and offers a comprehensive programme composed of a series of short episodes by well-known artists, promising young performers and noted *piaoyou* (non-professional artists), attracting a diverse audience including young people. The regular activities of *pingtan* societies feature both professional and non-professional performers. The venue that reaches the largest audience of different age groups has been radio and television, and certain channels in the region have been providing set time-slots for *pingtan* programmes. More stories on contemporary themes have been added to the *pingtan* repertoire. While performing a traditional story, the storyteller often uses his/her narrative skills to refer to various phenomena of the contemporary society for comments, satire and comic relief.

Further reading

Bender, Mark (2003). *Plum and Bamboo. China's Suzhou Chantefable Tradition*. Chicago: University of Illinois Press.

Jiangsusheng quyijia xiehui (ed.) (1991). *Pingtan yishu* (*Pingtan Arts*) 13. Suzhou: Xinhua chubanshe.

—— (1991–). *Pingtan yishu* (*Pingtan Arts*) 14 on. Suzhou: Jiangsu wenyi chubanshe.

Suzhou pingtan yanjiuhui (ed.) (1982–5). *Pingtan yishu* (*Pingtan Arts*) 1–4. Beijing: Zhongguo quyi chubanshe;

—— (1986–90). *Pingtan yishu* (*Pingtan Arts*) 5–11, Suzhou: Zhongguo quyi chubanshe.

—— (1991). *Pingtan yishu* (*Pingtan Arts*) 12. Suzhou: Xinhua chubanshe;

Wu, Zongxi (ed.) (1996). *Pingtan wenhua cidian* [Encyclopedia of Pingtan Culture]. Shanghai: Hanyu da cidian chubanshe.

DU WENWEI

swimming and diving

China is the world's undisputed powerhouse of springboard and platform diving. With disciplined elegance, technical finesse and explosive style, Chinese men and women perennially sweep competitions in the sport. Chinese swimming, on the other hand, has been a source of great embarrassment, with outstanding performances by women in the first half of the 1990s irretrievably tainted by drug scandals.

Chinese women won three gold swimming medals at the 1992 Barcelona Olympics and took an astonishing twelve of sixteen golds at the 1994 world championships, but suspicions proved justified when seven Chinese swimmers tested positive for drug use at the 1994 Asian Games and four more were caught at the 1998 world championships. One of China's top female swimmers was found with human growth hormones in her luggage. In all, some three dozen Chinese swimmers have tested positive for banned substances over the past two decades. Despite government resolve and considerable effort to clean up the sport, the repercussions of the scandal linger. Nevertheless, China shows continued strength in women's swimming and respectable results among the men. In the 2002 Asian Games, Chinese men and women won twenty swimming events.

In diving, meanwhile, Chinese athletes are unstoppable; they took five of eight gold medals at the 2000 Sydney Olympics, and all twelve golds, as well as men's and women's team titles, at the 2001 university games. Internationally, Russia and the USA provide some serious competition to China's dominance in diving – but Chinese divers' main rivals are each other. The near-legendary springboard diva Fu Mingxia, who earned a record fourth Olympics title at Sydney, has retired and married a Hong Kong businessman. But a new generation of young divers is upholding the tradition. With Tian Liang's victory in the men's 10-metre platform at the 2002 Asian Games, China has added to its record by taking every diving gold for the last six Asiads.

JUDY POLUMBAUM

T

T-shirts and their culture

In 1991 Beijing was swept by a fad for logo-emblazoned T-shirts, or 'cultural shirts' (*wenhua shan*), which carried ironic and tongue-in-cheek silk-screened statements and illustrations. The invention of a frustrated artist and cultural gadfly, Kong Yongqian, the shirts sold at street stalls and in shops throughout the city. Similar to 'attitude T-shirts' in other countries, in the oppressive urban atmosphere of post-4 June Beijing, the 'cultural shirts' proved to be a runaway popular success. They were a reflection of the temper of the times; resulting in numerous imitations; some people even claimed that the shirts gave rise to a 'T-shirt culture' that has flourished ever since.

Slogan T-shirts had appeared on the mainland as far back as the 1950s bearing legends like 'Oppose the US, Support Korea, and Protect the Motherland', or 'Oppose Revisionism, Prevent Revisionism'. Universities and schools also produced shirts bearing their names, either in print or in the calligraphy of Mao (if they were so privileged).

Kong's 1991 T-shirts had their greatest impact in Beijing, a city where sardonic wit and straight-faced irony that often verged on gallows humour were appreciated perhaps more than anywhere else in China. The most famous sayings on his shirts, which soon entered everyday language, included: 'Life's a bore' (*zhen lei*) and 'I'm pissed, leave me alone' (*fanzhe ne, bie li wo*). Others parodied old Party slogans, like 'I'm not afraid of hardship, nor afraid of dying; and I'm not afraid of you' (*yi bupa ku, er bupa si, ye bupa ni*). Still others expressed the frustrated commercial spirit of many in the days before Deng Xiaoping launched a new wave of economic reforms in early 1992, like 'A total failure: I'd like to be a smuggler but don't have the nerve/Wanna be a bureaucrat but ain't sly enough/If I slack off at work I'll be canned/Wanna start a stall but don't have the cash' (*Yishi wu cheng: yao zousi mei dan'r/xiang dangguan'r shao xinyan'r/hun rizi za fanwan'r/qu liantan'r mei ben'r*). The shirts were soon banned, Kong was detained and fined. Soon all that was left of the summer craze of 1991 were innocent and anodyne imitations, as well as the constant use of T-shirts as mobile billboards for brand products.

As Gregor Benton pointed out in an essay on political humour in China:

> **political jokes** are revolutions only metaphorically. They are moral victories, not material ones. To be sure, officials whose pride is wounded will smart for a while and may lash out at those responsible for the hurt. But the more cynical and far-sighted among them know that political jokes and the other small freedoms that irritate some zealots are a useful means of dissipating tensions and of keeping people happy, and that it would be foolish to deal with them too harshly ... To permit jokes against the state is a clever insurance against more serious challenges to the system.

After a stint in Australia and the USA in 1992–4, Kong returned to China and involved himself in a series of unsuccessful get-rich-quick schemes. With the coming of the new century, he, like so many others, turned his attention to the Internet.

Further reading

Barmé, Geremie R. (1999). 'Consuming T-shirts in Beijing'. In *idem*, *In The Red: On Contemporary Chinese Culture*. New York: Columbia University Press, 145–78.

Benton, Gregor (1988). 'The Origins of the Political Joke'. In Chris Powell and George E. C. Paton (eds), *Humor in Society: Resistance and Control*. London: Macmillan, 41.

GEREMIE R. BARMÉ

table tennis

Table tennis played the main role in China's sportive interactions with the outside world until other sports began to overshadow it in the 1990s. After the founding of the PRC, Chinese players quickly entered the ranks of the world's best with a gold medal in the men's singles in the 1959 World Cup. In the 1961 World Cup, the first world sports championships ever held in the PRC, China won three gold medals. Both events stimulated a great deal of patriotic fervour amidst the hardships of the times. 'Ping Pong Diplomacy' in 1971 and 1972 was instrumental in the restoration of Sino-US diplomatic relations. Table tennis was added to the Olympic programme in 1988, and Chinese players took home two gold medals and have dominated the sport since then.

Multiple world champion Deng Yaping became a member of the International Olympic Committee (IOC) in 1997 when an Athletes' Commission was added to give representation to athletes. When Deng played a Taiwanese for the gold medal in the 1996 Atlanta Olympic Games, two Taiwanese fans unfurled a Taiwanese flag, which was forbidden by the 1979 IOC resolution that allows Taiwan to compete in the Olympic Games only if it does not use the symbols of the Republic of China. When

they would not desist, they were led away in handcuffs by the police. Because of its importance in international relations, table tennis is known as 'the little ball that moved the big ball [the world]'.

SUSAN BROWNELL

Tai (Dai), culture of

The Tai live almost entirely in Yunnan. They speak a language that belongs to the Zhuang-Dong Branch of the Sino-Tibetan family (see **Sino-Tibetan language speakers**) and they have their own writing system. The 1990 census showed the Tai with a population of 1,025,128. There are two main Tai branches. The first is the Shui (Water) Tai concentrated in Sipsongpanna (Xishuangbanna), who are close culturally and linguistically to the Thais of Thailand. The second is the Han Tai, who live mainly in Dehong to the northwest of Sipsongpanna and are identical culturally and linguistically to the Shan of Burma.

The prevailing religion is Theravada Buddhism. The Water Splashing Festival, with its religious significance of washing away personal disaster through cleansing the Buddha statues with water, is still prevalent, although it is now more secular than formerly. One reason for boys to enter the temples for a period is to master their own written language, which is yielding to Chinese in the schools. Tai houses are frequently built on stilts with bamboo poles, floors of bamboo mats and livestock and farm tools below. The basic family unit is nuclear. Premarital contacts between men and women are comparatively free. Tai literature is rich in poetry and folk stories. The peacock dance imitates the movements and elegance of the peacock, a bird symbolizing good fortune and happiness for the Tai, and is a good example of the dance tradition. There is a Tai drama, the music being almost entirely Tai, though the costumes and stories are heavily influenced by **Jingju** (Peking opera). Tai drama survives but is in decline, especially in the cities.

See also: Theravada Buddhism among minority groups

COLIN MACKERRAS

Tam, Alan

(né Tam Wing Lun/Tan Yonglun)

b. 1950, Hong Kong

Pop musician

Nicknamed 'The Headmaster' of **pop music in Hong Kong**, Alan Tam was the most popular Cantonese singer in the 1980s. He reached his first career peak in the early 1970s as the lead singer in his band The Wynners, which mainly jammed English-language songs of the era. Yet the unassailable success of Alan was achieved after he left The Wynners in 1978. Since his first Cantonese album, *Naughty Star* (*Fandou xing*, 1979), Alan has released more than a hundred albums in twenty years. Romantic love songs are his trademark, especially 'The Root of Love' (*Ai di genyuan*, 1984), 'Mid-Autumn Romance' (*Aizai shenqiu*, 1984) and the popular 'The Trap of Love' (*Aiqing xianjing*, 1985), which also initiated the disco culture in East Asia. Alan was the biggest winner of Hong Kong pop music awards in the 1980s, until he set an example, soon followed by Anita **Mui** and Leslie **Cheung**, of declining further awards in 1988.

Alan is the most ambitious singer of his generation and has expanded his musical triumphs into other arenas. From the 1980s onwards, he began his own businesses, ranging from restaurants and entertainment enterprises to telecommunications and the Internet. He was among the 800 elite voters who were asked to select the Chief Executive of Hong Kong in 1997 and, in 2002, one of only eight representatives invited to endorse the re-election of the incumbent ruler. Alan Tam's legacy is one of constant upward mobility.

SIMON SHEN

Tamen

(They)

Poets, poetry magazine

'Tamen' is the name both of a group of poets and of a magazine established in 1985 in Nanjing that printed nine issues between 1985 and 1996. Founders of the group were Han Dong, Ding Dang, **Yu Jian** and Yu Xiaowei, young poets born in the 1950s and 1960s who followed regular studies and hold university degrees. Later on, Zhu Wen, Wu Chenjun, Liu Ligan, Yi Sha, Zhu Zhu joined the group. Some of them also became well known as fiction writers (Han Dong, Zhu Wen, Wu Chenjun). Since the beginning, the poet, writer and essayist Han Dong has been the editor of the magazine and, theoretically, the leader of the group.

'Tamen' poets claim to be a pure literary group, open to external contributions and based on literary exchange and mutual growth, such as the literary societies established in China in the 1930s. A true passion for poetry and a spiritual affinity that binds all its members finds its roots in the friendship shared by Li Bai and Du Fu in the Tang dynasty. The group has not put forward poetic theories or a manifesto, refuses literary schemes and opposes a joint method of writing, emphasizing the importance of diversity and the uniqueness of individual experience as starting points of poetic creation as well as a way to resist the homologization of post-industrial society. Their aim is to free Chinese contemporary poetry both from the burden of classical culture and tradition and from the influence of Western culture.

It is possible to find a few aspects shared by the members of the group: a tendency to use simple colloquial language, which represents a serious attack on and a provocation to the ideology of the dominant (poetic) culture; the decision to embody in their poetry themes tied to ordinary daily life, trivial scenarios and insignificant things in order to break ties with the existing value system. It is an anti-heroic and unconventional poetry, one that refuses allusions, quotations and the cultural sedimentation of an elitist language. The intent is to go back to an uncontaminated language, free from established significance in order to express authentic experiences, and extrapolate from the colloquial language the pure musicality of words, because language is not merely a means used by the poet but his companion in the act of poetic creation. The result is poetry that is often prosaic, tends to the narrative, listing facts and objects of daily life in an anti-lyrical style. In this way it succeeds in frustrating the reader's expectations and becomes an expedient able to break down and dissolve the musicality of the verse and its evocative strength.

They also claim that poetry should not live in the illusion of the past but should return to daily life in order to discover its poetic significance, and reveal the beauty of triviality and the absurdity of existence.

See also: Third Generation (poets)

ROSA LOMBARDI

Tan Dun

b. 1957, Simao village, Hunan

Composer, conductor

One of the most internationally famous of contemporary Chinese composers, Tan Dun has received the Grawemeyer and Grammy Awards, and an Oscar for his film score to *Crouching Tiger, Hidden Dragon* (2000, see **China Philharmonic Orchestra**). He has resided in New York City since 1986.

When Tan graduated from the first post-Cultural Revolution composition class of Beijing's Central Conservatory of Music, he had already received national attention as one of the leading 'New Wave' composers, along with fellow classmates **Qu Xiaosong**, **Guo Wenjing** and **Chen Qigang** (see **Third Generation (composers)**). In 1986, at the invitation of Chou Wen-chung, Tan enrolled at Columbia University for postgraduate studies. Almost as soon as he arrived in New York, he was active in the downtown music scene, with performances at the La MaMa Experimental Theatre. His subsequent success as composer and conductor included commissions and conducting engagements with the world's best-known orchestras, including the Boston Symphony and the BBC Symphony. He has also served as artistic director for new music festivals worldwide.

Tan's compositional output to date might appear stylistically disparate, but his search for the core of global musical and artistic experience, and his eagerness to challenge the concert-going convention reveal a composer dedicated to looking beyond the boundaries of avant-garde, folk, popular and classical music styles. Early works such as *On Taoism* (1985) and *Nine Songs* (1989) already incorporated spiritual elements and non-traditional orchestral sounds. His *Orchestral Theatre* series began to involve audience, multi-media and video images. The fourth of the series, *The Gate* (1999), tells the story of three women in a Rashomon-style narrative. Tan has written three other operas, *Marco Polo* (1995), *Peony Pavilion* (1998) and *Tea* (2002), in addition to film scores and *Water Passion after St Matthew* (2000), a commission by the Bach Academy on the occasion of the 250th anniversary of Bach's death. *The Map* (2003) uses video recordings of ethnic minority music-making that Tan recorded on a return trip to his native Hunan province. The video excerpts are played in conjunction with the orchestra and cello soloist, in dialogue or as concurrent musical commentary to each other, revolutionizing the concert convention.

Further reading

Kouwenhoven, Frank (1991/2). 'Composer Tan Dun: The Ritual Fire Dancer of China's New Music'. *China Information* 7.1: 17–39.

Putten, Bas van (1996). 'Tan Dun's *Marco Polo*: A Multi-cultural Journey'. *Chime* 9 (Autumn): 57–62.

Utz, Christian (1998). '"Extreme Cross-Over, Extremely Personal Music" – Interview with Tan Dun'. *Chime* 12/13 (Spring/Autumn): 142–50.

http://www.shirmir.com/composers/Tan_works.html
http://www.tandun.com/

JOANNA C. LEE

Tang Danian

b. 1968, Taiyuan, Shanxi

Screenwriter, director, producer

One of the most talented screenwriters of the Sixth Generation (see **Sixth Generation (film directors)**), Tang brought a new edgy urban sensibility to his depiction of Chinese society, especially its lost misguided youth. A graduate of the **Beijing Film Academy** (1989), Tang was immediately noticed as the writer of **Zhang Nuanxin**'s *Good Morning, Beijing* (*Beijing nizao*, 1990) – a film showing young Beijingers having casual sex, listening to rock music and contemplating abortion.

Tang was one of the three screenwriters involved in **Zhang Yuan**'s **Beijing Bastards** (*Beijing zazhong*, 1993) – with Zhang Yuan and the rock star **Cui Jian** – that goes even further in exploring the dislocation of society as evidenced by a nascent 'counter-culture' of marginal living and rock 'n' roll. After the film was banned, Tang worked in television – writing, producing and directing several dramatic series, including *Where Do You Stay?* (*Ni zai nali douliu*, 1997) and the documentary, *Alley People* (*Hutong renjia*, 1994).

In 1996, *Crazy Guy* (*Qiaozhe ge ren*) won a NHK/Sundance award for Best Screenplay, but was never produced as a film. In 1998, Tang wrote and directed *Jade* (*Yù*), as part of the made-for-TV film series *Super City* (*Chaoji chengshi*), produced by **Lou Ye** for the Shanghai Film Studio. *City Paradise* (*Dushi tiantang*, 2000), his first underground feature, describes the plight and broken dreams of a young peasant leaving his mother and wife in the country while hoping for a better, more 'modern' life in Beijing. Tang also collaborated on the screenplay of Wang Xiaoshuai's award-winning *Beijing Bicycle* (*Shiqisui de danche*, 2000).

BÉRÉNICE REYNAUD

Tang dress

(Tangzhuang)

The craze for *Tangzhuang* (Tang[-dynasty] dress) – a fad for wearing Chinese traditional clothing – swept China around the New Year of 2002, unexpectedly creating an economy of scale. By a conservative estimate, over 2 million Beijing residents alone spent 200–1,000 yuan per person, resulting in a total of 500 million yuan that benefited retailers, wholesalers, tailors, manufacturers, silk factory owners, silkworm farmers and even dry cleaners. Some were even saved from bankruptcy. The fad was attributed to the Asia-Pacific Economic Cooperation (APEC) forum convened on 21 October 2001 in Shanghai, where twenty world leaders were dressed, as they customarily do, in the traditional apparel of the host country. China provided *Tangzhuang*, so named by its designers after 'People of the Tang [dynasty]', the

self-designation of the Cantonese (and Cantonese immigrants who settled Western Chinatowns, called *Tangrenjie*). A group photo of the leaders in *Tangzhuang* lent great beauty to the attire and simultaneously fuelled the pride of the Chinese in their culture – a pride generated by their country's economic success and the prospect of reliving the glory of the great Tang dynasty.

The appeal of *Tangzhuang* lies in the marriage of a traditional theme with fashionable style. Based on the vest worn during the Qin dynasty (221–206 BC), *Tangzhuang* is characterized by a propped collar, sleeves seamlessly integrated with the body, and a buttoned front with knotted decorations. The garment material is mostly silk – blue, red or brown in colour – with elaborate designs of dragons, peonies or the Chinese characters for *fu* (happiness) or *shou* (longevity).

See also: Shanghai Tang

YUAN HAIWANG

Tashi Dawa

(Mandarin: Zhaxi Dawa)

b. 1955, Batang, Sichuan

Writer

One of the most prominent Tibetan authors writing in Chinese, Tashi Dawa was born to a Tibetan father and a Han Chinese mother in the Tibetan region of Kham in Sichuan province. He began to write stories in 1979 and has published several volumes of fiction and essays and produced a Tibetan-language documentary film. His translated works are found in most of the major languages, and scholarly studies of him began to emerge overseas in the mid 1990s.

The story 'Tibet: A Soul Knotted on a Leather Thong' (*Xizang, xizai pisheng koushang de hun*, 1985) was a path-breaking text that is at one and the same time realistic and magical, historical and futuristic. The tortuous path of Tibet's entrance into the modern world unfolds in the daily confusion with technology, in conflicts of belief and value systems, and in the story's structure, which encompasses contradictory notions of time and existence. He continued to explore this theme in its variations, culminating in the novel *The Tumultuous Shambhala* (*Saodong de xiangbala*, 1993). Although raised in a modern environment, Tashi Dawa draws inspiration from various Tibetan traditions and folk culture. Yet his deep concern with the complex issues facing modern Tibet leaves him with no illusions for a Shangri-la that never existed nor seems likely to come. As chairman of the Tibetan Writers' Association, his own career tells the story of a Tibetan intellectual simultaneously searching for roots and modernity and exploring faith and fate, only to embody the dilemma of embracing both.

See also: Root-seeking school

Further reading

Taxi, Dawa (2001). 'Tibet: A Soul Knotted on a Leather Thong', 'For Whom the Bell Tolls' and 'The Glory of the Wind'. Trans. Herbert Batt. In *idem* (ed.), *Tales of Tibet: Sky Burials, Prayer Wheels, and Wind Horses*. Lanham, MD: Rowman and Littlefield.

YUE GANG

Tat Ming Pair

(Daming yipai)

Pop musicians

First emerging onto the Hong Kong popular music scene in 1985, Tat Ming Pair captured and contributed to the cultural ferment and sense of political urgency that characterized the decade following the Sino-British Joint Declaration of 1984. This influential duo, pairing instrumentalist Tats Lau (Liu Yida) with vocalist Anthony Yiu-Ming Wong (Huang Yaoming), positioned itself (along with alternative rock acts such as **Beyond**) in opposition to the Hong Kong star system and mainstream Canto-pop balladry (see **pop music in Hong Kong**). Inspired by the modernist aesthetics and the synthesizer-driven sounds of British new wave bands of the 1980s such as Japan, Ultravox and the Pet Shop Boys, Tat Ming's music

represented a serious and sustained attempt to come to grips with the vagaries of Hong Kong's colonial identity and political predicament in the uncertain years before the handover to the mainland.

The duo's first long-playing album, *The Story of the Stone* (*Shitou ji*, 1987) already exhibited many of the qualities that would garner the band an appreciative following: driving electronic rhythms, strong melodies, literate lyrics packed with cinematic and literary allusions, and a concern for those relegated to Hong Kong's political and social margins. With their ironically titled record, *I'm Waiting for Your Return* (*Wo dengzhe ni huilai*, 1987), the band created Hong Kong's first 'concept' album: sandwiched between a melancholy sonic collage of airline departures (Hong Kong people migrating to the USA and Canada) and arrivals (from the mainland), Tat Ming offered a lyrically complex and wide-ranging suite of songs about the dilemmas of identity in a city doomed to decolonization and political powerlessness – aptly figured in one protest song about the construction of a nuclear power plant in Daya Bay, just across the border with China.

The duo released three more politically challenging and critically acclaimed albums in the ensuing years, allegorically addressing issues as diverse as the Tiananmen massacre and the repression of alternative sexualities in Hong Kong society, before splitting to pursue solo careers in 1991. A reunion album *Viva! Viva! Viva!* (*Wansui wansui wansui!*) was released to much fanfare in 1996, and Tat Ming's legacy continues to inform and inspire both mainstream and alternative musical production in Hong Kong.

ANDREW F. JONES

teahouses

(chaguan)

Before 1949, teahouses were popular social and cultural places for people to pass the time. A teahouse where one enjoyed book-reading or storytelling was called a 'book teahouse' (*shu chaguan*); a house where one tasted only tea in a quiet atmosphere was called a 'pure teahouse' (*qing chaguan*); a house where one enjoyed both wine and tea was called a 'wine teahouse' (*jiu chaguan*); a pavilion or traditional house in an open space where one appreciated the beauty of nature was called a 'wild teahouse' (*ye chaguan*); and finally, a teahouse large enough to perform opera and acrobatics was called a *chalou*. Teahouses of various styles have been revived or re-invented as places for socializing, holding business meetings, or appreciating, or exhibiting, cultural sophistication (especially on 'dates'). Many are very expensive by Chinese standards. Teahouses became fashionable during the 'culture craze' of the 1980s and pervasive since the economic growth of the early 1990s. Tianqiaole chaguan [Happiness at Heaven's Bridge Teahouse], in business from 1933 to 1952, reopened in 1992 with 180 seats, and Laoshe chaguan, named after the author of *Tea House*, was established in Beijing in 1988 with 250 seats. Both entertain people with traditional opera, book-reading, acrobatics and martial arts, serving 'old-Beijing style' tea and snacks or delicacies enjoyed by Qing emperors. Visited by national and foreign political figures, both have also become major tourist attractions. But there are numerous teahouses for young people to enjoy traditional music, or even electronic games and the Internet, and, of course, tea of high quality from southern China served in modern or classic-style pottery.

KIM KWANG-OK

television celebrities

The idea of television celebrity (*zhiming renshi*) took hold in the 1990s. Probably the most widely respected celebrities are Zhao Zhongxiang and Ni Ping, longstanding hosts of the annual *Spring Festival Variety Show* (*Chunjie lianhuan wanhui*). Zhao has hosted this annual event since 1986. He also fronted the magazine show *Zhengda Magazine* (*Zhengda zongyi*) during the early 1990s. A first-generation veteran of **CCTV (Chinese Central Television)**'s *National News Broadcast* (*Xinwen lianbo*), Zhao has presented the high-rating shows *People and Nature* (*Ren yü ziran*) and *Animal World* (*Dongwu shijie*) broadcast on CCTV. He is invariably called upon to host auspicious national events, such as the forty-fifth and fiftieth anniversaries of China's National Day, and

the festive celebrations surrounding the handover of Hong Kong and Macao. His Spring Festival co-host Ni Ping has been the stalwart of *Arts Kaleidoscope* (*Zongyi daguan*) since 1990. However, she has been less successful with her own CCTV talk show called *Chat* (*Liaotian*).

Another well-known celebrity from the early 1990s is Yang Lan, who was the original host of *Zhengda Magazine* until 1994. Yang later hosted a show on Shanghai TV in the mid 1990s called *Yan Lan's Viewpoint* (*Yan Lan shixian*), before moving to Phoenix Satellite Television (Fenghuang weishi). In 2001 she returned to prominence, producing documentary content for Hong Kong-based Sun Satellite Ltd, fronted by herself and Hong Kong film and TV producer Xu Xiaoming. One of the most popular celebrities currently working with CCTV is Cui Yongyuan, the witty and affable presenter of the talk show *Tell It Like It Is* (*Shihua shishuo*).

Further reading

Zhao, Bin (1998). 'Popular Family Television and Party Ideology – the Spring Festival Eve Happy Gathering'. *Media, Culture and Society* 20.1: 43–58.

MICHAEL KEANE

television formats

The most notable trend in Chinese television programming during the late 1990s was the phenomenon of cloning (*kelong*) television formats (*jiemu xingshi*). The need for new domestic programmes had been made acute by the advent of multichannelling and the expansion of cable television stations during the 1990s. Producers on the lookout for new programming ideas that deliver ratings were quick to recognize the advantages of replicating successful formats, even if they originated from a neighbouring television station. The rise in format cloning is significant for the internationalization of Chinese television and the diversification of Chinese culture. Despite criticisms that format cloning signifies a lack of cultural imagination, it nonetheless demonstrates the capacity to integrate and localize global media trends. While television formats, in particular trade in 'reality television', have been a feature of global television industries, Chinese variations have, with a few notable exceptions, been unlicensed. As with international trends, most format cloning occurs in game shows and talk shows. However, there is also considerable evidence of copying of television dramas.

Examples of licensed formats include *Sesame Street* (*Zhima jie*) and *Joy Luck Street* (*Xingfu jie*). The former was produced by Shanghai Television in conjunction with New York-based Children's Television Workshop. The parent company and Shanghai television producers localized the global *Sesame Street* format to suit the expectations of Chinese educators and to accommodate local cultural idioms. *Sesame Street* was first broadcast in February 1998. *Joy Luck Street* represents collaboration between the UK media company Granada and the Beijing-based Yahuan Cable Company. *Joy Luck Street* was based on the English soap *Coronation Street* and was syndicated in a special 6.30 theatre time slot to Chinese **cable television** stations.

In contrast to the few licensed formats, unlicensed formats predominate. Many come from SAR Hong Kong and Taiwan where they have been successful. The sudden proliferation of dating shows in 1998 can be attributed to the success of the Taiwanese-format *Special Man and Woman* (*Feichang nannü*) distributed by Phoenix Satellite Television to Chinese cable stations. Within two years there were dozens of imitations on the mainland. In 2001 the influence of international reality television formats extended to the Chinese media. *Expedition to Shangrila* (*Zouru Xianggelila*) was produced by the Beijing-based production company Beijing Weihan Culture and Media Company, in collaboration with eighteen provincial Chinese television stations. This adaptation of the wilderness reality format drew heavily on the original European *Survivor* but with sufficient localization to make it politically correct and culturally appropriate. Rather than contestants seeking to outwit each other for an ultimate prize, two teams challenge each other to perform thirty tasks in the harsh environment of Tibet. The format also allowed audience voting and feedback through branded websites. Even the well-known international format *Who Wants to be a Millionaire?* has had Chinese clones, such as *Millionaire* (*Baiwan fuweng*) and CCTV's *The Dictionary of*

Happiness (*Kaixin cidian*). While the prizes are more modest than their Western counterparts there is the same fascination with winners and losers, a sure sign of the times in China.

Further reading

Keane, Michael (2001). 'Send in the Clones: Television Formats and Content Creation in the People's Republic of China'. In Michael Keane and Yin Hong (eds), *Media in China: Consumption, Content, and Crisis*. London: Curzon Press, 176–202.
—— (2002). 'As a Hundred Television Formats Bloom, a Thousand Television Stations Contend'. *Journal of Contemporary China* 11.30: 5–16.

MICHAEL KEANE

television magazines

The television magazine format has become a feature of Chinese television schedules, offering a window on to contemporary society. Magazine shows can be broadly classified as investigative news/current affairs or info-tainment formats. The first daily national TV magazine in China was *Oriental Horizon* (*Dongfang shikong*). This began broadcasting on CCTV 1 as a forty-minute morning programme on 1 May 1993, and was revamped in 2000 to a two and a half hour format to compete with increasing competition from imitators.

Oriental Horizon was followed on 1 April 1994 by the harder-edged, primetime evening news magazine show *Focus* (*Jiaodian fangtan*), which has consistently achieved ratings of between 20 and 30 per cent. *Focus* follows the **CCTV (Chinese Central Television)** national news (*Xinwen lianbo*) and features a style of investigative reporting that has been called 'watchdog journalism' in China. The programme closely monitors social problems in China, including environmental vandalism, local government corruption and consumer protection issues. Despite its image of ruthless investigating, it has a normative function of promoting the Chinese Communist Party line on social reform.

Zhengda zongyi, an info-tainment magazine programme sponsored by the Thailand-based Zhengda Fertilizer Company, began production in April 1990. It features participants from different backgrounds interacting with audiences drawn from 'work units'. Throughout the 1990s it maintained consistently high ratings and gained fulsome praise from China's leaders for its innovative travelogue-style format that provided information about other cultures and societies, not to mention its traditional celebration of socialist values. By the late 1990s its audience share had faltered with increasing competition from its many imitators.

Further reading

Chan, A. (2002). 'From Propaganda to Hegemony: *Jiaodian fangtan* and China's Media Policy'. *Journal of Contemporary China* 16.30: 35–51.

Li, Xiaoping (2002). ' "Focus" (*Jiaodian fangtan*) and the Changes in the Chinese Television Industry'. *Journal of Contemporary China* 16.30: 17–34.

MICHAEL KEANE

television programmes

(a weekly programme schedule – CCTV 1)

The first TV broadcast in China occurred in May 1958. However, TV did not become the most important mass medium until the last two decades of the twentieth century, when television sets became more commonly available. Until 1993, only **CCTV (Chinese Central Television)** had national coverage, while provincial and municipal stations were technically restricted to local broadcasting. The situation changed in 1993 when local stations began to transmit their programmes through satellite, which has increased the number of channels available to each region from an average of five in the early 1980s to the present number of over thirty.

The number of TV programmes multiplied in the 1990s due to the adaptation of programme concepts from Euroamerican countries (see **television formats**). For example, news programmes in the form of a combination of journalistic reportage and commentaries *Oriental Horizon* (*Dongfang shikong*) and an in-depth report and commentary on current social issues *Focus Interview* (*Jiaodian fangtan*) were introduced in 1993 and 1994 respectively (see **television magazines**); in 1996 talk shows like *Tell It Like It Is* (*Shihua shishuo*) were added (see **television talk shows**); and in 1999 a programme designed to spread legal knowledge regarding everyday situations, *Today's Legal Advice* (*Jinri shuofa*), began. There has also been an increase in specialized programmes. CCTV alone now has increased to twelve channels. Only CCTV 1 still attempts to provide a full variety of programmes while the others each have their special area of coverage.

This weekly programme schedule offered below is based on CCTV 1, a channel that supplies a majority of programming formats currently used in China. CCTV 1 programmes are divided into 'fixed programmes' (*guding jiemu*) and variable programmes. The 'fixed' programmes are the same regardless of which day of the week it is, while, of course, other programmes vary. The 'fixed' programmes are divided into early morning, early afternoon and prime-time slots.

The CCTV 1 fixed morning programme includes: *Morning News Update* (*Gundong xinwen: Zao xinwen*, 6.00–6.30); *Fitness* (*Baixing jianshen*, 6.30–7.00); *Oriental Horizon* (7.00–7.45 and 7.00–8.00 on Sundays); *Eight O'Clock News* (*Xinwen zao badian*, 8.00–8.35); *Focus Interview* (8.35–8.50); and a programme for the elderly, *Evening Sun* (*Xiyang hong*, 8.50–9.25). Some local stations also have morning newscasts, such as *Good Morning Beijing* (*Beijing, ninzao*) by Beijing Station, but local news programmes are less comprehensive. The 'fixed' afternoon programmes on CCTV 1 start with *News in 30 Minutes* (*Xinwen 30 fen*, 12.00–12.30), followed by *Today's Legal Advice* (*Jinri shuofa*, 12.40–13.00); a relay of *Oriental Horizon* (13.00–13.40); *Cartoon City* (*Donghua cheng*, 17.30–18.06); and *Big Pinwheel* (18.09–18.59). The last is designed for and performed by children. Prime-time starts at 19.00 with a national and international news bulletin *CCTV News* (*Xinwen lianbo*, 19.00–19.30). *CCTV News* still represents the authoritative voice of the state and the Communist Party. Local stations generally start with *CCTV News* and continue with local news. The newscast is followed by the weather forecast (19.31–19.38), *Focus Interview* (19.38–19.54) and *Science and Technology* (*Keji bolan*, 19.55–20.04). As a form of family-oriented entertainment, TV drama enjoys a prestigious position among TV programmes. Popular and newly released TV dramas are presented during prime-time (20.05–21.00). CCTV 1 prime-time finishes with *Evening News* (*Xianzai bopao*, 21.00–21.14), except on Sundays when it ends with *Tell It Like It Is* (21.15–21.59).

The variable programmes include variable morning, evening and late evening broadcasts. They change depending on whether it is Monday–Saturday or Sunday, as well as among the weekdays themselves. Monday's programmes can be contrasted with Sunday's as an example of these differences, with the understanding that such programmes do change from day to day. CCTV 1 variable morning and afternoon broadcasting consists mainly of educational programmes, life skills and entertainment. On Monday morning CCTV 1 provides: *Highlights from Cinema* (*Yinmu caifeng*, 9.20–9.49); *Science and Technology* (9.50–9.59); *News Update* (10.00–10.10); the children's game show *Open Sesame* (10.10–10.22); TV drama (10.23–11.09); cooking demonstrations on *Everyday Gourmet* (*Tiantian yinshi*, 11.10–11.09); a programme for university students *The Twelfth Broadcasting Studio* (*Shi'er yanboshi*, 11.20–11.54); and finally a programme designed to popularize a new song each week called *The Song of the Week* (*Meizhou yige*, 11.55–11.59).

CCTV 1 late Sunday morning broadcasting consists of: *You, Me, He or She* (*Ni, wo, ta*, 9.50–10.25), a programme featuring audience participation in the analysis of selected programmes from all the CCTV channels; *Three-Star Knowledge Express* (*Sanxing zhili kuaiche*), a game show for middle school students; *Weekend Health* (*Zhoumo jiankang zhilu*); and finally *This Week* (*Benzhou* 11.40–11.59), a review of major social and cultural events of the week. Local stations tend to use this time slot for TV drama, MTV and other light entertainment.

Variable Monday afternoon programmes (14.10–18.59) include many from the fixed schedule, but also include TV drama, sports programmes and other forms of entertainment; a replay of *Science and Technology*, *The Song of the Week* and *Daily Gourmet*. Sunday afternoon programming includes: *A World of Fine Arts* (*Meishu xinkong*, 14.00–14.34); *The Second Starting Line* (*Di'er qipaoxian*, 14.35–15.29), a programme for middle school students; *Zhengda Theatre* (*Zhengda juchang*, 15.30–17.20),

introducing film and theatrical work mostly authored by artists of foreign countries; and *Zhengda Showbits* (*Zhengda zongyi*, 17.21–18.00), a comprehensive programme of cultural and artistic appreciation.

Late evening shows are mainly intended for mature viewers. On one particular Monday during the World Cup, the programme included international news, sports news and World Cup history (22.00–23.05); followed by a *Special Sports Programme: I Love the World Cup* (*Tiyu zhuangti: wo ai shijiebie*). The Sunday programme also includes: *Arts Viewpoint* (*Yiyuan fengjingxian*, 00.22–00.50); and *Three-Star Knowledge Express* (*Sanxing zhili kuaiche*, 01.22–01.35). At other times, the late evening may include a TV drama (approximately 23.00–1.22). CCTV 1 broadcasting finishes around 2.00 while some local stations run around the clock. Apart from the fact that there are no religious or explicitly sexual programmes on Chinese TV, Chinese TV programming is becoming more similar in content and format to programming internationally.

Further reading

Donald, Stephanie H., Keane, Michael and Yin, Hong (eds) (2002). *Media in China: Consumption, Content and Crisis*. London: Routledge.

Hong, Junhao (1998). *The Internationalization of Television in China: The Evolution of Ideology, Society, and Media Since the Reform*. Westport: Praeger.

Lull, James (1991). *China Turned On: Television, Reform, and Resistance*. London: Routledge.

HE DONGHUI

television ratings and surveys

TV ratings and demographic surveys are familiar territory to the institutions of quantitative reporting on the media industries. The need to scope potential and actual audiences for their viewing expectations and preferences has long been part of the competitive commercial and public broadcasting systems in the Western world. In China, however, CCTV has had an absolute monopoly for much of the past forty years, and audiences have had little chance of biting back by switching channel. That situation has altered. The television market in China, while still dominated by the hugely subsidized and privileged CCTV, has nonetheless grown to accommodate large regional stations with multi-industry interests. These corporations have made deals with offshore television giants, such as Pearson-Granada, Newscorp and the smaller players such as the Australian Seven-Asia. It is now imperative to have accurate and in-depth feedback on audience preference. There are both local and international organizations working the new industry, with key players AC Nielson and CVSC-Sofres looming large in the business of counting heads. In 2000, the first National People Meter (CSM) was launched with the collaboration of Chinese academic experts in the social sciences. Indeed, given the history and statistical reach of the China State Statistical Bureau it is not surprising that a mechanism for counting the Chinese people should be put together efficiently in response to a newly perceived counting challenge! There are, of course, many heads to count. The National People Meter claims a national TV population over the age of four years as 1,154,000,000, and that the average viewer watches for three hours a day. By the end of 2000, 95 per cent of Chinese households had a television, and 15 per cent had more than one set. As is true of many Eastern bloc and newly developed economies, black-and-white television is rare during the start-up period. In rural areas, the poorest viewing demographic, 60 per cent have colour sets. It is a complex task. Channel availability differs from province to province and city to city. Some areas can access Hong Kong television, while in Beijing it is possible to view as many as seventy-two channels, including those broadcast from Yunnan in the extreme south. That said, the number of channels is declining as success in the market becomes tougher over time and as the government advances regulations to control unmanageable growth in the sector. Audience ratings for the past two years (1999–2001) suggest that drama serials (those akin to soap operas) are popular, as are talk/game shows where audiences have a chance to join in and 'do the television experience' for themselves. In 2000 the big crowd-puller was the Olympic Games, and it may be that this is a taster for the huge pull of sporting events that feature Chinese athletes. At the time of writing it is likely that the soccer World Cup in Korea and Japan will send the National People Meter into the stratosphere!

Further reading

Luo, Ming *et al.* (eds) (1998). *Zhongguo dianshi guanzhong xianzhuang baogao* [Report on the Current State of Television Viewership in China]. Beijing: Shehui kexue wenxian.

People's Daily (2000). 'China's Satellite TV having Wider Coverage'. Available at http://www.peopledaily.co.jp/english/200011/09/print20001109-54778.html

Wanning, Sun (2001). 'Media Events or Media Stories? Time, Space and Chinese (Trans) nationalism'. *International Journal of Cultural Studies* 2.2: 25–44.

And see issues of *Screen Digest*, *Sofres*, *Zenith*

STEPHANIE HEMELRYK DONALD

television talk shows

Television talk shows have become very popular in China since the mid 1990s. This trend is evidence of the evolving nature of television from Chinese Communist Party mouthpiece to popular entertainment medium. It also demonstrates the extent to which Chinese media is now influenced by international styles and formats. Most television channels present talk formats, ranging from interviews with celebrities about their lives and work, and discussions with leading experts and academics about social issues, to formats that allow audience members to interact with guests. As well as being relatively cheap to produce, they fulfil broadcasters' obligations to reflect social reform issues while disseminating the guiding principles of the Chinese Communist Party. Well-known **CCTV (Chinese Central Television)** talk shows include *Tell It Like It Is (Shihua shishuo)*, *Friends (Pengyou)* and *Dialogue (Duihua)*.

Tell It Like It Is first debuted in 1996 and by 2000 was the highest rated programme on national television. People are invited on to the show to join host Cui Yongyuan and his audience in discussing a range of popular topics ranging from the role of women in society to **HIV/AIDS and STIs**.

Viewers can also participate in on-line discussion following the show.

Friends is hosted by Wang Gang and airs on CCTV 2. It follows the format of introducing a well-known celebrity who reminisces with family, friends and acquaintances. Live talk shows such as CCTV 2's *Dialogue* and its studio-recorded English-language counterpart on CCTV 9 provide a vehicle for experts, including foreign academics and business persons, to exchange views about economics, international relations and social issues.

See also: radio and TV hotlines (rexian) and call-in shows

MICHAEL KEANE

temple fairs

Temple fairs (*miaohui*) or 'competitive celebrations to welcome the gods' (*yingshen saihui*) take place in temples dedicated to local gods throughout rural China, and in a few closely regulated urban temples. The pantheon of gods worshipped in China extends into the thousands. These include many historical individuals who received a cult after their death. Other gods are nature gods, astral deities or figures from mythology and theatre. Each portion of the earth has a tutelary deity, and many towns and cities have a City god. A number of gods have achieved a trans-regional or even a nationwide cult. Each of the hundreds of local cultures of China has its own pantheon of gods, including many that are exclusive to each locale. Temples dedicated to the worship of particular or multiple gods can be found throughout China. Surveys conducted in the 1990s in southeast China show that most villages along the Fujian coast have over three temples, each with an average of three or four deities. Rituals (see **Jiao**; **Gongde**) and sometimes festivals are celebrated on major annual festivals such as the **Lantern Festival**, as well as on the birthdate of each god. In some especially densely populated and ritually intensive rural areas, rituals and festivities can take place over 250 days a year. However, many poorer inland regions have seen a marked decline in ritual activity, as workers have emigrated to urban centres (see **migration and settlement patterns**),

temples have been robbed and closed, and village solidarity has declined. Where communal ritual life is still active, village temples often merge into larger ritual alliances, so villagers are involved in rituals and processions involving a multitude of temples and a large variety of local gods (see **processions (religious)**). Festivals usually include rituals in the temple, opera on a stage facing the temple, processions of the gods around the ritual boundaries of the village, and the blessing of offerings prepared by each family in the village. Festivals are occasions of sensory overload – firecrackers explode, incense smoke fills the air, several competing musical and ritual troupes perform simultaneously, and participation is virtually total. Increasingly, these festivals also include performances by possessed **spirit-mediums**, who were once ubiquitous in Chinese village ritual events. The ritual processions provide a venue for the many different local performing arts troupes unique to each local cultural region. Each family in a village celebrating a festival provides a set amount (per capita) to the temple committee, which posts its accounts, showing income from the members of the village and individual donations, along with annual temple oil-lamp and incense income. Expenses are also scrupulously posted. These include costs of ritual performances (**Daoist priests**, Buddhist monks, sectarian ritual specialists, 'Confucian' masters of ceremony, and so forth can all provide ritual services). The opera performances are usually the primary expense. In some areas, these temple committees have already formed a secondary tier of local governance, providing many services to their communities.

Geography and local custom lead to wide differences in the nature of festivals dedicated to local gods. In northern China, large temples located in mountainous sites attract crowds in the tens of thousands to week-long temple fairs (see **pilgrimage**; **sacred mountains**). In southern China, mountains and valleys surround clusters of villages each with their own group of active temples, which are much more integrated into everyday life. Different regions have re-established temples at a different pace since 1980, depending on many local historical factors, in addition to current economic and political pressures (see **Minsu quyi (Min-su ch'ü-i)**). The greatest activity seems to be in southeast China, while northern and central

Chinese villages are still slowly rebuilding their temples, many of which were destroyed in Republican and CCP anti-'feudal superstition' campaigns (see **religion, recent history of**; **religious policies of the state**). Festivals, temples and rituals specific to many different minorities have also revived considerably in recent years (see **Daoism among minority nationalities**).

Further reading

Dean, Kenneth (1993). *Taoist Ritual and Popular Cults of Southeast China*. Princeton: Princeton University Press.

—— (2003). 'Local Religion in Contemporary Southeast China'. *China Quarterly* 174 (June): 338–58.

Overmyer, Daniel (ed.) (2002). *Ethnography in China Today*. Taipei: Yuan-Liou Publishing.

KENNETH DEAN

Teng Ge'er

b. 1960, Inner Mongolia

Pop musician, composer

A musician of Mongolian origin, living in Beijing, famous in China for his powerful and rough voice and for his many pop/rock songs, particularly his songs about Mongolia, many of which he not only performs but also wrote and composed. He has also composed Western-style serious music as well as the music for Xie Fei's film *Love in the Grassland Sky* (*Ai zai caoyuan de tiankong*), in which he also played the leading role.

Teng Ge'er graduated in 1985 from the Tianjin Music Conservatory and joined the Central Nationalities Song and Dance Troupe (Zhongyang minzu gewutuan). Since the late 1980s he has released more than ten solo albums in Chinese and Mongolian and has won numerous prizes in China and abroad. With their references to the stereotypical images of pastoralism and incorporation of elements from traditional Mongolian music, many of Teng Ge'er's songs conform to the long tradition in the PRC of minority songs that exoticize and idealize the lives of minority people. Nevertheless, several of

his songs also challenge this tradition in articulating a nationalistic minority voice that problematizes the life and status of Mongols in the PRC. This is best illustrated in 'The Land of the Blue Wolf (*Canglangdadi*), in which he expresses nostalgia for the time when the Mongols dominated China and protest over the loss of Mongolian tradition and land. Other famous songs include 'The Mongols' (*Mengguren*), 'Paradise' (*Tiantang*), and 'Gadameilin' (*Gadameiren*).

See also: minority pop musicians: the new generation; representations of minorities

Further reading

Baranovitch, Nimrod (2003). *China's New Voices: Popular Music, Ethnicity, Gender, and Politics, 1978–1997*. Berkeley: University of California Press, 72–83.

NIMROD BARANOVITCH

terms of address

Terms of address are used to index social relations between the addresser and the addressee. Since China is traditionally known to have put much emphasis on social hierarchy, it is no coincidence that Chinese possesses a sophisticated system of address forms. In the complex Chinese system of kinship terms, many remote relationships receive lexical coding. The use of kinship terms is so pervasive that the terms are also applied to strangers. For example, a child can be expected to address a female stranger as *jiejie* (elder sister) or *ayi* (auntie). The common prefixes of *lao* (old) and *xiao* (little/young) in a surname mark both age relation and perceived seniority.

Perhaps the areas most clearly reflecting changes in social structure and social values are the forms of address concerning non-kin. While in the pre-1949 era honorific forms such as *xiansheng* (mister) and *xiaojie* (miss) were widespread, the Communist Party actively promoted the use of *tongzhi* (comrade), a term inspired by their Soviet counterparts. *Tongzhi*, however, like many other high-profile terms of address, has undergone changes in status along with the society in which it is used, with the most recent change being the revival of old honorific forms in place of *tongzhi*. While honorific terms of address come and go, a common tendency in recent Chinese history has been to use appreciative terms that refer to craftsmanship and/or educatedness. Thus, *shifu* (master/teacher), *laoban* (boss/business owner) and *laoshi* (teacher) are some of the recent terms employed to address strangers who are not necessarily professionals.

TAO HONGYIN

theatre criticism (journals and periodicals)

Books of theatre criticism on contemporary Chinese drama and theatre since 1979 are rare. While some published books do contain chapters on this period, they can never stay on top of current developments. Therefore, theatre journals and periodicals are the best vehicle for understanding the contemporary performing arts. Although quite diverse in scope, the journals can be categorized by certain characteristics. For instance, some cover all of China while others emphasize individual regions, and while most cover both **Huaju** (spoken drama) and **Xiqu** (sung-drama/opera), a couple are devoted solely to the latter. Journals and periodicals can be further categorized into those that feature long and critical articles, those that contain short theatre reviews combined with a discussion/analysis of aspects of specific productions, and those that mainly publish newly written scripts. The following annotated bibliography introduces the reader to the nature and scope of theatre criticism via journals and periodicals in China. Each entry provides information by Chinese title (and English translation); place of publication; frequency of publication; the region(s) covered; and the type of materials included.

Anhui xinxi [Anhui New Drama], Hefei; bimonthly; Anhui province; short articles and scripts.

Da wutai [Big Stage], Shijiazhuang; monthly; Hebei province; short articles and scripts.

Dangdai xiju [Contemporary Theatre], Xi'an; bimonthly; Shaanxi province; short articles and scripts.

Dianshi yu xiju [Television and Theatre], Shenyang; monthly; Liaoning province; short articles and scripts.

Fujian yishu [Fujian Arts], Fuzhou; bimonthly; Fujian province; short articles on theatre and fine art.

Guangdong yishu [Guangdong Arts], Guangzhou; bimonthly; Guangdong province; short articles on theatre and fine art.

Henan xiju [Theatre in Henan], Zhengzhou; monthly; Henan province; short articles and scripts; replaced by *Nanqiang beidiao* [Mixed Accent] in the 1990s.

Jilu yitan [Theatre Forum in Shangdong], Jinan; monthly; articles on theatre and fine art.

Juben [Play Scripts], Beijing; monthly; China; mainly scripts with short articles.

Juying yuebao [Drama and Film Monthly], Nanjing; monthly; Jiangsu province; short articles on drama and film.

Juzuojia [Playwright], Haerbin; bimonthly; Heilongjiang province; scripts and long articles.

Nanguo hongdou [Red Bean in Southern Country], Guangzhou; bimonthly; Guangdong province; short articles.

Nanqiang beidiao [Mixed Accent], continued from *Henan xiju*; containing short articles on other subjects, too.

Puju yishu [Pu Opera Arts], Linfen; quarterly, Shanxi province; short articles and scripts.

Shanghai xiju [Shanghai Drama], Shanghai; monthly; Shanghai; short articles and scripts.

Shanghai yishujia [Shanghai Artists], Shanghai; bimonthly; Shanghai; articles on theatre and fine art.

Sichuan xiju [Sichuan Drama], Chengdu; monthly; Sichuan province; short articles and scripts.

Wenyi yanjiu [Literature and Art Studies], Beijing; China; long articles on all genres of literature, theatre and art.

Xiju [Drama], the journal of the Central Academy of Drama; quarterly; China; long articles on non-Chinese drama, Huaju and Xiqu.

Xiju chunqiu [Theatre Annals], Changsha; monthly; Hunan province; short articles and scripts.

Xiju congkan [Drama Series], Jinan; bimonthly; Shandong province; short articles and scripts.

Xiju wenxue [Dramatic Literature], Changchun; monthly; Jilin province; short articles and scripts.

Xiju yishu [Theatre Art], journal of Shanghai Academy of Theatre; long articles on non-Chinese drama, Huaju and Xiqu.

Xijujia [Dramatist], Chengdu; quarterly; Sichuan province; scripts and short articles.

Xin juben [New Play Script], Beijing; bimonthly; mainly scripts with short articles.

Xiqu yanjiu [Theatre Studies], Beijing; indefinite; China; long articles exclusively on Xiqu theatre.

Xiqu yishu [Art of Chinese Traditional Opera], journal of Chinese Academy of Traditional Theatre; Beijing; quarterly; China; articles exclusively on Xiqu theatre.

Xiwen [Zhejiang Drama], Hangzhou; monthly; Zhejiang province; short articles and scripts.

Yihai [All Arts], Changsha; quarterly; Hunan province; scripts and articles on theatre and fine art.

Yingju yishu [Art of Film and Drama], Nanning; monthly(?); Guangxi province; short articles on theatre and film.

Yishu baijia [Hundred Schools in Art], Nanjing; quarterly; China; long articles on theatre and fine art.

Yunnan xiju [Yunnan Drama], Kunming; bimonthly(?); Yunan province; short articles and scripts.

Zhongguo dianshi xiqu [Chinese Traditional Theatre on TV], Beijing; periodic; China; articles exclusively about Xiqu on TV.

Zhongguo jingju [Beijing Opera of China], Bejing; bimonthly; China; short articles and memoirs.

Zhongguo xiju [Chinese Theatre], Beijing; monthly; China; short articles on all forms of theatre.

Zhonghua xiqu [Chinese Theatre], Beijing; indefinite; China; long articles exclusively on Xiqu theatre.

DU WENWEI

theme parks

A theme park integrates exhibits, performance and commerce into a built environment. Theme parks have become a significant cultural industry in the Chinese economy. Since the establishment of the first modern theme park, Splendid China, in 1989, a 'theme park' (*zhuti gongyuan*) fever has emerged and more than 300 amusement and theme parks have been constructed. As most of the theme parks continue to upgrade their facilities, new theme parks are being established all over China each year. The best-known and most successful theme parks in China are those that focus on cultural displays. Examples include: Splendid China, China Folk Culture Villages, and Window on the World, all in Shenzhen, the Yuanming Xinyuan in Zhuhai, the World Park and the Chinese Ethnic Culture Park in Beijing, the World Landscape Park and the Wonderland of the Southwest in Chengdu, and Yunnan Nationalities Villages in Kunming.

These parks generally focus on three leitmotifs. The first of these are represented by those parks featuring stories, legends and folk tales such as Monkey King's *Journey to theWest* and *The Dream of the Red Chamber*. The second features notable world sites, displaying selected countries and cultures in Africa, Asia, Europe, North and South America, and the South Pacific, including architecture, scenic spots, landmarks and government buildings. Architecture such as Notre Dame and the Egyptian pyramids, tourist spots such as the Niagara Falls and the Grand Canyon, urban landmarks such as the Eiffel Tower and New York's Manhattan, governmental buildings such as the Kremlin in Moscow and the White House in Washington, DC, and others such as African tribal villages and Maori houses. The third showcases ethnic minorities in China, who are used to represent the culturally diverse but politically unified Chinese nation.

Although the popularity of Chinese theme parks is a recent phenomenon, theme parks as cultural forms do have historical roots in China. The original **Yuanming Yuan**, built from 1709 to 1744 and destroyed by British and French soldiers in 1860, may be seen as one of the earliest prototypes of the modern theme park, at least a hundred years before the Scandinavian 'folk museum' model of the late nineteenth century. The park integrated nature (gardens with pools, fountains, paths and hills), architecture (both traditional Chinese and European styles), displays (artifacts from China and other countries) and performances of daily life, all within a built retail urban environment linked to festivals (particularly the **Lantern Festival**). In Beijing during the early part of the twentieth century, the New World and South City Amusement

Parks offered entertainment, performances and games in connection with market days and **temple fairs**. In Shanghai, the Great World (1916–49) was the most influential and popular amusement centre and included variety shows, food shops and cinemas. Chinese theme parks are now part of the international tourist industry. China Travel Service (Holdings) Hong Kong Limited, a Chinese state-owned transnational corporation, established Splendid China in Florida in 1993. Through participation in international tourism, Chinese companies have also learned from theme parks in other countries.

See also: leisure culture; parks and squares; representations of minorities

Further reading

Stanley, Nick and Siu, King Chung (1995). 'Representing the Past as the Future: The Shenzhen Chinese Folk Culture Villages and the Making of Chinese Identity'. *Journal of Museum Ethnography* 7: 25–40.

Ren, Hai (1998). 'Economies of Culture: Theme Parks, Museums, and Capital Accumulation in China, Hong Kong, and Taiwan'. PhD diss., University of Washington.

REN HAI

Theravada Buddhism among minority groups

Theravada Buddhism, the 'Doctrine of the Elders', claims to be the oldest tradition of Buddhist teaching. Also called Hinayana, or the Lesser Vehicle, it is widely dispersed in mainland Southeast Asia, especially Thailand and Burma, but also in parts of Yunnan province. Among its teachings is renunciation of the world. The tradition is that boys and men spend at least part of their lives in temples, and the people are obliged to feed the monks. Several ethnic groups of Yunnan province still practise Theravada Buddhism, most importantly, the Tai (Dai), but also the De'ang, Achang, Blang and Jingpo.

Buddhism suffered persecution during the **Cultural Revolution**, but has revived since the early 1980s (see **religion, recent history of;**

religious policies of the state). Most Tai still follow Buddhism, and most rural families have house shrines. However, Buddhism is much stronger among the Shui Dai of Sipsongpanna than in Dehong among the Han Tai. About half of the Sipsongpanna villages still have temples, though not all have resident monks, and most boys go into the temples as 'little monks', at least for short periods. In Dehong there were 642 Theravada Buddhist temples in 1998. Though religious activities took place in all of them, only thirty-seven were homes to monks. Less than 1 per cent of boys still entered temples as 'little monks', though men often sought the monastic life as they grew older. There are still Theravada Buddhist temples in the villages of the De'ang, who adopted Buddhism from the Tai, and the people still feed the monks.

See also: Tai (Dai), culture of

COLIN MACKERRAS

Third Generation (composers)

The 'Third Generation' composers refers to those who entered the conservatories in 1978 when universities again began to recruit students after the **Cultural Revolution**. The best-known names among the 'Third Generation' composers are: **Qu Xiaosong**, **Zhou Long**, **Chen Yi**, **Zhang Xiaofu**, **Ye Xiaogang**, **Chen Qigang**, **Guo Wenjing**, **Su Cong** and **Tan Dun** of the Central Conservatory of Music in Beijing; **Ge Ganru**, **Sheng Zongliang** (Bright Sheng) and **Xu Shuya** of the Shanghai Conservatory; He Xuntian and Jia Daqun of the Sichuan Conservatory of Music; and Tang Jianping of the Shenyang Conservatory.

Their education in these **music conservatories** consisted of a standard Western music curriculum in harmony, counterpoint, form and analysis, and orchestration, as well as many Chinese music courses. However, there was no twentieth-century Western music in the curriculum. This was partly because China's policy of isolationism from the West in the previous three decades, which kept music professors from becoming expert in this area, and partly because the official ideology had discouraged the study of modernism. The exploration of modern

Western music, therefore, was left to the students themselves, generally through studying scores and listening to recordings. This might explain why, aside from cultural and aesthetic reasons, most of the composers have taken an eclectic approach in their assimilation and adoption of the language of modern Western music, instead of adhering to a single system, such as serialism.

The media called the music composed by the 'Third Generation' in the 1980s 'New Wave Music' (*Xinchao yinyue*). The music began to attract attention in the early 1980s when Tan Dun's string quartet won a composition competition in East Germany. Several symposia were held in Beijing to discuss the phenomenon of New Wave Music, which received both praise and criticism. In the second half of the 1980s, Tan Dun, Ye Xiaogang, Qu Xiaosong, Xu Shuya and Guo Wenjing gave a series of highly publicized concerts devoted to their own music in Beijing; this period was the heyday of New Wave Music.

Most New Wave Music compositions are not programmatic, although they usually bear titles that evoke the general mood or feeling of the music. The composers often draw their inspiration from classical Chinese literature and folklore, rather than patriotic or revolutionary themes as the older generation did. In general, their music expresses personal thoughts and feelings instead of conveying political messages. Although many modern Western elements can be found in their music, such as atonality, unorthodox use of harmony, dissonance, tone-clusters, spatial effects and irregular rhythm, everything is filtered through Chinese aesthetics and feelings. The composers use material from regional opera, folksongs and classical Chinese music. One of the most important achievements of the 'Third Generation' is their elevation of Chinese instrumental music to a completely new level and the creation of a new repertoire in the genre. Since 1990, many 'Third Generation' composers have developed and established careers abroad as well as in China, and their music has evolved in more personal and individual directions.

See also: He Xuntian; Fourth Generation (composers); musicology

JIN PING

Third Generation (poets)

Vaguely denoting a collective identity of younger poets in the mid 1980s, the term 'Third Generation poets' (*Disandai shiren*) was first used in a 1985 essay by Wan Xia in *Contemporary Poetry* (*Xiandai shi*, Chengdu). Defined by Wan Xia, the 'first generation' included Ai Qing, Guo Xiaochuan, Shao Yanxiang and others who had dominated the poetic realm in the 1950s and 1960s. The 'Second Generation' referred to those survivors of the Cultural Revolution, such as **Bei Dao**, **Jiang He** and **Yang Lian**, and the 'Third Generation' to those who had grown up in the 1970s and whose voices began to be heard in the mid 1980s. Wan Xia's periodization is supported by the fact that in the mid 1980s several new poetry groups simultaneously emerged in Beijing, Shanghai, Nanjing, Hangzhou and Sichuan, each linked to their own 'underground poetry publications' (*dixia shikan*). Among their publications the most notable were: *Contemporary Poetry*, *On the Sea* (*Haishang*), *They* (**Tamen**), *The Continents* (*Dalu*), and *Not-Not* (*Feifei*, see **Zhou Lunyou**). Representatives of this generation are Hu Dong, **Yu Jian**, **Zhai Yongming**, Wan Xia, Wang Yin, Meng Lang, Mo Mo, Hei Dachun, **Xi Chuan**, Lü De'an and Liang Xiaoming.

Eagerly distinguishing themselves from their precedents, especially from the established **Misty poetry** (of the 'Second Generation'), these poets searched for a new poetic identity based on a collective understanding of the unique and multiple capacities in the Chinese language; their techniques and aesthetic codes were indebted to various new literary theories, including poststructuralism and postmodernism; and their work, while offering diverse individual styles, shared several common features: textual complexity, a focus on everyday life, ordinary language and local colour, and irrationality.

Further reading

Crespi, John (2003). 'Form and Reform: New Poetry and the Crescent Moon Society'. In [Joshua Mostow (ed.) and Kirk Denton (ed. China section),] *Columbia Companion to Modern East Asian Literatures*. New York: Columbia University Press, 364–70.

Li, Fukan and Hung, Eva (1992). 'Post-Misty Poetry'. *Renditions* 37: 93–8.

Li, Xia (1999). 'Confucius, Playboys and Rusticated Glasperlenspieler: from Classical Chinese Poetry to Postmodernism' *Interlitteraria* (Tartu, Estonia) 4: 41–60.

Tao, Naikan (1995/1996). 'Going Beyond: Post-Menglong Poets.' *Journal of the Oriental Society of Australia* 27/28: 146–53.

Twitchell, Jeffrey and Huang, Fan (1997). 'Avant-Garde Poetry in China: The Nanjing Scene 1981–1992'. *World Literature Today* 71.1: 29–35.

CHEN JIANHUA

Three-Self Patriotic Movement (TSPM)

The Chinese Christian Three-Self Patriotic Movement (Zhongguo jidujiao sanzi aiguo yundong) is the full name of this organization, led by a National Committee in Shanghai. It counts its start from the signing and publication of the so-called *Christian Manifesto* (*Sanzi gexin xuanyan*) on 23 September 1950 in the **People's Daily** (*Renmin ribao*). A preparatory committee of the 'Chinese Christian Resist-America-Aid-Korea Three-Self Reform Movement' was set up in 1951, and the TSPM was officially formed at the first National Christian Meeting in 1954. The chairman of the TSPM during its first thirty years was Wu Yaozong (Y. T. Wu), who also founded the Christian magazine **Tianfeng**.

'Three-self' stands for 'self-governing' (*zizhi*), 'self-supporting' (*ziyang*) and 'self-propagating' (*zichuan*), and is an idea found among Chinese Christians before 1949. After 1949, however, the autonomy enshrined in the 'three-self' principle was compromised by the strict control of the state and the Party through the **Religious Affairs Bureau (State Administration for Religious Affairs)** and the United Front Work Department of the CCP. Most Chinese Christians, including those in the **house churches**, support the 'three-self' principle, but the house churches have sharply criticized the TSPM as a government- and Party-controlled church. The TSPM led campaigns against house-church leaders in the 1950s and

1960s and has condemned non-TSPM groups. The conflict has continued in the 1990s.

The TSPM is organized into local committees all over the PRC and it was the only Protestant organization before the **China Christian Council** (CCC) was formed in 1980. Now the CCC and local Christian councils have taken over much of the responsibility for church affairs, while the TSPM has become more an ideological counterpart to the authorities. The TSPM National Committee still exerts considerable power and its fundamental but double-edged role in shaping Protestant Christianity (see **Christianity (Protestantism)**) in the PRC is undeniable.

Further reading

Wickeri, P. (1988). *Seeking the Common Ground: Protestant Christianity, the Three-Self Movement, and China's United Front. Maryknoll*. New York: Orbis Books.

FREDERIK FÄLLMAN

Tian Liming

b. 1955, Beijing

Traditional Chinese painter

Tian Liming, an artist in the ink-painting mode, is a member of the Chinese Artists' Association. He grew up in Beijing. As a sixteen-year-old, he enlisted in the PLA where, owing to his talents, he served as an artist; he was even dispatched to Tibet to depict 'the true life of the highland people'. In the following years, he was invited to participate in numerous exhibitions and secured a valid place on the national art scene. In the meantime, he received a comprehensive art education in the Ink-painting Department of the **Central Academy of Fine Arts** (1982–5) under Lu Chen (b. 1935) and remained in the department after graduation. His paintings from this early period were composed of fast *pomo* (splash) brushstrokes, resulting in a spontaneous style known as *da xieyi* (very loose and watery brushstrokes). In 1989, after enrolling in a graduate course at the Department of Ink-painting, he began to diverge from the model set by Lu Chen.

Attracted by the **New Literati Painting**, he participated in most of their annual exhibitions until 1997, when the movement dissolved. In the late 1990s, he became the Deputy Head of the Ink-painting Department at the Central Academy.

At first sight, Tian Liming's paintings may not be suggestive of Chinese ink-painting, and some critics have pointed to Western influence. He does not restrict himself to the mere use of ink-painting techniques, employing, for example, colours in the manner of water-colouring. His are predominantly figure paintings and he is best known for a series of diluted, archetypal figures rendered in pastel colours and transparent washes. His favourite theme, however, is water, be it as background for at times naïve-looking figures, or as subject in its own right, deep and transparent, tinted with light colours. He is particularly suggestive in the rendition of the play of light and shadows, unknown in traditional Chinese art.

Further reading

Olivová, Lucie (2001). *Contemporary Chinese Ink Painting: Tradition and Experiment*. Prague: The National Gallery in Prague, 58–64.

LUCIE OLIVOVÁ

Tian Qinxin

b. 1969

Huaju (spoken drama) director

Tian Qinxin became the youngest director of the National Theatre Company of China (Zhongguo guojia huajuyuan) and, while being one of the few female spoken-drama directors in China, is hailed as having great potential in the field. Tian graduated from Beijing xiqu xuexiao, a Beijing traditional theatre school, in 1988 and from the Directing Department of the Central Drama Academy (Zhongyang xiju xueyuan) in 1996. In contrast to most spoken-drama directors, she received a combination of physical, performance and arts training since childhood. She trained in gymnastics for four years before attending Beijing xiqu xuexiao at age twelve, where she studied physical, vocal and spoken performance techniques.

In 1989–90, she began the study of film and art at the **Beijing Film Academy** and the renamed Academy of Arts and Design (Zhongyang gongyi meishu xueyuan) at **Qinghua University**. In 1997, she worked for a Hong Kong advertising company as an 'innovation planner' before entering the Peking Opera Troupe of Beijing (Beijing jing-juyuan) as a director in 1998. From 1999, however, she was hired as a director for the Central Experimental Drama Theatre (the predecessor of the National Theatre Company of China) where she continues today.

Tian is motivated by a desire to create strong visual theatrical effects while invoking passionate scenes on stage, which also guides her choice of subject matter. She is fond of national and historical subject matter, and many of her works carry a strong nationalist slant. Tian is skilled in creating visual effects by emphasizing physical movement, the beauty of scenery and costume, and poetic dialogue. Most of her work also has a strong experimental character, such that she is considered one of the foremost **avant-garde/ experimental theatre** directors in China. Her first play, *The Severance* (*Duanwan*, 1997), blended spoken drama form with traditional theatre performance, dance, film and gymnastics. Her most famous play, however, is *Between the Living and the Dead* (*Shengsichang*, 1999), adapted from the novel of the same name by Xiao Hong, an eminent female novelist of the 1930s. The play created a new style of presenting Chinese rural people and life. *Between the Living and the Dead* received the 'Highest Ticket Sales' award among the one hundred participating productions from China and overseas at the First Shanghai International Arts Festival. The triumph of *Shengsichang* made Tian one of the most important contemporary Chinese directors in spoken drama.

The Riddler (*Mige*, 2002), a music theatre production staged in Hong Kong, is Tian's latest work. In place of the usual emphasis on plot, character and language in spoken drama, Tian uses remarkable visual effects, gorgeous scenery, advanced multimedia technology and music sung by the well-known Chinese international singer Dadawa as the basis of the creation. In contemporary Chinese modern theatre, *The Riddler* is the only one of its kind. Her other works include *Peach Blossoms at the*

Stagecoach Station (*Yizhan tiaohua*, 1998, spoken drama), *The Hurricane* (*Kuangbiao*, 2001, spoken drama) and *The Hunchback Prime Minister* (*Zaixiang Liu Luoguo*, 2000), a **Jingju** (Peking opera) co-directed with **Lin Zhaohua**.

LIN WEI-YÜ

Tian Zhuangzhuang

b. 1952, Beijing

Film director/producer

A key figure of the **Fifth Generation (film directors)**, Tian Zhuangzhuang has contributed to the creation of China's 'New Wave' cinema. As with his peers, **Chen Kaige** and **Zhang Yimou**, Tian's life experience and journey to filmmaking reflect the historical and political conditions of his time. Born to a family whose members were all associated with film, he grew up with motion pictures as part of daily life. During the **Cultural Revolution**, like many urban youth Tian was 'sent down' to work in Jilin province and later joined the People's Liberation Army. Fortunately, admission to the **Beijing Film Academy** in 1978 enabled him to redirect his life towards filmmaking.

On the Hunting Ground (*Liechang zhasa*, 1985) and *Horse Thief* (*Dao mazei*, 1987) are the two early films that attracted critical attention. Both films establish a curious **Han** vision from which the dislocated spaces and marginal cultures of Inner Mongolia and Tibet unfold. The films' ethnographic observations and visual revelations bring the rituals and customs of the minorities to contrast the Han majorities (see **representations of minorities**). Tian's representations of life in Tibet and Mongolia failed to attract a mass audience, however. He then returned to narrative film and made *Blue Kite* (*Lan fengzhen*, 1992). Together with Chen Kaige's *Farewell My Concubine* and Zhang Yimou's *To Live*, *Blue Kite* forms a historical trilogy of the 'Fifth Generation'. The film uses a child's perspective and the sequential deaths of his three fathers to reveal how political history disrupts and damages private family life. Because of the politically sensitive subject matter and an international screening prior to receiving the censor's permission, the government

prohibited Tian from filmmaking until 1996. During the years of probation, however, Tian continued in his profession by opening a film workshop and acting as a producer. The workshop became the cradle in which a younger generation of film directors began their careers: for instance, **Lu Xuechang**'s *The Making of Steel* (1998) and Wang Xiaoshuai's *So Close to Paradise* (1998). Tian's first feature after he resumed directing was a remake of *Springtime in a Small Town* (*Xiaocheng zhichun*, 2002), a 1940s classic by Fei Mu. The return to the film of poetics and Chinese aesthetics indicates Tian's insistence on seeking the perfection of film art.

Further reading

Gladney, Dru (1995). 'Tian Zhuangzhuang, the Fifth Generation, and Minorities Films in China'. *Public Culture* 8: 161–75.

Lu, Tonglin (2002). 'Allegorical and Realistic Portrayals of the Cultural Revolution: Tian Zhuanzhuang, *On the Hunting Ground*, *Horse Thief*, *Blue Kite*'. In *idem*, *Confronting Modernity in the Cinemas of Taiwan and Mainland China*. Cambridge: Cambridge University Press, 58–92.

Tam, Kwok-kan, and Dissanayake, Wimal (1998). 'Tian Zhuangzhuang: Reconfiguring the Familiar and the Unfamiliar'. In *idem*, *New Chinese Cinema*. New York: Oxford University Press.

Wang, Ban (1999). 'Trauma and History in Chinese Film: Reading *The Blue Kite* against Melodrama'. *Modern Chinese Language and Culture* 11.1 (Spring): 125–56.

CUI SHUQIN

Tiananmen Square

(guangchang)

Across the more than 440,000 square metres (100 acres) of cement expanse and among the monumental edifices of Chinese socialist *neuesattlichkeit*, hundreds of tourists and city residents saunter; three-wheeled bicycle pedlars hawk their wares; anticipatory lines of spectators are seated around the northern core of the square for the start of the evening flag ceremony; friends jostle to have their photographs taken against the backdrop of Chairman Mao's portrait; multicoloured dragon and fish kites extend upward above the yellow glazed tile double-eaves of the rostrum at the Gate of Heavenly Peace (Tiananmen). This is where on 1 October 1949 Mao Zedong proclaimed the founding of the People's Republic and on 18 August 1966 reviewed more than a million Red Guards, and, urging them on with chants of '*zaofan youyi*' (to rebel is justified), launched the ten-year civil war against the Chinese Communist Party known as the Great Proletarian **Cultural Revolution**. It is the close of another day at Tiananmen *guangchang*, or more simply *guangchang*, 'the Square'. This is Tiananmen Square today, once a strategically constructed public space designed for the celebration of the Party and its revolution, as well as the southern entrance to the former locus of the imperial cult of China's 'galactic polity'.

The gate itself (Tian'an) is a ubiquitous national symbol, its bright-gold image emblazoned on the red lapel pins worn by each of the Party's 65 million members. The entire complex of gate and square is physically imposing. A cursory glance at any map reveals that it has long been the central frame of the Beijing urban landscape, a vast space at the foot of the Ming Imperial Palace (Gugong) that has been the site for mass rallies, parades, political campaigns and the popular anti-government protests (against an array of changing governments, all autocratic) of 4 May 1919 (May Fourth Movement); 10 June 1925 (Shameen Massacre Protest); 18 March 1926 (protest against the acceptance of Japanese imperialist demands by the northern warlord, Zhang Zuolin); 9 December 1935 (December Ninth Movement); 5 April 1976 (Tiananmen Incident); December 1978–March 1979 (Democracy Wall Movement); 1 January 1987 (Student Democracy Protests); and April through June of 1989 (Democracy Movement). The Tiananmen of tourists and petty capitalists is at the same time the seismic centre of the nation's political geology, the history of which breathes popular protest as well as public acclaim for the legitimacy of the People's Republic. However, following two decades of hypergrowth, politics has yielded to commerce; now the tourist guide is the reference tool for situating Tiananmen. According to any of the

Baedekkers carried by the site's 10,000 daily visitors, Tiananmen's proximity to both the Imperial Palace – with its mazes of walls, gates and halls – and adjacent Beihai makes it the preferred site for beginning the adventitious exploration of the *xiang* and *hutong* (residential alleys and courtyards) of the great northern capital.

Tiananmen is an artifact of modern nationhood and bears the traces of each of the upheavals from which China was forged. Mao's oft-quoted Cultural Revolution dictum, 'without destruction there can be no construction', is exemplified in every inch of the Square's 14 hectares, carved out of the bricks and mortar of old imperial Beijing to create a modern democratic plaza that dwarfed the Red Square of China's competitive international socialist ally. Successively built and rebuilt from the fifteenth to the late nineteenth centuries, Tiananmen was, until Mao's colossal choreographed remaking of it, a gate and not a square; in fact, for most of its pre twentieth-century history, it was not even known as Tiananmen but as Chengtianmen (Conforming with Heaven Gate). Tiananmen remained, but the inner and outer walls of the original Imperial City (*huangcheng*) were the casualties of urban renewal.

Since the third Ming emperor Yongle (r. 1403–24) moved the imperial capital from Nanjing on the Yangtze River to Beijing, the 'Gate of Heavenly Peace' has marked the southern entrance to the dynastic family's compound known as the Forbidden City (*Zijincheng*) and it has been a stage of diverse dramaturgy, the ritual pivot of the imperial kingdom. The gate mysteriously marked the outer limit of the Ming dynastic compound and beckoned family members, consorts, advisers and selected officials in through one of the four passageways to the Forbidden City on either side of the central gate. But for the last six decades the gate has opened out onto the massive parade ground and the broad Avenue of Eternal Peace (Chang'anjie) that were made by the voluntary labour of thousands in the early years of People's Republic.

Revolutionary banners proclaim 'Long Live the People's Republic of China' (*Zhonghua renmin gongheguo wansui*) and 'Long Live the Great Unity of the Peoples of the World' (*Shijie renmin datuanjie wansui*) to either side of the Gate of Heavenly Peace, through which one proceeds towards the Meridian Gate (Wumen) and the labyrinth of halls, gates and rooms of the Imperial Palace. The massive painted image of a vacant, implacable Mao has long hung above the Gate, at the north end of the Square, following a practice begun in the 1920s when an enlarged portrait of Sun Yat-sen was suspended from the same site. Given that in imperial times only the emperor himself could pass through this barrel-vaulted passage on his way to the Temple of Heaven at the southern reach of the old outer city, the hanging of revolutionary leaders' portraits indicates the curious commingling of the authoritarian and popular significances of the Square, something also conveyed by the rhetorical axes of the two revolutionary banners. At Tiananmen Square these meanings are inextricably, if undecidably, linked, a product of the history of this iconic site and of the revolutionary redesign of the capital that followed from the founding of the Chinese nation.

The architecture of the Square has not been modified since 1977 when the Mao Zedong mausoleum was constructed just to the south of the Monument to the People's Heroes, but an architectural plan for a new national construction project adjacent to the Great Hall of the People has been approved, if not yet implemented. The French architect Paul Andreu (designer of the Shanghai International Airport) forwarded a controversial proposal to build a National Grand Theatre on 120,000 square metres of land that will resemble 'an otherworldly giant bubble made of titanium and glass'. If and when this postmodern monument is completed, its 2,500-seat opera house, 2,000-seat music hall, 1,200-seat theatre, 500-seat auditorium will dwarf the revolutionary monuments that have long punctuated the Square and broadcast the legacy of China's reform generation.

Located virtually in the heart of central Beijing, at the base of a vertical axis linking heaven to earth, Tiananmen Square has long been the site for grand orchestrated revolutionary display. From its reviewing stand, thousands of Party luminaries have conferred favour on the drilled armies and the latest farming equipment and mobile weapons, regarded the numberless and often contradictory political banners, and received many an exalted state guest. It is the public architectural product of careful planning: a space self-consciously re-functioned so

that the imperial presence of China's last native dynasty serves as the stage for the revolutionary production of the people's republic. After liberation, the city's walls that shielded the inner compound from the aleatory effects of the winds of the four directions were removed, as were the symbolic gates of the cardinal points. Its architecture is ineluctably a strange hybrid of the demotic and the despotic with its wide, flat, cement parade ground and the imposing imperial roof tiles of the Forbidden City.

The conception of the Square since the revolution was horizontal, in contravention of the geomantic and theocratic principles of imperial architecture's requisite verticality. For the founders of the People's Republic the overweening impulse of the redesign was to defy the imperial conception by building out, not up – by constructing a counter-axis to the vertical north–south orientation of the Forbidden City. As if to violate the geomancy (see **fengshui**) of the cruciform *ya*-shaped construction of the imperial palace buildings, gardens and arteries explicitly attested to in pre-revolutionary maps of the city, the remade Square concentrates mass movement and visual attention within its vast space of horizontal flatness and obscures perception of the theologically inspired vertical architecture of the Imperial Palace. Indeed, as Rudolf Wagner has noted, Mao's mausoleum furthered this subversive architectural realignment through its conscious confutation of the Square's north/south symmetry: the memorial hall, like its symbolic ally the Monument to the People's Heroes, faces north towards the Gate.

Today's touristic and entrepreneurial square is a far cry from the heady days of peaceful democratic protest and celebration in 1989. Then, for more than six weeks as the world watched, Tiananmen Square obtained a revolutionary significance outside the reach of the Party-state. Millions – city-dwellers, peasants, students and workers – filled the Square and its adjoining arterial streets, yet were violently cast out by the despotic belch of tanks, trucks, jeeps and personnel carriers, leaving the 'broad field' empty of people but filled with shell casings, burning hulks, twisted wrecks of bicycles, and the scattered detritus of tents, make-do shelters, personal effects and the 'Goddess of Democracy' (*Minzhu zhi shen*).

In the minds of some, perhaps many, who drift along the avenues of today's state-sponsored nostalgia, the Square remains synonymous with those days of joy and sorrow, but this Tiananmen is a memory or a murmur barely audible beneath the din of tour-guide patter breathlessly reciting the documented data of the size of the space, the years and hundreds of thousands of workers it required to construct it, the physical dimensions of the Great Hall of the People (Renmin dahuitang), the Museum of Chinese History and the Chinese Revolution (Zhongguo geming lishi bowuguan), the Mao Zedong (the Square's only permanent resident) Mausoleum (Mao zhuxi jiniantang), and the tons of Qingdao marble sculpted to form the 36-metre tall obelisk of the Monument to the People's Heroes (Renmin yingxiong jinianbei), and the 9,600 rooms, pavilions, offices, that housed the families, servants and officials of the last two imperial dynasties, Ming (1368–1644) and Qing (1644–1911).

Yet because the powerful pageantry of its past is embedded in its stone, the Square has a risky polysemousness that cannot be overcome by the escalating volume of commercial pulp produced in honour of its capacity to generate revenue for the nation's most successful growth industry. Soldiers are always in evidence and agents of the Public Security Bureau are never far away, appearing suddenly when banners bearing the incendiary words 'zhen–shan–ren' (truth–goodness–forbearance) are unfurled or visitors begin to perform the first movements of the singular callisthenics of **Falun gong**, as has occurred periodically since the spiritual practice was deemed an 'evil cult' in the summer of 1999.

Today, the physical evidence of the massacre (most of which occurred offsite along Chang'an Avenue, just south of the gate and the parade grounds) has been expunged, the shell casings collected and bullets removed from their lodgings in the stone of monument and museum, and the space beckons numberless tourists scurrying towards the Forbidden City. It is a compelling, grandiose, apparently empty space peopled by tourists, guards, schoolchildren, but which for the 2008 **Olympics** will become the historically significant venue for beach volleyball. For the history that has been lived there, etched into its rough cement paving stones whose numberless bloodstains have long been scrubbed clean, and the myth that reaches far beyond it, Tiananmen frames the architecture of modern Chinese political life. For this alone the Square will always resonate with the triumph and tragedy of the nation's struggle with itself as if the vertical and horizontal planes of its hybrid architectural history meet in an unstable fault that runs the full length of its 14 hectares.

Further reading

(1993). *Beijing fengpo jishi* [The Truth about the Beijing Turmoil]. Beijing: Beijing chubanshe.

Arlington, L. C. and Lewisohn, William (1991). *In Search of Old Peking*. New York: Oxford University Press (reprint).

Boulanger, Robert (ed.) (1989). *Les Guides Bleus: China*. New York: Prentice Hall.

Brook, Timothy (1999). *Quelling the People: The Military Suppression of the Beijing Democracy Movement*. Stanford: Stanford University Press.

Fox, Richard G. (1977). *Urban Anthropology: Cities in their Cultural Settings*. Englewood Cliffs, NJ: Prentice Hall.

Lan, Peijin (ed.) (2001). *Beijing*. Beijing: Foreign Language Press.

Rowe, Peter G. and Seng Kuan (2002). *Architectural Encounters with Essence and Form in Modern China*. Cambridge, MA: MIT Press.

Schell, Orville (1995). *Mandate of Heaven: The Legacy of Tiananmen Square and the Next Generation of China's Leaders*. New York: Touchstone.

Sheehan, Sean (2002). *Fodor's Citypack Beijing*, 2nd edn. New York: Fodor's Travel Publications.

Spence, Jonathan (1982). *The Gate of Heavenly Peace: The Chinese and their Revolution, 1895–1980*. New York: Viking Press.

Steinhardt, Nancy Shatzman (1990). *Chinese Imperial City Planning*. Honolulu: University of Hawaii Press.

Wagner, Rudolf G. (1992). 'Reading the Chairman Mao Memorial Hall in Peking: The Tribulations of the Implied Pilgrim'. In Susan Naquin and Chün-fang Yü (eds), *Pilgrims and Sacred Sites in China*. Berkeley: University of California Press, 378–423.

Wheatley, Paul (1971). *The Pivot of the Four Quarters: A Preliminary Enquiry into the Origins and Character of the Ancient Chinese City*. Edinburgh: Edinburgh University Press.

Wu, Liangyong (1979). 'Tiananmen guangchang de guihua chuyi' [Plan and Construction of Gate of Heavenly Peace Square]. *Jianzhushi lunwenji* 2: 14–50.

LIONEL M. JENSEN

Tiananmen Square (1991)

(Tiananmen guanchang)

Video series (eight episodes)

Invited to be screened at the Hong Kong International Film Festival, the series had to be pulled following pressure from Beijing, but was eventually shown in various Western countries. The series was produced by the 'Structure, Wave, Youth, Cinema Experimental Group of China' (SWYC) (Zhongguo 'Jiegou, Lanchao, Qingnian, Dianying' shiyan xiaozu), an informal collective of young filmmakers founded in 1989 and devoted to the production of documentaries (see also **New Documentary Movement**). The SWYC includes the series director Shi Jian and Chen Jue, as well as screenwriters (Guang Yi) and cinematographers (Wang Hongyou, Zhao Baohong), among others (Meng Weidong, Wang Fei).

Based on interviews with more than a hundred people conducted between 1988 and 1991 (with a six-month gap after June 1989), the series documents various aspects of life in the streets, alleys and courtyards surrounding the Square: survivors of the imperial era, street performers, grandmothers cooking for their families, small entrepreneurs, young women in modelling schools, foreigners, and so forth. Starting with a close-up of a giant portrait of Mao being painted and hung over the Square, the series is a collage of archival footage and documentary material, weaving a permanent dialectic between the present and the past, daily life and history.

Other productions of the SWYC include *Life in Beijing* (*Jingcheng sanji*, 1988–91), *Juvenile Delinquent* (*Gong du sheng*, 1992) and the much-acclaimed *I Graduated!* (*Wobiyele*, 1992), in which eight recent graduates, who were attending China's most prestigious universities in June 1989, are interviewed about various topics: love, sex, the prospect of employment, philosophy of life, desire to travel abroad (ambivalent) and memories of the student movement. One of the most romantic, and also the most intimate, works ever inspired by the Tiananmen Square massacre, *I Graduated!* movingly captures the sense of loss experienced by a whole generation.

See also: Jia Zhangke

Further reading

Reynaud, B. (1996). 'New Visions/New Chinas – Video: Art, Documentation and the Chinese Modernity in Question'. In M. Renov and E. Suderburg (eds), *Resolutions: Essays on Contemporary Video Practices*. Minneapolis: Minnesota University Press.

BÉRÉNICE REYNAUD

Tianfeng

[Heavenly Wind]

Protestant journal

Tianfeng was founded in February 1945 as a liberal Christian journal published by the YMCA press. Among the founders was the famous Wu Yaozong (Y. T. Wu), chairman after 1950 of the **Three-Self Patriotic Movement (TSPM)**. Wu also published in *Tianfeng* some of his most important theological articles that laid the foundation for the TSPM. After 1949 the magazine became the official organ of the TSPM and its contents were very politicized during the 1950s and the 1960s, reflecting the ongoing political turmoil in society. *Tianfeng* stopped publishing in 1964, only to start again in late 1980s as a monthly. It has been the leading and sometimes only Christian journal available in China, and it is the only Protestant magazine officially to be sold abroad. Today, the national committee of the TSPM and the **China Christian Council** (CCC) publishes *Tianfeng* jointly in Shanghai. The magazine conveys official information from the TSPM and the CCC, disseminates government religious affairs policies, and also publishes spiritual and devotional articles that cater to the needs of ordinary congregation members. *Tianfeng* also carries news briefs from congregations around China.

See also: Christianity (Protestantism)

FREDERIK FÄLLMAN

Tianya

[Frontiers]

Literary periodical

When first published in Haikou, now the capital of Hainan province, in 1980, *Tianya* was just an average literary bimonthly, but it was transformed after 1996 when its editorial staff was changed and the writer **Han Shaogong** became chief editor. It is now regarded as the most important intellectual as well as literary magazine in south China. As with many other literary quarterlies, *Tianya*'s format is 16 mo, but the publishing capacity of each issue is only 192 pages at present, with approximately 30,000 subscribers (2001). Publishing short stories, poems and essays, *Tianya* has also featured two special columns since 1996, which have strongly attracted the sight line of the society: one is 'Zuojia lichang' [Writers' Stands], usually the lead, in which the writers and scholars from across the country and overseas express their views on literary or cultural subjects, and even on economic and political situations in China and the world; another is 'Minjian yüwen' [Popular Language] that publishes various informal, 'non-official' writing, including private letters, diaries, wall slogans and local slang (see **minjian**).

Probably because of its location in Hainan, the southernmost province of China, *Tianya* has been freer to publish what it wants than comparable periodicals in Shanghai or other central cities. It was the first magazine on the mainland to publish a post-1989 essay by **Bei Dao**, the famous exiled poet whose work had been banned, and the first to publish those of his writings that originally appeared on the Web.

WANG XIAOMING

Tibetan Buddhism among minority groups

Tibetan Buddhism is the esoteric or Tantric form of Buddhism which became prominent in India in the seventh century and spread quickly to Tibet. Other than the Tibetans, followers of Tibetan Buddhism are still found among such ethnic groups as the Mongols, the Tu of Qinghai, the Yugurs of Gansu, and the Moinba of Tibet. Many Chinese know this religion as 'lamaism' (*lamajiao*). The Cultural Revolution attempted to destroy the immense power of Buddhism, including the many monasteries. However, the religion has revived since the early 1980s, and the great majority of Tibetans are still dedicated followers of Tibetan Buddhism, though it is much weaker among the Mongolians. Quite a few Tibetan boys have again entered the monastic life, though not nearly as many as before 1950. An official count in 2000 gave a figure of 46,000 monks and lamas in the Tibet Autonomous Region. CCP authorities control all religious activities, but watch those associated with Tibetan Buddhism in Tibet with special care because of its association with Tibetan separatism, and suppress all signs of subversion. Some of Tibet's major political controversies since 1990 have involved the religion. In selecting the Eleventh Panchen Lama in 1995, the Chinese authorities conflicted with the Dalai Lama's choice. And in 1999, the highly influential Karmapa Lama fled to India and was given refugee status in 2001, to China's embarrassment.

See also: Buddhism in Inner Mongolia; Buddhist monasteries (Tibetan)

Further reading

Goldstein, M. C. and Kapstein, M. T. (eds) (1998). *Buddhism in Contemporary Tibet, Religious Revival and Cultural Identity*. Berkeley: University of California Press.

COLIN MACKERRAS

Tibetan theatre

Tibetan theatre features China's oldest ethnic drama style, arising independently of Chinese theatre in the fifteenth century, as well as the quasi-dramatic temple dances and other forms. Tibetan drama integrates singing, dialogue, dance, acrobatics, mime and colourful costumes. The musical accompaniment consists only of drum, cymbal and chorus. Both Tibetan drama and temple dance feature masks designating character. There are three sections to a Tibetan drama: a masked dance forming the prologue, the drama itself, and a farewell blessing. Content concerns Tibetan history and mythology, and a few are based on Indian literary works. Characterization is stark, with positive and negative features clearly shown. Tibetan dramas are performed during the day under special tents, with the audience all around the performance area, with only a narrow passage for the actors to enter or exit.

Chinese authorities established the professional Tibet Drama Troupe of Tibet in 1960, but during the **Cultural Revolution** only propaganda themes based on Han Chinese revolutionary stories were allowed. In the period of reform, the traditional theatre has revived strongly. Although dramas with modern content are still found, Tibetans find them boring and greatly prefer the traditional. In 1997 a Tibetan cultural official gave a figure of 150 professional and folk performing arts troupes for the Tibet Autonomous Region. Of these about half are folk drama troupes. Performances are still very common on festival days and enthusiastically patronized by ordinary Tibetans, who appear to regard their theatre as a symbol of their identity. Although there are also performances in modern theatres, most take place under the traditional tent or in any open space.

Further reading

Mackerras, C (1999). 'Tradition and Modernity in the Performing Arts of the Tibetans'. *International Journal of Social Economics* 26.1, 2, 3: 58–78.

COLIN MACKERRAS

Tibetans, culture of

The Tibetans, whose homeland is among the highest-lying of any people's, have two languages and many dialects, belonging to the Tibetan-Burmese branch of the Sino-Tibetan family. They have their own script, of seventh-century origin, and in 1988 a special commission was established to promote the use of the Tibetan language in the public sphere in the Tibet Autonomous Region (TAR). The 1990 census showed just over 2 million Tibetans in the TAR (95.46 per cent of the total), and 4,593,330 in all China. The 2000 census had the Tibetan population in the TAR as 2,411,100 (92.2 per cent of the total). Other than Tibet, the provinces with the most Tibetans are, in order, Sichuan, Qinghai, Gansu and Yunnan.

Tibetan culture is heavily influenced by Tibetan Buddhism (see **Tibetan Buddhism among minority groups**). To this day, the great majority of houses have shrines, especially in the countryside. Tibetan medicine is also religiously based, and is still much in use. Religious themes permeate the rich Tibetan tradition of paintings, scrolls, sculpture and statues. Masked religious dancing, performed by monks, still takes place in the monasteries. The gigantic Potala Palace, now a museum, stands atop a mountain towering over the Tibetan capital Lhasa, and is among the world's greatest old buildings. One of the few fully secular works of art in Tibet is the tale of the great King Gesar, fighter against evil, which said to be the world's longest epic (see **ethnic minority literary collections**). In addition to the classical arts, there is a modern tradition emerging in literature, painting and storytelling. More professionalized and secular, the content reflects conditions in modern Tibet and contemporary Tibetan history. However, Tibetans still prefer traditional themes. The epic of King Gesar is still sung by bards as well as being dramatized, and retains great popularity.

Formerly monasteries dominated the education system and Tibetan learning. Religious education survives in the monasteries, but there is also a comprehensive secular education system. Although most children now go to school, the literacy rate in the TAR for people aged over fourteen is only 52.7 per cent (2000 census), much lower than the national average (see **literacy (and illiteracy)**). Since the 1990s, attention has been given to devising Tibetan-language textbooks, and at primary level most instruction uses Tibetan, although it changes to Chinese higher in the education system.

Most marriages are monogamous. However, polyandrous and polygamous marriages still exist, especially the former – a 1996 survey showing polyandrous marriages at about 15 per cent of the total. The aim of polyandry, which usually sees brothers sharing a wife, and of polygyny, with sisters sharing a husband, is to avoid splitting inheritance.

Tibetan culture has changed significantly under Chinese pressure. It has, however, shown astonishing resilience, even conservatism, and no signs of extinction.

Further reading

Barnett, R. and Akiner, S. (eds) (1994). *Resistance and Reform in Tibet*. London: C. Hurst.

Snellgrove, D. and Richardson, H. (1968). *A Cultural History of Tibet*. London: Weidenfeld and Nicolson.

COLIN MACKERRAS

Tie Ning

b. 1957, Beijing

Writer

The vice president of the Chinese Writers' Association since 1996, Tie Ning represents an important strand of post-Mao era writing by women writers. Tie experienced the 'Rustification Movement' during the **Cultural Revolution** and did editorial work for a literary magazine before becoming a professional writer. She first published in 1975 and won fame for 'Ah, Fragrant Snow' (*O, Xiangxue*), which was awarded 'Best Short Story' in 1982, and for the film adaptation of her novel *A Red Pullover* (*Meiyou niukou de hongchenshan*, 1983). Tie positions her own literature as an alternative to the highly political literature of the 1980s. She emphasizes the unique perspective of her teenage female protagonists. The standpoint of the socially inexperienced is employed as a critique of cultural, moral and, in her later work, political observations.

Rose Gate (*Meigui men*, 1989) marks a transition to a more explicit treatment of sexuality. Based on the experience of three generations of women during the Cultural Revolution, the novel both questions female identity as a collective attribute in a broad social and political context and reveals hidden connections among these women. Though the perspective is still that of a young woman, the novel presents a picture of an adult world of violence, turbulence and power struggles. Tie's exploration of female sexuality strikes a more mellow note in the late 1990s. *Big Bathers* (*Da yunü*,1999; a.k.a. *Woman Showering*) was written for the *Cloth Tiger Series* (*Bulaohu congshu*), a project designed by the Laoning Literature and Arts Press to promote reader-friendly, optimistic and entertaining fiction for an emerging middle-class readership.

Further reading

Chen, Xiaoming (2002). 'The Extrication of Memory in Tie Ning's *Woman Showering*: Privacy and the Trap of History'. In Bonnie McDougall and Anders Hansson (eds), *Chinese Concepts of Privacy*. Leiden: Brill.

Tie, Ning (1999). 'Ah, Fragrant Snow'. Trans. Zha Jianya. In Tam Kwok-kan *et al.* (eds), *A Place of One's Own: Stories of Self in China, Hong Kong, and Singapore*. New York: Oxford University Press, 311–22.

HE DONGHUI

TOEFL and GRE

TOEFL (Test of English as a Foreign Language) tests one's English proficiency, while the GRE (Graduate Record Examination) tests one's verbal, analytical and quantitative skills. To be enrolled in a North American university, foreign students need to attain a threshold score, determined by each university, on both the TOEFL and GRE. When Beijing opened its first TOEFL testing centre in 1981, only 285 students sat for the exam. By the late 1980s, Beijing alone had seventeen testing centres that could test 35,000 people per year, but even with this new capacity, students still have to line up overnight just to get an application form. The TOEFL craze has been sustained into the 1990s. Its importance to Chinese students can be seen from a recent survey, which revealed that 45.5 per cent of the students in five major Beijing universities have taken or are preparing to take TOEFL and GRE. Preparation schools for TOEFL and GRE tests have also mushroomed. The most famous is the New East (Xindongfang). These training programmes have so inflated the scores that the tests are no longer a good measure of Chinese students' real proficiency, and it has been a headache for North American universities.

TOEFL has also great political significance. During the 1989 Democracy Movement, students who were preparing for TOEFL were much less likely to participate in the demonstrations. In the 1990s, Beijing students could pass the test with much higher scores than Shanghai and Guangzhou students because the southern students were distracted by, and attracted to, careers in their booming local economies. During the 1999 anti-US demonstrations which followed the US bombing of the Chinese Embassy in Belgrade, Beijing students followed many kinds of anti-US slogans but not slogans such as 'Down with TOEFL' and 'Down with Xindongfang'. The attraction of studying in America has created a safety valve for the Chinese government and in the meantime has also made it difficult for truly anti-US feelings to take root in the hearts of young Chinese. The Chinese translation of TOEFL is *tuofu*, literally 'thanks to good fortune'. The translation is telling.

Further reading

Hayhoe, Ruth (1989). *China's Universities and the Open Door*. Armonk, NY: M. E. Sharpe.

Orleans, Leo A. (1988). *Chinese Students in America: Policies, Issues, and Numbers*. Washington, DC: National Academy Press.

Rosen, Stanley (1991). 'The Role of Chinese Students at Home and Abroad as a Factor in Sino-American Relations'. In William T. Tow (ed.), *Building Sino-American Relations*. New York: Paragon House, 162–202.

Zhao, Dingxin (1996). 'Foreign Study as a Safety-Valve: The Experience of China's University Students Going Abroad in the Eighties'. *Higher Education* 31: 145–63.

—— (2002). 'The 1999 Anti-US Demonstrations and the Nature of Student Nationalism in China Today'. *Problems of Post-Communism* 49 (November/December): 16–28.

ZHAO DINGXIN

tombs and cremation

Since ancient times, tombs in China have most commonly consisted of a simple mound over the coffin, sometimes with a rectangular stone tablet identifying the deceased at the head or foot end. Mounds are found in different shapes, and are often covered over with mortar. Tombs must be located according to geomantic principles (see **fengshui**); the ideal tomb site has high ground behind it and water in front. In more elaborate tombs, the mound is surrounded by a horseshoe-shaped embankment built of stone or concrete, which protects the grave from falling rainwater if there really is high ground behind the tomb, and simulates a mountain if there is not. There is much regional variation: tombs in north China tend to be of the simple mound type, and coffins may be stored above ground to await final interment after the death of the spouse, while people in some parts of south China practise secondary burial, in which remains are disinterred after several years, then reburied in a jar at a permanent tomb.

Since 1956, the Chinese government has promoted cremation over tomb burial, citing concerns about superstitious practices, deforestation for coffins, and encroachment on arable land. But a strong cultural preference for burial persists. It is estimated that 50–70 per cent of Chinese dead are still buried in tombs, with higher proportions in rural areas. Some elderly urban residents return to their native village to await death, so that they can avoid compulsory cremation in the city. There are now over 100,000 public cemeteries in urban and rural areas, which sell rights to small burial plots, but especially in the countryside many people continue to build tombs illicitly, either separately or in family or lineage cemeteries. In the reform era, elaborate private tombs with large terraces, stone staircases and stone sepulchres have reappeared in the countryside, many built by overseas Chinese and residents of Taiwan or Hong Kong. Some kinship groups have also rebuilt putative graves of their distant ancestors in order to promote cohesiveness and build networks (see **ancestral halls/lineage temples**). The sweeping of tombs of ancestors and the offering of paper money and food are the central rituals of the Clear and Bright Festival (**Qingming Festival**). Recent government initiatives to reduce expenditure on tombs and tomb rituals include campaigns to plant trees over buried cremated remains, and the creation of Internet memorials.

MICHAEL SZONYI

Tongue

(Shetou)

Rock group

Tongue has the distinction of being the only Chinese rock band from Xinjiang province. In this region of western China, populated by the Muslim Uighurs, Islamic culture is a major influence on musical life. For the six members of Tongue, whose Han Chinese parents were relocated to the provincial capital of Urumuqi as part of the post 1949 frontier population project, the Uighur cultural environment exposed them to musical sensitivities alien to mainstream Han culture. From such an unusual set of musical valences Tongue was formed in 1997 to 'create some new music', and in the summer of that year they moved to Beijing. By 1999 Tongue's sound had solidified into an eccentric sonic blend of contrapuntal guitar fuzz, horror-flick karaoke keyboards, thunderbottom sprints and dirges, and beatnik hallucination rap. The band quickly developed a following which led to a two-record deal with Modern Sky's Badhead label (see **New Sound Movement, Modern Sky Records**). Their first record, *Little Chicken Hatches* (*Xiaoji chuke liao*), was released in early 2000. Their second was mired in conflict between the band, who had entitled the work *The Painter* (*Youqijiang*), and their new management company, Beijing Pulay Music, who spent an exorbitant sum on mastering the record in England and retitling the work *This Is You...* (*Zhe jiushi ni...*), all without the band's approval. Tongue has seen almost no money from both record releases. Thus, while remaining one of

the most respected entities in the Beijing live-music scene, success remains elusive for the band, whose hampered potential is indicative of so many musical artists living at the mercy of a dysfunctional Chinese music industry. Tongue includes: Wu Tun (b. 1972) on vocals, Wu Junde (b. 1972) on bass, Guo Dagang (b. 1970) on keyboards, Zhu Xiaolong (b. 1973) on guitar, Li Hongjun (b. 1970) on guitar, and Li Dan (b. 1975) on drums.

MATTHEW CLARK

tourism

Tourism has come a long way. China had gingerly guarded against foreigners until the early 1980s. The initial influx plagued the country's poor infrastructure. In two decades, however, its economic miracle has created one of the world's largest superhighway systems and airline fleets. Five- and four-star hotels are omnipresent. Trains have been speeded up so that a night's sleep will take a tourist from Beijing to Shanghai. Competition has helped introduce the idea of seasonal discounts and aggressive advertisement.

China's five-day work-week, adopted in 1995, and week-long paid vacations in both May and October have contributed to a surge in domestic tourism. Moreover, as the Chinese become richer and the government makes passports more available, outgoing Chinese tourists outnumbered incoming foreign tourists for the first time in 2002, when 7.35 million Chinese went to 226 countries and regions, with Hong Kong, Macau, Thailand, Japan and Russia the most popular destinations. Meanwhile, 6.14 million tourists visited China from 234 countries, mostly from Japan, South Korea, Russia, the United States, Malaysia, the Philippines, Singapore, Mongolia, Thailand and Britain. The number of people going in and out of China's ports hit a record high of 107.9 million at the same time. Incidentally, the government does not regard Taiwan, Hong Kong and Macau as 'abroad'.

Some tour guides accept tips in violation of government regulations. Other abuses include their receiving kickbacks from souvenir dealers that may short-change the tourists. Despite harsh crackdowns on prostitution, visitors may still be surprised by phone solicitations in many hotels.

Further reading

Oakes, Tim (1998). *Tourism and Modernity in China*. London: Routledge.

Tan, Chee-Beng, Cheung, Sidney and Yang, Hui (eds) (2001). *Tourism, Anthropology and China*. Bangkok: White Lotus Press.

YUAN HAIWANG

towns and townships

One sometimes sees references to China's 'counties and townships' as if the two words were interchangeable. In fact they are not. In each of China's 2,079 counties there is at least one major town (the county seat) and often several other smaller towns called *zhen*. In national census publications (Lu 1998) the population is given for some 4,720 different cities or *shi* and counties or *xian*. Although referring to the Pearl River Delta, Lin's (1997) description is fairly applicable across the country. He describes the administrative (and spatial) hierarchy as usually having five components: 'county' (*xian*), 'township' (*xiang*), 'towns' found within a township (*zhen*), 'administrative districts', replacing the former 'brigades' (*guanliqu*), and 'administrative villages' (*cun*) and/or 'village communities' (*cunmin weiyuanhui*), in lieu of the former 'production teams'. The name of the county seat town is almost always the same as the name of the county. Townships were created after 1980 to replace the 'communes'. Each township has a seat of local government that normally is designated with a 'town' (*zhen*) status, although the overall population and land area of the township are predominantly agricultural in nature (Lin 1997: 137). In eastern, densely populated China, a township can have a population well in excess of 50,000 covering an area of less than 100 sq. km. while at the other extreme in the far west – in southern Qinghai, for example – a township can have an area of 20,000 sq. km. or more with a population under 10,000.

See also: cities

Further reading

Fei, Hsiao Tung (1986). *Small Towns in China: Functions, Problems and Prospects*. Beijing: New World Press.

Lin, George C. S. (1997). *Red Capitalism in South China*. Vancouver: UBC Press.

Lu, Chenhung (1998). *China Population Statistics Yearbook*. Beijing: China Statistics Press.

PETER M. FOGGIN

traditional music

The term 'Chinese music' (*Zhongguo yinyue*) is used primarily to designate instrumental music, though sometimes it is used more broadly to include folksong and other minor vocal genres. Opera music (**Xiqu**) and narrative song (**quyi**), however, are usually considered to belong to different domains, since both are based upon literary sources. This entry will attempt to define some basic socio-functional distinctions in Chinese music, notably between the dichotomies of traditional and modern, sacred and secular, amateur and professional, male and female, and urban and rural.

The term 'traditional music' (*chuantong yinyue*) is commonly employed to designate a very broad range of surviving music, including genres (and actual repertoire) cited in pre tenth-century Tang dynasty literature (e.g. **qin** zither music), other genres which may be nearly as old (e.g. **Chaozhou-Hakka sixian** or **string ensemble music**), and even some early twentieth-century works by known composers (e.g. *Guangdong yinyue* or Cantonese instrumental music; see **Cantonese music**). While some sources refer to these latter types as 'folk music' (*minzu yinyue*), the term is not so appropriate in the Chinese context, since some traditions (e.g. **Jiangnan sizhu**, **Minnan nanyin**) display the sophistication of 'classical' art music. Musical developments before the Tang period are generally referred to as 'ancient' (*gudai*), while developments dating from the mid-twentieth century onward (mostly syncretic and Western-influenced compositions) are said to be 'modern' (*xiandai*).

Among the principal dichotomies in traditional music, the widespread concepts of sacred and secular are basic. String ensemble traditions of central-eastern and southern China (e.g. Jiangnan sizhu, Chaozhou sixian) are primarily thought to be entertainment genres, since they are usually performed in music clubs and teahouses for appreciative audiences. Wind and percussion ensemble traditions of northern China (e.g. **Beijing yinyue**, **Xi'an guyue**) are primarily ritual genres, since they are performed in **Buddhist monasteries** and temples, at **funerals** and other auspicious occasions, in tribute to gods and ancestors (see **Buddhist music**; **Daoist music**; **temple fairs**). It must be noted, however, that these two domains are not mutually exclusive, for in south China string ensemble music is also performed at ritual events (as is Minnan nanyin music at local temples on auspicious days). Conversely, wind ensemble music of north China is also performed for entertainment purposes (as at the end of funeral ceremonies when attendees request their favourite pieces). Related to the above duality, and in some ways underpinning it, are the ancient concepts of yin and yang ('dark' vs 'bright' in the instance of music).

The amateur–professional dichotomy is another problematic one. The traditional (largely Confucian) ideology disapproved of professional activity in the fine arts, notably the acceptance of payment for performance and the gratuitous display of virtuosity. The arts of poetry, painting and music were thought to be suitable (even necessary) for self-cultivation and reinforcement of the old values, but decidedly not for the type of specialization that might lead to cultural blindness. This so-called 'amateur ideal' has been maintained unevenly among the many regional music genres – strongly embraced by **qin**-playing literati of northern China and among the culturally conservative Minnan people of Fujian province (Minnan nanyin), but relatively weak in the eclectic tradition of the Cantonese. In some wind band traditions of rural areas surrounding Beijing, the highest quality of performance is believed to be maintained by ensembles claiming amateur status (e.g. the *guanzi*-led 'music associations', or *yinyue hui*). Indeed, professional wind bands are also active in this area (notably the *suona*-led **drumming and blowing**

musicians (*chuigushou*), but their music is thought to be of lower quality. Thus, in the Chinese context, it is commonly said that amateur performers have superior 'style' (*fengge*), while professional performers have better 'technique' (*jichao*).

Traditional instrumental ensemble music tends to be dominated by male performers. In the music clubs of most regional genres (e.g. Jiangnan sizhu, Beijing yinyue), performance of instruments is restricted (by custom) to male performers. Among younger conservatory-trained musicians, however, this gender orientation is slowly changing, especially in performance of the solo **zheng** (zither) and **pipa** (lute) repertoires, where women are now as active as men. In vocal music (e.g. local opera traditions, narrative song genres), both males and females sing, though here women often play the dominant role – notably in Yueju (Cantonese opera; see **Yueju (Guangdong, Guanxi opera)**) song where women routinely sing male parts.

The last dichotomy to be considered is that of urban vs rural. In China, as in much of the world, music has tended to become highly standardized in cities. In Shanghai, for example, where there is a major conservatory of music and a state-supported Chinese ensemble of international fame, established arrangements of the local **Silk and Bamboo** music (Jiangnan sizhu) have become performance ideals, especially among aspiring young urban musicians who rely heavily upon notated versions. Among the many amateur music clubs in Shanghai and the nearby countryside, however, the influence of the Shanghai professional ensembles has been weaker and greater diversity in the repertoire is found. The most standardized instrumental tradition in China is **Cantonese music** (Guangdong yinyue), centred in the southern port cities of Hong Kong and Guangzhou. Owing to the urbanizing forces of unification, but more significantly to the activity of numerous composer/performers who, beginning in the 1920s, composed new music and standardized arrangements of older pieces, Cantonese music today is performed in very nearly the same way in all Cantonese communities, urban or rural. Minnan nanyin music of nearby southern Fujian province, which is not centred in large urban areas, stands in contrast to the Cantonese tradition. Here there are noticeable structural differences in the repertoire between one village and another, differences great enough that musicians from different areas must resolve these local variants before performing together.

See also: folksongs (Han Chinese); traditional music composers; traditional music performers

Further reading

Jones, Stephen (1995). *Folk Music of China: Living Instrumental Traditions*. Oxford: Clarendon Press (rpt 1998).

Thrasher, Alan R. (1993). 'East Asia: China'. In Helen Myers (ed.), *Ethnomusicology: Historical and Regional Studies*. London: Macmillan.

—— (2000). *Chinese Musical Instruments*. Hong Kong: Oxford University Press.

Witzleben, J. Lawrence (1995). *Silk and Bamboo Music in Shanghai*. Kent, O: Kent State University Press.

—— (ed.) (2002). 'China'. In *The Garland Encyclopedia of World Music, vol. 7: East Asia: China, Japan and Korea*. New York: Routledge.

ALAN R. THRASHER

traditional music composers

When instrumental music moved from teahouse to concert hall in the mid twentieth century, musicians became aware of the need to rearrange traditional repertoire to satisfy the new ticket-buying public. Short pieces were lengthened by adding introductions and contrasting middle sections, performance volumes were increased, and textures thickened for concert-hall projection. A good amount of new music was also composed by creative artists who, for the first time in Chinese history, actually signed their compositions. Most of this body of music (known as *guoyue*, or 'national music', and by other names) was composed for traditional instruments, and employed traditional melodic styles but with Western-influenced harmonies.

Abing (né Hua Yanjun, 1893–1950) was the most famous Daoist traditional composer of the twentieth century. He was born in Wuxi, Jiangsu province, and his father, Hua Qinghe, was a Daoist priest as well as a famous musician. Abing began learning music from his father when he was seven years old. At eighteen he became a famous Daoist musician and played in local Daoist ceremonial bands (see **Daoist music**). The turning point in Abing's career came in his thirties. Since he became blind, he could not play in ceremonial bands any longer and became a street musician playing **erhu** and **pipa**, and singing ballads for a living until his death. It is said that he composed over two hundred pieces, but among them only six were recorded and published, including three erhu solos: 'Moon Reflected in the Second Spring' (*Erquan yingyue*), 'Listening to the Pines' (*Tingsong*), 'Cold Spring Wind' (*Hanchun fengqu*) and three pipa solos: 'Dragon Boats' (*Longchuan*), 'Great Waves Washing the Sand' (*Dalang taosha*) and 'Zhaojun Crosses the Border' (*Zhaojun chusai*). In his compositions, influenced by Daoist philosophy, nature is the most important subject. His music expresses inner emotion, and its style is linked with the local traditional music genres such as folksongs and Wuxi opera. While his total number of works is small, each one is tightly organized, but also song-like and poetic.

Gu Guanren (b. 1942) is a famous composer. He was born in Haimen, Jiangsu, and started to play pipa when he was a boy. In 1957, after having become a pipa player in the Shanghai Chinese Orchestra, he began to compose. From 1961 to 1965, Gu studied composition at the Shanghai Conservatory, and after graduation he composed for the orchestra for thirty years. In his music, he tried to mix Chinese traditional melodies with Western harmony. 'Melody of Beijing Opera' (*Jingdiao*) and the ensemble piece 'Fishermen's Song of the Eastern Sea' (*Donghai yuge*) are two of his well-known compositions.

Hu Dengtiao (1926–94) was a composer and teacher, and, in a quiet way, one of the most influential musicians of his time. Hu was born in Ninghai, Zhejiang, and started to learn erhu when he was a high school student. In 1948, he entered the Shanghai Conservatory and from 1964 he taught composition there for over thirty years. He wrote the first textbook on orchestration for Chinese orchestra. He is most noted for having composed forty quintets for Chinese strings.

Liu Mingyuan (1931–96) was one of the most versatile of contemporary musicians, being a composer, teacher and fiddle virtuoso of outstanding quality. Liu was born in Tianjin. His father was a medical doctor and a good musician. Liu started to play the *banhu* and *jinghu* at the age of five. At eleven he had already became famous in the city and played in concerts and was featured on the radio. In 1951, he became first chair in the Beijing Film Studio Philharmonic. From 1982 to 1996, as founder of the modern method of *banhu*, he taught in the Conservatory of China. His compositions include many solo pieces for various Chinese fiddles and orchestra. Best known are: 'Year of Happiness' (*Xingfunian*) and 'Jubilance' (*Xiyangyang*). Liu was a gifted melodist and his music is always light and gracious, never violent or deeply tragic.

Liu Tianhua (1895–1932) was one of the most important Chinese composers of the twentieth century. Born in Jiangyin, Jiangsu, Liu adopted music as his life work when he was very young. In 1909, he started to learn Western brass winds in Changzhou and joined a band in Shanghai three years later. In 1914, he returned to his home town and taught music in several middle schools. During that time, he learned to play the erhu and pipa from local virtuosos and started to compose. From 1922 to 1932, he taught Chinese instruments in the Music School of Peking University. During that period he studied violin and Western music theory and spent much time doing fieldwork, listening to traditional instrumental music and Peking opera, transcribing the original melodies and, later researching them. From 1922 to 1932, he composed ten erhu solo pieces, three pipa solos and two pieces for Chinese ensemble. Among the erhu pieces 'Beautiful Moonlight Eve' (*Yueye*), 'Melody of Brightness' (*Guangming xing*), 'A Short Song of New Year's Eve' (*Chuye xiaochang*) and 'Birds' Song in a Desolate Gorge' (*Kongshan niaoyu*) are his representative works. Under the influence of his brother, one of the pioneers of the 'New Culture' Movement (May Fourth Movement), his ideal was the use of Western music techniques and theory to improve Chinese traditional music. His erhu compositions are a successful fusion of Chinese melody with Western violin technique. In his music there is narrative song (**quyi**), which has been stylistically worked into the compositions.

Liu Wenjing (b. 1937) is the most important erhu composer of our time. Liu was born in Tangshan, where he studied composition with Lin Chaoxia and Huang Xiaofei. After graduation in 1961, he has worked in the Central Chinese Philharmonic Orchestra. His most important compositions are the erhu solos, 'Ballad of Northern Henan Province' (*Yubei xushiqu*) and 'Fantasy of Sanmenxia' (*Sanmenxia changxiangqu*) and the erhu concerto 'The Great Wall' (*Changcheng suixiang*).

Lü Wencheng (1898–1981) was a famous Cantonese composer. He was born in Zhongshan, Guangdong, but when he was three his parents moved to Shanghai. There the young man started his career as an erhu player. He joined the Shanghai Chinese Music Association in 1919, and also performed Cantonese music for radio and cut records. He and his teacher Situ Mengyan co-invented the *gaohu*, and so changed the instrumentation of Cantonese music. In 1932, he moved to Hong Kong and lived there for fifty years. He composed 125 pieces, the most famous of which are 'Higher Step by Step' (*Bubu gao*) and 'Autumn Moon on the Peaceful Lake' (*Pinghu qiuyue*). Since he lived in Shanghai for almost thirty years and learned traditional music there, his compositions also show a strong influence from the music of the area.

Peng Xiuwen (1931–96) was a famous composer and conductor. Peng was born in Wuhan, Hubei. He loved music and learned to play the erhu when he was a boy, though he was trained to be an accountant. In 1950, he was invited to be the music editor of a radio station, which established his future in music rather than in business. In 1952, Peng went to Beijing and started playing and composing in the Chinese orchestra of the Central Broadcasting Station. In 1957, he stopped playing and started to conduct and compose. Peng rearranged over 400 pieces for orchestra, which included folksongs, arias for Peking opera, pieces for traditional instruments, and foreign compositions. His ideal was to set up a Chinese symphonic orchestra. His famous compositions are 'Symphony No 1: Nanjing', the symphonic suite 'December' (*Shiyue*) and the erhu concerto 'Crane in the Clouds' (*Yunzhong he*).

Sun Wenming (?1928–62?) was a blind erhu player and composer. Little is known of his musical training, although it is possible that he studied with many folk musicians in the area near Shanghai. Sun was born in Shangyu, Zhejiang. He lost his sight when he was four years old and became a street musician at fourteen. In 1951, he started to compose, and from 1959 to 1961 he taught at the Shanghai Conservatory. He composed over ten erhu pieces, among which 'Flowing Wave' (*Liubo qu*), describing his vagrant life, is the most famous.

Zhang Shiye (b. 1931?) is a composer and conductor of the Chinese orchestra. He was born in Nanjing and learned to play violin when he was a boy. In 1955, he organized a Chinese instrumental orchestra and composed for it until the early 1990s. His famous compositions are a symphonic suite, 'Recollecting the Long March' (*Changzheng yishi*), and a symphonic poem, 'Mount Yimeng' (*Yimingsong*).

Zhou Dafeng (b. 1923?) is a composer and musicologist. He was born in Zhenhai, Zhejiang. As a boy in the 1930s, he loved music and started to compose songs. In 1943, one of his songs won him a prize that resulted in national fame and prestige. From 1952 to 1989, he was the composer for the Zhejiang Opera Company and composed many operas. He also wrote many articles about Zhejiang opera music (see **Yueju (Zhejiang opera)**) and the fundamentals of Chinese traditional music. Among his many compositions, the dance music 'Picking Tea Leaves' (*Caicha wuqu*) is well known.

Zhu Guangqing (b. 1932?) is a famous composer and conductor. He was born in Jinxian, Liaoning. At the age of fourteen, he started to compose and was accepted as a student at Shenyang Conservatory, where he stayed for four years studying piano, theory and composition. Since the late 1950s he has been working in the Jilin Chinese Philharmonic Orchestra and has composed many orchestra pieces based on Manchurian folk customs, such as 'Running in Fire' (*Paohuochi*) and 'The Manchurian Dance Mangshi' (*Mangshi wuqu*).

See also: erhu; modern Chinese orchestra; pipa; zheng; musicology

Further reading

Du, Yaxiong (1981). 'Abing zhuanlue' [A Short Biography of Abing]. *Nanyi xuebao* 4: 32–3.

Huang, Shengquan (1998). *Zhongguo yinyuejia cidian* [A Dictionary of Chinese Musicians]. Beijing: Renmin Chubanshe.

Liang, Maochun (1996). 'Tianhua Liu, A Contemporary Revolutionary of the *Erhu*'. *Sonus* 17.1: 44–52.

Stock, Jonathan (1996). *Musical Creativity in Twentieth-Century China: Abing, His Music, and Its Changing Meanings*. Rochester : University of Rochester Press.

Wang, Yuhe (1994). *Zhongguo jinxiandai yinyueshi* [History of Chinese Music in Modern Times]. Beijing: Renmin yinyue chubanshe.

Wu, Ganbo (2002). *Ershi shiji zhonghua guoyue renwu zhi* [Annals of Chinese Traditional Musicians of the Twentieth Century]. Shanghai: Yinyue chubanshe.

Wu, Ganbo and Zhou, Hao (1986). *Sun Wenming erhu quji* [Erhu Pieces of Sun Wenming]. Hong Kong: Shanghai shuju.

Yang Yinliu (1980). 'Abing qiren qishi' [Abing – His Personality and Story]. *Renming yinyue* 3: 31–4.

Zhongguo yinyue yanjiusuo (ed.) (1983). *Abing quji* [Abing's Music Pieces]. Renming yinyue chubanshe.

DU YAXIONG

traditional music performers

The following music performers have been among the most influential style setters of the mid and late twentieth century. All were trained in the performance of traditional music, subsequently moving into prestigious positions in the new conservatories and onto concert hall stages.

Liu Dehai (b. 1937) is one of the greatest **pipa** virtuosos, teachers and composers. Born in Shanghai, he started to learn pipa at the age of ten. In 1955, he became a student at the Central Conservatory in Tianjin, where he studied pipa with Lin Shicheng, who developed his musical skill and sensitivity. From 1964, he has been teaching in the Conservatory of China and has invented many new techniques, including the technique of striking the strings with two fingers simultaneously, and using the thumb of the left hand to hold down the strings (*shuangyao*). He has composed over twenty pipa solo pieces, including 'Swan' (*Tianya*),

'Childhood' (*Tongnian*), 'Old Boy' (*Laotong*) and 'Golden Dream' (*Jinse de meng*). His composition style is directly related to his innovations in pipa technique.

Lu Chunling (b. 1921) is a well-known **dizi** (bamboo flute) player. Born in Shanghai, Lu loved local **Silk and Bamboo** music (Jiangnan sizhu) from childhood and learned dizi from one of his neighbours. Before 1952, he was a taxi driver, but in that year he joined the Shanghai Folk Ensemble and became a professional dizi player. Lu's playing is highly personal, poetic, fine and smooth. He rearranged many traditional pieces and also composed some dizi pieces. His compositions are often based on simple folk-like themes that are harmonized with Western chords. His best-known pieces are 'Today and Yesterday' (*Jinxi*) and 'Spring in Jiangnan' (*Jiangnan chun*).

Lü Peiyuan/Lui Pui-yuen (b. 1933) is a well-known pipa player, better known by the latter, Cantonese spelling. He was born in Suzhou and grew up in Shanghai, where he started to play pipa when he was ten with several virtuosos, including Wang Yuting, Li Tingsong and Xia Baosen. In 1951, he moved to Hong Kong with his family. After quitting his job in his uncle's factory, he started to teach and promote Chinese traditional music in Hong Kong. During the 1960s, Lü taught in several high schools and organized a Chinese Music Association, a society where Chinese traditional music lovers could come together to perform. The Association held frequent performances and competitions. After Lü emigrated to the USA in 1973, he has been teaching and promoting Chinese traditional music throughout North America.

Selaxi (1887–1967) was a virtuoso of the Mongolian fiddle (*morinhur*). He was born in Darhan, Inner Mongolia, where his father and grandfather were famous morinhur players. He started to learn the instrument at age nine. After he became a Buddhist lama at nineteen, he kept studying with Renqin, a local morinhur master. He left the temple and became a musician, performing in eastern Inner Mongolia from the 1920s to the end of the 1940s. In 1949, he joined the Inner Mongolian Ensemble, and from 1957 to 1967 was a professor at the School of Music at the Inner Mongolian University. Selaxi's morinhur technique

was prodigious. He popularized many traditional Mongolian pieces, among them 'Bayin', 'Wind in the Sky' and 'A Girl called Nonjiya'.

Turdi Akhong (1881–1956) was an outstanding virtuoso of the Uighur string instrument, the *satar*. He was born in Yinjisha, southern Xinjiang. Turdi's family was musical, and when he was eleven he started to learn the *mukam* from his father. After 1900, he performed mukam music in Kashgar, Hotan and Yerqiang. In 1950, he became a music teacher in the Yerqiang Song and Dance Ensemble. The mukam, a kind of Uighur palace music created in the fifteenth century, consists of twelve suites with each suite lasting about two hours. In the 1950s, Turdi was the only musician who could play all twelve suites. He collaborated with Chinese musicologists to record and transcribe the mukam, and thanks to his contribution, the twelve suites were published for the first time in 1960.

Wei Zhongle (1908–97) was a famous pipa, **qin**, **erhu** and *xiao* (vertical flute) player. The son of a worker, he was born in Shanghai. He was interested in Chinese traditional music from early childhood, studying first the dizi, then the erhu, pipa and qin. In spite of a haphazard music education, Wei's talents were so great that he began to build a reputation as a virtuoso instrumentalist in Shanghai. In the 1920s and 1930s, he held many pipa and qin recitals, made records, and taught Chinese instruments at several universities and colleges. In 1936, the Russian composer Avshalomov, living in Shanghai at the time, composed an erhu concerto, which Wei played with a Western orchestra. In 1938, he made a tour of the USA, performing in more than thirty cities, and made four records including pieces on pipa, erhu, qin, dizi and xiao. In 1940 he started teaching Chinese instruments at Hujiang University, and in 1941 he and several friends established the Chinese Orchestra in Shanghai and performed many traditional pieces. In 1949, Wei became a professor at the Shanghai Conservatory; in 1956 the Conservatory set up the Department of Chinese Music and Wei became the department chair for almost thirty years. Many outstanding Chinese instrument players were his students. His playing style is sincere and honest. 'The Great Ambuscade' (*Shimian maifu*) is his best-known piece.

Wu Jinglue (1907–87) was one of the most important qin zither players and teachers of the twentieth century. Wu was born in Changshu, a small town near Shanghai. In the 1920s he went to Jiangyin to learn the pipa, **zheng** and xiao from famous virtuosos Zhou Shaomei (see below) and Wu Mengfei. In 1930, he learned the qin from Wang Ruipu in Tianjin. In 1936, he attended meetings of the Jinyu Qin Society (Jinyu qinshe) in Suzhou and learned many pieces from other members of the Society. In 1939, he started to teach qin in Shanghai, and in 1956 he became professor of the Central Conservatory in Beijing, where he became chair of the Chinese Instrument Department and wrote a qin textbook.

Xiang Sihua (1939–) is one of the best-known zheng zither players of our time. Xiang was born in Kunming, Yunnan. After ten years of private piano lessons with Xie Fuxin and other teachers, she entered Shanghai Conservatory in 1956 and studied zheng with Wang Xuanzhi, the famous virtuoso of the Zhejiang school. From 1965 to 1981, she worked in Beijing, performed in several ensembles, and taught in conservatories. In 1981, she moved to Hong Kong and taught at the Chinese University of Hong Kong. In 1993, she emigrated to Canada. She continues the ornate style of the Zhejiang zheng school and also attempts to imitate traditional singing styles, making her performances colourful.

Zha Fuxi (1895–1976) was an important qin player and educator. Like most of other qin players, Zha was not professionally trained. He studied the qin when he was a boy, but his primary desire was to become a specialist in aeronautic sciences. In 1921, he went to Guangdong Aviation School, and after graduation worked for several airline companies for over two decades, spending his free time promoting qin music, collecting ancient pieces and their literature. In 1932, Zha founded the Jinyu Qin Society (Jinyu qinshe) in Suzhou and published its journal, *Jinyu Qin Publication*. The publication contained a series of articles on finger techniques, modal theories, aesthetics and, most importantly, documentation on the state of qin musicians, their photos, and compositions then being performed. In 1950, he quit his job with China Air, and started to work in the Musicology Institute of the Central Conservatory. During the 1950s, he taught in the Conservatory and was active in giving qin recitals and in organizing qin musicians from various existing schools. He did fieldwork in over ten cities, and as a result published 262 qin pieces played by eighty-six different musicians.

Zhao Songting (1924–2001) was a famous dizi player, composer and teacher. Born in Dongyang, Zhejiang, Zhao started to play dizi with his father when he was nine. He studied **Kunqu** with Ye Xiaoxun, and taught music in Dongyang Middle School for several years. In 1949, he joined a military ensemble. In 1956, he was with the Song and Dance Ensemble of Zhejiang province as a dizi soloist. In 1976, he started to teach in the Arts School of Zhejiang. As an outstanding player, Zhao invented many new techniques, including how to use circular breathing. As a composer, he composed many dizi solo pieces, among them 'Morning' (*Zaochen*), 'Three, Five, Seven' (*Sanwuqi*) and 'View of Wujiang River' (*Wujiang fenguang*), now considered classics of the 'Zhao' style.

Zhou Shaomei (1885–1938) was a respected erhu and pipa player and teacher. Zhou was born in Jiangyin, Jiangsu. His father was a famous erhu and pipa virtuoso in the area. Like many other musicians, he was first taught by his father. In 1898, he went to Suzhou where he studied **Jiangnan sizhu** from local musicians. In 1906, he became the first teacher in twentieth-century China to teach traditional music in a school. Many of his students became famous musicians. From 1925 to 1937, he taught Chinese music in several high schools and teachers' training schools in Wuxi, Suzhou and Changzhou. In 1930, he founded the Xiangshan Silk and Bamboo Music Society, and in 1935 he set up the Research Association of Chinese Music in Zhenjiang. He collected many traditional instrumental and operatic pieces and used them in his textbooks. He also composed a number of pieces for his students. He redesigned the erhu, making the neck longer than before, and improved erhu playing technique. These important contributions have made him the most important erhu teacher of the twentieth century.

See also: dizi; erhu; modern Chinese orchestra; music conservatories; pipa; qin; traditional music; traditional music composers; zheng

Further reading

Lang, Miriam (1993). 'Swan Songs: Traditional Musicians in Contemporary China - Observations from a Film'. *East Asian History* 5 (June).

Liu, Dehai (1996). *Liu Dehai chuantong pipa quji* [Liu Dehai's Traditional Pipa Pieces]. Taiyuan: Shanxi jiaoyu chubanshe.

Miao, Tianrui, Ji, Liankang and Guo, Naian (eds) (1985). *Zhongguo yinyue cidian* [Dictionary of Chinese Music]. Beijing: Renming yinyue chubanshe.

Wu, Ganbo (2002). *Ershishiji zhonghua guoyue renwuzhi* [Annals of Chinese Traditional Musicians of the Twentieth Century]. Shanghai: Yinyue chubanshe.

DU YAXIONG

train stations

Train stations occupy a key position in China's transport network architecture. They play a major role as inland gateways for the transfer of freight and passengers. Information technology and intermodality are transforming China's train stations. Train stations have introduced computer enquiry systems, large-screen route information, ticket booking and purchasing services, luggage checking services and electronics monitoring devices. Networking systems have improved service quality, facilities and operating management. The participation of China in the global market economy is transforming freight railway stations into major goods flow centres. Changes are manifest in the development of intermodal rail stations for the handling and distribution of domestic and international containers. The growth in mobility among the Chinese population appears to be associated with the modernization of train stations. Passenger railway stations are playing a greater role in connecting intra-urban mass transit systems with the emerging inter-urban high-density rail passenger corridors. They are increasingly being integrated with public buses, passenger ferries and airports. Passenger railway stations have always been a major landmark in the Chinese urban landscape. They are public places and have performed an important economic function. Train stations have been favourable for attracting itinerant pedlars,

fixed-pitch stall and small retail outlets selling market produce, cooked food, sundry goods and services. They have led to the expansion of hotels, restaurants and tourist information centres in their vicinity. The expansion, modernization and relocation of train stations remain major features of the morphological changes of Chinese cities.

CLAUDE COMTOIS

translation industry

The translation industry in China must be seen as consisting of two essentially divided branches: the publishing sector and the commercial translation sector. Of all published translated publications in the PRC, more than half are translations of English-language fiction and non-fiction. Japanese and French are a distant second and third. As a rule, translators are not employees of the publisher but freelancers, many of them university teachers in foreign languages. Publishing companies still are state owned. Under the WTO, the wholesale as well as the retail publishing sector will open up, which will undoubtedly influence translation practices. Decisions about the translation of a foreign publication now lie with the editorial board of a publishing company. For these, as for any other publication, the publisher must apply for a book number (**shuhao**, a kind of national ISBN) from the central authority (Xinwen chuban zongshu), where also the number of copies is set. Each publisher has a yearly quota of book numbers it can obtain. In practice, smaller publishers buy unused book numbers from bigger publishing houses. Copyright is handled between the Chinese and the foreign publisher through an intermediary agent representing the main Western publishers. Professionals consider most translations to be of poor quality because of the speed with which they are produced, especially foreign bestsellers, as well as because of the poor qualifications of many translators. In historical perspective, the waves of literary movements have been accompanied by the translation of foreign literary works on a large scale, often bringing about a fusion of Chinese and foreign literary trends. Literary translation in China began with the translation of Buddhist classics during the Eastern Han (25–211).

The translation of Buddhist works had an enormous impact on the syntax, lexicon and phonology of the Chinese language. Liang Qichao (1873–1929), who recognized the potential political and social impact of foreign literature on an isolated Chinese society, encouraged foreign translation. After the **Cultural Revolution**, a new wave of translated foreign literature introduced influential writers such as Marquez and Kundera to the Chinese public.

The commercial translation sector is almost entirely independent of the literary. Translation companies employ translators and work with freelancers, often university graduates with a technical degree and proficient in the foreign language. Translators' fees in the commercial translation sector are substantially higher. Translation business was traditionally seen as a sensitive area and is difficult to grasp. For example: officially, 400 translation companies are registered in Beijing. In practice, probably more than double that number are active in the field, while also offering peripheral services such as interpretation and the organization of conferences. Many are spin-offs of universities. State-owned translation companies hold only a small market share and cater mainly to governmental institutions. For foreign companies, this segment of the services sector still is highly regulated, and competition with the practically unregulated local market is fierce. Most of the demand is for translations of English into Chinese.

Further reading

Murphy, C. (1995). '"Ulysses" in Chinese. The Story of an Elderly Pair of Translators and Their Unusual Bestseller'. *Language* (September).

Xu, Jun (ed.) (1999). *Theory and Practice of Translation in China*. Special issue of *Meta* 44.1.

MARTINE TORFS

Transmigration (a.k.a Samsara)

(*Lunhui*, 1988)

Film

Together with *The Black Cannon Incident* (1985) and *Dislocation* (1986), this film belongs to **Huang Jianxin**'s first urban trilogy. Adapted from a **Wang Shuo** novel, the film concerns disillusioned youth in a post-socialist China that is undergoing rapid cultural and economic change. The protagonist, Shiba (played by Lei Han), is alienated from the past yet disaffected about the present. The search for a self-identity involves a painful process of self-exploration and denial. To outsiders, Shiba is the beneficiary of a revolutionary elite family and a successful entrepreneur. From his perspective, however, his dead parents' background is no longer meaningful, and his illegal business brings him money but also threats. The question of his self-identity also figures in the relationship between Shiba and a female dance student (played by Tan Xiaoyan). Shiba is hardly an ideal man to the young woman, but she is attracted to his anti-heroic persona.

Their marriage is short-lived as Shiba fails to find a place in proper society and wallows in cynicism. The film uses colour to suggest his moments of psychological confusion. Shiba paints the walls of his house red to indicate his love towards the woman and then black as disillusion overwhelms him. A compelling mise-en-scène at the end of the film finishes the failed soul-searching journey. Shiba adjusts a lamp to project his shadow on the black wall. With two fists rising up from a lean masculine body, his silhouette appears larger than life. After a series of shots/reverse shots of Shiba and the moon, he jumps over the rail and plummets into the darkness. The death of the man, as the subtitles indicate, is followed by the birth of his son – hence the transmigration of the soul.

Further reading

Kuoshu, Harry H. (1997). 'Beyond the Yellow Earth: The Postsocialist City as a Cinematic Space of Anxiety'. *American Journal of Chinese Studies* 4.1 (April): 50–72.

Pickowicz, Paul (1994). 'Huang Jianxin and the Notion of Postsocialism'. In Nick Browne, Paul G. Pickowicz, Vivian Sobchack and Esther Yau (eds), *New Chinese Cinemas*. New York: Cambridge University Press: 57–87.

Wang, Yuejin (1991). 'The Rhetoric of Mirror, Shadow, and Moon: *Samsara* and the Problem of Representation of Self in China'. *East–West Film Journal* 5.2: 69–92.

CUI SHUQIN

transportation patterns (urban)

The Chinese urban landscape is characterized by different forms of mobility. Under the socialist regime, Chinese cities were initially designed for pedestrians and bicycles. The urban transportation pattern was undertaken in the context of proximity space where place of residence and employment were integrated. China's cities' narrow street system was not built to accommodate modern transportation. Bicycles were the main users of road capacity. The flow of hundreds of thousands of bicycles was the main contributor to urban traffic congestion. China has chosen to reduce the transport demand by a functional integration of urban space. Rapid economic growth led to new forms of spatial organization where the most important phenomena in terms of urban transportation patterns are expansion in road capacity and motorization.

The introduction of market-based reforms led to the planning, development and expansion of a new urban road system. A new pattern of road network is emerging from the foundation of the old dense street layout. Chinese cities are expanding their transportation network and modernizing portions of the system by building new facilities and widening street segments. China's urban transportation infrastructure comprises networks of **ring roads**, radial routes and high-performance expressways superimposed over the pattern of intricate narrow street system. The emerging road network changes the land use pattern of Chinese cities through the multiplication of specialized urban districts and the expansion of economic space towards peripheral areas. Various aspects of urban life are undertaken outside the spatial and organizational limits of the work unit. Traffic generation and attraction are gradually separated to induce increase in trip length. The urban road hierarchy defines the traffic function of each street and segregates motorized and non-motorized transport. Movements by bicycle and collective public transport remain the most important in terms of passengers carried. But the increasing income of urban residents is stimulating the demand for mobility.

A growing proportion of trips rely on minibuses, taxis, motorcycles and personal vehicles. The motorization of individual trips is stimulated by the Chinese government policy for the development of an automobile industry. Much of the new urban transport infrastructures are inscribed within the framework of increasing the flow of motorized vehicles. China already recognizes that the passage towards motorized mobility is creating negative environmental impacts. Several models of urban transport pattern are being planned to manage the soaring demand for the use of road space. The management of the massive flow of vehicles is stimulating the quest for high technology, such as intelligent transport systems, as a solution to urban transport problems. Some Chinese cities are already seeking the development of a comprehensive public transport system as an alternative to cars and motorcycles. Improvements in urban transportation demand is also offered by underground metro lines and powerful urban rail transit schemes being planned or under construction. Adapting the different mobility behaviour of Chinese urban citizens to the transformation of the urban landscape is becoming the key challenge for China's urban policy-makers.

See also: cars and taxis

CLAUDE COMTOIS

True Jesus Church

The True Jesus Church (Zhen yesu jiaohui) is a charismatic indigenous Protestant group that emerged in the early decades of the twentieth century, along with the **Little Flock** and the **Jesus Family**. Formally established in Beijing in 1917, the group developed primarily in the central interior provinces during the 1920s, especially Henan and Hunan. The church's founders were strongly influenced by the Apostolic Faith Mission of the American Pentecostal Church, and established the church on its charismatic practices and doctrines, especially baptism of the Holy Spirit and supernatural gifts such as prophecy, healing and speaking in tongues. The church was also exclusivist, upholding Seventh-day Sabbath, and mobilized by highly millenarian beliefs. Despite its strongly anti-foreign stance, the TJC nevertheless came under attack in 1953. Its leader, Isaac Wei, was arrested, and authorities forcibly dissolved its organizational structure and assimilated it into the **Three-Self Patriotic Movement (TSPM)**. Several prominent members relocated the TJC's headquarters to Taiwan, and then to Los Angeles in 1985. In the reform era, the TJC has experienced a dramatic revival on the mainland, mostly in central inland provinces, and has evangelized aggressively abroad, particularly among overseas Chinese. The church now claims a membership of over 1 million within China, and a total of 1.5 million in thirty-nine countries.

Further reading

Deng, Zhaoming (2001). 'Indigenous Chinese Pentecostal Denominations'. *China Study Journal* 16. 3: 5–22.

JASON KINDOPP

Ts'ai Ming-liang

(Cai Mingliang)

b. 1958, Kuching, Malaysia

Film director

Ts'ai Ming-liang graduated in 1982 in drama and cinema from the Chinese Culture University of Taiwan, and is regarded as the foremost second-generation filmmaker of Taiwan's 'New Cinema movement' (see **cinema in Taiwan**). A series of five films have all featured a single three-member (highly dysfunctional) family and set of performers: *Rebels of the Neon God* (1992), *Vive l'Amour* (1994, winner of the Venice Film Festival Golden Lion award), *The River* (1997), *The Hole* (1998), *What Time Is It There?* (2001). Profound alienation matched with a dry, black humour is the watchword of these films. Obsession and repression, physical pollution, lengthy silences and endless repetition, claustrophobic apartments drenched in overflowing water, and gigantic communication gaps between husband, wife and child are all combined with a monumentally slow pace to define a distinctive cinematic style that comments with exaggerated understatement on modern urban

alienation in Taipei. Action, when it comes, is sudden and vengeful. Sexuality, including masturbation and incestuous homosexuality, is neurotic but also embraces Taiwan's recent championing of gay rights. With the son, Hsiao-kang, performed by Lee Kang-sheng, Ts'ai has created a comic character as ironic as Jacques Tati's Mr Hulot and as identifiable to a committed Taiwan audience as Charlie Chaplin. Ts'ai's most recent film is *Goodbye Dragon Inn* (2003), about the few people who drifted in one evening to see the King Hu film, *Dragon Inn*.

Further reading

Berry, Chris (1999). 'Where is Love? The Paradox of Performing Loneliness in Ts'ai Ming-liang's *Vive L'Amour*'. In Lesley Stern and George Kouvaros (eds), *Falling for You: Essays on Cinema and Performance*. Sydney: Power Publications.

Martin, Fran (2003). '*Vive l'Amour*: Eloquent Emptiness'. In Chris Berry (ed.), *Chinese Films in Focus, 25 New Takes*. London: BFI, 175–82.

Rehm, Jean-Pierre, Joyard, Olivier and Rivière, Danièle (1999). *Tsai Ming-liang*. Paris: Dis voir.

Rojas, Carlos (2003). '"Nezha Was Here": Structures of Dis/placement in Tsai Ming-liang's *Rebels of a Neon God*'. *Modern Chinese Literature and Culture* 15.1 (Spring): 63–89.

Wang, Ban (2003). 'Black Holes of Globalization: Critique of the New Millennium in Taiwan Cinema'. *Modern Chinese Literature and Culture* 15.1 (Spring): 90–119.

JEROME SILBERGELD

Tsui Hark

(Xu Ke)

b. 1951, Vietnam

Film director, producer, screenwriter, actor

A versatile, original filmmaker, Tsui Hark has been a major figure in Hong Kong cinema since the 1980s. Like his colleagues of the 'Hong Kong New Wave' (see **Fong, Allen**), one of his first films, *Dangerous Encounters – 1st Kind* (*Diyi leixing weixian,*

1980), was a realistic drama, but he quickly switched to more commercial genres – action comedy and martial arts fantasy. After studying in Texas and working in New York's Chinatown, Tsui worked for the TV station TVB (1977–9) before turning to feature directing. His most significant influence is on **martial arts films**: the combination of Chinese mythology and dazzling special effects imported from Hollywood became his trademark after *Zu: Warriors from the Magic Mountain* (*Xin shushan jianxia*, 1983).

In 1984, with his wife, Nansun Shi, he founded The Film Workshop, becoming his own producer: *Peking Opera Blues* (*Dao Ma Dan*, 1986), the highly successful series *Once Upon a Time in China* (*Huang feihong*, 1991, 1992, 1993, 1994) and *The Blade* (*Dao*, 1995). He also produced the work of others: John **Woo**'s *A Better Tomorrow* (*Yingxiong bense*, 1986) and the brilliant martial arts series directed by his close collaborator, Ching Siu-tung, *A Chinese Ghost Story* (*Qiannü youhun*, 1987, 1990) and *Swordsman* (*Xiao'ao jianghu*, 1990, 1992, 1993). In 1997, in Hollywood, he directed *Double Team* and *Knock Off*, which generated mixed reviews. Meanwhile, he started producing feature-length **animation** films. He came back to Hong Kong with a violent yet stylish action film, *Time and Tide* (*Shunliu niliu*, 2000) and a return to the fantastic martial arts genre, *The Legend of Zu* (*Shushan zhengshuan*, 2001).

See also: He Jiping

Further reading

Ho, S. (ed.) (2002). *The Swordsman and His Jiang Hu: Tsui Hark and Hong Kong Film*. Hong Kong: Hong Kong Film Archives.

Teo, Stephen (2001). 'Tsui Hark: National Style and Polemic'. In Esther Yau (ed.), *At Full Speed: Hong Kong Cinema in a Borderless World*. Minneapolis: University of Minnesota Press, 143–58.

Zou, John (2003). 'A Chinese Ghost Story: Ghostly Council and Innocent Men'. In Chris Berry (ed.), *Chinese Films on Focus: 25 New Takes*. London: BFI, 39–46.

BéRéNICE REYNAUD

Tujia, culture of

The Tujia, who number some 6 million people, inhabit mountainous areas of Hunan, Hubei and Guizhou provinces, and southeastern Chongqing. The region is rich in rare medicinal herbs, minerals, aquatic products and giant salamanders. Glutinous rice cakes and rice balls are the favourite food, and their dishes are often spicy. Oil tea soup is a speciality. Weaving and embroidery are women's traditional line of work. Climbing the blade ladder is one of men's traditional sports which demonstrates their bravery and power. The spoken language is close to that of the Yi (see **Yi, culture of**), but they use Han Chinese characters for writing and many speak the local Han dialect. Tujia epics, which are rather imaginative, tell of humankind's origins and the Tujia migrations and aspirations in dramatic and poetic ways. The Tiaonian Meeting, Zhongwu Holiday and Guozu Festival are the three most important festivals. Among their dances, a hand-waving dance with over seventy ritual gestures to indicate war, hunting, farming and teasing and other behaviour is the most popular. They also perform a folk play called *Maogusi* as part of *Nuoxi* (the evil-dispelling drama). The play features monologues, sometimes interwoven with a chorus or musical dialogue in memory of their ancestors' achievements in exploring the wilderness, fishing, marriage and working. *Nuoxi* can last as long as six days, which is rare among other ethnic groups. It has attracted much attention from dramatists and dancers in and outside of China, and is regarded as the living fossil of ancient art and culture once prevalent throughout China. There are also festivals for tourists, including piglet running, as entertainment.

HELEN XIAOYAN WU

Tungusic language speakers

As a language group, Tungusic is a branch of Altaic. It includes two branches: one includes Ewenki and Oroqen, and the other Manchu, Sibo (or Xibe) and Hoche (or Hezhe/Hezhen). The speakers of Oroqen and Ewenki in China are mainly distributed over Inner Mongolia and Heilongjiang. The two languages do not have writing systems in China, and in school children learn Chinese or Mongolian. The population of Oroqen speakers is about 4,000 and that of Ewenki speakers in China about 20,000. Both the Oroqen and Ewenki people like singing and dancing. They are mainly engaged in hunting and animal husbandry.

The languages of Manchu and Sibo are so closely related that some scholars regard Sibo as a dialect of Manchu. There are about 10 million Manchu people in China, mainly distributed over north (especially northeast) China. The Manchu nationality ruled over China between 1644 and 1911; the people started to learn Chinese after they occupied China, and now only a number of old people in remote villages can speak Manchu. The Sibo people include two groups: one is distributed over northeast China and speaks Chinese or Mongolian, and the other lives in northwest China and speaks the Sibo language. The population of Sibo speakers is about 30,000. The Hoche people have a total population of about 4,500, living in Heilongjiang. The Hoche language does not have a writing system. Most Hoche people speak Chinese and only a few old people can speak Hoche. As for religion, Tungusic language speakers used to follow a form of shamanism, but most have given up the religion.

YANG LAN

Turkic language speakers

As a branch of Altaic, Turkic is a big group of languages and has about 10 million speakers in China. Turkic languages in China consist of two groups: the first includes Uighur, Kazak, Sala, Uzbek and Tatar, and the second Kirgiz and Yugur. Most of these languages have writing systems, which are based on the Arabic alphabet. Some Turkic languages are only spoken languages, and they adopt the writing systems of other languages, such as Uighur and Chinese. Turkic speakers are generally Muslims, but some follow Lamaism, such as Yugurs, and others follow forms of shamanism, such as some of the Kazaks.

Uighur in China has three main dialects and the pronunciation of Yili and Wulumuqi (Urumqi) is regarded as standard. Uighur speakers number over 7 million and they mainly live in Xinjiang. Kazak speakers in China, with a population of over

1 million, are distributed mainly in Xinjiang (with some in Gansu). Salas, living in Qinghai and Gansu, have a population of about 90,000. A number of Sala speakers can speak Chinese and/or Tibetan. Uzbek speakers in China live scattered in Xinjiang and the population is about 20,000. They use the Uighur writing system. There are about 5,000 Tatars in China. They live scattered among the Uighurs and Kazaks in Xinjiang and they now mainly use the language and writing system of Uighur or Kazak. Kirgiz speakers, with a population of over 140,000, are distributed in Xinjiang and Heilongjiang. Yugur speakers live in Gansu. A number of Yugurs speak Mongolian languages and the population of Yugur speakers is only about 10,000.

YANG LAN

two studies, two competitions

(shuangxue shuangbi huodong)

Social policy

The 'two studies, two competitions' activities were formally launched in 1989 as a distinctive Chinese variant of gender and development. The initiative built upon earlier grassroots work of the **All-China Women's Federation** in promoting the role of rural women in economic development, especially work to encourage the courtyard economy (*tingyuan jingji*) conducted in the mid 1980s. The 'two studies, two competitions' provided a structure for linking this work of the Women's Federations with the support and resources of those government departments connected to the rural economy through the institution of 'two studies, two competitions coordinating groups' (*shuangxue shuangbi xietiao zuzhi*) at all levels of government. The goal is to position rural women in the mainstream of rural economic development, to the benefit of both women and economic development. Literally, the 'two studies, two competitions' consist of adult basic education, technical training, competition among local women in achieving economic success and recognition, and competition in making social contributions. As implemented, the core of the programme has been short-term technical training oriented towards the market. A longer-term goal has been improvement in **women's quality**, with an initial focus on literacy training and a later focus (from the second five-year phase, beginning in 1994) on technical training. This approach has continued familiar practices of nurturing and promoting models of success, while also assisting less-advantaged women to access training and resources. It departs from earlier initiatives in its use of state structures to promote women's involvement in the market.

Further reading

Judd, Ellen (2002). *The Chinese Women's Movement Between State and Market*. Stanford: Stanford University Press.

ELLEN R. JUDD

U

Uighurs (Weiwu'er), culture of

The Uighurs are a Turkic people, the population in 1990 being 7,209,675, all but a few thousand living in Xinjiang. In 1999, they made up approximately 46.5 per cent of Xinjiang's total. They speak a language belonging to the Turkic branch of the Altaic family, and use Arabic script. Most Uighurs are Muslims and to this day their culture and livelihood remain deeply affected by their faith. Since 1990, when there was an uprising inspired by the Muslim doctrine of the 'holy war' in Baren township, Akto county, southern Xinjiang, the government has been suspicious of Islam among the Uighurs, believing it to be the source of ethno-nationalist separatism. In the south, Islam is especially strong, but in places like the capital Ürümqi and nearby Turpan, there are intellectuals interested in more secular ideas, often also strongly nationalist.

The Uighur arts reflect their Turkic ethnicity, with song and dance a major genre. Many dances accelerate, rising to a climactic and excited conclusion. Percussion and string instruments dominate the orchestras that accompany song-and-dance performances, the players normally being exclusively male. The Uighurs have a significant literary tradition. A very fine example among contemporary writers is Abdurehim Ötkür (d. 1995), author of several historical novels set in Xinjiang and with the theme of Uighur identity.

Further reading

Rudelson, Justin Jon (1997). *Oasis Identities, Uyghur Nationalism Along China's Silk Road*. New York: Columbia University Press.

COLIN MACKERRAS

Uncle Doggie's Nirvana

[Gou'er ye niepan, 1986]

Huaju (spoken drama)

Uncle Doggie's Nirvana, also referred to in English-language publications as both *Doggy Man Nirvana* and *The Nirvana of Dog's Father*, is a **Huaju** (spoken drama) by Liu Jinyun (a.k.a. Jin Yun, b. 1938). Widely regarded as the most significant Chinese drama of the 1980s, it premiered at the **Beijing People's Art Theatre** (directed by **Lin Zhaohua**) in 1986 and won the National Best Play Award. Peasant Chen Hexiang is nicknamed 'Dog' after his father eats a live dog upon a dare by a landlord promising land. The play chronicles Dog's efforts to retain ownership of his land throughout three decades of political movements and social upheavals. Theatrically, socialist-realist and experimental expressionist techniques are combined, with a non-linear plot featuring flashbacks. First translated into English by **Ying Ruocheng** and premiered in the USA under his direction at Virginia Commonwealth University in 1993, it was also translated and adapted as *Dog and His Master* by Wang Luoyong and Michael Johnson-Chase and staged in 1996 at the Lark Theatre Company in Wisconsin. Ying's translation was published in a 1997 Oxford anthology and in a side-by-side Chinese/English version by China Translation Publishing Corp. in 1999. Shiao-ling Yu's translation (*The Nirvana of Grandpa Doggie*) is included in her anthology.

Further reading

Jin, Yong (1996). 'The Nirvana of Grandpa Doggie'. In Yu Shiao-ling (ed. and trans.), *Chinese Drama after the Cultural Revolution*. Lewiston: Edwin Mellen Press, 349–422.

——(1997). 'Uncle Doggie's Nirvana', Trans. Ying Ruocheng. In Martha Cheung and Jane Lai (eds), *An Oxford Anthology of Contemporary Chinese Drama*. Hong Kong: Oxford University Press.

Pan, P. (1999). 'Triumphant Dancing in Chains: Two Productions of Huaju Plays in the Late 1980s'. *Asian Theatre Journal* 1: 107–21.

CLAIRE CONCEISON

university entrance examinations

University entrance exams have dominated the PRC secondary education system since the late 1970s, as they do in Taiwan and Hong Kong. Only a miniscule percentage of the students who participate do well enough to be admitted to an elite university, though a somewhat larger percentage are able to gain admission to either a non-elite four-year university or a technically oriented tertiary institution. Students who do not do well enough to get into the university of their choice the first time around sometimes choose to retake their senior year of high school in order to resit the exams.

University places are allocated through provinces and provincial-level cities. Consequently, students from those provinces with relatively few tertiary places but a strong secondary education system, like Hubei, require higher entrance exam scores than students from cities like Beijing and Shanghai to gain entrance to a same-tier university. This discrepancy leads to much resentment. Academic high schools devote themselves almost exclusively to preparing students for the exams, regularly keeping students in classes or study sessions eleven hours a day, six days a week. Though the number of university places expanded during the 1980s and 1990s, the number of students qualified to sit for the exams has grown even more quickly. The resulting competition is so tough that students liken gaining admittance to university to 'crossing a single-log bridge' (*dumuqiao*) and refer to the month in which the exams take place as 'Black July.' Occasional cheating scandals remind everyone of the stakes involved.

Further reading

Kipnis, A. (2001). 'The Disturbing Educational Discipline of "Peasanto"'. *The China Journal* 46: 1–24.

Thogersen, S. (1990). *Secondary Education in China after Mao: Reform and Social Conflict*. Aarhus: Aarhus University Press.

ANDREW KIPNIS

urban fashion trends

While different Chinese cities display dissimilar configurations of fashion cultures and different regional urban centres have developed distinctive fashion cultures, it is still possible to identify some of the common contours of fashion among young women in the largest Chinese metropolises.

A small number of young women pursue brandname high fashion. They come from disparate social backgrounds (e.g. children of high-ranking officials or successful businessmen, hostesses of expensive nightclubs, members of the fashion industry, and the girlfriends, mistresses and wives of the rich), and tend to gather in certain consumption spaces in the city – exclusive malls, restaurants and dance clubs. Other women prefer 'professional wear' (*zhiyefu*) for its fashion-neutrality and propriety, in contrast to trendy or sporty casual wear. Worn not only in the context of office and work but on all kinds of leisurely occasions as well, 'professional wear' wasoriginally composed of matching suit-like jacket and skirt (or trousers) in plain colours and style, but has gradually come to incorporate a variety of fashion elements. A large number of urban young women subscribe to 'casual wear' (*xiuxianfu*). Made up mainly of T-shirts, sweaters, jeans and sneakers, casual wear is not dissimilar to that found in the West. However, foreign-trained designers notice that Chinese consumers display certain local preferences in casual wear such as bright colours and the crowding of features. Hip-hop influenced 'street wear', offering a conspicuous and affordable stylistic alternative to elitist high fashion, has captured many Chinese teenagers in the past few years. Koreanized 'street wear' is more stylistically radical and is popular in northern cities, whereas Japanized 'street wear' centres more on brandnames and is popular in the south. China has not yet generated a very distinctive local version of 'street wear'. Finally, there are at least two commercially successful and interesting contemporary local urban fashion trends: the 'hostess look' and 'ladies' wear' (*shunufu*). The 'hostess look' juxtaposes high fashion with feminine, gaudy and erotic elements. 'Ladies' wear' combines Chinese traditional and Victorian sartorial features with whatever is currently in vogue in the West.

Although the clothes that most contemporary urban Chinese normally wear contain few traditional sartorial elements and should appear largely familiar to Western observers, they display numerous local features upon closer scrutiny. Many of these features developed out of unintended local mutations of Western dress. The most widespread is probably the exposure of the neck of stockings beneath the hemline. Exposing the neck of stockings may evoke images of untidiness, eroticism or indecency by Western conventions, but it assumes neutral or positive meanings in urban China, not to mention the warmth it provides. Exposed short stockings emerged in the early 1980s and are still often seen in urban China, but the social profile of their wearers has changed. Young and fashion-conscious metropolitan women have abandoned the practice as they internalized Western sartorial conventions (through the globalized fashion media in coastal metropolises) or as they were stigmatized for wearing exposed stockings (through personal contacts with globalized people and institutions in the coastal metropolises). Another widespread local fashion practice involves retaining brandname labels on, for example, the sleeve of men's jackets or the limb of sunglasses. Like exposed stockings, the display of brandname labels gradually retreated to older and provincial patrons as they came to be regarded as low-status fashion symbols in Chinese metropolises of the 1990s. Other local fashion practices that show signs of going through similar stages include handbags on successful middle-aged men and ponytails on fashionable young women.

See also: fashion designers; Mao Zedong and Sun Yatsen suits; qipao, cheongsam; Shanghai Tang; T-shirts and their culture; Tang dress

Further reading

Chew, Matthew (2003). 'The Dual Consequences of Cultural Localization: How Exposed Short Stockings Subvert and Sustain Global Cultural Hierarchy'. *positions: east asia cultures critique* 11.2 (special issue).

Hua, Mei (2000). *Fushi qinghuai* [Sartorial Impressions]. Tianjin: Tianjin renmin chubanshe.

——(2002). *Dingwei Shishang* [Positioning Fashion]. Tianjin: Baihua Literature and Art Publishing House.

Zhang, Jingqiong (2002). *Xifu Dongjian: Ershi Shiji Zhongwai Fushi Jiaoliu* [Eastern Diffusion of Western Dress: A History of Sartorial Exchange between China and Foreign Countries in the Twentieth Century]. Hefei: Anhui Arts Publisher.

MATTHEW CHEW

urban planning/renewal

Urban planning in China has undergone a sea-change in the past quarter-century. Many assumptions associated with planning's links to socialist, top-down paradigms of economic development, spatial uniformity and social egalitarianism have been shelved. Similarly, assumptions characterizing the 1949–79 period, when national leaders sought to transform cities from places of capitalist consumption to centres of socialist production, have increasingly been undermined as the reforms of the Deng era have proliferated. Local autonomy has become more commonplace, land markets have been de-tethered from central control, foreign direct investment has mushroomed, and urban planning has facilitated an ever-wider diversity of urban spaces, forms and contexts.

As Chinese cities increasingly become foci of social change and magnets attracting millions of rural migrants, they are being reconfigured according to both master plans (mandated under the State Council's City Planning Ordinance of 1985) and private initiatives. One key aspect of this widespread urban reconfiguration is associated with 'renewal' (*zaisheng*) Often this ideal has been tantamount to demolition and rebuilding, as sites perceived to be obsolete and stultifying have been transformed into places more suited to progress and profit. In fewer cases, local planners are beginning to broaden their notions of what constitutes 'renewal' by taking into consideration how best to thread new designs into older spaces. In 2003 examples of this more amplified approach can be seen in larger cities such as Beijing, Shanghai and Guangzhou, and (as often occurs in Chinese urban development), these are likely to be harbingers of ever-more diverse instances of urban design experimentation throughout China.

Further reading

Leaf, Michael (1998). 'Urban Planning and Urban Reality under Chinese Economic Reforms'. *Journal of Planning, Education, and Research* 18: 145–53.

Yan, Xiaopei, Jia Li, Li, Jianping and Weng, Jizhuan (2002). 'The Development of the Chinese Metropolis in the Period of Transition'. In John R. Logan (ed.), *The New Chinese City: Globalization and Market Reform*. Oxford: Blackwell, 37–55.

Yeh, Anthony Gar-on, Xu, Xueqiang and Yan, Xiaopei (eds) (1997). *Urban Planning and Planning Education under Economic Reform in China*. Hong Kong: University of Hong Kong, Centre of Urban Planning and Environmental Management.

JEFFREY W. CODY

urban slang

As a colourful vocabulary used in colloquial speech, slang is known to be the language use below the level of stylistically neutral language usages. Although the stylistic difference between 'colloquial' and 'literary' exists in a large number of Chinese words and expressions, Chinese is not as rich in specific slang words and expressions as many other languages, such as English. Some examples of slang expressions popular in Beijing are: *pi* (nonsense), *zhua po lian* (fall out with somebody), *ai goupi ci* (get a dressing down), *huo shao pigu* (a matter of the utmost urgency) and *cai ji bozi* (making an unpleasant sound, especially singing unpleasantly). Nonetheless, the use of slang has developed noticeably in Chinese urban areas since the 1980s. This may be attributed to a number of social changes. The social and economic reforms of the post-Mao period have given rise to a more liberal environment in which young people, especially, have greater freedom to choose their modes of informal, unconventional or emotional expression. The marketing economy, too, has brought to the great metropolises people, along with their slang, of differing social classes or circles, and from areas where different **dialects** are spoken, including the countryside, or from abroad. Moreover, a number of slang expressions are revivals of the slang found in older popular literature. Finally, contemporary literature and the arts have shown increasing freedom whereby writers and performers try to produce a range of expressive styles, including informality, humour and vulgarity, and consciously adopt or create slang expressions.

YANG LAN

V

van Dijk, Hans

(Johannes Gerardus Adrianus Wilhelmus Cloeck)

b. 1946, Deventer, Netherlands; d. 2002

Art curator

Hans van Dijk began his career as an artist studying at the Arnhem Arts Academy and at the Eindhoven Design Academy, where he graduated in 1970. In the early 1980s, van Dijk began to take an interest in classical Chinese furniture design, elements of which he integrated in his own Western European constructivist art. Gradually he broadened his interests to modern Chinese art and decided to study Chinese language and Chinese culture. In 1984, he left the Netherlands for China, where he would devote the rest of his life to document, archive and promote the work of Chinese contemporary artists with incessant zeal until the time of his early death in 2002.

Van Dijk studied at Nanjing University and at the Nanjing Art Academy (Nanjing yishu xueyuan; see **art academies**) where he was first introduced to the local art scene. Between 1991 and 1993 he was curator in Berlin for the Haus der Kulturen der Welt [House of World Cultures] in preparation for the exhibition **China Avant-Garde**. Back in China, after many years of official hindrance often resulting in moving venues and temporary disruption of operation, he founded the New Amsterdam Art Consultancy (NAAC) in 1993. From 1998 in collaboration with **Ai Weiwei** and Frank Uytterhaegen he formed the China Art Archives and Warehouse (CAAW) which

survives him and remains a critical centre for the promotion, exhibition and archiving of experimental art in China.

Van Dijk curated over forty shows in and outside of China, promoting artistic exchanges through the organization of joint exhibitions that often presented the work of both Chinese and European artists. Among the most important are: China Avant-Garde in Berlin (1993) which was the first ever to showcase Chinese experimental art in Europe; a joint exhibition by the **New Measurement Group** (Xin Kedu) and German installation artist Günther Ücker at the Neuer Berliner Kunstverein, Berlin in 1995; '"The Arts" Environment, Eighty Photographs of Artists in Beijing 1992–95' at the Gallery of the Central Institute of Fine Arts, Beijing and at the Goethe Institute, Hong Kong in 1995–6; 'China – Aktuelles aus 15 Ateliers' (China – Recent Works from 15 Studios) in Munich, Basel and Tokyo, 1996–7; 'Mondrian in China – A Documentary Exhibition with Chinese Originals', which toured Beijing, Shanghai and Canton in 1998; the exhibition of the Modern China Art Foundation Collection in Gent, Belgium in 1999.

Moreover, through his various activities in Beijing he promoted and showcased the works of emerging artists, many of whom found in his support their first opportunity to make themselves known to a larger international public. Among these are **Ai Weiwei**, **Chen Danqing**, Chen Shaoxiong (see **Big-Tailed Elephant**), **Ding Yi**, **Gu Dexin**, **Hai Bo**, **Han Lei**, **Hong Hao**, **Li Yongbin**, **Su Xinping**, **Sui Jianguo**, **Wang Xingwei**, **Zhang Hai'er**, Zhang Lei and

Zhou Tiehai. During his last years van Dijk concentrated on the promotion of new media art, particularly photography and video, making a substantially contribution to the emergence and visibility of this genre on the Chinese artistic scene.

Further reading

Noth, Jochen, Pöhlmann, Wolfger and Reschke, Kai (eds) (1994). *China Avant-Garde: Counter-Currents in Art and Culture*. Hong Kong, New York: Oxford University Press.

van Dijk, Hans (1991–2). 'Painting in China after the Cultural Revolution: Style Developments and Theoretical Debates (Part I: 1979–1985)'. *China Information* 5.3 (Winter): 1–21.

—— (1992). 'Painting in China after the Cultural Revolution: Style Developments and Theoretical Debates (Part II: 1985–1991)'. *China Information* 5.4 (Spring): 1–17.

—— (1994). 'Yishulilun bushi yishu' [Art-Theory is no Art]. *Jiangsu huakan* (June).

—— (1995). 'Politik, Dollar, Wiedergutmachung und Ruhm'. In *Configura 2 Dialog der Kulturen* (exhibition catalogue). Erfurt: Thueringen [translated as 'Zhengzhi, meiyuan, shuzui xinli he rongyu', *Hualang* (November) 1995].

—— (1995). 'Meishushi de shenhua' [The Myth of Modern Art History]. *Jiangsu huakan* (August).

—— (1996). 'Kunstgeschichte–Dollar–Wiedergutmachung–Ruhm' [Art History–Dollars–Rectification–Fame]. In *China – Aktuelles aus 15 Ateliers, Performances, Installationen*. Munich: Hahn Produktion, 124–7 [with English translation].

—— (1998). 'Modern Chinese Art and the Reaction to Non-Realistic Tendencies'. In *Mondrian in China – A Documentary Exhibition with Chinese Originals* (exhibition catalogue), Beijing.

—— (1999). 'From Piggy-Banks to "The Testimony of the Hare" and What Had Gone Before'. In *Modern Chinese Art Foundation* (exhibition catalogue). Provincieraad Oost-Vlaanderen, Belgium.

van Dijk, Hans and Schmid, Andreas (1994). 'The Fine Arts after the Cultural Revolution: Stylistic Development and Culture Debate'. In Jochen Noth, Wolfger Pöhlmann and Kai Reschke (eds), *China Avant-Garde: Counter-Currents in Art and Culture*. Hong Kong, New York: Oxford University Press, 14–39.

ROBERT BERNELL AND
FRANCESCA DAL LAGO WITH
BEATRICE LEANZA

vernacular priests (Daoist/Buddhist)

The term 'vernacular priests' refers to married Daoist and, in some cases Buddhist, priests who perform rituals in local temples and homes at the request of people or communities who are best referred to as their 'clients'. In the more common, Daoist case, the rituals performed belong to family traditions and are transmitted to disciples who have undergone a period of apprenticeship and, usually, a ritual of ordination, during which they are given a ritual name that defines their generational position in the tradition. In modern Chinese, such priests are described as *huoju* (hearth-dwelling) or *sanju daoshi* (scattered Daoists: that is, living at home, not in a temple or monastery). The names by which such priests are referred to traditionally varies a great deal from place to place, but one of the most commonly encountered is *shigong*, or 'master'.

In the most typical case, a future master is the son of a Daoist priest who learns the trade naturally, by following his father around. Frequently, however, he will also have to 'recognize a master' (*baishi*) – that is, in the company of local Daoists, officially and ritually become the apprentice of a Daoist master. As with many traditional occupations, that of vernacular priest normally requires a three-year apprenticeship during which the disciple lives in the home of his master and performs menial tasks for him while gradually learning the métier. At the end of the apprenticeship period, the disciple, having copied by hand the ritual manuscripts transmitted to him by his master, will undergo a public ritual of ordination which provides the kind of community recognition necessary to becoming a master in his own right. Often, this ritual involves 'ordeals', like the ascension of a ladder of swords or running barefoot across red-hot coals, demonstrating to the community his 'magic' power, and thereby attracting clients.

If, in contrast to a **spirit-medium** or Buddhist monk, such individuals become priests not by vocation but by heredity, and if their work may be described most appropriately in the economic terms of a 'trade', it must be underlined that their trade is a most peculiar one. Once admitted to the confraternity of local Daoists, their job is to worship the gods and drive away demons on behalf of those who request and pay for their services. This is considered to be extremely dangerous work, and it is therefore surrounded by a great number of prohibitions and rules that can best be described as 'religious'. Frequently, such Daoists must not eat beef, for their patron saint, Taishang laojun (Lord Lao, the Most High), is said to have ridden a buffalo. As mistakes in the preparation of ritual documents or in the execution of rituals will be punished severely by the gods, these masters must go about their work with great care. Particularly dangerous rituals are often preceded by the 'hiding of their souls', lest the demons being fed or driven away attack them and cause them to fall ill or even die. Personal names and above all birth dates are not communicated to fellow Daoists, lest this information be used to injure the priest who may be a rival as well as a collaborator. Most such Daoists, finally, engage in regular worship at their home altars, so as to maintain their contractual relationship with the gods, who, in their tradition, protect them personally and help ensure the efficacy of their rituals.

See also: Daoist priests; Lüshan jiao (Sannai jiao); temple fairs

Further reading

Lagerwey, John. (1987). *Taoist Ritual in Chinese Society and History*. New York: Macmillan.

Schipper, Kristofer. (1993). *The Taoist Body*. Trans. Karen C. Duval. Berkeley: University of California Press.

JOHN LAGERWEY

village schools

Village schools in contemporary China are as diverse as **villages** themselves. Even what constitutes a village in China is a tricky question. There are natural villages (*ziran cun*); there are administrative villages (*xingzheng cun*) that provide governmental functions for otherwise dispersed households or hamlets; and there are former rural areas that have been swallowed up by China's rapidly expanding towns and **cities**, but retain the governmental structure of a village. Villages also vary in terms of wealth, ethnic make-up and numerous other attributes. The schools that exist in 'village' settings reflect this diversity.

Village schools have historical links to the lineage schools and arrangements for private tutoring that existed in the Qing dynasty, but are primarily a legacy of Mao's effort to eliminate illiteracy in the countryside. Under Maos rule most villages in China came to have their own primary schools. Teachers were usually recruited from within the village even when that meant that these teachers were barely more educated than the students. The schools were called *minban* (literally, 'people run'), which meant that the funding came out of village coffers and that teacher salaries were quite low. Despite these shortcomings, the system was quite successful in raising literacy rates in rural China (see **literacy (and illiteracy)**). Relatively well-educated villagers did not usually have the opportunity to leave their villages, so the education levels of new *minban* teachers steadily progressed over the decades of Mao's rule.

During the post-Mao period there has been a general attempt to regularize village schools. This has involved replacing *minban* teachers with ones trained in the standardized teacher-training colleges, paying them a regular salary from the county government's payroll, and urging villages to invest more in school equipment and facilities. In many places this has been accomplished by consolidating the schools from a number of neighbouring villages, so that some villages are now without their own primary schools. In general these reforms have worked best in the relatively wealthy areas of the countryside, many of which have witnessed an improvement in educational standards. In many poorer areas, however, the policy has been a failure. Poorer counties are not able to fund teacher salaries, and the poorer villages in these counties have difficulty finding anyone to teach at the minimal salaries that they can offer.

Further reading

Gao, M. C. F. (1999). *Gao Village: A Portrait of Rural Life in Modern China*. Bathurst: Crawford House Publishing.

Li, S. (1999). *Cunluo Zhong De Guojia: Wenhua Bianqian Zhong De Xiangcun Xuexiao* [The State in the Village: Rural Schools in the Midst of Cultural Change]. Hangzhou: Zhejiang renmin chubanshe.

Ma, R. and Long, S. (eds) (1999). *Zhongguo Nongcun Jiaoyu Fazhande Quyu Chayi* [Regional Diversity in the Development of Chinese Village Education]. Fuzhou: Fujian jiaoyu chubanshe.

Paine, L. (1998). 'Making Schools Modern: Paradoxes of Educational Reform'. In A. Walder (ed.), *Zouping in Transition: The Process of Reform in Rural North China*. Cambridge: Harvard University Press.

Thogersen, S. (2001). 'Learning in Lijiazhuang: Education, Skills, and Careers in Twentieth-Century Rural China'. In G. Peterson, R. Hayhoe and Y. Lu (eds), *Education, Culture, and Identity in Twentieth-Century China*. Ann Arbor: University of Michigan Press.

Zhang, Yimou (1999). *The Road Home (Wode baba mama)* [film]

ANDREW KIPNIS

villages

As the basic community in rural China, a village occupies a definite physical space and performs many social functions. But the size, structure and formation of villages vary greatly with different geographical locations and socioeconomic settings. For example, villages in north China are relatively large. The average size of a north China village is easily exceeding one hundred households, who live closely together in a compact settlement. Villages in the Yangtze delta and the Sichuan basin, however, are usually much smaller, with fewer than twenty households.

In rural China, the village is not only a community of residence, but also one of consanguinity. People living in a village are often agnate kin, descending from a common ancestor or from several common ancestors. Significant disparities can be found among different regions of the country in this regard. In south and southeast China (in Guangdong and Fujian provinces), for example, the single-surname village dominates the rural setting, suggesting the coincidence of lineage and village, i.e. of residential and consanguineous communities. In many other parts of the country, the multi-surname village is the general norm. In these villages, the residential community encompasses several surnames, hence descent groups, but consanguinity is still a significant factor in village society. The prevalence of surname exogamy and village exogamy in many places also reinforces the sense of a village as a consanguineous community (see **marriage**).

A village performs many social functions for and by its members. These include economic cooperation (e.g. the reciprocal exchange of labour and technology and collective efforts at water control and the maintenance of public facilities), collective defence, religious and cultural activities, as well as the administration of domestic affairs and dealings with outside world. To fulfil these tasks, necessary institutional arrangements were and are made in the village. Among them the most important is the one that takes the role of village governance. Before the twentieth century, village governance was basically an informal arrangement, assumed by indigenous leaders who emerged from among the villagers. In the twentieth century, however, villages were enlisted by the state to fulfil its various modernization goals. This has changed village society significantly. The natural village was reorganized to fit into various administrative frameworks designed by the state, and informal village governance was transformed into a formal one. The village, no longer a self-governing entity, became the lowest echelon of the state edifice, and was required to serve various state needs. Deeper intrusion into village society in the course of the twentieth century allowed the state to mobilize and exploit rural resources to a much greater extent, but also increased the tensions between the state and the village and contributed to the deterioration of village politics.

State intrusion reached its apex under the Communist regime. From 1956 to 1980, agriculture was collectivized and the village was eventually turned into either a 'production brigade' or a team belonging to a 'people's commune' which encompassed a dozen or more villages and served simultaneously as an economic corporation and an administrative unit of the state. This commune system also made every villager a dependent of his/her commune. The rural reforms since the 1980s have dissolved the commune system, decollectivized agriculture and loosened state control over the village. But the reforms have not led to a total restoration of the old village community (see **villages (social organization)**). Recent developments in China's countryside, especially the commercialization of the rural economy and large-scale emigration of the rural population, have eroded older communal ties and made village society more open and integrated into the larger society of towns and cities, market and nation (see **migration and settlement patterns**).

LIU CHANG

villages (social organization)

The social organizations in villages range from official, state-mandated organizations to non-registered, villager-organized **minjian** (popular, non-official) institutions. Both state and *minjian* organizations oversee such varied activities as traditional rituals, village recreation and entertainment, and provision of public services. State directives require villages with sufficient resources to set up institutions that provide services and implement state policy. 'Village small groups' (*cunmin xiaozu*), for example, assist village cadres with administrative responsibilities such as collecting state and local taxes, carrying out birth control policies, mobilizing villagers to participate in village elections (see **democracy and elections**), and allocating land and housing. Villages also have a representative of the **All-China Women's Federation** (*fulian*) and may have women 'small group' leaders (*funu zuren*) who help township and village officials implement state **birth control and contraception** policies and disseminate information about women's health (see **reproductive health**). Other state-mandated village social institutions include 'associations for the elderly' (*laoren xiehui*), which are supposed to provide social activities and welfare subsidies, and councils called *hongbai lishihui*, organized by village cadres to standardize and oversee **weddings (rural)** and **funerals** and prevent villagers from going to great expense, an ancient concern of the Chinese state.

According to the 'Regulations on the Registration and Management of Social Organizations', approved by the State Council in September 1998, social organizations must find a sponsoring unit within the government and register with the Ministry of Civil Affairs or relevant department. Most rural *minjian* institutions, however, remain unregistered and located in villages where local authorities look the other way. At the village level, the line between state and society is often blurred as both official and *minjian* institutions cooperate with one another to finance and organize such community services as dispute mediation (see **People's Mediation Committees**), road and irrigation repair, mutual aid in agricultural production, movie screenings, opera performances, **basketball** tournaments, **temple fairs** and annual festivals (see **Dragon-Boat Festival**; **Ghost Festival**; **Lantern Festival**; **New Year Festival**; **Qingming Festival**). Moreover, officially permitted organizations, such as the Laoren xiehui and the Hongbai lishihui, often serve as fronts for unregistered *minjian* organizations.

Villager-organized *minjian* institutions include lineage organizations (see **ancestral halls/ lineage temples**), temple associations, community councils and rural folk-singing and dancing groups. Many of these traditional institutions were disbanded and banned during the **Cultural Revolution**, but revived again in the mid 1980s. Throughout the 1990s, *minjian* institutions often re-emerged where economic and political liberalization advanced more quickly or in areas far from metropolitan centres where local governments do not strictly enforce state regulations. In areas such as Guangdong and Fujian provinces, newly rebuilt temples and lineage halls have mushroomed with the influx of donations from overseas Chinese to their home villages.

Village temple and lineage organizations range from informal groups of several people who manage the upkeep of a temple or organize the New Year Festival to more formal associations with a clear division of labour and with members elected or appointed by the community at large. Different members will take responsibility for organizing religious rituals, social activities and public projects. Formal temple and lineage associations often have an accountant and/or cashier who will publicize the association's yearly expenses and income from donations. Lineage and religious institutions may also evolve into broader community organizations, such as community councils or village elders (*laoda*). In such communities, village cadres allow such organizations to take over the governmental responsibilities of providing public services and allocating village resources, such as land. State-registered churches, as well as underground **house churches**, are also common in parts of the countryside (see **Catholic villages**; **Christianity (Protestantism)**). However, because church organizations are more heavily regulated by the state than other village social organizations, they are far less likely to extend their activities into the social and public service domain.

See also: Guanxi; recreational associations; village schools; villages

Further reading

Jing, J. (1996). *The Temple of Memories: History, Power, and Morality in a Chinese Village*. Stanford: Stanford University Press.

Saich, T. (2000). 'Negotiating the State: The Development of Social Organizations in China'. *China Quarterly* 161: 124–41.

Tsai, L. (2002). 'Cadres, Temple and Lineage Organizations, and Governance in Rural China'. *China Journal* 48.

Yan, Y. (1996). *The Flow of Gifts: Reciprocity and Social Networks in a Chinese Village*. Stanford: Stanford University Press.

L. L. TSAI

virginity and premarital sexuality

In contrast with pre-socialist standards of chastity that applied almost exclusively to women, Maoist educational and administrative practices attempted to enforce a new norm of premarital chastity for both sexes. Chinese youth who engaged in consensual premarital sex could be dismissed from school, sent to reform schools, sanctioned by work units or imprisoned for hooliganism, rape or prostitution. During the reform era, Chinese youth experienced a revolution in sexual attitudes, often described as an 'opening up' to liberal ideas from abroad. In contrast to ten years before, a majority of youth surveyed in the late 1990s approved of premarital sexual intercourse in a dating relationship that involved romantic feelings. This new romantic standard represented a break with traditional norms of virginity that applied only to women. Young men began to accept the idea that their wives might have had previous sexual partners. Surveys in the late 1990s found that 70 to 80 per cent of young people had engaged in sexual intercourse before marriage, although sexual intercourse was still relatively uncommon among teenagers and high school students. Public policy changed more slowly. Secondary schools still prohibited dating, and universities still occasionally expelled students for engaging in sexual intercourse, usually in cases of pregnancy. An increasingly open media allowed space for criticisms of state policies, however. In one widely reported case in October 2002 the parents of two students dismissed after the girl became pregnant publicly argued that the university violated the students' rights to privacy and education, an argument that was rejected by the judges but received much support from editorialists and youth in Internet chat rooms.

See also: dating; sexual attitudes; sexuality and behaviour

Further reading

Evans, Harriet (1997). *Women and Sexuality in China: Female Sexuality and Gender since 1949*. London: Chiron Publications.

Farrer, James (2002). *Opening Up: Youth Sex Culture and Market Reform in Shanghai*. Chicago: University of Chicago Press.

JAMES FARRER

volleyball

The victory of the national women's volleyball team in the World Cup in 1981 was arguably the most significant event in public culture after the death of Mao and before the 1989 Tiananmen demonstrations. It was China's first world championship in an Olympic sport (table tennis was not then on the Olympic programme). The tournament took place in Japan and the final match pitted China against Japan, which had reigned over the volleyball world for two decades. When the live broadcast ended, people flooded the streets all over China, setting off firecrackers and weeping openly. Approximately 30,000 letters were mailed to the team, many of them written in blood. Thousands of letters were written to editors of newspapers and magazines; a feature film was made by director **Zhang Nuanxin** (*Seagull* or *Sha'ou*); the **CCTV (Chinese Central Television)** commentator Song Shixiong became a national icon (see **television celebrities**); and an ongoing national debate began over why 'the yin waxes and the yang wanes', i.e. why Chinese women were seemingly superior to Chinese men. 'Learn from womens volleyball' was a guiding slogan at political-study sessions nationwide. Their presence in the national consciousness continued through a string of five world titles, including the gold medal at the 1984 Los Angeles Olympic Games, until they were finally defeated at the 1988 Seoul Olympic Games. By the mid 1990s, professional leagues were established in men's **football (soccer)** and **basketball**, and the flow of capital into mens sports has led to the eclipse of womens sports in public culture.

SUSAN BROWNELL

Wang Anyi

b. 1954, Shanghai

Writer

After establishing herself as a writer on childhood, Wang was drawn to the cultural and aesthetic expression which became known as the **Root-seeking school** (*Xungenpai*) and is exemplified in her novella *Bao Town* (*Xiaobaozhuang*, 1985), inspired by Garcia-Marquez's *One Hundred Years of Solitude*. She then turned to depicting female sexuality, first in a trilogy of novellas entitled *Love in a Small Town* (*Xiaocheng zhi lian*), *Love on a Barren Mountain* (*Huangshan zhi lian*) and *Love in a Brocade Valley* (*Jinxiugu zhi lian*), and then in the homoerotic *Brothers* (*Dixiongmen*, 1989). By the early 1990s Wang had embarked on even longer projects focused on inventing first a past for her parents, and then one for the city of Shanghai. Her father's involvement in the Communist revolution is the topic of 'Grieving over the Pacific Ocean' (*Shangxin taipingyang*, 1992); *Fact and Fiction* (*Jishi yü xugou*, 1993) is filled with a mock genealogy tracing the maternal ancestry of her mother, the noted writer Ru Zhijuan. The history of Shanghai is told through the life of a woman in *Song of Enduring Regret* (*Changhen ge*, 1995), which is a tribute to the style of writer Zhang Ailing, while the novella *Meitou* (2000) presents an assertive woman of Shanghai through familiar scenes of a vanishing cityscape and the unusually frequent use of the Shanghai dialect.

Further reading

Wang, Anyi (1985). *Baotown*. Trans. Martha Avery. New York: Viking Penguin.

—— (1988). *Love in a Small Town*. Trans. Eva Hung. Hong Kong: Renditions.

—— (1991). *Love on a Barren Mountain*. Trans. Eva Hung. Hong Kong: Renditions.

—— (1992). *Brocade Valley*. Trans. Bonnie McDougall and Chen Maiping. New York: New Directions.

—— (2001). *Brothers*. Trans. Zhang Jingyuan. In Patricia Sieber (ed.), *Red is Not the Only Color: Contemporary Chinese Fiction on Love and Sex Between Women, Collected Stories*. Lanham, MD: Rowman and Littlefield, 93–142.

—— (2004). 'Tales of Gender'. In Wang Chaohua (ed.), *One China, Many Paths*. London: Verso, 250–6.

EDWARD GUNN

Wang Gongxin

b. 1960, Beijing

Video and installation artist

Graduating in 1992 from Beijing Capital Normal University, and subsequently a visiting scholar at the State University of New York (Cortland and Albany) in 1997, Wang began his career as a video artist with *The Sky of Brooklyn – Digging a Hole in Beijing* (1995), which emerged out of his experience travelling and living between China and the USA. A monitor with a shot of the Brooklyn sky was placed in a 3-metre well dug into his Beijing house, while a voice-over dissuaded the viewer from looking inside. This 'apparatus of myth-making' (Val Wang) reveals the artist's humour and melancholy with respect to the sense of loss framing notions of individualism in a rapid changing urban environment and the importance attributed to a tradition that is being replaced by an empty and obtuse curiosity with Western things. Later works like *Old Bench* (1996), *Baby Talk* (1997) and *Public Hallway* (1997) touch upon similar themes, minimizing the power of the myth of tradition as a misleading trail. Wang's video installations are characterized by a high operatic texture and present a critique of the essence of contemporary urban life. He often works in collaboration with his wife, installation artist **Lin Tianmiao**. His works have been shown at P.S.1 (New York), MoMA (San Francisco), 'MAAP 2000' (Brisbane, Australia), 'Documentation of Chinese Avant-Garde Art in the 90s' at the Fukuoka Asian Art Museum in Japan (2000), the Guangzhou Triennial (2002), and the Sao Paulo Biennial (2002).

Further reading

Dal Lago, Francesca (2000). 'The Fiction of Everyday Life: Video Art in the People's Republic of China'. *ART AsiaPacific* 27 (Summer): 52–7.

Macham, Kim (2000) 'Kara Oke in Brisbane. Exhibiting Digital New Media and Gongxin Wang'. In *MAAP-Multimedia Art AsiaPacific* (exhibition catalogue). Brisbane.

Smith, Karen (1996). 'Notes on China's Video Installation Art'. *AsiaPacific Sculpture News* 2.4 (Autumn): 19–21.

Wang, Val (2000). 'Wang Gongxing'. *Chinese Type-Contemporary Art Online Magazine* 1.2.

BEATRICE LEANZA

Wang Guangyi

b. 1957, Harbin, Heilongjiang

Painter

After graduating in oil painting at the **China Academy of Fine Arts** in 1984, Wang Guangyi became a leading member of the **Northern Art Group** (Beifang yishu qunti) active in the second half of the 1980s. He championed rationalism in his compositions of grey planes presenting outlines of people and scenes deprived of emotional quality. In 1988 he became the first Chinese artist to

appropriate Mao's standard portraits superimposed by square patterns. By the time of his participation in the **China Avant-Garde** exhibition (1989) in Beijing, he was already well known inside China, but it was not until 1993 that he made his name with the *Great Criticism* (*Da pipan*) series, which became a trademark of the trend known as **Political Pop**. That year Chinese contemporary art made its first large-scale appearance on the world stage with three exhibitions – 'China Avant-Garde' (Berlin), 'China's New Art Post-1989' (Hong Kong) and the 45th Venice Biennale – all of which displayed works by Wang Guangyi (see **China's New Art, Post-89 (Hong Kong, 1993) and China Avant-Garde (Berlin, 1993)**).

Wang's pastiches derived from the propaganda language of the **Cultural Revolution** which juxtaposed proletarian icons with symbols of capitalist consumer culture. The canonized postures of the people's heroes remain unaltered, but the subjects of their fierce battle have become the brand names of commercial products such as Marlboro or Coca-Cola. These paintings have enjoyed much success, particularly because they have actively served to nourish Western Don Quixote-like fantasies about the stereotype of an unadulterated nation ruled by diehard ideology. Though Wang has tried other subjects since, his main focus and style remain unchanged, even in his recent sculptures. Wang Guangyi has been honoured with four solo exhibitions, including one at Littmann Kulturprojekte in Basel (1997).

See also: Lei Feng; political icons (and art); poster art and artists; posters and education

Further reading

Dal Lago, Francesca (2001). 'Images, Words and Violence: Cultural Revolutionary Influences on Chinese Avant-Garde Art'. In Wu Hong (ed.), *Chinese Art at the Crossroads: Between Past and Future*. Hong Kong: New Art Media, 32–9.

Li, Xianting (1994) 'Wang Guangyi and "Political Pop"'. In *Wang Guangyi* (exhibition catalogue). Beijing: Hanart T Z Gallery.

Lü, Peng and Yi Dan (1992). *Zhongguo xiandai yishushi* [A History of Modern Art in China]. Changsha: Hunan meishu chubanshe, 157–68.

Smith, Karen, Yan, Shanchen and Merewether, Charles (eds) (2002). *Wang Guangyi*. Hong Kong: Timezone 8.

TANG DI

Wang Hui

b. 1959, Yangzhou

Intellectual, professor

From his origin in intellectual and literary history, Wang Hui has travelled across the broad academic and intellectual spectrum to become a leading social theorist in the Chinese-speaking world. A professor at the **Chinese Academy of Social Sciences** and **Qinghua University**, he is one of the two editors-in-chief of **Dushu** [Reading]. His essays in this prestigious forum have led to the redefinition of the major issues facing China today. He has held numerous visiting positions and is affiliated with a number of academic journals overseas. Some of his work has been published in English, French, Japanese and Korean.

Underlying his scholarship on early-modern Chinese thought is an intellectual tension, which he historically reconstructs, between discourse and subjectivity, and/or between history and interpretation. The past is made to face squarely with the present, so that historical inquiry becomes part of any theoretical dialogue across time and place. His award-winning book on Lu Xun makes a soul-searching call for intellectuals to 'resist despair' in the aftermath of 1989. His critique of 'scientism' foregrounds the question of the 'scientific interpretive paradigm' and delineates how that paradigm has shaped and limited the production of knowledge in the twentieth century. In 1997 he published *Contemporary Chinese Thought and the Question of Modernity* (*Dangdai Zhongguo sixiang zhuangkuang yu xiandaixing wenti*). A cornerstone in the transformation of contemporary Chinese thought, it has become a benchmark for the **New Left**. A series of debates followed between leftist and neo-liberal intellectuals and pushed him even more to the centre of intellectual life.

See also: liberalism

Further reading

Wang, Hui (1998). 'Contemporary Chinese Thought and the Question of Modernity' *Social Text* 55 (Summer): 9–44.
—— (1998). 'PRC Cultural Studies and Cultural Criticism in the 1990s.' Trans. Nicholas Kaldis. *positions: east asia cultures critique* 6.1: 239–51.
—— (2002). 'Challenging the Eurocentric, Cold-war View of China and the Making of a Post-Tiananmen Intellectual Field.' Ed. Zhang Xudong. *East Asia* 19.1/2 (Spring/Summer): 3–57.
—— (2003). *China's New Order: Society, Politics, and Economy in Transition*. Ed. Theodore Huters. Cambridge: Harvard University Press.
—— (2004). 'The New Criticism'. In Wang Chaohua (ed.), *One China, Many Paths*. London: Verso, 55–86 [interview].

YUE GANG

Wang Jianwei

b. 1958, Suining, Sichuan

Multimedia artist

Wang Jianwei received his MA in Painting from the Zhejiang Academy of Fine Arts in Hangzhou. He has held numerous solo and group exhibitions worldwide. In the 1980s, Wang's paintings explored realistic representations of the lives of Red Guards in the **Cultural Revolution**. Since the 1990s, Wang has become a leading expert in multimedia art. He uses multimedia (videos, slide projectors and mechanical structures) to construct what he calls a 'grey space', a non-determinative multimedia space that eliminates the authority of linear logic.

Linking multimedia art to sites of daily life, Wang comprehends the world of everyday life as ambiguous, non-fixed and multi-layered – a world full of possibilities. The setting for *Production* (1996), for example, is a Sichuan teahouse, where the place, environment, and human conversation and behaviour are the 'products'. The teahouse becomes a place depicting a conditioned way of life, a place where information is transmitted and communicated, a place where daily conversation and modes of thinking are transformed one by another, a place allowing interaction between the public and the private. Moreover, Wang Jianwei also explicitly addresses issues of social change. His 140-minute video *Living Elsewhere* (2000), for example, documents the daily life of four peasants living in villas along Chengdu's Airport Road which were built, but left unfinished, during the period of the bubble economy. In this project, Wang explores how everyday experience is related to the past and present of a built environment.

See also: New Documentary Movement

REN HAI

Wang Jin

b. 1962, Datong, Shanxi

Performance, installation artist

After gaining admission to the China Art Academy (see **art academies**) in 1983, Wang graduated in 1987 with a specialization in traditional figurative painting. He began teaching at the Beijing Institute of Fashion Design, quitting in 1992 to start a career as an independent artist. From the very beginning, his works focused on social change as reflected by China's course towards market reform, commenting on the effects of massive commercialization in Chinese urban life by means of performance art. His first work, *Wall* (1992), proved to be his most powerful visual trope and critical vehicle. Wang's oeuvre, in fact, is an individual response to the complex dilemmas of modern civilization, as expressed in *Knocking at the Door* (1993), where he painted the image of the US currency on seven original bricks from the Forbidden City on site, thus juxtaposing materialistic and cultural symbols. In 1994 he realized *Battling the Flood – Red Flag Canal* and *Red: Beijing–Kowloon*, where red is used as a central concept embedding past, present and future. The first is an environmental project where he poured 25 kg of red mineral pigment into the irrigation canal in Lin county, Henan, while the second was performed by covering with red paint a 200-metre section of the railroad outside of Beijing. Later works show his ongoing investigation of the

effect of rapid social changes and the transitory nature of traditions, like *Ice. Central Plain* (1996), a monumental installation consisting of a 30-metre-long wall made of 600 ice blocks containing a survival kit of desirable goods that he built across a newly opened shopping mall in the city of Zhengzhou. His works have been featured in 'Inside Out: New Chinese Art' at Asia Society, New York and San Francisco MoMA in 1998, 'Contemporary Chinese Art' at the Watari Museum of Contemporary Art, Tokyo (1997), 'A Chinese Dream', Yanhuang Museum of Contemporary Art, Beijing (1997) and the Guangzhou Triennial, Guangzhou (2002).

Further reading

Dematté, Monica (1999). 'Wang Jin'. In *La Biennale di Venezia, 48a Esposizione d'Arte, d'Apertutto, Aperto Over All*. La Biennale di Venezia: Marsilio, 186–9.

Dewar, Susan (1997). 'In the Eye of the Beholder: The Art of Wang Jin and Feng Jiali'. *ART Asia-Pacific* 15: 66–73.

Gao, Minglu (1998). 'From Elite to Small Man: The Many Faces of a Transitional Avant-Garde in Mainland China'. In *idem* (ed.), *Inside Out: New Chinese Art* (exhibition catalogue). Berkeley: University of California Press, 149–66.

BEATRICE LEANZA

Wang Jinsong

b. 1963, Heilongjiang

Oil and traditional Chinese painter, photographer

Wang Jinsong is an artist working in different media whose artistic explorations have consistently focused on the rapidly changing phenomena of contemporary society. Wang graduated from the Chinese Academy of Fine Art in Hangzhou (1987) with a degree in Chinese Traditional Painting; his earliest artistic endeavours were produced in this medium. However, it was his dense, carnival-like oil paintings that helped put him in the forefront of the Chinese art scene in the early 1990s. His paintings often depict street scenes, crowded with eclectic characters posing in front of recognizable historical and political sites around Beijing. Some of the characters' faces are left unpainted, or only slightly drawn, which gives the paintings a ghostly quality. Wang Jinsong began his photography project, *Standard Family*, in 1997. The project is comprised of 200 photographs of Beijing parents, in front of a red backdrop, with their only child posed between them. The piece gained international recognition as an acute reflection of the **one-child policy** in China (and see **little emperors**). His *Parent* series, which consists of images of aging couples in their own environments, also reflects the changing dynamics of family life in China.

Wang Jinsong has also continued to exhibit ink and watercolour works throughout his career. He teaches in the Fine Arts Department of the Institute of Education in Beijing. His work has been exhibited in 'China's New Art Post-1989' (Hong Kong and other venues), 'Inside/Out: New Chinese Art' (Asia Society, New York and San Francisco MoMA), and '50 Years Inside the People's Republic of China' (Aperture Foundation, USA), and is also in the collection of the International Center of Photography, New York.

Further reading

Doran, Valerie C. (ed.) (1993). *China's New Art, Post-1989, with a Retrospective from 1979 to 1989.* Hong Kong: Hanart T Z Gallery (exhibition catalogue). Reprinted in 2001 by Asia Art Archive, Hong Kong. Exhibition catalogue.

Smith, Karen (2001). 'Wang Jinsong'. *Chinese-art.com* 4.3, available at http://www.chinese-art.com/artists/WangJinsong/index.htm

MATHIEU BORYSEVICZ

Wang Keping

b. 1949, Hebei

Sculptor

One of the founder-participants of the **Stars** group, Wang Keping's wooden sculptures are outstanding for their emotional intensity and biting wit. A Red Guard member of an acting troupe during the **Cultural Revolution**, Wang tried his hand at writing plays, admiring the Theatre of the Absurd in particular. However, it was in woodcarving that he really found his medium. A self-taught sculptor, he has a feeling for deducing what kind of image a given piece of wood would best yield. *Silence* (*Chenmo*, 1979) uses a knot of wood where a branch has been lopped off to portray a corked-up mouth, symbolic of the lack of freedom of speech. *Backbone of Society* (*Shehui zhongjian*) makes use of a chunk of wood with a hole in the top to portray brainless, incompetent bureaucrats. His masterpiece is no doubt *Idol* (*Ouxiang*, 1979), a winking Buddha-like head wearing a Communist star insignia on his hat, with features reminiscent of Mao. Wang's sense of social responsibility and formal playfulness is summed up in his statement: 'Käthe Kollwitz is our banner, and Picasso is our pioneer. But for us Kollwitz is more important.' Indeed, he was one of the main organizers of the Stars demonstration for exhibition space on 1 October 1979, the Thirtieth Anniversary of the founding of the People's Republic of China, and expressed his need to sculpt as a way to vent pent-up feelings. In 1984 he moved to France, where he now lives and sculpts.

See also: China Art Gallery; political icons (and art)

Further reading

Andrews, Julia F. (1994). *Painters and Politics in the People's Republic of China 1949–1979.* Berkeley: University of California Press, 377–405.

Galikowski, Maria (1998). *Art and Politics in China, 1949–1984.* Hong Kong: Chinese University Press, 193–207.

Hui Ching-shuen, Janny (ed.) (1989). *The Stars: Ten Years* (exhibition catalogue). Hong Kong: Hanart T Z Gallery 2.

Sullivan, Michael (1996). *Art and Artists of 20th Century China.* Berkeley: University of California Press, 267–71.

EDUARDO WELSH

Wang Lei

b. 1971, Pengzhou, Tongji county, Sichuan

Rock musician

China's best-kept rock music secret is Wang Lei. Often referred to as the '**Cui Jian** of the south', Wang Lei's catalogue of four records was not widely distributed until 2000, when Jing Wen Records released a special reissue compendium of *Journey Man* (*Chumenren*, 1994), *Night* (*Ye*, 1996), *Everything Comes from Love* (*Yiqie cong aiqing kaishi*, 1998) and *Spring Is Here* (*Chuntian laile*, 1999). Wang Lei's father was an amateur painter, and his mother sang in a local cultural troupe. As a child he received training in the theatre, **martial arts** and **Chuanju** (Sichuan opera). At age seventeen, he left home to go walkabout in southwest China, eventually ending up in Guangzhou, where he began making records. In the last half of the 1990s, when Wang Lei released most of his catalogue, he also participated in various collaborative projects with foreign and domestic television and performance artists. He owned the 'Unplugged' bar in Guangzhou between 1997 and 2000. In 2001, he assembled a group of friends from his home town, taught them to play instruments, and moulded them into a live electronica outfit called Pump (Beng). In 2002, Wang Lei returned to Sichuan with Pump, who released their record *10 Brothers* through Beijing Pulay Music, though it was never widely available as a commercial release.

MATTHEW CLARK

Wang Meng

b. 1934, Beijing

Writer, editor, minister

The editor of *People's Literature* from 1983 to 1986 (see **literary periodicals**) and the Minister of Culture from 1986 to 1989, Wang Meng was central to the formation of a 'middlebrow' (neither too didactic nor purely entertaining) literature. His writing promotes a positive outlook and is constantly up to date, using stylistic experiments drawn from changing literary trends. Although Wang still employs the standardized literary language of the 1950s, his verbosity creates a sense of playfulness. These satirical elements are accentuated through the adoption of Beijing dialect in his publications of the late 1980s.

Wang's post-Mao writing takes on the thematic interests first announced in his 1956 novella *The Young Newcomer in the Organization Department* (*Zuzhibu lailege nianqingren*): to critique the bureaucracy and rejuvenate the Party. This ambiguous political allegiance was not tolerated and resulted in Wang's removal from the Beijing literary circle in 1957. After seventeen years of exile in Xinjiang (1962–79), he returned to Beijing and immediately resumed his form of constructive social criticism in a series of short stories, including 'Kite Streamer' (*Fengzheng piaodai*, 1980) and 'The Song of the Spring' (*Chun zhi sheng*, 1980), which received attention for their new stylistic technique and especially for their psychological realism. Wang's early work is concerned with concrete social interaction and relations, but he began to experiment with more abstract ideas and themes in the mid 1980s. *The Man with Moveable Parts* (*Huadong bianxingren*, 1985), for example, is an existential exploration in response to the 'cultural exploration movement'. The 1990s saw Wang switching to popular genres, in order to appear more approachable and less didactic: *Adventures of a Soccer Star* (*Qiuxing qiyu ji*, 1988) and *Murder 3322* (*Ansha 3322*, 1994) are two examples of his effort to respond to changes in consumer taste.

See also: Humanistic Spirit, 'Spirit of the Humanities'

Further reading

Xu, Zidong (1997). *Dangdai xiaoshuo yuedubiji* [Notes on Contemporary Novels]. Shanghai: Huadong shifan daxue chubanshe.

HE DONGHUI

Wang Mingdao

b. 1900; d. 1991

Protestant pastor

Wang Mingdao was an immensely popular independent Beijing-based Protestant pastor from the 1920s to the 1940s, and remains today one of the most important Protestant symbols of resistance to the CCP's repressive religious policies. Wang's rigidly fundamentalist theology – which posited a sharp division between the goodness of God and the depravity of man, and hence between believers and unbelievers – drew him into conflict with secular authorities, first with the occupying Japanese forces, and later with China's Communist rulers. Leaders of the **Three-Self Patriotic Movement (TSPM)** tried to recruit the popular Wang, but he refused on grounds that the TSPM accepted the CCP as its head. In an influential tract, *We, Because of Faith*, Wang criticized the TSPM leaders Wu Yaozong and **Ding Guangxun** by name, calling them 'unbelievers' and declaring that he would 'not unite in any way' with them, 'nor join any of their organizations'. The TSPM denounced Wang during the 'anti-Hu Feng' campaign in 1954. Wang was arrested in August 1955, the day after he preached a sermon entitled 'They in This Manner Betrayed Jesus'. Wang was released for a short period in 1956 after agreeing to write a self-criticism. He quickly retracted his self-criticism, however, and was re-imprisoned, where he remained until 1979. After his release, Wang moved to Shanghai, where he continued to preach and receive guests until his death in 1991.

See also: itinerant evangelists (Protestant)

Further reading

Wang, Mingdao (1955). 'We, Because of Faith' [pamphlet]. Beijing (June). Reprinted in Francis P. Jones (ed.) (1963), *Documents of the Three-Self Movement: Source Materials for the Study of Protestant Church in Communist China*. New York: National Council of the Churches of Christ in the USA.

JASON KINDOPP

Wang Nanming

b. 1962

Art critic, artist

Wang Nanming studied Law at the Huadong College of Politics and Law (Huadong zhengfa

xueyuan) in Shanghai. In 1988, he left the legal profession to become an independent artist, art critic and curator. He has also worked to set up artist residencies and exhibitions for overseas artists in China.

Since the mid 1980s, the focus of his critical work has been the modernization of Chinese traditional art practices. By combining deconstructionist and critical theory, he has targeted the views held by neo-conservatives in publications such as 'Understanding Modern Calligraphy' and 'From Chinese Painting to Modern Ink and Wash Painting'. Since the early 1990s, Wang Nanming has written numerous critical essays on art, including cultural and social criticism. On the subject of post-modernism and 'art concepts' that are 'effective' within contemporary art practice, he has written several critical essays on the **85 New Wave [Art] Movement** and its underlying ideas. On the subject of Chinese contemporary art practice and the stifling effects of an outdated art infra-structure and the perversions brought about by Western hegemonic practices, his best-known essay remains 'Chinatown Culture: Chinese Contemporary Art on the International Art Stage', originally presented as a symposium paper at the British Museum. In more recent years, he has curated exhibitions like 'Critical Dimensions: Art that Oversees Society', which looked carefully and critically at the dynamics of indigenous social, political and cultural development. He is presently working on two new publications, 'The Honour of the Post-colonials' and 'After the Concept: Art and Criticism'.

For the past ten years, Wang Nanming has continued to create new artworks in his *Calligraphy Ball Assemblages* series which were recently exhibited at the British Museum.

Further reading

Wang, Nanming (2000). 'The Shanghai Art Museum Should Not Become a Market Stall in China for Western Hegemonism – A Paper Delivered at the 2000 Shanghai Biennale'. In Wu Hong (ed.) (2001), *Chinese Art at the Crossroads: Between Past and Future, Between East and West*. Hong Kong: New Art Media, 265–8.

ROBERT BERNELL

Wang Quan'an

b. 26 October 1965, Yan'an

Independent filmmaker

Wang Quan'an is a 1991 graduate of the **Beijing Film Academy** and emerged as an independent filmmaker in 1999, after years of prolific script-writing in Xi'an. His debut film, *Lunar Eclipse* (*Yueshi*), received several prizes at national and international film festivals and established him as a stylist among the **Sixth Generation (film directors)**. *Lunar Eclipse* tells of the chance encounter between a young engaged woman and an amateur photographer, who claims to have known a girl with an uncanny resemblance to her. While she explores the life of her double, she comes to an understanding of her own anguish and of the process of her emotional development. The movie intertwines several stories and time frames, past and present, imagination and reality, but it is nevertheless constructed with ease. His second feature film, *The Wakening of Insects* (*Jingzhe*), depicts the psychology of a change in environment from the perspective of a rural girl coming to the city to establish a new life (see **migration and settlement patterns**).

Wang's films represent a unique combination of elements of cinematic art with depictions of the depth of human feeling. The suspenseful and subtle spiritual element, the proficient and authentic dialogue, the unique subjective spectator's viewpoint, the urban ambience, and the realistic lighting result in a carefully crafted style. Wang's films tend more towards the mystical than the social, and as such have added 'art film' to the national allegories of the **Fifth Generation (film directors)** and the urban realism of the 'Sixth'.

BIRGIT LINDER

Wang Renjie

b. 1942, Quanzhou, Fujian

Xiqu (sung-drama/opera) playwright

A native of Quanzhou, Wang Renjie has been mainly writing for **Liyuanxi** (Pear Garden Theatre), the regional sung-drama (opera) of his home town and one of the oldest living theatres in China,

preserving the tradition of the early Nanxi of the Song–Yuan period. His plays, which have been produced successfully on the Liyuanxi stage since the late 1980s, are *The Lament of a Chaste Woman* (*Jiefu yin*), *Tutor Dong and Widow Li* (*Dong sheng yü Li shi*), *Love under Evening Maple Trees* (*Fenglin wan*), *Chen Zhongzi*, and *Woman Thief and Her Male Escort* (*Zaoli yü nüzei*) – now collected in his *A Collection of Plays of the Sanwei Study* (*Sanwei zhai jugao*, Zhongguo xiju chubanshe, 2000). The first three plays are about widows in traditional or contemporary society, and Wang was subsequently nicknamed the 'Three-Widow Playwright'. *The Lament of a Chaste Woman* and *Tutor Dong and Widow Li* earned him two 'Cao Yu Awards' for Dramatic Literature. As he became a well-known playwright, theatrical troupes of other **Xiqu** (sung-drama) forms commissioned him to write plays for their productions. For the Shanghai Kunqu Opera troupe, he has adapted the complete version of Tang Xianzu's *Peony Pavilion* (*Mudan ting*) and Bai Juyi's ballad poetry 'Song of Pipa' (*Pipa xing*) into **Kunqu** of the same titles. He has also written for **Geju** (sung plays) and for **Huju** (Shanghai/Shaoxing opera).

Two prevailing themes in Wang's plays are, perhaps, man's culturally imposed repression of himself and woman's yearning for freedom, which take the form of tragedy in some plays and comedy in others. Wang's lyrics have been praised as containing the flow and rhythm of classical poetry, and his dialogue is full of witticisms, which is partly characteristic of the genre of Liyuanxi. Wang is considered to be one of the most important Xiqu playwrights since the late 1970s. A four-day symposium was held in December 2000 for the study of his plays, attracting some one hundred scholars and critics from Beijing, Shanghai, Sichuan province, Taiwan and Hong Kong, as well as from various places within his native province of Fujian province. Thirty-six articles were presented, some of them later published in theatre journals. The event marked a new trend of recognizing the contributions made by contemporary playwrights in the various regional Xiqu genres.

See also: theatre criticism (journals and periodicals); Xiqu playwrights

DU WENWEI

Wang Shuo

b. 1958, Nanjing/Beijing

Writer

After service in the navy, Wang Shuo began by contributing short fiction to periodicals in 1978, but found his distinctive voice when he adopted the fashionable idioms and local language of Beijing to create characters caught in illicit or absurd situations during the late 1980s, when the economic reforms had taken hold. Several novellas were rapidly adapted as films. Most successful as both fiction and film was *The Troubleshooters* (*Wanzhu*, 1987), in which young people venturing into the market economy offer personal services to relieve people of their ennui and sense of responsibility. A depiction of the black market, *Rising Out of the Sea* (*Fouchu haimian*), was adapted under the title **Transmigration** (*Lunhui*, 1988). In the novella *Half Flame, Half Brine* (*Yiban shi huoyan, yiban shi haishui*) and its film version (1989), a girl is driven to suicide after she plays the part of a prostitute in a blackmailing scheme. By 1994 a half-dozen or more of Wang's stories had resulted in films, a trend that peaked with the adaptation of his *Fierce as Animals* (*Dongwu xiongmeng*) as **In the Heat of the Sun**. Wang's grimmest fictional treatments of contemporary society may be found in the complex exploration of subjectivity within the murder mystery *Playing for Thrills* (*Wande jiushi xin tiao*, 1989) and in the fantasy of a cynical company determined to create a national idol in *Please Don't Call Me Human* (*Qianwan bie bei wo dang ren*, 1989). In the early 1990s Wang played a role in conceiving, and/or writing for, successful television productions, among them the sentimental story of an adoptive mother, **Yearnings, Aspirations** (*Kewang*, 1990), the comedy **Stories from an Editorial Office** (*Bianjibu de gushi*, 1991) and the love story *No Question, I Love You* (*Ai ni mei shangliang*, 1992). His creativity and controversial popularity faded after the rise of an affirmative new **nationalism**.

See also: dakou culture

Further reading

Barmé, Geremie (1999). 'The Apotheosis of the Liumang [Hooligans]'. In *idem*, *In The Red: On Contemporary Chinese Culture*. New York: Columbia University Press, 62–98.

Braester, Yomi (2003). 'Memory at a Standstill: From Maohistory to Hooligan History'. In *idem*, *Witness Against History: Literature, Film, and Public Discourse in Twentieth-Century China*. Stanford: Stanford University Press, 192–205.

Noble, Jonathan (2003). 'Wang Shuo and the Commercialization of Literature'. In Joshua Mostow (ed.) and Kirk Denton (ed. China section), *Columbia Companion to Modern East Asian Literatures*. New York: Columbia University Press, 598–603.

Rosen, Stanley (ed.) (1998). ' "The Troubleshooters" by Wang Shuo'. *Chinese Education and Society* 31.1 (January–February). [filmscript]

Wang, Jing (1996). 'Wang Shuo: "Pop Goes the Culture?" '. In *idem*, *High Culture Fever: Politics, Aesthetics, and Ideology in Deng's China*. Berkeley: University of California Press, 261–86.

Wang Shuo (1998). *Playing for Thrills*. Trans. Howard Goldblatt. New York: William Morrow.

—— (2000). *Please Don't Call Me Human*. Trans. Howard Goldblatt. New York: Hyperion East.

EDWARD GUNN

Wang Tong

(Wang T'ung)

b. 1942, Taihe, Anhui

Film director

Since 1949, Wang has lived in Taiwan, where he became a major proponent of 'nativist cinema'. After graduating from the National Taiwan College of Arts in 1964, Wang entered the Central Motion Pictures Corporation in 1966 and worked in stage design on many productions. His directorial debut, *If I Were for Real* (*Jiaru wo shi zhende*, 1981), is based on a true event that scandalized Shanghai in 1979 in which a young man obtained many illegal favours by pretending to be the son of a high-level cadre. The script was banned on the mainland before being taken up by the Taiwan studio. Wang proceeded to direct another politically sensitive script censored by the CCP, *Kulian* (*Unrequited Love*, 1982). While these two films addressed mainland issues, Wang's subsequent films focused on Taiwan.

A Flower in the Rainy Night (*Kan hai de rizi*, 1983), based on a story by nativist writer Huang Chunming, was followed the trilogy *Strawman* (*Daocaoren*, 1987), *Banana Paradise* (*Xiangjiao tiantang*, 1989) and *Hill of No Return* (*Wuyan de shanqiu*, 1992). Set during the last years of the Japanese occupation of Taiwan and the first years of the KMT rule, the films explore a key transitional moment in Taiwanese history. *Hill of No Return*, which focuses on Fumiko, an abandoned Japanese orphan who ends up as a prostitute, presents the devastating effect of Japanese colonialism for all people concerned. A sweeter tone is achieved in Wang's later *Red Persimmon* (*Hong shizi*, 1996).

See also: cinema in Taiwan; literature in Taiwan

YOMI BRAESTER

Wang Wenxing

b. 1939, Taiwan

Writer

A graduate of National Taiwan University and the University of Iowa, Wang was a leading voice among the young writers who developed a modernist literary movement in the 1960s. After a series of experiments with point of view in provocative stories of childhood and violence that explored existential themes, Wang introduced a controversy with the novel *Family Catastrophe* (*Jiabian*, 1972). Depicting the evolution of a boy's relationship with his parents, especially his growing dismay with his father that culminates in his abusiveness and the father's disappearance, the novel presents alternating points of view in varying styles. The absence in the novel of an explicit moral vision puzzled or angered many readers, as did the innovative form. After nearly a decade, Wang produced a novel that again disturbed many readers, the first volume of *Backed Against the Sea* (*Bei hai de ren*, 1981), the often amusing and frequently vulgar monologue of a demobilized soldier turned fortune-teller commenting freely and explicitly on society and his life. Only in 1999 did the second volume of this novel appear, extending the author's unique concern to effect a musical style through the written word. A professor at National Taiwan University, Wang's

criticism of literature and film is collected in *Books and Images* (*Shu he ying*, 1988).

See also: Bai Xianyong; literature in Taiwan; Ouyang Zi

Further reading

Lupke, Christopher (1998). 'Wang Wenxing and the "Loss" of China'. *Boundary 2* 25.2 (Fall): 97–128.

Wang, Wenxing (1993). *Backed Against the Sea*. Trans. Ed Gunn. Ithaca: Cornell University Press.

—— (1995). *Family Catastrophe: A Modernist Novel*. Trans. Susan Wan Dolling. Honolulu: University of Hawai'i Press.

EDWARD GUNN

Wang Xiao-yen

b. 1959, Beijing

Film director

Living in San Francisco but shooting her films in both the United States and China, Wang Xiao-yen gracefully treads between two cultures and may be the only 'Fifth Generation' director (see **Fifth Generation (film directors)**) to have become a 'Chinese-American filmmaker'. Wang was among the younger students attending the **Beijing Film Academy** when it reopened in 1978. She completed her studies at the San Francisco Academy of Arts (1985–6), arriving in the USA with $38 in her pocket (the amount allowed by the Chinese government) and partaking of the 'immigrant experience' through a variety of menial, illegal jobs.

In 1989 she created the Beijing–San Francisco Film Group, a small independent production company. For her first film, she chose to shoot in English and to express novel cross-cultural concerns. *The Blank Point* (1991) is a sensitive documentary about the lives of three transsexuals, but also a meditation on the filmmaker's bewilderment at the possibility of sex-change operations in the West. In 1993, without a permit, she returned to Beijing to shoot *The Monkey Kid* (*Hou San'r*, completed in 1995), based on her experiences as a mischievous nine-year-old during the **Cultural**

Revolution while her parents had been 'sent down' for 're-education'. After years of fundraising, she was able to direct the second part of her autobiography, *Discombobbled* (*Wo, Yun La*, 2003): a young artist is torn between her old life in China and her new life in the United States, between memories and hope – floating, fighting and finding herself between two worlds.

BÉRÉNICE REYNAUD

Wang Xiaobo

b. 1952; d. 1997, Beijing

Writer, essayist, screenwriter

Wang Xiaobo was one of the most important writers of the mid to late 1990s and became a veritable cultural phenomenon after his untimely death in 1997. Wang had a rich and diverse background, spending time as an agricultural worker in Yunnan, an 'educated youth' in Shandong, and a worker in an instrument factory, before earning a degree in trade economics from People's University in 1982. After two years as an instructor at his alma mater, Wang went to America where he earned an MA in East Asian Studies at the University of Pittsburgh. Returning to China in 1988, Wang held teaching posts in sociology and accounting until 1992, at which point he became a fulltime freelance writer.

Wang Xiaobo is best known for his 'trilogy of the ages': *The Golden Age* (*Huangjin shidai*), *The Silver Age* (*Baiyin shidai*) and *The Copper Age* (*Qingtong shidai*). His novels are marked by black humour, absurdist rhetoric and an attention to the plight of the intellectual which seems ever-present whether he is writing about the Tang dynasty, the **Cultural Revolution** or a science fiction future. In *The Golden Age* an 'educated youth' sent to the countryside for education through labour ends up with a sexual education instead, through his affair with a nurse. The novella's existential absurdity, however, proved to effectively deconstruct traditional narratives of the Cultural Revolution. Wang was also a talented essayist whose sensitive, sharp and highly perceptive collections, such as *My Spiritual Garden* (*Wo de jingshen jiayuan*) and *The Silent Majority* (*Chenmo de daduoshu*), won him just as many readers as his fiction.

Wang is also credited for several firsts. He was the first PRC writer to twice win Taiwan's prestigious Unitas Literary Award for outstanding novella; he co-authored (with his sociologist wife, Li Yinhe) the first serious study of homosexuality in China, entitled *Their World* (*Tamen de shijie*); and he was the first Chinese screenwriter to win a best screenplay award at a major international film festival – the film, **Zhang Yuan**'s *East Palace, West Palace* (*Donggong, xigong*) was also the first gay film in China. Many of Wang's major works were only published posthumously after his tragic death from a heart attack at the age of forty-five. In the wake of his death he became a bestselling author and virtual cultural phenomenon, inspiring such memorial books as *Wang Xiaobo: A Life in Pictures* (*Wang Xiaobo huazhuan*), *Romantic Warrior – Remembering Wang Xiaobo* (*Langman qishi – Jiyi Wang Xiaobo*) and *No Longer Silent* (*Buzai chenmo*).

MICHAEL BERRY

Wang Xiaodong

(a.k.a Shi Zhong)

b. 1955

Culture critic

The changing international order and the loosening of political control in China after 1992 facilitated the rise of **Liberal**, '**New-Leftist**' and **Neo-Conservative** intellectuals. These intellectuals debate with each other and have created a forum somewhat independent of the state. Wang Xiaodong is a major writer in the Neo-Conservative, nationalist camp.

Wang obtained a BS in mathematics from **Peking University** in 1982. After dropping out of a graduate programme in Japan, he returned to China and became a major nationalist writer. His views are not always coherent, but the recently published co-authored book, *China's Path in the Shadow of Globalization*, clearly shows the core of his nationalistic thought. He believes that China's national interests can be promoted in an open global market that shows a certain degree of tolerance towards China's protection of its infant industries. He thinks that some US politicians have seen China's booming economy as a threat and that there are strong anti-China forces developing in America. While he considers such a US reaction understandable, he suggests that the USA give China the space for development in exchange for China's long-term support of the US-dominated international order. As for the current international order, Wang believes that, now that the collapse of the Soviet Union has made the USA the only superpower and the US democracy cannot effectively check the US policy-makers in the foreign policy domain, unilateralism is the (natural) consequence. In response to US unilateralism, Wang recommends that China increase defensive military spending and insists that the prospects for a constructive partnership with the USA will improve when China acquires the economic and military power that the USA respects. As for domestic politics, Wang advocates democracy, arguing that no true nationalism can be developed without human rights and democracy.

Further reading

Fang, Ning, Wang, Xiaodong and Song, Qiang (eds) (1999). *Quanqiuhua yinying xia de zhongguo zhilu* [China's Path in the Shadow of the Globalization] Beijing: Zhongguo shehui kexue chubanshe.
—— (2000). 'Dangdai zhongguo minzu zhuyi lun' [On Contemporary Chinese Nationalism] *Zhuanlüe yü guanli* [Strategy and Management] 42: 69–82.
—— (2001). 'Ziyou bingfei qiangquan enci erlai: huida He Jiadong xiansheng de piping' [Freedom is Not a Gift of the Hegemons: A Rejoinder to Mr He Jiadong]. *Zhuanlüe yü guanli* 44: 82–4.

ZHAO DINGXIN

identify emerging issues, formulate new questions and define the terms for further inquiry. He writes in a style that is engaging yet candid, free of jargon but sophisticated in thought. At East China Normal University in Shanghai he has trained some of the best students in the field. Currently he directs the Centre for Contemporary Cultural Studies at Shanghai University.

A proponent of rewriting the literary history of modern China, Wang's scholarship has deepened the public understanding of a dozen major authors, best represented by *The Cold Face of Reality: A Biography of Lu Xun* (*Wufa zhimian de rensheng: Lu Xun zhuang*). His author-centred approach combines solid historiography with philosophical probing into the intellectual quandaries and ordeals of the author under question. By re-enacting the tensions between history and subjectivity, between social conditions and human desire, he allows historical truth to reveal its significance for the present. Consistent with this historical-intellectual approach are his analyses of contemporary authors and thought. In this domain, he is best known for his critiques of **Zhang Xianliang**, **Ah Cheng**, and the **Root-seeking school** (*Xungen pai*). He has also played a central role in some of the high-profile debates of the 1990s, including the 'humanistic-spirit' debate (see **Humanistic Spirit, 'Spirit of the Humanities'**).

Further reading

Wang, Xiaoming (2003). 'A Manifesto for Cultural Studies'. Trans. Robin Visser. In Wang Chaohua (ed.), *One China, Many Paths*. London: Verso, 274–91.

YUE GANG

Wang Xiaoming

b. 1955, Shanghai

Literary critic

A leading scholar of twentieth-century Chinese literature, Wang Xiaoming embraces the independent spirit of the intellectual and leads by defying the trendy. At major crossroads of social change since the late 1980s, he is among the earliest to

Wang Xingwei

b. 1969, Shenyang, Liaoning

Oil painter

Wang Xingwei graduated from the Fine Art Department of Shenyang Normal University (1990). His work is most often associated with its high degree of theatricality and kitsch performativity. Posing as one of the protagonists of his paintings, Wang shamelessly adopts all kind of visual references from both Chinese and Western visual and art historical practices, tossing them together in hyper-realistic pastiches of excess. One of his confessed intentions is to restrict the agency of the artist as much as possible: by using well-known artistic references, Wang wishes to establish a kind of independence for the work of art. Of his own artistic practices he has said:

> I am very interested in outmoded conventions. I believe that these are the areas in which people are most lacking in vigilance ... I try to make a surprise attack on this habit, or else to quietly change a certain element contained within, the better to make people feel a certain subtle unease.

Wang Xingwei lives and works in Haicheng. Exhibitions of his work include: 'China – Aktuelles aus 15 Ateliers' in Munich (1996); 'The Dust of the Romantic History of Male Heroism' at the Cifa Gallery in Beijing (solo exhibition, 1997); 'Biennial of Contemporary Art of Lyon' (1998); and the 48th Venice Biennale (1999).

Further reading

Dal Lago, Francesca (1999). 'Personal Mao: Reshaping an Icon in Contemporary Chinese Art'. *Art Journal* 58.2 (Summer): 46–59.

Dematté, Monica (1999). 'Wang Xingwei'. In *La Biennale di Venezia, 48a Esposizione d'Arte, d'Apertutto, Aperto Over All*. Marsilio: La Biennale di Venezia.

Knight, Juliet, Murray, Graeme, and Syme, Meg (eds) (1996). *Reckoning with the Past. Contemporary Chinese Painting* (exhibition catalogue). Edinburgh: The Fruitmarket Gallery.

FRANCESCA DAL LAGO

Wang Yong

b. 1964, Beijing

Rock musician

Wang Yong belongs to the first generation of Chinese rock musicians in the PRC and is now active in the broader field of world-music. He began learning the 24-string *guzheng* (zither, see **zheng**) at age nine under his father, a renowned *guzheng*-master himself, and in 1983 enrolled at the Central Music Conservatory to study the instrument. Around that time he joined Beijing's early rock formation Tumbler (Budaoweng) as a keyboard player. After graduation in 1987, he continued to emphasize his traditional music background and won several awards on national music contests. Meanwhile, he started to work with rock musicians such as **Cui Jian**, **Zang Tianshuo** and the heavy metal band Tang Dynasty (Tang Chao). A meeting with Laurie Anderson in Beijing turned his focus in the direction of midi-technology and led to his famous Buddhist-inspired composition 'Requiem March' (*Anhun jinxingqu*, 1993). This spirituality, together with his striving for a synthesis of tradition and modernity, East and West, influenced the album *Samsara* (*Wangsheng*, 1996). Apart from giving solo as well as band performances inside and outside the PRC, Wang is one of the very few Chinese musicians engaged in the international experimental jazz scene and continues to pursue his interest in Chinese string and wind instruments, all of which might lead him to further experiments and larger orchestral works.

See also: jazz; rock music, rock bands

Further reading

Steen, Andreas (1998). 'Buddhism and Rock Music – A New Music Style?' *Chime* 12/13 (Spring/Autumn): 151–64.

ANDREAS STEEN

Wang Youshen

b. 1964, Beijing

Installation and conceptual artist

Wang Youshen graduated from the **Central Academy of Fine Arts** in 1988. He continued his studies in the Department of Folk Art, majoring in illustration and graphic art and experimenting with various materials and media, mostly drawn from daily life. His job as an editor of the *Beijing Youth Daily* also became a source of inspiration for his art, which explores the limitations a media-filtered culture imposes on the human mind. In his *Newspaper* series (1992–3) Wang tries to reproduce such cultural and media games by plastering an entire portion of the Great Wall with disjointed news clippings from one issue of the *Beijing Youth Daily*. Wang's work also investigates the physical and psychological response of audiences to historical issues. *Washing: 1941 – Datong, Ten Thousand Men in a Ditch* (1995) is an installation where two enlarged photos taken from a report on the brutalities of the Japanese invasion of the 1930s are placed in two bath tubs and washed under running water until they gradually disappear. The interplay between audience and art is a crucial element in Wang's work. In *Dark Room* (1998), he built a photo lab in which images at different stages of developing were left floating in the water, and the public were invited to print copies of their personal photographic material. Wang has taken part in several international shows: 'Mao Goes Pop' at the Australian Contemporary Art Museum in Sydney (1993); the 45th Venice Biennale – 'Aperto' (1993); 'In and Out – Contemporary Chinese Art of Mainland and Diaspora' at the LaSalle SIA College of the Arts in Singapore (1997–2000); and 'Polypolis: Art from Asian Pacific Megacities' at the Kunsthaus in Hamburg, Germany (2001).

Further reading

(1997). *In and Out: Contemporary Art from China and Australia*. Singapore: LaSalle-SIA College of Art, Singapore.

Chiu, Melissa (1996). 'Everyday Sightings: Melissa Chiu Interviews the Chinese Artist Wang Youshen'. *ART AsiaPacific* 3.2: 50–4.

Doran, Valerie C. (ed.) (1993). *China's New Art, Post-1989* (exhibition catalogue). Hong Kong: Hanart T Z Gallery.

Thomas, Bronwyn (1992). 'Art and the Critic in Contemporary China'. *Orientations* 23.7 (July): 59–61 [based on an interview with Wang Youshen].

BEATRICE LEANZA

Wang Zengqi

b. 1920, Gaoyou, Jiangsu; d. 1997, Beijing

Writer

During the war and Japanese occupation, Wang Zengqi moved to Kunming (Yunnan), where he attended the lectures of Shen Congwen, whose views on literature had a deep influence. During the **Cultural Revolution**, Wang was assigned to write texts for revolutionary theatre (see **Xiqu**). After Mao's death, he published short stories, including 'A Tale of Big Nur' (*Danao jishi*, 1981) and 'Ordination' (*Shoujie*, 1980), which are considered masterpieces and stand as major steps in the rebirth of Chinese literature in the New Culture era. He advocates a kind of 'cultural literature', by which he builds a bridge, through personal remembrances, between the past and present, as a way to assist people in the reconsideration of their Chinese cultural inheritance, and focuses on human relationships and feelings, such as generosity, loyalty, purity. Wang is also famous for his creative and theoretical essays. His taste for the Chinese language, after years of rigidification and impoverishment, is now highly appreciated, and his contribution with respect to this is significant. He also created a narrative form that broke through the strict barrier between stories and essays, and was willing to write in a natural, highly visual way, close in fact to some concepts of Chinese painting.

Further reading

Wang, Zengqi (1985). 'A Tale of Big Nur'. Trans. Xu Qiaoqi. In *Prize-winning Stories from China, 1980–81*. Beijing: Foreign Language Press, 240–61.

—— (1989). *Les trois amis de l'hiver*. Trans. Annie Curien. Paris: Gallimard.

—— (1995). 'Buddhist Initiation'. In Fang Zhihua (ed., trans.), *Chinese Stories of the Twentieth Century*. New York: Garland, 173–201.

ANNIE CURIEN

Wang Zhenhe

b. 1940, Taiwan; d. 1990

Writer

Educated at National Taiwan University and the Writers' Workshop at the University of Iowa, Wang was a staff writer for Taiwan Television for most of his career. While drawn to the techniques of the modernist fiction he studied, Wang was also an acute observer of vulgarity and of the basic needs of many Taiwanese, all the while writing scripts for popular and socially acceptable television productions. Wang's fiction developed as a conflictual response to these varied aesthetic demands. In his earlier short fiction, Wang used modernist techniques in a series of intimate portrayals of socially neglected characters. In 'An Oxcart for a Dowry' (*Jiazhuang yi niuche*, 1967) he humorously combined linguistic registers in depicting a helplessly degraded peasant couple, establishing himself as a writer of social concern in the nativist 'homeland literature' movement; the story was adapted into film in 1987. Wang then turned to satirizing the rising middle class and its disregard for the needy – in 'Xiao Lin in Taipei' (*Xiao Lin lai Taibei*, 1973) and the novel, *The Beauty Trap* (*Meiren tu*, 1981), he saturated his socially respectable characters with vulgar language and puns. Local Taiwanese language is heavily used in the satirical novel *Rose, Rose, I Love You* (*Meigui, meigui, wo ai ni*, 1984), which depicts the involvement of educated professionals during the 1960s in organizing and training prostitutes for American servicemen on leave from the Vietnam war.

See also: literature in Taiwan

Further reading

Huang, I-min (1986). 'A Postmodern Reading of *Rose, Rose I Love You*'. *Tamkang Review* 17.1: 27–45.

Kinkley, Jeffrey (1992). 'Mandarin Kitsch and Taiwanese Kitsch in the Fiction of Wang Chen-ho'. *Modern Chinese Literature* 6.1/2: 85–114.

Wang, Zhenhe (1998). *Rose, Rose I Love You*. Trans. Howard Goldblatt. New York: Columbia University Press.

EDWARD GUNN

web literature

There are three types of web literature (*wangluo wenxue*) in China: the first are Internet sites with downloadable pre-modern and modern literature; the second type are Internet magazines that offer literature edited for 'publication' on the Internet, most notable among them *Olive Tree*; the third category consists of so-called 'pure web literature'

(*wangluo yuanchuan wenxue*) that includes unedited items from personal web pages, emails and chat rooms and is intended for Internet use only.

The third type is by far the most inexhaustible phenomenon and has a wide readership. It first developed through overseas Chinese students. In 1998, Taiwanese student Cai Zhiheng wrote an influential short story called 'First Intimate Encounter' (*Di yici de qinmi jiechu*) which introduced 'net language' (*wangluo yuyan*) to describe Internet life. Influenced by Cai, Li Xunhuan became the prize-winning vanguard of web literature on the mainland in 1998. Since then, web literature has flooded the Chinese Internet, not only on specific websites but also through main **Internet portals** such as 'Xinlang' (New Wave) and 'Wangyi' (Netease). By 2000, web literature surpassed 10,000 volumes of published articles of printed matter. Although most of the writing is short-lived and anonymous and the quality of writing is extremely uneven, it is popular for its immediacy, subjectivity, equality and accessibility. In 2001, at least 87 per cent of readers were under thirty years of age, and to them web literature has become an inexpensive and relatively safe venue for self-expression, spontaneity and exchange.

See also: Internet (content)

Further reading

Hockx, Michel (2004). 'Links with the Past: Mainland China's Online Literary Communities and their Antecedents'. *Journal of Contemporary China* 13.8 (February): 105–27.

BIRGIT LINDER

weddings (rural)

Chinese weddings serve to build and reinforce social networks, in addition to joining a man and a woman. As in other communities with a dominant pattern of patrilocal postmarital residence, marriage inducts new members into the family and village – namely, women from other villages. Contemporary Chinese weddings are based to some degree on the 'six rites' from the Confucian

Book of Rites (*Liji*): inquiries made by the matchmaker; gathering of genealogical and horoscopic data of the bride and groom; matching the couple's horoscope; transfer of brideprice, dowry or other gifts; fixing the date of the wedding; and the transfer of the bride. While there are differences as to what constitutes the six rites, postsocialist accounts of marriage still have six events: engagement (*dingqin*); receiving the betrothal gifts (silk) (*nacai*); welcoming the bride (*yingqin*); worshipping the ancestors (*baitang*); clowning around the nuptial suite (*naodongfang*); and the third-day visit of the bride to her natal home (*zuosanchao*).

Traditionally, marriage was a family concern, for the production of male heirs and the maintenance of the economic well-being of the family. The traditional ideal of marriage, with an adult bride moving to the home of her adult groom's home, results in the establishment of new alliances between different families and lineages. (Note that there are other forms of marriage, including uxorilocal and *sim-pua* or 'little daughter-in-law' marriages that deviate from this norm, for which see below.) In the traditional major form of marriage, the bride and the groom may not have laid eyes on each other prior to the transfer of the bride. There is a Chinese saying that 'marriage is based on the commands of parents and the arrangements of a matchmaker' (*fumu zhi ming, meishuo zhi yan*). In contemporary practice, however, marriage is increasingly the concern of the individuals, preceded by an extended acquaintance or **dating**. Contemporary Chinese weddings reflect this shift, yet still contain ritual elements that emphasize the familial aspect.

Weddings are ideally a series of events occurring over three days, ending with the bride's third-day visit to her natal home. Prior to the wedding, the couple will have scheduled the shooting of wedding photos with a studio, where the bride may wear a Western-style white wedding dress. On the first day, the bride and her dowry are transferred from her natal home to the groom's home (the brideprice and other gifts would already have been transferred following the engagement). Wearing a red dress, the bride is picked up by a group of the groom's family and friends and placed in a sedan (in the past, it would have been a sedan chair). Some female friends and relatives usually accompany the bride

on the journey to the groom's village. Upon her arrival at the village, firecrackers are set off, and the bride is rushed into the conjugal bedroom (later containing displays of her dowry). The bride is then presented to the ancestors, where the bride and groom kneel before the ancestors (for Chinese Catholics or Christians, a cross may be substituted for ancestral tablets). The bride is then presented to her new relatives, and instructed as to the proper kin terms to use with each relative. The bride and groom together serve tea or wine to each relative, and in exchange the bride is given a gift – a red envelope containing money (*hongbao*). In contemporary practice, this is followed by one or two wedding banquets; for those with the means to have multiple wedding banquets, one is primarily a family and village concern (held in the groom's home), while a second (held outside the home in a restaurant) is primarily for the concerns of the nuptial couple. The home wedding banquet is attended primarily by relations and friends of the groom's family; some female members of the bride's family may also attend. At some point during the banquet, the bride and groom will visit each table, pouring wine, tea or sodas, and making toasts with them. At the end of the banquet, gifts will be given to representatives of the bride's natal family to take back home. If there is a restaurant banquet, the guests are friends and former classmates of the bride and groom. The bride and groom stand outside and greet each guest as he or she enters the restaurant. In exchange, the couple receive another *hongbao*. As in the earlier wedding banquet, the bride and groom will visit each table and make a toast with each group. As a result, contemporary Chinese weddings reflect wider changes in marriage patterns and social concerns such as a growing emphasis of individual over family concerns; the increased social influence of the youth and young adults; and the commodification of cultural practices.

Although rural wedding celebrations, when compared to urban weddings, reflect differences in urban and rural lifestyles and social concerns, rural weddings in contemporary China are increasingly mirroring modern urban weddings. Through multiple forms of media, including widely circulated bridal and women's magazines, movies and television, a modern, Western-influenced and highly commodified wedding celebration is also becoming the standard for rural weddings. Nonetheless, rural Chinese weddings reflect the social concerns of villagers such as the need to produce male heirs and the stronger lineage and family ties in the countryside. Unlike urban areas, where financial and political limitations on the number of children are stronger, rural families may have more than one child.

Wedding celebrations, as we have said, are mostly held for the major form of marriage, where the adult bride moves into the adult groom's home. There are, however, other forms of marriage that address specific economic and demographic concerns and for which an elaborate wedding celebration may not be organized. One example of such a marriage is uxorilocal marriage, where the adult groom moves into the adult bride's home – a marriage form that meets the needs of families who only have girls. Children resulting from such a marriage will then become the heirs of the bride's father. Uxorilocal marriage, however, is not preferable for both bride and groom in the countryside, where patrilineal kinship relations form the dominant structure of rural communities. Another kind of marriage that would not have an elaborate wedding celebration is one common in south China prior to 1949. This is *sim-pua* or 'little daughter-in-law' marriage, where a juvenile bride is transferred to the home of her future groom's family to be raised by her future mother-in-law. *Sim-pua* marriages were much more affordable for poorer families, as they did not incur the considerable expense, including brideprice and marriage gifts, that are required by the major form of marriage.

See also: marriage; weddings (urban)

Further reading

Freedman, Maurice (1970). 'Ritual Aspects of Kinship and Marriage'. In *idem* (ed.), *Family and Kinship in Chinese Society*. Stanford: Stanford University Press: 163–89.

Judd, Ellen R. (1989). '*Niangjia*: Chinese Women and Their Natal Families'. *Journal of Asian Studies* 48. 3: 525–44.

Stockard, Janice E. (1989). *Daughters of the Canton Delta: Marriage Patterns and Economic Strategies in South China, 1860–1930*. Stanford: Stanford University Press.

Watson, Rubie S. and Ebrey, Patricia Buckley (eds) (1991). *Marriage and Inequality in Chinese Society*. Berkeley: University of California Press.

Wolf, Margery (1972). *Women and the Family in Rural Taiwan*. Stanford: Stanford University Press.

ERIBERTO P. LOZADA JR

weddings (urban)

A modern wedding celebration in urban China is a hybrid of traditions and new practices. A lucky day has to be chosen for the occasion. Next is to get the bridal chamber and the wedding ready. When the time comes, the groom's envoys pick up the bride in a car procession, a practice institutionalized in the 1980s and a job mostly taken over by commercial fleets today. Upon her arrival, the groom will escort the bride home amid a salvo of festive firecrackers. At the ceremony, traditionally known as *bai Tiandi*, they must bow to Heaven and Earth, their parents and each other. Even though their marriage has already been legalized by government certificates, only the ceremony will make it official. Then comes the feast, followed by a spree in which close friends participate. Most celebrations now occur in restaurants. Usually, the groom and his parents foot the bill for the wedding, furnishings and the couple's daily necessities, if not luxuries. The amount of the bride's dowry is decided by the bride's family. The cost of weddings has risen constantly – around 10,000 yuan in the 1980s and triple that today. Local governments used to intervene by encouraging mass marriage ceremonies to help cut the cost. From the 1990s, most brides in China's cities prefer wearing Western-style wedding gowns, though traditionally the Chinese consider white a colour of mourning. Now an expensive album of glamour shots in both Western and traditional Chinese wedding dresses has become an essential part of the urban wedding celebrations.

YUAN HAIWANG

Wei Hua

(Wayhwa)

Pop singer

Wei Hua was one of few female rock/pop stars of the 1990s. She had worked as an English-language newscaster at **CCTV (Chinese Central Television)** from 1987 to 1989. She resigned from CCTV because the Chinese government did not allowed her to appear on television after the 1989 student movements. She reinvented herself as a rock singer just at the time when rock music became popular in the early 1990s. She changed her appearance after becoming a rock star: She stopped wearing business power suits, and dyed her black hair with other colours – first purple and blue, then blonde.

Her music takes a strong position on the conventional rock themes of freedom, self and truth. She began to record music in 1990. In March 1993, she wrote the song 'Fresh' (*Xian*) to remind her audience of the unstoppable growth of life in the spring. Her most famous album is *Modernization* (*Xiandaihua*, 1995). Such songs as 'Forbidden City' (*Lao gugong*), 'Gossip' (*Xianhua*) and 'Modernization' (*Xiandaihua*) reveal the tension of a cultural identity caught between tradition and modernity, past and future, the inner world of the self and the external world of the other. Other songs show a close connection between self-expression and consumption. 'Sunday' (*Xingqitian*) links leisure to such places as Pizza Hut and Kentucky Fried Chicken. The English song 'Visa' describes a trip overseas: 'walk the streets of Rome and LA' and 'buy a few things: coffee, cheese, books, clothes, perfume'.

Further reading

Baranovitch, Nimrod (2003). *China's New Voices: Popular Music, Ethnicity, Gender, and Politics, 1978–1997*. Berkeley: University of California Press, 176–86.

REN HAI

Wei Minglun

b. 1940, Neijiang, Sichuan

Xiqu (sung-drama/opera) playwright

Wei Minglun is one of Sichuan's most successful and innovative dramatists and has created a considerable impact on the country's dramatic circles, particularly during the 1980s, with a number of his plays. Born in Sichuan province, Wei learned the craft of Sichuan opera from a very early age and joined the Zigong Sichuan Opera Troupe at the age of ten as a *xiao sheng* (young man) and *xiao chou* (small clown) actor (see **Xiqu role types**). Wei left the stage in 1962 and turned to playwriting. His contemporary operas, *Girl Four* (*Si Guniang*) and the *Courageous Yang* (*Yi Danda*), won him the National Best Drama Award in 1980/1. His 'newly written historical drama', *The Scholar of Bashan* (*Bashan Xiucai*), premiered in Beijing in 1983 and was highly recommended for depicting the oppression of the people by the ruling classes.

His most successful, but also most controversial play is **Pan Jinlian**, which premiered in Zigong (Sichuan) in 1985. Described in the title as 'a Sichuan opera of the absurd', it captured the attention of Chinese and foreign theatre experts due to its experimental approach in 'modernizing' the form and content of **Chuanju** (Sichuan opera). Pan Jinlian, traditionally condemned as a wanton woman who killed her husband for her lover, is here shown to be a victim of the patriarchal society. Wei experimented with the interweaving of different temporal and spatial dimensions. Characters include divergent women such as Empress Wu Zetian, a contemporary female judge and Tolstoy's Anna Karenina. *Pan Jinlian* has been praised for its social relevance, touching on the important issue of female emancipation in modern China and posing the provocative question whether or not a 'modern' Pan Jinlian would actually be free in her choices.

In 1993 Wei Minglun was invited to adapt Puccini's *Turandot* for **Jingju** (Peking opera) and later brought the production to Italy. Wei has also worked as a writer for film and for television series. His most recent success is *Face Changing* (*Bianlian*). Originally written as a screenplay and produced in Hong Kong in 1995, Wei adapted itas a Sichuan opera in 1997, creating once again a Chuanju that is innovative in style and socially relevant to today's audiences.

See also: Xiqu; Xiqu playwrights

Further reading

Dauth, Ursula (1997). 'Strategies of Reform in Sichuan Opera since 1982: Confronting the Challenge of Rejuvenating a Regional Opera'. PhD diss. Brisbane: Griffith University.

Zhang, Yunchu (1988). ' "Wei Minglun xianxiang" – xiandai yishide xiqu wenhua xianxiang' [The 'Wei Minglun Phenomenon' – the Phenomenon of a Modern Consciousness in Traditional Chinese Theatrical Culture]. *Juben* 5: 34–5, 53.

URSULA DAUTH

Wei Wei

b. 1964, Hohohot, Inner Mongolia

Pop singer

Wei Wei had a resonant mezzo-soprano voice when young. As girl of eight, she returned to her mother's home town in Guangxi where she learned ballet and local opera, which cultivated her talent for the performing arts. At fifteen, she managed to enrol in Beijing's Central Conservatory of Music, and did chores on the side until she became a household name with her debut, *The Magic of Love* (*Ai de fengxian*). Her subsequent success won her the name of 'Queen of the Chinese Pop Singers', being invited to sing the theme songs for the Asian Games in 1990, the East Asian Games in 1993, and the 7th National Games of China. Wei Wei was also one of the first Chinese to compete in international pop-singing contests, winning the Best-Focused Beauty Prize at the 24th Poland Nabot International Music Festival. She performed at Carnegie Hall in New York, at the Atlanta Olympic Games in 1996, and at Caesar's Palace in Las Vegas in 1999. In 1992, Wei Wei met Dr Michael Smith, a Swedish cultural emissary and later instructor at the Central Conservatory of Music in Beijing. Ten years of marriage and three sons later, they have become an example among Chinese of the ideal international marriage: Wei Wei has managed the roles of good mother and wife while remaining a successful pop singer. Her latest albums include *I Believe in China* (*Xiangxin Zhongguo*) (composed by her husband) and *Wei Wei's Devotion* (*Wei Wei's fengxian*).

HU MINGRONG

welfare and poverty relief

In China, welfare or *fuli* evokes a rich connotation of meanings and perceptions. In the broad sense, welfare refers to benefits and entitlements associated with employment, and in particular the collective amenities provided at the workplace for urban workers. In the socialist economy, a typical occupational package included a pension, health care, housing, child care and living support and is a core part of the social wage. In the narrow sense, welfare refers to financial aid, welfare services (e.g. old-age homes, children's homes, shelter/work for the disabled) and emergency relief for people with special needs: childless elders, disabled persons and orphans who have no ability for work, no family support and no means of livelihood (the 'three nos'), poor households (*pinkunhu*), victims of natural disasters and poor veterans. The responsible agencies are state civil affairs departments and local communities. It is within the narrow perspective that 'poverty relief' (*pinkun jiuji*) is most closely associated with welfare. Indeed, the two terms are commonly used together. Poverty relief is usually given on a temporary basis; long-term or regular relief is confined to the 'three nos'.

The old forms of welfare and poverty relief have been severely challenged by decollectivization, market liberalization and the privatization of social services (notably health care and education) which strips away collective support for peasants, unemployed state workers, employees in the private sector, and migrant workers without urban registration. In particular, rising unemployment and the erosion of welfare accompanying state-enterprise restructuring has increased vulnerability and urban poverty. In the countryside, notwithstanding remarkable reductions in rural poverty (from 250 million persons in 1978 to 30 million in 2001 according to official estimates), poverty is still a serious problem in under-developed areas and among peasants lacking social capital. Likewise, the migration of 100 million rural workers, the lack of formal social security (see **migration and settlement patterns**) and the under-supply of social services have also increased rural demands for social support. Additionally, rapid aging and the one-child policy compound the pressures.

To cope with the new challenges, wide-ranging reforms have been adopted. Welfare reforms include introducing new welfare services, extending service access to paying users, expanding community services, encouraging commercial provision and promoting philanthropy. To alleviate poverty and avoid social instability, a multi-pronged approach was adopted. Rural initiatives include the introduction of micro-credit, work relief schemes and aid packages to poor regions. In the cities, the state has regularized a system of poverty alleviation comprising unemployment insurance (since 1986), living allowances for 'laid off' workers (from 1998) (see **xiagang**), and means-tested social assistance, known as the 'minimum living security allowance' (*zuidi shenghuo baozhang*) (from 1997). Social assistance is expected to serve as the final safety net. At the end of 2001, some 12 million urban residents received relief. Extension to rural areas is envisaged.

See also: disabilities; medical insurance; medical doctors; mental health; iron rice bowl

Further reading

Wong, Linda (1998). *Marginalization and Social Welfare in China*. London and New York: Routledge and LSE.

Tang, Jun, Cook, Sarah and Ren, Zhenxing (2002). *The Final Safety Net – Poverty and the Scheme of Minimum Living Standard in Urban China*. Beijing: China Academy of Social Science.

LINDA WONG

Wen Hui

b. 1960, Yunnan

Choreographer

Wen Hui is one of the great modern dance choreographers in China. Originally a Chinese folk dancer in Yunnan, she attended the Department of Choreography of the Beijing Dance Academy from 1985 to 1989, and has since been a choreographer and dancer in the Oriental Song and Dance Ensemble of China (Dongfang gewutuan). In 1994, Wen Hui and the filmmaker **Wu Wenguang** co-founded China's first independent dance theatre company, Living Dance Studio (Wudao shenghuo guangcuoshi).

The use of documentary film, dance theatre style, and creative sources and subject matters from Chinese daily life feature highly in most of Wen Hui's works. Her first modern dance work, *100 Verbs* (*Yibai ge dongci*, 1994) brings together dancers and non-dancers in a structured improvisational piece in which the main idea is to show human life as composed of different verbs. *Toilet/Living Together* (*Tongju shenghuo/Matong*, 1995), performed by Wen Hui and Wu Wenguang, is a self-documenting dance relating Wen and Wu's unmarried life. During the performance, they project pictures of their daily life in a documentary style. *Report on Giving Birth* (*Shengyu baogao*) premiered in 1999 at the **Little Theatre** of **Beijing People's Arts Theatre**. The piece was a collective creation of Wen Hui and her dancers, and based on four years' research – interviewing mothers, doctors, journalists, athletes and midwives about their opinions and experiences of giving birth. These interviews were documented and displayed during the performance. *Dance with Farm Workers* (*He mingong tiaowu*), which premiered in 2001 at the East Modern Art Centre, was performed by thirty construction workers and ten professional artists. Wen Hui's basic idea for this piece was to present the bodies of rural workers as indispensable to Beijing's development. They documented the entire process of the eight-day rehearsal, in which construction workers developed a way of expressing themselves by communicating with the artists. In her latest production, *Report on the Body* (*Shenti baogao*), which premiered in 2002 at Beijing Qiseguang Children's Theatre, Wen Hui continues her documentary dance theatre style. By presenting a rural girl using her body as a means of survival, Wen Hui points out that a Chinese woman's body remains a commodity, a victim of the consumer and male-dominated society.

In place of choreographed dance movements, Wen Hui is fond of improvisation based on the movements of people's daily life, and she is highly interested in the movements that result from juxtaposing trained and untrained dancers. In addition to being a choreographer and dancer, Wen Hui also worked as an actor in *File O* (*Lingdangan*, 1994), one of the best-known works of **avant-garde/experimental theatre**, directed by **Mou Sen**. Although Wen Hui's works are culturally rooted in China, the technique and spirit of Western modern dance has without a doubt deeply influenced her creations. She studied Western modern dance at the Limon Institute, the Erick Haukins School of Dance, the Trisha Brown Company Workshop, the Foikwang-Hochschüle Dance School and Pina Bausch's dance company in 1994 and 1995. With the support of the Asian Cultural Council, she also studied aspects of modern dance in New York in 1997. Since 1995, Wen Hui and Wu Wenguang have been invited regularly to perform in the USA, UK, France, Holland, Belgium, Portugal, Korea, the Philippines and other countries. Other works of note include *Breath with Earth* (1996), *Dining with 1997* (1996), *Skirt* (1996), *Go Out and Come In* (1997), *Face* (1997), *Scene: Skirt, Video* (1998), and *Dining with 1999* (1999).

LIN WEI-YÜ

wenhua shuiping

(cultural level)

Social concept

This phrase is most commonly used to refer to a person's level of formal education. A person's level is considered high if he or she went to college and low if he or she only finished grade school. Although the formal translation refers to one's years of schooling, the term also has a wider social usage that refers to elocution, etiquette, self-presentation and family background. For instance, employers of college graduates and others with post-secondary education or special skills often use the term to refer to an employee's potential to make money for a corporation, their ability to make important connections in industry and government, and their skills at self-presentation in an increasingly professionalized work environment. As such, the phrase is similar to how the terms *suzhi* (quality) and

wenming (civilized) are used to distinguish between people and to suggest social classes.

Glorification of the term *wenhua* (culture) in the post-Mao era must be seen in contrast to the way *wenhua* and those identified with it (i.e. intellectuals; see **intellectuals and academics**) were castigated during the **Cultural Revolution**. The popular and official reappraisal of the role of culture and quality in national development means that those with educational credentials may be identified as valuable sources of modernizing strength. In the post-Mao era, *wenhua* has been transformed to fit the needs of contemporary modernization, so that now people believe it is reasonable and legitimate for someone with a high cultural level to get ahead.

See also: popular culture, mass culture; university entrance examinations

LISA M. HOFFMAN

Western theatre

Before the **Cultural Revolution** most of the Western plays performed in China were Russian. This tradition was interrupted by the Cultural Revolution, though afterwards the tradition resumed but with significant changes in the selection of plays and the way they were adapted for the Chinese stage. In the late twentieth century, with only a few exceptions – for example, the nostalgic and issue-based staging of Gogol's *The Inspector General* in 2000 – Chinese directors have generally preferred Euroamerican writers to Russian playwrights, and absurdist or abstract rather than realistic theatre.

The staging of Brecht's *The Life of Galileo* constituted a highlight of the late 1970s. The director invited the audience to imagine that the scientist persecuted for pursuing truth was a metaphor for their own experiences under Mao. The director also modified Brecht's ambivalent ending to underline the inevitable victory of truth and historical progress. An appreciation for Western culture and the desire to broaden the modes of theatrical expression determined the selection and staging of Western plays in the 1980s. For example, academics and artists jointly organized Shakespeare festivals (1986 and 1994) and an O'Neill festival (1988). Interest also extended to Miller, Brecht, Beckett, Ionesco and Ibsen. Since the late 1980s, Western plays have become increasingly associated with the avant-garde. The repertoire has expanded to include Dürrenmatt, Fo, Pinter, Genet and Frisch to express a growing scepticism. Performances frequently mix Chinese operatic traditions and traditions related to modernist theatre in the West. An example is *Three Sisters Waiting for Godot*, combining Chekhov's *Three Sisters* with Beckett's *Waiting for Godot*, or **Wild Man**.

See also: avant-garde/experimental theatre; Huaju

Further reading

Chen, Xiaomei (1995). *Occidentalism: A Theory of Counter-Discourse in Post-Mao China*. New York: Oxford University Press.

Meng, Jinghui (2000). *Xianfeng xiju dang'an* [An Archive of Avant-garde Drama]. Beijing: Zuojia chubanshe.

HE DONGHUI

Western-style Chinese medicine

For centuries, traditional Chinese medicines were manufactured as bolus, powder, plaster, pellet, decoction and liquor out of herbs, insects and animal parts that proved to have medicinal effectiveness. Without modern technology, these potent preparations were voluminous, unrefined and hard to administer. As early as 1957, manufacturers of traditional Chinese medicine, like Tongrentang in Beijing, attempted manufacturing 'Western-style Chinese medicine' (*Zhongyao xizhi*).

Not until the 1990s did traditional Chinese medicine manufacturers realize the urgency of modernizing their industry. Facing an increasing need for alternative medicines in the world, Chinese medicine manufacturers were disappointed that their products did not measure up to Western standards. Chinese medicines claimed only 2 per cent of the global traditional-medicine market. Chinese manufacturers realized the importance of applying the principles of Western pharmaceutics

to manufacturing traditional Chinese medicines; of employing the technology of drying, pellicular coating and the mass production of powdered injection via assembly lines; and of implementing quality control under modernized management. The State Council therefore pronounced its strategic plan for modernizing Chinese medicines in 1997 and promulgated 'An Outline for Modernizing Traditional Chinese Medicines' a few years later. Research institutes, medical schools and manufacturers are now collaborating in extracting effective elements from medicinal herbs and preparing them for manufacture in the Western style to battle cancer, heart disease, hypertension, diabetes and other illnesses. 'Kanggan chongtengpian' (Instantly Soluble Anti-Cold Tablets) and 'Shuanghuanglian qiwuji' (Four-Herb Spray), an eradicator of respiratory disorder, are two examples of a large array of newly manufactured Western-style Chinese medicines.

See also: herbal medicine

YUAN HAIWANG

Wild Children

Folk-music duo

Hailing from the western city of Lanzhou, Wild Children is the project of singer/songwriter/guitar duo Zhang Quan (b. 1968) and Xiao Suo (b. 1970). Zhang Quan describes his family background as 'part worker, part peasant and part hobo'. He left home at the age of fourteen to live in different parts of southwest and northeast China. Quan and Suo joined forces in 1994 to develop their own guitar tunings and vocal harmonization, gravitating towards the pentatonic scales of the traditional Chinese zither (see **qin**) and the dissonant harmonies of Buddhist incantation (see **Buddhist music**). Their music is informed by almost twenty years of living and working in peasant communities, where singing and music were prominent and the Chinese folk music tradition could be heard at its source. Having engaged this essentially Maoist project of 'going down to the countryside' to learn from the people (see **xiafang, xiaxiang**), Wild Children's proletarian credentials were firmly in place when they arrived in the nation's capital in

1999. After an initial year of playing around Beijing and establishing a presence on the local music scene, Quan and Suo purchased a tiny bar on Beijing's South Sanlitun Street and in no time were spinning delicate webs of down-home groove from the tiny stage of the River Bar. In 2003 Wild Children became a five-piece collective that shrinks and grows as the raucous late-night jam sessions dictate.

See also: Yang Yi

Further reading

http://www.wildchildren.net

MATTHEW CLARK

Wild Man

[Yeren, 1985]

Huaju (spoken drama)

Wild Man, written by **Gao Xingjian**, was directed by **Lin Zhaohua** and premiered by the **Beijing People's Art Theatre** in 1985. Although it first received mixed responses from both critics and audiences, *Wild Man* remains arguably one of the Nobel laureate's most important works. In *Wild Man*, Gao departed from his own experiments with Western modernist theatre as seen in *The Alarm Signal* (*Juedui xinhao*, 1982) or **Bus Stop** (*Chezhan*, 1983), and attempted to realize his ideal of establishing a new modern theatre that draws on traditional Chinese opera and involves song, speech, acting and acrobatics. As Gao declared in the play's 'Postscript', these non-verbal techniques compose a 'dramatic symphony' that consists of several themes to create a structure of multi-vocality and realize a total theatrical effect. Contrary to Aristotelian theatre with its beginning, middle and end, *Wild Man* consists of a series of diverse episodes without an obvious storyline. Set in the vanishing forest of contemporary Sichuan province, the play depicts an ecologist who is looking for a wild man yet is frustrated by the loggers and local officials who make their living by destroying the forest and environment. A schoolteacher devotes his time to rescuing a **Han** epic from a dying epic singer.

A devoted girl from the local village falls hopelessly in love with the ecologist, who is trapped in an unhappy marriage. Although the play attempts to integrate these realistic concerns with the issues of love, marriage, ethics, custom, tradition, corruption and environmental protection in contemporary China, Gao made it clear that his play should remind his audiences that it is a play, not real life, demonstrating the influence of the Brechtian 'alienation effect', which is to break down the conventional notion of theatre as a representation of real life. Gao achieved this end by asking the ecologist several times in the play to take off his mask to assume his identity as an actor and asking him also to play the role of stage director at the same time. *Wild Man* can thus be seen as one of the most innovative dramas in contemporary China which freely combines the theatrical traditions of East and West.

See also: avant-garde/experimental theatre; Huaju; Western theatre

Further reading

Chen, Xiaomei (1995). 'A *Wildman* between the Orient and the Occident: Retro-Influence in Comparative Literary Studies'. In *idem*, *Occidentalism: A Theory of Counter-Discourse in Post-Mao China*. New York: Oxford University Press, 99–118.

Gao, Xingjian (1990). *Wild Man*. Trans. Bruno Boubicek. *Asian Theatre Journal* 7.2: 195–249.

CHEN XIAOMEI

WM (W[o]m[en])

[We (Us), 1985]

Huanju (spoken drama)

This spoken drama by Wang Peigong (b. 1943) presents the disillusionment of a group of 'educated youth' (*zhiqing*) sent down to the countryside during the **Cultural Revolution** (see **xiafang, xiaxiang**). Seven irreverent young people, bound together by their collective hardships in Act I, turn in Act II towards individual dreams as they prepare for the newly reinstated **university entrance**

examinations, and reunite briefly in Act III to share news of their lives and recall the distance from their youthful ideals. Although one member of the group, Yue Yang, demonstrates a continuing commitment to socialist ideals, he does not dominate the play or inspire others. Although the inhumanity of the Cultural Revolution is portrayed, the dispirited attitudes of the characters in later years leave the suggestion that social problems are not confined to that earlier era. For these reasons, conservative members of the Communist Party attacked the play for failing to offer a positive evaluation of contemporary society. However, others defended, performed and published the play in an unprecedented act of defiance of these Party authorities, who did, however, subsequently stage a cultural purge in 1987 (see **cultural purges**). Wang Peigong, who was then in the People's Liberation Army, transferred to the Beijing Youth Art Theatre, and thereafter continued to write avant-garde plays and film scripts.

See also: avant-garde/experimental theatre; Huaju

Further reading

Wang, Peigong (1998). 'WM'. In Yan Haiping (ed.), *Theater and Society: An Anthology of Contemporary Chinese Drama*. New York: East Gate Book Publishing, 60–122.

EDWARD GUNN

women (the condition of)

Socially, the PRC government has promulgated a series of statutes to promote women's status and gender equality. The Marriage Law of 1950 backed by Mao prohibited arranged marriages, concubinage, foot-binding and child marriages. The Marriage Law of 1981, which stipulated that a breakdown in a relationship between husbands and wives was sufficient grounds for a divorce, made the procedures easier. The amendments to the second Marriage Law in 2001 reiterates that bigamy (*chonghun*, commonly called **bao ernai**) is illegal and those who violate it will be punished. The same amendments define family violence as a serious offence or crime that should be stopped.

Politically, there were 382 women delegates to the Sixteenth National Congress of the Party in November 2002, accounting for 18.1 per cent of the total 2,118 delegates. There were over 650 women deputies to the fifth session of the Ninth National People's Congress in March 2002, accounting for more than 22 per cent of the total. The percentage is on a par with or even surpasses that of many developed countries. By the late 1990s, the number of female cadres in government ministries and departments, state-owned enterprises and institutions had reached nearly 14 million or about 35 per cent of the total number of cadres across China.

Economically, female workers account for 38.8 per cent of urban employees and 65.6 per cent of rural labourers, though two-thirds of the laid-off workers in urban areas are women. 'Women can hold up half of the sky', a political slogan of Mao times to emphasize women's participation in all aspects of life, is far from being true. In fact, this aspiration is seldom mentioned during the reform era. While women now have greater opportunities for education, their 'sky' seems smaller and less bright. Some officials proposed that 'a generation of women be sacrificed to speed up the economic development'. There have been debates among economists as to whether women should 'return home'. One argument is that countries with lower rates of female employment would have higher rates of economic growth, thus it would be better off if women stayed at home. In practice, many women have been forced to take prolonged 'vacations' or maternity leave with little pay or have been pressured into early retirement. Officials in some localities practise 'periodical employment for women' to formally extend maternity leave to several years to relieve unemployment. The government admits that more girls drop out of school; that more women workers are laid off; and that almost all high-profile **corruption** committed by top state leaders is related to women as mistresses and accomplices. For some ordinary cadres, their attitude is reflected in a **shunkouliu** (doggerel verse):

Zhao qingren tai lei,
Zhao xiaojie tai gui,
Zhao xiagang nügong zui shihui.

To search for a mistress is too tiring;
To search for a 'Miss [Three Accompanies]' is
   too costly;
To search for a laid-off woman is most practical.

As for those laid-off women, they have their own response:

Xiagang nügong bu luolei,
Tingxiong zoujin yezonghui,
Shei shuo women wu diwei,
Zuotian hai pei shuji shui?

Laid-off women workers don't drop tears.
Throwing out our chests, we enter nightclubs
   proudly.
Who said that we don't have social status?
Just yesterday I accompanied the Party Secretary
   sleeping.

HELEN XIAOYAN WU

women's quality

(nüren suzhi)

Political/social concept

'Women's quality' emerged as a major issue in the 1980s with the decision of the **All-China Women's Federation** to emphasize raising women's quality as the cornerstone of their strategy to raise the status of women. The strategy was based on the premise that the main obstacle for women was low quality – primarily understood to refer to women's disadvantages in literacy, education and training, but also extending to work and leadership experience and to familiarity with and skills in the marketplace. Organized initiatives were proposed and implemented to improve women's quality, most notably the **two studies, two competitions** activities for rural women, as well as a programme to systematically improve the quality of all personnel in the Women's Federations or of those linked with them (most notably village women's heads). Con-current initiatives promoted women's strengths in the family, in character, and in political life.

The call to raise women's quality should also be understood within the context of wider calls to raise the overall quality of the Chinese nation and pursue both material and spiritual civilization (see

socialist spiritual civilization). In this broader sense it is connected with long-standing ideals of self-cultivation, both in Confucian and Communist variants. As the Women's Federations apply this approach within their own mandate, the emphasis is upon the internal strengthening of women in order to enable women to raise their social and political status. In terms of the socialist market, there is also a strong implication of preparing and encouraging women to compete successfully in the market.

ELLEN R. JUDD

women's script

(nüshu)

For at least a few centuries up until the early 1990s, in the rice-farming villages in and around Shang-jiangxu township, Jiangyong county (Hunan province), where most people were illiterate in the standard Chinese script, women wrote in a script men could not read. Girls and women used *nüshu* (women's script), a syllabic, phonetic representation of the local language, spoken by men and women alike, to write letters, autobiographies, narratives of local and national events, prayers, and translations of stories and morality manuals popular throughout China – all of these in highly formulaic verse easily memorized and transmitted orally as well as in writing. While the people living in the *nüshu* area are **Han**, the language they speak and some of their customs suggest non-Han heritage or contact. Girls used *nüshu* to write letters to establish an age mate relationship known as *laotong* (longtime same). The standard form of marital residence in the area is 'delayed transfer' marriage, in which a bride returns to her natal home a few days after the wedding and resides there until the birth of her first child is imminent, visiting her marital home only on special occasions. Associated with non-Han cultures, these social arrangements are or were also practised in other parts of the south. The texts and practices associated with 'women's script' are important as cultural traces of the historical Sinicization of the south, as an example of one of China's many regional or dialect popular literatures, and as an instance of rural women's expressive culture.

Further reading

McLaren, Anne (1998). 'Crossing Gender Boundaries in China: Nüshu Narratives'. *Intersections* (September).

Rainey, Lee (1996). 'The Secret Writing of Chinese Women: Religious Practices and Beliefs'. *Annual Review of Women in World Religions* 4: 130–63.

Silber, Cathy (1994). 'From Daughter to Daughter-in-Law in the Women's Script of Southern Hunan'. In C. Gilmartin, G. Hershatter, L. Rofel and T. White (eds), *Engendering China: Women, Culture, and the State*. Cambridge: Harvard University Press.

Smith, Norman (1996/1997). 'Women and Religion in Jiangyong County: Views from Nüshu'. *British Columbia Asian Review* 10: 121–78.

CATHY SILBER

women's studies

There are several trends in the contemporary cycle of women's studies in China. One is associated with the **All-China Women's Federation** (ACWF), a semi-governmental organization. In 1979, the first research office of the history of women's movement was set up as an affiliate of the ACWF, and in 1984, the first conference on women's issues in China was organized by ACWF. Later on, similar conferences would be held every two or three years. In 1994, the first women's studies journal, *Collection of Women's Studies*, was initiated by the Institute of Women's Studies, affiliated with the ACWF. The theoretical orientation within this stand of women's studies is Marxist, emphasizing the impact of economics on women's liberation and status. The research focus is on 'women's work', and tends to clarify and support government policy (Wang 2001). A second trend is derived from the university women scholars. Pioneering feminist scholars, such as Li Xiaojiang and a few others, are teaching in the university, and have been exposed to Western feminism. They started to review women's status and women's issues in the Chinese context from a feminist perspective, and have found the Marxist perspective to be inadequate in explaining and analysing women's inequality with men in China, where more and more women have gained economic independence

(Li 1989; Liu 1999). Gender analysis was introduced and applied in women's studies from the mid 1990s, and women scholars have since published books and papers from a gender perspective (Tong 2000; Liu 2000; Wang 2001). Nonetheless, there are barriers to this trend. While many women's research centres have been set up in universities, which serve as the base for these women scholars, women's studies is still marginalized in universities, and there is no department of women's studies nor any degree-granting programmes in women's studies in any university except for the National Women's University of China, which established the first department in China in 2001. Moreover, there is such a large gap between these few bastions of theoretical research and social reality that the research findings cannot yet serve as a basis for social change (Liu 1999). A third trend is also found in academia. Scholars who are interested in women's issues have conducted empirical research on women. However, 'women' is only a variable in this research. It is a gender-blind research (Li 1998; Wang 2000), and women have been depicted as passive subjects, women's rights have been violated in the research processes, and the findings are against women's interests (Wang 2000). This has been criticized as a form of 'patriarchal women's studies' (Wang 2000). To sum up, the development of women's studies in China still has a long way to go, as it needs more space and resources to develop in the mainstream society. Also, there is an urgent need for university women to connect with social change and women's movements.

Further reading

Barlow, Tani (2001). 'Spheres of Debt and Feminist Ghosts in Area Studies of Women in China'. *Traces: A Multilingual Journal of Cultural Theory and Translation* 1: 195–226.

Li, Xiaojiang (1989). *Women's Way Out*. Shenyang: Liaoning People's Press.

—— (1998). 'Women and Gender Issues in Development Research'. *Sociological Research* 3.

Li, Xiaojiang and Zhang, Xiaodan (1995). 'Creating a Space for Women: Women's Studies in China'. In Anna Gerstlacher and Margit Miosga (eds), *China for Women: Travel and Culture*. New York: Feminist Press.

Liu, M. (1999). 'Equality and Control: the Politics of Wife Abuse in Rural and Urban China'. PhD diss., University of Hong Kong.

—— (2000). 'Re-victimization: An Analysis of a Hotline Service for Battered Women in China'. *Asian Journal of Women's Studies* 7.2.

Roberts, Rosemary (1999). 'Women's Studies in Literature and Feminist Literary Criticism in Contemporary China'. In Antonia Finnane and Ann McLaren (eds), *Dress, Sex and Text in Chinese Culture*, Clayton: Monash Asia Institute, 225–40.

Tong, X. (2000). 'Production and Reproduction of Unequal Gender Relationships'. *Sociological Research* 1.

Wang, J. L. (2000). 'Gendering the Society'. Unpublished research reports.

—— (2001). 'Women's Studies within the Sociological Framework'. *Zhejiang xuekan* 2.

Wei, Guoying (ed.) (2000). *Nuxing xue gailun* [Overview of Women's Studies]. Beijing: Peking University Press.

LIU MENG

women's work

Social concept

While the CCP defined women's liberation as participation in public, productive labour, 'women's work' includes paid and unpaid activities associated with femaleness and women's roles in homes, factories, state and non-state entities. In post-Mao times many identify these roles, like that of the 'virtuous wife–good mother' (*xianqi liangmu*; see **good wife and mother**) as 'natural', in contrast to the stated 'unnatural' sameness of genders under Mao (e.g. 'iron girls'). This encourages urban women to find 'suitable' jobs, meaning they have flexible hours so that they may take care of the family, do not involve travel, and are inside offices. The inside/outside (*nei/wai*) dichotomy frames notions of work through symbolic and spatial ideas about female sexuality, morality and reputation. Work done inside is considered more appropriate for women, while work outside is deemed better suited for men (see **xiahai**). Families claim inside work is safe and secure for young women, evoking images of jobs inside air-conditioned buildings,

one's own city or town, and preferably in the state system.

Economic reforms have brought new occupational opportunities for women, however, like the feminized roles of secretary (**xiaomi**), public relations, domestic work, bank teller and multinational 'nimble fingers' production. Unmarried women from rural areas migrate to development zones (see **development zones (urban)**) to find production jobs, often being compensated less than men because their jobs are classified as less skilled and light (vs. heavy or dirty). Foreign companies also hire women for their language abilities, traditionally a female subject of study in college. If career women ignore their gendered home roles they may be called **nuqiangren, chiruanfan**.

See also: marriage; gender roles

Further reading

Gao, Xiaoxian (1994). 'China's Modernization and Changes in the Social Status of Rural Women'. In Christina Gilmartin, Gail Hershatter, Lisa Rofel and Tyrene White (eds), *Engendering China: Women, Culture, and the State*. Cambridge: Harvard University Press, 80–97.

Woo, Margaret Y. K. (1994). 'Chinese Women Workers: The Delicate Balance between Protection and Equality'. In Christina Gilmartin, Gail Hershatter, Lisa Rofel and Tyrene White (eds), *Engendering China: Women, Culture, and the State*. Cambridge: Harvard University Press, 279–95.

LISA M. HOFFMAN

Wong Fei

(a.k.a. Faye Wong)

b. 1969, Beijing

Pop singer

Wong Fei moved to Hong Kong in 1987 to become the city's – and later, Greater China's – biggest pop diva of the 1990s. Emerging in the era of the Four Heavenly Kings (see **pop music in Hong Kong**), her self-adopted name, 'Fei', stands for 'princess', staging her as the first woman to claim the royal title in Cantopop and thereby, like her male colleagues, inscribing herself into the long feudalist past of Chinese culture.

Wong Fei has generally been considered one of the most innovative stars with respect to both her music and her image. Her music moves from the more melodic love songs to complex arrangements in which her high-pitched voice accompanies the eerie score of a synthesizer. She has worked with the Cockteau Twins as well as with Beijing rock singer Dou Wei, her former husband and father of her daughter. Both her highly publicized status as a single mother and her liaison with the much younger pop star Nicolas Tse attest to her unusual ability to escape the moral judgement common in Hong Kong's popular press and society at large, probably due to her successful aura of being divine, not of this world, cool and beyond. Like Anita **Mui**, Wong Fei is a chameleon-like celebrity who moves between music and acting. She received international critical acclaim with her role (and music) in **Wong Kar-wai**'s *Chunking Express*. Wong Fei is emblematic for pop stardom in Greater China: both her music and her identity are, like the city, in constant flux. She is singer, actress, mother, celebrity, royalty, sex symbol and diva all at the same time. Her strength lies in her cosmopolitan, supernatural ambiguity.

See also: Zhang Yadong

JEROEN DE KLOET

Wong Kar-wai

(Wang Jiawei)

b. 1958, Shanghai

Film director

The Hong Kong film director Wong Kar-wai is best known for his innovative uses of cinema to capture experiences of urban life and their relations to Hong Kong's historical connections with mainland China and Britain. Wong moved with his family to Hong Kong when he was five years old. He studied Graphic Design at the Hong Kong Polytechnic and worked as a production assistant at Hong Kong Television Broadcast (HKTVB). In the 1980s, Wong first worked as a scriptwriter and then as a film director. Wong left HKTVB in 1982, and over the next five years scripted about ten feature films, ranging from comic romances to violent melodramas.

Wong has been hailed as one of Hong Kong's most innovative contemporary directors. *As Tears Go By* (1988), his directorial debut, was conceived in 1986, during work on Patrick Tam's *The Final Victory* (1987). Rapturously received by critics, the film firmly established Wong Kar-wai as a talent to watch. This promise was more than fulfilled by *Days of Being Wild* (1991), his second feature as director and screenwriter, which boasted a phenomenal cast and created a great deal of interest on the international film festival circuit, receiving numerous awards. Since 1994, he has completed seven more pictures: *Ashes of Time* (1994), *Chungking Express* (1994), *Fallen Angels* (1995), *Happy Together* (1997), *In the Mood of Love* (2000), *The Follow* (2001) and *2046* (2001).

Further reading

Abbas, Ackbar (1997). *Hong Kong: Culture and the Politics of Disappearance*. Minneapolis: University of Minnesota Press.

Chow, Rey (1999). 'Nostalgia of the New Wave: Structure in Wong Kar-wai's *Happy Together*'. *Camera Obscura* 42: 30–49.

Dissanayake, Wimal and Wong, Dorothy (2003). *Wong Kar-Wai's Ashes of Time*. Hong Kong: Hong Kong University Press.

Lalanne, Jean-Marc, Martinez, D., Abbas, A. and Ngai, J. (1997). *Wong Kar-Wai*. Paris: Editions Dis Voir.

Payne, Robert (2001). 'Ways of Seeing Wild: The Cinema of Wong Kar-Wai'. *Jump Cut* 44 (Fall) (online journal). Available at http://www.ejumpcut.org/ejumpcut.org/archive/jc44.2001/index.html

Tambling, Jeremy. *Wong Kar-Wai's Happy Together*. Hong Kong: Hong Kong University Press.

Tong, Janice (2003). 'Chungking Express: Time and its Dsplacements'. In Chris Berry (ed.), *Chinese Films in Focus: 25 New Takes*. London: BFI, 47–55.

Yue, Audrey (2003). 'In The Mood For Love: Intersections of Hong Kong Modernity'. In Chris Berry (ed.), *Chinese Films in Focus: 25 New Takes*. London: BFI, 128–36.

REN HAI

Woo, John

(né Ng Yu-sum/Wu Yusen)

b. 1946, Guangzhou

Director, producer, screenwriter

Worshipped by international movie fans since *The Killer* (*Diexue shuangxiong*, 1989), John Woo brilliantly succeeded in relocating to Hollywood – with the collaboration of Terence Chang (Chang Jia Tsun/ Zhang Jiazhen), his producer since the late 1980s. A complex *auteur* with an uncanny sense of style and a seductive romanticism, he often wrote and edited his own films while in the Hong Kong film industry.

Woo's family fled China for the slums of Hong Kong in 1951. In the 1960s, he wrote film criticism, founded a cine-club and directed experimental films. In 1969, he became a production assistant at the Cathay Film Company, then assistant to **martial arts films** director Zhang Che at the Shaw Brothers Studio, before directing his first feature, *The Young Dragons* (*Tiehan rouqing*, 1975). He worked in a variety of genres, from kung fu (*Countdown in Kung-Fu/ Shaolinmen*, 1976, which launched the careers of Jackie **Chan** and Sammo Hung Kam-bo) to opera (*Princess Chang-Ping/Dinü Hua*, 1976) to action films (*Heroes Shed No Tears/ Yingxiong wulei*, 1986) to comedies (*Plain Jane to the Rescue/Bacai Lin Azhen*, 1982) and even 'sexy' flicks.

In 1986, **Tsui Hark**'s Film Workshop produced *A Better Tomorrow* (*Yingxiong bense*) which changed his career and triggered a series of highly successful action films starring **Chow Yun-fat**, some produced by Woo's and Chang's independent company. His most ambitious film at the time was the hyper-violent *Bullet in the Head* (*Diexue jietou*, 1990), about young Chinese men tragically caught in the Vietnam War. After *Hard-Boiled* (*Lashou shentan*, 1992), Woo and Chang moved to Hollywood, where Woo directed *Hard Target* (1993), *Broken Arrow* (1996), *Face/Off* (1997), *Mission Impossible 2* (2000) and *Windtalkers* (2001).

Further reading

An, Jinsoo (2001). '*The Killer*: Cult Film and Transcultural (Mis)reading'. In Esther Yau (ed.), *At Full Speed: Hong Kong Cinema in a Borderless World*. Minneapolis: University of Minnesota Press, 95–114.

Ciecko, Anne (2001). 'Transnational Action: John Woo, Hong Kong, and Hollywood'. In Lu Sheldon (ed.), *Transnational Chinese Cinema: Identity, Nationhood, Gender*. Honolulu: University of Hawai'i Press.

Williams, Tony (2000). 'Space, Place, and Spectacle: The Crisis Cinema of John Woo'. In Poshek Fu and David Dresser (eds), *The Cinema of Hong Kong: History, Arts, Identity*. Cambridge: Cambridge University Press.

Steintrager, James (2003). 'Bullet in the Head: Trauma, Identity, and Violent Spectacle'. In Chris Berry (ed.), *Chinese Films in Focus: 25 New Takes*. London: BFI, 21–30.

BÉRÉNICE REYNAUD

World Heritage sites

China has twenty-eight sites inscribed on the World Heritage List, a global inventory of 730 properties (as of January 2003) that meet a set of criteria established by the 'Convention concerning the Protection of the World Cultural and Natural Heritage' adopted by the 17th General Conference of UNESCO in November 1972. China's National People's Congress ratified the Convention in 1985. Two years later, six sites were added to the List: the Great Wall, Mount Taishan, the Imperial Palace of the Ming and Qing dynasties in Beijing, the Mogao Caves, the Mausoleum of the first Qin emperor, and the site of Peking Man at Zhoukoudian. (For a complete inventory, see www.unesco.org/heritage.htm)

Three significant effects have resulted from China's decision to ratify the Convention. First, China has been progressively integrating its heritage protection practices with those of other countries (172 as of 2003) that have also ratified the Convention. China's acceptance of international standards can be seen in documents such as 'Principles for the Conservation of Heritage Sites in

China' (*Zhongguo wenwu guji baohu zhunze*), confirmed by the State Administration of Cultural Heritage of China in October 2000. Second, because of the global prestige stemming from World Heritage listing, provincial authorities have been urged by those at the national level to meet the criteria for listing of other sites that fall within their jurisdictions. Third, because both domestic and foreign tourists have visited World Heritage sites in mounting numbers, administrators of these sites have had to find ways to mitigate the many harmful effects of intensifying tourism. China's World Heritage sites – artifacts of recent heritage conservation reforms as well as relics of past cultural achievements – pose sharp challenges for the country's heritage professionals. Heightened awareness and clearer standards for protection have been matched by the perils of too many visitors and the effects of rampant tourism.

Further reading

Agnew, Neville and Demas, Martha (eds) (2002). *Principles for the Conservation of Heritage Sites in China*. Los Angeles: Getty Conservation Institute. Available at http://www.getty.edu/conservation/
Logan, William S. (ed.) (2002). *The Disappearing 'Asian' City: Protecting Asia's Urban Heritage in a Globalizing World*. Hong Kong: Oxford University Press.

JEFFREY W. CODY

World Trade Organization (WTO) debate

Should China join the WTO? Attitudes towards China's accession to the WTO reflected the diverse interests of Chinese in an era of globalization. Central leaders saw the WTO primarily as a way to formalize multilateral solutions to trade disputes with major export markets (especially eliminating the contentious annual review of bilateral agreements with the United States), and indirectly as a means to use foreign competition to dismantle the planned economy. Local government leaders and heads of central state-owned enterprises viewed it as

a way to push Chinese corporations in competitive sectors (electronics, appliances, telecommunications, chemicals and energy, but not media, which are excluded from WTO agreements) to 'go abroad' and compete with multi-national corporations in emerging markets. Many scholars of **liberalism** saw the WTO as part of an inevitable, albeit painful, process of integration with the global economy, although **New Left** intellectuals argued that the uniquely strict conditions negotiated with WTO members constituted a new form of economic imperialism. Although knowing little about the conditions of accession, the average Chinese will directly feel the pressure from increasing foreign competition at the workplace.

Further reading

Lardy, N. (2002) *Integrating China into the Global Economy*. Washington, DC: Brookings Institution Press.
Pearson, M. (2001). 'The Case of China's Accession to GATT/WTO'. In D. Lampton (ed.), *The Making of Chinese Foreign and Security Policy in the Reform Era*. Palo Alto: Stanford University Press.

STEVEN W. LEWIS

writing reform movements

Movements in the twentieth century aiming to modernize China and to increase literacy have frequently focused their attention on China's writing system. There have been three principal means by which writing reform has been approached: closer approximation of writing to the spoken language (in the May Fourth Movement of 1919), replacement of characters by roman letters (*pinyin*), and simplification of the existing script. Replacement has died away as a plausible mechanism, and simplification is less politically significant in the early twenty-first century than it was in the mid twentieth. Two lists of simplified characters were instituted in the PRC, one in 1955 and one in 1977. These often involved using popular handwritten abbreviations for characters, replacing complex components with simpler forms, or mandating a simplification. These simpler forms have become standard in the PRC and Singapore. Hong Kong and Taiwan do not use them. (Some forms are recognizable in Japan, though not most.) Even in the PRC in the 1990s some traditional characters have been brought back in, used on signs, on name cards and in books published in classical Chinese. Computers can easily use characters, though input is often in roman script. Support for eradication of characters has slipped quietly away.

See also: simplified characters

Further reading

DeFrancis, John (1950). *Nationalism and Language Reform in China*. Princeton: Princeton University Press.

—— (1984). *The Chinese Language: Fact and Fantasy*. Honolulu: University of Hawai'i Press.

Seybolt, Peter J. and Chiang, Gregory Kuei-ke (eds) (1979). *Language Reform in China: Documents and Commentary*. White Plains, New York: M. E. Sharpe.

SUSAN D. BLUM

One of the most admired aspects of some ethnic minorities is the existence of an indigenous writing system. Those most widely known for such systems are the Uighurs, Manchus, Naxi, Yi and Tai. Roman scripts also have been designed for ethnic minorities without their own script. Scripts designed by missionaries have been replaced by more 'scientific' Roman scripts. In cases where an indigenous script, such as Old Thai, has been replaced by a new Roman script, resistance has often forced the restoration of the old one.

See also: ethnicity, concepts of; writing reform movements

Further reading

DeFrancis, John (1984). *The Chinese Language: Fact and Fantasy*. Honolulu: University of Hawai'i Press.

—— (1989). *Visible Speech: The Diverse Oneness of Writing Systems*. Honolulu: University of Hawai'i Press.

SUSAN D. BLUM

writing systems

Chinese characters (sinographs, logographs), have a known history of approximately 3,200 years, with the earliest forms visible on the so-called oracle bones used by Shang diviners to query the future. At origin somewhat pictographic, this aspect of the script is only vestigial. As they now exist, characters typically have both a phonetic component and a signific component, together giving clues to pronunciation and category of meaning. Though over 100,000 characters have been used at some time in China's long literary past, for most purposes only 6,000 to 8,000 characters are used in high-level contemporary writing (such as newspapers and novels), and a vocabulary of approximately 4,000 characters is considered adequate for basic literacy. The lengthy process required to learn characters has been blamed for China's historically low literacy rates, leading to writing reform movements. These have largely been discarded and the writing system remains a beloved symbol of civilization, education and Chineseness.

Wu Guanzhong

b. 1919, Yixing, Jiangsu

Oil and traditional Chinese painter

An artist of a much earlier generation than most discussed in this book, Wu broke the **Cultural Revolution**-imposed taboo on abstract painting with his May 1979 article 'The Formal Beauty of Painting' (*Huihuade xingshi mei*), which argued that painting should exist independently of political content and be appreciated on the basis of its formal character. The ensuing debate on form and abstraction was crucial in developing a more tolerant atmosphere in the transitional period immediately following the end of the Cultural Revolution. Wu was active in the Beijing Oil Painting Research Association (Beijing youhua yanjiuhui), a popular organization with diverse membership, which began to hold a series of daring exhibitions starting from October 1979. Despite championing abstraction, Wu always retained a figurative element in his painting, stating that the line connecting artist and reality is like a kite's string that must never be broken.

Wu's foray in the early 1980s was backed by a solid and respectable career. He studied at the China Academy of Art in Hangzhou between 1937 and 1942, and in France from 1946 to 1950. After returning to China in 1950 he taught at the Central Academy of Fine Arts, Qinghua University, Beijing Academy of Arts, and at the Central Institute of Arts and Crafts. During the Cultural Revolution, like most artists of his background, he was sent to the countryside and forbidden to paint. Though his distinctive style in oil painting was already mature, it was in the 1980s that he found a propitious atmosphere for his bold experiments in large semi-abstract *Zhongguohua* (traditional Chinese) paintings. His *Zhongguohua* is untraditional for its absence of focus on brushwork and brushstrokes, substituted instead by an innovative use of long, rhythmic lines and energizing dots.

Further reading

Farrer, Anne (1992). *Wu Guanzhong: A Twentieth Century Chinese Painter*. London: British Museum Press.
Lim, Lucy (ed.) (1989). *Wu Guanzhong. A Contemporary Chinese Artist*. San Francisco: Chinese Culture Foundation.
Wu, Guanzhong (1979). 'Huihuade xingshi mei' [The Formal Beauty of Painting]. *Meishu* (May).

EDUARDO WELSH

Wu He

b. 1951, Tainan, Taiwan

Writer

Wu He [Dancing Crane] began creative writing in 1974 with the publication of his award-winning short story 'Peony Autumn' (*Mudan qiu*). A handful of assorted works of short fiction followed, continuing until 1979 when he began a thirteen-year period of reclusion. Throughout the 1980s, Wu He left publishing and mainstream society, spending several years of secluded life in Danshui, delving deep into the tribal societies of Taiwan's aboriginal

peoples (see **music in Taiwan**). Wu He returned to creative writing in the early 1990s with a string of brilliant works of fiction, including the novels *Meditative Thoughts on A Bang and Kalusi (Sisuo Abang Kalusi*) and *Remains of Life (Yusheng*), both of which were based on his experience living among aboriginal tribes. The latter novel gained critical attention not only for its radical structure, which consisted of a single paragraph written in stream-of-consciousness style, but also for its literary excavation of the Musha Incident, a violent aboriginal uprising against the Japanese that occurred in 1930 and was swiftly and brutally suppressed by the colonial government. *Remains of Life* went on to win more than seven major literary awards in Taiwan after its publication in 1999.

Wu He followed his pair of aboriginal novels with a contemporary fable of lust and sexual deviance, *Ghost and Goblin (Gui'er yü ayao*). From the politics of brutality to the politics of the body, and from the politics of nation to the politics of the novel, Wu He's powerful visions and literary innovations have led critic David Der-wei Wang to declare that, 'when the history of Taiwanese literature of the twenty-first century is written, the first page will inevitably start with Wu He'.

MICHAEL BERRY

Wu Meichun

b. 1969, Xiamen, Fujian

Art critic, curator

Graduating from the Department of Oil Painting at the China National Academy of Fine Arts in Hangzhou in 1994, Wu Meichun found her mission as a curator with an interest in new media in 1996. That year she organized at the gallery of her alma mater the first major Chinese video art exhibition, 'Image and Phenomena', which helped to create a heightened attention for video works in China. Most of the fifteen artists participating in the show were novices in this medium but have since become well-known videomakers. In the same period she co-wrote a thoughtful essay with artist **Qiu Zhijie**, providing the theoretical terrain and a broad international context for this emerging art form.

Curating and writing have since been her major activities, resulting in the organization of as many as four exhibitions a year, including 'Demonstration of Chinese Video Art 97' at the Gallery of the Central Academy of Fine Arts in Beijing; the Chinese participation at the Eleventh Video Festival 'Transmediale 98' in Berlin; and 'Beijing in London' at the ICA London in 1999. Wu also masterminded a number of events in alternative spaces, including the one-day controversial exhibition 'Post-Sense Sensibility: Alien Bodies and Delusion' in a Beijing basement in 1999 that displayed dead animals and human corpses as art objects. In autumn 2001, just after being appointed Curator and Professor of Art Theory at the newborn New Media Art Research Centre at the China National Academy of Fine Arts, she organized a new media festival entitled 'Non-Linear Narrative' at the Academy's gallery.

Further reading

Wu, Meichun (1999). 'Yixing yü wangxiang' [Alien Bodies and Delusion]. In *Post-Sense Sensibility. Alien Bodies and Delusion* (exhibition catalogue). Beijing, 1–4.

—— (2001). 'Electronic Conscience – Cultural Awareness in Chinese Video Art'. In Johnson Chang Tsong-zung (ed.) (1999), *Fast Forward New Chinese Video Art*. Hong Kong: Hanart T Z Gallery.

Wu, Meichun and Qiu, Zhijie (1996). 'Luxiang Shixue: Wenhua, Xinli, Jishu, Zhuangzhi' [The Poetics of Video Art: Its Cultural, Psychological, Technical Context and Installation Context] *Art Gallery Magazine* 58/59: 27–31.

TANG DI

Wu Nien-chen

(Nianzhen)

b. 1952, Taiwan

Writer, screenwriter, film director, actor

Working his way out of a working-class life through night school, Wu had just established himself as a short story writer with such collections as *Take Hold of a Springtime* (*Zhuazhu yige chuntian*, 1977) when he

was employed to write a script for the film *Oath* (*Xianghuo*, 1979). In the Taiwan 'New Cinema' movement that followed shortly, Wu became much in demand, beginning with the pioneering productions *Sandwich Man* (*Erzi de da wanou*, 1983), directed by Hou Xiaoxian and others, and *That Day on the Beach* (*Haitan de nayi tian*, 1983), directed by Edward **Yang**. Among his most recognized achievements are the scripts for Hou Xiaoxian's *City of Sadness* (*Beiqing chengshi*, 1989) and for **Zhu Tianwen** and Xu Anhua's *Song of Exile* (*Ke tu qiu hen*, 1990). Wu was especially active in bringing the local Southern Min dialect of Taiwan into print, but he has been equally valued for the range of his styles. He has worked for such directors as Hu Jinquan on *All the King's Men* (*Tianxia diyi*, 1982), for Chen Kunhou on *Osmanthus Alley* (*Guihuaxiang*, 1987), and for Hou Xiaoxian on *The Puppetmaster* (*Ximeng rensheng*, 1993). He played the leading role in Edward Yang's critically acclaimed *Yiyi* (2000).

Further reading

Davis, Darrell (2001). 'Borrowing Postcolonial: Wu Nien-chen's *Dou-san* and the Memory Mine'. *Post Script* 20.2/3 (Winter/Spring): 94–114.

—— (2003). 'A New Taiwanese Person? A Conversation with Wu Nien-chen'. *positions: east asia cultures critique* 11.3 (Winter): 717–34.

Lu, Tonglin (2002). 'A Postcolonial Reflection: Buddha Bless America'. In *idem, Confronting Modernity in the Cinemas of Taiwan and Mainland China*. Cambridge: Cambridge University Press, 191–205.

EDWARD GUNN

Wu Tianming

b. 1939

Film director, producer, actor

One of the most important figures in Chinese film industry in the 1980s, Wu Tianming entered the **Xi'an Film Studio** as an actor in 1960. Wu studied in the Department of Film Directing at the **Beijing Film Academy** from 1974 to 1976. He was elected as the Director of the Xi'an Film Studio in 1983. Wu recruited new graduates from the Beijing Film Academy and elsewhere and, under his tutelage, the Xi'an Film Studio became the most successful and respected film studio in China. Xi'an Studio produced blockbuster commercial films which subsidized the avant-garde (experimental) filmmaking of the 'Fifth Generation'. The film-makers at the Xi'an Studio also formulated a new film genre – the 'Chinese Western' – which succeeded both commercially and aesthetically.

Wu Tianming is himself an accomplished actor and filmmaker. His early films, *Reverberations of Life* (*Shenghuo de chanyin*, 1979) and *River Without Buoys* (*Meiyou hangbiao de heliu*, 1983), focused on the devastation of the **Cultural Revolution**. His most successful films of the mid 1980s, like *Life* (*Rensheng*, 1984) and *Old Well* (*Laojing*, 1987), established his international reputation. The latter has become a contemporary film classic in Chinese film history. Wu left China after the 1989 Tiananmen Event and lived in the United States for seven years, working as a visiting scholar and artist at New York University, the University of California at Davis, and the University of Southern California. In 1996, he returned to China and directed the inter-nationally acclaimed *King of Masks* (*Bianlian*). He now lives and works in Beijing.

Further reading

Luo, Xueying (1989). 'Wu Tianming's Rise to Fame'. *Chinese Literature* 3: 188–95.

Wang, Yuejin (1988). 'The Old Well: A Womb or Tomb? The Double Perspective in Wu Tianming's *Old Well*'. *Framework* 35: 73–82.

WANG CHANG

Wu Wenguang

b. 1956, Yunnan

Independent videomaker, writer

The most influential figure of the **New Documentary Movement**, Wu Wenguang sponta-neously recreated the aesthetics of cinema vérité through his long takes, intimate mode of filming, and extended duration of his pieces. As a writer and editor, he is a tireless advocate of documentary and digital media. In 1991, he founded the Wu Wengguang Documentary Studio (Wu Wenguang jilupian gongzuoshi).

After high school, Wu spent the last years of the **Cultural Revolution** (1974–8) as a farmer. From 1978 to 1982, he studied literature at Yunnan University, and later became a television journalist (1985–9). His first independent videos were a series on *Chinese People* (*Zhongguoren*, 1989), but his aesthetic breakthrough came with the epoch-making *Bumming in Beijing – The Last Dreamers* (*Liulang Beijing – Zuihou de mengxiangzhe*, 1990) and its follow-up, *At Home in the World* (*Shihai weijia*, 1995). Starting with the portrait of five young marginalized artists, Wu powerfully depicts the existential angst, creativity and cultural displacement that characterized his generation after June 1989. His video *1966, My Time in the Red Guards* (*1966, Wo de hongweibing shidai*, 1993) recalls the memories of former teenage Red Guards swept up by history. For the ambitious *Jiang Hu: On the Road* (*Jiang Hu*, 1999), Wu lived for months with the members of an impoverished 'Song and Dance Company' as they lived and performed throughout China.

In 1994, Wu co-founded the Living Dance Studio (Wudao shenghuo) with his partner, the dancer/choreographer **Wen Hui**, with whom he often collaborates – as a playwright, actor and video artist. He conceived the performance *Dance with Farm Workers* (*Hemingong tiaowu*), which she directed in 2001, and he reworked as a video in 2002. He published a desk-top magazine, *Documentary Scene* (*Jilu shouce*, 1996–7), then founded/edited the independent monthly art magazine *New Wave* (*Xinchao*, 2001). He has also written three books inspired by his videos, and edited two collections of critical texts, *Document* (*Xianchang*, 2000 and 2001). He was also the executive producer of Zhu Wen's **Seafood** (*Haixian*, 2001).

See also: Cobra

Further reading

Wu, Wenguang (2001). *Jiang Hu baogao* [Report on Jiang Hu]. Beijing: China Youth Publishing House.
—— (ed.) (2001/2002). *Document: Xianchang*. [Document: The Scene], vols. 1 and 2. Tianjin: Tianjin Institute of Social Sciences.

—— (2002). 'Just on the Road: A Description of the Individual Way of Recording Images in the 1990s'. In Wu Hung (ed.), *The First Guangzhou Triennial: Representation, A Decade of Experimental Chinese Art (1990–2000)*. Guangzhou: Guangzhou Museum of Art/Chicago: Art Media Resources: 132–8.

BÉRÉNICE REYNAUD

Wu Zhao

b. 18 December 1935, Suzhou, Jiangsu

Qin (seven-stringed zither) master, music historian

Wu Zhao studied **qin** under Zha Fuxi and Wu Jinglue. After graduating from Nankai University in Tianjin with a degree in history in 1959, he entered the National Music Institute of the Central Conservatory of Music in Beijing and studied Chinese music history under Yang Yinliu. In 1985 he became the associate research fellow at the Research Institute of Music, China Academy of Arts, and in 1991, a fellow. From 1981 until 1989 he was also the chair of the Chinese music history division of the same institute and in 1993 began to direct doctoral dissertations. As a qin expert, he was secretary and later director of the Beijing Guqin Research Society. Wu Zhao has been invited to lecture at the University of the Philippines (1988), the University of Michigan (1990) and the National Institute of the Arts, Taiwan (1994). In addition, he has been an external examiner of the Hong Kong Performing Arts Academy, the Chinese University of Hong Kong, and the Central Conservatory of Music in Beijing. He has presented papers and performed qin in international conferences in France, Germany, Holland, the United States, Korea and Japan.

In addition to numerous research articles in scholarly journals, he has also published the following: *Retracing the Lost Footprints of Music* (iconographical history of Chinese music), *A Short History of Chinese Music* (co-author Liu Dongseng), *Gems of Chinese Guqin* (ed.), *An Anthology of Qin Music* (ed.), *Guqin Teaching Fundamentals* (5-VCD), *Remembering an Old Friend* (qin performance, CD), *Autumn Moon Over the Han Palace* (qin performance, CD), to mention only a few.

HAN KUO-HUANG

Wu Ziniu

b. 1952, Sichuan

Film director

Wu Ziniu is a 'Fifth-Generation' film director best known for his war epics. A graduate of the Sichuan Leshan Art Institute, Wu worked in both a creative and on-stage capacity with the Leshan Song and Dance Troupe until 1978, when he was admitted into the historic class of 1982 at the **Beijing Film Academy**. Assigned to the Xiaoxiang Film Studio after graduation, Wu's first film, *Reserve Team Member* (*Houbu yanyuan*, 1983), was an interesting account of children's lives in contemporary China. His second feature, *Secret Decree* (*Diexue heigu*, 1984), was set during the War of Resistance; it was commercially successful and established Wu's trajectory as a director of war films. The film actually predates Zhang Junzhao's *One and Eight* (*Yige he bage*), which has led some film historians to credit *Secret Decree* as the first 'Fifth-Generation' film.

Wu Ziniu went on to direct more than half a dozen war films, including *The Last Day of Winter* (*Zuihou de dongri*), *Evening Bell* (*Wanzhong*), *Joyous Heroes* (*Hunaleyingxiong*), *Between the Living and the Dead* (*Yinyang jie*) and the Vietnam War epic personally banned by Deng Xiaoping, *The Dove Tree* (*Gezi shu*). Throughout his career Wu has had a tense relationship with the Chinese censors, who withdrew *The Big Mill* (*Da mofang*, 1990) from competition at the Berlin Film Festival. In 1993 Wu made *Sparkling Fox* (*Huohu*), an avant-garde film about the pursuit by two hunters of a mythical fox. The culmination of Wu's decade-long exploration of war was the epic *Nanjing 1937* (1994), a Taiwan co-production about a Chinese doctor and his Japanese wife who struggle to keep their family together during the 'Rape of Nanjing'. After a five-year hiatus, Wu Ziniu returned to directing with *National Anthem* (*Guoge*, 1999), a biographical film about the life of the legendary playwright Tian Han, who also penned the lyrics for China's national anthem. The film's didactic political message marks a dramatic departure from Wu's earlier iconoclastic trajectory and was even described as party propaganda by several critics.

Further reading

Zhang, Yingjin (2003). 'Evening Bell: Wu Ziniu's Vision of History, War and Humanity'. In Chris Berry (ed.), *Chinese Films in Focus: 25 New Takes*. London: BFI, 81–8.

MICHAEL BERRY

Wuju

(dance drama)

'Dance drama' is a comparatively new Chinese theatrical form, which integrates Chinese dance with Western ballet techniques and Chinese melodies and styles with Western harmony. Western instruments usually predominate in a fairly large orchestra. The décor is elaborate, and pieces are structured so as to reach a climax and dénouement and to last a full evening. These features apply also to ballets that have adopted Chinese melodies and characteristics. Soviet artists introduced ballet into China in the late 1950s, including such classical works as *Swan Lake* and *Giselle*. The PRC set up a dancing school in 1954 and a ballet company in 1959. Meanwhile, the Central Ethnic Song-and-Dance Troupe (Zhongyang minzu gewutuan), which also collected, preserved, adapted and performed ethnic dances, was established in September 1952.

The piece that launched the dance drama as a new large-scale performing art was the ballet-influenced *The Precious Lotus Lamp* (*Baolian deng*, 1957), a fantasy based on an old Chinese legend in which the hero, born of a goddess and a mortal, rescues his mother, who has been imprisoned for marrying the mortal. Another early dance drama was *The Small Sword Society* (*Xiaodao hui*), about an incident in Shanghai during the Taiping uprising (1850–64). Though Mao's wife, Jiang Qing (1913–91), had traditional themes banned during

the **Cultural Revolution**, two of her 'model plays' were ballets: *The White-Haired Girl* (*Baimao nü*) and *The Red Detachment of Women* (*Hongse niangzijun*). The dancing style and movements were clearly ballet, but also had strong Chinese elements: both stories were set in China, the CCP propaganda content was very strong, and the melodies were Chinese. After 1976, older pieces that pre-dated the Cultural Revolution were restaged and many new items created. Traditional themes proved most popular: *Tales of the Silk Road* (*Silu huayu*) is set in the Tang dynasty (618–907) and its movements copy images found in the famous Dunhuang Caves, in the west of Gansu province, while the classic novel *A Dream of the Red Chamber* (*Honglou meng*) became a fertile source of material for dance drama.

Since most of China's minorities have distinguished dance traditions (see **dance (ethnic)**), choreographers were happy to use stories based on their experiences to create new dance dramas. A good example was *Princess Wencheng* (*Wencheng gongzhu*), about the marriage of a Tang-dynasty princess to a seventh-century Tibetan king. The first dance drama actually to be written, choreographed and performed by an ethnic minority troupe was *Zhao Shudeng and Nanmu Nuonuo*c – a Tai piece from the late 1970s concerning the love between a mythical prince and a peacock princess. Some dance dramas have contemporary themes, including those featuring the minorities. In addition, there are dramas in which dance and song are of approximately equal importance, termed *gewuju* (song and dance dramas). Though ballet is not a particularly popular genre, it is still professionally performed and has produced some innovative items. In 2001, the National Ballet of China premiered **Zhang Yimou**'s adaptation of his own film *Raise the Red Lantern* (1991). The piece is called a ballet. It includes **Jingju** (Peking opera) music with a score composed by **Chen Qigang**, and has numerous other stylistic elements that are recognizably Chinese, as well as a Chinese story set in China and a Chinese choreographer, Wang Xinpeng.

See also: dance troupes; Geju

COLIN MACKERRAS

Xi Chuan

(né Liu Jun)

b. 1963, Xuzhou, Jiangsu

Poet, essayist, playwright, professor

Xi Chuan studied in the English Department of **Peking University** from 1981 to 1985 and became a professor at the **Central Academy of Fine Arts** in Beijing in the 1990s. He began poetry writing in 1981 and very quickly established himself as one of the most important new poets in the 1980s. His early poems, such as 'Gazing into the Starry Sky at Ha'ergai' (*Zai Ha'ergai yangwang xingkong*, 1986), are short, lyrical and meditative, even sublime. They are concerned mainly with an almost cosmic correspondence between nature, the universe, history, tradition and the individual. In the spring of 1989, his poet-friend **Haizi** committed suicide, while his other poet-friend, Luo Yihe, died later that year. These events had a profound impact upon Xi Chuan, whose own poetry took a radically different turn in the 1990s. In works such as 'Salute' (*Zhijing*, 1992) and 'Discourse of an Eagle' (*Ying de huayü*, 1999), he experiments with various hybrid forms of prose and poetry to convey what he now calls a 'pseudo-philosophy' (*wei zhexue*), inquiring into the absurdities and previously overlooked dark shadows of history, human consciousness and reason. Xi Chuan is the winner of many literary prizes. He has published four books of poetry and two books of essays and has been widely translated.

Further reading

Van Crevel, Maghiel (1999). 'Xi Chuan's "Salute": Avante-Garde Poetry in a Changing China'. *Modern Chinese Literature and Culture* 11.2 (Fall): 107–49.

Xi, Chuan (2003). 'What the Eagle Says'. Trans. Maghiel van Crevel. *Seneca Review* 33.2: 28–41.

HUANG YIBING

Xi Shu

(né Xi Xiaoping)

b. 1963, Nanchang, Jiangxi

Bookseller

Xi Shu is a book retailer and tycoon and the most prominent master of ink-pen calligraphy. His name 'Xi Shu' is a homophone for 'learning calligraphy'. A mathematics graduate from Fuzhou Normal School in Jiangxi, Xi gave up his two-year teaching career for ink-pen calligraphy. In October 1985, he initiated the first national ink-pen calligraphy exhibition in Beijing which brought him instant fame. Two years later, Xi returned to Nanchang, his home town, to become the editor for a well-known humanities journal published by the Jiangxi College of Social Sciences.

In 1992, Xi started the Ink-Pen Handwriting Institute in Jiangxi, promoting his unique technique, dubbed the 'Three-S System', which won the Jiangxi Social Science Research Award. His slogan

'Learning how to write? Look nowhere but to Xi' triggered a nation-wide craze for learning ink-pen calligraphy. In only five years, his followers numbered over 1 million. Xi became the first person to commercialize ink-pen calligraphy in China.

In 1995, Xi founded Beijing Xi Shu Booksellers, which soon grew into China's first private chain of bookstores, and second only to the Xinhua Bookstore. His success won him a nomination as one of the 'Ten Most Outstanding Youth of China' in 1996. In July 1997, Xi Shu established China's first national book club, the 'Good Book Club', which claims over 140,000 members. In March 2000, Xi set up the Jingqi Online Bookstore, the largest in China, and the first to solve the issue of online payment and distribution. Along with the book club and network of over 300 bookstores, the online outlet caught the attention of the well-established Hong Kong distributor, the Tianjuan Holding Company Ltd. In November 2001, Xi and the company formed a joint-venture, and he became its CEO. By the end of May 2002, Xi Shu Booksellers had opened 689 bookstores in over 300 cities, through either direct or licensed retailing arrangements.

HU MINGRONG

Xi Xi

(neé Zhang Yan)

b. 1938, Shanghai

Writer

Xi Xi received her primary education in Shanghai, but came to Hong Kong from Guangdong in 1950, where she graduated from college and lives today. She worked as a primary school teacher until 1979, but then decided to involve herself full time with writing. Since her first publication in 1965, she has written short stories and novels, but is also a poet, scriptwriter and film and art critic. She reads a lot of foreign literature and is also interested in the visual arts. She has published many books, including *My City* (*Wocheng*, 1979), *Marvels of a Floating City* (*Fucheng zhiyi*, 1986) and the

collection of short stories *A Girl Like Me* (*Xiangwo zheyang de yige nüzi*, 1982). Her writing, at once humorous and acute, is situated at the intersection of city life and individual feeling. Protagonists often try to escape from reality and the coercive urban environment, engaging objects more than human beings, playing with toys as adults, alternating between moods of fresh, childlike joy and of disillusion and derision, all within routine perceptions of daily life.

Further reading

Ng, Daisy S. Y. (2003). 'Xi Xi and Tales of Hong Kong'. In Joshua Mostow (ed.) and Kirk Denton (ed. China section), *Columbia Companion to Modern East Asian Literatures*. New York: Columbia University Press, 578–83.

Xi, Xi (1993). *My City: A Hong Kong Story*. Trans. Eva Hung. Hong Kong: Renditions.

—— (1997). *Marvels of a Floating City and Other Stories: An Authorized Collection*. Trans. Eva Hung. Hong Kong: Renditions.

—— (1997). *Une fille comme moi*. Trans. Véronique Woillez. Paris: Éditions de l'Aube.

ANNIE CURIEN

Xia Gang

b. 1953, Beijing

Film director

Xia Gang is a unique member of the 'Fifth Generation' of directors (see **Fifth Generation (film directors)**). His films are representative of the new kind of urban film reflecting modern Chinese life, and he laid the foundation for the 'Sixth Generation' (see **Sixth Generation (film directors)**). Xia Gang graduated from **Beijing Film Academy** in 1982 and began working at Beijing Film Studio. He directed his first film, *When We Are Still Young*, at graduation. The 1990s became the most productive period of his film career.

Xia Gang's films generally fall between art films and commercial films. While his Fifth Generation classmates, such as **Zhang Yimou**, made art films set in traditional rural China and were all grappling with issues such as *xungen* (see **Root-seeking school**), Xia Gang focused his films on modern urban daily life. Also, unlike many of his Fifth Generation contemporaries, Xia Gang's films are primarily for domestic consumption and garner good box office receipts. Xia Gang insists on making films about the 'feelings of urban people'. He is interested in creating a new type of character in response to the changing demands of modern life, as capitalism takes hold in China. His films are filled with humour, and skilfully maintain a light atmosphere while conveying the hardships of city life. Some of his best-known films are: *Encounter Passion* (*Zaoyu jiqing*, 1990), *After Separation* (*Da shaba*, 1992), *No One Applauds* (*Wuren hecai*, 1993) and *Toast the Past* (*Yu wangshi ganbei*, 1995). At the Thirteenth Golden Rooster Awards Xia Gang was named Best Director for *After Separation*.

MICHAEL WEIDONG WAN

xiafang, xiaxiang

(sent-down)

Social/political concept

Xiafang, or 'sent-down', refers to the process or state in which a person is or has been transferred from a high-ranking unit to a low-ranking unit, or from a large city to a smaller city, or from the city to the countryside. When a cadre is 'sent down' in one of the above manners, he or she is referred to as a *xiafang ganbu*, a 'sent-down cadre'.

In the context of Chinese youth, however, *xiafang* has a special significance. It began in 1955 when elementary- or middle-school urban graduates were sent to work in villages. On 22 December 1968, following the zenith of the **Cultural Revolution**, Mao launched the Rustication Movement, whereby 'urban educated youth' (*zhishi qingnian*) were to be sent to the countryside to receive re-education from the poor and lower-middle peasants. It has been estimated that 17 million city youth were sent to the countryside in this manner. These 'sent-down youths' (*zhiqing*) were typically sent to two different kinds of locations: to remote villages or to border regions such as Heilongjiang, Hainan Island, southern Yunnan, Xinjiang and Inner Mongolia. In

the former, the sent-down youths lived and worked with the peasants; in the latter, they lived a military-style life in Construction and Production Corps. It was not until 1979 that the educated youth were formally allowed to return to their city homes. The Rustication Movement was a disaster, both for that generation and for the nation as a whole, though many writers, filmmakers and musicians have since drawn on their experiences in their work.

See also: Cultural Revolution (education); laosanjie; Native Soil Painting; Scar literature; Scar art

Further reading

Ballew, Ted (2001). 'Xiaxiang for the 1990s: The Shanghai TV Rural Channel and Post-Mao Urbanity and Global Swirl'. In Nancy Chen, Constance D. Clark, Suzanne Z. Gottschang and Lynn Feffery (eds), *China Urban: Ethnographies of Contemporary Culture*. Durham: Duke University Press.

Louie, Kam (1989). 'Educated Youth Literature: Self-Discovery in the Chinese Villages'. In *idem*, *Between Fact and Fiction: Essays on Post-Mao Chinese Literature and Society*. Sydney: Wild Peony, 1–13.

LEUNG LAIFONG

xiagang

(laid off)

Social concept

This neologism literally translates as 'off the post', which means 'laid off'. It is a euphemism for urban unemployment (*shiye*). The concept used to be that unemployment was a feature of capitalism and was non-existent under socialism. Therefore, a neologism *daiye* (waiting for a job) was coined in the late 1970s. Since 1994, the concept has been changed, but there is still a difference between being 'laid off' and unemployment. 'Laid-off' workers still retain their relationship with their state-owned enterprises (SOEs) and receive a minimum subsidy for two years. The government, however, does not count them in the unemployment statistics for two years, not to mention the hundreds of millions of unemployed rural Chinese. According to Cai Rifang's *Green Paper on Population and Labour* (*Laodong yü renkou lupishu*, 2002), published by the Academy of Social Sciences Archive Press, the actual unemployment rate in urban areas already had reached the 7 per cent warning line (at which social unrest is considered probable), much higher than the 4.5 per cent that the government hoped to have achieved by 2002. In 2001, in fact, the government only admitted to an unemployment rate of 3.6 per cent. With the dissolution of most SOEs, tens of millions of more workers, especially women, have been and are being victimized. WTO membership may force farmers to join the already large 'floating population', who now compete with the urban poor for limited jobs. Some 'laid-off' workers have or will **xiahai** (go entrepreneurial), but most of them are unskilled, and unreported protests occur often. The state is now trying to address the status of 'laid-off' workers and establish sound social security measures.

Further reading

Chan, Anita (2001). *China's Workers Under Assault: The Exploitation of Labor in a Globalizing Economy.* New York: M. E. Sharpe.

HELEN XIAOYAN WU

xiahai

(jumping into the sea [of commerce])

Social concept

From 1985, when the late Vice-Premier Deng Xiaoping was alleged to have informed the masses that 'to get rich is glorious', the post-Mao, state capitalist phase of the revolution was identified as 'socialism with Chinese characteristics'. The annual Gross Domestic Product grew markedly throughout the 1980s and the national economy boasted annual increments of up to 12 per cent. At roughly the same time, the *Wall Street Journal* produced an entire supplement devoted to China's 'economic miracle' and the bright prospects for foreign investment. By the late 1980s, even as the Chinese

government and private entrepreneurs inked a historic number of joint-venture agreements with Western enterprises, domestic economic triumphalism was undermined by political dissent that culminated in the protests at **Tiananmen Square** in May and June 1989. Indeed, following the 4 June Massacre (*Liusi*), the events of which were broadcast to hundreds of millions worldwide, China found that foreign investment in its rapid development virtually dried up and the economy stagnated. Although many Japanese and Taiwanese investors returned after a few weeks or months, economic growth was stifled through 1990 and 1991; domestic despair threatened, as the government remained an international pariah.

As he did in 1985, Deng confronted the problem head on through political ritual and rhetoric, by embarking on his now celebrated 'Nanxun' or 'Southern Tour', strengthened by his belief that China was like 'red meat' for the hungry foreign investor. With his faithful daughter Deng Maomao at his side, Deng was nearly ninety when he travelled south in February 1992 to reinvigorate the national spirit for profit. He was said to have exhorted the masses he encountered 'to be more audacious', to take the rapacious commercial transformation of Shenzhen as the model, and renew their commitment to the prosperity juggernaut by *xiahai* – going overboard for profit, 'jumping into the sea of commerce', or 'going entrepreneurial'. There was in the unabashed quality of this recommendation a vestige of the perilous voluntarism of Mao Zedong's canon of revolutionary praxis, *Shixing lun* [On Practice], where human agency is pushed to the brink – 'a fall in the pit is a leap in your wit'. Except for Deng's grandiose exhortation the outcome was not vague, but assured. From 1992 forward, in a curious parallel trajectory with the United States' decade of IPO excess and over-inflated dot.com stock options, *xiahai* assumed linguistic prominence as the colloquial reference for individual pursuit of profit of the *getihu* (private household), as many Chinese left the security of state-owned enterprise work to set up private business. *Xiahai* quickly became, and has endured as, China's cultural icon of excess unconstrained by law, becoming the mantra of both township enterprise and the regional party cadre. The Party-sanctioned abandon of 'going overboard' turned the phrase into an inexorable law of profit to which even the contemporary intelligentsia and university professors succumbed, as signalled in other popular variants such as *wenren xiahai* ('literati jump into the sea' or 'cast a line out on the sea'), with many taking private employment as cab drivers, restaurateurs and salespeople to supplement the insufficiently remunerative employment of university positions.

Now, a long decade beyond Deng's travels in the south, *xiahai* stands for the national maximization of self-interest consequent upon the collapse of the Party's once persuasive ethical dictates and the exigent, wildly democratic demands for spending and acquiring derived from popular worship of the commodity form, and its concomitant obliteration of the prospects for democratic reform.

See also: intellectuals and academics; 4 June [1989] esprit; Southern Excursion Talks (Deng Xiaoping, 1992)

LIONEL M. JENSEN

Xiamen Dada

Artist group

Xiamen Dada is an art group founded in 1986 by **Huang Yongping**, Cha Lixiong, Liu Yiling, Lin Chun and Jiao Yaoming. Antagonistic to pre-conceived notions of art, they found similarities between Chan Buddhism and Dada in the recognition of the impossibility of truth. The group was primarily identified with the ideas of Huang Yongping, set out in 'Xiamen Dada – a Kind of Postmodernism?' (*Xiamen Dada – yizhong houxiandai?*) in 1986. Works in the Xiamen Dada exhibition of the same year were characterized by the use of modern styles and found objects. The artists publicly burned some of the works at the end of the exhibition as an act of self-liberation, and were consequently barred from holding further public events.

Huang had previously organized 'A Modern Art Exhibition of Five Artists' (*Wuren xiandai huazhan*, 1983) in Xiamen (Fujian province) where he showed his *Haystack* (*Duocao*). This work – a copy of Bastien Lepage's *Les Foins* with a plaster mask

placed on the peasant woman's face – ridiculed the tendency to ape Western art without real understanding. In *Non-Expressive Painting* (*Fei biaoda huihua*, 1985), he used a roulette to determine the colour and composition of his paintings. **Gao Minglu** identified this as the second of Huang's four periods: anti-artistic affectation; anti-self expression/anti-formalism; anti-art; and anti-history. '*A History of Chinese Painting*' and '*A Concise History of Modern Painting*' *Washed in a Washing Machine for Two Minutes* (*Zhongguo huihuashi yü xiandai huihua jianshi*, 1987) is representative of the latter phase. In this work the quintessential doctrines of Eastern and Western high art are compounded to form a pile of mulch. Huang moved to France in 1989.

Further reading

Gao, Minglu (1998). 'From Elite to Small Man: The Many Faces of a Transitional Avant-Garde in Mainland China'. In Gao Minglu (ed.), *Inside/Out New Chinese Art*. Berkeley: University of California Press, 149–66.

Huang, Yongping (1983). 'Tan wode jizhang hua' [On a Few of My Paintings]. *Meishu* (January): 22–6.

—— (1986). 'Xiamen Dada – yizhong houxiandai?' [Xiamen Dada – A Kind of Post-Modernism?] *Zhongguo meishubao* 46: 1.

Lü, Peng and Yi, Dan (1992). 'Xiamen xin dada'. In *Zhongguo xiandai yishushi* [A History of Modern Art in China]. Changsha: Hunan meishu chubanshe, 281–7.

van Dijk, Hans (1994). 'The Fine Arts after the Cultural Revolution: Stylistic Development and Theoretical Debate'. In Jochen Noth, Wolfger Puhlmann, Kai Reschke and Andreas Schmid (eds), *China Avant-Garde Counter-Currents in Art and Culture*. Oxford: Oxford University Press, 14–39.

EDUARDO WELSH

Xi'an Film Studio

One of the major film studios in China, Xi'an Film Studio was established on 23 August 1958. During its first decade, the studio produced nineteen films, including *Peach Blossom Fan* (*Taohua shan*, 1963). The film featured the talented actress Wang Danfeng and was acclaimed by audiences in China, Hong Kong and Southeast Asia. Film production at the studio was prohibited during the **Cultural Revolution**, but resumed in 1979 with **Wu Tianming**'s *The Reverberations of Life* (*Shenghuo de chanyin*). *The Xi'an Incident* (1981) marked a breakthrough in bringing a major historical event to the screen. In the early 1980s, Xi'an Studio became the cradle of 'Chinese New Film' by recruiting recent **Beijing Film Academy** graduates and encouraging experimental filmmaking. Under the direction of the studio director Wu Tianming, such 'Fifth-Generation' directors (see **Fifth Generation (film directors)**) as **Zhang Yimou**, **Chen Kaige**, **Tian Zhuangzhuang** and **Huang Jianxin** produced their early work and helped the studio establish an international reputation. In 1987, Xi'an Studio reached the height of its creativity with Wu Tianming's *Old Well* (*Laojing*) and Zhang Yimou's *Red Sorghum* (*Hong Gaoliang*) which won a series of international prizes and became domestic blockbusters. In the 1990s, like all other major film studios in China, Xi'an Studio faced serious financial hardship after a cut in government subsidies. The studio therefore began to engage in international co-productions, while building the impressive Xi'an Film Production City (Xi'an Cinecitta). In August 2000, Xi'an Studio and its adjunct businesses were incorporated as the Xi'an Film Studio Company.

WANG CHANG

Xi'an guyue

Regional traditional music genre

Xi'an guyue (Old Music of Xi'an) is a traditional **drumming and blowing** genre which is popular in the Xi'an area. The genre includes Buddhist, Daoist and village styles. The Buddhist style is mainly represented by the Xicang and Dongcang bands in Xi'an city; the Daoist style by the bands of Chenghuang miao and Yingxiang guan (temples); and the village style by the bands of Hejiaying village of Chang'an country, and Nanjixian village of Zhouzhi county. The village style differs from the

religious styles in that it has absorbed more folk elements and has a distinctive suite-form.

The bands typically have as many as forty musicians. Forms include 'sitting' and 'processional'. The structure of 'sitting music' is very complex; usually the suite includes two parts with many different *qupai* ('fixed/labelled melodies'). The leading instruments are bamboo flutes and mouth-organs, followed by **zheng**, **pipa** and *yunluo* (two sets of ten small pitched gongs hung from two frames). The bands use four different drums as well as cymbals, gongs and wooden clappers (see **luogu**). There are two main formats: 'eight-beat sitting music' and 'lay sitting music'. The 'processional music' uses bamboo flutes, mouth-organs, cylindrical double reeds and *yunluo*. It also has two formats: *gaobazi* and *luanbaxian*. Both use individual melodies from the 'sitting music' repertory accompanied by a modified percussion section. One of the most important traditional occasions to play Xi'an guyue is the **pilgrimage** to the southern Wutai and Zhongnan mountains on the first day of the sixth month. The genre is also played during rain ceremonies, **funerals**, the Spring Festival (i.e. **New Year Festival**) and after the summer harvest.

Further reading

Jones, Stephen (1995). *Folk Music of China: Living Instrumental Traditions*. Oxford: Clarendon.

Miao, Tianrui *et al.* (eds) (1985). *Zhongguo yinyue cidian* [Dictionary of Chinese Music]. Beijing: Renming yinyue chubanshe.

DU YAXIONG

xiangsheng

(cross-talk, comic dialogue)

Xiangsheng is a traditional form of Chinese comic dialogue which can traced back to the Ming dynasty (1368–1644). It is translated as 'cross-talk', but because it refers to two performers talking to each other in a comic way, it is also translated as 'comic dialogue'. *Xiangsheng* usually consist of a story or stories with one or several subjects.

Sometimes *xiangsheng* is performed by one person (*dankou xiangsheng*), sometimes by a group of people (*qunkou xiangsheng*). Unlike Western standup comedy, which often consists of a string of one-liners that switch from topic to topic, a *xiangsheng* piece has a beginning, development and ending. This popular linguistic art tends to be more reserved and conservative than Western comedy. Its puns, homonyms, homophones, neologisms, cultural code words and phrases, use of dialect, and other language-based humour also make *xiangsheng* very difficult to translate with any degree of satisfaction. *Xiangsheng* reflects history and everyday life. It can be used to praise the CCP and government policies or to satirize social maladies. A piece called 'Yaogun **shunkouliu**' [Rock'n'roll Doggerel] satirizes **corruption**. *Xiangsheng* performers are almost all men, but women have also appeared, first in Taiwan and now on the mainland. On 8 March 1992, over forty pairs of women participated in the first 'Spark Cup' female *xiangsheng* competition in Beijing, marking International Women's Day. The oldest were two grandmothers in their seventies, the youngest a first-grade pupil. Occasionally you may still catch Mark Rowswell, or **Dashan** (Big Mountain), a Canadian fluent in the Beijing vernacular, cross-talking with his Chinese partner.

See also: quyi; Performance Workshop Theatre; xiaopin

Further reading

Kaikonen, Marja (1990). *Laughable Propaganda: Modern Xiangsheng as Didactic Entertainment.* Stockholm: Institute of Oriental Languages.

HELEN XIAOYAN WU

Xiao Lu

b. 1962, Hangzhou

Multi-media artist

Xiao Lu and her male partner Tang Song (b. 1960, Hangzhou), both graduates of the Zhejiang Academy of Art (now China Academy of Art, see **art academies**), rose to international prominence when Xiao Lu unexpectedly fired two bullets into her installation at the China National Gallery on 5 February 1989. The installation, entitled *Dialogue* (*Duihua*), was comprised of two telephone booths, separated by mirror glass, and was part of the '**China Avant-Garde**' exhibition. Conceived as action art, the event had far-reaching repercussions. The exhibition was closed, and the couple were taken into custody. According to the critic **Li Xianting**, Xiao Lu's gunshots signalled the close of the ten year period of 'New Wave Art' (*Xinchao meishu*). After the 4 June Massacre, Xiao Lu and Tang Song left China. From December 1989 until 1997 Xiao Lu lived in Sydney, Australia. Tang Song was held in a refugee camp in Hong Kong from 1989 until May 1991 when he fled by ship to Sydney. In Sydney he was held in detention until November 1991. Since then, Xiao Lu and Tang Song have continued to collaborate, creating confrontational works that reflect upon the surreality of life. *Us in New York* (*Women zai Niuyüe*), dating from June 2002, is a performance piece that documents Xiao Lu, accompanied by a fibreglass cast of Tang Song, visiting key sights in New York, including the former site of the World Trade Center, Brooklyn Bridge and Times Square.

CLAIRE ROBERTS

xiaomi

(keeping a female secretary-cum-lover)

Probably originating in Beijing in the 1980s, the term *xiaomi* refers to a young female secretary hired by a male boss in a private company more for her looks and sexual companionship than for her skills as a worker. It is unclear how common the practice was in reality, but the term was widely employed in conversation, fiction and humour. As a stereotype about gender relations in the reform era, the character of the *xiaomi* represents a sexualization of female labour also connoted in other terms, such as the *xiaojie* (miss, hostess or waitress), the *nü gongguan* (public relations girl), or even the *bailing nüxing* (white-collar woman). *Xiaomi* is also one of several popular names for mistresses of rich men, including *jinsiniao* (caged bird or kept woman) and *ernai* (second wife). These terms reflect both the reality of women's sexual commodification in the market economy and a popular interest in the various new sexual strategies of young Chinese women. Less apparent perhaps, the *xiaomi* also represents stereotypes about male sexuality in the reform era, particularly the uncontrolled sexual appetite of the private entrepreneur, often derogatively referred to as the *dakuan* (big money). Such stereotypes were part of a larger moral dialogue about the unrestrained nature of personal choices in the market era. Chinese employed such labels to negotiate the boundaries between acceptable strategies of self-promotion and dating and unacceptable strategies that bordered on prostitution or sexual exploitation.

See also: bao ernai; xiahai

Further reading

Farrer, James. 2002. *Opening Up: Youth Sex Culture and Market Reform in Shanghai*. Chicago: University of Chicago Press.

JAMES FARRER

xiaopin

(small performance, skit)

Performing art

Xiaopin is the shortened form of *xiju xiaopin* (comedic small performances). Believed to originate from *lachangxi*, a **quyi** show popular in the Tieling region of northeast China, it inherited the rustic humour of the local populace. *Xiaopin* emerged at a time when **xiangsheng** (cross-talk) saw its charm fading. A hybrid of the one-act play and *xiangsheng*, *xiaopin* appeared first on the stage and then the television.

Comedian Chen Peisi and Zhu Shimao performed their *Eating Noodles* (*Chimian*) at the 1984 Chinese New Year Celebration Gala, broadcast to millions of television viewers. Chen played an uncouth lad dreaming of being an actor. He was asked to improvise noodle-eating at a solicited interview. Out of his eagerness, he ended up

finishing a whole bucket of noodles before knowing what he was expected to do. His excellent pantomime established him as an icon of early Chinese *xiaopin*, which included the memorable *Unlicensed Pregnancy* (*Chaosheng youjidui*) by Huang Hong; *A Rice Pedlar* (*Huan dami*) by Guo Da; and *Packaged to Cheat* (*Ruci baozhuang*) by Gong Hanlin and Zhao Lirong. Zhao's untimely death saddened the whole nation.

In the 1990s, a 'northeast wind' dominated the limelight with the success of Zhao Benshan, Pan Changjiang and Gao Xiumei – all from northeast China. Their famous skits included *A New Year's Call* (*Bainian*) and *Cross the River* (*Guohe*). But, like *xiangsheng*, *xiaopin* is running out of steam due to lack of originality. Nevertheless, together with *xiangsheng* and pop music, it still counts as one of the most popular forms of entertainment.

Further reading

Du, Wenwei (1998). '*Xiaopin*: Chinese Theatrical Skits as Both Creatures and Critics of Commercialism'. *China Quarterly* 154 (June): 382–99.

YUAN HAIWANG

Xie Jin

b. 1923, Shaoxing, Zhejiang

Film director, producer

Xie Jin is little known in the West but is an unparalleled phenomenon in Chinese film, an institution unto himself. His success is built upon a skilful and distinctive blending (popularly called the 'Xie Jin model') of two features usually segregated in mainland film: politically propagandist ('educational') subject matter and an emotionally appealing, melodramatic style associated with 'entertainment' film.

A graduate of the National Nanjing School of Theatre in the late 1940s, his prize-winning films go back to the mid 1950s with *Girl Basketball Player No. 5* (1957) and *Red Detachment of Women* (1961), the latter winning China's first 'Hundred Flowers' award for most popular feature film. During the **Cultural Revolution**, Xie's *Stage Sisters* (1965) was severely criticized for characters and environment rather than the depiction of class and class struggle that dictated the plot, and Xie Jin was badly persecuted. He made no more films until filming Jiang Qing's model opera, *On the Docks*, with Xie Tieli in 1973.

After the Cultural Revolution, Xie's films began to offer limited but significant criticism of the government from within the film establishment itself, prior to the emergence of the so-called 'Fifth Generation' of directors. These films were the most popular of the year in six different years during the 1980s, including: *Legend of Tianyun Mountain* (1980), which won the film industry's first 'Golden Rooster' awards for best film, director, script, cinematography and art design and dared to criticize official motives during the Anti-Rightist Movement of 1957; *Garlands at the Foot of the Mountain* (1984), which censured bureaucratism in the PLA itself during China's 1979 border war with Vietnam; and the still-popular *Hibiscus Town* (1986), which documented self-serving radicalism during the Cultural Revolution. In the free market of the 1990s, having long dominated the government's powerful Shanghai Film Studio, Xie formed his own film company, the Xie Jin Hengtong Corporation. In 1997, to celebrate the handing over of Hong Kong, Xie's *Opium War* (1997) was produced on a record budget of US$12 million, but lacked the dramatic force of his better films of the 1980s.

See also: Fifth Generation (film directors)

Further reading

Chi, Robert (2003). 'The Red Detachment of Women: Resenting, Regendering, Remembering'. In Chris Berry (ed.), *Chinese Films in Focus: 25 New Takes*. London: BFI, 152–9.

Hayford, Charles (2003). '*Hibiscus Town*: Revolution, Love, and Bean Curd'. In Chris Berry (ed.), *Chinese Films in Focus: 25 New Takes*. London: BFI, 120–7.

Karl, Rebecca (2001). 'The Burdens of History: *Lin Zexu* (1959) and *The Opium War* (1997)'. In Zhang Xudong (ed.), *Whither China? Intellectual Politics in Contemporary China*. Durham: Duke University Press, 229–62.

Xiao, Zhiwei (2000). 'The Opium War in the Movies: History, Politics, and Propaganda'. *Asian Cinema* 11.1 (Spring): 68–83.

JEROME SILBERGELD

Xinhua News Agency

The Xinhua [New China] News Agency is the official state and Party news agency in China charged with collecting and supplying news, information and analysis to news organizations throughout the country and overseas. It officially exists as a department of the State Council, but it is also answerable to the Central Propaganda Committee of the Chinese Communist Party (CCP) and its primary function is the promulgation of propaganda for the CCP and the government.

Xinhua, by far the largest news agency in China, was originally launched as the Red China News Service to report the First Congress of Workers, Peasants and Soldiers organized by the CCP in Jiangxi province in 1931. According to CCP theory, Xinhua is conceived as having a dual role – to supply news to the people but also to canvass views of the population about government policy and social developments and feed these views back to the Party leadership. However, in general the transfer of information has been from the government to the people, and the Agency is still conceived as the principle mouthpiece of the Party.

In the 1990s, considerable investment in the Agency from the central government has seen it grow and develop to offer a professional and commercial, as well as politically motivated, news service. It has 106 overseas bureaus in addition to its thirty-six domestic bureaus and numerous sub-bureaus throughout the country. The balance of its foreign news within its news reporting has steadily increased over the post-Mao reform period and currently stands at approximately 60:40 in favour of domestic news. In the late 1990s the Agency launched its own comprehensive news website in Chinese, English, French, Russian, Spanish, Japanese and Arabic.

See also: Internet (content); newspapers; state control of media

KEVIN LATHAM

Xinhua zidian, Xinhua cidian

Dictionaries

Both *zidian* and *cidian* may translated as 'dictionary'. A *zidian*, however, lists single-characters as entries only, while a *cidian* lists multi-character words and phrases as sub-entries under a single-character entry.

(1998, rev. ed.) *Xinhua zidian* [Xinhua Dictionary] (Beijing: Commercial Press). With just over 10,000 characters, this was the only standard dictionary in the PRC for two decades. Most Chinese families have at least one copy. Between 1957 and 1998, nine editions and over a hundred printings were published. Some 400 million copies have been distributed since its first edition. Though small in size, it has nine useful appendices, and is especially good in indicating characters belonging to complex characters or which categories of variants are defined in the PRC. This is a feature that other authoritative dictionaries lack. It is very useful for anyone who deals with different groups of characters.

Yi Ken'ichiro, Dong Jingru and Yamada Runko (1999). *Xinhua zidian Hanyu pinyin ban* [Xinhua Dictionary: Hanyu Pinyin Edition] (Taiyuan: Shanxi Education Press). Two Japanese and a Chinese scholar romanized all characters in the definitions and examples based on the original editions of 1979 and 1992.

Yao Naiqiang *et al.* (2000). *Ying-Han shuangjie Xinhua zidian* [Xinhua Dictionary with English Translation]. Beijing: Commercial. Everything in the 1998 edition is kept, including the *Zhuyin fuhao* (National Phonetic Symbols) next to pinyin in the entry, and is translated. Pinyin is added to all examples under the definitions, a useful function for learners.

(2001, rev. ed.) *Xinhua cidian* [Xinhua Word Dictionary] (Beijing: Commercial.) This is mainly a language dictionary of 47,231 compound-words, but is also a compact encyclopedia. The third edition has sixteen appendices and lists all variant characters clearly, a weak point of the *Xiandai Hanyu cidian* [Modern Chinese Dictionary].

HELEN XIAOYAN WU

Xinmin Evening News

[Xinmin wanbao]

Xinmin or 'new people' was a neologism in the early twentieth century in response to Western cultural influence. Originally founded in 1929 as the *Xinminbao* (*Xinmin News*), which had both day and evening editions, only the evening edition continued to publish after 1949 and changed its name to the *Xinmin Evening News* (*Xinmin wanbao*) in 1958. The newspaper was closed down by the Nationalist government in the 1940s and during the **Cultural Revolution** (1966–76) and was not re-launched until 1982. In 1996, it was the first evening newspaper that established an office in California for the American edition, which periodically publishes its last page (page 32) in English. In 1998, the *Xinmin Evening News* and the *Wenhui Daily*, established in 1938, teamed up to form the core of the Wenhui Xinmin United Press Group. The new company owns many periodicals as well as the English-language newspaper, *Shanghai Daily*. The *Xinmin Evening News* is probably the most popular evening daily with a circulation of 1,700,000 copies in Shanghai, Beijing, Guangzhou, Xi'an, Shenzhen, etc. Its fictionalized newspaper office appears frequently and prominently in **Wong Kar-wai**'s film *In the Mood for Love* (2000): the lead actor works for the *Xinmin yebao*, which is exactly the Shanghainese spoken version of the newspaper's actual name, and even the calligraphy for the film's newspaper title is in the same style. Many columns of the *Xinmin Evening News* are thoughtfully written, e.g. 'Reading is Pleasant' (*Dushule*) and 'New Book Corridor' (*Xinshulang*). From time to time, the newspaper sponsors **literary awards**.

HELEN XIAOYAN WU

Xiqu

('theatre [of] sung-verse'/sung-drama/opera)

Xiqu (often called 'traditional Chinese theatre', 'Chinese music-drama' or 'Chinese opera' in English) is the primary genre of indigenous Chinese theatre, and the only major genre in existence prior to the twentieth century (other contemporary genres include **Geju**, **Huaju** and **Wuju**).

Historically, Xiqu has been fundamentally performer-centred, and this remains true today, despite the importance of playwrights and the Western-inspired personnel added to the genre in the early 1950s, including directors, composers and designers. Performers specialize in portraying characters of a specific role type (see **Xiqu role types**) through the display of four stylized performance skills: song (*chang*), speech (*nian*), dance-acting (*zuo*) and combat (*da*). The synthesis of these skills in performance, and the presence of both prose and rhymed verse and both comic and serious elements in almost all Xiqu plays, are other defining characteristics of the genre.

Originating as early as the third century BC, Xiqu reached maturity in the 'Nanxi' and 'Zaju' forms of the tenth to fifteenth centuries. Each form of Xiqu develops in a particular region, and some become sufficiently widespread to be considered national forms. **Kunqu Xiqu** was the predominant form in the sixteenth to eighteenth centuries, and **Jingju** has been the leading form nationally since the nineteenth century. The number of individual forms of Xiqu has varied dramatically during the twentieth century, from lows of just over a hundred in the wakes of WWII and the **Cultural Revolution**, to a high of almost 400 during the peak of government support in the 1950s and 1960s. There have been well over 300 forms since the early 1980s.

Xiqu is highly theatrical, employing conventions that allow for remarkably mutable presentation and use of time and space. Aesthetic emphasis is placed upon beauty, a concept that almost invariably includes the attributes of round and effortless performance. This shared aesthetic makes the hundreds of forms of contemporary Xiqu generally similar to the eye, with each form of Xiqu distinguished primarily by its aural characteristics, including the language of the region in which it arose, and the vocal and instrumental music of the form. Each of the four primary Xiqu musical systems employs one of two styles of characterizing **Xiqu musical structure**.

Extensive government intervention during the second half of the twentieth century has perhaps forever altered the course of Xiqu. During the 1950s, Xiqu was highly institutionalized under the newly established PRC, leading to the growth of ever-larger companies organized along socialist/military lines and completely dependent upon the state. Xiqu plays were taxonomized in three categories: 'traditional plays' (*chuantongxi*), created before 1949, and 'newly written historical plays' (*xinbian lishiju*), created after 1949 – both set either in pre-twentieth-century or mythological eras; and 'modern plays' (*xiandaixi*), set after the nineteenth century.

During the Cultural Revolution, only modern plays with revolutionary themes were allowed. In the late 1970s first newly written historical and then traditional plays returned to the stage, and since then most new creative work has taken the form of newly written historical plays (though the term itself is often not used). An outstanding example is **Cao Cao and Yang Xiu** (*Cao Cao yü Yang Xiu*), first staged in 1988. The modern Xiqu play has seemed inseparably linked to political propaganda, and since the Cultural Revolution has rarely served as a vehicle for creative experimentation. However, several major exceptions could be seen at the Sixth China Art Festival held in autumn 2000, when three modern plays adapted from earlier twentieth-century works won top honours: the **Chuanju** (Sichuan opera) *Mask* (*Bianlian*), from **Wei Minglun**'s film by the same name; the Chuanju play *Jinzi* (named for the play's title role and based on Cao Yu's Huaju *Wilderness* (*Yuanye*)); and the Jingju play *Rickshaw Boy* (*Luotuo Xiangzi*), based on Lao She's novel of the same name. Additionally, some experimental work has transcended these taxonomies. A prime example is Wei Minglun's Chuanju **Pan Jinlian (1985)**, the eponymous, controversial wife from the traditional novel *Tales of the Water Margin* (*Shuihu zhuan*) – a play that includes historical and fictional characters from the ancient past through the late twentieth century who explore together the ways in which women are, and have been, judged.

In general, since the early 1980s traditional plays have been presented on decorated but essentially bare stages, while a wide range of scenic experimentation inspired primarily by the practices of Huaju has been carried out for newly written historical and modern plays. On the other hand, Huaju, which emerged from the Cultural

Revolution confined by Socialist Realism, has repeatedly turned to Xiqu during the same period as a primary source of theatrical, presentational inspiration.

Since the early 1980s, Xiqu has also seen a steady decline in audience numbers due to changing societal attitudes, and a progressive decline in government support. The large companies that developed from the 1950s to the 1970s have been faced with radical reorganization and an emphasis on box-office value and private corporate sponsorships. Though widely regarded as the most representative Chinese performing art, Xiqu continues to face prejudice at home, especially among urban populations – the early twentieth-century perception of the genre as backward, 'feudal' and old-fashioned has re-emerged. And modernization (including Westernization) continues to have a wide-ranging and substantial impact upon it.

ELIZABETH WICHMANN-WALCZAK

Xiqu musical structure

Musical structure is the most fundamental aspect of music in **Xiqu** (sung-drama/opera). There are two main styles of musical structure: the *lianquti* ('joined song style', also called *qupai liantaoti*, 'fixed-melody joined set style'); and the *banqiangti* ('beat [and] tune style', also called *banshi bianhuati*, 'metrical-type change style').

Lianquti structure is employed in Xiqu music from the playwright-centred musical systems: *kunshanqiang* ('tunes of Kunshan') and *yiyangqiang* ('tunes of Yiyang', also called *gaoqiang*, 'high tunes'). Following *lianquti* structure, vocal music in these systems is derived from a large number of 'fixed-melodies' (*qupai*), usually arranged in a specific order in sets; each fixed-melody conveys both emotional and structural sense. In creating new plays, playwrights first select and arrange fixed-melodies, and then write lyrics to fit them. Xiqu forms employing this playwright-centred compositional process tend to be more elite. Kunqu is the principal contemporary form of Xiqu in the *kunshanqiang* system (see **Kunqu Xiqu**), while **Chuanju**, **Minju** and **Liyuanxi** employ *lianquti* structured music from both elite musical systems.

Banqiangti structure is employed in Xiqu music from the actor-centred musical systems: *bangziqiang* ('tunes of the **Bangzi** clapper') and *pihuang* (named for its two principal modes, [*xi*]*pi* and [*er*]*huang*). Following *banqiangti* structure, vocal music in these systems is based upon modes and metrical-types, which provide rhythmic and melodic patterns that convey atmospheric and emotional sense. In creating new plays, actors select modes and metrical-types, and then apply these patterns in composing melodies to fit lyrics. Xiqu forms employing this actor-centred compositional process tend to be popular rather than elite. The late twentieth-century introduction of composers to the creative process has perhaps increased popularity problems in these forms. **Jingju** (Peking opera) is one of the principal forms of Xiqu in the *pihuang* system, while there are numerous Bangzi forms in the *bangziqiang* system. **Yueju** (**Guangdong**, **Guangxi opera**) and Chuanju (Sichuan opera) employ music from both popular musical systems, and **Huangmeixi** and **Pingju** both include *banqiangti* structured music.

Further reading

Wichmann, Elizabeth (1991). *Listening to Theatre: The Aural Dimension of Beijing Opera*. Honolulu: University of Hawai'i Press.

ELIZABETH WICHMANN-WALCZAK

Xiqu on television

While television has created and popularized new forms of entertainment since the mid 1980s, old forms of **Xiqu** (spoken drama/opera) are also using television to reach a broader audience and to adapt to more contemporary tastes. Most central and local TV stations in China have either a designated channel or a fixed time slot for Xiqu theatre. There have been four forms of TV theatrical adaptations. To illustrate the characteristics of these forms, different versions of *The Western Wing* (*Xixiangji*) are used here as a case in point. The first form is called *wutai shikuang zhuanbo*, a 'live televised version', including reruns, of a particular stage production, such as the 1980s **Jingju** (Peking opera) *Hongniang* with Song Changrong in the title role. The next category is called *wutai xiqu yishupian*, a version, similar to operatic films, which preserves the style of a stage production, using a realistic setting shot from different angles. An example is Tian Han's 1950s Jingju version adapted for television in the 1980s with the famous singer Zhang Junqiu as Cui Yingying. The third category is termed *xiqu dianshi lianxuju*, a TV series in which actors perform as they do on stage, but in a realistic environment that does not allow for certain stage conventions such as pantomimic gestures. An example is Wu Chen's 1988 four-segment adaptation of Su Xue'an's 1950s **Yueju (Zhejiang opera)** *The Western Wing*. This TV series was in fact followed in 1988 by the fourth type of musical TV drama termed *xiqu yinyue dianshiju*, in which characters in a realistic setting speak and act naturally, but sing in the style of a particular regional opera: the **Huangmeixi** (Hubei opera) *yinyue dianshiju* of *The Western Wing* directed by Hu Liancui. The main difference between a traditional stage production and these four types of TV adaptations is that the theatrical concepts of time and space have been increasingly modified and transformed by cinematic modes.

The recent marriage between traditional theatre and television is significant for four reasons: the Western-influenced television culture is made more Chinese, while some of the old theatrical forms are preserved or modernized, for better or for worse; young members of the television audience are exposed to Xiqu theatre; the range of dramatic topics is broadened through cinematic techniques, and more playwrights are engaged in the production of Xiqu theatre; and different regional styles of the traditional theatre become known and appreciated by a national audience.

Further reading

Meng, Fanshu. (1999). *Xiqu dianshiju yishu lun* [On the Art of Xiqu TV Drama]. Beijing: Beijing guangbo xueyuan chubanshe.

Zhong, Yibing and Huang, Wangnan. (eds) (1994). *Zhongguo dianshi yishu fazhanshi* [A History of the Development of Chinese Television Arts]. Hangzhou: Zhejiang renmin chubanshe, 249–90.

DU WENWEI

Xiqu playwrights

One of the recent developments in **Xiqu** (sung-drama/ opera) is the increased emphasis on the role and importance of playwrights. In the past, most authors of the plays of 'regional music dramas' (*difangxi*), including Peking opera, remained either anonymous or unrecognized. Despite the fact that authors' names began to appear in published scripts in the 1950s and 1960s, scholars and critics seldom studied playwrights while discussing plays. Furthermore, audiences rarely knew about Xiqu playwrights except for a few well-known literary figures like Tian Han who had mainly made their names known in other genres. During the **Cultural Revolution**, the names of authors of the 'model plays' were largely suppressed and replaced by impersonal names of collective authorship. Since the late 1970s, the role of the playwrights of the 1950s and 1960s, such as Xu Jin, Chen Renjian and Wen Mu, have been gradually recognized and studied. As the old generation of playwrights continued to write in the 1980s, a new generation who write exclusively for Xiqu emerged and has remained active and influential on the contemporary stage. Scholars and critics began to study them as subject matter and, accordingly, audiences began paying attention to the authors of respective plays. The successful playwrights, old and young, in contemporary Xiqu circles include: **Wei Minglun, Yu Xiaoyu, Xu Fen, Wang Renjie**, Zheng Huaixing, Chen Ya-xian, Wu Zhaofen, Gu Xidong, Guo Dayu, Peng Zhigan, Zeng Zhaohong, among others. While some of these writers have been providing scripts exclusively for a specific regional theatre, others like **Guo Qihong** and **Luo Huaizhen** have been writing for a variety of music dramas. The latter is itself a new phenomenon in the New Period.

The subject matter of these playwrights' work is largely traditional. It consists of three categories: (1) newly written historical plays (*xinbian lishiju*) whose stories are based upon historical events, such as Chen Yaxian's **Cao Cao and Yang Xiu**; (2) reinterpretation of well-known historical, literary or legendary figures, which often negates or rever-ses the traditional moral judgment on these char-acters, such as Wei Minglun's **Pan Jinlian** and Xu Fen's *Sister Tian and Zhuangzi* (*Tian Jie yü Zhuang Zhou*); and (3) invention of new legends set in the real historical past, which are often critical of traditional culture or allude to the present social conditions, such as Luo Huaizhen's *Golden Dragon and Mayfly* (*Jinlong yü fuyou*). Although most of these new plays are set in the remote past, they are all characterized by a strong linkage between the historical and the contemporary. The contemporaneity of these traditional themes is usually conveyed through emphasis on the emancipation of women (*nüxing*), humanity (*renxing*) and individuality (*gexing*).

From time to time, there have also appeared exciting plays reflecting modern and contemporary life and society, known as *Xiqu xiandaixi* (modern plays). Resident playwrights of certain theatrical troupes, like those performing **Huju** (Shanghai opera), tend to write more such plays on contemporary themes. Those troupes specializing in older theatrical forms have, however, also produced modern plays. Almost all Xiqu forms have had 'modern plays' since the late 1970s. **Jingju** (Peking opera) has, for example, even produced such successful modern plays as *Wrapped Honey* (*Yibao mi*), *Lofty Petroleum Towers* (*Gaogaode lianta*), *Legends of the Temple of the Medicine God* (*Yaowang miao chuanqi*) and *Camel Xiangzi* (a.k.a. *Rickshaw Boy*; *Luotuo Xiangzi*). Playwrights noted for 'modern plays' include Yang Chunlan, Yu Yonghe, Chen Wu and Xiao Shang.

Unlike most old plays of regional theatres which had less literary value and depended more on actors' skills, these new Xiqu plays of both traditional and modern themes tend to be richer in literary or philosophical content and more elaborate in dramatic structure, which partly reflects an influence from Western thoughts and dramaturgy introduced into China since the early 1980s. Contemporary Xiqu playwrights have begun to be a subject of scholarly and critical studies.

See also: Shi Yukun

Further reading

Guo, Qihong (1992). *Guo Qihong juzuo xuan* [Selected Plays by Guo Qihong]. Beijing: Zhongguo xiju chubanshe.

Luo, Huaizhen (1990). *Xi Shi gui Yue – Luo Huaizhen tansuo xiqu ji* [Xi Shi Returns to the Kingdom of Yue – A Collection of Luo Huaizhen's Exploratory Plays]. Shanghai: Xuelin chubanshe.

—— (1993). *Jinlong yü Fuyou* [Golden Dragon and Mayfly]. *Shanghai Yishujia* 6: 25–36.

Xu, Fen (1993). *Mulian zhi mu* [Mulian's Mother]. *Sichuan xiju* 4: 53–62.

—— (1996). *Sishui weilan* [Billows out of Dead Waters]. *Juben* 4: 2–18.

Yu, Xiaoyu and Li, Yunyan (1992). *Famen zhongsheng xiang* [All Living Creatures at the Famen Temple]. *Juben* 6: 7–22.

Yu, Xiaoyu, Xie, Lu and Peng, Zhigan (1989). *Gaoyao Zhang* [Zhang the Dogskin-Plaster Seller]. *Xin Juben* 2.

DU WENWEI

Xiqu role types

(hangdang)

Character portrayal in **Xiqu** (sung-drama/opera) is based upon a system of role types. Each specific role type is indicative of a particular gender, age and level of dignity, and is distinguished by makeup and costume conventions together with patterns of vocal and physical stylization. Each character is portrayed as a specific role type, and actors specialize in one or more specific role types.

Four general role types appear in contemporary Xiqu: *sheng*, dignified male characters; *dan*, female characters; *jing*, larger-than-life, 'painted-face' (*hualian*) male characters; and *chou*, often comic, earthy male characters. Each specific role type is a subcategory of one of these four general types, and some are unique to one or a few forms of Xiqu. Most contemporary forms include both young (*xiao*) and old (*lao*) subcategories in the *sheng* and *dan* role types, and, in all four general role types, one or more civil (*wen*) subcategories featuring song, speech and dance-acting skills, and one or more martial (*wu*) subcategories especially featuring combat, acrobatics and other martial skills.

Role types help actors portray characters not of their own age and/or gender, as in **Yueju (Zhejiang opera)**, in which women generally portray male as well as female leads, and **Jingju** (Peking opera), in which some individual performers portray characters not of their own gender, including the male *dan* star Mei Baojiu and the female *jing* performer Qi Xiaoyun. Role types have been the focus of much historical and contemporary creativity. They are also deeply woven into the fabric of Chinese culture, and even today provide a widely used means of personal description.

ELIZABETH WICHMANN-WALCZAK

Xper.Xr

Experimental composer and performer

One of a handful of experimental musicians to emerge in musically conservative Hong Kong in the 1980s, the cryptically named Xper.Xr gained a measure of notoriety as arguably the first Chinese 'industrial noise' musician. His confrontational, electronically generated sound works, described by one reviewer as 'techno-disco-karaoke-noise', are characterized by harsh timbres, extremes of volume and dynamics, and satirical deconstructions of familiar pop music. Although his work is known only to a small specialized audience, it nevertheless marks a significant departure from Chinese musical precedent in its disregard for established musical forms and preoccupation with themes of alienation and sexuality.

Xper.Xr made his self-financed debut recording, *Murmur*, in 1989, and went on to give infrequent performances at Hong Kong arts festivals and galleries. In 1992 he released his first full-length CD, *Voluptuous Musick*, on the city's adventurous but short-lived Sound Factory label. During this period he also published the Hong Kong experimental arts magazine *Cacophon*.

Disappointed with hostile public response to his sound experiments in Hong Kong, in the early 1990s Xper.Xr moved to the more musically receptive environment of London, where he continues to test the boundaries between noise and music as both a solo artist and collaborator with a wide range of international avant-garde musicians. In 1997 he formed his own Vaseline label and released the more conventionally structured *Lun Hsiao Shuai*. Subsequent recordings have included *Golden Wonder, Look Left/Right, Because I'm Worth It*, and contributions to numerous international compilations.

DENNIS REA

Xu Bing

b. 1955, Chongqing

Printmaker, installation artist

Xu Bing was a self-taught artist and an 'intellectual youth', sent during the **Cultural Revolution** to work with peasants in suburban Beijing, when he was admitted in 1977 to the Print-making Department of the **Central Academy of Fine Arts**, where he received his BA (1981) and MFA (1987) degrees and remained as a member of the faculty until 1990, when he moved to the United States. *A Book from the Sky* (1988), an installation of a series of prints of thousands of fake Chinese characters, exhibited at his first solo show at the **China Art Gallery** (Zhongguo meishuguan), won him nationwide and then international recognition as one of the prominent (and famous) Chinese avantgarde artists. It also won Xu an invitation to the United States as a visiting artist at the University of Wisconsin at Madison (1990), his first exposure at the Venice Biennale (1993), and the extremely prestigious 'Genius Prize' from the MacArthur Foundation (1999).

In 1996, Xu exhibited his *New English Calligraphy* at the Pace Art Foundation in Texas, a project he had been working on since 1994. In this installation, presented in the form of a classroom, Xu attempts to teach his audience how to use a Chinese brush and ink to write English words employing the structure of Chinese characters. Ever since the mid 1990s, Xu has been busy exhibiting his works around the world. Major shows include solo shows at the Boston College of Art (1995), the Konstmuseum Uppsala in Sweden (1996), the ICA in London (1997), New Museum of Contemporary Art in New York (1998), as well as important group shows like the South Africa Biennale (1997), Kwangju Biennale (1999) and Sydney Biennial, Australia (2000). Xu's obsession with language, Chinese characters and calligraphy in particular, was on display in his retrospective show at the Arthur M. Sackler Gallery in Washington, DC (2001).

Xu Bing's attitude towards language is multidimensional. On one hand, he seems to doubt the reliability of the written word – the thousands of seemingly rigorous characters in his *A Book from the Sky* turn out to be nothing but nonsense. On the other hand, he tries to create a kind of written language that may help people from different cultural backgrounds better understand each other – the character-words in his *New English Calligraphy* look familiar to both Chinese and English readers. In still other cases, he seems to believe that language is aggressive – in his *Cultural Animals* (1994), the body of a live mating male pig is printed with English words while the body of a live mating female pig is printed with Chinese characters. Xu Bing has been working and living in Brooklyn, New York, since 1998.

Further reading

Abe, Stanley (2000). 'No Questions, No Answers: China and *A Book from the Sky*'. In Ray Chow (ed.), *Modern Chinese Literary and Cultural Studies in the Age of Theory: Reimagining a Field*. Durham: Duke University Press, 227–50.

—— (2000). 'Reading the Sky'. In Yeh Wen-hsin (ed.), *Cross-Cultural Readings of Chineseness: Narratives, Images, and Interpretations of the 1990s*. Berkeley: Center for Chinese Studies, 53–79. [See also Patricia Berger, 'Pun Intended: A Response to Stanley Abe', in the same volume, 80–99].

Erickson, Britta (2001). *Words Without Meaning, Meaning Without Words The Art of Xu Bing* (exhibition catalogue). Washington, DC: Arthur M. Sackler Gallery.

Yang, Alice (1998) 'Xu Bing: Rewriting Culture'. In idem, *Why Asia? Contemporary Asian and Asian American Art*. New York: New York University Press, 24–9.

QIAN ZHIJIAN

Xu Fen

b. 1933, Chongqing, Sichuan

Xiqu (sung-drama/opera) playwright

In 1961, Xu Fen became the first female playwright in the history of **Chuanju** (Sichuan opera). Since then she has written more than thirty plays. Her most representative work before the **Cultural Revolution** was *Yanyan*, a revision, from a feminist point of view, of the characterization of the leading character of Guan Hanqing's Yuan-dynasty farce *A Girl Tricked into Amorous Relations* (*Zha nizi tiao fengyue*), in which Yanyan accepts her position as a concubine even after she has been taken advantage of, betrayed and ridiculed by her man. Since the late 1970s, Xu's revision has been adapted by different regional theatre troupes and has also been produced on television. Since Reform, but in the same vein, she has written a series of plays focusing on new portrayals of women: *Sister Tian and Zhuangzi* (*Tianjie yü Zhuang Zhou*), *Interrupted Dream of Red Chamber* (*Honglou jing meng*) and *Mulian's Mother* (*Mulian zhi mu*). She has also turned to modern and contemporary themes, producing such plays as *Gentle Waves of Dead Waters* (*Sishui weilan*), *Governor's Wife* (*Dudu furen*), and *The Raging Tide in the Sea of Desire* (*Yuhai kuangchao*). *Gentle Waves of Dead Waters*, adapted from a novel of the same title, tells the story of a countrywoman who rebels against feudal ethics and pursues her own love in the last years of the Qing Dynasty. *Governor's Wife* is based on an autobiography by Dong Zhujun, a woman entrepreneur who had escaped from her life as a sing-song girl at the age of fifteen and, following a failed marriage to a governor of Sichuan, started a Sichuanese restaurant in Shanghai which later developed into the famous Jinjiang Hotel. *The Raging Tide in the Sea of Desire* is a transformation of Eugene O'Neill's *Desire Under the Elms*, turning the concept of sexual desire into a concrete and vivid image on stage.

Like **Wei Minglun**, Xu Fen has written mainly for Sichuan opera. These two playwrights have been most innovative and, sometimes, controversial of the Chuanju stage. Xu is undoubtedly one of the most important female playwrights in the contemporary scene. Her works have also appeared in **Jingju** (Peking opera) (i.e. *The One and Only*, or *Qiangu yiren*), **Huaju** (spoken drama) (i.e. *The Tide of the Xinhai Revolution*, or *Xinhai chao*), and **Wuju** (dance drama) (i.e. *Flowers of Distant Mountains*, or *Yuanshan de huaduo*).

See also: Xiqu playwrights

DU WENWEI

Xu Hong

b. 1957, Shanghai

Painter, art critic

In 1981, Xu Hong enrolled in the Faculty of Art Education at Shanghai Normal University, graduating in 1986. She has taken part in many national and international exhibitions, including: the seminal **China Avant-Garde** exhibition at the **China Art Gallery** in Beijing (1989), *China New Art* in Australia (1992), *Chinese Women Painters* in Washington (1995), and the important *Century Woman* at the China Art Gallery in Beijing (1998). Since 1986 she has been working at the Art Research and Acquisition Department of the Shanghai Art Museum and has also published a number of essays on the development of modern art and women artists in China.

Originally trained as an oil painter, Xu was a member of the Shanghai modern art movement in the 1980s and among the first Chinese artists to experiment with mixed media works (*cailiaore*). This form of expression was part of a trend in the mid 1980s concerned with transforming the use and meanings of materials and redefining aspects of traditional Chinese culture. Xu was also one of the few women artists who showed a strong interest in exploring abstraction, a style shunned during ideologically saturated times for its associations with 'bourgeois' and liberal Western ideals. Xu's *Himalayan Wind*, a series of seven large mixed media canvases, partly exhibited in the 'China Avant-Garde' exhibition, used juxtaposed layers of Chinese traditionally hand-made paper pasted over black-painted canvases studded with crushed sharp-edged stones. Inverting the traditional idea of black brush strokes on white background, this non-objective series is part of an exploration that rethinks the self in relation to the cosmos, a fundamental association in Chinese philosophy.

Further reading

Xu, Hong (1994). 'The Spotted Leopard: Seeking Truth from History and Reality: Trends in the Development of Chinese Art'. *ART AsiaPacific* 1.2 (April): 31–5.

—— (1995). 'China – Dialogue: The Awakening of Women's Consciousness'. *ART AsiaPacific* 2.2: 44–51.

ALICE MING WAI JIM

Xu Jilin

b. 1957, Shanghai

Intellectual historian

A prominent historian of modern Chinese thought, Xu Jilin has authored numerous essays and books on intellectual trends and individuals in twentieth-century China. Since the mid 1990s, he has also become an influential critical commentator on Chinese intellectual concerns in the contemporary, post-1978 period.

Xu is Professor of History at East China Normal University, where he heads the Contemporary Chinese Thought and Culture Research Institute. He has been a councillor of the Academy of Chinese History (PRC) since 1998. Xu is commonly regarded by his intellectual peers as a moderate advocate of **liberalism** in relation to the debate between **liberalism** and the **New Left** which has ensued since the late 1990s. This debate, widely seen as having divided the elite Chinese intellectual world of Beijing and Shanghai, has led Xu to focus his research on the liberal tradition within modern Chinese thought and to propose an inclusive 'Third Way' which will allow Chinese critical thought to move beyond the ideological impasse that has resulted from the ongoing debate.

Since 2000, Xu has presented numerous seminars and conference papers in the United States, Europe and Asia. His influential books include: *A Spiritual Purgatory: Chinese Intellectuals in Cultural Transition* (*Jingshen de lianyu: wenhua bianqianzhong de Zhongguo zhishifenzi*. Taipei: Shulin chubanshe, 1995) and *Another Kind of Enlightenment* (*Ling yizhong qimeng*. Guangzhou: Huacheng chubanshe, 1999). His essay 'The Fate of an Enlightenment: Twenty Years in the Chinese Intellectual Sphere 1978–1998' ('Qimeng de mingyun: ershinian laide Zhongguo sixiangjie' (1999), translated by Geremie Barmé with Gloria Davies, *East Asian History* 20 (December 2000): 169–86), provides an insightful critical survey of contemporary Chinese intellectual politics.

GLORIA DAVIES

Xu Kun

b. 1965, Shenyang, Dongbei

Writer, literary critic

Representative of the post-Cultural Revolution generation, Xu Kun has attracted great attention since her emergence in the early 1990s. Her stories embody vividly the mood of Chinese society at this time, especially the rise of popular culture and the decline of elitism. In characteristically witty, playful and sarcastic language, Xu subverts the conventional image of Chinese intellectuals, particularly males, as in 'The Vernacular Language' (*Baihua*) and 'The Avant-Garde' (*Xianfeng*). The former mocks the hypocrisy and psychological dislocation of a group of Chinese intellectuals during a short stay in the countryside, while the latter satirizes the predicament and degradation of Chinese artists in an increasingly commercialized society. Xu is skilful in using a male narrator to subvert male characters.

Xu's second major theme is her sensitive but darkly humorous and sardonic delineation of the misunderstandings and disappointments in contemporary relations between the sexes. This theme is particularly evident in her stories 'Misty Dreams' (*Ruyan rumeng*), 'Kitchen' (*Chufang*) and 'Encountering Love' (*Zaoyu aiqing*). The first depicts the sexual adventure of an unhappily married career woman; the second mocks the romantic illusions of a female art agent; and the third shows the mutual manipulation of the sexes in the pursuit of profit. Xu is a researcher at the Modern Chinese Literature Division of the **Chinese Academy of Social Sciences** in Beijing. Her scholarly book, *Night Boat Journey* (*Yexingchuan*, 1999), is a provocative study of works by contemporary Chinese women writers.

Further reading

Huot, Claire (2000). 'Literary Experiments: Six Files, "Xu Kun's Theme Parks"'. In *idem*, *China's New Cultural Scene*. Durham: Duke University Press, 41–8.

LEUNG LAIFONG

Xu Shuya

b. 1961, Changchun, Jilin

Composer

Xu Shuya is now residing in France. A formidable influence in his musical career were his experiences during the **Cultural Revolution**, when he became a member of a Literary and Arts Troupe (*Wenyidui*). His entire family had been sent to the countryside in the northeast between 1969 and 1973. There, he watched performances of *yangge* (rice-planting dances) and heard music of the *suona* (Chinese oboe) and *sheng* (mouth-organ). Back in the city, he began to play the piano and cello and started to compose. In 1978, he entered the Shanghai Conservatory and studied composition with **Zhu Jian'er** and Ding Shande. After graduation he served as a lecturer at the Conservatory. In 1988, he received a French scholarship to attend the École Normale de Musique de Paris. In 1989 he was admitted to the Conservatoire National Supérieur de Musique to study composition and electro-acoustical music with Ivo Malec and Laurent Cuniot. Already in his earliest compositions – in the string quartet *Song of the Miao* (*Miaoge*, 1982) and *Violin Concerto* (1982) – he had experimented with microtonality and other contemporary compositional techniques. In this he was inspired, like many composers of his generation, by the particular qualities of Chinese folk and traditional music: in his cello concerto *Search* (*Suo*, 1984), for example, he makes the cellist use glissando and pull the strings, as is done in **qin**-playing to inflect the pitch, while also alienating the pentatonic melody employed in the piece.

His compositions are expressionist studies in anti-melody, made up of small units of climax/anti-climax, as in his First Symphony *Curves* (*Huxian*, 1986) and in *Choc* (1989) for four cellos. He prefers harsh dissonances and is a master of orchestration. In *Choc*, Xu makes use of the full range of modernist string-technique: Bartók pizzicato, collegno playing, overpressuring. So, although he chooses a uniform body of sound, four instruments of essentially the same timbre, he achieves unforeseen effects. Chinese themes continue to dominate his music: in *The Great Void II* (*Taiyi II*, 1991) he enters the realm of *musique concrète*, the 'concrete material' here being a piece of *xiao*-music. His opera, *Snow in August*, was co-produced with **Gao Xingjian** in December 2002, and centres on the life of the Chan monk Huineng.

See also: folksongs (Han Chinese); traditional music

BARBARA MITTLER

Xu Xing

b. 1956, Beijing

Writer

Xu Xing lives in Beijing, having spent several years in Germany in the 1990s. Left by himself as a child, and with no schooling during the **Cultural Revolution** (his parents had been sent far away for re-education), his mind was oriented towards feelings of loneliness, bitterness and humour, and he has travelled and wandered in many distant places of China. These feelings also stand as the main topics of his literary explorations. He lives at the edge of main and established streams. He wrote several short stories in the mid 1980s which gave him notoriety – the most well-known are collected in *Variations Without a Theme* (*Wu zhuti biancou*, 1985). These stories, which are considered to be characteristic of the new modernist current, express a quest for spatial and individual freedom, a taste for humour and fantasy, and an ability to picture common people in a vision which, however, emerges out of official schemes. Through an 'on the road' mood, individuality appears as a disintegrated entity in his writings. As a man who likes to travel in foreign countries as well as in his own, Xu Xing also explores popular culture. He has made some works for television and cinema, and a documentary film about an old woman painter in the economically poor and remote countryside of Shaanxi, where he lived for two years during the Cultural Revolution and to which he returned in 2002.

Further reading

Xu, Xing (1997). '*Variations Without a Theme' and Other Stories*. Trans. Maria Galikowski and Lin Min. Sydney: Wild Peony.

—— (1992). *Le Crabe à lunettes*. Trans. Sylvie Gentil. Paris: Éditions Julliard.

Lin, Min and Galikowski, Maria (1999). 'Absurdity, Senselessness, and Alienation: Xu Xing's Literary Reflections on the Contemporary Human Condition'. In *idem*, *The Search for Modernity: Chinese Intellectuals and Cultural Discourse in the Post-Mao Era*. New York: St Martin's Press, 103–22.

ANNIE CURIEN

Xu Ying

b. 1962, Hunan

Theatre librettist

Xu Ying is a prolific librettist, actor and director, whose work ranges from adaptations of classics to avant-garde productions. After studying *Huaguxi* (Flower Drum opera) in Changsha in his native Hunan, he studied at Beijing's Academy of Chinese Traditional Theatre. As a visiting lecturer at UCLA in 1998, he staged the **Wuju** (dance drama) *Ah Q*, co-written with choreographer Victoria Marks. Xu is currently resident playwright at the China National Opera and Dance Theatre Company in Beijing.

Xu brings out the human dimensions of quasi-mythical heroes: the military strategist Sun Wu in *Sun Wu, the Supreme Military Strategist* (*Bingsheng Sun Wu* 2002); the poet Li Bai in an opera of the same name (co-written with Diana Liao, with music composed by **Chen Yi**): and the heroine Hua Mulan, who joins the army as a man and falls in love, in *Magnolia Mulan* (co-written with Qiu Yupu, 2001). Xu often reinterprets traditional stories and characters. His bilingual opera, *Wenji: Eighteen Songs of a Nomad Flute* (music by **Lam Bun-ching**), departs from Chinese tradition in its depiction of the unresolved inner conflict over cultural identity of the exiled poetess Cai Wenji, while *Tea* (music by **Tan Dun**), an opera in progress, relocates the life of tea-master Lu Yu from the Song (960–1279) to the Tang dynasty (618–907) so as to emphasize the cross-cultural exchanges between China and Japan. Many of Xu's librettos for experimental artists, such as composers Chen Yi, Lam Bun-ching and Tan Dun, and choreographers Victoria Marks and Yin

Mei, are funded and produced outside of China. Xu, along with other playwrights, organized the first independent Beijing International Drama Festival in 2003.

ISABELLE DUCHESNE

Xu Zhen

b. 1977, Shanghai

Performance, video, installation artist

Xu Zhen graduated in Graphic Design at the Shanghai School of Arts and Crafts in 1996. Although he has only formally produced art for five years, Xu has attained a striking level of international success. Since 1998, he has been in seminal group exhibitions, including the now legendary 'Art for Sale (Supermarket)' at the Shanghai Square Shopping Centre (1999) and 'Fuck Off' (Buhezuo fangshi), a 'fringe' exhibition at the Shanghai Biennale (2000). In 2001, he was the youngest of the Chinese artists to participate in the 49th Venice Biennale with *Rainbow* (*Caihong*, 1998), a video showing a human back gradually reddening under the strain of heard but unseen slaps against the body's surface.

Using animal corpses and human flesh as artistic materials, nearly all of Xu's works deal with the body, its physicality – skin, nudity and desire, often revealing the extent of moral taboos still held with respect to distinctions between art and life, beauty and violence, private and public acts. In 1999, he produced *From Inside of the Body*, a three-monitor video installation showing, respectively, a man and woman sniffing themselves, and the same man and woman undressed sniffing each other. While social taboos in China rarely extend to using animals or human bodies in art, a practice now gaining currency among some experimental artists, the corporeal violence contained in Xu's works has not been without controversy. In his performance video, *I'm Not Doing Anything* (1999), the artist swings a dead cat against the ground for forty-five minutes. Xu currently collaborates with BizArt, an art centre in Shanghai, as art director, designer and events organizer.

Further reading

Dal Lago, Francesca (2002). 'The Fiction of Everyday Life: Video Art in the People's Republic of China'. *ART AsiaPacific* 27 (Summer).

Pederson, Amy (2002). 'Contemporary Art with Chinese Characteristics: Shen Fan, Ding Yi, and Xu Zhen'. *Yishu: Journal of Contemporary Chinese Art* 1.3 (Fall/Nov.): 27–43.

ALICE MING WAI JIM

Y

Yan Xin

b. 1949, Sichuan

Qigong master

Yan Xin is one of the best known contemporary Qigong masters. He promoted the practice of Qigong in China between 1986 and 1990. Yan Xin began to learn martial art techniques at the age of ten and between 1974 and 1979 he studied traditional Chinese medicine in college. Yan Xin began his career as a teacher, then worked as a doctor in Chongqing, Sichuan. In 1984, he was reported to be a 'miraculous Qigong doctor' by local media and caught the attention of the public. In 1986, Yan Xin's Qigong power was tested in a series of scientific experiments at several universities in Beijing. He was qualified by the government officials as a master of 'scientific Qigong', and became the first to launch 'qi-emitting conferences' (*daigong baogao*) in 1987. In one year, Yan Xin gave over two hundred of these conferences nationwide, which usually included a performance by Yan Xin of miraculous healing along with a collective trance. Since 1990, Yan Xin has been participating in Qigong research and promoting 'Yan-Xin Qigong' in North America. In September 1991, practitioners in the United States founded the International Yan-Xin Qigong Association, and are still organizing Qigong workshops across North America today.

See also: Qigong (history); Qigong (masters)

Further reading

International Yan Xin Qigong Association (1999). *Yan Xin Qigong Collectanea*. St-Bruno (Quebec): Les éditions lotus.
Tie, Cheng and Ming, Zhen (eds) (1988). *Guibao zhi guang: Yan Xin yü Qigong* [Light of Treasures: Yan Xin and Qigong]. Beijing: Gongren chubanshe.

MENG QING

Yang, Edward

(né Yang Dechang)

b. 1947, Shanghai

Film director

Yang Dechang moved to Taiwan two years after his birth, received a degree in engineering from Chiao-tung University twenty years later, and then left for the United States. He received an MA in computer science at the University of Florida in 1979 and briefly studied film at the University of Southern California. He worked as a computer specialist in Seattle before returning to Taiwan in 1981.

Yang contributed to the four-part film *In Our Time* (1982) which helped launch Taiwan's 'New Cinema' movement. *That Day on the Beach* (1983) and *Taipei Story* (1984) established Yang's cinematic focus on Taiwan's emerging urban modernity which stands in contrast to fellow-director **Hou Hsiao-hsien**'s emphasis on Taiwan's old and vanishing village culture. *The Terrorizer* (1986) confirmed Yang's stature as a complex and brilliant director interested in the psychological diversity of Taiwanese people coping with the transition from traditional to global values. Through the story of a female mystery author's writing block that is resolved only when fiction and fact become hopelessly entangled, Yang explores the roles of technology and art in isolating and terrorizing the urban individual. *Confucian Confusion* (1995) turned to cinematic density and Oscar Wilde-like rapid-fire humour to convey the chaos of a younger generation, for whom traditional loyalties and personal friendships are sabotaged by the pursuit of economic success. *Mahjong* (1996) continued this satirical critique. In the gently humourous *Yi Yi* (2000), Yang's first international success, he appeared more optimistic, juxtaposing two families in adjacent apartments, one fated for tragedy but the other held together after various personal experiments with extra-marital romance and religious retreats by a return to fundamental family values. Throughout his career, Yang's film art has sympathized neither with Confucian authority nor with modern materialism. It constructs neither an essentially Chinese nor a distinctly Taiwanese identity, but rather emphasizes the diversity of situations and personalities that constitute Taiwan's rapidly changing society.

See also: cinema in Taiwan; Wu Nien-chen

Further reading

Austerlitz, Saul (2002). 'Edward Yang'. *Senses of Cinema: Great Directors – A Critical Database.* Available at http://www.sensesofcinema.com/contents/directors/02/yang.html

Chiao, Peggy (1996). '*Mahjong*: Urban Travails'. *Cineyama* 33: 24–7.

Huang, Jianye (1995). *Yang Dechang dianying yanjiu – Taiwan xindianying de zhixing sibianjia* [Studies on the Films of Yang Dechang – A Critical Thinker in Taiwan's New Cinema]. Taipei: Yuanliu.

Li, David Leiwei (2003). '*Yi Yi*: Reflexions on Reflexive Modernity in Taiwan'. In Chris Berry (ed.), *Chinese Films in Focus: 25 New Takes*. London: BFI, 198–205.

Tam, Kwok-kan and Dissanayake, Wimal (1998). 'Edward Yang: Visions of Taibei and Cultural Modernity'. In *idem* (eds), *New Chinese Cinema*. Oxford: Oxford University Press.

JEROME SILBERGELD

Yang Fudong

b. 1971, Beijing

Video artist, filmmaker

Yang Fudong graduated from the **Central Academy of Fine Arts** in Beijing in 1995 (see **art academies**) and moved to Shanghai three years later to pursue his studies and interest in photography and film which, along with video and installation, have remained at the centre of his artistic endeavours. In 1997 he realized *An Estranged Paradise*, a 35 mm 76-minute film shot in black and white and ultimately presented at 'Documenta 11' in Kassel (2002). The piece tells the story of the frustration and restlessness undermining the life of a young Chinese man. Its flimsy narrative structure is constructed through intimate and censored views of events, involves leaps in time and the intrusion of alien elements, including reflections on boredom, melancholy and the search for peace, and combines classical stereotypes and role models with newly acquired images, like Western fashion statements, in a personal aesthetic language. In 2000 he took part in the controversial show 'Fuck Off' (*Bu hezuo fangshi*), held concurrently with the 3rd Shanghai Biennale, while *Tonight Moon* (2000) was featured at the Istanbul Biennale in 2001. In *City Lights* (2000), *Backyard* (2001) and *Flatter Flatter Jasmine Jasmine* (2002) he builds abstract imagery which suggest that the artist's main task is to achieve a transformation in the viewer's critical standpoint, creating an interaction between the urban environment and popular, romantic feelings. Yang's videos have been featured in several international shows: the 4th Shanghai Biennale (2002), the 50th Venice Biennale (2003) and 'Chinese Contemporary Photography from the Haudenschild Collection', sponsored by San Diego State University and the San Diego Museum of Art.

Further reading

(2000). *Useful Life/Youxiaoqi* (exhibition catalogue). Shanghai.

(2002). *China Art Now – Out of the Red* (exhibition catalogue). Milan: Marella Arte Contemporanea Gallery.

Kee, Joan (2002). 'Yang Fudong'. *Tema Celeste* 92 (July/August).

BEATRICE LEANZA

Yang Jiang

(née Yang Jikang)

b. 1911

Writer

Yang began writing familiar essays and fiction while in graduate school at Qinghua University, where she met and married **Qian Zhongshu**. She studied overseas in Europe, and the couple returned to China in 1938. During the Japanese occupation of Shanghai she contributed comedies and dramas to the lively theatre boom there: among them were *As You Desire* (*Chenxin ruyi*, 1944), *Cheat* (*Nongzhen cheng jia*, 1944) and *Windswept Blossoms* (*Fengxu*, 1945). In 1952 she joined the **Chinese Academy of Science** (later, the **Chinese Academy of Social Sciences**). Her selected short fiction was collected in *Inverted Images* (*Daoyingji*, 1981), her familiar essays in *Taking Tea* (*Jiangyin cha*, 1987) and her critical essays in *Spring Soil* (*Chunniji*, 1979). Yang's best-remembered fiction is her novel about the educated elite during the early years of Maoism, *Cleansing* (*Xizao*, 1988), while her best-remembered non-fiction work is her account of life during the Cultural Revolution, *Six Chapters on a Cadre School* (*Ganxiao liuji*, 1981). Her work is noted for its understatement and irony. Her studies of picaresque fiction resulted in translations of *Gils Blas*, *La Vida de Lazarillo de Tormes* and *Don Quixote*, which was presented as a state gift to Juan Carlos of Spain.

Further reading

Dooling, Amy (1994). 'In Search of Laughter: Yang Jiang's Feminist Comedy'. *Modern Chinese Literature* 8.12: 41–68.

Goldblatt, Howard (1980). 'The Cultural Revolution and Beyond: Yang Jiang's *Six Chapters from My Life Down Under*'. *Modern Chinese Literature* 6.2: 1–11.

Yang, Jiang (1989). *Lost in the Crowd: A Cultural Revolution Memoir*. Trans. Geremie Barmé. Melbourne: McPhee Gribble.

EDWARD GUNN

Yang Jiechang

b. 1956, Foshan, Guandong

Painter, multimedia installation artist

Yang Jiechang's oeuvre consists of a variety of artistic media: painting, collage, installation, site-specific works, performance and sculpture. For Yang painting is a way of contemplation, not a means of representation. The concepts inspiring his painting, such as repetition and the overlapping of images, re-occur in his work with other media, such as his multi-media installations *Zaizao Dong Cunrui* [Recreate Dong Cunrui, 1999–2002] and *I Saw It in the Sky* (2002). Yang was trained in the techniques of paper mounting, calligraphy and traditional Chinese painting at the Fine Arts Academy Guangzhou (1978–82), where he taught until 1988. Living in Paris and Heidelberg since 1989, he has participated in numerous international exhibitions. Together with **Gu Dexin** and **Huang Yongping**, he was one of the Chinese artists participating in the exhibition 'Magiciens de la terre' at the Centre Pompidou in Paris (1989). Other exhibitions include 'Chine demain pour hier' (France 1990), 'Silent Energy' (MoMA Oxford, 1993), 'Shenzhen International Ink Biennial' (1998, 2000, 2002), 'Pause – Gwanju Biennial 2002' (Korea) and 'Zone of Urgency – Venice Biennial 2003'. In Yang's work – the *One Hundred Layers of Ink* (*Qianceng mo*) series or *Eye of the Storm*, (2000), for example – Chinese tradition and contemporary art form a stirring blend. One of his main concerns is to find ways of implanting Chinese traditional painting, aesthetics and thought into a contemporary context. Daoist thought, post-structuralist strategies and an iconoclast attitude, which Yang inherited from his time as a Red Guard, are important vehicles used by the artist to attempt such integration.

Further reading

Hou, Hanru (1999). 'Malpositioning'. In *Yang Jiechang – Dong Cunrui*. Taipei: Cherngpiin Gallery.

Köppel-Yang, Martina (2002). '*Zaofan Youli*/Revolt is Reasonable: Remanifestations of the Cultural Revolution in Chinese Contemporary Art of the 1980s and 1990s'. *Yishu: Journal of Contemporary Chinese Art* 1.2 (Summer/August): 66–75.

MARTINA KÖPPEL-YANG

Yang Lian

b. 1955, Switzerland

Poet

Yang Lian was the son of a diplomat and grew up in Beijing. He began to write poetry in the 1970s as an 'educated youth' in the countryside. On his return to the capital, he co-founded – with **Bei Dao**, Mang Ke and others – the influential literary magazine *Today* (*Jintian*). As a result of the 'cleansing spiritual pollution' campaign in 1983, his poems were banned in China. In 1989, while visiting New Zealand, Yang Lian received the news of the 4 June Massacre. Sad and furious, he expressed his protest by organizing a memorial for the dead of Tiananmen; he then claimed himself a 'Chinese poet in exile'. After sojourns in Australia, Germany and the United States, he settled in London.

One of the most prolific and innovative of contemporary Chinese poets, Yang Lian has been widely hailed in Europe and America as a 'highly individual voice' in world literature. He has published seven books of poetry and two of essays; his works have been translated into many languages. Haunted by the traumatic experiences in his past, Yang Lian often deals with themes of death and inner darkness; his poetry is saturated with horrible images and disturbing voices. The enchanting, often eerie imagination evidenced in his works is embedded in a humanitarian concern for the everyday desires of the common people. In search for new form, Yang Lian experiments with style, and has self-consciously expanded the aesthetic territory of Chinese poetic language. His highly modernistic style is sometimes reminiscent of Western masters such as Yeats, Pound or Eliot, but he has also mined the spiritual sources of the Chinese cultural tradition, as shown by his book-length poem entitled *Yi*, which was inspired by **Yijing** [Book of Changes]. In his 1999 collection, *Where the Sea Stands Still*, Yang Lian presents a myriad of poetic expression in a style at once serene and complex. This collection won a British book award in the same year.

Further reading

Cayley, John (2002). 'John Cayley with Yang Lian'. *positions: east asia cultures critique* 10.3: 773–84.

Yang, Lian (1999) *Where the Sea Stands Still: New Poems*. Trans. Brian Holton. Newcastle upon Tyne: Bloodaxe Books.

—— (2002). *Notes of a Blissful Ghost*. Trans. Brian Holton. Hong Kong: Renditions [anthology].

CHEN JIANHUA

Yang Liqing

b. 1942, Sichuan

Composer, pianist, music theorist

In 1970, Yang received his BA degree from Shenyang Conservatory of Music, where he was appointed Assistant Professor after graduation. In 1978 he went on to study composition at the Shanghai Conservatory of Music and earned his MA degree in 1980. Yang then went to Hanover, West Germany, to study composition with Alfred Koerppen at the Hochschule für Musik und Theater and to study piano with Kurt Bauer at the Hochschule für Musik. In 1983 he received a 'Solistenklasse' diploma and a 'Ausbildungsklasse' diploma for composition and piano, respectively. He returned to China in the same year and has taught composition at the Shanghai Conservatory of Music ever since.

Viewed as an expert in Western contemporary music, Yang made his unique contribution by disseminating modern Western composition and its techniques to Chinese composers in the 1980s. His lectures on the music of such composers as Ligeti, Rzewski and Rochberg were especially influential among composition students. Yang is one of the leading theorists in China specializing in instrumentation and orchestration. His scholarly work includes *The Compositional Techniques of Olivier Messiaen* and two influential essays, 'Style Evolution in Orchestration' and 'On Neo-Romanticism in Recent European Music'. Among his important compositions are a symphonic ballade for **pipa** and large orchestra, *Grievances at Wujiang*, the quintet *Si*, and a vocal work entitled *Four Poems from Tang Dynasty*. Yang has been the president of the Shanghai Conservatory of Music since 2000.

JIN PING

Yang Yi

b. 1969, Wengcheng, Guangdong

Folksinger

Acclaimed by some media as the 'Chinese Bob Dylan' or 'minstrel in quasi-capitalist China', Yang Yi is a Beijing-based folksinger. Having quit high school at age sixteen, he has been trying to live outside the institutional system of Chinese society. He first attempted various jobs, such as electronics repairman, graphic designer and bar singer, before being inspired by an American who introduced him to Bob Dylan and the American Folksong Movement in 1992. Bored by the over-commercialized life in Guangzhou, he then chose a life on the road, singing periodically outside the National Art Gallery in Beijing. Since 1993, he has also begun roving and collecting folksongs in the Chinese hinterland, especially in northern Shaanxi province, and writes songs about the life of the 'floating population', in which he includes himself.

Technically and spiritually, Yang draws on the heritage of both the American folksong revival and traditional Chinese folksong. To the accompaniment of a guitar and a harmonica attached to his head, he sings about the daily life and concerns of China's common people: a roast sweet-potato vendor who tries to avoid policemen and taxmen, migrant workers looking for jobs everywhere, personal memories of life in a small Hakka town, and so forth. He also sings folksongs collected from Shaanxi in the local style. Having attracted

extremely diverse audiences, Yang has nevertheless refused to associate with any established record company, maintaining his independence. Instead, in 2000, he personally produced his first CD, *Neibu cankao (For Internal Reference Only*; also called *Minstrel in Tune with Life*), whose limited copies were sold mainly on the spot during street performances. Yang Yi has been invited to perform at a folk music festival in Frankfurt, Germany, and performed on college campuses in Beijing and Shanghai in 2001.

Further reading

Shi, Anbin (2003). 'Rock-and-Roll on the Road of a Post-Socialist "Long March": A "Chinese Bob Dylan" and His Quest for a New Socio-Cultural Identity'. In *idem*, *A Comparative Approach to Redefining Chinese-ness in the Era of Globalization*. Lewiston: Mellen Press, 79–128.

BAO YING

Yang Zhengzhong

b. 1968, Hangzhou

Video and installation artist

Yang graduated from the Fashion Design Department of the Zhejiang Institute of Silk Textiles in 1990. He continued his studies in oil painting at the China Academy of Fine Arts in Hangzhou (see **art academies**). Despite a traditional training, he soon began experimenting with both performance (*Happy Birthday* and *Christmas Gift*, 1994) and video art (*Shower* and *45° as a Reason*, 1995). Ever since, he has focused on the production of video installations that examine ordinary subjects, present extraordinary situations and evoke the puzzling anxiety and paradoxical impressions of the inhabitants of modern urban spaces. In such a mode is *Fish Tank* (1996), in which the video image of a large mouth is shown underwater in a fish tank, with a recorded voice obsessively repeating 'we are not fish'. Yang's video assemblages highlight the whimsical effects produced by the accurate coordination of sound and image, where repetition becomes a kind of expressive power. Such is the case in *I Will Die* (2000) and *922 Rice Corns* (2002), where a digital counter synchronized with male and female voices counts the number of rice grains greedily pecked by a hen and a cock. *Let's Puff* (2002) was presented at the 50th Venice Biennale (2003) and the 4th Shanghai Biennale (2002*)*. This video installation consists of two facing projections in which a girl on one screen energetically blows air out of her chest and seemingly affects the movement of an urban crowd projected on the other screen. Yang's work has been featured in 'Art for Sale' in Shanghai (1999), 'Living in Time' at the Hamburger Bahnhof in Berlin (2001), and the 1st Guangzhou Triennial (2002).

Further reading

Chen, Xiaoyun (2001). 'Artist of the Week: Chen Xiaoyun interviews Yang Zhengzhong'. *Chinese Type-Contemporary Art Online Magazine* 4.3.

Dal Lago, Francesca (2000). 'The Fiction of Everyday Life: Video Art in the People's Republic of China'. *ART AsiaPacific* 27 (Summer): 52–7.

Smith, Karen (1996). 'Notes on China's Video Installation Art'. *Asia-Pacific Sculpture News* 2.4 (Autumn): 19–21.

BEATRICE LEANZA

Yangcheng Evening News

The *Yangcheng Evening News* is probably China's best-known local evening newspaper with a nationwide distribution. Produced in Guangzhou as the flagship newspaper of the Yangcheng Evening News Group, the paper has had a long-standing reputation for being relatively critical and independent-minded, offering lively news coverage of issues close to people's everyday lives. Although it is not an official party organ, it is nonetheless subject to careful Party supervision under the Guangzhou city Party Propaganda Bureau because of its large circulation and popularity.

One of several evening newspapers founded by the Party in the late 1950s and early 1960s, the paper was launched on 1 October, 1956 and was specifically intended to offer lighter news coverage than the heavily political morning dailies. The *Yangcheng Evening News* was closed down during the Cultural Revolution period, but reopened in 1980 with a renewed commitment to social news reporting. Circulation of the newspaper in 2000 reached approximately 1.2 million nationwide, putting it among the country's leading titles, although the majority of papers are still sold in Guangdong province. The *Yangcheng Evening News* has been a commercial success in the post-Mao reform period and has expanded its operations, establishing the Yangcheng Evening News Group, home to five other daily and weekly titles, a book-publishing house, and a number of other business interests.

See also: evening newspapers and weekend editions; journalism; newspapers; state control of media

KEVIN LATHAM

Yao, culture of

With a population of over 2.2 million, the Yao live in mountainous villages scattered over 130 counties in the Guangxi Autonomous Region and the provinces of Hunan, Yunnan, Guangdong, Guizhou and Jiangxi. Most are farmers, but some manage forests. There are many small- and medium-sized factories in their areas, making farm machines, chemicals and cement, and processing timber. Half of the Yao speak the Yao language, while the rest speak the languages of the Miao, Dong, Zhuang or **Han** Chinese. They cherish a magnificent oral literature, and singing is an indispensable part of their life. During the spring ploughing or when people open up wasteland or engage in any form of communal work, one or two selected persons will stand aside, beat their drums and sing. Young people often sing in antiphonal tones through the night. Some folksongs are beautiful love songs, others recount Yao history, legends about the creation of the world, and ask questions of each other or tell humourous stories. The Yao waist-drum dance is frequently performed in China and abroad, while 'The Yao Dance' (*Yaozu wuqu*) has long been part of the repertory of many orchestras in China. The largest Yao festival is the King Pan Festival on 16 October, during which they worship their king and ancestors with long drums and sing for three days in celebration of the birth of their king. Their religion is heavily influenced by Daoism.

See also: autonomous regions, prefectures, counties and banners; Daoism among minority nationalities

Further reading

Litzinger, Ralph A. (2000). *Other Chinas: The Yao and the Politics of National Belonging.* Durham: Duke University Press.

HELEN XIAOYAN WU

Yaoshi-Ziyue

Rock band

The black comedian of Chinese rock music is Qiu Ye (b.1966), leader of the Beijing art rock ensemble Yaoshi-Ziyue (English name: You.Me.It.). Originally founded as Ziyue (The Master Says, a.k.a. Sperm & Egg) the band began playing Beijing bars in 1996 and developed a reputation for high-calibre musicianship in a scene essentially devoid of musical technique. Ziyue were quickly discovered by Chinese rock legend **Cui Jian**, who produced and released their first record, *Volume I*, in 1997. The association with Cui Jian brought the band immediate attention, and their debut record was hailed by the Chinese media as a major work. However, a misunderstanding with Cui Jian's publishing company in 1999 led Ziyue to re-form under the name Yaoshi (translation: 'a transcendent explanation from the basic units of reality'). By 2002 the dispute was finally resolved, and a second record, *Volume II*, was released under the hybrid moniker Yaoshi-Ziyue. The band has long since stepped out from under the shadow of its former mentor and is well established as a top act in Beijing nightclubs. Yaoshi-Ziyue's songs run the gamut from funk comic narrations of daily life to melancholic crooning about lost love and youth. Between songs, as Qiu Ye banters with the audience in the vernacular Beijing dialect, the band's live set takes on the tone of a Vegas lounge act, betraying the irony and emotion at the heart of Yaoshi-Ziyue's iconoclastic musings. In 2003 the band reports

playing more shows in the provinces and shaking its reputation as a strictly Beijing phenomenon. However, Yaoshi-Ziyue remains a central fixture of the Beijing live-music scene.

See also: rock music, rock bands

Further reading

http://www.yaoshiziyue.com

MATTHEW CLARK

Yau Ching

b. 1966, Hong Kong

Video/filmmaker, writer, educator, activist

An active, enthusiastic, articulate female voice, Yau Ching's self-chosen task is to express the plight of the queer subject in the post-colonial, multi-cultural landscape of Hong Kong and the Chinese diaspora. Raised in Hong Kong, where she is a noted published author, Yau started working in video collaboratively, then made *Inscape* (*Neijing*, 1989). From 1990 to 1999, she was studying, teaching and producing work in the United States and Great Britain. During that time, she worked with the Gay Men Health Crisis Center and Dyke TV in New York, made several videotapes and short films dealing with the issues of immigration, displacement and identity – *Flow* (*Liu*, 1993) and *Diasporama: Dead Air* (*Ling Qi Lu Zao Zhi Er Zai Tong*, 1997) – and wrote a PhD dissertation on the work of legendary Hong Kong female filmmaker Tang Shu Shuen.

Back in Hong Kong, she started teaching at Hong Kong Polytechnic University, published three books, including a collection of poetry, *The Impossible Home* (*Bukeneng di jia*, 2001), and resumed making queer media work, such as the short video *Suet Sin's Sisters* (*Bai Xuexian de meimei*, 1999), about the 'invisible' queer female tradition in Hong Kong. In 2002, she completed her first feature film, *Ho Yuk – Let's Love Hong Kong* (*Hao Yu*), shot in DV, guerilla-style (without permit) in real locations and self-described as 'the first movie made in Hong Kong by a woman about women in love with each other' (production notes).

Further reading

Yau, C (ed.) (2002). *Ho Yuk – Let's Love Hong Kong – Script and Critical Essays (Hao Yu – Ju Ben Ji Ping Luen Ji)*. Hong Kong: Youth Literary Bookstore.

BÉRÉNICE REYNAUD

Ye Xiaogang

b. 1955, Shanghai

Composer

Ye Xiaogang is one of the most active and best-known composers in China. He was admitted to the Central Conservatory of Music in 1978, where he studied composition with Du Mingxin. Ye joined the Central Conservatory's composition faculty in 1983. In 1985, Ye became one of the first 'New Wave' composers to give concerts in Beijing. The programme included *Horizon (Dipingxiang)*, scored for soprano, baritone and orchestra, among others of his works. This piece became one of the representative works of the New Wave Music.

Ye came to the United States in 1987 to pursue a master's degree at the Eastman School of Music, where his teachers included Samuel Adler and Joseph Schwantner. His important works while in the United States include *The Last Paradise*, *The Winter* and *The Silence of Sakyamuni*, which won the 'first-composition competition' prize in Taiwan in 1992. In 1994, Ye returned to China to continue his teaching at the Central Conservatory. He received a number of high-profile commissions from the Chinese government, including the orchestral work *The Story of Spring*, the ballet *The Story of Shenzhen*, and most notably the *Great Wall Symphony*, written for voice, piano, Chinese instruments and orchestra. Ye is the leading advocate for the creation of contemporary music ensembles in China, and the founder of Ensemble Eclipse. He has served as Artistic Director of the China Contemporary Music Forum, an international modern music festival in Shanghai.

See also: Third Generation (composers)

JIN PING

Ye Zhaoyan

b. 1957, Nanjing

Writer

Ye Zhaoyan came to prominence on the PRC literary scene in the early 1980s along with **Mo Yan**, **Su Tong** and **Wang Anyi**. Hailing from a literary family that includes his father, Ye Zicheng, a noted writer, and his grandfather, Ye Shengtao, a famed educator and writer of the Republican period, Ye Zhaoyan began writing in the late 1970s. He earned his MA from **Nanjing University** in 1986. After graduation, Ye worked as an editor for the Jiangsu Arts and Literature Publishing House. In 1991, he left the publishing world to pursue writing full-time and has since produced an astounding twenty-eight books, including a seven-volume set of collected works.

An extremely versatile writer, Ye Zhaoyan has attempted endless narrative and literary experiments in his body of work, which ranges from historical fiction to the Mandarin Duck and Butterfly tradition (see **Butterfly literature**) and from **detective fiction** to the avant-garde. His major works include *Evening Moor on the Qinhuai (Yebo Qinhuai)*, a series of four novellas set in Republican-era Nanjing; *Flower Demon (Huasha)*, a fascinating story about a Western missionary in China; and *Nanjing 1937: A Love Story (Yijiusanqinian de aiqing)*, a historical novel which juxtaposes the fall of the ancient capital with a love story that is as unlikely as it is epic. His novel *The Flower's Shadow (Huaying*, 1994), a decadent tale of incest and addiction, was the basis for **Chen Kaige**'s film *Temptress Moon (Fengyue)*.

MICHAEL BERRY

Yearnings, Aspirations

[Kewang, 1989]

Television serial

Kewang [Yearnings] is a fifty-episode TV series produced in 1989. Directed by Lu Xiaowei and adapted by Ling Xiaoming from **Wang Shuo**'s original story, it was the first soap opera in Chinese TV history, apparently a response to the Brazilian soap operas then dominating the TV screens. Nevertheless, it was very much a product of its time. In that 'innocent' era when people yearned for love and sincerity, the theme of *Kewang* found its echo in the hearts of millions. As China had just survived the ten-year **Cultural Revolution** that ruined many lives, stories of sufferings and forbearance easily captivated sympathetic viewers. *Kewang* thus made history by 'emptying the streets' during its show time.

The story is set in Beijing from the 1960s through the 1980s. Huifang, a beautiful and kindhearted young worker, adopts an abandoned girl, Xiaofang, and marries a persecuted college student, Husheng. Her secret admirer, Dacheng, has had to marry someone else. Rehabilitated after the Cultural Revolution, Husheng resumes his relations with his college sweetheart. Divorced, Huifang continues her motherly care for Xiaofang. Dacheng's concern for Huifang makes his wife jealous, setting a chain of events which cause Huifang to be paralysed in a car accident. Learning that Xiaofang was actually his own niece, Husheng wants to be reconciled with Huifang. But she refuses, and so on and so forth. The leading actress Kai Li won the top prize at the Third Top Ten Actors Awards for her excellent performance as 'the perfect wife'. *Kewang* won the Sixth Feitian Award and the First Prize for the Ninth 'Golden Eagle Award'.

Further reading

Keane, Michael (2001). 'Television Drama in China: Engineering Souls for the Market'. In Richard King and Tim Craig (eds), *Global Goes Local: Popular Culture in Asia*. Vancouver: University of British Columbia Press, 176–202.

Lu, Sheldon (2002). 'Soap Opera in China: The Transnational Politics of Visuality, Sexuality, and Masculinity'. In *idem, China, Transnational Visuality, Global Postmodernity*. Stanford: Stanford University Press, 213–38.

Rofel, Lisa (1994). 'Yearnings: Televisual Love and Melodramatic Politics in China'. *American Ethnologist* 21.4: 700–22.

Zha, Jianying (1995). *China Pop: How Soap Operas, Tabloids, and Bestsellers are Transforming a Culture*. New York: The New Press.

HU MINGRONG

Yellow Earth

[Huang tudi, 1984]

Film

Yellow Earth, produced by the **Xi'an Film Studio**, is one of China's most famous films. Directed by **Chen Kaige** with **Zhang Yimou** as cinematographer, it launched China's 'Fifth Generation' cinema onto the global scene. The film's plot is a parody of revolutionary stories. A handsome Party cadre, Gu Qing, arrives in an impoverished Shaanxi region during the Anti-Japanese War to collect folksongs. He stays with a peasant family: father, daughter (Cuiqiao) and son (Hanhan). Cuiqiao and Hanhan are romanced by Gu's revolutionary message. However, Cuiqiao drowns crossing the river to Yan'an and the peasants return to age-old rituals against drought and famine. The story therefore subverts the Yan'an myth of the Communist Party as the people's saviour.

The film is famous for its ravishing cinematography. Panoramic shots of the vast yellow earth, of the Yellow River, and of the empty sky at day and night, re-envision the cradle of Chinese civilization, whether ancient or revolutionary. *Yellow Earth* returns a concealed Daoist yin–yang iconography as integral to the symbolic world of modern China. In this sense, *Huang tudi* belongs to the **Root-seeking school** in 1980s fiction and film.

Further reading

Berry, Chris and Farquhar, Mary Ann (1994). 'Post-Socialist Strategies: An Analysis of *Yellow Earth* and *Black Cannon Incident*'. In Kinda Erlich and David Desser (eds), *Cinematic Landscapes: Observations on the Visual Arts and Cinema of China and Japan*. Austin: University of Texas, 81–116.

Leung, Helen Hok-Sze (2003). '*Yellow Earth*: Hesitant Apprenticeship and Bitter Agency'. In Chris Berry (ed.), *Chinese Films in Focus: 25 New Takes*. London: BFI, 191–7.

McDougall, Bonnie S., (1991). *The Yellow Earth: A Film by Chen Kaige, with a Complete Translation of the Filmscript*. Hong Kong: Chinese University Press.

Yingjin, Zhang and Zhiwei, Xiao and Xiao Zhiwei Zhang, Yingjin (eds) (1998). *Encyclopaedia of Chinese Film*. London and New York, Routledge, 382.

MARY FARQUHAR

Yeoh, Michelle

(née Yeoh Chu-kheng; Yeung Chi-king; Yang Ziqiong)

b. 6 August 1962, Ipoh, Perak, Malaysia

Film actress

Michelle Yeoh (Michelle Khan in her first films), grew up in Malaysia speaking English and Malay; she later learned Cantonese and some Mandarin, but does not read Chinese. Yeoh studied dance and drama in college in England, became Miss Malaysia in 1983, and made her first movie in 1984. Her second, *Yes, Madam!* (*Huangjia shijie*, 1985), a policewoman-gangster picture, amplified Yeoh's celebrity and inspired other Hong Kong action movies starring women. Yeoh made four more films, married, retired, divorced, and then came back to co-star alongside Jackie **Chan** in *Supercop: Police Story III* (*Jingcha gushi III: Chaoji jingcha*, 1992). This was directed by Stanley Tong, the former stuntman who helped Yeoh make her initial transition from dance to chop socky (Yeoh does her own impressive stunts). The imaginary heroines Yeoh has created include an invisible woman in *Heroic Trio* (*Dongfang sanxia*, 1992), a Ming-dynasty martial artist in *Wing Chun* (*Yongchun*, 1994) and the 'Bond girl' Wai Lin in *Tomorrow Never Dies* (1997). She played Song Ailing in *The Soong Sisters* (*Songjia huangchao*, 1997). In *Wing Chun* and *Crouching Tiger, Hidden Dragon* (*Wohu canglong*, 2000), Yeoh is teamed with Cheng Pei Pei (Zheng Peipei), one of Hong Kong's first fighting females of film. In the latter, Yeoh plays the dignified, determined swordswoman Yu Shu Lien (Yu Xiulian), who comes across as both traditionally female and anachronistically feminist. In March 2003, Yeoh was reportedly preparing for the role of Hua Mulan, the most famous woman warrior of them all.

Further reading

Lu, Sheldon H. and Chieko, Anne T. (2002). 'The Heroic Trio: Anita Mui, Maggie Cheung, Michelle Yeoh – Self-Reflexivity and the Globalization of the Hong Kong Action Heroine'. In Sheldon Lu (ed.), *China, Transnational Visuality, Global Postmodernity*. Stanford: Stanford University Press, 122–38.

Williams, Tony (2001). 'Michelle Yeoh: Under Western Eyes'. *Asian Cinema* 12.2 (Fall/Winter): 119–31.

THOMAS MORAN

Yi, culture of

The Yi total nearly 7 million people who live mainly in Yunnan, Sichuan and Guizhou provinces; some are in Guangxi. Other than farming, animal rearing is also important. They have made great achievements in agriculture, astronomy, the calendar, meteorology and medicine, e.g. the renowned 'Yunnan White Medicine', which stops bleeding and reduces inflammation, is produced according to an ancient Yi recipe. Among the Yi living in Liangshan prefecture, Sichuan, the old custom of 'snatching the bride' is still common. Before a wedding, the bridegroom's villagers go to meet the bride. The bride's family members pour water on them to prevent them from entering, but the men press on. Once they have touched her clothes, her family cannot resist any more. The bride, nonetheless, starts 'wailing' to show her reluctance to leave her parents. The Yi have their own spoken and written languages, and have produced important historical and literary works, e.g. the epic *Ashima* is popular in Yunnan and known all over China thanks to the film of the same name. The Torch Festival is the most widespread holiday, usually on 24 or 25 June, celebrated with song and dance, horse-racing and wrestling competitions. Songs such as 'Guest from Afar, Please Stay' and 'Axi Dancing under the Moon' are known and loved by all Chinese. In October 2002, the expansion of the Liangshan Slave Society Museum was completed, exhibiting over 2,000 cultural relics and artifacts.

Further reading

Harrell, Steven (1990). 'Ethnicity, Local Interests, and the State: Yi Communities in Southwest China'. *Comparative Studies in Society and History* 32.3 (July): 515–48.

—— (1995). 'A History of the History of the Yi'. In *idem* (ed.), *Cultural Encounters on China's Ethnic Frontiers*. Seattle: University of Washington Press, 63–91.

Teng, Xing (2001). *Wenhua Bianqian yü Shuangyu Jiaoyu: Liangshan Yizu Shequ Jiaoyu Renleixue de Tianye Gongguo yü Wenben Zhuanshu* [Cultural Change and Bilingual Education: Field Work and Text Writing on Anthropology of Education in the Yi Ethnic Community in Liangshan]. Beijing: Education and Science Press.

Yagare,Wei Pengfei, Qi, Chonghai *et al.* (2000). *One Country Many Peoples: 56 Nationalities of China* (with VCDs, bilingual). Beijing: Minzu chubanshe.

HELEN XIAOYAN WU

Yiguan Dao

Sectarian religion

The Yiguan Dao (Way of Unity) is a popular sect, which was founded in Shandong province in the 1920s by Zhang Tianran (Zhang Guangbi, 1889–1947). While Zhang gave it a new shape and organizational structure, the Yiguan Dao is rooted in an older sectarian tradition, active throughout the Ming and Qing dynasties. Its key teachings include the belief in an imminent apocalypse and the advent of a saviour who would open up a path of salvation in this final world period. Zhang Tianran was believed to be an incarnation of the Living Buddha Jigong, who had been dispatched by the cosmic goddess (the Eternal Mother – Wuji Laomu) to transmit the Dao to human beings, who are none other than her lost and confused children. All who received the Dao in the Yiguan Dao initiation ritual would count among the saved and be assured to return to the Mother's paradise, from which they had once fallen due to their attachments to the illusory world of samsara.

In the midst of the political unrest and military conflict of the Republican period, this eschatology found an echo in the religious needs of many. As a result, the sect spread rapidly across China after it had moved its centre of activity to Tianjin in 1935. Several officials of the Japanese-controlled Northern puppet government joined the sect and it thus came to flourish in particular in regions of China that were under Japanese control. These political ties caused problems for the movement after 1945, as it came under pressure from both the Nationalists and the Communists. After Zhang's death in 1947, the sect effectively split up into a number of separate branches (conventionally said to be eighteen) that continued to develop more or less independently. Thus, there exists today no central leadership for the sect, which has become a 'family' of closely related yet autonomous branch associations. This decentralized structure gave it a certain amount of protection under adverse political conditions, but ultimately could not shield it against the PRC government's determined opposition. In 1951 a bloody campaign was conducted against the sect, in the course of which many of its leading functionaries were executed. By the end of the decade, the Yiguan Dao had ceased to exist on the Chinese mainland.

Some leaders had fled the mainland and established new bases in Hong Kong and Taiwan. While the sect was allowed to operate without much government interference in the British colony, it suffered persecution in KMT-controlled Taiwan, until its proscription was formally lifted in 1987. In 1988 an umbrella organization was established in Taipei (Zhonghua minguo Yiguan Dao zonghui), which consists of representatives of the major branches. In addition, the sect continues to maintain a strong presence in Hong Kong even after the colony's return to China, and it is proselytizing actively and successfully among overseas Chinese communities in Southeast Asia, Australia, North America and Europe. In the PRC the Yiguan Dao remains illegal, but since the 1980s it has gradually been re-establishing itself as an underground movement through the efforts of missionaries from outside the mainland and in particular from Taiwan. In the face of widespread government crackdowns on unauthorized religious activities, these missionary endeavours are conducted in great secrecy and it is not clear how large a following the sect has regained in the PRC.

See also: religion, recent history of; sectarian religion

Further reading

Bosco, Joseph (1994). 'Yiguan Dao: "Heterodoxy" and Popular Religion in Taiwan'. In Murray A.

Rubinstein (ed.), *The Other Taiwan: 1945 to the Present*. Armonk, New York: M. E. Sharpe, 423–44.

Clart, Philip (2000). 'Opening the Wilderness for the Way of Heaven: A Chinese New Religion in the Greater Vancouver Area'. *Journal of Chinese Religions* 28: 127–44.

DuBois, Thomas (2001). 'The Sacred World of Cang County: Religious Belief, Organization and Practice in Rural North China During the Late Nineteenth and Twentieth Centuries', PhD dissertation, University of California, Los Angeles, ch. 8.

Jordan, David K. and Overmyer, Daniel L. (1986). *The Flying Phoenix: Aspects of Chinese Sectarianism in Taiwan*. Princeton: Princeton University Press.

Skoggard, Ian A. (1996). 'Inscribing Capitalism. Belief and Ritual in a New Taiwanese Religion'. In Gösta Arvastson and Mats Lindqvist (eds), *The Story of Progress*. Uppsala: Acta Universitatis Upsaliensis. (Studia Ethnologica Upsaliensia 17), 13–26.

Soo, Khin Wah (1997). 'A Study of the Yiguan Dao (Unity Sect) and Its Development in Peninsular Malaysia'. PhD dissertation, University of British Columbia.

PHILIP CLART

Yijing

[Classic of Changes]

For more than two thousand years the *Yijing* or *Classic of Changes* (also transliterated *I Ching* and often known as *Book of Changes*) was viewed as the 'first of the [Chinese] Classics', a divination manual and repository of abstruse wisdom that had a profound effect on virtually every aspect of traditional Chinese culture – from language, philosophy, religion, art and literature to politics, social life, mathematics, science and medicine. In the twentieth century, however, the *Changes* came to be stigmatized as a 'feudal' relic that reflected 'superstitious' practices and reflected a discredited ideology (Confucianism). This was especially true after the Chinese Communists came to power in 1949.

But from 1978 onward, thanks to the 'Open Policy' inaugurated in that year, the *Yijing* has made a remarkable comeback. 'Traditional' beliefs and practices are no longer stigmatized in the way that they had been prior to Mao Zedong's death, and China's ongoing 'spiritual crisis' (*jingshen weiji*) has prompted many Chinese to look for intellectual stimulation, spiritual inspiration or divinatory guidance in the *Yijing*.

Meanwhile, the *Changes* emerged as an object of intense scholarly interest. An historic 1984 conference in Wuhan, for example, produced 120 papers and five specialized volumes, generating much enthusiasm and material for further research by Chinese and foreign scholars alike. Even the *People's Daily* got into the act, publishing three successive articles (18, 19 and 21 November, 1988) designed to introduce readers to new developments in *Yijing* research. A year later, Professor Liu Zheng, writing in the journal *Zhexue yanjiu* [Philosophical Research], pointed out that 'Within the last decade, our country's publishers, large and small, have published and republished thirty to forty works on the study of the *Yijing*, and two to three hundred articles on the subject have ... [appeared] in our scholarly journals.' Such articles now number in the thousands.

One prominent theme in Chinese scholarship during the 1980s and 1990s was the idea that the *Changes* was a 'scientific' document, which anticipated many modern developments in mathematics, physics, biology and computer theory. Feng Youlan, for example, maintained that the *Yijing* contained an incipient 'algebra of the universe'; and Xie Qiucheng went so far as to claim that the hexagrams of the classic were originally designed as a high efficiency information transfer system analogous to contemporary computer coding based on optimal units of two (the number of basic trigrams in each hexagram) and three (the number of lines in each trigram). Tang Mingbang, drawing on the writings of Xie and other contemporary Chinese scholars, asserted that the forms of atomic structure in nuclear physics, the genetic code in molecular biology, the eight-tier matrix in linear algebra, all seem to be related to the logic of the *Yijing*. These arguments seem to be motivated at least in part by Chinese national pride.

Further reading

Liu, Zheng (1993). 'The Dilemma Facing Contemporary Research in the *I-ching*'. *Chinese Studies in Philosophy* 24.4 (Summer).

Smith, Richard J. (1998). 'The Place of the *Yijing* (Classic of Changes) in World Culture: Some Historical and Contemporary Perspectives'. *Journal of Chinese Philosophy* (Winter): 391–422

Tang, Mingbang (1987). 'Recent Developments in Studies of the *Book of Changes*'. *Chinese Studies in Philosophy* (Fall): 46–63.

RICHARD J. SMITH

expunge personal guilt and pursue legal justice in a manner more Western than traditionally Chinese. Shot through with Oedipal tensions, the film explored symbolically the conflicting ties between the Chinese fatherland and the British heritage that still threaten to tear Hong Kong apart.

Further reading

Richie, Donald (1996). '*The Day the Sun Turned Cold*: Some Aspects of Yim Ho's Film'. *Cineyama* 31: 16–18.

JEROME SILBERGELD

Yim Ho

b. 1952, Hong Kong

Film director

Yim Ho was an early contributor to the 'New Wave' movement in Hong Kong cinema. After studying at the London Film School (1973–5), he worked in Hong Kong television, then entered film in 1978. A stylistic innovator and thoroughly conversant with Western film and culture, Yim's films emphasize social realism, psychological drama and occasional sardonic humour. They also take a strong thematic interest in Hong Kong's position with respect to Chinese culture, PRC politics and parallels with Taiwan.

Yim's second film, *The Happening* (1980), dealt with the explosive violence of Hong Kong's alienated youth in a shocking manner reminiscent of America's contemplation of juvenile delinquency in the 1950s. In *King of Chess* (1992), co-directed with **Tsui Hark**, Yim cross-cut scenes of China plunging frighteningly backwards during the Cultural Revolution while Taiwan raced into an equally frightening cyber-modernity. In his most sophisticated film, *The Day the Sun Turned Cold* (1995), awarded Best Film and Director at the Tokyo Film Festival, Yim explored an authentic Chinese crime story in which a young man accused his mother of poisoning his father ten years earlier. Less important than whether this crime really happened was the question of why anyone Chinese would cause their family such public shame in order to

Yin Ji'nan

b. 1958

Art historian, critic and curator

Yin Ji'nan graduated from the History Department of Beijing University with a BA in Archaeology in 1982. In 1987, he earned an MA from the Art History Department at the **Central Academy of Fine Arts**, where he studied Classical Painting and Calligraphy Authentication. In 1991, he curated the exhibition 'New Generation' at the China History Museum. In 1993, he was engaged by the National Relics Bureau to train graduate students in the field of Chinese painting and calligraphy authentication. He authored a column in the magazine **Dushu** in 1996. That same year, he worked as programme advisor for the TV art programme *Meishu xingkong* [New Space for Art] on **CCTV (Chinese Central Television)** and wrote a monthly column for the magazine *Dongfang*. From 1997 to 1999, Yin Ji'nan organized and led a pro-seminar, 'Research in Chinese Contemporary Art Practice and Criticism'. In 2000, he was invited to give a presentation on 'Chinese Contemporary Art and Women's History' at Cornell, Harvard and New York Universities. In 2001, he gave a paper on the subject of Gu Kaizhi's *Nüshi jiantu* [Admonitions to the Palace Instructress] at the British Museum. Books that he has authored include: *Duzi Koumen* [Knocking on a Door Alone, 1993] and *Hou-niangzhuyi* [Post-Motherism, 2002] both published by the Joint Publishing Company. Yin Ji'nan is presently Director of the Art History Department at the Central Academy of Art, where he is also a professor and a member of the Board of Academic Advisors.

Further reading

Yin, Ji'nan (2001). 'What Next, Ultra-Postmodernism?'. In John Clark (ed.), *Chinese Art at the End of the Millennium*. Hong Kong: New Media, 52–4.

ROBERT BERNELL

Further reading

Gao, Minglu (ed.) (1999). *Inside Out: New Chinese Art*. San Francisco and New York: San Francisco Museum of Modern Art and Asia Society Galleries, New York [for *Woollen Sweaters*].

Wu, Hung (2000). *Transience: Chinese Experimental Art at the End of the Twentieth Century*. Chicago: Smart Museum of Art/University of Chicago Press [for *Suitcase, Ruined City, Transformation*].

Yin, Xiuzhen and Song, Dong (2002). *Kuaizi/Chopsticks*. New York: Chambers Fine Art.

ROBIN VISSER

Yin Xiuzhen

b. 1963, Beijing

Artist

Trained in academy painting at Capital Normal University (BFA, 1989), Yin Xiuzhen has produced installation and performance art since the mid 1990s. Her early works emphasized tensions between separation and connection. In her installation *Door* (1994), she placed outline sketches of a male and a female figure on either side of a common household door, and in her performance *Woollen Sweaters* (1995) she deconstructed clothing by unravelling and reknitting male and female sweaters.

Yin's socially charged works in relation to the environment gained her an international audience. In 1996 she inaugurated a collaborative series, *The Chinese and American Artists Group Project: Protectors of Water Source*. The first work, an installation of polluted ice bricks from a river outside of Chengdu, contrasts sharply with the second, a performance washing clothes in pristine waters near Lhasa. In the installation *Ruined City* (1996), Yin filled an exhibition hall with fragments and personal effects gathered around Beijing, covered with dry cement, evoking the dusty urban chaos of contemporary Beijing. Her installation, *Transformation* (1997), consists of rows of roof tiles filling a now-empty courtyard, to which she attached photos of the houses demolished for new development.

Ying Ruocheng

b. 21 June 1929, Beijing

Spoken-drama actor, director, translator, administrator

Born into a family of Catholic Manchu intellectuals (his grandfather founded Furen University), Ying Ruocheng is the best-known Chinese actor of the later twentieth century. Raised in English-speaking missionary schools and a graduate of **Qinghua University**, Ying married Wu Shiliang (d. 1987) in 1950 and became an actor at the **Beijing People's Art Theatre** upon graduation. Imprisoned from 1968 to 1971, Ying became a translator for *China Reconstructs* after the Cultural Revolution ended in 1976, and returned to the theatre in 1979. In 1983, Ying served as translator for, and played the part of Willy Loman in, Arthur Miller's famed direction of *Death of a Salesman* at the Beijing People's Art Theatre. Ying was appointed China's Vice Minister of Culture in 1986 and resigned in 1990. As Vice Minister, he promoted artistic collaborations with Western nations and travelled to the USA in 1982, 1984 and 1993 to direct university and repertory theatre productions of modern Chinese plays in English translation. Ying has translated dozens of Chinese and foreign classics, eight of which were published by the China Translation Publishing Corp. in 1999. Italian director Bernardo Bertolucci cast Ying in his films *The Last Emperor* (1987) and *Little Buddha* (1994). Ying was diagnosed with cirrhosis of the liver in 1990. His son, Ying Da, is a prominent actor and television director/producer.

Further reading

Miller, A. (1983). *Salesman in Beijing.* New York: Viking.

CLAIRE CONCEISON

Yu Hong

b. 1966, Beijing

Painter

Yu Hong graduated from the Department of Oil Painting at the **Central Academy of Fine Arts**, where she currently teaches. So far she has been the only mainland Chinese female artist to have participated in the Venice Biennale. In her early paintings she showed a clear interest in the description of the life of her contemporary urban youth. The figures, hard-edged and monochrome, were captured in playful moods against an empty background. The movements frozen in the moment, appeared pointless and weird, signalling hesitation. These works were exhibited at 'The World of Woman Artists' (*Nühuajia de shijie*) at the Museum of the Central Academy of Fine Arts in 1990 and at 'The New Generation' at the Museum of Chinese History in 1991, among other venues.

After becoming a mother in 1994, Yu Hong began to address her own life and that of her daughter as the main art subjects. She created a large body of oil paintings depicting the personal episodes that she considers as the most meaningful in each of her first thirty-six years. When exhibited in a solo show, 'Witness Growth' (*Mujie chengzhang*), held at the East Modern Art Centre in Beijing in 2002, these realistic, colourful and diary-like works were juxtaposed with photographs marking the most important historical events relevant to the year to which the painting referred. As a whole they serve as a record of the much broader growth experienced by youth of Yu Hong's generation.

Further reading

Dal Lago, Francesca (1993). 'Il realismo critico della giovane arte cinese' [The Critical Realism of Young Chinese Art]. In *Punti Cardinali dell'Arte, Catalogo della XLV Esposizione Internazionale d'Arte.* Marsilio: La Biennale di Venezia, 538.

Hess, Nicole. (2002). *Witness Growth* (exhibition catalogue). Beijing: Modern Art Publishing, 87–9.

Wei, Qimei. (2002). 'Chenzhong de chanshi: du Yu Hong de "Mujie chengzhang"' [Deep Interpretation – A Review of the Exhibition 'Witness Growth' by Yu Hong]. *Meishu yanjiu* 4: 22–4.

TANG DI

Yu Hua

b. 1960, Hangzhou

Writer

Yu Hua, originally a dentist by profession, came to public notice as a writer of **avant-garde/experimental fiction** in the latter half of the 1980s. He has since established himself as a professional writer of short fiction and novels and as an authority in literary criticism and music theory. Yu Hua first came to fame in 1986 with his short stories 'On the Road at Eighteen' (*Shibasui chumen yuanxing*) and 'One Kind of Reality' (*Shishi ru yan*). These and other stories are marked by an intensity of style and content. His detached and controversial depictions of violence are coupled with his own experimental language. The combination of the fantastic and the realistic form a disconcerting picture of reality and compel the reader to see the presence of suppression, the force of instinct and the depth of social woundedness.

The publication of his novel *To Live* (*Huozhe*) marked a shift from experimental to more traditional storytelling. It was made into a movie by **Zhang Yimou** in 1994. After the publication of two more novels, Yu Hua devoted himself to essay writing, publishing mainly in the magazine **Dushu** [Reading]. Of particular influence were his literary analyses of works from various literary traditions and writers in China and the West. Yu Hua is a writer-intellectual whose penetrating style, originality of imagination, graphic art of description and intellectual pursuits paved a new way in Chinese narrative art and contributed to a renewal of Chinese literature and learning.

Further reading

Jones, Andrew (1994). 'The Violence of the Text: Reading Yu Hua and Shi Zhicun'. *positions: east asia cultures critique* 2.3: 570–602.

Knight, Deirdre Sabina (2002). 'Capitalist and Enlightenment Values in 1990s Chinese Fiction: The Case of Yu Hua's *Blood Seller*'. *Textual Practice* 16.3 (November): 547–68.

Yu, Hua (1996). *Pain and Punishments*. Trans. Andrew Jones. Honolulu: University of Hawai'i Press.

—— (2003). *Chronicle of a Blood Merchant*. Trans. Andrew Jones. New York: Pantheon.

Zhao, Yiheng (1991). 'Yu Hua: Fiction as Subversion'. *World Literature Today* (Summer).

BIRGIT LINDER

Yu Jian

b. 1954, Kunming

Poet

Yu Jian, a contemporary poet with a strong interest in experimentation, is a leading figure of the **Third Generation (poets)**, also referred to as the **minjian** ('popular space'/folk) group. Characteristic features of his poetry include a rejection of highly metaphorical language, romantic individuality, lyricism and idealism. For Yu Jian, poetry 'must be firmly planted in the soil of contemporary life'. Although he is occasionally accused of writing 'non-poetry' by conservative critics, Yu Jian's work is generally free of the coarseness and triviality encountered in the writing of other 'Third Generation' poets. Over twenty years, he has experimented with a range of styles in a quest for an effective blending of the empirical, the speculative and the aesthetic. Many poems take a fact of everyday life and use it to 'unfold' unforeseen cultural implications.

Sixty Poems (*Shiliushi shou*), his first significant collection, was published in 1989. This was followed by *The Naming of a Crow* (*Dui yi zhi wuya de mingming*)

and *A Nail Through the Sky* (*Yi mei chuanguo tiankong de dingzi*). A representative self-selection of his poetry appeared in *The Poetry of Yu Jian* (*Yu Jian de shi*, 2000). This contains definitive versions of two controversial long poems: 'File 0' (*Ling dang'an*, 1992, made into a play by **Mou Sen**), an extended meditation on the personal dossier and its pervasive influence on Chinese life; and 'Flight' (*Feixing*, 2000), an ambitious summation of many of the styles and themes of his work which deals at length with the destructive effects of modernization.

See also: Misty poetry; poetry

Further reading

Huot, Clair (2000). 'Away from Literature II: Words Acted Out'. In *idem*, *China's New Cultural Scene: A Handbook of Changes*. Durham: Duke University Press, 72–90.

Van Crevel, Maghiel (2000). 'Fringe Poetry, but Not Prose: Works by Xi Chuan and Yu Jian'. *Journal of Modern Literature in Chinese* 3.2: 7–42.

Yu, Jian (2001). 'File 0'. Trans. Maghiel van Crevel. *Renditions* 56: 24–57.

—— (2001). 'Extracts from Yu Jian's *Feixing*'. Trans. Simon Patton. *Mantis* 2: 8–29.

SIMON PATTON

Yu Jie

b. 1963, Pujiang

Culture critic

Yu Jie represents himself as offering a critical, independent and marginal perspective on contemporary Chinese culture. He portrays his writing as 'drawer literature' (*chuti wenxue*), that is, written for self-reflection instead of for publication. His work has nevertheless become widely available in print after 1997, and appears in many different forms: maxims, reminiscences, book reviews, social and literary criticism. He writes in a highly personal, almost lyrical style, as if he were writing in an anti-academic way. In fact, Yu is quite critical of the recent professionalism in Chinese cultural criticism, and wants to restore the tradition associated with

Lu Xun, Cai Yuanpei and the humanism of **Peking University**. His criticism is driven by a sense of the moral responsibility that he believes intellectuals should feel towards history.

For example, Yu's best-known literary criticism is directed at Yu Qiuyu, a well-known writer of cultural/historical essays. In an article entitled 'Yu Qiuyu, Why Don't You Confess?' (*Yu Qiuyu, ni weihe bu chanhui?*), Yu Jie takes issue with retrospective writings about the **Cultural Revolution**. He charges that such writing lacks self-reflection and recommends self-reflection as a tool to criticize cultural production. In Yu's cultural criticism there is a tendency to de-contextualize Chinese culture. He compares the monolithic notion of 'Chinese culture' to the ideas of dissident writers such as the Czech playwright Vaclav Havel. Havel's determined resistance to cultural totalitarianism is presented as a positive model that Yu believes the Chinese intelligentsia ought to follow.

Further reading

Barmé, Geremie R. (1999). *In the Red: On Contemporary Chinese Culture*. New York: Columbia University Press, 351–4, 357, 361.

HE DONGHUI

Yu Xiaoyu

b. 1935, Hubei

Xiqu (sung-drama/opera) director, playwright, actor

Yu Xiaoyu started to perform on stage at three years old and grew up in the theatrical world of Chuju, one of the regional theatre genres in Hubei province. Since 1970, he has served as playwright, director and artistic leader for the Beijing Opera Troupe of Hubei Province (Hubeisheng jingjutuan). He has played an extremely important role in making this once unknown troupe in the mid 1970s into a present-day nationally renowned troupe. Under his leadership, the style of the troupe's productions since the late 1970s has been recognized as 'Hubei Style' (*E'pai*), equally distinctive as 'Beijing Style' (*Jingpai*) and 'Shanghai Style' (*Haipai*) – the

two leading styles on the Beijing opera stage since the early twentieth century. He has authored and co-authored successful plays such as *Wrapped Honey* (*Yibao mi*), *Zhang the Dogskin-Plaster Seller* (*Gaoyao Zhang*), and *All Living Creatures at the Famen Temple* (*Famen zhongsheng xiang*). More importantly, he guided the troupe's other playwrights in writing other well-known plays of which *Xu Jiujing's Promotion* (*Xu Jiujing shengguanji*) and *Legends of the Temple of Medicine God* (*Yaowang miao chuanqi*) are among the best of **Jingju** (Peking opera) plays created since the late 1970s. Yu directed all five aforementioned plays, receiving five national awards in succession. His contribution to the contemporary Beijing opera stage has been manifested in at least four areas: (1) he has established a system of creating a different stage design for each individual play that goes beyond the traditional one-desk, two-chair set, while still keeping the aesthetic concept of a bare stage; (2) he has created a series of new conventions for actors' gestures and body movements, as seen in the 'Wheel-Chair Dance' in *Legends of the Temple of Medicine God* which employs older physical skills to reflect a new body language; (3) he cast Zhu Shihui, who specializes in *wenchou* (civil clown) roles, as the lead role in a series of successful plays, thus broadening the range of *wenchou*'s capability of expression and promoting this secondary role type to the level of *laosheng* (male lead); and (4) he has championed the absorption of the best elements from other regional theatres to vivify Beijing opera.

Yu is better known as a **Xiqu** (sung-drama/opera) director. He has been invited by various troupes of other regional theatres as renowned guest director. His artistic influence in directorship has touched **Hanju**, Chuju, Quju, Guiju, Yuju, Jingzhou huaguxi, **Huangmeixi** and Cantonese opera (see **Yueju (Guangdong, Guanxi opera)**).

DU WENWEI

Yu Youhan

b. 1943, Shanghai

Painter

Yu Youhan, a protagonist of the **Political Pop** art current, graduated from the Central Academy of Art and Design in Beijing (1970). He is now an instructor at the Shanghai School of Art and Design. After adopting abstract, mostly monochrome painting in the late 1980s, Yu shifted to compositions employing notorious images of Communist iconography as an ironical commentary on the ideological changes in contemporary society. A member of a generation of painters who were young adults during the **Cultural Revolution**, Yu Youhan appropriates Mao's official photographs to create grotesque or ridiculing effects. In the painting *Mao Discussing with the Peasants of Shao Shan* (1991), Yu reproduces a well-documented encounter between Mao and a peasant family in his native village. The scene is repainted in garish colours, and a sense of the grotesque is achieved through the addition of floral patterns, used as a reference to the language of folk and popular art, which was promoted by Mao as a major source of high-culture inspiration in his '1942 Yan'an Talks' on art. By pushing this folk mood to excess, Yu mocks the leader (and his ideology) through the paradoxical distortion of the principles he once advocated.

Yu Youhan has participated in various international exhibitions, such as : **China Avant-Garde** in Beijing (1989); **China's New Art, Post-89 (Hong Kong, 1993) and China Avant-Garde (Berlin 1993)**; the 45th Venice Biennale, Italy; and the 1st Asia-Pacific Triennial of Contemporary Art in Brisbane, Australia.

Further reading

Dal Lago, Francesca (1999). 'Personal Mao: Reshaping an Icon in Contemporary Chinese Art.' *Art Journal* (Summer): 46–59.

Doran, Valerie C. (ed.) (1993*). China's New Art, Post-1989*. Hong Kong: Hanart T Z Gallery.

Knight, Juliet *et al.* (eds) (1996). *Reckoning with the Past* (exhibition catalogue). Edinburgh: The Fruitmarket Gallery.

FRANCESCA DAL LAGO

Yuanming Yuan

(The Garden of Perfect Brightness)

The Yuanming Yuan, the Garden of Perfect Brightness, was a garden palace to the northwest of Beijing, created as a summer retreat by early emperors of the Qing dynasty.

Over the years, as pavilions were added and the landscape of the marshy area remoulded according to imperial fiat creating a fantasy realm for the imperial family, the Yuanming Yuan also became the de facto seat of government for much of the year. As the gardens expanded, themes taken from poetry, myths and stories were used to create themed areas and vistas to create what the architectural historian Charles Moore names as one of the great theme parks, along with Hadrian's villa at Tivoli and Walt Disney's modern fantasy at Anaheim.

In the mid eighteenth century the Qianlong emperor – the most celebrated ruler of the dynasty – instructed the Jesuit missionaries who had been sent from Rome to convert the Chinese court to design a series of European-style marble palaces within the precinct of the garden-palace. He wanted to-scale copies of the rococo structures he had seen in the books that the missionaries had used to illustrate the grandeur of Western civilization. Now the emperor bent the Jesuits' strategy to his own will – he wanted European follies for his diversion; they were obliged to keep their message of salvation to themselves.

A series of syncretic mock-rococo pavilions was thereby erected in the northeastern reaches of the Yuanming Yuan, their marble facades supporting bright *liuli*-tiled roofs. Called the 'Western Palaces' (*Xiyang Lou*) they included a maze, gazebos, a mosque, loggia, galleries, banquet halls, throne rooms and elaborate fountains and water works. The palaces were filled with the tributes the throne received from European envoys: tapestries, paintings and all manner of precious objects.

In 1860, however, this marvellous palace complex, the largest and most elaborate garden ever built in China, was reduced to a devastated ruin when an Anglo-French imperial force under the command of Lord Elgin (the son of the man who had stripped the Athenian Parthenon of its marble frieze) invaded Beijing. They were there to force the Chinese imperial government to sign a peace treaty following its defeat in the Second Opium War.

This calamitous event, the invasion of the sacred imperial capital and the looting of the palaces, more perhaps than the defeat in the Opium Wars itself, symbolically marked the absolute degradation and humiliation of the Manchu-Chinese government. For later generations the burning of the Yuanming Yuan sounded the death knell of the imperial system itself and marked the beginning of the end of old China. Many of the remaining structures in the grounds were dismantled when the nearby Qingyi Yuan (later known as the Yihe Yuan, or the Summer Palace in English) was rebuilt for the pleasure of the Empress Dowager Cixi in the late nineteenth century.

After 1949, the university district grew up around the remains of the Yuanming Yuan palace in Haidian District. Elite institutions like the Qinghua Attached Middle School and Number 101 Middle School abutted it. Under the People's Republic, and after decades of neglect and plunder – many of Beijing's public parks were built using stones and trees taken from the imperial gardens – the Yuanming Yuan was cordoned off for preservation. Nonetheless, it remained a desolate and forsaken spot; the only palpable evidence of its former glory was the marble ruins of the Western Palaces. Once a discrete corner in the palace complex, they became its centrepiece.

As China's official ruin, a symbol of national humiliation, the Western Palaces were the place where students were educated in patriotic fervour. The original Red Guards of 1966 and their classmates had all visited or read about the Yuanming Yuan and the national shame that its destruction marked. It was this place more than any other that elicited the outrage, anger and ire of youth. The ruins were also the place where new China, the socialist revolution and the Communist cause had their earliest symbolic roots. For, as the authorities told it, it was the awakening that came with the destruction of the Yuanming Yuan that had sparked the will for national renewal among Han Chinese.

Following the Cultural Revolution concerted efforts were made to turn the area into a public part with patriotic significance (and by default a place for avant-garde art events), and the Western Palaces became a focus for officially orchestrated displays of nationalist ardour (and glitz) from 1990. At various stages moneymaking enterprises, like fun-fair rides and shooting galleries, were also a feature of the grounds. From the 1980s, the nearby village of Fuyuan cun was home to rogue artists, and it was raffishly dubbed the 'East Village'.

In recent years, debates about the future of this monument to the past have centred on whether various long-destroyed pavilions or 'scenes' (*jing*) within the demesne should be rebuilt, a sign to all of a revenant multi-ethnic although Han-centred civilization.

See also: 798

GEREMIE R. BARMÉ

Yueju (Guangdong, Guangxi opera)

Sung-drama, opera

The main regional drama style of Guangdong, Guangxi, Hong Kong and Macau, and very popular among many originally Cantonese Chinese living outside China, Yueju is one of the largest in scale of Chinese regional styles. It is usually called Cantonese Opera in English. This avoids the confusion with Zhejiang Opera, which has the same sound (*Yueju*) but different characters. Cantonese Opera arose in the eighteenth century, belonging to the *pihuang* system of Chinese regional drama (see **Xiqu**). Its proximity to Hong Kong ensured outside impact in music, costumes and staging, and from the cinema. Musically, the Cantonese Opera has adopted local folk music as well as a few Western influences. Musical instruments are mainly traditional wind, string and percussion, including the *yangqin* (dulcimer), but Western instruments such as the saxophone, violin and violoncello have been added and remain in use.

Under the PRC, Cantonese Opera has done well, other than during the Cultural Revolution. The main professional troupe is the Guangdong Provincial Cantonese Opera Company (Guangdongsheng Yuejuyuan), established in 1958. However, there are many others in Guangzhou and the other main cities of Guangdong and Guangxi. The new and rising city of Shenzhen has aspirations as a cultural centre, and the Shenzhen Municipal Cantonese Opera Company (Shenzhenshi Yuejutuan), dating from 1980, has shown itself especially active and innovative in producing new Cantonese operas, on both traditional and contemporary themes. Probably, however, the most innovative work is carried out in Hong Kong.

Further reading

Yung, Bell (1989). *Cantonese Opera: Performance as Creative Process.* Cambridge: Cambridge University Press.

COLIN MACKERRAS

Yueju (Zhejiang opera)

Sung-drama, opera

Formed by peasant balladeers in Shaoxing in eastern Zhejiang, it was brought to Shanghai about 1916. The orchestration, initially only percussion, became more complex, with string instruments absorbed from other styles. A girls' school set up in 1923 trained actresses for the style, and by the late 1920s all-female troupes competed with all-male. By the mid 1930s virtually all Yueju troupes were entirely female. As a result, content tends strongly to be romantic or social, or to feature women, with very few military plots. The music, orchestration and singing are quite gentle in tone, and the costumes accord with the style's romantic feel.

The PRC was active in promoting the Zhejiang Opera from the start. Several items featured in the 1952 government-sponsored First Festival of Traditional Drama, including the famous love story *Liang Shanbo and Zhu Yingtai*, the tragic story of the couple in the title. They are transformed into butterflies after death, hence the name by which the drama is usually known, *The Butterfly Lovers*. The Shanghai Zhejiang Opera Company, still the best representative of the genre and very active in promoting it, was established in 1955.

During the **Cultural Revolution**, all-female casts went out of fashion and romantic themes succumbed to crass propaganda featuring class struggle. Since the late 1970s, however, the old themes have returned, being supplemented by newly written dramas also with romantic or social themes. Men play evil roles, but women again perform the scholar-lover characters. There are exceptions. In Su Leici's adaptation of *Hamlet*, entitled *A Record of a Prince's Revenge* (*Wangzi fuchou ji*), performed at the 1994 Shanghai Shakespeare Festival, a man plays the prince. The item is set in ancient China and is a particularly innovative example of Shakespeare in Chinese theatre. Because of the flexibility shown in this example, Yueju has weathered the challenges of modernization better than most traditional styles.

Further reading

(1962). *Yueju congkan* 1 and 2. Shanghai: Shanghai wenyi chubanshe.

(1983). *Zaoqi yueju fazhanshi.* Hangzhou: Zhejiang renmin chubanshe.

Chen, Zhiqing (1999). *Nanyin yue'ou de cilu quyun.* Hong Kong: Xianggang wenxue baoshe.

Fan, Jingfen (1986). *Yueju xikao.* Hangzhou: Zhejiang wenyi chubanshe.

Zhou, Dafeng (1995). *Yueju yinyue gailun.* Beijing: Renmin yinyue chubanshe.

COLIN MACKERRAS

Z

Zang Tianshuo

b. 1964, Beijing

Rock musician

Zang Tianshuo began the piano at age six and belongs to the first generation of rock musicians in the PRC. Today, he is a major figure in the field of Chinese pop-rock. Around 1983, he worked with groups such as the Coal Mine Culture Group and the Railway Culture Group, and acquired experience singing and playing the piano. His career as a rock musician began in 1984, when he joined one of Beijing's earliest bands, Tumbler (Budaoweng). Besides composing his own songs, Zang also co-founded the band White Angel (Bai tianshi) in 1987 before organizing his own band two years later (1989). He was the main organizer of Beijing's Concert of Modern Music (1990), which was later regarded as a milestone in PRC rock history. Between 1991 and 1993 he was the keyboard-player for **Cui Jian**. By the end of 1993 he had recorded his own album, *My Ten Years* (*Wode shinian*), which was released in July 1995 and earned him nationwide fame with the song 'Friend' ('*Pengyou*', 1985). He is also engaged in film music. In 1997 he had his personal debut concert at Beijing's Workers' Stadium. Zang's message emphasizes friendship, underscored by his personal engagement in volunteer concerts for anti-flood donations. Zang is regularly invited to play large-scale concerts throughout the PRC. He states that he does not have any musical ideals, but merely combines rap, rock and popular light music as his feelings dictate.

See also: rock music, rock bands

Further reading

Baranovitch, Nimrod (2003). *China's New Voices: Popular Music, Ethnicity, Gender, and Politics, 1978–1997*. Berkeley: University of California Press, 243–51 and passim.

ANDREAS STEEN

Zeng Fangzhi

b. 1964, Wuhan, Hubei

Oil painter

A graduate of the Department of Oil Painting at the Hubei Academy of Fine Arts (see **art academies**), Zeng Fangzhi exhibited his first series of paintings – triptychs of hospital interiors – in a solo-show at the Academy's gallery in 1990. The expressionistic brushstrokes (inspired by the work of German expressionist Max Beckmann), the cool hue of pigments and the rough treatment of bloody tones laid the psychological foundation for his entire oeuvre and conveyed his pessimistic view of life and human weakness. Blood and exposed flesh appear as powerful metaphors in the series *Meat* (1992), evoking scepticism towards man's freedom and dignity. The human propensity to violence is abstracted in portraits of exposed flesh on slaughtering tables, graphically reviving the theme of psychological wounding that recurs in **Scar art**. One year after moving to Beijing in 1993, Zeng began his signature series of masked portraits which made him a central figure in the artistic current known as **Cynical Realism** (Popi). In the earlier works of this series (1994–2000), the deterioration of interpersonal relationships in the process of modernization, as witnessed in the frantic urban milieu, is rendered by means of a grey palette, while human solitude is represented as individuals donning white masks with stereotyped expressions. Since 1997 landscapes have been added to the composition.

Zeng Fangzhi has exhibited extensively in international shows: 'Out From the Middle Kingdom: Chinese Avant-Garde Art' at the Santa Mónica Arts Centre in Barcelona (1995); 'Quotation Marks' at the Singapore Art Museum (1997); and 'Paris-Pekin' at the Espace Pierre Cardin in Paris (2002). In 1993 he was the subject of a ten-year retrospective at the Shanghai Art Museum.

Further reading

(1993/1994). 'Zeng Fangzhi fangtan lu' [An Interview with Zeng Fangzhi]. *Meishu shichang* [Art and Market]: 8–10.

(2003). *'I/We' 1991–2003: The Painting of Zeng Fanzhi* (exhibition catalogue). Shanghai: Shanghai Art Museum.

Jin, Yan (2001). 'Far, Fashionable and Restless'. *Xiandai yishu* [Contemporary Art] 10: 68–70.

Leng, Lin (1998). *It's Me: A Profile of Chinese Contemporary Art in the 1990s* (catalogue). Beijing: Contemporary Art Centre Co.

Li, Xianting (1998). *Zeng Fanzhi by Beijing Art Critic Li Xianting*. ShangArt Gallery website, available at http://www.shanghart.com (19 February).

Pi, Li (ed.) (1998). *Zeng Fangzhi* (exhibition catalogue). Beijing: Beijing Yumutang Design and Photography [with essays by Li Xianting, Feng Boyi, Peng De].

BEATRICE LEANZA

Zeng Hao

b. 1963, Kunming, Yunnan

Painter

In 1993, four years after graduating from the Department of Oil Painting at the **Central Academy of Fine Arts**, Zeng Hao was hired by the Guangzhou Academy of Fine Arts. In 1996, he moved back to Beijing as an independent artist. As a student, his style had followed very much the line of **Cynical Realism** (Popi) popular at the time. It was only after his three-year sojourn in Guangzhou, a city preoccupied with the search for wealth and comfort, that he found his own painting idiom. In 1994 he started concentrating on describing indoor life. His initial work placed people and objects in an arbitrary perspective, but remained, ironically, rather realistic. Soon, however, he moved his attention away from detail. With a detached gaze, he begun creating a rarefied universe in which carefully silhouetted miniature human figures and interior objects are dispersed in a random order to resemble cosmic dust: weightless, meaningless but spellbinding. The various unrelated figures and objects are juxtaposed against beautiful monochromatic backgrounds. This literal objectification and depersonalization of people has since become Zeng Hao's signature style. Zeng Hao had his first solo show at the Gallery of the Central Academy of Fine Arts (1999), and has participated in many exhibitions, including 'Transience' at the Smart Museum of Art in Chicago (1999), and the First Guangzhou Triennial (2002).

Further reading

Li, Xianting (1997). 'Pingmian'er shuli de richang jingguan: Zeng Hao zuoping jiqi xiangguan huati' [Two Dimensionality and Alienation of the Everyday Experience: Regarding Zeng Hao's Work and Related Topics]. In *Zeng Hao* (exhibition catalogue). Beijing: The Gallery of the Central Academy of Fine Arts.

Wu, Hung (1999). 'Interior Time/Space'. In Wu Hung, *Transience. Chinese Experimental Art at the End of the 20th Century*. Chicago: David and Alfred Smart Museum of Art.

TANG DI

Zhai Yongming

b. 1955, Chengdu, Sichuan

Poet

Zhai Yongming worked in the 209 Institute of Arms Industry Bureau from 1974. In 1977 she entered the Chengdu College of Telecommunication and Construction. After graduation in 1980, she returned to the Institute and began writing poetry. Her debut, *Women Series* (*Nüren zushi*), appeared in 1984, and was immediately acclaimed by critics for its daring feminist perspective and unique style. From the late 1980s she became a full-time writer in the Chengdu Academy of Literature. Her published anthologies are *The Women* (*Nüren*) and *Expressions in Darkness* (*Hei'anli de biaoxian*).

In her work, Zhai Yongming explores the female voice and poetic space through a combination of complex self-reflection and bold formal experiment. In the poetic landscape of the 1990s, she stood out for a distinctive style that departed from the lyricism pervasive in the previous decade. In a poetic language that is inventive, dense and mysterious, she depicts tragic, evocative and rebellious emotions. In her preface to *Women Series*, she declares, 'As a half of the human race, a woman faces a totally different world from the moment of her birth ... In fact, every woman faces her own abyss where the pains in her inner heart are incessantly destroyed and recognized.' With her 'consciousness of darkness' Zhai Yongming probes the realms of eroticism, voyeurism and madness, and opens new possibilities for aesthetic creation. Based on her individual experience, she creates a poetic world saturated with nightmare, dream, delirium, fantasy and hallucination. It is a dark world that is, nonetheless, imbued with a feminist concern for the fate of Chinese women in the past and present.

See also: Third Generation (poets)

Further reading

Tao, Naikan (1999). 'Building a White Tower at Night: Zhai Yongming's Poetry'. *World Literature Today* 73.3: 409–16.

Zhang, Jeanne H. (2002). 'Zhai Yongming's "Woman" – With Special Reference to its Intertextual Relations with the Poetry of Sylvia Plath'. *Journal of Modern Literature in Chinese* 5.2: 109–30.

CHEN JIANHUA

Zhang Chengzhi

b. 1948, Beijing

Writer

Zhang Chengzhi began studying history at **Peking University** in 1972, and subsequently continued his studies at the **Chinese Academy of Social Sciences**. But the more definitive period for Zhang as a writer was the time he spent in rural Mongolia from 1967 through 1972. In the early 1980s, Zhang began publishing stories about the life of rural Mongolians which were later synthesized into the novel *Golden Pastureland* (*Jin muchang*, 1987). The most celebrated of these stories, 'Black Horse' (*Hei junma*, 1982), depicts the cultural gap separating a modernizing Han majority from rural minorities, through the tale of a Han boy raised by a Mongolian woman on the plains who leaves his fiancée to study in the city. In the late 1980s, Zhang turned his attention to the impoverished Sufi Islamic religious minority that represented his own family background. The result was *Spiritual History* (*Xinlingshi*, 1990), a controversial, impassioned study of their history and a declaration on their behalf of a spirituality in opposition to Han Chinese culture. Throughout the 1990s Zhang continued to argue against the commercialization of the educated elite and in favour of representing the less fortunate in a series of essays collected in *The Barren Road of the Hero* (*Huangwu yingxiong lu*, 1994) and *The Pen as a Banner* (*Yibi wei qi*, 1999), among other books.

Further reading

Liu, Xinmin (2000). 'Deciphering the Populist Gadfly: Cultural Polemic around Zhang Chengzhi's "Religious Sublime"'. In Martin Woesler (ed.), *The Modern Chinese Literary Essay: Defining the Chinese Self in the 20th Century*. Bochum: Bochum University Press, 227–37.

Xu, Jian (2002). 'Radical Ethnicity and Apocryphal History: Reading the Sublime Object of History in Zhang Chengzhi's Late Fiction'. *positions: east asia cultures critique* 10.3 (Winter): 526–46.

Zhang, Chengzhi (1990). 'The Black Steed'. In *Love That Burns on a Summer's Night*. Beijing: Chinese Literature Press, 137–230.

—— (2002). 'Statue of a Dog'. Trans. Andrew Jones. *positions: east asia cultures critique* 10.3 (Winter): 511–24.

EDWARD GUNN

Zhang Dali

b. 1963, Harbin, Heilongjiang

Graffiti and performance artist, photographer

Zhang Dali graduated from the National Academy of Fine Arts and Design in 1987. He lived briefly in Beijing's **Dongcun** (East Village) artist community, until he left for Bologna shortly before the political turmoil of 1989. In Italy he was exposed to Europe's graffiti art. After experimenting with oil painting and many installations, he began spray painting the simple outline of a human head in profile on walls around Bologna. In 1995 he returned to a Beijing that was in the process of radical change as a result of government policies of urban modernization. Zhang promptly began employing his human-headed 'tag' as a form of dialogue with the city's transformation. When the head appeared as the first and only form of graffiti in the city, it quickly became a scandal among the public and in the press which helped to extend the 'dialogue' concept. After distributing the image throughout the city, Zhang proceeded to photograph the heads, out of which he formed light-boxes. He also printed the images on canvas, thus returning the graffiti to the realm of fine art. Next, Zhang took his work into the sculptural realm when he orchestrated performance pieces in which hired construction workers chiselled the spray-painted heads out of the house walls still standing at Beijing's many demolition sites. His graffiti was covered on international television by such agencies as Reuters (China) and Associated Press. His light-box works were exhibited in 'Urbanity' at the China Art Museum (Beijing, 1998), 'Demolition and Dialogue' at the Courtyard Gallery (Beijing, 1999), 'Food for Thought' at the Mu Art Foundation Eindhoven (Holland, 1999) and 'Green Dog and Masters' at the Chinese Contemporary Gallery in London.

Further reading

(1999). *Zhang Dali* (exhibition catalogue). Beijing: Courtyard Gallery

Borysevicz, Mathieu (1999). 'Zhang Dali's Conversation with Beijing'. *ART AsiaPacific* 22: 52–8.

Fathers, Frankie (1999) 'Democracy Walls'. *Asiaweek* (April). Available at http://www.asiaweek.com/asiaweek/99/0423/feat3.html

Yu, Zhong (1998). 'Someone's Graffiti on Ping'an Avenue' *Beijing Youth Daily* (24 February).

MATHIEU BORYSEVICZ

Zhang Guangtian

b. 1966, Shanghai

Musician, playwright, culture critic

Zhang Guangtian is an independent musician, critic, playwright, director and poet. His art is highly politicized and controversial, and while many praise him for his idealism, there are others who accuse him of being a radical Maoist and nationalist. Through much of his art, he actively engages in social criticism. His art conveys his sympathy for the common people as well as his view that there is a continuing need for revolution to correct the social injustices brought about by Deng Xiaoping's economic reforms. Because of these views, he is often referred to as a member of the **New Left**. Another major theme in his art and written articles is the resistance to Americanization and the promulgation of pride in China's traditional culture, with particular emphasis on folk music.

Zhang spent four years at the Shanghai College of Chinese Medicine (1982–6). In 1986 he was sentenced to three years of re-education through labour for political and moral misconduct. In the early 1990s he moved to Beijing. Since then he has released several albums and has composed music for numerous plays, TV series and films, including **Zhang Yimou**'s *Shanghai Triad*. Zhang has also published numerous articles, mainly on popular music. His diverse artistic activity reached a peak between 2000 and 2002. During this period he wrote, composed and directed a series of four experimental plays, integrating his diverse talents and political views. These were: *Che Guevara* (*Qie-Gewala*, co-directed with Shen Lin, Huang Jisu and Wang Huiqing); *Mr Lu Xun* (*Lu Xun xiansheng*), *Red Star Beauty* (*Hongxing meinü*) and *Sage Confucius* (*Shengren Kongzi*).

Further reading

Wang, Abby (2002). 'Minstrel, Confucian, Scholar, Poet'. *City Weekend* (7 February). Available at http://www.cityweekend.com

NIMROD BARANOVITCH

Zhang Hai'er

b. 1957, Guangzhou

Photographer

Zhang Hai'er began his artistic career in 1978 as a student of stage design at the Shanghai Drama Institute. He then worked as an art director and set designer for the Guangdong Television Network before deciding to continue his education in photography at the Guangzhou College of Fine Arts. Zhang Hai'er has photographed numerous subjects throughout his career, most often in his native Guangzhou, but also as far away as Denmark and Africa. His coal-miner series and beauty-pageant work show not only his journalistic vigour but also his artistic bent. His signature expressionistic style is accentuated by a preference for the wide-angle lens and high-contrast prints which help to portray his subjects in an often glamorized or theatrical manner.

Some of his earliest work had its solo debut in 1988 at the Provincial Library of Guangdong Province, Guangzhou, from where it travelled to Germany ('Fotografien Aus China: 1986–1989'). His series of Guangzhou prostitutes is perhaps his best-known and most widely exhibited work. Using call-girls as models, Zhang poses his subjects in a manner akin to fashion photography. The girls, in various states of undress, stare unassumingly at the camera as if in a dream state. Zhang Hai'er also works as a photo journalist and fashion photographer for Agence Vu (Paris). He splits his time between Guangzhou and Paris. His work has been featured in 'China – Fifty Years in the People's Republic' (Aperture Foundation, New York, 2000), 'Zhang Hai'er – Solo Exhibition' (Image Photo Gallery, Aarhus, Denmark) and 'Contemporary Photo Art from the People's Republic of China' (Neuer Berliner Kunstverein, Berlin and other venues in Germany).

See also: Lu Zhirong; Zhuang Hui

Further reading

Clark, John and van Dijk, Hans (1999). *Modern Chinese Art Foundation* (exhibition catalogue). Netherlands: Provincieraad Oost-Vlaanderen, 82–5.

Kunz, André (1994) 'Contemporary Chinese Photography: From a "Correct" to a "Fragmentary" World View'. In Jochen Noth, Wolfger Puhlmann, Kai Reschke and Andreas Schmid (eds) (1994), *China Avant-Garde: Counter-Currents in Art and Culture*. Berlin and Hong Kong: Haus der Kulturen der Welt and Oxford University Press, 93–100.

MATHIEU BORYSEVICZ

Zhang Hongtu

b. 1943, Pingliang, Gansu

Painter, conceptual artist

The art of Zhang Hongtu, a member of the Hui nationality, is among the most widely disseminated of all contemporary Chinese artists outside of China. His personal experience and engagement with socialist realism, traditional Chinese art and contemporary Western art lend his imagery a distinctive insight into the cultural boundaries and peculiarities inherent in both Chinese and Western art. He received a BFA from the Central Academy of Arts and Crafts (Gongyi meishu xueyuan), where he studied between 1964 and 1969. Thereafter he was 'sent down' to 'The Contemporaries' (Tongdairen), an artist group active in Beijing in the late 1970s and early 1980s. Later, he emigrated to the United States and has lived in New York City since 1982.

Among his most influential artworks are a series of humorous and sometimes disturbing pieces exploring Mao's image in the Chinese and Western psyche. Beginning with the *Quaker Oats Mao* series in 1987, his subsequent explorations include the *Last Banquet* (1989), which borrows from Da Vinci's *Last Supper* to evoke Mao's virtual deification among disciples, who made themselves in his image. The creation of satirical and imaginary artworks in *Christie's Catalogue Pages* began in 1998 as a parody of the values and conventions of Chinese and Western art. *Repainting Shanshui*, begun in 1998, is a series of oil paintings based on compositions of Chinese landscape paintings executed in the styles of various European Impressionists. The series remains faithful to literati philosophy regarding copying and the mastery of brush technique, while exploring the nature of modernism and the artistic encounter between China and the West. His work may be found in many private and public collections and exhibitions, including the Princeton University Art Museum, the Bronx Museum of Art, the Yale-China Association, and the Guangzhou Triennial.

Further reading

Dal Lago, Francesca (1999). 'Personal Mao: Reshaping an Icon in Contemporary Chinese Art'. *The Art Journal* 58: 46–59.

Hay, Jonathan (1994). 'Zhang Hongtu/ Hongtu Zhang: An Interview'. In John Hay (ed.), *Boundaries in China*. London: Reaktion Books, 281–300.

Perkins, Morgan (2003). 'The Supple Vision of Zhang Hongtu'. In *Icons and Innovations: The Cross-Cultural Art of Zhang Hongtu* (exhibition catalogue). New York: Roland Gibson Gallery, State University of New York, Potsdam, 4–6.

Wu, Hung (1999). 'Nothing Beyond the Gate'. In idem (ed.), *Transience: Chinese Experimental Art at the End of the Twentieth Century*. Chicago: David and Alfred Smart Museum of Art, University of Chicago, 43–8.

Zhang Hongtu's website: www.momao.com

MORGAN PERKINS

Zhang Huan

b. 1965, Anyang, Henan

Performance artist

Zhang Huan was trained as an oil painter, first in the Department of Fine Arts of Henan University (1984–8) and then at the **Central Academy of Fine Arts** in Beijing (1991–3). He was banned from public spaces after his first performance (*Angel*, 1993) with the **Dongcun** (East Village) group, causing the cancellation of the show planned at the **China Art Gallery**. For the following five years Zhang organized his performances in informal spaces in Beijing – such as old suburban houses, village toilets, rural fish ponds, etc. – documenting them through video and photography. After moving to New York in 1998 he quickly gained international recognition with his on-site performance, *New York Fengshui*, at the 'Inside-Out' show (1998) at P.S.1 where he lay naked on a slab of ice placed on a traditional Chinese bed. Ever since he left China all his performances have been carried out publicly. Zhang has shown at important New York galleries like Deitch Projects (2000) and Luhring Augustine (2001), and has taken part in international exhibitions including the 1999 Venice Biennale and the 2002 Whitney Biennial.

Zhang Huan's early performances focused on the spiritual as well as physical pressures experienced at an individual level by exposing or torturing the body to often shocking situations of physical coercion. In his performance *65 KG* (1994) in Beijing he tied his body with an iron chain to a beam and let his own blood drip through a clinic tube onto an electrically heated pan. In his more recent works, Zhang has explored the relationship between his own and other bodies by organizing group performances featuring dramatic choreographies with people from different cultural backgrounds. In *My*

America (2000) naked men and women followed him in Qigong practice. Zhang Huan lives and works in New York.

Further reading

(2002). *Zhang Huan* (exhibition catalogue). Madrid: Xunda de galicia and Cotthem Gallery.

Gao, Minglu (1998). 'From Elite to Small Man: The Many Faces of a Transitional Avant-Garde in Mainland China'. In Gao Minglu (ed.), *Inside/Out. New Chinese Art*. Berkeley: University of California Press, 149–66.

Qian, Zhijian (1999). 'Performing Bodies: Performance Art in China'. *Art Journal* 58.2: 60–81.

QIAN ZHIJIAN

Zhang Jianya

b. May 1951, Shanghai

Film director, producer

A member of China's 'Fifth Generation' of filmmakers (see **Fifth Generation (film directors)**) and a stalwart of the contemporary Shanghai film industry, Zhang Jianya spent five years as a carpenter after graduating from junior high school in 1968. In 1975 he joined the Shanghai Film Studio Actors Troupe. From 1978 to 1982, Zhang studied in the directing department of the **Beijing Film Academy** together with **Chen Kaige** and **Tian Zhuangzhuang**, among other well-known directors.

Zhang's debut film at the Shanghai studio was *Ice River* (*Binghe shengsixian*, 1986), a story of a country ferry trapped in ice on the Yellow River. The film was more typical of the harsh naturalism of **Yellow Earth** (Chen Kaige, dir.) than the usual gloss of a Shanghai film. Zhang then assisted studio head Wu Yigong on *Tribulations of a Chinese Gentleman* (*Shaoye de monan*, 1987), a Sino-West German co-production based on a Jules Verne story. Zhang established his métier in comedy with *Kidnapping von Karajan* (*Bangjia Kalayang*, 1988), a story about a group of young people who plot against the conductor on a China visit and a satire on China's feverish Westernization. With *San Mao Joins the Army* (*San Mao congjun*, 1994), Zhang turned to a much-loved satirical cartoon

strip of the 1940s. Following his appointment as head of the newly formed Third Creative Group at the Shanghai Film Studio in 1985, Zhang also became a producer and a major artistic leader at the studio. His action film, *Crash Landing* (*Jinji jialuo*, 1999), made more money at the box-office than any film produced in China. Skilful development of tension and world-class computer-assisted special effects distinguished the film. Zhang has continued in this successful adventure/disaster/special effects vein in *Red Snow* (*Jidi jingjiu*, 2002), set in the spectacular Tibetan landscape.

PAUL CLARK

Zhang Jie

b. 1937, Manchuria

Writer

Winner of **literary awards** and an author whose works have been translated into a dozen languages, Zhang Jie is renowned for her brave probing of social problems. Zhang earned a degree in economics and worked as a statistician in an industrial ministry in Beijing until she was sent to a labour camp in 1968. After returning to Beijing, she published her first story in 1978. She has since produced a large body of poignant psychological fiction concerned with pragmatic and ethical dilemmas posed by social and political change.

Best known for portraying the difficult social position of women, Zhang also addresses the legacy of political trauma, the loneliness of isolated individuals, and the ineptitude and irrationality of various institutions, from factories to hospitals. In her celebrated but controversial story 'Love Must Not Be Forgotten' (*Ai, shi bu neng wangji de*, 1979), Zhang challenged compulsory marriage through a daughter's reflections on her mother's unfulfilled love. She won the Mao Dun prize for *Heavy Wings* (*Chenzhong de chibang*, 1981), a novel confronting industrial modernization, corruption and personal compromise. Her path-breaking novella 'The Ark' (*Fangzhou*) describes the everyday trials, discrimination and patent harassment endured by three female roommates as they struggle to carry on their lives and professions after a divorce or separation.

Published between 1998 and 2001, Zhang's epic four-volume novel, *Without Words* (*Wuzi*), spans the violent twentieth century. Author's notes help the reader navigate the stream-of-consciousness narration and the frequent shifts in narrative perspective as characters from different walks of life pursue, then assess, their values.

Further reading

Chong, Woei Lien (1995). 'The Position of Women in China: A Lecture by Woman Writer Zhang Jie'. *China Information* 10.1 (Summer): 51–8.

Muller, Eva (2001). 'Die Schrifstellerein Zhang Jie: vom grossen politischen Roman zum weilblichen Psychogramm'. In Christina Neder *et al.* (eds), *China in Seinen Biographischen Dimension: Gedenkscrift fur Helmut Martin*. Weisbaden: Harrassowitz.

Zhang, Jie (1985). *Die Arche.* Trans. Nelly Ma. Munich: Frauenoffensive.

—— (1987). *Leaden Wings.* Trans. Gladys Yang. New York: Random House.

—— (1989). *Heavy Wings.* Trans. Howard Goldblatt. New York: Grove Press.

DEIRDRE SABINA KNIGHT

Zhang Kangkang

b. 1950, Hangzhou

Writer

Zhang Kangkang is a representative of the generation of writers who were Red Guards and 'sent-down youth'. Her fiction is characterized by lively characterization and vivid diction, as well as a keen grasp of the social mood.

Zhang volunteered to go to the 'Great Northern Wilderness' as an 'educated youth' in 1969. Her novel *The Demarcation* (*Fenjiexian*, 1975) deals with 'educated youth' and is a work of propaganda. After Mao's death, however, she was among the first writers to call for liberation from dogmatic thinking. In February 1979, she published 'The Right to Love' (*Ai de quanli*) and in 1980 'The Northern Lights' (*Beijiguang*), both of which received great attention. In the early 1980s, several stories about the confrontations between Chen Lang, an independent-minded female student, and society, as represented by the college authority, further dismantled hypocrisy and dogmatism. Zhang's first real novel, *The Invisible Companion* (*Yinxiang banlu*, 1986), is a skilful use of internal monologue, flashback and stream of consciousness. It probes into the split personalities of 'educated youth', who have been shaped by propaganda and lies. *The Red* (*Chitong danzhu*) is a biographical account of her parents' devotion to the Communist Party and their subsequent suffering, while *Love Corridor* (*Qing'ai hualang*) is a call for beauty and love in an increasingly commercialized environment.

See also: Cultural Revolution; Cultural Revolution (education); xiafang, xiaxiang

Further reading

Leung, Laifong (1994). 'Zhang Kangkang: Sensing the Trends'. In *idem, Morning Sun: Interviews with Chinese Writers of the Lost Generation*. New York: M. E. Sharpe, 229–39.

Zhang, Kangkang (1987). 'The Right to Love'. Trans. R. A. Roberts and Angela Knox. In *One Half the Sky: Selections from Contemporary Women Writers*. London: Heinemann, 51–81.

—— (1988). 'Northern Lights'. Trans. Daniel Bryant. *Chinese Literature* (Winter): 51–81.

—— (1996). *The Invisible Companion.* Trans. Daniel Bryant. Hong Kong: New World Press.

LEUNG LAIFONG

Zhang Nuanxin

b. 27 October 1940, Hohhot, Inner Mongolia; d. 28 May 1995, Beijing

Film director, theorist

Daughter of a doctor who was also a connoisseur of literature and art, Zhang studied directing in at the **Beijing Film Academy** from 1968 to 1972. She married the Beijing writer and critic **Li Tuo**, and taught directing at her alma mater. Zhang first drew attention in 1979, when she co-authored 'On the Modernization of the Language of Film', arguing against the prevailing focus on content over form, and arguing for the director as auteur and for cinematic realism as a means to achieve filmic lyricism rather than merely capturing external reality on screen. In her own work, Zhang sought to express subjectivity by recreating dominant features of her inner landscape.

Assigned as a director of the Beijing Film Academy's Youth Film Studio, Zhang's early work, *The Seagull* (*Sha Ou*, 1981) and *The Drive to Win* (1981), won two domestic awards. But it was **Sacrificed Youth** (*Qingchunji*, 1985) that brought her international acclaim and an invitation to Paris as a visiting researcher. Domestically, she is best known for *Good Morning, Beijing!* (*Beijing nin zao*, 1991), which won the PRC's Best Picture and Hong Kong's Best Chinese Language Film awards. Her most recent work is *A Yunnan Story* (*Yunnan gushi*, 1994).

Further reading

Berry, Chris (1988). 'Interview with Zhang Nuanxin'. *Camera Obscura* 18 (September): 20–5.

Semsel, George (ed.) (1987). *Chinese Film: The State of the Art in the People's Republic*. New York: Praeger.

Zhang, Nuanxin with Li Tuo (1979). 'On the Modernization of the Language of Film'. In *Dianying Yishu* [Film Art]. Beijing: publisher not known. Translated in George Semsel, Xia Hong and Hou Jianping (eds) (1990), *Chinese Film Theory: A Guide to the New Era*. New York: Praeger.

CYNTHIA Y. NING

Zhang Peili

b. 1957, Hangzhou

Oil, conceptual and video artist

Zhang Peili is a pioneer of Chinese video art and one of its most acclaimed practitioners. He is currently Director of the New Media Art Centre at the China Academy of Art in Hangzhou. In 1984 Zhang Peili graduated from the oil painting department of the Zhejiang Academy of Fine Arts, later renamed the China Academy of Art (Zhongguo meishu xueyuan). He organized and participated in the exhibition '85 New Space'

(*85 Xin kongjian*), which developed out of the Youth Art Group (Qingnian chuangzuoshe) that was established in 1984 and comprised graduates from the Academy. He was also a founding member of the **Pond Society** (Chishe, 1986–7), which was responsible for a series of significant art events, happenings and installations in Hangzhou.

His early works were oil paintings inspired by daily life and urban modernization, rendered in a cool, analytical style described as 'grey humour' (*huise youmo*). Since the late 1980s, Zhang Peili has created a series of multi-media works concerned with language, communication and the absurd. He has focused primarily on video art, favouring it as a popular medium that also provides access to the dimensions of movement, sound and time. Zhang Peili's video works are conceived as installations. He often takes banal events and transforms them into highly stylized meditations on society. Since the early 1990s, Zhang Peili has participated in many important international art exhibitions. His works have been collected by institutions in Asia, Australia, Europe and North America.

CLAIRE ROBERTS

Zhang Wang

b. 1962, Beijing

Sculptor, installation artist

Zhang Wang graduated in 1981 from the Academy of Applied Arts (Gongyi meishu xueyuan) in Beijing and in 1988 from the Department of Sculpture of the **Central Academy of Fine Arts**, where he now teaches. Zhang Wang's oeuvre acting is in close interchange with its cultural and physical space of production, intervening in the relentless flow of changes affecting urban spaces and functioning as a commentary on the artificial and awkward position seemingly assigned to traditional cultural values in contemporary China.

In 1994 Zhang produced a performance, *Ruin Cleaning Project*, in which he set out to temporarily clean and refurbish the ruins of an old building during a pause in its demolition process. This act functioned as a response to his sense of personal helplessness in the face of the irreversible process of urban modernization.

Zhang's most famous series, *Jiashanshi* [Artificial Mountain Stones] – begun in 1995 – employs the classic *topos* of the scholar's rock, embossed from the real stones now decoratively displayed in the streets of Beijing. The shiny, reflective rocks thus produced are then repositioned in public spaces where they explicitly comment on the artificial redeployment of traditional motifs, now so ubiquitous in the cultural and visual sphere of China's cities.

Zhang Wang has taken part in numerous exhibitions both in China and overseas, such as the 'Kongling Kong Seduction Series', a solo exhibition at the Gallery of the Central Academy of Fine Arts in Beijing (1994); 'Crack in the Continent' at the Watari Museum of Contemporary Art in Tokyo; and the travelling exhibition 'Cities on the Move' in Vienna (1997).

Further reading

Dal Lago, Francesca (2000). 'Space and Public: Site Specificity in Beijing'. *Art Journal* (Spring): 75–87.

Erickson, Britta (2001). 'Material Illusion: Adrift with the Conceptual Sculptor Zhan Wang'. *Art Journal* (Summer): 72–81.

Wu, Hung (1998). 'Ruins, Fragmentation, and the Chinese Modern/Postmodern'. In Gao Minglu (ed.), *Inside Out: New Chinese Art*. Berkeley: University of California Press.

FRANCESCA DAL LAGO

a mystical style. His first and still most influential novel is *The Ancient Boat* (*Guchuan*, 1986). In an atmospheric and tale-like style, the novel creates a panoramic description of China's historical reality and development from the first land reform of the 1940s to the economic reforms of the 1980s. Zhang's other celebrated novel, *September's Fable* (*Jiuyue yuyan*, 1992), is a mystical tale of the changing lives of several generations of inhabitants of a small village on the north Chinese seacoast. Zhang's other major fiction includes *Seven Kinds of Mushrooms* (*Mogu qizhong*, 1988) and *Bai Hui* (1994). *Seven Kinds of Mushrooms*, a novella drawing upon the author's dreams of childhood, tells the story of a forest king and his subjects in an experimental style. *Bai Hui* represents the author's agitation over an age of commercialism which is conveyed through the long monologues of the protagonist. The novel provoked a contentious debate in intellectual and literary circles. In addition to novels, Zhang Wei's short stories, essays and poems have increasingly drawn the attention of audiences. Many again echo China's social changes and the author's feelings about them.

Further reading

Lu, Jie (2000). 'Nostalgia without Memory: Reading Zhang Wei's Essays in the Context of Fable of September'. In Martin Woesler (ed.), *The Modern Chinese Literary Essay: Defining the Chinese Self in the 20th Century*. Bochum: Bochum University Press, 211–25.

YANG LAN

Zhang Wei

b. 1956, Shandong

Writer

Zhang Wei has received more than thirty literary awards for work renowned for its cultural perspective on social reality. Zhang studied creative writing at Yantai Normal Institute around 1979 and 1980. Since 1980, he has published over seventy individual volumes of writings, including fiction, poetry and essays.

Zhang's fiction is known for its shadings of romanticism and idealism interwoven with

Zhang Xian

b. 1955, Shanghai

Playwright, screenwriter

Born in Shanghai to cadre parents, Zhang Xian spent a decade in Yunnan during the **Cultural Revolution** from the age of fifteen. Upon his return, he entered the Shanghai Theatre Academy, but was expelled after two years for political reasons. Never attached to an official work unit, Zhang works independently, scripting experimental dramas while earning income from more conventional scripts for television and film. His play *Owl in the House* (*Wuli de maotouyin*, 1986) broke new ground at the Nanjing Little Theatre Festival in 1989. An independent revival of the work in Shanghai was thwarted by local officials in the summer of 2000. After a stay in the USA sponsored by the Asian Cultural Council in 2000, Zhang became artistic director of the Hard Han Café, Shanghai's first café-theatre. Notable works include *Fashion Street* (*Shizhuang jie*, 1987), *The Wife from America* (*Meiguo lai de qizi*, 1993), *The Margin Upstairs* (*Loushang de majin*, 1994), *Crowded* (*Yongji*, 1994), *Mother Tongue* (*Muyü*, 1996), *Men and a Jar* (*Wantanzhe shuo*, 1996) and *Back Room* (*Baofang*, 2002). Zhang's career and body of work reflect the artistic dilemma of producing experimental drama with social commentary while also prospering in a decentralizing market economy driven by popular mainstream consumer preferences. Zhang Xian is married to writer Tang Ying; they returned to Shanghai from Singapore in 2002.

See also: Little Theatre

Further reading

Kaye, L. (1994). 'Shanghai Fables'. *Far Eastern Economic Review* (14 April): 50–1.

CLAIRE CONCEISON

Zhang Xianliang

b. 1936, Nanjing

Writer

Zhang Xianliang is representative of writers who were persecuted in the Anti-Rightist Campaign of 1957. He was imprisoned for almost twenty years in northwest China, and re-emerged in 1979 with semi-autobiographical stories focusing on the suffering of intellectuals in labour camps, including: the short story 'Soul and Flesh' (*Ling yü rou*, 1980), which was made into a film entitled *The Herdsman* (*Mumaren*); the novellas *Love in Prison* (*Tulao qinghua*, 1981), *Mimosa* (*Luhuashu*, 1984) and *Half of Man Is Woman* (*Nanren de yiban shi nüren*, 1985); and the novels *Getting Used to Dying* (*Xiguan siwang*, 1989) and *Nettle Soup* (*Wode puti shu*, 1989). While writing about the suffering of Chinese intellectuals, he also wrote stories in the 1980s calling for economic reform, such as 'Dragon Seed' (*Longzhong*) and 'Man of Character' (*Nanren de fengge*).

Zhang reveals in frank detail, emotion and occasional black humour the harsh conditions under so-called labour reform and its devastating effect on all aspects of human life, including the degradation of human dignity through psychological emasculation. His boldness in depicting sexual deprivation aroused heated debate, along with accusations of male chauvinism. Zhang has visited many countries and his writing has been translated into many languages. Since the late 1990s he has also been in charge of a big enterprise in his home town of Yinchuan, Ningxia.

Further reading

Yue, Gang (1999). 'Postrevolutionary Leftovers: Zhang Xianliang and Ah Cheng'. In *idem*, *The Mouth That Begs: Hunger, Cannibalism, and the Politics of Eating in Modern China*. Durham: Duke University Press, 184–221.

Zhang, Xianliang (1985). *Mimosa*. Trans. Gladys Yang. Beijing: China Books and Periodicals.

—— (1988). *Half a Man Is Woman*. Trans. Martha Avery. New York: W. W. Norton.

—— (1995). *Grass Soup* (2nd ed.). Trans. Martha Avery. Boston: David Godine.

Zhong, Xueping (1994). 'Male Suffering and Male Desire: The Politics of Reading *Half a Man Is Woman*'. In C. K. Gilmartin, G. Hershatter, L. Rofel and T. White (eds), *Engendering China: Women, Culture, and the State*. Cambridge: Harvard University Press, 175–91.

LEUNG LAIFONG

Zhang Xiaofu

b. 1954, Changchun

Composer

Zhang Xiaofu, the most important figure in electronic music in China, is a professor at the Central Conservatory of Music. At the age of sixteen he joined his home town's song and dance troupe (*gewutuan*), playing bassoon and **erhu**, as well as acting as conductor and staff composer. In 1977 he was admitted to the Central Conservatory of Music where he studied composition under Wu Zuqiang. In 1988, after five years on the faculty of the Central Conservatory, where he primarily taught harmony, Zhang was selected by the **Ministry of Culture** to go to France for advanced studies at the École Normal de Musique Paris and the Conservatoire Edgar Varèse. He was subsequently invited to work at La Muse en Circuit and INA-GRM.

After returning to the Central Conservatory in 1993, Zhang founded the Centre of Electroacoustic Music of China (CEMC), which subsequently hosted a series of high-profile national and international electronic-music conferences and festivals, including the 94 Musicacoustica and 96 Musicacoustica. The Centre maintains an active academic exchange programme with its European and American counterparts. Zhang has been the driving force in the formation of the Electroacoustic Music Association of China and of the master's programme in electronic music at the Central Conservatory. Zhang's electronic music works include *Dialogues entre des Mondes Différents* and *Nuo Ri Lang*. *Yaluzangbu*, scored for three Tibetan singers, electronic music and a full orchestra, integrates different media and cultural elements.

JIN PING

Zhang Xiaogang

b. 1958, Kunming, Yunnan

Oil painter

Zhang Xiaogang's oeuvre constitutes one of the most significant contributions to the language of Chinese oil painting since the mid 1980s. After graduating from the Sichuan Academy of Fine Arts in Chongqing in 1982 (see **art academies**), Zhang founded the **Southwest Art Research Group** (Xinan yishu qunti) together with artist Pen Dehai and Mao Xuhui. The conceptual research of these artists carried more surrealist and less political overtones than groups in Hong Kong and Beijing, exploring human desire in a period when the once-suppressed humanism was taking up new

meanings and relevance. In Zhang's early work *Eternal Life* (1988), depicting minority people surrounded by animals, emerges the concern for the purity of simple and rustic life as opposed to that of the 'modern man'. In his two most famous series of paintings, *Amnesia and Memory* and *Bloodline: The Big Family* (both begun in 1993), Zhang captures the historical dimension of a rising consumer society by adopting the format and visual texture of the family album and by portraying ordinary Chinese persons in a form reminiscent of portraiture typical of the late Qing and the early Republican period. The smooth, brushless quality of the finish and the placement of the figures, often wearing Mao suits, on dim flattening backgrounds are distorted by the veering strokes of vivid colour and by the addition of physical blemishes to the faces, an expression of the struggle of the individual in the face of the power of collective and family ties, which is represented by the ubiquitous red line linking the various figures in the paintings. Zhang's work has been shown worldwide. Among other venues he has figured in: *Mao Goes Pop* at the Sydney Museum of Contemporary Art (1993); *Sao Paolo Biennale* (1994); *Venice Biennale* (1995); *Inside Out: New Chinese Art*, Asia Society, New York (1998); and *Paris-Pekin*, Espace Cardin, Paris (2002).

Further reading

(1997). *Faces and Bodies of the Middle Kingdom* (exhibition catalogue). Prague: Galerie Rudolfinum.

Chang, Tsong-zung and He, Xiangning (2002). 'Zhang Xiaogang – Between Reality and Illusion'. Museum talk on 21 November 2002; partly available at http://www.Chinese-art.com, 'Artist of the Week' (9 January 2003).

Gao, Minglu (1998). 'From Elite to Small Man: The Many Faces of a Transitional Avant-Garde in Mainland China'. In *idem* (ed.), *Inside Out: New Chinese Art* (exhibition catalogue). Berkeley: University of California Press.

Pollack, Barbara (1998). 'PoMaoism'. *Art & Auction* (March): 110–15.

Zhang, Xiaogang (1997). *Bloodline: The Big Family* (exhibition catalogue). Beijing: Gallery of the Central Academy of Fine Arts.

BEATRICE LEANZA

Zhang Xinxin

b. 1953, Beijing

Writer

Raised in Beijing, Zhang was sent to rural China to work during the **Cultural Revolution**, first as a peasant, then as a nurse. In 1978 she was admitted to the Central Academy of Theatre to study directing, but spent her spare time writing fiction. Her novellas of the early 1980s were innovative, modernist depictions of the subjectivity of young women who attempt to resolve the conflict of marriage and a career, as in *On the Same Horizon* (*Zai tongyi dipingxian shang*, 1981), or to reconcile the experience of youth in the Maoist era with that of adulthood in the reform period, as in *The Dreams of Our Generation* (*Women zhege nianji de meng*, 1982). She co-authored with **Sang Ye** an extensive series of interviews with Chinese from all walks of life, collectively entitled *Chinese Lives* or *Chinese Profiles* (*Beijingren*, 1985), establishing a popular form, derived from Studs Terkel, that inspired several similar projects by other writers over the next decade. Zhang also continued her modernist experiments, such as the fact-fiction treatment of a bicycle journey along the Grand Canal in *On the Road* (*Zailushang*, 1987). Repeatedly subject to official criticism, in 1988 Zhang Xinxin emigrated to the USA, where she subsequently became a web-based columnist.

Further reading

Jiang, Hong (2001). 'The Masculine-Feminine Woman: Transcending Gender Identity in Zhang Xinxin's Fiction'. *China Information* 15.1: 138–65.

Kinkley, Jeffrey C. (1987–8). 'Modernism and Journalism in the Works of Chang Hsin-hsin'. *Tamkang Review* 18.1–4: 97–123.

Wakeman, Carolyn and Yue, Daiyun (1989). 'Fiction's End: Zhang Xinxin's New Approaches to Creativity'. In Michael S. Duke (ed.), *Modern Chinese Women Writers: Critical Appraisals*. New York: M. E. Sharpe, 196–216.

Zhang Xinxin (1992). 'A "Bengal Tigress" Interviews Herself' and 'The "June 4 Syndrome": Spiritual and Ideological Schizophrenia'. In Helmut Martin (ed.), *Modern Chinese Writers: Self-Portrayals*. Armonk: M. E. Sharpe, 137–46 and 165–7.

EDWARD GUNN

Zhang Yadong

b. 1965, Shanxi

Record producer

With well over a hundred productions to his credit, Zhang Yadong is China's most prolific record producer. Yadong grew up in a family of musicians and began his musical training early, mastering instruments such as the **erhu** and Chinese dulcimer. Later training in cello and Western classical music led him to learn guitar and experiment with pop music. In 1993 Zhang Yadong moved to Beijing in search of bigger things and got his wish when Cantopop-diva and Beijing-native Wang Fei (Faye Wong, see **Wong Fei**) invited him to produce several tracks on her album *Restless* (1996), a record which generated the quirky 'out-of-line' chic that is now the trademark of Wang Fei's musical persona. Riding on the acclaim that came with his association with Wang Fei, Zhang Yadong was hired to produce a string of ground-breaking rock and pop records for the Beijing record company Jingwen Records. His first solo album, *Zhang Yadong* (1998), prompted the Hong Kong Standard to proclaim it, '1998's most important record of new Chinese music'. In recent years, Yadong has focused on television and movie soundtracks. He maintains a working partnership with Wang Fei, and his second solo album is due out in 2004 on Warner Music.

Further reading

http://www.zhangyadong.net

MATTHEW CLARK

Zhang Yang

b. 1967, Beijing

Film director, scriptwriter

After completing his undergraduate education in Chinese literature at Zhongshan University (now Sun Yat-sen University) in 1988, Zhang Yang pursued film directing and graduated from the Central Drama Academy in 1992. Young and independent, Zhang Yang and his peers have been described as a new generation of film directors determined to create a genre of urban cinema and innovative filmmaking. Their works are markedly different from the Fifth Generation's national allegories (see **Fifth Generation (film directors)**) as well as from official mainstream narratives.

Zhang Yang has made three feature films to date, each produced by Imar Film Co., an independent film production company founded by Peter Loehr, who is also as a producer. *Spicy Love Soup* (*Aiqing malatang*, 1997) is a romantic comedy that uses montage to assemble five episodes about different relationships into a meta-narrative. Although the fragments bear no connection to each other, collectively they present a picture of the reality of urban life in contemporary China. *Shower* (*Xizao*, 1999) has attracted audiences inside and outside China. Using the setting of a traditional public bathhouse to consider father–son relationships, the film captures a moment of transition in China when tradition fades out while modernity asserts itself.

A later work, *Quitting* (*Zuotian*, 2001), depicts the story of a real person, Jia Hongsheng, a cult film actor who struggles to recover from drug addiction with the help of his loving parents. The story is personal and compelling as the actor and his parents play themselves. Realistic yet not truly a documentary, the film reveals different aspects of the actor's journey as Zhang Yuan juxtaposes various episodes like a stage director.

Further reading

Kuo, Kaiser. *Shower Power: An Interview with Shower Director Zhang Yang*. Available at http://www.chinanow.com

Rayns, Tony (2001). 'Reviews'. *Sight and Sound* 11: 4 and 58.

CUI SHUQIN

Zhang Yimou

b. 14 November 1951, Xi'an

Film director, cinematographer, actor

Perhaps the 'Fifth-Generation' filmmaker best known in the West, Zhang Yimou spent ten years at manual labour during the **Cultural Revolution**: a significant influence, since he developed an intense dislike for the effeteness of China's coastal 'sophisticated' culture. Zhang graduated in cinematography from the **Beijing Film Academy** in 1982, along with classmates **Tian Zhuangzhuang** and **Chen Kaige**. His earliest work was as cinematographer for *One and Eight* (*Yige he bage*, 1984), *Yellow Earth* (*Huang tudi*, 1984) and *The Big Parade* (*Da yuebing*, 1985). Returning to Xi'an in 1987, he was both cinematographer and male lead for *The Old Well* (*Laojin*), which won Best Film and Best Actor awards at the Tokyo Film Festival. That year, Zhang directed his first feature, *Red Sorhum* (*Hong gaoliang*), featuring actress **Gong Li** in her debut. It won the Golden Bear award at the Berlin Film Festival – China's first. *Code Name Puma* (*Daihao meizhoubao*, 1988) was a commercial effort that Zhang would prefer to overlook, but his films since then have assured him an international following. *Judou* (1989), a visually gorgeous film about sexual torture and illicit love, was nominated for an Oscar for Best Foreign Film, while *Raise the Red Lantern* (*Da hong denglong gaogao gua*, 1991), about intrigues in a household of four wives under one manipulative man, won the Silver Lion at the Venice Film Festival. Both films, however, were panned at home for 'exoticizing and eroticizing China'. *The Story of Qiu Ju* (*Qiuju da guansi*, 1992) was Zhang's response to his critics. The story of a simple rural woman, it was filmed in a more realist style, using hidden cameras to shoot a number of public scenes, and won the Golden Lion at the Venice Film Festival. The epic *To Live* (*Huozhe*, 1994) won the Grand Jury and Best Actor awards at the Cannes Film Festival, and is perhaps the best-loved of Zhang's offerings domestically. The gangster film *Shanghai Triad* (*Yao a yao, yao dao waipoqiao*, 1995) was the last made in collaboration with Gong Li, who had held the female lead in all the other films Zhang had directed. The 1995 Hawaii International Film Festival honoured Zhang with a Lifetime Achievement Award, which he accepted in person. *Keep Cool* (*You hua haohao shuo*, 1997), Zhang's first post-Gong Li offering, was a frenetic urban comedy, shot largely with a hand-held camera, that failed to make an impact on audiences anywhere. His subsequent two films returned to his rural roots: *Not One Less* (*Yige dou bu neng shao*, 1999) focuses on the educational needs of China's poorest regions, and *The Road Home* (*Wode baba mama*, 1999) pays homage to Zhang's own parents. Following a brief hiatus, he returned to directing with a star-studded **martial arts** feature called *Hero* (*Yingxiong*, 2002).

Although Zhang has visited cities in Europe and the USA on many occasions, he insists that he is a simple-minded Chinese man who does not cater and has never catered to Western sensibilities, citing as proof, for example, that he cannot and will likely never learn to speak English, or any foreign language.

See also: Fifth Generation (film directors); Zhang Ziyi; Zhao Jiping

Further reading

Chow, Rey (2003). 'Not One Less: The Fable of a Migration'. In Chris Berry (ed.), *Chinese Films in Focus: 25 New Takes*. London: BFI, 144–51.

Farquhar, Mary (2002). 'Zhang Yimou'. In *Senses of Cinema: Great Directors – A Critical Database*. Available at http://www.sensesofcinema.com/contents/directors/02/zhang/html

Gateward, Frances (2001). *Zhang Yimou: Interviews*. Jackson: University Press of Mississippi.

Lu, Sheldon (2002). 'Zhang Yimou'. In Yvonne Tasker (ed.), *Fifty Contemporary Filmmakers*. London: Routledge, 412–17.

Yue, Mingbao (1996). 'Visual Agency and Ideological Fantasy in Three Films by Zhang Yimou'. In Wimal Dissanayake (ed.), *Narratives of Agency: Self-Making in China, India, and Japan*. Minneapolis: University of Minnesota Press, 56–73.

Zhang, Yingjin and Xiao, Zhiwei (1998). *Encyclopedia of Chinese Film*. London: Routledge.

CYNTHIA Y. NING

Zhang Yiwu

b. 1962, Beijing

Culture critic

A noted postmodernist critic, Zhang Yiwu locates post-Mao Chinese culture in relation to globalization. He bases his poetics and politics on a postcolonial celebration of the margin, as developed in his first book on contemporary Chinese literature, *Exploring the Periphery* (*Zai bianyuanchu zhuxun*, 1993). He argues that modernist discourse characterized Chinese literature from the 1920s to the early 1980s, and was embedded in a colonial discourse. By contrast, some newly emerging genres of the late 1980s defy the colonial discourse. The subversion of modernism is exemplified in experimental fiction, neo-realistic fiction, films by the Sixth Generation of directors, and soap operas.

Zhang's monograph *From Modernity to Postmodernity* (*Cong xiandaixing dao houxiandaixing*, 1997) pursues the relocation of Chinese culture in global capitalism by addressing debates among literary critics in the mid 1990s. Such debates included discussions about the loss of the 'humanistic spirit' (*renwen jingshen*) and the rise of 'latter-day **National Studies**' (*hou guoxue*). Zhang argues in favour of embracing the 'new condition' (*xin zhuangtai*) of post-Cold War market culture. Zhang criticizes the anxiety over the loss of the 'humanist spirit' as an elitist resistance to mass culture; at the same time, he categorizes this anxiety as a form of Westernization. He also warns that the reassertion of National Studies as 'essentially Chinese' only reinforces the concept of Chinese culture as the 'Oriental other'. Ultimately, Zhang's postmodernist theorizing faces the question of how to work from the margin without reinforcing the traditional view of Chinese culture as marginal.

See also: Humanistic Spirit, 'Spirit of the Humanities'; postmodernism (houxiandai zhuyi) and 'post-ism' (houxue)

Further reading

Wang, Hui and Yu, Guoliang (eds) (1998). *90 niandai de 'houxue' lunzheng* ['Post-ism' in the Nineties], Hong Kong: Chinese University Press [includes two of Zhang Yiwu's essays originally published in *Ershiyi shiji* 28 and 38].

HE DONGHUI

Zhang Yuan

b. 1963, Nanjing, Jiangsu

Film director

Zhang Yuan graduated in 1989 from the **Beijing Film Academy** in cinematography. He rejected an official assignment to the August First Film Studio, raised just over US$1,000 himself, and produced his first film, *Mama* (*Mum*, 1991), about an autistic boy and his mother. It won awards in Nantes, Switzerland, Edinburgh and Berlin. Subsequently, Zhang produced music videos and commercials in Hong Kong, and was the first Asian director to win an MTV award.

In 1993 he collaborated with the rock artist **Cui Jian** to make **Beijing Bastards** (*Beijing zazhong*), a semi-documentary underground film about a rock band, their music and its expression of urban angst. It was acclaimed at the Rotterdam, Locarno and Singapore Film Festivals, but shortly thereafter Zhang was banned from filmmaking by the government. Nevertheless, he completed a documentary, *The Square* (*Guangchang*, 1994), in which the lack of commentary underlines the silence surrounding the 1989 Tiananmen Incident. In 1995, he followed with *Sons* (*Erzi*), a docudrama about a dysfunctional Beijing family, which won a Tiger Award at the Rotterdam Film Festival, and in 1996, with what has been called China's first gay movie, *East Palace West Palace* (a.k.a. *Behind the Forbidden City*; *Donggong xigong*), about a Beijing policeman's fury at his own attraction to a gay prisoner.

By 1997 Zhang Yuan had been officially reinstated as a director. *Seventeen Years* (*Guonian huijia*, 1999), his first film to be distributed domestically through formal channels, won international acclaim, including a Special Director's Award at the Venice Film Festival. In 1999 he also directed *Crazy English* (*Fengkuang yongyu*). Zhang's latest product, *I Love You* (*Wo Ai Ni*, 2002) – based on a **Wang Shuo** novel and script with music by **Zhang Yadong** – was scheduled for release in 2003.

Further reading

Barmé, Geremie (1999). *In the Red: On Contemporary Chinese Culture*. New York: Columbia University Press, 189–97.

Reynaud, Bérénice (1997). 'Gay Overtures: Zhang Yuan's *Dong Gong, Xi Gong*'. *Cineyama* 36: 31–3.

Zhang, Zhen (2002). 'Zhang Yuang'. In Yvonne Tasker (ed.), *Fifty Contemporary Filmmakers*. London: Routledge, 418–29.

CYNTHIA Y. NING

Zhang Ziyi

b. 9 February 1980, Beijing

Actress

A Beijing native and performing arts graduate of the China Central Drama Academy, Zhang Ziyi achieved international fame after her debut in *The Road Home* (*Wode fuqin he muqin*, 1999), directed by **Zhang Yimou**. The film won the Jury Grand Prix Silver Bear at the 2000 Berlin Film Festival. Her performance won her Best Actress at China's Golden Horse (*Jinma*) awards. She has been pitched as 'little **Gong Li**' and 'Zhang Yimou's little girlfriend'.

Her foray into Hollywood came with her second film, *Crouching Tiger, Hidden Dragon* (*Wohu canglong*, 2000), directed by Ang **Lee**. She was elected Best Supporting Actress by the Toronto Film Critics Association. Her international visibility expanded in 2001 when she played in four films originating from three national or regional industries. They were *Rush Hour 2*, *Warrior* (*Musa*, Korea), *2046* and *Legend of Zu* (*Shushan zhenzhuan*), the last two directed by **Wong Kar-wai** and **Tsui Hark**, respectively. These conspicuous roles contributed to her selection in 2001 as one of the 'Fifty Most Beautiful' by *People's Magazine*. In her most recent film, *Hero* (*Yingxiong*), she collaborates once again with Zhang Yimou. She plays opposite Jet Li (Li Lianjie), continuing her previous work with other action movie stars, including **Chow Yun-fat**, Michelle **Yeoh** and Jackie **Chan**. Zhang's success hinges upon the trend of transnational filmmaking. It remains to be seen how this trend will redefine Chinese cinema and whether Zhang's career will continue to be shaped by it.

See also: Lou Ye

Further reading

http://uk.geocities.com/lisiulung_zhangziyi/index.
  htm

http://www.dreamwater.net/ziyicorner/links.htm

WANG YIMAN

Zhao Bandi

b. 1963, Beijing

Painter, photographer, installation artist

Zhao Bandi's first exposure to the art scene was in 1993 when, after graduation from the Oil Painting Department of the **Central Academy of Fine Arts** (see also **art academies**) in 1988, his oil paintings were displayed in 'China Avant-Garde', an exhibition organized by Hans **van Dijk** for the Haus Der Kulturen der Welt in Berlin which toured Europe for two years. In his first solo-show, 'Moonflight' at the Hanmo Art Centre in Beijing (1994), Zhao addressed issues of social concern in such installations as *The Big Rumour, Spreading until Today*, in which a plexiglass cut-out in the form of a human silhouette was suspended from iron chains. Zhao's early painterly work fell within the current of **Cynical Realism**, fusing black humour with ironical wit. In *Zhao Bandi and Qian Qian* (1996), a series of calendar photos realized in cooperation with the singer Zhang Qianqian, quotations from **Cultural Revolution**, visual imagery and a contemporary photo album are juxtaposed to depict the whimsical and existential landscape of modern urban life. His later work increasingly engages in a satire of notions of history and reality, country, culture and law. In the series *Zhao Bandi and the Panda*, for example, the photographic medium mimics the language of public-issue advertising. Begun in 1998, it was used in 2000 for a public art installation in which 300 light-boxes were scattered at different locations in Beijing's subway stations and trains, each depicting the artist and a toy panda bear engaged in a dialogue marked by cartoon balloons and creating feelings of absurdity by mimicking public awareness campaigns. Zhao's work has been shown at the 48th Venice Biennale (1999), 'The Sun Rises in the East' at the Arles Photo Festival in France (2000), and the Shanghai Biennale at the Shanghai Museum (2000), among other venues.

Further reading

de Matté, Monica (1999). 'Zhao Bandi'. In *La Biennale di Venezia, 48a Esposizione d'Arte, d'Apertutto, Aperto Over All*. Marsilio: La Biennale di Venezia: 212–15.

Dewar, Susan (1995). 'Moonflight in Beijing'. *ART Asia Pacific* 2.1: 34–5 [review of *Moonflight*].

Pollack, Barbara (2004). 'Chinese Photography: Beyond Stereotypes'. *ARTnews* 103.2 (February): 98–103.

van Dijk, Hans and Lindermann, Inge (1996). *China, China – Aktuelles aus 15 Ateliers* (exhibition catalogue). Munich: Herausgeber Hahn Produktion.

Zhao, Bandi (1995). *Configura 2 – Dialog der Kulturen – Die Frage 40 Antworten Band 2*. Erfuhrt: Configura Projekt GbR.

BEATRICE LEANZA

Zhao Jiping

b. 1945, Shulu, Hebei

Composer

Zhao Jiping became internationally known as a composer for such 'Fifth-Generation' filmmakers as **Chen Kaige**, **Zhang Yimou** and **He Ping**. Among his most famous film scores are those for *Raise the Red Lantern* (1991), *To Live* (1993) and *Farewell My Concubine* (1993). He is also a noted composer for the concert stage.

Son of the painter Zhao Wangyun, Zhao Jiping was trained at the Xi'an Conservatory of Music, majoring in composition and graduating in 1970. When the Central Conservatory reopened after the Cultural Revolution in 1978, Zhao was accepted there for postgraduate studies. Zhao entered the limelight as a film composer when Chen Kaige invited him to write music for **Yellow Earth** (1984). The music, close to its folk roots, was highly crafted and evocative of Chen's cinematic expanse. In *To Live* and *Raise the Red Lantern*, Zhao's colourful use of Chinese instruments, such as the *banhu*, *xun* and *sheng*, in combination with a Western orchestra met with critical acclaim. The incorporation of regional opera, especially operatic percussion passages, added even more brilliance and dramatic context to *Farewell My Concubine*, a story about two **Jingju** (Peking opera) stars. In 2000, Zhao received a commission from Yo Yo Ma and the Silk Road Project to write a chamber work. *Moon over Guan Mountains* (scored for **pipa**, sheng, cello and tabla) was premiered at Tanglewood, and remained in the Silk Road Ensemble's international repertory throughout 2002.

See also: Fifth Generation (film directors); China National Symphony Orchestra

JOANNA C. LEE

Zhao Puchu

b. 1907, Taihu, Anhui; d. 2000, Beijing

Buddhist, political activist

A well-known social activist and one of the religious leaders in China, Zhao Puchu enrolled in Soochow University, but discontinued his studies one year later because of illness. Recuperating at home, Zhao began studying the doctrines of Buddhism. In the early 1930s, Zhao served as chief secretary of the Chinese Buddhist Association based in Shanghai. During the War of Resistance against Japan, he went to Shanghai to participate in charity work. In 1945 Zhao Puchu, together with Ma Xulun, Xu Guangping and Lei Jieqiong, founded the China Association for Promoting Democracy (CAPD).

After 1949, Zhao Puchu engaged in more social and political work. Among his numerous official titles were Secretary of the Chinese Writers' Association, Vice-Chairman of the Sino-Japan Friendship Association, President of the Chinese Buddhist Association, Honorary President of the Red Cross Society in China, and Vice-Chairman of the Chinese People's Political Consultative Conference. For his efforts at promoting peace and Buddhism, Zhao won the Buddhist Evangelic Credit Award from the Japan Buddhist Evangelist

Association, an honorary doctorate from the Japanese University of Buddhism and an international Peace Award in 1985. Accomplished in classical poetry and calligraphy, Zhao has left two collections of poems, *A Collection of Drops of Water* (*Dishui ji*) and *A Collection of Stone Pieces* (*Pianshi ji*), both warmly received. His calligraphy is much sought after by visitors.

FU HONGCHU

Zhao Wei

(a.k.a. Vicky Chiu)

b. 12 March 1976, Wuhu

Actress

A graduate of the Performance Department at the **Beijing Film Academy**, Zhao Wei has become an idol among young audiences in Hong Kong, Taiwan, Southeast Asia, as well as in mainland China. Her first three films, *Le peinter* (*Huahun*, **Huang Shuqin**, dir., 1994), *A Young Girl's Valley* (*Nü'er gu*, **Xie Jin**, dir., 1995) and *East Palace, West Palace* (*Donggong xigong*, **Zhang Yuan**, dir., 1996), did not bring her much attention. However, she achieved tremendous success with, and henceforth became known as, 'Little Swallow' (*Xiao yanzi*), the character she played in the TV mini-series *Princess Pearl* (*Huanzhu gege*, 1997), adapted from a novel by **Qiong Yao**. Her performance won her a Golden Eagle award.

Her career has since diversified. She acts in films and TV serials, performs in concert, and records CDs. Her 'cute' image, established in *Princess Pearl*, was radically refashioned when she was invited by the Hong Kong comic star Stephen **Chow** (Chow Sing Chi/Zhou Xingchi) to play a scar-faced girl in a film combining martial arts and soccer, entitled *Kungfu Soccer* (*Shaolin zuqiu*) – Hong Kong's highest-grossing film ever, which was released in the USA in 2003. This was followed by her first foray into Hollywood with *So Close* (*Xiyang tianshi*, originally entitled *Virtual Twilight*, 2002), a Columbia Pictures (Asia) production directed by Corey Yuan.

WANG YIMAN

Zhao Xiaosheng

b. 1945, Shanghai

Composer

Zhao studied piano at the primary and middle schools of the Shanghai Conservatory. Already during the **Cultural Revolution**, he was writing adaptations for piano of 'model revolutionary plays' (*yangbanxi*, see **Xiqu**). Between 1978 and 1981 he studied in the composition department of the Shanghai Conservatory. He continued his studies, particularly of computer music, at Columbia University and Missouri State University from 1981 to 1984.

In his compositions, Zhao attempts to retain Chinese sonorities within contemporary idioms. In Chinese style, he provides titles for all of his compositions. In his first dance suite, *Tune of the Earth* (*Diqu*, 1990–1), he includes Chinese instruments and singing in Peking-opera style. His third dance suite, *Heavenly Sacrifice* (*Tianji*, 1990–1), features elements from Chinese ritual music. His ballet music, *Sun Over the Wasteland* (*Dahuang de taiyang*, 1992), is a collage incorporating pop-bass rhythms, a vocalizing choir and alienated Chinese orchestral playing, which includes **pipa**s sounding like the banjos in American country music. While his numerous piano compositions are primarily studies in virtuosity, those compositions in particular that combine Western and Chinese instruments are full of unique sound effects.

In 1987, Zhao created his own Chinese-style serialism, the so-called Taiji System of Composition (*Taiji zuoqufa*). It is based on a very complicated symmetrical scale. The notes of this Taiji scale form two six-tone rows with characteristic pentatonic intervals which are exact mirror images of each other. From these rows, tone-groups are selected according to the hexagrams of the ancient *Book of Changes* (**Yijing**) which restricts the number of notes to be used at any given time. One of Zhao's earliest compositions applying this system is *Three Poems on Yin and Yang* (*Yinyang sanque*, 1987) for any sixteen performers.

Further reading

Mittler, Barbara (1997). *Dangerous Tunes. The Politics of Chinese Music in Hong Kong, Taiwan and the*

People's Republic of China since 1949. Wiesbaden: Harrassowitz, 362–4.

Zhao, Xiaosheng (1987). 'Taiji yuelun' [On Taiji Music] *Yinyue yishu* 2: 60–74.

—— (1990). *Taiji zuoqu xitong* [The Taiji Composition System]. Guangdong: Guangdongsheng xinhua shudian.

BARBARA MITTLER

zheng

Musical instrument

The zheng is a board zither with strings running along its length over individual movable bridges. It appears in different sizes with a varying number of strings. In ancient times, the instrument was small and portable, about three feet in length and with six to sixteen strings made of silk. The modern zheng, in contrast, may be as long as five feet and have from twenty-one to twenty-five strings made of either steel or silk wound with nylon.

In the traditional way of playing the instrument, plectra are attached to the thumb, index and third fingers of the right hand and these pluck the strings at the right of the bridges while three fingers of the left hand press the strings to their left, producing pitch glides and subtle tonal embellishments. In the 1950s, new techniques of playing were developed in an effort to expand the capabilities of the instrument and enable it to imitate the piano and the harp in musical effect. These involved the use of the left hand in plucking or strumming the strings and providing a kind of harmonic accompaniment to the melody played by the right hand. Hand in hand with the development of new playing techniques was the development of bigger instruments, with a wider range, and capable of withstanding percussive techniques.

There are four traditional 'schools' of zheng-playing. These can be divided into the Northern and the Southern schools. The Northern schools consist of the zheng traditions of Henan and Shandong. The pieces in the repertoire of both schools are derived from the music of sung-narratives (**quyi**) and are often based on the 'labelled melodies' (*qupai*) called the 'old six-beats' (*lao liuban*, also known as 'eight beats' or *baban*). The Southern schools consist of the zheng traditions of the Chaozhou region and of the Hakka (Kejia) people, who are concentrated in Meixian in northeastern Guangdong. Their repertoires are derived from the instrumental interludes of the regional operas. Compared with the Northern styles, the Southern zheng styles are more lyrical and place greater emphasis on the ornamentation of individual notes.

MERCEDES M. DUJUNCO

Zheng Xiaoying

b. 1929, Yongding, Fujian

Conductor, music educator

Zheng Xiaoying began her music career in the early 1950s and has been the best-known female conductor for half a century. She was once the chief conductor of the National Central Opera Theatre and Director of the Conducting Department at the China Music Academy. She initiated the idea of a women's philharmonic, establishing the Beijing Women's Philharmonic Orchestra at the beginning of the 1990s. She also founded the Xiamen Philharmonic Orchestra, which was organized in 1998.

In 1952, Zheng Xiaoying became a student, pursuing composition courses at the China National Central Academy of Music. She learned to be a chorus-conductor from N. Dumashev, the teacher of Veronica Doudarova, the first female conductor in the world and People's Artist of the USSR. In 1960, Zheng Xiaoying went to the USSR to study at the Tchaikovsky Music Institute, majoring in philharmonic-conducting.

As a conductor, Zheng Xiaoying's artistic activities won recognition in musical circles both in China and abroad. She was well known for conducting Puccini's *Tosca* at the Russian National Musical Theatre in Moscow in 1962. Around 1978, she conducted a number of influential performances of Chinese and foreign operas, including *The God of Flowers*, *La Traviata*, *Carmen*, *Le Nozze di Figaro* and *Madam Butterfly*. Since the beginning of the 1990s, Zheng Xiaoying's repertoire has included the works of Haydn, Mozart, Beethoven, Mendelssohn, Strauss, Chopin, Tchaikovsky, Rimsky-Korsakov and Prokofiev, and some of the finer Chinese symphonies.

GE CONGMIN

Zheng Yi

b. 1947, Chongqing, Sichuan

Writer

Zheng Yi is a dissident writer. He attended the middle school attached to **Qinghua University**, the originating place of the Red Guard movement. When the **Cultural Revolution** broke out, he became the Red Guard leader of a rebel faction. In 1968, he volunteered to go to the countryside in the area of the Luliang Mountains in Shanxi province as an educated youth. He entered Yuci Teachers' Training college in 1978, and became an editor for the literary magazine *Yellow River* (*Huanghe*) after graduation.

Zheng Yi's fiction concentrates on two areas: the Cultural Revolution and the peasants. His short story 'Maple' (*Feng*, 1979) was the first work to expose the violent fights among Red Guard factions. The death of two young Red Guards epitomizes the victimization of youth by Mao's personality cult. His novella *Old Well* (*Laojing*) is a symbolic rendering of Chinese peasants' Sisyphean struggle for survival, through generations of well-digging in search of water. Similarly, 'Distant Village' (*Yuancun*) depicts an awkward and painful marriage arrangement due to poverty.

Zheng was active in the pro-democracy movement in the spring of 1989. He was under arrest after the 4 June Massacre, and escaped to Hong Kong in March 1993. 'Scarlet Memorial' (1996), a piece of 'reportage literature' (*baogao wenxue*), documents the cannibalism in Guangxi province during the Cultural Revolution. He now lives in Washington, DC.

Further reading

Leung, Laifong (1994). 'Zheng Yi: Well-Digging and Root-Searching'. In Leung, Laifong, *Morning*

Sun: Interviews with Chinese Writers of the Lost Generation. New York: M. E. Sharpe: 259–69.

Zheng, Yi (1990). *Old Well*. Trans. David Kwan. San Francisco: China Books and Periodicals.

—— (1998). *Scarlet Memorial: Tales of Cannibalism in Modern China*. Trans. and ed. T. P. Sym. Boulder: Westview Press.

LEUNG LAIFONG

Zhong Xiaoyang

b. 1962, Guangzhou

Writer

A contemporary Hong Kong writer, Zhong Xiaoyang is known for her precociousness. She began to write at the age of fourteen and published her first novel, *Stopping by the Roadside* (*Tingche zhan jiewen*, 1982) by the age of eighteen. The work was praised and compared to the early work of Eileen Chang. Zhong is also known for her legendary friendship with the young literary talents in Taiwan in the 1980s, including Zhu Tianxin and Ding Yamin. While her publications over the past twenty years include two novels, five volumes of collected short stories, and two volumes of essays and poems, Zhong's literary activity decreased significantly after the mid 1980s.

A doctor's daughter, Zhong Xiaoyang grew up in Hong Kong. She studied film as a college student in the USA, and emigrated to Australia in 1993. In her early stage of writing, Zhong Xiaoyang's image as a prodigy, her unsophisticated adolescent poems and short stories set in northern China captured the cultural imagination of some Taiwan writers nostalgic for the lost mainland. Among them was the noted novelist Zhu Xining and the young contributors to the *Sansan Magazine*. Zhong's later works, however, have been largely viewed as 'obsessive romances' (*qiqing xiaoshuo*), and the potential depth of her work has been undermined by overly melodramatic storylines consisting of adultery, incest, murder, suicide, kidnapping, financial battles, disease, madness and death. Zhong Xiaoyang's collections of fiction and prose include: *The Passing Years* (*Liunian* 1983), *In Detail* (*Xishuo*, 1983), *Spring in the Green Wilderness* (*Chun zai luwuzhong*, 1983), *Beloved Wife* (*Aiqi*, 1986), *Eulogy* (*Aige*, 1986), *After the Flame* (*Ranshao zhihou*, 1992), *An Ordinary Life* (*Putongde shenghuo*, 1992) and *A Romance of Unending Sorrow* (*Yihen chuanqi*, 1996).

Further reading

Zhang, Xiaoyang (1991). 'Greensleeves'. Trans. Michael S. Duke. In *idem, Worlds of Modern Chinese Fiction*. Armonk: M. E. Sharpe, 206–21.

—— (1993). 'The Wedding Night'. Trans. Samuel Cheung. In Kao Hsin-sheng (ed.), *Nativism Overseas: Contemporary Chinese Women Writers*. Albany: SUNY Press, 211–20.

MING FENGYING

Zhongguo keyi shuo bu

[China Can Say No]

Book

China Can Say No: The Choice Between Politics and Emotion in the Post-Cold-War Period (*Zhongguo keyi shuo bu: Lengzhan hou shidai de zhengzhi yu qinggang jueze*) is a book of protest against China's treatment by the West and Japan. It was written by Song Qiang, Zhang Zangzang and Qiao Bian and published in May 1996 by the Chinese Industrial and Commercial Combined Press in Beijing.

The theme of the book is China's annoyance at the way in which Western powers, especially the United States but also Japan, formed a hostile bloc against China, criticizing it on such matters as human rights, Tibet, Taiwan and world trade. The authors believe this policy to be inspired by a renewal of the containment policy of the past. The Foreword specifies the book's overarching theme as China's demand for dialogue in an atmosphere of equality. It denies that the book is nationalist, but its tone is definitely strident. If anything, the feeling against Japan expressed here is even stronger than that against the United States. A fifth reprinting of the book with a total of 160,000 copies appeared in September 1996. Soon after, several other books followed on similar themes, with the phrase 'China Says No' included in the titles. The series is part of the general nationalistic trend of the 1990s.

Its inspiration comes in part from pride in China's strategic rise in international affairs, and in part from the perception of an exaggerated Western condemnation of China's human rights record and of its policies with respect to Taiwan and Tibet.

See also: nationalism; Olympics

Further reading

Gries, Peter (1997). 'Review' of *China Can Say No. The China Journal* 37 (Jan.): 180–5.

Zhou, Yi (1996). 'Before and After the Publication of *China Can Say No*'. *China Strategic Review* 1.7: 19–21.

COLIN MACKERRAS

Zhongguo meishubao

[Fine Arts in China 1985–9]

Art journal

Fine Arts in China was China's sole weekly art publication in the 1980s and provided a both broader and faster coverage of events than its competitors. It was a particularly stimulating source of news for the up-and-coming artists of the New Wave Art Movement. Established in July 1985, it was a publication of the Fine Art Department of the Chinese Art Research Institute (Zhongguo yishu yanjiuyuan meishu yanjiusuo) and was therefore able to put together a superb talent pool. Zhang Qiang was its director, and Liu Xiaochun, its chief editor. The deputy editors Yang Gengxi, Zhang Zuying and Zhai Mo were joined by Shui Tianzhong in 1987. In editorial direction it sought tolerance towards contending academic viewpoints to allow for intellectual exploration and dialogue. The editorial board emphasized collective expertise, but also tried to maintain a different approach in each issue, which was edited by a different critic each week. Both the issue editor and its sub-editors were granted a high degree of autonomy. Among its numerous members, the editorial team included: **Li Xianting**, Chen Weihe, Tao Yongbai, **Liao Wen**, Xu Wencun and **Ding Fang**. A lively publication, it carried reports on current trends and

exhibitions, including topics such as environmental art and architectural culture. It was also a forum for theoretical debate on issues such as the future of Chinese painting and postmodernism in China. Reports on the art world's involvement in the student movement of 1989 resulted in the journal being shut down at the end of the year.

Further reading

Galikowski, Maria (1998). *Art and Politics in China, 1949–1984*. Hong Kong: Chinese University Press, 187–98.

EDUARDO WELSH

Zhongshan

[Zhong Mountain]

Literary periodical

Zhongshan is one of the so-called 'four most famous magazines' in the literary field. It began publication as a quarterly in January 1979 in Nanjing, and changed to a bimonthly in January 1982. It has a format of 16 mo and a capacity of 200 pages per issue. In the beginning, *Zhongshan* was sponsored by the Jiangsu People's Publishing House, but in 1982 the Jiangsu Writers' Association, a department of the provincial government, become the new sponsor. Today, however, the magazine receives strong financial support from a local cigarette factory because the government subsidy has been continuously reduced since the early 1990s.

Since the early 1980s, almost every writer of note, especially authors of fiction and prose, has published his or her work in *Zhongshan*, including Gao Xiaosheng, Lu Wenfu, **Su Tong**, Ye Zhaoyan and Zhu Sujin. The editors have paid great attention to so-called **avant-garde/experimental literature** (*xianfeng wenxue*), especially in the mid 1980s. A special one-year column called 'Great Show of New Realistic Fiction' (*Xin xieshi xiaoshuo de lianzhan*, 1989–90) was both a timely response to, and influence on, the literary changes of the day.

WANG XIAOMING

Zhou Li

b. 1950, Shanghai

Writer

Zhou Li's autobiography, *A Chinese Woman in Manhattan* (*Manhadun de zhongguo nüren*, 1992), is one of the bestselling examples from the 1990s of 'overseas student literature', a genre which also includes Cao Guilin's *Beijingren zai niuyue*, Chen Yanni's *Gaosu ni yige zhen meiguo*, Qian Ning's *Liuxue meiguo* and Tang Ying's *Meiguo laide qizi*. The first chapter of the book was first published in the renowned literary journal *October* (*Shiyue*) in early 1992. The book was published by the Beijing Press in July. Unlike other overseas student literature, which focuses on life experiences abroad, Zhou Li combines her memories of growing up in the Mao era with her overseas experiences in America, whereby the strong-willed former Red Guard turned out to be a successful New York businesswoman. Zhou Li depicts America as a land of opportunity, open to anyone with determination, courage and innovation, willing to break through conventional barriers. Despite the minute biographical details of her life in Maoist and early post-Maoist China and many personal observations of American society and culture, the large and most significant portion of the book is devoted to reflections on the taste and fate of Mao-era intellectuals, who are represented by the three men she fell in love with during her adolescent and young-adult years – a university teacher, a painter and an amateur musician. These personal random reflections convey to us a faithful picture of the elite cultural configuration of the Mao era, and Zhou Li's book can be recommended as a useful resource for studying the period.

LU HONGWEI

Zhou Long

b. 1953, Beijing

Composer

Zhou Long is best known for the sensitive and intelligent way he integrates Chinese and Western musical elements. He enrolled in the Central Conservatory of Music in 1977. After graduating in 1983 he served as the Composer-in-Residence with the China Broadcasting Symphony. Zhou came to the United States in 1985 to study composition at Columbia University under Chou Wen-Chung, Mario Davidovsky and George Edwards. He received his doctorate in 1993.

Zhou's music is imbued with the elegant, sensitive and tranquil spirit of classical Chinese art and literature. Yet he is also a master at exploiting limited material to its maximum potential. *The Ineffable*, written for mixed Western and Chinese instruments, is a perfect blend of these two aspects. For over a decade, Zhou has served as music director of the Chinese instrument ensemble Music From China in New York City, and he received ASCAP's Adventurous Programming Award in 1999. He was the Music Alive! Composer-in-Residence for the Seattle Symphony's 'Silk Road Project' Festival with Yo-Yo Ma in 2002. Zhou's music has been recorded on major labels, as well as performed by major orchestras and ensembles all over the world. He has won the Masterprize (BBC, EMI, London Symphony) and the CalArts/Alpert Award in the Arts, as well as the Barlow International Competition. Zhou has been Visiting Professor of Composition at the University of Missouri–Kansas City Conservatory of Music since 2001.

JIN PING

Zhou Lunyou

b. 1952, Chengdu

Poet, editor and critic

Zhou Lunyou is the principal founder and leading member of the 'Not Not' (*Feifei*) poetry society, established in 1985. Zhou's poetic and theoretical work may be described as an effort to strip language down to its essence. This manoeuvre marked a distinct departure from the grandiose lyricism and powerful sense of mission of **Misty poetry** (*Menglongshi*), and immediately established Zhou's reputation as an innovative critical force. In Zhou's estimation, poetry should be self-sufficient and ideally independent of the symbolic structures that pervade social systems. The deconstructive thrust of Zhou's theoretical writings and his poetry is also indicative of the influence of Western critical theorists, particularly Jacques Derrida.

Zhou's major poems include 'Free Blocks', 'Twenty Poems on a Knife's Edge' and 'Escape'. Though his poems vary considerably in structure, running in length from ten lines to as many pages, Zhou's style is highly consistent in its terse phrasing and quotidian diction. 'Escape' is exemplary of his highly complex meditations on metaphor and signification couched in plain language. Zhou's other major poetic and theoretical works are collected in the magazines *Feifei* [Not-Not] and *Feifei pinglun* [Not-Not Theory], of which he is editor-in-chief. The journals, both inaugurated in 1986, have been largely sustained by personal contributions from writers. A collection of Zhou Lunyou's poems and theoretical articles entitled *Opening the Door of the Flesh: Not-Not-ism, From Theory to Practice* (*Dakai ruoti de men/Feifei zhuyi: cong lilun dao zuopin*), was published by Dunhuang Press in 1994.

See also: Third Generation (poets)

PAUL MANFREDI

Zhou Tiehai

b. 1966, Shanghai

Artist

Zhou Tiehai graduated from the School of Fine Arts at Shanghai University in 1987. His career took off after his first solo show, 'Too Materialistic, Too Spiritualized', opened at the Gallery of the **Central Academy of Fine Arts** in 1996 (see **art academies**). While Chinese critics were bemoaning the hegemonic power of Western cultural practices in China, Zhou frankly declared his acceptance of the trend. He created large gouaches on paper, reminiscent of the big character posters of the **Cultural Revolution**, in order to comment on the complex psychology of coming to terms with the Western art system as Chinese artists pursued success and fame for themselves. He even created a series of montages for the covers of well-known international

magazines as an exercise in unabashed boosterism. Intentionally and without irony, Zhou's appropriation and manipulation of images coldly deconstruct the aura of Western contemporary art as an industry sustained, like any commercial venture, by a systemic consensus created between curators, institutions, the market and the media. Seemingly uncritical appropriations are indeed Zhou's distinctive trait, exploited to the full in his prints, gouaches and, more recently, airbrushed compositions. In these works he exposes the power of the powerful, from movie stars to Chinese and Western icons recurrent in our visual library. Zhou's works have been widely exhibited at home and abroad, including the exhibition 'Cities on the Move' that toured Europe and the USA between 1997 and 1999; the Venice Biennale in 1999; and a solo show at the Hara Museum in Japan in 2000.

See also: poster art and artists

Further reading

De Matté, Monica (1999). 'Zhou Tiehai'. In *d'Apertutto Aperto Over All* (exhibition catalogue). Marsilio: La Biennale di Venezia, 272–3.

Pi, Li (2001). 'Dangdai yishu bushi anweiyao' [Contemporary Art is Not a Placebo]. *Diancang* [Art and Collecting] 107: 40–4.

Szeemann, Harald (2000). 'Zhou Tiehai'. In John Clark (ed.), *Chinese Art at the End of the Millennium*. Hong Kong: New Art Media, 246–7. [Reprinted in *Zhou Tiehai* (exhibition catalogue). Tokyo: Hara Museum of Contemporary Art.]

Tasch, Stephanie (2000). 'Zhou Tiehai: The Artist as a Young Man – Ambivalent'. In John Clark (ed.), *Chinese Art at the End of the Millennium*. Hong Kong: New Art Media, 248–9.

TANG DI

Zhou Xiaowen

b. 1954, Beijing

Film director, cinematographer

The transition from military service to film study at the **Beijing Film Academy** in 1973 marked a turning point in Zhou Xiaowen's professional life.

After two years of training in cinematography, he was assigned to the **Xi'an Film Studio**, where discussions of film art and experimentation were considered politically dangerous at the time. Nonetheless, Zhou Xiaowen refused to subordinate himself to the mainstream and even tried to become a film director. His chance finally came in 1984 when Wu Tianming, the new head of the Xi'an Film Studio, allowed Zhou to assist director Yan Xueru in the shooting of *Wild Mountain*.

While **Chen Kaige** and **Zhang Yimou** were engaged in filming national allegories, Zhou Xiaowen created films that spoke to contemporary themes while achieving commercial success. The success of *Desperation* (*Zuihou de fengkuang*, 1987) and *The Price of Frenzy* (*Fengkuang de daijia*, 1988) demonstrated a possible alternative to having to choose between art and commercial film. International recognition did not occur until 1994, however, when *Ermo* attracted critical attention. In this film, Zhou turns his camera from urban scenes to a rural village to follow a peasant woman as she relentlessly pursues ownership of a 29-inch television that she takes as the symbol of modernity. The clash of socialist value systems with emerging commercial culture is treated ironically, as the film emphasizes how social and economic changes drive ordinary Chinese into the arms of material capitalism. The success of *Ermo* brought Zhou Xiaowen the capital necessary to finish a historical epic, *The Emperor's Shadow* (*Qin Song*), in 1996.

Further reading

Ciecko, Anne and Lu, Sheldon (2002). 'Televisuality, Capital, and the Global Village: *Ermo*'. In Sheldon Lu (ed.), *China, Transnational Visuality, Global Postmodernity*. Stanford: Stanford University Press, 122–38.

Notar, Beth (2001). 'Blood Money: Women's Desire and Consumption in *Ermo*'. *Asian Cinema* 12.2 (Fall/Winter): 131–53.

Fu, Ping (2003). '*Ermo*: (Tele)Visualizing Urban/ Rural Transformation'. In Chris Berry (ed.), *Chinese Films in Focus: 25 New Takes*. London: BFI, 73–80.

Tang, Xiaobing (2003). 'Rural Women and Social Change in New China Cinema: From

Li Shuangshuang to *Ermo*'. *positions: east asian cultures critique* 11.3 (Winter): 647–74.

CUI SHUQIN

Zhu Fadong

b. 1960, Dongchuan village, Yunnan

Performance and conceptual artist

Before entering the Yunnan Academy of Fine Arts, Zhu Fadong was an amateur painter earning a living as a farmer and gardener. After graduating in 1985, Zhu got a job as an editor in Zhaotong, but soon left his native region to seek his fortune in Haikou (Hainan) as part of the large economic migration then taking place as a result of reform, a phenomenon which raised questions to the artist about the dispersion of collective identity and personal values. Consequently, in Zhu Fadong's work the artist's 'state of being' becomes both subject and medium of the art itself, and the act of performing visualizes the chronicling of the search for a lost Self. In his first paintings – *Black Square* (1990) and *Missing Missing* (1993), for example – the canvas is filled with personal ads, notices of missing people, and abstract human silhouettes reduced to minimal graphic lines. In *Big Business Card* (1993) and *Looking for a Missing Person* (1993) Zhu Fadong's ID photo and words, cut out from magazines, are printed on commercial posters and hung here and there on the walls of Kunming, expanding the piece from 'himself to society'.

Among other projects is the video *This Person is For Sale* (1994), realized in cooperation with Zhang Xuejun, who filmed Zhu's walks through Beijing dressed in a Mao jacket that bore a rectangular piece of white cloth on the back with the sentence 'This Person Is For Sale, Price Negotiable' – a reminder of the status of migrating peasant workers in the urban environment. Zhu Fadong has performed in Shanghai, Nanjing and major Chinese cities in Hunan and Yunnan, and has been featured in various shows: 'It's Me! A Profile of Chinese Contemporary Art in the 1990s' at the Tai Miao in the Forbidden City, Beijing (1998); 'Transience: Chinese Experimental Art at the End of the Twentieth Century' at the University of Chicago and USA (1999); 'Documentation of China Avant-Garde Artists' at the Fukuoka Museum of Art in Japan (2000); and 'Money Funny Money', Taikang Building, Beijing (2001).

Further reading

(1994). 'Jinri xianfen: Shiyan yishujia Zhu Fadong Zhuang Hui tanhua' [Today's Pioneers: A Conversation Between Zhu Fadong and Zhuang Hui] (ms, Beijing, 16 November).

Jia, Wei (1994). 'Xingwei de meili. Ji yishujia Zhu Fadong' [The Power of Action. On the Artist Zhu Fadong]. *Shidai fengcai* [Modern Elegance] 43: 43–5.

Wu, Hong (1999). 'State of Being'. In *idem* (ed.), *Transience: Chinese Experimental Art at the End of the Twentieth Century*. Chicago: University of Chicago Press, 137–41.

Yang, Alice (1998). 'Beyond Nation and Tradition: Art in Post-Mao China'. In *Why Asia? Contemporary Asian and Asian-American Art*. New York: New York University, 107–18.

BEATRICE LEANZA

Zhu Jian'er

b. 1922, Tainjin

Composer, educator

Zhu Jan'er grew up in Shanghai and taught himself to play the piano during his middle school years. Even before receiving a formal music education, he began composing and worked in a 'Literature and Arts Troupe' (*wengongtuan*) in the 1940s. From 1949 he served as a composer for the Shanghai and Beijing National Film Studios. He was sent to the Tchaikovsky Conservatory in Moscow (1955–60). Since 1975 he has worked for the Shanghai Symphony as a composer-in-residence. In the late 1990s he went to New York as a visiting scholar, studying contemporary music.

His stylistic development is remarkable. His early works, such as the overture *The Holiday* (*Jieri*, 1958), a symphonic cantata based on words by Mao Zedong (1959), and a Fugato for string quartet, based on the model ballet *The White-haired Girl* (*Baimaonü*, 1972)

and composed together with Shi Yongkang, are all characterized by a tonal, pentatonic idiom. As composer-in-residence at the Shanghai Symphony, he attended many classes on **New Music** held at the Shanghai Conservatory. This, along with field-trips to Guizhou province, are reflected in his numerous symphonies and symphonic poems written in short succession since the mid 1980s. Each explores new dimensions in compositional technique and instrumental make-up. Zhu writes symphonies for *suona* (Chinese cornet), musical saws and percussion, in twelve-tone, aleatoric and expressionist styles. He incorporates melodies, rhythmic patterns and other structural elements from China's folk musical traditions. And many of his symphonic works are programmatic. His *First Symphony* (1986) and his *Second Symphony* (1987), for example, two studies in manipulated twelve-tone-technique, both deal with the Cultural Revolution. They are pieces of 'Scar music' (see **Scar literature**). Work on his *First Symphony* actually began in early 1977, when Zhu felt enthusiastic about the ending of the 'ten years of stagnation', as the Cultural Revolution would come to be called. Yet completion of the symphony took him nine years. During this period, he researched the Cultural Revolution and wrote *In Memory* (1979), a 'symphonic fantasy'.

Further reading

Luo, Zhongrong (ed.) (1996).*Xiandai yinyue xinshang cidian* [Dictionary for the Appreciation of Contemporary Music]. Beijing: Gaodeng jiaoyu, 697–706.

Mittler, Barbara (1997). *Dangerous Tunes. The Politics of Chinese Music in Hong Kong, Taiwan and the People's Republic of China since 1949*. Wiesbaden: Harrassowitz, 97–105 and 151–2.

BARBARA MITTLER

Zhu Tianwen

b. 1956, Taiwan

Writer

Raised in Taiwan, Zhu began publishing short stories while in high school and continued while at

Tamkang University. In 1982 she sold the film rights to her short story 'Growing Up' (*Xiaobi de gushi*, 1982) and joined in scripting the film. This began a long working association with the director **Hou Hsiao-hsien**, writing novellas that she then scripted for films following Hou's suggestions. Among these were *Boys from Fenggui* (*Fenggui laide ren*, 1983), *The Time to Live and the Time to Die* (*Tongnian wangshi*, 1985), *Dust in the Wind* (*Lianlian fengchen*, 1987) and *Daughter of the Nile* (*Nilohe nü'er*, 1987). Most celebrated has been the script she co-authored with Wu Nien-chen for *City of Sadness* (*Beiqing chengshi*, 1989), which recreated Taiwanese society at the time of the 28 February Massacre in 1947, an incident that had remained virtually banned from public discourse until shortly before the film was released. Zhu has also secured a leading place in the fiction of Taiwan in the 1990s, first with the stories collected in *Fin-de-siècle Splendour* (*Shijimo de huali*, 1990) and then with *Notes of a Desolate Man* (*Huangren shouji*, 1995), an account of a gay's experience in Taipei.

See also: cinema in Taiwan; literature in Taiwan; Wu Nien-chen (Nianzhen)

Further reading

Martin, Fran (2003). 'Postmodern Cities and Viral Subjects: *Notes of a Desolate Man*'. In *idem*, *Situating Sexualities: Queer Representation in Taiwanese Fiction, Film and Public Culture*. Hong Kong: Hong Kong University Press, 101–16.

Zhu, Tianwen (1999). *Notes of a Desolate Man*. Trans. Howard Goldblatt and Sylvia Li-Chuan Lin. New York: Columbia University Press.

EDWARD GUNN

Zhuang, culture of

The Zhuang, the largest minority in China, number over 18 million. Two sub-groups, the northern and southern Zhuang, are by far the most numerous, accounting for 62 and 23 per cent, respectively. Most live in the Guangxi-Zhuang Autonomous Region where they make up roughly a third of the total population. Significant numbers of Zhuang are also found in the nearby provinces of Guizhou, Hunan and Guangdong, as well as in southeastern Yunnan, where close to a million share with the Miao the distinction of having an autonomous prefecture named after them (Wenshan). In many ways the Zhuang are similar to their **Han** Chinese neighbours who share the land – they look alike, dress alike, grow rice and seek out the same ecological conditions for agriculture as the Han, and are generally comfortable speaking whatever variety of Chinese is spoken locally. However, the southern and northern Zhuang languages are quite different from Mandarin and from each other, the latter being very close to Bouyei. Some of the numerous southern Zhuang dialects (officially seven, but estimated by some linguists to be as many as fifty) are more accurately classified as distinct languages. Nevertheless, many of the southern Zhuang can also speak a general form of northern Zhuang. Although ancient Zhuang ideographs appeared during the Southern Song period (1127–1276), they never made an inroad, and today a romanized script, introduced in 1950, is used to protect and preserve Zhuang culture.

For more than 2,000 years, the Zhuang have had close ties with both the Chinese and the Vietnamese. However, their historical records go back only as far as the Song dynasty when they first became known as Zhuang. There are, of course, certain features that distinguish them from the Han. For example, the role of women in their culture seems to be more important, and much of this is discernible in the content of their famous antiphonal singing. One of their most important festivals is sometimes called the 'singing fest' when ballads are sung antiphonally in rice fields or outside caves by day, and in the villages by night. Common accompanying musical instruments include the *suona* (a cornet), bronze drums, cymbals, gongs, the *lusheng* (wind pipes) – used also by the Miao and the Yi – the *xiao* (vertical bamboo flutes), and the *huqin* (a stringed instrument made of horse bone). Their distinctive opera (dating back to Tang times) combines Zhuang folk literature, music, dance and other art forms. Very few Zhuang wear traditional clothing on a regular basis, but they enjoy wearing it at festivals and other special occasions. The majority of Zhuang now live in houses that resemble those of the Han. However, in remote mountain villages many have kept their traditional (*ganlan*-type) two-storey wood dwellings where the upper level serves as living quarters and the lower as stables and storerooms. These structures are similar to the housing that is characteristic of the Dong, Bouyei (Buyi) and Miao.

Further reading

Holm, David (2003). *Killing a Buffalo for the Ancestors: A Zhuang Cosmological Text from Southwest China.* Northern Illinois University Monograph Series on Southeast Asia 5. Illinois: Southeast Asia Publications.

Kaup, K. P. (2000). *Creating the Zhuang: Ethnic Politics in China.* Boulder: Lynne Rienner.

Lin, Guozhi (1992). *Une terre, des peoples: Us et coutumes des ethnies minoritaires chinoises.* Beijing: Éditions de l'Art photographique des nationalités de la Chine.

PETER M. FOGGIN

Zhuang Hui

b. 1963, Yumen, Gansu

Photographer

Zhuang Hui grew up in Luoyang, Henan. He attributes his early interest in photography and the arts to his father, who worked as an itinerant photographer. Throughout Zhuang's artistic work the search for identity in a changing society is central.

Zhuang's career began with oil painting and then moved to performance art in the early 1990s with works that often involved travel. It was, however, Zhuang's photographic endeavours that launched him into the spotlight. His *One and Thirty* series of 1995–6 shows the artist posed full length with thirty different individuals of a particular social or vocational group. Each piece consists of thirty individual portraits arranged in a grid, with the artist as the common denominator across different socially constructed identities. In 1997 Zhuang began a series of group portraits with an antique banquet camera that requires arduous preparation and that produces an elongated horizontal image. The groups he photographed were sometimes as large as 350 people. Each photograph was inscribed with the name and location of the group as well as the date of the photograph. *Shuangyuan Energy Source Construction Company, 26 March 1997* shows hardhatted workers posed in front of a nuclear reactor. In each of these photographs the artist himself stands at one end of the group, helping to confound the boundaries between group portraiture and self-portraiture. Zhuang Hui has exhibited his work in 'Contemporary Photo Art from the People's Republic of China' (Kunstverein, Berlin and other venues in Germany, 1997), 'Revelation Series III: Falling Apart Together' (Amsterdam, 1999), and 'dAPERTutto, the 48th Venice Biennial' (1999).

See also: Lu Zhirong; Zhang Hai'er

Further reading

Borysevicz, Mathieu (1998). 'The Conductor of Grand Theatre, Zhuang Hui's Photographic Portraits'. *ART AsiaPacific* 19: 74–9. [Reprinted in John Clark (ed.) (2000), *Chinese Art at the End of the Millennium.* Hong Kong: New Art Media, 250–4.]

De Matté, Monica (1999). 'Zhou Tiehai'. In *dApertutto Aperto Over All* (exhibition catalogue). Venezia: Edizioni La Biennale di Venezia/Marsilio, 216–17.

Nowald, Inken and Tolnay, A. (eds) (1997). *Zeitgenössische Fotokunst aus der Volksrepublic China.* Heidelberg: Edition Braus, 104–13.

MATHIEU BORYSEVICZ

Zuni Icosahedron

Theatre troupe

Zuni Icosahedron, a legendary performing group established in 1982, has pioneered experimental performing arts in Hong Kong. The name Zuni Icosahedron, according to Zuni's interpretation, represents the aspirations in the combination of two expressions. Zuni stands both for a colour between green and blue and for a Native American tribe famous for its handcrafted art. Icosahedron is a twenty-sided object as well as the name of a kind of virus. The company undertakes a variety of activities encompassing workshops that tour among secondary schools, video art, an arts policy study group that initiates public forums, and a prolific performance schedule. All of this has been achieved without significant government funding.

Following their production of *The Opium War* in 1984, Zuni began independently operating a small theatre in Causeway Bay. Since establishing its popularity in 1987 with *Romance of the Rock*, Zuni has performed *One Hundred Years of Solitude Series* (1982–96), *Mirage, Vanity Fair – A Love Story in Glamorous Costume* (1986), *The Decameron* (1988), *The Deep Structure of Chinese Culture* (1990), *Two or Three Things...Hong Kong* (1993–5), *Feeding the Hungry Ghost* (1996), *The Book of Mountain and Ocean* (1996–7)

and *Journey to the East '97* (1997). Zuni's performances rely on the careful repetition of images, gestures and words to create a metamorphosing network of associations designed to suggest arenas of social knowledge and feeling that are believed to be inarticulable.

Further reading

Lilley, R. (1990). *Staging Hong Kong: Gender and Performance in Transition.* Honolulu: University of Hawai'i Press.

REN HAI

Index

Note: Page numbers in **bold** refer to main subject entries. Bold page numbers after a person's name indicate entries written by this person.